# GEOGRAPHICAL SYMBOLS

| | |
|---|---|
| **A** | **UNITED STATES** |
| AA | Regions |
| AS | States (A-Z) (Counties and cities are under appropriate state without further division) |
| | e.g., **ASA** - Alabama, Arizona, Alaska |
| | **ASC** - California, Colorado, Connecticut |
| | (For Hawaii see **P**) |
| | |
| **C** | **CANADA** |
| CA | Regions |
| CP | Provinces (A-Z) |
| | e.g., **CPN** - New Brunswick |
| | |
| **D** | **LATIN AMERICA** |
| DC | Central America |
| DM | Mexico |
| DS | South America |
| DSA | Argentina |
| DSB | Bolivia |
| | Brazil |
| DSC | Chile |
| | Colombia |
| DSE | Ecuador |
| DSG | Guiana |
| DSP | Paraguay |
| | Peru |
| DSU | Uruguay |
| DSV | Venezuela |
| DW | West Indies |
| | |
| **E** | **EUROPE** |
| EA | Regions |
| EB | Great Britain. British Isles. Any two parts of Great Britain or England alone |
| EBC | British Empire. Commonwealth. Colonies in general ( For individual members see appropriate country) |
| EBE | English towns or cities |
| EBI | Ireland. Northern Ireland. Irish Free State. Eire, including individual towns or cities (See **EB** when discussed with any other part of Great Britain) |
| EBS | Scotland, including individual towns or cities (See **EB** when discussed with any other part of Great Britain) |
| EBW | Wales, including individual towns or cities (See **EB** when discussed with any other part of Great Britain) |
| | **Other countries, A-Z** |
| ECA | Austria. Austria-Hungary |
| ECB | Belgium |
| | Bulgaria |
| ECC | Czechoslovakia. Bohemia |
| ECF | Finland |
| EE | Estonia. Latvia. Livonia |

| | |
|---|---|
| EF | France |
| EG | Germany |
| EGr | Greece |
| EH | Hungary |
| | (For Austria-Hungary see **ECA**) |
| EI | Italy |
| EL | Lithuania |
| | Livonia <u>see</u> **EE** |
| EN | Netherlands |
| EP | Poland |
| ER | Soviet Union. Russia |
| ERA | Soviet Bloc |
| | (For individual countries in the bloc see appropriate country) |
| ERu | Rumania |
| ES | Scandinavia. Sweden |
| ESD | Denmark |
| ESI | Iceland |
| ESN | Norway |
| ESp | Spain. Portugal |
| ESw | Switzerland |
| EY | Yugoslavia. Serbia |
| | |
| **F** | **ASIA** |
| FA | Regions, including Southeast Asia, Far East, Indochina (For Middle East see **M**) |
| FAf | Afghanistan |
| FC | China. Formosa (See **ERA** when discussed with other countries of the Soviet Bloc) |
| FH | Hongkong |
| FI | India, including Pakistan before partition. Burma |
| FIC | Ceylon |
| FIN | Indonesia |
| FIP | Pakistan (Before partition see **FI**) |
| FJ | Japan |
| FK | Korea |
| FM | Malaya |
| FMo | Mongolia. Outer Mongolia |
| FP | Philippines |
| FT | Thailand. Siam |
| FV | Vietnam |
| | |
| **H** | **AFRICA**, including regions and individual countries not noted below (For Egypt and the Sudan see **ME**) |
| HSA | South Africa |
| | |
| **M** | **MIDDLE EAST**, including individual countries not noted below |
| ME | Egypt and the Sudan |
| MI | Israel. Palestine |
| | |
| **N** | **AUSTRALIA. NEW ZEALAND** |
| | |
| **P** | **PACIFIC ISLANDS**, including Hawaii |
| | |
| **R** | **ARCTIC and ANTARCTIC REGIONS** (For Alaska see **ASA**) |

# INDEX OF ECONOMIC JOURNALS

# INDEX OF
# ECONOMIC JOURNALS

## Volume III • 1940-1949

*Prepared under the Auspices of*

THE AMERICAN ECONOMIC ASSOCIATION

*Committee:*

JOHN PERRY MILLER, *Chairman*
ROBERT L. BISHOP — EARL J. HAMILTON
FRITZ MACHLUP — JOSEPH J. SPENGLER

*Staff:*

DOROTHY F. LIVINGSTON, *Director*
TRUUS W. KOOPMANS, *Chief of Classification*

1961

RICHARD D. IRWIN, INC.

HOMEWOOD, ILLINOIS

First Printing, August, 1962
Second Printing, March, 1964

Library of Congress Catalogue Card No. 61-8020

Printed in the United States of America

# TABLE OF CONTENTS

# INTRODUCTION

"The correction of Textual Errors (Courteous Reader)
is a work of time, and that hath taken wing. The more
faults thou findest, the larger field is presented to thy
humanity to practise in. Be indulgent in thy censure,
and remember that Error, whether Manual or Mental,
is an inheritance, descending upon us, from the first
of our Race." Errata leaf in Francis Bacon's Of the
Advancement and Proficience of Learning. Oxford,
1640.

## SCOPE

This index lists by author and subject English language articles in major professional economic
journals published during the period 1886-1959. The use of geographical symbols makes it possible to locate easily all major empirical studies of principal geographical areas. The industry
classification in 15.5 includes all major studies of each industry, whether concerned with prices,
production, trade, labor conditions, etc.

Journals Included. The Committee has included those professional journals which it believes will
be of widest use to teachers and scholars of economics. Government publications and some specialized journals are excluded. Journals indexed are listed on pages xvii-xx with bibliographical
description. An alphabetical list of abbreviations used in citing the journals will be found on the
inside front cover. An asterisk (*) indicates that coverage of English articles is selective. No
articles in foreign languages are indexed.

The Publications of the American Economic Association 1886 to 1910 are not indexed herein because this series includes monographs as well as articles. An index to these Publications appeared in the American Economic Review Supplement, Volume 7, no. 4, December, 1917.

For the early part of the period covered by volume I of the Index many significant articles on economics appeared in more general journals not included, e.g., the Political Science Quarterly. For
more detailed coverage of the literature during this period users are referred to the standard volumes on the history of economic thought, the Encyclopaedia of the Social Sciences, and the standard periodical indexes.

Scope of Each Index Volume. In each volume of the Index articles falling within the calendar years
of the volume are included. When a volume of a journal overlaps two calendar years, e.g., October 1939-July 1940, articles are divided between the two Index volumes according to date. Where
individual issues are not dated, they have been divided according to our best judgment. There is
one exception to these principles: when successive parts of the same article fall in two Index
volumes, the entire entry for both parts appears in each volume. Errata are listed only with the
entry for the original article, regardless of date published.

## COVERAGE OF MATERIAL

In this section the general rules for inclusion of material in all journals are set forth. In particular cases we have not hesitated to violate the rules where our judgment indicated this was desirable. In doubtful cases the decision usually has been in favor of inclusion rather than the contrary.

Material Indexed. The following have been included: articles whether signed or unsigned; comments, replies, rejoinders, and corrections of articles; papers at meetings of professional associations and discussion of such papers; reports of symposia, round tables, and similar group discussions; substantive reports of committees; signed notes and communications; signed editorials;
obituaries containing biographical or bibliographical material whether signed or unsigned; special
subject bibliographies; book reviews and notes about them only when not in a book review section.

Regular features appearing over a substantial period of time have been included if we judged them
useful; when signed they have usually been included. Such features have been summarized in a
single entry in the classified index and listed under the various authors or editors in the author
index.

<u>Material Not Indexed</u>.  Material not generally indexed includes abstracts of papers presented at professional meetings; abstracts of theses; book reviews and notes about them appearing in a book review section; unsigned notes and editorials; routine or administrative reports of committees; reports of proceedings of meetings; obituaries without biographical or bibliographical material; general bibliographies which are regular features.  In addition, in the case of selective journals (indicated by * in the list of journals) we have excluded noneconomic material such as articles on politics, sociology, statistical theory, and population which are not of primary significance for economists.

ARRANGEMENT

Each volume of the Index is in two parts:  1) a classified index in which material is arranged by subject according to a classification scheme developed by the Committee in consultation with other experts; 2) an author index.

The author index is strictly a personal author file.  All items which could not be assigned a personal entry are listed only in the classified index, under the heading "Anonymous."  These include, in addition to unsigned items, articles signed with indefinite pseudonyms (e.g. "Mercator"; "A stockbroker"), and items for which a corporate body has been responsible.  An item signed with initials which have been identified is entered under the author's name in both the classified and author indexes.  Where the initials have not been identified, the item is listed <u>only</u> in the classified index under the surname initial.  Arrangement of titles under each author is chronological in both the classified and author indexes.

<u>Classified Index</u>.  In the classified index authors are usually listed alphabetically under each subclass.  Anonymous entries are listed under the heading "Anonymous" which is interfiled in alphabetical place with authors' names.  Articles of joint authorship are listed under the first-named author only.  The names of joint authors are indicated up to three; for more than three, the name of the first author only is given, followed by "[and others]."  Committee reports are listed only under the name of the chairman, where known.  Comments on an article or discussions of a paper which follow it immediately are included in the entry for the article or paper.  When a discussion covers two or more papers, it is listed separately under the name of the discussant and is not noted in the entry for each paper discussed.

There are two exceptions to the alphabetical author arrangement under each subclass:  first, in subclass <u>4.8 - Individuals</u>, where arrangement is alphabetical by the person who is the subject of the article, note, or obituary; second, in class <u>5 - Economic History</u>, class <u>6 - General Contemporary Economic Conditions</u>, <u>Policy</u>, <u>and Planning</u>, and some subdivisions of other classes where a geographical arrangement is used (see p. xv).

<u>Author Index</u>.  In the author index titles are listed under each author in chronological order.  For journals which do not use month of issue we have determined the chronological order arbitrarily within each year, listing all items with months first.  The names of all joint authors of articles are included, each such article being listed under the name of each of its authors.  Discussions are listed under the name of each discussant up to three; where there are more than three the discussion appears, if at all, under the first-named discussant only.  Exception is made for discussions in the <u>Papers and Proceedings of the American Economic Association</u>, which generally have been fully indexed regardless of this rule.  Anonymous articles and those signed with initials which have not been identified are not listed in the author index.  Translators are not indexed, but are usually mentioned in the entry under the author's name.

Authors are listed in the author index of all volumes under the latest form of name when known.  References are made from alternate or obsolete forms.  (In the classified index the name follows the form which appears in the particular issue of the journal, in order to facilitate the location of the item.)  The Library of Congress catalog has been the authority for form of name wherever possible.  It has been our practice to make special search only for women's names, questionable forms (compound and prefix names and those with variant spellings), and names where the first forename was not available from the journals themselves.  If the first forename was given, no search was made to establish the complete name.

Where authors were not identified in the Library of Congress or the Yale catalogs, other obvious reference books have sometimes been consulted.  But we have by no means exhausted such sources.  Many authors have not been identified; we have had to use our best judgment in determining the appropriate form for entry, consulting specialists on foreign names when possible.  Full names are given only in the author index; in the classified index forename initials are used.

viii

Alphabetizing of names follows general American library practice. Prefix names are arranged as if spelled as one word; names beginning with "M'," "Mc," and "Mac" are interfiled as if spelled "Mac"; diacritical marks are ignored, e.g. Müller is filed as Muller, not as Mueller. We have solved the problem of variations in transliteration of Indian and similar names by interfiling them under one spelling without altering the entry itself. Where variant spellings have been used for the same author, we have chosen the spelling most frequently used in the journals or the latest spelling, when no other authority was available. We have followed the Western practice of entry under surname (or family name) with reference from forename where called for.

## CONTENT AND FORM OF ENTRIES

Titles have been given exactly as in the journals except that obvious typographical errors have been corrected without transcribing the incorrect form. Occasionally, when titles have not indicated the subject of the article, we have inserted explanatory material in the classified index. In general, such insertion has been enclosed in brackets.

Review articles which were easily identified as such are indicated by the symbol "R." Obituaries are specified by "[obit.]." Notes and other types of material are not specified.

## CLASSIFICATION SCHEDULE

The classification system consists of 23 main classes with a total of nearly 700 subclasses. It represents an amplification of the system used for classifying books and articles in the American Economic Review. The Committee developed the present system after many discussions and consultations with various specialists. It is the result of the adoption of certain principles based on our understanding of the past development and present status of the body of economic knowledge, tempered by our sense of the future. However, logical principles have been modified in the interest of usability of the Index, resulting in a classification which is in some respects a compromise between principle and practice. We cannot hope that users of the Index will find it ideal, nor can we hope that the decisions of the classifiers in individual cases will always be approved. In fact, during our prolonged discussions of the principles and practice of classification it became clear to members of the Committee that even experts in various aspects of economic knowledge cannot always reach agreement. In practice, the limitation of resources, particularly of human resources, often made it impracticable to employ experts or to delay too long in arriving at firm decisions in individual cases. The most that the Committee can hope is that the classified index will make more readily available to economists the wealth of material in the journals covered. We believe that users will generally be able to find what they want with the aid of various cross references, experience, and a certain amount of ingenuity.

The same classification system has been used throughout the five volumes. The change in the character of economics and in the nature of research is reflected in the changing number of items appearing in various subclasses.

The classification schedule, based on analysis of the materials for the whole period 1886-1959, is published in each volume of the Index on pages xxi-xlvi. Where there are no items in a given subclass for a given volume, the title of the subclass is omitted from the classified index in that volume but not from the classification schedule. In only two cases have the materials in various subclasses been consolidated because the amount of material in some volumes of the Index was small while in others it was so large as to require a more detailed breakdown: in 2.34 - Growth and Development Theory, where the amount of material is substantial only in recent years; and in 13 - War and Defense Economics, where the schedule was devised for the large amount of material in the 1940-49 volume.

Generally items have been classified once only. Where a group of items is relevant to more than one subclass, it has usually been placed in one, with a cross reference from the alternative subclass indicated in the classification schedule. However, 15 to 20 per cent of the items have been classified in two or, occasionally, three or more subclasses. In particular, major studies of individual industries or commodities have been listed in the appropriate subclasses of 15.5 or 16.01 and also under the appropriate function, such as international trade.

Serious problems arise in determining the place of items in the various subclasses. These problems are inherent in the structure of economic thinking and research. Differences of opinion and even errors are inevitable. Users of the Index are urged to take note of the cross references provided in the Classification Schedule, which should help to overcome many of the deficiencies of classification.

In each class or subclass which is further subdivided, the first subdivision is called "General." Into this goes all material which is relevant to the class or subclass but is not primarily related to a single subdivision thereof; thus, it includes not only material on two or more of the subdivisions but also more specific material for which special subdivisions have not been established. Consequently, a user interested in exhausting the material for any specific subdivision should look also at material in the "General" category of its class and subclasses. For example: material on the theory of building cycles might be found in all of the following subclasses: 2.335 - Building Cycles; 2.330 - General Cycle Theory; 2.30 - General Aggregative and Monetary Theory, Cycles, and Growth, and possibly in 2.0, the most general class under 2 - Economic Theory.

Although the classification schedule is largely self-explanatory, a brief statement of some classification principles governing the individual classes will help to orient the reader more quickly.

1. Scope and Method of Economics

This class includes general discussions of the scope and method of economics and of economic research. Subclass 1.3 - Teaching of Economics contains all material on the teaching of economics, including teaching in secondary schools, business schools, and other professional and technical schools. It does not include material on general professional training of businessmen, industrial relations experts, agricultural economists, or city and regional planners. All material concerning professional economic societies and journals and all general bibliographies are classified in 1.5 and 1.4, respectively.

2. Economic Theory, including Monetary Theory

All economic theory since 1870 except the theory of international trade, fiscal theory, and the theory of population has been included in class 2. It covers the major divisions of contemporary theory: value, price, and allocation theory; factors of production and distributive shares; aggregative theory, including the theory of money, cycles, and economic development and growth. The various subdivisions of class 2 have their empirical counterparts in other classes. Material relevant to certain topics, e.g. wages, may be found in two or more of the subclasses in the theory class and also in the applied class (19).

3. Economic Systems. Planning

This class is concerned with general discussions of alternative economic systems and of the role of government in economic life. Descriptions and analyses of specific economic systems such as the United States, Soviet Union, Fascist Italy, or Nazi Germany, will be found either in 5 - Economic History, or 6 - General Contemporary Economic Conditions, Policy, and Planning. Discussions of particular institutions or policies under various systems will be found in the appropriate functional class, e.g. cartels in Fascist Italy in the appropriate subclass of 15. However, all studies of cooperation and cooperative societies (except agricultural cooperatives) are classified in 3.4.

4. History of Economic Thought

Subclasses 4.0-4.7 for various periods or schools of thought include general discussions or those concerned with three or more individuals. All material on a single individual is classified under his name in 4.8, regardless of the period in which he lived or the school to which he belonged. Articles on two individuals appear under each name. Discussions of a particular theory of a period, school, or individual, and views on special topics are classified in 4. For the period since 1870 they are also listed under the appropriate subdivision of another class. An item written by a well-known economist and published posthumously in any of the journals has been classified in 4.8 along with articles about him if it is of interest for the history of economic thought. Such items are listed first under his name and usually do not appear in the author index except under the name of the editor if there is one.

It should also be noted that shifts in the chronology of the various volumes of the Index lead to variations in the inclusion of individuals in this class. For example, a discussion of John A. Hobson's theory of distribution published in 1904 will appear only in 2.20; a similar article written about Hobson today would appear also in 4.8.

All obituaries are included in this class, regardless of the place of the individual in economic science; however, except for obituaries, biographical and critical material in 4.8 is restricted to recognized economists; others are classified according to the fields of their activity, e.g. bankers in 9; businessmen in 14; labor leaders in 19.

The history of economic societies and journals is classified in 1.5.

## 5. Economic History

General articles on economic history and historical articles discussing three or more functions, e.g. production, prices, and trade, are included in 5. This class is subdivided by period and by country except that the ancient period (5.1) has no country breakdown. Works that significantly overlap two periods are double-classed. Historical articles discussing one or two functions in the ancient or medieval period are double-classed in 5.1 or 5.2 and under the appropriate function. For the later periods, material discussing one or two functions is classified in the History subdivision of the appropriate functional class or classes, not in 5, e.g. "Prices and wages in Paris during the French Revolution" in 9.61 and 19.31.

The dividing line between historical and contemporary discussion has been determined arbitrarily. In general, only articles concerned primarily with a period 20 years or more earlier than the beginning date of the volume have been considered historical. Accordingly, the cut-off date varies for the volumes of the Index as follows:

<pre>
          Vol. I.    1886-1924 . . . . . . . . . . . . . . 1865
          Vol. II.   1925-1939 . . . . . . . . . . . . . . 1910
          Vol. III.  1940-1949 . . . . . . . . . . . . . . 1918
          Vol. IV.   1950-1954 . . . . . . . . . . . . . . 1930
          Vol. V.    1955-1959 . . . . . . . . . . . . . . 1935
</pre>

This pertains not only to material in 5.4 but also to material in the History subdivisions under each functional class. Articles dealing with both a historical and contemporary period, e.g. "the last hundred years," have been classified according to the emphasis and purpose of the author, e.g. in 5 or 6 or both.

The number of History subclasses in the functional classes varies with the amount of material. The digit 1 after the class number signifies historical material wherever this category is established (see below). The History subdivision under any class or subclass number includes articles on the historical aspect of any of its subdivisions. For example, 19.41 - Trade Union Organization. History includes historical material on any subdivision of 19.4, such as 19.44 - Union Security or 19.46 - Finances.

Below is a list of all the History classes and subclasses throughout the schedule:

### HISTORY CLASSES AND SUBCLASSES

4.0-4.8  HISTORY OF ECONOMIC THOUGHT
5.0-5.4  ECONOMIC HISTORY

8.1  SOCIAL ACCOUNTING. STATISTICAL DATA
8.21  National Income and Wealth
8.51  Statistical Data (not elsewhere classified)

9.1  MONEY, CREDIT, AND BANKING
9.21  Money. Currency. Monetary Standards
9.31  Commercial Banks
9.41  Financial Intermediaries
9.51  Security and Money Markets
9.61  Prices. Inflation. Deflation
9.71  Portfolio Selection
9.81  Consumer Finance
9.91  Monetary Policy. Central Banks

10.1  PUBLIC FINANCE
10.21  Fiscal Policy for Economic Stabilization and Growth
10.31  Public Expenditure
10.41  Taxation and Other Revenue
10.51  Public Debt and Debt Policy

11.1  INTERNATIONAL ECONOMICS
11.21  Structure of International Trade
11.31  Balance of Payments. Mechanisms of Adjustment

19.71 Labor Legislation and Regulation. Public Employees

20.1 CONSUMER ECONOMICS

21.1 HEALTH. EDUCATION. WELFARE

22.1 REGIONAL PLANNING AND DEVELOPMENT. HOUSING

6. General Contemporary Economic Conditions, Policy, and Planning
This class is restricted to general discussions of the contemporary economic situation, or of
three or more functions. It is subdivided by country. Material on one or two functions is
classified in the appropriate functional classes, e.g. wages and prices in England in 9 and 19.
Discussions of general problems of underdeveloped areas are classified in 2.34 but discussions
of specific underdeveloped countries, in 6.

7. Mathematical, Statistical, and Other Tools of Analysis
This class is restricted to methods and tools of analysis. In general, methodological articles
in the statistical journals, where coverage has been selective, have been excluded. Only applications of methods to economic phenomena have been included from these journals.

8. Social Accounting. Statistical Data
Material on social accounting including national income and wealth, flow of funds, and input-
output is classified here. The mathematical structure of input-output models is in 7.11. Much
statistical data not elsewhere classified is also in class 8, including indexes of prices, production, or profit covering a sector of the economy, in contrast to those covering a single industry. Material on survey methods and the theory of index numbers is in 7.2.

9. Money, Credit, and Banking
This class covers empirical studies of money, credit, and banking as well as discussions of
monetary and banking policy. Monetary theory is classified in 2.32.

10. Public Finances
All material on public finance and on general fiscal policy (excluding monetary policy) is
classified in 10. Material on the theory of the effects of taxes on product prices is in 2.1338;
on the welfare effects of tax and expenditure policies, in 2.163. Discussion of government
procurement in war is classified in 13.21; of the administration of public enterprise, in 15.42
or the appropriate subdivision of 15.5-15.9.

11. International Economics
This class includes the theory of international trade and finance, empirical studies in the whole
field of international economics, and all discussions of international trade and financial policies.
The distinction between trade policy (11.23) and quantitative trade and exchange restrictions
(11.34) has presented unusually difficult classification problems because of changes in the objectives of particular trade or exchange restrictions. This is especially true for the period
since 1945.

12. Economic Fluctuations. Stabilization Policy
This class includes discussions of general economic fluctuations and of two or more instruments of stabilization policy. Discussions of a particular instrument for economic stabilization such as monetary policy or fiscal policy will be found in the appropriate class, e.g. 9 or
10. Stabilization in war or mobilization is classified in 13; general economic policy not concerned with stabilization, in 3 or 6.

13. War and Defense Economics
This class draws together material on the economics of the defense establishment and military
operations, as well as material relating to economic mobilization and stabilization during periods of war, of rapid mobilization, and of demobilization. The line between material in 13
and that in other classes is necessarily arbitrary. During periods covering World Wars I and II
this class has been used rather heavily. However, discussions of stabilization policy during the
recent period of prolonged military expenditure incident to the cold war are not generally included in 13. In volumes II and V material in the various subclasses has been consolidated
into fewer categories than indicated in the classification schedule because the amount of material is small. Articles covering a long period, a portion of which includes a war, are classified in 5 or 6 or an appropriate functional class, not in 13.

14. Business Organization. Managerial Economics
    This class includes material on the business firm and its _internal_ operations, including education for business in its various aspects.

15. Industrial Organization and Public Policy
    This class is concerned primarily with the _external_ relations of the business firm. 15.5 includes all the articles of major interest on individual industries (manufacturing, distributive, extractive, construction, and service). General studies of public enterprise are classified in 15.42 but studies of particular public enterprises will be found in the appropriate subdivision of 15.5-15.9.

16. Agriculture
    This class includes articles relating to the production and initial distribution of agricultural products. The processing of agricultural products except milk is classified in 15.526 or 15.528. The economics of land (tenure, utilization, and policy) is classified in 17.3.

17. Natural Resources. Land Economics
    This class is concerned with problems of basic natural resources and conservation. A distinction is made between the supply and utilization of natural resources in 17 and the cultivation or processing of the resources which is classified in 15 or 16. Forestry and fishing are classified in 17 as long as the processing does not go beyond the cutting and gathering of timber and the catching and unloading of fish.

18. Population
    All articles on population have been included in full coverage journals, but in the selective journals only articles concerned with the theory of population and the relation of population to economic growth have been included. Persons interested in a fuller coverage of demographic material are referred to the _Population Index_, published at Princeton, N.J., by the Office of Population Research, Princeton University and Population Association of America, Inc.

19. Labor Economics
    "Labor" in this class covers primarily the industrial labor force and its supervisory personnel. Material dealing with managers and executives is classified in 14.33; with sales personnel, in 14.56; with agricultural labor, in 16.3. Subclass _19.7 - Labor Legislation. Public Employees_ includes only _general_ laws and legislation on labor and industrial relations. Laws on particular topics and the effect of a general law on a particular topic are classified with the topic, e.g. wage legislation, in 19.35, strike legislation, in 19.6, effect of Taft-Hartley law on the open shop, in 19.44.

20. Consumer Economics
    This class includes primarily empirical and policy studies. The theory of consumer choice is classified in 2.11; of the consumption function, in 2.315. Consumer price indexes are classified in 8.54; consumer finance, in 9.8.

21. Health. Education. Welfare
    This class draws together material on all kinds of social welfare programs, private and public. For convenience, material on all phases of _Medical Economics_ and of the _Economics of Education_ is classified in 21.7 and 21.8, respectively.

22. Regional Planning and Development. Housing
    This class includes all studies of regional problems and planning, as well as the growing body of literature on the theory of regional science. "Region" is used here to denote a geographical area which is a part of a larger national area. It does not refer to regional blocs of nations. _22.5 - Housing_ includes all material on housing, housing markets, and housing policy, except for the construction industry which is classified in 15.55.

23. Unclassified
    This class includes a small group of articles appearing in the full-coverage journals which could not be fitted appropriately into any category in the classification scheme.

# TOPICAL INDEX TO THE CLASSIFICATION SCHEDULE

The topical index to the classification schedule (see pp. xlvii-lv at the end of the volume) is designed to assist users in locating major topics within the schedule. Included are all the topics which appear in the class or subclass headings; topics or concepts not appearing therein are generally not listed in the topical index.

## GEOGRAPHICAL SYMBOLS

Alphabetical symbols appearing in the left-hand margin of the Classified Index indicate material relating to particular countries or other geographical areas. A table of these symbols appears on the first flyleaf. When two countries are discussed in the same article two symbols are given; for more than two a regional symbol is used, if any. Where the symbol is not sufficiently specific, the area covered is indicated in the title, enclosed in brackets.

In two classes, 5 - Economic History and 6 - General Contemporary Economic Conditions, Policy, and Planning, and in some subdivisions of other classes, entries are arranged geographically by the symbols in order to bring together material on the same area. The name of the country (United States) or continent (Europe, Asia, etc.) is used as a heading, preceding the articles relating to the area. The symbol appears in the margin opposite the first entry only for each geographical division and pertains to the following entries without repetition until a different symbol appears. When the same symbol applies to different areas, e.g. states of the United States which begin with the same letter, the entries are arranged alphabetically by the area covered and the symbol is repeated for each different area. An article pertaining to two areas is listed under each, unless they are contiguous. Subclasses employing a geographical arrangement are not necessarily the same in all volumes of the Index, since the amount of material in various subclasses varies considerably in different time periods. Readers are cautioned that the assignment of geographical symbols is not infallible, depending as it has on the judgment of individual classifiers as to the geographical significance of particular items.

## ACKNOWLEDGMENTS

The Index was prepared under the auspices of the American Economic Association by a special committee appointed for this purpose. Financial support for the project was provided by the Ford Foundation and the American Economic Association. The Committee in charge is responsible for the general plan of the work and the classification scheme. The Chairman of the Committee and the staff were necessarily responsible for most of the detailed decisions.

The Committee is indebted to many for making the Index possible. We are particularly indebted to Mrs. Dorothy F. Livingston, Director of the project, who has played a major part from the early planning stage. Her ability to organize and her concern for detail together with her wide experience in library classification and bibliographical work have been invaluable. We are likewise deeply indebted to Mrs. Truus W. Koopmans, Chief of Classification, for her devoted and careful work in helping to develop the classification system and in supervising the classification of material.

Invaluable aid in solving problems of classification was given to the staff and Committee by Professors Charles H. Berry, Henry W. Broude, Tjalling C. Koopmans, Mark W. Leiserson, Jacob Marschak, Raymond P. Powell, and Robert Triffin of the Yale Department of Economics, and Professors Irving S. Fellows of the University of Connecticut and George G. Judge of the University of Illinois. Useful comments on the classification scheme were also received from Professors Otto H. Ehrlich of New York University and Bernard F. Haley of Stanford University. John Fall and Paul B. Kebabian of the New York Public Library contributed important bibliographic information and helpful advice on editorial matters.

Mrs. Koopmans was ably assisted in the classification of material by Thomas F. Wise and the following graduate students in economics at Yale: Shane Hunt, Robert W. Kilpatrick, Charlotte D. Phelps, Judith V. Reppy, Timothy E. Rice, and Edward J. Stevens, III. Devoted secretarial and clerical assistance was rendered by Barbara Alderman, Mrs. Elizabeth Baskin, Richard C. Carr, Mrs. Anne Granger, Mary McNulty, Mrs. Edith Owen, and Mrs. Frances Tarson. The prodigious task of proofreading was accomplished with meticulous care by Mary C. Withington, formerly Executive Secretary of the Yale University Library.

Our gratitude extends also to Miss Gertrude Tait, Executive Secretary of the American Economic Association, who was responsible for the many details of the project's fiscal affairs, and to Mrs. Louise S. Stevens, of the Irwin Editorial Staff, who supervised and largely performed the arduous feat of transforming the thousands of entries on individual paper slips into the finished pages which follow.

Finally, we are greatly indebted to Mr. James T. Babb, Librarian of Yale University, for providing convenient and pleasant working quarters for the project, and to Mr. John H. Ottemiller, Associate Librarian, for extensive advice on printing and for facilitating the use of the library's resources.  Our obligation extends also to many other members of the library staff, in particular to Harry P. Harrison, Head of the Circulation Department, Robert J. Olson and Mrs. Marjorie T. Garber of the Reference Department, Elizabeth H. Butler, Regina A. McPartland and Mrs. Anne Whelpley of the processing departments, for exceptional service in expediting the collecting of journals as they were needed.

**THE COMMITTEE**

# JOURNALS INDEXED

(*Indicates selective coverage of English articles.  No foreign language material is included.)
Unless otherwise indicated, coverage of each journal includes the latest issue of 1959.


*AGRICULTURAL HISTORY. v.1-    Jan. 1927-    Published for the Agricultural History
Society. [Champaign, Ill.]
AMERICAN ECONOMIC ASSOCIATION.  PAPERS AND PROCEEDINGS of the annual meeting,
23rd, 1910-    [Evanston, Ill.] (American Economic Review. Supplement, v.1-    )
Prior to 1910, issued in the "Publications," and "Economic Studies." For Index to the Pub-
lications, 1886-1910, see American Economic Review. Supplement, v.7, no. 4, Dec. 1917.
THE AMERICAN ECONOMIC REVIEW. v.1-    March, 1911-    Menasha, Wis.
American Economic Association
*AMERICAN STATISTICAL ASSOCIATION. JOURNAL. v.1-    March, 1888-    Washington,
D.C.
Title 1888-1919, Publications; 1920, Quarterly publication.
*APPLIED STATISTICS; a journal of the Royal Statistical Society. v.1-    March, 1952-
London.
*ARTHA VIJÑĀNA. v.1-    March, 1959-    Poona, Gokhale Institute of Politics and Economics.
ARTHANITI. v.1-    Nov., 1957-    Calcutta, Calcutta University, Department of Economics.
*ASIAN AFFAIRS. v.1-    March, 1956-    Tokyo, Asia Kyokai.
Suspended after v.3, no. 1, March, 1958; resumed Oct., 1959.


BANCA NAZIONALE DEL LAVORO. REVIEW. v.1-    Apr., 1947-    Rome.
BUSINESS HISTORY. v.1-    Dec., 1958-    Liverpool, Liverpool University Press.
*BUSINESS HISTORY REVIEW. v.1-    June, 1926-    Boston, Graduate School of Business
Administration, Harvard University.
Title  1926-1953, Bulletin of the Business Historical Society.

*THE CANADIAN JOURNAL OF ECONOMICS AND POLITICAL SCIENCE; the journal of the
Canadian Political Science Association. v.1-    Feb., 1935-    Toronto, University of
Toronto Press.
*THE CEYLON ECONOMIST. v.1-    Aug., 1950-    Dehiwela, Ceylon Economic Research
Association.
*CONTEMPORARY CHINA; economic and social studies. v.1-    1955-    Hongkong, University
of Hongkong.
*CONTRIBUTIONS TO CANADIAN ECONOMICS. v.1-7. 1928-34. Toronto, The University Li-
brary. (University of Toronto Studies.  History and Economics)
Superseded by The Canadian Journal of Economics and Political Science.

*EAST AFRICAN ECONOMICS REVIEW; journal of the Economics Club of Kenya and the Uganda
Economics Society. v.1-    July, 1954-    Nairobi.
ECONOMETRICA; journal of the Econometric Society. v.1-    Jan., 1933-    Amsterdam.
ECONOMIA INTERNAZIONALE; revista dell' Istituto di Economia Internazionale. v.1-
Genn., 1948-    Genova.
ECONOMIC DEVELOPMENT AND CULTURAL CHANGE. v.1-    March, 1952-    Chicago,
University of Chicago Research Center in Economic Development and Cultural Change.
ECONOMIC HISTORY (a supplement to the Economic Journal). v.1-4 (no.1-15) Jan., 1926-Feb.,
1940. London, New York, Royal Economic Society.
Combined with Economic Journal April, 1940.
ECONOMIC HISTORY ASSOCIATION. THE TASKS OF ECONOMIC HISTORY: papers presented
at the 1st-10th annual meeting of the Economic History Association, 1941-50. New York.
Supplementary issue of the Journal of Economic History; included in the Journal after 1950.
THE ECONOMIC HISTORY REVIEW. v.1-18, Jan., 1927-[Apr.?] 1948; Second Series, v.1-
[July] 1948-    Published for the Economic History Society. Utrecht.
THE ECONOMIC JOURNAL; the journal of the Royal Economic Society. v.1-    March, 1891-
London.
Issues for 1891-1902 were the journal of the Society under its earlier name:  British
Economic Association.

(*Indicates selective coverage of English articles. No foreign language material is included.)

JOURNAL OF REGIONAL SCIENCE. v.1-    1958-    Philadelphia, Institute of Regional
    Science.

*KOBE ECONOMIC & BUSINESS REVIEW. v.1-    1953-    [Kobe, Japan], Research Institute
    for Economics and Business Administration, Kobe University.
KOBE UNIVERSITY ECONOMIC REVIEW. v.1-    1955-    Kobe, Faculty of Economics,
    Kobe University.
*KYKLOS; internationale Zeitschrift für Sozialwissenschaften. v.1-    1947-    Basel.
    Subtitle also in French and English.
*KYOTO UNIVERSITY ECONOMIC REVIEW. v.1-    , July, 1926-    Kyoto, Department of
    Economics, University of Kyoto.


LAND ECONOMICS; a journal of planning, housing & public utilities. v.1-    Jan., 1925-
    Madison, University of Wisconsin.
    Title 1925-1947, Journal of Land and Public Utility Economics.
LLOYDS BANK REVIEW. no. 1-    July, 1946-    London.
    Supersedes The Monthly review of Lloyds Bank, Ltd.

MALAYAN ECONOMIC REVIEW. (The journal of the Malayan Economic Society). v.1-
    June, 1956-    Singapore.
*THE MANCHESTER SCHOOL OF ECONOMIC AND SOCIAL STUDIES. v.1-    1930-
    Manchester, Faculty of Economic and Social Studies, University of Manchester.
    Title 1930-31, The Manchester School of Economics, Commerce, and Administration; 1932-
    38, The Manchester School.
METROECONOMICA; revista internazionale di economica. v.1-    luglio, 1949-    Trieste.
    Subtitle also in French and English.
MIDDLE EAST ECONOMIC PAPERS 1954-    [Beirut], Economic Research Institute, American
    University of Beirut.

NATIONAL TAX JOURNAL. v.1-    March, 1948-    Chicago, National Tax Association.
    Succeeds the Bulletin of the National Tax Association.
NORDISK TIDSSKRIFT FOR TEKNISK ØKONOMI. 1.-16. aargang (nr.1-42) Sept., 1935-1955.
    Oslo.
    Suspended publication 1949-1950.


OSAKA ECONOMIC PAPERS. v.1-    May, 1952-    Osaka University, Department of Eco-
    nomics. Toyonaka, Osaka.
OXFORD ECONOMIC PAPERS. no.1-8, Oct., 1938-Nov., 1947; New Series, v.1-    Jan, 1949-
    Oxford.
*OXFORD. UNIVERSITY. INSTITUTE OF STATISTICS. BULLETIN. v.1-    Nov., 1939-
    Oxford.

*PAKISTAN ECONOMIC JOURNAL. The journal of the Pakistan Economic Association. v.1-
    July, 1949-    Dacca.
*PROBLEMS OF ECONOMICS. v.1-    May, 1958-    New York, International Arts and Sciences
    Press.
    Subtitle, May, 1958-Oct., 1959: English translation of USSR journal, Voprosy Ekonomiki;
    Nov., 1959-    Selected articles from Soviet economics journals in English translation.
PUBLIC FINANCE; international quarterly journal devoted to the study of fiscal policy and re-
    lated problems. v.1-    1946-    Amsterdam.
    Title 1946-49, Openbare financiën.

THE QUARTERLY JOURNAL OF ECONOMICS. v.1-    Oct., 1886-    Cambridge, Mass.,
    Harvard University.

REGIONAL SCIENCE ASSOCIATION. PAPERS AND PROCEEDINGS [of the] annual meeting.
    1st-    1954-    Chambridge, Mass.
THE REVIEW OF ECONOMIC STUDIES. v.1-    Oct., 1933-    Cambridge, Eng., Economic
    Study Society.
THE REVIEW OF ECONOMICS AND STATISTICS. v.1-    Jan., 1919-    Cambridge, Harvard
    University, Department of Economics.
    Title 1919-47, The Review of Economic Statistics.

# CLASSIFICATION SCHEDULE
## SYNOPSIS

*For pages of particular classes in the <u>Classified Index</u> see Table of Contents, p. v.

1. SCOPE AND METHOD OF ECONOMICS

    1.0  GENERAL
    1.1  METHODOLOGY
       1.10  General
       1.11  Philosophy
       1.12  Use of Mathematics
          (For mathematical and econometric tools  see 7)
       1.13  Empirical Research
       1.14  Historicism. Institutionalism
          (For Historical and Institutionalist Schools  see 4.6)
       1.15  Marginalism
          (For marginal cost analysis  see 2.123; full cost vs. marginal cost controversy, 2.1334)
       1.16  Catholic Economics
       1.17  Relation of Economics to Other Disciplines
       1.18  Relation of Economics to Policy
          (For economic systems  see 3)

    1.2  ROLE OF THE ECONOMIST
    1.3  TEACHING OF ECONOMICS
       (For business education  see 14.231; education of agricultural economists, 16.031; teaching of industrial relations, 19.52; education of city and regional planners, 22.0)
    1.4  RESEARCH. BIBLIOGRAPHY
       (For research and bibliographies on special subjects  see subject)
    1.5  ECONOMIC SOCIETIES. PERIODICALS


2. ECONOMIC THEORY, INCLUDING MONETARY THEORY
    (For fiscal theory  see 10; international trade theory, 11; theory of population, 18.0)

    2.0  GENERAL
       2.01  Motivation
          (For utility maximization  see 2.111; profit maximization of the firm, 2.1311)
       2.02  Uncertainty and Expectations. Decision Making under Uncertainty
          (For utility theory and decision making under certainty  see 2.111; business expectations, 2.1312; theory of speculation, 2.1322; investment decisions by the individual firm, 2.213; mathematical treatment, 7.12)
       2.03  Game Theory
          (For oligopoly and bilateral monopoly  see 2.1333)
       2.04  Statics and Dynamics

    2.1  VALUE, PRICE, AND ALLOCATION THEORY
       2.10  General
       2.11  Utility. Demand. Theory of the Household
         2.110  General
         2.111  Utility and Indifference Analysis
            (For general maximization problems  see 2.01; measurable utility connected with decision theory, 2.02; interpersonal comparisons and group decisions, 2.162; theory of index numbers, 7.22)
         2.112  Consumer's Surplus
         2.113  Demand Analysis
            (For consumption function  see 2.315; studies of demand for a particular commodity, 15.5-15.9 and 16.23; empirical studies of consumption, 20.2)
         2.114  Elasticity of Demand
         2.115  Rationing
            (For empirical studies and public policy  see 13.43 and 15.443)
       2.12  Production. Cost. Supply
          (For theory of the firm  see 2.131; the business firm, 14; empirical studies of particular firms and industries, 15 and 16)
         2.120  General
         2.121  Production Functions of Firm and Industry
            (For production function of the economy as a whole  see 2.14 and 2.201)
         2.122  Economies of Scale, Internal or External
            (For empirical studies  see 15.24 and 16.44)

2. ECONOMIC THEORY, INCLUDING MONETARY THEORY (Cont.)
  2.1 VALUE, PRICE, AND ALLOCATION THEORY (Cont.)
    2.12 Production. Cost. Supply (Cont.)
      2.123 Cost and Supply
      2.124 Joint Production. Joint Cost
          (For multiproduct price relations  see 2.1335)
    2.13 Price and Market. Theory of Firm and Industry
        (For empirical studies  see 14, 15, and 16)
      2.130 General
      2.131 The Firm and its Equilibrium
          (For cost analysis  see 2.12; full-cost pricing, 2.1334; investment by the firm,
          2.213)
        2.1310 General
        2.1311 Profit Maximization and Business Behavior
        2.1312 Business Expectations
        2.1313 Theory of Organization
      2.132 Market Equilibrium
          (For competition and monopoly  see 2.133; general equilibrium, 2.14)
        2.1320 General
        2.1321 Stability of Market Equilibrium
        2.1322 Speculation. Forward Markets
            (For uncertainty  see 2.02; stock market speculation, 9.52; foreign exchange
            market, 11.3310; hedging, 14.6; agricultural commodity exchanges, 16.52)
        2.1323 Price Control and Black Market
            (For empirical studies  see 13.4 and 15.44)
      2.133 Competition and Monopoly
          (For empirical studies  see 15 and 16)
        2.1330 General
        2.1331 Monopoly. Degree of Monopoly
        2.1332 Competition: Pure, Monopolistic, Imperfect. Entry
        2.1333 Oligopoly. Bilateral Monopoly
            (For game theory  see 2.03)
        2.1334 Full-Cost Pricing
        2.1335 Price Discrimination.   Multiproduct Price Relations
            (For joint production  see 2.124; spatial price discrimination, 2.1337; govern-
            ment policy, 15.342)
        2.1336 Product Differentiation. Sales Effort
            (For empirical studies  see 14.5 and 15.26)
        2.1337 Spatial Competition. Basing-Point
            (For location theory  see 2.15; basing-point policy, 15.341; regional economics,
            22.2)
        2.1338 Tax Shifting and Product Prices
            (For welfare aspects of taxation  see 2.163; empirical studies, 10.4)
        2.1339 Innovation and Competition
            (For technological change and adaptation  see 2.344; empirical studies, 14.335
            and 15.27)
    2.14 General Equilibrium
        (For partial equilibrium  see 2.13)
      2.140 General
      2.141 Input-Output Models
          (For mathematical structure  see 7.11; empirical studies, 8.3)
    2.15 Location Theory
        (For spatial equilibrium  see 2.1337; empirical studies, 15.501; regional planning and
        development, 22)
    2.16 Welfare Economics
        (For welfare problems of international trade  see 11.231)
      2.160 General
      2.161 Allocative Efficiency
          (For pricing and investment policies in a socialist system  see 3.2; in the USSR
          and other communist countries, 6)
        2.1610 General
        2.1611 Public Utilities. Public Enterprise
            (For empirical studies  see 15.42, 15.43, and 15.6-15.9)

2. ECONOMIC THEORY INCLUDING MONETARY THEORY (Cont.)
   2.1 VALUE, PRICE, AND ALLOCATION THEORY (Cont.)
      2.16 Welfare Economics (Cont.)
         2.162 Social Choice. Distributive Justice
         2.163 Welfare Analysis of Taxation and Government Expenditure
            (For empirical studies see 10.2-10.4)

**2.2** FACTORS OF PRODUCTION AND DISTRIBUTIVE SHARES
     (For elasticity of substitution of factors of production see 2.123; distributive justice, 2.162; factor proportions in growth theory, 2.3402; national income and its distribution, 8.2; labor productivity, 19.01)
   2.20 General
      2.201 Production Function and Income Distribution
         (For production function of the individual firm see 2.121)
      2.202 Effect of Innovation on Factor Shares
         (For effects of technological change see 2.223 and 19.597)
   2.21 Capital and Interest
      (For saving and investment in the theory of income and employment see 2.31; monetary theories of interest, 2.325; investment theories of the cycle, 2.332; investment as a factor of economic growth, 2.342; saving and investment as a component of national income, 8.2; security and money markets, 9.5; empirical studies of saving, 14.42 and 20.21)
      2.210 General
      2.211 Capital
        2.2110 General
        2.2111 Depreciation. Obsolescence. Replacement
           (For depreciation in relation to growth theory see 2.3422; depreciation accounting, 14.341)
      2.212 Interest. Rates of Return
         (For monetary interest theory see 2.325; investment policies in a socialist system, 3.2; in the USSR and other communist countries, 6)
        2.2120 General
        2.2121 Supply of Savings
           (For the savings function see 2.315)
        2.2122 Loanable Funds. Natural Rate of Interest
      2.213 Investment by Individual Firm. Inventories
         (For empirical studies see 14.336 and 14.338)
   2.22 Labor and Wages
      (For aggregate theory of employment and wages see 2.318; wage aspects of stabilization policy, 12.32; empirical studies, 19)
      2.220 General
      2.221 Wage Differentials
         (For empirical studies see 19.33)
      2.222 Collective Wage Determination
         (For collective bargaining see 19.5)
      2.223 Technological Unemployment
         (For empirical studies see 19.202 and 19.597)
      2.224 Minimum Wages
         (For empirical studies see 19.32 and 19.35)
   2.23 Land and Rent
      (For tenure systems, land use and conservation see 17.3)
   2.24 Entrepreneurship and Profit
      (For entrepreneurship and growth see 2.341; empirical studies of dividends and profits, 14.43)
      2.240 General
      2.241 Entrepreneurship
         (For concept of the entrepreneur in historical research see 14.1; empirical studies, 14.2; in specific industries, 15.5-15.9 and 16.4)
      2.242 Profit
         (For empirical studies see 8.55 and 14.43)
      2.243 Incidence of Taxes on Profits
         (For empirical studies see 10.4)

2. ECONOMIC THEORY INCLUDING MONETARY THEORY (Cont.)
  2.3 AGGREGATIVE AND MONETARY THEORY, CYCLES, AND GROWTH
      (For theory of economic policy see 3.01; general stabilization policies and fluctuations, 12)
    2.30 General
    2.31 Income and Employment Theory
        (For appraisals of Keynes see also 4.8. For business cycle theory see 2.33; empirical studies of employment and unemployment, 19.202)
      2.310 General
      2.311 Underemployment. Full Employment
      2.312 Effective Demand. Aggregate Supply
      2.313 Relation of Saving and Investment
      2.314 Investment Function
          (For capital and interest see 2.21 and 2.342; liquidity preference, 2.322)
      2.315 Consumption Function
          (For demand analysis see 2.113; empirical studies of consumption and saving, 20.2)
      2.316 Multiplier
          (For balanced budget multiplier see 10.22; foreign trade multiplier, 11.322)
      2.317 Accelerator
      2.318 Wage and Price Aspects of Employment Theory
          (For wage theory see 2.22; wage aspects of stabilization policies, 12.32; price flexibility, 15.251; empirical studies of wages, 19.3)
    2.32 Monetary Theory
        (For utility of money see 2.111; general equilibrium models including money, 2.14; monetary explanation of the business cycle, 2.331; monetary institutions and policy, 9)
      2.320 General
      2.321 Supply of Money and of Bank Credit
          (For empirical studies see 9.22 and 9.32)
      2.322 Demand for Money. Liquidity Preference. Hoarding
      2.323 Velocity of Circulation
      2.324 Quantity Theory and Price Level
          (For empirical studies of price level see 9.6)
      2.325 Monetary Interest Theories
          (For natural rate of interest see 2.2122; empirical studies of interest rates, 9)
      2.326 Structure of Interest Rates
      2.327 Inflation. Deflation
          (For inflation and growth see 2.3424; empirical studies, 9.6; stabilization policies, 12.3)
    2.33 Cycle Theory
        (For growth and cycles see 2.30; income and employment theories, 2.31; economic fluctuations and stabilization policy, 12)
      2.330 General
        2.3301 Models
      2.331 Monetary Theories
      2.332 Investment Theories
      2.333 Overproduction and Underconsumption Theories
      2.334 Inventory Cycles
      2.335 Building Cycles
      2.336 International and Interregional Propagation
    2.34 Growth and Development Theory
        (For cycles and growth see 2.30; empirical studies of particular countries, 5 and 6; international aspects of economic development, 11.3; industrialization, 15.0; regional planning and development, 22)
      2.340 General
        2.3401 Growth Models
        2.3402 Factor Proportions
        2.3403 Structural Aspects of Growth
            (For structural unemployment see 2.343)
        2.3404 Developed Economies. Stagnation
        2.3405 Underdeveloped Economies
      2.341 Entrepreneurship and Growth
          (For entrepreneurship and profit see 2.24; studies of particular entrepreneurs and business firms, 14 and 15)

2. ECONOMIC THEORY, INCLUDING MONETARY THEORY (Cont.)
  2.3 AGGREGATIVE AND MONETARY THEORY, CYCLES, AND GROWTH (Cont.)
    2.34 Growth and Development Theory (Cont.)
      2.342 Capital Formation and Growth
        (For capital and interest see 2.21; income and employment theory, 2.31; industrial
        development corporations, 9.47 and 15.42; international investment, 11.35)
        2.3420 General
        2.3421 Capital-Output Ratios
        2.3422 Depreciation and Growth
          (For depreciation, obsolescence, and replacement see 2.2111)
        2.3423 Underdeveloped Areas
        2.3424 Inflation and Growth
          (For theory of inflation see 2.327; empirical studies, 9.6)
      2.343 Population. Labor Force. Wages
        (For theory of labor and wages see 2.22; population, 18; labor economics, 19)
      2.344 Technological Change and Adaptation
        (For innovation and competition see 2.1339; effect of technological change on fac-
        tor shares, 2.202; technological unemployment, 2.223, 19.202, and 19.597; research
        and innovation, 15.27)
        2.3440 General
        2.3441 Underdeveloped Areas
      2.345 Natural Resources and Agriculture
        (For empirical studies see 16 and 17)
      2.346 Industrialization
        (For empirical studies see also 15.0. For labor's attitude toward industrializa-
        tion, see 2.343 and 19.597; studies of cottage and small-scale industry, 14.223 and
        15.24; particular industries, 15.5-15.9)
      2.347 Government Development Policy
        (For particular policies see other sections of 2.34; planning and theory of economic
        policy, 3.01; empirical studies, 5 and 6; fiscal policy, 10.2-10.4; regional planning,
        22)
        2.3470 General
        2.3471 Underdeveloped Countries
      2.348 Noneconomic Factors

3. ECONOMIC SYSTEMS. PLANNING
  (For welfare economics see 2.16; empirical studies of particular countries, 6; international
  systems of economic power, 11.5)

  3.0 GENERAL
    3.01 Planning, Policy Making
      (For theory of government development policy see 2.347; regional planning. 22)
    3.02 Government and the Economy
      (For particular aspects of government policy see appropriate class [e.g. money and
      banking 9])

  3.1 CAPITALIST SYSTEM
  3.2 SOCIALIST AND COMMUNIST SYSTEMS
    (For schools of thought see 4.5)
  3.3 CORPORATIVE SYSTEM
  3.4 COOPERATION. COOPERATIVE SOCIETIES
    (For agricultural cooperatives see 16.6; cooperative housing, 22.5)
  3.5 SOLIDARISM

4. HISTORY OF ECONOMIC THOUGHT

  4.0 GENERAL
  4.1 ANCIENT. MEDIEVAL
  4.2 PRE-CLASSICAL
    4.20 General
    4.21 Mercantilists

4. HISTORY OF ECONOMIC THOUGHT (Cont.)
   4.2 PRE-CLASSICAL (Cont.)
      4.22 Physiocrats
      4.23 Other

   4.3 CLASSICAL SCHOOL
   4.4 AUSTRIAN, LAUSANNE, MARSHALLIAN, NEO-CLASSICAL SCHOOLS
   4.5 SOCIALIST, MARXIST, COMMUNIST SCHOOLS
      (For systems see 3.2; Karl Marx, 4.8)
      4.50 General
      4.51 Non-Marxist Socialism

   4.6 HISTORICAL AND INSTITUTIONALIST SCHOOLS
      (For methodology see 1.14; methodology of economic history, 5.01)
   4.7 OTHER GROUPS SINCE 1800
      (For Keynesian economics see 2.3; J. M. Keynes, 4.8)
      4.70 General
      4.71 Swedish School

   4.8 INDIVIDUALS (A-Z)


5. ECONOMIC HISTORY
   (For dividing line between history and contemporary studies see Introduction p. xi. For history of special subjects see History sections under each class as listed on pp. xi-xiii.)

   5.0 GENERAL
      5.01 Discipline of Economic History
      5.02 Empirical Studies

   5.1 ANCIENT
   5.2 MEDIEVAL (to 1500)
   5.3 PRE-INDUSTRIAL REVOLUTION (1500-1760)
   5.4 AFTER 1760


6. GENERAL CONTEMPORARY ECONOMIC CONDITIONS, POLICY, AND PLANNING
   (For particular conditions and policies see appropriate class: e.g. national income and wealth, 8; fluctuations and stabilization policy, 12; war and defense economics, 13; regional planning and development, 22)


7. MATHEMATICAL, STATISTICAL, AND OTHER TOOLS OF ANALYSIS
   (For statistical data see 8)

   7.0 GENERAL
   7.1 MATHEMATICAL TOOLS
      (For methodology of use of mathematics see 1.12)
      7.10 General
      7.11 Linear Equations and Inequalities. Non-Negative Matrices. Mathematical Structure of Input-Output Model
         (For input-output applications see 2.141, 2.3, 8.3, and other appropriate classes; related properties of matrices relevant to stability conditions, 7.13)
      7.12 Maximization Under Restraints
        7.120 General
        7.121 Mathematical Programming
           (For operations research and mathematical programming see 14.339)
      7.13 Difference, Differential, and Integral Equations. Stability Conditions in Dynamic Systems
         (For stability of general equilibrium see 2.14)

7.  MATHEMATICAL, STATISTICAL, AND OTHER TOOLS OF ANALYSIS (Cont.)
    7.2 STATISTICAL AND ECONOMETRIC METHODS
        7.20 General
        7.21 Survey Methods
             (For market research see also 14.52)
             7.210 General
             7.211 Survey Design
             7.212 Consumer Surveys
                   (For empirical studies see 20.2)
        7.22 Theory of Index Numbers and Aggregation
             (For aggregation in input-output see 7.11; index number series, 8.5)
             7.220 General
             7.221 Consumer Price Indexes
             7.222 Other Price Indexes
             7.223 Production Indexes
             7.224 Measurement of Productivity
                   (For labor productivity see 19.01)
             7.225 Other Indexes
        7.23 Identification and Estimation of Parameters.  Tests of Hypotheses.  Prediction
             (For business indicators including methods see 12.21)
             7.230 General
             7.231 Analysis of Variance.  Design of Experiments
             7.232 Regression and Correlation.  Multivariate Analysis.  Analysis of Covariance
                   7.2320 General
                   7.2321 Simultaneous Equations
                          (For general equilibrium models see 2.14; models of growth and cycles, 2.3)
             7.233 Single Time Series Analysis
             7.234 Distributed Lags
             7.235 Graphic Methods
        7.24 Statistical Decision Making.  Quality Control.  Sequential Analysis

    7.3 COMPUTATION.  INFORMATION PROCESSING.  ANALOGUES
        (For computation in mathematical programming see 7.121)


8.  SOCIAL ACCOUNTING.  STATISTICAL DATA
    (For statistical methods see 7)

    8.0 GENERAL
    8.1 HISTORY
    8.2 NATIONAL INCOME AND WEALTH
        (For corporate saving see 14.42; personal savings, 20.21)
        8.20 General
        8.21 History
        8.22 Distribution of Personal Income and Wealth
        8.23 International Comparisons
             (For comparisons of the economies of different countries see 6)

    8.3 INPUT-OUTPUT
        (For general equilibrium models see 2.141 and 2.3; input-output method, 7.11)
    8.4 FINANCING ACCOUNTS.  FLOW OF FUNDS
    8.5 STATISTICAL DATA (not elsewhere classified)
        8.50 General
        8.51 History
        8.52 Census
             (For particular censuses see appropriate class, e.g. population, 18.5)
        8.53 Production.  Trade Volume
             (For labor productivity see 19.01)
        8.54 Price
        8.55 Profit

9.  MONEY, CREDIT, AND BANKING
    (For monetary theory see 2.32; income and employment theory, 2.31; financing accounts and flow of funds, 8.4)

    9.0  GENERAL
    9.1  HISTORY
    9.2  MONEY.  CURRENCY.  MONETARY STANDARDS
        9.20  General
        9.21  History
        9.22  Money Supply.  Velocity of Circulation
        9.23  Monetary Standards
            (For international aspects see 11.3)
            9.230  General
            9.231  Gold
                (For gold mining see 15.533)
            9.232  Silver and Bimetallism
            9.233  Other Standards
        9.24  Currency and Currency Reform

    9.3  COMMERCIAL BANKS
        (For consumer finance see 9.8; bank regulation and supervision, 9.95)
        9.30  General
        9.31  History
        9.32  Assets and Liabilities

    9.4  FINANCIAL INTERMEDIARIES
        (For investment banking and security markets see 9.52; consumer credit institutions, 9.8)
        9.40  General
        9.41  History
        9.42  Savings Banks.  Savings and Loan Associations
        9.43  Insurance Companies
            (For medical insurance see also 21.7)
        9.44  Pension Funds
        9.45  Investment Companies
        9.46  Agricultural Credit Institutions
            (For cooperative agricultural credit institutions see 16.6)
        9.47  Industrial Development Banking.  Mercantile Credit Institutions
        9.48  Housing Credit Institutions.  Mortgage Market
            (For mortgages in portfolios see appropriate institution)

    9.5  SECURITY AND MONEY MARKETS
        9.50  General
        9.51  History
        9.52  Security Markets
            9.520  General
            9.521  Security Prices and Yields
            9.522  Regulation of Security Markets
                (For margin controls see 9.924)
        9.53  Money Markets
            (For brokers' loans see 9.520)

    9.6  PRICES.  INFLATION.  DEFLATION
        (For theory of inflation see 2.327; inflation and growth, 2.3424; price series, 8.5; economic fluctuations and stabilization, 12)
        9.60  General
        9.61  History

    9.7  PORTFOLIO SELECTION
        (For portfolio selection of particular institutions see 9.3 and 9.4)
        9.70  General
        9.71  History

9. <u>MONEY, CREDIT, AND BANKING</u> (Cont.)
   9.8 CONSUMER FINANCE
     (For central bank control see 9.924; rural credit and finance, 16.46; consumer economics, 20)
     9.80 <u>General</u>
     9.81 <u>History</u>

   9.9 MONETARY POLICY. CENTRAL BANKS
     (For regulation of financial intermediaries and government credit institutions see 9.4;
     regulation of the securities market, 9.522; regulation of consumer finance, 9.8; public
     debt policy, 10.5; international monetary policy, 11.3; stabilization policies, 12.3)
     9.90 <u>General</u>
     9.91 <u>History</u>
     9.92 <u>Tools of Monetary Policy</u>
       9.920 General
       9.921 Reserve Requirements
       9.922 Rediscounts and Rediscount Rate
       9.923 Open Market Operations
       9.924 Selective Controls
       9.925 Other Tools
     9.93 <u>Monetary Aspects of Public Debt Management</u>
     9.94 <u>Deposit Insurance</u>
     9.95 <u>Bank Regulation and Supervision</u>

10. <u>PUBLIC FINANCE</u>
   (For war finance see 13.3)

   10.0 GENERAL
     10.01 <u>Budgets and Budget Administration</u>
     10.02 <u>State and Local Finance</u>
       (For specific aspects see 10.3-10.5)
     10.03 <u>Intergovernmental Relations</u>
       (For relations between state and local governments see 10.02; intergovernmental tax
       relations, 10.4)

   10.1 HISTORY
   10.2 FISCAL POLICY FOR ECONOMIC STABILIZATION AND GROWTH
     (For aggregative and monetary theory, cycles and growth see 2.3; monetary policy, 9.9;
     expenditure policy, 10.301; taxation policy, 10.402; general stabilization policies, 12.3)
     10.20 <u>General</u>
       10.201 Underdeveloped Countries
     10.21 <u>History</u>
     10.22 <u>Fiscal Policy and the Multiplier</u>

   10.3 PUBLIC EXPENDITURE
     (For welfare theory of government expenditures see 2.163; military expenditure, 13.20;
     public enterprise, 15.42 and 15.43; highway finance, 15.85; agriculture, 16.7; veterans'
     benefits, 21.5; education, 21.8; public housing, 22.53)
     10.30 <u>General</u>
       10.301 Expenditure Policy for Stabilization and Growth
         (For general fiscal policy see 10.20)
     10.31 <u>History</u>
     10.32 <u>Subsidies</u>
       (For export subsidies see 11.230; subsidies to special industries, 15.5-15.9)

   10.4 TAXATION AND OTHER REVENUE
     (For tariffs see 11; discriminatory taxation, 15.35; social security taxes, 21.21. For
     taxation of public utilities see 15.65; of railroads, 15.825; for roads and highways, 15.85;
     of agriculture, 16.75)
     10.40 <u>General</u>
       10.401 Theory
         (For theory of shifting and incidence see also 2.1338; welfare theory of taxation,
         2.163; theory of incidence of taxes on profits, 2.243; shifting and incidence of
         specific taxes, 10.42-10.44)

11. INTERNATIONAL ECONOMICS (Cont.)
  11.3 BALANCE OF PAYMENTS. MECHANISMS OF ADJUSTMENT
    11.30 General
      11.301 Sterling Area
        (For individual countries see 11.30)
      11.302 Dollar Shortage
        (For dollar problems of specific countries see 11.30; of the Sterling Area, 11.301)
    11.31 History
    11.32 Balance of Payments Theory
      11.320 General
      11.321 Accounting Framework
      11.322 Theory of Price, Income, and Employment
        (For international propagation of business cycles see 2.336 and 12.23; comparative cost and price theory, 11.22; transfer problem, 11.351)
    11.33 International Adjustment Mechanisms
      (For payments arrangements within the Sterling Area see 11.301)
      11.330 General
      11.331 Exchange Rates
        11.3310 General
        11.3311 Flexible Rates
        11.3312 Stabilized Rates
        11.3313 Revaluation
          (For revaluation under the gold standard see also 11.3321)
      11.332 Automatic Schemes
        (For monetary standards see also 9.23; revaluation of exchange rates, 11.3313)
        11.3320 General
        11.3321 Gold
        11.3322 Silver. Bimetallic
        11.3323 Other Schemes
      11.333 Negotiated Schemes
        (For customs unions see 11.4)
        11.3330 General
        11.3331 International Monetary Fund. Bank for International Settlements
        11.3332 International Trade Organization. General Agreement on Tariffs and Trade
        11.3333 Regional Schemes
        11.3334 Movements toward Convertibility
          (For sterling convertibility see 11.301)
    11.34 Quantitative Trade and Exchange Restrictions
      (For trade policy not designed to affect the balance of payments see 11.23; control of capital movements, 11.35)
    11.35 Capital Movements. Foreign Assistance
      11.350 General
      11.351 Theory. Transfer Problem
      11.352 Private Capital Movements
      11.353 Government Capital Movements
        11.3530 General
        11.3531 International Loans and Investments
        11.3532 Relief. Assistance
        11.3533 Reparations. War Debts
          (For theory of transfer problem see 11.351)
      11.354 Technical Assistance
        (For programs which include both capital movements and technical assistance see 11.350)

  11.4 ECONOMIC INTEGRATION. CUSTOMS UNIONS
    11.40 General
    11.41 History

  11.5 ECONOMIC POWER. IMPERIALISM
    11.50 General
    11.51 History

## 12. ECONOMIC FLUCTUATIONS. STABILIZATION POLICY
(For aggregative and monetary theory, cycles and growth see 2.3; inflation, 9.6)

12.0 GENERAL
12.1 HISTORY
12.2 FLUCTUATIONS. FORECASTING
    (For theory of cycles see 2.33)
    12.20 General
    12.21 Indicators. Statistical Series
    12.22 Forecasts
        (For long term forecasts see 6)
    12.23 International Propagation
        (For theory see 2.336)

12.3 STABILIZATION POLICIES
    (For planning and policy making see 3.01; monetary policy, 9.9; fiscal policy for stabili-
    zation, 10.2; balance of payments and trade policy, 11.3; wartime stabilization, 13.3 and
    13.4; direct controls, 15.44; agricultural stabilization, 16.7)
    12.30 General
    12.31 Employment Aspects of Stabilization Policies
    12.32 Wage Aspects of Stabilization Policies
        (See also 19.591-19.592)

## 13. WAR AND DEFENSE ECONOMICS
(For particular problems during demobilization and reconversion see 13.9; veterans' pensions
and benefits, 21.5)

13.0 GENERAL
13.1 HISTORY
13.2 ECONOMICS OF THE DEFENSE ESTABLISHMENT
    13.20 General
    13.21 Procurement. Renegotiation. Contract Termination
    13.22 Surplus Disposal
    13.23 Military and Intelligence Operations

13.3 WAR FINANCE AND STABILIZATION POLICIES
    (For reparations and debts see 11.3533; general stabilization policies, 12.3)
    13.30 General
    13.31 Taxation
    13.32 Monetary Policy
    13.33 Prices. Inflation
        (For inflation see 2.327 and 9.6; price control, 13.41)
    13.34 Insurance. War Damage Compensation

13.4 PRICE CONTROL AND RATIONING
    (For theory see 2.115 and 2.1323; controls in peacetime, 15.44)
    13.40 General
    13.41 Price Control
        (For price control in specific industries except food see 13.7)
    13.42 Rent Control
        (For housing see 13.75)
    13.43 Rationing
        (For rationing of specific goods except food see 13.7)

13.5 PRODUCTION POLICIES AND CONTROL
    (For specific industries see 13.7)
    13.50 General
    13.51 Raw Materials Control
    13.52 Expansion of Facilities
    13.53 Small Business and Defense Contracts

13. WAR AND DEFENSE ECONOMICS (Cont.)

13.6 LABOR FORCE. CONSUMPTION
    13.60 General
    13.61 Labor and Manpower
        (For labor problems in specific industries see 13.7)
    13.62 Wartime Consumption
        (For price control and rationing see 13.4; nutrition standards, 20.22)

13.7 SPECIFIC INDUSTRIES
    13.70 General
    13.71 Manufacturing
    13.72 Distributive Trades
        (For food price controls and rationing see 13.4)
    13.73 Extractive Industries
    13.74 Transportation. Communications. Public Utilities
    13.75 Construction. Housing
        (For rent control see 13.42)
    13.76 Agriculture
        (For food requirements and food stocks see 13.62)

13.8 INTERNATIONAL ECONOMIC RELATIONS
13.9 DEMOBILIZATION. RECONVERSION
    (For war debts and reparations see 11.3533; postwar stabilization policy, 12.3)


14. BUSINESS ORGANIZATION. MANAGERIAL ECONOMICS
    (For role of the business economist see 1.2; theory of firm and market, 2.13; theory of
    entrepreneurship, 2.241; entrepreneurship and theory of growth, 2.341; industrial organiza-
    tion and public policy, 15; farm management, 16.4; labor relations and policy, 19)

14.0 GENERAL
14.1 HISTORY
    (For teaching of business history see 14.231)
14.2 THE FIRM. THE BUSINESSMAN
    (For particular entrepreneurs see the industry concerned)
    14.20 General
    14.21 History
        (For the discipline of entrepreneurial and business history see 14.1)
    14.22 The Firm
        (For theory of the individual firm see 2.131; role of board of directors, 14.32)
        14.220 General
        14.221 Stockholder Relations
        14.222 Public and Community Relations
            (For trade associations see 15.235)
        14.223 Small Business
            (For defense contracts see 13.53; determinants of market structure, 15.24)
    14.23 The Businessman
        (For management function see 14.33)
        14.230 General
        14.231 Education for Business
            (For executive development programs see 14.332)

14.3 INTERNAL ORGANIZATION AND OPERATION OF THE FIRM
    14.30 General
    14.31 History
    14.32 Board of Directors
    14.33 Management Function
        14.330 General
        14.331 Executive Compensation
        14.332 Executive Development
            (For business schools see 14.231)
        14.333 Administrative Organization and Procedures
            (For theory of organization see 2.1313)

14. **BUSINESS ORGANIZATION.  MANAGERIAL ECONOMICS** (Cont.)
  14.3 INTERNAL ORGANIZATION AND OPERATION OF THE FIRM (Cont.)
    14.33 <u>Management Function</u> (Cont.)
      14.334 Decision-Making and Forecasting
        (For decision theory see 2.02; sales forecasting, 14.522)
      14.335 Research and Development
        (For theory of innovation and competition see 2.1339; technological change and adaptation, 2.344; role of research and innovation in market structure and behavior, 15.27; effect of technological change on the labor force, 19.597)
      14.336 Capital Expenditure and Investment Policy
        (For theory of investment by individual firm see 2.213; business finance, 14.4)
      14.337 Production Management.  Quality Control
        (For job standards and evaluation see 19.598)
      14.338 Inventory Policies
        (For theory see 2.213)
      14.339 Operations Research.  Mathematical Programming
        (For theory of mathematical programming see 7.121)
    14.34 <u>Tools of Management</u>
      (For quality control see 14.337; operations research and mathematical programming, 14.339)
      14.340 General
      14.341 Accounting
        (For theory of depreciation, obsolescence, and replacement see 2.2111; accelerated amortization, 10.4222)
      14.342 Statistical Tools
        (For statistical methods see 7.2)
      14.343 Break-Even Analysis

  14.4 BUSINESS FINANCE
    (For theory of investment by the firm see 2.213; financing of expansion for war production, 13.52; teaching of business finance, 14.231; management investment policy, 14.336)
    14.40 <u>General</u>
    14.41 <u>History</u>
    14.42 <u>Sources of Funds</u>
      (For mercantile credit institutions see 9.47; new issues and regulation of security markets, 9.5)
    14.43 <u>Profits.  Dividend Policies</u>
      (For theory of profit see 2.24; profit data, 8.55)
    14.44 <u>Reorganization</u>

  14.5 MARKETING
    (For survey methods see 7.21; teaching of marketing, 14.231; distributive trades, 15.54)
    14.50 <u>General</u>
    14.51 <u>History</u>
    14.52 <u>Market Research</u>
      14.520 General
      14.521 Consumer Motivation.  Brand Preference
      14.522 Sales Forecasting
    14.53 <u>Product Policies</u>
    14.54 <u>Price Policies</u>
      (For price theory see 2.13; internal transfer pricing, 14.333; price behavior, 15.25; policies in individual industries, 15.5-15.9)
    14.55 <u>Advertising</u>
      (For advertising theory see 2.1336; government control of advertising, 15.46; advertising as a business, 15.56)
    14.56 <u>Sales Personnel</u>
    14.57 <u>Other Distribution Policies</u>

  14.6 PURCHASING
    (For theory of speculation and forward markets see 2.1322)
    14.60 <u>General</u>
    14.61 <u>History</u>

15. **INDUSTRIAL ORGANIZATION AND PUBLIC POLICY**
(For theory of industrialization in economic growth see 2.346; industrial classification systems, 8.52)

15.0 GENERAL
15.1 HISTORY
15.2 MARKET STRUCTURE AND BEHAVIOR
   (For theory see 2.13)
   15.20 General
      15.201 Economic Blocs. Countervailing Power
   15.21 History
   15.22 Business Population
   15.23 Monopoly. Concentration. Competition
      (For government policy see 15.3)
      15.230 General
      15.231 Measurement
      15.232 Combinations. Mergers
      15.233 Collusion. Cartels
         (For international cartels see 11.24; collusive behavior of trade associations, 15.235)
      15.234 Rationalization. Reorganization
         (For financial reorganization of the firm see 14.44)
      15.235 Trade Associations
         (For other business groups see 14.222)
   15.24 Determinants of Market Structure
      (For theory of economies of scale see 2.122)
   15.25 Price Behavior
      (For price control see 2.1323, 13.41, and 15.341; discrimination, 2.1335 and 15.342; basing point, 2.1337 and 15.341; wage and price aspects of employment theory, 2.318; inflation and deflation, 2.327 and 9.6; collusive price behavior, 15.233; effects of wage policies on prices, 19.591 and 19.592)
      15.250 General
      15.251 Price Flexibility
   15.26 Non-Price Competition
      (For theory see 2.1336)
   15.27 Research. Innovation
      (For theory of innovation and competition see 2.1339; of technological unemployment, 2.223; technological change and adaptation, 2.344; research and development in the firm, 14.335; effect of technological change on the labor force, 19.597)

15.3 GOVERNMENT POLICY TOWARD MONOPOLY AND COMPETITION
   (For theory of competition and monopoly see 2.13; market structure and behavior, 15.2)
   15.30 General
   15.31 History
   15.32 Monopoly. Combinations. Mergers
      (For public utility holding companies see 15.66)
   15.33 Restrictive Agreements. Trade Associations
   15.34 Other Competitive Practices
      15.340 General
      15.341 Basing Point
         (For theory see 2.1337)
      15.342 Discrimination
         (For theory see 2.1335)
      15.343 Resale Price Maintenance. Fair Trade
      15.344 Tying and Exclusive Dealing Contracts
   15.35 Discriminatory Taxation
   15.36 Patents. Trade-Marks
   15.37 Intranational Trade Barriers

15.4 OTHER GOVERNMENT POLICIES TOWARD THE MARKET. PUBLIC ENTERPRISE
   (For government development policy see 2.347; role of government in the economy, 3.02; subsidies, 10.32; public utilities, 15.6; communications, 15.7; transportation, 15.8; atomic industries, 15.9; agriculture, 16.5 and 16.7)

15. INDUSTRIAL ORGANIZATION AND PUBLIC POLICY (Cont.)
    15.4 OTHER GOVERNMENT POLICIES TOWARD THE MARKET. PUBLIC ENTERPRISE (Cont.)
        15.40 General
        15.41 History
        15.42 Public Enterprise
              (For public enterprise in specific industries see the appropriate industry in 15.5-
              15.9. For theory see 2.1611; multipurpose projects, 15.43, post office, 15.7)
        15.43 Multipurpose Projects
              (For single aspect of a project see 15.6, 15.83, and 17. For welfare economics see
              2.16)
        15.44 Direct Controls
              (For controls in specific industries see 15.5-15.9 and 16. For theory of price control
              and black market see 2.1323; direct controls in war, 13.4 and 13.5)
            15.440 General
            15.441 Price Control
                   (For milk price control see 16.541)
            15.442 Rent Control
            15.443 Rationing
                   (For theory see 2.115)
        15.45 National Recovery Administration
        15.46 Consumer Protection
        15.47 Licensing

    15.5 INDUSTRY STUDIES
         (For production, price, and profit series covering the industrial sector see 8.5; public
         utilities, 15.6; communications, 15.7; transportation, 15.8; atomic industry, 15.9; labor
         productivity, 19.01)
        15.50 General
            15.501 Location of Industry
                   (For theory see 2.15; industrial dispersion and diversification, 22.23)
        15.51 History
        15.52 Manufacturing Industries
              (For general production function of manufacturing see 2.201)
            15.520 General
            15.521 History
            15.522 Metals
                15.5220 General
                15.5221 History
                15.5222 Iron and Steel
                        (For European Coal and Steel Community see 11.40)
                15.5223 Other Metals
            15.523 Machinery. Tools. Electrical Equipment and Appliances. Castings
                15.5230 General
                15.5231 History
            15.524 Transportation Equipment
                15.5240 General
                15.5241 History
            15.525 Chemicals. Drugs. Plastics. Ceramics. Glass. Rubber
                   (For fertilizers and munitions see 15.529)
                15.5250 General
                15.5251 History
            15.526 Textiles. Leather. Clothing
                   (For fur trade see 17.0)
                15.5260 General
                15.5261 History
            15.527 Forest Products. Building Materials
                   (For construction industry, see 15.55; furniture, 15.529; forestry, 17.4)
                15.5270 General
                15.5271 History
            15.528 Food Processing. Tobacco. Beverages
                   (For milk see 16; fisheries, 17.5)
                15.5280 General
                15.5281 History

15. <u>INDUSTRIAL ORGANIZATION AND PUBLIC POLICY</u> (Cont.)
   15.5 INDUSTRY STUDIES (Cont.)
      15.52 <u>Manufacturing Industries</u> (Cont.)
         15.529 Miscellaneous Manufacturing
            15.5290 General
            15.5291 History
      15.53 <u>Extractive Industries</u>
         (For mineral deposits see 17.7)
         15.530 General
         15.531 History
         15.532 Coal Mining
            (For European Coal and Steel Community see 11.40)
         15.533 Other Mining
         15.534 Oil. Gas
      15.54 <u>Distributive Trades</u>
         (For cooperative societies see 3.4; marketing by the firm, 14.5; marketing by manufacturer, 15.52; service industries, 15.56; agricultural marketing, 16.5)
         15.540 General
         15.541 History
         15.542 Wholesaling
            (For wholesale price index see 8.54)
         15.543 Retailing
            (For retail price index see 8.54; gasoline sales, 15.534; shopping centers, 22.33)
         15.544 Retail Food
            (For milk distribution see 16.541)
         15.545 Chain Stores
            (For discriminatory taxation see 15.35)
      15.55 <u>Construction Industry</u>
         (For building materials see 15.527; construction of highways, railroads, dams and ports, 15.8)
         15.550 General
         15.551 History
      15.56 <u>Service Industries</u>
         (For financial institutions see 9; insurance, 9.43; radio and television, 15.7; parking, 15.86; medical service, 21.7; education, 21.8)
         15.560 General
         15.561 History

15.6 PUBLIC UTILITIES. ELECTRICITY. GAS. WATER
      (For welfare theory of public utility pricing see 2.1611; multipurpose projects, 15.43; communications, 15.7; transportation, 15.8; atomic industries, 15.9)
      15.60 <u>General</u>
         15.601 Public Regulation and Ownership
            (For specific aspects of regulation see 15.62-15.66)
      15.61 <u>History</u>
      15.62 <u>Demand</u>
      15.63 <u>Rate Level. Rate Base. Rate of Return</u>
      15.64 <u>Rate Structure</u>
      15.65 <u>Taxation</u>
      15.66 <u>Holding Companies</u>

15.7 COMMUNICATION INDUSTRIES
      (For communication equipment see 15.523; newspapers, magazines, films, and books, 15.56)
      15.70 <u>General</u>
      15.71 <u>History</u>

15.8 TRANSPORTATION
      (For location theory see 2.15; welfare theory of public utility pricing, 2.1611; discussion of public utilities and transportation jointly, 15.6)
      15.80 <u>General</u>
      15.81 <u>History</u>

15. INDUSTRIAL ORGANIZATION AND PUBLIC POLICY (Cont.)
   15.8 TRANSPORTATION (Cont.)
      15.82 Railroads
         15.820 General
         15.821 History
         15.822 Demand
         15.823 Rate Level. Rate Base. Rate of Return
         15.824 Rate Structure
         15.825 Taxation
         15.826 Labor
      15.83 Water Transportation
         (For shipbuilding see 15.524; multipurpose projects, 15.43)
         15.830 General
         15.831 History
      15.84 Air Transportation
         (For aircraft construction see 15.524)
         15.840 General
         15.841 History
      15.85 Road Transportation. Highways
         15.850 General
         15.851 History
      15.86 Urban Transportation
         15.860 General
         15.861 History

   15.9 ATOMIC INDUSTRIES
      (For military uses of atomic energy see 13.2)


16. AGRICULTURE
   (For agriculture in economic development theory see 2.345; agriculture in war, 13; manufacturing industries, 15.5; conservation, 17; rural planning and development, 22.4)

   16.0 GENERAL
      16.01 Agricultural Situation
         16.010 General
         16.011 Food Crops
         16.012 Livestock. Dairy Products
            (For general food situation see 16.011)
         16.013 Fiber Crops
         16.014 Other Crops
      16.02 Agricultural Outlook
         (For forecasting see 16.26)
      16.03 Agricultural Economics and Research
         16.030 General
         16.031 Education of Agricultural Economists
      16.04 Agricultural Information and Education Services
      16.05 Agricultural Statistics
      16.06 Farmers' Organizations
         (For agricultural cooperatives see 16.6)

   16.1 HISTORY
   16.2 AGRICULTURAL SUPPLY AND DEMAND ANALYSIS
      (For agricultural marketing see 16.5)
      16.20 General
      16.21 History
      16.22 Agricultural Productivity and Technological Change
         (For resource combination and allocation in farm management see 16.42)
      16.23 Demand Analysis
         (For consumer expenditure on agricultural products see 20.2)
      16.24 Supply Analysis
         (For production estimates see 16.20)
      16.25 Price Analysis

16. <u>AGRICULTURE</u> (Cont.)
  16.2 AGRICULTURAL SUPPLY AND DEMAND ANALYSIS (Cont.)
    16.26 <u>Forecasting</u>
      (For agricultural outlook see 16.02; productivity estimates, 16.22)

  16.3 FARM POPULATION. LABOR FORCE. INCOME
    (For land settlement programs see 17.342; rural population, 18.4)
    16.30 <u>General</u>
    16.31 <u>History</u>
    16.32 <u>Population. Employment. Labor Force</u>
      (For farm labor in wartime see 13.76; use of labor in farm management, 16.422;
      social security and other welfare programs, 21)
    16.33 <u>Migratory Workers</u>
    16.34 <u>Income. Wages. Budgets. Cost and Standard of Living</u>
      (For national income originating in agricultural sector see 8.2)

  16.4 FARM MANAGEMENT
    16.40 <u>General</u>
    16.41 <u>History</u>
    16.42 <u>Resource Combination and Allocation</u>
      (For aggregative studies of agricultural productivity and technological change see
      16.22; resource use under uncertainty, 16.43)
     16.420 General
     16.421 Land. Water. Fertilizer
      (For fertilizer industry see 15.529; conservation, 17; irrigation projects, 17.33;
      land utilization, 17.35)
     16.422 Labor
      (For agricultural labor force see 16.32)
     16.423 Feeds and Forage
      (For feed processing industry see 15.529; grazing land, 17.3)
     16.424 Machinery and Buildings
      (For farm machinery industry see 15.523)
    16.43 <u>Resource Use under Uncertainty</u>
      (For agricultural forecasting see 16.26)
    16.44 <u>Farm Size</u>
      (For family farm see 16.40)
    16.45 <u>Accounting. Cost Analysis</u>
    16.46 <u>Finance. Credit</u>
      (For agricultural credit institutions and farm debt legislation see 9.46; cooperative
      agricultural credit, 16.6)

  16.5 AGRICULTURAL MARKETING
    (For distributive trades see 15.54; cooperative marketing, 16.6)
    16.50 <u>General</u>
    16.51 <u>History</u>
    16.52 <u>Commodity Exchanges</u>
      (For theory of speculation and forward markets see 2.1322; price analysis, 16.25;
      forecasting, 16.26)
    16.53 <u>Marketing Margins</u>
    16.54 <u>Specific Markets and Market Control</u>
      (For marketing aspects of government price and income policies see 16.72)
     16.540 General
     16.541 Milk and Dairy
     16.542 Fruits. Vegetables. Nuts
     16.543 Cotton. Wool
     16.544 Livestock. Poultry. Eggs
     16.545 Grains. Cereals
     16.546 Other Markets
    16.55 <u>Transportation</u>

  16.6 AGRICULTURAL COOPERATIVES
    16.60 <u>General</u>
    16.61 <u>History</u>

16. AGRICULTURE (Cont.)

16.7 GOVERNMENT PROGRAMS AND POLICIES
(For government credit institutions see 9.46; war policies, 13.76; rural electrification, 15.6; agricultural information and education services, 16.04; policies to increase efficiency of marketing operations or bargaining power of producers, 16.54; conservation other than as an adjunct of price policy, 17; land policies, 17.3; reclamation and irrigation, 17.33; rural relief, 21)
  16.70 General
  16.71 History
  16.72 Price and Income Policies
    16.720 General
    16.721 Price Supports and Stabilization Policies
      (For processing tax see 16.75)
    16.722 Production Controls and Adjustment
    16.723 Surplus Disposal
      (For food subsidies see 21.31)
  16.73 International Aspects of Domestic Agricultural Policies
    (For agricultural aspects of foreign trade policy see 11.23 and 11.35; international commodity agreements, 11.241; surplus disposal, 16.723)
  16.74 Agricultural Insurance
    (For insurance companies see 9.43)
  16.75 Taxation
    (For property tax see 10.43)
  16.76 Administration

17. NATURAL RESOURCES. LAND ECONOMICS
(For natural resources and agriculture in development theory see 2.345; raw materials in war, 13.51; extractive industries, 15.53; agriculture, 16; regional development, 22)

17.0 GENERAL
17.1 HISTORY
17.2 CONSERVATION
(For multipurpose projects see 15.43; conservation of a specific resource, 17.3-17.7)
  17.20 General
  17.21 History

17.3 LAND ECONOMICS
(For theory of land and rent see 2.23; property taxation, 10.43; regional planning and development, and housing, 22)
  17.30 General
    17.301 Government Policy
      (For specific aspects see 17.32-17.36)
  17.31 History
  17.32 Conservation
  17.33 Reclamation. Irrigation
    (For irrigation on the individual farm see 16.421)
  17.34 Ownership and Tenure
    (For financial aspects of farm ownership and leasing see 16.46)
    17.340 General
    17.341 Land Tenure Reform
    17.342 Government Acquisition, Ownership, and Administration
      17.3420 General
        (For railroad land grants see 15.820; highway land acquisition, 15.85)
      17.3421 Veterans' Settlement
        (For veterans' housing see 22.53)
  17.35 Utilization
    17.350 General
    17.351 Land Use Policy

  17.36 Land Market and Values
    (For tax appraisal see 10.43; housing, 22.5)

17. NATURAL RESOURCES. LAND ECONOMICS (Cont.)

17.4 FORESTS
(For forest products industries see 15.527)
17.40 General
17.41 History

17.5 FISHERIES
(For fishery products industries see 15.528)
17.50 General
17.51 History

17.6 WATER RESOURCES
(For multipurpose projects see 15.43; water utilities, 15.6; water transport, 15.83; watershed management and flood control, 17.2; reclamation and irrigation, 17.33)
17.60 General
17.61 History

17.7 MINERALS
(For extractive industries see 15.53)
17.70 General
17.71 History

18. POPULATION
(For population in economic development theory see 2.343; farm population, 16.3)

18.0 GENERAL
18.1 HISTORY
18.2 POLICY
(For land settlement policy see 17.342; family allowances, 21.30)
18.3 SIZE AND COMPOSITION
(For labor force see 19.2; occupational distribution, 19.201)
18.4 GEOGRAPHICAL DISTRIBUTION. MIGRATION
(For immigration policy see 18.2; immigrant labor, 19.224; internal labor migration, 19.23)
18.5 CENSUS. REGISTRATION

19. LABOR ECONOMICS
(For theory of labor and wages see 2.22; labor as a factor in growth and development theory, 2.343; stabilization policies, 12.3; labor in wartime, 13.6; agricultural labor, 16.3; social security, 21.2)

19.0 GENERAL
19.01 Labor Productivity
(For measurement of productivity see 7.224; agricultural productivity, 16.22; wages and productivity, 19.301)

19.1 HISTORY
19.2 LABOR SUPPLY. LABOR MARKET
(For aggregate theory of employment see 2.31)
19.20 General
19.201 Occupational Classification
(For theory of occupational choice see 2.22; labor supply in individual industries and trades, 19.226; occupational mobility, 19.23)
19.202 Employment. Unemployment
(For theory of technological unemployment see 2.223; components of the labor force, 19.221-19.226; unemployment assistance, 21.6)
19.21 History
19.22 Components of the Labor Force
(For general discussions of the labor force see 19.20)
19.221 Women. Children

19. LABOR ECONOMICS (Cont.)
  19.2 LABOR SUPPLY. LABOR MARKET (Cont.)
    19.22 Components of the Labor Force (Cont.)
      19.222 Older Workers
          (For retirement and pensions see 19.596 and 21.4)
      19.223 Racial, Ethnic, and Social Groups
          (For union membership see 19.42)
      19.224 Immigrants
      19.225 Slave Labor. Forced Labor
      19.226 Individual Trades and Occupations
    19.23 Labor Turnover. Mobility
      (For farm migratory labor see 16.33; immigrant labor, 19.224)
    19.24 Recruiting and Training

  19.3 WAGES AND HOURS
    (For wage aspects of aggregate theory see 2.318; of development theory, 2.343; of stabilization policies, 12.32. For wage share of national income see 8.2; systems of wage payments, 19.593; guaranteed annual wage, 19.594)
    19.30 General
      19.301 Wages and Productivity
          (For labor productivity see also 19.01)
    19.31 History
    19.32 Wage Levels
    19.33 Wage Differentials. Wage Structures
      (For theory of wage differentials see 2.221; racial wage differentials, 19.223; impact of collective bargaining, 2.222 and 19.591; family allowances, 21.30)
      19.330 General
      19.331 Occupational
          (For government employees see 19.72)
      19.332 Industrial
      19.333 Geographical
      19.334 Age. Sex
      19.335 Union vs. Non-Union
    19.34 Hours
    19.35 Legislation and Regulation
      (For theory of minimum wage see 2.224; minimum wage legislation for women and children, 19.334)

  19.4 TRADE UNION ORGANIZATION
    (For farm labor unions see 16.32; collective bargaining, 19.5; wage and employment policies, 19.592; government employees, 19.72)
    19.40 General
      19.401 Theory
      19.402 International Labor Movement
          (For legislation see 19.70)
      19.403 Political Aspects
      19.404 Inter-Union Relations
    19.41 History
    19.42 Membership. Organizing Activities
    19.43 Structure. Organization. Administration
    19.44 Union Security
      (For union employment policies see 19.592)
    19.45 Labor Leaders
    19.46 Finances
      (For labor banks see 9.30; union welfare funds, 19.596)
    19.47 Educational Programs of Unions
    19.48 Individual Unions
      (For special activities of individual unions see other sections of 19 (e.g. strikes, 19.64). For farm labor unions see 16.31; foremen, 19.572; government employees, 19.72)

19. LABOR ECONOMICS (Cont.)

19.5 INDUSTRIAL RELATIONS. COLLECTIVE BARGAINING
(For industrial relations in individual industries or companies see 19.58, in government employment, 19.72; in regulated industries, 19.74. For legislation and regulation of industrial relations and collective bargaining see 19.7)

19.50 General
19.51 History
19.52 Research. Education
(For educational programs of unions see 19.47)
19.53 Union-Management Relations
19.54 Bargaining Systems
(For laws concerning appropriate bargaining unit see 19.7)
19.55 Collective Agreements
19.56 Employee Participation in Management
(For producers' cooperatives and guild socialism see 3.4; company unions, 19.575; co-partnership, 19.595)
19.57 Personnel Management
(For special industries and companies see 19.58; special issues, 19.59)
19.570 General
19.571 Selection. Testing. Training and Promotion
(For executive development see 14.332; salesmen, 14.56; technical and vocational education, 19.24; foremen and supervisors, 19.572)
19.572 Foremen. Supervisors
19.573 Safety. Health. Workmen's Compensation
(For union sick benefits see 19.596; contributory health insurance and pre-paid medical care, 21.7)
19.5730 General
19.5731 Workmen's Compensation
19.574 Human Relations. Morale
(For utilization of older workers see 19.222; grievance procedures, 19.55; foremen and supervisors, 19.572; retirement policies, 19.596)
19.575 Company Unions
19.576 Company Towns and Related Benefits
19.58 Case Studies
(For specific issues see other sections of 19 (e.g. Pensions, 19.596); cases in public employment, 19.72; in regulated industries, 19.74)
19.59 Selected Issues
19.591 Impact of Collective Bargaining
(For theory see 2.222)
19.592 Wage and Employment Policies
(For wage aspects of stabilization policies see 12.32)
19.593 Systems of Wage Payments. Incentives
19.594 Guaranteed Annual Wage. Dismissal Compensation
19.595 Profit-Sharing
19.596 Pensions. Fringe Benefits
(For management of pension funds see 9.44; retirement adjustment programs, 19.574; social security, 21.20; contributory pension plans, 21.4)
19.597 Technological Change and Innovation
(For theory of technological unemployment see 2.223; technological change and adaptation, 2.344; research and innovation, 15.27; technological unemployment, 19.202; occupational rehabilitation of displaced workers, 19.23)
19.598 Job Standards and Evaluation. Work Rules
(For production management and control see 14.337)
19.599 Seniority

19.6 STRIKES. DISPUTES. METHODS OF SETTLEMENT
(For wartime disputes see 13.61; union jurisdictional disputes, 19.404)
19.60 General
19.61 History
19.62 Emergency Disputes
19.63 Mediation and Arbitration
(For in-plant arbitration of disputes see 19.55)
19.64 Case Studies

19.  LABOR ECONOMICS (Cont.)

    19.7  LABOR LEGISLATION AND REGULATION.  PUBLIC EMPLOYEES
        (For laws relating to specific aspects of industrial relations see other sections of 19;
        fair employment practices legislation, 19.223; anti-trust laws applied to unions, 19.591)
        19.70  General
        19.71  History
        19.72  Government Labor.  Public Employees
            (For individual unions in public enterprises see 19.48; strikes, 19.6; work relief pro-
            grams, 21.6)
        19.73  Labor on Government Contracts
            (For strikes see 19.6)
        19.74  Labor in Regulated Industries
            (For strikes see 19.6)


20.  CONSUMER ECONOMICS
    (For theory of the household see 2.11; theory of consumption function and saving, 2.315; con-
    sumer cooperatives, 3.4; consumer price index, 7.221 and 8.54; distribution of personal in-
    come, 8.22; consumer finance, 9.8; wartime consumption, 13.62; consumer motivation, 14.521;
    farm families, 16.34; housing, 22.5)

    20.0  GENERAL
    20.1  HISTORY
    20.2  EMPIRICAL STUDIES
        20.20  General
        20.21  Saving
        20.22  Food Consumption
            (For wartime price control and rationing see 13.4; demand analysis of agricultural
            products, 16.23; food subsidies, 21.31)
        20.23  Consumption of Other Individual Goods or Services


21.  HEALTH.  EDUCATION.  WELFARE
    (For employers' health and safety measures and workmen's compensation see 19.573)

    21.0  GENERAL
    21.1  HISTORY
    21.2  CONTRIBUTORY PUBLIC INSURANCE.  SOCIAL SECURITY
        21.20  General
        21.21  Methods of Financing

    21.3  NON-CONTRIBUTORY WELFARE PROGRAMS
        21.30  General
            (For unemployment assistance see 21.6)
        21.31  Food Subsidies
            (For disposal of agricultural surpluses see 16.723; food subsidies for unemployed,
            21.6)

    21.4  OLD AGE ECONOMICS AND ASSISTANCE
        (For statistics of the aged population see 18.3; older workers, 19.222; employers' retire-
        ment policies and pensions, 19.596; budgets and living standards, 20.2)
    21.5  VETERANS' BENEFITS
        (For land settlement programs see 17.3421; housing policy, 22.53)
    21.6  UNEMPLOYMENT ASSISTANCE
        (For public works expenditure see 10.3)
    21.7  MEDICAL ECONOMICS
        (For insurance companies see 9.43)
    21.8  ECONOMICS OF EDUCATION
    21.9  OTHER NONPROFIT ORGANIZATIONS

## 22. REGIONAL PLANNING AND DEVELOPMENT. HOUSING
(For spatial competition and transportation see 2.1337; location theory, 2.15; empirical studies of regional economic conditions, 6; land economics, 17.3; population distribution, 18.4)

22.0 GENERAL
22.1 HISTORY
22.2 REGIONAL ECONOMICS
(For international economic integration see 11.4)
  22.20 General
  22.21 Theory
  22.22 Interregional Relations
    (For intranational trade barriers see 15.37)
  22.23 Industrial Dispersion and Diversification
    (For location of industry see 15.501)

22.3 URBAN-METROPOLITAN STUDIES
(For housing see 22.5)
  22.30 General
  22.31 Redevelopment
  22.32 Zoning
  22.33 Industrial and Shopping Centers

22.4 RURAL STUDIES
(For agriculture see 16; housing, 22.5)
  22.40 General
  22.41 Zoning

22.5 HOUSING
(For mortgage credit institutions see 9.4; property tax, 10.43; wartime housing, 13.75; construction industry, 15.55; consumer housing expenditure, 20.23)
  22.50 General
  22.51 Demand and Supply
    (For land market and values see 17.36)
  22.52 Rentals
    (For rent controls see 13.42 and 15.442; rent expenditure, 20.23)
  22.53 Government Policy
    (For rental policy see 22.52)


## 23. UNCLASSIFIED

# CLASSIFIED INDEX

# I. SCOPE AND METHOD OF ECONOMICS

1.0 GENERAL

Bhatnagar, B. G. [and others] Discussions of the scope and method of economics. IJE 20:810-21 Apr 40

-- Scope of economics. IJE 20:645-47 Apr 40

Bhide, H. B. Scope of economics. IJE 20:423-32 Apr 40

Chand, M. Scope and method of economics. IJE 20:531-34 Apr 40

Chopra, V. K. The scope of economics. IJE 20:459-73 Apr 40

Clark, J. M. Educational functions of economics after the war. AER/S 34:58-67 Mar 44

Daly, F. St.L. The scope and method of economics. CJE 11:165-76 May 45

Govindarow, B. Scope and method of economics. IJE 20:475-83 Apr 40

Hawtrey, R. G The need for faith. EJ 56:351-65 Sep 46

Karve, D. G. Towards progress in economics: a plea for strengthening its foundations and broadening its scope. IJE 26:685-715 Apr 46

Karwal, G. D. The scope of economics: economics and practice. IJE 20:749-59 Apr 40

La Nauze, J. A. The modern use of "economist." ER 16:125-26 Jun 40

Lange, O. The scope and method of economics. REStud 13:19-32 no.1, 45

Mehta, J. K. The scope of economics. IJE 20:395-404 Apr 40

Qureshi, A. I. The scope of economics. IJE 20:433-42 Apr 40

Rothschild, K. W. The meaning of rationality: a note on Professor Lange's article. REStud 14:50-52 no.1, 46

Salz, A. The present position of economics. AER/S 34:15-24 Mar 44

Samad, S. A. The relativity of economic phenomena. IJE 20:443-50 Apr 40

Tewari, J. N. What is economics? IJE 27:421-25 Apr 47

1.1 METHODOLOGY

1.10 GENERAL

Allin, B. W. Theory: definition and purpose. JFE 31:409-17 Aug 49

Bhatia, B. The method of study. IJE 20:505-12 Apr 40

Friedman, M. Lange on price flexibility and employment: a methodological criticism. AER 36:613-31 Sep 46

Hayek, F. A. von. The use of knowledge in society. AER 35:519-30 Sep 45

Heady, E. O. Implications of particular economics in agricultural economics methodology. JFE 31,pt.2:837-50 Nov 49

Knight, F. H. Immutable law in economics: its reality and limitations. AER/S 36:93-111 May 46

Lutz, F. A. History and theory in economics. R. Ec N.S.11:210-14 Nov 44

Marschak, J. A discussion of methods in economics. R. JPE 49:441-48 Jun 41

Mills, F. C. Economics in a time of change. AER 31:1-14 Mar 41

Parsons, K. H. The logical foundations of economic research. JFE 31:656-86 Nov 49

Prasad, P. S. N. Economics and political economy. IJE 20:485-504 Apr 40

Robertson, D. H. On sticking to one's last. EJ 59:505-09 Dec 49

Schuller, G. J. Isolationism in economic method. QJE 63:439-75 Nov 49

Schumpeter, J. A. Science and ideology. AER 39:345-59 Mar 49

Sinding, T. Some remarks on objectivity and subjectivity. NTTO 12:241-46 no.37, 48

1.11 PHILOSOPHY

Agarwala, S. N. A religious interpretation of economics. IJE 26:299-302 Oct 45

Bittermann, H. J. Adam Smith's empiricism and the law of nature. Pt.I-II. JPE 48:487-520; 703-34 Aug,Oct 40

Divine, T. F. The nature of economic science and its relation to social philosophy. RSE 6:106-17 May 48

Hayek, F. A. von. Scientism and the study of society. Pt.I-III. Ec N.S.9:267-91; 10:34-63; 11:27-39 Aug 42, Feb 43, Feb 44

Hutchison, T. W. The significance and basic postulates of economic theory: a reply to Professor Knight [followed by F. H. Knight's rejoinder]. JPE 49:732-53 Oct 41

Karwal, G. D. Is economics non-moral? IJE 24:75-80 Jul 43

Kaufmann, F. On the postulates of economic theory. SR 9:379-95 Sep 42

Knight, F. H. "What is truth" in economics? R. JPE 48:1-32 Feb 40

-- Salvation by science: the gospel according to Professor Lundberg. R. JPE 55:537-52 Dec 47

Lowe, A. A reconsideration of the law of supply and demand. SR 9:431-57 Nov 42

Murray, A. H. Professor Hayek's philosophy. Ec N.S.12:149-62 Aug 45

Northrop, F. S. C. The impossibility of a theoretical science of economic dynamics. QJE 56:1-17 Nov 41

Salz, A. Economic liberalism reinterpreted. SR 8:373-89 Sep 41

# 1. SCOPE AND METHOD OF ECONOMICS

## 1.1 METHODOLOGY (Cont.)
### 1.11 PHILOSOPHY (Cont.)

Scoon, R. Professor Robbins' definition of economics. R. JPE 51:310-21 Aug 43

Stonier, A. W. [Note on F. A. Hayek's "Scientism and the study of society," with rejoinder by Hayek.] Ec N.S.10: 188-89 May 43

Tagliacozzo, G. Croce and the nature of economic science. QJE 59:307-29 May 45

## 1.12 USE OF MATHEMATICS

Boulding, K. E. Samuelson's Foundations: the role of mathematics in economics. R. JPE 56:187-99 Jun 48

Datta, B. The continuity-assumption in economic analysis. IJE 20:779-86 Apr 40

Pigou, A. C. Newspaper reviewers, economics and mathematics. EJ 51:276-80 Jun-Sep 41

## 1.13 EMPIRICAL RESEARCH

Johnson, V. W. Problem research. JFE 30:576-78 Aug 48

Usher, A. P. The significance of modern empiricism for history and economics. JEH 9:137-55 Nov 49

## 1.14 HISTORICISM. INSTITUTIONALISM

Buchanan, D. H. The use of economic history in the solution of current economic problems. SEJ 13:370-77 Apr 47

Higgins, B. The economic man and economic science. R. CJE 13:587-99 Nov 47

Pinney, H. The institutional man. JPE 48: 543-62 Aug 40

Popper, K. The poverty of historicism. Pt.I-III. Ec N.S.11:86-103; 119-37; 12:69-89 May,Aug 44, May 45

## 1.15 MARGINALISM

Blum, F. H. Marginalism and economic policy: a comment. AER 37:645-52 Sep 47

Hague, D. C. Economic theory and business behavior. REStud 16:114-57 no.3, 49

Lester, R. A. Shortcomings of marginal analysis for wage-employment problems. AER 36:63-82 Mar 46

-- Marginalism, minimum wages, and labor markets. AER 37:135-48 Mar 47

-- Equilibrium of the firm. AER 39:478-84 Mar 49

Machlup, F. Marginal analysis and empirical research. AER 36:519-54 Sep 46

-- Rejoinder to an antimarginalist. AER 37: 148-54 Mar 47

Stigler, G. J. Professor Lester and the marginalists. AER 37:154-57 Mar 47

## 1.16 CATHOLIC ECONOMICS

Berger, A. V. Problems of a Catholic economic science. RSE 7,no.2:39-42 Sep 49

Cronin, J. F. Implementing the social encyclicals in American economic life. RSE 5:1-18 Jun 47

Dempsey, B. W. Economics implicit in the social encyclicals [with discussion by J. L. Shea]. RSE 1:12-22 Dec 42

Dirksen, C. F. The Catholic philosopher and the Catholic economist. RSE 4: 14-20 Jan 46

Killeen, E. C. Ethics, data for the economist. RSE 7,no.1:8-21 Mar 49

McAvoy, B. L. A philosopher's comment on philosophico-economic relations. RSE 4:25-30 Jan 46

Ryan, J. A. Two objectives for Catholic economists. RSE 1:1-5 Dec 42

Sheehan, J. H. An economist's comment on philosophico-economic relationships. RSE 4:21-24 Jan 46

## 1.17 RELATION OF ECONOMICS TO OTHER DISCIPLINES

Anderson, W. Political science, economics, and public policy. AER/S 34:77-85 Mar 44

Beckwith, B. P. Comments on Professor Spengler's article "Sociological presuppositions in economic theory" [followed by J. J. Spengler's reply]. SEJ 7:398-401 Jan 41

Divine, T. F. On yoking the economic forces to the social car. RSE 1:6-11 Dec 42

Ginzberg, E. The conference on science, philosophy and religion in their relation to the democratic way of life. AER 31: 108-09 Mar 41

Herskovits, M. J. Economics and anthropology: a rejoinder. JPE 49:269-78 Apr 41

Joshi, T. M. The functions of economic analysis. IJE 20:773-78 Apr 40

Katona, G. Contribution of psychological data to economic analysis. JASA 42: 449-59 Sep 47

Knight, F. H. Anthropology and economics. R. JPE 49:247-68 Apr 41

-- Professor Heimann on religion and economics. R. JPE 56:480-97 Dec 48

Lisman, J. H. C. Econometrics and thermodynamics: a remark on Davis' theory of budgets. Em 17:59-62 Jan 49

Malhotra, P. C. Scope of economics: a discussion of the relation between economics and ethics. IJE 20:451-58 Apr 40

Schauder, H. The economist and the engineer: an analysis and a synthesis. SAJE 12:303-12 Dec 44

Sharfman, I. L. Law and economics. AER 36:1-19 Mar 46

## 1.17  RELATION OF ECONOMICS TO OTHER DISCIPLINES (Cont.)

Spengler, J. J.  Sociological presuppositions in economic theory.  SEJ 7:131-57 Oct 40

Weisskopf, W. A.  Psychological aspects of economic thought.  JPE 57:304-41 Aug 49

## 1.18  RELATION OF ECONOMICS TO POLICY

Dillard, D.  A note on methodology in modern economic theory.  AER 34: 856-62 Dec 44

-- Pragmatism and economic theory: rebuttal.  AER 35:665-67 Sep 45

Mering, O. von.  Some problems of methodology in modern economic theory.  AER 34:87-97 Mar 44

-- Pragmatism and economic theory: a rejoinder [and a final word].  AER 35: 145-47; 667 Mar,Sep 45

Smith, H. R.  The role of science in the formulation of economic policy.  SEJ 12: 331-47 Apr 46

Spiegel, H. W.  Economic theory and economic policy.  R.  JB 18:56-59 Jan 45

Viner, J.  The short view and the long in economic policy.  AER 30:1-15 Mar 40

## 1.2  ROLE OF THE  ECONOMIST

Abramson, A. G.  Opportunities of the economist in an industrial company. HBR 20:389-90 no.3, 42

Browne, G. W. G.  Economists and government.  SAJE 14:188-201 Sep 46

Crick, W. F.  What's the use of economists? SAJE 14:17-21 Mar 46

Dewey, D. J.  Notes on the analysis of socialism as a vocational problem. MS 16:269-88 Sep 48

Frisch, R.  The responsibility of the econometrician.  Em 14:1-4 Jan 46

Goldenweiser, E. A.  Research and policy. JASA 39:1-9 Mar 44

-- The economist and the state.  AER 37: 1-12 Mar 47

Johnston, E. A.  Economists and the economy.  JPE 52:160-63 Jun 44

Little, I. M. D.  The economist and the state.  REStud 17:75-76 no.1, 49

Lonigan, E.  The professors versus the people:  comment.  AER 34:356-58 Jun 44

Micoleau, H. L.  The economist and management.  HBR 20:380-81 no.3, 42

Nourse, E. G.  Economics in the public service.  AER/S 37:21-30 May 47

Nussbaum, F. L. and Schweitzer, A.  The professors versus the people.  AER 33: 906-07 Dec 43

Ottman, A. H.  The economist's reports. HBR 20:388-89 no.3, 42

Robbins, L.  The economist in the twentieth century.  Ec N.S.16:93-105 May 49

Schoenfeldt, L.  The departmental economist.  HBR 20:386-88 no.3, 42

Smith, B. B.  Functions of the economist. HBR 20:375-79 no.3, 42

Snider, J. L.  Symposium on the industrial economist.  [Introduction] HBR 20: 375 no.3, 42

Weber, P. J.  The economics department of one industrial company.  HBR 20:381-85 no.3, 42

Whitney, N. R.  The economist as adviser. HBR 20:379-80 no.3, 42

Wright, W.  The industrial economist as staff officer.  HBR 20:385-86 no.3, 42

Young, C. E.  Duties of the economist. HBR 20:391-92 no.3, 42

## 1.3  TEACHING OF ECONOMICS

Abramson, A. G.  Fellowships in industry. AER 38:142-44 Mar 48

Anonymous.  Teaching of economics in the
ER  Soviet Union, from the Russian journal Pod Znamenem Marxizma.  Translated by R. Dunayevskaya.  AER 34:501-30 Sep 44

Blodgett, R. H., chairman.  Round table on problems in the teaching of economics. AER/S 30,no.5:416-21 Feb 41

Blum, L.  The elementary course.  JFE 29: 278-82 Feb 47

Bowen, H. R.  The teaching of money and banking.  JF 4:231-33 Sep 49

Bowman, M. J.  Undergraduate teaching of
A  economics: discussion.  AER/S 36: 857-60 May 46

Bronfenbrenner, M.  The introductory course: comment.  AER 32:557-58 Sep 42

-- Letter to the editor [on economics curriculum].  Em 17:251-52 Jul-Oct 49

Bye, R. T., chairman.  Round table on problems in the teaching of economics. AER/S 30:106-11 Mar 40

Carlson, V.  A plea for new texts in beginning economics.  AER 31:102-03 Mar 41

Clark, J. M.  Educational functions of economics after the war.  AER/S 34:58-67 Mar 44

Clemence, R. and Doody, F. S.  Modern economics and the introductory course. AER 32:334-47 Jun 42

Copeland, M. A.  Interdepartmental courses in the social sciences: discussion.  AER/S 35:148-49 May 45

Cronin, J. F.  The place of economics in liberal arts colleges and seminaries. RSE 7,no.1:1-7 Mar 49

Donoghue, M.  Economics a living subject. RSE 6:101-05 May 48

1.3 TEACHING OF ECONOMICS (Cont.)

Dunayevskaya, R. A new revision of
ER    Marxian economics. AER 34:531-37
Sep 44

-- Revision or reaffirmation of Marxism?
ER    A rejoinder. AER 35:660-64 Sep 45

Dunkman, W. E. The teaching of money
and banking. JF 4:234-37 Sep 49

Elkinton, C. M. A study of student values
and inconsistent reasoning. AER 31:
557-59 Sep 41

Froman, L. A. Graduate students in eco-
A    nomics, 1904-1940. AER 32:817-26
Dec 42

Hacker, L. M. The contemporary civiliza-
A    tion course at Columbia College.
AER/S 35:137-47 May 45

Harbeson, R. W. The case for an introductory course in economic theory.
AER 33:121-25 Mar 43

[Hayek, F. A. von] The London School of
EB    Economics 1895-1945. Ec N.S.13:1-31
Feb 46

Hewett, W. W. The use of economic principles in the teaching of applied subjects.
AER 30:333-38 Jun 40

-- Some problems in teaching elementary
economics. AER/S 36:853-56 May 46

Hudson, P. G. Principles of economics
prerequisite to courses in public
finance. AER 30:582 Sep 40

Kapp, K. W. Teaching of economics: a
new approach. SEJ 12:376-83 Apr 46

-- Methods of visual presentation and the
teaching of economics. AER 37:652-54
Sep 47

Kenkel, J. B. Teaching economics in college [with discussion by J. E. Norton].
RSE 6:85-96 May 48

Kirkland, E. C. The place of theory in
teaching American economic history.
JEH/S 9:99-102 '49

Knight, F. H. Economics, political science,
and education. AER/S 34:68-76 Mar 44

Leont'ev, L. A. [and others] Political econ-
ER    omy in the Soviet Union. [Translated by
H. F. Mins, Jr.] S&S 8:115-25 no.2, 44

Machlup, F. The teaching of money and
banking. JF 4:227-30 Sep 49

Marget, A. W. Monetary theory at the
textbook level. AER 32:775-90 Dec 42

Marshall, A. R. College courses in con-
A    sumption economics. JM 5:26-34 Jul 40

Mendershausen, H. Concept and teaching
of economics. AER 36:376-84 Jun 46

Mills, M. C. Principles and practice in
public finance. AER 31:101 Mar 41

Mitchell, B. Treatment of controversial
questions in the teaching of political
economy. AER 30:339-43 Jun 40

Neisser, H. Concept and teaching of economics: comment. AER 36:906-08
Dec 46

Newcomer, M., chairman. Report of the
A    Subcomittee on the Undergraduate Economics Curriculum and Related Areas
of Study. AER/S 36:845-47 May 46

O'Leary, E. B. The teaching of economics.
RSE 1:54-55 Dec 42

O'Leary, J. M. The teaching of economics
A    in public high schools. QJE 54:502-18
May 40

Parrish, J. B. "Principles of economics
prerequisite to courses in public
finance": a rejoinder. AER 31:102
Mar 41

Pertinax [pseud]. Letter to the editor [on
lack of mathematics in economics cur-
riculum]. Em 17:90-92 Jan 49

Polanyi, M. Economics by motion symbols.
REStud 8:1-19 Oct 40

Puffer, C. E. Indifference curves versus
marginal utility. AER 30:118 Mar 40

Quigley, T. J. The place of economics in
the common school curriculum. RSE 7,
no.2:43-47 Sep 49

Reedman, J. N. Some reflections on the
teaching of business cycle theory. R.
SAJE 13:52-57 Mar 45

Robinson, R. I. The teaching of money and
banking. JF 4:237-42 Sep 49

[Schumpeter, J.] Statement on the choice
of textbooks. AER 38:626 Sep 48

Shilland, P. D. Problems in the teaching
of economics. AER 30:350 Jun 40

Spengler, J. J. Undergraduate teaching of
A    economics: discussion. AER/S 36:
860-63 May 46

Tolles, N. A. Conference on the teaching
of economics. AER 36:908-10 Dec 46

Vakil, C. N. Teaching of economics:
FI    change in outlook. IJE 27:331-32 Jan 47

Wintergalen, E. H. Teachers' cooperative
A    training courses. RSE 7,no.1:82-85
Mar 49

Wolfe, A. B. Undergraduate teaching of
A    economics: discussion. AER/S 36:
848-52 May 46

Zvavich, I. Economic education and eco-
ER    nomic research in the Soviet Union.
EJ 53:415-18 Dec 43

1.4 RESEARCH. BIBLIOGRAPHY

Agarwala, A. N. Recent economic literature. IJE 23:373-87 Apr 43

Bladen, V. W. Provision for social research. R. CJE 13:287-92 May 47

Copeland, M. A. Economic research in the
federal government. AER 31:526-36
Sep 41

Ellis, H. S. Research as seen in a survey
of contemporary economics. AER/S 39:
427-39 May 49

Ensley, G. W. Suggested lines of economic
research needed to carry out objectives
of the Employment Act. AER/S 39:
453-63 May 49

## 1.4 RESEARCH. BIBLIOGRAPHY (Cont.)

Goldenweiser, E. A. Research and policy. JASA 39:1-9 Mar 44

Hamer, P. M. Round table on economic research: discussion. AER/S 37:700 May 47

Hoffman, P. G. Planning for post-war opportunity. JM 8:33-40 Jul 43

-- Business plans for postwar expansion. AER/S 35:85-89 May 45

Homan, P. T., chairman. Round table on economic research. AER/S 30,no.5: 409-15 Feb 41

-- Research in prices, wages, and profits. AER/S 39:440-43 May 49

Hoover, E. M. Research in the area of productive capacity and investment. AER/S 39:444-52 May 49

Hunsberger, W. S. Economic research of interest to the Department of State. AER/S 37:681-89 May 47

Hutt, W. H. Plan for economic research in the Union. SAJE 12:81-100 Jun 44

Leland, S. E., chairman. Round table on economic research. AER/S 37:649-50 May 47

Nourse, E. G. Developments concerning the National Research Foundation. AER/S 36:789-92 May 46

Pumphrey, L. Material in the national archives of especial interest for economists. AER 31:344-45 Jun 41

Rush, R. H. A case study of postwar planning by business. JM 8:150-55 Oct 43

Saulnier, R. J. The financial research program of the National Bureau of Economic Research. JF 2,no.1:4-14 Apr 47

Schwartz, H. Official criticism of Soviet Economics Institute. AER 37:190-91 Mar 47

Spengler, J. J. [and others] Round table on economic research: discussion. AER/S 39:464-72 May 49

## 1.5 ECONOMIC SOCIETIES. PERIODICALS

Agnew, H. E. The history of the American Marketing Association. JM 5:374-79 Apr 41

Anonymous. George S. Wehrwein January 31, 1883-January 10, 1946. [Influence on editorial policy of the Journal] LE 21: 1 Feb 45

-- Inauguration of the Francis A. Walker and John Bates Clark awards. AER/S 38: [xi-xiv] May 48

-- [Explorations in Entrepreneurial History.] Editorial report. EEH 2:44-46 Nov 49

Applebaum, W. The Journal of Marketing: the first ten years. JM 11:355-63 Apr 47

Bates, G. E. Twenty years [of Harvard Business Review]. HBR 21:1-4 no.1, 42

Bodfish, M. Translating research into progress through the Journal of Land and Public Utility Economics. LE 18:82-84 Feb 42

Butlin, S. J. The Australian Economic Association, 1887-1898. ER 23:20-31 Jun 47

Clough, S. B. The economic history of a young corporation [the Economic History Association]. JEH/S 1:110-11 Dec 41

Dewey, D. R. Dewey dinner and testimonial. Remarks of Davis Rich Dewey [retiring editor of the American Economic Review] at testimonial dinner. AER/S 30, no.5:v-xi Feb 41

Edwards, C. D., chairman. Report of the Subcommittee on Consensus and recommendations as to Association policy. AER/S 36:832-41 May 46

Edwards, E. E. Objectives for the Agricultural History Society during its second twenty-five years. AH 18:187-92 Oct 44

Giblin, L. F. The Record and its editors (1925-1946). ER 23:1-4 Jun 47

Hardy, C. O. Economic opinion and public policy: discussion. AER/S 36:842-44 May 46

Heaton, H. The early history of the Economic History Association. JEH/S 1: 107-09 Dec 41

[Keynes, J. M.] The [Royal Economic] Society's jubilee 1890-1940. EJ 50: 401-09 Dec 40

Matherly, W. J. The history of the Southern Economic Association, 1927-1939. SEJ 7: 225-40 Oct 40

Peterson, A. G. The Agricultural History Society's first quarter century. AH 19: 193-203 Oct 45

R[ichards], C. S. Note on the design for the "Pearsall Memorial Founders Medal" and new monogram for the Journal. SAJE 13:136 Jun 45

Roos, C. F. A future role for the Econometric Society in international statistics. Em 16:127-34 Apr 48

Spengler, J. J., chairman. Final report of the Committee on Development of Economic Thinking and Information. AER/S 36:922-33 May 46

-- and Burns, E. M. The proposed publication of a periodic review of economics. [Precis of the round table discussion] AER/S 36:784-88 May 46

# 2. ECONOMIC THEORY, INCLUDING
# MONETARY THEORY

## 2.0 GENERAL

Allen, R. G. D.  The mathematical foundations of economic theory.  QJE 63: 111-27 Feb 49

Atkinson, L. J.  Recent developments in economic thinking.  JFE 29:261-77 Feb 47

Baumol, W. J.  Relaying the foundations.  R. Ec N.S.16:159-68 May 49

Boulding, K. E.  Professor Tarshis and the state of economics.  AER 38:92-102 Mar 48

Friedman, M.  Lerner on The economics of control.  R.  JPE 55:405-16 Oct 47

Galletti, R.  Pure economics and social engineering.  IJE 23:319-63 Apr 43

Haney, L. H.  Professor Bowman's review of Value and distribution.  AER 30: 582-83 Sep 40

Keirstead, B. S.  A note on "equilibrium in process."  CJE 9:235-42 May 43

Lerner, A. P.  Professor Hicks' dynamics. R.  QJE 54:298-306 Feb 40

McCracken, H. L.  Economic contradictions.  SEJ 13:343-59 Apr 47

Machlup, F.  Professor Hicks' statics. R.  QJE 54:277-97 Feb 40

McQueen, R.  The approach to economics. R.  CJE 6:79-85 Feb 40

Marrama, V.  Some observations on Professor Lange's analysis.  Ec N.S.14: 120-33 May 47

Marschak, J.  Identity and stability in economics: a survey.  Em 10:61-74 Jan 42

Meade, J. E.  Mr. Lerner on "The economics of control."  R.  EJ 55:47-69 Apr 45

Morgenstern, O.  Professor Hicks on Value and capital.  R.  JPE 49:361-93 Jun 41

Mukerjee, R.  The sociological elements in price economics.  IJE 21:109-30 Oct 40

Neisser, H.  The economics of the short run: remarks on John R. Hicks' "Value and capital."  SR 7:32-44 Feb 40

Reder, M. W.  Professor Samuelson on the foundations of economic analysis. R.  CJE 14:516-30 Nov 48

Timlin, M. F.  The economics of control. R.  CJE 11:285-93 May 45

## 2.01 MOTIVATION

Chapman, S.  The profit motive and the economic incentive.  EJ 56:51-56 Mar 46

Kapp, K. W.  Rational human conduct and modern industrial society.  SEJ 10: 136-50 Oct 43

Keirstead, B. S.  Economic man in relation to his natural environment.  R.  CJE 15: 231-36 May 49

Knight, F. H.  Professor Parsons on economic motivation [followed by T. Parsons' reply].  CJE 6:460-72 Aug 40

Parsons, T.  The motivation of economic activities.  CJE 6:187-202 May 40

Powicke, F. M.  The economic motive in politics.  EHR 16:85-92 no.2, 46

Samuelson, P. A.  Comparative statics and the logic of economic maximizing.  REStud 14:41-43 no.1, 46

Schuetz, A.  The problem of rationality in the social world.  Ec N.S.10:130-49 May 43

Spiegel, H. W.  The war economy and the economic man.  JB 16:1-6 Jan 43

Walker, K. F.  The psychological assumptions of economics.  ER 22:66-82 Jun 46

## 2.02 UNCERTAINTY AND EXPECTATIONS. DECISION MAKING UNDER UNCERTAINTY

Black, D.  On the rationale of group decision-making.  JPE 56:23-34 Feb 48

-- The elasticity of committee decisions with alterations in the members' preference schedules.  SAJE 17:88-102 Mar 49

Boulding, K. E.  The theory and measurement of price expectations: discussion.  AER/S 39:167-68 May 49

Friedman, M. and Savage, L.  The utility analysis of choices involving risk.  JPE 56:279-304 Aug 48

-- [and others]  Liquidity and uncertainty: discussion.  AER/S 39:196-210 May 49

Graaff, J. de V. and Baumol, W.  Three notes on "Expectation in economics." II.  R.  Ec N.S.16:338-42 Nov 49

Hart, A. G.  Uncertainty and inducements to invest.  REStud 8:49-53 Oct 40

Hirshleifer, J.  A note on expectations.  AER 36:901-03 Dec 46

Lachmann, L. M.  The role of expectations in economics as a social science.  Ec N.S.10:12-23 Feb 43

-- A note on the elasticity of expectations.  Ec N.S.12:248-53 Nov 45

Marschak, J.  Lack of confidence.  SR 8: 41-62 Feb 41

Norton, L. J.  The theory and measurement of price expectations: discussion.  AER/S 39:168-70 May 49

Shackle, G. L. S.  The nature of the inducement to invest.  REStud 8:44-48 Oct 40

-- A reply to Professor Hart.  REStud 8: 54-57 Oct 40

-- A theory of investment-decisions.  OEP 6:77-94 Apr 42

-- The expectational dynamics of the individual.  Ec N.S.10:99-129 May 43

## 2.02 UNCERTAINTY AND EXPECTATIONS. ETC. (Cont.)

Shackle, G. L. S. (Cont.)
-- Three notes on "Expectation in economics." III. <u>R</u>. Ec N.S.16:343-46 Nov 49
-- Probability and uncertainty. Met 1: 161-73 Dec 49
-- A non-additive measure of uncertainty. REStud 17:70-74 no.1, 49
Tintner, G. The pure theory of production under technological risk and uncertainty. Em 9:305-12 Jul-Oct 41
-- The theory of choice under subjective risk and uncertainty. Em 9:298-304 Jul-Oct 41
-- A contribution to the non-static theory of choice. QJE 56:274-306 Feb 42
Turvey, R. Three notes on "Expectation in economics." I. <u>R</u>. Ec N.S.16:336-38 Nov 49
Working, H. The investigation of economic expectations. AER/S 39:150-66 May 49

## 2.03 GAME THEORY

Hurwicz, L. The theory of economic behavior. AER 35:909-25 Dec 45
Kaysen, C. A revolution in economic theory? <u>R</u>. REStud 14:1-15 no.1, 46
Leunbach, G. The theory of games and economic behaviour, Johann v. Neumann and Oscar Morgenstern. <u>R</u>. NTTO 12: 175-78 no.37, 48
Marschak, J. Neumann's and Morgenstern's new approach to static economics. <u>R</u>. JPE 54:97-115 Apr 46
Morgenstern, O. Economics and the theory of games. Kyk 3:294-308 fasc.4, 49
Stone, R. The theory of games. <u>R</u>. EJ 58: 185-201 Jun 48

## 2.04 STATICS AND DYNAMICS

Bode, K. Plan analysis and process analysis. AER 33:348-54 Jun 43
Caplan, B. Some Swedish stepping stones in economic theory: a comment. CJE 7:559-62 Nov 41
Fellner, W. Period analysis and timeless equilibrium. QJE 58:315-22 Feb 44
Hood, W. C. Some aspects of the treatment of time in economic theory. CJE 14: 453-68 Nov 48
Lerner, A. P. Some Swedish stepping stones in economic theory. <u>R</u>. CJE 6: 574-91 Nov 40
Samuelson, P. A. The stability of equilibrium: comparative statics and dynamics. Em 9:97-120 Apr 41
-- Dynamics, statics, and the stationary state. REStat 25:58-68 Feb 43
-- The relation between Hicksian stability and true dynamic stability. Em 12: 256-57 Jul-Oct 44

Smithies, A. Process analysis and equilibrium analysis. Em 10:26-38 Jan 42

## 2.1 VALUE, PRICE, AND ALLOCATION THEORY
## 2.10 GENERAL

Ayres, C. E. Addendum to The theory of economic progress. AER 35:937-40 Dec 45
Dillard, D. The status of the labor theory of value. SEJ 11:345-52 Apr 45
Evinitsky, A. Value theory and socialism. S&S 9:260-63 no.3, 45
Lowe, A. A reconsideration of the law of supply and demand. SR 9:431-57 Nov 42
Morgenstern, O. Demand theory reconsidered. QJE 62:165-201 Feb 48
Niebyl, K. H. The need for a concept of value in economic theory. QJE 54: 201-16 Feb 40
Paulson, W. E. Diagrammatic economics. JFE 28:687-722 Aug 46
Prasad, P. S. N. Disinterring the labour theory of value. IJE 21:175-83 Oct 40
Rao, K. V. Value in a socialistic state. IJE 21:476-87 Apr 41
Surányi-Unger, T. The concept of elasticity in economics. WA 62:11-25 Hft.1, 49
Tintner, G. Homogeneous systems in mathematical economics. Em 16: 273-94 Oct 48

## 2.11 UTILITY. DEMAND. THEORY OF THE HOUSEHOLD
## 2.110 GENERAL

Becker, A. P. Psychological production and conservation. QJE 63:577-83 Nov 49
Knight, F. H. Realism and relevance in the theory of demand. JPE 52:289-318 Dec 44
Kozlik, A. Conditions for demand curves whose curves of total revenue, consumers' surplus, total benefit, and compromise benefit are convex. Em 8:263-71 Jul 40
Surányi-Unger, T. Individual and collective wants. JPE 56:1-22 Feb 48

## 2.111 UTILITY AND INDIFFERENCE ANALYSIS

Anantachar, V. S. The determinateness of the utility function. IJE 28:577-79 Apr 48
-- Utility and its place in economics. IJE 29:1-15 Jul 48
Armstrong, W. E. Uncertainty and the utility function. EJ 58:1-10 Mar 48
Bishop, R. L. Professor Knight and the theory of demand [followed by F. H. Knight's comment]. JPE 54:141-76 Apr 46
Clark, J. M. Realism and relevance in the theory of demand. JPE 54:347-53 Aug 46

## 2. ECONOMIC THEORY, ETC.

211. UTILITY. DEMAND. ETC. (Cont.)

2.111 UTILITY AND INDIFFERENCE
ANALYSIS (Cont.)

Coppock, J. D. Indifference curve analysis applied to the food stamp plan. AER 35: 99-110 Mar 45

Divine, T. F. The derivation of the Marshallian curve from the Paretian indifference curves. AER 33:125-29 Mar 43

Hart, A. G. Peculiarities of indifference maps involving money. REStud 8: 126-28 Feb 41

Hayek, F. A. von. The geometrical representation of complementarity. REStud 10:122-25 no.2, 43

Howell, L. D. Does the consumer benefit from price instability? QJE 59:287-95 Feb 45

Kemp, A. A terminological note on indifference curves. SEJ 8:88-92 Jul 41

-- Professor Whittaker on indifference curves. AER 31:569-70 Sep 41

Little, I. M. D. A reformulation of the theory of consumer's behavior. OEP N.S.1:90-99 Jan 49

Lovasy, G. [Does the consumer benefit from price instability?] Further comment. QJE 59:296-301 Feb 45

Malan, G. H. T. An objective ordinal theory of value. SAJE 13:117-28 Jun 45

Marx, W. The law of diminishing marginal utility of income: an investigation of its validity. Kyk 3:254-72 fasc.3, 49

Morgan, J. N. Can we measure the marginal utility of money? Em 13:129-52 Apr 45

-- The measurement of gains and losses. QJE 62:287-308 Feb 48

Puffer, C. E. Indifference curves versus marginal utility. AER 30:118 Mar 40

Samuelson, P. A. Consumption theory in terms of revealed preference. Ec N.S.15:243-53 Nov 48

-- Some implications of "linearity." REStud 15:88-90 no.2, 48

Scitovszky, T. Some consequences of the habit of judging quality by price. REStud 12:100-05 no.2, 45

Stark, W. Diminshing utility reconsidered. Kyk 1:321-44 fasc.4, 47

Vickrey, W. Measuring marginal utility by reactions to risk. Em 13:319-33 Oct 45

Wald, A. The approximate determination of indifference surfaces by means of Engel curves. Em 8:144-75 Apr 40

Waugh, F. V. Does the consumer benefit from price instability? QJE 58:602-14 Aug 44

-- ---- Reply. QJE 59:301-03 Feb 45

Whittaker, E. Professor Whittaker on indifference curves: a rejoinder. AER 31:835-36 Dec 41

Wilson, E. B. On notation for utility theory. QJE 58:647-50 Aug 44

-- Hicks on perfect substitutes. QJE 59: 134-40 Nov 44

-- Consumption in fixed proportion. QJE 59:635-39 Aug 45

2.112 CONSUMER'S SURPLUS

Bishop, R. L. Consumer's surplus and cardinal utility. QJE 57:421-49 May 43

Boulding, K. E. The concept of economic surplus. AER 35:851-69 Dec 45; Errata. 36:393 Jun 46

Henderson, A. Consumer's surplus and the compensating variation. REStud 8: 117-21 Feb 41

Hicks, J. R. The rehabilitation of consumers' surplus. REStud 8:108-16 Feb 41

-- Consumers' surplus and index-numbers. REStud 9:126-37 no.2, 42

-- The four consumer's surpluses. REStud 11:31-41 no.1, 43

-- The generalised theory of consumer's surplus. REStud 13:68-74 no.2, 46

Kozlik, A. Note on consumer's surplus. JPE 49:754-62 Oct 41

Mishan, E. J. Realism and relevance in consumer's surplus. REStud 15:27-33 no.1, 47

Tharakhan, K. J. M. 'Consumer's surplus': a rejoinder. IJE 21:307-19 Jan 41

2.113 DEMAND ANALYSIS

Court, L. M. Entrepreneurial and consumer demand theories for commodity spectra. Pt.I-II. Em 9:135-62; 241-97 Apr, Jul-Oct 41

Friedman, M. The Marshallian demand curve. JPE 57:463-95 Dec 49

Hicks, J. R. A comment [on O. Lange's Complementarity and interrelations of shifts in demand]. REStud 8:64-65 Oct 40

Horner, F. B. The demand equation for a raw material in empirical studies. ER 25,(no.48):85-91 Jun 49

Kozlik, A. The use of per capita figures for demand curves. JASA 36:417-22 Sep 41

-- Note on the integrability condition for interrelated demand. REStud 10:73-74 no.1, 42

-- Application of the indifference curves analysis to rising demand curves. AER 33:129-30 Mar 43

Lange, O. Complementarity and interrelations of shifts in demand. REStud 8: 58-63 Oct 40

Lewis, H. G. The nature of the demand for steel. JASA 36:110-15 Mar 41

Li, C. M. A note on Professor Hicks' value and capital. REStud 9:74-76 Nov 41

Marschak, J. Money illusion and demand analysis. REStat 25:40-48 Feb 43

2.113 DEMAND ANALYSIS (Cont.)

Marschak, J. (Cont.)

-- Income inequality and demand studies: a note. Em 11:163-66 Apr 43

Maverick, L. A. Demand and supply curves. QJE 54:307-13 Feb 40

Mosak, J. L. Some theoretical implications of the statistical analysis of demand and cost functions for steel. JASA 36:100-10 Mar 41

Prest, A. R. Notes on the history of the Giffen paradox: comment [followed by G. J. Stigler's reply]. JPE 56:58-62 Feb 48

-- Some experiments in demand analysis. REStat 31:33-49 Feb 49

Robertson, D. H. The inter-relations of shifts in demand [followed by comments by J. R. Hicks and O. Lange]. REStud 12:71-78 no.1, 44

Roos, C. F. and Von Szeliski, V. S. The demand for durable goods. Em 11: 97-122 Apr 43

Stigler, G. J. Notes on the history of the Giffen paradox. JPE 55:152-56 Apr 47

Stone, R. The analysis of market demand [with discussion]. JRSS 108:286-391 pt.3-4, 45

-- The analysis of market demand: an outline of methods and results. RIIS 16: 23-34 no.1-4, 48

Weintraub, S. The foundations of the demand curve. AER 32:538-52 Sep 42

Wilson, E. B. Pareto on Marshall's demand curve. QJE 58:141-45 Nov 43

-- Notes on utility theory and demand equations. QJE 60:453-60 May 46

Wold, H. O. A. On Giffen's paradox. NTTO 12:283-93 no.37, 48

2.114 ELASTICITY OF DEMAND

Gallego-Diaz, J. A note on the arc elasticity of demand. REStud 12:114-15 no.2, 45

Girshick, M. A. The application of the theory of linear hypotheses to the coefficient of elasticity of demand. JASA 37:233-37 Jun 42

Holt, C. C. and Samuelson, P. A. The graphic depiction of elasticity of demand. JPE 54:354-57 Aug 46

Hyson, C. D. and Hyson, W. P. Geometrical measurement of elasticities. AER 39: 728-29 Jun 49

Lange, O. Theoretical derivation of elasticities of demand and supply: the direct method. Em 10:193-214 Jul-Oct 42

Leontief, W. Elasticity of demand computed from cost data. AER 30:814-17 Dec 40

Lerner, A. P. Geometrical comparison of elasticities. AER 37:191 Mar 47

Leser, C. E. V. Family budget data and price-elasticities of demand. REStud 9: 40-57 Nov 41

Lester, R. A. Absence of elasticity considerations in demand to the firm. SEJ 14:285-89 Jan 48

Marschak, J. Demand elasticities reviewed. Em 11:25-34 Jan 43

Oliver, H. M., Jr. Average cost and long-run elasticity of demand. JPE 55: 212-21 Jun 47

Staehle, H. Elasticity of demand and social welfare. QJE 54:217-31 Feb 40

Sumner, J. D. A note on cyclical changes in demand elasticity. AER 30:300-08 Jun 40

Wolff, P. de. Income elasticity of demand, a micro-economic and a macro-economic interpretation. EJ 51:140-45 Apr 41

Woolley, H. B. The general elasticity of demand. Em 15:226-30 Jul 47

2.115 RATIONING

Carter, C. F. The dual-currency problem. EJ 58:586-94 Dec 48

Dowsett, W. T. A note on minimum standards for rationed necessities. ER 21: 89-94 Jun 45

Graaff, J. de V. Towards an austerity theory of value. SAJE 16:35-50 Mar 48

-- Rothbarth's "virtual price system" and the Slutsky equation. REStud 15:91-95 no.2, 48

Haraldson, W. C. Welfare economics and rationing. QJE 58:146-48 Nov 43

Henderson, A. A note on the theory of rationing. REStud 15:42-45 no.1, 47

Holben, R. E. General expenditure rationing with particular reference to the Kalecki plan. AER 32:513-23 Sep 42

Makower, H. Rationing and value theory. REStud 13:75-80 no.2, 46

Nicholson, J. L. Rationing and index numbers. REStud 10:68-72 no.1, 42

Polak, J. J. Rationing of purchasing power to restrict consumption. Ec N.S.8: 223-38 Aug 41

Reder, M. W. Welfare economics and rationing. QJE 57:153-59 Nov 42

Rothschild, K W. Rationing and the consumer. OEP 7:67-82 Mar 45

Worswick, G. D. N. Points, prices and consumers' choice. OIS 6:33-39 Feb 26, 44

2.12 PRODUCTION. COST. SUPPLY
2.120 GENERAL

Amoroso, L. The transformation of value in the productive process. Em 8:1-11 Jan 40

Jantzen, I. Laws of production and cost. Em 17,suppl.:58-67 Jul 49

2. ECONOMIC THEORY, ETC.

2.12 PRODUCTION. COST. SUPPLY (Cont.)
2.120 GENERAL (Cont.)

Marschak, J. and Andrews, W. H., Jr.
Random simultaneous equations and the
theory of production. Em 12:143-205
Jul-Oct 44; Errata. 13:91 Jan 45

Tintner, G. The pure theory of production
under technological risk and uncertainty.
Em 9:305-12 Jul-Oct 41

-- The theory of production under nonstatic
conditions. JPE 50:645-67 Oct 42

Verhulst, M. J. J. The pure theory of production applied to the French gas industry. Em 16:295-308 Oct 48

2.121 PRODUCTION FUNCTIONS OF FIRM
AND INDUSTRY

Bronfenbrenner, M. Production functions:
Cobb-Douglas, interfirm, intrafirm.
Em 12:35-44 Jan 44

Chenery, H. B. Engineering production
functions. QJE 63:507-31 Nov 49

Lerner, J. Constant proportions, fixed
plant and the optimum conditions of
production. QJE 63:361-70 Aug 49

Reder, M. W. A reconsideration of the
marginal productivity theory. JPE 55:
450-58 Oct 47

Smith, V. E. Nonlinearity in the relation
between input and output: the Canadian
automobile industry, 1918-1930. Em 13:
260-72 Jul 45

Tintner, G. A note on the derivation of
production functions from farm records.
Em 12:26-34 Jan 44

2.122 ECONOMIES OF SCALE, INTERNAL OR
EXTERNAL

Blair, J. M. Technology and size.
AER/S 38:121-52 May 48

Boulding, K. E. [and others] Does large-
scale enterprise lower costs: discussion. AER/S 38:165-71 May 48

Chamberlin, E. H. Proportionality, divisibility and economies of scale. QJE 62:
229-62 Feb 48

Ellis, H. S. and Fellner, W. External economies and diseconomies. AER 33:
493-511 Sep 43

Klein, L. R. The relationship between total
output and man-hour output: comment.
QJE 56:342-43 Feb 42

McLeod, A. N. and Hahn, F. H. Proportionality, divisibility, and economies of
scale: two comments [followed by E. H.
Chamberlin's reply]. QJE 63:128-43
Feb 49

Mehta, M. M. Relation between size and
efficiency. IJE 30:61-67 Jul 49

Oliver, H. M., Jr. The relationship of total
output to man-hour output: reply.
QJE 59:640-41 Aug 45

2.123 COST AND SUPPLY

Apel, H. Marginal cost constancy and its
implications. AER 38:870-85 Dec 48

Bauer, P. T. Rubber production costs during the Great Depression. EJ 53:361-69
Dec 43

-- Notes on cost. Ec N.S.12:90-100 May 45

Beach, E. F. The use of polynomials to
represent cost functions. REStud 16:
158-69 no.3, 49

Bishop, R. L. Cost discontinuities, declining costs, and marginal analysis.
AER 38:607-17 Sep 48

Bray, F. S. An accountant's comments on
the subjective theory of value and accounting cost. Ec N.S.13:295-99 Nov 46

Court, L. M. and Lewis, H. G. Production
cost indices. REStud 10:28-42 no.1, 42

Daly, M. C. The effect of overhead costs
upon the structure of the American
economy. SEJ 8:22-39 Jul 41

Dean, J. Cost structures of enterprises
and break-even charts. AER/S 38:
153-64 May 48

-- Cost forecasting and price policy.
JM 13:279-88 Jan 49

Eiteman, W. J. Factors determining the
location of the least cost point. AER 37:
910-18 Dec 47

-- The least cost point, capacity, and
marginal analysis: a rejoinder. AER 38:
899-904 Dec 48

Erdman, H. E. Interpretation of variations
in cost data for a group of individual
firms. JFE 26:388-91 May 44

Ezekiel, M. and Wylie, K. H. Cost functions
for the steel industry. JASA 36:91-99
Mar 41

Haines, W. W. Capacity production and the
least cost point. AER 38:617-24 Sep 48

-- --- Reply. AER 39:1287-89 Dec 49

Hurwicz, L. Some problems arising in
estimating economic relations. Em 15:
236-40 Jul 47

Lange, O. Theoretical derivation of elasticities of demand and supply: the direct
method. Em 10:193-214 Jul-Oct 42

Larson, A. L. The fixity gradient: a tool
for fixed and variable cost analysis.
JFE 28:825-34 Aug 46

Lerner, A. P. User cost and prime user
cost. AER 33:131-32 Mar 43

Maverick, L. A. Demand and supply curves.
QJE 54:307-13 Feb 40

Mehta, J. K. Diagrammatical representation of marginal, average and total prime
and supplementary costs. IJE 21:74-79
Jul 40

Mosak, J. L. Some theoretical implications
of the statistical analysis of demand and
cost functions for steel. JASA 36:
100-10 Mar 41

2.123  COST AND SUPPLY (Cont.)

Nichol, A. J.  Production and the probabilities of cost.  QJE 57:69-89 Nov 42

Noyes, C. R.  Certain problems in the empirical study of costs.  AER 31: 473-92 Sep 41

Oliver, H. M., Jr.  The relationship between total output and man-hour output in American manufacturing industry.  QJE 55:239-54 Feb 41

Paulson, W. E.  Characteristics of the marginal cost curve.  JFE 30:467-99 Aug 48

Robinson, J.  Rising supply price.  Ec N.S.8:1-8 Feb 41

Rowntree, R. H.  Note on constant marginal cost.  AER 31:335-38 Jun 41

Ruggles, R.  The concept of linear total cost-output regressions.  AER 31: 332-35 Jun 41

Schumpeter, J. A., chairman.  Round table on cost and demand functions of the individual firm.  (Report of three main papers and discussion)  AER/S 32: 349-50 Mar 42

Smith, C. A.  The cost-output relation for the U.S. Steel Corporation.  REStat 24: 166-76 Nov 42

Staehle, H.  The measurement of statistical cost functions: an appraisal of some recent contributions.  AER 32:321-33 Jun 42

Stigler, G. J.  A note on discontinuous cost curves.  AER 30:832-35 Dec 40

Straus, E.  Cost accounting and statistical cost functions.  AER 35:430-32 Jun 45

Thirlby, G. F.  The subjective theory of value and accounting "cost."  Ec N.S.13: 32-49 Feb 46

Vatter, W. J.  Accounting measurements of incremental cost.  JB 18:145-56 Jul 45

-- Cost accounting and statistical cost functions.  AER 35:940-42 Dec 45

Woolley, H. B.  The anomalous case of the shifting cost curve.  QJE 57:646-56 Aug 43

Yntema, T. O., chairman.  Round table on cost functions and their relation to imperfect competition.  AER/S 30:400-02 Mar 40

2.124  JOINT PRODUCTION. JOINT COST

Ciriacy-Wantrup, S. v.  Economics of joint costs in agriculture.  JFE 23:771-818 Nov 41

2.13  PRICE AND MARKET. THEORY OF FIRM AND INDUSTRY

2.130  GENERAL

Boulding, K. E.  A liquidity preference theory of market prices.  Ec N.S.11: 55-63 May 44

Mehta, J. K.  The representative firm and its place in the study of dynamic economics.  IJE 24:126-34 Oct 43

Mills, F. C.  Elasticity of physical quantities and flexibility of unit prices in the dimension of time.  JASA 41:439-67 Dec 46

2.131  THE FIRM AND ITS EQUILIBRIUM

2.1310  GENERAL

Boulding, K. E.  The theory of the firm in the last ten years.  AER 32:791-802 Dec 42

Court, L. M.  Invariable classical stability of entrepreneurial demand and supply functions.  QJE 56:134-44 Nov 41

Dingwall, J.  Equilibrium and process analysis in the traditional theory of the firm.  CJE 10:448-63 Nov 44

Halvorson, H. W. and Waite, W. C.  Relative importance of changes in demand and quantity on producer revenues.  JFE 22:776-79 Nov 40

Katona, G.  Psychological analysis of business decisions and expectations.  AER 36: 44-62 Mar 46

Neal, A. C.  Marginal cost and dynamic equilibrium of the firm.  JPE 50:45-64 Feb 42

Otsuka, I.  On the liquidity of industrial enterprise.  Kyo 19,no.1:20-43 Jan 44

Preinreich, G. A. D.  The mathematical theory of the firm.  EI 2:492-508 Mar 49

Reder, M. W.  Inter-temporal relations of demand and supply within the firm.  CJE 7:25-38 Feb 41

2.1311  PROFIT MAXIMIZATION AND BUSINESS BEHAVIOR

Dickson, H.  A note on business planning and interest rates.  NTTO 12:75-81 no.37, 48

Enke, S.  Resource malallocation within firms.  QJE 63:572-76 Nov 49

Hurwicz, L.  Theory of the firm and of investment.  Em 14:109-36 Apr 46

Myrvoll, O.  The profit motive and the theory of partial equilibrium of the firm.  NTTO 12:179-86 no.37, 48

Nichol, A. J.  Probability analysis in the theory of demand, net revenue and price.  JPE 49:637-61 Oct 41

Scitovszky, T.  A note on profit maximisation and its implications.  REStud 11: 57-60 no.1, 43

2.1312  BUSINESS EXPECTATIONS

Coase, R. H. and Fowler, R. F.  The analysis of producers' expectations.  Ec N.S.7:280-92 Aug 40

Heflebower, R. B.  The effect of dynamic forces on the elasticity of revenue curves.  QJE 55:652-66 Aug 41

# 2. ECONOMIC THEORY, ETC.

## 2.1312 BUSINESS EXPECTATIONS (Cont.)
Lange, O. A note on innovations.
RGStat 25:19-25 Feb 43

## 2.1313 THEORY OF ORGANIZATION
Cooper, W. W. Theory of the firm: some
suggestions for revision. AER 39:
1204-22 Dec 49

## 2.132 MARKET EQUILIBRIUM
## 2.1320 GENERAL
Aoyama, H. On the extension of the con-
cept of a commodity: a note on Hicks'
theory of the "group of commodities."
Kyo 18,no.2:48-68 Apr 43
Davies, G. R. Pricing and price levels.
Em 14:219-26 Jul 46
Mehta, J. K. The conception of market in
economic theory. IJE 23:364-71 Apr 43
Radford, R. A. The economic organisation
of a P.O.W. camp. Ec N.S.12:189-201
Nov 45

## 2.1321 STABILITY OF MARKET EQUILIB-
RIUM
Coase, R. H. and Fowler, R. F. The analy-
sis of producers' expectations.
Ec N.S.7:280-92 Aug 40
Pabst, W. R., Jr. Unstable conditions of
competition and monopoly in exhaustible
resource industries. JPE 50:739-49
Oct 42
Smithies, A. The stability of competitive
equilibrium. Em 10:258-74 Jul-Oct 42
Tinbergen, J. Unstable and indifferent
equilibria in economic systems.
RIIS 9:36-50 no.1-2, 41

## 2.1322 SPECULATION. FORWARD MARKETS
Blau, G. Some aspects of the theory of
futures trading. REStud 12:1-30 no.1, 44
Dow, J. C. R. Addenda to Mr. Kaldor's
note [on the theory of the forward mar-
ket]. REStud 7:201-02 Jun 40
-- A theoretical account of futures markets.
REStud 7:185-95 Jun 40
-- The inaccuracy of expectations. A sta-
tistical study of the Liverpool cotton
futures market, 1921-22, 1937-38.
Ec N.S.8:162-75 May 41
Hawtrey, R. G. Mr. Kaldor on the forward
market. REStud 7:202-05 Jun 40
Kaldor, N. A note on the theory of the
forward market. REStud 7:196-201
Jun 40
Leeman, W. A. An evaluation of organized
speculation. SEJ 16:139-46 Oct 49
Shackle, G. L. S. An analysis of specula-
tive choice. Ec N.S.12:10-21 Feb 45
Working, H. Quotations on commodity
futures as price forecasts. Em 10:39-52
Jan 42

-- The investigation of economic expectations. AER/S 39:150-66 May 49
-- The theory of price of storage. AER 39:
1254-62 Dec 49

## 2.1323 PRICE CONTROL AND BLACK
MARKET
Boulding, K. E. A note on the theory of
the black market. CJE 13:115-18
Feb 47
Bronfenbrenner, M. Price control under
imperfect competition. AER 37:107-20
Mar 47
-- Regressus in black market demand: a
reply. AER 37:934-36 Dec 47
-- Price control under imperfect competi-
tion: the joint production problem.
CJE 15:210-16 May 49
Nordin, J. A. and Moore, W. R. Bronfen-
brenner on the black market. AER 37:
933-34 Dec 47
Plumptre, A. F. W. The theory of the
black market: further considerations.
CJE 13:280-82 May 47
Polak, J. J. On the theory of price control.
REStat 27:10-16 Feb 45

## 2.133 COMPETITION AND MONOPOLY
## 2.1330 GENERAL
Bain, J. S. Market classifications in
modern price theory. QJE 56:560-74
Aug 42
Barfod, B. Polysony, polypoly. NTTO 12:
31-39 no.37, 48
Beach, E. F. Triffin's classification of
market positions. CJE 9:69-74 Feb 43
Boulding, K. E. In defense of monopoly.
QJE 59:524-42 Aug 45
Chamberlin, E. H. [Various views on the
monopoly problem.] Some final com-
ments. REStat 31:123-29 May 49
Holben, R. E. In defense of monopoly:
comment [followed by K. W. Rothschild's
further comment and K. E. Boulding's
reply]. QJE 60:612-21 Aug 46
Mason, E. S. [Various views on the
monopoly problem.] Introduction.
REStat 31:104-06 May 49
Nichol, A. J. Monopoly supply and monopsony demand. JPE 50:861-79 Dec 42
Nicholls, W. H. Social biases and recent
theories of competition. QJE 58:1-26
Nov 43
Nicols, A. The rehabilitation of pure
competition. QJE 62:31-63 Nov 47
Rothschild, K. W. Monopsony, buying costs,
and welfare expenditure. REStud 10:
62-67 no.1, 42
Scitovszky, T. Prices under monopoly and
competition. JPE 49:663-85 Oct 41
Weintraub, S. The classification of market
positions: comment [followed by R.
Triffin's reply]. QJE 56:666-77 Aug 42

2.133 COMPETITION AND MONOPOLY
(Cont.)

2.1330 GENERAL (Cont.)

Wolfe, A. B. Price-making in a democracy.
R. JPE 53:73-78 Mar 45

Yntema, T. O. Competition as a norm of
economic behavior. JB 14:270-83 Jul 41

2.1331 MONOPOLY. DEGREE OF MONOPOLY

Anderson, T. J., Jr. Note on "The rise of
monopoly." AER 30:118-20 Mar 40

Bain, J. S. Measurements of the degree of
monopoly: a note. Ec N.S.10:66-68
Feb 43

Balakrishna, R. Monopolistic influences in
capitalistic economy. IJE 24:368-73
Apr 44

Bauer, P. T. A note on monopoly.
Ec N.S.8:194-202 May 41

Duncan, A. J. Monopoly adjustments to
shifts in demand. Em 10:75-79 Jan 42

Kalecki, M. Mr. Whitman on the concept of
"degree of monopoly": a comment.
EJ 52:121-27 Apr 42

Morgan, T. A measure of monopoly in
selling. QJE 60:461-63 May 46

Papandreou, A. G. Market structure and
monopoly power. AER 39:883-97 Sep 49

Rothschild, K W. The degree of monopoly.
Ec N.S.9:24-39 Feb 42

-- A further note on the degree of monopoly.
Ec N.S.10:69-70 Feb 43

Triffin, R. Monopoly in particular-equilibrium and in general-equilibrium economics. Em 9:121-27 Apr 41

Weintraub, S. Monopoly equilibrium and
anticipated demand. JPE 50:427-34
Jun 42

-- Monopoly pricing and unemployment.
QJE 61:108-24 Nov 46

Whitman, R. H. A note on the concept of
"degree of monopoly." EJ 51:261-69
Jun-Sep 41

2.1332 COMPETITION: PURE, MONOPOLIS-
TIC, IMPERFECT. ENTRY

Chamberlin, E. H. An experimental imperfect market. JPE 56:95-108 Apr 48

-- A supplementary bibliography on monopolistic competition. QJE 62:629-38
Aug 48

Clark, J. M. Toward a concept of workable
competition. AER 30:241-56 Jun 40

Cochran, T. C. Historical aspects of imperfect competition: theory and history.
JEH/S 3:27-32 Dec 43

Copeland, M. A. Competing products and
monopolistic competition. QJE 55:1-35
Nov 40

Enke, S. Profit maximization under
monopolistic competition. AER 31:
317-26 Jun 41

Fog, B. Dynamic price problems under
monopolistic competition. NTTO 11:
257-70 no.36, 47

Gregory, P. M. Fashion and monopolistic
competition. JPE 56:69-75 Feb 48

Hawkins, E. R. Marketing and the theory
of monopolistic competition. JM 4:
382-89 Apr 40

Hawtrey, R. G. Competition from newcomers. Ec N.S.10:219-22 Aug 43

Kalecki, M. The supply curve of an industry under imperfect competition.
REStud 7:91-112 Feb 40

Levy, M. J., Jr. Note on some Chamberlinian solutions. AER 30:344-46 Jun 40

Lynch, E. S. A note on Mr. Higgins'
"Indeterminancy in non-perfect compe-
tition" [followed by B. Higgins' reply].
AER 30:347-50 Jun 40

Machlup, F. Competition, pliopoly, and
profit. Pt.I-II. Ec N.S.9:1-23; 153-73
Feb, May 42

Mehta, J. K. Competition and the demand
curve. IJE 28:547-54 Apr 48

Mund, V. A. Monopolistic competition
theory and public price policy. AER 32:
727-43 Dec 42

Nicols, A. The development of monopolistic
competition and the monopoly problem.
REStat 31:118-23 May 49

Renwick, C. The equilibrium of the firm in
monopolistic and imperfect competition
theories. ER 24:32-41 Jun 48

Smithies, A. Equilibrium in monopolistic
competition. QJE 55:95-115 Nov 40

-- An addendum. QJE 56:332-36 Feb 42

Stolper, W. F. The possibility of equilibrium under monopolistic competition.
QJE 54:519-26 May 40

Yntema, T. O., chairman. Round table on
cost functions and their relation to imperfect competition. AER/S 30:400-02
Mar 40

2.1333 OLIGOPOLY. BILATERAL MONOPOLY

Adelman, M. A. The large firm and its
suppliers. REStat 31:113-18 May 49

Bain, J. S. Output quotas in imperfect
cartels. QJE 62:617-22 Aug 48

-- Pricing in monopoly and oligopoly.
AER 39:448-64 Mar 49

Brems, H. Some notes on the structure of
the duopoly problem. NTTO 12:41-74
no.37, 48

Bronfenbrenner, M. Applications of the
discontinuous oligopoly demand curve.
JPE 48:420-27 Jun 40

Dowdell, E. G. Oligopoly and imperfect
competition. OEP N.S.1:217-26 Jun 49

Efroymson, C. W. A note on kinked demand
curves. AER 33:98-109 Mar 43

Fellner, W. Prices and wages under bilateral monopoly. QJE 61:503-32 Aug 47

## 2. ECONOMIC THEORY, ETC.

### 2.1333 OLIGOPOLY. BILATERAL MONOPOLY (Cont.)

Henderson, A. M. A further note on the problem of bilateral monopoly. JPE 48: 238-43 Apr 40

Heyward, E. J. R. H. von Stackelberg's work on duopoly. ER 17:99-106 Jun 41

Jaffé, W. [and others] The economic theory of imperfect competition, oligopoly, and monopoly: discussion. AER/S 38:19-32 May 48

Kaysen, C. A dynamic aspect of the monopoly problem. REStat 31:109-13 May 49

Leontief, W. W. Multiple-plant firms: comment. QJE 61:650-51 Aug 47

Lewis, H. G. Some observations on duopoly theory. AER/S 38:1-9 May 48

Lindblom, C. E. "Bargaining power" in price and wage determination. QJE 62: 396-417 May 48

Morgan, J. N. Bilateral monopoly and the competitive output. QJE 63:371-91 Aug 49

Morgenstern, O. Oligopoly, monopolistic competition, and the theory of games. AER/S 38:10-18 May 48

Morin, A. J. A note on bilateral monopoly, with special reference to seasonal agricultural labor. JFE 31:101-15 Feb 49

Patinkin, D. Multiple-plant firms, cartels, and imperfect competition. QJE 61: 173-205 Feb 47

-- Note on the allocation of output. QJE 61: 651-57 Aug 47

Pigou, A. C. A comment on duopoly. Ec N.S.15:254-58 Nov 48

Reynolds, L. G. Cutthroat competition. AER 30:736-47 Dec 40

Rothschild, K. W. Price theory and oligopoly. EJ 57:299-320 Sep 47

Smith, V. E. Note on the kinky oligopoly demand curve. SEJ 15:205-10 Oct 48

Smithies, A. and Savage, L. J. A dynamic problem in duopoly. Em 8:130-43 Apr 40

Stigler, G. J. Notes on the theory of duopoly. JPE 48:521-41 Aug 40

-- The kinky oligopoly demand curve and rigid prices. JPE 55:432-49 Oct 47

Weintraub, S. Price cutting and economic warfare. SEJ 8:309-22 Jan 42

### 2.1334 FULL-COST PRICING

Andrews, P. W. S. A reconsideration of the theory of the individual business. OEP N.S.1:54-89 Jan 49

Due, J. F. A theory of retail price determination. SEJ 7:380-97 Jan 41

Fellner, W. Average-cost pricing and the theory of uncertainty. JPE 56:249-52 Jun 48

Fog, B. Price theory and reality. NTTO 12:89-94 no.37, 48

Gordon, R. A. Short-period price determination in theory and practice. AER 38:265-88 Jun 48

Hague, D. C. Economic theory and business behavior. REStud 16:144-57 no.3, 49

Lester, R. A. Equilibrium of the firm. AER 39:478-84 Mar 49

Oliver, H. M., Jr. Average cost and long-run elasticity of demand. JPE 55: 212-21 Jun 47

-- Marginal theory and business behavior. AER 37:375-83 Jun 47

### 2.1335 PRICE DISCRIMINATION. MULTI-PRODUCT PRICE RELATIONS

Cassady, R., Jr. Some economic aspects of price discrimination under non-perfect market conditions. JM 11:7-20 Jul 46

-- Techniques and purposes of price discrimination. JM 11:135-50 Oct 46

Clemens, E. W. Price discrimination in decreasing cost industries. AER 31: 794-802 Dec 41

-- The marginal revenue curve under price discrimination. AER 38:388-90 Jun 48

Coase, R. H. Monopoly pricing with inter-related costs and demands. Ec N.S.13: 278-94 Nov 46

Colberg, M. R. Monopoly prices under joint costs: fixed proportions. JPE 49: 103-10 Feb 41

Copeland, M. A. A social appraisal of differential pricing. JM 6,no.4,pt.2:177-84 Apr 42

Edwards, C. D. Types of differential pricing. JM 6,no.4,pt.2:156-67 Apr 42

Leontief, W. The theory of limited and unlimited discrimination. QJE 54:490-501 May 40

Machlup, F. [Differential pricing and the general welfare]: discussion. JM 6, no.4,pt.2:184-85 Apr 42

Maroni, Y. R. Discrimination under market interdependence. QJE 62:95-117 Nov 47

Peries, H. E. Dynamical equilibrium with two alternative uses. IJE 22:87-91 Jul 41

Simkin, C. G. F. Some aspects and generalisations of the theory of discrimination. REStud 15:1-13 no.1, 47

Weldon, J. C. The multi-product firm. CJE 14:176-90 May 48

Worcester, D. A., Jr. Justifiable price "discrimination" under conditions of natural monopoly: a diagrammatic representation. AER 38:382-88 Jun 48

2.133  COMPETITION AND MONOPOLY
(Cont.)
2.1336  PRODUCT DIFFERENTIATION. SALES
EFFORT
Brems, H.  The interdependence of quality
variations, selling effort and price.
QJE 62:418-40 May 48
Bronfenbrenner, M.  Price control under
imperfect competition: the joint production problem.  CJE 15:210-16 May 49
Buchanan, N. S.  Advertising expenditures:
a suggested treatment.  JPE 50:537-57
Aug 42
Chamberlin, E. H.  Advertising costs and
equilibrium: a correction.  REStud 12:
116-20 no.2, 45
Hayes, J. P.  A note on selling costs and
the equilibrium of the firm.  REStud 12:
106-09 no.2, 45
Jastram, R. W.  Advertising outlays under
oligopoly. (Various views on the monopoly problem)  REStat 31:106-09 May 49
Nordin, J. A.  Spatial allocation of selling
expenses.  JM 7:210-19 Jan 43
Rothschild, K. W.  A note on advertising.
EJ 52:112-21 Apr 42
Silcock, T. H.  Professor Chamberlin and
Mr. Smith on advertising.  REStud 15:
34-39 no.1, 47
Smith, H.  Advertising costs and equilib-
rium: a reply.  REStud 15:40-41
no.1, 47
Zingler, E. K.  Advertising and the maxi-
misation of profit.  Ec N.S.7:318-21
Aug 40

2.1337  SPATIAL COMPETITION. BASING-
POINT
Ackley, G.  Spatial competition in a dis-
continuous market.  QJE 56:212-30
Feb 42
Clark, J. M.  Imperfect competition theory
and basing-point problems.  AER 33:
283-300 Jun 43
Coase, R. H.  The economics of uniform
pricing systems.  MS 15:139-56 May 47
Enke, S.  Space and value.  QJE 56:627-37
Aug 42
Fetter, F. A.  Exit basing point pricing.
AER 38:815-27 Dec 48
Mund, V. A.  Reply to Professor Clark on
Imperfect competition theory and basing-
point problems [followed by J. M. Clark's
rejoinder].  AER 33:612-19 Sep 43
Nelson, S.  Basing-point problems: com-
ment.  AER 33:620-22 Sep 43
Salera, V.  Aspects of the basing-point
system: comment [followed by A.
Smithies' reply].  AER 33:900-02 Dec 43
Smithies, A.  Monopolistic price policy in
a spatial market.  Em 9:63-73 Jan 41
-- Optimum location in spatial competition.
JPE 49:423-39 Jun 41

-- Aspects of the basing-point system.
AER 32:705-26 Dec 42
Stigler, G. J.  A theory of delivered price
systems.  AER 39:1143-59 Dec 49

2.1338  TAX SHIFTING AND PRODUCT PRICES
Arnold, S.  Forward shifting of a payroll
tax under monopolistic competition.
QJE 61:267-84 Feb 47
Due, J. F.  Ad valorem and specific taxes.
QJE 54:679-85 Aug 40
Fagan, E. D.  Tax shifting in the market
period.  AER 32:72-86 Mar 42; Correc-
tion. 356 Jun 42
Gilbert, D. W.  [The incidence of sales
taxes]: rejoinder.  QJE 54:686-93
Aug 40
Higgins, B.  The incidence of sales taxes:
a note on methodology.  QJE 54:665-72
Aug 40
Holden, G.  Incidence of taxation as an
analytical concept.  AER 30:774-86
Dec 40
Jastram, R. W.  The shifting of sales taxes.
QJE 54:673-78 Aug 40
Kendrick, M. S.  Comment on incidence of
taxation.  AER 31:110 Mar 41
Mehta, J. K.  Taxation of monopoly.
IJE 25:124-29 Oct 44
Pritchard, L. J.  The effects of specific
and ad valorem taxes.  QJE 58:149-52
Nov 43
Reilly, E. E.  The use of the elasticity
concept in economic theory; with special
reference to some economic effects of
a commodity tax.  CJE 6:39-55 Feb 40
Shephard, R. W.  A mathematical theory of
the incidence of taxation.  Em 12:1-18
Jan 44

2.1339  INNOVATION AND COMPETITION
Lange, O.  A note on innovations.
REStat 25:19-25 Feb 43

2.14  GENERAL EQUILIBRIUM
2.140  GENERAL
Champernowne, D. G.  A note on J. v.
Neumann's article on "A model of economic equilibrium."  REStud 13:10-18
no.1, 45
Fort, D. M.  A theory of general short-run
equilibrium.  Em 13:293-310 Oct 45
Frisch, R.  Overdeterminateness and optimum equilibrium.  NTTO 12:95-105
no.37, 48
Gloerfelt-Tarp, B.  The marginal productivity function and the Walras-Cassel
system of equations.  NTTO 12:111-21
no.37, 48
Hicks, J. R.  Recent contributions to general equilibrium economics.  R.
Ec N.S.12:235-42 Nov 45

## 2. ECONOMIC THEORY, ETC.

### 2.14 GENERAL EQUILIBRIUM (Cont.)
### 2.140 GENERAL (Cont.)

Mehta, J. K. The concepts of static and dynamic equilibria in the general theory of value. IJE 26:1-10 Jul 45

Metzler, L. A. Stability of multiple markets: the Hicks conditions. Em 13: 277-92 Oct 45

Neisser, H. A note on Pareto's theory of production. Em 8:253-62 Jul 40

Patinkin, D. Relative prices, Say's law, and the demand for money. Em 16: 135-54 Apr 48

-- The indeterminacy of absolute prices in classical economic theory. Em 17:1-27 Jan 49

Reder, M. W. Monopolistic competition and the stability conditions. REStud 8: 122-25 Feb 41

Roy, P. On Marshall's statics and dynamics. IJE 20:761-71 Apr 40

Singer, K. Robot economics; a critical introduction to Von Neumann's theory of general equilibrium. ER 25,(no.48): 48-73 Jun 49

Timlin, M. F. General equilibrium analysis and public policy. CJE 12:483-95 Nov 46

-- General equilibrium analysis and public policy: a rejoinder. CJE 13:285-87 May 47

Triffin, R. Monopoly in particular-equilibrium and in general-equilibrium economics. Em 9:121-27 Apr 41

Tyndall, D. G. A note on "General equilibrium analysis and public policy." CJE 13:118-20 Feb 47

Von Neumann, J. A model of general economic equilibrium (translated by G. Morgenstern). REStud 13:1-9 no.1, 45

Williams, B. R. Further note on a homogeneous system. ER 24:104-08 Jun 48

### 2.15 LOCATION THEORY

Balakrishna, R. Limitations of the deductive theories of industrial location. IJE 27:117-21 Oct 46

Converse, P. D. New laws of retail gravitation. JM 14:379-84 Oct 49

Hammond, S. Location theory and the cotton industry. JEH/S 2:101-17 Dec 42

Helburn, S. Location of industry. LE 19: 253-63 Aug 43

Hutchinson, K. D. Traffic and trade correlations: a technique in store location. JM 5:137-42 Oct 40

Isard, W. The general theory of location and space-economy. QJE 63:476-506 Nov 49

Paranjpe, V. M. Theory of location of industry. IJE 27:131-39 Oct 46

Ramanadham, V. V. Railways and industrial location. Pt.I-II. IJE 27:163-76; 28:237-43 Oct 46, Oct 47

Robinson, A. A problem in the theory of industrial location. EJ 51:270-75 Jun-Sep 41

Rodwin, L. Two approaches to industrial location analysis. LE 21:23-33 Feb 45

Smith, G. C., Jr. Lorenz curve analysis of industrial decentralization. JASA 42: 591-96 Dec 47

### 2.16 WELFARE ECONOMICS
### 2.160 GENERAL

Christenson, C. L. Note on national income measurement; a supplement to Professor Whittaker on "Wealth and welfare." AER 31:107-08 Mar 41

Fleming, J. M. A new synthesis of welfare economics. R. MS 14,no.3:1-18 Sep 46

Frisch, R. Overdeterminateness and optimum equilibrium. NTTO 12:95-105 no.37, 48

Jastram, R. W. Economic welfare: a comment. EJ 50:156-57 Mar 40

Lange, O. The foundations of welfare economics. Em 10:215-28 Jul-Oct 42

Lazere, M. Welfare economics a misnomer. AER 30:346-47 Jun 40

Little, I. M. D. The foundations of welfare economics. OEP N.S.1:227-46 Jun 49

-- The economist and the state. REStud 17: 75-76 no.1, 49

Radomysler, A. Welfare economics and economic policy. R. Ec N.S.13:190-204 Aug 46

Roy, P. On the conception of collective wants. IJE 26:11-28 Jul 45

Samuelson, P. A. Further commentary on welfare economics. AER 33:604-07 Sep 43

Stigler, G. J. The new welfare economics. AER 33:355-59 Jun 43

Surányi-Unger, T. Analytical notes on economic systems. ZN 12:171-97 Dec 49

Timlin, M. F. Theories of welfare economics. R. CJE 15:551-59 Nov 49

Tintner, G. A note on welfare economics. Em 14:69-78 Jan 46

Whittaker, E. Wealth and welfare. AER 30: 580-82 Sep 40

### 2.161 ALLOCATIVE EFFICIENCY
### 2.1610 GENERAL

Boulding, K. E. The concept of economic surplus. AER 35:851-69 Dec 45; Errata. 36:393 Jun 46

Coase, R. H. The marginal cost controversy. Ec N.S.13:169-82 Aug 46

-- The marginal cost controversy: some further comments. Ec N.S.14:150-53 May 47

Dey, H. L. Socialist economy and the problem of pricing. IJE 21:723-30 Apr 41

2.16  WELFARE ECONOMICS (Cont.)
2.161  ALLOCATIVE EFFICIENCY (Cont.)
2.1610  GENERAL (Cont.)

Enke, S.  Consumer cooperatives and economic efficiency.  AER 35:148-55 Mar 45

Gopal, M. H.  The role of cost in socialist pricing.  IJE 21:435-55 Apr 41

Haraldson, W. C.  Welfare economics and rationing.  QJE 58:146-48 Nov 43

Hutt, W. H.  The concept of waste. SAJE 11:1-10 Mar 43

Koopmans, T. C.  Optimum utilization of the transportation system.  Em 17, suppl.:136-45 Jul 49; Errata.  19:227 Apr 51

Krishna Murthy, T.  Output and price in a socialist economy.  IJE 21:470-75 Apr 41

Lange, O.  The practice of economic planning and the optimum allocation of resources.  Em 17,suppl.:166-70 Jul 49

Lewis, W. A.  Fixed costs.  Ec N.S.13: 231-58 Nov 46

Nordin, J. A.  The marginal cost controversy: a reply.  Ec N.S.14:134-49 May 47

Reder, M. W.  Welfare economics and rationing.  QJE 57:153-59 Nov 42

Ruggles, N.  The welfare basis of the marginal cost pricing principle.  REStud 17: 29-46 no.1, 49

Satyanarayanarao, T.  Saving, investment and enterprise in a socialistic state. IJE 21:488-96 Apr 41

Scitovszky, T. de.  A note on welfare propositions in economics.  REStud 9: 77-88 Nov 41

Staehle, H.  Elasticity of demand and social welfare.  QJE 54:217-31 Feb 40

Stafford, J.  The optimal utilization of national resources.  Em 17,suppl.: 157-64 Jul 49

Thirlby, G. F.  The ruler.  SAJE 15:253-76 Dec 46

-- The marginal cost controversy: a note on Mr. Coase's model.  Ec N.S.14:48-53 Feb 47

Tirumalachar, B.  Allocation of resources in a socialist economy.  IJE 21:511-25 Apr 41

Vickrey, W.  Some objections to marginal-cost pricing.  JPE 56:218-38 Jun 48

Wilson, T.  Private enterprise and the theory of value.  MS 16:165-91 May 48

Worcester, D. A., Jr.  Justifiable price "discrimination" under conditions of natural monopoly: a diagrammatic representation.  AER 38:382-88 Jun 48

2.1611  PUBLIC UTILITIES. PUBLIC ENTERPRISE

Balakrishna, R.  Rate structure of public utilities in a socialist state.  IJE 21: 383-94 Apr 41

Coase, R. H.  Price and output policy of state enterprise: a comment.  EJ 55: 112-13 Apr 45

Gopal, M. H.  A new basis for railway rates: the social benefit of service principle.  IJE 26:441-51 Jan 46

Henderson, A. M.  The pricing of public utility undertakings.  MS 15:223-50 Sep 47

-- Prices and profits in state enterprise. REStud 16:13-24 no.1, 48

Jantzen, I.  Social production theory. NTTO 12:141-50 no.37, 48

Little, I. M. D.  Welfare and tariffs. REStud 16:65-70 no.2, 49

Meade, J. E. and Fleming, J. M.  Price and output policy of state enterprise.  A symposium.  EJ 54:321-39 Dec 44

Norris, H.  State enterprise price and output policy and the problem of cost imputation.  Ec N.S. 14:54-62 Feb 47

Ramanadham, V. V.  Road-owners and road-hauliers.  IJE 25:520-32 Apr 45

Sveistrup, P. P.  Some problems in laying out a new traffic line.  NTTO 12:255-64 no.37, 48

Troxel, E.  Demand elasticity and control of public utility earnings.  AER 38: 372-82 Jun 48

Wilson, T.  Price and outlay policy of state enterprise.  EJ 55:454-61 Dec 45

2.162  SOCIAL CHOICE. DISTRIBUTIVE JUSTICE

Adarkar, B. P.  Interpersonal comparisons of utility.  IJE 20:513-30 Apr 40

Baumol, W. J.  Community indifference [followed by N. Kaldor's comment]. REStud 14:44-49 no.1, 46

Black, D.  The decisions of a committee using a special majority.  Em 16:245-61 Jul 48

-- The elasticity of committee decisions with an altering size of majority.  Em 16: 262-70 Jul 48

Bowen, H. R.  The interpretation of voting in the allocation of economic resources. QJE 58:27-48 Nov 43

Fisher, A. G. B.  "Full employment" and income inequality.  EJ 56:18-26 Mar 46

Hicks, J. R.  The valuation of the social income.  Ec N.S.7:105-24 May 40

-- The valuation of the social income: a comment on Professor Kuznets' reflections.  Ec N.S.15:163-72 Aug 48

Hutt, W. H.  The concept of consumers' sovereignty.  EJ 50:66-77 Mar 40

-- Distributive justice.  SAJE 9:219-34 Sep 41

## 2. ECONOMIC THEORY, ETC.

### 2.16 WELFARE ECONOMICS (Cont.)
### 2.162 SOCIAL CHOICE. DISTRIBUTIVE JUSTICE (Cont.)

Krishnaswami Ayyangar, **A. A.** Inequalities [of incomes]. IJE 24:65-70 Jul 43    C

Kuznets, S. On the valuation of social income: reflections on Professor Hicks' article. Pt.I-II. Ec N.S.15: 1-16; 116-31 Feb,May 48

Little, I. M. D. The valuation of the social income. Ec N.S.16:11-26 Feb 49

Neal, A. C. The "planning approach" in public economy. QJE 54:246-54 Feb 40    A

Worcester, D. A., Jr. Economics, politics, and consumer subsidies. SEJ 11:56-62 Jul 44

### 2.163 WELFARE ANALYSIS OF TAXATION AND GOVERNMENT EXPENDITURE

Allen, J. E. A fairer income tax. EJ 50: 475-81 Dec 40

Bach, G. L. War financing and the distribution of income. AER 32:352-54 Jun 42

Green, A. R. Social reconstruction by the regulation of incomes. EJ 52:37-44 Apr 42

Henderson, **A.** The case for indirect taxation. EJ 58:538-53 Dec 48

Preinreich, G. A. D. Progressive taxation and proportionate sacrifice. AER 38: 103-17 Mar 48

Rolph, E. R. and Break, G. F. The welfare aspects of excise taxes. JPE 57:46-54 Feb 49

Wald, H. P. The classical indictment of indirect taxation. QJE 59:577-96 Aug 45

### 2.2 FACTORS OF PRODUCTION AND DISTRIBUTIVE SHARES
### 2.20 GENERAL

Gelting, J. On redistribution of income. NTTO 12:107-09 no.37, 48

Gloerfelt-Tarp, B. The marginal productivity function and the Walras-Cassel system of equations. NTTO 12:111-21 no.37, 48

Kalecki, M. A theory of long-run distribution of the product of industry. OEP 5: 31-41 Jun 41

Oakes, E. E. The incidence of the general income tax. AER/S 32:76-82 Mar 42

### 2.201 PRODUCTION FUNCTION AND INCOME DISTRIBUTION

Bronfenbrenner, M. Production functions: Cobb-Douglas, interfirm, intrafirm. Em 12:35-44 Jan 44

Browne, G. W. G. The production function for South African manufacturing industry. SAJE 11:258-68 Dec 43    HSA

Daly, P.; Olson, E. and Douglas, P. H. The production function for manufacturing in    A the United States, 1904. JPE 51:61-65 Feb 43

-- and Douglas, P. H. The production function for Canadian manufactures. JASA 38:178-86 Jun 43    C

Douglas, P. H. Are there laws of production? AER 38:1-41 Mar 48

Gunn, G. T. and Douglas, P. H. Further measurements of marginal productivity. QJE 54:399-428 May 40

-- and Douglas, P. H. The production function for American manufacturing in 1919. AER 31:67-80 Mar 41    A

-- and Douglas, P. H. A reply to Dr. Mendershausen's criticism [followed by his rejoinder]. AER 31:564-69 Sep 41

-- and Douglas, P. H. The production function for Australian manufacturing. QJE 56:108-29 Nov 41    N

-- and Douglas, P. H. The production function for American manufacturing for 1914. JPE 50:595-602 Aug 42    A

Lomax, K. S. An agricultural production function for the United Kingdom, 1924 to 1947. MS 17:146-62 May 49    EB

Mendershausen, H. On the significance of another production function: a comment. AER 31:563-64 Sep 41

Reder, M. W. An alternative interpretation of the Cobb-Douglas function. Em 11:259-64 Jul-Oct 43

Smith, V. E. The statistical production function. QJE 59:543-62 Aug 45

Tinbergen, J. Professor Douglas' production function. RIIS 10:37-47 no.1-2, 42

Williams, J. Professor Douglas' production function. ER 21:55-63 Jun 45    N

### 2.202 EFFECT OF INNOVATION ON FACTOR SHARES

Belfer, N. Implications of capital-saving inventions. SR 16:353-65 Sep 49

Bloom, G. F. A note on Hicks's theory of invention. AER 36:83-96 Mar 46

Brown, W. M. "Labor-saving" and "capital-saving" innovations. SEJ 13: 101-14 Oct 46

Graue, E. Inventions and production. REStat 25:221-23 Aug 43

Kalecki, M. A theorem on technical progress. REStud 8:178-84 Jun 41

Keirstead, B. S. Technical advance and economic equilibria. CJE 9:55-68 Feb 43

Sullam, V. B. Scientific progress as a cause of maladjustment. SEJ 8:391-95 Jan 42

### 2.21 CAPITAL AND INTEREST
### 2.210 GENERAL

Scitovszky, T. A study of interest and capital. Ec N.S.7:293-317 Aug 40

## 2.211 CAPITAL
### 2.2110 GENERAL
Anderson, M. D. Investment and the valuation of capital. Em 10:159-68 Apr 42

Fellner, W. and Ellis, H. S. Hicks and the time-period controversy. JPE 48: 563-78 Aug 40

Hagen, E. E. Capital theory in a system with no agents fixed in quantity. JPE 50: 837-59 Dec 42

Hawtrey, R. G. Professor Hayek's Pure theory of capital. R. EJ 51:281-90 Jun-Sep 41

Knight, F. H. Professor Mises and the theory of capital. R. Ec N.S.8:409-27 Nov 41

Lachman, L. M. Complementarity and substitution in the theory of capital. Ec N.S.14:108-19 May 47

Neisser, H. Capital gains and the valuation of capital and income. Em 9: 198-220 Jul-Oct 41

Paish, F. W. Capital value and income. Ec N.S.7:416-18 Nov 40

Prest, W. The pure theory of capital. R. ER 19:71-77 Jun 43

Smithies, A. Professor Hayek on The pure theory of capital. AER 31:767-79 Dec 41

Thirlby, G. F. Permanent resources. Ec N.S.10:238-50 Aug 43

### 2.2111 DEPRECIATION. OBSOLESCENCE. REPLACEMENT
Benson, C. B. and Kimball, B. F. Mortality characteristics of physical property based upon location life table and re-use ratios. Em 13:214-24 Jul 45

Caplan, B. The premature abandonment of machinery. REStud 7:113-22 Feb 40

Dobrovolsky, S. P. The effect of replacement investment on national income and employment. JPE 55:352-58 Aug 47

Froehlich, W. The role of income determination in reinvestment and investment. AER 38:78-91 Mar 48

Hayek, F. A. von. Maintaining capital intact: a reply. Ec N.S.8:276-80 Aug 41

Hicks, J. R. Maintaining capital intact: a further suggestion. Ec N.S.9:174-79 May 42

Jeming, J. Estimates of average service life and life expectancies and the standard deviation of such estimates. Em 11: 141-50 Apr 43

Kimball, B. F. General theory of plant account subject to constant mortality law of retirements. Em 11:61-82 Jan 43

-- A system of life tables for physical property based on the truncated normal distribution. Em 15:342-60 Oct 47; Errata. 21:370 Apr 53

Moonitz, M. The risk of obsolescence and the importance of the rate of interest. JPE 51:348-55 Aug 43

Pigou, A. C. Maintaining capital intact. Ec N.S.8:271-75 Aug 41

Preinreich, G. A. D. The economic life of industrial equipment. Em 8:12-44 Jan 40

-- Note on the theory of depreciation [followed by K. G. Hagstroem's reply]. Em 9:80-92 Jan 41

## 2.212 INTEREST. RATES OF RETURN
### 2.2120 GENERAL
Haavelmo, T. The effect of the rate of interest on investment: a note. REStat 23:49-52 Feb 41

Hayek, F. A. Time-preference and productivity: a reconsideration. Ec N.S.12: 22-25 Feb 45

Knight, F. H. Diminishing returns from investment. JPE 52:26-47 Mar 44

Lutz, F. A. Professor Hayek's theory of interest [followed by F. A. von Hayek's comment]. Ec N.S.10:302-11 Nov 43

-- The interest rate and investment in a dynamic economy. AER 35:811-30 Dec 45

Morgan, T. Interest, time preference, and the yield of capital. AER 35:81-98 Mar 45; Correction. 437 Jun 45

Roos, C. F. and Von Szeliski, V. The determination of interest rates. JPE 50: 501-35 Aug 42

-- The demand for investment goods. AER/S 38:311-20 May 48

Shackle, G. L. S. The nature of interest-rates. OEP N.S.1:100-20 Jan 49

Wright, D. M. Professor Knight on limits to the use of capital. QJE 58:331-58 May 44

### 2.2121 SUPPLY OF SAVINGS
Bergson, A. The incidence of an income tax on saving. QJE 56:337-41 Feb 42

Machlup, F. Forced or induced saving: an exploration into its synonyms and homonyms. REStat 25:26-39 Feb 43

Shenoy, B. R. The classical theory of saving. IJE 28:223-36 Oct 47

Tucker, D. S. The interest rate and saving. JASA 38:101-02 Mar 43

### 2.2122 LOANABLE FUNDS. NATURAL RATE OF INTEREST
Bronfenbrenner, M. The role of money in equilibrium capital theory. Em 11: 35-60 Jan 43

Higgins, B. A diagrammatic analysis of the supply of loan funds. Em 9:231-40 Jul-Oct 41

Neisser, H. Monetary equilibrium and the natural rate of interest. SR 8:454-68 Nov 41

## 2. ECONOMIC THEORY, ETC.

### 2.213 INVESTMENT BY INDIVIDUAL FIRM. INVENTORIES

Andrews, P. W. S. A further inquiry into the effects of rates of interest. OEP 3: 33-73 Feb 40

Buchanan, N. S. Anticipations and industrial investment decisions. AER/S 32: 141-55 Mar 42

Caplan, B. Reinvestment and the rate of interest. AER 30:561-68 Sep 40

Hahn, D. Investment repercussions: a comment [followed by L. M. Lachmann's reply]. QJE 63:430-34 Aug 49

Hamilton, E. J. [and others] The determinants of investment decision: discussion. AER/S 32:156-64 Mar 42

Hart, A. G. Uncertainty and inducements to invest. REStud 8:49-53 Oct 40

-- Assets, liquidity, and investment. AER/S 39:171-81 May 49

Hildreth, C. A note on maximization criteria. QJE 61:156-64 Nov 46

Hoover, E. M. Research in the area of productive capacity and investment. AER/S 39:444-52 May 49

Hurwicz, L. Theory of the firm and of investment. Em 14:109-36 Apr 46

Lachmann, L. M. Investment repercussions. QJE 62:698-713 Nov 48

Lutz, F. A. The criterion of maximum profits in the theory of investment. QJE 60:56-77 Nov 45

Oliver, H. M. Expectations, lags, and labor-saving bias. SEJ 16:80-81 Jul 49

Peries, H. E. A note on the problem of a durable good. IJE 21:207-09 Oct 40

Sanderson, G. B. A note on the theory of investment. Ec N.S.8:176-93 May 41

Sayers, R. S. Business men and the terms of borrowing. OEP 3:23-31 Feb 40

Schackle, G. L. S. The nature of the inducement to invest. REStud 8:44-48 Oct 40

-- A reply to Professor Hart. REStud 8: 54-57 Oct 40

-- Interest-rates and the pace of investment. EJ 56:1-17 Mar 46

Shaw, E. S. Elements of a theory of inventory. JPE 48:465-85 Aug 40

Wilson, J. S. G. Investment in a monetary economy. Ec N.S.16:321-35 Nov 49

### 2.22 LABOR AND WAGES
### 2.220 GENERAL

Barna, T. Note on the productivity of labour: its concept and measurement. OIS 8:205-16 Jul 46

Bloom, G. F. A reconsideration of the theory of exploitation. QJE 55:413-42 May 41

Bowman, M. J. Theories of income distribution: where do we stand? R. JPE 56: 533-38 Dec 48

Dempsey, B. W. Ability to pay. [Presidential address] RSE 4:1-13 Jan 46

-- "Ability to pay." [Based on the presidential address before the Catholic Economic Association] QJE 60:351-64 May 46

Dewey, D. J. Occupational choice in a collectivist economy. JPE 56:465-79 Dec 48

Dunlop, J. T. and Higgins, B. "Bargaining power" and market structures. JPE 50: 1-26 Feb 42

-- The demand and supply functions for labor. AER/S 38:340-50 May 48

Gini, C. Evolution of the psychology of work and of accumulation. BNL 1: 207-19 Jan 48

Goode, R. The income tax and the supply of labor. JPE 57:428-37 Oct 49

Lester, R. A. Shortcomings of marginal analysis for wage-employment problems. AER 36:63-82 Mar 46

Lindblom, C. E. "Bargaining power" in price and wage determination. QJE 62: 396-417 May 48

Machlup, F. Marginal analysis and empirical research. AER 36:519-54 Sep 46

-- Rejoinder to an antimarginalist. AER 37: 148-54 Mar 47

Maclaurin, W. R. [and others] The determination of wages: discussion. AER/S 32:302-06 Mar 42

Mikesell, R. F. Oligopoly and the short-run demand for labor. QJE 55:161-66 Nov 40

-- The possibility of a positively sloped demand curve for labor. AER 30: 829-32 Dec 40

Miller, J. D., Jr. Wages-fund theory and the popular influence of economists. AER 30:108-12 Mar 40

Mosak, J. L. Wage increases and employment. AER 31:330-32 Jun 41

Reynolds, L. G. Relations between wage rates, costs, and prices. AER/S 32: 275-89 Mar 42

-- The supply of labor to the firm. QJE 60:390-411 May 46

-- Toward a short-run theory of wages. AER 38:289-308 Jun 48

Rothschild, K. W. Wages and risk-bearing. OIS 7:193-98 Sep 1, 45

Shackle, G. L. S. Some theoretical aspects of payment by results. EI 2:841-53 Nov 49

Stigler, G. J. Professor Lester and the marginalists. AER 37:154-57 Mar 47

Sufrin, S. C. Wage increases and employment: reply. AER 31:838 Dec 41

Winton, E. M. "Wages fund theory and the popular influence of economists": a reply. AER 31:343-44 Jun 41

## 2.2 FACTORS OF PRODUCTION AND DISTRIBUTIVE SHARES (Cont.)
## 2.22 LABOR AND WAGES (Cont.)
## 2.220 GENERAL (Cont.)

Yoder, D. The structure of the demand for labor. AER/S 32:261-74 Mar 42

## 2.221 WAGE DIFFERENTIALS

Lester, R. A. Wage diversity and its theoretical implications. REStat 28: 152-59 Aug 46

## 2.222 COLLECTIVE WAGE DETERMINATION

Austin, R. C. Effects of unionization in monopolistic competition on the southern worker. SEJ 16:81-84 Jul 49

Bloom, G. F. and Belfer, N. Unions and real labor income. SEJ 14:290-303 Jan 48

Boulding, K. E. Collective bargaining and fiscal policy. IRRA 2:52-68 Dec 49

Dunlop, J. T. Wage policies of trade unions. AER/S 32:290-301 Mar 42

-- [and others] Collective bargaining, wages and the price level: discussion. IRRA 1:51-61 Dec 48

Heimann, E. On strikes and wages. SR 15: 82-98 Mar 48

Hochwald, W. Collective bargaining and economic theory. SEJ 13:228-46 Jan 47

Leontief, W. The pure theory of the guaranteed annual wage contract. JPE 54:76-79 Feb 46

Lester, R. A. The influence of unionism upon earnings: comment [followed by A. M. Ross's reply]. QJE 62:783-90 Nov 48

Lindblom, C. E. Collective bargaining and the competitive system. CJE 11:566-77 Nov 45

-- The union as a monopoly. QJE 62: 671-97 Nov 48

Phelps, O. W. Collective bargaining, Keynesian model. AER 38:581-97 Sep 48

Reyburn, H. A. Wage and price movements. SAJE 8:183-84 Jun 40

Reynolds, L. G. Wage bargaining, price changes, and employment. IRRA 1: 35-50 Dec 48

Ross, A. M. The trade union as a wage-fixing institution. AER 37:566-88 Sep 47

-- The dynamics of wage determination under collective bargaining. AER 37: 793-822 Dec 47

-- The influence of unionism upon earnings. QJE 62:263-86 Feb 48; Addendum. 791 Nov 48

Shister, J. Collective bargaining and the competitive system: a comment. CJE 12:176-78 May 46

Slichter, S. The responsibility of organized labor for employment. AER/S 35: 193-208 May 45

-- Wage-price policy and employment. AER/S 36:304-18 May 46

## 2.223 TECHNOLOGICAL UNEMPLOYMENT

Belfer, N. The theory of the automatic reabsorption of technologically displaced labor. SEJ 16:35-43 Jul 49

Graham, B. National productivity: its relationship to unemployment-in-prosperity. AER/S 37:384-96 May 47

Hagen, E. E. Saving, investment and technological unemployment. AER 32: 553-55 Sep 42

Neisser, H. P. "Permanent" technological unemployment; "demand for commodities is not demand for labor." AER 32: 50-71 Mar 42

-- The concept of technological unemployment: a reply to Mr. Hagen's criticism. AER 32:555-57 Sep 42

Staehle, H. Employment in relation to technical progress. REStat 22:94-100 May 40

## 2.224 MINIMUM WAGES

Bronfenbrenner, M. Minimum wages, unemployability, and relief: a theoretical note. SEJ 10:52-59 Jul 43

Brown, W. M. Some effects of a minimum wage upon the economy as a whole. AER 30:98-107 Mar 40

-- --- Reply to Messrs. Mikesell, Hagen and Sufrin. AER 30:578-79 Sep 40

Hagen, E. E. Elasticity of demand and a minimum wage. AER 30:574-76 Sep 40

Hamberg, D. Minimum wages and the level of employment. SEJ 15:321-36 Jan 49

Lester, R. A. Marginalism, minimum wages, and labor markets. AER 37: 135-48 Mar 47

Mikesell, R. F. A note on the effects of minimum wages on the propensity to consume. AER 30:574 Sep 40

Stigler, G. J. The economics of minimum wage legislation. AER 36:358-65 Jun 46

Sufrin, S. C. The effects of minimum wages. AER 30:576-78 Sep 40

## 2.23 LAND AND RENT

Aggarwala, K. C. Marshall's concept of quasi-rent. IJE 28:555-61 Apr 48

Anderson, T. J., Jr. Competition and monopoly in land markets. AER 31: 341-43 Jun 41

Baker, J. A. Toward a theory of land income. LE 21:160-66 May 45

Bloom, G. F. Technical progress, costs and rent. Ec N.S.9:40-52 Feb 42

Brown, H. G. Economic rent: in what sense a surplus? AER 31:833-35 Dec 41

## 2. ECONOMIC THEORY, ETC.

### 2.23  LAND AND RENT (Cont.)

Galletti, R.  Making sense of land utilization figures.  IJE 25:465-91 Apr 45

Hammar, C. H.  Reconsideration of rent theory as it applies to agricultural land.  JFE 23:145-60 Feb 41

Hasan, M. A.  The theory of rent.  IJE 28:571-76 Apr 48

Hendrickson, C. I.  [Reconsideration of rent theory as it applies to agricultural land]: discussion.  JFE 23:170-71 Feb 41

Ise, J.  Monopoly elements in rent.  AER 30:33-45 Mar 40

Keirstead, B. S. and Coore, D. H.  Dynamic theory of rents.  CJE 12:168-72 May 46

Mehta, J. K.  Rent in economic theory.  IJE 23:59-67 Jul 42

Pribram, K.  Residual, differential, and absolute urban ground rents and their cyclical fluctuations.  Em 8:62-78 Jan 40

Rochester, A.  On the nature of rent.  S&S 4:57-69 no.1, 40

Simon, H. A.  The incidence of a tax on urban real property.  QJE 57:398-420 May 43

Singer, H. W.  An index of urban land rents and house rents in England and Wales 1845-1913.  Em 9:221-30 Jul-Oct 41

Sinha, B. C.  The basis of land tax: a problem in applied economics.  IJE 21:158-66 Oct 40

Skovgaard, K.  Utilisation of productive capacity and the problem of intensity in agriculture.  NTTO 12:247-54 no.37, 48

Spengler, J. J.  Monopolistic competition and the use and price of urban land service.  JPE 54:385-412 Oct 46

Tiwari, J. N.  Marshall and the theory of rent.  IJE 26:290-95 Oct 45

Worcester, D. A., Jr.  A reconsideration of the theory of rent.  AER 36:258-77 Jun 46

-- The dynamic theory of rents: a comment [followed by B. S. Keirstead's rejoinder].  CJE 13:283-85 May 47

Zeuthen, F.  A note about capital values.  Met 1:53-56 Apr 49

### 2.24  ENTREPRENEURSHIP AND PROFIT
### 2.240  GENERAL

Divine, T. F.  On the place of "profit" in a capitalistic economy.  RSE 2:57-67 Jan 44

Schumpeter, J. A.  The creative response in economic history.  JEH 7:149-59 Nov 47

Weston, J. F.  Profit as the payment for the function of uncertainty-bearing.  JB 22:106-18 Apr 49

-- Enterprise and profit.  JB 22:141-59 Jul 49

### 2.241  ENTREPRENEURSHIP

Aitken, H. G. J.  The analysis of decisions.  EEH 1,no.2:17-23 Feb 49

-- Parameters: a reply.  EEH 1,no.3:23-24 Mar 49

-- The problem of entrepreneurial freedom.  EEH 1,no.4:1-8 Apr 49

-- The religious sanction.  EEH 1,no.4:29-30 Apr 49

Clark, J. M.  Relations of history and theory.  (Symposium on profits and the entrepreneur)  JEH/S 2:132-42 Dec 42

Cole, A. H.  Entrepreneurship as an area of research.  JEH/S 2:118-26 Dec 42

-- An approach to the study of entrepreneurship: a tribute to Edwin F. Gay.  JEH/S 6:1-15 '46

Easterbrook, W. T.  The climate of enterprise.  AER/S 39:322-35 May 49

Evans, G. H., Jr.  A theory of entrepreneurship.  JEH/S 2:142-46 Dec 42

-- The entrepreneur and economic theory: a historical and analytical approach.  AER/S 39:336-48 May 49

Goodrich, C. [and others]  Possibilities for a realistic theory of entrepreneurship: discussion.  AER/S 39:349-55 May 49

Jenks, L. H.  Methodological problems of typologies.  EEH 1,no.1:3-7 Jan 49

Knight, F. H.  Profit and entrepreneurial functions.  JEH/S 2:126-32 Dec 42

Passer, H. C.  Entrepreneurial history and economics.  EEH 1,no.1:21-25 Jan 49

Redlich, F.  The origin of the concepts of "entrepreneur" and "creative entrepreneur."  EEH 1,no.2:1-7 Feb 49

Stauss, J. H.  The entrepreneur: the firm.  JPE 52:112-27 Jun 44

Steindl, J.  On risk.  OEP 5:43-53 Jun 41

-- Capitalist enterprise and risk.  OEP 7:21-45 Mar 45

Stykolt, S.  A note on the parametric approach.  EEH 1,no.2:25-26 Feb 49

Wohl, R. R.  [Aitken's Analysis of business decisions.]  EEH 1,no.3:26-29 Mar 49

-- A further note on Aitken's parametric approach.  EEH 2:51-53 Nov 49

### 2.242  PROFIT

Buchanan, N. S.  Toward a theory of fluctuations in business profits.  AER 31:731-53 Dec 41

Chenault, L. R.  Buchanan's theory of fluctuations in business profits.  AER 32:840-42 Dec 42

Hahn, F. H.  A note on profit and uncertainty.  Ec N.S.14:211-25 Aug 47

Kalecki, M.  A theory of profits.  EJ 52:258-67 Jun-Sep 42

Kirkenfeld, T.  The paradox of profit.  S&S 12:33-41 no.1, 48

2.242  PROFIT (Cont.)

Lacey, K.  Profit measurement and the
trade cycle.  EJ 57:456-74 Dec 47

Machlup, F.  Competition, pliopoly and
profit.  Pt.I-II.  Ec N.S.9:1-23; 153-73
Feb,May 42

Norris, H.  Profit: accounting theory and
economics.  Ec N.S.12:125-33 Aug 45

Singer, H. W.  Profit measurement and the
trade cycle.  EJ 58:594-96 Dec 48

Streeten, P.  The theory of profit.  MS 17:
266-96 Sep 49

2.243  INCIDENCE OF TAXES ON PROFITS

Boulding, K. E.  The incidence of a profits
tax.  AER 34:567-72 Sep 44

Bowen, H. R.  The incidence of the corpo-
ration income tax: a reply [followed by
R. Goode's rejoinder].  AER 36:146-48
Mar 46

Domar, E. D. and Musgrave, R. A.  Proportional income taxation and risk-
taking.  QJE 58:388-422 May 44

Goode, R.  The corporate income tax and
the price level.  AER 35:40-58 Mar 45

Macy, C. W.  Incidence or effects of the
corporation income tax?  AER 36:
903-06 Dec 46

Munshi, M. C.  Incidence and effects of
corporation taxes.  IJE 27:503-11 Apr 47

Shoup, C.  Incidence of the corporation income tax: capital structure and turnover rates.  NTJ 1:12-17 Mar 48

Weston, J. F.  Incidence and effects of the
corporate income tax.  NTJ 2:300-15
Dec 49

2.3  AGGREGATIVE AND MONETARY THEORY,
CYCLES, AND GROWTH
2.30  GENERAL

Mirkowich, N.  Schumpeter's theory of
economic development.  AER 30:580
Sep 40

Sweezy, P. M.  Professor Schumpeter's
theory of innovation.  REStat 25:93-96
Feb 43

2.31  INCOME AND EMPLOYMENT THEORY
2.310  GENERAL

Ames, E. and Ferguson, A. R.  Technological change and the equilibrium level of
the national income.  QJE 62:441-58
May 48

Anderson, M. D.  Dynamic theory of employment.  SEJ 7:37-50 Jul 40

Ayzenshtadt, A.  The learned handmaidens
of American capital.  A survey of literature.  Translated by E. D. Domar.
AER 39:930-45 Sep 49

Benoit-Smullyan, E.  Net investment, consumption and full employment [followed
by A. R. Sweezy's reply and Benoit-
Smullyan's rejoinder].  AER 34:871-79
Dec 44

Chandler, L. V.  In reply to Mr. Hicks.
SEJ 7:556-57 Apr 41

Copeland, M. A.  Keynesian economics:
savings, investment, and wage rates:
discussion.  AER/S 38:351-53 May 48

De Vegh, I.  Savings, investment, and consumption.  AER/S 30,no.5:237-47 Feb 41

Dobrovolsky, S. P.  The effect of replacement investment on national income and
employment.  JPE 55:352-58 Aug 47

Doody, F. S.  Keynesian policies and
Christian social teaching.  RSE 7,no.2:
1-9 Sep 49

Ellis, H. S.  The state of the "new economics."  AER 39:465-77 Mar 49

Fels, R.  Warburton vs Hansen and Keynes.
AER 39:923-29 Sep 49

Fossati, E.  Vilfredo Pareto and John
Maynard Keynes: one or two economic
systems?  Met 1:126-30 Oct 49

Gilbert, J. C.  Professor Polanyi's Full
employment and free trade.  R.
MS 14,no.2:85-97 May 46

Gordon, R. A.  Keynesian economics:
savings, investment, and wage rates:
discussion.  AER/S 38:354-56 May 48

Grayson, H.  The econometric approach:
a critical analysis.  JPE 56:253-57
Jun 48

Hahn, L. A.  The effects of saving on employment and consumption.  JM 11:35-43
Jul 46

Kalecki, M.  Professor Pigou on "The
classical stationary state": a comment.
EJ 54:131-32 Apr 44

Lerner, A. P.  Some Swedish stepping
stones in economic theory.  R.  CJE 6:
574-91 Nov 40

Littler, H. G.  A pure theory of money.
CJE 10:422-47 Nov 44

Moulton, H. G. [and others]  Capital expansion, employment, and economic stability: a reply to H. H. Villard.  AER 31:
110-12 Mar 41

Neisser, H.  The new economics of spending: a theoretical analysis.  Em 12:
237-55 Jul-Oct 44

Pigou, A. C.  Models of short-period equilibrium [followed by N. Kaldor's reply].
EJ 52:250-58 Jun-Sep 42

-- The classical stationary state.  EJ 53:
343-51 Dec 43

-- Some considerations on stability conditions, employment and real wage rates.
EJ 55:346-56 Dec 45

Poduval, R. N.  Multiplier, "pump-priming"
and "acceleration."  IJE 23:271-76
Jan 43

Rasmussen, P. N.  Some remarks on the
joint effects of simultaneous relations
between economic variables.  NTTO 12:
215-22 no.37, 48

## 2. ECONOMIC THEORY, ETC.

### 2.31 INCOME AND EMPLOYMENT THEORY (Cont.)

#### 2.310 GENERAL (Cont.)

Reder, M. W. Interest and employment. JPE 54:243-57 Jun 46

Samuelson, P. A. The stability of equilibrium: comparative statics and dynamics. Em 9:97-120 Apr 41

-- Professor Pigou's Employment and equilibrium. R. AER 31:545-52 Sep 41

Simpson, P. B. Neoclassical economics and monetary problems. AER 39:861-82 Sep 49

Smithies, A. Process analysis and equilibrium analysis. Em 10:26-38 Jan 42

Tintner, G. Static macro-economic models and their econometric verifications. Met 1:48-52 Apr 49

Villard, H. H. Reply to H. G. Moulton and associates. AER 31:570-72 Sep 41

Wolfe, A. B. "Full utilization," equilibrium, and the expansion of production. QJE 54: 539-65 Aug 40

Wright, D. M. The future of Keynesian economics. AER 35:284-307 Jun 45

#### 2.311 UNDEREMPLOYMENT. FULL EMPLOYMENT

Bennion, E. G. Unemployment in the theories of Schumpeter and Keynes. AER 33:336-47 Jun 43

-- Is unemployment chronic? HBR 23: 115-28 no.1, 44

Benoit-Smullyan, E. On the meaning of full employment. REStat 30:127-34 May 48

Feiler, A. "Full employment of resources" and war economy. SR 9:141-45 Feb 42

Hansen, A. H. Cost functions and full employment. AER 37:552-65 Sep 47

Isles, K. S. Employment and equilibrium: a theoretical discussion. R. ER 19: 212-24 Dec 43

Lydall, H. F. Unemployment in an unplanned economy. EJ 56:366-82 Sep 46

Oliver, H. M., Jr. The analytical value of employment-equilibrium models. SEJ 16:129-38 Oct 49

Reder, M. W. Service industries and the volume of employment. AER 31:512-19 Sep 41

Stone, R. and Jackson, E. F. Economic models with special reference to Mr. Kaldor's system. EJ 56:554-67 Dec 46

Trachtenberg, I. Soviet comment on Keynesian theories of full employment. S&S 10:405-09 no.4, 46

#### 2.312 EFFECTIVE DEMAND. AGGREGATE SUPPLY

Higgins, B. To save or not to save? R. CJE 14:98-107 Feb 48

Klein, L. R. Theories of effective demand and employment. JPE 55:108-32 Apr 47

Kreps, T. J. Consumption: a vast underdeveloped economic frontier. AER/S 30, no.5:177-99 Feb 41

Patinkin, D. Involuntary unemployment and the Keynesian supply function. EJ 59:360-83 Sep 49

Wilson, T. A reconsideration of the theory of effective demand. Ec N.S.14:283-95 Nov 47

#### 2.313 RELATION OF SAVING AND INVESTMENT

Abramovitz, M. Savings and investment: profits vs prosperity? AER/S 32,no.2: 53-88 Jun 42

Altman, O. L. Private investment, full employment, and public funds. AER/S 30,no.5:228-36 Feb 41

Anderson, M. D. A formula for total savings. QJE 58:106-19 Nov 43

Aoyama, H. A critical note on D. H. Robertson's theory of savings and investment. Pt.I-II. Kyo 16,no.1:49-73; no.2:64-81 Jan,Apr 41

Hansen, A. H. A note on savings and investment. REStat 30:30-33 Feb 48

Heilbroner, R. L. Savings and investment: dynamic aspects. AER 32:827-28 Dec 42

Neisser, H. Government net contribution and foreign balance as offset to savings. REStat 26:216-20 Nov 44

#### 2.314 INVESTMENT FUNCTION

Ezekiel, M. The statistical determination of the investment schedule [followed by L. R. Klein's reply]. Em 12:89-92 Jan 44

Haavelmo, T. A note on the theory of investment. REStud 16:78-81 no.2, 49

Klein, L. R. Pitfalls in the statistical determination of the investment schedule. Em 11:246-58 Jul-Oct 43

-- Notes on the theory of investment. Kyk 2:97-117 fasc.2, 48

Pedersen, J. Interest rates, employment and changes in population. Kyk 2:1-16 fasc.1, 48

Tsiang, S. C. Rehabilitation of time dimension of investment in macrodynamic analysis. Ec N.S.16:204-17 Aug 49

Tucker, D. S. Capital money and revenue funds. AER 32:468-85 Sep 42

Wilson, J. S. G. Investment in a monetary economy. Ec N.S.16:321-35 Nov 49

#### 2.315 CONSUMPTION FUNCTION

Baer, W. Equality and prosperity. SR 10: 118-22 Feb 43

Bassie, V. L. Woytinsky on consumption and savings. REStat 30:298-300 Nov 48

2.31 INCOME AND EMPLOYMENT THEORY (Cont.)

2.315 CONSUMPTION FUNCTION (Cont.)

Bean, L. H. Relation of disposable income and the business cycle to expenditures. REStat 28:199-207 Nov 46

Bennion, E. G. The consumption function: cyclically variable? REStat 28:219-24 Nov 46

Boulding, K. E. The consumption concept in economic theory. AER/S 35:1-14 May 45

Brady, D. S. Expenditures, savings, and income. REStat 28:216-18 Nov 46

Bronfenbrenner, M. The consumption function controversy. SEJ 14:304-20 Jan 48

Friend, I. Relationship between consumers' expenditures, savings, and disposable income. REStat 28:208-15 Nov 46

-- Consumption-saving function: comments. REStat 30:301-03 Nov 48

Garvy, G. The role of dissaving in economic analysis. JPE 56:416-27 Oct 48

Graaff, J. de V. Fluctuations in income concentration; with special reference to changes in the concentration of super-taxable incomes in South Africa: July, 1915-June, 1943. SAJE 14:22-39 Mar 46

Haavelmo, T. Methods of measuring the marginal propensity to consume. JASA 42:105-22 Mar 47

-- Family expenditures and the marginal propensity to consume. Em 15:335-41 Oct 47

Jones, M. V. Secular and cyclical saving propensities. JB 17:1-15 Jan 44

Katona, G. and Likert, R. Relationship between consumer expenditures and savings: the contribution of survey research. REStat 28:197-99 Nov 46

-- Effect of income changes on the rate of saving. REStat 31:95-103 May 49

Koffsky, N. An additional view on the consumption function. REStat 30:55-56 Feb 48

Lawler, P. J. The consumption function. ER 25,suppl.:93-122 Aug 49

Livingston, S. M. Forecasting postwar demand: II. Em 13:15-24 Jan 45

-- [and others] Consumption economics: discussion. AER/S 35:56-66 May 45

Mack, R. P. The direction of change in income and the consumption function. REStat 30:239-58 Nov 48

Metzler, L. A. Effects of income redistribution. REStat 25:49-57 Feb 43

Mosak, J. L. Forecasting postwar demand: III. Em 13:25-53 Jan 45

Musgrave, R. A. and Painter, M. S. The impact of alternative tax structures on personal consumption and saving. QJE 62:475-99 Aug 48

O'Leary, J. J. Consumption as a factor in postwar employment. AER/S 35:37-55 May 45

Quantius, F. Sales taxes and the propensity to consume. SEJ 11:269-73 Jan 45

Roos, C. F. [and others] Forecasting postwar demand: discussion. Em 13:54-59 Jan 45

Rosa, R. V. Use of the consumption function in short run forecasting. REStat 30:91-105 May 48

Schneider, E. A note on the consumption function. NTTO 12:223-27 no.37, 48

Smithies, A. Forecasting postwar demand: I. Em 13:1-14 Jan 45

Woytinsky, W. S. Relationship between consumers' expenditures, savings and disposable income. REStat 28:1-12 Feb 46

-- Consumption-saving function: its algebra and philosophy. REStat 30:45-55 Feb 48

2.316 MULTIPLIER

Anderson, M. D. Employment, investment, and the multiplier. Em 8:240-52 Jul 40

Bode, K. A note on the mathematical coincidence of the instantaneous and the serial multiplier. REStat 26:221-22 Nov 44

Cohn, S. M. Keynesian economics: the propensity to consume and the multiplier: discussion. AER/S 38:308-10 May 48

Dowdell, E. G. The multiplier. OEP 4:23-38 Sep 40

Fellner, W. Period analysis and timeless equilibrium. QJE 58:315-22 Feb 44

Garvy, G. Keynesian economics: the propensity to consume and the multiplier: discussion. AER/S 38:306-08 May 48

Goodwin, R. M. The multiplier as matrix. EJ 59:537-55 Dec 49

Iyengar, S. K. The investment multiplier [followed by B. N. Adarkar's reply]. IJE 23:80-84 Jul 42

Lange, O. The theory of the multiplier. Em 11:227-45 Jul-Oct 43

Samuelson, P. A. A fundamental multiplier identity. Em 11:221-26 Jul-Oct 43

Schelling, T. C. Income determination: a graphic solution. REStat 30:227-29 Aug 48

Smithies, A. The multiplier. AER/S 38:299-305 May 48

Tew, B. A note on the multiplier. ER 24:109-11 Jun 48

Turvey, R. The multiplier. Ec N.S.15:259-69 Nov 48

2.317 ACCELERATOR

Manne, A. S. Some notes on the acceleration principle. REStat 27:93-99 May 45

# 2. ECONOMIC THEORY, ETC.

## 2.31 INCOME AND EMPLOYMENT THEORY (Cont.)

### 2.317 ACCELERATOR (Cont.)

Wright, D. M. A neglected approach to the acceleration principle. REStat 23: 100-01 May 41

### 2.318 WAGE AND PRICE ASPECTS OF EMPLOYMENT THEORY

Arndt, H. W. Recent discussion of Keynes's theory of wages. R. ER 25,(no.49): 77-83 Dec 49

Bangs, R. B. Wage reductions and employment. JPE 50:251-71 Apr 42

Bergson, A. Prices, wages, and income theory. Em 10:275-89 Jul-Oct 42

-- Price flexibility and the level of income. REStat 25:2-5 Feb 43

Bissell, R. M., Jr. Price and wage policies and the theory of employment. Em 8: 199-239 Jul 40

-- Prices, costs, and investment. AER/S 30,no.5:200-27 Feb 41

Carroll, J. M. The distribution of efficiency savings. QJE 55:517-20 May 41

Dunlop, J. T. Wage-price relations at high level employment. AER/S 37:243-53 May 47

-- The demand and supply functions for labor. AER/S 38:340-50 May 48

Edwards, C. D. [and others] Wage-price relations at high level employment: discussion. AER/S 37:254-64 May 47

Engle, N. H. Wages, prices, and profits. JB 20:121-30 Jul 47

Fields, R. H. Lord Keynes's theory of wages. ER 22:284-89 Dec 46

Franszen, D. G. Methodological issues in the theory of price flexibility. SAJE 15: 87-115 Jun 47

Friedman, M. Lange on price flexibility and employment: a methodological criticism. AER 36:613-31 Sep 46

Hahn, L. A. Wage flexibility upwards. SR 14:148-67 Jun 47

Higgins, B. H. The optimum wage rate. REStat 31:130-39 May 49

-- Reder on wage-price policy [followed by M. W. Reder's further comment]. CJE 15: 203-10 May 49

Hildebrand, G. H., Jr. The Nathan Report and its critics. AER 37:386-91 Jun 47

Jones, M. V. Wage-rate reductions as a stimulus to recovery. JB 14:68-82 Jan 41

Oliver, H. M., Jr. Does wage reduction aid employment by lowering prices? SEJ 6: 333-43 Jan 40

Patinkin, D. Price flexibility and full employment. AER 38:543-64 Sep 48

Reder, M. W. The theoretical problems of a national wage-price policy. CJE 14: 46-61 Feb 48

Reynolds, L. G. Relations between wage rates, costs, and prices. AER/S 32: 275-89 May 42

Schelling, T. C. Raise profits by raising wages? Em 14:227-34 Jul 46

-- The dynamics of price flexibility. AER 39:911-22 Sep 49

Scitovszky, T. Capital accumulation, employment and price rigidity. REStud 8: 69-88 Feb 41

Slichter, S. H. Wage-price policy and employment. AER/S 36:304-18 May 46

-- Raising the price of labor as a method of increasing employment. (Comments on the steel report) REStat 31:283-88 Nov 49

Sloan, D. Full employment measures and the real wage rate. SAJE 16:306-08 Sep 48

Somers, H. M. Money wage cuts in relation to unemployment: a rejoinder to Mr. Kaldor [followed by N. Kaldor's comment]. REStud 7:136-37 Feb 40

Stein, H. Price flexibility and full employment: comment [followed by D. Patinkin's reply]. AER 39:725-28 Jun 49

Straus, E. M. Prices, income flow and employment. QJE 60:600-11 Aug 46

Swan, T. W. Price flexibility and employment. R. ER 21:236-53 Dec 45

Sweezy, A. Wages and investment. JPE 50: 117-29 Feb 42

Timlin, M. F. Price flexibility and employment. CJE 12:204-13 May 46

Tobin, J. A note on the money wage problem. QJE 55:508-16 May 41

Tsiang, S. C. Prof. Pigou on the relative movements of real wages and employment. EJ 54:352-65 Dec 44

Unterberger, S. H. and Henig, H. Theory of wage control in the transition period. SEJ 12:283-89 Jan 46

Weintraub, S. Monopoly pricing and unemployment. QJE 61:108-24 Nov 46

Williams, B. R. Mr. Swan's theory of price flexibility [followed by T. W. Swan's rejoinder]. ER 22:275-84 Dec 46

-- Types of competition and the theory of employment. OEP N.S.1:121-44 Jan 49

## 2.32 MONETARY THEORY

### 2.320 GENERAL

Amoroso, L. Prices and money. Em 17, suppl.:334-40 Jul 49; Errata. 19:227 Apr 51

Hicks, J. R. The monetary theory of D. H. Robertson. R. Ec N.S.9:53-57 Feb 42

Kemp, M. C. Interest and the money supply in Keynes' economics. ER 25,(no.49): 64-73 Dec 49

Krishnaswamy, A. Marshall's theory of money and interest. IJE 22:121-43 Oct 41

2.32 MONETARY THEORY (Cont.)
2.320 GENERAL (Cont.)

Marget, A. W. Monetary theory at the textbook level. AER 32:775-90 Dec 42

Marschak, J. Wicksell's two interest rates. SR 8:469-78 Nov 41

Modigliani, F. Liquidity preference and the theory of interest and money. Em 12: 45-88 Jan 44

Neisser, H. Monetary equilibrium and the natural rate of interest. SR 8:454-68 Nov 41

Shackle, G. L. S. Myrdal's analysis of monetary equilibrium. OEP 7:47-66 Mar 45

Takata, Y. Money, the economic veil. Kyo 15,no.4:25-43 Oct 40

Thirlby, G. F. Demand and supply of money. EJ 58:331-55 Sep 48

Warburton, C. Monetary theory, full production, and the Great Depression. Em 13:114-28 Apr 45

2.321 SUPPLY OF MONEY AND OF BANK CREDIT

Poindexter, J. C. A critique of functional finance through quasi-free bank credit. AER 36:311-23 Jun 46

Pritchard, L. J. The nature of bank credit: a comment. AER 37:399-402 Jun 47

Robinson, R. I. Money supply and liquid asset formation. AER 36:127-33 Mar 46

Vining, R. A process analysis of bank credit expansion. QJE 54:599-623 Aug 40

Whittlesey, C. R. Retirement of internally held debt. AER 33:602-04 Sep 43

-- Memorandum on the stability of demand deposits. AER 39:1192-1203 Dec 49

2.322 DEMAND FOR MONEY. LIQUIDITY PREFERENCE. HOARDING

Boulding, K. E. A liquidity preference theory of market prices. Ec N.S.11: 55-63 May 44

Bronfenbrenner, M. Some fundamentals in liquidity theory. QJE 59:405-26 May 45

Duncan, A. J. "Free money" of large manufacturing corporations and the rate of interest [followed by A. Kisselgoff's reply]. Em 14:251-54 Jul 46

Fellner, W. Monetary policies and hoarding in periods of stagnation. JPE 51:191-205 Jun 43

-- Monetary policy and the elasticity of liquidity functions. REStat 30:42-44 Feb 48

Friedman, M. [and others] Liquidity and uncertainty: discussion. AER/S 39: 196-210 May 49

Hahn, A. Anachronism of the liquidity preference concept. Kyk 1:203-20 fasc.3, 47

Jones, Homer. The optimum rate of investment, the savings institutions, and the banks. AER/S 38:321-39 May 48

Kennedy, C. Period analysis and the demand for money. REStud 16:41-49 no.1, 48

Kisselgoff, A. Liquidity preference of large manufacturing corporations (1921-1939). Em 13:334-46 Oct 45

Leser, C. E. V. The consumer's demand for money. Em 11:123-40 Apr 43

McKean, R. N. Liquidity and a national balance sheet. JPE 57:506-22 Dec 49

Marschak, J. Role of liquidity under complete and incomplete information. AER/S 39:182-95 May 49

Ou, P. S. Ex-ante saving and liquidity-preferences. REStud 11:52-56 no.1, 43

Philip, K. A statistical measurement of the liquidity preference of private banks. REStud 16:71-77 no.2, 49

Tobin, J. Liquidity preference and monetary policy. REStat 29:124-31 May 47

Wallich, H. C. The current significance of liquidity preference. QJE 60:490-512 Aug 46

Wright, D. Internal inconsistency in D. H. Robertson's "Saving and hoarding" concepts [followed by Robertson's comment]. EJ 51:334-38 Jun-Sep 41

2.323 VELOCITY OF CIRCULATION

Behrman, J. N. The short-term interest rate and the velocity of circulation. Em 16:185-90 Apr 48; Addendum. 370 Oct 48

Franchini-Stappo, A. Components and significance of the circular velocity of money. [Translated by O. R. Agresti] EI 2:236-49 Feb 49

Geren, P. The role of velocity of circulation in the present rise of prices. IJE 24:99-116 Oct 43

Gordon, R. A. Period and velocity as statistical concepts. QJE 55:306-13 Feb 41

Oliver, H. M., Jr. A note on velocity. REStat 31:153-54 May 49

Salant, W. S. The demand for money and the concept of income velocity. JPE 49: 395-421 Jun 41

Warburton, C. Monetary velocity and monetary policy [followed by J. Tobin's rejoinder]. REStat 30:304-17 Nov 48

2.324 QUANTITY THEORY AND PRICE LEVEL

Craig, J. I. Money and prices in Egypt (preliminary note). EgC 34:327-33 Apr-May 43

2.325 MONETARY INTEREST THEORIES

Adarkar, B. P. and Ghosh, D. Mr. Keynes's theory of interest. IJE 21:285-300 Jan 41

## 2. ECONOMIC THEORY, ETC.

### 2.325 MONETARY INTEREST THEORIES
(Cont.)

Fellner, W. and Somers, H. M. Alternative monetary approaches to interest theory. REStat 23:43-48 Feb 41

-- and Somers, H. M. Comment on Dr. Lerner's note [on interest theory]. REStat 26:92 May 44

-- and Somers, H. M. Note on "stocks" and "flows" in monetary interest theory. REStat 31:145-46 May 49

Goodwin, R. M. Keynesian and other interest theories. REStat 25:6-12 Feb 43

Judd, P. R. Indifference curves and the rate of interest on government securities. ER 17:232-39 Dec 41

Kafka, A. Professor Hicks's theory of money interest. AER 31:327-29 Jun 41

Kalecki, M. The short-term rate of interest and the velocity of cash circulation. REStat 23:97-99 May 41

Lerner, A. P. Interest theory: supply and demand for loans or supply and demand for cash. REStat 26:88-91 May 44

Mehta, J. K. The negative rate of interest. IJE 21:301-06 Jan 41

Morgan, E. V. Some thoughts on the nature of interest. OEP N.S.1:182-90 Jun 49

Robertson, D. H. What has happened to the rate of interest? TBR 1:15-31 Mar 49

Smithies, A. The quantity of money and the rate of interest. REStat 25:69-76 Feb 43

Somers, H. M. Monetary policy and the theory of interest. QJE 55:488-507 May 41

Swan, T. W. Some notes on the interest controversy. ER 17:153-65 Dec 41

Tinbergen, J. Some problems in the explanation of interest rates. QJE 61:397-438 May 47

Wallich, H. C. The changing significance of the interest rate. AER 36:761-87 Dec 46

### 2.326 STRUCTURE OF INTEREST RATES

Daniel, J. L. Interest rates: long-term vs. short-term. Em 8:272-78 Jul 40

Kalecki, M. The short-term rate and the long-term rate. OEP 4:15-22 Sep 40

Lusher, D. W. The structure of interest rates and the Keynesian theory of interest. JPE 50:272-79 Apr 42

Lutz, F. A. The structure of interest rates. QJE 55:36-63 Nov 40

Marcus, E. The interest-rate structure. REStat 30:223-26 Aug 48

Max, D., Jr. The structure of interest rates: comment. QJE 56:152-56 Nov 41

### 2.327 INFLATION. DEFLATION

Craig, J. I. The definition of "inflation." EgC 36:35-46 Jan-Feb 45

Dowsett, W. T. Delayed action inflation. ER 19:64-70 Jun 43

Dunlop, J. T. [and others] Collective bargaining, wages and the price level: discussion. IRRA 1:51-61 Dec 48

Ensley, G. W. and Goode, R. Mr. Warburton on the gap. AER 33:897-99 Dec 43

Hirst, R. R. Inflation: its impact on enterprises. ER 25,(no.49):24-30 Dec 49

Johnson, A. The theory of the nth wages round. SR 16:416-24 Dec 49

Kalecki, M. What is inflation? OIS 3: 159-64 Jun 7, 41

Koopmans, T. The dynamics of inflation. REStat 24:53-65 May 42

Lerner, A. P. The inflationary process: some theoretical aspects. REStat 31: 193-200 Aug 49

Machlup, F. The inflationary process: comments. REStat 31:210-12 Aug 49

Mitnitzky, M. Some monetary aspects of government borrowing. AER 33:21-37 Mar 43

Mosak, J. L. and Salant, W. S. Income, money and prices in wartime. AER 34: 828-39 Dec 44

Pigou, A. C. Types of war inflation. EJ 51: 439-48 Dec 41; [Errata]. 52:131 Apr 42

Röpke, W. Repressed inflation. Kyk 1: 242-53 fasc.3, 47

Salant, W. S. The inflationary gap. AER 32: 308-20 Jun 42

Smithies, A. The behavior of money national income under inflationary conditions. QJE 57:113-28 Nov 42

-- The dynamics of inflation: a comment [followed by T. Koopmans' reply]. REStat 24:189-90 Nov 42

Somers, H. M. The inflationary process: comments. REStat 31:212-13 Aug 49

Spero, H. and Leavitt, J. A. Inflation as a post-war problem. JPE 51:356-60 Aug 43

Turvey, R. The inflationary gap. ET 50: 10-17 Mar 48

-- A further note on the inflationary gap. ET 51:92-97 Jun 49

-- Period analysis and inflation. Ec N.S.16: 218-27 Aug 49

Villard, H. H. The inflationary process: comments. REStat 31:213-16 Aug 49

Warburton, C. Measuring the inflationary gap. AER 33:365-69 Jun 43

-- Who makes the inflationary gap? AER 33:607-12 Sep 43

-- Monetary expansion and the inflationary gap. AER 34:303-27 Jun 44

-- Messrs. Mosak and Salant on wartime inflation: a rejoinder. AER 35:658-60 Sep 45

Wright, D. M. Inflation and equality. AER 38:892-97 Dec 48

Youngson, A. J. Inflation and the flight from cash. YB 1:33-42 Sep 49

## 2.33 CYCLE THEORY
### 2.330 GENERAL

Adams, W. Accounting practices and the business cycle. JB 22:119-33 Apr 49

Åkerman, J. Political economic cycles. Kyk 1:107-17 fasc.2, 47

-- Structural limits in economic development. DeEc 97:785-98 Nov 49

Ames, E. A theoretical and statistical dilemma: the contributions of Burns, Mitchell, and Frickey to business-cycle theory. Em 16:347-69 Oct 48

Angell, J. W. [and others] Current research in business cycles: discussion. AER/S 39:73-88 May 49

Bakke, E. W. The economists and unemployment. AER/S 30,no.5:294-300 Feb 41

Bernhard, R. C. Myths and illogic in popular notions about business cycles. JPE 51:53-60 Feb 43

Bernstein, E. M. War and the pattern of business cycles. AER 30:524-35 Sep 40

Briefs, G. Business cycles. A methodological approach. ZN 12:465-74 Dec 49

Chait, B. Les fluctuations économiques et l'interdépendance des marchés: a reply [to S. E. Hotelling's review followed by her rejoinder]. JPE 48:740-46 Oct 40

Garvy, G. Kondratieff's theory of long cycles. REStat 25:203-20 Aug 43

Goodwin, R. Innovations and the irregularity of economic cycles. REStat 28: 95-104 May 46

Gordon, R. A. Business cycles in the interwar period: the "quantitative-historical" approach. AER/S 39:47-63 May 49

Graaff, A. de. Price disparity and business cycles. Kyk 1:358-69 fasc.4, 47

Haberler, G. The present cyclical situation of the American economy in the light of business cycle theory. EI 1:235-39 Jan 48

Kalecki, M. A new approach to the problem of business cycles. REStud 16:57-64 no.2, 49

Kirty, V. S. R. The classical theory of equilibrium and the monetary theory of the trade cycle. IJE 22:177-88 Oct 41

Koopmans, T. C. Measurement without theory. R. REStat 29:161-72 Aug 47

Kuznets, S. Schumpeter's business cycles. AER 30:257-71 Jun 40

Marschak, J. A cross section of business cycle discussion. AER 35:368-81 Jun 45

Metzler, L. A. Business cycles and the modern theory of employment. AER 36: 278-91 Jun 46

Morgenstern, O. Unemployment: analysis of factors. AER/S 30,no.5:273-93 Feb 41

Nazmy, A. A. H. The land is a bottomless sink for Egyptian capital. EgC 35: 239-41 Mar-Apr 44

Reedman, J. N. Some reflections on the teaching of business cycle theory. R. SAJE 13:52-57 Mar 45

Robertson, D. H. A Spanish contribution to the theory of fluctuations. Ec N.S.7: 50-65 Feb 40

Rose, A. Wars, innovations and long cycles: a brief comment. AER 31:105-07 Mar 41

Shaw, E. S. Burns and Mitchell on business cycles. R. JPE 55:281-98 Aug 47

Tinbergen, J. Critical remarks on some business-cycle theories. Em 10:129-46 Apr 42

Tsiang, S. C. A note on speculation and income stability. Ec N.S.10:286-96 Nov 43

Vining, R. Koopmans on the choice of variables to be studied and of methods of measurement [followed by T. Koopman's reply and Vining's rejoinder]. REStat 31:77-94 May 49

### 2.3301 MODELS

Baumol, W. J. Notes on some dynamic models. EJ 58:506-21 Dec 48

Clark, C. A system of equations explaining the United States trade cycle, 1921 to 1941. Em 17:93-124 Apr 49

Goodwin, R. M. Dynamical coupling with especial reference to markets having production lags. Em 15:181-204 Jul 47

Haavelmo, T. The inadequacy of testing dynamic theory by comparing theoretical solutions and observed cycles. Em 8: 312-21 Oct 40

-- Statistical testing of business-cycle theories. REStat 25:13-18 Feb 43

Hubbard, J. C. A model for the forty-month or trade cycle. JPE 50:197-225 Apr 42

Kaldor, N. A model of the trade cycle. EJ 50:78-92 Mar 40

Koopmans, T. C. The degree of damping in business cycles. Em 8:79-89 Jan 40

-- The logic of econometric business-cycle research. JPE 49:157-81 Apr 41

-- The econometric approach to business fluctuations. AER/S 39:64-72 May 49

Marrama, V. Short notes on a model of the trade cycle. REStud 14:34-40 no.1, 46

Sumner, J. D. A note on cyclical changes in demand elasticity. AER 30:300-08 Jun 40

Tinbergen, J. Econometric business cycle research. REStud 7:73-90 Feb 40

-- On a method of statistical business-cycle research. A reply [followed by J. M. Keynes's comment]. EJ 50:141-56 Mar 40

Tintner, G. A "simple" theory of business fluctuations. Em 10:317-20 Jul-Oct 42

-- The "simple" theory of business fluctuations: a tentative verification. REStat 26: 148-57 Aug 44

## 2. ECONOMIC THEORY, ETC.

### 2.33 CYCLE THEORY (Cont.)

### 2.331 MONETARY THEORIES

Harwood, E. C. Comment on review of cause and control of the business cycle. AER 30:832 Dec 40

Kirty, V. S. R. The beginnings of monetary explanation of the trade cycle. IJE 25: 491-502 Apr 45

Knight, F. H. The business cycle, interest, and money: a methodological approach. REStat 23:53-67 May 41

Stolper, W. F. Monetary equilibrium, and business-cycle theory. REStat 25:88-92 Feb 43

Warburton, C. Volume of savings, quantity of money, and business instability. JPE 55:222-33 Jun 47

-- Bank reserves and business fluctuations. JASA 43:547-58 Dec 48

### 2.332 INVESTMENT THEORIES

Bennion, E. G. The multiplier, the acceleration principle, and fluctuating autonomous investment. REStat 27:85-92 May 45

Dobrovolsky, S. P. Corporate retained earnings and cyclical fluctuations. AER 35:559-74 Sep 45

Domar, E. D. Capital accumulation and the end of prosperity. Em 17,suppl.:307-12 Jul 49

Hawtrey, R. G. The trade cycle and capital intensity. Ec N.S.7:1-15 Feb 40

Hayek, F. A. von. The Ricardo effect. Ec N.S.9:127-52 May 42

-- A comment [on N. Kaldor's "Professor Hayek and the concertina-effect"]. Ec N.S.9:383-85 Nov 42

Kaldor, N. The trade cycle and capital intensity: a reply. Ec N.S.7:16-22 Feb 40

-- Professor Hayek and the concertina-effect. Ec N.S.9:359-82 Nov 42

Lachmann, L. M. A reconsideration of the Austrian theory of industrial fluctuations. Ec N.S.7:179-96 May 40

Mises, L. von. "Elastic expectations" and the Austrian theory of the trade cycle. Ec N.S.10:251-52 Aug 43

Roos, C. F. and Von Szeliski, V. S. The demand for durable goods. Em 11:97-122 Apr 43

Towle, H. L. The new type of business cycle: an industrial interpretation. JB 13:360-86 Oct 40

Warburton, C. Monetary theory, full production, and the Great Depression. Em 13:114-28 Apr 45

-- The misplaced emphasis in contemporary business-fluctuation theory. JB 19: 199-220 Oct 46

Wilson, T. Capital theory and the trade cycle. REStud 7:169-79 Jun 40

### 2.333 OVERPRODUCTION AND UNDERCONSUMPTION THEORIES

Adarkar, B. N. A simplified version of the trade cycle theory. Pt.I-II. IJE 21: 250-68; 22:38-67 Jan,Jul 41

Johnson, A. The theory of the nth wages round. SR 16:416-24 Dec 49

### 2.334 INVENTORY CYCLES

Lacey, K. Commodity stocks and the trade cycle. Ec N.S.11:12-18 Feb 44

-- --- A reply. Ec N.S.11:140-42 Aug 44

-- Some implications of the first in-first out method of stock valuation. Ec N.S.12: 26-30 Feb 45

Metzler, L. A. The nature and stability of inventory cycles. REStat 23:113-29 Aug 41

-- Factors governing the length of inventory cycles. REStat 29:1-15 Feb 47

Norris, H. Commodity stocks and the trade cycle; 1. A note. Ec N.S.11:138-40 Aug 44

Paradiso, L. J. Significance of inventories in the current economic situation. JASA 43:361-76 Sep 48

### 2.335 BUILDING CYCLES

Bowen, I. Building output and the trade cycle (U.K. 1924-38). OEP 3:110-30 Feb 40

-- The future output of the constructional industries in the United States. EJ 56: 208-29 Jun 46

Derksen, J. B. D. Long cycles in residential building: an explanation. Em 8: 97-116 Apr 40

Grebler, L. Housing policy and the building cycle. REStat 24:66-74 May 42

Isard, W. A neglected cycle: the transport-building cycle. REStat 24:149-58 Nov 42

-- Transport development and building cycles. QJE 57:90-112 Nov 42

-- and Isard, C. The transport-building cycle in urban development: Chicago. REStat 25:224-26 Aug 43

Pribram, K. Residual, differential, and absolute urban ground rents and their cyclical fluctuations. Em 8:62-78 Jan 40

Stolper, W. F. British monetary policy and the housing boom. QJE 56,no.1,pt.2: 1-166 Nov 41

### 2.336 INTERNATIONAL AND INTERREGIONAL PROPAGATION

Garvy, G. [and others] Interregional variations in economic fluctuations: discussion. AER/S 39:120-34 May 49

Krishna, V. S. International co-operation for controlling trade cycles. IJE 25: 301-06 Jan 45

2.33 CYCLE THEORY (Cont.)

2.336 INTERNATIONAL AND INTERREGIONAL PROPAGATION (Cont.)

Morgenstern, O. On the international spread of business cycles. JPE 51: 287-309 Aug 43

Neff, P. Interregional cyclical differentials: causes, measurement, and significance. AER/S 39:105-19 May 49

Vining, R. Regional variation in cyclical fluctuation viewed as a frequency distribution. Em 13:183-213 Jul 45

-- The region as a concept in business-cycle analysis. Em 14:201-18 Jul 46

-- Measuring state and regional business cycles. R. JPE 55:346-51 Aug 47

-- The region as an economic entity and certain variations to be observed in the study of systems of regions. AER/S 39: 89-104 May 49

2.34 GROWTH AND DEVELOPMENT THEORY

2.340 GENERAL

Ayres, C. E. Addendum to The theory of economic progress. AER 35:937-40 Dec 45

Clark, C. Theory of economic growth. Em 17,suppl.:112-14 Jul 49

Domar, E. D. The "burden of the debt" and the national income. AER 34:798-827 Dec 44

-- --- A rejoinder. AER 35:414-18 Jun 45

Giblin, L. F. Economic progress. R. [followed by C. Clark's note and Giblin's comment]. ER 16:262-70 Dec 40

Gini, C. Savings, technical progress and unemployment. [Translated by O. R. Agresti] EI 2:187-205 Feb 49

Kuznets, S. Economic progress. R. MS 12:28-34 Apr 41

-- Measurement of economic growth. JEH/S 7:10-34 '47

Merlin, S. The theory of economic change. QJE 59:185-205 Feb 45

Pigou, A. C. Economic progress in a stable environment. Ec N.S.14:180-88 Aug 47

Ratchford, B. U. Mr. Domar's "Burden of the debt." AER 35:411-14 Jun 45

Rosen, M. M. Population, growth, investment, and economic recovery. AER 32: 122-25 Mar 42

Schumpeter, J. A. Theoretical problems of economic growth. JEH/S 7:1-9 '47

2.3401 GROWTH MODELS

Baumol, W. J. Formalisation of Mr. Harrod's model. EJ 59:625-29 Dec 49

Champernowne, D. G. A note on J. v. Neumann's article on "A model of economic equilibrium." REStud 13:10-18 no.1, 45

Domar, E. D. Expansion and employment. AER 37:34-55 Mar 47

Hicks, J. R. Mr. Harrod's dynamic theory. R. Ec N.S.16:106-21 May 49

Higgins, B. Towards a dynamic economics. R. ER 24:173-90 Dec 48

Hildebrand, G. H., Jr. Monopolization and the decline of investment opportunity. AER 33:591-601 Sep 43

Robinson, J. Mr. Harrod's dynamics. EJ 59:68-85 Mar 49

Von Neumann, J. A model of general economic equilibrium. (Translated by G. Morgenstern) REStud 13:1-9 no.1, 45

2.3403 STRUCTURAL ASPECTS OF GROWTH

Fisher, A. G. B. Tertiary production as a postwar international economic problem. REStat 28:146-51 Aug 46

Simon, H. A. Effects of increased productivity upon the ratio of urban to rural population. Em 15:31-42 Jan 47

Solomon, M. R. The structure of the market in undeveloped economies. QJE 62: 519-41 Aug 48

2.3404 DEVELOPED ECONOMIES. STAGNATION

Adler, H. A. Absolute or relative rate of decline in population growth? QJE 59: 626-34 Aug 45

EA Arndt, H. W. Savings in a state with a stationary population: comment. QJE 62:623-28 Aug 48

A Carter, J. P. The prospect for economic growth: comment. AER 37:926-30 Dec 47

A Colm, G. Comments on W. I. King: "Are we suffering from economic maturity?" JPE 48:114-18 Feb 40

Fellner, W. The technological argument of the stagnation thesis. QJE 55:638-51 Aug 41

Franzsen, D. G. The secular stagnation-thesis and the problem of economic stability. SAJE 10:282-94 Dec 42

EA Goldenberg, L. Savings in a state with a stationary population. [France, Germany, Great Britain] QJE 61:40-65 Nov 46

Hansen, A. H. Extensive expansion and population growth. JPE 48:583-85 Aug 40

A -- Some notes on Terborgh's "The bogey of economic maturity." REStat 28:13-17 Feb 46

A Higgins, B. The doctrine of economic maturity. R. [followed by G. Terborgh's note]. AER 36:133-41 Mar 46

Hudson, P. G. The possibility of maintaining a positive rate of physical production growth. SEJ 8:191-200 Oct 41

EB Jervis, F. R. J. The handicap of Britain's early start. MS 15:112-22 Jan 47

Neisser, H. The economics of a stationary population. SR 11:470-90 Nov 44

## 2. ECONOMIC THEORY, ETC.

### 2.34 GROWTH AND DEVELOPMENT THEORY (Cont.)
#### 2.3404 DEVELOPED ECONOMIES. STAGNATION (Cont.)

A    Noyes, C. R. The prospect for economic growth. AER 37:13-33 Mar 47
-- --- Rejoinder. AER 38:394-96 Jun 48
A    Reed, H. L. Economists on industrial stagnation. JPE 48:244-50 Apr 40
A    Schiff, E. Family size and residential construction. AER 36:97-112 Mar 46
Smith, H. R. The status of stagnation theory. Pt.I-II. SEJ 15:191-204; 289-302 Oct 48, Jan 49
Sweezy, A. R. Population growth and investment opportunity. QJE 55:64-79 Nov 40
A    Terborgh, G. Dr. Hansen on "The bogey of economic maturity." REStat 28:170-72 Aug 46
Towle, H. L. Economic maturity: an industrial view. JB 19:224-31 Oct 46
Tsiang, S. C. The effect of population growth on the general level of employment and activity. Ec N.S.9:325-32 Nov 42
A    Wright, D. M. "The great guessing game": Terborgh versus Hansen. R. REStat 28: 18-22 Feb 46

#### 2.3405 UNDERDEVELOPED ECONOMIES
Gregory, Sir T. The problems of the underdeveloped world. LBR 10:39-56 Oct 48
HSA   Krige, E. J. Economics of exchange in a primitive society. SAJE 9:1-21 Mar 41
Singer, H. W. Economic progress in underdeveloped countries. SR 16:1-11 Mar 49

#### 2.341 ENTREPRENEURSHIP AND GROWTH
AA   Baughn, W. H. Capital formation and entrepreneurship in the South. SEJ 16:161-69 Oct 49
Taymans, A. C. George Tarde and Joseph A. Schumpeter: a similar vision. EEH 1,no.4:9-17 Apr 49

#### 2.342 CAPITAL FORMATION AND GROWTH
#### 2.3420 GENERAL
Alexander, S. S. The accelerator as a generator of steady growth. QJE 63: 174-97 May 49
AA   Baughn, W. H. Capital formation and entrepreneurship in the South. SEJ 16:161-69 Oct 49
Domar, E. D. Capital expansion, rate of growth, and employment. Em 14:137-47 Apr 46
-- The problem of capital accumulation. AER 38:777-94 Dec 48
Schelling, T. C. Capital growth and equilibrium. AER 37:864-76 Dec 47
Stern, E. H. Capital requirements in progressive economies. Ec N.S.12:162-71 Aug 45

-- The problem of capital accumulation [followed by E. D. Domar's rejoinder]. AER 39:1160-72 Dec 49

#### 2.3423 UNDERDEVELOPED AREAS
Sarkar, N. K. Subjective cost of financing industrialisation. IJE 29:27-35 Jul 48
FI   Sengupta, S. Capital requirements of the Bombay plan for economic development of India. IJE 25:56-63 Jul 44
Wu, Y. L. International capital investment and the development of poor countries. EJ 56:86-101 Mar 46

#### 2.343 POPULATION. LABOR FORCE. WAGES
EI   Marrama, V. Some aspects of Italian economy and the theory of full employment. BNL 1:220-27 Jan 48
Moore, W. E. Primitives and peasants in industry. SR 15:44-81 Mar 48
-- Theoretical aspects of industrialization. SR 15:277-303 Sep 48
Peltzer, E. Industrialization of young countries and the change in the international division of labor. SR 7:299-325 Sep 40
EI   Pietranera, G. Note about the "Survey of current inflationary and deflationary tendencies" prepared by the United Nations Department of Economic Affairs. BNL 1:260-63 Jan 48

#### 2.345 NATURAL RESOURCES AND AGRICULTURE
A    Danhof, C. H. Farm-making costs and the "safety valve": 1850-60. JPE 49:317-59 Jun 41
HSA   Franklin, N. N. Economic welfare and the development of the Native Reserves. SAJE 10:1-15 Mar 42
EBC   Lewis, W. A. Developing colonial agriculture. TBR 2:3-21 Jun 49

#### 2.346 INDUSTRIALIZATION
EBC   Ady, P. Colonial industrialisation and British employment. REStud 11:42-51 no.1, 43
FI   Agarwal, A. N. The case for cottage industries in planned economy. IJE 25:545-51 Apr 45
Balogh, T. Note on the deliberate industrialisation for higher incomes. EJ 57: 238-41 Jun 47
Belshaw, H. Observations on industrialisation for higher incomes. EJ 57:379-87 Sep 47
Buchanan, N. S. Deliberate industrialisation for higher incomes. EJ 56:533-53 Dec 46
Frankel, H. Industrialisation of agricultural countries and the possibilities of a new international division of labour. EJ 53: 188-201 Jun-Sep 43

## 2.34 GROWTH AND DEVELOPMENT THEORY (Cont.)

### 2.346 INDUSTRIALIZATION (Cont.)

Qureshi, A. I. International economic co-operation. IJE 25:274-82 Jan 45

Rahmer, B. A. Note on "The industrialisation of backward areas." EJ 56:657-62 Dec 46

EA Rosenstein-Rodan, P. N. Problems of industrialisation of eastern and south-eastern Europe. EJ 53:202-11 Jun-Sep 43

Wu, Y. L. A note on the post-war industrialisation of "backward" countries and centralist planning. Ec N.S.12:172-78 Aug 45

### 2.347 GOVERNMENT DEVELOPMENT POLICY

#### 2.3471 UNDERDEVELOPED COUNTRIES

FI Krishnamurti, B. V. The state under the Bombay plan. IJE 26:243-61 Oct 45

EI Saraceno, P. Public expenditure, savings and foreign loans in the development of southern Italy. BNL 2:146-58 Jul-Sep 49

Spengler, J. J. The role of the state in shaping things economic. JEH/S 7: 123-43 '47

### 2.348 NON-ECONOMIC FACTORS

FI Adams, W. Some factors in Indian economic development. IJE 29:17-26 Jul 48

FI -- A political force in Indian economic development. IJE 30:1-18 Jul 49

AA Snavely, T. R. The place of education in the developing economic structure of the South. SEJ 13:404-15 Apr 47

# 3. ECONOMIC SYSTEMS. PLANNING

## 3.0 GENERAL

Ayzenshtadt, A. The learned handmaidens of American capital. A survey of literature. Translated by E. D. Domar. AER 39:930-45 Sep 49

Beckerath, H. von. Interrelations between moral and economic factors in the post-war world. AER/S 34:25-40 Mar 44

Brand, R. H. Private enterprise and socialism. EJ 58:315-30 Sep 48

Bye, R. T. Some criteria of social economy. AER/S 34:1-8 Mar 44

Callard, K. B. To plan or not to plan: the debate continues. R. CJE 15:416-20 Aug 49

Cox, G. V. Free enterprise vs. authoritarian planning. JB 20:59-66 Apr 47

Hardy, C. O. Schumpeter on Capitalism, socialism, and democracy. R. JPE 53: 348-56 Dec 45

Heimann, E. Industrial society and democracy. SR 12:43-59 Feb 45

-- Recent literature on economic systems. R. SR 13:103-16 Mar 46

Hoover, C. B. Keynes and the economic system. JPE 56:392-402 Oct 48

Machlup, F. Capitalism and its future appraised by two liberal economists. R. AER 33:301-20 Jun 43

Mitchell, W. C. [and others] Political science, political economy, and values: discussion. AER/S 34:48-57 Mar 44

Mukerjee, R. Typology of contrasted economic systems: a clue to the methods of analysis of Indian economic conditions. IJE 22:290-306 Jan 42

Prasad, P. S. N. Market mechanism under control: its implications for economic theory. IJE 24:395-402 Apr 44

Qureshi, A. I. The state and economic life: a reply to some of the criticisms. IJE 21:30-48 Jul 40

Shils, E. A. Some remarks on "The theory of social and economic organization." R. Ec N.S.15:36-50 Feb 48

Spengler, J. J. Political science, political economy, and values: discussion. AER/S 34:9-12 Mar 44

Surányi-Unger, T. Analytical notes on economic systems. ZN 12:171-97 Dec 49

Taylor, H. Political science, political economy, and values: discussion. AER/S 34: 12-14 Mar 44

Taylor, O. H. Economic theory and the age we live in. R. REStat 29:102-07 May 47

-- The economics of a "free" society: four essays. R. QJE 62:641-70 Nov 48

Wilson, F. G. Ethics in the study of democratic politics. AER/S 34:41-47 Mar 44

Wolfe, A. B. Economy and democracy. AER 34:1-20 Mar 44

Zebot, C. Evaluation of economic systems. RSE 7,no.2:48-63 Sep 49

## 3.01 PLANNING. POLICY MAKING

Anderson, B. M., Jr. Governmental economic planning. AER/S 30:247-62 Mar 40

Balogh, T. The planning and control of investment. OIS 7:244-51 Oct 13, 45

Beckerath, H. von. Economic planning in the welfare state. WA 63:49-79 Hft.1, 49

Bonn, M. J. Planning for peace. AER/S 30: 272-80 Mar 40

# 3. ECONOMIC SYSTEMS. PLANNING

## 3.01 PLANNING. POLICY MAKING (Cont.)

Bouvier, E. Economic trends in China, and
EA   in central and western Europe. RSE 7,
FC   no.1:22-29 Mar 49

Copland, D. B. Professor Jewkes and the
alternative to planning. R. ER 24:
191-203 Dec 48

Devons, E. Economic planning in war and
EB   peace. MS 16:1-28 Jan 48

Durbin, E. F. M. Professor Hayek on economic planning and political liberty. R.
EJ 55:357-70 Dec 45

Eucken, W. On the theory of the centrally
EG   administered economy: an analysis of
the German experiment. (Translated by
T. W. Hutchison). Pt.I-II. Ec N.S.15:
79-100; 173-93 May,Aug 48

Frisch, R. Repercussion studies at Oslo.
ESN   AER 38:367-72 Jun 48

Grayson, H. The econometric approach: a
critical analysis. JPE 56:253-57 Jun 48

Hoover, C. B. Economic planning and the
problem of full employment. AER/S 30:
263-71 Mar 40

Jewkes, J. Variety among the planners.
EB   MS 15:93-111 Jan 47

Kahn, R. F. Professor Meade on planning.
R. EJ 59:1-16 Mar 49

Karve, D. G. Ranade and economic plan-
FI   ning. IJE 22:235-44 Jan 42

Keirstead, B. S. Liberty and a planned
economy. R. CJE 11:281-85 May 45

Klein, L. R. The use of econometric models
as a guide to economic policy. Em 15:
111-51 Apr 47

Knight, F. H. Freedom under planning. R.
JPE 54:451-54 Oct 46

Landauer, C. Literature on economic planning. R. SR 7:496-508 Nov 40

-- Economic planning and the science of
economics: comment [followed by D. F.
Pegrum's rejoinder]. AER 31:825-33
Dec 41

Lange, O. The practice of economic planning and the optimum allocation of resources. Em 17,suppl.:166-70 Jul 49

Meade, J. E. Planning without prices.
Ec N.S.15:28-35 Feb 48

Mitchell, C. C. A comment on "planning
and control." JFE 31:708-11 Nov 49

Musgrave, R. A. The planning approach in
public economy: a reply. QJE 55:
319-24 Feb 41

Neuman, A. M. Real economies and the
EB   balance of industry. EJ 58:373-84 Sep 48

Pegrum, D. F. Economic planning and the
science of economics. AER 31:298-307
Jun 41

-- Economic planning in a democratic
society. LE 19:18-27 Feb 43

Pigou, A. C. Central planning and Professor Robbins. Ec N.S.15:17-27 Feb 48

Polanyi, M. Planning and spontaneous
order. MS 16:237-68 Sep 48

Prest, W. War-time controls and post-war
planning. ER 18:211-17 Dec 42

Robertson, D. H. The economic outlook.
EB   EJ 57:421-37 Dec 47

Schumpeter, J. A. English economists and
the state-managed economy. R. JPE 57:
371-82 Oct 49

Schwartz, G. L. Planning and economic
privileges. (The notion of equity in economics) MS 14,no.1:53-71 Jan 46

Shibata, K. Economic theory of planning.
R. Kyo 18,no.4:19-41 Oct 43

Shirras, G. F. The British Association
conference and economic planning.
EJ 51:515-23 Dec 41

-- Planning towards recovery. ZN 12:
EB   475-82 Dec 49

Simon, H. A. The planning approach in
public economy: further comment.
QJE 55:325-30 Feb 41

Singh, A. Can we plan under Indian capital-
FI   ism? IJE 26:305-11 Oct 45

Surányi-Unger, T. Economic structure and
planning. ZS 105:251-82 Hft. 2, 49

Tinbergen, J. Central planning in the
EN   Netherlands. REStud 15:70-77 no.2, 48

-- [and others] Theory of choice and utilization of resources: discussion. Em 17,
suppl.:173-78 Jul 49

Tress, R. C. The practice of economic
planning. MS 16:192-213 May 48

Wright, D. M. How much can planning do?
JPE 56:337-41 Aug 48

## 3.02 GOVERNMENT AND THE ECONOMY

Abbott, C. C. and Spencer, M. J. Government and private enterprise: discussion. AER/S 33:39-44 Mar 43

Arnold, T. Must 1929 repeat itself?
A   HBR 26:32-45 Jan 48

Bain, J. S. The normative problem in industrial regulation. AER/S 33:54-70
Mar 43

Balakrishna, R. Public enterprise in a
mixed economy. IJE 30:167-74 Oct 49

Bell, J. W., chairman. What should be the
A   relative spheres of private business and
government in our postwar American
economy? Symposium by past presidents
of AEA. AER/S 34:288-309 Mar 44

-- The function of government in postwar
A   American economy; a report on an experiment by an ad hoc consensus committee. AER/S 35:422-47 May 45

Berle, A. A., Jr. Government function in
a stabilized economy. AER/S 33:27-38
Mar 43

Blumer, H. Group tension and interest
organizations. IRRA 2:150-64 Dec 49

Brebner, J. B. Laissez faire and state in-
EB   tervention in nineteenth-century Britain.
JEH/S 8:59-73 '48

## 3.02 GOVERNMENT AND THE ECONOMY (Cont.)

Brown, L. H. Using private business agencies to achieve public goals in the postwar world. AER/S 33:71-81 Mar 43

EB Burrows, H. R. "Plan for reconstruction." R. SAJE 12:1-12 Mar 44

A Bursk, E. C. Selling the idea of free enterprise. HBR 26:372-84 May 48

Clark, J. M. The relation of government to the economy of the future. JPE 49: 797-816 Dec 41

Commons, J. R. Legislative and administrative reasoning in economics. JFE 24: 369-91 May 42

De Chazeau, M. G. Employment policy and organization of industry after the war. AER 35:629-39 Sep 45

Dewhurst, J. F. Economic claims of government and of private enterprise: discussion. AER/S 33:105-07 Mar 43

Dickinson, Z. C. Incentive problems in regulated capitalism. AER/S 34:151-62 Mar 44

A Durr, C. J. The postwar relationship between government and business. AER/S 33:45-53 Mar 43

Easterbrook, W. T. Political economy and enterprise. CJE 15:322-33 Aug 49

Fainsod, M. Economic interests and the political process. IRRA 2:165-73 Dec 49

Fisher, A. G. B. A liberal new order. R. Ec N.S.10:176-87 May 43

Flanders, R. E. Economics collides with ethics. AER/S 38:357-67 May 48

Garver, F. B. Government and private enterprise: discussion. AER/S 33:82-83 Mar 43

Gordon, R. A. Government and private enterprise: discussion. AER/S 33:83-86 Mar 43

-- Economic theory in relation to the long-run postwar situation: discussion. AER/S 34:163-65 Mar 44

Gras, N. S. B. The growth of rigidities. HBR 18:322-36 no.3, 40

Hoffman, P. G. The survival of free enterprise. HBR 25:21-27 no.1, 46

Hutt, W. H. The sanctions for privacy under private enterprise. Ec N.S.9:237-44 Aug 42

A Jacoby, N. H. The American economy during and after the war: a look ahead. JB 15:289-305 Oct 42

A Lansing, J. B. Comments on the economists' opinion survey. AER 36:143-46 Mar 46

Lyon, L. S. The private-enterprise system confronts emergency. JB 14:259-69 Jul 41

A -- Government and American economic life. JB 22:83-91 Apr 49

Machlup, F. The division of labor between government and private enterprise. AER/S 33:87-104 Mar 43

A Meriam, R. S. The question of controls. HBR 26:454-67 Jul 48

FI Rao, R. V. Mixed economy in theory and practice: with special reference to India. IJE 30:193-96 Oct 49

A Smith, R. Government and the economy. JFE 29:77-83 Feb 47

A Speier, H. [and others] Economic power blocs and American capitalism: discussion. IRRA 2:192-202 Dec 49

A Spengler, J. J. Power blocs and the formation and content of economic decision. IRRA 2:174-91 Dec 49

Wright, D. M. Hopes and fears: the shape of things to come. R. REStat 26:106-15 Nov 44

## 3.1 CAPITALIST SYSTEM

Ayres, C. E. Capitalism in retrospect. SEJ 9:293-301 Apr 43

Baerwald, F. The economics of control. RSE 5:35-48 Jun 47

Chand, G. Capitalism in flux: recent changes in the structure of capitalism. IJE 24:374-86 Apr 44

Ellis, H. S. Competition and welfare. CJE 11:554-65 Nov 45

Gopal, M. H. The role of the excess profits tax in modifying capitalism. IJE 24: 387-94 Apr 44

Gras, N. S. B. Capitalism: concepts and history [with discussion by R. De Roover and H. M. Larson]. BHR 16:21-42 Apr 42

-- What is capitalism in the light of history? BHR 21:79-120 Oct 47

-- Behavior of business men in a changing world. BHR 23:1-65 Mar 49

Hardy, C. O. Liberalism in the modern state: the philosophy of Henry Simons. R. JPE 56:305-14 Aug 48

Harrod, R. F. Professor Hayek on individualism. R. EJ 56:435-42 Sep 46

Henderson, H. D. The price system. EJ 58: 467-82 Dec 48

Knight, F. H. The role of the individual in the economic world of the future. JPE 49:817-32 Dec 41

Lachmann, L. M. Finance capitalism? Ec N.S.11:64-73 May 44

Rao, T. H. Structural changes in capitalistic economy: ideas of Keynes and Karl Marx. IJE 24:418-43 Apr 44

Salz, A. Economic liberalism reinterpreted. SR 8:373-89 Sep 41

S[chlesinger], R. The discussions on E. Varga's book on capitalist war economy. SovS 1:28-40 Jun 49

Sriram, P. Some aspects of the recent structural changes in the capitalistic economy. IJE 24:444-50 Apr 44

## 3. ECONOMIC SYSTEMS. PLANNING

### 3.1 CAPITALIST SYSTEM (Cont.)

Venkatasubbiah, H. Structural changes in the capitalist economy in relation to its rationale. IJE 24:403-08 Apr 44

Wolfe, A. B. Price-making in a democracy. R. JPE 53:73-78 Mar 45

### 3.2 SOCIALIST AND COMMUNIST SYSTEMS

Anjaria, J. J. The problem of valuation in a socialist state. IJE 21:361-82 Apr 41

Anonymous. On misunderstanding Soviet political economy. S&S 8:342-45 no.4, 44

Atkinson, F. J. Saving and investment in a socialist state. REStud 15:78-83 no.2, 48

Balakrishna, R. Rate structure of public utilities in a socialist state. IJE 21:383-94 Apr 41

Butani, D. H. The problem of value in a socialist state. IJE 21:395-419 Apr 41

Chand, G. Value and socialism. IJE 21:703-15 Apr 41

Dewey, D. J. Notes on the analysis of socialism as a vocational problem. MS 16:269-88 Sep 48

-- Occupational choice in a collectivist economy. JPE 56:465-79 Dec 48

Dey, H. L. Socialist economy and the problem of pricing. IJE 21:723-30 Apr 41

D'Souza, V. L. Economic valuation in a socialist state. IJE 21:420-34 Apr 41

Gopal, M. H. The role of cost in socialist pricing. IJE 21:435-55 Apr 41

Halévy, E. The age of tyrannies. [Translated by M. Wallas] Ec N.S.8:77-93 Feb 41

Hayek, F. A. von. Socialist calculation: the competitive solution. Ec N.S.7:125-49 May 40

Heimann, E. Professor Hayek on German socialism. II. AER 35:935-37 Dec 45

Hoselitz, B. F. Socialist planning and international economic relations. AER 33:839-51 Dec 43

-- Professor Hayek on German socialism. I. AER 35:929-34 Dec 45

Hunter, H. The planning of investments in the Soviet Union. REStat 31:54-62 Feb 49

Hutt, W. H. Economic institutions and the new socialism. R. Ec N.S.7:419-34 Nov 40

Karve, D. G. Value in a socialistic state. IJE 21:456-69 Apr 41

Knight, F. H. Professor Heimann on religion and economics. R. JPE 56:480-97 Dec 48

Krishna Murthy, T. Output and price in a socialist economy. IJE 21:470-75 Apr 41

Leont'ev, L. A. [and others] Political economy in the Soviet Union. [Translated by H. F. Mins, Jr.] S&S 8:115-25 no.2, 44

M[iller], J. Some recent developments in Soviet economic thought. SovS 1:119-27 Oct 49

Ostrovitianov, K. Basic laws of development of socialist economy. S&S 9:232-51 no.3, 45

Rao, K. V. Value in a socialistic state. IJE 21:476-87 Apr 41

Rudra, S. K. Value in the socialist state. IJE 21:716-22 Apr 41

Satyanarayanarao, T. Saving, investment and enterprise in a socialistic state. IJE 21:488-96 Apr 41

Schnierer, F. Economics of socialism. R. ER 17:258-62 Dec 41

Shafi, S. M. Problem of value in a socialist state. IJE 21:731-33 Apr 41

Tirumalachar, B. Allocation of resources in a socialist economy. IJE 21:511-25 Apr 41

### 3.3 CORPORATIVE SYSTEM

Brady, R. A. Modernized cameralism in the
EG    Third Reich: the case of the National Industry Group. JPE 50:65-97 Feb 42

Haight, F. A. The nature and significance of fascism. SAJE 8:224-42 Sep 40

Harris, A. L. Sombart and German (na-
EG    tional) socialism. JPE 50:805-35 Dec 42

Wunderlich, F. The National Socialist conception of landed property. SR 12:60-76 Feb 45

### 3.4 COOPERATION. COOPERATIVE SOCIETIES

Ali, Ch. I. Co-operative multipurpose
FIP    societies. PEJ 1,no.2:38-41 Oct 49

Bekenstein, A. L. A theoretical analysis of consumer co-operatives: the managerial problem. JPE 51:251-57 Jun 43

Bennett, V. W. Consumers and the Green-
ASM    belt Cooperative [in Maryland]. JM 6:3-10 Jul 41

Bradley, W. L. Taxation of cooperatives.
A    HBR 25:576-86 no.4a, 47

Canoyer, H. G. A study of consumer co-
AA    operative associations in the north central states. JM 9:373-80 Apr 45

Clark, L. The cooperative one-half of one
A    per cent. QJE 56:321-31 Feb 42

Enke, S. Consumer cooperatives and economic efficiency. AER 35:148-55 Mar 45

Halpern, D. B. The co-operative movement
EB    since the outbreak of war. OIS 3:318-24 Oct 11, 41; Erratum. 358 Nov 1, 41

Hough, J. A. Retail sales per employee.
EB    MS 17:49-66 Jan 49

Khan, K. M. B. A. Co-operation in
FIP    Pakistan: multipurposes societies (with special reference to West Punjab). PEJ 1,no.1:78-95 Jul 49

Khan, M. Y. Review of co-operation in
FIP    N.W.F.P. PEJ 1,no.2:42-47 Oct 49

Miller, G. W. Wages and hours in con-
A
EB    sumers' cooperatives in Great Britain and the United States. QJE 55:294-305 Feb 41

## 3.4 COOPERATION. COOPERATIVE SOCIETIES (Cont.)

EB   Murphy, M. E. Centenary of the British cooperative movement. JM 10:270-78 Jan 46

ASU   Olsen, A. B. Mormon mercantile cooperation in Utah. JM 6:136-42 Oct 41

D   Ribas, A. F. The Catholics of the Americas and cooperation. RSE 7,no.1:30-54 Mar 49

FC   Sen Gupta, R. N. China's Indusco. IJE 23: 277-81 Jan 43

FIP   Sharif, M. R. The role of co-operation in Pakistan. PEJ 1,no.2:32-37 Oct 49

FJ   Yagi, Y. The co-operative movement under wartime economic control. Kyo 15,no.3: 25-40 Jul 40

## 3.5 SOLIDARISM

Higgins, G. G. Social action program of the National Catholic Welfare Conference. RSE 7,no.2:34-38 Sep 49

Mueller, F. H. The principle of solidarity in the teachings of Father Henry Pesch, S.J. RSE 4:31-39 Jan 46

# 4. HISTORY OF ECONOMIC THOUGHT

## 4.0 GENERAL

Bladen, V. W. The history of economic ideas. R. CJE 7:100-08 Feb 41

Evans, G. H., Jr. The entrepreneur and economic theory: a historical and analytical approach. AER/S 39:336-48 May 49

Gopal, M. H. The return to classicism and after. IJE 20:405-21 Apr 40

Grampp, W. D. A re-examination of Jeffersonian economics. SEJ 12:263-82 Jan 46

Gray, A. Economics: yesterday and tomorrow. EJ 59:510-30 Dec 49

Grossman, H. The evolutionist revolt against classical economics. Pt.I-II. JPE 51:381-96; 506-22 Oct,Dec 43

Heimann, E. The central theme in the history of economics. SR 11:202-15 May 44

Hicks, J. R. History of economic doctrine. R. EHR 13:111-15 no.1-2, 43

Knight, F. H. Heimann's History of doctrine and current issues. R. JPE 54:363-67 Aug 46

Lamontagne, M. Some French contributions to economic theory. CJE 13:514-32 Nov 47

Moos, S. Laissez-faire, planning and ethics. EJ 55:17-27 Apr 45

Polanyi, M. The growth of thought in society. Ec N.S.8:428-56 Nov 41

Spengler, J. J. The problem of order in economic affairs. SEJ 15:1-29 Jul 48

Wolfe, A. B. The economic mind in American civilization: a review. R. JPE 55: 65-68 Feb 47

## 4.1 ANCIENT. MEDIEVAL

Hozumi, F. The Chinese ideas of money. Kyo 18,no.1:34-57 Jan 43

Welles, C. B. The economic background of Plato's communism. JEH/S 8:101-14 '48

## 4.2 PRE-CLASSICAL
### 4.21 MERCANTILISTS

De Roover, R. What is dry exchange? A contribution to the study of English mercantilism. JPE 52:250-66 Sep 44

Grampp, W. D. The third century of mercantilism. SEJ 10:292-302 Apr 44

Roy, P. The mercantilist view of money in relation to public finance. IJE 23:257-70 Jan 43

-- On the definition of mercantilism. IJE 25:130-40 Oct 44

### 4.22 PHYSIOCRATS

Maverick, L. A. The Chinese and the physiocrats: a supplement. EH 4:312-18 Feb 40

Neill, T. P. The physiocrats' concept of economics. QJE 63:532-53 Nov 49

Spengler, J. J. The physiocrats and Say's law of markets. Pt.I-II. JPE 53:193-211; 317-47 Sep,Dec 45

## 4.3 CLASSICAL SCHOOL

Black, R. D. Trinity College, Dublin, and the theory of value, 1832-1863. Ec N.S.12: 140-48 Aug 45

Checkland, S. G. The Birmingham economists, 1815-1850. EHR II:1-19 no.1, 48

-- The propagation of Ricardian economics in England. Ec N.S.16:40-52 Feb 49

Crane, R. S. Montesquieu and British thought. R. JPE 49:592-600 Jun 41

Daugherty, M. R. The currency-banking controversy. Pt.I-II. SEJ 9:140-55; 241-51 Oct 42, Jan 43

Fain, J. T. Ruskin and the orthodox political economists. SEJ 10:1-13 Jul 43

Grampp, W. D. On the politics of the classical economists. QJE 62:714-47 Nov 48

Johnson, H. G. Demand for commodities is not demand for labour. EJ 59:531-36 Dec 49

# 4. HISTORY OF ECONOMIC THOUGHT

## 4.3 CLASSICAL SCHOOL (Cont.)

Kennet, [E. H. Young, baron]. What did Mr. Malthus say in 1798? LBR 2:18-24 Oct 46

Kirty, V. S. R. The classical theory of equilibrium and the monetary theory of the trade cycle. IJE 22:177-88 Oct 41

May, K. The structure of classical value theories. REStud 17:60-69 no.1, 49

Miller, J. D., Jr. Wages-fund theory and the popular influence of economists. AER 30:108-12 Mar 40

Mukerjee, R. The sociological assumptions and norms of classicism. IJE 20:303-20 Jan 40

Myint, H. The welfare significance of productive labour. REStud 11:20-30 no.1, 43

-- The classical view of the economic problem. Ec N.S.13:119-30 May 46

Natarajan, B. Economic ideas behind the Permanent Settlement. IJE 22:708-23 Jan 42

Neisser, H. P. "Permanent" technological unemployment: "demand for commodities is not demand for labor." AER 32:50-71 Mar 42

Niebyl, K. H. A reexamination of the classical theory of inflation. AER 30:759-73 Dec 40

Patel, S. J. British economic thought and the treatment of India as a colony. IJE 27:367-71 Apr 47

Robertson, H. M. Reflexions on Malthus and his predecessors. SAJE 10:295-306 Dec 42

Shenoy, B. R. The classical theory of saving. IJE 28:223-36 Oct 47

Walker, K. O. The classical economists and the factory acts. JEH 1:168-77 Nov 41

Winton, E. M. "Wages fund theory and the popular influence of economists": a reply. AER 31:343-44 Jun 41

## 4.4 AUSTRIAN, LAUSANNE, MARSHALLIAN, NEO-CLASSICAL SCHOOLS

Bladen, V. W. Mill to Marshall: the conversion of the economists. JEH/S 1:17-29 Dec 41

Robertson, R. M. Mathematical economics before Cournot. JPE 57:523-36 Dec 49

Simpson, P. B. Neoclassical economics and monetary problems. AER 39:861-82 Sep 49

## 4.5 SOCIALIST, MARXIST, COMMUNIST SCHOOLS
### 4.50 GENERAL

Anonymous. Teaching of economics in the Soviet Union, from the Russian journal Pod Znamenem Marxizma. Translated by R. Dunayevskaya. AER 34:501-30 Sep 44

Baran, P. A. New trends in Russian economic thinking? AER 34:862-71 Dec 44

Dobb, M. H. "Vulgar economics" and "vulgar Marxism": a reply [followed by A. P. Lerner's further note]. JPE 48:251-60 Apr 40

Dunayevskaya, R. A new revision of Marxian economics. AER 34:531-37 Sep 44

-- Revision or reaffirmation of Marxism? A rejoinder. AER 35:660-64 Sep 45

Evinitsky, A. Value theory and socialism. S&S 9:260-63 no.3, 45

Hayek, F. A. von. The counter-revolution of science. Pt.I-III. Ec N.S.8:9-36; 119-50; 281-320 Feb,May,Aug 41

Hoselitz, B. F. Socialism, communism, and international trade. JPE 57:227-41 Jun 49

Landauer, C. From Marx to Menger: the recent development of Soviet economics. AER 34:340-44 Jun 44

Lange, O. Marxian economics in the Soviet Union. AER 35:127-33 Mar 45

Lerner, A. P. Marxism and economics: Sweezy and Robinson. R. JPE 53:79-87 Mar 45

McConnell, J. W. [and others] The sociology and economics of class conflict: discussion. AER/S 39:37-46 May 49

May, K. Value and price of production: a note on Winternitz' solution. EJ 58:596-99 Dec 48

Mills, F. C. Round table in commemoration of the centenary of the Communist Manifesto: the sociology and economics of class conflict: opening remarks. AER/S 39:13-15 May 49

Ostrovitianov, K. Basic laws of development of socialist economy. S&S 9:232-51 no.3, 45

Otis, B. The communists and the labor theory of value. AER 35:134-37 Mar 45

Parsons, T. Social classes and class conflict in the light of recent sociological theory. AER/S 39:16-26 May 49

Patel, S. J. Marxism and recent economic thought. S&S 11:52-65 no.1, 47

Rogin, L. Marx and Engels on distribution in a socialist society. AER 35:137-43 Mar 45

Schumpeter, J. A. The Communist Manifesto in sociology and economics. JPE 57:199-212 Jun 49

Schwartz, H. Recent activities of Soviet economists. AER 36:650-58 Sep 46

Shove, G. F. Mrs. Robinson on Marxian economics. R. EJ 54:47-61 Apr 44

Sweezy, P. M. Marxian and orthodox economics. S&S 11:225-33 no.3, 47

Winternitz, J. Values and prices: a solution of the so-called transformation problem. EJ 58:276-80 Jun 48

4.5 SOCIALIST, MARXIST, COMMUNIST
SCHOOLS (Cont.)
4.50 GENERAL (Cont.)
Wright, D. M. The economics of a classless
society. AER/S 39:27-36 May 49
Zauberman, A. Economic thought in the
Soviet Union. Pt.I-III. REStud 16:1-12;
102-16; 189-200 no.1, 48, no.2-3, 49

4.51 NON-MARXIST SOCIALISM
Murphy, M. E. The role of the Fabian
Society in British affairs. SEJ 14:14-23
Jul 47
Sweezy, P. M. Fabian political economy.
JPE 57:242-48 Jun 49

4.6 HISTORICAL AND INSTITUTIONALIST
SCHOOLS
Venkatasubbiah, H. A note on Institution-
alism in Indian economic thought.
IJE 22:394-99 Jan 42

4.7 OTHER GROUPS SINCE 1800
4.70 GENERAL
Ayres, C. E. The impact of the Great De-
pression on economic thinking.
AER/S 36:112-25 May 46
Bronfenbrenner, M. The dilemma of lib-
eral economics. JPE 54:334-46 Aug 46
Butani, D. H. The quality and perspective of
Indian economic thought. IJE 22:280-89
Jan 42
Chamberlin, E. H. [and others] New fron-
tiers in economic thought: discussion.
AER/S 36:139-53 May 46
Clark, J. M. Some current cleavages among
economists. AER/S 37:1-11 May 47
Ellis, H. S. Research as seen in a survey
of contemporary economics. AER/S 39:
427-39 May 49
Gordon, L. Libertarianism at bay. R.
AER 39:976-78 Sep 49
Honjō, E. The formation of "Japanese
political economy." Kyo 17,no.2:1-19
Apr 42
-- The original current of "Japanese po-
litical economy." Kyo 17,no.3:1-19
Jul 42
Joshi, T. M. A critique of "Indian eco-
nomics." IJE 22:276-79 Jan 42
Kellock, J. Ranade and after: a study of
the development of economic thought in
India. IJE 22:245-60 Jan 42
Knight, F. H. Truth and relevance at bay.
AER 39:1273-76 Dec 49
Lazere, M. Welfare economics a misnomer.
AER 30:346-47 Jun 40
Melville, L. G. Where are we going?
ER 22:193-98 Dec 46
Munshi, M. C. Protectionism and Indian
economic thought. IJE 22:331-56 Jan 42
Roll, E. The social significance of recent
trends in economic theory. CJE 6:448-59
Aug 40

Sen, K. N. Economic thinking in the Indian
National Congress. IJE 22:689-707
Jan 42
Stigler, G. J. A survey of contemporary
economics. R. JPE 57:93-105 Apr 49
Wright, D. M. Business and the radical
indictment. HBR 23:393-414 no.4, 45

4.71 SWEDISH SCHOOL
Caplan, B. Some Swedish stepping stones
in economic theory: a comment. CJE 7:
559-62 Nov 41
Lerner, A. P. Some Swedish stepping
stones in economic theory. R. CJE 6:
574-91 Nov 40

4.8 INDIVIDUALS (A-Z)
ADAMS, HENRY CARTER
Anonymous. Henry Carter Adams.
AER 32:[234a] Jun 42
ADDIS, Sir CHARLES
Hawtrey, R. G. Sir Charles Addis (1861-
1945). [obit.] EJ 56:507-10 Sep 46
ALLEN, WILLIAM
B[ooth], J. F. William Allen, 1892-1941.
[obit.] JFE 23:694-95 Aug 41
ALSBERG, CARL L.
V[oorhies], E. C. Carl L. Alsberg, 1877-
1940. [obit.] JFE 23:535-36 May 41
ARMSTRONG, CLEMENT
Bindoff, S. T. Clement Armstrong and his
treatises of the commonweal. EHR 14:
64-73 no.1, 44
ASHLEY, Sir PERCY
L[eak], H. Sir Percy Ashley, K.B.E., C.B.
[obit.] JRSS 108:479-80 pt.3-4, 45
AYRES, LEONARD P.
Burgess, W. R. Leonard P. Ayres: an
appreciation. JASA 42:128-33 Mar 47
BALCOM, ALFRED BURPEE
M[acKeigan], I. M. Alfred Burpee Balcom,
1876-1943. [obit.] CJE 10:79 Feb 44
BARBON, NICHOLAS
Williams, E. Nicholas Barbon: an early
economic realist. SEJ 11:45-55 Jul 44
BASTABLE, CHARLES FRANCIS
Smith, J. G. C. F. Bastable. [obit.]
EJ 55:127-30 Apr 45
BENTHAM, JEREMY
[Anonymous] [On the repairs recently
made to the auto-ikon of Jeremy Ben-
tham: an extract from the Annual report
of the Provost of University College,
London.] EJ 50:365-66 Jun-Sep 40
Stark, W. Liberty and equality or: Jeremy
Bentham as an economist. Pt.I-II.
EJ 51:56-79; 56:583-608 Apr 41, Dec 46
Viner, J. Bentham and J. S. Mill: the
utilitarian background. AER 39:360-82
Mar 49
BERGLUND, ABRAHAM
Snavely, T. R. Abraham Berglund, 1875-
1942. [obit.] AER 33:238-40 Mar 43

## 4. HISTORY OF ECONOMIC THOUGHT

### 4.8 INDIVIDUALS (A-Z) (Cont.)

BLOCH, MARC
  Debien, G. Marc Bloch and rural history. [Translated by H. E. Hart] AH 21: 187-89 Jul 47
  Postan, M. M. Marc Bloch: an obituary note. EHR 14:161-62 no.2, 44

BONAR, JAMES
  MacG[ibbon], D. A. Dr. James Bonar. [obit.] CJE 7:283-84 May 41
  P[rice], L. L. James Bonar, M.A., LL.D. [obit.] JRSS 104:91-94 pt.1, 41
  Shirras, G. F. James Bonar (1852-1941). [obit.] EJ 51:145-56 Apr 41

BOSS, ANDREW
  P[ond], G. A. and J[esness], O. B. Andrew Boss, 1867-1947. [obit.] JFE 29: 355-57 Feb 47

BRAY, JOHN FRANCIS
  Carr, H. J. John Francis Bray [1809 -1897]. Ec N.S.7:397-415 Nov 40

BURKE, EDMUND
  Dunn, W. C. Adam Smith and Edmund Burke: complementary contemporaries. SEJ 7:330-46 Jan 41

CABOT, PHILIP
  Anonymous. Philip Cabot. [obit.] BHR 16:64-66 Jun 42

CAIRNES, JOHN ELLIOTT
  -- A letter from J. E. Cairnes to W. S. Jevons [with introductory note by A. N. Agarwala]. IJE 25:80-82 Jul 44
  O'Brien, G. J. S. Mill and J. E. Cairnes. Ec N.S.10:273-85 Nov 43

CANTILLON, RICHARD
  Hone, J. Richard Cantillon, economist: biographical note. EJ 54:96-100 Apr 44

CAREY, MATHEW
  Selekman, B. M. and Selekman, S. K. Mathew Carey. HBR 19:326-41 no.3, 41

CASSEL, GUSTAV
  Ellis, H. S. Gustav Cassel 1866-1945. [obit.] AER 35:508-10 Jun 45
  Englund, E. Gustav Cassel's Autobiography. R. QJE 57:466-93 May 43
  Montgomery, A. Gustav Cassel (1866-1945). [obit.] EJ 57:532-42 Dec 47

CHALMERS, THOMAS
  Roberts, R. O. Thomas Chalmers on the public debt. Ec N.S.12:111-16 May 45

CHAPMAN, JOHN H.
  C[ondliffe], J. B. John H. Chapman. [obit.] ER 25,(no.48):92-93 Jun 49

CHASTELLUX, FRANÇOIS JEAN de
  Stark, W. A forerunner of Marxism: François-Jean de Chastellux. Ec N.S.8: 203-07 May 41

CHERINGTON, PAUL TERRY
  Thorp, W. L. Paul T. Cherington, 1876-1943. [obit.] JASA 38:471-72 Dec 43

CHIEN, SSU-MA
  Hozumi, F. Ssu-ma Chien's economic outlook. Kyo 15,no.1:16-29 Jan 40

CLAPHAM, Sir JOHN HAROLD
  Postan, M. M. Sir John Clapham. [obit. and bibliography] EHR 16:56-59 no.1, 46
  Trevelyan, G. M. John Harold Clapham (1873-1946). [obit.] EJ 56:499-507 Sep 46

CLARK, JOHN BATES
  Anonymous. John Bates Clark. AER 31: [730a] Dec 41
  Mirkowich, N. The place of J. B. Clark and E. R. A. Seligman in American economic science. IJE 21:67-74 Jul 40

CLARK, VICTOR SELDEN
  Durand, E. D. Dr. Victor Selden Clark. [obit.] JASA 41:390-92 Sep 46

CLERC, JACQUES OLIVIER
  A[shley], C. A. Jacques Olivier Clerc, 1917-1944. [obit.] CJE 11:268-69 May 45

COGHLAN, Sir TIMOTHY AUGUSTINE
  Arndt, H. W. A pioneer of national income estimates. EJ 59:616-25 Dec 49

COHEN, JOSEPH LOUIS
  Anonymous. J. L. Cohen. [obit.] EJ 51: 157 Apr 41

COLLET, CLARA ELIZABETH
  Mahalanobis, P. C. Clara Elizabeth Collet. [obit.] JRSS 111:254 pt.3, 48
  T., C. Clara Elizabeth Collet. [obit.] JRSS 111:252-53 pt.3, 48

COMMONS, JOHN ROGERS
  Cranfill, S. E. Recent contributions of John R. Commons to economic thought. SEJ 7:63-79 Jul 40
  Gruchy, A. G. John R. Commons' concept of twentieth-century economics. JPE 48:823-49 Dec 40
  Parsons, K. H. John R. Commons' point of view. LE 18:245-66 Aug 42
  Perlman, S. John Rogers Commons 1862-1945. [obit.] AER 35:782-86 Sep 45

COPELAND, CHARLES
  Anonymous. Charles Copeland, 1867-1944. [obit.] BHR 18:69 Jun 44

COYAJEE, Sir JAHANGIR COOVERJEE
  Chatterjee, A. Jahangir Cooverjee Coyajee. [obit.] EJ 53:453-56 Dec 43

CUDMORE, SEDLEY ANTHONY
  L[eak], H. Sedley Anthony Cudmore. [obit.] JRSS 109:169-70 pt.2, 46
  Marshall, H. Sedley Anthony Cudmore 1878-1945. [obit.] JASA 41:75-76 Mar 46
  M[ichell], H. Sedley Anthony Cudmore, 1878-1945. [obit.] CJE 12:93-95 Feb 46

DALY, FREDERICK ST. LEGER
  G. H. C. Frederick St. Leger Daly, 1905-1944. [obit.] CJE 10:391-92 Aug 44

DARWIN, LEONARD
  K. M. E. Leonard Darwin. [obit.] EJ 53: 439-48 Dec 43
  K[eynes, J. M.] Leonard Darwin (1850-1943). [obit.] EJ 53:438-39 Dec 43

4.8 INDIVIDUALS (A-Z) (Cont.)

DAVENPORT, HERBERT JOSEPH
Anonymous. Herbert Joseph Davenport.
AER 37:[79a] Dec 47

DAY, JOSEPH PAUL
Anonymous. Joseph P. Day. [obit.]
BHR 18:142 Nov 44

DEL MAR, ALEXANDER
Hicks, E. Alexander del Mar, critic of
metallism. SEJ 6:314-32 Jan 40

DEWEY, DAVIS RICH
Rogers, B. A. and Tucker, D. S. Davis
Rich Dewey, 1858-1942. [obit.]
AER 33:236-38 Mar 43
-- and Tucker, D. S. Davis Rich Dewey,
1858-1942. [obit.] JASA 38:107-09
Mar 43

DORMER, DIEGO JOSÉ
Smith, R. S. Spanish antimercantilism of
the seventeenth century: Alberto
Struzzi and Diego José Dormer.
JPE 48:401-11 Jun 40

DOTEN, CARROLL WARREN
Armstrong, F. E. Carroll W. Doten,
1871-1942. [obit.] JASA 37:543 Dec 42

DUCKWORTH, ARTHUR
Butlin, S. J. Arthur Duckworth. [obit.]
EJ 54:443-45 Dec 44

DUNBAR, CHARLES FRANKLIN
Anonymous. Charles Franklin Dunbar.
AER 31:[472a] Sep 41

EBERSOLE, JOHN FRANKLIN
Gras, N. S. B. J. Franklin Ebersole,
1884-1945. [obit.] BHR 19:177-78
Nov 45

ELY, RICHARD THEODORE
Anonymous. Richard Theodore Ely.
AER 32:[704a] Dec 42
Taylor, H. C. and Wehrwein, G. S.
Richard T. Ely. [obit.] LE 19:389-90
Nov 43
-- Richard Theodore Ely (Apr 13, 1854-
October 4, 1943). [obit.] EJ 54:132-38
Apr 44
Woodbury, C. Richard T. Ely and the be-
ginnings of research in urban land and
housing economics. LE 25:55-66 Feb 49

EVANS, MERCER GRIFFIN
Bryan, M. H. Mercer Griffin Evans, 1901-
1939. [obit.] SEJ 6:557-60 Apr 40

FARNAM, HENRY WALCOTT
Anonymous. Henry Walcott Farnam.
AER 34:[706a] Dec 44

FARRELL, JAMES AUGUSTINE
Anonymous. James A. Farrell, 1863-1943.
[obit.] BHR 17:102 Dec 43

FERRARA, FRANCESCO
Weinberger, O. The importance of
Francesco Ferrara in the history of
economic thought. JPE 48:91-104
Feb 40

FETTER, FRANK ALBERT
Brown, J. D. Frank Albert Fetter 1863-
1949. [obit.] AER 39:979-81 Sep 49

Howard, S. E. and Kemmerer, E. W.
Frank Albert Fetter. A birthday note.
AER 33:230-35 Mar 43

FINLAY, THOMAS ALOYSIUS
O'Brien, G. Rev. Professor T. A. Finlay,
S. J. [obit.] EJ 50:157-59 Mar 40

FISHER, IRVING
Anonymous. Irving Fisher. AER 37:
[286a] Jun 47
-- Irving Fisher. [obit.] IJE 28:581-82
Apr 48
Douglas, P. H. [Irving Fisher. obit.]
AER 37:661-63 Sep 47
Frisch, R. Tribute to Irving Fisher [fol-
lowed by Fisher's response]. JASA 42:
2-5 Mar 47
-- --- [idem.] Em 15:71-74 Apr 47
H[awtrey], R. G. Irving Fisher. [obit.]
JRSS 110:85 pt.1, 47
Sasuly, M. Irving Fisher and social sci-
ence. Em 15:255-78 Oct 47
Schumpeter, J. A. Irving Fisher's econo-
metrics. Em 16:219-31 Jul 48
Shirras, G. F. Irving Fisher (1867-1947).
[obit.] EJ 57:393-98 Sep 47
Thorp, W. L. Irving Fisher 1867-1947.
[obit.] JASA 42:311 Jun 47
Westerfield, R. B. Irving Fisher. [obit.]
AER 37:656-61 Sep 47

FLUX, Sir ALFRED WILLIAM
B[laden], V. W. Sir William Flux, 1867-
1942. [obit.] CJE 9:74-75 Feb 43
Chapman, S. J. Sir Alfred Flux. [obit.]
EJ 52:400-03 Dec 42
L[eak], H. Sir Alfred William Flux, C.B.
[obit.] JRSS 105:144-47 pt.2, 42

FOX, ABRAHAM MANUEL
Durand, E. D. A. Manuel Fox, 1889-1942.
[obit.] JASA 38:105-06 Mar 43

FRANKLIN, BENJAMIN
Aldridge, A. O. Franklin as demographer.
JEH 9:25-44 May 49
Grampp, W. D. The political economy of
Poor Richard. JPE 55:132-41 Apr 47

GANDHI, MOHANDAS KARAMCHAND
Anjaria, J. J. The Gandhian approach to
Indian economics. IJE 22:357-66
Jan 42

GARDNER, HENRY BRAYTON
Anonymous. Henry Brayton Gardner.
AER 37:[534a] Sep 47

GAREY, LEWIS FARR
F[illey], H. C. Lewis F. Garey, 1886-
1941. [obit.] JFE 23:936-37 Nov 41

GAY, EDWIN FRANCIS
Gras, N. S. B. Edwin Francis Gay.
EHR 16:60-62 no.1, 46
Hamilton, E. J. Edwin Francis Gay.
[obit.] AER 37:410-13 Jun 47
Heaton, H. The making of an economic
historian. JEH/S 9:1-18 '49

GESELL, SILVIO
Dillard, D. Silvio Gesell's monetary theory
of social reform. AER 32:348-52 Jun 42

# 4. HISTORY OF ECONOMIC THOUGHT

## 4.8 INDIVIDUALS (A-Z) (Cont.)

GILL, CORRINGTON CALHOUN
Myers, H. B. Corrington Calhoun Gill
1898-1946. [obit.] JASA 41:393-94
Sep 46

GLAZEBROOK, ARTHUR JAMES
I[nnis], H. A. Arthur James Glazebrook.
[obit.] CJE 7:92-94 Feb 41

GOBBI, ULISSE
Loria, A. Ulisse Gobbi. [obit.] EJ 50:
364-65 Jun-Sep 40

GOKHALE, GOPAL KRISHNA
Lokanathan, P. S. The economics of
Gokhale. IJE 22:225-34 Jan 42

GRAY, JOHN HENRY
Robinson, J. S. John Henry Gray 1859-
1946. [obit.] AER 36:664-66 Sep 46

GRIMES, WALDO ERNEST
H[odges], J. A. Waldo E. Grimes. [obit.]
JFE 29:797-98 Aug 47

GROSSKOPF, JOHANNES FRIEDRICH
WILHELM
De S[wardt], S. J. Johannes Friedrich
Wilhelm Grosskopf 1885-1948. [obit.]
SAJE 16:219-20 Jun 48

HADLEY, ARTHUR TWINING
Anonymous. Arthur Twining Hadley.
AER 32:[450a] Sep 42

HALLE, HIRAM J.
Anonymous. Hiram J. Halle: a memorial.
BHR 19:211-12 Dec 45

HAMMOND, JOHN LAWRENCE LE BRETON
Anonymous. Dr. J. L. Hammond. [obit.]
EHR II.1:143 no.2-3, 49

HEARN, WILLIAM EDWARD
La Nauze, J. A. Two notes on Hearn.
ER 17:255-58 Dec 41

HIGGS, HENRY
Collet, C. E. Henry Higgs (March 4, 1864-
May 21, 1940). [obit.] EJ 50:546-61
Dec 40
Keynes, J. M. Henry Higgs (March 4,
1864-May 21, 1940). [obit.] EJ 50:
555-58 Dec 40

HILTON, JOHN
Fay, C. R. Professor John Hilton (1880-
1943). [obit.] EJ 53:449-50 Dec 43
R[hodes], E. C. Professor John Hilton.
[obit.] JRSS 106:293-94 pt.3, 43

HOBSON, JOHN ATKINSON
Cole, G. D. H. J. A. Hobson (1858-1940).
[obit.] EJ 50:351-60 Jun-Sep 40
Mirkowich, N. The economics of John A.
Hobson. IJE 23:175-85 Oct 42

HOLLANDER, JACOB HARRY
Anonymous. Jacob Harry Hollander.
AER 38:[244a] Jun 48

ISAACS, NATHAN
Mace, M. L. Nathan Isaacs. [obit.]
BHR 16:19-20 Feb 42

JAMES, EDMUND JANES
Anonymous. Edmund Janes James.
AER 34:[456a] Sep 44

JENKS, JEREMIAH WHIPPLE
Anonymous. Jeremiah Whipple Jenks.
AER 33:[790a] Dec 43

JESSEN, JENS PETER
Schmölders, G. Jens Jessen (1896-1944).
[obit.] EJ 58:135-36 Mar 48

JEVONS, WILLIAM STANLEY
La Nauze, J. A. Jevons in Sydney. ER 17:
31-45 Jun 41

KALE, VAMAN GOVIND
Karve, D. G. The late Prof. V. G. Kale
of Poona. [obit.] IJE 27:335-37 Jan 47
Row, B. G. V. G. Kale: his industrial
outlook. IJE 27:323-30 Jan 47
Thomas, P. J. The late Professor V. G.
Kale. [obit.] IJE 27:333-34 Jan 47

KEIRSTEAD, WILFRED CURRIER
P[etrie], J. R. Wilfred Currier Keirstead,
1871-1944. [obit.] CJE 11:111-14
Feb 45

KEMMERER, EDWIN WALTER
Anonymous. Edwin Walter Kemmerer.
AER 39:[1142a] Sep 49
Howard, S. E. [and others] Edwin Walter
Kemmerer 1875-1945. [obit.] AER 36:
219-21 Mar 46
Shirras, G. F. Edwin Walter Kemmerer
(1875-1945). [obit.] EJ 56:325-28
Jun 46

KEYNES, JOHN MAYNARD
Alexander, S. S. Mr. Keynes and Mr.
Marx. REStud 7:123-35 Feb 40
Angell, J. W. Keynes and economic analy-
sis today. R. REStat 30:259-64 Nov 48
Anonymous. [Report of dinner by mem-
bers of the Council of the Royal Eco-
nomic Society in honor of Lord Keynes.]
EJ 55:298-300 Jun-Sep 45
Arndt, H. W. Recent discussion of
Keynes' theory of wages. R. ER 25,
(no.49):77-83 Dec 49
Beveridge, W. H. [Communication on
Lord Keynes's elevation to the Peer-
age.] EJ 52:267-68 Jun-Sep 42
-- ; H[arrod], R. F. and R[obinson], E. A.
G. The editorship. [Resignation of Lord
Keynes]. EJ 55:1 Apr 45
Browne, G. W. G. The Keynesian revolu-
tion in economics. SAJE 14:237-52
Dec 46
Burns, A. F. Keynesian economics once
again [followed by A. H. Hansen's re-
joinder]. REStat 29:252-68 Nov 47
Chandler, L. V. [and others] A consideration
of the economic and monetary theories
of J. M. Keynes: discussion. AER/S 38:
291-98 May 48
Dillard, D. Keynes and Proudhon. JEH 2:
63-76 May 42
-- The pragmatic basis of Keynes's political economy. JEH 6:121-52 Nov 46
-- The Keynesian revolution and economic
development. R. JEH 8:171-77 Nov 48

4.8 INDIVIDUALS (A-Z) (Cont.)
KEYNES, JOHN MAYNARD (Cont.)

Elliott, G. A. The significance of The general theory of employment, interest, and money. CJE 13:372-78 Aug 47

Fields, R. H. Lord Keynes's theory of wages. ER 22:284-89 Dec 46

Fossati, E. Vilfredo Pareto and John Maynard Keynes: one or two economic systems? Met 1:126-30 Oct 49

Giblin, L. F. John Maynard Keynes. (Some personal notes) ER 22:1-3 Jun 46

Gruchy, A. G. J. M. Keynes' concept of economic science. SEJ 15:249-66 Jan 49

Haberler, G. The place of The general theory of employment, interest, and money in the history of economic thought. REStat 28:187-94 Nov 46

Hansen, A. H. Keynes and the General theory. REStat 28:182-87 Nov 46

-- Dr. Burns on Keynesian economics. REStat 29:247-52 Nov 47

Harrod, R. F. and R[obinson], E. A. G. John Maynard Keynes. [obit.] EJ 56: 171 Jun 46

-- John Maynard Keynes. REStat 28: 178-82 Nov 46

H[awtrey], R. G. Lord Keynes. [obit.] JRSS 109:169 pt.2, 46

Hoover, C. B. Keynes and the economic system. JPE 56:392-402 Oct 48

Kahn, E. Keynes' influence on theory and public policy. R. SAJE 16:70-74 Mar 48

Labini, P. S. The Keynesians (a letter from America to a friend). [Translated by O. R. Agresti] BNL 2:238-42 Oct-Dec 49

Mackintosh, W. A. Keynes as a public servant. CJE 13:379-83 Aug 47

Neisser, H. Keynes as an economist. SR 13:225-35 Jun 46

O'Leary, J. J. Malthus and Keynes. JPE 50:901-19 Dec 42

Plumptre, A. F. W. Keynes in Cambridge. [obit.] CJE 13:366-71 Aug 47

Rao, T. H. Structural changes in capitalistic economy: ideas of Keynes and Karl Marx. IJE 24:418-43 Apr 44

Robinson, A. John Maynard Keynes (1883-1946). [obit.] EJ 57:1-68 Mar 47

Rueff, J. The fallacies of Lord Keynes' General theory. QJE 61:343-67 May 47

Samuelson, P. Lord Keynes and the General theory. Em 14:187-200 Jul 46

Schumpeter, J. A. John Maynard Keynes 1883-1946. AER 36:495-518 Sep 46

-- Keynes and statistics. REStat 28: 194-96 Nov 46

Scott, I. O., Jr. Professor Leontief on Lord Keynes [followed by W. Leontief's

comment and G. Haberler's further comment.] QJE 63:554-71 Nov 49

Sweezy, P. M. John Maynard Keynes. S&S 10:398-405 no.4, 46

Tarshis, L. An exposition of Keynesian economics. AER/S 38:261-72 May 48

Timlin, M. F. John Maynard Keynes. [obit.] CJE 13:363-65 Aug 47

Tobin, J. The fallacies of Lord Keynes' General theory: comment [followed by J. Rueff's reply]. QJE 62:763-82 Nov 48

Williams, J. H. An appraisal of Keynesian economics. AER/S 38:273-90 May 48

Wilson, E. B. John Law and John Keynes. QJE 63:381-85 May 48

KHALDUN, IBN

Qadir, M. A. The economic ideas of Ibn Khaldun [1332-1406]. IJE 22:898-907 Apr 42

KINLEY, DAVID

Anonymous. David Kinley. AER 35: [518a] Sep 45

Litman, S. David Kinley 1861-1844. [obit.] AER 35:1041-44 Dec 45

KIRSTEIN, LOUIS EDWARD

Anonymous. Louis Edward Kirstein. [obit.] BHR 17:57-62 Jun 43

KRZYZANOWSKI, ADAM

Lange, O. Adam Krzyzanowski. [obit.] EJ 50:159-61 Mar 40

KUCZYNSKI, ROBERT RENÉ

Carr-Saunders, A. M. Robert René Kuczynski (1876-1947). [obit.] EJ 58: 434-38 Sep 48

LAUDERDALE, JAMES MAITLAND, 8th earl of

Fetter, F. A. Lauderdale's oversaving theory. AER 35:263-83 Jun 45

Paglin, M. Fetter on Lauderdale. AER 36: 391-93 Jun 46

LAUGHLIN, JAMES LAURENCE

Mitchell, W. C. J. Laurence Laughlin. R. [of Bornemann's biography]. JPE 49: 875-81 Dec 41

LAW, JOHN

Wilson, E. B. John Law and John Keynes. QJE 62:381-95 May 48

LEACOCK, STEPHEN BUTLER

D[ay], J. P. Professor Leacock at McGill. [obit.] CJE 10:226-30 May 44

I[nnis], H. A. Stephen Butler Leacock (1869-1944). [obit.] CJE 10:216-26 May 44

LEDERER, EMIL

Anonymous. Emil Lederer, 1882-1939: I. The sociologist. II. The economist [with bibliography]. SR 7:337-58; 8:79-105, Sep 40, Feb 41

LIVINGSTON, ROBERT R.

McAnear, B. Mr. Robert R. Livingston's reasons against a land tax. JPE 48: 63-90 Feb 40

4. HISTORY OF ECONOMIC THOUGHT

4.8 INDIVIDUALS (A-Z) (Cont.)
LORIA, ACHILLE
Einaudi, L. Achille Loria (1857-1943).
[obit.] EJ 56:147-50 Mar 46
LUXTON, EDWARD ARTHUR GEORGE
S[tewart], A. Edward Arthur George
Luxton, 1914-1945. [obit.] CJE 11:
478-79 Aug 45
McLEAN, SIMON JAMES
C[oats], R. H. Simon James McLean,
1871-1946. [obit.] CJE 13:121-22
Feb 47
MACLEOD, ALAN GROVER
Anonymous. Alan Macleod. [obit.]
JFE 29:796 Aug 47
McQUEEN, ROBERT
MacG[ibbon], D. A. Robert McQueen,
1896-1941. [obit.] CJE 7:278-81
May 41
W[aines], W. J. [Robert McQueen, 1896-
1941]. Bibliography. CJE 7:281-83
May 41
MACROSTY, HENRY WILLIAM
G[reenwood], M. H. W. M. [obit.]
JRSS 104:85-90 pt.1, 41
Smith, H. L. H. W. Macrosty. [obit.]
EJ 51:156-57 Apr 41
MALTHUS, THOMAS ROBERT
Johnson, H. G. Malthus on the high price
of provisions. CJE 15:190-202 May 49
O'Leary, J. J. Malthus and Keynes.
JPE 50:901-19 Dec 42
-- Malthus's general theory of employ-
ment and the post-Napoleonic depres-
sions. JEH 3:185-200 Nov 43
Spengler, J. J. Malthus's total population
theory: a restatement and reappraisal.
Pt.I-II. CJE 11:83-110; 234-64 Feb,
May 45
Zinke, G. W. Six letters from Malthus to
Pierre Prévost. JEH 2:174-89 Nov 42
MARSHALL, ALFRED
Aggarwala, K. C. Marshall's concept of
quasi-rent. IJE 28:555-61 Apr 48
Anonymous. The centenary of the birth of
Alfred Marshall July 26, 1842-July 13,
1942. EJ 52:289 Dec 42
Friedman, M. The Marshallian demand
curve. JPE 57:463-95 Dec 49
Guillebaud, C. W. The evolution of Mar-
shall's Principles of economics.
EJ 52:330-49 Dec 42
Krishnaswami, A. Marshall's theory of
money and interest. IJE 22:121-43
Oct 41
-- Marshall's contribution to Indian eco-
nomics. IJE 22:875-97 Apr 42
Macgregor, D. H. Marshall and his book.
Ec N.S.9:313-24 Nov 42
Macmillan, D. Marshall's Principles of
economics: a bibliographical note.
EJ 52:290-93 Dec 42
Roy, P. On Marshall's statics and dynam-
ics. IJE 20:761-71 Apr 40

Schumpeter, J. A. Alfred Marshall's
Principles: a semi-centennial apprai-
sal. AER 31:236-48 Jun 41
Shove, G. F. The place of Marshall's
Principles in the development of eco-
nomic theory. EJ 52:294-329 Dec 42
Tiwari, J. N. Marshall and the theory of
rent. IJE 26:290-95 Oct 45
Viner, J. Marshall's economics, in rela-
tion to the man and to his times.
AER 31:223-35 Jun 41
Wilson, E. B. Pareto on Marshall's de-
mand curve. QJE 58:141-45 Nov 43
MARSHALL, MARY PALEY
Keynes, J. M. Mary Paley Marshall
(1850-1944). [obit.] EJ 54:268-84
Jun-Sep 44
MARX, KARL
Alexander, S. S. Mr. Keynes and Mr.
Marx. REStud 7:123-35 Feb 40
Bladen, V. W. The centenary of Marx and
Mill. JEH/S 8:32-41 '48
Bloom, S. F. Man of his century: a re-
consideration of the historical signifi-
cance of Karl Marx. JPE 51:494-505
Dec 43
Bober, M. M. Marx and economic calcu-
lation. AER 36:344-57 Jun 46
Irvine, W. George Bernard Shaw and Karl
Marx. JEH 6:53-72 May 46
Robinson, J. Marx on unemployment.
EJ 51:234-48 Jun-Sep 41
Rosenberg, B. Veblen and Marx. SR 15:
99-117 Mar 48
MENGER, KARL
Bloch, H. S. Carl Menger: the founder of
the Austrian school. JPE 48:428-33
Jun 40
MESTON, JAMES SCORGIE MESTON, baron
S[hove], G. F. Lord Meston 1865-1943.
[obit.] JRSS 106:294-96 pt.3, 43
MILL, JOHN STUART
-- A correspondence [with John Rae].
Ec N.S.10:253-55 Aug 43
-- Notes on N. W. Senior's Political econ-
omy [reproduced from an interleaved
copy of the first (quarto) edition of N.
W. Senior's Outline of the science of
political economy. Edited by F. A.
Hayek]. Ec N.S.12:134-39 Aug 45
Bladen, V. W. The centenary of Marx and
Mill. JEH/S 8:32-41 '48
-- John Stuart Mill's Principles: a cen-
tenary estimate. AER/S 39:1-12 May 49
Hyde, F. E. Utility and radicalism, 1825-
1837: a note on the Mill-Roebuck
friendship. EHR 16:38-44 no.1, 46
LeRossignol, J. E. Mill on machinery.
AER 30:115-16 Mar 40
O'Brien, G. J. S. Mill and J. E. Cairnes.
Ec N.S.10:273-85 Nov 43
Pigou, A. C. Mill and the wages fund.
EJ 59:171-80 Jun 49

4.8 INDIVIDUALS (A-Z) (Cont.)

MILL, JOHN STUART (Cont.)

Viner, J. Bentham and J. S. Mill: the utilitarian background. AER 39:360-82 Mar 49

MILLIS, HARRY ALVIN

Brown, E. C. [and others] Harry Alvin Millis 1873-1948. [obit.] AER 39: 742-50 Jun 49

MIRKOVICH, NICHOLAS

Fisher, A. G. B. Nicholas Mirkovich (1915-1944). [obit.] EJ 56:510-11 Sep 46

MITCHELL, WESLEY CLAIR

Dorfman, J. Wesley C. Mitchell (1874-1948). EJ 59:448-58 Sep 49

Hansen, A. H. Wesley Mitchell, social scientist and social counselor. REStat 31:245-55 Nov 49

H[arrod], R. F. Wesley Mitchell in Oxford. EJ 59:459-60 Sep 49

Hayek, F. A. Wesley Clair Mitchell, 1874-1948. [obit.] JRSS 111:254-55 pt.2, 48

Kuznets, S. Wesley Clair Mitchell, 1874-1948: an appreciation. JASA 43:126-31 Mar 49

Mills, F. C. Wesley Clair Mitchell 1874-1948. [obit.] AER 39:730-42 Jun 49

MORGAN, JOHN PIERPONT

Anonymous. John Pierpont Morgan, 1867-1943. [obit.] BHR 17:92-96 Nov 43

MUNZER, EGBERT

Ballantyne, M. The late Egbert Munzer: a tribute. [obit.] CJE 15:409-11 Aug 49

NAIDOO, V. SIRKARI

Anonymous. V. Sirkari Naidoo. [obit.] SAJE 16:108 Mar 48

NEILL, CHARLES PATRICK

Hinrichs, A. F. Charles P. Neill, 1865-1942. [obit.] JASA 38:110-11 Mar 43

NEWTON, Sir ISAAC

Shirras, G. F. and Craig, J. H. Sir Isaac Newton and the currency. EJ 55:217-41 Jun-Sep 45

OLSEN, NILS ANDREAS

Anonymous. Nils A. Olsen, 1886-1940. [obit.] JFE 22:828-29 Nov 40

OPPENHEIMER, FRANZ

Guelfat, I. Franz Oppenheimer. [obit.] EJ 55:132-37 Apr 45

Heimann, E. Franz Oppenheimer's economic ideas. SR 11:27-39 Feb 44

OSEROV, T. CHR.

Tverdokhlebov, V. T. Chr. Oserov. [obit.] EJ 55:297-98 Jun-Sep 45

OTIS, DANIEL H.

S[chaars], M. A. Daniel H. Otis. [obit.] JFE 24:555 May 42

PALMER, HORSLEY

Horsefield, J. K. The opinions of Horsley Palmer, Governor of the Bank of England, 1830-33. Ec N.S.16:143-58 May 49

PARETO, VILFREDO

Clerc, J. O. Walras, and Pareto: their approach to applied economics and social economics. CJE 8:584-94 Nov 42

Fossati, E. Vilfredo Pareto and John Maynard Keynes: one or two economic systems? Met 1:126-30 Oct 49

Schumpeter, J. A. Vilfredo Pareto (1848-1932). QJE 63:147-73 May 49

Spengler, J. J. Pareto on population. Pt.I-II. QJE 58:571-601; 59:107-33 Aug,Nov 44

Wilson, E. B. Pareto on Marshall's demand curve. QJE 58:141-45 Nov 43

PATTEN, SIMON NELSON

Anonymous. Simon Nelson Patten. AER 34:[226a] Jun 44

PATTON, HARALD SMITH

MacG[ibbon], D. A. Harald Smith Patton, 1889-1945. [obit.] CJE 11:614-15 Nov 45

PEARL, RAYMOND

Dunn, H. L. Raymond Pearl, 1879-1940. [obit.] JASA 36:120-21 Mar 41

PERKINS, JAMES HANDASYD

Anonymous. James Handasyd Perkins. [obit.] BHR 14:93 Dec 40

PESCH, HEINRICH

Harris, A. L. The scholastic revival: the economics of Heinrich Pesch. JPE 54: 38-59 Feb 46

Mueller, F. H. The principle of solidarity in the teachings of Father Henry Pesch, S.J. RSE 4:31-39 Jan 46

Mulcahy, R. E. The welfare economics of Heinrich Pesch. QJE 63:342-60 Aug 49

PETERSON, GEORGE MARTIN

T[inley], J. M. George Martin Peterson, 1897-1940. [obit.] JFE 22:827-28 Nov 40

PIROU, GAËTAN

Bloch, H. S. Gaëtan Pirou. [obit.] AER 37:192-93 Mar 47

PLAYFAIR, WILLIAM

Grossman, H. W. Playfair, the earliest theorist of capitalist development. EHR 18:65-83 no.1-2, 48

PLEHN, CARL COPPING

Anonymous. Carl Copping Plehn, AER 38: [776a] Dec 48

POWER, EILEEN

Clapham, J. H. Eileen Power, 1889-1940. [obit.] Ec N.S.7:351-59 Nov 40

Tawney, R. H. Dr. Eileen Power. [obit.] EHR 10:92-94 Nov 40

Webster, C. K. Eileen Power (1889-1940). [obit.] EJ 50:561-72 Dec 40

PROUDHON, PIERRE JOSEPH

Dillard, D. Keynes and Proudhon. JEH 2: 63-76 May 42

Watkins, F. M. Proudhon and the theory of modern liberalism. CJE 13:429-35 Aug 47

# 4. HISTORY OF ECONOMIC THOUGHT

## 4.8 INDIVIDUALS (A-Z) (Cont.)

PUGLIESE, MARIO
[Anonymous] Mario Pugliese. [obit.]
EJ 50:365 Jun-Sep 40

RAE, JOHN
-- A correspondence [with John Stuart
Mill]. Ec N.S.10:253-55 Aug 43

RANADE, MAHADEV GOVIND
Anantaram, K. Ranade, the economist.
IJE 22:387-93 Jan 42
Coyajee, Sir J. C. Ranade's work as an
economist. IJE 22:307-30 Jan 42
Datta, B. The background of Ranade's
economics. IJE 22:261-75 Jan 42
Karve, D. G. Ranade and economic plan-
ning. IJE 22:235-44 Jan 42
Kellock, J. Ranade and after: a study of
the development of economic thought
in India. IJE 22:245-60 Jan 42

RICARDO, DAVID
Johnson, H. G. An error in Ricardo's
exposition of his theory of rent.
QJE 62:792-93 Nov 48
Roberts, R. O. Ricardo's theory of public
debts. Ec N.S.9:257-66 Aug 42

RICCI, UMBERTO
Einaudi, L. Umberto Ricci. [obit.]
AER 36:666-68 Sep 46

RICH, GEORGE AVERY
Anonymous. George Avery Rich. [obit.]
BHR 18:171 Dec 44

RICHTER, LOTHAR
Bates, S. Lothar Richter (1894-1948).
[obit.] CJE 15:543-45 Nov 49

ROBINSON, MARJORIE EVE
Henderson, H. D. Marjorie Eve Robinson. [obit.] EJ 50:161-62 Mar 40

ROGERS, NORMAN McLEOD
M[ackintosh], W. A. Norman McLeod
Rogers, 1894-1940. [obit.] CJE 6:
476-78 Aug 40

ROTHBARTH, ERWIN
Champernowne, D. G. and Kaldor, N.
Erwin Rothbarth. [obit.] EJ 55:130-32
Apr 45
Kalecki, M. The work of Erwin Rothbarth.
REStud 12:121-22 no.2, 45

RUSKIN, JOHN
Fain, J. T. Ruskin and the orthodox
political economists. SEJ 10:1-13
Jul 43

SAINT-SIMON, CLAUDE HENRI, comte de
Stark, W. Saint-Simon as a realist.
JEH 3:42-55 May 43
-- The realism of Saint-Simon's spiritual
program. JEH 5:24-42 May 45

SALTER, LEONARD AUSTIN, Jr.
Clark, N. An appreciation of Leonard A.
Salter, Jr. LE 22:302-03 Aug 46
Fred, E. B. In memoriam to Leonard A.
Salter, Jr. [obit.] LE 22:117-18 May 46
P[arsons], K. H. and P[enn], R. J. Leonard
A. Salter, Jr. [obit.] JFE 28:885 Aug 46

-- The development of Salter's conception of research. LE 24:175-78 May 48

SCHULZE-GAEVERNITZ, GERHART von
Rosenbaum, E. Gerhart von Schulze-
Gaevernitz (July 25, 1864-July 10,
1943). [obit.] EJ 53:450-53 Dec 43

SCOTT, WILLIAM AMASA
Morton, W. A. William A. Scott 1862-
1944. [obit.] AER 35:786-87 Sep 45

SCOTT, WILLIAM ROBERT
Clapham, J. H. William Robert Scott
(Born August 31, 1868. Died April 10,
1940). [obit.] EJ 50:347-51 Jun-Sep 40
Tawney, R. H. Professor W. R. Scott.
[obit.] EHR 10:91-92 Nov 40

SEAGER, HENRY ROGERS
Anonymous. Henry Rogers Seager.
AER 38:[494a] Jun 48

SECRIST, HORACE
Deibler, F. S. Horace Secrist, 1881-1943.
[obit.] JASA 38:365-66 Sep 43

SELIGMAN, EDWIN ROBERT ANDERSON
Anonymous. Edwin Robert Anderson
Seligman. AER 33:[246a] Jun 43
Mirkowich, N. The place of J. B. Clark
and E. R. A. Seligman in American eco-
nomic science. IJE 21:67-74 Jul 40

SERING, MAX
Hibbard, B. H., chairman. Max Sering.
[obit.] JFE 22:409 Feb 40

SHAW, GEORGE BERNARD
Irvine, W. George Bernard Shaw and
Karl Marx. JEH 6:53-72 May 46

SHAW, WILLIAM ARTHUR
Hawtrey, R. W. A. Shaw. [obit.] EJ 53:
290 Jun-Sep 43

SIEVEKING, HEINRICH
Stark, W. Heinrich Sieveking. [obit.]
EJ 56:329-30 Jun 46

SILBERLING, NORMAN JOHN
Anonymous. Norman John Silberling,
1892-1942. [obit.] JASA 38:112 Mar 43;
A correction. 249 Jun 43

SIMIAND, FRANÇOIS
Keirstead, B. S. and Mankiewicz, R. H.
The works of François Simiand. R.
CJE 14:249-54 May 48

SIMONS, HENRY CALVERT
Hardy, C. O. Liberalism in the modern
state: the philosophy of Henry Simons.
R. JPE 56:305-14 Aug 48
Lewis, H. G. Henry Calvert Simons.
[obit.] AER 36:668-69 Sep 46

SKELTON, OSCAR DOUGLAS
M[ackintosh], W. A. O. D. Skelton, 1878-
1941. [obit.] CJE 7:270-78 May 41

SMITH, ADAM
Anonymous. The Adam Smith collection
at the Harvard School of Business Administration. BHR 19:26-28 Feb 45
Bittermann, H. J. Adam Smith's empiricism and the law of nature. Pt.I-II.
JPE 48:487-520; 703-34 Aug,Oct 40

4.8  INDIVIDUALS (A-Z) (Cont.)

SMITH, ADAM (Cont.)

Dunn, W. C.  Adam Smith and Edmund Burke: complementary contemporaries. SEJ 7:330-46 Jan 41

Grampp. W. D.  Adam Smith and the economic man. JPE 56:315-36 Aug 48

Jones, C.  Adam Smith's library: some additions. EH 4:326-28 Feb 40

La Nauze, J. A.  A manuscript attributed to Adam Smith. EJ 55:288-91 Jun-Sep 45

MacGarvey, C. J.  Notes on Adam Smith's library and the Bonar catalogue 1932. EJ 59:259-64 Jun 49

Romanes, J. H.  [Communication relating to the Muir portrait of Adam Smith.] EJ 55:465-66 Dec 45

Salomon, A.  Adam Smith as sociologist. SR 12:22-42 Feb 45

SMITH, Sir HUBERT LLEWELLYN

Beveridge, W. H.  Sir Hubert Llewellyn Smith (1864-1945). [obit.] EJ 56: 143-47 Mar 46

Bowley, A. L.  Sir Hubert Llewellyn Smith, G.C.B. [obit.] JRSS 108:480-81 pt.2-4, 45

Collet, C. E.  Charles Booth, the Denison Club and H. Llewellyn Smith. [obit.] JRSS 108:482-85 pt.3-4, 45

SNYDER, CARL

Burgess, W. R.  Carl Snyder: an appreciation. [obit.] JASA 41:244-46 Jun 46

SOMBART, WERNER

Epstein, M.  Werner Sombart (January 19, 1863-May 13, 1941). [obit.] EJ 51: 523-26 Dec 41

Harris, A. L.  Sombart and German (national) socialism. JPE 50:805-35 Dec 42

Rogin, L.  Werner Sombart and the uses of transcendentalism. AER 31:493-511 Sep 41

STACKELBERG, HEINRICH von

Eucken, W.  Heinrich von Stackelberg (1905-1946). [obit.] EJ 58:132-35 Mar 48

STAMP, JOSIAH CHARLES STAMP, baron

Bowley, A. L.  Lord Stamp. JRSS 104: 193-96 pt.2, 41

Henderson, H. D.  Josiah Charles Stamp, Baron Stamp of Shortlands (June 21, 1880, to April 16, 1941). [obit.] EJ 51: 338-47 Jun-Sep 41

Willcox, W. F.  Josiah Charles Stamp, 1880-1941. [obit.] JASA 36:546-47 Dec 41

STEUART, Sir JAMES

Sen, S. R.  Sir James Steuart's general theory of employment, interest and money. Ec N.S.14:19-36 Feb 47

Stettner, W. F.  Sir James Steuart on the public debt. QJE 59:451-76 May 45

STOKDYK, ELLIS ADOLPH

K[napp], J. G.  Ellis A. Stokdyk. [obit.] JFE 28:886 Aug 46

STRAUS, PERCY SELDEN

Anonymous.  Percy Selden Straus. [obit.] BHR 18:172-73 Dec 44

STRIGL, RICHARD von

Hayek, F. A.  Richard von Strigl. [obit.] EJ 54:284-86 Jun-Sep 44

STRUVE, PETER BERNHARDOVICH

Struve, G.  Peter Struve. [obit. and bibliography] EJ 54:438-43 Dec 44

STRUZZI, ALBERTO

Smith, R. S.  Spanish antimercantilism of the seventeenth century: Alberto Struzzi and Diego José Dormer. JPE 48:401-11 Jun 40

TARDE, GEORGE

Taymans, A. C.  George Tarde and Joseph A. Schumpeter: a similar vision. EEH 1,no.4:9-17 Apr 49

TAUSSIG, FRANK WILLIAM

-- My father's business career. HBR 19: 177-84 no.2, 41

Anonymous.  Frank William Taussig. AER 33:[492a] Sep 43

Ellis, H. S.  Frank William Taussig, 1859-1940. [obit.] AER 31:209-11 Mar 41

Opie, R.  Frank William Taussig (1859-1940). [obit.] EJ 51:347-68 Jun-Sep 41

Prest, W.  Taussig's Principles. R. ER 16:270-75 Dec 40

Schumpeter, J. A.; Cole, A. H.; and Mason, E. S.  Frank William Taussig. [obit.] QJE 55:337-63 May 41

TAYLOR, CHARLES HENRY

Anonymous.  Charles H. Taylor. [obit.] BHR 15:59-61 Oct 41

TAYLOR, JOHN

Grampp, W. D.  John Taylor: economist of southern agrarianism. SEJ 11: 255-68 Jan 45

THÜNEN, JOHANN HEINRICH von

Leigh, A. H.  Von Thünen's theory of distribution and the advent of marginal analysis. JPE 54:481-502 Dec 46

URWICK, EDWARD JOHNS

I[nnis], H. A.  Edward Johns Urwick, 1867-1945. [obit.] CJE 11:265-68 May 45

VEBLEN, THORSTEIN

Davis, A. K.  Sociological elements in Veblen's economic theory. JPE 53: 132-49 Jun 45

Oshima, H. T.  Veblen on Japan. SR 10: 487-94 Nov 43

Rosenberg, B.  Veblen and Marx. SR 15: 99-117 Mar 48

VERDIER, JAMES WILLIAM

G[eorge], R. F.  James William Verdier. [obit.] JRSS 111:376 pt.4, 48

VERRIJN STUART, COENRAAD ALEXANDER

G[eorge], R. F.  Conrad Alexander Verrijn Stuart. [obit.] JRSS 112:346 pt.3, 49

## 4. HISTORY OF ECONOMIC THOUGHT

4.8 INDIVIDUALS (A-Z) (Cont.)
WALKER, CHARLES EDGAR
   S[mails], R. G. C. E. Walker, 1880-1942.
      [obit.] CJE 9:75-76 Feb 43
WALKER, FRANCIS AMASA
   Anonymous. Francis Amasa Walker.
      AER 31:[222a] Mar 41
WALRAS, LÉON
   Clerc, J. O. Walras and Pareto: their
      approach to applied economics and
      social economics. CJE 8:584-94
      Nov 42
WALWYN, WILLIAM
   Schenk, W. A seventeenth-century radical.
      EHR 14:74-83 no.1, 44
WEAVER, FREDERICK PATTISON
   L[ininger], F. F. Frederick Pattison
      Weaver, 1882-1940. [obit.] JFE 22:
      829 Nov 40
WEBB, BEATRICE
   Cole, G. D. H. Beatrice Webb as an econ-
      omist. [obit.] EJ 53:422-37 Dec 43
   Woolf, L. Beatrice Webb. (1858-1943).
      [obit.] EJ 53:284-90 Jun-Sep 43
WEBB, SIDNEY
   Beveridge, Sir W. H. Sidney Webb (Lord
      Passfield 1859-1947). [obit.] EJ 58:
      428-34 Sep 48
   Tawney, R. H. In memory of Sidney Webb.
      [obit.] Ec N.S.14:245-53 Nov 47
WEBER, MAX
   Fischoff, E. The Protestant ethic and the
      spirit of capitalism: the history of a
      controversy. SR 11:53-77 Feb 44
   Honigsheim, P. Max Weber as historian
      of agriculture and rural life. AH 23:
      179-213 Jul 49

Riemersma, J. C. Max Weber's "Protes-
      tant ethic": an example of historical
      conceptualization. EEH 1,no.6:11-19
      Jun 49
WEHRWEIN, GEORGE SIMON
   Anonymous. George S. Wehrwein, Janu-
      ary 31, 1883-January 10, 1945. LE 21:
      1 Feb 45
   -- Exemplar: George S. Wehrwein.
      LE 21:191-93 May 45
   H[ibbard], B. H. George Simon Wehrwein.
      [obit.] JFE 27:232 Feb 45
   S[alter], L. A., Jr. George S. Wehrwein,
      1883-1945. [obit.] AER 35:511 Jun 45
WHEATLEY, JOHN
   Fetter, F. W. The life and writings of
      John Wheatley. JPE 50:357-76 Jun 42
WICKSELL, KNUT
   Marschak, J. Wicksell's two interest
      rates. SR 8:469-78 Nov 41
WILLCOX, WALTER FRANCIS
   Durand, E. D. Tribute to Walter F. Will-
      cox [followed by Willcox's response].
      JASA 42:5-10 Mar 47
WILSON, Sir DUNCAN
   H[ill], A. B. Sir Duncan Wilson, C.B.E.,
      C.V.O. [obit.] JRSS 108:245 pt.1-2, 45
WOOD, STUART
   Stigler, G. J. Stuart Wood and the mar-
      ginal productivity theory. QJE 61:
      640-49 Aug 47
YOUNG, ALLYN ABBOTT
   Anonymous. Allyn Abbott Young. AER 39:
      [860a] Sep 49
ZAITZEV, ALEXANDER
   Tverdokhlebov, V. A. Zaitzev (1888-1942).
      [obit.] EJ 54:138-39 Apr 44

# 5. ECONOMIC HISTORY

(For list of other history classes and subclasses see pp. xi-xiii)

5.0 GENERAL
5.01 DISCIPLINE OF ECONOMIC HISTORY
   Ashton, T. S. The relation of economic
      history to economic theory. Ec N.S.13:
      81-96 May 46
   Clark, J. M. Relations of history and
      theory (Symposium on profits and the
      entrepreneur). JEH/S 2:132-42 Dec 42
   Cochran, T. C. Historical aspects of im-
      perfect competition: theory and history.
      JEH/S 3:27-32 Dec 43
   Cole, A. H. A report on research in eco-
      nomic history. JEH 4:49-72 May 44
   -- Business history and economic history.
      JEH/S 5:45-53 Dec 45
   Feuer, L. S. The economic factor in his-
      tory. S&S 4:168-92 no.2, 40
   Fischoff, E. The Protestant ethic and the
      spirit of capitalism: the history of a
      controversy. SR 11:53-77 Feb 44

Gay, E. F. The tasks of economic history.
      JEH/S 1:9-16 Dec 41
Gilfillan, S. C. Invention as a factor in
      economic history. JEH/S 5:66-85 Dec 45
Honjo, E. The development of the study of
      the economic history of Japan subsequent
      to the Meiji restoration. Kyo 16,no.1:
      18-31 Jan 41
Innis, H. A. On the economic significance
      of culture. JEH/S 4:80-97 Dec 44
Johnson, E. A. J. New tools for the eco-
      nomic historian. JEH/S 1:30-38 Dec 41
Kirkland, E. C. The place of theory in
      teaching American economic history.
      JEH/S 9:99-102 '49
Kuznets, S. Statistics and economic history.
      JEH 1:26-41 May 41
MacIver, R. M. History and social causa-
      tion. JEH/S 3:135-45 Dec 43
Malin, J. C. Space and history; reflections

5.01 DISCIPLINE OF ECONOMIC HISTORY
(Cont.)

Malin, J. C. (Cont.)
on the closed-space doctrines of Turner
and Mackinder and the challenge of those
ideas by the air age. Pt.I-II. AH 18:
65-74; 107-26 Apr,Jul 44

Nef, J. U. The responsibility of economic
historians. JEH/S 1:1-8 Dec 41

-- What is economic history? JEH/S 4:
1-19 Dec 44

Postan, M. M. The rise of a money economy. EHR 14:123-34 no.2, 44

Powicke, F. M. The economic motive in
politics. EHR 16:85-92 no.2, 46

Renier, G. J. History and ourselves.
Ec N.S.15:270-75 Nov 48

Riemersma, J. C. Max Weber's "Protestant
ethic": an example of historical conceptualization. EEH 1,no.6:11-19 Jun 49

Robertson, H. M. Panaceas, past and present: the history of some current ways of
thought and plans for economic reform.
SAJE 12:251-62 Dec 44

-- Economic historians and their colleagues.
SAJE 14:202-11 Sep 46

Ross, E. D. and Tontz, R. L. The term
"agricultural revolution" as used by
economic historians. AH 22:32-38
Jan 48

Schumpeter, J. A. The creative response
in economic history. JEH 7:149-59
Nov 47

Shryock, R. H. [What is economic history?]
Comment. JEH/S 4:20-24 Dec 44

Spengler, J. J. Laissez faire and intervention: a potential source of historical
error. JPE 57:438-41 Oct 49

Usher, A. P. Institutional methodology in
economic history. R. JEH 1:88-96
May 41

-- The significance of modern empiricism
for history and economics. JEH 9:137-55
Nov 49

Williamson, H. F. [What is economic history?] Comment. JEH/S 4:25-28 Dec 44

5.02 EMPIRICAL STUDIES

Bloch, K. Whither Japan? SR 8:173-88
FJ    May 41

Brinton, C. The manipulation of economic
unrest. JEH/S 8:21-31 '48

Leuilliot, P. Recent French writings in the
EF    social and economic history of modern
France. [Pt.I-II] EHR II.1:61-72;
II.2:200-05 no.1, 48, no.2, 49; [Bibliogra-
phy] II.5:400-11 no.3, 53

Parker, A. Contemporary Scandinavia:
ES    historical foreword. LBR 8:13-19 Apr 48

5.1 ANCIENT

Anonymous. A traveling merchant opens to
the West the trade and culture of the
Orient, 67 A.D. R. BHR 16:80-81 Oct 42

Bromberg, B. Temple banking in Rome.
EHR 10:128-31 Nov 40

-- The origin of banking: religious finance
in Babylonia. JEH 2:77-88 May 42

Clark, G. Forest clearance and prehistoric
farming. EHR 17:45-51 no.1, 47

Dubs, H. H. An ancient Chinese stock of
FC    gold. JEH 2:36-39 May 42

Einaudi, L. Greatness and decline of
planned economy in the Hellenistic
world. R. [Translated by R. H. F.
Dalton] Pt.I-II. Kyk 2:193-210; 289-316
fasc.3,4, 48

Gruber, J. W. Irrigation and land use in
ancient Mesopotamia. AH 22:69-77
Apr 48

Hammer, J. Rostovtzeff's "Social and
economic history of the Hellenistic
world." R. JEH 3:70-81 May 43

Hammond, M. Economic stagnation in the
early Roman empire. JEH/S 6:63-90
'46

Heichelheim, F. M. Professor Rostovtzeff's
history of the Hellenistic world. R.
EJ 52:59-61 Apr 42

Jasny, N. The breads of Ephesus and their
prices. AH 21:190-92 Jul 47

Kirchberger, H. An ancient experience
with price control. JFE 24:621-36
Aug 42

Michell, H. Economic history of the Hellenistic world. R. CJE 8:247-60 May 42

-- The impact of sudden accessions of
treasure upon prices and real wages.
CJE 12:1-17 Feb 46

-- The Edict of Diocletian: a study of price
fixing in the Roman Empire. CJE 13:
1-12 Feb 47

Srikantan, K. S. Labour in ancient India.
FI    IJE 20:639-43 Apr 40

Tirumalachar, B. Economic organisation
FI    in ancient India. IJE 22:367-86 Jan 42

Wells, C. B. The economic background of
Plato's communism. JEH/S 8:101-14 '48

Westermann, W. L. Industrial slavery in
Roman Italy. JEH 2:149-63 Nov 42

White, K. D. The neglect of economic factors in the study of Roman history.
Pt.I-III. SAJE 16:422-29; 17:194-201;
18:196-204 Dec 48, Jun 49, Jun 50

Wilbur, C. M. Industrial slavery in China
FC    during the former Han Dynasty (206B.C.-
A.D.25). JEH 3:56-69 May 43

5.2 MEDIEVAL (TO 1500)
EUROPE

De Roover, F. E. Francesco Sassetti and
E    the downfall of the Medici banking house.
BHR 17:65-80 Oct 43

Deutsch, K. W. Medieval unity and the economic conditions for an international
civilization. CJE 10:18-35 Feb 44

# 5. ECONOMIC HISTORY

## 5.2 MEDIEVAL (TO 1500) (Cont.)
### EUROPE (Cont.)

E Gras, N. S. B. The growth of rigidity in business during the Middle Ages. AER/S 30:281-89 Mar 40

Helleiner, K. F. Population movement and agrarian depression in the later Middle Ages. CJE 15:368-77 Aug 49

Larson, H. M. The armor business in the Middle Ages. BHR 14:49-64 Oct 40

Lennard, R. The agrarian life of the Middle Ages. R. EJ 52:45-53 Apr 42

-- An early fulling-mill: a note. EHR 17: 150 no.2, 47

Lestocquoy, J. The tenth century. EHR 17: 1-14 no.1, 47

Stephenson, C. In praise of medieval tinkers. JEH 8:26-42 May 48

Thrupp, S. L. Social control in the medieval town. JEH/S 1:39-52 Dec 41

-- Medieval gilds reconsidered. JEH 2: 164-73 Nov 42

EA Brutzkus, J. Trade with eastern Europe, 800-1200. EHR 13:31-41 no.1-2, 43

Turner, R. E. Economic discontent in medieval western Europe. JEH/S 8: 85-100 '48

EB Carus-Wilson, E. M. An industrial revolution of the thirteenth century. EHR 11: 39-60 no.1, 41

-- The English cloth industry in the late twelfth and early thirteenth centuries. EHR 14:32-50 no.1, 44

Dodwell, B. The free tenantry of the Hundred Rolls. EHR 14:163-71 no.2, 44

Hilton, R. H. Peasant movements in England before 1381. EHR II.2:117-36 no.2, 49

Lennard, R. The origin of the fiscal carucate. EHR 14:51-63 no.1, 44

-- The destruction of woodland in the eastern counties under William the Conqueror. EHR 15:36-43 no.1-2, 45

-- The economic position of the Domesday villani. EJ 56:244-64 Jun 46

-- The economic position of the Domesday sokemen. EJ 57:179-95 Jun 47

-- The destruction of woodland in the eastern counties, 1066-1086. [Note] EHR II.1:144 no.2-3, 49

Mollat, M. Anglo-Norman trade in the fifteenth century. EHR 17:143-50 no.2, 47

Oschinsky, D. Medieval treatises on estate accounting. EHR 17:52-61 no.1, 47

Postan, M. M. Some social consequences of the Hundred Years' War. EHR 12: 1-12 no.1-2, 42

Ruddock, A. A. Alien hosting in Southampton in the fifteenth century. EHR 16: 30-37 no.1, 46

Schlauch, M. The revolt of 1381 in England. S&S 4:414-32 no.4, 40

Smith, R. A. L. Marsh embankment and sea defence in medieval Kent. EHR 10: 29-37 Feb 40

Taylor, E. G. R. The surveyor. EHR 17: 121-33 no.2, 47

ECB De Roover, R. Money, banking, and credit in medieval Bruges. JEH/S 2:52-65 Dec 42

Redlich, F. Banking in mediaeval Bruges. R. BHR 23:109-12 Jun 49

EF Mollat, M. Anglo-Norman trade in the fifteenth century. EHR 17:143-50 no.2, 47

Postan, M. M. Some social consequences of the Hundred Years' War. EHR 12: 1-12 no.1-2, 42

EG Carsten, F. L. Slavs in north-eastern Germany. EHR 11:61-76 no.1, 41

EI Cipolla, C. M. The trends in Italian economic history in the later Middle Ages. EHR II.2:181-84 no.2, 49

De Roover, F. E. The business records of an early Genoese notary, 1190-1192. BHR 14:41-46 Jun 40

-- Partnership accounts in twelfth century Genoa. BHR 15:87-92 Dec 41

Lane, F. C. Venture accounting in medieval business management. BHR 19:164-73 Nov 45

Lopez, R. S. The English and the manufacture of writing materials in Genoa. EHR 10:132-37 Nov 40

-- The life of the Genoese woolworkers as revealed in thirteenth-century notarial records. BHR 16:101-05 Dec 42

-- Italian leadership in the medieval business world. R. JEH 8:63-68 May 48

Nelson, B. N. The usurer and the merchant prince: Italian businessmen and the ecclesiastical law of restitution, 1100-1550. JEH/S 7:104-22 '47

Reynolds, R. L. In search of a business class in thirteenth-century Genoa. JEH/S 5:1-19 Dec 45

ESp Smith, R. S. Life insurance in fifteenth-century Barcelona. JEH 1:57-59 May 41

Verlinden, C. The rise of Spanish trade in the Middle Ages (Studies in sources and bibliography, VII). EHR 10:44-59 Feb 40

### ASIA

FA Lopez, R. S. European merchants in the medieval Indies: the evidence of commercial documents. JEH 3:164-84 Nov 43

FC Hozumi, F. On the monetary ideas as seen in the Records of economics and finance in the Sung history. Kyo 17,no.3:36-59 Jul 42

FI Ataullah, S. A fourteenth century experiment in price control. IJE 24:340-47 Apr 44

## 5.3 PRE-INDUSTRIAL REVOLUTION (1500-1760)

### UNITED STATES

A Hesseltine, W. B. Regions, classes and sections in American history. LE 20: 35-44 Feb 44

### OTHER COUNTRIES

E Nef, J. U. Industrial Europe at the time of the Reformation (ca.1515-ca.1540). [Pt.I-II] JPE 49:1-40; 183-224 Feb, Apr 41

-- War and economic progress 1540-1640. EHR 12:13-38 no.1-2, 42

-- Wars and the rise of industrial civilization, 1640-1740. CJE 10:36-78 Feb 44

EB Kuehn, G. W. The novels of Thomas Deloney as source for "climate of opinion" in sixteenth-century economic history. JPE 48:865-75 Dec 40

Stone, L. The anatomy of the Elizabethan aristocracy. EHR 18:1-53 nos.1/2, 48

Tawney, R. H. The rise of the gentry, 1558-1640. EHR 11:1-38 no.1, 41

Wilson, J. H. Industrial activity in the eighteenth century. Ec N.S.7:150-60 May 40

EG Clapham, J. H. Charles Louis, Elector Palatine, 1617-1680: an early experiment in liberalism. Ec N.S.7:381-96 Nov 40

EN Riemersma, J. C. Calvinism and capitalism in Holland, 1550-1650. EEH 1,no.3:19-22 Mar 49

ESp Hamilton, E. J. Monetary disorder and economic decadence in Spain, 1651-1700. JPE 51:477-93 Dec 43

FJ Honjo, E. The economic thought in the middle period of the Tokugawa era. Kyo 15,no.2:1-33 Apr 40

Horie, Y. An outline of economic policy in the Tokugawa period. Kyo 15,no.4:44-65 Oct 40

HSA Robertson, H. M. The economic development of the Cape under Van Riebeek. Pt.I-IV. SAJE 13:1-17; 75-90; 170-84; 245-62 Mar,Jun,Sep,Dec 45

## 5.4 AFTER 1760

Heaton, H. Other wests than ours. JEH/S 6: 50-62 '46

### UNITED STATES

A Crippen, H. R. Conflicting trends in the Populist movement. S&S 6:133-49 no.2, 42

Danhof, C. H. Economic validity of the safety-valve doctrine. JEH/S 1:96-106 Dec 41

Freund, R. Turner's theory of social evolution. AH 19:78-87 Apr 45

Grampp, W. D. A re-examination of Jeffersonian economics. SEJ 12:263-82 Jan 46

Havens, R. M. Laissez-faire theory in presidential messages during the nineteenth century. JEH/S 1:86-95 Dec 41

Henrich, F. K. The development of American laissez faire: a general view of the age of Washington. JEH/S 3:51-54 Dec 43

Hesseltine, W. B. Regions, classes and sections in American history. LE 20: 35-44 Feb 44

Mood, F. The concept of the frontier, 1871-1898: comments on a select list of source documents. AH 19:24-30 Jan 45

Pegrum, D. F. Economic contributions of the United States to civilization. SEJ 11: 157-68 Oct 44

Ross, E. D. Agriculture in our economic history. AH 22:65-69 Apr 48

Saloutos, T. The agricultural problem and nineteenth-century industrialism. AH 22: 156-74 Jul 48

Usher, A. P. Institutional methodology in economic history. R. JEH 1:88-96 May 41

AA Anderson, R. H. Advancing across the eastern Mississippi Valley. AH 17: 97-104 Apr 43

Loehr, R. C. Moving back from the Atlantic seaboard. AH 17:90-96 Apr 43

ASG Heath, M. S. Laissez-faire in Georgia, 1732-1860. JEH/S 3:78-100 Dec 43

ASI Carter, H. L. Rural Indiana in transition, 1850-1860. AH 20:107-21 Apr 46

ASM Handlin, O. Laissez-faire thought in Massachusetts, 1790-1880. JEH/S 3:55-65 Dec 43

Useem, J. Changing economy and rural security in Massachusetts. AH 16:29-40 Jan 42

ASP Hartz, L. Laissez-faire thought in Pennsylvania, 1776-1860. JEH/S 3:66-77 Dec 43

### OTHER AMERICAN COUNTRIES

C Clark, S. D. Economic expansion and the moral order. CJE 6:203-25 May 40

-- The religious sect in Canadian economic development. CJE 12:439-53 Nov 46

-- The religious factor in Canadian economic development. JEH/S 7:89-103 '47

Innis, H. A. Decentralization and democracy. CJE 9:317-30 Aug 43

CA Sharp, P. F. The American farmer and the "last best West." AH 21:65-75 Apr 47

DM Aubrey, H. C. Deliberate industrialization. SR 16:158-82 Jun 49

DSV Rasmussen, W. D. Colonia Tovar, Venezuela. AH 17:156-66 Jul 43

### EUROPE

E Nef, J. U. The industrial revolution reconsidered. JEH 3:1-31 May 43

## 5. ECONOMIC HISTORY

### 5.4  AFTER 1760 (Cont.)
#### EUROPE (Cont.)

EB — Ashton, T. S.  Some statistics of the industrial revolution in Britain.  MS 16:214-34 May 48

Aydelotte, W. O.  The England of Marx and Mill as reflected in fiction.  JEH/S 8: 42-58 '48

Brebner, J. B.  Laissez faire and state intervention in nineteenth-century Britain. JEH/S 8:59-73 '48

Hamilton, E. J.  Profit inflation and the industrial revolution, 1751-1800. QJE 56:256-73 Feb 42

Robertson, D. H.  New light on an old story.  R.  Ec N.S.15:294-300 Nov 48

Wilson, J H.  Industrial activity in the eighteenth century.  Ec N.S.7:150-60 May 40

EBW — Hodges, T. M.  The peopling of the hinterland and the port of Cardiff.  EHR 17: 62-72 no.1, 47

EF — Clough, S. B.  The crisis in French economy at the beginning of the Revolution.  R. JEH 6:191-96 Nov 46

-- Retardative factors in French economic development in the nineteenth and twentieth centuries.  JEH/S 6:91-102 '46

#### ASIA

FA — Lattimore, O.  Inner Asian frontiers: Chinese and Russian margins of expansion.  JEH 7:24-52 May 47

FJ — Honjo, E.  Economic thought in the latter period of the Tokugawa era.  Kyo 15, no.4:1-24 Oct 40

Horie, Y.  An outline of economic policy in the Tokugawa period.  Kyo 15,no.4:44-65 Oct 40

-- Development of economic policy in the closing days of the Tokugawa period.  Kyo 17,no.4:48-63 Oct 42

Oshima, H. T.  Veblen on Japan.  SR 10: 487-94 Nov 43

#### AFRICA

HSA — Kahn, E.  The study of economic history in South Africa and the concept of the "frontier spirit."  R.  SAJE 10:36-46 Mar 42

# 6. GENERAL CONTEMPORARY ECONOMIC CONDITIONS, POLICY, AND PLANNING

#### GENERAL

Backman, J. and Gainsbrugh, M. R.  Productivity and living standards.  ILRR 2: 163-94 Jan 49

Benham, F.  The muddle of the thirties. Ec N.S.12:1-9 Feb 45

Clark, C.  The fruits of economic progress. EI 1:239-46 Jan 48

Frankel, S. H.  World economic solidarity. SAJE 10:169-92 Sep 42

Hartley, Sir H.  Limiting factors in world development, or what is possible? SAJE 16:260-73 Sep 48

Landuyt, B. F.  Economic upheaval in the Pacific basin.  RSE 4:40-53 Jan 46

Malin, J. C.  Space and history; reflections on the closed-space doctrines of Turner and Mackinder and the challenge of those ideas by the air age.  Pt.I-II.  AH 18: 65-74; 107-26 Apr,Jul 44

Mitchell, W. C.  Economics in a unified world.  SR 11:1-10 Feb 44

Olson, E. C.  Factors affecting international differences in production.  AER/S 38: 502-22 May 48

Qureshi, A. I.  Some structural changes in the post-war world economy.  IJE 24: 409-17 Apr 44

Robinson, A.  Five economic surveys.  R. EJ 59:629-38 Dec 49

Rostas, L.  Industrial production, productivity and distribution in Britain, Germany and the United States.  EJ 53: 39-54 Apr 43

Tinbergen, J.  Colin Clark's "Economics of 1960."  RIIS 12:1-4 no.1-4, 44

#### UNITED STATES

A — Arndt, H. W.  Productivity in manufacturing and real income per head in Great Britain and the United States.  OEP 8: 65-80 Nov 47

Arnold, T.  Must 1929 repeat itself? HBR 26:32-45 Jan 48

Boulding, K. E.  Desirable changes in the national economy after the war.  JFE 26: 95-100 Feb 44

Brady, R. A.  Government control after the war.  JFE 25:807-21 Nov 43

Brogan, D. W.  The American Negro problem.  R.  EHR 15:73-78 no.1-2, 45

Chew, A. P.  Postwar planning and the rural-urban balance.  JFE 27:664-75 Aug 45

Cox, G. V.  The American economy in the interwar period: discussion.  AER/S 36: 28-32 May 46

Ezekiel, M.  Desirable changes in the national economy for the postwar period. JFE 26:101-09 Feb 44

Gideonse, H. D.  The relation of American foreign-trade policy to New Deal domestic policy.  AER 30:87-97 Mar 40

Gini, C.  Apparent and real causes of American prosperity.  BNL 1:351-64 Jul 48

UNITED STATES (Cont.)

Hagen, E. E. and Kirkpatrick, N. B. The
A    national output at full employment in
1950. AER 34:472-500 Sep 44

Herring, J. W. Trails to new America:
reply to W. I. King. AER 31:345-46
Jun 41

Hirsch, J. Productivity in war and peace.
AER/S 37:397-411 May 47

McLaughlin, G. E. [and others] The changing structure of the American economy:
discussion. AER/S 36:80-92 May 46

Means, G. C. The American economy in
the interwar period: discussion.
AER/S 36:32-35 May 46

Rothbarth, E. Causes of the superior efficiency of U.S.A. industry as compared
with British industry. EJ 56:383-90
Sep 46

Schumpeter, J. A. The decade of the
twenties. (The American economy in
the interwar period) AER/S 36:1-10
May 46

Slichter, S. H. The conditions of expansion.
AER 32:1-21 Mar 42

Smith, E. R. and Himmel, C. Some major
recent market changes. JM 9:225-33
Jan 45

Smithies, A. The American economy in the
thirties. AER/S 36:11-27 May 46

Stauss, J. H. The Supreme Court and the
architects of economic legislation.
JPE 56:138-56 Apr 48

Stewart, W. B. Shifts in the geographical
and industrial pattern of economic activity. AER/S 36:36-51 May 46

Warburton, C. Normal production, income,
and employment 1945 to 1965. SEJ 11:
219-45 Jan 45

Watkins, M. W. "Post-war plan and program." R. JPE 51:397-414 Oct 43

Griffith, E. C. Some aspects of the South's
AA    financial development, 1929-1946.
SEJ 15:162-70 Oct 48

Harris, S. E. New England's decline in the
American economy. HBR 25:348-71
no.3, 47

Harvill, R. A. The economy of the South.
JPE 48:33-61 Feb 40

Hulse, A. E. and DeTuro, P. J. Economic
problem of the Southeast. HBR 27:34-52
Jan 49

Hyson, C. D. and Neal, A. C. New England's
economic prospects. HBR 26:156-80
Mar 48

Lee, M. W. Appraisal of the Pacific
Northwest. HBR 26:282-304 May 48

Martin, B. F. Southern industrial development. HBR 19:159-76 no.2, 41

-- The cellulose South. HBR 20:43-52
no.1, 41

Salter, L. A., Jr. Transition in the northern
lake states. LE 18:92-96 Feb 42

Van Sickle, J. V. Industrialization and the
South. SEJ 15:412-24 Apr 49

Grether, E. T. The postwar market and
ASC    industrialization in California. JM 12:
311-16 Jan 48

Culliton, J. W. Massachusetts prepares
ASM    for tomorrow. HBR 21:298-308 no.3, 43

Conklin, H. E. The rural-urban economy of
ASN    the Elmira-Corning region. LE 20:1-19
Feb 44

OTHER AMERICAN COUNTRIES

Fowke, V. C. On some appendices to the
C    Rowell-Sirois report: II. The economic
background. CJE 7:73-78 Feb 41

Harris, K. S. Canada's industrial transformation. HBR 22:155-66 no.2, 44

Mackintosh, W. A. Canada and the world
economy in the making. LBR 12:12-28
Apr 49

Surveyer, A. The Canadian economy and
the encyclicals. RSE 7,no.1:61-72
Mar 49

Irving, J. A. The evolution of the social
CPA    credit movement. CJE 14:321-41 Aug 48

Mallory, J. R. Disallowance and the national interest: the Alberta social
credit legislation of 1937. CJE 14:
342-57 Aug 48

Woods, H. D. The Dawson Report on Nova
CPN    Scotia. R. CJE 12:495-505 Nov 46

Carson, J. S. The commercial and eco-
D    nomic background of marketing in Latin
America. JM 6,no.4,pt.2:137-41 Apr 42

Spiegel, H. W. [and others] Present issues
of the Latin-American economy: discussion. AER/S 39:406-14 May 49

Wallich, H. C. The outlook for Latin America. HBR 23:65-78 no.1, 44

W[urm], F. J. Note on the French posses-
DA    sions in South & Central America.
OIS 2,no.7:21-22 Sep 40

Foster, G. M. The folk economy of rural
DM    Mexico with special reference to marketing. JM 13:153-62 Oct 48

Ebenstein, W. Land and politics: Eastern
DS    Europe and South America. R. LE 22:
59-65 Feb 46

Spiegel, H. W. The prospects of business
DSB    in Brazil. JB 20:33-43 Jan 47

EUROPE

Hirsch, J. Productivity in war and peace.
E    AER/S 37:397-411 May 47

Hoover, C. B. What can Europe do for itself? [with discussion]. JF 3,no.1:
16-40 Feb 48

Hovde, B. J. The economic and social crisis
of Europe. SR 16:271-88 Sep 49

Joseph, J. J. European recovery and
United States aid. S&S 12:293-383
no.3, 48

## 6. GENERAL CONTEMPORARY ECONOMIC CONDITIONS, ETC.

EUROPE (Cont.)

Morgan, D. J. The economy of Europe. R.
E   Ec N.S.16:255-62 Aug 49

Bouvier, E. Economic trends in China, and
EA   in central and western Europe. RSE 7
no.1:22-29 Mar 49

Ebenstein, W. Land and politics: Eastern
Europe and South America. R. LE 22:
59-65 Feb 46

Einzig, P. Hitler's "new order" in theory
and practice. EJ 51:1-18 Apr 41

Guillebaud, C. W. Hitler's new economic
order for Europe. EJ 50:449-60 Dec 40

Anonymous. Statistics relating to the
EB   North-West. MS 17:97-109; 218-30;
328-40 Jan,May,Sep 49

Arndt, H. W. Productivity in manufacturing and real income per head in Great
Britain and the United States. OEP 8:
65-80 Nov 47

Balogh, T. Britain's economic problem.
QJE 63:32-67 Feb 49

Brown, A. S. Prospects of United Kingdom
recovery. ER 25,suppl.:3-28 Aug 49

Burchardt, F. A. and Worswick, G. D. N.
Britain in transition: output and financial policy. OIS 9:74-103 Mar,Apr 47

-- Cuts in capital expenditure. R. OIS 10:
1-8 Jan 48

Clay, Sir H. The economic outlook of the
United Kingdom. AER/S 37:12-20 May 47

Daly, M. C. An approximation to a
geographical multiplier. EJ 50:248-58
Jun-Sep 40

Devons, E. The British four year plan?
MS 16:94-127 Jan 48

Henderson, Sir H. The moral of the British
crisis. REStat 31:256-60 Nov 49

Henderson, P. D. Some comparisons of
pre-war and post-war productivity.
OIS 9:347-51 Oct 47

Hicks, J. R. The empty economy. LBR 5:
1-13 Jul 47

Hood, A. L. Great Britain's economic
problem. HBR 25:625-36 no.4a, 47

Kalecki, M. The third quarter. OIS 2,
no.10:1-5 Nov 23, 40; Erratum. 2,no.11:
21 Dec 40

Meyer, F. V. Economic change in the
North-West. MS 17:1-11 Jan 49

Murphy, M. E. The British Labor Party
and domestic reform. JPE 54:522-37
Dec 46

Paish, F. W. Britain's economic problem.
AER 38:118-21 Mar 48

Robbins, L. Economic prospects. LBR 3:
21-32 Jan 47

Robertson, D. H. The economic outlook.
EJ 57:421-37 Dec 47

Rogers, J. F. Aims and limitations of
British planning. S&S 13:97-117 no.2, 49

Rothbarth, E. Causes of the superior efficiency of U.S.A. industry as compared

with British industry. EJ 56:383-90
Sep 46

Seers, D. British industrial recovery.
OIS 11:100-06 Apr 49

Singer, H. W. and Leser, C. E. V. Industrial productivity in England and Scotland [with discussion]. JRSS 111:309-30
pt.4, 48

Waterhouse, S. G. British marketing today.
JM 13:289-94 Jan 49

Wensley, A. J. and Florence, P. S. Recent
industrial concentration, especially in
the Midlands. REStud 7:139-58 Jun 40

Steindl, J. The economic position of
ECA   Austria. OIS 9:1-15 Jan 47

De Ridder, A. V. The Belgian monetary
ECB   reform: an appraisal of the results.
REStud 16:25-40 no.1, 48

Pâquet, R. The economic recovery of
Belgium. MS 17:202-07 May 49

Henderson, P. D. and Seers, D. The tech-
ECC   nique and progress of Czechoslovakia's
two-year plan. OIS 9:357-74 Nov 47

Clough, S. B. Retardative factors in French
EF   economic development in the nineteenth
and twentieth centuries. JEH/S 6:91-102
'46

Jolly, P. Aspects of the French economy.
HBR 26:257-66 May 48

Rosa, R. V. The problem of French recovery. EJ 59:154-70 Jun 49

Dobb, M. Aspects of Nazi economic policy.
EG   S&S 8:97-103 no.2, 44

Eucken, W. On the theory of the centrally
administered economy: an analysis of
the German experiment. (Translated
by T. W. Hutchison) Pt.I-II. Ec N.S.15:
79-100; 173-93 May,Aug 48

Havens, R. M. Note on effect of denazification upon property rights in Germany.
SEJ 13:158-61 Oct 46

Johnson, A. and Hamburger, E. The economic problem of Germany. SR 13:
135-82 Jun 46

Lutz, F. A. The German currency reform
and the revival of the German economy.
Ec N.S.16:122-42 May 49

Mendershausen, H. Prices, money and the
distribution of goods in postwar Germany.
AER 39:646-72 Jun 49

Merlin, S. Trends in German economic
control since 1933. QJE 57:169-207
Feb 43

Paechter, H. Recent trends in the German
Command economy. JPE 52:217-33
Sep 44

Robinson, N. German foreign trade and industry after the First World War.
QJE 58:615-36 Aug 44

Schweitzer, A. Big business and the Nazi
party in Germany. JB 19:1-24 Jan 46

-- Big business and private property under
the Nazis. JB 19:99-126 Apr 46

EUROPE (Cont.)

Schweitzer, A. (Cont.)
-- Profits under Nazi planning. QJE 61:
EG    1-25 Nov 46

Beattie, T. E. Observations on southern
EI    Italy. AH 19:120-26 Apr 45

Bresciani-Turroni, C. Economic reconstruction in Italy. LBR 7:19-32 Jan 48

Cosmo, G. Unemployment and emigration in Italy in the light of the E.R.P. and O.E.E.C. BNL 1:434-40 Oct 48

Marrama, V. Some aspects of Italian economy and the theory of full employment. BNL 1:220-27 Jan 48

Molinari, A. Southern Italy. BNL 2:25-47 Jan-Mar 49

Saraceno, P. Public expenditure, savings and foreign loans in the development of southern Italy. BNL 2:146-58 Jul-Sep 49

Schüller, R. Trieste. SR 13:399-409 Dec 46

Tremelloni, R. The Italian long-term program submitted to the O.E.E.C. BNL 2: 12-24 Jan-Mar 49

Tinbergen, J. Central planning in the
EN    Netherlands. REStud 15:70-77 no.2, 48
-- Government budget and central economic plan. PF 4:195-99 no.3, 49

Baran, P. A. The economy of the U.S.S.R.:
ER    discussion. AER/S 37:646-48 May 47

Bergson, A. The economy of the U.S.S.R.: discussion. AER/S 37:643-46 May 47

Devons, E. The Soviet economic system. R. MS 14,no.3:54-59 Sep 46

Dobb, M. H. Economic planning in the Soviet Union. S&S 6:305-14 no.4, 42
-- Post-war economic prospects in the U.S.S.R. OIS 8:190-98 Jun 46

East, W. G. The economic history of U.S. S.R. R. EHR 16:141-44 no.2, 46

Hunter, H. The planning of investments in the Soviet Union. REStat 31:54-62 Feb 49

Hutt, W. H. The development of the Soviet economic system. R. SAJE 14:215-19 Sep 46

Rao, B. R. S. Determination of prices in Soviet Russia. IJE 21:497-510 Apr 41

Cederwall, G. An economic suvey for
ES    Sweden. OIS 10:245-54 Jul-Aug 48

Heckscher, G. Pluralist democracy: the Swedish experience. SR 15:417-61 Dec 48

Lundberg, E. Economic prospects and the risk of inflation in Sweden. OIS 9:37-43 Feb 47

Montgomery, A. Post-war economic problems in Sweden. LBR 8:20-34 Apr 48

Ohlsson, I. and Cederwall, G. Sweden's economy 1946-1949. OIS 11:53-58 Feb-Mar 49

Schlauch, M. Scandinavia: the dilemma of the middle way. S&S 9:97-124 no.2, 45

Iversen, C. Post-war economic problems
ESD    in Denmark. LBR 10:22-38 Oct 48

Holben, R. E. Planned economy in Norway:
ESN    comment. AER 39:1283-87 Dec 49

Keilhau, W. Main trends in Norway's economy. LBR 9:21-33 Jul 48

Klein, L. R. Planned economy in Norway. AER 38:795-814 Dec 48

ASIA

Lokanathan, P. S. Economic reconstruc-
F    tion of Asia and the Far East: presidential address. IJE 28:457-66 Jan 48

Holland, W. L. Postwar political economy
FA    of the Far East and the Pacific. AER/S 34:356-67 Mar 44

Bouvier, E. Economic trends in China,
FC    and in central and western Europe. RSE 7,no.1:22-29 Mar 49

Hozumi, F. A study of the character of current Chinese economy. Kyo 15,no.3: 41-66 Jul 40

Ou, P. S. and Wang, F. S. Industrial production and employment in pre-war China. EJ 56:426-34 Sep 46

Yu-Pin, P. The economic future of China. RSE 2:100-01 Jan 44

Adiseshiah, M. S. [and others] Discussion
FI    on economic planning. IJE 25:641-57 Apr 45

Agarwal, S. N. Gandhian economics. IJE 23:193-99 Oct 42

Agarwala, A. N. Economic conditions in Baroda and Hyderabad states. IJE 25: 83-89 Jul 44
-- The place of agriculture vis-a-vis industry in the industralists' plan. IJE 25: 117-23 Oct 44
-- Economic planning and agriculture. IJE 26:61-82 Jul 45

Agarwala, S. N. A critique of the Gandhian plan. R. IJE 26:262-70 Oct 45

Anjaria, J. J. The Gandhian approach to Indian economics. IJE 22:357-66 Jan 42

Butani, D. H. A socio-economic survey of Pano Akil Taulaka. IJE 21:328-35 Jan 41

Dubey, P. D. S. The place of agriculture in the proposed plans. IJE 25:551-56 Apr 45

Hassan, M. Gandhiji's economic ideals and creed. IJE 21:131-47 Oct 40

Iyengar, S. K. Rural co-operation and national planning in India. IJE 22:400-35 Jan 42
-- Industrialisation and agriculture in India post-war planning. EJ 54:189-205 Jun-Sep 44
-- Post-war economic planning in India: balances and weightages. IJE 25:47-55 Jul 44

Jain, L. C. Presidential address [before the Indian Economic Association]. IJE 20:797-809 Apr 40

## 6. GENERAL CONTEMPORARY ECONOMIC CONDITIONS, ETC.

ASIA (Cont.)

Krishnamurti, B. V.  The state under the
FI   Bombay Plan.  IJE 26:243-61 Oct 45

Lal, H.  Agriculture in the Bombay Plan.
IJE 26:43-60 Jul 45

Lalwani, K. C.  Reflections on future eco-
nomic order: international and national.
Pt.I-II.  IJE 25:450-65; 26:29-42 Apr,
Jul 45

-- Fundamentals of economic planning in
free India.  IJE 29:337-50 Apr 49

Malhotra, P. C.  How to raise the Indian
standard of living?  IJE 25:166-68
Oct 44

-- and Agarwala, A. N.  Agriculture in the
industrialists' plan.  IJE 25:502-10
Apr 45

Mehta, Sir C. B.  Planning and reconstruction.  IJE 25:41-46 Jul 44

Mukherjee, B. C.  Economy of the province
of West Bengal and its relations with
Pakistan.  IJE 29:45-54 Jul 48

Nag, D. S.  The Gandhian plan: a rejoinder
[followed by S. N. Agarwala's reply].
IJE 27:64-71 Jul 46

Narayanaswamy, B. V.  India and post-war
reconstruction: presidential address.
IJE 24:463-524 Apr 44

Prasad, P. S. N.  Some ambiguities in the
Bombay Plan.  IJE 25:24-40 Jul 44

Qureshi, A. I.  A planned economy for
Hyderabad.  IJE 26:83-100 Jul 45

Rao, K. V.  War to peace economy in India.
IJE 25:247-53 Jan 45

Rudra, S. K.  Post-war Indian economic
development.  IJE 25:423-35 Apr 45

Sen, K. N.  Economic thinking in the Indian
National Congress.  IJE 22:689-707
Jan 42

Sengupta, S.  Capital requirements of the
Bombay Plan for economic development
of India.  IJE 25:56-63 Jul 44

Singh, A.  Can we plan under Indian capitalism?  IJE 26:305-11 Oct 45

Sinha, J. C.  Recent economic policy in
India: presidential address.  IJE 29:
311-25 Jan 49

Steindl, J.  Industrialisation policy in India.
OIS 7:145-48 Jun 9, 45

Idris, S. M.  A bird's eye view of Pakistan
FIP   economy.  PEJ 1,no.2:55-66 Oct 48

Bloch, K.  Whither Japan?  SR 8:173-88
FJ   May 41

Johnston, B.  Japan: the race between food
and population.  JFE 31:276-92 May 49

AFRICA

Henry, J. A.  Some aspects of the economic
H   development of Northern Rhodesia.
SAJE 14:100-16 Jun 46

Richards, C. S.  Industrial possibilities and
potentialities of Northern Rhodesia.  R.
SAJE 13:203-14 Sep 45

Burrows, H. R.  Fundamentals of economic
HSA   policy in the Union: a comment [followed
by C. S. Richards' reply].  SAJE 10:
307-14 Dec 42

-- An approach to the Indian problem in
South Africa.  SAJE 15:157-77 Sep 47

Frankel, S. H.  Whither South Africa?  An
economic approach.  SAJE 15:27-39
Mar 47

Franklin, N. N.  Economic welfare and the
development of the Native Reserves.
SAJE 10:1-15 Mar 42

Hutt, W. H.  A critique of the first Report
of the Social and Economic Planning
Council.  SAJE 11:48-62 Mar 43

Kahn, E.  Whither our war-time Native
policy?  SAJE 10:126-52 Jun 42

Krige, E. J.  Economics of exchange in a
primitive society.  SAJE 9:1-21 Mar 41

Richards, C. S.  Fundamentals of economic
policy in the Union.  R.  SAJE 10:47-72
Mar 42

-- Economic incentives in the post-war
world.  SAJE 13:145-69 Sep 45

-- Some thoughts on the Union's economic
outlook.  SAJE 17:142-54 Jun 49

Thirlby, G. F.  The Industrial and Agricultural Requirements Commission (First
interim report).  (U.G. 33/1940) SAJE 8:
185-94 Jun 40

MIDDLE EAST

Bonné, A.  Movement of population and eco-
M   nomic expansion in the Middle East.
EgC 33:319-35 Apr 42

Weinryb, B. D.  Industrial development of
the Near East.  QJE 61:471-99 May 47

Lackany, S.  Post-war problems.  EgC 35:
ME   99-105 Jan-Feb 44

Johnson, A.  The economic position of
MI   Israel.  SR 15:395-402 Dec 48

Kahn, A. E.  Palestine: a problem in economic evaluation.  AER 34:538-60 Sep 44

AUSTRALIA.  NEW ZEALAND

Belshaw, H.  New Zealand in the post-war
N   world: reconstruction problems of a
vulnerable economy.  CJE 11:388-401
Aug 45

Copland, D.  Balance of production in the
Australian post-war economy.  ER 25,
(no.49):1-6 Dec 49

Melville, L. G.  Some post-war problems.
ER 22:4-22 Jun 46

Nazmy, A. A. H.  The Australian experience.  EgC 35:49-53 Jan-Feb 44

PACIFIC ISLANDS

Moscheles, J.  The South Seas in the mod-
P   ern world.  ER 18:82-87 Jun 42

Weitzell, E. C.  Resource development in
the Pacific Mandated Islands.  LE 22:
199-212 Aug 46

# 7. MATHEMATICAL, STATISTICAL, AND OTHER TOOLS OF ANALYSIS

## 7.0 GENERAL

Fisher, I. Mathematical method in the social sciences. Em 9:185-97 Jul-Oct 41

Samuelson, P. A. Some implications of "linearity." REStud 15:88-90 no.2, 48

## 7.1 MATHEMATICAL TOOLS
## 7.10 GENERAL

Baumol, W. J. Mathematics for economists. R. Ec N.S.14:310-13 Nov 47

Clark, J. M. Mathematical economists and others: a plea for communicability. Em 15:75-78 Apr 47

Frisch, R. On the zeros of homogeneous functions. Em 17:28-29 Jan 49

Henderson, J. S. Geometrical note on elasticity of demand. AER 36:662-63 Sep 46

Higgins, B. A diagrammatic analysis of the supply of loan funds. Em 9:231-40 Jul-Oct 41

Hyson, C. D. and Hyson, W. P. Geometrical measurement of elasticities. AER 39: 728-29 Jun 49

Kalecki, M. On the Gibrat distribution. Em 13:161-70 Apr 45

Kapp, K. W. Methods of visual presentation and the teaching of economics. AER 37: 652-54 Sep 47

Kozlik, A. Note on the terminology convex and concave. AER 31:103-05 Mar 41

Leontief, W. Introduction to a theory of the internal structure of functional relationships. Em 15:361-73 Oct 47

Lerner, A. P. Geometrical comparison of elasticities. AER 37:191 Mar 47

Marschak, J. On mathematics for economists. R. REStat 29:269-73 Nov 47

Maverick, L. A. Demand and supply curves. QJE 54:307-13 Feb 40

Paulson, W. E. Diagrammatic economics. JFE 28:687-722 Aug 46

Savage, L. J. Samuelson's Foundations: its mathematics. R. JPE 56:200-02 Jun 48

## 7.12 MAXIMIZATION UNDER RESTRAINTS
## 7.120 GENERAL

Tintner, G. Homogeneous systems in mathematical economics. Em 16:273-94 Oct 48

## 7.121 MATHEMATICAL PROGRAMMING

Dantzig, G. B. Programming of interdependent activities. II. Mathematical model. Em 17:200-11 Jul-Oct 49

Koopmans, T. C. Optimum utilization of the transportation system. Em 17,suppl.: 136-45 Jul 49; Errata. 19:227 Apr 51

Stigler, G. J. The cost of subsistence. JFE 27:303-14 May 45

Wood, M. and Dantzig, G. B. Programming of interdependent activities. I. General discussion. Em 17:193-99 Jul-Oct 49

## 7.13 DIFFERENCE, DIFFERENTIAL, AND INTEGRAL EQUATIONS. STABILITY CONDITIONS IN DYNAMIC SYSTEMS

Court, L. M. Entrepreneurial and consumer demand theories for commodity spectra. Pt.I-II. Em 9:135-62; 241-97 Apr,Jul-Oct 41

Hawkins, D. Some conditions of macroeconomic stability. Em 16:309-22 Oct 48

-- and Simon, H. A. Note: some conditions of macroeconomic stability. Em 17: 245-48 Jul-Oct 49

Koopmans, T. The degree of damping in business cycles. Em 8:79-89 Jan 40

-- Distributed lags in dynamic economics. Em 9:128-34 Apr 41

Samuelson, P. A. The stability of equilibrium: comparative statics and dynamics. Em 9:97-120 Apr 41

-- The stability of equilibrium: linear and nonlinear systems. Em 10:1-25 Jan 42

-- A fundamental multiplier identity. Em 11:221-26 Jul-Oct 43

-- The relation between Hicksian stability and true dynamic stability. Em 12: 256-57 Jul-Oct 44

Smithies, A. and Savage, L. J. A dynamic problem in duopoly. Em 8:130-43 Apr 40

-- The stability of competitive equilibrium. Em 10:258-74 Jul-Oct 42

Tintner, G. A "simple" theory of business fluctuations. Em 10:317-20 Jul-Oct 42

## 7.2 STATISTICAL AND ECONOMETRIC METHODS
## 7.20 GENERAL

Craig, J. I. Industry and statistics. EgC 39:39-43 Jan-Feb 48

Frisch, R. The responsibility of the econometrician. Em 14:1-4 Jan 46

Haavelmo, T. The probability approach in econometrics. Em 12,suppl.:1-115 Jul 44

Homeyer, P. G. and Heady, E. O. The role of modern statistics in analyzing farm management data. JFE 29:1241-49 Nov 47

Jones, H. L. Note on square-root charts. Em 14:313-15 Oct 46

Koopmans, T. C. Measurement without theory. R. REStat 29:161-72 Aug 47

Riefler, W. W. Government and the statistician. JASA 37:1-11 Mar 42

Robinson, A. The qualifications of statisticians. EJ 54:265-68 Jun-Sep 44

# 7. MATHEMATICAL TOOLS, ETC.

## 7.2 STATISTICAL AND ECONOMETRIC METHODS (Cont.)

### 7.20 GENERAL (Cont.)

Sinha, H. Teaching and research in economic statistics. IJE 24:221-24A Jan 44

Smith, J. H. Constant-amplitude scales for plotting stock prices. Em 14:316-19 Oct 46

Törnqvist, L. An attempt to analyze the problem of an economical production of statistical data. NTTO 12:265-74 no.37, 48

Vining, R. Koopmans on the choice of variables to be studied and of methods of measurement [followed by T. Koopmans' reply and Vining's rejoinder]. REStat 31: 77-94 May 49

Wilson, E. B. and Worcester, J. The normal logarithmic transform. REStat 27: 17-22 Feb 45

## 7.21 SURVEY METHODS

### 7.210 GENERAL

Andrews, R. B. Urban fringe studies of two Wisconsin cities: a summary. LE 21:375-82 Sep 45

Batson, E. The use of random sampling in sociographical research. SAJE 12:45-56 Mar 44

Bell, J. W. The function of government in postwar American economy: a report on an experiment by an ad hoc consensus committee. AER/S 35:422-47 May 45

Blankenship, A. B. The case for and against the public opinion poll. JM 5:110-13 Oct 40

Borg, L. E. The Minnesota poll. JM 9: 381-84 Apr 45

Breyer, R. F. Some preliminary problems of sample design for a survey of retail trade flow. JM 10:343-53 Apr 46

Brown, G. H. A comparison of sampling methods. JM 11:331-37 Apr 47

Brownlee, O. Memory errors as they affect survey data. JFE 22:495-97 May 40

Cassady, R., Jr. Statistical sampling techniques and marketing research. JM 9: 317-41 Apr 45

Colley, R. H. Some practical applications of precision sampling. JM 14:437-41 Oct 49

Cordell, W. N. The commercial use of probability samples. JM 14:447-49 Oct 49

Cornfield, J. On certain biases in samples of human populations. JASA 37:63-68 Mar 42

Crossley, A. M. Theory and application of representative sampling as applied to marketing. JM 5:456-61 Apr 41

Cunningham, L C. and Warren, S. W. Sampling methods in use in some of the farm management research at Cornell. JFE 29:1267-70 Nov 47

Deming, W. E. Some criteria for judging the quality of surveys. JM 12:145-57 Oct 47

Engene, S. A. Sampling procedures used in study of haymaking methods. JFE 29: 1271-74 Nov 47

Ghate, B. G. A scheme for the survey of rural indebtedness in India. IJE 21: 13-29 Jul 40

Ghiselli, E. E. Some further points on public opinion polls. JM 5:115-19 Oct 40

Hansen, M. H. and Hurwitz, W. N. Dependable samples for market surveys. JM 14: 363-72 Oct 49

Hauser, P. M. and Hansen, M. H. On sampling in market surveys. JM 9: 26-31 Jul 44

Hayes, S. P., Jr. Commercial surveys as an aid in the determination of public policy: a case study. JM 12:475-82 Apr 48

Iyengar, S. K. Survey of rural indebtedness in India: a comment. IJE 21:335-41 Jan 41

Katz, D. Good and bad practices in attitude surveys in industrial relations. IRRA 2: 212-21 Dec 49

Keyfitz, N. The sampling approach to economic data. CJE 11:467-77 Aug 45

King, A. J. and Simpson, G. D. New developments in agricultural sampling. JFE 22: 341-49 Feb 40

-- and McCarty, D. E. Application of sampling to agricultural statistics with emphasis on stratified samples. JM 5:462-73 Apr 41

Lansing, J. B. Comments on the economists' opinion survey. AER 36:143-46 Mar 46

Ludeke, H. C. A test of two methods commonly used in reader-interest surveys. JM 10:171-73 Oct 45

McConnell, J. Measurement of employee attitudes: discussion. IRRA 2:222-25 Dec 49

Malcolm, T. A new research tool. JM 5: 38-39 Jul 40

Nafziger, R. O. Problems in reader-interest surveys. JM 9:359-63 Apr 45

Osgood, O. T. Results of two sampling methods used in farm management research. JFE 31:157-68 Feb 49

Prindle, H. F. Sampling medical service charges: a new application of sampling method. JFE 31:357-60 May 49

Salter, L. A., Jr. Cross-sectional and case-grouping procedures in research analysis. JFE 24:792-805 Nov 42

Sanford, F. H. Measurement of employee attitudes: discussion. IRRA 2:225-27 Dec 49

Sarle, C. F. The possibilities and limitations of objective sampling in strengthening agricultural statistics. Em 8:45-61 Jan 40

7.21  SURVEY METHODS (Cont.)
7.210  GENERAL (Cont.)

Sarle, C. F. (Cont.)
-- The role of sampling in farm-management research. JFE 29:1229-40 Nov 47

Singh, A.  Principles of sampling as applied to investigations in agricultural economics. IJE 25:533-40 Apr 45

Smith, E. R., chairman. Design, size, and validation of sample for market research. [Report of Committee on Marketing Research Techniques] JM 10:221-34 Jan 46

Stephan, F. F.  Stratification in representative sampling. JM 6:38-46 Jul 41

Stepp, J. M.  Postwar planning survey at Anderson, S.C. LE 21:184-91 May 45

Warner, L.  Estimating the character of unsampled segments of a universe. JM 12:186-92 Oct 47

White, M. and Zeisel, J.  Reading indices. JM 6:103-11 Oct 41

7.211  SURVEY DESIGN

Andrews, L.  The interviewer problem in market research. JM 13:522-24 Apr 49

Bell, J. W.  Report of ad hoc Committee on Monetary Policy. (Economic opinion and public policy) AER/S 36:807-16 May 46

Bennett, A. S.  Some aspects of preparing questionnaires. JM 10:175-79 Oct 45

-- Toward a solution of the "cheater problem" among part-time research investigators. JM 12:470-74 Apr 48

Blankenship, A. B., chairman. Questionnaire preparation and interviewer technique. [Report of a sub-committee] JM 14:399-433 Oct 49

Clarkson, E. P.  Some suggestions for field research supervisors. JM 13:321-29 Jan 49

Frank, M.  Measurement and elimination of confusion elements in recognition surveys. JM 12:362-64 Jan 48

Greenberg, A.  A method for coding questionnaires in market surveys. JM 14:456-58 Oct 49

Hartkemeier, H. P.  The use of data collected by poorly trained enumerators. JPE 52:164-66 Jun 44

Lockley, L. C. and Watson, A. N.  Some fundamental considerations in the conduct of polls. JM 5:113-15 Oct 40

Snead, R. P.  Problems of field interviews. JM 7:139-45 Oct 42

Wallace, D.  Mail questionnaires can produce good samples of homogeneous groups. JM 12:53-60 Jul 47

7.212  CONSUMER SURVEYS

Barton, S. G.  The consumption pattern of different economic groups under war changes. JM 8:50-53 Jul 43

Blankenship, A.  Psychological difficulties in measuring consumer preference. JM 6,no.4,pt.2:66-75 Apr 42

Brady, D. S. and Williams, F. M.  Advances in the techniques of measuring and estimating consumer expenditures. JFE 27:315-44 May 45

Cawl, F. R.  The continuing panel technique. JM 8:45-50 Jul 43

Ferber, R.  Weekly versus monthly consumer purchase panels. JM 13:223-24 Oct 48

Goodman, R.  Sampling for the 1947 Survey of consumer finances. JASA 42:439-48 Sep 47

Katona, G. and Likert, R.  Relationship between consumer expenditures and savings: the contribution of survey research. REStat 28:197-99 Nov 46

Lewis, H. F.  A comparison of consumer responses to weekly and monthly purchase panels. JM 12:449-54 Apr 48; Erratum. 13:231 Oct 48

Madge, C. and Rothbarth, E.  Saving and spending in Leeds: a reply to Dr. Singer's criticisms. MS 13:80-88 Aug 44

Nicholson, J. L.  Variations in working class family expenditure [with discussion]. JRSS 112:359-418 pt.4, 49

Singer, H. W.  How widespread are national savings? A critique of the Madge enquiry. MS 13:61-79 Aug 44

Stonborough, T. H. W.  Fixed panels in consumer research. JM 7:129-38 Oct 42

Webber, H. H.  The consumer panel: a method of media evaluation. JM 9:137-40 Oct 44

Womer, S.  Some applications of the continuous consumer panel. JM 9:132-36 Oct 44

7.22  THEORY OF INDEX NUMBERS AND AGGREGATION
7.220  GENERAL

Allen, R. G. D.  The economic theory of index numbers. Ec N.S.16:197-203 Aug 49

Davies, G. R.  Pricing and price levels. Em 14:219-26 Jul 46

Klein, L. R.  Macroeconomics and the theory of rational behavior. Em 14:93-108 Apr 46

-- Remarks on the theory of aggregation. Em 14:303-12 Oct 46

Little, I. M. D.  A note on the interpretation of index numbers. Ec N.S.16:369-70 Nov 49

May, K.  The aggregation problem for a one-industry model. Em 14:285-98 Oct 46

-- Technological change and aggregation. Em 15:51-63 Jan 47

# 7. MATHEMATICAL TOOLS, ETC.

## 7.22 THEORY OF INDEX NUMBERS AND AGGREGATION (Cont.)
### 7.220 GENERAL (Cont.)

Pande, J. K. A formula for limits of variations in a weighted index due to a new series of weights. IJE 21:324-28 Jan 41

Pu, S. S. A note on macroeconomics. Em 14:299-302 Oct 46

Rothbarth, E. A note on an index number problem. REStud 11:91-98 no.2, 44

Williams, F. M. and Hoover, E. D. Measuring price and quality of consumers' goods. JM 10:354-69 Apr 46

### 7.221 CONSUMER PRICE INDEXES

Bowley, A. L. Earnings and prices, 1904, 1914, 1937-8. REStud 8:129-42 Jun 41

Ferger, W. F. Historical note on the purchasing power concept, and index numbers. JASA 41:53-57 Mar 46

Ghosh, D. Wage and the Indian cost of living index numbers. IJE 26:226-42 Oct 45

Kaldor, N. Rationing and the cost of living index. REStud 8:185-87 Jun 41

Karmel, P. H. The relation between Laspeyre's and Paasche's index numbers for measuring price changes. ER 21:261-64 Dec 45

Klein, L. R. and Rubin, H. A constant-utility index of the cost of living. REStud 15:84-87 no.2, 48

Mills, F. C., chairman. An appraisal of the U.S. Bureau of Labor Statistics cost of living index by a special committee. JASA 38:387-405 Dec 43

Mudgett, B. D. The cost-of-living index and Konüs' condition. Em 13:171-81 Apr 45

Nicholson, J. L. Rationing and index numbers. REStud 10:68-72 no.1, 42

Ostrander, F. T. The Mitchell Committee's report on the cost-of-living index: comments. AER 34:849-56 Dec 44

Rosen, J. On the calculation of cost-of-living index figures. Kyk 3:325-51 fasc.4, 49

Rothbarth, E. The measurement of changes in real income under conditions of rationing. REStud 8:100-07 Feb 41

Seers, D. The increase in the middle-class cost-of-living since before the war. OIS 10:255-68 Jul-Aug 48

Teper, L. Observations on the cost of living index of the Bureau of Labor Statistics [followed by notes by A. J. Wickens and F. M. Williams]. JASA 38:271-86 Sep 43

Ulmer, M. J. On the economic theory of cost of living index numbers. JASA 41:530-42 Dec 46

Wickens, A. J. What the cost-of-living index is. JB 17:146-61 Jul 44

Williams, F. M. Factors to be considered in measuring intercity and interregional differences in living costs. JASA 35:471-82 Sep 40

--; Rice, F. R. and Schell, E. D. Cost of living indexes in wartime. JASA 37:415-24 Dec 42

Woodbury, R. M. Quantity adjustment factors in cost-of-living ratios. Em 8:322-32 Oct 40

### 7.222 OTHER PRICE INDEXES

Allen, R. G. D. Wholesale prices, 1938-48. EJ 59:137-53 Jun 49

Epstein, R. C. Price dispersion and aggregative analysis. AER 37:402-07 Jun 47

Imperatori, M. The construction of wholesale price index numbers and wholesale price trend in Italy, May 1946-July 1949. BNL 2:172-78 Jul-Sep 49

Seers, D. The increase in the working-class cost-of-living since before the war. OIS 10:140-61 May 48

-- Is there bias in the Interim index of retail prices? OIS 11:1-8 Jan 49

Taylor, M. D. Appraisal of the BLS index of wholesale food prices in wartime. JM 9:32-42 Jul 44

### 7.223 PRODUCTION INDEXES

Brown, E. C. A note on the new Federal Reserve Board index of production. EJ 52:127-29 Apr 42

Geary, R. C. The concept of net volume of output, with special reference to Irish data [followed by H. Leak and A. Maizels' note]. JRSS 107:251-61 pt.3-4, 44

-- Rejoinder to Messrs. Leak and Maizels. JRSS 107:290-92 pt.3-4, 44

Hirsch, H. G. Crop yield index numbers. JFE 25:583-98 Aug 43

Siegel, I. H. The concept of productive activity. JASA 39:218-28 Jun 44

Stolper, G. and Doblin, E. M. The new Federal Reserve Board index of production. EJ 51:47-55 Apr 41

Working, E. J. Crop-yield index numbers. JFE 22:701-13 Nov 40

-- --- Some comments on Hirsch's views. JFE 25:874-81 Nov 43

### 7.224 MEASUREMENT OF PRODUCTIVITY

Barna, T. Note on the productivity of labour: its concept and measurement. OIS 8:205-16 Jul 46

Evans, W. D. and Siegel, I. H. The meaning of productivity indexes. JASA 37:103-11 Mar 42

-- Recent productivity trends and their implications. JASA 42:211-23 Jun 47

Goodrich, C. Productivity in the American economy: discussion. AER/S 37:421-22 May 47

7.224 MEASUREMENT OF PRODUCTIVITY (Cont.)

Mills, T. J.  Notes on the productivity conference.  AER 37:187-90 Mar 47

Stigler, G. J.  Labor productivity and size of farm: a statistical pitfall.  JFE 28: 821-25 Aug 46

Young, C. E.  Applications and problems of productivity data.  JASA 41:421-31 Dec 46

7.225 OTHER INDEXES

Baumgart, G.  Weekly index numbers, measuring business activity.  JB 13: 234-52 Jul 40

Buckatzsch, E. J.  An index of social conditions in the county boroughs in 1931.  OIS 8:365-74 Dec 46

Court, L. M. and Lewis, H. G.  Production cost indices.  REStud 10:28-42, no.1, 42

Haring, C. E.  The Haring indexes of local business conditions.  JM 9:217-24 Jan 45

7.23 IDENTIFICATION AND ESTIMATION OF PARAMETERS.  TESTS OF HYPOTHESES.  PREDICTION

7.230 GENERAL

Dodd, E. L.  Certain tests for randomness applied to data grouped into small sets.  Em 10:249-57 Jul-Oct 42

Neyman, J. and Scott, E. L.  Consistent estimates based on partially consistent observations.  Em 16:1-32 Jan 48

Wallis, W. A.  Compounding probabilities from independent significance tests.  Em 10:229-48 Jul-Oct 42

Wilson, E. B. and Worcester, J.  Frequency functions fitted by moments.  REStat 25: 97-100 Feb 43

7.231 ANALYSIS OF VARIANCE.  DESIGN OF EXPERIMENTS

Geiringer, H.  A new explanation of non-normal dispersion in the Lexis theory.  Em 10:53-60 Jan 42

Wallis, W. A.  The temporal stability of consumption patterns.  REStat 24:177-83 Nov 42

7.232 REGRESSION AND CORRELATION.  MULTIVARIATE ANALYSIS.  ANALYSIS OF COVARIANCE

7.2320 GENERAL

Adelman, M. A.  Correlations and forecasting.  AER 36:645-50 Sep 46

Bartlett, M. S.  A note on the statistical estimation of supply and demand relations from time series.  Em 16:323-29 Oct 48

Cobb, C. W.  A regression.  Em 11:265-67 Jul-Oct 43

Cochrane, D.  Measurement of economic relationships.  ER 25,(no.49):7-23 Dec 49

Ezekiel, M.  A check on a multiple correlation result.  JFE 22:766-68 Nov 40

Geary, R. C.  Determination of linear relations between systematic parts of variables with errors of observation the variances of which are unknown.  Em 17: 30-58 Jan 49

Georgescu-Roegen, N.  Further contribution to the scatter analysis.  Em 17, suppl.:39-42 Jul 49

Hurwicz, L.  Some problems arising in estimating economic relations.  Em 15: 236-40 Jul 47

Jensen, E.  Comparison of results of two methods of analysis.  JFE 22:769-72 Nov 40

Kendall, M. G.  The estimation of parameters in linear autoregressive time series.  Em 17,suppl.:44-56 Jul 49

Lienau, C. C.  Statistical method: forecasting electric energy demand and regulating supply.  LE 18:102-05 Feb 42

Metzler, L. A.  The assumptions implied in least squares demand techniques.  REStat 22:138-49 Aug 40

Prest, A. R.  Some experiments in demand analysis.  REStat 31:33-49 Feb 49

Rao, C. R.  Note on a problem of Ragnar Frisch.  Em 15:245-49 Jul 47; Correction.  17:212 Jul-Oct 49

Reiersøl, O.  Confluence analysis by means of lag moments and other methods of confluence analysis.  Em 9:1-24 Jan 41

Ruggles, R.  The concept of linear total cost-output regressions.  AER 31:332-35 Jun 41

Ruist, E.  Standard errors of the tilling coefficients used in confluence analysis.  Em 14:235-41 Jul 46

Samuelson, P. A.  A note on alternative regressions.  Em 10:80-83 Jan 42

Staehle, H.  The measurement of statistical cost functions: an appraisal of some recent contributions.  AER 32:321-33 Jun 42

Stephenson, C. A.  Methods of correlation analysis: reply.  AER 33:902-03 Dec 43

Stone, R.  The analysis of market demand [with discussion].  JRSS 108:286-391 pt.3-4, 45

-- The analysis of market demand: an outline of methods and results.  RIIS 16: 23-34 no.1-4, 48

Straus, E.  Cost accounting and statistical cost functions.  AER 35:430-32 Jun 45

Tinbergen, J.  The use of correlation analysis in economic research.  ET 49: 173-92 Sep 47

Tintner, G.  The analysis of economic time series.  JASA 35:93-100 Mar 40

-- An application of the variate difference method to multiple regression.  Em 12: 97-113 Apr 44

# 7. MATHEMATICAL TOOLS, ETC.

**7.232 REGRESSION AND CORRELATION.
MULTIVARIATE ANALYSIS. ANALYSIS
OF COVARIANCE (Cont.)**

**7.2320 GENERAL (Cont.)**

Tintner, G. (Cont.)
-- Some applications of multivariate analysis to economic data. JASA 41:472-500
Dec 46

Vatter, W. J. Cost accounting and statistical cost functions. AER 35:940-42
Dec 45

Waugh, F. V. Regressions between sets of variables. Em 10:290-310 Jul-Oct 42

Wold, H. O. A. Statistical estimation of economic relationships. Em 17,suppl.: 1-21 Jul 49; Errata. 19:227 Apr 51

Woolley, E. B. The method of minimized areas as a basis for correlation analysis. Em 9:38-62 Jan 41

**7.2321 SIMULTANEOUS EQUATIONS**

Cavin, J. P. Agricultural micro-economic studies: discussion. JFE 30:139-41
Feb 48

Cooper, G. The role of econometric models in economic research. JFE 30:101-16
Feb 48

Girshick, M. A. and Haavelmo, T. Statistical analysis of the demand for food: examples of simultaneous estimation of structural equations. Em 15:79-110
Apr 47

Haavelmo, T. The statistical implications of a system of simultaneous equations. Em 11:1-12 Jan 43
-- Statistical testing of business-cycle theories. REStat 25:13-18 Feb 43

Hurwicz, L. Stochastic models of economic fluctuations. Em 12:114-24 Apr 44

Koopmans, T. C. Statistical estimation of simultaneous economic relations.
JASA 40:448-66 Dec 45
-- Identification problems in economic model construction. Em 17:125-44
Apr 49

Kuznets, G. M. The use of econometric models in agricultural micro-economic studies. JFE 30:131-39 Feb 48

Mann, H. B. and Wald, A. On the statistical treatment of linear stochastic difference equations. Em 11:173-220 Jul-Oct 43

Marschak, J. and Andrews, W. H., Jr. Random simultaneous equations and the theory of production. Em 12:143-205
Jul-Oct 44; Errata. 13:91 Jan 45
-- Economic structure, path, policy, and prediction. AER/S 37:81-84 May 47

Stone, R.; Champernowne, D. G. and Meade, J. E. The precision of national income estimates. REStud 9:111-25 no.2, 42
-- Prediction from autoregressive schemes and linear stochastic difference systems. Em 17,suppl.:29-37 Jul 49; Errata. 19:227 Apr 51

Tintner, G. Multiple regression for systems of equations. Em 14:5-36 Jan 46

**7.233 SINGLE TIME SERIES ANALYSIS**

Anderson, T. W. A note on a maximum-likelihood estimate. Em 15:241-44
Jul 47

Burns, A. F. Frickey on the decomposition of time series. R. REStat 26:136-47
Aug 44

Dodd, E. L. The problem of assigning a length to the cycle to be found in a simple moving average and in a double moving average of chance data. Em 9: 25-37 Jan 41

Haavelmo, T. The inadequacy of testing dynamic theory by comparing theoretical solutions and observed cycles.
Em 8:312-21 Oct 40
-- A note on the variate difference method. Em 9:74-79 Jan 41

Hald, A. The decomposition of a series of observations composed of a trend, a periodic movement and a stochastic variable. NTTO 11:97-196 no.36, 47

Juliber, G. S. Relation between seasonal amplitudes and the level of production: an application to the production of steel ingots. JASA 36:485-92 Dec 41

Kalecki, M. and Tew, B. A new method of trend elimination. Em 8:117-29 Apr 40; Correction. 9:93-94 Jan 41

Knudsen, L. F. Interdependence in a series. JASA 35:507-14 Sep 40

Mann, H. B. Nonparametric tests against trend. Em 13:245-59 Jul 45

Simonsen, W. On the reproduction of the trend by the method of simple moving averages. NTTO 12:229-39 no.37, 48

Stone, J. R. N. Prediction from autoregressive schemes and linear stochastic difference systems. Em 17,suppl.:29-37
Jul 49; Errata. 19:227 Apr 51

Tintner, G. The analysis of economic time series. JASA 35:93-100 Mar 40
-- The variate difference method: a reply. Em 9:163-64 Apr 41

Vickery, C. W. Cyclically invariant graduation. Em 12:19-25 Jan 44

**7.234 DISTRIBUTED LAGS**

Alt, F. L. Distributed lags. Em 10:113-28
Apr 42

**7.235 GRAPHIC METHODS**

Bean, L. H. The use of the short-cut graphic method of multiple correlation: comment [followed by M. Ezekiel's further comment, J. D. Black and W. Malenbaum's rejoinder and Malenbaum's concluding remarks]. QJE 54:318-64
Feb 40

## 7.235 GRAPHIC METHODS (Cont.)

Waite, W. C. Place of, and limitations to the [graphic multiple correlation] method. JFE 23:317-22 Feb 41

Wellman, H. R. Application and uses of the graphic method of multiple correlation. JFE 23:311-16 Feb 41

Working, E. J. and Shepherd, G. S. Notes on the discussion of the graphic method of correlation analysis. JFE 23:322-23 Feb 41

## 7.24 STATISTICAL DECISION MAKING. QUALITY CONTROL. SEQUENTIAL ANALYSIS

Arrow, K. J.; Blackwell, D.; and Girshick, M. A. Bayes and minimax solutions of sequential decision problems. Em 17: 213-44 Jul-Oct 49

Samuelson, P. A. Exact distribution of continuous variables in sequential analysis. Em 16:191-98 Apr 48

Wald, A. Foundations of a general theory of sequential decision functions. Em 15: 279-313 Oct 47

## 7.3 COMPUTATION. INFORMATION PROCESSING. ANALOGUES

Boyajy, J. S., chairman. Tabulation planning and tabulation techniques. [Report of a sub-committee] JM 13:330-55 Jan 49

Bruner, N. Note on the Doolittle solution. Em 15:43-44 Jan 47

Leavens, D. H. Accuracy in the Doolittle solution. Em 15:45-50 Jan 47

Paton, M. R. Selection of tabulation method, machine or manual. JM 6:229-35 Jan 42

Zielske, H. Tabulation planning. JM 14: 458-59 Oct 49

# 8. SOCIAL ACCOUNTING. STATISTICAL DATA

## 8.0 GENERAL

ER  Bergson, A. A problem in Soviet statistics. REStat 29:234-42 Nov 47

EB  Bowley, A. L. Development of statistics in the United Kingdom. RIIS 14:52-61 no.1-4, 46

A  Burgess, R. W. Do we need a "bureau of standards" for statistics? JM 11:281-82 Jan 47

EB  Crump, N. Britain's new post-war economic guide. JASA 41:171-72 Jun 46

ER  Dobb, M. A comment on Soviet statistics. REStat 30:34-38 Feb 48

ER  -- Comment on Soviet economic statistics. SovS 1:18-27 Jun 49

ER  Harris, S. E. [Appraisals of Russian economic statistics.] Introduction. REStat 29:213-14 Nov 47

A  Hauser, P. M. The statistical program of the Census Bureau. JASA 42:24-30 Mar 47

HSA  Kelly, T. H. Social and economic statistics in the Union. R. SAJE 13:304-17 Dec 45

A  Moore, G. H. Accuracy of government statistics. HBR 25:306-17 no.3, 47

Nichols, C. K. The statistical work of the League of Nations in economic, financial and related fields. JASA 37:336-42 Sep 42

A  Novick, D. Statistical materials collected by the War Production Board. REStat 28: 131-34 Aug 46

A  Rice, S. A. Collection of economic statistics in the United States. RIIS 13:62-85 no.1-4, 45

-- The United Nations Statistical Commission. Em 14:242-50 Jul 46

EB  Robinson, A. Official Statistics. R. EJ 53: 418-22 Dec 43

ER  Schwartz, H. On the use of Soviet statistics. JASA 42:401-06 Sep 47

ER  -- A critique of "Appraisals of Russian economic statistics." REStat 30: 38-41 Feb 48

ER  Yogow, A. Economic statistics in the U.S.S.R. REStat 29:242-46 Nov 47

## 8.2 NATIONAL INCOME AND WEALTH
## 8.20 GENERAL

Aukrust, O. On the theory of social accounting. REStud 16:170-88 no.3, 49

Barber, C. L. The concept of disposable income. CJE 15:227-29 May 49

Beach, E. F. A measurement of the productive capacity of wealth. CJE 7:538-44 Nov 41

Bowley, A. L. The measurement of real income. MS 11:59-86 Apr 40

-- --- [Reply to J. M Keynes, followed by Keynes's rejoinder.] EJ 50:340-42 Jun-Sep 40

Brown, H. P. Some aspects of social accounting: interest and banks. ER 25, suppl.:73-92 Aug 49

Brown, W. M. Measuring physical inventories. JASA 43:377-90 Sep 48

Burk, M. Mr. Boulding's criticism of the net national product concept [followed by K. E. Boulding's Comment on Mr. Burk's note]. AER 38:897-99 Dec 48

Christenson, C. L. Note on national income measurement; a supplement to Professor Whittaker on "Wealth and welfare." AER 31:107-08 Mar 41

## 8.2 NATIONAL INCOME AND WEALTH (Cont.)
## 8.20 GENERAL (Cont.)

Colm, G. From estimates of national income to projections of the nation's budget. SR 12:350-69 Sep 45

Gilbert, M. Measuring national income as affected by the war. JASA 37:186-98 Jun 42

-- [and others] Measurement of national income: discussion. Em 17,suppl.: 255-72 Jul 49

Gini, C. The content and use of estimates of the national income. BNL 1:271-310 Apr 48

-- The valuation of commodities for direct consumption. BNL 2:108-10 Apr-Jun 49

-- National income estimates. RIIS 17: 119-28 no.3-4, 49

Goldberg, S. A. The concept of disposable income: a reply. CJE 15:539-42 Nov 49

Gruenbaum, L. National income and outlay with reference to savings, capital movements and investment. SAJE 12:28-45 Mar 44

Hagen, E. E. Dr. Mayer on postwar national income. JPE 54:177 Apr 46

Hicks, J. R. The valuation of the social income. Ec N.S.7:105-24 May 40

-- The valuation of the social income: a comment on Professor Kuznets' reflections. Ec N.S.15:163-72 Aug 48

Keynes, J. M. The concept of national income: a supplementary note. EJ 50: 60-65 Mar 40

Kuznets, S. National and regional measures of income. SEJ 6:291-313 Jan 40

-- Measurement of economic growth. JEH/S 7:10-34 '47

-- On the valuation of social income: reflections on Professor Hicks' article. Pt.I-II. Ec N.S.15:1-16; 116-31 Feb, May 48

Little, I. M. D. The valuation of the social income. Ec N.S.16:11-26 Feb 49

Loosmore, R. J. A note on the visual representation of national income statistics. MS 15:296-306 Sep 47

MacGregor, D. C. Recent studies on national income. Pt.I-II. R. CJE 11: 115-29; 270-80 Feb,May 45

May, G. O. Gross income. QJE 55:521-25 May 41

Mayer, J. Deficiencies in the gross-national-product concept as a national measure. JPE 53:357-63 Dec 45

-- Dr. Mayer on postwar national income: a reply. JPE 54:454 Oct 46

Meade, J. E. and Stone, R. The construction of tables of national income, expenditure, savings and investment. EJ 51: 216-33 Jun-Sep 41

Ou, P. S. International payments in national income. QJE 60:289-98 Feb 46

Pigou, A. C. The measurement of real income. EJ 50:524-25 Dec 40

-- Comparisons of real income. Ec N.S.10: 93-98 May 43

Radice, E. A. The national income. (Essays in bibliography and criticism III) EHR 14: 180-84 no.2, 44

Rolph, E. R. The concept of transfers in national income estimates. QJE 62: 327-61 May 48

Rothschild, K. W. Public expenditure in the national income: a note. Ec N.S.11: 19-22 Feb 44

Sandee, J. Independent applications of national accounts. Ec N.S.16:249-54 Aug 49

Seers, D. Social accounting. ER 22:117-32 Jun 46

-- A note on current Marxist definitions of the national income. OEP N.S.1:260-68 Jun 49

Stern, E. H. Public expenditure in the national income: a reply. Ec N.S.11: 23-26 Feb 44

Stone, R.; Champernowne, D. G. and Meade, J. E. The precision of national income estimates. REStud 9:111-25 no.2, 42

Tinbergen, J. and Derksen, J. B. D. Recent experiments in social accounting: flexible and dynamic budgets. Em 17,suppl.: 195-203 Jul 49

Tress, R. C. The diagrammatic representation of national income flows. Ec N.S.15: 276-88 Nov 48

UNITED STATES

Adamson, W. M. Measurement of income in small geographic areas. SEJ 8: 479-92 Apr 42

Ezekiel, M. Statistical investigations of saving, consumption, and investment. Pt.I-II. AER 32:22-49; 272-307 Mar, Jun 42

Friend, I. Ezekiel's analysis of saving, consumption, and investment. AER 32: 829-35 Dec 42

Gilbert, M. U.S. national income statistics [followed by R. Stone's comment]. EJ 53: 76-83 Apr 43

-- ; Staehle, H. and Woytinsky, W. S. National product, war and prewar: some comments on Professor Kuznets' study and a reply by Professor Kuznets. REStat 26:109-35 Aug 44

-- [and others] Objectives of national income measurement: a reply to Professor Kuznets. REStat 30:179-95 Aug 48

Hoffenberg, M. Estimates of national output, distributed income, consumer spending, saving, and capital formation. REStat 25:101-74 May 43; Correction. 201 Aug 43

8.2 NATIONAL INCOME AND WEALTH (Cont.)
8.20 GENERAL (Cont.)
  UNITED STATES (Cont.)
  Kalecki, M. Further comments on the De-
A  partment of Commerce series.
   REStat 30:195-97 Aug 48
  Kuznets, S. National income: a new ver-
   sion. (Discussion of the new Department
   of Commerce income series) REStat 30:
   151-79 Aug 48
  Malenbaum, W. The cost of distribution.
   QJE 55:255-70 Feb 41
  Mayer, J. National product distortions:
   war and postwar. SEJ 12:141-50 Oct 45
  Oliver, H. M., Jr. Income, region, com-
   munity-size and color. QJE 60:588-99
   Aug 46
  Stone, R. The national income, output and
   expenditure of the United States of
   America, 1929-41. EJ 52:154-75
   Jun-Sep 42
  -- Two studies on income and expenditure
   in the United States. R. EJ 53:60-75
   Apr 43
  Tucker, R. S. The composition of income
   and ownership of capital by income
   classes in the United States in 1936.
   JASA 38:187-200 Jun 43
  Wilcox, W. W. Capital in agriculture.
   QJE 58:49-64 Nov 43
  Wright, D. M. The interpretation of the
   Kuznets-Fabricant figures for "net"
   capital consumption. JPE 50:435-43
   Jun 42
  Stepp, J. M. Postwar planning survey at
ASS  Anderson, S.C. LE 21:184-91 May 45

  OTHER AMERICAN COUNTRIES
  Burton, G. L. Agriculture's share of the
C  national income: a comment. CJE 10:
   206-09 May 44
  Chang, T. C. A note on exports and national
   income in Canada. CJE 13:276-80 May 47
  Goldberg, S. A. The development of national
   accounts in Canada. CJE 15:34-52 Feb 49
  Hope, E. C. Agriculture's share of the na-
   tional income. CJE 9:384-93 Aug 43
  MacGregor, D. C. Gross and net investment
   in Canada: tentative estimates. CJE 7:
   39-68 Feb 41
  Skeoch, L. A. Agriculture's share of the
   national income further considered.
   CJE 10:210-12 May 44
  Studenski, P. On some appendices to the
   Rowell-Sirois report: III. The national
   income of Canada. CJE 7:78-84 Feb 41

  EUROPE
  Barna, T. Valuation of stocks and the na-
EB  tional income. Ec N.S.9:349-58 Nov 42
  Booker, H. S. The distribution of income
   under full employment. MS 15:75-92
   Jan 47

Bowley, A. L. Some constituents of the
  national income. JRSS 103:491-518
  pt.4, 40
-- Note on Mr. Barna's Valuation of stocks.
  Ec N.S.10:64-65 Feb 43
Brown, P. S. Prospective national income
  and capital formation in the United King-
  dom. AER 36:555-77 Sep 46
Champernowne, D. G. The national income
  and expenditure of the United Kingdom
  1938-1945. OIS 8:130-45 May 46
Dacey, W. M. The 1944 White Paper on
  national income and expenditure. EJ 54:
  177-88 Jun-Sep 44
-- National income in the transition.
  LBR 5:43-57 Jul 47
Gilbert, M. and Jaszi, G. The 1945 White
  Paper on national income and expendi-
  ture. R. EJ 55:444-454 Dec 45
Harrod, R. F. The fall in consumption.
  OIS 10:162-67 May 48
-- --- A rejoinder. OIS 10:235-44
  Jul-Aug 48
Henderson, P. D.; Seers, D. and Wallis,
  P. F. D. Notes on estimating national
  income components. OIS 11:59-70
  Feb-Mar 49
Jackson, E. F. Comments on Mr. Harrod's
  paper. OIS 10:209-13 Jun 48; Erratum.
  234 Jul-Aug 48
-- The fall in consumption: a further note.
  OIS 10:290 Sep 48
Kaldor, N. The White Paper on national
  income and expenditure. R. EJ 51:
  181-91 Jun-Sep 41
-- The 1941 White Paper on national in-
  come and expenditure. R. EJ 52:206-22
  Jun-Sep 42
-- and Barna, T. The 1943 White Paper on
  national income and expenditure. R.
  EJ 53:259-74 Jun-Sep 43
Kalecki, M. Wage bill and cash circulation.
  OIS 2,no.5:2-6 Aug 10, 40
-- --- A supplement. OIS 2,no.6:10-13
  Aug 31, 40
-- The share of wages in the national in-
  come. OIS 3:196-98 Jun 28, 41; Erratum.
  262 Aug 9, 41
-- The White Paper on the national income
  and expenditure in the years 1938-1943.
  OIS 6:137-44 Jul 1, 44
Mars, J. The integration of the balance of
  payments into national income accounts.
  YB 1:43-66 Sep 49
Prest, A. R. National income of the United
  Kingdom. EJ 58:31-62 Mar 48
Rothbarth, E. Bowley's Studies in national
  income. R. EJ 53:55-59 Apr 43
Seers, D. The 1947 national income White
  Paper. OIS 9:228-53 Jul 47
-- The national product before and after the
  war. OIS 10:309-31 Oct 48

# 8. SOCIAL ACCOUNTING. STATISTICAL DATA

## 8.2 NATIONAL INCOME AND WEALTH (Cont.)
### 8.20 GENERAL (Cont.)
#### EUROPE (Cont.)
Seers, D. (Cont.)

EB
-- and Wallis, P. F. D. Changes in real national income. OIS 11:163-76 Jun 49

-- and Wallis, P. F. D. A national income matrix. OIS 11:181-93 Jul-Aug 49

-- Quarterly estimates of the national income. OIS 11:293-306; 373-81 Oct, Dec 49

Shirras, G. F. The measurement of national wealth. Em 17,suppl.:247-53 Jul 49

Stern, E. H. Public expenditure in the national income. Ec N.S.10:166-75 May 43

Worswick, G. D. N. A fall in consumption: a reply. OIS 10:195-208 Jun 48

-- --- A further comment [followed by R. F. Harrod's rejoinder]. OIS 10:284-93 Sep 48

Youngson, A. J. Resources available for war: a comparison. OEP 3:1-22 Feb 40

EF
Barna, T. The French national accounts. OIS 10:73-83 Mar 48

EI
Gini, C. On national income. BNL 1:63-74 Jul 47

EN
Idenburg, P. J. and Derksen, J. B. D. Methods of evaluation of the national income of the Netherlands, 1921-1938. RIIS 8:13-30 no.1-2, 40

ER
Baran, P. A. National income and product of the U.S.S.R. in 1940. REStat 29:226-34 Nov 47

Clark, C. Russian income and production statistics. REStat 29:215-17 Nov 47

Jasny, N. Intricacies of Russian national-income indexes. JPE 55:299-322 Aug 47

Studenski, P. and Wyler, J. National income estimates of Soviet Russia: their distinguishing characteristics and problems. AER/S 37:595-610 May 47

Wyler, J. The national income of Soviet Russia. SR 13:501-18 Dec 46

#### ASIA
FC
Ou, P. S. A new estimate of China's national income. JPE 54:547-54 Dec 46

FI
Anstey, V. Social accounting in India. IJE 27:271-77 Jan 47

#### AFRICA
H
Shaul, J. R. H. and Irvine, A. G. The national income of Southern Rhodesia, 1946-1948. SAJE 17:511-15 Dec 49

HSA
Anonymous. Estimates of national income of the Union of South Africa, 1943-44 to 1946-47. [By the Office of Census and Statistics] SAJE 16:215-18 Jun 48

-- The net national income of the Union of South Africa, 1947-48. [By the Office of Census and Statistics] SAJE 17:205-14 Jun 49

Frankel, S. H. and Neumark, S. D. Note on the national income of the Union of South Africa. 1927/28, 1932/33, 1934/35. SAJE 8:78-80 Mar 40

-- Consumption, investment and war expenditure in relation to the South African national income [1938/39-1944/45]. SAJE 9:445-48; 11:75-77; 12:147-49; 13:132-35; 14:220-23 Dec 41, Mar 43, Jun 44, Jun 45, Sep 46

-- and Herzfeld, H. An analysis of the growth of the national income of the Union in the period of prosperity before the war. SAJE 12:112-38 Jun 44

-- Expenditure in relation to national income. SAJE 15:276-79 Dec 47

Franzsen, D. G. Some methodological problems raised by the calculation of the Union's national income, by income type. SAJE 16:157-67 Jun 48

Ravenscroft, A. P. National accounts and national income. Memorandum no.2. Union government public debt and interest. SAJE 16:296-305 Sep 48

Reedman, J. N. A note on the table of net investment in the Third interim report of the Industrial and Agricultural Requirements Commission. SAJE 10:82-84 Mar 42

#### AUSTRALIA. NEW ZEALAND
N
Arndt, H. W. A pioneer of national income estimates [T. A. Coghlan]. EJ 59:616-25 Dec 49

Brown, H. P. The composition of personal income. ER 25,(no.48):18-36 Jun 49

G[iblin], L. F. "Estimates of national income and public authority income and expenditure," presented by the Right Hon. J. B. Chifley for the information of honourable members on the occasion of the budget, 1945-46. R. ER 21:254-56 Dec 45

Neale, E. P. Recent New Zealand data regarding the incomes of individuals. ER 17:68-80 Jun 41

Oxnam, D. W. Some observations on changes in money and real incomes in Australia, 1938-39 to 1948-49. ER 25, (no.49):46-63 Dec 49

Rosenburg, W. New Zealand official estimates of national income. ER 25,(no.48): 74-81 Jun 49

Wilson, R. F. New Zealand production. ER 17:252-55 Dec 41

### 8.22 DISTRIBUTION OF PERSONAL INCOME AND WEALTH
Anantachar, V. S. Forces behind Pareto's law. IJE 26:302-05 Oct 45

Durand, D. A simple method for estimating the size distribution of a given aggregate income. REStat 25:227-30 Aug 43

## 8.22 DISTRIBUTION OF PERSONAL INCOME AND WEALTH (Cont.)

Marschak, J. Income inequality and demand studies: a note. Em 11:163-66 Apr 43

Rhodes, E. C. The Pareto distribution of incomes. Ec N.S.11:1-11 Feb 44

### UNITED STATES

Ames, E. A method for estimating the size
A   distribution of a given aggregate income. REStat 24:184-89 Nov 42

Bowman, M. J. A graphical analysis of personal income distribution in the United States. AER 35:607-28 Sep 45

Clark, E. and Fishman, L. Appraisal of methods for estimating the size distribution of a given aggregate income. REStat 29:43-46 Feb 47

Copeland, M. A. The social and economic determinants of the distribution of income in the United States. AER 37: 56-75 Mar 47

Crossley, A. M. The effect of the war on income changes. JM 7:355-59 Apr 43

Durand, D. An appraisal of the errors involved in estimating the size distribution of a given aggregate income. REStat 30:63-68 Feb 48

Garvy, G. Dr. Rhodes' analysis of the distribution of single incomes in the United States. Ec N.S.11:104-05 May 44

Rhodes, E. C. The distribution of incomes in the United States. Ec N.S.10:223-32 Aug 43

-- Comments on Dr. Garvy's note. Ec N.S.11:106 May 44

Smelker, M. W. Shifts in the concentration of income. REStat 30:215-22 Aug 48

Tucker, R. S. The National Resources Committee's report on distribution of income. REStat 22:165-82 Nov 40

-- Distribution of income in 1935-36. JASA 37:489-95 Dec 42

### OTHER COUNTRIES

Cockfield, F. A. The distribution of in-
EB   comes. Ec N.S.14:254-82 Nov 47

Nicholson, J. L. The distribution of incomes [1938-9 and 1941-2]. OIS 4: 225-28 Aug 29, 42

-- The distribution of incomes [1940-1 and 1941-2]. OIS 6:23-29 Feb 5, 44

Rhodes, E. C. The distribution of incomes. Ec N.S.9:245-56 Aug 42

-- The distribution of family incomes. Ec N.S.12:31-35 Feb 45

-- The distribution of earned and investment incomes in the United Kingdom. Ec N.S.16:53-65 Feb 49

Seers, D. Income distribution in 1938 and 1947. OIS 11:253-68 Sep 49

Mukherjee, M. M. A note on trend of con-
FI   centration ratio. IJE 28:291-92 Oct 47

Peries, H. E. Distribution of incomes. IJE 27:90-91 Jul 46

Frankel, S. H. and Herzfeld, H. European
HSA   income distribution in the Union of South Africa and the effect thereon of income taxation. SAJE 11:121-36 Jun 43

Graaff, J. de V. Fluctuations in income concentration; with special reference to changes in the concentration of super-taxable incomes in South Africa: July, 1915-June, 1943. SAJE 14:22-39 Mar 46

## 8.23 INTERNATIONAL COMPARISONS

Abraham, W. I. The comparability of national income statistics of English-speaking countries. REStat 30:207-14 Aug 48

Bowley, A. L. National income in America
A   and the United Kingdom. R. Ec N.S.9:
EB   227-36 Aug 42

Giblin, L. F. Economic progress. R. [followed by C. Clark's note and Giblin's comment]. ER 16:262-70 Dec 40

Kuznets, S. Economic progress. R. MS 12: 28-34 Apr 41

-- National income and industrial structure.
A/FC Em 17,suppl.:205-39 Jul 49

Olson, E. C. Factors affecting international differences in production. AER/S 38: 502-22 May 48

Smithies, A. The effect of the role of government on international comparisons of national income. Em 17,suppl.:242-46 Jul 49

Stone, R. National income in the United
A   Kingdom, and the United States of
EB   America. REStud 10:1-27 no.1, 42

-- The measurement of national income and expenditure: a review of the official estimates of five countries. EJ 57: 272-98 Sep 47

Wyler, J. The share of capital in national income: United States, United Kingdom and Germany. SR 10:436-54 Nov 43

## 8.3 INPUT-OUTPUT

Fabricant, S. [and others] Input-output analysis and its use in peace and war economies: discussion. AER/S 39: 226-40 May 49

Leontief, W. Output, employment, consump-
A   tion, and investment. QJE 58:290-314 Feb 44

-- Exports, imports, domestic output, and
A   employment. QJE 60:171-93 Feb 46; Correction. 469 May 46

-- Wages, profit and prices. QJE 61:26-39 Nov 46

-- Recent developments in the study of interindustrial relationships. AER/S 39: 211-25 May 49

# 8. SOCIAL ACCOUNTING. STATISTICAL DATA

## 8.3 INPUT-OUTPUT (Cont.)
Leontief, W. (Cont.)
-- Structural matrices of national economies. Em 17,suppl.:273-80 Jul 49

## 8.4 FINANCING ACCOUNTS. FLOW OF FUNDS
A   Copeland, M. A. Tracing money flows through the United States economy. AER/S 37:31-49 May 47
AA  Haroldson, W. C. Comments on regional dependency. JFE 25:701-04 Aug 43
A   Shapiro, S. The distribution of deposits and currency in the United States, 1929-1939. JASA 38:438-44 Dec 43

## 8.5 STATISTICAL DATA NOT ELSEWHERE CLASSIFIED
### 8.50 GENERAL
Kolesnikoff, V. S. Standard commodity classification. JASA 39:42-52 Mar 44
A   Reed, V. D. War time facts and peace time needs. JASA 39:144-54 Jun 44

### 8.51 HISTORY
EB  Hamilton, E. J. Sir William Beveridge's price history. R. EJ 52:54-58 Apr 42
EB  Hoffmann, W. The growth of industrial production in Great Britain: a quantitative study. EHR II.2:162-80 no.2, 49
ESp Sardà, J. Spanish prices in the nineteenth century. QJE 62:143-59 Nov 47

### 8.52 CENSUS
Beales, R. E. Industrial classification, national and international. JRSS 112: 316-30 pt.3, 49
A   Carson, D. Incomparabilities in "Census of manufactures" data. AER 31:559-60 Sep 41
A   Cherington, P. T. The uses of the Census of business. [Summary of a discussion] JASA 35:107-15 Mar 40
A   Kolesnikoff, V. S. Standard classification of industries in the United States. JASA 35:65-73 Mar 40
EB  Leak, H. Statistics of the censuses of production and distribution. JRSS 112: 67-80 pt.1, 49

### 8.53 PRODUCTION. TRADE VOLUME
EI  Battera, P. Index numbers of industrial production and capitalisation in Italy. BNL 2:118-23 Apr-Jun 49
EB  Bowley, A. L. The volume of industrial production. JRSS 106:167-70 pt.2, 43
ER  Clark, C. Russian income and production statistics. REStat 29:215-17 Nov 47
A   Garfield, F. R. Measurement of industrial production since 1939. JASA 39:439-54 Dec 44
EBI Geary, R. C. The concept of net volume of output, with special reference to Irish data [followed by H. Leak and A. Maizels' note]. JRSS 107:251-61 pt.3-4, 44

EBI -- --- Rejoinder to Messrs. Leak and Maizels. JRSS 107:290-92 pt.3-4, 44
ER  Gerschenkron, A. The Soviet indices of industrial production. REStat 29:217-26 Nov 47
A   Johnson, N. O. Federal Reserve Bank of New York indexes of production and trade. JASA 36:423-25 Sep 41
EB  Leak, H. Volume of industrial production. JRSS 106:60-63 pt.1, 43
ER  Nichols, R. T. Soviet production estimates [followed by H. Schwartz's comments]. JPE 57:249-50 Jun 49
ER  Schwartz, H. Soviet postwar industrial production. JPE 56:438-41 Oct 48
Snow, E. C. The international comparison of industrial output [with discussion]. JRSS 107:1-55 pt.1, 44

## 8.54 PRICE
A   Ascher, L. A statistical analysis of recent changes in commodity prices at wholesale. JASA 39:35-41 Mar 44
A   Bean, L. H. Wholesale prices and industrial stock prices during and immediately after the two world wars. REStat 29: 199-200 Aug 47
FI  Beri, S. G. Price trends during the last decade and their effects on Indian economy. IJE 21:734-84 Apr 41
FI  Bhan, R. K. Prices in India between the two great wars. IJE 21:785-97 Apr 41
Gilles, R. C. International comparison of wholesale prices. REStat 22:150-56 Aug 40
C   MacGregor, D. C. Studies of the cost of living in Canada. CJE 7:545-58 Nov 41
A   McIntyre, F. Wholesale price indexes. JASA 36:185-90 Jun 41
N   Neale, E. P. The New Zealand war-time prices index. ER 21:94-100 Jun 45
EB  Nicholson, J. L. The cost of living index. OIS 3:31-32 Feb 1, 41
EB  Seers, D. The increase in the working-class cost-of-living since before the war. OIS 10:140-61 May 48
EB  -- Is there bias in the Interim index of retail prices? OIS 11:1-8 Jan 49
EB  -- The cost of living, 1938-1948. OIS 11: 127-38 May 49

## 8.55 PROFIT
ME  Hussein, H. M. Mathematical analysis of company profits in Egypt. EgC 38: 115-21 Jan-Feb 47
ME  Issawi, C. and Rosenfeld, F. Company profits in Egypt 1929-1939. EgC 32: 679-86 Nov 41
ME  -- Company profits in Egypt, 1940-1941. EgC 33:577-80 May-Nov 42

# 9. MONEY, CREDIT, AND BANKING

## 9.0 GENERAL

Bowen, H. R. The teaching of money and banking. [Round table discussion] JF 4:231-33 Sep 49

Dunkman, W. E. The teaching of money and banking. [Round table discussion] JF 4:234-37 Sep 49

Gopal, M. H. The depositor and bank management. IJE 24:348-54 Apr 44

Machlup, F. The teaching of money and banking. [Round table discussion] JF 4:227-30 Sep 49

Robinson, R. I. The teaching of money and banking. [Round table discussion] JF 4:237-42 Sep 49

### UNITED STATES

A   Ballantine, A. A. When all the banks closed. HBR 26:129-43 Mar 48

Preston, H. H. [and others] Banking problems: discussion. AER/S 37:289-98 May 47

Reed, H. L. Principles of banking reform. AER/S 37:277-88 May 47

Seltzer, L. H. Postwar domestic monetary problems: discussion. AER/S 34: 280-87 Mar 44

-- The changed environment of monetary-banking policy. AER/S 36:65-79 May 46

Tongue, W. W. Postwar domestic monetary problems: discussion. AER/S 34: 278-80 Mar 44

Whittlesey, C. R. Problems of our domestic money and banking system. AER/S 34: 245-59 Mar 44

### OTHER COUNTRIES

Ortiz Mena, R. Monetary problems in
DM   Mexico. JB 20:1-8 Jan 47

Adler, H. A. The post-war reorganization
EG   of the German banking system. QJE 63: 322-41 Aug 49

Usoskin, M. Soviet banking system. PF 2:
ER   348-53 no.4, 47

Kojima, S. Special currency system of
FC   China: a study of the "Wei Wah" system in Shanghai. Kyo 16,no.3:16-50 Jul 41

-- The Wei Wah system as a special credit system of China. Kyo 16,no.4:1-19 Oct 41

-- Financial circles in Shanghai following the outbreak of the Greater East Asia War. Kyo 18,no.2:1-26 Apr 43

Tokunaga, K. The progress of monetary unification in the Meng Chiang provinces. Kyo 15,no.1:30-44 Jan 40

Bhat, A. R. Regulation of organisation and
FI   management of Indian joint stock banks. IJE 25:510-20 Apr 45

Gopalswamy, S. Co-ordination and control of banking in Mysore. IJE 24:38-58 Jul 43

Sengupta, S. Banking reform in India. IJE 24:59-65 Jul 43

Arndt, E. H. D. The proposed new banking
HSA   legislation. SAJE 9:274-311 Sep 41

-- The Union Banking Act, 1942. SAJE 11: 235-57 Dec 43

El Falaki, M. S. Post-war planning of cur-
ME   rency and the monetary market in Egypt. EgC 35:187-204 Jan-Feb 44

## 9.1 HISTORY

Daugherty, M. R. The currency-banking
EB   controversy. Pt.I-II. SEJ 9:140-55; 241-51 Oct 42, Jan 43

De Roover, R. Money, banking, and credit
ECB   in medieval Bruges. JEH/S 2:52-65 Dec 42

Roy, P. The mercantilist view of money in relation to public finance. IJE 23: 257-70 Jan 43

Schwartz, A. J. An attempt at synthesis
A   in American banking history. R. JEH 7:208-17 Nov 47

Venit, A. H. Isaac Bronson: his banking
A   theory and the financial controversies of the Jacksonian period. JEH 5:201-14 Nov 45

Walters, P. G. and Walters, R., Jr. The
A   American career of David Parish. JEH 4:149-66 Nov 44

## 9.2 MONEY. CURRENCY. MONETARY STANDARDS

### 9.20 GENERAL

Bratter, H. M. The Committee For the
A   Nation: a case history in monetary propaganda. JPE 49:531-53 Jun 41

De Kock, M. H. The concepts of money,
HSA   capital and credit. SAJE 12:13-27 Mar 44

Egle, W. P. Money as numéraire. AER/S 37:325-31 May 47

Ellis, H. S. The changing character of
A   money: summary and comments. AER/S 37:332-34 May 47

Graham, B. Money as pure commodity.
A   AER/S 37:304-07 May 47

Graham, F. D. The primary functions of money and their consummation in monetary policy. AER/S 30:1-16 Mar 40

Lerner, A. P. Money as a creature of the
A   state. AER/S 37:312-17 May 47

Malhotra, D. K. Indian currency: past,
FI   present and future. IJE 24:202-11 Jan 44

Murad, A. The nature of money. SEJ 9: 217-33 Jan 43

Niebyl, K. H. What rights should the holder
A   of money have? AER/S 37:299-303 May 47

Rolph, E. R. The payment of interest on
A   Series E bonds. AER/S 37:318-21 May 47

# 9. MONEY, CREDIT, AND BANKING

## 9.2 MONEY, CURRENCY, MONETARY STANDARDS (Cont.)
### 9.20 GENERAL (Cont.)

A   Simmons, E. C. The relative liquidity of money and other things. AER/S 37: 308-11 May 47

Triffin, R. International versus domestic money. AER/S 37:322-24 May 47

### 9.21 HISTORY

A   De Roover, F. E. Concerning the ancestry of the dollar sign. BHR 19:63-64 Apr 45

FC   Dubs, H. H. An ancient Chinese stock of gold. JEH 2:36-39 May 42

ESp   Hamilton, E. J. Monetary disorder and economic decadence in Spain, 1651-1700. JPE 51:477-93 Dec 43

ESp   -- Monetary problems in Spain and Spanish America 1751-1800. JEH 4:21-48 May 44

EB   Horsefield, J. K. Gibson and Johnson: a forgotten cause célèbre. Ec N.S.10: 233-37 Aug 43

FC   Hozumi, F. On the monetary ideas as seen in the Records of economics and finance in the Sung history. Kyo 17,no.3:36-59 Jul 42

EA   Nef, J. U. Silver production in central Europe, 1450-1618. JPE 49:575-91 Jun 41

E   Pond, S. The ducat: once an important coin in European business. BHR 14: 17-19 Apr 40

EF   -- The louis d'or. BHR 14:77-80 Nov 40

-- The Spanish dollar: the world's most famous silver coin. BHR 15:12-16 Feb 41

M   -- The Maria Theresa Thaler: a famous trade coin [in the Near East]. BHR 15: 26-31 Apr 41

Postan, M. M. The rise of a money economy. EHR 14:123-34 no.2, 44

A   Redlich, F. Bank money in the United States during the first half of the nineteenth century. SEJ 10:212-21 Jan 44

A   -- "Translating" economic policy into business policy: an illustration from the resumption of specie payments in 1879. BHR 20:190-95 Dec 46

### 9.22 MONEY SUPPLY. VELOCITY OF CIRCULATION

A   Angell, J. W., chairman. Round table on bank deposits and the business cycle. AER/S 30:80-82 Mar 40

A   Cooke, G. W. Savings deposits in mutual and nonmutual banks, 1911-40. JB 16: 195-203 Jul 43

Dice, C. A. and Schaffner, P. [Offset checks] A reply to Mr. Villard. AER 30: 113 Mar 40

-- --- Further reply. AER 30:825-27 Dec 40

Eiteman, W. J. Comment on "Offset checks

as a component of the money supply" by Mr. Villard. AER 30:114-15 Mar 40

EB   Goodwin, R. M. The supply of bank money in England and Wales, 1920-1938. OEP no.5:1-29 Jun 41

A   Hart, A. G. Postwar effects to be expected from wartime liquid accumulations. AER/S 35:341-51 May 45

Harwood, E. C. Comment on A neglected component of the money supply. AER 30: 115 Mar 40

A   Kähler, A. The public debt in the financial structure. SR 11:11-26 Feb 44

EB   Kalecki, M. The war-time trend of deposits. OIS 5:63-66 Mar 13, 43

FJ   Kojima, S. The origination and extinction of currency in the world of circulation. Kyo 18,no.4:1-18 Oct 43

FI   Malkani, H. C. Post-war currency system in India. IJE 26:388-91 Jan 46

M   Mikesell, R. F. Financial problems of the Middle East. JPE 53:164-76 Jun 45

A   Shapiro, S. The distribution of deposits and currency in the United States, 1929-1939. JASA 38:438-44 Dec 43

FI   Sinha, M. N. Indian currency and war. IJE 22:199-207 Oct 41

Tirana, R. Behavior of bank deposits abroad. AER/S 30:92-105 Mar 40

Villard, H. H. Further comment on "Offset checks." AER 30:823-25 Dec 40

N   Walker, E. R. and Beecroft, R. M. Changes in the stock of Australian money. ER 17: 210-17 Dec 41

A   Warburton, C. Quantity and frequency of use of money in the United States, 1919-45. JPE 54:436-50 Oct 46

A   -- The secular trend in monetary velocity. QJE 63:68-91 Feb 49

Whittlesey, C. R. Retirement of internally held debt. AER 33:602-04 Sep 43

-- Memorandum on the stability of demand deposits. AER 39:1192-1203 Dec 49

## 9.23 MONETARY STANDARDS
### 9.230 GENERAL

Graham, F. D. Achilles' heels in monetary standards. AER 30:16-32 Mar 40

Hicks, E. Alexander del Mar, critic of metallism. SEJ 6:314-32 Jan 40

### 9.231 GOLD

Anonymous. Who pays for the gold? AER 32:125-28 Mar 42

FI   Banerjee, P. C. Problem and policy of gold sales. IJE 26:271-89 Oct 45

Brown, W. A., Jr. Comments on gold and the monetary system. AER/S 30,no.5: 38-51 Feb 41

Busschau, W. J. The case for increasing the price of gold in terms of all currencies. SAJE 17:1-22 Mar 49

## 9.23 MONETARY STANDARDS (Cont.)

### 9.231 GOLD (Cont.)

Hardy, C. O. The price level and the gold problem: retrospect and prospect. AER/S 30,no.5:18-29 Feb 41

-- Professor Lester's questions on gold: two replies. [I] AER 31:560-62 Sep 41

Lehmann, F. The gold problem. SR 7: 125-50 May 40

Lester, R. A. Gold imports: cost and benefits. AER 31:340-41 Jun 41

Lichtenstein, W. Recent literature on the gold problem. R. JB 13:146-58 Apr 40

HSA Lowry, G. M. L. The timing and control of a rise in the South African price of gold. SAJE 17:202-04 Jun 49

A Machlup, F. Eight questions on gold: a review. AER/S 30,no.5:30-37 Feb 41

Neisser, H. P. The price level and the gold problem. AER/S 30,no.5:1-17 Feb 41

-- Professor Lester's questions on gold: two replies. [II] AER 31:562-63 Sep 41

Richards, C. S. The case for increasing the price of gold in terms of all currencies: a comment. SAJE 17:23-31 Mar 49

Shirras, G. F. The position and prospects of gold. EJ 50:207-23 Jun-Sep 40

### 9.232 SILVER AND BIMETALLISM

Leavens, D. H. Bullion prices and the gold-silver ratio "1929-1945." REStat 28: 160-64 Aug 46

### 9.233 OTHER STANDARDS

Atkins, D. A dimensional national economy: a reply [followed by R. W. Burgess's rejoinder]. JPE 52:267-70 Sep 44

Beale, W. T. M., Jr.; Kennedy, M. T.; and Winn, W. J. Commodity reserve currency: a critique. JPE 50:579-94 Aug 42

Calsoyas, C. D. Commodity currency and commodity storage. AER 38:341-52 Jun 48

Frommer, J. C. A price formula for multiple-commodity monetary reserve. Em 13:153-60 Apr 45

Graham, B. The critique of Commodity-reserve currency: a point-by-point reply. JPE 51:66-69 Feb 43

Graham, F. D. Transition to a commodity reserve currency. AER 31:520-25 Sep 41

-- Commodity-reserve currency: a criticism of the critique. JPE 51:70-75 Feb 43

-- Keynes vs. Hayek on A commodity reserve currency [followed by J. M. Keynes's note]. EJ 54:422-30 Dec 44

Hayek, F. A. A commodity reserve currency. EJ 53:176-84 Jun-Sep 43

Rosen, M. M. The demand for cigarettes ECA in Austria. SEJ 14:186-91 Oct 47

Rosenson, A. International commodity reserve standard reconsidered. REStat 30: 135-40 May 48

Winn, W. J. Commodity-reserve currency: a rejoinder. JPE 51:175-77 Apr 43

## 9.24 CURRENCY AND CURRENCY REFORM

Cross, I. B. A note on the use of the word "currency." JPE 52:362-63 Dec 44

### UNITED STATES

A Goldenweiser, E. A. Pritchard on the Federal Reserve bank note: comment [followed by L. J. Pritchard's reply]. JPE 55:359-61 Aug 47

Pritchard, L. J. The Federal Reserve bank note. JPE 55:157-66 Apr 47

### EUROPE

E Klopstock, F. H. Monetary reform in liberated Europe. AER 36:578-95 Sep 46

EBC Clauson, G. L. M. The British colonial currency system. EJ 54:1-25 Apr 44

ECB De Ridder, V. A. The Belgian monetary reform. REStud 15:51-69 no.2, 48

-- The Belgian monetary reform: an appraisal of the results. REStud 16:25-40 no.1, 48

EG Heller, W. W. Tax and monetary reform in occupied Germany. NTJ 2:215-31 Sep 49

Klopstock, F. H. Monetary reform in Western Germany. JPE 57:277-92 Aug 49

Lutz, F. A. The German currency reform and the revival of the German economy. Ec N.S.16:122-42 May 49

EH Nogaro, B. Hungary's recent monetary crisis and its theoretical meaning. AER 38:526-42 Sep 48

Vargo, S. Hungary's monetary crisis: comment [followed by B. Nogaro's rejoinder]. AER 39:956-60 Sep 49

Winklé, F. F. Some aspects of the recent inflation and stabilization of the Hungarian currency. SAJE 15:178-91 Sep 47

ER Baran, P. A. Currency reform in the USSR. HBR 26:194-206 Mar 48

Haensel, P. Soviet "inflation" reform. PF 3:107-08 no.2, 48

ESN Schjander, F. Norwegian savings banks and the state of the money market during and after the war. SAJE 15:73-77 Mar 47

### OTHER COUNTRIES

FA Matsuoka, K. The currency system in French Indo-China. Kyo 17,no.2:44-63 Apr 42

FC Tokunaga, K. Monetary and financial reorganization in North China. Kyo 15, no.2:71-100 Apr 40

# 9. MONEY, CREDIT, AND BANKING

## 9.24 CURRENCY AND CURRENCY REFORM (Cont.)
### OTHER COUNTRIES (Cont.)

FI    Leavens, D. H. Rupee circulation in India. AER 31:87-90 Mar 41

FIC    Shenoy, B. R. The new currency law in Ceylon. EJ 51:512-15 Dec 41

FJ    Morgan, A. The Japanese currency reform: a lesson in monetary experience. OIS 10:424-37 Dec 48

H    Wasserman, M. J. The new Ethiopian monetary system. JPE 54:358-62 Aug 46

## 9.3 COMMERCIAL BANKS
### 9.30 GENERAL

A    Carlson, V. Democratizing money. JF 2, no.2:68-71 Oct 47

A    Ebersole, J. F. Banks can make more postwar jobs. HBR 22:1-9 no.1, 43

A    -- Government can help banks make more jobs. HBR 22:167-77 no.2, 44

A    Floyd, J. S. The changing impact of national banking costs, 1921-43. SEJ 12:365-75 Apr 46

A    Henderson, J. S. Regional differentials in interest rates. SEJ 11:113-32 Oct 44

   Morton, W. A. A zero deposit rate. AER 30: 536-53 Sep 40

FIP    Muhajir, A. Banking in East Pakistan. PEJ 1,no.1:112-16 Jul 49

EI    Pietranera, G. and Zacchia, C. Recent banking developments in Italy: December 1947-September 1949. BNL 2:255-37 Oct-Dec 49

   Poindexter, J. C. Some misconceptions of banking and interest theory. SEJ 13: 132-45 Oct 46

AA    Popple, C. S. Group banking [in the 9th Federal Reserve District]. HBR 22: 191-98 no.2, 44

AA    Rapp, R. E. The Hamilton National Associates, Inc.: a case study in group banking. Pt.I-II. SEJ 9:1-14; 105-21 Jul, Oct 42

FC    Tokunaga, K. The Chinese banks in malformed transition, with a special reference to their movement in the early period of the republican regime. Kyo 17,no.1:53-69 Jan 42

FC    -- Adjustment of the Chinese banking business. Kyo 18,no.4:42-62 Oct 43

FIP    Uqaili, N. Resurrection of banking in Western Pakistan. PEJ 1,no.1:109-11 Jul 49

N    Wilson, J S. G. The future of banking in Australia. EJ 59:208-18 Jun 49

### 9.31 HISTORY

EB    Anonymous. The Three banks group. TBR 1:5-14 Mar 49

EB    -- The Royal Bank and the '45. TBR 2: 30-34 Jun 49

EBI    -- The 'Ireland' forgeries. TBR 4:34-39 Dec 49

EB    Ashton, T. S. The bill of exchange and private banks in Lancashire, 1790-1830. EHR 15:25-35 no.1-2, 45

ASC    Brayer, H. O. Boom town banker: Central City, Colorado, 1880. BHR 19:67-95 Jun 45

   Bromberg, B. Temple banking in Rome. EHR 10:128-31 Nov 40

   -- The origin of banking: religious finance in Babylonia. JEH 2:77-88 May 42

EB    Cope, S. R. The original security bank. Ec N.S.13:50-55 Feb 46

E    De Roover, F. E. Francesco Sassetti and the downfall of the Medici banking house. BHR 17:65-80 Oct 43

E    De Roover, R. The Medici Bank: organization and management. JEH 6:24-52 May 46

E    -- The Medici Bank: financial and commercial operations. JEH 6:153-72 Nov 46

E    -- The decline of the Medici Bank. JEH 7: 69-82 May 47

AA    Hammond, B. Banking in the early West: monopoly, prohibition, and laissez faire. JEH 8:1-25 May 48

EA    Helleiner, K. F. Deposit banking in Mediterranean Europe. CJE 12:214-18 May 46

EBW    Hodges, T. M. Early banking in Cardiff. EHR 18:84-90 no.1-2, 48

EB    Horsefield, J. K. The duties of a banker. Pt.I-II. Ec N.S.8:37-51; 11:74-85 Feb 41, May 44

EB    -- The cash ratio in English banks before 1800. JPE 57:70-74 Feb 49

AA    Lake, W. S. The end of the Suffolk system [New England]. JEH 7:183-207 Nov 47

A    Mellon, T. Selections from the autobiography of Thomas Mellon. Pt.I-II. BHR 18:145-54; 19:12-26 Dec 44, Feb 45

EA    Postan, M. M. Early banking. R. EHR 16: 63-67 no.1, 46

ECB    Redlich, F. Banking in mediaeval Bruges. R. BHR 23:109-12 Jun 49

E    Sapori, A. The Medici Bank. BNL 2: 195-210 Oct-Dec 49

ASP    Schwartz, A. J. The beginning of competitive banking in Philadelphia, 1782-1809. JPE 55:417-31 Oct 47

ASP    Tooker, E. C. A merchant turns to money-lending in Philadelphia. BHR 20:71-85 Jun 46

### 9.32 ASSETS AND LIABILITIES

A    Beckhart, B. H. Monetary policies and commercial bank portfolios. AER/S 30: 17-26 Mar 40

A    Cooke, H. J. M. Significance of bank capital ratios. JPE 57:75-77 Feb 49

9.3 COMMERCIAL BANKS (Cont.)
9.32 ASSETS AND LIABILITIES (Cont.)

A    Dunkman, W. E. Postwar commercial bank lending policies. JF 4:87-100 Jun 49

A    Ebersole, J. F. Protecting bank bond investments. HBR 18:410-16 no.4, 40

A    Froman, L. A. The adequacy of bank equities. JF 2,no.2:22-30 Oct 47

A    Hartwell, J. M., Jr. Interest rates by loan size and geographical region. JASA 42: 242-45 Jun 47

A    Jacoby, N. H. Government loan agencies and commercial banking. AER/S 32: 250-60 Mar 42

A    Machlup, F. Bank deposits and the stock market in the cycle. AER/S 30:83-91 Mar 40

EI    Mancini, M. Bank credits in Italy, classified by business branches and bank groups (1936-1946). BNL 1:184-96 Oct 47

A    Mors, W. P. Commercial banks and competitive trends in consumer instalment financing. JB 21:133-67 Jul 48

EB    Muller, C. British war finance and the banks. JB 16:77-99 Apr 43

A    Ostrolenk, B. A note on Mr. Silverstein's article [followed by N. L. Silverstein's reply and Ostrolenk's rejoinder]. JB 13: 420-23 Oct 40

ESD    Philip, K. A statistical measurement of the liquidity preference of private banks. REStud 16:71-77 no.2, 49

A    Prochnow, H. V. Bank liquidity and the new doctrine of anticipated income. JF 4: 298-314 Dec 49

EI    Rienzi, E. The distribution of share capital of Italian banking companies. BNL 1: 10-19 Apr 47

ASN    Rivel, R. B. Industrial composition of the business loans of the Chase National Bank, 1940-47. JB 22:50-59 Jan 49

A    -- The use of average maturity in the analysis of commercial bank investments. JF 4:342-47 Dec 49

A    Robinson, R. I. Bank capital and dividend policies. HBR 26:398-409 Jul 48

A    Seligman, H. L. The problem of excessive commercial bank earnings. QJE 60: 365-89 May 46

A    Silverstein, N. L. Some considerations on the management of commercial bank investments. JB 13:136-45 Apr 40

A    Smith, T. and Hengren, R. E. Bank capital: the problem restated. JPE 55:553-66 Dec 47

A    Willis, J. B. Postwar changes in commercial bank investments in U.S. government securities. JF 4:140-55 Jun 49

9.4 FINANCIAL INTERMEDIARIES
9.40 GENERAL

A    Jacoby, N. H. Government loan agencies and commercial banking. AER/S 32: 250-60 Mar 42

A    Jones, H. Investment prospects. JF 2, no.1:15-33 Apr 47

A    -- The optimum rate of investment, the savings institutions, and the banks. AER/S 38:321-39 May 48

A    -- The flow of savings. Pt.I-II. JF 3,no.3: 1-26; 4:28-46 Oct 48, Mar 49

A    Mann, F. K. The dual-debt system as a method of financing government corporations. JPE 55:39-56 Feb 47

ASC    Wendt, P. F. The availability of capital to small business in California in 1945-1946. JF 2,no.2:43-54 Oct 47

9.41 HISTORY

ASM    Anonymous. A note on marine insurance in Salem [Massachusetts]. BHR 14:30-32 Apr 40

EF    Arndt, H. W. Savings in a state with a stationary population: comment. QJE 62: 623-28 Aug 48

E    De Roover, F. E. Early examples of marine insurance. JEH 5:172-200 Nov 45

EF    Goldenberg, L. Savings in a state with a stationary population. QJE 61:40-65 Nov 46

A    Hazard, W. H. Marketing life insurance: its history in America. R. BHR 16: 1-7 Feb 42

EB    Hidy, R. W. The organization and functions of Anglo-American merchant bankers, 1815-1860. JEH/S 1:53-66 Dec 41

EB    Hodges, T. M. The history of the Newport and Caerleon Savings Bank (1830-1888). EHR II.2:188-99 no.2, 49

EB    James, F. G. Charity endowments as sources of local credit in seventeenth- and eighteenth-century England. JEH 8: 153-70 Nov 48

ASM    McCann, H. The business papers of Emerson Cole [of Minnesota]. BHR 14: 81-86 Dec 40

   Manes, A. Outlines of a general economic history of insurance. JB 15:30-48 Jan 42

EI    Nelson, B. N. The usurer and the merchant prince: Italian businessmen and the ecclesiastical law of restitution, 1100- 1550. JEH/S 7:104-22 '47

   Shackell, R. S. A short historical note on the marine policy. SAJE 17:306-19 Sep 49

ESp    Smith, R. S. Life insurance in fifteenth- century Barcelona. JEH 1:57-59 May 41

EB    Walker, C. H. Unincorporated investment trusts in the nineteenth century. EH 4: 341-55 Feb 40

## 9. MONEY, CREDIT, AND BANKING

### 9.42 SAVINGS BANKS. SAVINGS AND LOAN ASSOCIATIONS

Arndt, E. H. D. The building society move-
HSA  ment in the Union. SAJE 11:185-97
Sep 43

-- Pre-Union building society legislation.
HSA  SAJE 16:133-56 Jun 48

-- Building societies in South Africa.
HSA  SAJE 17:503-10 Dec 49

Ballaine, W. C. New England mutual sav-
AA  ings bank laws as interstate barriers to
the flow of capital. AER 35:155-59
Mar 45

Cooke, G. W. Savings deposits in mutual
A  and nonmutual banks, 1911-40. JB 16:
195-203 Jul 43

Greene, F. T. Significant post-depression
A  changes in savings and loan practices.
LE 16:30-36 Feb 40

Gregory, P. M. The mortgage portfolio of
A  mutual savings banks. QJE 61:232-66
Feb 47

Harold, G. The savings and loan associa-
A  tion as a refuge for trust funds. JB 15:
166-83 Apr 42

Moos, S. Building societies and building
EB  finance. OIS 7:149-59 Jun 30, 45

Schjander, F. Norwegian savings banks
ESN  and the state of the money market dur-
ing and after the war. SAJE 15:73-77
Mar 47

Steiner, W. H. The New York Mutual Sav-
ASN  ings Banks Fund. JPE 52:74-79 Mar 44

Strunk, N. The improved investment posi-
A  tion of savings and loan associations.
JF 2,no.2:1-21 Oct 47

Welfling, W. Some characteristics of sav-
ASN  ings deposits [in New York]. AER 30:
748-58 Dec 40

### 9.43 INSURANCE COMPANIES

Agarwala, A. N. The need for the study of
insurance finance. IJE 21:204-06 Oct 40

Alam, M. Insurance in U.S.S.R. PEJ 1,
ER  no.2:48-50 Oct 49

Berry, T. S. On measuring the cost of life
A  insurance. JASA 35:631-43 Dec 40

Campbell, G. C. Problems with sampling
procedures for reserve valuations.
JASA 43:413-27 Sep 48

Edmunds, S. The limits of the market for
A  ordinary life insurance. JM 11:117-28
Oct 46

-- Outlets for life insurance investment.
A  HBR 25:409-31 no.4, 47

Fulcher, G. S. Life insurance saving of
A  American families. REStat 26:93-94
May 44

Geren, P. The contribution of life insurance
A  to the savings stream. JPE 51:33-51
Feb 43

Hazard, W. H. The literature of life insur-
A  ance. HBR 19:123-32 no.1, 40

Johnson, R. B. The cost of legal reserve
A  life insurance. SEJ 8:351-65 Jan 42

Ketchum, M. D. Can life insurance companies use formula plans? JB 22:30-49
Jan 49

Lang, F. Insurance research. JM 12:66-71
Jul 47

McDiarmid, F. J. Life company investments
A  and the capital markets. JASA 43:265-73
Jun 48

-- Current trends in institutional invest-
A  ments. JF 4:119-28 Jun 49

Magee, J. H. The future of the commercial
A  insurance business. HBR 21:321-35
no.3, 43

Manes, A. Insurable hazards. JB 14:1-10
Jan 41

Nerlove, S. H. Common stocks as invest-
A  ments for American life insurance com-
panies: a non-academic view, I-II.
JF 3,no.3:39-51; 4:60-77 Oct 48, Mar 49

Parry, C. L. European insurance com-
E  panies and real estate: with particular
reference to housing. LE 16:294-305
Aug 40

Sawa, S. The organization of insurance
FJ  pools in Japan. Kyo 15,no.1:60-67
Jan 40

Stewart, M. C. Industrial assurance.
EB  OIS 5,suppl.4:18-24 Feb 20, 43

Tousaw, A. A. Taxation problems of life
C  insurance. CJE 6:440-47 Aug 40

### 9.45 INVESTMENT COMPANIES

Bosland, C. C. The Investment Company
A  Act of 1940 and its background. Pt.I-II.
JPE 49:477-529; 687-721 Jun,Oct 41

Carter, W. D. Mutual investment funds.
HBR 27:715-40 Nov 49

### 9.46 AGRICULTURAL CREDIT INSTITUTIONS UNITED STATES

Banfield, E. C. Ten years of the farm
A  tenant purchase program. JFE 31:
469-86 Aug 49

Benedict, M. R. The relation of public to
private lending agencies (in agriculture)
and recent trends in their development.
JFE 27:88-103 Feb 45

--, chairman. The federally sponsored
credit services to American agriculture;
suggestions for improvement and coordination. A report of a research committee [followed by discussion]. JFE 29:
1429-1516 Nov 47

Black, J. D. Agricultural credit policy in
the United States, 1945. JFE 27:591-614
Aug 45

-- The future of government in the farm
mortgage field. LE 23:1-11 Feb 47

Brinser, A. and Wheeler, R. G. Farm
planning as a basis for extending agricultural credit. JFE 30:243-58 May 48

## 9.46 AGRICULTURAL CREDIT INSTITUTIONS (Cont.)

### UNITED STATES (Cont.)

A  Burroughs, R. J.  Mortgage insurance for farm housing. JFE 27:676-82 Aug 45

Engberg, R. C.  Risks in agricultural lending [with discussion]. JFE 31,pt.2: 602-19 Feb 49

Horton, D. C.  Insurance aspects of extra-risk mortgage loans. JFE 23:855-66 Nov 41

Huston, J. M.  How can delinquent loans and foreclosed properties best be serviced and handled? JFE 22:277-84 Feb 40

Johnson, E. C.  What elements enter into a desirable resale policy? JFE 22: 285-91 Feb 40

Norton, L. J.  When and under what conditions should a mortgage on a farm be foreclosed? JFE 22:270-76 Feb 40

Pritchard, N. T.  Pricing of production credit to farmers. JFE 30:588-91 Aug 48

Stewart, C. E.  Can sufficient private credit be obtained for FHA insured farm real estate loans? JFE 30:561-66 Aug 48

AA  King, J. J.  FSA group services in the Pacific Northwest. HBR 22:475-76 no.4, 44

ASS  Fite, G. C.  South Dakota's rural credit system: a venture in state socialism, 1917-1946. AH 21:239-49 Oct 47

### OTHER COUNTRIES

ER  Katkoff, V.  Financing of agriculture in Russia. JFE 22:640-46 Aug 40

FI  Krishnaswami, A.  Rural credit. IJE 22: 908-32 Apr 42

Rao, A.  Loans and their classification. IJE 22:615-23 Jan 42

ME  Amer, A.  Agricultural and co-operative credit in Egypt. EgC 39:345-48 Mar 48

## 9.47 INDUSTRIAL DEVELOPMENT BANKING. MERCANTILE CREDIT INSTITUTIONS

A  Cross, J. S.  The volume and significance of mercantile credit. JM 14:391-98 Oct 49

A  Edwards, G. W.  The myth of the security affiliate. JASA 37:225-32 Jun 42

C  Fergusson, D. A.  The Industrial Development Bank of Canada. JB 21:214-29 Oct 48

A  Potter, A.  The financing of a product from producer to consumer: an important subject for research in the field of marketing. JM 10:66-67 Jul 45

A  Zinner, S. M.  The contribution of commercial receivable companies and factors to financing small- and medium-sized business. JF 2,no.1:76-90 Apr 47

## 9.48 HOUSING CREDIT INSTITUTIONS. MORTGAGE MARKET

A  Ashley, E. E., 3rd.  Government housing activities. HBR 19:230-42 no.2, 41

ESD  Bager, R.  A comparison of the respective conditions on which social and private building enterprises may be granted government loans. NTTO 12:23-30 no.37, 48

A  Grebler, L.  The home mortgage structure in transition. HBR 18:357-71 no.3, 40

A  -- Stabilizing residential construction: a review of the postwar test. AER 39: 898-910 Sep 49

A  Gregory, P. M.  Imperfect competition in the mortgage market. SEJ 10:275-91 Apr 44

A  -- An appraisal of mortgage advertising. HBR 23:32-45 no.1, 44

A  Hoyt, H.  The effect of cyclical fluctuations upon real estate finance. JF 2,no.1: 51-64 Apr 47

A  Husband, W. H.  Interest rates for home financing. AER 30:272-84 Jun 40

A  -- Loan terms and the rate of interest for home financing. LE 17:39-47 Feb 41

A  Kaplan, M.  A method of analyzing the elements of foreclosure risk. JASA 37: 247-55 Jun 42

A  Lintner, J.  Our tremendous mortgage debt. HBR 27:88-106 Jan 49

A  McFarland, C.  An economic evaluation of FHA's property improvement program. LE 23:399-416 Nov 47

A  Moore, W. H.  State experiments in mortgage lending. JB 22:169-77 Jul 49

E  Parry, C. L.  European insurance companies and real estate: with particular reference to housing. LE 16:294-305 Aug 40

A  Pease, R. H.  Today's real estate market. HBR 26:385-97 Jul 48

ASN  Posner, L. S.  The lesson of guaranteed mortgage certificates. HBR 26:560-71 Sep 48

A  Smith, R. S.  A method of comparing home-mortgage financing costs. JM 9:386-88 Apr 45

A  -- A note on mortgage loan interest. LE 24:185-86 May 48

A  Stoner, P. M.  The mortgage market: today and after World War I. LE 19: 224-30 May 43

A  Thompson, D. S.  Nonfarm real estate finance. JF 2,no.1:34-50 Apr 47

-- --- [idem] LE 23:105-16 May 47

A  Tierney, J. L.  "Fair value" and the deficiency judgment. LE 16:181-95 May 40

A  Weimer, A. M.  Federal inducements for small-house construction. LE 16: 101-02 Feb 40

A  Westerfield, R. B.  Amortization of mortgage premiums. LE 20:316-29 Nov 44

# 9. MONEY, CREDIT, AND BANKING

## 9.5 SECURITY AND MONEY MARKETS
### 9.50 GENERAL

EB  Morgan, E. V.  The future of interest rates.  EJ 54:340-51 Dec 44

Westerfield, R. B., chairman.  The future of interest rates.  Abstract of specialized conference discussion.  AER/S 32: 217-26 Mar 42

### 9.51 HISTORY

EB  Cope, S. R.  The Goldsmids and the development of the London money market during the Napoleonic wars.  Ec N.S.9: 180-206 May 42

A  Garvy, G.  Rivals and interlopers in the history of the New York security market.  JPE 52:128-43 Jun 44

EB  Gayer, A. D.; Jacobson, A.; and Finkelstein, I.  British share prices, 1811-1850.  REStat 22:78-93 May 40

A  Hammond, B.  The Chestnut Street raid on Wall Street, 1839.  QJE 61:605-18 Aug 47

EB  Hidy, R. W.  Cushioning a crisis in the London money market.  BHR 20:131-45 Nov 46

EF  Redlich, F.  Jacques Laffitte and the beginnings of investment banking in France.  BHR 22:137-61 Dec 48

### 9.52 SECURITY MARKETS
#### 9.520 GENERAL

A  Abbott, C. C.  The availability of new equity capital.  AER/S 32:129-40 Mar 42

A  --, chairman.  The changing outlook for investment banking.  Abstract of specialized conference discussion.  AER/S 32: 212 Mar 42

A  Brodie, H.  Odd-lot trading on the New York Stock Exchange and financial decentralization.  SEJ 6:488-97 Apr 40

A  Cherrington, H. V.  National Association of Securities Dealers.  HBR 27:741-59 Nov 49

Cowles, A.  Stock market forecasting.  Em 12:206-14 Jul-Oct 44

EI  Federici, L.  Causes of the decline in the stock exchange in Italy.  BNL 2:211-24 Oct-Dec 49

A  Hubbard, J. B.  Industrial bond and preferred stock refundings, 1933-1937 REStat 22:17-44 Feb 40

A  -- Nonrefunding security flotations and capital structures.  REStat 25:192-201 Aug 43

HSA  Lurie, R.  The company promotion boom in South Africa 1933-38: an analysis of new Johannesburg stock exchange quotations.  SAJE 9:265-73 Sep 41

A  Machlup, F.  Bank deposits and the stock market in the cycle.  AER/S 30:83-91 Mar 40

A  Madden, J. T. and Backman, J.  Public utility holding company common stocks.  JB 13:213-33 Jul 40

EI  Mancini, G.  Aspects and problems of the Italian stock market.  BNL 1:321-37 Apr 48

EB  Murphy, M. E.  The English approach to the distribution of securities.  JB 14: 372-83 Oct 41

A  Robbins, S. M.  Competitive bidding in sale of securities.  HBR 27:646-64 Sep 49

A  Smith, F. P.  Management-trading and stock-market profits.  JB 13:103-17 Apr 40

FC  Tokunaga, K.  Characteristics of the security market in China: its special relations with Chinese native capital.  Kyo 18,no.2:27-47 Apr 43

A  White, H. G., Jr.  Foreign trading in American stock-exchange securities.  JPE 48:655-702 Oct 40

A  Wilcoxen, L. C.  The market forecasting significance of market movements.  JASA 37:343-51 Sep 42

#### 9.521 SECURITY PRICES AND YIELDS

A  Bean, L. H.  Wholesale prices and industrial stock prices during and immediately after the two world wars.  REStat 29: 199-200 Aug 47

A  Benjamin, H. S.  The Dow theory of stock prices.  SR 9:204-24 May 42

A  Brown, B.  Common-stock price ratios and long-term interest rates.  JB 21:180-92 Jul 48

Kamm, J. O.  American security price movements compared to foreign security price movements.  JF 3,no.2:59-70 Jun 48

C  McDougall, J L.  The earning power of Canadian corporate capital, 1934-40.  CJE 8:557-65 Nov 42

A  Myers, J. H. and Bakay, A. J.  Influence of stock split-ups on market price.  HBR 26: 251-55 Mar 48

A  Roos, C. F. and Von Szeliski, V.  The determination of interest rates.  JPE 50: 501-35 Aug 42

Wachtel, S. B.  Certain observations on seasonal movements in stock prices.  JB 15:184-93 Apr 42

#### 9.522 REGULATION OF SECURITY MARKETS

A  Eiteman, W. J.  Security regulation and the volume of new issues.  SEJ 7:27-36 Jul 40

A  Howard, S. E.  The Trust Indenture Act of 1939.  LE 16:168-80 May 40

EG  Schweitzer, A.  Schacht's regulation of money and capital markets.  JF 3,no.2: 1-18 Jun 48

### 9.53 MONEY MARKETS

EB  Kalecki, M.  The 'mysteries' of the money market.  OIS 2,no.8:2-5 Oct 40

## 9.6 PRICES. INFLATION. DEFLATION
## 9.60 GENERAL

Clark, C. Public finance and changes in the value of money. EJ 55:371-89 Dec 45

Cobb, C. W. Price and volume. Em 13: 273-74 Jul 45

Director, A. Does inflation change the economic effects of war? AER/S 30:351-61 Mar 40

Nerlove, S. H. War expansion and price inflation. JB 15:95-130 Apr 42

Youngson, A. J. Inflation and the flight from cash. YB 1:33-42 Sep 49

### UNITED STATES

A Boulding, K. E. Price control in a subsequent deflation. REStat 30:15-17 Feb 48

Davis, J. S. Food prices. (Ten economists on the inflation) REStat 30:8-10 Feb 48

Haberler, G. Causes and cures of inflation. REStat 30:10-14 Feb 48

Harris, S. E. [Ten economists on the inflation.] Introduction. REStat 30:1-3 Feb 48

-- The inflationary process: in theory and recent history. REStat 31:200-10 Aug 49

Heflebower, R. B. Food prices, wage rates, and inflation. REStat 30:27-29 Feb 48

Kalecki, M. Determinants of the increase in the cost of living in the United States. (Ten economists on the inflation) REStat 30:22-24 Feb 48

Lerner, A. P. Rising prices. (Ten economists on the inflation) REStat 30:24-27 Feb 48

Machlup, F. Misconceptions about the current inflation. REStat 30:17-22 Feb 48. Correction. 230 Aug 48

Mills, F. C. Living costs, prices, and productivity. REStat 30:6-8 Feb 48

Rotwein, E. Post-World War I price movements and price policy. JPE 53:234-57 Sep 45

Slichter, S. H. The problem of inflation. REStat 30:3-5 Feb 48

Spengler, J. J. The future of prices. SEJ 13:1-35 Jul 46

Warburton, C. The volume of money and the price level between the World Wars. JPE 53:150-63 Jun 45

Wells, O. V. Significance of the "general price level" and related influences to American agriculture [followed by J. W. Tapp's and F. F. Hill's further comments]. JFE 31,pt.2:779-99 Nov 49

ASM Cobb, C. W. Employment and relative inflation in Massachusetts. Em 12:130-38 Apr 44

### OTHER AMERICAN COUNTRIES

C Buck, H. Means of payment and prices in Canada, 1900-46. CJE 13:197-207 May 47

MacGregor, D. C. The problem of price level in Canada. CJE 13:157-96 May 47

D Pazos, F. Inflation and exchange instability in Latin America. AER/S 39:396-405 May 49

DSB Spiegel, H. W. A century of prices in Brazil. REStat 30:57-62 Feb 48

### EUROPE

E Steindl, J. The problem of inflation in continental Europe. OIS 7:279-86 Nov 24, 45

EB Carter, C. F. British public finance and the progress of inflation. PF 4:28-48 no.1, 49

EH Winklé, F. F. Some aspects of the recent inflation and stabilization of the Hungarian currency. SAJE 15:178-91 Sep 47

EI Ceriani, L. Survey of the Italian monetary situation. BNL 1:121-34 Jul 47

Grampp, W. D. The Italian lira, 1938-45. JPE 54:309-33 Aug 46

Hirschman, A. O. Inflation and deflation in Italy. AER 38:598-606 Sep 48

Pietranera, G. Considerations on the dynamics of the Italian inflation. BNL 1: 20-52 Apr 47

-- Note about the "Survey of current inflationary and deflationary tendencies" prepared by the United Nations Department of Economic Affairs. BNL 1: 260-63 Jan 48

### ASIA

FC Huang, A. C. The inflation in China. QJE 62:562-75 Aug 48

Li, C. M. Inflation in wartime China. REStat 27:23-33 Feb 45

Matsuoka, K. The inflation of Chinese legal tender. Kyo 16,no.2:22-43 Apr 41

FI Ady, P. Inflation in India. OIS 6:9-16 Jan 15, 44

Bose, S. R. Some investigations in banking, currency and prices. IJE 24:20-37 Jul 43

Geren, P. The role of velocity of circulation in the present rise of prices. IJE 24:99-116 Oct 43

Kulkarni, N. K. Inflation and Indian monetary policy. IJE 30:175-84 Oct 49

Raturi, A. S. Liquidity preference, price movements, and deposits of Indian joint stock banks. IJE 27:85-89 Jul 46

Zacharias, C. W. B. Inflation and monetary policy with special reference to India. IJE 30:185-92 Oct 49

FIP Barari, B. Inflation in Pakistan and the way out. PEJ 1,no.2:12-24 Oct 49

FJ Kurihara, K. K. Post-war inflation and fiscal-monetary policy in Japan. AER 36: 843-54 Dec 46

### AFRICA

HSA Van der Horst, S. T. Inflation in South Africa: some comments on the annual address of the Governor of the Reserve Bank. SAJE 12:238-40 Sep 44

9. MONEY, CREDIT, AND BANKING

9.6 PRICES. INFLATION. DEFLATION (Cont.)
9.60 GENERAL (Cont.)
AFRICA (Cont.)
Van Waasdijk, T. Some notes on price in-
HSA  flation in South Africa 1938-1948. Pt.I-II.
SAJE 17:252-73; 380-415 Sep,Dec 49

MIDDLE EAST
Craig, J. I. The general rise of prices in
ME   Egypt. EgC 32:1-56 Jan-Feb 41

9.61 HISTORY
Hamilton, E. J. War and inflation in
ESp  Spain, 1780-1800. QJE 59:36-77 Nov 44
-- Use and misuse of price history.
JEH/S 4:47-60 Dec 44
Kristensson, R. The consequences of errors
ES   in accounting due to inflation 1914-18.
EH 4:371-83 Feb 40
Michell, H. The impact of sudden acces-
E    sions of treasure upon prices and real
wages. CJE 12:1-17 Feb 46
Mitchell, W. C. The role of money in eco-
nomic history. JEH/S 4:61-67 Dec 44
Niebyl, K. H. A reexamination of the classi-
EB   cal theory of inflation. AER 30:759-73
Dec 40
Woodcock, F. The price of provisions and
EB   some social consequences in Worcester-
shire in the eighteenth and nineteenth
centuries. JRSS 106:268-72 pt.3, 43
Working, H. War and commodity prices.
JASA 35:309-24 Jun 40

9.7 PORTFOLIO SELECTION
9.70 GENERAL
Cottle, C. S. Factors to be considered in
appraising formula plans. SEJ 16:62-79
Jul 49
Dulan, H. A. Common-stock investment as
an inflation hedge, 1939-46. JB 21:
230-38 Oct 48
Eiteman, W. J. Current investment tenden-
A    cies: discussion. JF 4:176-79 Jun 49
Hall, J. P. Current tendencies in college
A    investments. JF 4:129-39 Jun 49
Ketchum, M. D. Investment management
through formula timing plans. JB 20:
156-69 Jul 47
-- Adjustment for the secular trend of
stock prices in formula timing plans.
JB 21:29-49 Jan 48
Morrison, P. L. Trends in investment
A    policies of individuals. JF 4:156-76
Jun 49
Solomon, E. Are formula plans what they
seem to be? JB 21:92-97 Apr 48
Wallich, H. C. Effect of taxation on invest-
A    ment. HBR 23:442-50 no.4, 45
Weston, J. F. Some theoretical aspects of
formula timing plans. JB 22:249-70
Oct 49
Wilsey, H. L. The Investment Advisers Act
A    of 1949. JF 4:286-97 Dec 49

9.8 CONSUMER FINANCE
9.80 GENERAL
Cragg, A. Streamlined shopping credit.
JB 15:21-29 Jan 42
Dauer, E. A. Radical changes in industrial
banks. HBR 25:609-24 no.4a, 47

UNITED STATES
Blackburn, B. Can we avoid consumer
A    credit indigestion? [with discussion by
A. Haring]. JM 4,no.4,pt.2:100-10 Apr 40
Clark, L. Credit unions in the United
States. JB 16:235-46 Oct 43
-- The credit-union legal framework.
JB 17:51-66 Jan 44
Croteau, J. T. The credit union: legal
form versus economic function. RSE 7,
no.2:10-28 Sep 49
Foster, W. T. Consumer credit charges
after the war. JB 17:16-22 Jan 44
Grimes, W. H. Distribution and the finance
company. HBR 18:199-206 no.2, 40
Hagios, J A. Credit terms as an element
in merchandising competition. JM 4,
no.4,pt.2:70-78 Apr 40
Lorenz, O. C. Consumer credit costs:
what are they and who pays them.
JM 4,no.4,pt.2:79-88 Apr 40
Merriam, M. L. Influence of retail credit
upon the continuity of demand. JM 4,
no.4,pt.2:89-99 Apr 40
Mors, W. Rate regulation in the field of
consumer credit. Pt.I-II. JB 16:51-63;
124-37 Jan,Apr 43
-- Commercial banks and competitive
trends in consumer instalment financing.
JB 21:133-67 Jul 48
Neifeld, M. R. and Robichaud, A. E.
Lenders exchanges in the personal finance business. JM 4:268-73 Jan 40
-- Consumer credit: impact of the war.
JM 7:342-44 Apr 43
Phelps, C. W. Monopolistic and imperfect
competition in consumer loans. JM 8:
382-93 Apr 44
Robinson, R. I. The downward course of
consumer credit. JM 7:345-49 Apr 43
Schmaltz, C. N. Retail credit in the postwar
world. HBR 22:63-74 no.1, 43
Upton, M. Expanded cooperation between
commercial banks and finance companies
in financing consumer credits. JF 2,
no.2:55-67 Oct 47
Shapiro, E. Experience with reductions in
ASW  the small-loan rate in Wisconsin. JB 18:
209-18 Oct 45
-- Liquidation record of Wisconsin credit
unions. JB 19:82-98 Apr 46
-- The wartime experience of Wisconsin
credit unions. JB 20:201-11 Oct 47

9.8 CONSUMER FINANCE (Cont.)
9.80 GENERAL (Cont.)
ASIA
Gopal, M. H. An enquiry into indebtedness
FI    in a Mysore village. IJE 23:1-23 Jul 42
Srikantan, K. S. Indebtedness of the mill
worker. IJE 21:184-92 Oct 40

9.81 HISTORY
De Roover, R. The three golden balls of
the pawnbrokers. BHR 20:117-24
Oct 46

9.9 MONETARY POLICY. CENTRAL BANKS
9.90 GENERAL
Bopp, K. R. Central banking at the cross-
roads. AER/S 34:260-77 Mar 44
Ellis, H. S. Monetary policy and investment. AER/S 30:27-38 Mar 40
Fellner, W. Monetary policy and the elasticity of liquidity functions. REStat 30:
42-44 Feb 48
Graham, F. D. The primary functions of
money and their consummation in monetary policy. AER/S 30:1-16 Mar 40
Kriz, M. A. Central banks and the State
today. AER 38:565-80 Sep 48
Poduval, R. N. Monetary policy and the
trade cycle. IJE 24:192-201 Jan 44
Poindexter, J. C. A critique of functional
finance through quasi-free bank credit.
AER 36:311-23 Jun 46
-- Professors Pritchard and Benoit-Smullyan on bank-financed functional deficits:
a reply. AER 38:391-94 Jun 48
Pritchard, L. J. The nature of bank credit:
a comment. AER 37:399-402 Jun 47
Rao, B. R. S. Recent developments in cen-
tral bank technique. IJE 20:587-98
Apr 40
Rao, T. S. Easy money policy. IJE 20:
557-65 Apr 40
Robinson, R. I. Central banks and the state:
a comment. AER 39:494-96 Mar 49
Westerfield, R. B. [and others] The objec-
tives of monetary policy: discussion.
AER/S 30:39-43 Mar 40

UNITED STATES
Abbott, C. C. Governmental activity in the
A     financial field. BHR 20:51-56 Apr 46
-- Notes on Federal Reserve policy, August,
1945-June, 1948. JF 4:101-10 Jun 49
Bach, G. L. Bank supervision, monetary
policy, and governmental reorganization.
JF 4:269-85 Dec 49
-- The Federal Reserve and monetary
policy formation. AER 39:1173-91
Dec 49
Beckhart, B. H. Monetary policies and com-
mercial bank portfolios. AER/S 30:
17-26 Mar 40
Bell, J. W. Domestic and international

monetary policies. A summary of the
discussion of the results of a poll.
AER/S 36:214-40 May 46
-- Report of ad hoc Committee on Monetary
Policy. AER/S 36:807-16 May 46
Coleman, G. W. The effect of interest rate
increases on the banking system.
AER 35:671-73 Sep 45
Goldenweiser, E. A. Federal Reserve ob-
jectives and policies: retrospect and
prospect. AER 37:320-38 Jun 47
Hardy, C. O. Federal Reserve System
report for 1945. R. HBR 25:207-12
no.2, 47
Harris, S. E. A one per cent war? AER 35:
667-71 Sep 45
Link, A. S. The Federal Reserve policy
and the agricultural depression of
1920-1921. AH 20:166-75 Jul 46
Palyi, M. Interest rates in the managed
economy. LE 18:28-35 Feb 42
Preston, H. H. [and others] Banking problems: discussion. AER/S 37:289-98
May 47
Rosa, R. V. Some small business problems
indicated by the industrial loan experience of the Federal Reserve Bank of
New York. JF 2,no.1:91-100 Apr 47
Samuelson, P. A. The effect of interest
rate increases on the banking system.
AER 35:16-27 Mar 45
-- The turn of the screw. [The effect of
interest rate increases on the banking
system] AER 35:674-76 Sep 45
Saulnier, R. J. Institutional changes affect-
ing the exercise of monetary controls.
RSE 5:19-34 Jun 47
-- and Wills, J. H. Postwar monetary and
credit policies: discussion. JF 4:110-18
Jun 49
Sayers, R. S. Central banking in the light
of recent British and American experi-
ence. QJE 63:198-211 May 49
Sproul, A. Monetary management and
credit control. AER 37:339-50 Jun 47
Thomas, W. The heritage of war finance.
AER/S 37:205-15 May 47
Tobin, J. Liquidity preference and monetary policy. REStat 29:124-31 May 47
Warburton, C. Monetary velocity and
monetary policy [followed by J. Tobin's
rejoinder]. REStat 30:304-17 Nov 48
-- Monetary policy and business forecasting. Pt.I-II. JB 22:71-82; 178-87
Apr,Jul 49
Whittlesey, C. R. Federal Reserve policy
in transition. QJE 60:340-50 May 46
Williams, J. H. The implications of fiscal
policy for monetary policy and the banking system. AER/S 32:234-49 Mar 42
Willis, J. B. The case against the maintenance of the wartime pattern of yields
on government securities. AER/S 37:
216-27 May 47

# 9. MONEY, CREDIT, AND BANKING

## 9.9 MONETARY POLICY. CENTRAL BANKS (Cont.)

### 9.90 GENERAL (Cont.)

#### EUROPE

Dacey, W. M. The cheap money technique.
EB     LBR 3:49-63 Jan 47

    Paish, F. W. Cheap money policy.
    Ec N.S.14:167-79 Aug 47

    Robertson, D. H. What has happened to the rate of interest? TBR 1:15-31 Mar 49

    Sayers, R. S. Central banking in the light of recent British and American experience. QJE 63:198-211 May 49

    McQueen, R. Central banking in the
EBC   Dominions. R. CJE 6:599-610 Nov 40

    Borgatta, G. Interest rate policy and re-
EI    construction requirements. BNL 1:407-15 Oct 48

    Federici, L. Six months of Italian economic policy. BNL 1:246-59 Jan 48

    Gambino, A. Recent developments in banking activity in Italy. BNL 1:109-20 Jul 47

    Mancini, M. The banking year 1947 in Italy. BNL 1:381-89 Jul 48

    Miller, H. S. Italian monetary and exchange policies under fascism. AER 30:554-60 Sep 40

#### ASIA

    Anantaram, K. Limitations of cheap money
FI    policy. IJE 28:383-87 Jan 48

    Basu, S. K. Some aspects of cheap money policy. IJE 28:371-75 Jan 48

    Bhattacharya, K. N. Stabilisation of prices: an aspect of the post-war currency system in India. IJE 26:404-09 Jan 46

    Chand, G. The post-war monetary issues in India. IJE 26:472-87 Jan 46

    Dalal, K. N. Cheap money. IJE 28:377-82 Jan 48

    Dhar, B. Cheap money policy. IJE 28:95-103 Jul 47

    Iyengar, S. K. Central banking in Hyderabad. EJ 53:274-80 Jun-Sep 43

    -- Post-war currency system in India. IJE 26:499-507 Jan 46

    Kulkarni, N. K. Inflation and Indian monetary policy. IJE 30:175-84 Oct 49

    Malhotra, P. C. [Monetary policy of India]: discussion. IJE 20:822-23 Apr 40

    Misra, H. Cheap money and its place in the postwar economy of India. IJE 28:89-93 Jul 47

    Paranjpe, V. M. Cheap money policy. IJE 28:83-88 Jul 47

    Pillai, V. R. Post-war Indian monetary policy. IJE 26:392-403 Jan 46

    Poduval, R. N. Cheap money policy in India. IJE 28:365-69 Jan 48

    Rao, B. S. Cheap money policy. IJE 28:67-74 Jul 47

    Sahasrabudhe, V. G. Post-war monetary system for India. IJE 26:554-64 Jan 46

    -- Cheap money policy in free India. IJE 28:75-81 Jul 47

    Simha, S. L. N. The future of cheap money. IJE 28:113-20 Jul 47

    Sitaramayya, M. Cheap money policy. IJE 28:105-12 Jul 47

    Vaswani, M. H. Cheap money policy. IJE 28:61-66 Jul 47

    Zacharias, C. W. B. Inflation and monetary policy with special reference to India. IJE 30:185-92 Oct 49

    Ahmed, S. State Bank of Pakistan: its
FIP   constitution and functions. PEJ 1,no.1:102-08 Jul 49

    Khan, A. A. The State Bank of Pakistan. PEJ 1,no.1:96-101 Jul 49

#### MIDDLE EAST

    Berger, A. V. Consistent reflation in
ME   Egypt and the high costs of living. EgC 38:177-85 Mar-Apr 47

    El Falaki, M. S. Post-war planning of currency and the monetary market in Egypt. EgC 35:187-204 Jan-Feb 44

#### AUSTRALIA. NEW ZEALAND

    Simkin, C. G. F. The nationalization of the
N   Bank of New Zealand. ER 22:228-40 Dec 46

    Wilson, J. S. G. Australia's central bank. JPE 55:28-38 Feb 47

### 9.91 HISTORY

#### UNITED STATES

    Brown, K. L. Stephen Girard, promoter of
A   the second Bank of the United States. JEH 2:125-48 Nov 42

    Hammond, B. Jackson, Biddle, and the Bank of the United States. JEH 7:1-23 May 47

    Walters, R., Jr. The origins of the second Bank of the United States. JPE 53:115-31 Jun 45

    Wettereau, J. O. The branches of the first Bank of the United States. JEH/S 2:66-100 Dec 42

#### EUROPE

    Bopp, K. R. The Bank of England. R.
EB   CJE 11:616-27 Nov 45

    Clapham, J. H. The private business of the Bank of England, 1744-1800. EHR 11:77-89 no.1, 41

    Fetter, F. W. The Bullion report reexamined. QJE 56:655-65 Aug 42

    Horsefield, J. K. The Bank and its treasure. Ec N.S.7:161-78 May 40

    -- The origins of the Bank Charter Act, 1844. Ec N.S.11:180-89 Nov 44

    -- The bankers and the bullionists in 1819. JPE 57:442-48 Oct 49

## 9.9 MONETARY POLICY. CENTRAL BANKS (Cont.)
## 9.91 HISTORY (Cont.)
### EUROPE (Cont.)
Horsefield, J. K. (Cont.)
-- The Bank of England as mentor. EHR II. 2:80-87 no.1, 49

King, W. T. C. The Bank of England. R. EHR 15:67-72 no.1-2, 45

Viner, J. Clapham on the Bank of England. R. Ec N.S.12:61-68 May 45

Whale, P. B. A retrospective view of the Bank Charter Act of 1844. Ec N.S.11: 109-11 Aug 44

ESp Hamilton, E. J. The foundation of the Bank of Spain. JPE 53:97-114 Jun 45
-- The first twenty years of the Bank of Spain. Pt.I-II. JPE 54:17-37; 116-40 Feb,Apr 46
-- Spanish banking schemes before 1700. JPE 57:134-56 Apr 49
-- Plans for a national bank in Spain, 1701-83. JPE 57:315-36 Aug 49

### ASIA
FC Tokunaga, K. The first phase of the Bank of China as a note-issuing bank. Kyo 16, no.1:32-48 Jan 41

## 9.92 TOOLS OF MONETARY POLICY
## 9.921 RESERVE REQUIREMENTS
Brown, H. G. Objections to the 100 per cent reserve plan. AER 30:309-14 Jun 40

Graham, F. D. 100 per cent reserves: comment. AER 31:338-40 Jun 41

Higgins, B. Comments on 100 per cent money. AER 31:91-96 Mar 41

Riddle, J. H. and Reierson, R. L. An analysis of the certificate reserve plan. JF 1:27-51 Aug 46

Seltzer, L. H. The problem of our excessive banking reserves. JASA 35:24-36 Mar 40

Simmons, E. C. Treasury deposits and excess reserves. JPE 48:325-43 Jun 40

Thomas, R. G. 100 per cent money: the present status of the 100 per cent plan. AER 30:315-23 Jun 40

Villard, H. H. The problem of bank-held government debt: comment. AER 37: 936-37 Dec 47

Whittlesey, C. R. Reserve requirements and the integration of credit policies. QJE 58:553-70 Aug 44

Willis, J B. Secondary reserve requirements. JF 3,no.2:29-44 Jun 48

## 9.922 REDISCOUNTS AND REDISCOUNT RATE
Hartkemeier, H. P. Seasonal variation in the volume of bills discounted. Em 12: 125-29 Apr 44

## 9.924 SELECTIVE CONTROLS
Matherly, W. J. The regulation of consumer credit. SEJ 11:34-44 Jul 44

Mors, W. Rate regulation in the field of consumer credit. Pt.I-II. JB 16:51-63; 124-37 Jan,Apr 43

Nugent, R. Post-war-delivery installment sales and government controls. JM 7: 350-53 Apr 43

Simmons, E. C. The role of selective credit control in monetary management. AER 37:633-41 Sep 47

## 9.925 OTHER TOOLS
Mikesell, R. F. Gold sales as an anti-inflationary device. REStat 28:105-08 May 46

Tew, B. The direct control of interest rates. ER 23:198-205 Dec 47

## 9.93 MONETARY ASPECTS OF PUBLIC DEBT MANAGEMENT
A Abbott, C. C. Management of the federal debt. HBR 24:96-108 no.1, 45

A -- The commercial banks and the public debt. AER/S 37:265-76 May 47

A Aldrich, W. W. The management of the public debt. JF 4:1-12 Mar 49

Benoit-Smullyan, E. Interest-free deficit financing and full employment. AER 37: 397-99 Jun 47

A Bernstein, P. L. Federal Reserve policy and federal debt: a comment. AER 39: 1278-81 Dec 49

Carr, H. C. The problem of bank-held government debt. AER 36:833-42 Dec 46

A Chandler, L. V. Federal Reserve policy and the federal debt. AER 39:405-29 Mar 49

A Dolley, J. C. Ability of the banking system to absorb government bonds. JPE 51: 23-31 Feb 43

A Hansen, A. H. [How to manage the national debt.] Comments on the symposium. REStat 31:30-32 Feb 49

A Harris, S. E. [How to manage the national debt.] Introduction. REStat 31:15-17 Feb 49

A Leland, S. E. Management of the public debt after the war. AER/S 34,no.2: 89-132 Jun 44

A -- The government, the banks and the national debt. JF 1:5-26 Aug 46

EI Mancini, M. The Italian money market and the financing of the Treasury. BNL 1: 100-08 Jul 47

A Musgrave, R. A. Debt management and inflation. REStat 31:25-29 Feb 49

A Ratchford, B. U. The monetary effects of public debts. PF 4:5-16 no.1, 49

A Reinhardt, H. The great debt redemption, 1946-1947. SR 15:170-93 Jun 48

## 9.93 MONETARY ASPECTS OF PUBLIC DEBT MANAGEMENT (Cont.)

Riddle, J. H. and Reierson, R. L. An
A   analysis of the certificate reserve plan.
JF 1:27-51 Aug 46

Seltzer, L. H. [Management of the public
A   debt after the war]: discussion.
AER/S 34:134-38 Jun 44

-- [and others] The public debt: effects on
A   institutions and income: discussion.
AER/S 37:192-204 May 47

-- Notes on managing the public debt.
A   REStat 31:17-21 Feb 49

Simmons, E. C. Federal Reserve policy
A   and the national debt during the war
years. JB 20:84-95 Apr 47

Simons, H. C. On debt policy. JPE 52:
356-61 Dec 44

-- Debt policy and banking policy.
REStat 28:85-89 May 46

Smith, D. T. [Management of the public
A   debt after the war]: discussion.
AER/S 34,no.2:133-34 Jun 44

Villard, H. H. The problem of bank-held
government debt: comment. AER 37:
936-37 Dec 47

Wallich, H. C. Debt management as an instrument of economic policy. AER 36:
292-310 Jun 46

## 9.94 DEPOSIT INSURANCE

Ihlefeld, A. Reducing the bank deposit in-
A   surance premium. HBR 27:438-48 Jul 49

O'Leary, J. J. Should federal deposit in-
A   surance be extended? SEJ 10:41-51 Jul 43

## 9.95 BANK REGULATION AND SUPERVISION

Jones, H. An appraisal of the rules and pro-
A   cedures of bank supervision, 1929-39.
JPE 48:183-98 Apr 40

Pillai, V. R. Regulation of joint-stock bank-
FI   ing in India. IJE 24:355-60 Apr 44

Quantius, F. The insurance of bank loans
A   and its implications. JB 19:133-44 Jul 46

Robinson, R. I. The capital-deposit ratio
A   in banking supervision. JPE 49:41-57
Feb 41

Sailor, V. L. Bank supervision and the bus-
A   iness cycle. JF 3,no.3:65-77 Oct 48

Sengupta, S. Banking reform, with special
FI   reference to the draft bank bill proposed
by the Reserve Bank of India. IJE 24:
361-67 Apr 44

Trefftzs, K. L. The regulation of loans to
A   executive officers of commercial banks.
JPE 50:377-96 Jun 42

Watkins, L. L., chairman. Round table on
A   banking reform through supervisory
standards. AER/S 30:230-40 Mar 40

# 10. PUBLIC FINANCE

## 10.0 GENERAL

Buchanan, J. M. The pure theory of government finance: a suggested approach.
JPE 57:496-505 Dec 49

Clark, C. Public finance and changes in the
value of money. EJ 55:371-89 Dec 45

Colm, G. Why public finance? NTJ 1:
193-206 Sep 48

Gordon, N. N. The second session of the
United Nations Fiscal Commission.
NTJ 2:166-72 Jun 49

Houghton, D. H. Changing emphasis in
public finance. SAJE 15:60-67 Mar 47

Hudson, P. G. Principles of economics
prerequisite to courses in public finance.
AER 30:582 Sep 40

Koed, H. Some aspects of the rationalization of public administration. NTTO 12:
157-65 no.37, 48

Mann, F. K. Re-orientation through fiscal
theory. Kyk 3:116-29 fasc.2, 49

Mills, M. C. Principles and practice in
public finance. AER 31:101 Mar 41

Parrish, J. B. "Principles of economics
prerequisite to courses in public
finance": a rejoinder. AER 31:102
Mar 41

Somers, H. M. The impact of fiscal policy
on national income. CJE 8:364-85
Aug 42

UNITED STATES

Abbott, C. C. Administration of fiscal
A   policy. HBR 23:46-64 no.1, 44

Colm, G. Fiscal problems of transition
and peace: discussion. AER/S 35:
352-53 May 45

Crum, W. L. Postwar federal expenditures
and their implications for tax policy.
AER/S 35:329-40 May 45

Fairchild, F. R. The federal financial
system. AER 31:280-97 Jun 41

Goode, R. Federal finances in 1948.
NTJ 2:71-87 Mar 49

Maxwell, J. A. Fiscal program of the 80th
Congress. HBR 26:63-73 Jan 48

Mills, M. C. American government finance
1930-1940. SAJE 9:361-78 Dec 41

Upgren, A. R. Fiscal problems of transition and peace: discussion. AER/S 35:
353-54 May 45

Wueller, P. H. Public finance: trends and
issues. HBR 19:248-60 no.2, 41

10.0 GENERAL (Cont.)
OTHER COUNTRIES

Maxwell, J. A. On some appendices to the
C    Rowell-Sirois report: VI. Public finance.
CJE 7:244-49 May 41

George, C. O. British public finance in
EB    peace and war [with discussion].
JRSS 104:235-80 pt.3, 41

Kaldor, N. The Beveridge report. II. The
financial burden. EJ 53:10-27 Apr 43

Shiomi, S. The taxation system of China.
FC    Kyo 17,no.4:1-26 Oct 42

Iyengar, S. K. "British" & "Indian" finance.
FI    IJE 21:830-70 Apr 41

Joshi, T. M. Some economic and financial
problems of the transition from war to
peace. IJE 25:224-35 Jan 45

Lokanathan, P. S. The economics of
Gokhale. IJE 22:225-34 Jan 42

Thomas, P. J. "The growth of federal
finance." IJE 21:210 Oct 40

Wood, G. L. Federal finance in India. R.
ER 17:106-09 Jun 41

Sadie, J. L. Public finance and the business
HSA  cycle in South Africa, 1910-1940.
SAJE 14:132-60 Jun 46

King, H. W. The New Zealand government
N    finances, 1945-46; 1946-47; 1947-48;
1947-48 [i.e. 1948-49]. ER 22:293-98;
23:271-74; 24:254-56; 25,(no.49):97-99
Dec 46, Dec 47, Dec 48, Dec 49

Neale, E. P. The New Zealand government
finances, 1945-46 [i.e. 1944-45]. ER 21:
256-61 Dec 45

10.01 BUDGETS AND BUDGET ADMINISTRA-
TION

Colm, G. From estimates of national income to projections of the nation's
budget. SR 12:350-69 Sep 45

-- The government budget and the nation's
economic budget. PF 3:5-14 no.1, 48

Marchal, J. The state and its budget: from
the budget of the patrimonial state to the
budget of the Faustian state. PF 3:23-34
no.1, 48

Maxwell, J. A. The capital budget. QJE 57:
450-65 May 43

UNITED STATES

Anonymous. Federal budget on performance
A    basis. NTJ 2:284 Sep 49

Burkhead, J. The outlook for federal
budget-making. NTJ 2:289-99 Dec 49

Burrows, D. S. A program approach to
federal budgeting. HBR 27:272-85 May 49

Copeland, M. A. The capital budget and the
war effort. AER 33:38-49 Mar 43

Ensley, G. W. A budget for the nation.
SR 10:280-300 Sep 43

Gaston, H. E. The government as a business: a consideration of budget problems
in relation to the general welfare. SR 7:
434-46 Nov 40

Leiserson, A. Coordination of federal
budgetary and appropriations procedures
under the Legislative Reorganization
Act of 1946. NTJ 1:118-26 Jun 48

Mann, F. K. A fiscal testament of the New
Deal. PF 2:244-48 no.3, 47

Welcker, J. W. The Federal budget: a
challenge to businessmen. HBR 22:
431-42 no.4, 44

OTHER COUNTRIES

Balls, H. R. The development of govern-
C    ment expenditure control: the issue and
audit phases. CJE 10:464-75 Nov 44

Balogh, T. The budget: B. The budget
EB    proposals and technical progress.
OIS 6:104-07 May 20, 44

-- Reflections on the budget. OIS 7:253-62
Nov 3, 45

Carter, C. F. The structure of the British
budget 1947. PF 2:336-47 no.4, 47

-- The British budget, April 1948. PF 3:
231-34 no.3, 48

-- Problems of British public finance in
1949. PF 4:313-20 no.4, 49

Steindl, J. The budget and reconstruction.
OIS 8:121-29 May 46

Kozák, J. Czechoslovak budget economy
ECC  after the war. PF 3:329-46 no.4, 48

M., G. E. Italy's state budget, 1945-48.
EI    BNL 2:48-69 Jan-Mar 49

Tinbergen, J. Government budget and cen-
EN    tral economic plan. PF 4:195-99 no.3, 49

Haensel, P. Soviet finances. PF 1:38-51
ER    no.1, 46

Simkin, C. G. F. Budgetary reform [in
ES    Sweden]. ER 17:192-209 Dec 41

Roman, A. China's first post-war budget.
FC    PF 2:354-62 no.4, 47

Ali, A. Pakistan budgets: general and
FIP  provincial. PEJ 1,no.1:117-25 Jul 49

Simkin, C. G. F. Budgetary reform for
N    New Zealand. ER 18:16-30 Jun 42

10.02 STATE AND LOCAL FINANCE

Rao, K. V. The scope of local finance.
IJE 22:832-36 Jan 42

UNITED STATES

Gilbert, D. W. Cycles in municipal finance.
A    REStat 22:190-202 Nov 40

Morgan, H. D. Financing of state veterans'
bonuses. NTJ 1:233-40 Sep 48

Taylor, C. T. Population increase, municipal outlays, and debts. SEJ 9:327-34
Apr 43

Heer, C. State and local finance in the post-
AA  war plans of the South. SEJ 11:246-54
Jan 45

Ratchford, B. U. Public finances in the
southern region of the United States.
NTJ 1:289-310 Dec 48

# 10. PUBLIC FINANCE

## 10.02  STATE AND LOCAL FINANCE (Cont.)

### UNITED STATES (Cont.)

Davies, E. J.  The Louisiana Property Tax
ASL   Relief Fund: a source of financial assistance for local governments.  NTJ 1:
270-72 Sep 48

### OTHER COUNTRIES

Stewart, A. and Hanson, E. J.  Some aspects
CPA   of rural municipal finance.  CJE 14:
481-90 Nov 48

Macpherson, L. G.  Report of the Royal
CPM   Commission on the Municipal Finances
and Administration of the City of Winni-
peg, 1939.  CJE 6:68-72 Feb 40

Iyengar, S. K.  A note on the working of the
FI   departmentalisation scheme of finances
in Hyderabad State during eighteen years.
IJE 23:24-45 Jul 42

Joshi, T. M.  The "depression finance" of
the Bombay government.  IJE 21:605-17
Apr 41

Krishnamurthy, G. N.  Finances of district
boards in Mysore.  IJE 22:837-48 Jan 42

Madan, B. K.  Financial problems under
provincial autonomy.  IJE 21:689-702
Apr 41

Malhotra, D. K.  Finance of local bodies in
the Punjab.  IJE 22:933-45 Apr 42

Misra, S.  Five years of Orissa budget.
IJE 21:634-47 Apr 41

Narayanaswamy Naidu, B. V.  Finances of
the Madras Province, 1920-40.  IJE 21:
881-91 Apr 41

-- A review of Madras local finance.
IJE 22:637-48 Jan 42

Poduval, R. N.  Travancore finances during
the last decade.  IJE 23:68-79 Jul 42

Qureshi, A. I.  A note on the financial system of Hyderabad.  IJE 21:668-77 Apr 41

-- The new budget of Hyderabad.  IJE 25:
169-72 Oct 44

Rao, B. R. S.  State in relation to local
finance in Mysore.  IJE 22:649-57 Jan 42

Rao, T. S.  Reorganization of local finance
in India.  IJE 22:677-88 Jan 42

Rohatgi, B. N.  Some aspects of provincial
finance.  IJE 21:678-88 Apr 41

Seth, B. R.  Public revenue and expenditure
in the United Provinces 1921-41.
IJE 21:804-18 Apr 41

Srinivasamurthy, A. P.  Some aspects of
village panchayet finance in Mysore
State since 1927.  IJE 22:849-62 Jan 42

Srivastava, D. P.  Some aspects of municipal finance in Bihar.  IJE 22:667-76
Jan 42

Thomas, P. J.  The finances of Indian states.
IJE 21:819-29 Apr 41

Akhtar, S. M.  Pakistan's provincial finance:
FIP   West Punjab.  PEJ 1,no.2:1-11 Oct 49

Randall, R. J.  Municipal enterprise.  R.
HSA   SAJE 8:117-28 Jun 40

Rose-Innes, N. and Chambers, R. D.  Report of the Provincial Financial Resources Committee.  R.  SAJE 12:
263-78 Dec 44

## 10.03  INTERGOVERNMENTAL RELATIONS

Hicks, U. K.  National and local finance.
EJ 56:609-22 Dec 46

Wood, G. L.  Power or palsy in the federation?  R.  ER 23:90-95 Jun 47

-- Financial systems in federations.  R.
ER 24:235-37 Dec 48

### UNITED STATES

Blakey, R. G., chairman.  Co-ordination of
A   federal, state, and local fiscal systems.
Abstract of specialized conference dis-
cussion.  AER/S 32:214-15 Mar 42

B[lough], R.  Federal-state fiscal relations.
NTJ 1:273-74 Sep 48

Chatters, C. H.  The economic classification of cities and its fiscal implications.
NTJ 1:111-17 Jun 48

Cornell, F. G.  Grant-in-aid apportionment
formulas.  JASA 42:92-104 Mar 47

Martin, J. W.  Should the federal government tax state and local bond interest?
SEJ 8:323-35 Jan 42

Studenski, P.  Federal grants-in-aid.
NTJ 2:193-214 Sep 49

Tucker, R. H.  Some aspects of intergovernmental tax exemption.  SEJ 6:273-90
Jan 40

Armstrong, K. P.  Effect of federal owner-
ASD   ship of real estate upon local self-
government in the District of Columbia.
NTJ 2:343-48 Dec 49

### OTHER COUNTRIES

Birch, A. H.  Federalism and finance.
C   MS 17:163-85 May 49

Lutz, H. L.  The Canadian Royal Commission on Dominion-Provincial Relations.
JPE 49:111-16 Feb 41

Maxwell, J. A.  Canadian dominion-provincial relations.  QJE 55:584-610 Aug 41

Osborne, R. G. and Walker, E. R.  Federalism in Canada.  ER 16:245-59 Dec 40

Hicks, J. R. and Hicks, U. K.  The Beveridge
EB   plan and local government finance.
REStud 11:1-19 no.1, 43

Hicks, U. K.  The grant provisions of the
local government bill.  OIS 10:33-52
Feb 48

Ghosh, H.  Review of finances in Bengal
FI   (1937-41).  IJE 21:569-93 Apr 41

Maxwell, J. A.  The recent history of the
N   Australian Loan Council.  CJE 6:22-38
Feb 40

Moffat, R. E.  Financial relations between
the Australian Commonwealth and the
Australian states.  CJE 13:465-79 Aug 47

Wood, G. L.  The future of federal aid.
ER 21:197-211 Dec 45

## 10.1 HISTORY

EB Bromberg, B. The financial and administrative importance of the Knights Hospitallers to the English crown. EH 4:307-11 Feb 40

EB Lennard, R. The origin of the fiscal carucate. EHR 14:51-63 no.1, 44

Marchal, J. The state and its budget: from the budget of the patrimonial state to the budget of the Faustian state. PF 3: 23-34 no.1, 48

EB Wren, M. C. The Chamber of London in 1633. EHR II.1:46-53 no.1, 48

## 10.2 FISCAL POLICY FOR ECONOMIC STABILIZATION AND GROWTH
## 10.20 GENERAL

A Bowen, H. R. [and others] Federal expenditure and revenue policy for economic stability. [Statement drafted at a conference called by the National Planning Association, and adopted by those attending.] AER 39:1263-68 Dec 49

EB Carter, C. F. British public finance and the progress of inflation. PF 4:28-48 no.1, 49

Chamberlain, N. W. Professor Hansen's fiscal policy and the debt [followed by A. H. Hansen's note]. AER 35:400-10 Jun 45

Clark, J. M. Hansen's "Three methods of expansion through fiscal policy": comment [followed by A. H. Hansen's comment]. AER 35:926-28 Dec 45

EB Dacey, W. M. The budget, overseas borrowing and domestic investment. LBR 9:34-51 Jul 48

A De Vegh, I. Savings, investment, and consumption. AER/S 30,no.5:237-47 Feb 41

A Domar, E. D. The "burden of debt" and the national income. AER 34:798-827 Dec 44
-- --- A rejoinder. AER 35:414-18 Jun 45

A Dowling, E. The business of government. S&S 9:193-213 no.3, 45

A Galbraith, J. K. [and others] Problems of timing and administering fiscal policy in prosperity and depression: discussion. AER/S 38:443-51 May 48

Griffith, E. C. Deficit financing and the future of capitalism. SEJ 12:130-40 Oct 45

A Hagen, E. E. The problem of timing fiscal policy. AER/S 38:417-29 May 48

A Haley, B. F. The Federal budget: economic consequences of deficit financing. AER/S 30,no.5:67-87 Feb 41

Hansen, A. H. Three methods of expansion through fiscal policy. AER 35:382-87 Jun 45

Hardy, C. O. Fiscal policy and the national income. R. AER 32:103-10 Mar 42

A -- Fiscal operations as instruments of economic stabilization. AER/S 38:395-403 May 48

Hart, A. G. "Model-building" and fiscal policy. AER 35:531-58 Sep 45
-- National budgets and national policy: a rejoinder. AER 36:632-36 Sep 46

A -- Timing and administering fiscal policy: how to give relevant counsel. AER/S 38: 430-42 May 48

Howenstine, E. J., Jr. Some principles of compensatory action. QJE 61:165-68 Nov 46

Lerner, A. P. Functional finance and the federal debt. SR 10:38-51 Feb 43

MacGibbon, D. A. Fiscal policy and business cycles. R. CJE 9:77-82 Feb 43

Melville, L. G. Economics of new orders. ER 18:143-57 Dec 42

Mosak, J. L. National budgets and national policy. AER 36:20-43 Mar 46
-- --- A final reply. AER 36:637-41 Sep 46

Moulton, H. G. D. McC. Wright's character attack [followed by D. McC. Wright's reply and Moulton's rejoinder]. AER 34: 116-21 Mar 44

Musgrave, R. A. Alternative budget policies for full employment. AER 35:387-400 Jun 45
-- and Miller, M. H. Built-in flexibility. AER 38:122-28 Mar 48

A -- Fiscal policy in prosperity and depression. AER/S 38:383-94 May 48

Paranjpe, V. M. National budgets and economic planning. IJE 29:117-24 Oct 48

Pierson, J. H. G. The underwriting of aggregate consumer spending as a pillar of full-employment policy. AER 34: 21-55 Mar 44

Poduval, R. N. Budgeting for full employment. IJE 29:125-30 Oct 48

A Ratchford, B. U. Mr. Domar's "Burden of the debt." AER 35:411-14 Jun 45

A -- The monetary effects of public debts. PF 4:5-16 no.1, 49

A Salant, W. S. [and others] Fiscal policy in prosperity and depression: discussion. AER/S 38:404-16 May 48

A Seltzer, L. H. Direct versus fiscal and institutional factors [in deficit financing]. AER/S 30,no.5:99-107 Feb 41

EB Shackle, G. L. S. The deflative or inflative tendency of government receipts and disbursements. OEP 8:46-64 Nov 47

Shiomi, S. Economic fluctuations and public finance. Kyo 16,no.1:1-17 Jan 41

A Simons, H. C. Hansen on fiscal policy. R. JPE 50:161-96 Apr 42

A Smith, D. T. Economic consequences of deficit financing: a review. AER/S 30, no.5:88-98 Feb 41

A Smithies, A. The impact of the federal budget. REStat 29:28-31 Feb 47

Tirumalachar, B. Deficit financing. IJE 20: 567-86 Apr 40

# 10. PUBLIC FINANCE

## 10.2 FISCAL POLICY FOR ECONOMIC STABILIZATION AND GROWTH (Cont.)

### 10.20 GENERAL (Cont.)

Tyndall, D. G. A suggestion for the control of peacetime inflation. JF 4:315-27 Dec 49

Wald, H. P. Fiscal policy, military preparedness, and postwar inflation. NTJ 2: 51-62 Mar 49

A     Williams, J. H. Deficit spending. AER/S 30,no.5:52-66 Feb 41

Wright, D. M. Moulton's The new philosophy of public debt. R. AER 33:573-90 Sep 43

### 10.201 UNDERDEVELOPED COUNTRIES

FI   Balakrishna, R. Budgetary scope for planning in Madras. IJE 29:109-16 Oct 48

FI   Bhattacharya, K. N. Stabilisation of prices: an aspect of the post-war currency system in India. IJE 26:404-09 Jan 46

FI   -- Budgets and planning in India. IJE 29: 131-34 Oct 48

FI   Cirvante, V. R. Post-war planning and budgetary policy in India. IJE 29:147-54 Oct 48

FI   Ghosh, M. K. Inflation: a possible remedy. IJE 23:371-72 Apr 43

FI   -- Control of inflation. IJE 24:73-75 Jul 43

FI   Misra, B. Can the government of India finance a plan at present? IJE 29:243-47 Jan 49

### 10.21 HISTORY

A     Havens, R. M. Reactions of the federal government to the 1837-1843 depression. SEJ 8:380-90 Jan 42

### 10.22 FISCAL POLICY AND THE MULTIPLIER

Arndt, H. W. Public finance and the national income. ER 24:243-45 Dec 48

Gehrels, F. Inflationary effects of a balanced budget under full employment. AER 39:1276-78 Dec 49

Goodwin, R. M. Multiplier effects of a balanced budget: the implication of a lag for Mr. Haavelmo's analysis. Em 14: 150-51 Apr 46

Haavelmo, T. Multiplier effects of a balanced budget. Em 13:311-18 Oct 45

-- ---- Reply. Em 14:156-58 Apr 46

Haberler, G. Multiplier effects of a balanced budget: some monetary implications of Mr. Haavelmo's paper. Em 14: 148-49 Apr 46

Hagen, E. E. Multiplier effects of a balanced budget: further analysis. Em 14: 152-55 Apr 46

Norris, H. Fiscal policy and the propensity to consume: a note. EJ 56:316-18 Jun 46

Rosa, R. V. A multiplier analysis of armament expenditure. AER 31:249-65 Jun 41

Samuelson, P. A. Fiscal policy and income determination. QJE 56:575-605 Aug 42

Somers, H. M. The multiplier in a tri-fiscal economy. QJE 63:258-72 May 49

Sumberg, T. A. Leakage problems in flexible taxation. JPE 55:572-75 Dec 47

Wallich, H. C. Income-generating effects of a balanced budget. QJE 59:78-91 Nov 44

Williams, R. S., Jr. Fiscal policy and the propensity to consume. EJ 55:390-97 Dec 45

## 10.3 PUBLIC EXPENDITURE

### 10.30 GENERAL

A     Ballaine, W. C. How government purchasing procedures strengthen monopoly elements. JPE 51:538-46 Dec 43

Baumol, W. J. Notes on the theory of government procurement. Ec N.S.14:1-18 Feb 47

FI   Gopal, M. H. Public expenditure in Mysore: a review. IJE 21:594-604 Apr 41

A     Howenstine, E. J., Jr. Public works program after World War I. JPE 51:523-37 Dec 43

A     -- An inventory of public construction needs. AER 38:353-66 Jun 48

A     Johnson, V. W. and Timmons, J. F. Public works on private land. JFE 26:665-84 Nov 44

--; Timmons, J. F. and Howenstine, E. J., Jr. Rural public works. Pt.I-II. LE 23: 12-21; 132-41 Feb,May 47

AA   Macon, H. L. War and postwar developments in state expenditures for the Southeast. SEJ 15:30-42 Jul 48

Maisel, S. J. Timing and flexibility of a public works program. REStat 31:147-52 May 49

A     Miller, J. P. Military procurement in peacetime. HBR 25:444-62 no.4, 47

C     Urquhart, M. C. Public investment in Canada. CJE 11:535-53 Nov 45

### 10.301 EXPENDITURE POLICY FOR STABILIZATION AND GROWTH

Anderson, C. J. The development of the pump-priming theory. JPE 52:144-59 Jun 44

-- The compensatory theory of public works expenditure. JPE 53:258-74 Sep 45

Benoit-Smullyan, E. Public works in the depression. AER 38:134-39 Mar 48

Bratt, E. C. Timing pump-priming expenditure. AER 31:97-98 Mar 41

Hahn, L. A. Compensating reactions to compensatory spending. AER 35:28-39 Mar 45

A     Howenstine, E. J., Jr. Dovetailing rural public works into employment policy. REStat 28:165-69 Aug 46

A     -- Public works policy in the twenties. SR 13:479-500 Dec 46

10.3  PUBLIC EXPENDITURE (Cont.)
10.301  EXPENDITURE POLICY FOR STABILI-
ZATION AND GROWTH (Cont.)

Hutt, W. H.  A critique of the first Report
HSA  of the Social and Economic Planning
Council. SAJE 11:48-62 Mar 43

-- Public works and reconstruction. [Reply
HSA  to J. N. Reedman] SAJE 11:198-209
Sep 43

McLeod, A. N.  The financing of employment-maintaining expenditures. AER 35:
640-45 Sep 45

Margolis, J.  Public works and economic
stability. JPE 57:293-303 Aug 49

Reedman, J. N.  Public works and employ-
HSA  ment: a note on Professor Hutt's critique
of the first Report of the Social and Economic Planning Council. SAJE 11:152-57
Jun 43

Samuelson, P. A.  The theory of pump-
priming reëxamined. AER 30:492-506
Sep 40

Simkin, C. G. F.  Economic planning and the
N   N.Z. Ministry of Works. ER 23:103-07
Jun 47

Strayer, P. J.  Public expenditure policy.
A   AER 39:383-404 Mar 49

10.32  SUBSIDIES

Balogh, T.  The finance of scientific & ap-
EB  plied research. OIS 6:1-7 Jan 15, 44

Harris, S. E.  Subsidies and inflation.
AER 33:557-72 Sep 43

Lowry, R. E.  Municipal subsidies to indus-
AST  tries in Tennessee. SEJ 7:317-29 Jan 41

Maclaurin, W. R.  Federal support for sci-
A   entific research. HBR 25:385-96 no.3, 47

Morgan, C. S.  Aspects of the problem of
A   public aids to transportation. AER/S 30:
130-39 Mar 40

Pigou, A. C.  The food subsidies. EJ 58:
EB  202-09 Jun 48

10.4  TAXATION AND OTHER REVENUE
10.40  GENERAL

Benham, F.  "The taxation of war wealth."
R. Ec N.S.8:321-24 Aug 41

-- What is the best tax-system? Ec N.S.9:
115-26 May 42

Ciriacy-Wantrup, S. v.  Taxation and the
conservation of resources. QJE 58:
157-95 Feb 44

Dowsett, W. T.  The tax lag myth. ER 20:
214-17 Dec 44

Flood, M. M.  Recursive methods in business-cycle analysis. Em 8:333-53 Oct 40

Hicks, U. K.  The terminology of tax analysis. EJ 56:38-50 Mar 46

Jaszi, G. and Musgrave, R. A.  Taxation of
war wealth. R. CJE 8:260-72 May 42

Musgrave, R. A. and Painter, M. S.  The impact of alternative tax structures on personal consumption and saving. QJE 62:
475-99 Aug 48

Ruml, B.  Tax policies for prosperity.
AER/S 36:265-74 May 46

-- --- [idem] JF 1:81-90 Aug 46

Warburton, C.  A suggestion for post-war
taxes. AER 36:882-91 Dec 46

Wueller, P. H. [and others]  Problems of
taxation: discussion. AER/S 32:102-11
Mar 42

UNITED STATES

Anderson, W.  [Economic research and tax
A   policy]: discussion. AER/S 34,no.2:
22-24 Jun 44

Anonymous.  Exchange of information for
purposes of federal, state, and local tax
administration (prepared by Bureau of
Internal Revenue). NTJ 2:151-56 Jun 49

Blakey, R. G. and Blakey, G. C.  The two
federal revenue acts of 1940. AER 30:
724-35 Dec 40

-- and Blakey, G. C.  The Revenue act of
1941. AER 31:809-22 Dec 41

Blough, R.  Economic research and tax
policy. AER/S 34,no.2:1-21 Jun 44

Bronfenbrenner, M.  Diminishing returns
in federal taxation. JPE 50:699-717 Oct 42

Brownlee, O. H.  The C.E.D. on federal tax
reform. R. JPE 56:166-72 Apr 48

Butters, J. K.  An appraisal of postwar tax
plans. HBR 23:253-64 no.2, 45

-- Research project: effect of federal
taxes on business. NTJ 1:91-92 Mar 48

Colm, G.  [Revising the postwar federal
tax system]: discussion. AER/S 34,no.2:
39-41 Jun 44

Ferger, W. F.  The role of economics in
federal tax administration. NTJ 1:
97-110 Jun 48

Flanders, R. E.  [Revising the postwar
federal tax system]: discussion.
AER/S 34,no.2:41-43 Jun 44

Gerrish, C. R.  Treasury tax studies.
Pt.I-II. NTJ 1:144-53; 250-60 Jun,Sep 48

Groves, H. M.  Revising the postwar federal tax system. AER/S 34,no.2:27-38
Jun 44

Kuznets, S.  National income and taxable
capacity. AER/S 32:37-75 Mar 42

Martin, J. W.  American taxation and
World War II. PF 4:112-20 no.2, 49

Paul, R. E.  Redesigning federal taxation.
HBR 19:143-50 no.2, 41

Pettengill, R. B.  Division of the tax burden
among income groups in the United States
in 1936. AER 30:60-71 Mar 40

Phelps, O. W.  The Supreme Court and
regulatory taxation. JB 14:99-126
Apr 41

Poole, K. E.  The problem of simplicity in
the enactment of tax legislation, 1920-40.
JPE 49:895-905 Dec 41

Salant, W. S.  [Economic research and tax
policy]: discussion. AER/S 34,no.2:
24-26 Jun 44

# 10. PUBLIC FINANCE

**10.4 TAXATION AND OTHER REVENUE (Cont.)**
**10.40 GENERAL (Cont.)**

### UNITED STATES (Cont.)

Shoup, C. Three plans for post-war taxa-
A     tion. AER 34:757-70 Dec 44

### OTHER AMERICAN COUNTRIES

Tousaw, A. A. Taxation problems of life
C     insurance. CJE 6:440-47 Aug 40
Sherwood, W. T. Tax administration in
DM    Mexico. NTJ 2:63-70 Mar 49

### EUROPE

Balogh, T. and Burchardt, F. Taxation in
EB    the transition period. OIS 7:163-73
     Jul 21, 45
Edelberg, V. Flexibility of the yield of
     taxation: some econometric investiga-
     tions [with discussion]. JRSS 103:153-90
     pt.2, 40
Schwartz, G. L. The significance of fiscal
     statistics [with discussion]. JRSS 105:
     92-114 pt.2, 42
Heller, W. W. Tax and monetary reform in
EG    occupied Germany. NTJ 2:215-31 Sep 49
Newcomer, M. War and postwar develop-
     ments in the German tax system. NTJ 1:
     1-11 Mar 48
Cosciani, C. Italian tax policy. BNL 1:
EI    86-99 Jul 47
     -- A critical examination of the Italian tax
     system. BNL 1:311-20 Apr 48
Louwman, J. Netherlands: survey of the
EN    yield of state finances for the financial
     year 1946. PF 3:180-83 no.2, 48
     -- Tax revenues in the Netherlands in 1946,
     in 1947 and (as far as known) in 1948.
     PF 4:151-59 no.2, 49

### ASIA

Shiomi, S. The taxation system of China.
FC    Kyo 17,no.4:1-26 Oct 42
Malhotra, P. C. Reconstructing the Indian
FI    tax system: some broad considerations.
     IJE 27:250-55 Oct 46
Mundle, A. K. Trend of commerce and its
     effects on tax policy. IJE 28:389-95
     Jan 48
Sriram, P. Tax structure in India. IJE 27:
     264-69 Oct 46
Shavell, H. Postwar taxation in Japan.
FJ    JPE 56:124-37 Apr 48
     -- Taxation reform in occupied Japan.
     NTJ 1:127-43 Jun 48
Shiomi, S. The reform of the tax system.
     Kyo 15,no.2:34-70 Apr 40

### AUSTRALIA. NEW ZEALAND

Groves, H. M. Taxation in Australia and
N    New Zealand. NTJ 2:1-11 Mar 49
Laffer, K. Taxation reform in Australia.
     ER 18:168-79 Dec 42

**10.401 THEORY**

Abbott, C. C. and Zuckert, E. M. Venture
     capital and taxation. QJE 55:667-82
     Aug 41
Ballantine, A. A. Psychological bases for
     tax liability. HBR 27:200-08 Mar 49
Balogh, T. Taxation, risk-bearing and in-
     vestment. OIS 7:181-92 Sep 1, 45
Brown, H. G., chairman. Round table on
     the incidence of taxation. AER/S 30:
     241-46 Mar 40
Chambers, S. P. Taxation and incentives.
     LBR 8:1-12 Apr 48
Due, J. F. Ad valorem and specific taxes.
     QJE 54:679-85 Aug 40
Fagan, E. D. Tax shifting in the market
     period. AER 32:72-86 Mar 42; Correc-
     tion. 356 Jun 42
Fasiani, M. Tax distribution and Pareto's
     law in a recent theoretical study. R.
     EI 2:469-91 Mar 49
Ferger, W. F. The measurement of tax
     shifting: economics and law. QJE 54:
     429-54 May 40
Groves, H. M. Neutrality in taxation.
     NTJ 1:18-24 Mar 48
Henderson, A. The case for indirect taxa-
     tion. EJ 58:538-53 Dec 48
Higgins, B. Post-war tax policy. Pt.I-II.
     CJE 9:408-28; 532-56 Aug,Nov 43
Holden, G. Incidence of taxation as an
     analytical concept. AER 30:774-86
     Dec 40
Kendrick, M. S. Comment on Incidence of
     taxation. AER 31:110 Mar 41
Kuznets, S. National income and taxable
     capacity. AER/S 32:37-75 Mar 42
Mann, F. K. The threefold economic func-
     tion of taxation. PF 2:5-15 no.1-2, 47
Mehta, J. K. Taxation of monopoly. IJE 25:
     124-29 Oct 44
Nelson, R. W. How dead is the benefit
     theory? AER 30:117-18 Mar 40
Poduval, R. N. The economic effects of
     taxes. IJE 24:117-25 Oct 43
Pritchard, L. J. The effects of specific
     and ad valorem taxes. QJE 58:149-52
     Nov 43
Shephard, R. W. A mathematical theory of
     the incidence of taxation. Em 12:1-18
     Jan 44
Shirras, G. F. Methods of estimating the
     burden of taxation [with discussion].
     JRSS 106:214-49 pt.3, 43
Slitor, R. E. The measurement of progres-
     sivity and built-in flexibility. QJE 62:
     309-13 Feb 48
Studenski, P. Toward a theory of business
     taxation. JPE 48:621-54 Oct 40
Wald, H. P. The classical indictment of in-
     direct taxation. QJE 59:577-96 Aug 45

## 10.402 TAX POLICY FOR STABILIZATION AND GROWTH

Blum, W. J. Tax policy in a democratic society. NTJ 2:97-109 Jun 49

Clark, C. Public finance and changes in the value of money. EJ 55:371-89 Dec 45

Colm, G. Full employment through tax policy? SR 7:447-67 Nov 40

Gilbert, D. W. Taxation and economic stability. QJE 56:406-29 May 42

Hart, A. G. Use of flexible taxes to combat inflation. AER 32:87-102 Mar 42

Higgins, B. Post-war tax policy. Pt.I-II.
C    CJE 9:408-28; 532-56 Aug,Nov 43

Holt, C. C. Averaging of income for tax purposes: equity and fiscal-policy considerations. NTJ 2:349-61 Dec 49

Hubbard, J. C. Income creation by means of income taxation. QJE 58:265-89 Feb 44

-- The proportional personal-income tax as an instrument of income creation. EJ 59:56-67 Mar 49

Lindholm, R. W. Note on the effect of tax reduction. AER 36:910 Dec 46

Salera, V. Taxation and economic stability. QJE 57:323-25 Feb 43

Samant, D. R. Restrictive tax structure of
FI    the central government. IJE 27:256-63 Oct 46

Tobin, J. Taxes, saving, and inflation.
A    AER 39:1223-232 Dec 49

Wallich, H. C. Effect of taxation on invest-
A    ment. HBR 23:442-50 no.4, 45

## 10.403 STATE AND LOCAL

### UNITED STATES

Bird, F. L. The financial problems of
A    cities. AER/S 32:323-30 Mar 42

Donnahoe, A. S. Measuring state tax burden. JPE 55:234-44 Jun 47

Groves, H. M. Income versus property taxation for state and local governments. LE 22:346-50 Nov 46

Herzel, W. G. State tax legislation in 1947. NTJ 1:79-90 Mar 48

Logsdon, C. S. Taxation with misrepresentation. JM 4,no.4,pt.2:11-16 Apr 40

Macon, H. L. Payments in lieu of state and local taxes. SEJ 8:493-503 Apr 42

Manning, R. E. Burden of state and local taxes in 18 large cities. NTJ 2:173-78 Jun 49

Martin, J. W. State and local taxation in
AA    the Southeast and the war. SEJ 14: 376-86 Apr 48

-- The reorganization of revenue adminis-
ASC    tration in Colorado. SEJ 8:395-97 Jan 42

Williamson, K. M. Connecticut State Tax
ASC    Survey. NTJ 2:371-74 Dec 49

Armstrong, K. P. Effect of federal owner-
ASD    ship of real estate upon local self-gov-

ernment in the District of Columbia. NTJ 2:343-48 Dec 49

Allen, H. K. Illinois Commission studies
ASI    tax problems. NTJ 2:259-71 Sep 49

Borak, A. M. Tax equivalents versus taxes
ASM    of municipal and private utilities in Minnesota. LE 23:381-98 Nov 47

Spaulding, R. C. Pennsylvania amends
ASP    permissive local tax law. NTJ 2:272-77 Sep 49

Cartwright, P. W. Public attitudes toward
ASW    sources of state tax revenues [in the state of Washington]. NTJ 2:368-71 Dec 49

### OTHER COUNTRIES

Abell, A. S. Rural municipal difficulties in
CPA    Alberta. CJE 6:555-61 Nov 40

Clark, R. M. Report of the Commission to
CPN    Investigate Taxation in the City of Fredericton [New Brunswick]. CJE 14: 510-11 Nov 48

Datey, C. D. Municipal taxation in C.P. &
FI    Berar. IJE 22:658-66 Jan 42

Nanjundaiya, K. S. The tax system of Mysore State. IJE 21:648-67 Apr 41

Shiomi, S. The reform of the local tax
FJ    system. [Pt.I-II] Kyo 16,no.3:51-67; no.4:42-57 Jul,Oct 41

Burrows, H. R. [Financial policy of muni-
HSA    cipalities towards Natives.] A comment. SAJE 8:279-81 Sep 40

Randall, R. J. [Financial policy of municipalities towards Natives.] A reply. SAJE 8:282-93 Sep 40

Shepstone, D. G. Some reflections on the financial policy of certain municipalities toward the Natives within their boundaries. A criticism. SAJE 8:264-71 Sep 40

Smith, R. H. [Financial policy of municipalities towards Natives.] A criticiam. SAJE 8:272-78 Sep 40

## 10.41 HISTORY

Honjo, E. Views in the taxation on com-
FJ    merce in the closing days of Tokugawa age. Kyo 16,no.3:1-15 Jul 41

Ike, N. Taxation and landownership in the
FJ    westernization of Japan. JEH 7:160-82 Nov 47

McAnear, B. Mr. Robert R. Livingston's
ASN    reasons against a land tax [in New York State]. JPE 48:63-90 Feb 40

## 10.42 INCOME TAX
## 10.420 GENERAL

Allen, J. E. A fairer income tax. EJ 50: 475-81 Dec 40

Blakey, R. G. The federal income tax, a
A    reply to the review [followed by G. O. May's rejoinder]. JASA 35:698-700 Dec 40

10.42 INCOME TAX (Cont.)

10.420 GENERAL (Cont.)

Eichelgrun, G. Income-tax in British
EBC  colonies. EJ 58:128-32 Mar 48

G[oode], R. Investigation of the Bureau of
A  Internal Revenue. NTJ 1:261-69 Sep 48

Groves, H. M. Personal versus corporate
income taxes. AER/S 36:241-49 May 46

-- --- [idem] JF 1:52-60 Aug 46

Hotelling, H. Income-tax revision as proposed by Irving Fisher [followed by
Fisher's reply]. Em 11:83-94 Jan 43

Johnson, B. L. Income tax deductibility:
A  a reply [followed by H. E. Klarman's
rejoinder]. NTJ 2:88-90 Mar 49

Klarman, H. E. Income tax deductibility.
A  NTJ 1:241-49 Sep 48

Reed, E. W. Coordination of federal and
A  state income taxes. SEJ 15:458-72
Apr 49

Slitor, R. E. The flexibility of income-tax
yield under averaging. JPE 54:266-68
Jun 46

Tibbetts, F. C. The accounting period in
A  federal income taxation. SEJ 7:362-79
Jan 41

Van Sickle, J. V. Reform of the federal
A  taxes on personal and corporate income.
AER 34:847-49 Dec 44

Vickrey, W. The effect of averaging on the
cyclical sensitivity of the yield of the
income tax. JPE 53:275-77 Sep 45

Wasserman, M. J. and Tucker, J. F. The
A  U.S. tax treaty program. NTJ 2:33-50
Mar 49

Welinder, C. On the future of income tax.
NTTO 12:275-81 no.37, 48

10.4201 STATE AND LOCAL

Lasser, J. K. State income tax simplifica-
ASV  tion in Vermont. NTJ 1:62-66 Mar 48

10.421 PERSONAL

Bailey, K. H. The Uniform Income Tax
N  Plan (1942). ER 20:170-88 Dec 44

Barber, E. L. Modifying the federal income
A  tax to promote greater stability of farm
income. JFE 30:331-39 May 48

Booker, H. S. Income tax and incentive to
EB  effort. Ec N.S.12:243-47 Nov 45

Borden, S. Cost of living variations and
A  the personal exemption from the income
tax. NTJ 2:157-65 Jun 49

Bowley, A. L. Pay as you earn. OIS 5:
EB  257-60 Nov 20, 43

Bradley, P. D. Some effects of the personal
income tax. QJE 58:134-40 Nov 43

Carslaw, H. S. Federal and state income
N  tax. ER 17:19-30 Jun 41

-- The uniform income tax in Australia.
N  ER 18:158-67 Dec 42

-- Australian income tax, 1943. ER 19:
N  1-10 Jun 43

-- Australian income tax, 1945. ER 22:
N  40-49 Jun 46

-- The Australian Social Services Contri-
N  bution and Income Tax Acts, 1946-1947.
ER 22:219-27; 23:177-85 Dec 46, Dec 47

Domar, E. D. and Musgrave, R. A. Proportional income taxation and risk-taking.
QJE 58:388-422 May 44

Dowell, A. A. and Toben, G. E. Some eco-
A  nomic effects of graduated income tax
rates on investors in farm capital.
JFE 26:348-58 May 44

Dowsett, W. T. Child endowment and in-
N  come tax exemptions. ER 17:239-47
Dec 41

Farioletti, M. The 1948 audit control pro-
A  gram for federal individual income tax
returns. NTJ 2:142-50 Jun 49

Fisher, I. Rebuttal to Professor Crum and
Mr. Musgrave. [The double taxation of
saving] AER 32:111-17 Mar 42

-- Paradoxes in taxing savings. Em 10:
147-58 Apr 42

Goode, R. Federal tax legislative activities
A  in 1947. NTJ 1:67-78 Mar 48

-- The income tax and the supply of labor.
JPE 57:428-37 Oct 49

Green, A. R. The tax curve. EJ 50:
469-74 Dec 40

Holt, C. C. Averaging of income for tax
A  purposes: equity and fiscal-policy considerations. NTJ 2:349-61 Dec 49

Hood, W. C. Structural changes in the
C  Dominion personal income tax, 1932-49.
CJE 15:220-27 May 49

Hughes, G. E. Postwar changes in individ-
ual income taxes: United States, United
Kingdom, and Canada. NTJ 1:175-83
Jun 48

Hughes, W. J. Income tax allowances for
EB  dependents. EJ 51:502-07 Dec 41

Lent, G. E. Collection of the personal in-
A  come tax at the source. JPE 50:719-37
Oct 42

Martin, J. W. Should the federal govern-
A  ment tax state and local bond interest?
SEJ 8:323-35 Jan 42

Musgrave, R. A. and Thin, T. Income tax
A  progression, 1929-48. JPE 56:498-514
Dec 48

Nicholson, J. L. The changes in income
EB  tax. OIS 7:262-66 Nov 3, 45

Oakes, E. E. The incidence of the general
income tax. AER/S 32:76-82 Mar 42

Paish, F. W. Economic incentive in war-
time. Ec N.S.8:239-48 Aug 41

Sengupta, S. The proposed agricultural in-
FI  come tax in Bengal. IJE 24:212-18
Jan 44

Tucker, R. H. Some aspects of intergovernmental tax exemption. SEJ 6:273-90
Jan 40

10.42  INCOME TAX (Cont.)
10.421  PERSONAL (Cont.)

Vickrey, W.  Some limits to the income
elasticity of income tax yields.
REStat 31:140-44 May 49

White, M. I.  Personal income tax reduction
in a hypothetical contraction. REStat 31:
63-68 Feb 49

C Wilson, J R. M.  Report of the Royal Commission on the taxation of annuities and
family corporations, 1945.  CJE 12:
87-92 Feb 46

10.422  BUSINESS
10.4220  GENERAL

Blakey, R. G.  Post-war tax policy: discussion.  AER/S 36:275-79 May 46
-- --- [idem] JF 1:76-80 Aug 46

Boulding, K. E.  The incidence of a profits
tax.  AER 34:567-72 Sep 44

Bowen, H. R.  The incidence of the corpo-
ration income tax: a reply [followed by
R. Goode's rejoinder].  AER 36:146-48
Mar 46

Bradley, P. D.  The direct effects of a
corporate income tax.  QJE 56:638-54
Aug 42

Brown, E. C.  Pay-as-you-go corporate
taxes?  AER 37:641-45 Sep 47

Dobrovolsky, S. P.  Business income taxation and asset expansion.  JF 4:183-93
Sep 49

Goode, R.  The corporate income tax and
the price level.  AER 35:40-58 Mar 45

Guthmann, H. G.  The effect of the undistributed profits tax upon the distribution
of corporate earnings; a note [followed
by F. McIntyre's reply].  Em 8:354-60
Oct 40

Macy, C. W.  Incidence or effects of the
corporation income tax?  AER 36:903-06
Dec 46

Musgrave, R. J.  Business income taxation
and asset expansion: discussion.  JF 4:
193-96 Sep 49

Shoup, C.  Incidence of the corporation income tax: capital structure and turnover rates.  NTJ 1:12-17 Mar 48

Weston, J. F.  Incidence and effects of the
corporate income tax.  NTJ 2:300-15
Dec 49

UNITED STATES

A Ballantine, A. A.  The corporation and the
income tax.  HBR 22:277-90 no.3, 44

Bradley, W. L.  Taxation of cooperatives.
HBR 25:576-86 no.4a, 47

Buehler, A. G.  The taxation of small business.  AER/S 36:250-64 May 46
-- --- [idem] JF 1:61-75 Aug 46

Butters, J. K.  Taxation and new product
development.  HBR 23:451-59 no.4, 45

-- Federal income taxation and external
vs. internal financing.  JF 4:197-205
Sep 49

Calkins, F. J.  Federal income taxation
and external vs. internal financing: discussion.  JF 4:205-07 Sep 49

Howell, P. L.  The effects of federal income taxation on the form of external
financing by business.  JF 4:208-22
Sep 49

Ketchum, M. D.  The effects of federal income taxation on the form of external
financing: discussion.  JF 4:222-26
Sep 49

Lent, G. E.  Bond interest deduction and
the federal corporation income tax.
NTJ 2:131-41 Jun 49

May, G. O.  Corporate structures and
federal income taxation.  HBR 22:
10-18 no.1, 43

O'Leary, H. J.  Utility rate problems arising from recent and prospective income
tax legislation.  LE 18:184-87 May 42

O'Neil, W. G.  Do high corporate taxes
deter investment?  HBR 22:443-46
no.4, 44

Seghers, P. D.  Tax accounting compared
with recognized accounting principles.
NTJ 1:341-52 Dec 48

Shere, L.  Federal corporate income tax:
revenue and reform.  NTJ 2:110-21
Jun 49

Smith, D. T. and Mace, M.  Tax uncertainties in corporate financing.  HBR 20:
315-26 no.3, 42

OTHER COUNTRIES

EB Beck, M.  British anti-inflationary tax on
distributed corporate profits.  NTJ 1:
275-77 Sep 48

Chambers, S. P.  Taxation and the supply
of capital for industry.  LBR 11:1-20
Jan 49

Forge, F. W.  The taxation of industry.
TBR 4:24-33 Dec 49

FI Gopal, M. H.  Planning of production
through tax adjustments.  IJE 29:155-63
Oct 48

Munshi, M. C.  Incidence and effects of
corporation taxes.  IJE 27:503-11
Apr 47

10.4221  EXCESS PROFITS TAX

A Blough, R.  Measurement problems of the
excess profits tax.  NTJ 1:353-65 Dec 48

Gopal, M. H.  The role of the excess profits
tax in modifying capitalism.  IJE 24:
387-94 Apr 44

A Hellerstein, J. R.  Excess profits tax relief
for the electric utilities under Section
722 of the Internal Revenue Code.  LE 20:
149-56 May 44

## 10. PUBLIC FINANCE

10.42 INCOME TAX (Cont.)
10.4221 EXCESS PROFITS TAX (Cont.)
Kalecki, M. Notes on finance. OIS 3:51-53
EB    Feb 22, 41
-- Excess profits tax and government con-
EB    tracts. OIS 4:40-43 Jan 10, 42
-- The problem of profit margins. OIS 4:
EB    114-17 Apr 4, 42
-- Excess profits tax and post-war re-
EB    equipment. OIS 6:58-61 Mar 18, 44
Lacey, K. Commodity stock values and
EB    E.P.T. EJ 55:2-16 Apr 45
Lalwani, K. Tax relief vs. 100 o/o E.P.T.
FI    IJE 25:149-53 Oct 44
Leach, C. W. Excess profits taxation: II.
C     A business man's view. CJE 7:363-70
      Aug 41
Pruefer, C. H. The excess profits tax and
A     defense financing. SEJ 8:40-53 Jul 41
Ratchford, B. U. The Federal excess prof-
A     its tax. Pt.I-II. SEJ 12:1-16; 97-114
      Jul,Oct 45
Severson, L. General relief provisions of
A     the excess profits tax. NTJ 2:247-58
      Sep 49
Singhania, L. L. Section 6(4) of the Excess
FI    Profit Tax Act. IJE 25:164-65 Oct 44
Tolmie, J. R. Excess profits taxation: I.
C     The Canadian Act and its administration.
      CJE 7:350-63 Aug 41
Yamey, B. S. The excess profits duty in
HSA   South Africa. SAJE 10:263-81 Dec 42

10.4222 DEPRECIATION
Balet, J. W. Application of the LIFO inven-
A     tory method to income tax depreciation
      for public utilities. NTJ 1:322-29 Dec 48
Brown, E. C. Tax allowances for deprecia-
A     tion based on changes in the price level.
      NTJ 1:311-21 Dec 48
Manning, R. E. Depreciation in the tax laws
      and practices of the United States, Aus-
      tralia, Canada, Great Britain, New Zea-
      land, and South Africa. NTJ 1:154-74
      Jun 48; Erratum. 283 Sep 48

10.423 CAPITAL GAINS AND LOSSES
Somers, H. M. An economic analysis of the
A     capital gains tax. NTJ 1:226-32 Sep 48
Vickrey, W. The effects of federal revenue
A     acts of 1938, 1939, and 1940 on the reali-
      zation of gains and losses on securities:
      comment [followed by Q. F. Walker, W.
      T. Collins, and D. E. Higgins' rejoinder].
      JASA 36:431-35 Sep 41
Walker, Q. F.; Collins, W. T. and Higgins,
A     D. E. The effects of federal revenue
      acts of 1938, 1939, and 1940 on the real-
      ization of gains and losses on securities.
      JASA 35:602-14 Dec 40; A correction.
      36:122 Mar 41
Wells, A. Legislative history of treatment
A     of capital gains under the federal in-
      come tax, 1913-1948. NTJ 2:12-32 Mar 49

10.43 PROPERTY TAX
Simon, H. A. The incidence of a tax on
      urban real property. QJE 57:398-420
      May 43
Sinha, B. C. The basis of land tax: a prob-
      lem in applied economics. IJE 21:158-66
      Oct 40

UNITED STATES
Marquis, R. W. Severance taxes on forest
A     products and their relation to forestry.
      LE 25:315-19 Aug 49
Buehler, A. G., chairman. Improving the
AA    property tax: New England Tax Confer-
      ence. NTJ 1:369-72 Dec 48
Burkhead, J. V. Property tax as a burden
AS    on shelter. LE 20:255-63 Aug 44
Feldman, E. S. Exemption of house furn-
      ishings from property taxation. NTJ 2:
      334-42 Dec 49
Groves, H. M. The property tax in Canada
      and the United States. Pt.I-II. LE 24:
      23-30; 120-28 Feb,May 48
Jacobs, J. L. Systematic assessment of
      property for tax equalization. LE 17:
      71-81 Feb 41
-- Neighborhood and property obsolescence
      in the assessment process. LE 17:
      344-53 Aug 41
Mitchell, G. W. Using sales data to meas-
      ure the quality of property tax adminis-
      tration. NTJ 1:330-40 Dec 48
Reeves, H. C. and Pardue, B. L. Some
      reasons why property is poorly assessed
      for taxation. NTJ 1:366-68 Dec 48
Spengler, E. H The taxation of urban land-
      value increments. LE 17:54-58 Feb 41
Davies, E. J. The Louisiana Property Tax
ASL   Relief Fund: a source of financial as-
      sistance for local governments. NTJ 1:
      270-72 Sep 48
Rozman, D. Massachusetts forest tax law.
ASM   LE 18:363-65 Aug 42
Phillips, J. C. Tax exempt real estate in
ASP   Philadelphia. LE 17:361-66 Aug 41
Groves, H. M. and Goodman, A. B. A pat-
ASW   tern of successful property tax admin-
      istration: the Wisconsin experience.
      Pt.I-III. LE 19:141-52; 300-15;
      419-35 May,Aug,Nov 43

OTHER COUNTRIES
Groves, H. M. The property tax in Canada
CP    and the United States. Pt.I-II. LE 24:
      23-30; 120-28 Feb,May 48
Bowley, M. Local rates and housing sub-
EB    sidies. REStud 8:33-43 Oct 40
Daly, M. Regional differences in rates and
      rateable values in England and Wales,
      1921-1936. QJE 54:624-54 Aug 40
Ellis, A. W. T. Rents, rates and income in
EBE   Bristol. REStud 11:99-108 no.2, 44

10.43  PROPERTY TAX (Cont.)
   OTHER COUNTRIES (Cont.)
   Fogarty, M. P.  The incidence of rates on
EBE   houses [in Birmingham, England].
   REStud 10:81-105 no.2, 43
   Ward, R. L.  The taxation of land values in
HSA   the Transvaal by local authorities.
   SAJE 10:16-35 Mar 42
   -- A note on Cape Town's draft rating
   ordinance.  SAJE 11:69-75 Mar 43
   Groves, H. M.  Impressions of property
N   taxation in Australia and New Zealand.
   LE 25:22-28 Feb 49

10.44  OTHER TAXES
10.440  GENERAL
   Kaldor, N.  The income burden of capital
   taxes.  REStud 9:138-57 no.2, 42

10.441  SALES AND TURNOVER TAXES
   Barna, T.  The British purchase tax.  PF 1:
EB   234-42 no.3, 46
   Brady, M. J.  Retail sales taxation in the
A   United States.  ER 17:262-65 Dec 41
   Bronfenbrenner, M.  Sales taxation and the
A   Mints plan.  REStat 29:39-42 Feb 47
   Due, J. F.  A general sales tax and the
   level of employment: a reconsideration.
   NTJ 2:122-30 Jun 49
   Gilbert, D. W.  [The incidence of sales
   taxes]: rejoinder.  QJE 54:686-93 Aug 40
   Haygood, T. F.  How would a federal sales
A   tax affect farmers?  JFE 27:649-63
   Aug 45
   Higgins, B.  The incidence of sales taxes:
   a note on methodology.  QJE 54:665-72
   Aug 40
   Jastram, R. W.  The shifting of sales taxes.
   QJE 54:673-78 Aug 40
   Johnson, B. L.  Denver adopts local sales
ASC   tax.  NTJ 1:184-86 Jun 48
   McGrew, J. W.  Effect of a food exemption
A   on the incidence of a retail sales tax.
   NTJ 2:362-67 Dec 49
   Peterson, W. C.  The Los Angeles City
ASC   sales tax administration.  NTJ 2:232-46
   Sep 49
   Quantius, F.  Sales taxes and the propen-
   sity to consume.  SEJ 11:269-73 Jan 45
   Reilly, E. E.  The use of the elasticity con-
   cept in economic theory; with special
   reference to some economic effects of
   a commodity tax.  CJE 6:39-55 Feb 40
   Rolph, E.  Mr. Sumberg's interpretation of
ER   the Soviet turnover tax.  AER 36:661-62
   Sep 46
   Wald, H. P.  A comparative analysis of three
   variations of retail sales taxes.  AER 34:
   280-302 Jun 44

10.442  EXCISE TAXES
   Ghosh, H.  The rationale of salt tax in
FI   India.  IJE 27:493-501 Apr 47

Hall, J. K.  Excise tax incidence and the
   postwar economy.  AER/S 32:83-101
   Mar 42
Lent, G. E.  The admissions tax.  NTJ 1:
   31-50 Mar 48
Rolph, E. R. and Break, G. F.  The welfare
   aspects of excise taxes.  JPE 57:46-54
   Feb 49
Traylor, O. F.  State taxation of production
ASK   of blended spirits [in Kentucky].  NTJ 2:
   179-84 Jun 49

10.443  DEATH AND GIFT TAXES
   Barna, T.  The burden of death taxes in
   terms of an annual tax.  REStud 9:28-39
   Nov 41
   Chand, G.  The inheritance tax in India.
FI   IJE 25:436-50 Apr 45
   Hall, J. K.  Incidence of death duties.
   AER 30:46-59 Mar 40
   Harriss, C. L.  Federal estate taxes and
A   philanthropic bequests.  JPE 57:337-44
   Aug 49
   -- Wealth estimates as affected by audit of
A   estate tax returns.  NTJ 2:316-33 Dec 49
   Kahn, E.  Death duties in South Africa.
HSA   SAJE 14:81-99 Jun 46
   Oakes, E.  The Federal offset and the
A   American death tax system.  QJE 54:
   566-98 Aug 40
   Vickrey, W.  The rationalization of succes-
   sion taxation.  Em 12:215-36 Jul-Oct 44

10.444  CAPITAL LEVY
   Balogh, T.  The unimportance of a capital
EB   levy.  OIS 6:44-48 Feb 26, 44
   Gopal, M. H.  A neglected source of local
FI   revenues.  IJE 22:830-31 Jan 42
   Griziotti, B.  Three forms of capital levy
EI   in Italy.  BNL 1:149-56 Oct 47
   Rostas, L.  Capital levies in central
EA   Europe, 1919-24.  REStud 8:20-32 Oct 40
   Schouten, D. B. J.  Theory and practice of
EN   the capital levies in the Netherlands.
   OIS 10:117-22 Apr 48

10.445  OTHER TAXES
   Baker, J. A.  The graduated farm land
A   transfer stamp tax.  LE 16:21-29 Feb 40
   Brandt, L. K.  Mr. Floyd on Mississippi
ASM   corporate fees and taxes.  SEJ 15:
   339-40 Jan 49
   Bronfenbrenner, J.  An incentive tax pro-
A   posal for alleviation of the housing
   shortage.  NTJ 1:51-61 Mar 48
   Buehler, A. G.  Production taxes.  HBR 19:
A   458-69 no.4, 41
   Burkhead, J. and Steele, D. C.  Electric
ASN   rates and tax burdens in Pennsylvania
ASP   and New York.  NTJ 2:278-80 Sep 49
   Chand, G.  Local terminal taxation.  IJE 22:
FI   624-36 Jan 42

# 10. PUBLIC FINANCE

## 10.445 OTHER TAXES (Cont.)

Clark, R. M. The municipal business tax
CP  in Canada. CJE 14:491-501 Nov 48

Craine, L. E. Chain store taxes as revenue
A  measures. NTJ 2:280-83 Sep 49

Eiteman, W. J. Effect of franchise taxes
AS  upon corporate location. SEJ 9:234-40
Jan 43

Friedman, M. The spendings tax as a war-
time fiscal measure. AER 33:50-62
Mar 43

Harriss, C. L. Revenue implications of a
A  progressive-rate tax on expenditures.
A study of selected aspects of Irving
Fisher's proposal to eliminate savings
from the income tax base. REStat 25:
175-91 Aug 43

Poole, K. E. Problems of administration
and equity under a spendings tax.
AER 33:63-73 Mar 43

## 10.45 NON-TAX SOURCES OF REVENUE

Gopalaswamy, S. Non-tax revenue of
FI  Mysore. IJE 21:618-33 Apr 41

## 10.5 PUBLIC DEBT AND DEBT POLICY
## 10.50 GENERAL

Bach, G. L. and Musgrave, R. A. A stable
purchasing power bond. AER 31:823-25
Dec 41

Balogh, T. The burden of the national debt:
a comment. EJ 55:461-63 Dec 45

Benoit-Smullyan, E. Interest-free deficit
financing and full employment. AER 37:
397-99 Jun 47

Coleman, R. Government bonds and the
balanced budget. HBR 20:75-80 no.1, 41

Dalal, K. L. Measurement of the "burden"
of the public debt. IJE 29:135-46 Oct 48

Poindexter, J. C. Fallacies of interest-free
deficit financing. QJE 58:438-59 May 44

-- --- Rejoinder. QJE 60:154-65 Nov 45

-- A critique of functional finance through
quasi-free bank credit. AER 36:311-23
Jun 46

-- Professors Pritchard and Benoit-Smullyan on bank-financed functional deficits:
a reply. AER 38:391-94 Jun 48

Pritchard, L. J. The nature of bank credit:
a comment. AER 37:399-402 Jun 47

Ratchford, B. U. The burden of a domestic
debt. AER 32:451-67 Sep 42

Schmidt, E. P. Private versus public debt.
AER 33:119-21 Mar 43

Suiter, W. O. Divergent theories of national
debt. SEJ 13:53-64 Jul 46

Wright, D. M. The economic limit and economic burden of an internally held national debt. QJE 55:116-29 Nov 40

-- Mr. Ratchford on the burden of a domestic debt: comment. AER 33:115-19
Mar 43

-- Interest-free deficit financing: a reply.
QJE 58:637-46 Aug 44

## UNITED STATES

Abbott, C. C. Government debt and private
A  investment policy. REStat 31:21-25
Feb 49

Burkhead, J. V. Full employment and
interest-free borrowing. SEJ 14:1-13
Jul 47

Haley, B. F. The federal budget: economic
consequences of deficit financing.
AER/S 30,no.5:67-87 Feb 41

Hargreaves, H. W. The guaranteed security
in federal finance. JPE 50:559-77
Aug 42

Kähler, A. The public debt in the financial
structure. SR 11:11-26 Feb 44

Lanston, A. G. Crucial problem of the
federal debt. HBR 24:133-50 no.2, 46

Lerner, A. P. [Postwar federal interest
charge]: discussion. AER/S 34,no.2:
86-88 Jun 44

Ratchford, B. U. History of the federal
debt in the United States. AER/S 37:
131-41 May 47

-- The economics of public debts. PF 3:
299-310 no.4, 48

Reinhardt, H. On the incidence of public
debt. SR 12:205-26 May 45

Rolph, E. R. The payment of interest on
Series E bonds. AER/S 37:318-21
May 47

Shoup, C. Postwar federal interest charge.
AER/S 34,no.2, 44-85 Jun 44

Simmons, E. C. The position of the Treasury bill in the public debt. JPE 55:
333-45 Aug 47

Smith, D. T. Economic consequences of
deficit financing: a review. AER/S 30,
no.5:88-98 Feb 41

Tostlebe, A. S. Estimate of Series E bond
purchases by farmers. JASA 40:317-29
Sep 45

Wickens, A. J. The public debt and national
income. AER/S 37:184-91 May 47

Wilmerding, L., Jr. Public debt: history:
discussion. AER/S 37:151-56 May 47

Woodward, D. B. Public debt and institutions. AER/S 37:157-83 May 47

Ratchford, B. U. New forms of state debts.
AS  SEJ 8:459-78 Apr 42

## OTHER COUNTRIES

Fetter, F. W. History of public debt in
D  Latin America. AER/S 37:142-50 May 47

Kalecki, M. The fall in 'small' savings.
EB  OIS 4:290-93 Oct 31, 42; Erratum. 5:22
Jan 9, 43

-- The burden of the national debt. OIS 5:
76-80 Apr 3, 43

Paish, F. W. British floating debt policy.
Ec N.S.7:225-47 Aug 40

10.5 PUBLIC DEBT AND DEBT POLICY (Cont.)
10.50 GENERAL (Cont.)
OTHER COUNTRIES (Cont.)
EB Stettner, W. F. Sir James Steuart on the public debt. QJE 59:451-76 May 45
FI Bhojwani, N. K. The financial situation in Sind. IJE 21:892-900 Apr 41
Sarkar, K. C. Public debts in the U.P. 1921-37. IJE 21:871-80 Apr 41
Sitaramayya, M. Reserve bank and the management of public debt. Pt.I-II. IJE 26:597-621; 27:35-52 Apr,Jul 46
N Maxwell, J. A. The recent history of the Australian Loan Council. CJE 6:22-38 Feb 40
Neale, E. P. The growth of New Zealand's general government debt. ER 21:182-96 Dec 45

10.51 HISTORY
D Fetter, F. W. History of public debt in Latin America. AER/S 37:142-50 May 47
EB Hamilton, E. J. Origin and growth of the national debt in western Europe.
EF AER/S 37:118-30 May 47
A Ratchford, B. U. History of the federal debt in the United States. AER/S 37: 131-41 May 47
EB Sutherland, L. S. Samson Gideon and the reduction of interest, 1749-50. EHR 16: 15-29 no.1, 46
Wilmerding, L., Jr. and Abbott, C. C. Public debt: history: discussion. AER/S 37:151-56 May 47

# II. INTERNATIONAL ECONOMICS

11.0 GENERAL
Aldrich, W. W. The International Chamber of Commerce and the Economic and Social Council. EI 1:233-35 Jan 48
De Haas, J. A. World trade faces a new order. HBR 19:243-47 no.2, 41
Frankel, S. H. World economic welfare. SAJE 11:165-84 Sep 43; Errata. 296 Dec 43
Kantorovitz, P. P. The future of world trade: towards the International Trade Conference, 1946. EgC 36:609-762 Dec 45
Lalwani, K. Reflections on future economic order: international and national. Pt.I-II. IJE 25:450-65; 26:29-42 Apr,Jul 45
Marschak, J. Peace economics. SR 7: 280-98 Sep 40

11.2 STRUCTURE OF INTERNATIONAL TRADE
11.20 GENERAL
Blau, G. Wool in the world economy [with discussion]. JRSS 109:179-242 pt.3, 46
Chalmers, H. [Economic regionalism and multilateral trade]: discussion. AER/S 33:448-54 Mar 43
Chang, T. C. International comparison of demand for imports. REStud 13:53-67 no.2, 46
Ciriacy-Wantrup, S. von [and others] Natural resources and international policy: discussion. AER/S 35:130-36 May 45
Frankel, H. Industrialisation of agricultural countries and the possibilities of a new international division of labour. EJ 53:188-201 Jun-Sep 43
Glesinger, E. Forest products in a world economy. AER/S 35:120-29 May 45

Gordon, M. S. [Economic regionalism and multilateral trade]: discussion. AER/S 33:446-48 Mar 43
Hilgerdt, F. The case for multilateral trade. AER/S 33:393-407 Mar 43
Hirschman, A. O. The commodity structure of world trade. QJE 57:565-95 Aug 43
Johnson, A. R. Some international angles on postwar agricultural trade. JM 11: 174-78 Oct 46
Knorr, K. E. Access to raw materials in the postwar world. HBR 21:385-96 no.3, 43
Pasvolsky, L., chairman. Round table on bases of international economic relations. AER/S 33:455-65 Mar 43; A correction by G. Crowther. 625 Sep 43
Viner, J. The prospects for foreign trade in the post-war world. MS 15:123-38 May 47

UNITED STATES
A Adler, J. H. United States import demand during the interwar period. AER 35: 418-30 Jun 45
-- The postwar demand for United States exports. REStat 28:23-33 Feb 46
Bliss, C. A. Our trade to South America. HBR 20:107-15 no.1, 41
Brandt, K. The prospects of European agriculture and their implications for the United States. JFE 26:601-12 Nov 44
Hansen, A. H. and Upgren, A. R. Some aspects, near-term and long-term, of the international position of the United States. AER/S 30,no.5:366-72 Feb 41
Hunsberger, W. S. Economic research of interest to the Department of State. AER/S 37:681-89 May 47

# 11. INTERNATIONAL ECONOMICS

## 11.2 STRUCTURE OF INTERNATIONAL TRADE (Cont.)
### 11.20 GENERAL (Cont.)
#### UNITED STATES (Cont.)

A Kilduff, V. R. Economic factors in the development of Canadian-American trade. SEJ 8:201-17 Oct 41

Linville, F. A. Latin American aspects of post-war agricultural readjustments. JFE 24:42-51 Feb 42

Nelson, G. L. Volume of United States exports and imports of foods, 1909-43. JFE 26:399-405 May 44

Pasvolsky, L. Some aspects of our foreign economic policy. AER/S 30,no.5:320-37 Feb 41

Patterson, E. M. United States in the world economy, 1940: a summary. AER/S 30, no.5:328-43 Feb 41

Schwenger, R. B. The prospect for postwar agricultural exports from the United States. JFE 28:42-53 Feb 46

Skelton, D. A. Canada-United States trade relationships. JFE 24:35-41 Feb 42

Taylor, A. E. International economic problems; regional: discussion [of D. G. Munro's "Postwar problems in our Latin-American relations," pub. in the American Political Science Review]. AER/S 34: 370-71 Mar 44

Thomas, E. P. Shifting scenes in foreign trade. JM 4,no.4,pt.2:51-58 Apr 40

Walsh, R. M. Export market and price of lard. JFE 25:487-94 May 43

White, B. S., Jr. The shrinking foreign market for United States cotton. QJE 54: 255-76 Feb 40

Williamson, W. F. The place of coffee in trade with Latin America. JM 6,no.4, pt.2:149-51 Apr 42

Wythe, G. International economic problems; regional: discussion [of D. G. Munro's "Postwar problems in our Latin-American relations," pub. in American Political Science Review]. AER/S 34:368-70 Mar 44

AA Ratchford, B. U. The South's stake in international trade: past, present, and prospective. SEJ 14:361-75 Apr 48

Taylor, H. C. World conditions in the postwar period that will affect Mississippi Valley agriculture. JFE 26:1-9 Feb 44

AS Beckett, G. Comments on Alaska's trade. JM 10:291-93 Jan 46

#### OTHER AMERICAN COUNTRIES

C Kilduff, V. R. Economic factors in the development of Canadian-American trade. SEJ 8:201-17 Oct 41

Skelton, D. A. Canada-United States trade relationships. JFE 24:35-41 Feb 42

D De Haas, J. A. Buying Latin American loyalty. HBR 19:298-310 no.3, 41

Inman, S. G. Planning Pan-American trade. HBR 18:137-47 no.2, 40

Linville, F. A. Latin American aspects of post-war agricultural readjustments. JFE 24:42-51 Feb 42

Taylor, A. E. International economic problems; regional: discussion [of G. D. Munro's "Postwar problems in our Latin-American relations," pub. in the American Political Science Review]. AER/S 34:370-71 Mar 44

Williamson, W. F. The place of coffee in trade with Latin America. JM 6,no.4, pt.2:149-51 Apr 42

Wythe, G. International economic problems; regional: discussion [of D. G. Munro's "Postwar problems in our Latin-American relations," pub. in American Political Science Review]. AER/S 34:368-70 Mar 44

DS Bliss, C. A. Our trade to South America. HBR 20:107-15 no.1, 41

Rippy, J. F. South America's foreign trade and hemisphere defense. JB 14:89-98 Apr 41

#### EUROPE

E Brandt, K. The prospects of European agriculture and their implications for the United States. JFE 26:601-12 Nov 44

EA Moos, S. The foreign trade of west European countries. Pt.I-II. OIS 7:7-13; 56-60 Jan 13, Feb 24, 45

EB Anonymous. British television for export. TBR 3:22-28 Sep 49

Balogh, T. Britain's foreign trade problem: a comment [followed by G. D. A. McDougall's reply]. EJ 58:74-98 Mar 48

Barna, T. The British demand for imports: a comment [followed by T. C. Chang's reply]. EJ 56:662-66 Dec 46

Chang, T. C. The British demand for imports in the inter-war period. EJ 56: 188-207 Jun 46

Clay, H. The place of exports in British industry after the war. EJ 52:145-53 Jun-Sep 42

Fisher, A. G. B. Some essential factors in the evolution of international trade. MS 13:1-23 Oct 43

Lewis, W. A. The prospect before us. MS 16:129-64 May 48

McDougall, G. D. A. Britain's bargaining power. EJ 56:27-37 Mar 46

-- Britain's foreign trade problem. EJ 57: 69-113 Mar 47

-- Notes on Britain's bargaining power. OEP N.S.1:18-39 Jan 49

Macrosty, H. W. The overseas trade of the United Kingdom 1930-39 [with discussion]. JRSS 103:451-90 pt.4, 40

Maizels, A. The oversea trade statistics of the United Kingdom. JRSS 112:207-23 pt.2, 49

11.2 STRUCTURE OF INTERNATIONAL TRADE
(Cont.)

11.20 GENERAL (Cont.)

EUROPE (Cont.)

EB   Nash, E. F. Changes in external factors affecting British agriculture. LBR 8: 35-56 Apr 48

Robertson, D. H. The problem of exports. EJ 55:321-25 Dec 45

Snow, E. C. [and others] The statistical basis of export targets. JRSS 110: 169-86 pt.3, 47

EBI   Duncan, G. A. The foreign trade of the Irish Free State, 1924-47. EI 1:584-92 May 48

EG   Hillmann, H. C. Analysis of Germany's foreign trade and the war. Ec N.S.7: 66-88 Feb 40

EI   Tagliacarne, G. Italian foreign trade in the framework of world trade. BNL 1:228-39 Jan 48

ER   Sen Gupta, R. N. India's trade with U.S.S.R. IJE 24:145-49 Oct 43

ES   Cederwall, G. Post-war development of Sweden's foreign trade. OIS 9:307-14 Sep 47

ASIA

FA   Lockwood, W. W. Postwar trade relations in the Far East. AER/S 33:420-30 Mar 43

FI   Balakrishna, R. India in a world trading system. IJE 28:1-8 Jul 47

Murray, Sir A. R. Indian jute. LBR 5: 29-42 Jul 47

Oulton, P. G. Indian cotton. LBR 1:35-40 Jul 46

Sen Gupta, R. N. India's trade with U.S.S.R. IJE 24:145-49 Oct 43

FIP   Khalil, K. F. Pakistan's foreign trade: analysis and prospects. PEJ 1,no.1: 69-77 Jul 49

AFRICA

H   Robertson, C. J. Monoexport in Africa. SAJE 8:1-18 Mar 40

MIDDLE EAST

ME   El-Said, M. H. Seasonality of the Egyptian export trade. EgC 37:227-31 May-Dec 46

11.21 HISTORY

Cummings, R. O. American interest in world agriculture, 1861-1865. AH 23: 116-23 Apr 49

Gray, S. and Wyckoff, V. J. The international tobacco trade in the seventeenth century. SEJ 7:1-26 Jul 40

Mackintosh, W. A. Reciprocity. R. CJE 6: 611-20 Nov 40

Martin, K. and Thackeray, F. G. The terms of trade of selected countries, 1870-1938. OIS 10:373-94 Nov 48

UNITED STATES

Heaton, H. Non-importation, 1806-1812.

A   JEH 1:178-98 Nov 41

Smith, G. W. A rising industry's battle for the Morrill tariff [The American Screw Company of Providence, R.I.]. BHR 16: 106-11 Dec 42

OTHER COUNTRIES

Jones, R. L. The Canadian agricultural

C   tariff of 1843. CJE 7:528-37 Nov 41

Zimmern, W. H. Lancashire and Latin

D   America. MS 13:45-60 Aug 44

Heaton, H. A merchant adventurer in

DSB   Brazil 1808-1818 [John Luccock]. JEH 6: 1-23 May 46

Goebel, D. B. British-American rivalry in

DSC   Chilean trade, 1817-1820. JEH 2: 190-202 Nov 42

Mollat, M. Anglo-Norman trade in the

E   fifteenth century. EHR 17:143-50 no.2, 47

Usher, A. P. The role of monopoly in colonial trade and in the expansion of Europe subsequent to 1800. AER/S 38: 54-62 May 48

Wilson, C. Treasure and trade balances: the mercantilist problem. EHR II.2: 152-61 no.2, 49

Brutzkus, J. Trade with eastern Europe,

EA   800-1200. EHR 13:31-41 no.1-2, 43

Fisher, F. J. Commercial trends and

EB   policy in sixteenth-century England. EHR 10:95-117 Nov 40

Furber, H. The United Company of Merchants of England Trading to the East Indies, 1783-96. EHR 10:138-47 Nov 40

Imlah, A. H. Real values in British foreign trade, 1798-1853. JEH 8:133-52 Nov 48

Mosse, G. L. The Anti-League: 1844-1846. EHR 17:134-42 no.2, 47

Pesmazoglu, J. S. Some international aspects of British cyclical fluctuations, 1870-1913. REStud 16:117-43 no.3, 49

Ruddock, A. A. Alien hosting in Southampton in the fifteenth century. EHR 16: 30-37 no.1, 46

-- London capitalists and the decline of Southampton in the early Tudor period. EHR II.2:137-51 no.2, 49

Stone, L. Elizabethan overseas trade. EHR II.2:30-58 no.1, 49

Sutherland, L. S. The East India Company in eighteenth-century politics. EHR 17: 15-26 no.1, 47

Zimmern, W. H. Lancashire and Latin America. MS 13:45-60 Aug 44

Morazé, P. The Treaty of 1860 and the in-

EF   dustry of the Department of the North. EHR 10:18-28 Feb 40

Tagliacarne, G. Italian foreign trade in the

EI   framework of world trade. BNL 1:228-39 Jan 48

# 11. INTERNATIONAL ECONOMICS

## 11.2 STRUCTURE OF INTERNATIONAL TRADE (Cont.)

### 11.21 HISTORY (Cont.)

#### OTHER COUNTRIES (Cont.)

ESp    Verlinden, C. The rise of Spanish trade in the Middle Ages. (Studies in sources and bibliography, VII) EHR 10:44-59 Feb 40

FA    Lopez, R. S. European merchants in the medieval Indies: the evidence of commercial documents. JEH 3:164-84 Nov 43

FJ    Honjo, E. Facts and ideas of Japan's oversea development prior to the Meiji restoration. Kyo 17,no.1:1-13 Jan 42

N    La Nauze, J. A. Australian tariffs and imperial control. Pt.I-II. ER 24:1-17; 218-34 Jun,Dec 48

### 11.22 PRICE THEORY. COMPARATIVE COST

Baldwin, R. E. Equilibrium in international trade: a diagrammatic analysis. QJE 62:748-62 Nov 48

Balogh, T. Static models and current problems in international economics. OEP N.S.1:191-98 Jun 49

Benham, F. The terms of trade. Ec N.S.7: 360-76 Nov 40

Dasgupta, A. K. The elasticity of reciprocal demand and terms of international trade. IJE 22:164-76 Oct 41

Dorrance, G. S. The income terms of trade. REStud 16:50-56 no.1, 48

Ellsworth, P. T. A comparison of international trade theories. AER 30:285-89 Jun 40

Forchheimer, K. The role of relative wage differences in international trade. QJE 62:1-30 Nov 47

Henderson, A. M. A geometrical note on bulk purchase. Ec N.S.15:61-69 Feb 48

Lovasy, G. International trade under imperfect competition. QJE 55:567-83 Aug 41

Marsh, D. B. The scope of the theory of international trade under monopolistic competition. QJE 56:475-86 May 42

Meier, G. M. The theory of comparative costs reconsidered. OEP N.S.1:199-216 Jun 49

Qureshi, A. I. International economic cooperation. IJE 25:274-82 Jan 45

Raj, J. S. The rôle of national wage and income structures in international trade. IJE 21:233-49 Jan 41

Roberts, R. O. Comparative shipping and shipbuilding costs. Ec N.S.14:296-309 Nov 47

Robinson, J. The pure theory of international trade. REStud 14:98-112 no.2, 47

Samuelson, P. A. International trade and the equalisation of factor prices. EJ 58: 163-84 Jun 48

-- International factor-price equalisation once again. EJ 59:181-97 Jun 49

Stolper, W. F. and Samuelson, P. A. Protection and real wages. REStud 9:58-73 Nov 41

Tinbergen, J. The equalisation of factor prices between free-trade areas. Met 1: 39-47 Apr 49

### 11.23 TRADE POLICY

#### 11.230 GENERAL

Condliffe, J. B. The disposal of agricultural surpluses. JFE 24:434-46 May 42

Haberler, G., chairman. Problems of international economic policy. Abstract of specialized conference discussion. AER/S 32:206-11 Mar 42

Marsh, D. B. Fiscal policy and tariffs in post-war international trade. CJE 9: 507-31 Nov 43

Schultz, T. W. Supporting agricultural prices by concealed dumping. JPE 56: 157-60 Apr 48

Schwenger, R. B. World agricultural policies and the expansion of trade. JFE 27: 67-87 Feb 45

#### UNITED STATES

A    Allen, R. H. and MacFarlane, D. L. Trade reciprocity and agriculture: discussion. JFE 24:822-25 Nov 42

Bidwell, P. W., chairman. Round table on problems of American commercial policy. AER/S 30:118-23 Mar 40

-- Professor Litman's review of The invisible tariff. AER 30:353 Jun 40

Bryce, R. B. Basic issues in postwar international economic relations. AER/S 32:165-81 Mar 42

Chew, A. P. Nationalistic trends in agricultural policy. JFE 26:59-76 Feb 44

Copland, D. B. America's economic leadership. HBR 23:415-19 no.4, 45

Davis, J. S. A desirable foreign trade policy for American agriculture. JFE 22:430-39 May 40

Deimel, H. L., Jr. United States shipping policy and international economic relations. AER/S 36:547-60 May 46

Diebold, W., Jr. Oil import quotas and "equal treatment." AER 30:569-73 Sep 40

Ellsworth, P. T. An economic foreign policy for America. AER/S 30,no.5: 301-19 Feb 41

Fetter, F. W. Some neglected aspects of the wool duty. JFE 23:399-420 May 41

-- The economists' tariff protest of 1930. AER 32:355-56 Jun 42

Gideonse, H. D. The relation of American foreign-trade policy to New Deal domestic policy. AER 30:87-97 Mar 40

11.23  TRADE POLICY (Cont.)
11.230  GENERAL (Cont.)
  UNITED STATES (Cont.)
  Gordon, M. S.  International aspects of
A    American agricultural policy.  AER 36:
     596-612 Sep 46
  James, C. L.  Industrial concentration and
     trade barriers.  SEJ 14:163-72 Oct 47
  Johnson, D. G.  Reconciling agricultural
     and foreign trade policies.  JPE 55:
     567-71 Dec 47
  Kelley, D. N.  The McNary-Haugen Bills,
     1924-1928; an attempt to make the tariff
     effective for farm products.  AH 14:
     170-80 Oct 40
  Kreider, C.  Valuation for customs.
     QJE 56:157-59 Nov 41
  Loftus, J. A.  United States commercial
     policy.  JB 21:193-202 Jul 48
  Mighell, R. L.  Effects of American-
     Canadian trade reciprocity on agricul-
     ture.  JFE 24:806-21 Nov 42
  Nelson, R. S.  Export subsidies and agricul-
     tural income.  JFE 23:619-31 Aug 41
  Pendleton, W. C.  American sugar policy,
     1948 version.  JFE 30:226-42 May 48
  Sumberg, T. A.  The government's role in
     export trade.  HBR 23:157-73 no.2, 45
  -- Menace of export subsidies.  HBR 23:
     420-32 no.4, 45
  Thomsen, F. L.  Export-dumping plans.
     JFE 22:446-59 May 40
  Upgren, A. R.  Economic proposals for the
     peace settlement.  HBR 22:393-404
     no.4, 44
  Young, J. P.  Problems of international
     economic policy for the United States.
     AER/S.32:182-94 Mar 42
  Brandis, B.  Professor Fels and the dragon.
AA   [Rejoinder to R. Fels's "Free trade and
     southern progress."]  SEJ 16:86-88
     Jul 49
  Fels, R.  Free trade and southern progress.
     SEJ 16:84-86 Jul 49

  OTHER COUNTRIES
  Allen, R. H. and MacFarlane, D. L.  Trade
C    reciprocity and agriculture: discussion.
     JFE 24:822-25 Nov 42
  Bladen, V. W.  Tariff policy and employ-
     ment in depression.  CJE 6:72-78 Feb 40
  Mighell, R. L.  Effects of American-
     Canadian trade reciprocity of agriculture.
     JFE 24:806-21 Nov 42
  Wurm, F. J.  Argentine trade policy.
DSA   OIS 2,no.9:10-13 Nov 2, 40; Errata. 3,
     no.1:16 Jan 11, 41
  Furth, J. H.  Trade barriers in central
EA   Europe.  JM 4,no.4,pt.2:25-30 Apr 40
  Ashley, P.  An experiment in tariff making.
EB   MS 11:1-35 Apr 40
  Schumacher, E. F.  Tax incentives for ex-
     port.  OIS 7:124-28 May 19, 45

  Schiff, E.  Dutch foreign-trade policy and
EN   the infant-industry argument for protec-
     tion.  JPE 50:280-90 Apr 42
  Adams, W.  A political force in Indian eco-
FI   nomic development.  IJE 30:1-18 Jul 49
  Adarkar, B. P.  Fiscal policy muddles: a
     reply.  IJE 23:115-32 Oct 42
  Balakrishna, R.  Role of tariffs in economic
     expansion.  IJE 28:207-22 Oct 47
  Chatterji, R. N.  Essentials of a short-term
     commercial policy for India.  IJE 28:
     9-15 Jul 47
  Dasgupta, A. K.  The Indian fiscal policy.
     R.  IJE 23:101-14 Oct 42
  Habbu, R. K.  Commercial policy of India.
     IJE 28:397-402 Jan 48
  Hajela, P. D.  The foreign trade policy of
     the new India government.  IJE 28:
     293-96 Oct 47
  Mundle, A. K.  Trend of commerce and its
     effects on tax policy.  IJE 28:389-95
     Jan 48
  Rao, R. V.  Industrial policy of India with
     special reference to tariffs.  IJE 28:
     23-30 Jul 47
  Richards, C. S.  The task before us: with
HSA   special reference to industry.  SAJE 12:
     157-204 Sep 44
  Tinley, J. M. and Mirkowich, B. M.  Con-
     trol in the sugar-cane industry of South
     Africa.  JFE 23:537-49 Aug 41
  Sutch, W. B.  Changes in New Zealand's
N    import structure.  ER 19:203-11 Dec 43

11.231  THEORY OF TRADE BARRIERS
  Balogh, T.  A note on the economics of re-
     taliation.  REStud 11:86-90 no.2, 44
  Browne, G. W. G.  A note on tariffs and
     subsidies [followed by R. L. Threlfell's
     reply].  SAJE 14:224-25 Sep 46
  Denis, H.  A note on the theory of tariffs.
     REStud 12:110-13 no.2, 45
  Elliott, G. A.  The relation of protective
     duties to domestic production.  CJE 6:
     296-98 May 40
  Enke, S.  The monopsony case for tariffs.
     QJE 58:229-45 Feb 44
  -- Monopolistic output and international
     trade.  QJE 60:233-49 Feb 46
  Graaff, J. de V.  A note on the relative
     merits of tariffs and subsidies.  SAJE 15:
     149-50 Jun 47
  -- On optimum tariff structures.  REStud 17:
     47-59 no.1, 49
  Kahn, A. E.  The burden of import duties:
     a comment [followed by E. R. Rolph's
     rejoinder].  AER 38:857-69 Dec 48
  Kahn, R. F.  Tariffs and the terms of trade.
     REStud 15:14-19 no.1, 47
  Kaldor, N.  A note on tariffs and the terms
     of trade.  Ec N.S.7:377-80 Nov 40
  Little, I. M. D.  Welfare and tariffs.
     REStud 16:65-70 no.2, 49

# 11. INTERNATIONAL ECONOMICS

## 11.231 THEORY OF TRADE BARRIERS (Cont.)

Metzler, L. A. Tariffs, the terms of trade, and the distribution of national income. JPE 57:1-29 Feb 49

-- Tariffs, international demand, and domestic prices. JPE 57:345-51 Aug 49

Morgan, J. N. The burden of import duties: a comment. AER 37:407-09 Jun 47

Munshi, M. C. Protectionism and Indian economic thought. IJE 22:331-56 Jan 42

Myers, J. H. Tariffs and prices: a diagrammatic representation. AER 31: 553-57 Sep 41

Raj, J. S. A note on the changes in prices and imports occasioned by the imposition of a tariff. IJE 25:154-59 Oct 44

Rolph, E. R. The burden of import duties. AER 36:788-812 Dec 46

-- The burden of import duties with fixed exchange rates. AER 37:604-32 Sep 47

Roy, P. On the nature of mercantilist tariff. IJE 24:1-19 Jul 43

Scitovszky, T. A reconsideration of the theory of tariffs. REStud 9:89-110 no.2, 42

Stolper, W. F. and Samuelson, P. A. Protection and real wages. REStud 9:58-73 Nov 41

Threlfell, R. L. The relative merits of tariffs and subsidies as methods of protection. SAJE 14:117-31 Jun 46

## 11.232 INTERNATIONAL TRADE AGREEMENTS

A Beckett, G. The problem of reclassification in the reciprocal trade agreements. JPE 48:199-209 Apr 40

A -- Effect of the reciprocal trade agreements upon the foreign trade of the United States. QJE 55:80-94 Nov 40

-- A statistical note on the trade agreements program. JM 5:280-82 Jan 41

Elliott, F. F. A proposed world trade board for expanding international trade. JFE 27: 571-90 Aug 45

A Evans, J. W. United States foreign trade policy: a practical approach [with discussion by D. S. Anderson]. JFE 31, pt.2:504-18 Feb 49

EBC Glickman, D. L. The British imperial preference system. QJE 61:439-70 May 47

A  
EB Kreider, C. The Anglo-American cotton-rubber barter agreement. SEJ 7:216-24 Oct 40

-- The effect of American trade agreements on third countries: retrospect. AER 31:780-93 Dec 41

A Pino, N. Comment on "A statistical note on the trade agreement program." JM 6:48-50 Jul 41

N Rose, W. J. A "made to measure" tariff. ER 21:212-22 Dec 45

EBC Rossouw, G. S. H. The problem of imperial preference. SAJE 14:173-87 Sep 46

Snyder, R. C. Commercial policy as reflected in treaties from 1931 to 1939. AER 30:787-802 Dec 40

EG Staudinger, H. The future of totalitarian barter trade. SR 7:410-33 Nov 40

## 11.24 CARTELS. COMMODITY AGREEMENTS. STATE TRADING

Ady, P. Bulk purchasing and the colonial producer. OIS 9:321-40 Oct 47

Bladen, V. W. [and others] International cartels: discussion. AER/S 36:768-83 May 46

De Haas, J. A. Economic peace through private agreements. HBR 22:139-54 no.2, 44

Edwards, C. D. International cartels as obstacles to international trade. AER/S 34:330-39 Mar 44

Haley, B. F. The relation between cartel policy and commodity agreement policy. AER/S 36:717-34 May 46

Hamilton, W. H. The control of strategic materials. AER 34:261-79 Jun 44

-- The economic man affects a national role. AER/S 36:735-44 May 46

Hexner, E. American participation in the International Steel Cartel. SEJ 8:54-79 Jul 41

-- International cartels in the postwar world. SEJ 10:114-35 Oct 43

-- The political economy of international cartels: discussion. AER/S 35:321-24 May 45

Hoselitz, B. F. Socialist planning and international economic relations. AER 33: 839-51 Dec 43

C -- The cartel report. CJE 12:172-75 May 46

-- International cartel policy. JPE 55:1-27 Feb 47

-- Socialism, communism, and international trade. JPE 57:227-41 Jun 49

Kreps, T. J. Cartels, a phase of business haute politique. AER/S 35:297-311 May 45

A Landry, R. S. The Federal Trade Commission and "unfair competition" in foreign trade. AER 35:575-84 Sep 45

EG McGill, V. J. Cartels and the settlement with Germany. S&S 9:23-54 no.1, 45

A Mason, E. S., chairman. Consensus report on the Webb-Pomerene law. AER 37: 848-63 Dec 47

EB Meyer, F. V. Bulk purchases. Ec N.S.15: 51-60 Feb 48

FA Taniguchi, K. The trade policy of East Asia wider territory economy. Kyo 17, no.2:20-43 Apr 42

FA -- The formation of the Trade Corporation. Kyo 18,no.3:26-45 Jul 43

## 11.24 CARTELS. COMMODITY AGREEMENTS. STATE TRADING (Cont.)

Terrill, R. P. Cartels and the international exchange of technology. AER/S 36: 745-67 May 46

Tucker, R. S. [and others] The progress of concentration in industry: discussion. AER/S 38:109-20 May 48

Vernon, R. Postwar trends in international business organization. AER/S 38:94-108 May 48

Viner, J. International relations between state-controlled national economies. AER/S 34:315-29 Mar 44

Walters, A. The International Copper Cartel. SEJ 11:133-56 Oct 44

Weidenhammer, R. M. The political economy of international cartels: discussion. AER/S 35:324-28 May 45

### 11.241 COMMODITY AGREEMENTS

Bauer, P. T. The working of rubber regulation. EJ 56:391-414 Sep 46

-- Malayan rubber policies. Ec N.S.14: 81-107 May 47

Davis, J. S. International commodity agreements in the postwar world. AER/S 32: 391-403 Mar 42

--, chairman. Round table on international commodity agreements. AER/S 33: 466-72 Mar 43

-- Experience under intergovernmental commodity agreements, 1902-45. JPE 54:193-220 Jun 46

Haussmann, F. World oil control, past and future: an alternative to "international cartelization." SR 9:334-55 Sep 42

Riefler, W. W. A proposal for an international buffer-stock agency. JPE 54: 538-46 Dec 46

Silcock, T. H. A note on the working of rubber regulation [followed by P. T. Bauer's rejoinder]. EJ 58:228-43 Jun 48

Staley, E. Taussig on "international allotment of important commodities." AER 33:877-81 Dec 43

Tsou, S. S. and Black, J. D. International commodity arrangements. QEJ 58: 521-52 Aug 44

Tyszynski, H. Economics of the Wheat Agreement. Ec N.S.16:27-39 Feb 49

Zaglits, O. International price control through buffer stocks. JFE 28:413-43 May 46

## 11.3 BALANCE OF PAYMENTS. MECHANISMS OF ADJUSTMENT
### 11.30 GENERAL

[Anonymous.] Bretton Woods. ER 20: 141-51 Dec 44

Batheja, H. R. The ends and machinery of international economic co-operation. IJE 25:306-15 Jan 45

Bell, J. W. Domestic and international monetary policies. A summary of the discussion of the results of a poll. AER/S 36:214-40 May 46

Benham, F. Full employment and international trade. Ec N.S.13:159-68 Aug 46

Bentwich, N. From Geneva to Yalta: the foundations of the new international order. EgC 36:285-92 Mar 45

Bonnell, A. T. The post-war international economic order. SEJ 9:46-52 Jul 42

Crick, W. F. Free trade and planned economy. SAJE 15:40-46 Mar 47

Crowther, G. [and others] International economic relations: discussion. AER/S 33:332-35 Mar 43

De Haas, J. A. The future of world trade. HBR 21:100-08 no.1, 42

Edminster, L. R. International trade and postwar reconstruction. AER/S 33: 303-21 Mar 43

El Falaki, M. S. The Bretton Woods' international finance program. EgC 36: 157-201 Jan-Feb 45

Fellner, W. The commercial policy implications of the Fund and Bank. AER/S 35: 262-71 May 45

Froehlich, W. International economic problems of a postwar world. RSE 1: 31-53 Dec 42

Habbu, R. K. International economic relations. IJE 29:179-84 Oct 48

Hirschman, A. O. International aspects of a recession. AER 39:1245-53 Dec 49

Hula, E. The Dumbarton Oaks proposals. SR 12:135-56 May 45

Jesness, O. B. Foreign trade policy: which way? JFE 31,pt.2:814-24 Nov 49

Kalecki, M. and Schumacher, E. F. International clearing and long-term lending. OIS 5,suppl.5:29-33 Aug 7, 43

-- Multilateralism and full employment. CJE 12:322-27 Aug 46

Krishna, V. S. International co-operation for controlling trade cycles. IJE 25: 301-06 Jan 45

Kurihara, K. K. Toward a new theory of monetary sovereignty. JPE 57:162-70 Apr 49

Marsh, D. B. Fiscal policy and tariffs in post-war international trade. CJE 9: 507-31 Nov 43

Mikesell, R. F. International disequilibrium and the postwar world. AER 39:618-45 Jun 49

Mutyala, J. International economic relations. IJE 29:257-63 Jan 49

Nurkse, R. International monetary policy and the search for economic stability. AER/S 37:569-80 May 47

Rasminsky, L. Anglo-American trade prospects: a Canadian view. EJ 55:161-78 Jun-Sep 45

# 11. INTERNATIONAL ECONOMICS

## 11.3 BALANCE OF PAYMENTS. MECHANISMS OF ADJUSTMENT (Cont.)

### 11.30 GENERAL (Cont.)

Schüller, R. Commercial policy between the two wars: personal observations of a participant. SR 10:152-74 May 43

Scott, R. H. "Bretton woods." ER 23: 49-57 Jun 47

Simons, H C. Postwar economic policy: some traditional liberal proposals. AER/S 33:431-45 Mar 43

Sitaramayya, M. Recent developments in monetary practice. IJE 22:1-37 Jul 41

Stern, E. H. The agreements of Bretton Woods. Ec N.S.11:165-79 Nov 44

Sumberg, T. A. Financing international institutions. SR 13:276-306 Sep 46

Upgren, A. R. International trade: discussion. AER/S 34:354-55 Mar 44

Valk, W. L. The transfer problem and the idea of an international monetary union. EI 1:246-50 Jan 48

Viner, J. International finance in the postwar world. LBR 2:3-17 Oct 46

-- --- [idem] JPE 55:97-107 Apr 47

Wigglesworth, E. International balance of payments, 1941. JM 6:290-92 Jan 42

Witt, L. W. Some further world trade problems: a review of Professor Jesness' paper. JFE 31,pt.2:825-31 Nov 49

### UNITED STATES

**A**
Balogh, T. The United States and the world economy. OIS 8:309-23 Oct 46

Bidwell, P. W. A postwar commercial policy for the United States. AER/S 34: 340-53 Mar 44

Bloomfield, A. I. The mechanism of adjustment of the American balance of payments: 1919-1929. QJE 57:333-77 May 43

De Vegh, I. Imports and income in the United States and Canada. REStat 23: 130-46 Aug 41

Elkinton, C. M. Foreign trade problems: further comment. JFE 31,pt.2:832-36 Nov 49

Gardner, W. R. The future international position of the United States as affected by the Fund and Bank. AER/S 35:272-88 May 45

Hinshaw, R. American prosperity and the British balance-of-payments problem. REStat 27:1-9 Feb 45

Keynes, J. M. The balance of payments of the United States. EJ 56:172-87 Jun 46

Landis, J. M. Economic relationships between the United States and Egypt. EgC 36:217-27 Mar 45

Mikesell, R. F. United States international financial policy. CJE 12:313-21 Aug 46

Rostow, W. W. The political basis for U.S. foreign policy. LBR 6:39-49 Oct 47

Sternberg, F. The United States in the future world economy. SR 11:285-304 Sep 44

### OTHER AMERICAN COUNTRIES

**C**
Blyth, C. D. Some aspects of Canada's international financial relations. CJE 12: 302-12 Aug 46

Chang, T. C. A note on exports and national income in Canada. CJE 13:276-80 May 47

De Vegh, I. Imports and income in the United States and Canada. REStat 23: 130-46 Aug 41

Elliott, G. A. On some appendices to the Rowell-Sirois report: V. Dominion monetary policy, 1929-1934. CJE 7: 88-91 Feb 41

Gibson, J. D. The Canadian balance of international payments: a study of methods and results. CJE 6:282-88 May 40

Knox, F. A. Some aspects of Canada's postwar export problem. CJE 10:312-27 Aug 44

-- Canada's balance of international payments, 1940-5. CJE 13:345-62 Aug 47

Mackintosh, W. A. Canada and the world economy in the making. LBR 12:12-29 Apr 49

Munzer, E. Exports and national income in Canada. CJE 11:35-47 Feb 45

**D**
De Beers, J. S. Some aspects of Latin America's trade and balance of payments. AER/S 39:384-95 May 49

### EUROPE

**E**
Rodano, C. The economic future of Europe and the ERP. BNL 2:135-45 Jul-Sep 49

**EB**
Balogh, T. The importance of multilateral trade for Britain. OIS 6:183-88 Aug 12, 44

-- The problem of the British balance of payments. OIS 9:211-27 Jul 47

-- Britain, O.E.E.C. and the restoration of a world economy. OIS 11:35-52 Feb-Mar 49

Behrman, J. N. A reappraisal of the United Kingdom's balance of payments problem under full employment. SEJ 14:173-85 Oct 47

Bernstein, E. M. British policy and a world economy. AER 35:891-908 Dec 45

Brown, A. S. Prospects of United Kingdom recovery. ER 25,suppl.:3-28 Aug 49

Carter, C. F. and Chang, T. C. A further note on the British balance of payments. Ec N.S.13:183-89 Aug 46

Chang, T. C. The British balance of payments, 1924-1938. EJ 57:475-503 Dec 47

Clark, C. The value of the pound. EJ 59: 198-207 Jun 49

Friday, F. A. United Kingdom export target. OIS 8:169-77 Jun 46

Hinshaw, R. American prosperity and the British balance-of-payments problem. REStat 27:1-9 Feb 45

11.3 BALANCE OF PAYMENTS. MECHANISMS
OF ADJUSTMENT (Cont.)

11.30 GENERAL (Cont.)

EUROPE (Cont.)

Hinshaw, R. (Cont.)

EB -- and Metzler, L. A. World prosperity and the British balance of payments. REStat 27:156-70 Nov 45

Kahn, A. E. The British balance of payments and problems of domestic policy. QJE 61:368-96 May 47

Meade, J. E. Bretton Woods, Havana and the United Kingdom balance of payments. LBR 7:1-18 Jan 48

-- Financial policy and the balance of payments. Ec N.S.15:101-15 May 48

Morgan, D. J. Commentary on "Great Britain's trade policy" [followed by R. Schüller's rejoinder]. SR 12:370-77 Sep 45

-- The British commonwealth and European economic co-operation. EJ 59:307-25 Sep 49

Nash, E. F. Changes in external factors affecting British agriculture. LBR 8:35-56 Apr 48

Opie, R. A British view of postwar trade. AER/S 33:322-31 Mar 43

Paish, F. W. Britain's economic problem. AER 38:118-21 Mar 48

Robbins, L. Inquest on the crisis. LBR 6:1-27 Oct 47

-- The sterling problem. LBR 14:1-31 Oct 49

Schüller, R. Great Britain's trade policy. SR 11:268-84 Sep 44

Viner, J. An American view of the British economic crisis. LBR 6:28-38 Oct 47

EBC  Lewis, E. M. R. and Miller, K. W. Notes
EF on the balance of payments of the British and French empires with non-sterling countries. ER 16:114-18 Jun 40

EG Huber, J. R. The effects of German clearing agreements and import restrictions on cotton, 1934-1939. SEJ 6:419-39 Apr 40

EI Miller, H. S. Italian monetary and exchange policies under fascism. AER 30:554-60 Sep 40

ER Prince, C. The USSR's role in international finance. HBR 25:111-28 no.1, 46

ESN Holben, R. E. Planned economy in Norway: comment. AER 39:1283-87 Dec 49

Klein, L. R. Planned economy in Norway. AER 38:795-814 Dec 48

ESw Rappard, W. E. The economic position of Switzerland. LBR 11:21-36 Jan 49

ASIA

FC Liu, T. C. China's foreign exchange problems: a proposed solution. AER 31:266-79 Jun 41

FI Anantaram, K. Pathology of India's balance of payments. IJE 30:115-21 Oct 49

Bhattacharya, K. N. Some aspects of India's commercial policy. IJE 28:17-21 Jul 47

Bhojwani, N. K. Post-war implications of India's sterling credits. IJE 25:1-14 Jul 44

Gurtoo, D. N. Balance of payment of India. IJE 30:129-37 Oct 49

Idris, S. M. [and others] Discussion on "India and international economic co-operation." IJE 25:626-29 Apr 45

Krishna, V. S. India and the Sterling Area. IJE 26:508-16 Jan 46

Malhotra, D. K. Indian currency: past, present and future. IJE 24:202-11 Jan 44

Malhotra, P. C. India's balance of payments. IJE 30:109-14 Oct 49

Mishra, J. K. Price level and balance of payments of India in recent years. IJE 30:123-27 Oct 49

Narasimham, N. V. A. Terms of trade and commercial policy. IJE 28:39-48 Jul 47

Poduval, R. N. India's commodity balance of trade since the war. IJE 30:149-60 Oct 49

Saha, K. B. India's balance of payments. IJE 30:101-07 Oct 49

Sen, M. K. International economic relations. IJE 29:265-69 Jan 49

Sengupta, S. Essentials of an appropriate commercial policy for India. IJE 28:49-54 Jul 47

Sinha, M. N. Indian currency and war. IJE 22:199-207 Oct 41

FIP Alvi, H. A. Pakistan's system of payments. PEJ 1,no.1:126-37 Jul 49

AFRICA

H Anonymous. The balance of payments of Southern Rhodesia, 1939-1947. By the Central African Statistical Office. SAJE 16:388-404 Dec 48

HSA Garmany, J. W. South Africa and the Sterling Area. SAJE 17:480-91 Dec 49

MIDDLE EAST

M Lackany, S. From the Middle East Monetary Conference to Bretton Woods. EgC 36:95-109 Jan-Feb 45

Mikesell, R. F. Financial problems of the Middle East. JPE 53:164-76 Jun 45

ME El Falaki, M. S. Egypt and the organisation of the international finance to-day. EgC 38:101-14 Jan-Feb 47

Landis, J. M. Economic relationships between the United States and Egypt. EgC 36:217-27 Mar 45

Schumacher, E. F. Anglo-Egyptian currency relations. OIS 7:30-36 Feb 3, 45

# 11. INTERNATIONAL ECONOMICS

## 11.3 BALANCE OF PAYMENTS. MECHANISMS OF ADJUSTMENT (Cont.)
## 11.30 GENERAL (Cont.)
### AUSTRALIA. NEW ZEALAND

N   Simkin, C. G. F. Insulationism and the problem of economic stability. ER 22: 50-65 Jun 46

Wood, G. L. International economic co-operation and the Australian economy. ER 23:159-76 Dec 47

## 11.301 STERLING AREA
Balogh, T. Should sterling be devalued? BNL 2:90-102 Apr-Jun 49

-- --- [idem] OIS 11:228-42 Jul-Aug 49

Garmany, J. W. South Africa and the Sterling Area. SAJE 17:480-91 Dec 49

Harris, S. E. The official and unofficial markets for sterling. QJE 54:655-64 Aug 40

Hicks, J. R. Devaluation and world trade. TBR 4:3-23 Dec 49

Schumacher, E. F. Anglo-Egyptian currency relations. OIS 7:30-36 Feb 3, 45

Tew, B. Sterling as an international currency. ER 24:42-55 Jun 48

## 11.302 DOLLAR SHORTAGE
Balogh, T. The concept of a dollar shortage. BNL 2:83-89 Apr-Jun 49

-- --- [idem] MS 17:186-201 May 49

Bloomfield, A. I. Induced investment, overcomplete international adjustment, and chronic dollar shortage [followed by C. P. Kindleberger's rejoinder]. AER 39: 970-75 Sep 49

Ellis, H. S. The dollar shortage in theory and fact. CJE 14:358-72 Aug 48

Harris, S. E. Dollar scarcity: some remarks inspired by Lord Keynes' last article. EJ 57:165-78 Jun 47

Hirschman, A. O. Disinflation, discrimination, and the dollar shortage. AER 38: 886-92 Dec 48

Paranjpe, V. M. The dollar shortage and the international monetary co-operation. IJE 29:165-70 Oct 48

Robinson, J. The United States in the world economy. R. EJ 54:430-37 Dec 44

Stolper, W. F. American foreign economic policy, the dollar shortage, and Mr. Balogh. R. Kyk 3:160-72 fasc.2, 49

Tinbergen, J. Some considerations on the problem of dollar scarcity. EI 1:562-67 May 48

-- Some remarks on the problem of dollar scarcity. Em 17,suppl.:73-95 Jul 49

## 11.31 HISTORY
D/EB   Anonymous. British investments in Latin America. TBR 2:22-29 Jun 49

A   Brayer, H. O. The influence of British capital on the western range-cattle industry. JEH/S 9:85-98 suppl.:9 49

DSC   Centner, C. W. Great Britain and Chilian mining 1830-1914. EHR 12:76-82

EB   no.1-2, 42

Cooney, E. W. Capital exports, and invest-
A   ment in building in Britain and the U.S.
EB   A. 1856-1914. Ec N.S.16:347-54 Nov 49

E   De Roover, R. What is dry exchange? A contribution to the study of English mercantilism. JPE 52:250-66 Sep 44

H   Duncan, A. J. South African capital imports, 1893-8. CJE 14:20-45 Feb 48

EB   Henderson, W. O. British economic activity
H   in the German colonies, 1884-1914. EHR 15:56-66 no.1-2, 45

EG   -- German economic penetration in the
M   Middle East, 1870-1914. EHR 18:54-64 no.1-2, 48

EB   Hidy, R. W. A leaf from investment history. HBR 20:65-74 no.1, 41

EB   Jenks, L. H. British experience with foreign investments. JEH/S 4:68-79 Dec 44

A   Redlich, F. The business activities of Eric Bollmann: an international business promoter, 1797-1821. Pt.I-II. BHR 17:81-91; 103-12 Nov,Dec 43

E   Wilson, C. Treasure and trade balances: the mercantilist problem. EHR II.2: 152-61 no.2, 49

## 11.32 BALANCE OF PAYMENTS THEORY
## 11.321 ACCOUNTING FRAMEWORK
Aukrust, O. International accounting. NTTO 12:13-22 no.37, 48

Bell, H. H. Short-run equilibrium in the balance of payments. SEJ 8:366-79 Jan 42

Conan, A. R. Notes on some balance of payments figures. OIS 9:196-206 Jun 47

Hall, R. O. Some neglected relationships in the balance of payments. AER 31: 81-86 Mar 41

Lengyel, S. J. Insurance in the international balances of payments. JASA 39:428-38 Dec 44

McKinley, G. W. The residual item in the balance of international payments. AER 31:308-16 Jun 41

Mars, J. The integration of the balance of payments into national income accounts. YB 1:43-66 Sep 49

Ou, P. S. International payments in national income. QJE 60:289-98 Feb 46

## 11.322 THEORY OF PRICE, INCOME, AND EMPLOYMENT
Bloomfield, A. I. [and others] Domestic versus international equilibrium: discussion. AER/S 37:581-94 May 47

Booker, H. S. A note on deferred export credits. EJ 59:253-58 Jun 49

Bronfenbrenner, M. The Keynesian equations and the balance of payments. REStud 7:180-84 Jun 40

## 11.32 BALANCE OF PAYMENTS THEORY (Cont.)
## 11.322 THEORY OF PRICE, INCOME, AND EMPLOYMENT (Cont.)

Chipman, J. S. The generalized bi-system multiplier. CJE 15:176-89 May 49

Datta, A. International equilibrium in a complementary economy. IJE 23:221-56 Jan 43

Haberler, G. [The foreign trade multiplier]. Comment. AER 37:898-906 Dec 47

Harvie, C. H. A note on deferred export credits. EJ 58:425-28 Sep 48

Kindleberger, C. P. The foreign-trade multiplier, the propensity to import and balance-of-payments equilibrium. AER 39:491-94 Mar 49

Leontief, W. W. Exports, imports, domestic output, and employment. QJE 60: 171-93 Feb 46; Correction. 469 May 46

Marsh, D. B. Fiscal policy and tariffs in post-war international trade. CJE 9: 507-31 Nov 43

Meade, J. E. National income, national expenditure and the balance of payments. Pt.I-[II]. EJ 58:483-505; 59:17-39 Dec 48, Mar 49

Metzler, L. A. Underemployment equilibrium in international trade. Em 10: 97-112 Apr 42

Neisser, H. The significance of foreign trade for domestic employment. SR 13: 307-25 Sep 46

-- The nature of import propensities and the foreign trade multiplier. EI 2:573-87 Aug 49

Polak, J. J. The foreign trade multiplier. AER 37:889-97 Dec 47

-- and Haberler, G. [The foreign trade multiplier.] A restatement. AER 37:906-07 Dec 47

Raj, J. S. International equilibrium in a complementary economy. IJE 24:71-73 Jul 43

Smithies, A. Multilateral trade and employment. AER/S 37:560-68 May 47

Stolper, W. F. The volume of foreign trade and the level of income. QJE 61:285-310 Feb 47

## 11.33 INTERNATIONAL ADJUSTMENT MECHANISMS
## 11.330 GENERAL

Adiseshiah, M. S. International economic co-operation and an international standard. IJE 25:290-300 Jan 45

-- Some aspects of post-war Indian currency. IJE 26:452-71 Jan 46  [FI]

Arndt, H. W. The concept of liquidity in international monetary theory. REStud 15:20-26 no.1, 47

Balogh, T. A new view of the economics of international readjustment. REStud 14: 82-94 no.2, 47

Chand, G. The post-war monetary issues in India. IJE 26:472-87 Jan 46  [FI]

De Kock, M. H. World monetary policy after the present war. SAJE 9:113-37 Jun 41

Haberler, G. Comments on "National central banking and the international economy." EI 1:1117-32 Nov 48

Harrod, R. F. A comment [on R. Triffin's National central banking and the international economy]. REStud 14:95-97 no.2, 47

Henderson, H. D. The international economy [a comment on R. Triffin's National central banking and the international economy]. REStud 14:76-81 no.2, 47

Iyengar, S. K. Post-war currency system in India. IJE 26:499-507 Jan 46  [FI]

Kumar, K. International currency experience during the inter-war period. R. IJE 25:374-76 Jan 45

Lalwani, K. The future of gold vis-a-vis currency plans. Pt.I-II. IJE 25:15-23; 103-16 Jul,Oct 44

Matsuoka, K. The currency system in French Indo-China. Kyo 17,no.2:44-63 Apr 42  [FA]

-- Southern economy: its currency and financial problems. Kyo 17,no.4:27-47 Oct 42  [FA]

Pardasani, N. S. Post-war currency system in India. IJE 26:535-43 Jan 46  [FI]

Sahasrabuddhe, V. G. Post-war monetary system for India. IJE 26:554-64 Jan 46  [FI]

Triffin, R. International versus domestic money. AER/S 37:322-24 May 47

-- National central banking and the international economy. REStud 14:53-75 no.2, 47

## 11.331 EXCHANGE RATES
## 11.3310 GENERAL

Bernardelli, H. Some comment on a dynamic theory of foreign exchanges. IJE 23:301-18 Apr 43

Brovedani, B. Exchange rate structure and price levels in Italy: 1947-48. BNL 1: 369-80 Jul 48  [EI]

Chang, T. C. International comparison of demand for imports. REStud 13:53-67 pt.2, 46

-- A statistical note on world demand for exports. REStat 30:106-16 May 48

Ciano, J. L. D. The pre-war "black" market for foreign bank notes. Ec N.S.8: 378-91 Nov 41  [EB]

Dupriez, L. H. Postwar exchange-rate parities: comment. QJE 60:299-308 Feb 46

Ellis, H. S. The problem of exchange systems in the postwar world. AER/S 32: 195-205 Mar 42

Field, H. A note on exchange stability. REStud 15:46-49 no.1, 47

# 11. INTERNATIONAL ECONOMICS

## 11.331 EXCHANGE RATES (Cont.)
### 11.3310 GENERAL (Cont.)

Frisch, R. Prolegomena to a pressure-analysis of economic phenomena. Met 1:135-60 Dec 49

Garnsey, M. E. Postwar exchange-rate parities. QJE 60:113-35 Nov 45

Graham, F. D. Exchange rates: bound or free? JF 4:13-27 Mar 49

Haberler, G. The choice of exchange rates after the war. AER 35:308-18 Jun 45

-- The market for foreign exchange and the stability of the balance of payments: a theoretical analysis. Kyk 3:193-218 fasc.3, 49

Halasi, A. International monetary cooperation. SR 9:183-203 May 42

Hawtrey, R. G. The function of exchange rates. OEP N.S.1:145-56 Jun 49

Henderson, Sir H. The function of exchange rates. OEP N.S.1:1-17 Jan 49

-- A comment [on Hawtrey's "The function of exchange rates"]. OEP N.S.1:157-58 Jun 49

Koo, A. Y. C. Income elasticity of demand for imports and terms of trade. AER 39:966-70 Sep 49

Machlup, F. The theory of foreign exchanges. Pt.I-II. Ec N.S.6:375-97; N.S.7:23-49 Nov 39, Feb 40

FI Malkani, H. C. Post-war currency system in India. IJE 26:388-91 Jan 46

Metzler, L. A. Tariffs, international demand, and domestic prices. JPE 57:345-51 Aug 49

Mikesell, R. F. The determination of post-war exchange rates. SEJ 13:263-75 Jan 47

D Pazos, F. Inflation and exchange instability in Latin America. AER/S 39:396-405 May 49

Raj, J. S. A dynamic theory of the foreign exchanges. IJE 23:155-66 Oct 42

Sadie, J. L. Further observations on foreign exchange rates. SAJE 16:194-201 Jun 48

Salera, V. Exchange-rate parities: comment [followed by M. E. Garnsey's reply]. QJE 60:622-30 Aug 46

FI Sovani, N. V. The future of the rupee. IJE 26:410-19 Jan 46

Stolper, W. F. Purchasing power parity and the pound sterling from 1919-1925. Kyk 2:240-69 fasc.3, 48

Tamagna, F. M. The fixing of foreign exchange rates. JPE 53:57-72 Mar 45

Tinbergen, J. Some measurements of elasticities of substitution. REStat 28:109-16 Aug 46

-- Long-term foreign trade elasticities. Met 1:174-85 Dec 49

Wijnholds, H. W. J. Some observations on foreign exchange rates in theory and practice. SAJE 15:235-47 Dec 47

-- Further observations on foreign exchange rates. SAJE 16:309 Sep 48

Winton, J. R. The value of the rupee. FI LBR 4:42-48 Apr 47

Young, J. P. Exchange rate determination. AER 37:589-603 Sep 47

Youngson, A. J. Trade balances and exchange stability. OEP 6:57-75 Apr 42

FI Zacharias, C. W. B. The level of stabilization. IJE 27:21-34 Jul 46

### 11.3312 STABILIZED RATES

Bloomfield, A. I. Operations of the American exchange stabilization fund. REStat 26:69-87 May 44

Chand, G. The exchange stabilization funds: their function and future. IJE 20:535-43 Apr 40

D'Souza, V. L. Exchange equalisation. IJE 20:545-55 Apr 40

Jain, P. C. Recent monetary technique: [discussion]. IJE 20:824-25 Apr 40

EB Pumphrey, L. M. The exchange equalization account of Great Britain, 1932-1939: exchange operations. AER 32:803-16 Dec 42

### 11.3313 REVALUATION

Balogh, T. Exchange depreciation and economic readjustment. REStat 30:276-85 Nov 48

-- Should sterling be devalued? BNL 2:90-102 Apr-Jun 49

-- --- [idem] OIS 11:228-42 Jul-Aug 49

FI Bhattacharya, K. N. India's balance of trade: a case for devaluation. IJE 30:139-47 Oct 49

EB Burtle, J. L. and Liepe, W. Devaluation and the cost of living in the United Kingdom. REStud 17:1-28 no.1, 49

EB Harris, S. E. Devaluation of the pound sterling. HBR 27:781-90 Nov 49

Hicks, J. R. Devaluation and world trade. TBR 4:3-23 Dec 49

Hirschman, A. O. Devaluation and the trade balance: a note. REStat 31:50-53 Feb 49

Kähler, A. The British devaluation. SR 16:474-88 Dec 49

FI Kibe, M. V. Monetary policy and inflation in India: debasement of currency and its effect. IJE 30:197-98 Oct 49

DSA Luzzatto, G. The depreciation of the peso and trade between Italy and Argentina. EI BNL1:427-33 Oct 48

Meade, J. E. A geometrical representation of balance of payments policy. Ec N.S.16:305-20 Nov 49

N Neale, E. P. The N.Z. exchange alteration of August 1948. ER 24:245-49 Dec 48

E Polak, J. J. European exchange depreciation in the early twenties. Em 11:151-62 Apr 43

-- Exchange depreciation and international monetary stability. REStat 29:173-82 Aug 47

11.331 EXCHANGE RATES (Cont.)

11.3313 REVALUATION (Cont.)

Sahasrabudhe, V. G. Devaluation and infla-
FI    tion. IJE 30:199-204 Oct 49

Singh, B. Devaluation and India's balance
FI    of payments. IJE 30:205-09 Oct 49

11.332 AUTOMATIC SCHEMES

11.3320 GENERAL

Bernstein, E. M. Exchange rates under the
gold standard. JPE 48:345-56 Jun 40

Brown, W. A., Jr. Dr. Palyi on the meaning of the gold standard. JB 14:419-23
Oct 41

-- Gold as a monetary standard, 1914-1949.
JEH/S 9:39-49 '49

Fels, R. Gold and international equilibrium.
AER 39:281-83 Dec 49

Harris, S. E. Gold and the American econ-
A    omy. REStat 22:1-12 Feb 40

-- American gold policy and Allied war.
A    economics. EJ 50:224-30 Jun-Sep 40

Kahn, A. E. The burden of import duties:
a comment [followed by E. R. Rolph's
rejoinder]. AER 38:857-69 Dec 48

Knox, F. A. The international gold standard reinterpreted. R. CJE 10:502-07
Nov 44

Palyi, M. The meaning of the gold standard. R. JB 14:294-314 Jul 41

-- England versus gold: a rejoinder to
Professor Brown. JB 14:423-26 Oct 41

Reedman, J. N. Gold and post-war currency standards. SAJE 9:379-99 Dec 41

Rist, C. The measure of gold. R. SAJE 17:
371-79 Dec 49

Rolph, E. R. The burden of import duties
with fixed exchange rates. AER 37:
604-32 Sep 47

Whittlesey, C. R. Political aspects of the
gold problem. JEH/S 9:50-60 '49

11.333 NEGOTIATED SCHEMES

11.3330 GENERAL

Mikesell, R. F. Quantitative and exchange
restrictions under the ITO charter.
AER 37:351-68 Jun 47

11.3331 INTERNATIONAL MONETARY FUND.
BANK FOR INTERNATIONAL SETTLE-
MENTS

Agarwala, S. N. India and international
FI    currency plans. R. IJE 25:372-74 Jan 45

Anonymous. New plans for international
trade: lessons of the past [by the editor].
OIS 5,suppl.5:3-8 Aug 7, 43

-- An international Monetary Fund.
ER 20:81-91 Jun 44

Arndt, H. W. The International Monetary
Fund and the treatment of cyclical balance of payments disequilibria. ER 23:
186-97 Dec 47

Balogh, T. The foreign balance and full
employment. OIS 5,suppl.5:33-39
Aug 7, 43

-- New monetary agreements. OIS 7:
138-45 Jun 9, 45

Bernstein, E. M. A practical international
monetary policy. AER 34:771-84 Dec 44

-- Scarce currencies and the International
Monetary Fund. JPE 53:1-14 Mar 45

Bourneuf, A. E. Postwar international
monetary institutions [with discussion
by R. J. Saulnier]. RSE 2:68-80 Jan 44

-- Professor Williams and the Fund.
AER 34:840-47 Dec 44

-- [and others] International monetary and
credit arrangements: discussion.
AER/S 35:289-96 May 45

-- Lending operations of the International
Monetary Fund. REStat 28:237-47 Nov 46

Brown, E. E. The International Monetary
Fund: a consideration of certain objections. JB 17:199-208 Oct 44

Brown, W. A., Jr. The repurchase provisions of the proposed International
Monetary Fund. AER 35:111-20 Mar 45

Condliffe, J. B. Exchange stabilization and
international trade. (Symposium on the
International Monetary Fund) REStat 26:
166-69 Nov 44

Cover, J. H. [International financial relations after the war]: discussion.
AER/S 33:390-92 Mar 43

Crump, N. [and others] Post-war international monetary plans. JRSS 106:
201-13 pt.3, 43

De Vegh, I. The International Clearing
Union. AER 33:534-56 Sep 43

Dey, H. L. International Monetary Fund.
Pt.I-II. IJE 25:173-78; 413-22 Oct 44,
Apr 45

Ellis, H. S. Can national and international
monetary policies be reconciled?
AER/S 34:385-95 Mar 44

Graham, F. D. International monetary problems: discussion. AER/S 34:399-401
Mar 44

Gutt, C. Exchange rates and the International Monetary Fund. REStat 30:81-90
May 48

Haberler, G. Currency depreciation and
the International Monetary Fund.
REStat 26:178-81 Nov 44

-- Some comments on Professor Hansen's
note. (Symposium on the International
Monetary Fund) REStat 26:191-93 Nov 44

Haines, W. W. Keynes, White, and history.
QJE 58:120-33 Nov 43

Halm, G. N. The International Monetary
Fund. REStat 26:170-75 Nov 44

Hansen, A. H. A brief note on "fundamental
disequilibrium." (Symposium on the
International Monetary Fund) REStat 26:
182-84 Nov 44

## 11. INTERNATIONAL ECONOMICS

### 11.3331 INTERNATIONAL MONETARY FUND. BANK FOR INTERNATIONAL SETTLEMENTS (Cont.)

Harris, S. E. The contributions of Bretton Woods and some unsolved problems. (Symposium on the International Monetary Fund) REStat 26:175-77 Nov 44

Holloway, J. E. The Bretton Woods Conference and the International Monetary Fund. SAJE 12:205-22 Sep 44

Keynes, J. M. The objective of international price stability. EJ 53:185-87 Jun-Sep 43

Lachmann, L. M. Notes on the proposals for international currency stabilization. REStat 26:184-91 Nov 44

Lackany, S. From the Middle East Monetary Conference to Bretton Woods. EgC 36:95-109 Jan-Feb 45

Ladenburg, H. Plan for a postwar world clearing bank. SR 9:510-29 Nov 42

MacGibbon, D. A. International monetary control. CJE 11:1-13 Feb 45

Michell, H. Monetary reconstruction. CJE 8:339-50 Aug 42

Mikesell, R. F. The key currency proposal. QJE 59:563-76 Aug 45

-- The role of the international monetary agreements in a world of planned economies. JPE 55:497-512 Dec 47

-- The International Monetary Fund. JPE 57:395-412 Oct 49

Morgan, E. V. The plans for an international clearing system. Ec N.S.10:297-301 Nov 43

-- The joint statement by experts on the establishment of an international monetary fund. Ec N.S.11:112-18 Aug 44

Neisser, H. P. An international reserve bank: comments on the American and British plans. SR 10:265-79 Sep 43

Opie, R. International monetary problems: discussion. AER/S 34:396-99 Mar 44

Pillai, V. R. Money and the nations. IJE 25:282-89 Jan 45

Plumptre, A. F. W. [International financial relations after the war]: discussion. AER/S 33:388-90 Mar 43

Poole, K. E. National economic policies and international monetary cooperation. AER 37:369-75 Jun 47

Rao, B. S. Equilibrium exchange rates and the I.M.F. IJE 29:249-56 Jan 49

Robertson, D. H. The post-war monetary plans. EJ 53:352-60 Dec 43

Robinson, J. The international currency proposals. EJ 53:161-75 Jun-Sep 43

Salera, V. Mikesell on international monetary agreements and planned economies [followed by R. F. Mikesell's reply]. JPE 56:442-50 Oct 48

Schumacher, E. F. The new currency plans. OIS 5,suppl. 5:8-29 Aug 7, 43

-- and Baloch, T. An international monetary fund. OIS 6:81-93 Apr 29, 44

Sovani, N. V. The future of the rupee. IJE 26:410-19 Jan 46

White, H. D. Postwar currency stabilization. AER/S 33:382-87 Mar 43

Williams, J. H. The postwar monetary plans. AER/S 34:372-84 Mar 44

### 11.3332 INTERNATIONAL TRADE ORGANIZATION. GENERAL AGREEMENT ON TARIFFS AND TRADE

Balogh, T. The charter of the International Trade Organization and the Preparatory Committee of the United Nations Conference on Trade and Employment. OIS 9:104-28 Mar,Apr 47

EB -- Britain and the Geneva Tariff Agreements. OIS 9:417-29 Dec 47

Bidwell, P. W. International Trade Organization: discussion. AER/S 37:554-56 May 47

Coppola d'Anna, F. False aims in the I.T.O. Draft Charter. BNL 1:143-48 Oct 47

Earley, J. S. [and others] Problems of the ITO: discussion. AER/S 39:269-79 May 49

Ellsworth, P. T. The Havana Charter: comment. AER 39:1268-73 Dec 49

Furth, J. H. Short-run escape clauses of the Havana Charter. AER/S 39:252-60 May 49

Gerschenkron, A. International Trade Organization: discussion. AER/S 37:556-59 May 47

ER -- Russia and the International Trade Organization. AER/S 37:624-42 May 47

Gordon, M. S. The character and significance of the general commitments that nations will make under the ITO Charter. AER/S 39:241-51 May 49

Henderson, Sir H. A criticism of the Havana charter. AER 39:605-17 Jun 49

A Hopkins, J. A. Significance of the Geneva Trade Conference to United States agriculture. JFE 29:1055-71 Nov 47

Karve, D. G. Free trade among nations: American proposals. IJE 27:279-85 Jan 47

Knorr, K. E. The functions of an International Trade Organization: possibilities and limitations. AER/S 37:542-53 May 47

Loftus, J. A. Permanent exceptions to the commercial policy provisions of the ITO Charter. AER/S 39:261-68 May 49

Loveday, A. The Report for the trade discussions. R LBR 4:26-41 Apr 47

FI Paranjpe, V. M. Commercial policy for India. IJE 28:31-38 Jul 47

Schüller, R. Foreign trade policies of the United States and Soviet Russia. SR 14:135-47 Jun 47

11.3332 INTERNATIONAL TRADE ORGANIZA-
TION. GENERAL AGREEMENT ON
TARIFFS AND TRADE (Cont.)
Schüller, R. (Cont.)
-- The ITO Charter. SR 15:135-45 Jun 48
Urquhart, M. C. Post-war international
trade arrangements. CJE 14:373-85
Aug 48
Wilcox, C. The London draft of a charter
for an International Trade Organization.
AER/S 37:529-41 May 47

11.3333 REGIONAL SCHEMES
Balogh, T. Intra-European clearing.
OIS 10:281-83 Sep 48
Bean, R. W. European multilateral clear-
ing. JPE 56:403-15 Oct 48
Fels, R. Regional multilateral clearing.
JPE 56:342-43 Aug 48
Kahn, R. F. A possible intra-European
payments scheme. Ec N.S.16:293-304
Nov 49
Mikesell, R. F. Regional multilateral pay-
ments arrangements. QJE 62:500-18
Aug 48
Schumacher, E. F. Multilateral clearing.
Ec N.S.10:150-65 May 43

11.34 QUANTITATIVE TRADE AND EXCHANGE
RESTRICTIONS
Balogh, T. The League of Nations on post-
war foreign trade problems. R. EJ 54:
256-61 Jun-Sep 44
EB -- Discrimination: British trade problems
and the Marshall Plan. OIS 10:221-29
Jul-Aug 48
-- --- [idem] EI 1:1133-46 Nov 48
Bloomfield, A. I. Postwar control of inter-
national capital movements. AER/S 36:
687-709 May 46
Crowley, N. G. and Haddon-Cave, C. P.
The regulation and expansion of world
trade and employment. ER 23:32-48
Jun 47
Ekker, M. H. A scheme of international
compensation: postscript. Em 17:
150-53 Apr 49
Ellis, H. S. Exchange control in Germany.
EG QJE 54,no.4,pt.2:1-220 Aug 40
-- Exchange control and discrimination.
AER 37:877-88 Dec 47
Frisch, R. On the need for forecasting a
multilateral balance of payments.
AER 37:535-51 Sep 47
-- Outline of a system of multicompensa-
tory trade. REStat 30:265-71 Nov 48
Gini, C. Bilateral and multilateral trade.
BNL 2:3-11 Jan-Mar 49
Henderson, A. The restriction of foreign
trade. MS 17:12-35 Jan 49
Hinshaw, R. Professor Frisch on discrimi-
nation and multilateral trade.
REStat 30:271-75 Nov 48

Hoffman, M. L. Capital movements and
E international payments in postwar
Europe. REStat 31:261-65 Nov 49
Holzman, F. D. Discrimination in inter-
national trade. AER 39:1233-44 Dec 49
Klein, L. A scheme of international com-
pensation. Em 17:145-49 Apr 49
McDougall, G. D. A. Notes on non-dis-
crimination. OIS 9:375-94 Nov 47
Meade, J. E. A geometrical representa-
tion of balance of payments policy.
Ec N.S.16:305-20 Nov 49
Meier, G. M. The trade matrix: a further
comment on Professor Frisch's paper.
AER 38:624-26 Sep 48
Patterson, G. and Polk, J. The emerging
pattern of bilateralism. QJE 62:118-42
Nov 47
Polak, J. J. Balancing international trade:
a comment on Professor Frisch's paper.
AER 38:139-42 Mar 48
Rona, F. Objectives and methods of ex-
EB change control in the United Kingdom
during the war and post-war transition.
Ec N.S.13:259-77 Nov 46
Shannon, H. A. The British payments and
EB exchange control system. QJE 63:
212-37 May 49
Smith, A. H. Evolution of the exchange
EB control. Ec N.S.16:243-48 Aug 49
Stolper, W. F. American foreign economic
A policy, the dollar shortage, and Mr.
Balogh. R. Kyk 3:160-72 fasc.2, 49
Tokunaga, K. Monetary and financial re-
FC organization in North China. Kyo 15,
no.2:71-100 Apr 40

11.35 CAPITAL MOVEMENTS. FOREIGN
ASSISTANCE
11.350 GENERAL
Anantaram, K. The future of international
investment. IJE 29:171-78 Oct 48
Bloomfield, A. I. Postwar control of inter-
national capital movements. AER/S 36:
687-709 May 46
Hahn, L. A. Capital is made at home.
EG SR 11:242-58 May 44
Hoffman, M. L. Capital movements and
E international payments in postwar
Europe. REStat 31:261-65 Nov 49
Neisser, H. Comments on "Capital is made
EG at home." SR 11:367-71 Sep 44
Schoepperle, V. Future of international
A investment: private versus public
foreign lending. AER/S 33:336-41
Mar 43
Wallich, H. C. The future of Latin Ameri-
D can dollar bonds. AER 33:321-35 Jun 43
Wu, Y. L. International capital investment
and the development of poor countries.
EJ 56:86-101 Mar 46

## 11. INTERNATIONAL ECONOMICS

### 11.35 CAPITAL MOVEMENTS. FOREIGN ASSISTANCE (Cont.)

#### 11.351 THEORY. TRANSFER PROBLEM

Balogh, T. Some theoretical problems of post-war foreign investment policy. OEP 7:93-110 Mar 45

Bloomfield, A. I. Induced investment, over-complete international adjustment, and chronic dollar shortage [followed by C. P. Kindleberger's rejoinder]. AER 39: 970-75 Sep 49

Hinshaw, R. Foreign investment and American employment. AER/S 36:661-71 May 46

Kindleberger, C. P. Planning for foreign investment. AER/S 33:347-54 Mar 43

Knapp, J. The theory of international capital movements and its verifications. REStud 10:115-21 no.2, 43

Kurihara, K. K. Foreign investment and full employment. JPE 55:459-64 Oct 47

Lary, H. B. The domestic effects of foreign investment. AER/S 36:672-86 May 46

Leontief, W. The pure theory of transfer. [Outline of a paper presented at the] Round table on theory of international trade. AER/S 30:219-22 Mar 40

Martin, K. Capital movements, the terms of trade and the balance of payments. OIS 11:357-66 Nov 49

Metzler, L. A. The transfer problem reconsidered. JPE 50:397-414 Jun 42

Valk, W. L. The transfer problem and the idea of an international monetary union. EI 1:246-50 Jan 48

#### 11.352 PRIVATE CAPITAL MOVEMENTS

Bloomfield, A. I. The significance of outstanding securities in the international movement of capital. CJE 6:495-524 Nov 40

FC Hu, K. T. Investment in China's postwar industry. HBR 21:309-20 no.3, 43

EI Rienzi, E. The participation of foreign capital in Italian joint-stock companies at the outbreak of the Second World War. BNL 1:338-43 Apr 48

A
DS Rippy, J. F. South American investments and hemisphere defense. JB 14:345-55 Oct 41

DC
EG -- German investments in Quatemala. JB 20:212-19 Oct 47

DSA
EG -- German investments in Argentina. JB 21:50-54 Jan 48

D/EB -- British investments in Latin America, 1939. JPE 56:63-68 Feb 48

D/EG -- German investments in Latin America. JB 21:63-73 Apr 48

A
D -- Investments of citizens of the United States in Latin America. JB 22:17-29 Jan 49

Schiff, E. Direct investments, terms of trade, and balance of payments. QJE 56: 307-20 Feb 42

DM Zimmerman, R. W. Doing business in Mexico. HBR 20:508-16 no.4, 42

#### 11.353 GOVERNMENT CAPITAL MOVEMENTS
#### 11.3530 GENERAL

A
EF Balogh, T. French reconstruction and the Franco-U.S. loan agreement. Pt.I-II. OIS 8:261-77; 294-300 Aug,Sep 46

A Condliffe, J. B. The foreign loan policy of the United States. EI 1:568-83 May 48

EB Dacey, W. M. The budget, overseas borrowing and domestic investment. LBR 9:34-51 Jul 48

A/EB Henderson, H. D. The Anglo-American financial agreement. OIS 8:1-13 Jan 46

Jeal, E. F. Dollar despotism. SAJE 17: 111-13 Mar 49

Polak, J. J. Balance of payments problems of countries reconstructing with the help of foreign loans. QJE 57:208-40 Feb 43

A
EB Rosenson, A. The terms of the Anglo-American financial agreement. AER 37: 178-87 Mar 47

FI Sitaramayya, M. Reserve bank and the management of public debt. Pt.I-II. IJE 26:597-621; 27:35-52 Apr,Jul 46

#### 11.3531 INTERNATIONAL LOANS AND INVESTMENTS

Ala'i, H. The liquidity crisis abroad. AER 37:908-10 Dec 47

Balogh, T. The new plan for an international investment board. OIS 5: 254-56 Oct 30, 43

Buchanan, N. S. International investment: some post-war problems and issues. CJE 10:139-49 May 44

De Kock, M. H. International Bank for Reconstruction and Development. SAJE 12: 223-32 Sep 44

De Vegh, I. Peace aims, capital requirements, and international lending. AER/S 35:253-61 May 45

Fetter, F. W. The need for postwar foreign lending. AER/S 33:342-46 Mar 43

Hall, R. L. [and others] [The future of international investment]: discussion. AER/S 33:355-61 Mar 43

Kahn, R. F. The International Bank for Reconstruction and Development. R. EJ 59:445-47 Sep 49

A Korican, O. H. Aims of our foreign investment policy. HBR 24:498-511 no.4, 46

Mendershausen, H. Future foreign financing. REStat 31:266-79 Nov 49

Mikesell, R. F. [and others] International investment: discussion. AER/S 36: 710-16 May 46

Patterson, G. The Export-Import Bank. QJE 58:65-90 Nov 43

## 11.3531 INTERNATIONAL LOANS AND INVESTMENTS (Cont.)

Smithies, A. The International Bank for Reconstruction and Development. AER 34:785-97 Dec 44

Viner, J. International finance in the post-war world. JPE 55:97-107 Apr 47

-- --- [idem] JPE 55:97-107 Apr 47

Wallich, H. C. Financing the International Bank. HBR 24:164-82 no.2, 46

Weyl, N. and Wasserman, M. J. The International Bank, an instrument of world economic reconstruction. AER 37:92-106 Mar 47

## 11.3532 RELIEF. ASSISTANCE

A    Abbott, C. C. Economic penetration and power politics. HBR 26:410-24 Jul 48

A    -- Economic defense of the United States. HBR 26:613-26 Sep 48

E    Anonymous. ECA in action on the food and agriculture front. R. JFE 31:317-36 May 49

Balogh, T. Discrimination: British trade problems and the Marshall Plan. OIS 10:221-29 Jul-Aug 48

-- --- [idem] EI 1:1133-46 Nov 48

E    -- postscript on E.R.P. OIS 10:230-34 Jul-Aug 48

E    Berle, A. A., Jr. The Marshall Plan in the European struggle. SR 15:1-21 Mar 48

Brodsky, N. Some aspects of international relief. QJE 62:596-609 Aug 48

EI    Cosmo, G. Balance-sheet of the first year of ERP in Italy. BNL 2:111-17 Apr-Jun 49

Elliott, F. F. Redirecting world agricultural production and trade toward better nutrition. JFE 26:10-30 Feb 44

A    Farnsworth, H. C. The European recovery
E    program and the American farmer [with discussion by L. Bacon]. JFE 31,pt.2:519-36 Feb 49

FitzGerald, D. A. Coming readjustments in agriculture: the international phase. JFE 31:19-28 Feb 49

E    Freund, R. Methods of financing the European Recovery Program. SEJ 15:267-78 Jan 49

E    Gordon, L. ERP in operation. HBR 27:129-50 Mar 49

E    Haberler, G. Some economic problems of the European Recovery Program. AER 38:495-525 Sep 48

A    Harris, S. E. Cost of the Marshall Plan to the United States. JF 3,no.1:1-15 Feb 48

Henderson, H. D. The implications of the Marshall speech. OIS 9:274-82 Aug 47

E    Hoselitz, B. F. Four reports on economic aid to Europe. JPE 56:109-23 Apr 48

A/E    Joseph, J. J. European recovery and United States aid. S&S 12:293-383 no.3, 48

E    -- Trends in the Marshall Plan. S&S 13:1-21 no.1, 48-49

McCloy, J. J. Europe's hope for recovery.
E    EI 1:551-61 May 48

Malenbaum, W. [United States and world
A    needs]: discussion. JFE 29:1072-74 Nov 47

Medici, G. The E.R.P. and the problems
EI    of Italian agriculture. BNL 1:416-26 Oct 48

Rodano, C. The economic future of Europe
E    and the ERP. BNL 2:135-45 Jul-Sep 49

Shoup, C. S. Résumé of remarks at the conference of the International Institute of Public Finance. PF 2:387-88 no.4, 47

## 11.3533 REPARATIONS. WAR DEBTS

Burchardt, F. A. Reparations and reconstruction. OIS 7:199-212 Sep 1, 45

Cowles, W. B. Recovery in American
A    claims abroad. HBR 25:92-110 no.1, 46

Landauer, C. The German reparations
EG    problem. JPE 56:344-47 Aug 48

[Parker, A.]. Mantoux versus Keynes. R. LBR 3:1-20 Jan 47

## 11.4 ECONOMIC INTEGRATION. CUSTOMS UNIONS

## 11.40 GENERAL

Balogh, T. Britain, O.E.E.C. and the restoration of a world economy. OIS 11:35-52 Feb-Mar 49

Basch, A. European economic regionalism. AER/S 33:408-19 Mar 43

Bonn, M. J. Planning for peace. AER/S 30:272-80 Mar 40

Chalmers, H. [Economic regionalism and multilateral trade]: discussion. AER/S 33:448-54 Mar 43

De Beers, J. S. Tariff aspects of a federal union. QJE 56:49-92 Nov 41

Gordon, M. S. [Economic regionalism and multilateral trade]: discussion. AER/S 33:446-48 Mar 43

Grazzi, U. Some aspects of the Franco-Italian Customs Union in regard to the gradual manner of its achievement. BNL 1:365-68 Jul 48

Harrod, R. F. European Union. LBR 9:1-20 Jul 48

Lodewyckx, A. The Benelux Economic Union. ER 23:227-37 Dec 47

Loveday, A. Some reflections on Europe's trade. EI 2:179-86 Feb 49

Morgan, D. J. The British commonwealth and European economic co-operation. EJ 59:307-25 Sep 49

Papi, G. U. The dilemma of the O.E.E.C. BNL 2:103-07 Apr-Jun 49

Parker, A. Benelux. LBR 14:32-54 Oct 49

Robertson, D. H. Britain and European recovery. LBR 13:1-13 Jul 49

Rothschild, K. W. The small nation and world trade. EJ 54:26-40 Apr 44

Schüller, R. A free-trade area. SR 16:151-57 Jun 49

## 11. INTERNATIONAL ECONOMICS

### 11.4 ECONOMIC INTEGRATION. CUSTOMS UNIONS (Cont.)
### 11.40 GENERAL (Cont.)

Tremelloni, R. The Italian long-term program submitted to the O.E.E.C. BNL 2: 12-24 Jan-Mar 49

Weststrate, C. The economic and political implications of a customs union. QJE 62:362-80 May 48

### 11.5 ECONOMIC POWER. IMPERIALISM
### 11.50 GENERAL

A   Abbott, C. C. Economic penetration and power politics. HBR 26:410-24 Jul 48

A   -- Economic defense of the United States. HBR 26:613-26 Sep 48

EBC  Ady, P. Colonial industrialisation and British employment. REStud 11:42-51 no.1, 43

A   Condliffe, J. B. Economic power as an instrument of national policy. AER/S 34: 305-14 Mar 44

FI   Iyengar, S. K. "British" & "Indian" finance. IJE 21:830-70 Apr 41

A   Jaffe, P. J. Economic provincialism and American Far Eastern policy. S&S 5: 289-309 no.4, 41
FA

FI   Patel, S. J. British economic thought and the treatment of India as a colony. IJE 27:367-71 Apr 47

EBC  Speers, P. C. Colonial policy of the British Labour Party. SR 15:304-26 Sep 48

FJ   Sternberg, F. Japan's economic imperialism. SR 12:328-49 Sep 45

Taniguchi, K. The theory of wider territory economy. Kyo 16,no.4:20-41 Oct 41

### 11.51 HISTORY

EBC  Clapham, J. H. Imperial economics. R. EHR 14:84-88 no.1, 44

EBC  Davidson, J. W. The history of empire. R. EHR 16:68-73 no.1, 46

A   Duncan, B. Diplomatic support of the American rice trade, 1835-1845. AH 23:92-96 Apr 49

EBC  Fay, C. R. The growth of the new Empire, 1783-1870. R. EJ 51:80-91 Apr 41

E   Hamilton, E. J. The role of monopoly in the overseas expansion and colonial trade of Europe before 1800. AER/S 38: 33-53 May 48

EG  Henderson, W. O. German economic penetration in the Middle East, 1870-1914.
M   EHR 18:54-64 no.1-2, 48

E   Hutchins, J. G. B. [and others] The role of monopoly in the colonial trade and expansion of Europe: discussion. AER/S 38:63-71 May 48

Koebner, R. The concept of economic imperialism. EHR II.2:1-29 no.1, 49

EG  Townsend, M. E. The economic impact of imperial Germany: commercial and colonial policies. JEH/S 3:124-34 Dec 43

E   Usher, A. P. The role of monopoly in colonial trade and in the expansion of Europe subsequent to 1800. AER/S 38: 54-62 May 48

# 12. ECONOMIC FLUCTUATIONS AND STABILIZATION POLICY

### 12.0 GENERAL
### 12.1 HISTORY

EB   Beveridge, Sir W. The trade cycle in Britain before 1850. OEP 3:74-109 Feb 40

-- --- A postscript. OEP 4:63-76 Sep 40

A   Fels, R. The long-wave depression, 1873-97. REStat 31:69-73 Feb 49

EB   Fisher, F. J. Commercial trends and policy in sixteenth-century England. EHR 10:95-117 Nov 40

EB   Pesmazoglu, J. S. Some international aspects of British cyclical fluctuations, 1870-1913. REStud 16:117-43 no.3, 49

A   Rezneck, S. The influence of depression upon American opinion, 1857-1859. JEH 2:1-23 May 42

EA   Rosenberg, H. Political and social consequences of the great depression of 1873-1896 in central Europe. EHR 13: 59-73 no.1-2, 43

EB   Rostow, W. W. Explanations of the "great depression," 1873-96: an historian's view of modern monetary theory. EH 4: 356-70 Feb 40

-- Business cycles, harvests, and politics: 1790-1850. JEH 1:206-21 Nov 41

FJ   Tsuru, S. Economic fluctuations in Japan, 1868-1893. REStat 23:176-89 Nov 41

### 12.2 FLUCTUATIONS. FORECASTING
### 12.20 GENERAL

Åkerman, J. Discontinuities of employment cycles. NTTO 12:9-12 no.37, 48

### UNITED STATES

Åkerman, J. Political economic cycles.
A   Kyk 1:107-17 fasc.2, 47

Gordon, R. A. Business cycles in the interwar period: the "quantitative-historical" approach. AER/S 39:47-63 May 49

Moulton, H. G. [and others] Capital expansion, employment and economic stability: a reply to the review [followed by S. Fabricant's rejoinder]. JASA 35: 700-06 Dec 40

Neisser, H. The economic state of the nation. SR 16:320-31 Sep 49

12.2 FLUCTUATIONS. FORECASTING (Cont.)
12.20 GENERAL (Cont.)
UNITED STATES (Cont.)

A Paradiso, L. J. Significance of inventories in the current economic situation. JASA 43:361-76 Sep 48

Roose, K. D. The recession of 1937-38. JPE 56:239-48 Jun 48

Vining, R. Location of industry and regional patterns of business-cycle behavior. Em 14:37-68 Jan 46

OTHER COUNTRIES

EB Brown, J. A. The 1937 recession in England. HBR 18:248-60 no.2, 40

FI Beri, S. G. Price trends during the last decade and their effects on Indian economy. IJE 21:734-84 Apr 41

Bhan, R. K. Prices in India between the two great wars. IJE 21:785-97 Apr 41

Saksena, S. P. Price level in India with particular reference to agricultural prices. IJE 21:798-803 Apr 41

FM Bauer, P. T. Some aspects of the Malayan rubber slump 1929-33. Ec N.S.11: 190-98 Nov 44

HSA De Jongh, T. W. Monetary and banking factors and the business cycle in the Union. SAJE 9:138-53 Jun 41

Sadie, J. L. A note on the business cycle in South Africa, 1939-1940. SAJE 14: 70-75 Mar 46

12.21 INDICATORS. STATISTICAL SERIES

Baumgart, G. Weekly index numbers, measuring business activity. JB 13: 234-52 Jul 40

A Haring, C. E. The Haring indexes of local business conditions. JM 9:217-24 Jan 45

12.22 FORECASTS

Adelman, M. A. Correlations and forecasting. AER 36:645-50 Sep 46

Bratt, E. C. Business-cycle forecasting. JB 21:1-11 Jan 48

-- Data needed to forecast the business cycle. JB 21:168-79 Jul 48

-- The use of behavior classifications in business-cycle forecasting. JB 22: 209-24 Oct 49

Chaudhari, S. C. Business forecasting. IJE 25:160-64 Oct 44

Cowles, A. Stock market forecasting. Em 12:206-14 Jul-Oct 44

Flood, M. M. Recursive methods in business-cycle analysis. Em 8:333-53 Oct 40

Gilbert, R. V. and Perlo, V. The investment-factor method of forecasting business activity. Em 10:311-16 Jul-Oct 42; A correction. 11:94 Jan 43

Lebergott, S. Forecasting the national product. AER 35:59-80 Mar 45

Marschak, J. Economic structure, path, policy, and prediction. AER/S 37:81-84 May 47

Mills, F. C. The economic outlook of Friday and Edie and Ayres. AER/S 37: 50 May 47

Roos, C. F. [and others] Forecasting postwar demand: discussion. Em 13: 54-59 Jan 45

Stone, R. The fortune teller. R. Ec N.S.10: 24-33 Feb 43

UNITED STATES

A Balogh, T. Savings, the business cycle and the trend. OIS 7:114-15 May 19, 45

Barnes, L. How sound were private postwar forecasts? JPE 56:161-65 Apr 48

Bean, L. H. Postwar output in the United States at full employment. REStat 27: 202-03 Nov 45

Beckman, T. N. Large versus small business after the war. AER/S 34: 94-106 Mar 44

Brown, E. C. Some evidence on business expectations. REStat 31:236-38 Aug 49

Clark, C. Post-war savings in the U.S.A. OIS 7:97-103 May 19, 45

Colm, G. Fiscal problems of transition and peace: discussion. AER/S 35: 352-53 May 45

Garfield, F. R. Measuring and forecasting consumption. JASA 41:322-33 Sep 46

-- Transition forecasts in review. AER/S 37:71-80 May 47

Hagen, E. E. Postwar output in the United States at full employment. REStat 27: 45-59 May 45

-- The Brookings and Tucker estimates: further comments. REStat 27:196-201 Nov 45

-- The reconversion period: reflections of a forecaster. REStat 29:95-101 May 47

Hamill, C. The structure of postwar American business: discussion. AER/S 34:131-33 Mar 44

Hart, A. G. Postwar effects to be expected from wartime liquid accumulations. AER/S 35:341-51 May 45

Hirsch, J. Facts and fantasies concerning full employment. AER/S 34:118-27 Mar 44

Hoffman, P. G. Business plans for postwar expansion. AER/S 35:85-89 May 45

Klein, L. R. A post-mortem on transition predictions of national product. JPE 54: 289-308 Aug 46

Livingston, S. M. Forecasting postwar demand: II. Em 13:15-24 Jan 45

-- The measurement of postwar labor supply and its capacity to produce. JASA 40: 20-28 Mar 45

## 12.22 FORECASTS (Cont.)
### UNITED STATES (Cont.)

A  Mayer, J. [and others] Postwar national income: an appraisal of criticisms of the Brookings Institution estimate. REStat 27:189-91 Nov 45

Modigliani, F. Fluctuations in the saving ratio: a problem in economic forecasting. SR 14:413-20 Dec 47

Moll, W. J. Survey of consumer buying intent. JM 8:54-58 Jul 43

Mosak, J. L. Forecasting postwar demand: III. Em 13:25-53 Jan 45

Naess, R. D. The outlook for incomes and spending. AER/S 37:58-63 May 47

Nourse, E. G. The structure of postwar American business: discussion. AER/S 34:128-31 Mar 44

Rosa, R. V. Use of the consumption function in short run forecasting. REStat 30:91-105 May 48

Slichter, S. H. Postwar boom or collapse. HBR 21:5-42 no.1, 42

Smithies, A. Forecasting postwar demand: I. Em 13:1-14 Jan 45

-- Economic forecasts: discussion. AER/S 37:85 May 47

Snider, J. L. Looking ahead. HBR 26:1-10 Jan 48

-- What's ahead for prices and business? HBR 26:757-66 Nov 48

-- Facing the business future. HBR 27:449-58 Jul 49

Stein, H. Economic forecasts: discussion. AER/S 37:86 May 47

Steindl, J. Post-war employment in the United States. OIS 6:193-202 Sep 2, 44

-- Long-run changes in the propensity to save: a reply. OIS 7:103-13 May 19, 45

Temple, A. H. The business outlook. AER/S 37:64-70 May 47

Thomas, W. Planning and forecasting in the transition period. AER/S 37:51-57 May 47

Tucker, R. S. Postwar output at full employment: a rebuttal. REStat 27:192-96 Nov 45

Upgren, A. Fiscal problems of transition and peace: discussion. AER/S 35:353-54 May 45

Warburton, C. Monetary policy and business forecasting. Pt.I-II. JB 22:71-82; 178-87 Apr,Jul 49

Woytinsky, W. S. What was wrong in forecasts of postwar depression? JPE 55:142-51 Apr 47

### OTHER COUNTRIES

Bates, S. Government forecasting in Can-
C  ada. CJE 12:361-78 Aug 46

Gibson, J. D. Business prospects in Canada. CJE 15:394-401 Aug 49

EB  Brown, P. S. Prospective national income and capital formation in the United Kingdom. AER 36:555-77 Sep 46

Kalecki, M. Employment in the United Kingdom during and after the transition period. OIS 6:265-87 Dec 4, 44

ES  Lundberg, E. and Ohlsson, I. Models of the future national income in Sweden. OIS 8:301-03 Sep 46

N  Steindl, J. Employment in Australia: war and post-war. OIS 6:293-97 Dec 4, 44

## 12.23 INTERNATIONAL PROPAGATION

Forchheimer, K. The 'short cycle' in its international aspects. OEP 7:1-20 Mar 45

Hirschman, A. O. International aspects of a recession. AER 39:1245-53 Dec 49

Robinson, J. The United States in the world economy. R. EJ 54:430-37 Dec 44

## 12.3 STABILIZATION POLICIES
## 12.30 GENERAL

Ackley, G. Inflation and equality: comment [followed by D. McWright's rejoinder]. AER 39:960-66 Sep 49

Baker, J. G. The universal discount as a means of economic stabilization. Em 16:155-84 Apr 48

Balogh, T. The planning and control of investment. OIS 7:244-51 Oct 13, 45

Benoit-Smullyan, E. Seventeen post-war plans: the Pabst post-war employment awards. AER 35:120-27 Mar 45

Copeland, M. A. Business stabilization by agreement. AER 34:328-39 Jun 44

Ellis, H. S. Postwar economic policies. R. REStat 28:34-39 Feb 46

-- Comments on the Mints and Hansen papers. (A symposium on fiscal and monetary policy) REStat 28:74-77 May 46

Fisher, A. G. B. Less stabilisation: more stability. Kyk 1:1-18 fasc.1, 47

Friedman, M. A monetary and fiscal framework for economic stability. AER 38:245-64 Jun 48

Hansen, A. H. Notes on Mints' paper on monetary policy. (A symposium on fiscal and monetary policy) REStat 28:69-74 May 46

-- Needed: a cycle policy. ILRR 1:60-65 Oct 47

Hawtrey, R. G. Monetary aspects of the economic situation. AER 38:42-55 Mar 48

Kalecki, M. A comment on "Monetary policy." (A symposium on fiscal and monetary policy) REStat 28:81-84 May 46

Lerner, A. P. Monetary policy and fiscal policy. REStat 28:77-81 May 46

12.3 STABILIZATION POLICIES (Cont.)
12.30 GENERAL (Cont.)

Marschak, J. Lack of confidence. SR 8:
41-62 Feb 41

-- The task of economic stabilization.
SR 8:361-72 Sep 41

Mints, L. W. Monetary policy. REStat 28:
60-69 May 46

Neff, P. Professor Friedman's proposal:
a comment [followed by M. Friedman's
rejoinder and Neff's final comment].
AER 39:946-56 Sep 49

Pedersen, J. The control of the value of
money in a free economy. NTTO 12:
193-99 no.37, 48

Seltzer, L. H. Is a rise in interest rates
desirable or inevitable? AER 35:831-50
Dec 45

Shackle, G. L. S. A means of promoting
investment. EJ 51:249-60 Jun-Sep 41

Stafford, J. The optimal utilization of
national resources. Em 17,suppl.:
157-64 Jul 49

UNITED STATES

Anonymous. Economic studies by the Joint
A    Committee on the Economic Report.
AER 39:1289-90 Dec 49

Arndt, H. W. The monetary theory of
deficit spending: a comment on Dr.
Clark Warburton's article [followed by
Warburton's reply]. REStat 28:90-94
May 46

Bach, G. L. Monetary-fiscal policy, debt
policy, and the price level. AER/S 37:
228-42 May 47

-- Monetary-fiscal policy reconsidered.
JPE 57:383-94 Oct 49

Bottum, J. C. Stabilization of the general
price level. JFE 29:1107-21 Nov 47

Bronfenbrenner, M. Postwar political
economy: the President's reports. R.
JPE 56:373-91 Oct 48

Clark, J. D. Can government influence
business stability? JF 2,no.1:65-75
Apr 47

Colm, G. On the road to economic stabilization. SR 15:265-76 Sep 48

Ellis, H. S. The January 1949 economic
report of the President: appraisal.
REStat 31:174-76 Aug 49

Ensley, G. W. Suggested lines of economic
research needed to carry out objectives
of the Employment Act. AER/S 39:
453-63 May 49

Fetter, F. W. The economic reports of the
President and the problem of inflation.
R. QJE 63:273-81 May 49

Gilbert, M. Expanding civilian production
and employment after the war: discussion. AER/S 37:90-93 May 45

Hagen, E. E. The January 1949 economic
report of the President: appraisal.
REStat 31:178-81 Aug 49

Hansen, A. H. The first reports under the
Employment Act of 1946. REStat 29:
69-74 May 47

Harris, S. E. The inflationary process: in
theory and recent history. REStat 31:
200-10 Aug 49

-- The January 1949 economic report of
the President: introduction. REStat 31:
165-66 Aug 49

-- Effectiveness and coordination of monetary, credit, and fiscal policies. Met 1:
90-104 Oct 49

Hermens, F. A. Domestic postwar problems. RSE 1:23-30 Dec 42

Klein, L. R. The use of econometric
models as a guide to economic policy.
Em 15:111-51 Apr 47

Lloyd, I. S. Basic economese: new science
or new language? R. SAJE 17:74-87
Mar 49

Machlup, F. The inflationary process:
comments. REStat 31:210-12 Aug 49

Meyer, J. Trade union plans for post-war
reconstruction in the United States.
SR 11:491-505 Nov 44

-- The Latimer report. I. Some general
observations. ILRR 1:465-70 Apr 48

Neisser, H. Employment in 1947. SR 14:
95-103 Mar 47

Paish, F. W. The January 1949 economic
report of the President: appraisal.
REStat 31:172-74 Aug 49

Pierson, J. H. G. Expanding civilian production and employment after the war:
discussion. AER/S 35:93-96 May 45

Rotwein, E. Post-World War I price movements and price policy. JPE 53:234-57
Sep 45

Shere, L. Taxation and inflation control.
AER 38:843-56 Dec 48

Shields, M. A measure of purchasing power
inflation and deflation. JASA 35:461-71
Sep 40

Somers, H. M. The inflationary process:
comments. REStat 31:212-13 Aug 49

Sweezy, A. R. Fiscal and monetary policy.
AER/S 36:291-303 May 46

Terborgh, G. The January 1949 economic
report of the President: appraisal.
REStat 31:176-78 Aug 49

Upgren, A. R. Objectives and guides to
policy. (Expanding civilian production
and employment after the war)
AER/S 35:67-84 May 45

Vickrey, W. Limitations of Keynesian
economics. SR 15:403-16 Dec 48

Villard, H. H. The inflationary process:
comments. REStat 31:213-16 Aug 49

Warburton, C. The monetary theory of
deficit spending. REStat 27:74-84
May 45

Wilson, T. The January 1949 economic
report of the President: appraisal.
REStat 31:166-72 Aug 49

12.3 STABILIZATION POLICIES (Cont.)
12.30 GENERAL (Cont.)
UNITED STATES (Cont.)
Working, H. Reflections on the President's
A   economic report. R. AER 37:383-86
Jun 47
Wright, D. M. Inflation and equality.
AER 38:892-97 Dec 48

OTHER COUNTRIES
Kershaw, J. A. Postwar Brazilian eco-
DSB   nomic problems. AER 38:328-40 Jun 48
Klopstock, F. H. Western Europe's attack
EA   on inflation. HBR 26:597-612 Sep 48
Busschau, W. J. The hardships of Britain:
EB   Mr. Harrod's ideas. SAJE 15:248-55
Dec 47
Champernowne, D. G. Critique of the Eco-
nomic survey. R. OIS 9:57-73 Mar,
Apr 47
Devons, E. The Economic survey for 1949.
R. MS 17:111-27 May 49
Henderson, H. D. Cheap money and the
budget. EJ 57:265-71 Sep 47
Jewkes, J. and Devons, E. The Economic
survey for 1947. R. LBR 4:1-10 Apr 47
Thompson, C. H. "The United Kingdom
Economic survey for 1948." R.
SAJE 16:89-97 Mar 48
Snider, D. A. French monetary and fiscal
EF   policies since the liberation. AER 38:
309-27 Jun 48
Paranjape, V. M. A monetary system for
FI   India. IJE 26:544-53 Jan 46
Melville, L. G. Some post-war problems.
N   ER 22:4-22 Jun 46

12.31 EMPLOYMENT ASPECTS OF STABILI-
ZATION POLICIES
Abramson, A. G. The problem of full em-
ployment. HBR 22:337-45 no.3, 44
Anderson, R. V. Policy for full employ-
ment. R. CJE 12:192-203 May 46
Bauer, P. T. Lord Beveridge on full em-
ployment. R. Kyk 1:166-76 fasc.2, 47
Beveridge, Sir W. Life, liberty, and the
pursuit of happiness (1950 model). R.
REStat 28:53-59 May 46
Croome, H. Liberty, equality and full em-
ployment. LBR 13:14-32 Jul 49
Dobretsberger, J. Misunderstandings about
full-employment. EgC 36:129-55
Jan-Feb 45
-- A critical review of the discussions on
full-employment. Kyk 1:19-25 fasc.1, 47
Gaev, V. Plans for full employment after
the war. S&S 9:67-76 no.1, 45
Harrod, R. F. Full employment and securi-
ty of livelihood. EJ 53:321-42 Dec 43
Hawtrey, R. G. Livelihood and full employ-
ment. EJ 54:417-22 Dec 44
Kalecki, M. Full employment by stimulating
private investment? OEP 7:83-92 Mar 45

-- The maintenance of full employment
after the transition period: a rejoinder
to Mr. Woytinsky's note. AER 37:
391-97 Jun 47
Langer, H. C., Jr. Maintaining full employment. AER 33:888-92 Dec 43
Lindblom, C. E. Long-run considerations
in employment stabilization and unemployment compensation. QJE 56:145-51
Nov 41
-- Pay roll taxation and employment stabilization. QJE 57:657-58 Aug 43
Merry, D. H. and Bruns, G. R. Full employment: the British, Canadian and
Australian White Papers. ER 21:
223-35 Dec 45
Meyers, A. L. Some implications of full-
employment policy. JPE 54:258-65
Jun 46
Pierson, J. H. G. The underwriting approach
to full employment: a further explana-
tion. REStat 31:182-92 Aug 49
Pribram, K. Employment stabilization
through pay roll taxation. QJE 57:
142-52 Nov 42
Richardson, J. H. Livelihood and full employment. EJ 56:139-43 Mar 46
Smithies, A. Full employment in a free
society. R. AER 35:355-67 Jun 45
Sweezy, A. R. The government's responsibility for full employment. AER/S 33:
19-26 Mar 43
Van der Horst, S. T. Some reflections on
full employment. SAJE 14:1-16 Mar 46
Vaswani, M. H. Policy of full employment.
IJE 27:317-21 Jan 47
Wasson, R. G. Beveridge's "Full employment in a free society." R. HBR 23:
507-18 no.4, 45
Yntema, T. O. "Full" employment in a
private enterprise system. AER/S 34:
107-17 Mar 44

UNITED STATES
Apel, H. Self-liquidating wages. SR 10:
A   301-11 Sep 43
Copeland, M. A. How achieve full and stable
employment. AER/S 34:134-47 Mar 44
Courtney, C. J. How many jobs must we
provide for a balanced postwar economy
[with discussion by W. Froelich].
RSE 3:34-44 Dec 44
Fellner, W. Hansen on full-employment
policies. R. JPE 55:254-56 Jun 47
Fels, R. Warburton vs Hansen and Keynes.
AER 39:923-29 Sep 49
Gragg, C. I. and Teele, S. F. The proposed
full employment act. HBR 23:323-37
no.3, 45
Graham, B. The hours of work and full em-
ployment [followed by D. Yoder's com-
ment]. AER 35:432-37 Jun 45

12.31 EMPLOYMENT ASPECTS OF STABILI-
ZATION POLICIES (Cont.)

UNITED STATES (Cont.)

Haberler, G. Some observations on the
A   Murray Full Employment Bill. REStat 27:
106-09 Aug 45

Hansen, A. H. A new goal of national policy:
full employment. REStat 27:102-03
Aug 45

Harris, S. E. Some aspects of the Murray
Full Employment Bill. REStat 27:104-06
Aug 45

Hart, A. G. Facts, issues, and policies.
(The problem of "full employment")
AER/S 36:280-90 May 46

Hoover, C. B. Economic planning and the
problem of full employment. AER/S 30:
263-71 Mar 40

McCarthy, P. J. Employment policies and
the Employment Act. RSE 7,no.2:29-33
Sep 49

McFall, R. J. Can we stabilize purchasing
power at a high level? JM 8:61-74
Jul 43

McNair, M. P. Some practical questions
about the Murray Bill. REStat 27:
113-16 Aug 45

-- The full employment problem. HBR 2:
1-21 no.1, 45

Pierson, J. H. G. [How achieve full and
stable employment]: discussion.
AER/S 34:148-50 Mar 44

-- [and others] The problem of "full employment": discussion. AER/S 36:
319-35 May 46

Slichter, S. H. Comment on the Murray
Bill. REStat 27:109-12 Aug 45

Viner, J. The Employment Act of 1946 in
operation. REStat 29:74-79 May 47

Wallace, H. A. The use of statistics in the
formulation of a national full employment
policy. JASA 40:11-19 Mar 45

Warburton, C. Hansen and Fellner on full
employment policies. AER 38:128-34
Mar 48

Wellman, H. R. and Mehren, G. L. Some
theoretical aspects of agricultural parity
price policies and national employment.
JFE 28:563-71 May 46

Wirtenberger, H. J. Public policy and post-
war employment in the United States
[with discussion by T. A. Mogilnitsky].
RSE 3:45-54 Dec 44

Woytinsky, W. S. The maintenance of full
employment after the transition period:
notes on Mr. Kalecki's models. AER 36:
641-45 Sep 46

OTHER COUNTRIES

Beattie, J. R. Some aspects of the problem
C   of full employment. CJE 10:328-42
Aug 44

Åkerman, G. Unemployment and unemploy-
EB   ment policy in England. Kyk 3:23-35
fasc.1, 49

Beveridge, W. H. The Government's employment policy. EJ 54:161-76
Jun-Sep 44

Booker, H. S. Have we a full employment
policy? Ec N.S.14:37-47 Feb 47

De Chazeau, M. G. Employment policy and
organization of industry after the war.
AER 35:629-39 Sep 45

Jewkes, J. Second thoughts on the British
White Paper on employment policy.
MS 14,no.2:65-84 May 46

Joseph, M. F. W. The British White Paper
on employment policy. AER 34:561-67
Sep 44

Kalecki, M. The White Paper on employment policy. OIS 6:131-35 Jun 10, 44

McDougall, A. The White Paper on Employment Policy. RSE 3:18-33 Dec 44

Richardson, J. H. Some remedies for post-
war unemployment. EJ 51:449-57
Dec 41

Robinson, A. Sir William Beveridge on
full employment. R. EJ 55:70-76
Apr 45

Simons, H. C. The Beveridge program:
an unsympathetic interpretation. R.
JPE 53:212-33 Sep 45

Henry, J. A. Some comments on Profes-
HSA   sor Hutt's "Full employment and the
future of industry." SAJE 14:67-70
Mar 46

Hutt, W. H. Full employment and the
future of industry. SAJE 13:185-202
Sep 45

Schumann, C. G. W. Aspects of the problem
of full employment in South Africa.
SAJE 16:115-32 Jun 48

Garland, J. M. Some aspects of full em-
N   ployment. Pt.[I]-II. ER 20:152-69;
21:23-36 Dec 44, Jun 45

Wilson, J. S. G. Prospects of full employment in Australia. ER 22:99-116 Jun 46

12.32 WAGE ASPECTS OF STABILIZATION
POLICIES

Dunlop, J. T. A review of wage-price
A   policy. REStat 29:154-60 Aug 47

Harris, S. E. Some aspects of the wage
A   problem. REStat 29:145-53 Aug 47

-- [Symposium: wage policy.] Introduc-
A   tion. REStat 29:137-39 Aug 47

Mason, E. S. Some reflections on the wage-
A   price problem. IRRA 1:22-34 Dec 48

Richardson, J. H. Wage policy in full em-
EB   ployment [comment, followed by H. W.
Singer's rejoinder]. EJ 58:421-25
Sep 48

12.32 WAGE ASPECTS OF STABIL-
    IZATION POLICIES
    (Cont.)
    Singer, H. W.  Wage policy in full employ-
EB    ment.  EJ 57:438-55 Dec 47
    Slichter, S. H.  The problem of wage policy

A    in the spring of 1947.  REStat 29:139-45
    Aug 47
    Steindl, J.  Reconstruction and wage policy.
EB    OIS 8:285-93 Sep 46
    Worswick, G. D. N. and Martin, K.  Prices
EB    and wages policy. OIS 10:84-93 Mar 48

# 13. WAR AND DEFENSE ECONOMICS

## 13.0 GENERAL

Basch, A.  The new economic warfare: a
    reply.  AER 32:558-60 Sep 42

Bates, S.  The price system and the war
    economy.  CJE 7:324-37 Aug 41

Bernstein, E. M.  War and the pattern of
    business cycles.  AER 30:524-35 Sep 40

Butlin, S. J.  The political economy of war.
    R.  ER 16:96-108 Jun 40

Condliffe, J. B.  War and economics.  R.
    JPE 51:157-65 Apr 43

Director, A.  Does inflation change the eco-
    nomic effects of war?  AER/S 30:351-61
    Mar 40

Galbraith, J. K.  The disequilibrium system.
    AER 37:287-302 Jun 47

Gilbert, M.  Measuring national income as
    affected by the war.  JASA 37:186-98
    Jun 42

Hamilton, E. J., chairman.  The economic
    effects of war.  Abstract of specialized
    conference discussion.  AER/S 32:
    227-30 Mar 42

Hansen, A. H.  A general view of the insti-
    tutional effects of the war.  AER/S 32:
    351-59 Mar 42

Hardy, C. O., chairman.  Round table on
    the economics of war.  AER/S 30:
    362-65 Mar 40

Homan, P. T.  Economics in the war period.
    AER 36:855-71 Dec 46

Hutt, W. H.  Economic lessons of the
    Allied war effort.  SAJE 8:205-23 Sep 40

-- War demand, entrepreneurship and the
    distributive problem.  Ec N.S.8:341-60
    Nov 41

Isaacs, A. [and others] Effects of the war
    and defense program upon economic
    conditions and institutions: discussion.
    AER/S 32:426-31 Mar 42

Issawi, C.  To what extent are the costs of
    a war borne by future generations.
    EgC 31:39-44 Jan 40

Knight, B.  Postwar costs of a new war.
    AER/S 30:340-50 Mar 40

Lyon, L. S.  The private-enterprise system
    confronts emergency.  JB 14:259-69
    Jul 41

MacDougall, G. D. A.  World economic
    survey, 1941-1942.  R.  EJ 53:280-84
    Jun-Sep 43

Mitchell, W. C. [and others] Economic
    consequences of war since 1790: dis-
    cussion.  AER/S 30,no.5:362-65 Feb 41

Nerlove, S. H.  War expansion and price
    inflation.  JB 15:95-130 Apr 42

Nettels, C. P.  Economic consequences of
    war: costs of production.  JEH/S 3:
    1-8 Dec 43

Paish, F. W.  Economic incentive in war-
    time.  Ec N.S.8:239-48 Aug 41

Radford, R. A.  The economic organisa-
    tion of a P.O.W. camp.  Ec N.S:12:
    189-201 Nov 45

Rosenbaum, E. M.  War economics.  A
    bibliographical approach.  Ec N.S.9:
    64-94 Feb 42

Severson, L.  Some current books on the
    economics of total war.  R.  JPE 51:
    169-74 Apr 43

Spiegel, H. W.  The war economy and the
    economic man.  JB 16:1-6 Jan 43

Stafford, J.  Planning for war.  EJ 50:27-41
    Mar 40

Wright, W. [and others] Effects of the war
    and defense program upon economic con-
    ditions and institutions: discussion.
    AER/S 32:382-90 Mar 42

UNITED STATES

Bollinger, L. L.; Lilley, T. and Lombard,
A    A. E., Jr.  Preserving American air
    power.  HBR 23:372-92 no.3, 45

Copeland, M. A.  The defense effort and the
    national income response pattern.
    JPE 50:415-26 Jun 42

Crossley, A. M.  The effect of the war on
    income changes.  JM 7:355-59 Apr 43

Cutler, A. T.  War economics and the
    American people.  S&S 4:165-82 no.3, 40

Feiler, A.  Economic impacts of the war.
    SR 8:297-309 Sep 41

Gordon, L.  An official appraisal of the war
    economy and its administration.  R.
    REStat 29:183-88 Aug 47

Grether, E. T.  Preparedness for war and
    general economic policy.  AER/S 39:
    366-77 May 49

Hamer, P. M.  Round table on economic
    research: discussion.  AER/S 37:700
    May 47

Henderson, L. and Nelson, D. M.  Prices,
    profits, and government.  HBR 19:
    389-404 no.4, 41

13.0  GENERAL (Cont.)

UNITED STATES (Cont.)

A    Jacoby, N. H.  The American economy during and after the war:  a look ahead. JB 15:289-305 Oct 42

Lester, R. A.  War controls of materials, equipment, and manpower:  an experiment in economic planning.  SEJ 9: 197-216 Jan 43

Lewis, B. W.  The economics of preparedness for war:  discussion.  AER/S 39: 378-79 May 49

Machlup, F.  The economics of preparedness for war:  discussion.  AER/S 39: 379-83 May 49

Nelson, S.  Preservation of war records. AER/S 36:793-98 May 46

Robbins, S. M. and Murphy, T. E.  Industrial preparedness.  HBR 26:329-52 May 48

Rowe, H. B.  Use of wartime government records in economic research. AER/S 36:799-806 May 46

Rutherford, H. K.  Industrial preparedness. JM 4,no.4,pt.2:47-50 Apr 40

Schweitzer, A.  Must rearmament lead to regulation?  JB 21:203-13 Oct 48

Steindl, J.  The United States war economy. OIS 4:197-201 Jul 18, 42

-- The peak of the war effort in the United States?  OIS 6:7-9 Jan 15, 44

Watkins, R. J.  Statistical requirements for economic mobilization.  JASA 44:406-12 Sep 49

Wernette, J. P.  Guns and butter?  HBR 19: 286-97 no.3, 41

Wright, C. W.  American economic preparations for war, 1914-1917 and 1939-1941. CJE 8:157-75 May 42

AA   Hon, R. C.  The South in a war economy. SEJ 8:291-308 Jan 42


OTHER AMERICAN COUNTRIES

C    Keirstead, B. S.  The effects of the war on the concept of national interest.  CJE 8: 197-212 May 42

Petrie, J. R.  Business efficiency in the Canadian war effort.  CJE 9:357-65 Aug 43

CA   Fowke, V.  Economic effects of the war on the prairie economy.  CJE 11:373-87 Aug 45

DSC  Delaplane, W. H.  The war and an agricultural economy:  the case of Colombia. SEJ 9:33-45 Jul 42


EUROPE

EA   Pollock, F.  Economics of war:  influence of preparedness on western European economic life.  AER/S 30:317-25 Mar 40

EB   Balogh, T.  The economic effort.  OIS 2, no.9:1-4 Nov 2, 40

-- Economic mobilization.  OIS 2,no.10:5-8 Nov 23, 40

-- The role of compensation in the war-economic system.  OIS 3:99-103 Apr 5, 41

Burchardt, F.  Output and employment policy.  OIS 4:29-40 Jan 10, 42

Devons, E.  Economic planning in war and peace.  MS 16:1-28 Jan 48

Hicks, J. R.  Saving and the rate of interest in war-time.  MS 12:21-27 Apr 41

Kalecki, M.  War-time changes in employment and the wage bill.  OIS 3:294-98 Sep 20, 41

-- Employment, wage bill, and cash circulation.  OIS 4:67-70 Feb 21, 42

-- Wages and the national income in 1940 and 1941.  OIS 4:150-53 May 16, 42

-- Profits, salaries and wages.  OIS 5: 125-29 Jun 5, 43

Madge, C.  War-time saving and spending: a district survey.  EJ 50:327-39 Jun-Sep 40

Maizels, A.  Consumption, investment and national expenditure in wartime. Ec N.S.8:151-61 May 41

Nicholson, J. L.  The trend of wages. OIS 3:242-46 Aug 9, 41

-- Wages and prices.  OIS 4:319-25 Dec 12, 42

-- Employment and national income during the war.  OIS 7:230-44 Oct 13, 45; Corrigenda.  268 Nov 3, 45

Singer, H. W.  Some disguised blessings of the war.  MS 12:49-56 Oct 41

EBI  Duncan, G. A.  The first year of war:  its economic effects on twenty-six counties of Ireland.  EJ 51:389-99 Dec 41

EF   Anonymous.  The economic importance of the war zone in northern France. OIS 2,no.1:5-8 Feb 40

Balogh, T.  The economic problems of France.  OIS 7:61-78 Apr 7, 45

Baudin, L.  An outline of economic conditions in France under the German occupation.  EJ 55:326-45 Dec 45

EG   Kaldor, N.  The German war economy. REStud 13:33-52 no.1, 45

-- --- [idem] MS 14,no.3:19-53 Sep 46

Klein, B.  Germany's preparation for war: a re-examination.  AER 38:56-77 Mar 48

Mandelbaum, K.  Germany's wage bill and national income in the first year of the war.  OIS 3:223-25 Jul 19, 41

Paechter, H.  Recent trends in the German Command economy.  JPE 52:217-33 Sep 44

Singer, H. W.  The German war economy in the light of German economic periodicals. Pt.I-XII.  EJ 50:534-46; 51:19-35; 192-215; 400-21; 52:18-36; 186-205; 377-99; 53:221-39; 243-59; 370-80; 54:62-74; 206-16 Dec 40-Jun-Sep 44

Spiegel, H. W.  Wehrwirtschaft:  economics of the military state.  AER 30:713-23 Dec 40

## 13. WAR AND DEFENSE ECONOMICS

### 13.0 GENERAL (Cont.)

#### EUROPE (Cont.)

ER   Baykov, A. Remarks on the experience in the organisation of "war economy" in the U.S.S.R. EJ 51:422-38 Dec 41

-- Russia's economic losses. OIS 4:245-47 Sep 19, 42

ES   Kock, K. Swedish economic policy during the war. REStud 10:75-80 no.2, 43

#### ASIA

FC   Fong, H. D. Economic reconstruction in wartime China. HBR 20:415-26 no.4, 42

FI   Bhattacharya, K. N. Economic control in India during and after the war. IJE 25: 541-45 Apr 45

Iyengar, S. K. Economic control in India during the war. IJE 24:239-60 Apr 44

Steindl, J. The impact of the war on India. OIS 4:105-13 Apr 4, 42

#### AFRICA

H   Goldmann, J. The economic significance of French North Africa. OIS 4:308-10 Nov 21, 42

Leslie, R. Authority and economy in war. HSA   SAJE 9:208-09 Jun 41

Richards, C. S. Some economic and administrative aspects of South Africa's war effort. SAJE 8:325-63 Dec 40; Errata. 9:207 Jun 41

Robertson, H. M. Some problems in writing an official "civil" history of the war. SAJE 16:405-14 Dec 48

#### MIDDLE EAST

M   Ady, P. Some economic problems of the Middle East. OIS 5:14-20 Jan 9, 43

#### AUSTRALIA. NEW ZEALAND

N   Burton, H. The Australian war economy, May, 1943-May, 1945. ER 19:149-61; 20:1-17; 189-205; 21:1-22 Dec 43, Jun,Dec 44, Jun 45

Isles, K. S. The building of a war economy. ER 18:58-74 Jun 42

Simkin, C. G. F. Wartime changes in the New Zealand economy. ER 24:18-31 Jun 48

Sutch, W. B. New Zealand's war economy. ER 16:208-17 Dec 40

Walker, E. R. and Riley, M. E. Australia's war economy: developments from December, 1939, to May, 1940. ER 16: 78-81 Jun 40

-- War economy: the nature of the problem. ER 16:1-15 Jun 40

-- and Beecroft, R. M. New developments in Australia's war economy. ER 17:1-18 Jun 41

-- Total war, with reservations. (Australia's war economy, May to October, 1941) ER 17:166-79 Dec 41

Wilson, J. S. G. Further developments in Australia's war economy (October, 1941 to April, 1942). ER 18:43-57 Jun 42

-- The octopus of control. (Australia's war economy May to October, 1942) ER 18:192-208 Dec 42

-- The present versus the future. (Australia's war economy November, 1942, to May, 1943) ER 19:23-37 Jun 43

### 13.1 HISTORY

Burchardt, F. Allied control for Allied supplies: the case of shipping. OIS 4: 252-58 Sep 19, 42

Dulles, E. War and investment opportunities: an historical analysis. AER/S 32: 112-28 Mar 42

Gras, N. S. B. War and business: four century-long struggles. BHR 20:165-89 Dec 46

Hamilton, E. J. [and others] The determinants of investment decision: discussion. AER/S 32:156-64 Mar 42

Mitchell, W. C. [and others] Economic consequences of war since 1790: discussion. AER/S 30,no.5:362-65 Feb 41

Oliver, H. War and inflation since 1790 in England, France, Germany, and the United States. AER/S 30,no.5:344-51 Feb 41

Rotwein, E. Post-World War I price movements and price policy. JPE 53: 234-57 Sep 45

Sharp, M. W. Allied wheat buying in relationship to Canadian marketing policy, 1914-18. CJE 6:372-89 Aug 40

Thorp, W. L. Postwar depressions. AER/S 30,no.5:352-61 Feb 41

Wright, A. R. Food purchases of the Allies, 1917-1918. AH 16:97-102 Apr 42

#### UNITED STATES

A   Brand, C. J. Some fertilizer history connected with World War I. AH 19:104-13 Apr 45

Dickinson, F. G. An aftercost of the World War to the United States. AER/S 30: 326-39 Mar 40

Dickson, M. R. The Food Administration: educator. AH 16:91-96 Apr 42

Hardy, C. O. Adjustments and maladjustments in the United States after the first World War. AER/S 32:24-30 Mar 42

Howenstine, E. J., Jr. The Industrial Board, precursor of the N.R.A.: the price-reduction movement after World War I. JPE 51:235-50 Jun 43

-- Demobilization after the first World War. QJE 58:91-105 Nov 43

-- The domestic retreat after World War I. SR 10:480-86 Nov 43

-- Why "normalcy" failed. SR 11:363-66 Sep 44

13.1  HISTORY (Cont.)
  UNITED STATES (Cont.)
  Moore, W. H.  Termination of contracts
A   and disposal of surpluses after the first
   World War.  AER/S 33:138-49 Mar 43
  Peterson, A. G.  Governmental policy re-
   lating to farm machinery in World War I.
   AH 17:31-40 Jan 43
  Schwartz, H.  Agricultural labor in the
   first World War.  JFE 24:178-87 Feb 42
  -- Farm labor adjustments after World
   War I.  JFE 25:269-77 Feb 43
  Wright, A. R.  World War food controls
   and archival sources for their study.
   AH 15:72-83 Apr 41
  Wright, C. W.  American economic prepara-
   tions for war, 1914-1917 and 1939-1941.
   CJE 8:157-75 May 42
  -- The more enduring economic conse-
   quences of America's wars.  JEH/S 3:
   9-26 Dec 43
  Atherton, L. E.  Western foodstuffs in the
AA  Army provisions trade.  AH 14:161-69
   Oct 40
  Jorgenson, L. P.  Agricultural expansion
   into the semiarid lands of the west north
   central states during the first World
   War.  AH 23:30-40 Jan 49
  Bezanson, A.  Inflation and controls,
ASP  Pennsylvania, 1774-1779.  JEH/S 8:1-20
   '48


  OTHER COUNTRIES
  Deutsch, J. J.  War finance and the Canadian
C   economy, 1914-20.  CJE 6:525-42 Nov 40
  Knox, F. A.  Canadian war finance and the
   balance of payments, 1914-18.  CJE 6:
   226-57 May 40
  Sharp, M. W.  Allied wheat buying in rela-
   tionship to Canadian marketing policy,
   1914-18.  CJE 6:372-89 Aug 40
  Nef, J. U.  War and economic progress
E   1540-1640.  EHR 12:13-38 no.1-2, 42
  -- Wars and the rise of industrial civiliza-
   tion, 1640-1740.  CJE 10:36-78 Feb 44
  Gilbert, J. C.  Anglo-French financial co-
EB  operation during the war, 1914-18.
   REStud 7:159-68 Jun 40
  Hay, D.  The official history of the Minis-
   try of Munitions 1915-1919.  R.  EHR 14:
   185-90 no.2, 44
  Higgins, B. H.  Agriculture and war: a com-
   parison of agricultural conditions in the
   Napoleonic and World War periods.
   AH 14:1-12 Jan 40
  Pearce, B.  Elizabethan food policy and the
   armed forces.  EHR 12:39-46 no.1-2, 42
  Postan, M. M.  Some social consequences
   of the Hundred Years' War.  EHR 12:1-12
   no.1-2, 42
  Rostow, W. W.  Adjustments and maladjust-
   ments after the Napoleonic wars.
   AER/S 32:13-23 Mar 42

  Tawney, R. H.  The abolition of economic
   controls 1918-1921.  EHR 13:1-30
   no.1-2, 43
  Gilbert, J. C.  Anglo-French financial co-
EF  operation during the war, 1914-18.
   REStud 7:159-68 Jun 40
  Postan, M. M.  Some social consequences
   of the Hundred Years' War.  EHR 12:
   1-12 no.1-2, 42
  Zeitlin, L.  Merits and demerits of German
EG  price-control during the last war.  EJ 51:
   507-12 Dec 41
  Hamilton, E. J.  War and inflation in Spain,
ESp  1780-1800.  QJE 59:36-77 Nov 44
  Ataullah, S.  A fourteenth century experi-
FI   ment in price control.  IJE 24:340-47
   Apr 44
  Henderson, W. O.  The war economy of
H   German East Africa, 1914-1917.
   EHR 13:104-10 no.1-2, 43

13.2  ECONOMICS OF THE DEFENSE ESTAB-
   LISHMENT
13.20  GENERAL
  Black, R. F.  Wheels for defense.  HBR 19:
A   14-20 no.1, 40
  Bliss, C. A. and McNeill, R. B.  Manage-
A   ment control in uniform.  HBR 22:
   227-38 no.2, 44
  Brodsky, N.  A proposal for study of
   military distribution.  JM 14:88-90
   Jul 49
  Hoos, S.  The determination of military
   subsistence requirements.  JFE 28:
   973-88 Nov 46
  Macy, R. M.  Forecasting demand for U.S.
A   Army supplies in wartime.  JM 10:
   156-64 Oct 45
  Nathan, R. R.  Problems of statistical
A   control: economic aspects.  JASA 36:
   18-26 Mar 41
  Schmidt, L. A.  Navy accounting: a lesson
A   in adaptation.  HBR 25:243-54 no.2, 47
  Taitel, M.  Price indexes as viewed from
A   the standpoint of the national defense
   program.  JASA 36:201-09 Jun 41

13.21  PROCUREMENT. RENEGOTIATION.
   CONTRACT TERMINATION
  Parkin, N. C.  Renegotiation of war con-
   tract prices.  JB 17:91-103 Apr 44

  UNITED STATES
  Barton, F. L.  The freight-rate structure
A   and the distribution of defense contracts.
   SEJ 9:122-33 Oct 42
  Bollinger, L. L.  Dealing with Uncle Sam.
   HBR 19:211-20 no.2, 41
  Christenson, C. L.  Economic implications
   of renegotiation of government contracts.
   JPE 52:48-73 Mar 44
  George, H. B., Jr.  Buying perishables for
   the armed forces.  HBR 22:209-19 no.2, 44

# 13. WAR AND DEFENSE ECONOMICS

## 13.21 PROCUREMENT. RENEGOTIATION. CONTRACT TERMINATION (Cont.)

### UNITED STATES (Cont.)

A  Gragg, C. I.  Negotiated contracts. HBR 19: 221-29 no.2, 41

Hawes, A. B.  Issues and policies of contract termination.  AER/S 33:150-58 Mar 43

Lang, R. O.  Problems of statistical control: military aspects.  JASA 36:11-17 Mar 41

Lee, A. T. M.  Land acquisition program of the War and Navy Departments, World War II.  JFE 29:889-909 Nov 47

Miller, J. P.  Military procurement in peacetime.  HBR 25:444-62 no.4, 47

Nemmers, E. E.  Principles of war-contract termination.  JB 18:35-40 Jan 45

-- Economic aspects of termination of war contracts.  QJE 59:386-404 May 45

Nerlove, S. H.  Renegotiation of war contracts and the public interest.  JB 17: 104-10 Apr 44

Parkin, N. C.  Marketing aspects of the renegotiation of war contract prices. JM 9:207-16 Jan 45

-- Management statistics in war contract renegotiation.  JASA 40:504-19 Dec 45

-- Some economic concepts affecting the renegotiation of war contracts. JB 19: 31-42 Jan 46

-- Control of war contract profits. HBR 26:230-50 Mar 48

Parr, C. M.  Why the middleman?  JB 17: 23-36 Jan 44

Sanders, T. H.  Renegotiation of contract prices.  HBR 21:164-82 no.2, 43

### OTHER COUNTRIES

C  Mackintosh, W. A.  The price system and the procurement of essential supplies. CJE 7:338-49 Aug 41

EB  Balogh, T.  Compensation in practice. OIS 4:231-35 Aug 29, 42

-- Control over property.  OIS 5:196-99 Aug 28, 43

Kalecki, M.  Excess profits tax and government contracts.  OIS 4:40-43 Jan 10, 42

Steindl, J.  Economic incentive and efficiency in war industry.  OIS 3:164-69 Jun 7, 41

Worswick, G. D. N.  Costs and prices in government contracts.  OIS 4:185-89 Jun 27, 42

-- A survey of war contract procedure. OIS 7:79-90 Apr 7, 45

EG  Horniker, A. L.  German contracting in occupied Europe.  HBR 25:74-91 no.1, 46

FA  Matsuoka, K.  Southern economy: its currency and financial problems.  Kyo 17, no.4:27-47 Oct 42

N  Firth, G. G.  A note on supply.  ER 16: 111-14 Jun 40

## 13.22 SURPLUS DISPOSAL

A  Mack, C. E. and Knox, J.  Disposition of government property.  HBR 22:54-62 no.1, 43

A  McLean, J. G.  Sale of war surpluses to speculators.  HBR 23:229-45 no.2, 45

A  Sumner, J. D.  The disposition of surplus war property.  AER 34:457-71 Sep 44

A  Tosdal, H. R.  Disposal of war surpluses. HBR 22:346-57 no.3, 44

## 13.23 MILITARY AND INTELLIGENCE OPERATIONS

EG  Baran, P. A. and Galbraith, J. K.  Professor Despres on "Effects of strategic bombing on the German war economy." REStat 29:132-34 May 47

EI  Beattie, T. E.  The American soldier as a purchaser in southern Italy.  JM 9: 384-86 Apr 45

Coale, A. J.  The problem of reducing vulnerability to atomic bombs.  AER/S 37: 87-97 May 47

Lachmann, K.  War and peace economics of aviation.  SR 7:468-79 Nov 40

A  Ruggles, R. and Brodie, H.  An empirical approach to economic intelligence in World War II.  JASA 42:72-91 Mar 47

## 13.3 WAR FINANCE AND STABILIZATION POLICIES

## 13.30 GENERAL

Douglas, M.  Limitations of the financial factor in a war economy.  CJE 8:351-63 Aug 42

Gupta, D. L.  War and distribution of incomes.  IJE 27:409-15 Apr 47

Plumptre, A. F. W.  An approach to war finance.  CJE 7:1-12 Feb 41

Rosa, R. V.  A multiplier analysis of armament expenditure.  AER 31:249-65 Jun 41

### UNITED STATES

A  Bach, G. L.  War financing and the distribution of income.  AER 32:352-54 Jun 42

Buehler, A. G.  Compulsory loans in war financing.  HBR 21:115-23 no.1, 42

Copeland, M. A.  The capital budget and the war effort.  AER 33:38-49 Mar 43

Dolley, J. C.  Ability of the banking system to absorb government bonds.  JPE 51: 23-31 Feb 43

Haensel, P.  Financing World War II in the United States of America.  PF 1:329-56 no.4, 46

Hardy, C. O.  War finance, price control, and industrial mobilization.  JB 14: 222-34 Jul 41

Hermens, F. A. and Wallace, G. S.  Inflation and anti-inflation policies in the United States, 1939-1949.  ZS 105: 675-709 Hft. 4, 49

13.3 WAR FINANCE AND STABILIZATION
POLICIES (Cont.)

13.30 GENERAL (Cont.)

UNITED STATES (Cont.)

Kähler, A.  On the economics of war finance.  SR 9:458-75 Nov 42
A

Kazakévich, V. D.  The war and American finance.  S&S 4:153-67 no.2, 40

Lindeman, J.  The armaments program and national income.  AER 31:42-46 Mar 41

Mitnitzky, M.  Some monetary aspects of government borrowing.  AER 33:21-37 Mar 43

Sharpe, G. E.  Federal financing in the United States, 1941-1946.  SAJE 15: 1-26 Mar 47

Shoup, C.  Problems in war finance.  AER 33:74-97 Mar 43

Smithies, A.  Fiscal aspects of preparedness for war.  AER/S 39:356-65 May 49

Steindl, J.  War finance in the United States.  OIS 5:205-11 Sep 18, 43

-- The American financial position.  OIS 6: 65-68 Apr 8, 44

Taylor, C. T.  Voluntary savings and consumer behavior.  SEJ 10:239-45 Jan 44

Thomas, W.  The heritage of war finance.  AER/S 37:205-15 May 47

Tostlebe, A. S.  Estimate of Series E bond purchases by farmers.  JASA 40:317-29 Sep 45

Villard, H. H.  The effect of the war upon capital markets.  AER/S 32:369-81 Mar 42

Wernette, J. P.  Financing the defense program.  AER 31:754-66 Dec 41

Wheeler, W. C.  The victory merchandise bond plan.  JM 8:58-61 Jul 43

OTHER AMERICAN COUNTRIES

Chatters, C. H.  War-time problems of local government.  II.  The effect of war on municipal finance.  CJE 9:405-07 Aug 43
C

McIvor, R. C.  Canadian war-time fiscal policy, 1939-45.  CJE 14:62-93 Feb 48

Mackintosh, W. A.  Canadian war financing.  JPE 50:481-500 Aug 42

Parkinson, J. F.  Some problems of war finance in Canada.  CJE 6:403-23 Aug 40

Steindl, J.  Income and war finance in Canada.  OIS 3:37-44 Feb 22, 41

EUROPE

Allen, J E.  An alternative to the last two budgets.  EJ 51:498-502 Dec 41
EB

Anonymous.  The financing of the budget deficit in the period October 1939-February 1940.  OIS 2,no.1:1-5 Feb 40

-- Labour supply and war finance in the two fiscal years 1939/40 and 1940/41.  OIS 2,no.2:1-9 Jun 17, 40

Balogh, T.  The budget and economic mobilization.  OIS 3:113-18 Apr 26, 41

Bowen, I. and Worswick, G. D. N.  The controls and war finance.  OEP 4:77-104 Sep 40

George, C. O.  British public finance in peace and war [with discussion].  JRSS 104:235-80 pt.3, 41

Harris, S. E.  The British White Paper on war finance and national income and expenditure.  JPE 50:27-44 Feb 42

Holden, G.  Exchange control in British war finance: a correction.  QJE 54: 694-95 Aug 40

Kaldor, N.  The White Paper on national income and expenditure.  EJ 51:181-91 Jun-Sep 41

-- The 1941 White Paper on national income and expenditure.  EJ 52:206-22 Jun-Sep 42

Kalecki, M.  War finance in the first half of 1940.  OIS 2,no.7:7-18 Sep 40

-- The financial position on the eve of the budget.  OIS 3:61-65 Mar 15, 41

-- Recent trends in the financial situation.  OIS 3:389-93 Dec 13, 41

-- The burden of the war: B.  The burden on wages and other incomes.  OIS 4: 10-11 Jan 10, 42

-- The budget.  OIS 4:129-32 Apr 25, 42

-- War finance in 1940 and 1941.  OIS 4: 161-66 Jun 6, 42

-- The financial situation in the first half of 1942.  OIS 4:247-52 Sep 19, 42

-- The burden of the national debt.  OIS 5: 76-80 Apr 3, 43

-- The budget.  OIS 5:96-97 Apr 24, 43

-- War finance in 1940, 1941 and 1942.  OIS 5:137-42 Jun 26, 43

-- The financial situation in the first half of 1943.  OIS 5:216-20 Sep 18, 43

-- The problem of 'small' savings.  OIS 5: 260-65 Nov 20, 43

-- The budget: A.  The stabilisation policy.  OIS 6:101-04 May 20, 44

-- The White Paper on the national income and expenditure in the years 1938-1943.  OIS 6:137-44 Jul 1, 44

Madge, C.  Public opinion and paying for the war.  EJ 51:36-46 Apr 41

Musgrave, R. A.  White Paper on British war finance, 1938-41.  JPE 50:920-33 Dec 42

Nicholson, J. L.  The burden of the war: A.  Changes in real incomes, 1938 to 1940 [and 1938 to 1941].  OIS 4:5-10; 166-69 Jan 10, Jun 6, 42

-- The distribution of the war burden [1938 to 1942 and 1938 to 1943].  OIS 5:105-12; 6:153-61 May 15, 43, Jul 22, 44; Erratum. 6:192 Aug 12, 44

Niebyl, K. H.  The cynical Mr. Keynes.  S&S 4:234-39 no.3, 40

# 13. WAR AND DEFENSE ECONOMICS

## 13.3 WAR FINANCE AND STABILIZATION POLICIES (Cont.)
### 13.30 GENERAL (Cont.)
#### EUROPE (Cont.)

Radice, E. A. Consumption, savings, and
EB    war finance. OEP 4:1-14 Sep 40

Stafford, J. War finance. MS 11:36-46
Apr 40

Weintraub, S. Compulsory savings in Great
Britain. HBR 20:53-64 no.1, 41

Doblin, E. The German "profit stop" of
EG    1941. SR 9:371-78 Sep 42

Lindholm, R. W. German finance in World
War II. AER 37:121-34 Mar 47

Singer, H. W. The sources of war finance
in the German war economy. REStud 10:
106-14 no.2, 43

Sumberg, T. A. The Soviet Union's war
ER    budgets. AER 36:113-26 Mar 46

#### ASIA

Tamagna, F. M. The financial position of
FC    China and Japan. AER/S 36:613-27
May 46

Sinha, M. N. Indian currency and war.
FI    IJE 22:199-207 Oct 41

Tamagna, F. M. The financial position of
FJ    China and Japan. AER/S 36:613-27
May 46

#### AFRICA

Randall, R. J. War finance and the South
HSA    African war budgets 1941-42 and 1942-43.
SAJE 9:348-60 Dec 41

Reedman, J. N. and Guénault, P. H. The
war and the budget. SAJE 8:364-71
Dec 40

Van der Horst, S. T. Financing the South
African war effort. SAJE 9:66-84
Mar 41

#### AUSTRALIA. NEW ZEALAND

Isles, K. S. Some aspects of war finance.
N    ER 16:191-207 Dec 40

King, H. W. H. The New Zealand budget,
1941-1942, 1942-1943, 1943-1944.
ER 17:265-71; 18:217-22; 19:237-40
Dec 41, Dec 42, Dec 43

Neale, E. P. New Zealand general government finances, 1944-45. ER 20:222-26
Dec 44

Nimmo, J. F. Reports of Commonwealth
Parliamentary Joint Committee on
Profits. R. ER 18:226-28 Dec 42

Swan, T. W. Australian war finance and
banking policy. ER 16:50-67 Jun 40

## 13.31 TAXATION
### UNITED STATES

Allen, E. D. Treasury tax policies in 1943.
A    AER 34:707-33 Dec 44

Blakey, R. G. and Blakey, G. C. The two
federal revenue acts of 1940. AER 30:
724-35 Dec 40

Friedman, M. The spendings tax as a war-
time fiscal measure. AER 33:50-62
Mar 43

Lee, M. W. Taxation, defense, and consumer purchasing power. JM 6:11-15
Jul 41

Macy, C. W. Social security taxes in the
war finance program. JPE 51:135-47
Apr 43

Newcomer, M. Congressional tax policies
in 1943. AER 34:734-56 Dec 44

Poole, K. E. Problems of administration
and equity under a spendings tax.
AER 33:63-73 Mar 43

Pruefer, C. H. The excess profits tax and
defense financing. SEJ 8:40-53 Jul 41

Ratchford, B. U. The Federal excess
profits tax. Pt.I-II. SEJ 12:1-16;
97-114 Jul,Oct 45

Rosenson, A. M. Monetary effects of war-
time social security taxes. JPE 50:
881-900 Dec 42

Wald, H. P. A comparative analysis of
three variations of retail sales taxes.
AER 34:280-302 Jun 44

#### OTHER COUNTRIES

Leach, C. W. Excess profits taxation: II.
C    A business man's view. CJE 7:363-70
Aug 41

MacGibbon, D. A. The administration of
the Income War Tax Act. CJE 12:75-78
Feb 46

Morgan, L. The impact of war taxation on
eighty Canadian corporations. CJE 8:
566-83 Nov 42

Tolmie, J. R. Excess profits taxation: I.
The Canadian act and its administration.
CJE 7:350-63 Aug 41

Benham, F. "The taxation of war wealth."
EB    R. Ec N.S.8:321-24 Aug 41

Goldmann, J. Taxation of tobacco, beer,
and cinema attendances. OIS 5:35-39
Jan 30, 43

Hicks, U. K. Lags in tax collection: a
neglected problem in war finance.
REStud 8:89-99 Feb 41

Jaszi, G. and Musgrave, R. A. Taxation of
war wealth. R. CJE 8:260-72 May 42

Kalecki, M. Notes on finance. OIS 3:51-53
Feb 22, 41

-- The problem of profit margins. OIS 4:
114-17 Apr 4, 42

Lacey, K. Commodity stock values and
E.P.T. EJ 55:2-16 Apr 45

Nicholson, J. L. Wages and income tax.
OIS 4:87-89 Mar 14, 42

Yamey, B. S. The excess profits duty in
HSA    South Africa. SAJE 10:263-81 Dec 42

Carslaw, H. S. Australian income tax, 1943.
N    ER 19:1-10 Jun 43

## 13.3 WAR FINANCE AND STABILIZATION POLICIES (Cont.)

### 13.32 MONETARY POLICY

A    Bach, G. L. Rearmament, recovery and monetary policy. AER 31:27-41 Mar 41

A    Coleman, G. W. The effect of interest rate increases on the banking system. AER 35:671-73 Sep 45

FI    Dhar, B. Cheap money policy. IJE 28: 95-103 Jul 47

A    Harris, S. E. A one per cent war? AER 35:667-71 Sep 45

EB    Kalecki, M. The war-time trend of deposits. OIS 5:63-66 Mar 13, 43

FC    Kojima, S. Financial circles in Shanghai following the outbreak of the Greater East Asia War. Kyo 18,no.2:1-26 Apr 43

A    Matherly, W. J. The regulation of consumer credit. SEJ 11:34-44 Jul 44

A    Mors, W. Rate regulation in the field of consumer credit. Pt.I-II. JB 16:51-63; 124-37 Jan,Apr 43

EB    Muller, C. British war finance and the banks. JB 16:77-99 Apr 43

A    Neifeld, M. R. Consumer credit: impact of the war. JM 7:342-44 Apr 43

A    Robinson, R. I. The downward course of consumer credit. JM 7:345-49 Apr 43

A    Samuelson, P. A. The effect of interest rate increases on the banking system. AER 35:16-27 Mar 45

-- The turn of the screw. [The effect of interest rate increases on the banking system.] AER 35:674-76 Sep 45

ESN    Schjander, F. Norwegian savings banks and the state of the money market during and after the war. SAJE 15:73-77 Mar 47

ASW    Shapiro, E. The wartime experience of Wisconsin credit unions. JB 20:201-11 Oct 47

A    Simmons, E. C. Federal Reserve policy and the national debt during the war years. JB 20:84-95 Apr 47

N    Weller, G. A. Control of banking in wartime. ER 18:87-93 Jun 42

### 13.33 PRICES. INFLATION

Dowsett, W. T. Delayed action inflation. ER 19:64-70 Jun 43

Fellner, W. War finance and inflation. AER 32:235-54 Jun 42

Harris, S. E. Subsidies and inflation. AER 33:557-72 Sep 43

Oliver, H. War and inflation since 1790 in England, France, Germany, and the United States. AER/S 30,no.5:344-51 Feb 41

Pigou, A. C. War finance and inflation. EJ 50:461-68 Dec 40

Swanson, E. W. Some aspects of value and capital in a war economy. AER 33: 852-67 Dec 43

Working, H. War and commodity prices. JASA 35:309-24 Jun 40

### UNITED STATES

A    Angell, J. W. Defense financing and inflation: some comments on Professor Hansen's article. Taxation, inflation, and the defense program. REStat 23: 78-82 May 41

Clark, J. M. Further remarks on defense financing and inflation. REStat 23:107-12 Aug 41

Dowling, L. Comments on inflation. S&S 7:52-55 no.1, 43

Fellner, W. J. Postscript on war inflation: a lesson from World War II. AER 37: 76-91 Mar 47

Galbraith, J. K. Defense financing and inflation: some comments on Professor Hansen's article. The selection and timing of inflation controls. REStat 23: 82-85 May 41

Hansen, A. H. Defense financing and inflation potentialities. REStat 23:1-7 Feb 41

-- Some additional comments on the inflation symposium. REStat 23:91-93 May 41

Hart, A. G. Defense financing and inflation: some comments on Professor Hansen's article. Safeguards against inflation. REStat 23:85-87 May 41

-- Use of flexible taxes to combat inflation. AER 32:87-102 Mar 42

-- What it takes to block inflation. REStat 24:101-13 Aug 42

Kähler, A. The prospects of inflation. SR 8:156-72 May 41

Shoup, C. Defense financing and inflation: some comments on Professor Hansen's article. Choice of tax measures to avert inflation. REStat 23:88-90 May 41

### OTHER COUNTRIES

EB    Burchardt, F. The Trade Union Congress and inflation. OIS 3:298-300 Sep 20, 41

Dacey, W. M. Inflation and its aftermath. LBR 1:24-34 Jul 46

-- Inflation under controls. LBR 4,suppl.: 2-8 Apr 47

Kalecki, M. The budget and inflation. OIS 3:112-13 Apr 26, 41

Nicholson, J. L. Signs of inflation. OIS 3: 65-67 Mar 15, 41

FC    Matsuoka, K. The inflation of Chinese legal tender. Kyo 16,no.2:22-43 Apr 41

FI    Adiseshiah, M. S. [and others] Currency expansion during the war: discussion. IJE 24:545-60 Apr 44

Rao, T. S. The control of inflation in India. IJE 24:308-13 Apr 44

HSA    Guénault, P. H. [and others] Financing the South African war effort. I. The inflation danger in the Union: a comment [followed by S. T. Van der Horst's reply]. SAJE 9:176-89 Jun 41

# 13. WAR AND DEFENSE ECONOMICS

## 13.34 INSURANCE. WAR DAMAGE COMPENSATION

Balogh, T. Compensation for war-damage.
EB    OIS 2,no.7:18-20 Sep 40
-- The new bill for war damage compensa-
EB    tion. OIS 2,no.11:16-18 Dec 40
Wood, G. L. Economic aspects of war
N    damage compensation. ER 18:77-82
   Jun 42

## 13.4 PRICE CONTROL AND RATIONING
## 13.40 GENERAL

Walker, E. R. War-time economic controls.
   QJE 58:503-20 Aug 44

### UNITED STATES

Clark, J. M. General aspects of price con-
A    trol and rationing in the transition pe-
   riod. AER/S 35:152-62 May 45
Enke, S. Price control and rationing.
   AER 32:842-43 Dec 42
Grether, E. T. Price control and rationing
   under the Office of Price Administration:
   a brief selective appraisal. JM 7:300-18
   Apr 43
Heflebower, R., chairman. Content and re-
   search uses of price control and ration-
   ing records. [Report of a subcommittee]
   AER/S 37:651-66 May 47
Hobart, D. M. Probable effects of a
   national emergency on marketing func-
   tions and policies. JM 4,no.4,pt.2:59-65
   Apr 40
Mikesell, R. F. and Galbreath, C. E. Sub-
   sidies and price control. AER 32:524-37
   Sep 42
Rostow, W. W. Some aspects of price con-
   trol and rationing. AER 32:486-500
   Sep 42
Steindl, J. The problem of price and wage
   control. OIS 4:269-74 Oct 10, 42
Wallis, W. A. How to ration consumers'
   goods and control their prices. AER 32:
   501-12 Sep 42

### OTHER COUNTRIES

Stewart, S. I. Statutes, orders, and official
C    statements relating to Canadian war-
   time economic controls: [bibliography].
   CJE 13:99-114 Feb 47
Bowen, I. and Worswick, G. D. N. The con-
EB    trols and war finance. OEP 4:77-104
   Sep 40
Hartley, H. British war controls: the legal
   framework. MS 11:163-76 Oct 40
Kalecki, M. Rationing and price control.
   OIS 6:29-32 Feb 5, 44
Keezer, D. M. Observations on rationing
   and price control in Great Britain.
   AER 33:264-82 Jun 43
Stafford, J. British war controls: an eco-
   nomic comment. MS 11:142-62 Oct 40

Ataullah, S. Need for war time control of
FI    food stuffs in India. IJE 24:330-39
   Apr 44
Qureshi, A. I. Some thoughts on the Indian
   food problem. IJE 26:359-69 Jan 46
Row, B. G. Some aspects of economic con-
   trol in India during the war. IJE 24:
   314-22 Apr 44
Shenoy, B. R. [and others] Economic con-
   trols during the war: discussion. IJE 24:
   535-44 Apr 44
Sutch, W. B. New Zealand's war controls.
N    SAJE 8:136-44 Jun 40

## 13.41 PRICE CONTROL

Downing, R. I. Prices in wartime. ER 20:
   206-14 Dec 44
Rao, K. V. Economics of price control.
   IJE 24:300-07 Apr 44

### UNITED STATES

Abramson, V. Price freezing under the
A    Office of Price Administration. AER 32:
   760-74 Dec 42
-- and Phillips, C. F. Retail price control.
   HBR 20:184-98 no.2, 42
Backman, J. Price control: discussion.
   AER/S 33:272-76 Mar 43
Benham, F. Wartime control of prices. R.
   Ec N.S.9:58-63 Feb 42
Burley, O. E. [Price control]: discussion.
   JM 8:302-06 Jan 44
Fainsod, M. and Thompson, W. The OPA
   economy for victory program. JM 7:
   319-24 Apr 43
Galbraith, J. K. Price control: some les-
   sons from the first phase. AER/S 33:
   251-59 Mar 43
-- Reflections on price control. QJE 60:
   475-89 Aug 46
Gilliatt, N. Marketing implications in the
   OPA community pricing program. JM 9:
   101-08 Oct 44
Hardy, C. O. War finance, price control,
   and industrial mobilization. JB 14:
   222-34 Jul 41
Harrell, G. D. Prices paid by farmers:
   their use in administering wartime price
   control programs. JFE 25:338-50 Feb 43
Hirsch, J. Evaluation of our wartime price
   control. JM 8:281-88 Jan 44
Humphrey, D. D. Price control in outline.
   AER 32:744-59 Dec 42
MacFarlane, D. L. Ceiling over ceiling
   pricing. JFE 26:800-03 Nov 44
Miller, J. P. The tactics of retail price
   control. QJE 57:497-521 Aug 43
Morris, B. R. Price control at the retail
   level. QJE 58:323-24 Feb 44
Ratchford, B. U. Some preliminary obser-
   vations on price control. SEJ 10:99-113
   Oct 43

13.41  PRICE CONTROL (Cont.)
    UNITED STATES (Cont.)
    Reitz, J. W.  War-time price control of
A    fresh citrus fruits.  JFE 27:553-70
    Aug 45
    Segal, S. A. and Hoffman, A. C.  Food price
    control:  policy and mechanics [with
    discussion by G. Shepherd].  JFE 25:
    19-35 Feb 43
    Sumner, J. D.  The effects of the war on
    price policies and price making.
    AER/S 32:404-15 Mar 42
    Wallis, W. A.  Price control: discussion.
    AER/S 33:276-78 Mar 43
    Working, E. J.  Some problems in the con-
    trol of food prices.  JM 6,no.4,pt.2:29-36
    Apr 42
    -- Price control and the wartime pricing of
    farm products [with discussion by A. C.
    Hoffman].  JFE 26:110-23 Feb 44
    Pettengill, R. B.  Comparative retail
ASC  grocery ceiling prices in Los Angeles.
    JM 8:145-49 Oct 43

    OTHER AMERICAN COUNTRIES
    Aikenhead, J. T. E.  Practical problems of
C    the retail price ceiling: I.  Problems of
    the administrator.  CJE 8:433-40 Aug 42
    Elliott, G. A.  Price ceilings and inter-
    national trade theory.  CJE 8:186-96
    May 42
    Heywood, P. K.  Practical problems of the
    retail price ceiling: II.  Problems of the
    retailer.  CJE 8:440-45 Aug 42
    MacFarlane, D. L.  Ceiling over ceiling
    pricing.  JFE 26:800-03 Nov 44
    Taylor, K. W.  Canadian war-time price
    controls, 1941-6.  CJE 13:81-98 Feb 47
    Wagner, L. C.  Price control in Canada.
    JM 7:107-14 Oct 42

    EUROPE
    Bowen, I. and Worswick, G. D. N.  The
EB    Prices of Goods Act.  Pt.I-II.  OIS 2,no.6:
    2-5; no.7:2-7 Aug 31, Sep 21, 40
    Brandis, B.  British prices and wage rates:
    1939-1941.  QJE 57:543-64 Aug 43
    Hargreaves, E. L.  Price control of (non-
    food) consumer goods.  OEP 8:1-11
    Nov 47
    Richter-Altschaffer, J. H.  War-time price
    control in the United Kingdom.  JFE 22:
    680-90 Nov 40
    Smith, H.  Reflections on the war-time con-
    trol of food prices.  OEP 8:12-17 Nov 47
    Burchardt, F.  German price policy.  OIS 4:
EG    117-21 Apr 4, 42
    Doblin, E.  The German "profit stop" of
    1941.  SR 9:371-78 Sep 42
    Schwartz, H.  Prices in the Soviet war
ER    economy.  AER 36:872-82 Dec 46

    ASIA
    Bhattacharya, K. N.  Price stabilisation.
FI    IJE 26:296-99 Oct 45
    Bose, S. R.  Price control.  IJE 20:631-38
    Apr 40
    -- Price policy in war-time.  IJE 24:225-38
    Apr 44
    Qureshi, A. I.  Control of prices.  IJE 24:
    272-80 Apr 44
    Ram, V. S.  Price control in the U.P.
    IJE 24:281-90 Apr 44
    Tilak, V. R. K.  Some aspects of price con-
    trol in India.  IJE 24:323-29 Apr 44

    AFRICA
    Burrows, H. R., Halliday, I. G. and Smith,
HSA  R. H.  Price control in war-time. [Pt.I
    of a three-part survey, completed by
    Smith alone.]  SAJE 8:400-30 Dec 40
    Smith, R. H.  War-time control of prices
    in South Africa [Pt.II-III].  SAJE 9:
    400-15; 11:11-23 Dec 41, Mar 43

    AUSTRALIA.  NEW ZEALAND
    Airey, C. R.  The scope of price regulation
N    [followed by W. Prest's comment].
    ER 16:121-24 Jun 40
    -- --- A reply.  ER 16:280-81 Dec 40
    Downing, R. I.  The costs and achievements
    of price stabilization.  ER 20:38-57
    Jun 44
    Kelly, W. S.  Primary products prices.
    ER 19:162-70 Dec 43
    Nimmo, J. F.  Reports of Commonwealth
    Parliamentary Joint Committee on
    Profits.  R.  ER 18:226-28 Dec 42
    Sutch, W. B.  Marketing and price control
    in New Zealand.  ER 16:68-77 Jun 40
    Walker, E. R. and Linford, R. J.  War-time
    price control and price movements in
    an open economy:  Australia 1914-20
    and 1939-40.  REStat 24:75-86 May 42
    Wise, H. L.  War-time price control in
    New Zealand.  ER 17:180-91 Dec 41
    -- Some aspects of price stabilization in
    New Zealand.  ER 18:180-91 Dec 42
    -- Price stabilization in New Zealand.
    ER 19:38-45 Jun 43
    -- Stabilization of land values in New Zea-
    land.  ER 19:225-30 Dec 43

13.42  RENT CONTROL
    Ady, P.  Rents and rent restriction.
EB    OIS 5:248-54 Oct 30, 43
    Borders, K.  The problems of determining
A    fair rents.  JASA 37:34-40 Mar 42
    Downs, J. C., Jr.  Rent control.  LE 17:
A    406-09 Nov 41
    Gage, D. D.  Wartime experiment in federal
A    rent control.  LE 23:50-59 Feb 47
    Redlich, F.  Rental analysis in wartime.
A    JPE 55:245-53 Jun 47

## 13. WAR AND DEFENSE ECONOMICS

### 13.43 RATIONING

#### UNITED STATES

A   Abramson, V. and Phillips, C. F. The rationing of consumer goods. JB 15:1-20 Jan 42

Derber, M. Gasoline rationing policy and practice in Canada and the United States. JM 8:137-44 Oct 43

Gettell, R. G. Rationing: a pragmatic problem for economists. AER/S 33:260-71 Mar 43

Goldmann, J. Consumption and rationing in the United States. OIS 5:221-25 Oct 9, 43

Kaplan, J. J. Rationing objectives and allotments, illustrated with sugar data. JFE 24:647-64 Aug 42

-- Some problems in rationing meats. REStat 24:159-65 Nov 42

Maxwell, J. A. and Balcom, M. N. Gasoline rationing in the United States. Pt.I-II. QJE 60:561-87; 61:125-55 Aug,Nov 46

Neisser, H. P. Theoretical aspects of rationing. QJE 57:378-97 May 43

Phillips, C. F. Some observations on rationing. JB 18:9-20 Jan 45

Sweezy, P. M. Rationing and the war economy. S&S 7:64-71 no.1, 43

Taylor, M. D. Allocation of scarce consumers' goods to retailers. JM 8:123-32 Oct 43

Waite, W. C. The pressure of red point rationing. JM 8:422-24 Apr 44

Weintraub, S. Rationing consumer expenditure. HBR 21:109-14 no.1, 42

#### OTHER COUNTRIES

C   Derber, M. Gasoline rationing policy and practice in Canada and the United States. JM 8:137-44 Oct 43

EB   Ady, P. The statistical background of clothes rationing, 1941-44. Pt.I-III. OIS 6:209-19; 225-31; 256-64 Sep 23, Oct 14, Nov 4, 44

Andrews, P. W. S. Food rationing and the present emergency. OIS 2,no.4:2-7 Jul 40

-- Food policy. OIS 3:48-51 Feb 22, 41

Anonymous. Fuel rationing. OIS 4:145-47 May 16, 42

Brandis, B. Control of consumption in Britain. JFE 24:845-56 Nov 42

Burchardt, F. and Worswick, G. D. N. Point rationing. OIS 3:183-89 Jun 28, 41

Goldmann, J. Differential rationing in practice. OIS 4:274-76 Oct 10, 42

Kalecki, M. A scheme of curtailment of consumption. OIS 2,no.3:7-9 Jun 30, 40

-- General rationing. OIS 3:1-6 Jan 11, 41

-- Notes on general rationing. OIS 3:103-05 Apr 5, 41

-- Towards comprehensive rationing. OIS 3:269-72 Aug 30, 41

-- Differential rationing. OIS 4:215-17 Aug 8, 42

-- Some problems of non-food rationing. OIS 4:325-28 Dec 12, 42

MacGregor, J. J. Britain's wartime food policy. JFE 25:384-96 May 43

Richardson, J. H. Consumer rationing in Great Britain. CJE 8:69-82 Feb 42

Rothschild, K. W. and Goldmann, J. Point rationing of foodstuffs. OIS 5:129-33 Jun 5, 43

Rutherford, R. S. G. The consumption and rationing of butter and margarine. OEP 3:131-43 Feb 40

-- and Rutherford, M. E. E. The consumption and rationing of meat and cheese. OEP 5:74-87 Jun 41

Steindl, J. Rationing and surplus goods. OIS 3:346-48 Nov 1, 41

Worswick, G. D. N. Notes on rationing. OIS 4:44-52 Jan 10, 42

FI   Chatterji, R. Food rationing in India. IJE 26:622-30 Apr 46

Rajalakshman, D. V. Cereal rationing in the Madras Presidency. IJE 26:116-24 Jul 45

Rudra, S. K. Rationing of foodgrains in the U.P. during World War II. IJE 26:716-33 Apr 46

FJ   Smith, H. F. Food controls in occupied Japan. AH 23:220-23 Jul 49

Yagi, Y. Japan's current rice policy. Kyo 16,no.2:1-21 Apr 41

### 13.5 PRODUCTION POLICIES AND CONTROL
### 13.50 GENERAL

Allen, R. G. D. International programming of the distribution of resources: II. Statistics and combined planning. JASA 39:286-90 Sep 44

Batt, W. L. International programming of the distribution of resources: I. The problem of combined planning. JASA 39:281-85 Sep 44

Feiler, A. Conscription of capital. SR 8:1-23 Feb 41

Walker, E. R. The co-ordination problem in war economy. JPE 51:149-55 Apr 43

#### UNITED STATES

A   Arnold, T. and Livingston, J. S. Antitrust war policy and full production. HBR 20:265-76 no.3, 42

Baruch, B. M. Priorities: the synchronizing force. HBR 19:261-70 no.3, 41

Blaisdell, T. C., Jr. Industrial concentration in the war. AER/S 33:159-61 Mar 43

Browder, E. Centralized control of war production. S&S 7:56-63 no.1, 43

Brown, T. H. Business approaches to rearmament production control. JASA 36:27-35 Mar 41

Brunsman, H. G. The sample census of congested production areas. JASA 39:303-10 Sep 44

Burns, A. R. Concentration of production. HBR 21:277-90 no.3, 43

13.5  PRODUCTION POLICIES AND CONTROL
(Cont.)

13.50  GENERAL (Cont.)

UNITED STATES (Cont.)

Copeland, M. A.; Jacobson, J. and Lasken, H.
The WPB index of war production.
JASA 40:145-59 Jun 45

Davis, S. C.  Coordinating production for
war.  JASA 38:417-24 Dec 43

Gilbert, H. N. From industrial mobilization
to war production. HBR 21:124-36
no.1, 42

Gordon, L. Government controls in war and
peace. BHR 20:42-51 Apr 46

Gragg, C. I.; Grimshaw, A. and Teele, S.
F. Competition under rationing. HBR 20:
141-55 no.2, 42

Johnson, S. Y. Expediting in wartime.
HBR 21:344-57 no.3, 43

Martin, J. H. Present status of priorities.
HBR 19:271-85 no.3, 41

-- Administration of priorities. HBR 19:
419-28 no.4, 41

-- Priorities and allocation. HBR 20:
406-14 no.4, 42

-- Interim report on CMP. HBR 21:472-84
no.4, 43

Moore, G. H.  Industrial materials production, World Wars I and II. JASA 39:
335-44 Sep 44

Myers, C. A. Wartime concentration of
production. JPE 51:222-34 Jun 43

Novick, D. Research opportunities in the
War Production Board records.
AER/S 37:690-99 May 47

-- and Steiner, G. A. The War Production
Board's statistical reporting experience.
Pt.I-VI. JASA 43:201-30; 463-88;
575-96; 44:413-43 Jan 48-Sep 49

Robbins, S. M. and Murphy, T. E. Economics of scheduling for industrial
mobilization. JPE 57:30-45 Feb 49

Siegel, I. H. The measurement of capacity
utilization. JASA 37:430-36 Dec 42

Steindl, J. Problems of defence production
in the United States. OIS 4:11-20
Jan 10, 42

Stern, B. J. Science and war production.
S&S 7:97-114 no.2, 43

Taitel, M. Business-reporting under the
defense program. JB 14:284-93 Jul 41

OTHER COUNTRIES

Ady, P. Utility goods. OIS 4:281-87
EB   Oct 31, 42

Balogh, T. and Burchardt, F. Concentration in the 'non-essential' industries.
OIS 3:68-71 Mar 15, 41

-- Money incentive and the production
drive. OIS 3:311-14 Oct 11, 41

Murphy, M. E. Wartime concentration of
British industry. QJE 57:129-41 Nov 42

Steindl, J. The Production Executive's
regional boards. OIS 3:272-78
Aug 30, 41

Worswick, G. D. N. Concentration: success or failure? OIS 3:359-64
Nov 22, 41

-- Dual capacity. OIS 5:80-85 Apr 3, 43

Shenfield, A. and Florence, P. S. The
EBE  economies and diseconomies of industrial concentration: the wartime experience of Coventry. REStud 12:79-99
no.2, 45

Block, H. Industrial concentration versus
EG   small business: the trend of Nazi
policy. SR 10:175-99 May 43

Grajdanzev, A. J. Japan's wartime pro-
FJ   duction: comment. AER 33:905-06
Dec 43

Yagi, Y. The co-operative movement
under wartime economic control.
Kyo 15,no.3:25-40 Jul 40

Rosenberg, W. Second report of the N.Z.
N    National Service Department. R. ER 20:
218-21 Dec 44

13.51  RAW MATERIALS CONTROL

Block, H. German methods of allocating
EG   raw materials. SR 9:356-70 Sep 42

Gordon, R. A. International programming
of the distribution of resources: III. The
Combined Raw Materials Board.
JASA 39:291-96 Sep 44

Halpern, D. B. The salvage of waste mate-
EB   rial. OIS 4:235-41 Aug 29, 42; Erratum.
260 Sep 19, 42

Hamilton, W. The control of strategic materials. AER 34:261-79 Jun 44

Hurstfield, J. The control of British raw
EB   material supplies, 1919-1939. EHR 14:
1-31 no.1, 44

Moos, S. The accumulation of raw material
EB   surpluses. OIS 2,no.11:11-14 Dec 40;
Errata. 3:16 Jan 11, 41

Watkins, M. W. Scarce raw materials: an
analysis and a proposal. AER 34:227-60
Jun 44

Worswick, G. D. N. British raw material
EB   controls. OEP 6:1-41 Apr 42

13.52  EXPANSION OF FACILITIES

Abramson, A. G. Industrial adjustment at
A    the end of the war: discussion.
AER/S 33:137 Mar 43

Andrews, P. W. S. Development-projects
EB   in Great Britain during the war. OIS 3:
22-25 Feb 1, 41

-- A survey of industrial development in
EB   Great Britain planned since the com-
mencement of the war. OEP 5:55-71
Jun 41

Bower, M. Gearing a business for national
A    defense. HBR 19:66-71 no.1, 40

13.61  LABOR AND MANPOWER (Cont.)
UNITED STATES (Cont.)

Hawkins, E. D., chairman. Technical as-
A     pects of applying a dismissal wage to
      defense workers. Abstract of special-
      ized conference discussion. AER/S 32:
      215-16 Mar 42

Henig, H. and Unterberger, S. H. Wage
      control in wartime and transition.
      AER 35:319-36 Jun 45

Hinrichs, A. F. The defence programme
      and labour supply in the United States.
      CJE 7:414-25 Aug 41

Joseph, J. J. The mobilization of man-
      power. S&S 7:2-13 no.1, 43

Keezer, D. M. Observations on the opera-
      tions of the National War Labor Board.
      AER 36:233-57 Jun 46

Lester, R. A. Effects of the war on wages
      and hours. AER/S 33:218-37 Mar 43

Levine, L. The impact of war on labor
      supply and labor utilization. JASA 37:
      54-62 Mar 42

McNatt, E. B. Wage policy in the defense
      program. SEJ 8:504-12 Apr 42

-- Toward a national wartime labor policy:
      the union-security issue. JB 16:64-69
      Jan 43

-- Toward a national wartime
      labor policy: the wage issue. JPE 51:
      1-11 Feb 43

Mautz, W. H. and Durand, J. D. Population
      and war labor supply. JASA 38:31-42
      Mar 43

Myers, H. B. Defense migration and labor
      supply. JASA 37:69-76 Mar 42

Myers, R. J. and Ober, H. Statistics for
      wage stabilization. JASA 38:425-37
      Dec 43

-- Wartime changes in urban wage rela-
      tionships. JASA 40:175-86 Jun 45

O'Leary, J. J. A general wage ceiling.
      SEJ 9:24-32 Jul 42

Opdyke, W. K. Training within industry.
      HBR 20:348-57 no.3, 42

Parrish, J. B. Impact of World War II on
      internal wage rate structures. SEJ 15:
      134-51 Oct 48

Record, J. C. The War Labor Board: an
      experiment in wage stabilization.
      AER 34:98-110 Mar 44

Robbins, E. C. War-time labor productivity.
      HBR 19:99-105 no.1, 40

Shishkin, B. Labor problems: discussion.
      AER/S 33:249-51 Mar 43

Shister, J. The National War Labor Board:
      its significance. JPE 53:37-56 Mar 45

Shryock, H. S., Jr. Internal migration and
      the war. JASA 38:16-30 Mar 43

Steindl, J. Labour in the war industries of
      Britain and U.S.A.: B. The U.S. war effort
      in terms of manpower. OIS 5:11-14
      Jan 9, 43

-- Wage structure and wage policy in the
      United States. OIS 5:157-62 Jul 17, 43

-- The U.S. war effort in terms of man-
      power in 1942. OIS 5:178-81 Aug 7, 43

Stewart, C. D. Degree and character of
      the wartime expansion of the national
      labor force. AER/S 33:207-17 Mar 43

Stone, R. W. Labor problems: discussion.
      AER/S 33:252-53 Mar 43

Walsh, J. R. Labor's contribution to the
      war. S&S 7:72-79 no.1, 43

Witte, E. E. Wartime handling of labor
      disputes. HBR 25:169-89 no.2, 47

Wolf, H. D., chairman. Wartime materials
      in the field of labor. [Report of a sub-
      committee] AER/S 37:671-80 May 47

Wright, W. Impact of the war on technical
      training and occupational mobility.
      AER/S 33:238-48 Mar 43

Henderson, S. and Upchurch, M. L. Relo-
ASW  cation of manpower and zoning [in Wis-
      consin]. LE 19:1-17 Feb 43

OTHER AMERICAN COUNTRIES

Amos, J. L. Vocational rehabilitation dur-
C     ing and after the war. CJE 9:164-74
      May 43

Steindl, J. Canada's labour reserve.
      OIS 3:144-47 May 17, 41

Stewart, B. M. War-time labour problems
      and policies in Canada. CJE 7:426-46
      Aug 41

EUROPE

Anonymous. Labour supply and war finance
EB   in the two fiscal years 1939/40 and
      1940/41. OIS 2,no.2:1-9 Jun 17, 40

Bowley, A. L. Relative wages and earnings
      in different occupations. Pt.I-II. OIS 3:
      383-89; 4:1-4 Dec 13, 41, Jan 10, 42;
      Erratum. 55 Jan 31, 42

Brandis, B. British prices and wage rates:
      1939-1941. QJE 57:543-64 Aug 43

Bunn, M. Mass Observation: a comment
      on People in production. R. MS 13:
      24-37 Oct 43

Burchardt, F. The White Paper on indus-
      trial and labour policy. OIS 3:235-42
      Aug 9, 41

Crippen, H. R. Workers and jobs in war-
      time Britain. S&S 6:208-26 no.3, 42

Daniel, G. H. War-time release of labour
      from consumption-goods industries.
      OIS 2,no.4:7-9 Jul 40

Forchheimer, K. War-time changes in
      industrial employment: a comparison
      between the two world wars. OIS 7:
      269-78 Nov 24, 45

Frankel, H. Quantitative and qualitative
      full employment. OIS 3:342-46 Nov 1,
      41; Erratum. 381 Nov 22, 41

-- The employment of married women.
      OIS 4:183-85 Jun 27, 42

## 13.61 LABOR AND MANPOWER (Cont.)
### EUROPE (Cont.)

Gomberg, E. L. Strikes and lock-outs in

EB    Great Britain. QJE 59:92-106 Nov 44

Ince, G. H. Mobilisation of man-power in Great Britain for the second great war. MS 14,no.1:17-52 Jan 46

Kalecki, M. Labour in the war industries of Britain and U.S.A.: A. Sources of manpower in the British war sector. OIS 5:2-11 Jan 9, 43

-- Sources of manpower in the British war sector in 1941 and 1942. OIS 5:173-78 Aug 7, 43

Murphy, M. E. The war and British workers. HBR 20:92-106 no.1, 41

Needham, J. The utilization of scientists in England. S&S 7:32-35 no.1, 43

Nicholson, J. L. Earnings of workpeople in 1938 and 1942. OIS 5:31-35 Jan 30, 43

-- Substitution of women for men in industry. OIS 5:85-87 Apr 3, 43

-- Earnings in January 1943. OIS 5:193-95 Aug 28, 43

-- Wages during the war. OIS 6:232-35 Oct 14, 44

-- Earnings, hours, and mobility of labour. OIS 8:146-63 May 46

Reubens, B. G. Unemployment in war-time Britain. QJE 59:206-36 Feb 45

Schulz, T. Labour and industrial output. OIS 4:89-93 Mar 14, 42

Steindl, J. The problem of price and wage control. OIS 4:269-74 Oct 10, 42

Wilson, T. Programmes and allocations in the planned economy. OEP N.S.1:40-53 Jan 49

Shenfield, A. and Florence, P. S. Labour

EBE   for the war industries: the experience of Coventry. REStud 12:31-49 no.1, 44

Balogh, T. and Mandelbaum, K. Manpower

EG   policy in Germany. OIS 3:279-81 Aug 30, 41

Block, H. Man-power allocation in Germany. HBR 21:259-68 no.2, 43

Grunfeld, J. Mobilization of women in Germany. SR 9:476-94 Nov 42

### ASIA

Bose, S. R. Labour in wartime. IJE 24:

FI   179-91 Jan 44

Qadir, M. A. Industrial disputes during war time and their settlement. IJE 24: 266-71 Apr 44

### AFRICA

Franklin, N. N. and Yamey, B. S. An en-

HSA   quiry into some effects of a wage determination in Grahamstown. SAJE 9: 416-22 Dec 41

Guénault, P. H. Labour supply. SAJE 8: 388-99 Dec 40

Randall, R. J. Full employment in wartime. SAJE 10:121-25 Jun 42

### AUSTRALIA. NEW ZEALAND

Rosenberg, W. Second report of the N.Z.

N   National Service Department. R. ER 20: 218-21 Dec 44

Wise, H. L. Price [and wage] stabilization in New Zealand. ER 19:38-45 Jun 43

## 13.62 WARTIME CONSUMPTION

Davis, J. S. Food in a world at war. HBR 19:133-42 no.2, 41

-- The world's food position and outlook. HBR 21:43-49 no.1, 42

Schulz, T. Food consumption in the United Kingdom, the United States and Canada. R. OIS 6:145-50 Jul 1, 44

### UNITED STATES

Barton, S. G. The consumption pattern of

A   different economic groups under war changes. JM 8:50-53 Jul 43

Bassie, V. L. Consumers' expenditures in war and transition. REStat 28:117-30 Aug 46

Black, J. D. The food situation, May, 1943. HBR 21:397-414 no.4, 43

Cavin, J. P. Aspects of wartime consumption. AER/S 35:15-36 May 45

Crossley, A. M. The impact of war on American families. JM 8:41-45 Jul 43

Gilboy, E. W. Changes in consumption expenditures and the defense program. REStat 23:155-64 Nov 41

Goldmann, J. Consumption and rationing in the United States. OIS 5:221-25 Oct 9, 43

Howell, L. D. Internal trade barriers for margarine. JFE 25:793-806 Nov 43

Johnson, R. N. Facts and trends of government control affecting consumer economy. JM 8:5-12 Jul 43

Jones, W. O. Impact of the war on United States flour consumption. JFE 30: 518-36 Aug 48

Ruderman, A. P. Wartime food-consumption patterns and the cost of living. JB 17: 244-49 Oct 44

Williams, F. M.; Rice, F. R. and Schell, E. D. Cost of living indexes in wartime. JASA 37:415-24 Dec 42

### OTHER COUNTRIES

Stocking, S. B. Recent trends in consump-

C   tion. CJE 7:371-81 Aug 41

Barna, T. Indirect taxes, subsidies and the

EB   cost-of-living index. REStud 10:53-61 no.1, 42

Burchardt, F. A. Sales and stocks of nonfood goods 1944. OIS 7:13-16 Jan 13, 45

Daniel, G. H. War-time consumption of food. OIS 2,no.3:5-6 Jun 30, 40

-- War-time food requirements of the United Kingdom. OIS 2,no.5:6-7 Aug 10, 40

13.  WAR AND DEFENSE ECONOMICS

13.73  EXTRACTIVE INDUSTRIES (Cont.)
Moos, S. (Cont.)
-- Incentives to the development of mineral
EB      resources.  OIS 4:302-08 Nov 21, 42

.3.74  TRANSPORTATION.  COMMUNICATION.
PUBLIC UTILITIES
Perry, H. S.  Ocean shipping.  HBR 19:
438-50 no.4, 41

UNITED STATES
Dowell, A. A.  Wartime transportation of
A      farm products [with discussion by H. M.
Haag].  JFE 26:159-80 Feb 44
Eastman, J. B.  Public administration of
transportation under war conditions.
AER/S 34:86-93 Mar 44
Gates, J. E.  Problems in administering
war-time shortages of electric energy.
LE 17:477-82 Nov 41
Hammerberg, D. O.  Wartime problems of
conservation of transportation [with dis-
cussion by C. M. Hardin].  JFE 25:
147-65 Feb 43
Jones, H. F.  Midwest Power Conference.
LE 18:224-25 May 42
Melamerson-Vandenhaag, E. R.  A ration-
ing rate structure.  LE 19:243-45 May 43
Northrup, H. R.  The Railway Labor act and
railway labor disputes in wartime.
AER 36:324-43 Jun 46
Perry, H. S.  Ocean rate regulation, World
War II.  HBR 21:238-52 no.2, 43
Ruggles, C. O., chairman.  The impact of
national defense and the war upon public
utilities.  Abstract of specialized confer-
ence discussion.  AER/S 32:216-17
Mar 42
Simpson, F. R.  The war's impact on urban
transit systems.  HBR 23:460-68 no.4, 45
Sorrell, L. C.  Transportation and national
defense.  JB 14:235-58 Jul 41
Talmage, G. E., Jr.  Transportation for
war.  HBR 21:336-43 no.3, 43
Wilson, G. L.  Freight rates in wartime.
HBR 21:230-37 no.2, 43
Murray, V. M.  Grand Coulee and Bonne-
AA      ville power in the national war effort.
LE 18:134-39 May 42

OTHER COUNTRIES
Allen, G. H.  Wartime changes in English
C      and Canadian radio.  JM 7:220-26 Jan 43
Block, H.  European transportation under
E      German rule.  SR 11:216-41 May 44
Allen, G. H.  Wartime changes in English
EB      and Canadian radio.  JM 7:220-26 Jan 43
Balogh, T.  The shipping balance.  OIS 5:
25-31 Jan 30, 43
Buckatzsch, E. J.  The canals.  OIS 3:71-74
Mar 15, 41
-- War transport.  OIS 4:81-86 Mar 14, 42
-- Reorganisation of inland transport.
OIS 4:297-301 Nov 21, 42

Burchardt, F.  Shipping: the bottleneck.
OIS 4:193-97 Jul 18, 42
Kendall, M. G.  Losses of U.K. merchant
ships in World War II.  Ec N.S.15:289-93
Nov 48
Macgregor, D. H.  Aspects of the shipping
question.  OIS 2,no.11:7-10 Dec 40
Moos, S.  The shipping situation.  OIS 3:
74-76 Mar 15, 41
Stewart, M.  The new railway agreement.
OIS 3:300-04 Sep 20, 41
Moos, S. and Buckatzsch, E. J.  The Balkan
EG      war and the blockade of Germany.  OIS 3:
141-44 May 17, 41
Ramanadham, V. V.  War and road trans-
FI      port.  IJE 24:291-99 Apr 44

13.75  CONSTRUCTION.  HOUSING
Bryant, L. C. and Feldstein, M. J.  Organ-
A      ization of occupancy in critical war lo-
calities.  LE 18:339-49 Aug 42
Dennis, S. J.  Housing in relation to national
A      defense.  JASA 36:36-44 Mar 41
Diehl, L. F.  Ordnance causes ordinance in
ASP    Crawford County, Pennsylvania.  LE 18:
357-63 Aug 42
Elsas, M. J.  War and housing.  EJ 50:42-50
EB      Mar 40
Fitzpatrick, F. S.  Defense housing.  LE 16:
A      344-45 Aug 40
Goldmann, J.  The new building programme.
EB      OIS 4:228-30 Aug 29, 42
Hoagland, H. E.  Housing and national de-
A      fense.  LE 16:377-81 Nov 40
Lapin, B. B.  Occupancy of housing in war-
A      production centers.  LE 19:222-24
May 43
Mendelsohn, R.  Australian housing policy:
N      war and post-war.  ER 17:57-67 Jun 41
Moos, S.  Building materials and building
EB      policy.  OIS 5:112-17 May 15, 43
Nurnberg, M.  Housing between boom and
A      bottlenecks.  SR 8:189-212 May 41
Pribram, K.  Housing policy and the de-
A      fense program.  AER 31:803-08 Dec 41
Rowlands, D. T.  Defense housing insur-
A      ance.  LE 17:357-61 Aug 41
Russell, H.  Defense housing and the Lan-
A      ham Bill.  LE 16:457-59 Nov 40
Strunk, N.  Progress in defense housing.
A      LE 17:92-97 Feb 41
A      -- Housing priorities.  LE 17:484-88 Nov 41
Tierney, J. L.  War housing: the Emer-
A      gency Fleet Corporation experience.
Pt.I-II.  LE 17:151-64; 303-12 May,
Aug 41
Weimer, A. M.  Potential effects of the de-
A      fense program on housing.  LE 17:207-15
May 41
Weintraub, R. G. and Tough, R.  Federal
A      housing and World War II.  LE 18:155-62
May 42
Wood, E.  The role of the government in de-
A      fense housing.  LE 16:382-85 Nov 40

# 13. WAR AND DEFENSE ECONOMICS

## 13.76 AGRICULTURE
### UNITED STATES

A Allbaugh, L. G. Working with farmers to achieve maximum production [with discussion by G. A. Pond]. JFE 26:214-31 Feb 44

Arant, W. D. Wartime meat policies. JFE 28:903-19 Nov 46

Becker, J. A. Problems in estimating food production in wartime. JASA 39:30-34 Mar 44

Bennett, J. B. A desirable wartime land policy. JFE 25:166-75 Feb 43

Black, J. D. American agriculture in the new war and defense situation. JFE 23: 28-36 Feb 41

-- Agricultural price policy, January 1943 [with discussion by G. Shepherd and H. Working]. JFE 25:1-18 Feb 43

-- and Gibbons, C. A. The war and American agriculture. REStat 26:1-55 Feb 44

Borg, W. T. Food administration experience with hogs, 1917-19. JFE 25:444-57 May 43

Bunce, A. C. War and soil conservation. LE 18:121-33 May 42

Canning, J. B. Foods for defense. JFE 23: 697-711 Nov 41

Ciriacy-Wantrup, S. von. The relation of war economics to agriculture, with particular reference to the effects of income and price inflation and deflation. AER/S 30:366-82 Mar 40

-- A discussion of "Food production policies in wartime" by Sherman E. Johnson. JFE 25:869-74 Nov 43

Craig, G. H. War developments in land utilization and policy in the Northern Plains [with discussion by V. L. Hurlburt]. JFE 25:176-89 Feb 43

Curtiss, W. M. Farm labor and food production. JFE 25:301-04 Feb 43

Dowell, A. A. Wartime transportation of farm products [with discussion by H. M. Haag]. JFE 26:159-80 Feb 44

Elliott, F. F. Agriculture when the war ends [with discussion by M. R. Benedict]. JFE 25:309-25 Feb 43

Foote, R. J. Wartime dairy policies. JFE 29:679-90 Aug 47

Ham, W. T. Wage stabilization in agriculture. JFE 27:104-20 Feb 45

Hobson, A. War adjustments for American agriculture. JFE 22:269-78 Feb 40

Horton, D. C. and Larsen, H. C. Agricultural finance guides in wartime. LE 19: 59-68 Feb 43

-- Finance and effective wartime use of agricultural resources. SEJ 10:14-26 Jul 43

Jesness, O. B. Newly developing international situation and American agriculture. JFE 23:1-14 Feb 41

Johnson, N. W. Wartime experience in production adjustment research and future possibilities [with discussion by C. A. Pond and J. B. Andrews]. JFE 27: 903-27 Nov 45

Johnson, S. E. Adapting agricultural programs for war needs. JFE 24:1-16 Feb 42

--; Tetro, R. C. and Johnson, N. W. Resources available for agricultural production in 1943. JFE 25:65-83 Feb 43

-- Food production policies in wartime. JFE 25:545-59 Aug 43

Johnston, P. E. Farm labor situation and its effect on agricultural production in the corn belt. JFE 25:278-86 Feb 43

Kaufman, J. J. Farm labor during World War II. JFE 31:131-42 Feb 49

Kling, W. A nutritional guide to wartime use of agricultural resources. JFE 25: 683-91 Aug 43

-- Food waste in distribution and use. JFE 25:848-59 Nov 43

Lee, A. T. M. Use of military land for agriculture during World War II. LE 23: 349-59 Nov 47

Levin, G. Government egg programs during wartime, a review and appraisal. JFE 28:887-902 Nov 46

Linville, F. A. An agricultural policy for Hemisphere defense. JFE 23:726-42 Nov 41

Mighell, R. L. and Christensen, R. P. Measuring maximum contribution to food needs by producing areas [with discussion]. JFE 26:181-96 Feb 44

Patton, H. S. The war and North American agriculture. CJE 7:382-96 Aug 41

Regan, M. M. The farm real estate market in war time. LE 18:140-45 May 42

Schickele, R. War-time adjustments in farm tenure. LE 18:163-68 May 42

-- Farm tenure under the strain of war. JFE 25:235-44 Feb 43

Schwartz, H. Hired farm labor in World War II. JFE 24:826-44 Nov 42

-- Farm labor policy, 1942-1943. JFE 25: 691-701 Aug 43

Smith, R. C. Social effects of the war and the defense program on American agriculture. JFE 23:15-27 Feb 41

Thomsen, F. L. The impact of war on marketing farm products [with discussion by C. M. Clark]. JFE 25:120-46 Feb 43

Tinley, J. M. Behavior of prices of farm products during World Wars I and II. JFE 24:157-67 Feb 42

Uhlmann, R. The war and the wheat market. JB 15:131-39 Apr 42

Waite, W. C. Price fixing of agricultural products. JASA 37:13-21 Mar 42

13.76 AGRICULTURE (Cont.)
UNITED STATES (Cont.)

Warren, S. W. and Hardin, L S. Maintain-
A   ing farm output with a scarcity of production factors. JFE 25:95-100 Feb 43

Wilcox, W. W. The wartime use of manpower on farms. JFE 28:723-41 Aug 46

Working, H. Agricultural price policies in
war time. JFE 24:557-70 Aug 42

Case, H. C. M. Problems of achieving
AA   maximum food and fiber production in
the Mississippi Valley [with discussion].
JFE 26:197-213 Feb 44

Saunderson, M. H. Adjustments in western
beef cattle production and marketing during the war and post-war periods.
JFE 26:789-94 Nov 44

Ward, R. E. Adjusting wheat acreage in the
northern Great Plains to wartime demand. LE 20:344-60 Nov 44

Kaldor, D. R. Farm labor situation in Iowa.
ASI   JFE 25:295-97 Feb 43

Pine, W. H. A study of farm labor in two
ASK   years of war [in Kansas]. JFE 26:563-65
Aug 44

Morison, F. L. Ohio farm labor situation.
ASO   JFE 25:298-300 Feb 43

OTHER AMERICAN COUNTRIES

Booth, J. F. The economic problems of
C   Canadian agriculture in the war and
post-war period. CJE 8:446-59 Aug 42

Britnell, G. E. The war and Canadian
wheat. CJE 7:397-413 Aug 41

Coke, J. Farm labour situation in Canada.
JFE 25:287-94 Feb 43

Haythorne, G. V. Agricultural man-power.
CJE 9:366-83 Aug 43

Lattimer, J. E. Canadian agricultural
post-war planning [with discussion by H.
S. Patton]. JFE 25:326-37 Feb 43

Patton, H. S. The war and North American
agriculture. CJE 7:382-96 Aug 41

-- Wartime wheat policy in Canada. JFE 24:
772-91 Nov 42

Shefrin, F. Administration of Canadian
wartime agricultural policies. LE 21:
167-80 May 45

Linville, F. A. An agricultural policy for
D   Hemisphere defense. JFE 23:726-42
Nov 41

EUROPE

Jensen, E. Rehabilitation of agriculture in
E   German-occupied Europe. JFE 26:31-45
Feb 44

Blair, I. D. Wartime problems of English
EB   agriculture. AH 15:12-19 Jan 41

Brandis, B. Control of consumption in
Britain. JFE 24:845-56 Nov 42

Goldmann, J. Meat and wheat. OIS 5:73-76
Apr 3, 43

MacGregor, J. J. Britain's wartime food
policy. JFE 25:384-96 May 43

Marley, J. G. A statistical and economic
survey of certain aspects of the beef
producing, milk producing and cattle
rearing industries in Great Britain between 1939 and 1945 [with discussion].
JRSS 110:187-256 pt.3, 47

Skilbeck, D. War-time changes in British
farming. LBR 5:60-80 Jul 47

Stafford, J. Agriculture in wartime. MS 12:
1-20 Apr 41

Whetham, E. H. War-time changes in agricultural marketing. LBR 7:33-46 Jan 48

Strauss, F. The food problem in the German
EG   war economy. QJE 55:364-412 May 41

OTHER COUNTRIES

Desai, M. B. War and rural indebtedness
FI   in Gujarat. IJE 26:101-11 Jul 45

Gadre, R. N. The effects of war on the
agricultural production and crop planning in the C.P. & Berar. IJE 28:
269-80 Oct 47

Patel, S. K. J. An inquiry into the effect
of war-time prices on agricultural indebtedness. IJE 25:561-65 Apr 45

Yagi, Y. The planning of agricultural pro-
FJ   duction in wartime. Kyo 15,no.1:1-15
Jan 40

-- Japan's current rice policy. Kyo 16,
no.2:1-21 Apr 41

Neumark, S. D. The war and its effect on
HSA   agricultural prices and surpluses in
South Africa. SAJE 8:431-45 Dec 40

13.8 INTERNATIONAL ECONOMIC RELATIONS

Ady, P. The U.K.C.C. in the Middle East.
M   OIS 5:97-103 Apr 24, 43

Allen, R. G. D. Mutual aid between the U.S.
A   and the British Empire, 1941-45 [with
EB   discussion]. JRSS 109:243-77 pt.3, 46

Avison, T. L. The Canadian Foreign Ex-
C   change Control Board. CJE 6:56-60
Feb 40

Balogh, T. Foreign exchange and export
EB   trade policy. EJ 50:1-26 Mar 40

-- The drift towards a rational foreign ex-
EB   change policy; an example of economic
war organisation in Britain. Ec N.S.7:
248-79 Aug 40

-- The new Order in foreign exchange con-
EB   trol. OIS 2,no.5:12-14 Aug 10, 40

-- Fixing exchange rates in war. OIS 6:
EB   73-76 Apr 8, 44

Buckatzsch, E. J. Aircraft from North
A/EB   America. OIS 2,no.5:14-15 Aug 10, 40

-- War material from the U.S.A. OIS 2,
A/EB   no.10:8-11 Nov 23, 40

Cover, J. H. [International financial relations after the war]: discussion.
AER/S 33:390-92 Mar 43

# 13. WAR AND DEFENSE ECONOMICS

## 13.8 INTERNATIONAL ECONOMIC RELATIONS (Cont.)

Elliott, G. A. Price ceilings and international trade theory. CJE 8:186-96 May 42

A Ellsworth, P. T. An economic foreign policy for America. AER/S 30,no.5: 301-19 Feb 41

N Firth, G. G. Article seven: a programme for prosperity? ER 18:1-15 Jun 42

FI Govil, K. L. U.K.C.C. and India. R. IJE 25:376 Jan 45

H Gundry, H. Some features of wartime finance and exchange control in the South-West African karakul trade. SAJE 13: 318-25 Dec 45

A
EB Harris, S. E. External aspects of a war and a defense economy: the British and American cases. REStat 23:8-24 Feb 41

EG Hillmann, H. C. Analysis of Germany's foreign trade and the war. Ec N.S.7: 66-88 Feb 40

EB Holden, G. Rationing and exchange control in British war finance. QJE 54:171-200 Feb 40; A correction. 694-95 Aug 40

DW Hubert, G. A. War and the trade orientation of Haiti. SEJ 13:276-84 Jan 47

N Janes, C. V. History of exchange control in Australia. ER 16:16-33 Jun 40

A Katz, M. A case study in international organization. HBR 25:1-20 no.1, 46

EB
EF Lachmann, K. The Franco-British bloc. (Economic and social developments through the European war.) SR 7:229-42 May 40

C/EB Lattimer, J. E. The British bacon agreement. CJE 6:60-67 Feb 40

N Low, A. R. Exchange control in New Zealand. ER 16:218-35 Dec 40

EB McCurrach, D. F. Britain's U.S. dollar problems 1939-45. EJ 58:356-72 Sep 48

MacFarlane, D. L. The UNRRA experience in relation to developments in food and agriculture. JFE 30:69-77 Feb 48

Moos, S. International commodity control. OIS 3:7-11 Jan 11, 41

EY -- Yugoslavia's foreign trade during the first year of war. OIS 3:124-29 Apr 26, 41

-- Some features of British cotton exports. OIS 4:93-98 Mar 14, 42

A Pasvolsky, L. Some aspects of our foreign economic policy. AER/S 30,no.5:320-37 Feb 41

A
C Pierce, S. D. and Plumptre, A. F. W. Canada's relations with war-time agencies in Washington. CJE 11:402-19 Aug 45

Plumptre, A. F. W. [International financial relations after the war]: discussion. AER/S 33:388-90 Mar 43

FI Poduval, R. N. War-time control of foreign exchanges in India. IJE 24:261-65 Apr 44

A Polk, J. The future of frozen foreign funds. AER 32:255-71 Jun 42

N Randerson, H. R. Import reduction and Australia's war effort. ER 16:34-49 Jun 40

EBC -- Maximum and equity in relation to the Empire's war effort. ER 16:177-90 Dec 40

FI Rao, A. S. War and recent trends in India's foreign trade. Pt.I-II. IJE 25:64-71; 25:141-48 Jul,Oct 44

HSA Reedman, J. N. Exchange policy and import control. SAJE 8:372-87 Dec 40

DS Rippy, J. F. South America's foreign trade and hemisphere defense. JB 14:89-98 Apr 41

Rostow, E. V. Two aspects of lend-lease economics. AER/S 33:377-81 Mar 43

EG Schweitzer, A. The role of foreign trade in the Nazi war economy. JPE 51: 322-37 Aug 43

Staley, E. The economic implications of lend-lease. AER/S 33:362-76 Mar 43

N Sutch, W. B. Changes in New Zealand's import structure. ER 19:203-11 Dec 43

HSA Thirlby, G. F. A note on Dr. J. N. Reedman's remarks upon the balance of external payments. SAJE 9:100-02 Mar 41

A Wigglesworth, E. International balance of payments, 1941. JM 6:290-92 Jan 42

EB Worswick, G. D. N. Export policy since the outbreak of war. OIS 3:17-21 Feb 1, 41

## 13.9 DEMOBILIZATION. RECONVERSION

Bye, R. T. [and others] Economic adjustments after wars: discussion. AER/S 32:31-36 Mar 42

Cairncross, A. K. League of Nations studies of transition problems. R. EJ 54:252-56 Jun-Sep 44

Chand, G. Shadows of the peace. IJE 25: 254-61 Jan 45

Clark, J. M. Economic adjustments after wars: the theoretical issues. AER/S 32: 1-12 Mar 42

Davis, J. S. International commodity agreements in the postwar world. AER/S 32: 391-403 Mar 42

De Haas, J. A. The democratic new order. HBR 19:470-81 no.4, 41

Glenday, R. G. [and others] Economic reconstruction after the war: discussion. JRSS 105:17-35 pt.1, 42

Hicks, J. R. World recovery after war: a theoretical analysis. EJ 57:151-64 Jun 47

Lachmann, K. The shipping problem at the end of the war. SR 10:52-75 Feb 43

Malhotra, P. C. Transition from war to peace economy. IJE 25:261-65 Jan 45

Ryan, J. A. Some economic aspects of European relief and rehabilitation. RSE 3:1-8 Dec 44

## 13.9 DEMOBILIZATION. RECONVERSION (Cont.)

Saulnier, R. J. The transition to peace under military government. RSE 3: 9-17 Dec 44

Shenoy, B. R. The three phases of the transition from war to peace economy. IJE 25:201-07 Jan 45

Staley, E. Taussig on "International allotment of important commodities." AER 33:877-81 Dec 43

Staudinger, H. The United States and world reconstruction. SR 8:283-96 Sep 41

Sumner, J. D. [and others] Economic problems of foreign areas: discussion. AER/S 36:650-60 May 46

Taylor, A. E. Five postwar trade problems. HBR 21:150-63 no.2, 43

Wood, G. L. American thought on reconstruction. R. ER 18:228-31 Dec 42

## UNITED STATES

Abramson, A. G. Industrial adjustment at
A   the end of the war: discussion. AER/S 33:137 Mar 43

Anderson, J. T. The relation of market research to post-war planning. JM 7: 115-24 Oct 42

Bean, L. H. Wholesale prices and industrial stock prices during and immediately after the two world wars. REStat 29: 199-200 Aug 47

Black, J. D. Transitions to the post-war agricultural economy. JFE 24:52-70 Feb 42

-- and Hyson, C. D. Postwar soldier settlement. QJE 59:1-35 Nov 44

Booth, J. F. Post-war economy: discussion. JFE 24:70-74 Feb 42

Burchardt, F. A. Manpower in the reconversion period in U.S.A. and U.K. OIS 7: 303-05 Dec 15, 45

Canning, J. B. The demand for agricultural commodities in the period of transition from war to peace. JFE 26:709-24 Nov 44

Clark, J. M. General aspects of price control and rationing in the transition period. AER/S 35:152-62 May 45

Davenport, D. H. and Hitchcock, D. Swords and plowshares. HBR 20:307-14 no.3, 42

Fainsod, M. Political and administrative aspects of price control in the war-peace transition. AER/S 35:175-85 May 45

George, E. B. and Landry, R. J. Policy suggestions, January 1947-June 1948. REStat 29:24-28 Feb 47

Haber, W. Manpower and employment problems in transition from war to peace. REStat 26:57-68 May 44

-- and Welch, E. The labor force during reconversion. Estimated changes in employment and labor force distribution during transition period. REStat 26: 194-205 Nov 44

Hall, J. K. Excise tax incidence and the postwar economy. AER/S 32:83-101 Mar 42

Henig, H. and Unterberger, S. H. Wage control in wartime and transition. AER 35:319-36 Jun 45

Hirose, A. P. Market research as a practical help in reconversion problems. JM 9:342-49 Apr 45

Hitch, C. Lessons of reconversion. REStat 29:16-20 Feb 47

Hoffman, C. T. A guide to postwar planning for the manufacturer. JM 9:5-10 Jul 44

Hubbard, J. B. Reconversion. REStat 29: 31-38 Feb 47

Johnson, A. The coming peace crisis. SR 11:305-11 Sep 44

Koopmans, T. Durable consumers' goods and the prevention of post-war inflation. AER 33:882-88 Dec 43

Lauterbach, A. From rationing to informed consumption. JB 17:209-19 Oct 44

Livingston, S. M. Economic policy in the transition. REStat 29:20-24 Feb 47

Martin, E. M. The disposition of government financed industrial facilities in the postwar period. AER/S 33:128-36 Mar 43

Marx, D., Jr. The Merchant Ship Sales Act of 1946. JB 21:12-28 Jan 48

Meehan, M. J. Economic dimensions of postwar readjustments. RSE 2:81-86 Jan 44

-- Industry and business statistics. The federal government's statistical program for reconversion and postwar adjustment: a round table [with discussion by R. S. Tucker]. JASA 40:229-31 Jun 45

O'Leary, P. M. Price control and rationing in the war-peace transition: discussion. AER/S 35:186-88 May 45

Phillips, C. F. Price control in immediate postwar economy. JM 8:289-95 Jan 44

Renne, R. R. [and others] Programs for post war: discussion. JFE 24:26-34 Feb 42

Rosenson, A. Proposal for cushioning the transition to a peacetime economy. AER 32:117-22 Mar 42

Schiff, E. Employment during the transition period, in prospect and retrospect. REStat 28:231-36 Nov 46

Schultz, T. W. Transition readjustments in agriculture [with discussion by W. E. Grimes and E. A. Starch]. JFE 26: 77-94 Feb 44

Seltzer, L. H. Is a rise in interest rates desirable or inevitable? AER 35:831-50 Dec 45

## 13.9 DEMOBILIZATION. RECONVERSION
(Cont.)

UNITED STATES (Cont.)

A  Shoup, E. C.  Post-war marketing responsibilities need changed marketing executives.  JM 7:125-28 Oct 42

Slichter, S. H.  Adjustment of wages during conversion.  HBR 24:57-74 no.1, 45

Staats, E. B.  Price control and rationing in the war-peace transition: discussion. AER/S 35:188-92 May 45

Steindl, J.  The transition in the United States.  OIS 7:213-17 Sep 22, 45

Taeuber, C.  Farm wage statistics for a full employment program.  (The federal government's statistical program for reconversion and postwar adjustment: a round table.)  JASA 40:234-35 Jun 45

Terborgh, G.  Postwar surpluses and shortages of plant and equipment. AER/S 32:360-68 Mar 42

Tolles, N. A.  Labor statistics for a full employment program.  (The federal government's statistical program for reconversion and postwar adjustment: a round table.)  JASA 40:235-36 Jun 45

Tolley, H. R. [and others]  Agriculture in the transition from war to peace. AER/S 35:390-404 May 45

Truesdell, L. E.  Population.  (The federal government's statistical program for reconversion and postwar adjustment: a round table.)  JASA 40:232-33 Jun 45

Wallace, D. H.  Price control and rationing in the war-peace transition: introduction. AER/S 35:150-51 May 45

Wilcox, C.  Price control policy in the post-war transition.  AER/S 35:163-74 May 45

Wynne, W. H.  Industrial adjustment at the end of the war: discussion.  AER/S 33: 162 Mar 43

AA  Ormsby, H. F.  Postwar industrial planning on the Pacific Coast.  JM 8:156-58 Oct 43

### OTHER AMERICAN COUNTRIES

C  Brady, A.  Reconstruction in Canada: a note on policies and plans.  CJE 8:460-68 Aug 42

### EUROPE

E  Frankel, H.  Reconstruction in Europe.  R. OIS 9:44-50 Feb 47

Klopstock, F. H.  Monetary reform in liberated Europe.  AER 36:578-95 Sep 46

Loveday, A.  The progress of European recovery.  R.  EJ 58:601-05 Dec 48

Robinson, N.  Problems of European reconstruction.  QJE 60:1-55 Nov 45

EB  Balogh, T. and Burchardt, F. A.  Taxation in the transition period.  OIS 7:165-73 Jul 21, 45

Burchardt, F. A.  Manpower in the reconversion period in U.S.A. and U.K.  OIS 7: 303-05 Dec 15, 45

Devons, E.  The progress of reconversion. MS 15:1-25 Jan 47

Finer, H.  Post-war reconstruction in Great Britain.  CJE 8:493-513 Nov 42

Hitch, C. J.  The controls in post-war reconstruction.  OEP 6:43-56 Apr 42

Kalecki, M.  Employment in the United Kingdom during and after the transition period.  OIS 6:265-87 Dec 4, 44

-- Excess profits tax and post-war re-equipment.  OIS 6:58-61 Mar 18, 44

Koopmans, T.  Durable consumers' goods and the prevention of post-war inflation. AER 33:882-88 Dec 43

Kovacs, L.  An instalment plan for post-war deliveries.  EJ 51:492-98 Dec 41

Murphy, M. E.  Trends and conflicts in the British economy.  AER/S 36:628-41 May 46

Opie, R.  A British view of postwar trade. AER/S 33:322-31 Mar 43

Pigou, A. C.  1946 and 1919.  LBR 1:9-23 Jul 46

Steindl, J.  The budget and reconstruction. OIS 8:121-29 May 46

Worswick, G. D. N.  The T.U.C. and reconstruction.  R.  OIS 6:287-92 Dec 4, 44

-- Price stabilisation.  OIS 7:173-80 Jul 21, 45

ECB  Bareau, P.  Reconstruction in the low countries.  LBR 3:33-48 Jan 47

EF  Balogh, T.  French reconstruction and the Franco-U.S. loan agreement.  Pt.I-II. OIS 8:261-77; 294-300 Aug,Sep 46

Bareau, P.  The economic regeneration of France.  LBR 4:11-25 Apr 47

Walch, J. W.  A survey of the problems of reconstruction facing the Fourth Republic.  JB 20:67-83 Apr 47

EG  Burchardt, F. A. and Martin K.  Western Germany and reconstruction.  OIS 9: 405-16 Dec 47

Einzig, P.  A plan for Germany's economic disarmament.  EJ 52:176-85 Jun-Sep 42

Hoover, C. B.  The future of the German economy.  AER/S 36:642-49 May 46

Mendershausen, H.  Prices, money and the distribution of goods in postwar Germany. AER 39:646-72 Jun 49

Stamp, M.  Germany without incentive. LBR 5:14-28 Jul 47

EN  Bareau, P.  Reconstruction in the low countries.  LBR 3:33-48 Jan 47

Tinbergen, J.  The economic situation in the Netherlands in autumn, 1945.  OIS 7: 266-68 Nov 3, 45

Verdoorn, P. J.  Problems of recovery in the Netherlands.  OIS 9:15-18 Jan 47

ER  Haensel, P.  Soviet finances.  PF 1:38-51 no.1, 46

Schwartz, H.  Soviet economic reconversion, 1945-46.  AER/S 37:611-23 May 47

ES  Lundberg, E.  Readjustment problems in Sweden.  OIS 8:81-87 Mar 46

13.9 DEMOBILIZATION. RECONVERSION
(Cont.)
EUROPE (Cont.)
Petersen, K. Economic conditions in Nor-
ESN way. OIS 8:112-16 Apr 46
Angehrn, O. The Swiss economy in the
ESw transition period. OIS 8:51-54 Feb 46
Boehi, A. The reconstruction boom in
Switzerland. OIS 9:18-20 Jan 47

ASIA
Remer, C. F. Economic reconstruction in
FA the Far East. AER/S 36:603-12 May 46
Bhattacharya, K. N. Will India face a
FI slump? An aspect in transition economy.
IJE 25:242-47 Jan 45
Hasan, A. [and others] Discussion on
transition from war to peace economy.
IJE 25:629-34 Apr 45
Joshi, T. M. Some economic and financial
problems of the transition from war to
peace. IJE 25:224-35 Jan 45
Rao, K. V. War to peace economy in India.
IJE 25:247-53 Jan 45
Sovani, N. V. Transition from war to peace
economy in India. IJE 25:207-23 Jan 45
Sriram, P. Some aspects of the transition
from war to peace economy. IJE 25:
235-42 Jan 45

Kurihara, K. K. Post-war inflation and
FJ fiscal-monetary policy in Japan.
AER 36:843-54 Dec 46

AFRICA
Hutt, W. H. and Leslie, R. The price fac-
HSA tor and reconstruction. SAJE 9:441-44
Dec 41
Smith, R. H. The organisation of employ-
ment in the transition from war to
peace. SAJE 13:91-116 Jun 45

AUSTRALIA. NEW ZEALAND
Belshaw, H. New Zealand in the post-war
N world: reconstruction problems of a
vulnerable economy. CJE 11:388-401
Aug 45
Burton, H. The transition to a peace econ-
omy: the Australian economy, May-
October, 1945. ER 21:149-64 Dec 45
Firth, G. G. Article seven: a programme
for prosperity? ER 18:1-15 Jun 42
Wood, G. L. The economic implications of
peace for Australia. ER 16:82-95
Jun 40

# 14. BUSINESS ORGANIZATION.
## MANAGERIAL ECONOMICS

14.0 GENERAL
14.1 HISTORY
Aitken, H. G. J. The analysis of decisions.
EEH 1,no.2:17-23 Feb 49
-- Parameters: a reply. EEH 1,no.3:23-24
Mar 49
-- The problem of entrepreneurial free-
dom. EEH 1,no.4:1-8 Apr 49
-- The religious sanction. EEH 1,no.4:
29-30 Apr 49
-- A note on partial analyses. EEH 1,no.6:
30 Jun 49
Anonymous. Send me a business historian.
BHR 17:44-46 Apr 43
-- The corporation and the historian.
BHR 18:155-62 Dec 44
-- A select bibliography on entrepreneur-
ship. EEH 1,no.2:27-29 Feb 49
Bishop, P. W. Some problems of research
methods. EEH 2:46-49 Nov 49
Budd, R. [The corporation and the histor-
A ian.] Comment. JEH/S 4:38-42 Dec 44
Cochran, T. C. New York City business
ASN records: a plan for their preservation.
BHR 18:59-62 Jun 44
-- The New York Committee on Business
ASN Records. JEH 5:60-64 May 45

-- The economics in a business history.
JEH/S 5:54-65 Dec 45
-- The empirical approach. EEH 1,no.3:
24-25 Mar 49
Cole, A. H. Business manuscripts: a
pressing problem: JEH 5:43-59 May 45
-- An approach to the study of entrepreneur-
ship: a tribute to Edwin F. Gay.
JEH/S 6:1-15 '46
-- Dales' "Approaches." EEH 1,no.2:24
Feb 49
Dales, J. H. Approaches to entrepreneurial
history. EEH 1,no.1:10-14 Jan 49
Deutsch, K. W. A note on the history of
entrepreneurship, innovation and deci-
sion-making. EEH 1,no.5:8-16 May 49
Gay, L. S. A new approach to local business history. BHR 21:3-9 Feb 47
Gras, N. S. B. Are you writing a business
history? BHR 18:73-110 Oct 44
-- What type of business history are you
writing? BHR 20:146-58 Nov 46
Hidy, R. W. Problems in collaborative
writing of business history. BHR 23:
67-77 Jun 49
Hower, R. M. Problems and opportunities
in the field of business history. BHR 15:
17-26 Apr 41

## 14. BUSINESS ORGANIZATION, ETC.

### 14.1 HISTORY (Cont.)

Landes, D. S. Dales' "Approaches." EEH 1, no.4:28-29 Apr 49

Larson, H. M. Danger in business history. HBR 22:316-27 no.3, 44

A   -- The Business History Foundation, Inc. BHR 21:51-54 Jun 47

-- Business history: retrospect and prospect. BHR 21:173-99 Dec 47

A   -- Availability of records for research in the history of large business concerns. BHR 22:12-21 Feb 48

A   McKenzie, C. H. An experiment in the retention and preservation of corporate records. BHR 17,no.1,suppl.:3-23 Feb 43

Miller, W. The problems [of research methods] resolved. EEH 2:49-51 Nov 49

A   Pargellis, S. The corporation and the historian. JEH/S 4:29-37 Dec 44

Passer, H. C. Economic factors in entrepreneurial history. EEH 1,no.5:29-30 May 49

Schumpeter, J. A. The creative response in economic history. JEH 7:149-59 Nov 47

Stykolt, S. A note on the parametric approach. EEH 1,no.2:25-26 Feb 49

Taymans, A. C. Facts and theory in entrepreneurial history. EEH 1,no.1:15-20 Jan 49

A   Warne, C. E. [The corporation and the historian.] Comment. JEH/S 4:42-46 Dec 44

A   Wasson, R. G. Another view of the historian's treatment of business. BHR 18: 62-68 Jun 44

Wohl, R. R. An historical context for entrepreneurship. EEH 1,no.2:8-16 Feb 49

-- [Aitken's Analysis of business decisions.] EEH 1,no.3:26-29 Mar 49

-- An historical context for entrepreneurship: III. EEH 1,no.6:1-10 Jun 49

-- A further note on Aitken's parametric approach. EEH 2:51-53 Nov 49

### 14.2 THE FIRM. THE BUSINESSMAN

Hamilton, W. H. The economic man affects a national role. AER/S 36:735-44 May 46

ER   Schwarz, S. M. The industrial enterprise in Russia. HBR 23:265-76 no.3, 45

Strauss, J. H. The entrepreneur: the firm. JPE 52:112-27 Jun 44

A   Sweezy, P. M. The illusion of the "managerial revolution." S&S 6:1-23 no.1, 42

### 14.21 HISTORY
#### UNITED STATES

A   Anonymous. The petty capitalist in American business history. BHR 15:72-73 Nov 41

-- Selections from de Tocqueville's Democracy in America: a Frenchman assays the spirit behind American business ex-

pansion in the 1830's. BHR 19:202-11 Dec 45

Cochran, T. C. The legend of the robber barons. EEH 1,no.5:1-7 May 49

Davis, J. S., chairman. The history of American corporations: abstract of specialized conference discussion. AER/S 32:211-12 Mar 42

Destler, C. M. Entrepreneurial leadership among the "robber barons": a trial balance. JEH/S 6:28-49 '46

East, R. A. The business entrepreneur in a changing colonial economy, 1763-1795. JEH/S 6:16-27 '46

Evans, G. H., Jr. Business incorporations: their nature and significance. JEH/S 1: 67-85 Dec 41

Gras, N. S. B. Shifts in public relations. BHR 19:97-148 Oct 45

Handlin, O. and Handlin, M. F. Origins of the American business corporation. JEH 5:1-23 May 45

Hidy, R. W. Importance of the history of the large business unit. BHR 22:4-11 Feb 48

Larson, H. M. "Plutarch's lives" of trade: the first series of American business biographies. BHR 20:28-32 Feb 46

Miller, W. American historians and the business elite. JEH 9:184-208 Nov 49

Mills, C. W. The American business elite: a collective portrait. JEH/S 5:20-44 Dec 45

Wexler, H. J. How to succeed in business, 1840-1860. EEH 1,no.1:26-29 Jan 49

-- Business opinion and economic theory, 1840-1860. EEH 1,no.3:10-18 Mar 49

AA   Kessler, W. C. Incorporation in New England: a statistical study, 1800-1875. JEH 8:43-62 May 48

ASM   Taussig, F. W. My father's business career [in St. Louis, Missouri]. HBR 19: 177-84 no.2, 41

ASN   Friedman, L. M. The first chamber of commerce in the United States [the Chamber of Commerce of the State of New York]. BHR 21:137-43 Nov 47

Kessler, W. C. A statistical study of the New York General Incorporation Act of 1811. JPE 48:877-82 Dec 40

ASP   Miller, W. A note on the history of business corporations in Pennsylvania, 1800-1860. QJE 55:150-60 Nov 40

#### EUROPE

EB   Anonymous. A proposal for schools of business administration in seventeenth-century England. BHR 15:43-46 Jun 41

Fry, R. The British business man: 1900-1949. EEH 2:35-43 Nov 49

Rix, M. S. Company law: 1844 and today. EJ 55:242-60 Jun-Sep 45

14.2 THE FIRM. THE BUSINESSMAN (Cont.)
14.21 HISTORY (Cont.)
　　EUROPE (Cont.)

　　Gras, N. S. B. Sir Andrew Freeport, a
EBE　merchant of London [in Addison's Spec-
　　tator]. BHR 19:159-62 Nov 45
　　Landes, D. S. A note on cultural factors in
EF　entrepreneurship. EEH 1,no.1:8-9 Jan 49
　　-- French entrepreneurship and industrial
　　growth in the nineteenth century. JEH 9:
　　45-61 May 49
　　De Roover, F. E. The business records of
EI　an early Genoese notary, 1190-1192.
　　BHR 14:41-46 Jun 40
　　-- Partnership accounts in twelfth century
　　Genoa. BHR 15:87-92 Dec 41
　　Lane, F. C. Family partnerships and joint
　　ventures in the Venetian Republic.
　　JEH 4:178-96 Nov 44
　　Lopez, R. S. Italian leadership in the
　　medieval business world. R. JEH 8:
　　63-68 May 48
　　Reynolds, R. L. In search of a business
　　class in thirteenth-century Genoa.
　　JEH/S 5:1-19 Dec 45
　　Shimkin, D. B. The entrepreneur in Tsarist
ER　and Soviet Russia. EEH 2:24-34 Nov 49


14.22 THE FIRM
14.220 GENERAL
　　Coppola d'Anna, F. Italian joint stock com-
EI　panies from 1938 to 1948. BNL 2:159-71
　　Jul-Sep 49
　　Murphy, M. E. Revision of British com-
EB　pany law. AER 36:659-60 Sep 46
　　Richards, C. S. The Report of the Company
HSA　Law Amendment Enquiry Commission.
　　R. SAJE 17:229-51 Sep 49
　　Rix, M. S. Company law: 1844 and today.
EB　EJ 55:242-60 Jun-Sep 45

14.221 STOCKHOLDER RELATIONS
　　Bradley, J. F. Voting rights of preferred
A　stockholders in industrials. JF 3,no.3:
　　78-88 Oct 48
　　Florence, P. S. The statistical analysis of
EB　joint stock company control [with discus-
　　sion]. JRSS 110:2-26 pt.1, 47
　　Rienzi, E. Distribution of shareholders
EI　among Italian joint stock companies.
　　BNL 1:390-95 Jul 48


14.222 PUBLIC AND COMMUNITY RELATIONS
　　Aldrich, W. W. The International Chamber
　　of Commerce and the Economic and
　　Social Council. EI 1:233-35 Jan 48
　　Ballaine, F. K. Businessmen and the com-
A　munity forum. HBR 25:372-84 no.3, 47
　　Cleveland, A. S. NAM: spokesman for in-
A　dustry? HBR 26:353-71 May 48
　　Gras, N. S. B. Shifts in public relations.
A　BHR 19:97-148 Oct 45
　　-- Leadership, past and present. HBR 27:
A　419-37 Jul 49

　　Roper, E. The public looks at business.
A　HBR 27:165-74 Mar 49
　　Welcker, J. W. The community relations
A　problem of industrial companies.
　　HBR 27:771-80 Nov 49
　　Wood, R. The corporation goes into
A　politics. HBR 21:60-70 no.1, 42


14.223 SMALL BUSINESS
　　Abbott, C. C. Small business: a community
A　problem. HBR 24:183-96 no.2, 46
　　Adams, Q. Marketing aspects of postwar
A　small business. JM 9:350-53 Apr 45
　　Buehler, A. G. The taxation of small busi-
A　ness. AER/S 36:250-64 May 46
　　-- --- [idem] JF 1:61-75 Aug 46
　　Clark, T. D. Records of little businesses as
A　sources of social and economic history.
　　BHR 19:151-58 Nov 45
　　Comish, N. H. Retail store operating re-
ASO　sults as guides for small merchants [in
　　Oregon]. JM 11:62-64 Jul 46
　　-- The model stock plan in small stores.
A　JM 11:402-07 Apr 47
　　Forbes, G. The passing of the small oil
AA　man [in the Southwest]. SEJ 7:204-15
　　Oct 40
　　Ketchum, M. D. The financial problem of
A　small business. Pt.I-II. JB 17:67-90;
　　162-85 Apr,Jul 44
　　Lawler, P. F. A note on control in small
A　businesses. HBR 25:521-26 no.4, 47
　　Mace, M. L. Management assistance for
A　small business. HBR 25:587-94 no.4a, 47
　　Mayer, K. Small business as a social in-
A　stitution. SR 14:332-49 Sep 47
　　Reubens, E. P. Small-scale industry in
FJ　Japan. QJE 61:577-604 Aug 47
　　Robbins, I. D. Management services for
A　small business through trade associa-
　　tions. HBR 26:627-40 Sep 48
　　Rosa, R. V. Some small business problems
A　indicated by the industrial loan experi-
　　ence of the Federal Reserve Bank of New
　　York. JF 2,no.1:91-100 Apr 47
　　-- Small business and depression. HBR 26:
A　58-62 Jan 48
　　Rosenthal, R. L. $R_X$ for smaller business.
A　HBR 24:22-31 no.1, 45
　　Stoddard, W. L. Small business wants
A　capital. HBR 18:265-74 no.3, 40
　　Turnbull, J. G. The small business enter-
A　prise and the management prerogative
　　issue. ILRR 2:33-49 Oct 48
　　Welsh, C. A. The Murray Report on small
A　business. ILRR 1:94-103 Oct 47
　　Wendt, P. F. The availability of capital to
ASC　small business in California in 1945-
　　1946. JF 2,no.2:43-54 Oct 47
　　-- Term loans to small business in Califor-
ASC　nia, 1945-46. JF 3,no.2:45-58 Jun 48
　　Woosley, J. B. The capital problem of
A　small and medium-sized businesses.
　　SEJ 7:461-74 Apr 41

## 14. BUSINESS ORGANIZATION, ETC.

### 14.223 SMALL BUSINESS (Cont.)

Zinner, S. M. The contribution of commer-
A   cial receivable companies and factors to
financing small- and medium-sized
business. JF 2,no.1:76-90 Apr 47

### 14.23 THE BUSINESSMAN
### 14.230 GENERAL

Aitken, H. G. J. Taussig and Joslyn on
A   business leaders. R. EEH 1,no.3:29-32
Mar 49

Bursk, E. C. and Clark, D. T. Reading
A   habits of business executives. HBR 27:
330-45 May 49

Cole, A. H. Business and the stream of
A   social thought. HBR 23:203-10 no.2, 45
-- The evolving perspective of businessmen.
A   HBR 27:123-28 Jan 49

Culliton, J. W. Business and religion.
HBR 27:265-71 May 49

Dempsey, B. W. The roots of business re-
A   sponsibility. HBR 27:393-404 Jul 49

Duddy, E. A. The moral implications of
business as a profession. JB 18:63-72
Apr 45

Flanders, R. E. The moral dilemma of an
industrialist. HBR 23:433-41 no.4, 45

Fry, R. The British business man: 1900-
EB   1949. EEH 2:35-43 Nov 49

Gras, N. S. B. The social implications of
business administration. BHR 17:2-5
Feb 43
-- Religion and business. BHR 18:27-32
Apr 44

Green, C. M. What has the business ad-
A   ministrator contributed to society?
BHR 17:22-26 Feb 43

Kittridge, G. W. Services for sale. JM 5:
125-27 Oct 40

Larson, H. M. Some general considerations
A   [on business administration]. BHR 17:
27-31 Feb 43
-- Business men as collectors. BHR 18:
A   162-70 Dec 44

Meadows, P. Professional behavior and
industrial society. JB 19:145-50 Jul 46

Miller, J. D., Jr. The academic mind in
business. JB 20:146-55 Jul 47

Navin, T. R., Jr. Evaluating the methods
A   of the business administrator. BHR 17:
11-14 Feb 43

Porter, K. W. The business man in Ameri-
A   can folklore. BHR 18:113-30 Nov 44

Stykolt, S. A note on economic activity in
A   the administrative state. EEH 1,no.1:
30-31 Jan 49

Tomajan, J. S. But who is to lead the
A   leader? HBR 23:277-82 no.3, 45

### 14.231 EDUCATION FOR BUSINESS

Calkins, F. J. University courses in fi-
A   nance. JF 4:244-65 Sep 49

Calkins, R. D. Business education after the
A   war. JB 18:1-8 Jan 45

-- A challenge to business education.
A   HBR 23:174-86 no.2, 45
-- Objectives of business education.
A   HBR 25:46-57 no.1, 46

Chenault, L. R. A note on business concepts and economic theory. AER 31:
98-101 Mar 41

Clark, R. W. Investment Bankers Associa-
A   tion training courses. JF 1:91-92 Aug 46

Coman, E. T., Jr. The status of business
ASC   history at the Stanford Graduate School
of Business. BHR 20:17-21 Feb 46

Holton, H. Survey of the teaching of busi-
A   ness history. BHR 23:96-103 Jun 49

Kennedy, C. J. Introducing college fresh-
A   men to business history. BHR 22:57-63
Apr 48

Rose, J. R. Business education in a uni-
A   versity. JB 20:183-90 Oct 47

Seelye, A. L. The importance of economic
theory in marketing courses. JM 11:
223-27 Jan 47

Smith, D. T. Education for administration.
HBR 23:360-71 no.3, 45

Upton, R. M. Conference on the teaching
A   of business finance. JF 4:243 Sep 49

### 14.3 INTERNAL ORGANIZATION AND OPERA-
TION OF THE FIRM
### 14.31 HISTORY

Anonymous. Freeman Hunt on the science
A   of business. BHR 18:9-10 Feb 44

Jucius, M. J. Historical development of
uniform accounting. JB 16:219-29
Oct 43

Kristensson, R. The consequences of er-
ES   rors in accounting due to inflation
1914-18 [in Sweden]. EH 4:371-83
Feb 40

Lane, F. C. Venture accounting in medie-
EI   val business management. BHR 19:
164-73 Nov 45

Murphy, M. E. Arthur Lowes Dickinson:
A   pioneer in American professional ac-
countancy. BHR 21:27-38 Apr 47

Puffer, E. H. A great business lawyer
A   [Daniel Webster]. BHR 16:61-62 Jun 42

Yamey, B. S. Scientific bookkeeping and
the rise of capitalism. EHR II.1:99-113
no.2-3, 49

### 14.32 BOARD OF DIRECTORS

Bates, G. E. The board of directors.
A   HBR 19:72-87 no.1, 40
-- and Zuckert, E. M. Directors' indem-
A   nity: corporate policy or public policy?
HBR 20:244-64 no.2, 42

Weinberg, S. J. A corporation director
A   looks at his job. HBR 27:585-93 Sep 49

### 14.33 MANAGEMENT FUNCTION
### 14.330 GENERAL

Barnard, C. I. Comments on the job of the
A   executive. HBR 18:295-308 no.3, 40

## 14.33 MANAGEMENT FUNCTION (Cont.)
### 14330 GENERAL (Cont.)

A   Brown, T. H. The business consultant. HBR 21:183-89 no.2, 43

A   Chapple, E. D. and Donald, G., Jr. A method for evaluating supervisory personnel. HBR 24:197-214 no.2, 46

A   Copeland, M. T. The job of an executive. HBR 18:148-60 no.2, 40

A   Donham, R. Management consultants deal with people. HBR 19:33-41 no.1, 40

A   Given, W. B., Jr. Freedom within management. HBR 24:427-37 no.4, 46

A   Hower, R. M., chairman. The effect of managerial policy upon the structure of American business. Abstract of specialized conference discussion. AER/S 32:226-27 Mar 42

A   -- The effect of managerial policy upon the structure of American business. [Abridgement] BHR 16:42-52 Apr 42

Jensen, A. Stochastic processes applied to a simple problem of administrative economy. NTTO 12:151-55 no.37, 48

A   Learned, E. P. Problems of a new executive. HBR 27:362-72 May 49

A   Littler, R. M. C. Managers must manage. HBR 24:366-76 no.3, 46

A   Mace, M. L. Management assistance for small business. HBR 25:587-94 no.4a, 47

A   Martin, B. F. What business learns from war. HBR 21:358-68 no.3, 43

Murphy, C. D. Simplification as a business policy and procedure. JB 16:230-34 Oct 43

A   Olson, J. C. Is your company prepared for rough weather? HBR 25:595-608 no.4a, 47

A   Perkins, J. S. Management research. HBR 18:488-95 no.4, 40

ER   Schwarz, S. M. Heads of Russian factories: a sociological study. SR 9:315-33 Sep 42

A   Selekman, B. M. Wanted: mature managers. HBR 24:288-44 no.2, 46

Swope, G. Some aspects of corporate management. HBR 23:314-22 no.3, 45

Tannenbaum, R. The manager concept: a rational synthesis. JB 22:225-41 Oct 49

## 14.331 EXECUTIVE COMPENSATION

A   Baker, J. C. Pensions for executives. HBR 18:309-21 no.3, 40

A   -- Stock options for executives. HBR 19:106-22 no.1, 40

A   -- Executive compensation by small textile companies. HBR 20:81-91 no.1, 41

A   -- A "just gauge" for executive compensation. HBR 22:75-87 no.1, 43

A   -- Payments to senior corporation executives. QJE 59:170-84 Feb 45

A   Gordon, R. A. Ownership and compensation as incentives to corporation executives. QJE 54:455-73 May 40

## 14.332 EXECUTIVE DEVELOPMENT

Barnard, C. I. Education for executives. JB 18:175-82 Oct 45

Beckley, D. K. Appraising professional training for retailing. JM 14:38-45 Jul 49

A   Haldane, B. A pattern for executive placement. HBR 25:652-63 no.4a, 47

## 14.333 ADMINISTRATIVE ORGANIZATION AND PROCEDURES

A   Bliss, C. A. and McNeill, R. B. Management control in uniform. HBR 22:227-38 no.2, 44

A   Brooks, J. B. The organization of the selling function in a department store. JM 13:189-94 Oct 48

A   Henderson, R. D. Company response to coupon inquiries. JM 13:368-71 Jan 49

Johnson, R. W. Executive myopia. JB 19:63-66 Apr 46

Kristensson, R. Division of labour as an optimum problem in organization and management. NTTO 12:167-74 no.37, 48

A   Lewis, H. T. Evaluating departmental efficiency. HBR 26:313-28 May 48

Marshall, L. C. Groups and their co-ordination: backgrounds of administration. JB 14:205-21 Jul 41

O'Donnell, C. Control of business forms. JB 19:176-82 Jul 46

Phelps, O. W. A theory of business communication. JB 15:343-60 Oct 42

A   Roethlisberger, F. J. The foreman: master and victim of double talk. HBR 23:283-98 no.3, 45

## 14.334 DECISION-MAKING. FORECASTING

McNeal, D. The development and use of economic information and forecasts by industry. JFE 31,pt.2:646-50 Feb 49

ASC   Oxenfeldt, G. E. and Oxenfeldt, A. R. Businessmen's information about profitability of local enterprises [in Boulder, Colorado]. JPE 55:257-61 Jun 47

## 14.336 CAPITAL EXPENDITURE. INVESTMENT POLICY

EB   Andrews, P. W. S. A further inquiry into the effects of rates of interest. OEP 3:33-73 Feb 40

Hart, A. G. Assets, liquidity, and investment. AER/S 39:171-81 May 49

## 14.337 PRODUCTION MANAGEMENT. QUALITY CONTROL

Adelman, M. A. "Equilibrium in multiprocess industries": further comments. QJE 60:464-68 May 46

Cowden, D. J. and Connor, W. S. The use of statistical methods for economic control of quality in industry. SEJ 12:115-29 Oct 45

## 14. BUSINESS ORGANIZATION, ETC.

**14.337 PRODUCTION MANAGEMENT.**
**QUALITY CONTROL (Cont.)**

Eiteman, W. J. The equilibrium of the firm in multi-process industries. QJE 59:280-86 Feb 45   A

Henriksen, E. K. Simultaneous operation of several machines by one person. Application of a method of probability. NTTO 12:133-40 no.37, 48

Lalwani, K. Cost and efficiency in Indian
FI   business. Pt.I-II. IJE 26:579-96; 27:1-20 Apr,Jul 46

Marcuse, S. An application of the control chart method to the testing and marketing of foods. JASA 40:214-22 Jun 45

O'Donnell, C. Problems in the organization of multiplant production control. JB 18:140-44 Jul 45

Rice, W. B. Quality control applied to business administration. JASA 38: 228-32 Jun 43

Schrock, E. M. Matters of misconception concerning the quality control chart. JASA 39:325-34 Sep 44

Simon, L. E. On the initiation of statistical methods for quality control in industry. JASA 36:53-60 Mar 41

Trickett, J. M. Planning and controlling sales and production. JM 10:331-35 Apr 46

Vaswani, M. H. Scientific management and rationalisation. IJE 27:401-07 Apr 47

**14.338 INVENTORY POLICIES**

Cahen, A. Measuring the merchandise flow
A   of men's clothing. JM 14:67-71 Jul 49

Deming, W. E. and Simmons, W. On the design of a sample for dealers' inventories. JASA 41:16-33 Mar 46

Engquist, E. J., Jr. and Miller, W. S. Measuring retailers' inventories. JM 9: 49-52 Jul 44

Gorgas, N. The storage and issuance of hospital supplies. Pt.I-II. JB 13: 172-204; 275-315 Apr,Jul 40

**14.34 TOOLS OF MANAGEMENT**
**14.340 GENERAL**

Anderson, E. H. The meaning of scientific
A   management. HBR 27:678-92 Nov 49

Drager, W. The interpretation of ratios used in cost analyses. JM 8:424-25 Apr 44

Hart, J. K. The management of figures.
A   HBR 27:24-33 Jan 49

Schiller, I. P. A program for the manage-
A   ment of business records. BHR 21:44-48 Apr 47

**14.341 ACCOUNTING**

Adams, W. Accounting practices and the business cycle. JB 22:119-33 Apr 49

Bailey, G. D. Concepts of income. HBR 26: 680-92 Nov 48

Balet, J. W. Application of the LIFO in-
A   ventory method of income tax deprecia- tion for public utilities. NTJ 1:322-29 Dec 48

Bliss, C. A. The reality of inventory profits. HBR 26:527-42 Sep 48

Bornemann, A. Accounting profits: an institution. JPE 51:166-68 Apr 43

Bray, F. S. An accountant's comments on the subjective theory of value and ac- counting cost. Ec N.S.13:295-99 Nov 46

Brown, E. C. Tax allowances for deprecia-
A   tion based on changes in the price level. NTJ 1:311-21 Dec 48

Butters, J. K. Management considerations
A   on Lifo. HBR 27:308-29 May 49

Garner, S. P. Application of burden in wartime industries. SEJ 11:360-68 Apr 45

Hartwig, J. D. Should the accountant de- preciate investment buildings held by trustees under testamentary trusts? JB 18:41-55 Jan 45

Jeal, E. F. Accounting and the price level. SAJE 17:105-10 Mar 49

Jucius, M. J. Historical development of
A   uniform accounting. JB 16:219-29 Oct 43

-- Uniform accounting and pricing policies.
A   JB 17:37-50 Jan 44

Kimball, B. F. The failure of the unit- summation procedure as a group method of estimating depreciation. Em 13:225-44 Jul 45

Kircher, P. Common dollar accounting for investments. JB 22:242-48 Oct 49

Lacey, K. Commodity stocks and the trade cycle. Ec N.S.11:12-18 Feb 44

-- --- A reply. Ec N.S.11:140-42 Aug 44

-- Some implications of the first in-first out method of stock valuation. Ec N.S.12: 26-30 Feb 45

-- Commodity stock values and E.P.T. EJ 55:2-16 Apr 45

Lawson, E. W. The choice of capitalization
A   ratios in practice. SEJ 9:335-49 Apr 43

Lowenstern, E. S. A uniform act for the
A   certified public accountant. JB 20:14-20 Jan 47

Massel, M. S. Reappraisal of depreciation
A   and obsolescence. HBR 24:85-95 no.1, 45

Murphy, M. E. British company law reform:
EB   implications for accounting practice. JB 19:151-60 Jul 46

Norris, H. Commodity stocks and the trade cycle: 1. A note. Ec N.S.11:138-40 Aug 44

-- Notes on the relationship between econ- omists and accountants. EJ 54:375-83 Dec 44

-- Profit: accounting theory and economics. Ec N.S.12:125-33 Aug 45

14.341 ACCOUNTING (Cont.)

Saliers, E. A. Depreciation inventoried [followed by R. L. Dixon, Jr.'s rejoinder]. JB 13:87-89 Jan 40

EB Sanders, T. H. British accounting practices and the profession. HBR 18:161-76 no.2, 40

A -- Government by "accounting principles." R. HBR 22:265-76 no.3, 44

A -- Depreciation and 1949 price levels. HBR 27:293-307 May 49

A -- Two concepts of accounting. HBR 27:505-20 Jul 49

A Schmidt, L. A. Navy accounting: a lesson in adaptation. HBR 25:243-54 no.2, 47

A Seghers, P. D. Tax accounting compared with recognized accounting principles. NTJ 1:341-52 Dec 48

Sevin, C. H. Some aspects of distribution cost analysis. JM 12:92-98 Jul 47

Silcock, T. H. Accountants, economists and the valuation of fixed assets. EJ 59:343-59 Sep 49

Thirlby, G. F. The subjective theory of value and accounting "cost." Ec N.S.13:32-49 Feb 46

Vatter, W. J. Accounting measurements of incremental cost. JB 18:145-56 Jul 45

Walker, R. G. Explorations in accounting. HBR 18:384-96 no.3, 40

14.342 STATISTICAL TOOLS

A Alger, P. L. The importance of the statistical viewpoint in high production manufacturing. JASA 36:50-52 Mar 41

A Bliss, C. A. Statistics takes a second breath. HBR 18:510-19 no.4, 40

Brown, T. H. Scientific sampling in business. HBR 20:358-68 no.3, 42

A Catlin, J. B. Opportunities for statisticians in industry. JASA 40:75-79 Mar 45

Donnahoe, A. S. Presenting seasonal variation to the business executive. JASA 41:468-71 Dec 46

Fagerholt, G. and Hald, A. A few remarks on the application of statistical methods in industry. NTTO 12:83-88 no.37, 48

A Perkins, J. S. A critical appraisal of business statistics. JASA 37:220-24 Jun 42

A Roos, C. F. Business planning and statistical analysis. Em 17,suppl.:69-70 Jul 49

Weeks, H. T. [and others] Statistics and the statistician in industry. JRSS 110:95-107 pt.2, 47

14.343 BREAK-EVEN ANALYSIS

Dean, J. Cost structures of enterprises and break-even charts. AER/S 38:153-64 May 48

14.4 BUSINESS FINANCE
14.40 GENERAL

A Abbott, C. C. Working capital during the transition. HBR 22:291-98 no.3, 44

A Bailey, G. D. Problems in reporting corporation income. HBR 26:513-26 Sep 48

A Butters, J. K. Research project: effect of federal taxes on business. NTJ 1:91-92 Mar 48

Duncan, A. J. "Free money" of large manufacturing corporations and the rate of interest [followed by A. Kisselgoff's reply]. Em 14:251-54 Jul 46

A England, W. H. The Federal Trade Commission's corporation reports. JASA 42:22-24 Mar 47

Greenwood, H. Reform in published accounts. SAJE 11:137-44 Jun 43

Hirst, R. R. Inflation: its impact on enterprises. ER 25,(no.49):24-30 Dec 49

A Hubbard, J. B. Easy money: doctrine and results. HBR 19:52-65 no.1, 40

Hunt, P. The financial policy of corporations. QJE 57:303-13 Feb 43

A Kisselgoff, A. Liquidity preference of large manufacturing corporations (1921-1939). Em 13:334-46 Oct 45

Otsuka, I. On the liquidity of industrial enterprise. Kyo 19,no.1:20-43 Jan 44

A Sanders, T. H. The annual report: portrait of a business. HBR 27:1-12 Jan 49

A Smith, D. T. and Mace, M. Tax uncertainties in corporate financing. HBR 20:315-26 no.3, 42

14.41 HISTORY

EB Jefferys, J. B. The denomination and character of shares, 1855-1885. EHR 16:45-55 no.1, 46

14.42 SOURCES OF FUNDS

A Abbott, C. C. The availability of new equity capital. AER/S 32:129-40 Mar 42

A -- Sources of business funds; selected statistics, 1930-44. REStat 28:135-45 Aug 46

EI Battera, P. Index numbers of industrial production and capitalisation in Italy. BNL 2:118-23 Apr-Jun 49

A Brandt, L. K. Note on corporate expansion since 1940. AER 36:141-43 Mar 46

A -- Sources of funds for corporate plant expansion, 1946-1948. SEJ 15:279-88 Jan 49

A Butters, J. K. Tax revisions for reconversion needs. HBR 22:299-315 no.3, 44

A Cary, W. L. Sale and lease-back of corporate property. HBR 27:151-64 Mar 49

EB Chambers, S. P. Taxation and the supply of capital for industry. LBR 11:1-20 Jan 49

# 14. BUSINESS ORGANIZATION, ETC.

## 14.4 BUSINESS FINANCE (Cont.)
## 14.42 SOURCES OF FUNDS (Cont.)

Dirks, F. C. The rising liquidity of manu-
A  facturing companies and its implications
for financing postwar conversion.
JASA 39:207-17 Jun 44

Froehlich, W. The role of income determination in reinvestment and investment.
AER 38:78-91 Mar 48

Grunwald, K. Industrial credit survey
1919-1939. EgC 33:143-314 Feb-Mar 42

Guthmann, H. G. Dilution and common
stock financing. HBR 23:246-52 no.2, 45

Henderson, R. F. The significance of the
EB  new issue market for the finance of industry. EJ 58:63-73 Mar 48

Hersey, A. B. Sources and uses of corporation funds. JASA 36:265-74 Jun 41

Jacoby, N. H. The demand for funds by
A  American business enterprises: retrospect and prospect. Pt.I-II. JF 3,no.3:
27-38; 4:47-59 Oct 48, Mar 49

Ketchum, M. D. Plant financing in a war
A  economy. JB 16:28-50 Jan 43

-- The financial problem of small business.
A  Pt.I-II. JB 17:67-90; 162-85 Apr,Jul 44

McFerrin, J. B. Resources for financing
AA  industry in the South. SEJ 14:46-61
Jul 47

Miller, S. L. The equity capital problem.
HBR 26:671-79 Nov 48

Rienzi, E. The participation of foreign
capital in Italian joint-stock companies
at the outbreak of the second World War.
BNL 1:338-43 Apr 48

Robbins, S. M. Competitive bidding in sale
A  of securities. HBR 27:646-64 Sep 49

Rosa, R. V. Some small business problems
A  indicated by the industrial loan experi-
ence of the Federal Reserve Bank of New
York. JF 2,no.1:91-100 Apr 47

Sayers, R. S. Business men and the terms
EB  of borrowing. OEP 3:23-31 Feb 40

Silverman, H. R. Factoring as a financing
A  device. HBR 27:594-611 Sep 49

Wendt, P. F. The availability of capital to
ASC  small business in California in 1945-
1946. JF 2,no.2:43-54 Oct 47

-- Term loans to small business in Cali-
ASC  fornia, 1945-46. JF 3,no.2:45-58 Jun 48

Wilsey, H. L. The use of sinking funds in
A  preferred stock issues. JF 2,no.2:31-42
Oct 47

Woosley, J. B. The capital problem of
A  small and medium-sized businesses.
SEJ 7:461-74 Apr 41

Zinner, S. M. The contribution of commercial receivable companies and factors to
financing small- and medium-sized business. JF 2,no.1:76-90 Apr 47

## 14.43 PROFITS. DIVIDEND POLICIES

Barna, T. Those 'frightfully high' profits.
EB  OIS 11:213-27 Jul-Aug 49

Burr, S. S. Problems in providing adequate
A  statistics on business profits. JASA 42:
432-38 Sep 47

Crum, W. L. The current improvement in
A  business profits. REStat 22:157-60
Nov 40

Dobrovolsky, S. P. Corporate retained
A  earnings and cyclical fluctuations.
AER 35:559-74 Sep 45

Hope, R. Profits in British industry from
EB  1924 to 1935. OEP N.S.1:159-81 Jun 49

Lacey, K. Profit measurement and the
trade cycle. EJ 57:456-74 Dec 47

Lalwani, K. Dividend policy in Indian bus-
FI  iness. IJE 28:261-68 Oct 47

Lawrence, J. S. Profits and progress.
A  HBR 26:480-91 Jul 48

Ravenscroft, A. P. Dividends on industrial
HSA  shares 1947-48. SAJE 17:349-57 Sep 49

Robinson, L. R. Corporate earnings on
A  share and borrowed capital in percent-
ages of gross income (1918-1940).
JASA 36:253-64 Jun 41

Singer, H. W. Profit measurement and the
trade cycle. EJ 58:594-96 Dec 48

Slichter, S. H. Profits in a laboristic so-
A  ciety. HBR 27:346-61 May 49

Smith, D. T. Business profits during inflation. HBR 26:216-29 Mar 48

Spal, S. G. The treatment of noncumula-
A  tive preferred shareholders with regard
to dividends. JB 15:248-65 Jul 42

Spear, H. M. Dividend policies under chang-
A  ing price levels. HBR 27:612-21 Sep 49

Sweezy, M. Y. German corporate profits:
EG  1926-1938. QJE 54:384-98 May 40

Welcker, J. W. Fair profit? HBR 26:
A  207-15 Mar 48

-- Divergent views on corporate profits.
A  HBR 27:250-64 Mar 49

## 14.44 REORGANIZATION

Bates, G. E., chairman. Economic aspects
A  of reorganization under the Chandler
act. Abstract of specialized conference
discussion. AER/S 32:230-31 Mar 42

Calkins, F. J. Corporate reorganization
A  under chapter X: a post-mortem.
JF 3,no.2:19-28 Jun 48

Panuch, J. A. Investor protection in reor-
A  ganization. HBR 19:21-32 no.1, 40

## 14.5 MARKETING
## 14.50 GENERAL

Adams, Q. Marketing aspects of postwar
A  small business. JM 9:350-53 Apr 45

Alderson, W. The marketing viewpoint in
A  national economic planning. JM 7:326-32
Apr 43

-- and Cox, R. Towards a theory of marketing. JM 13:137-52 Oct 48

Alexander, R. S., chairman. Report of the
Definitions Committee. JM 13:202-17
Oct 48

14.5  MARKETING (Cont.)
14.50  GENERAL (Cont.)

Bartels, R. D. W.  Marketing principles. JM 9:151-57 Oct 44

EI  Beattie, T. E.  Comments on marketing in southern Italy.  JM 9:269-74 Jan 45

Brown, L. O.  Toward a profession of marketing.  JM 13:27-31 Jul 48

Converse, P. D.  The development of the science of marketing: an exploratory survey.  JM 10:14-23 Jul 45

A  -- Fred Clark's bibliography as of the early 1920's.  JM 10:54-57 Jul 45

A  Coutant, F. R.  Marketing's part in getting back to sound prosperity.  JM 11:285-87 Jan 47

Cowan, D. R. G.  Trends in industrial mar-
A  keting.  JM 6,no.4,pt.2:12-13 Apr 42

A  -- Requisites of a successful sales program. JM 10:244-52 Jan 46

Cox, R.  [Commodity marketing: going where?]  General synthesis.  AER/S 39: 421-23 May 49

Culliton, J. W.  The management challenge
A  of marketing costs.  HBR 26:74-88 Jan 48

A  Evans, M. J.  Case study in industrial mar-keting.  JM 5:443-45 Apr 41

Freeland, W. E.  Scientific management in marketing [with discussion by J. Mee]. JM 4,no.4,pt.2:31-38 Apr 40

Fullbrook, E. S.  The functional concept in marketing.  JM 4:229-37 Jan 40

Gragg, C. I.  Marketing and the defense
A  program.  JM 5:423-30 Apr 41

Haynes, E.  Industrial production and mar-
A  keting.  JM 8:13-20 Jul 43

Hill, L.  Marketing and employment.
A  JM 11:65-66 Jul 46

Hobart, D. M.  Probable effects of a national
A  emergency on marketing functions and policies.  JM 4,no.4,pt.2:59-65 Apr 40

Hurley, N. C.  Industrial marketing under
A  the defense program.  JM 5:450-55 Apr 41

Johnson, A. H.  Advertising and marketing
A  opportunities in the postwar period. JM 10:113-27 Oct 45

Jones, F. M.  A new interpretation of mar-keting functions.  JM 7:256-60 Jan 43

Jones, G. S., Jr.  Salesmanship's responsi-
A  bility for the future.  JM 8:75-78 Jul 43

Lebow, V.  New outlooks for marketing. JB 22:160-68 Jul 49

Livingston, S. M.  The marketing viewpoint
A  in planning for the business enterprise. JM 7:332-36 Apr 43

Norton, L. J.  Market and marketing re-
AA  search in the Midwest.  JFE 31:350-55 May 49

Phillips, C. F.  A critical analysis of recent literature dealing with marketing effi-ciency.  JM 5:360-65 Apr 41

A  -- Impact of shortages on marketing. HBR 21:432-42 no.4, 43

A  Reed, V. D.  Governmental activity in marketing.  JM 6,no.4,pt.2:18-19 Apr 42

Schultz, W. J.  The credit man in market-
A  ing conferences.  JM 11:73-77 Jul 46

Shoup, E. C.  Post-war marketing responsi-
A  bilities need changed marketing execu-tives.  JM 7:125-28 Oct 42

Tosdal, H. R.  Significant trends in sales
A  management.  JM 5:215-18 Jan 41

A  -- Significant current trends in sales man-agement.  JM 6,no.4,pt.2:14-16 Apr 42

A  -- Sales management: restrospect and prospect.  HBR 21:71-82 no.1, 42

Vaile, R. S.  Towards a theory of market-ing: a comment.  JM 13:520-22 Apr 49

Waterhouse, S. G.  An Englishman looks at
A  American marketing and distribution
EB  policies.  JM 12:305-10 Jan 48

EB  -- British marketing today.  JM 13:289-94 Jan 49

Watson, A. N.  Wartime incomes and con-
A  sumer markets.  JM 8:231-37 Jan 44

Wilson, J. M.  How the National Cash Reg-
A  ister Company views the responsibilities of sales management.  JM 10:283-88 Jan 46

14.51  HISTORY

Atherton, L. E.  Predecessors of the com-
AA  mercial drummer in the old South. BHR 21:17-24 Feb 47

Bacon, E. M.  Marketing sewing machines
A  in the post-Civil War years.  BHR 20: 90-94 Jun 46

Coolsen, F. G.  Pioneers in the develop-
A  ment of advertising.  JM 12:80-86 Jul 47

Friedman, L. M.  The drummer in early
A  American merchandise distribution. BHR 21:39-44 Apr 47

Marburg, T. F.  Manufacturer's drummer,
A  1832.  BHR 22:40-56 Apr 48

A  -- Manufacturer's drummer, 1852, with comments on western and southern mar-kets.  BHR 22:106-14 Jun 48

14.52  MARKET RESEARCH
14.520  GENERAL

Alderson, W.  Marketing classification of
A  families.  JM 6:143-46 Oct 41

A  --, chairman.  Report of sub-committee on dollar classification of incomes.  JM 6: 383-86 Apr 42

Anderson, J. T.  The relation of market
A  research to post-war planning.  JM 7: 115-24 Oct 42

Arnold, P.  Woman's role in market re-search.  JM 12:87-91 Jul 47

Atwood, P. W.  Marketing research as a tool of management in industrial goods problems.  JM 12:295-304 Jan 48

Barton, S. G.  A working system for the
A  socio-economic classification of a na-tional sample of families.  JM 11:364-66 Apr 47

14. BUSINESS ORGANIZATION, ETC.

14.52  MARKET RESEARCH (Cont.)
14.520  GENERAL (Cont.)

Blankenship, A. B.  Needed: a broader concept of marketing research. JM 13: 305-10 Jan 49

Borton, W. M.  Marketing research by Los
ASC  Angeles industrial concerns.  JM 14: 450-52 Oct 49

Brown, W. F.  The broader concept of marketing research.  JM 13:527-28 Apr 49

Cherington, P. T.  Current progress in
A  market research.  JM 5:225-27 Jan 41
-- Trends in marketing research.  JM 6,
A  no.4,pt.2:17-18 Apr 42

Cheskin, L. and Ward, L. B.  Indirect ap-
A  proach to market reactions.  HBR 26: 572-80 Sep 48

Cowan, D. R. G.  Commercial research for post war activities.  JM 7:49-56 Jul 42

Crossley, A. M., chairman.  Report of sub-
A  committee on descriptive classification of income levels.  JM 6:379-82 Apr 42

Dichter, E.  Psychology in market research.
A  HBR 25:432-43 no.4, 47

Dirksen, C. J. and Forman, L. W.  Oppor-
A  tunities in marketing research.  JM 13: 37-43 Jul 48

Eckler, A. R. and Staudt, E. P.  Marketing
A  and sampling uses of population and housing data.  JASA 38:87-92 Mar 43

Elder, R. F.  What sales management expects from research.  JM 13:52-55 Jul 48

Engle, N. H.  Gaps in marketing research. JM 4:345-53 Apr 40

Ferber, R.  The disproportionate method of market sampling.  JB 19:67-75 Apr 46

Fisk, G.  Methods of handling certain field research problems.  JM 12:382-84 Jan 48

Franzen, R. and Teilhet, D.  A method for measuring product acceptance.  JM 5: 156-61 Oct 40

Frothingham, R. S., chairman.  Preparation and presentation of the research report. [Report of a sub-committee, written by G. W. Robbins] JM 13:62-72 Jul 48

Galbraith, J. K.  Appraisal of marketing
A  research. [Abstract] AER/S 39:415-16 May 49

Ghent, M. D.  Selection and training of commercial research analysts.  JM 14: 22-26 Jul 49

Goldsen, J. M. and Curtis, A.  Montclair
ASN  studies the shopping experiences and attitudes of its residents.  JM 10:165-70 Oct 45

Heusner, W. W., chairman.  Marketing re-
A  search in American industry.  Pt.I-II. [Report by the Committee on Marketing Research] JM 11:338-54; 12:25-37 Apr,Jul 47

Hirose, A. P.  Market research as a prac-
A  tical help in reconversion problems. JM 9:342-49 Apr 45

Hobart, D. M.  Occupational classification
A  for market research.  JM 7:367-73 Apr 43

Luck, D. J.  Education for marketing re-
A  search.  JM 14:385-90 Oct 49

Maledon, W. J.  Research in retail distri-
A  bution: its methods and problems. JM 4:238-48 Jan 40

Nyman, C. R.  Visual analysis: a new method in market research.  JM 8: 249-52 Jan 44

Phillips, C. F., chairman.  Major areas for marketing research. [Report of three conferences] JM 11:21-26 Jul 46

Przeworska, Z. M.  A market research
EB  method and its application to war-time problems.  OIS 3:370-74 Nov 22, 41

Rebensburg, G. A.  Market analysis: a
A  case study [in the electric appliance field].  JM 9:141-43 Oct 44

Reed, V. D., chairman.  Selection, training, and supervision of field interviewers in marketing research. [Report of a committee] JM 12:365-78 Jan 48

Sellers, M.  Pre-testing of products by
A  consumer juries.  JM 6,no.4,pt.2:76-80 Apr 42

Smith, E. R.  Buying power classifications:
A  introduction.  JM 7:354-55 Apr 43
--, chairman.  Report of AMA Committee
A  on Buying Power Classifications. JM 8: 329-30 Jan 44
--, chairman.  Design, size, and validation
A  of sample for market research. [Report of Committee on Marketing Research Techniques] JM 10:221-34 Jan 46

Stehman, J. H., ed.  Research in market-
A  ing. [Regular feature edited successively by Stehman, R. S. Vaile, R. Breyer, and O. E. Burley] JM 4-14 Jun 40-Oct 49

Strohkarck, F. and Phelps, K.  The mechanics of constructing a market area map.  JM 12:493-96 Apr 48

Thomsen, F. L.  How good is marketing
A  research?  HBR 24:453-65 no.4, 46

Watson, A. N.  Use of small area census
A  data in marketing analysis.  JM 6,no.4, pt.2:42-47 Apr 42

Weld, L. D. H.  The place of marketing re-
A  search during a national emergency. JM 4,no.4,pt.2:66-69 Apr 40
--, chairman.  Report of the Committee on
A  Income Classifications.  JM 6:375-79 Apr 42

White, J. H.  Measuring local markets.
A  JM 12:220-33 Oct 47
-- Discretionary spending power at multi-
A  ple levels.  JM 13:1-11 Jul 48

Whittinghill, D. C.  Manufacturer's sales
A  research helps large customers to grow. JM 7:203-05 Jan 43

Wood, R.  Market research and industrial
A  development.  JM 12:503-04 Apr 48

14.52  MARKET RESEARCH (Cont.)
14.521  CONSUMER MOTIVATION. BRAND
       PREFERENCE
    Alexander, R. S.  Some aspects of sex dif-
      ferences in relation to marketing.
      JM 12:158-72 Oct 47
    Brew, M. L.  A home economist looks at
      marketing.  JM 14:72-76 Jul 49
    Brown, G. H. and Hadary, G.  Beverage
ASI   preference of industrial workers: a
      study in consumer preference ratings
      [in the Chicago area].  JB 17:111-17
      Apr 44
    Cassady, R., Jr.  [Consumer preference
      studies]: discussion.  JM 6,no.4,pt.2:
      87-88 Apr 42
    Church, D. E.  The consumer market for
A     canned vegetables, fruits, and juices.
      JM 11:44-54 Jul 46
    Duncan, D. J.  What motivates business
A     buyers?  HBR 18:448-54 no.4, 40
    Furbush, F.  Farm family income and ex-
A     penditures.  JM 4:264-67 Jan 40
    Hadary, G.  The use of taste response tests
      in market research.  JM 10:152-55
      Oct 45
    McGregor, D.  "Motives" as a tool of mar-
A     ket research.  HBR 19:42-51 no.1, 40
    McMurry, R. N.  Psychology in selling.
      JM 9:114-18 Oct 44
    Moll, W. J.  Survey of consumer buying
A     intent.  JM 8:54-58 Jul 43
    Nybroten, N.  Rate of commodity disap-
      pearance and consumer preference.
      JFE 31:346-50 May 49
    O'Connell, J. S.  A study in selling sterling
A     silver.  JM 10:64-66 Jul 45
    Schreier, F. T. and Wood, A. J.  Motivation
      analysis in market research.  JM 13:
      172-82 Oct 48
    -- --- Reply to criticism by Lazare Teper.
      JM 14:453-56 Oct 49
    Steele, E. A.  Some aspects of the Negro
A     market.  JM 11:399-401 Apr 47
    Sullivan, D. J.  The Negro market today
A     and postwar.  JM 10:68-69 Jul 45
      Errata.  10:179 Oct 45
    Teper, L.  "Motivation analysis in market
      research": a criticism.  JM 13:524-27
      Apr 49
    Wolfe, H. D.  Techniques of appraising
A     brand preference and brand conscious-
      ness by consumer interviewing.  JM 6,
      no.4,pt.2:81-87 Apr 42

14.522  SALES FORECASTING
    Johnson, A. H.  Market potentials, 1948.
A     HBR 26:11-31 Jan 48
    MacGowan, T. G.  Forecasting sales.
A     HBR 27:760-70 Nov 49
    Newbury, F. D.  A forecast of business
A     prospects.  HBR 25:273-88 no.3, 47

    Wallace, I.  Individual firm sales forecast-
A     ing.  JM 13:183-88 Oct 48

14.53  PRODUCT POLICIES
    Butler, R.  Growth patterns for new spe-
      cialty products: a case study.  JM 11:
      27-34 Jul 46
    Cunningham, R. M.  Locating and appraising
      product ideas.  JM 7:41-48 Jul 42
    Dameron, K.  Labeling terminology.  JB 18:
      157-66 Jul 45
    Gregory, P. M.  A theory of purposeful
      obsolescence.  SEJ 14:24-45 Jul 47
    -- An economic interpretation of women's
      fashions.  SEJ 14:148-62 Oct 47
    Johnson, G. C.  Effective marketing begins
      on the design board.  JM 13:32-36 Jul 48
    Kebker, V. W.  Will grade labeling pay?
ASK   [A study made in Lawrence, Kansas]
      JM 8:185-88 Oct 43
    Simmons, F. E.  Packaging aids to market-
      ing.  JM 13:512-17 Apr 49
    Walker, S. B.  Developing products to fit
      market needs.  JM 8:268-73 Jan 44
    White, M.  Ideal conditions for product
      testing.  JM 11:55-61 Jul 46

14.54  PRICE POLICIES
    Abramson, A. G.  Price policies.  SEJ 12:
      39-47 Jul 45
    Alt, R. M.  The internal organization of the
A     firm and price formation: an illustrative
      case.  QJE 63:92-110 Feb 49
    Dean, J.  Cost forecasting and price policy.
      JM 13:279-88 Jan 49
    Hawkins, E. R.  Marketing and the theory
      of monopolistic competition.  JM 4:
      382-89 Apr 40
    Katona, G. and Leavens, D. H.  Price in-
A     creases and uptrading: the change in
      advertised prices of apparel and house
      furnishings.  JB 17:231-43 Oct 44
    Knauth, O.  Considerations in the setting of
A     retail prices.  JM 14:1-12 Jul 49
    Lockley, L. C.  Theories of pricing in mar-
      keting.  JM 13:364-66 Jan 49

14.55  ADVERTISING
    Banks, S.  The use of incremental analysis
      in the selection of advertising media.
      JB 19:232-43 Oct 46
    Belley, B.  Toward a measure of pharma-
A     ceutical advertising effectiveness.  JB 16:
      107-14 Apr 43
    Berreman, J. V.  Advertising and the sale
      of novels.  JM 7:234-40 Jan 43
    Beville, H. M., Jr.  Surveying radio
A     listeners by use of a probability sample.
      JM 14:373-78 Oct 49
    Borden, N. H.  Findings of the Harvard
A     study on the economic effects of adver-
      tising.  JM 6,no.4,pt.2:89-99 Apr 42

# 14. BUSINESS ORGANIZATION, ETC.

## 14.55 ADVERTISING (Cont.)

Borden, N. H. (Cont.)

A -- Use of newspapers by national advertisers. HBR 24:295-305 no.3, 46

A -- Selling newspaper space to national advertisers. HBR 24:438-52 no.4, 46

A -- Advertising branded parts to consumers. HBR 25:129-44 no.1, 46

A Branch, F. T. A comparison of direct-mail and magazine cost in pharmaceutical advertising. JB 18:78-95 Apr 45

A Canoyer, H. G. National brand advertising and monopolistic competition. JM 7: 152-57 Oct 42

Cassady, R., Jr. and Williams, R. M.
ASC Radio as an advertising medium [in California]. HBR 27:62-78 Jan 49

A Dameron, K. Advertising and the consumer movement. JM 5:234-47 Jan 41

A -- Information in advertising. HBR 20: 482-95 no.4, 42

A Deckinger, E. L. The network radio advertiser and summer policy. JM 13: 23-26 Jul 48

Dichter, E. A psychological view of advertising effectiveness. JM 14:61-66 Jul 49

A Edsall, R. L. A method of measuring effectiveness of business and trade paper advertising. JM 7:208-09 Jan 43

A Edwards, C. D. Antitrust policy toward advertising. JM 6,no.4,pt.2:106-11 Apr 42

A Franzen, R. Inequalities which affect scores of advertisements. JM 6,no.4, pt.2:128-32 Apr 42

A Gardner, E. H. The business view of advertising policy. JM 6,no.4,pt.2:112-17 Apr 42

A Gregory, P. M. An appraisal of mortgage advertising. HBR 23:32-45 no.1, 44

A Hollander, S., Jr. A rationale for advertising expenditures. HBR 27:79-87 Jan 49

A Hotchkiss, G. B. Consumer economists in glass houses. JM 5:228-33 Jan 41

A -- Evaluation of the Harvard study. JM 6, no.4,pt.2:100-05 Apr 42

A Jastram, R. W. Advertising ratios planned by large-scale advertisers. JM 14:13-21 Jul 49

A Jeuck, J. E. Direct-mail advertising to doctors. JB 13:17-38 Jan 40

A Laybourn, G. P. and Longstaff, H. P. Certain correlates of attitudes toward radio commercials. JM 13:447-58 Apr 49

A Lockley, L. C. Trade associations as advertisers. JM 8:189-93 Oct 43

Lucas, D. B. A controlled recognition technique for measuring magazine advertising audiences. JM 6,no.4,pt.2: 133-36 Apr 42

A Margolis, C. Traceable response as a method of evaluating industrial advertising: a case study. JM 12:202-10 Oct 47

D Mateyo, G. Latin American consumers: some problems in reaching them by advertising. JM 6,no.4,pt.2:142-48 Apr 42

EB Moos, S. Statistics of advertising. OIS 5: 181-87 Aug 7, 43; Erratum. 204 Aug 28, 43

A Moses, L B. Merchandising the advertising campaign. JM 9:124-26 Oct 44

A Mullen, W. H. Measurement of national advertising. HBR 27:622-45 Sep 49

A Neilsen, A. C. Trends toward mechanization of radio advertising. JM 6:217-28 Jan 42

A -- Two years of commercial operation of the audimeter and the Neilsen radio index. JM 9:239-55 Jan 45

A Oehler, C. M. Measuring the believability of advertising claims. JM 9:127-31 Oct 44

A Rand, R. B. Pharmaceutical advertising to doctors. JB 14:150-68 Apr 41

Reed, V. D. Promotion and research. JM 11:367-70 Apr 47

Roberts, H. V. The measurement of advertising results. JB 20:131-45 Jul 47

Root, A. R. and Welch, A. C. The continuing consumer study: a basic method for the engineering of advertising. JM 7: 3-21 Jul 42

EB Rothschild, K. W. Advertising in war-time. OIS 4:169-75 Jun 6, 42

A Salisbury, P. Has advertising come of age? JM 8:25-32 Jul 43

A Scott, J. D. Advertising when consumers cannot buy. HBR 21:207-29 no.2, 43

A -- Advertising when buying is restricted. HBR 21:443-54 no.4, 43

Shepard, T. M. The Starch application of the recognition technique. JM 6,no.4, pt.2:118-24 Apr 42

A Simmons, H. H. Building an industrial advertising campaign. JM 5:446-49 Apr 41

A Wagner, L. C. Advertising and the business cycle. JM 6:124-35 Oct 41

A Zeisel, H. and Harper, V. E. The advertising value of different magazines. JM 13: 56-61 Jul 48

## 14.56 SALES PERSONNEL

A Chamberlain, S. D. The use of "aptitude tests" in sales management. JM 8: 159-64 Oct 43

A Flemming, E. G. and Flemming, C. W. test-selected salesmen. JM 10:336-42 Apr 46

A Hilgert, J. R. Use of sales aptitude tests. HBR 23:484-92 no.4, 45

A Osborne, D. S. Sales training for the new type of selling. JM 8:79-82 Jul 43

A -- Trends in the selection and training of salesmen. JM 11:70-73 Jul 46

14.56  SALES PERSONNEL (Cont.)

Stokes, J. W.  The new projective-type
A    tests for selection of salesmen.  JM 10:
58-59 Jul 45

14.57  OTHER DISTRIBUTION POLICIES

Applebaum, W.  A case history of sales
A    quotas [for bread in a retail grocery
chain].  JM 7:200-03 Jan 43

Burgoyne, J., Jr.  Conducting sales tests.
JM 9:158-59 Oct 44

Bursk, E. C.  Low-pressure selling.
A    HBR 25:227-42 no.2, 47

Francisco, L. M.  The talking picture: an
example of the machine method applied
to selling.  JM 9:119-23 Oct 44

Frederick, J. H.  How air transportation
A    may affect marketing and product development.  JM 8:274-80 Jan 44

Grimes, W. H.  Distribution and the finance
A    company.  HBR 18:199-206 no.2, 40

Hankins, F. W.  Arithmetic for sales management.  JM 7:59-64 Jul 42

Hansen, H. L.  Premium merchandising.
A    HBR 19:185-96 no.2, 41

Hart, L. C.  Essentials of successful mar-
A    keting: a case history in manufacturer-
distributor collaboration.  JM 13:195-201
Oct 48

Lebow, V.  Our changing channels of dis-
A    tribution.  JM 13:12-22 Jul 48

McNeill, R. B.  The lease as a marketing
A    tool.  HBR 22:415-30 no.4, 44

Nordin, J. A.  Spatial allocation of selling
expenses.  JM 7:210-19 Jan 43

Wormser, A. R.  A case study in the costs
of distribution [in a wholesale grocery
company].  JM 9:19-25 Jul 44

14.6  PURCHASING
14.60  GENERAL

Malott, D. W.  Does futures trading in-
A    fluence prices?  HBR 18:177-90
no.2, 40

Schwieger, A. J.  Subcontracting: a
device for expansion.  HBR 22:88-92
no.1, 43

Lewis, H. T.  This business of procure-
A    ment.  HBR 24:377-93 no.3, 46

# 15. INDUSTRIAL ORGANIZATION
# AND PUBLIC POLICY

15.0  GENERAL

El-Gritly, A. A. I.  The structure of mod-
ME    ern industry in Egypt.  EgC 38:363-582
Nov-Dec 47

Kolesnikoff, V. S.  Standard commodity
A    classification.  JASA 39:42-52 Mar 44

Leser, C. E. V.  Industrial specialisation
EB    in Scotland and in regions of England
and Wales.  YB 1:19-30 Dec 48

Molinari, A.  Future responsibilities of the
EI    Italian industry.  BNL 1:3-9 Apr 47

Oppenheimer-Bluhm, H.  Industrialization
MI    in Palestine.  SR 8:438-53 Nov 41

Richards, C. S.  The task before us: with
HSA    special reference to industry.  SAJE 12:
157-204 Sep 44

Samant, D. R.  The new industrial policy of
FI    the government of India.  IJE 26:631-40
Apr 46

Worsdale, J. E. The task before us: with
HSA    special reference to industry: a com-
ment [followed by C. S. Richards' reply].
SAJE 13:63-67 Mar 45

15.1  HISTORY

Anonymous.  Growth of rigidity in business.
[Résumé of papers and discussion which
are published in AER/S 30] BHR 14:
1-9 Feb 40

Aubrey, H. G.  Deliberate industrialization.
DM    SR 16:158-82 Jun 49

Barbour, V.  Rigidities affecting business
in the sixteenth and seventeenth centuries.  AER/S 30:290-97 Mar 40

Clemen, R. A.  The growth of rigidity in
business: discussion.  AER/S 30:
314-15 Mar 40

Gras, N. S. B.  The growth of rigidity in
business during the Middle Ages.
AER/S 30:281-89 Mar 40

Hamilton, E. J.  The growth of rigidity in
business during the eighteenth century.
AER/S 30:298-305 Mar 40

Heaton, H. Rigidity in business since the
industrial revolution.  AER/S 30:306-13
Mar 40

Tucker, R. S.  The growth of rigidity in
business: discussion.  AER/S 30:
315-16 Mar 40

15.2 MARKET STRUCTURE AND BEHAVIOR
15.20  GENERAL

Bober, M. M.  Price and production policies.
A    AER/S 32,no.2:23-52 Jun 42

Brady, R. A.  Modernized cameralism in
EG    the Third Reich: the case of the National
Industry Group.  JPE 50:65-97 Feb 42

-- Reports and conclusions of the Temporary National Economic Committee
A    (U.S.A.).  R.  EJ 53:409-15 Dec 43

Crumbaker, C.  Note on concentration of
A    economic power.  R.  JPE 50:934-44
Dec 42

# 15. INDUSTRIAL ORGANIZATION AND PUBLIC POLICY

## 15.2 MARKET STRUCTURE AND BEHAVIOR (Cont.)

### 15.20 GENERAL (Cont.)

Heflebower, R. B. The effects of the war
A   on the structure of commodity and labor
markets. AER/S 36:52-64 May 46

Hoffman, A. C. Current institutional trends
A   in business. JFE 31,pt.2:1132-40 Nov 49

Leak, H. and Maizels, A. The structure of
EB   British industry [followed by discussion].
JRSS 108:142-207 pt.1-2, 45

### 15.201 ECONOMIC BLOCS. COUNTERVAILING POWER

Nourse, E. G. Collective bargaining and
the common interest. AER 33:1-20
Mar 43

### 15.21 HISTORY

Horie, Y. Clan monopoly policy in the
FJ   Tokugawa period. Kyo 17,no.1:31-52
Jan 42

### 15.22 BUSINESS POPULATION

Adams, Q. Notes on business population
A   data. JM 10:173-75 Oct 45

Bowen, H. R. Turnover of business enter-
A   prises. JB 18:73-77 Apr 45

-- Significance of recent changes in the
A   business population. JM 10:24-34 Jul 45

Burd, H. A. Mortality of men's apparel
ASW   stores in Seattle, 1929-1939. JM 6:
22-26 Jul 41

McGarry, E. D. The mortality of inde-
ASN  pendent grocery stores in Buffalo and
ASP  Pittsburg, 1919-1941. JM 12:14-24
Jul 47

Steiner, W. H. Changing composition of the
ASG  Savannah business community 1900-1940.
SEJ 10:303-10 Apr 44

### 15.23 MONOPOLY. CONCENTRATION. COMPETITION

### 15.230 GENERAL

Anderson, T. J., Jr. Note on "The rise of
monopoly." AER 30:118-20 Mar 40

Ballaine, W. C. How government purchas-
A   ing procedures strengthen monopoly
elements. JPE 51:538-46 Dec 43

Berge, W. Monopoly and the South. SEJ 13:
AA  360-69 Apr 47

Boulding, K. E. In defense of monopoly.
QJE 59:524-42 Aug 45

Clark, J. M. Toward a concept of workable
competition. AER 30:241-56 Jun 40

Holben, R. E. In defense of monopoly: comment [followed by K. W. Rothschild's
further comment and K. E. Boulding's
reply]. QJE 60:612-21 Aug 46

Lalwani, K. Combination as a form of
FI   business organisation in India. IJE 26:
191-225 Oct 45

Means, G. C. Big business, administered

A   prices, and the problem of full employment. JM 4:370-78 Apr 40

Mund, V. A. Monopolistic competition
theory and public price policy. AER 32:
727-43 Dec 42

-- and Schmidt, E. P. Monopoly and competition: discussion. AER/S 36:205-13
May 46

Papandreou, A. G. Market structure and
monopoly power. AER 39:883-97 Sep 49

Stigler, G. J. The extent and bases of
A   monopoly. AER/S 32,no.2:1-22 Jun 42

### 15.231 MEASUREMENT

Bain, J. S. The profit rate as a measure
of monopoly power. QJE 55:271-93
Feb 41

Haddon-Cave, C. P. Trends in the concen-
N   tration of operations of Australian secondary industries, 1923-1943. ER 21:
65-78 Jun 45

Houghton, H. F. The growth of big busi-
A   ness. AER/S 38:72-93 May 48

James, C. L. Industrial concentration and
A   trade barriers. SEJ 14:163-72 Oct 47

Livermore, S. Concentration of control
A   now as compared with 1890. JM 4:
362-69 Apr 40

Schmidt, C. T. Concentration of joint-stock
EI   enterprise in Italy. AER 30:82-86
Mar 40

Tucker, R. S. Concentration and competi-
A   tion. JM 4:354-61 Apr 40

-- The degree of monopoly. QJE 55:167-69
Nov 40

-- [and others] The progress of concentration in industry: discussion.
AER/S 38:109-20 May 48

### 15.232 COMBINATIONS. MERGERS

Block, H. Industrial concentration versus
EG   small business: the trend of Nazi policy.
SR 10:175-99 May 43

Lachmann, K. The Hermann Göring Works.
EG   SR 8:24-40 Feb 41

-- More on the Hermann Göring Works.
EG   SR 9:396-401 Sep 42

### 15.233 COLLUSION. CARTELS

Bain, J. S. Output quotas in imperfect
cartels. QJE 62:617-22 Aug 48

Brady, R. A. The role of cartels in the
current cultural crisis. AER/S 35:
312-20 May 45

Brown, W. F. and Cassady, R., Jr. Guild
AS   pricing in the service trades. [State
laws relating to barbering] QJE 61:
311-38 Feb 47

Dowdell, E. G. The concerted regulation of
price and output. EJ 58:210-27 Jun 48

Garver, F. B. Cartels, combinations and
the public interest. JFE 26:613-30
Nov 44

## 15.233 COLLUSION. CARTELS (Cont.)

James, L. M. Restrictive agreements and practices in the lumber industry, 1880–1939. SEJ 13:115-25 Oct 46

EG Newman, P. C. Key German cartels under the Nazi regime. QJE 62:576-95 Aug 48

EI Pitigliani, F. R. The development of Italian cartels under fascism. JPE 48:375-400 Jun 40

Terrill, R. P. Cartels and the international exchange of technology. AER/S 36: 745-67 May 46

## 15.234 RATIONALIZATION. REORGANIZATION

EB Allen, G. C. An aspect of industrial reorganisation. EJ 55:179-91 Jun-Sep 45

Smith, R. H. A note on the meaning of the term "rationalisation." SAJE 11:210-17 Sep 43

## 15.235 TRADE ASSOCIATIONS

A Brand, C. J. Experiences of a trade association in an antitrust suit. JM 7:227-33 Jan 43

A Constantine, E. Trade associations and government statistics. JASA 42:20-22 Mar 47

A Hays, J. S. and Ratzkin, J. L. Trade association practices and antitrust law. HBR 25:501-20 no.4, 47

A Lockley, L. C. Trade associations as advertisers. JM 8:189-93 Oct 43

A Meyers, E. S. Some observations on the trade associations and the law. JM 12: 379-81 Jan 48

A Robbins, I. D. Management services for small business through trade associations. HBR 26:627-40 Sep 48

## 15.24 DETERMINANTS OF MARKET STRUCTURE

A Alexander, S. S. The effect of size of manufacturing corporation on the distribution of the rate of return. REStat 31: 229-35 Aug 49

A Anthony, R. N. Effect of size on efficiency. HBR 20:290-306 no.3, 42

A Beckman, T. N. Large versus small business after the war. AER/S 34:94-106 Mar 44

A Blair, J. M. The relation between size and efficiency of business. REStat 24:125-35 Aug 42

A -- Technology and size. AER/S 38:121-52 May 48

A Bressler, R. G., Jr. Research determination of economies of scale. JFE 27: 526-39 Aug 45

Coonley, H. How big should a business be? JM 5:102-09 Oct 40

Davenport, R. How big should a business be? JM 5:97-102 Oct 40

Engle, N. H. Measurement of economic and marketing efficiency. JM 5:335-49 Apr 41

EB Jewkes, J. Is British industry inefficient? MS 14,no.1:1-16 Jan 46

EB Lomax, K. S. A note on the size of establishments in factory trades. MS 17: 317-27 Sep 49

FI Mehta, M. M. Corporate size and rate of profit. IJE 29:365-73 Apr 49

FI -- Relation between size and efficiency. IJE 30:61-67 Jul 49

FIP Qureshi, A. I. The future of cottage industries. PEJ 1,no.1:62-68 Jul 49

FJ Reubens, E. P. Small-scale industry in Japan. QJE 61:577-604 Aug 47

A Siegel, I. H. The measurement of capacity utilization. JASA 37:430-36 Dec 42

A Smith, B. [Significance of size in our economic system.] Discussion. JM 4: 378-81 Apr 40

HSA Smith, R. H. The size of the South African industrial unit. SAJE 13:263-303 Dec 45

A Yntema, T. O. The future role of large-scale enterprise. JPE 49:833-48 Dec 41

## 15.25 PRICE BEHAVIOR
## 15.250 GENERAL

N Cheek, B. M. Economic theory and industrial pricing. ER 25,suppl.:140-57 Aug 49

A Grether, E. T. Current trends affecting pricing policies. JM 5:222-23 Jan 41

-- Price policy trends, 1941. JM 6,no.4, pt.2:16-17 Apr 42

EB Jones, E. Price leadership in the rayon industry. MS 12:80-96 Oct 41

A Keim, W. G. Prices and wages. JASA 37: 377-82 Sep 42

A Nicholls, W. H. Dr. Nourse on low-price policy. R. [followed by E. G. Nourse's Addendum] JFE 26:754-74 Nov 44

A Nickerson, C. B. The cost element in pricing. HBR 18:417-28 no.4, 40

Nourse, E. G. The meaning of "price policy." QJE 55:175-209 Feb 41

ASN Rodgers, R. and Luedicke, H. E. Dynamic competition [applied to a study of price movements of petroleum products in the New York marketing area]. HBR 27: 237-49 Mar 49

A Wein, H. H. Wages and prices: a case study [of the U.S. Steel Corporation]. REStat 29:108-23 May 47

## 15.251 PRICE FLEXIBILITY

Alt, R. M. Statistical measurement of price flexibility. QJE 56:497-502 May 42

A Backman, J. The causes of price inflexibility. QJE 54:474-89 May 40

A -- Price inflexibility: war and postwar. JPE 56:428-37 Oct 48

## 15.251  PRICE FLEXIBILITY (Cont.)

Doblin, E. M.  Some aspects of price flex-
A   ibility. REStat 22:183-89 Nov 40

Neal, A. C.  Comment on Review of Industrial concentration and price inflexibility.
AER 33:622-25 Sep 43

Thorp, W. L. and Crowder, W. F.  Concen-
A   tration and product characteristics as
factors in price-quantity behavior.
AER/S 30,no.5:390-408 Feb 41

## 15.26  NON-PRICE COMPETITION

Anderson, K. L.  Terms of sale. JM 11:
250-57 Jan 47

Canoyer, H. G.  National brand advertising
A   and monopolistic competition. JM 7:
152-57 Oct 42

Cox, R.  Non-price competition and the
measurement of prices. JM 10:370-83
Apr 46

Hagios, J. A.  Credit terms as an element
A   in merchandising competition. JM 4,
no.4,pt.2:70-78 Apr 40

Lewis, W. A.  Notes on the economics of
EB   loyalty. Ec N.S.9:333-48 Nov 42

## 15.27  RESEARCH. INNOVATION

Balogh, T.  The finance of scientific & ap-
EB   plied research. OIS 6:1-7 Jan 15, 44

-- The budget proposals and technical
EB   progress. OIS 6:104-07 May 20, 44

Bright, A. A., Jr. and McLaurin, W. R.
A   Economic factors influencing the development and introduction of the fluorescent lamp. JPE 51:429-50 Oct 43

Butters, J. K.  Taxation and new product
A   development. HBR 23:451-59 no.4, 45

Conant, J. B.  The place of research in our
A   national life. HBR 26:46-57 Jan 48

Hughes, F.  Soviet invention awards. EJ 55:
ER   291-97 Jun-Sep 45

-- Incentive for Soviet initiative. EJ 56:
ER   415-25 Sep 46

Maclaurin, W. R., chairman.  Economics
of industrial research. Abstract of specialized conference discussion.
AER/S 32:231-32 Mar 42

-- Federal support for scientific research.
A   HBR 25:385-96 no.3, 47

Shirras, G. F.  The British Association con-
EB   ference and the place of science in industry. EJ 55:121-27 Apr 45

Terrill, R. P.  Cartels and the international
exchange of technology. AER/S 36:
745-67 May 46

## 15.3  GOVERNMENT POLICY TOWARD MONOP-
OLY AND COMPETITION

## 15.30  GENERAL

### UNITED STATES

Bain, J. S.  The Sherman Act and "The
A   bottlenecks of business." R. JM 5:
254-58 Jan 41

Ballantine, A. A.  The Supreme Court and
business planning. HBR 24:151-65
no.2, 46

Berge, W.  Problems of enforcement and
interpretation of the Sherman Act.
AER/S 38:172-81 May 48

Comer, G. P.  The outlook for effective
competition. AER/S 36:154-71 May 46

Daggett, S.  Railroad traffic associations
and antitrust legislation. AER/S 38:
452-64 May 48

Edwards, C. D.  Can the antitrust laws
preserve competition? AER/S 30:
164-79 Mar 40

-- Antitrust policy toward advertising.
JM 6,no.4,pt.2:106-11 Apr 42

-- An appraisal of the antitrust laws.
AER/S 36:172-89 May 46

-- [and others]  The Sherman Act and the
enforcement of competition: discussion.
AER/S 38:203-14 May 48

Ezekiel, M.  Is government intervention or
planning consistent with antitrust policy?
AER/S 36:190-204 May 46

Feldman, G. J.  Anti-trust paradoxes.
JM 6:147-51 Oct 41

Homan, P. T.  In what areas should antitrust policy be replaced? AER/S 30:
180-93 Mar 40

Ise, J.  The futility of trust-busting.
AER/S 38:488-501 May 48

Keezer, D. M., chairman.  The effectiveness of the federal antitrust laws: a
symposium. AER 39:689-724 Jun 49

Kefauver, E.  Needed changes in [anti-
trust] legislation. AER/S 38:182-202
May 48

Mason, E. S., chairman.  Round table on
preserving competition versus regulating monopoly. AER/S 30:213-18 Mar 40

Nicholls, W. H.  Constitutional aspects of
public regulation of business price
policies. JFE 25:560-82 Aug 43

Stauss, J. H.  The Supreme Court and the
architects of economic legislation.
JPE 56:138-56 Apr 48

Wallace, D.  Kinds of public control to replace or supplement antitrust laws.
AER/S 30:194-212 Mar 40

Watkins, M. W.  Present position and prospects of antitrust policy. AER/S 32,
no.2:89-135 Jun 42

### OTHER COUNTRIES

Bladen, V. W.  The Combines Investigation
C   Commission and post-war reconstruction. CJE 10:343-54 Aug 44

Froehlich, W. Changes in the central Euro-
EA   pean retail trade. JM 4:258-63 Jan 40

-- Aid for the independent retail trade: a
step toward fascism? JM 5:276-79
Jan 41

## 15.3 GOVERNMENT POLICY TOWARD MONOPOLY AND COMPETITION (Cont.)

### 15.30 GENERAL (Cont.)

OTHER COUNTRIES (Cont.)

EA    Reisner, E. Aid for the independent retail trade: a step toward fascism? JM 5: 163-66 Oct 40

EB    Cohen, R. The new British law on monopoly. AER 39:485-90 Mar 49

Lewis, W. A. The British Monopolies Act. MS 17:208-17 May 49

Plant, Sir A. Monopolies and restrictive practices. LBR 10:1-21 Oct 48

ESw    Ucker, P. Swiss retail trade and fascism. JM 6:50-53 Jul 41

FJ    Hadley, E. M. Trust busting in Japan. HBR 26:425-40 Jul 48

### 15.31 HISTORY

AA    Hayter, E. W. The western farmers and the drivewell patent controversy. AH 16: 16-28 Jan 42

EB    Ramsay, G. D. Industrial laisser-faire and the policy of Cromwell. EHR 16: 93-110 no.2, 46

EB    Stone, L. State control in sixteenth-century England. EHR 17:103-20 no.2, 47

### 15.32 MONOPOLY. COMBINATIONS. MERGERS

A    Adelman, M. A. The A&P case: a study in applied economic theory. QJE 63:238-57 May 49

A    -- The economic consequences of some recent antitrust decisions: the A & P case. AER/S 39:280-83 May 49

A    Edwards, C. D. [and others] The economic consequences of some recent antitrust decisions: discussion. AER/S 39:311-21 May 49

A    Nicholls, W. H. The Tobacco case of 1946. (Economic consequences of recent antitrust decisions) AER/S 39:284-96 May 49

A    Oxenfeldt, A. R. Monopoly dissolution: a proposal outlined. AER 36:384-91 Jun 46

### 15.33 RESTRICTIVE AGREEMENTS. TRADE ASSOCIATIONS

A    Brand, C. J. Experiences of a trade association in an antitrust suit [in the fertilizer industry]. JM 7:227-33 Jan 43

AA    Compton, W. The Southern Pine case. LE 16:214-16 May 40

A    Hays, J. S. and Ratzkin, J. L. Trade association practices and antitrust law. HBR 25:501-20 no.4, 47

A    Landry, R. S. The Federal Trade Commission and "unfair competition" in foreign trade. AER 35:575-84 Sep 45

A    Meyers, E. S. Some observations on the trade associations and the law. JM 12: 379-81 Jan 48

## 15.34 OTHER COMPETITIVE PRACTICES

### 15.341 BASING POINT

AA    Bliss, C. A. Some field notes on freight absorption [in New England]. HBR 26: 656-70 Nov 48

A    Clark, J. M. Law and economics of basing points. AER 39:430-47 Mar 49

A    -- Machlup on the basing-point system. R. QJE 63:315-21 Aug 49

A    Clark, T. C. New basing point problems. HBR 24:109-18 no.1, 45

A    Edwards, C. D. The effect of recent basing point decisions upon business practices. AER 38:828-42 Dec 48

A    Fetter, F. A. Exit basing point pricing. AER 38:815-27 Dec 48

A    Head, N. C. The basing point cases. HBR 26:641-55 Nov 48

A    Kaysen, C. Basing point pricing and public policy. QJE 63:289-314 Aug 49

A    Mund, V. A. The "freight allowed" method of price quotation. QJE 54:232-45 Feb 40

A    Nicols, A. The cement case. (Economic consequences of recent antitrust decisions) AER/S 39:297-310 May 49

A    Vaile, R. S. Federal Trade Commission v. Cement Institute. JM 13:224-26 Oct 48

A    Wooden, W. B. The cement basing point case. JM 13:220-22 Oct 48

### 15.342 DISCRIMINATION

A    Cassady, R., Jr. Legal aspects of price discrimination: federal law. JM 11: 258-72 Jan 47

AS    -- Legal aspects of price discrimination: state law. JM 11:377-89 Apr 47

### 15.343 RESALE PRICE MAINTENANCE. FAIR TRADE

A    Behoteguy, W. C. Resale price maintenance in the tire industry. JM 13:315-20 Jan 49

ASW    Burd, H. A. "Cost" under the Unfair Practices Act. [Case study of the state of Washington vs. the Great Atlantic and Pacific Tea Co.] JM 7:146-51 Oct 42

A    Edwards, C. D. Appraisal of "fair trade" and "unfair practices" acts. JM 5:3-15 Jul 40

A    Grether, E. T., chairman. Round table on price control under "fair trade" legislation. AER/S 30:112-17 Mar 40

A    -- Long run postwar aspects of price control. JM 8:296-301 Jan 44

A    -- The Federal Trade Commission versus resale price maintenance. JM 12:1-13 Jul 47

A    -- [In defense of "fair trade"]: rejoinder. JM 13:85-88 Jul 48

A    Griffiths, F. J. Further comments on prices under fair trade. JM 13:381-83 Jan 49

15.3 GOVERNMENT POLICY TOWARD MONOP-
OLY AND COMPETITION (Cont.)
15.343 RESALE PRICE MAINTENANCE.
FAIR TRADE (Cont.)
Kebker, V. W. Operation of the Unfair
ASK   Trade Practices Act in the large cities
of Kansas. JM 7:22-31 Jul 42
Peak, G. W. Administration of the Montana
ASM   Unfair Practices Act. JB 15:140-59
Apr 42
Phillips, C. F. Fair trade and the retail
A   drug store. JM 6:47-48 Jul 41
Seelye, A. L. Drug prices in cities with
ASK   and without a fair trade law [Kansas
ASM   City, Kansas and Kansas City, Missouri].
JM 6:16-21 Jul 41
Tannenbaum, R. Developments affecting
A   cost under the unfair practices acts.
JB 13:118-35 Apr 40

15.344 TYING AND EXCLUSIVE DEALING
CONTRACTS
Chambers, R. W. Block booking: blind
A   selling [in the motion picture industry].
HBR 19:496-507 no.4, 41

15.35 DISCRIMINATORY TAXATION
Brown, G. H. A note on federal taxation of
A   chain stores. JB 13:74-86 Jan 40
Craine, L. E. Chain store taxes as revenue
A   measures. NTJ 2:280-83 Sep 49
Due, J. F. The incidence of chain store
A   taxes. JM 5:128-36 Oct 40
Hardin, C. M. Are state margarine taxes
AS   constitutionally vulnerable? JFE 25:
677-83 Aug 43
Lee, M. W. Recent trends in chain-store
A   tax legislation. JB 13:253-74 Jul 40
Nicholls, W. H. Some economic aspects of
A   the margarine industry. JPE 54:221-42
Jun 46
Pabst, W. R., Jr. Interstate trade barriers
AS   and state oleomargarine taxes. SEJ 7:
505-17 Apr 41

15.36 PATENTS. TRADEMARKS
Borden, N. H. The new trade-mark law.
A   HBR 25:289-305 no.3, 47
Davis, W. H. Our national patent policy.
A   AER/S 38:235-44 May 48
Folk, G. E. [and others] Patent policy:
A   discussion. AER/S 38:245-60 May 48
Fox, H. G. Patents in relation to monopoly.
C   CJE 12:328-42 Aug 46
-- --- A rejoinder. CJE 13:68-80 Feb 47
Hutchinson, K. D. Design piracy. HBR 18:
A   191-98 no.2, 40
Kahn, A. E. Fundamental deficiencies of
A   the American patent law. AER 30:475-91
Sep 40
MacKeigan, I. M. Notes on "Patents in re-
C   lation to monopoly." CJE 12:470-82
Nov 46

Phelps, D. M. Certification marks under
A   the Lanham Act. JM 13:498-505 Apr 49
Plant, Sir A. Patent and copyright reform.
EB   TBR 3:3-21 Sep 49
Polanyi, M. Patent reform. REStud 11:
61-76 no.2, 44
Reik, R. Compulsory licensing of patents.
AER 36:813-82 Dec 46
Rewoldt, S. H. Assignment of trade marks.
A   JM 12:483-87 Apr 48
Vaughan, F. L. Patent policy. AER/S 38:
A   215-34 May 48

15.37 INTRANATIONAL TRADE BARRIERS
Ballaine, W. C. New England mutual sav-
AA   ings bank laws as interstate barriers to
the flow of capital. AER 35:155-59
Mar 45
Cassady, R., Jr. Trade barriers within
A   the United States. HBR 18:231-47
no.2, 40
-- Municipal trade barriers. HBR 19:
A   364-76 no.3, 41
Holzman, R. S. Interstate tax barriers to
A   marketing. JM 12:72-79 Jul 47
Howell, L. D. Internal trade barriers for
A   margarine. JFE 25:793-806 Nov 43
Logsdon, C. S. Taxation with misrepre-
A   sentation. JM 4,no.4,pt.2:11-16 Apr 40
Mickle, W. T. Margarine legislation.
A   JFE 23:567-83 Aug 41
Pabst, W. R., Jr. Interstate trade barriers
AS   and state oleomargine taxes. SEJ 7:
505-17 Apr 41
Salisbury, P. Planning sales campaigns in
A   forty-eight sovereignties. JM 4,no.4,
pt.2:17-24 Apr 40
Taylor, G. R. State laws which limit com-
AS   petition in agricultural products.
JFE 22:241-48 Feb 40
Waugh, F. V. State protectionism as a
AS   menace to a sound agricultural program.
JM 4,no.4,pt.2:5-10 Apr 40

15.4 OTHER GOVERNMENT POLICIES
TOWARD THE MARKET. PUBLIC
ENTERPRISE
15.40 GENERAL
Barker, J. M. Surveying the boundary
line between government and private
enterprise in the field of business.
AER/S 33:1-18 Mar 43
Courtauld, S. An industrialist's reflections
EB   on the future relations of government
and industry. EJ 52:1-17 Apr 42
Gordon, L. Government controls in war
A   and peace. BHR 20:42-51 Apr 46
Nicholls, W. H. Federal regulatory agen-
A   cies and the courts. AER 34:56-75
Mar 44
Ruggles, C. O. Government control of
A   business. HBR 24:32-50 no.1, 45

## 15.4 OTHER GOVERNMENT POLICIES TOWARD THE MARKET. PUBLIC ENTERPRISE (Cont.)

### 15.40 GENERAL (Cont.)

A   Watkins, M. W. Cushman on independent regulatory commissions. R. JPE 51: 547-50 Dec 43

### 15.41 HISTORY

EG   Brady, R. A. The economic impact of imperial Germany: industrial policy. JEH/S 3:108-23 Dec 43

Gras, N. S. B. Historical background [of government control]. BHR 20:36-42 Apr 46

Kirchberger, H. An ancient experience with price control. JFE 24:621-36 Aug 42

Michell, H. The edict of Diocletian: a study of price fixing in the Roman Empire. CJE 13:1-12 Feb 47

### 15.42 PUBLIC ENTERPRISE

EB   Angel, A. D. British use of public corporations. SR 14:321-31 Sep 47

Balakrishna, R. Public enterprise in a mixed economy. IJE 30:167-74 Oct 49

Balogh, T. Compensation and public boards. OIS 5:277-80 Dec 11, 43

EB   Brand, R. H. Nationalization. LBR 12: 1-11 Apr 49

Chowdhury, R. C. Nationalisation. IJE 27: 373-87 Apr 47

EB   Eastham, J. K. Compensation terms for nationalised industry. MS 16:29-45 Jan 48

EF   Einaudi, M. Nationalization in France and Italy. SR 15:22-43 Mar 48
EI

M   Grunwald, K. State and industry in the Middle East. EgC 31:225-31 Mar 40

Kumar, G. A note on some problems arising out of payment of compensation. IJE 29:399-402 Apr 49

EB   Neuman, A. M. Private profits and extra-budgetary revenue. OIS 6:178-83 Aug 12, 44

EB   Pegrum, D. F. The public corporation as a regulatory device. LE 16:335-43 Aug 40

A   Pray, K. L. Financial status of federal corporations. HBR 25:158-68 no.2, 47

FI   Rao, R. V. Mixed economy in theory and practice: with special reference to India. IJE 30:193-96 Oct 49

FI   Vaswani, M. H. Mixed economy in theory and practice. IJE 30:161-66 Oct 49

FI   Venkatesan, S. Nationalisation of industries: the role of local bodies (with special reference to Hyderabad State). IJE 29:301-06 Jan 49

### 15.43 MULTIPURPOSE PROJECTS

ASC   Angel, A. D. Wanted: one responsible administration for the Greater Central

Valley Project of California. LE 21: 136-43 May 45

ASC   -- Who will pay for the Central Valley Project of California? LE 22:266-72 Aug 46

EG   Brook, W. F. The German TVA. LE 20: 217-22 Aug 44

AA   Clapp, G. R. Problems of union relations in public agencies [illustrated by the case of TVA]. AER/S 33:184-96 Mar 43

AA   Gaston, T. L. A conservationist's appraisal of the Missouri development program. JFE 31,pt.2:1024-29 Nov 49

ASC   Goodall, M. R. Land and power administration of the Central Valley Project [of California]. LE 18:299-311 Aug 42

FI   -- River valley planning in India: the Damodar. LE 21:371-75 Sep 45

A   Kelso, H. "Navigable waters" as a legal fiction. LE 17:394-405 Nov 41

ASC   Moulton, J. S. Who will pay for the Central Valley Project of California? A reply [followed by R. A. Wehe's reply and A. D. Angel's rejoinder]. LE 23:86-90 Feb 47

AA   Renne, R. R. An economist's appraisal of the Missouri River development program. JFE 31,pt.2:1017-23 Nov 48

FIP   Salim, P. B. A. Irrigation and power development in Pakistan. PEJ 1,no.1: 33-39 Jul 49

AA   Schwartz, D. S. Investigations of the Columbia Basin project and their procedural significance. LE 23:83-86 Feb 47

AA   Short, J. A. An engineer's appraisal of the Missouri Basin development program. JFE 31,pt.2:1030-34 Nov 49

AA   Steele, H. A. The Missouri River development program. JFE 31,pt.2:1010-16 Nov 49

### 15.44 DIRECT CONTROLS

#### 15.440 GENERAL

EB   Hurstfield, J. The conrrol of British raw material supplies, 1919-1939. EHR 14: 1-31 no.1, 44

#### 15.441 PRICE CONTROL

A   Boulding, K. E. Price control in a subsequent deflation. (Ten economists on the inflation) REStat 30:15-17 Feb 48

Bronfenbrenner, M. Price control under imperfect competition: the joint production problem. CJE 15:210-16 May 49

A   Burley, O. E. [Price control]: discussion. JM 8:302-06 Jan 44

A   Galbraith, J. K. Reflections on price control. QJE 60:475-89 Aug 46

A   Grether, E. T. Long run postwar aspects of price control. JM 8:296-301 Jan 44

A   Isaacs, N. Price control by law. HBR 18: 504-09 no.4, 40

## 15. INDUSTRIAL ORGANIZATION AND PUBLIC POLICY

### 15.441 PRICE CONTROL (Cont.)

Lloyd, E. M. H.  Price control and control
of inflation.  REStat 27:149-55 Nov 45

Phillips, C. F.  Price control in immediate
A    postwar economy.  JM 8:289-95 Jan 44

Pitt, R. F.  Government price fixing in
EI    Italy, 1922-1940.  SEJ 8:218-37 Oct 41

Weintraub, S.  Inflation and price control.
HBR 18:429-36 no.4, 40

Wolff, R. P.  Foreign experience with re-
E    tail price controls.  JM 5:143-47 Oct 40

Worswick, G. D. N. and Martin, K.  Prices
EB    and wages policy.  OIS 10:84-93 Mar 48

### 15.442 RENT CONTROL

Bloomberg, L. N.  Rent control and the
A    housing shortage.  LE 23:214-18 May 47

### 15.443 RATIONING

Chossudowsky, E. M.  Rationing in the
ER    U.S.S.R.  REStud 8:143-65 Jun 41

-- De-rationing in the U.S.S.R.  REStud 9:
ER    1-27 Nov 41

Lloyd, E. M. H.  Some notes on point
rationing.  REStat 24:49-52 May 42

Scitovszky, T.  The political economy of
consumers' rationing.  REStat 24:
114-24 Aug 42

Smith, H. F.  Food controls in occupied
FJ    Japan.  AH 23:220-23 Jul 49

### 15.45 NATIONAL RECOVERY ADMINISTRA-
TION (U.S.)

Bernstein, I.  Labor and the recovery program, 1933.  QJE 60:270-88 Feb 46

Guthrie, J. A.  Price regulation in the
paper industry.  QJE 60:194-218 Feb 46

### 15.46 CONSUMER PROTECTION

Bader, L. and Hotchkiss, G. B.  Attitudes
A    of teachers of marketing toward con-
sumer grade labeling.  JM 6:274-79
Jan 42

Bayard, C. C.  The defective United States
A    retail price structure.  SEJ 11:1-19
Jul 44

Brown, W. F.  The Federal Trade Commis-
A    sion and false advertising.  Pt.I-II.
JM 12:38-46; 193-201 Jul,Oct 47

Coles, J. V. and Erdman, H. E.  Some aspects of the arguments against grade
labeling.  JM 9:256-61 Jan 45

Douglas, E.  Protection offered to con-
ASN    sumers by the North Carolina state government.  JM 7:32-40 Jul 42

Freer, R. E.  Informative and nondeceptive
A    advertising.  JM 13:358-63 Jan 49

Hotchkiss, G. B.  Some fundamental objec-
A    tions to mandatory A B C grades.
JM 10:128-34 Oct 45

Kebker, V. W.  Will grade labeling pay?
ASK    [A study made in Lawrence, Kansas]
JM 8:185-88 Oct 43

Mossman, F. H.  Grade labeling for canned
A    fruits and vegetables.  JM 7:241-44
Jan 43

Payne, H.  Standardized description, a
A    form of specification labeling.  JM 12:
234-41 Oct 47

Tousley, R. D.  The Federal Food, Drug,
A    and Cosmetic Act of 1938.  JM 5:259-69
Jan 41

Wadsworth, H. E.  Utility cloth and clothing
EB    scheme.  REStud 16:82-101 no.2, 49

Williams, F. M. and Hoover, E. D.  Measuring price and quality of consumers'
goods.  JM 10:354-69 Apr 46

Yolande, M., sister.  Some economic and
ethical considerations for legislation
protecting the consumer.  RSE 7,no.1:
73-81 Mar 49

### 15.5 INDUSTRY STUDIES
### 15.50 GENERAL

Baykov, A.  Development of industrial pro-
ER    duction in the U.S.S.R.  Ec N.S.8:94-103
Feb 41

Gerschenkron, A.  The rate of industrial
ER    growth in Russia since 1885.  JEH/S 7:
144-74 '47

Kazakevich, V. D.  The economic strength
ER    of the Soviet Union.  S&S 5:385-89
no.4, 41

Thirlby, G. F.  The Report of the Rural
HSA    Industries Commission. (U.G. no.27,
1940)  SAJE 8:303-11 Sep 40

### 15.501 LOCATION OF INDUSTRY

Anantaram, K.  The future of industrial
FI    location.  IJE 27:157-62 Oct 46

Baykov, A.  The location of heavy industry
ER    in the U.S.S.R.  OIS 3:252-56 Aug 9, 41

Hammond, S.  Location theory and the cotton industry.  JEH/S 2:101-17 Dec 42

Isard, W.  Some locational factors in the
iron and steel industry since the early
nineteenth century.  JPE 56:203-17
Jun 48

-- and Capron, W. M.  The future locational
A    pattern of iron and steel production in
the United States.  JPE 57:118-33 Apr 49

Rao, R. V.  Location of industry in India.
FI    IJE 27:140-48 Oct 46

Row, B. G.  The theory of location of indus-
FI    tries with reference to India.  IJE 27:
122-30 Oct 46

Vaswani, M. H.  The theory of location of
FI    industries.  IJE 27:149-56 Oct 46

### 15.51 HISTORY

Gerschenkron, A.  The rate of industrial
ER    growth in Russia since 1885.  JEH/S 7:
144-74 '47

Horie, Y.  The development of the domes-
FJ    tic market in the early years of Meiji.
Kyo 15,no.1:45-59 Jan 40

## 15.5 INDUSTRY STUDIES (Cont.)
### 15.51 HISTORY (Cont.)

EG   Kuczynski, J. Productivity and exploitation under German capitalism. S&S 9: 55-66 no.1, 45

EF   Morazé, P. The Treaty of 1860 and the industry of the Department of the North. EHR 10:18-28 Feb 40

### 15.52 MANUFACTURING INDUSTRIES
#### 15.520 GENERAL

AA   Bonham, H. D. The prospect for heavy industry in the South. SEJ 13:395-403 Apr 47

HSA   Busschau, W. J. The expansion of manufacturing industry in the Union. R. SAJE 13:215-31 Sep 45

A   Carson, D. Incomparabilities in "Census of manufactures" data. AER 31:559-60 Sep 41

A   Chawner, L. J. Some recent changes in industrial markets. JM 6,no.4,pt.2:53-65 Apr 42

ECC   Goldmann, J. Czechoslovak industry after nationalization. OIS 8:88-90 Mar 46

EB   Hill, W. Planning industry's future in Britain. HBR 22:129-38 no.2, 44

EB   -- Whither British industry? HBR 22: 328-36 no.3, 44

C   MacGregor, D. C. Manufacturers' expenses, net production, and rigid costs in Canada. REStat 27:60-73 May 45

FC   Sen Gupta, R. N. China's Indusco. IJE 23: 277-81 Jan 43

A   Spengler, J. J. Regional differences and the future of manufacturing in America. SEJ 7:475-93 Apr 41

HSA   Threlfell, R. L. Some comments on secondary industry in South Africa. SAJE 14: 288-304 Dec 46

#### 15.521 HISTORY

A   Gibb, G. S. The pre-industrial revolution in America: a field for local research. BHR 20:103-16 Oct 46

FI   Gras, N. S. B. A great Indian industrialist: Jamsetji Nusserwanji Tata, 1839-1904. BHR 23:149-51 Sep 49

FJ   Horie, Y. The encouragement of kokusan or native products in the Tokugawa period. Kyo 16,no.2:44-63 Apr 41

#### 15.522 METALS
##### 15.5221 HISTORY

EB   Burn, D. L. Recent trends in the history of the steel industry. EHR 17:95-102 no.2, 47

EB   Chaloner, W. H. Further light on the invention of the process for smelting iron ore with coke. EHR II.2:185-87 no.2, 49

Isard, W. Some locational factors in the iron and steel industry since the early nineteenth century. JPE 56:203-17 Jun 48

A   Marburg, T. F. Imperfect competition: in brass manufacturing during the 1830's. JEH/S 3:33-37 Dec 43

A   -- Manufacturer's drummer, 1832. BHR 22:40-56 Apr 48

A   -- Manufacturer's drummer, 1852, with comments on western and southern markets. BHR 22:106-14 Jun 48

##### 15.5222 IRON AND STEEL

Hexner, E. American participation in the International Steel Cartel. SEJ 8:54-79 Jul 41

Isard, W. Some locational factors in the iron and steel industry since the early nineteenth century. JPE 56:203-17 Jun 48

Tew, B. Reports on the iron and steel industry. R. EJ 56:487-99 Sep 46

UNITED STATES

A   Barloon, M. The question of steel capacity. HBR 27:209-36 Mar 49

Blair, J. M. Price discrimination in steel: a reply. AER 33:369-70 Jun 43

Ezekiel, M. and Wylie, K. H. Cost functions for the steel industry. JASA 36: 91-99 Mar 41

Harris, S. E. [Comments on the steel report.] Introductory remarks. REStat 31: 280-82 Nov 49

Isard, W. and Capron, W. M. The future locational pattern of iron and steel production in the United States. JPE 57: 118-33 Apr 49

Juliber, G. S. Relation between seasonal amplitudes and the level of production; an application to the production of steel ingots. JASA 36:485-92 Dec 41

Leontief, W. Elasticity of demand computed from cost data. AER 30:814-17 Dec 40

Lewis, H. G. The nature of the demand for steel. JASA 36:110-15 Mar 41

Mosak, J. L. Some theoretical implications of the statistical analysis of demand and cost functions for steel. JASA 36:100-10 Mar 41

Nathan, R. R. Comments of Sumner H. Slichter [on the steel report]. REStat 31: 288-91 Nov 49

Slichter, S. H. Raising the price of labor as a method of increasing employment. (Comments on the steel report) REStat 31:283-88 Nov 49

Smith, C. A. The cost-output relation for the U.S. Steel Corporation. REStat 24: 166-76 Nov 42

Stigler, G. J. A note on Price discrimination in steel. AER 32:354-55 Jun 42

Tower, W. S. Steel to meet our needs. HBR 20:34-42 no.1, 41

15.52 MANUFACTURING INDUSTRIES (Cont.)
15.5222 IRON AND STEEL (Cont.)
UNITED STATES (Cont.)

Wein, H. H. Wages and prices: a case
A   study [of the U.S. Steel Corporation].
REStat 29:108-23 May 47

Wylie, K. H. and Ezekiel, M. The cost
curve for steel production. JPE 48:
777-821 Dec 40

Northrup, H. R. The Negro and unionism
ASA   in the Birmingham, Ala., iron and steel
industry. SEJ 10:27-40 Jul 43

OTHER COUNTRIES

Shone, R. M. The iron and steel develop-
EB   ment plan: some statistical considerations [with discussion]. JRSS 110:
283-309 pt.4, 47

Worswick, G. D. N. Steel prices. OIS 5:
151-55 Jun 26, 43

-- Note on steel prices. OIS 5:284-88
Dec 11, 43

Lachmann, K. The Hermann Göring Works.
EG   SR 8:24-40 Feb 41

Sinigaglia, O. The future of the Italian iron
EI   and steel industry. BNL 1:240-45 Jan 48

Fetter, F. A. The pricing of steel in South
HSA   Africa. R. SAJE 9:235-50 Sep 41

15.5223 OTHER METALS

Anderson, K. L. The pricing of copper and
A   copper alloy scrap and of brass and
bronze ingot. AER/S 33:295-302 Mar 43

Backman, J. and Fishman, L. British war-
EB   time control of copper, lead, and zinc.
QJE 55:210-38 Feb 41

-- and Fishman, L. British war time con-
EB   trol of aluminum. QJE 56:18-48 Nov 41

Brewer, A. L. The beryllium industry: a
A   case study in monopolistic competition.
EG   SEJ 8:336-50 Jan 42

Engle, N. H. The Pacific Northwest light
AA   metals industry. JM 8:253-59 Jan 44

Fishman, L. Wartime control of tin in
EB   Great Britain, 1939-41. JPE 54:413-35
Oct 46

Goldstein, M. D. War-time aluminum sta-
A   tistics. JASA 41:34-52 Mar 46

Kemp, A. Chromium: a strategic material.
A   HBR 20:199-212 no.2, 42

Moos, S. Aluminium prices. OIS 5:280-83
Dec 11, 43

-- The change in non-ferrous metal prices.
OIS 6:117-24 Jun 10, 44

-- Price formation and price maintenance
on the aluminium market. MS 16:66-93
Jan 48

-- The structure of the British aluminium
EB   industry. EJ 58:522-37 Dec 48

Muller, C. Aluminum and power control.
A   LE 21:108-24 May 45

Sumner, J. D. Differential pricing in non-
A   ferrous metals. AER/S 33:279-86 Mar 43

Walters, A. The International Copper
Cartel. SEJ 11:133-56 Oct 44

15.523 MACHINERY. TOOLS. ELECTRICAL
EQUIPMENT AND APPLIANCES.
CASTINGS
15.5230 GENERAL

Anonymous. British television for export.
EB   TBR 3:22-28 Sep 49

Bright, A. A., Jr. and MacLaurin, W. R.
A   Economic factors influencing the development and introduction of the fluorescent lamp. JPE 51:429-50 Oct 43

-- and Exter, J. War, radar, and the radio
industry. HBR 25:255-72 no.2, 47

Crowder, W. F. Market outlook for ma-
A   chines and equipment. [Abstract]
AER/S 39:420-21 May 49

Dean, J. Direct control of machinery
A   prices. HBR 20:277-89 no.3, 42

Gustin, R. P. and Holme, S. A. An approach
A   to postwar planning [by the General
Electric Company]. HBR 20:459-72
no.4, 42

Hart, C. W. M. The Hawthorne experi-
C   ments [in the Western Electric Company's plant]. CJE 9:150-63 May 43

Neiswanger, W. A. Price control in the
A   machinery industries. AER/S 33:287-94
Mar 43

Rebensburg, G. A. Market analysis: a case
A   study [in the electric appliance field].
JM 9:141-43 Oct 44

Tremelloni, R. Premises and tasks of the
EI   special fund for financing the Italian
engineering industry. BNL 1:169-83
Oct 47

Walker, C. L., Jr. Education and training
A   at International Harvester. HBR 27:
542-58 Sep 49

15.5231 HISTORY

Cule, J. E. Finance and industry in the
EB   eighteenth century: the firm of Boulton
and Watt. EH 4:319-25 Feb 40

Larson, H. M. An early industrial capital-
ASC   ist's labor policy and management
[Samuel Watkinson Collins, manufacturer
of cutting tools in Connecticut]. BHR 18:
132-41 Nov 44

Loehr, R. C. Saving the kerf: the intro-
A   duction of the band saw mill. AH 23:
168-72 Jul 49

Navin, T. R., Jr. The Wellman-Woodman
A   patent controversy in the cotton textile
machinery industry. BHR 21:144-52
Nov 47

Passer, H. C. E. H. Goff: an entrepreneur
A   who failed. EEH 1,no.5:17-25 May 49

Perry, J. M. Sketch of the life and work of
ASM   Milton Prince Higgins, 1842-1912 [of
Worcester, Massachusetts]. BHR 18:
33-54 Jun 44

15.52  MANUFACTURING INDUSTRIES (Cont.)
15.523  MACHINERY.  TOOLS.  ELECTRICAL
EQUIPMENT AND APPLIANCES.
CASTINGS (Cont.)
15.5231  HISTORY (Cont.)

Peterson, A. G.  Governmental policy relat-
A    ing to farm machinery in World War I.
AH 17:31-40 Jan 43

Redlich, F.  The leaders of the German
EG    steam-engine industry during the first
hundred years. JEH 4:121-48 Nov 44

Smith, G. W.  A rising industry's battle for
ASR    the Morrill tariff [The American Screw
Company of Providence, R.I.].  BHR 16:
106-11 Dec 42


15.524  TRANSPORTATION EQUIPMENT
15.5240  GENERAL

Bailer, L. H.  The Negro automobile worker.
A    JPE 51:415-28 Oct 43

Bollinger, L. L. and Lilley, T.  Maintain-
A    ing a strong aircraft industry. HBR 22:
178-90 no.2, 44

-- Marketing personal airplanes.  HBR 23:
A    217-28 no.2, 45

Burden, W. A. M.  Postwar status of the
A    aircraft industry.  HBR 23:211-16
no.2, 45

Gilbert, H. N.  The emergency in aircraft
A    manufacture.  HBR 19:508-19 no.4, 41

-- The expansion of shipbuilding.  HBR 20:
A    156-70 no.2, 42

Haddon-Cave, C. P.  Shipping and ship-
N    building.  ER 23:274-76 Dec 47

Knox, J. M.  Private enterprise in ship-
A    building.  HBR 24:75-84 no.1, 45

Lewis, H. T. and Livesey, C. A.  Materials
A    management in the airframe industry.
HBR 22:477-94 no.4, 44

Leyland, N. H.  A note on price and quality
EB    [in the bicycle industry].  OEP N.S.1:
269-72 Jun 49

Lloyd, I. S.  The environment of business
EB    decision; some reflections on the history
of Rolls-Royce.  SAJE 17:457-79 Dec 49

Lovett, R. W.  The Thompson Products col-
A    lection [on the company's labor rela-
tions].  BHR 23:191-95 Dec 49

McDiarmid, O. J.  Some aspects of the
C    Canadian automobile industry.  CJE 6:
258-74 May 40

Northrup, H. R.  Negroes in a war industry:
A    the case of shipbuilding.  JB 16:160-72
Jul 43

Reder, M. W.  The significance of the 1948
A    General Motors agreement.  REStat 31:
7-14 Feb 49

Roberts, M. J.  Recent innovations in rail-
A    road freight and passenger equipment.
JB 13:56-73 Jan 40

Ross, A. M.  The General Motors wage
A    agreement of 1948.  REStat 31:1-7
Feb 49

Smith, V. E.  Nonlinearity in the relation
C    between input and output: the Canadian
automobile industry, 1918-1930.  Em 13:
260-72 Jul 45

Stokes, R. S.  A shipyard from within.
EB    MS 17:88-96 Jan 49

Tremelloni, R.  Premises and tasks of the
EI    special fund for financing the Italian
engineering industry.  BNL 1:169-83
Oct 47

Weaver, R. C.  Negro employment in the
A    aircraft industry.  QJE 59:597-625
Aug 45

Worswick, G. D. N.  Aircraft production.
EB    OIS 5:211-16 Sep 18, 43


15.5241  HISTORY

Chapman, D.  The New Shipwright Building
EBS    Company of Dundee, 1826 to 1831.
EHR 10:148-51 Nov 40

Condron, H. D.  The Knapheide Wagon Com-
ASI    pany 1848-1943 [of Quincy, Illinois].
JEH 3:32-41 May 43

Gibb, G. S.  Three early railroad equipment
ASM    contracts [of the Locks and Canals Company of Lowell, Massachusetts].  BHR 21:
10-17 Feb 47

Woodwell, W. H.  The Woodwell shipyard,
ASM    1759-1852 [in Newburyport, Massachu-
setts].  BHR 21:58-74 Jun 47


15.525  CHEMICALS.  DRUGS.  PLASTICS.
CERAMICS.  GLASS.  RUBBER
15.5250  GENERAL

Baldwin, W. H.  The McKesson & Robbins
A    reorganization.  HBR 20:473-82 no.4, 42

Bauer, P. T.  Rubber and foreign exchange.
EB    EJ 50:231-41 Jun-Sep 40

-- Future competition between natural and
synthetic rubber.  MS 14,no.2:40-64
May 46

Behoteguy, W. C.  Resale price maintenance
A    in the tire industry.  JM 13:315-20 Jan 49

Belley, B.  Toward a measure of pharma-
A    ceutical advertising effectiveness. JB 16:
107-14 Apr 43

Bloor, W. F.  Postwar rubber industry
A    capacities and implications.  JM 10:
279-81 Jan 46

Branch, F. T.  A comparison of direct-
A    mail and magazine cost in pharmaceutical advertising.  JB 18:78-95 Apr 45

Copeland, M. T.  Price trends of industrial
A    chemicals.  HBR 18:437-47 no.4, 40

Dymond, W. R.  Union-management co-op-
CPO    eration at the Toronto factory of Lever
Brothers Limited.  CJE 13:26-67 Feb 47

Friedlaender, H. E.  The story of the nit-
EF    rogen process in France: an experiment
in post-war planning.  JB 16:247-52
Oct 43

Gaffey, J. D.  Labor productivity in tire
A    manufacturing: a reply to L. G. Reynolds.
AER 31:837-38 Dec 41

# 15. INDUSTRIAL ORGANIZATION AND PUBLIC POLICY

15.52 MANUFACTURING INDUSTRIES (Cont.)
15.525 CHEMICALS. DRUGS. PLASTICS.
        CERAMICS. GLASS. RUBBER (Cont.)
15.5250 GENERAL (Cont.)

    Gettell, R. G. Changing competitive condi-
A   tions in the marketing of tires. JM 6:
    112-23 Oct 41

    Halpern, D. B. The plastic industry.
    OIS 6:125-30 Jun 10, 44

    Howard, F. A. Synthetic rubber. HBR 20:
A   1-9 no.1, 41

    Kellett, W. G. G. International rubber sta-
    tistics. JRSS 112:419-35 pt.4, 49

    Knorr, K. E. World rubber problems.
    HBR 24:394-404 no.3, 46

    MacGowan, T. G. Trends in tire distribu-
A   tion. JM 10:265-69 Jan 46

    Moos, S. Natural versus synthetic rubber.
    OIS 5:51-55 Feb 20, 43; Erratum. 72
    Mar 13, 43

    Rand, R. B. Pharmaceutical advertising to
A   doctors. JB 14:150-68 Apr 41

    Schalk, A. F., Jr. Significant merchandis-
A   ing trends of the independent tire dealer.
    JM 12:462-69 Apr 48

    Smith, A. G. Synthetics versus Singapore.
    LE 24:89-94 Feb 48

    Wendt, P. The control of rubber in World
A   War II. SEJ 13:203-27 Jan 47

    Winters, R. A. Aspects of joint bargaining
A   in the rubber industry. ILRR 3:3-16
    Oct 49

    Wood, R. C. The control of rubber: a case
A   study. JM 7:99-106 Oct 42

    Worswick, G. D. N. The Pottery Working
EB   Party Report. R. OIS 8:217-31 Jul 46

15.5251 HISTORY

    Clow, A. and Clow, N. L. Vitriol in the
EB   industrial revolution. EHR 15:44-55
    no.1-2, 45

    Pounds, N. J. G. The discovery of china
E    clay. EHR II.1:20-33 no.1, 48

    Schauder, H. The chemical industry in
HSA  South Africa: before union (1910).
    SAJE 14:277-87 Dec 46

    Scoville, W. C. Technology and the French
EF   glass industry, 1640-1740. JEH 1:153-67
    Nov 41

    -- State policy and the French glass indus-
EF   try, 1640-1789. QJE 56:430-55 May 42

    -- Large-scale production in the French
EF   plate-glass industry, 1665-1789. JPE 50:
    669-98 Oct 42

    -- Growth of the American glass industry
A    to 1880. [Pt.I-II] JPE 52:193-216;
    340-55 Sep, Dec 44

15.526 TEXTILES. LEATHER. CLOTHING
15.5260 GENERAL

    Halpern, D. B. The rayon industry and the
    war. OIS 4:136-42 Apr 25, 42

    Hammond, S. Location theory and the cot-
    ton industry. JEH/S 2:101-17 Dec 42

    Hyson, C. D. Maladjustments in the wool
    industry and need for new policy.
    JFE 29:425-56 May 47

## UNITED STATES

    Allen, C. L. Rayon staple fiber: its past
A   and its prospects. SEJ 13:146-57
    Oct 46

    Backman, J. The budget approach to wage
    adjustments: a case study [in the textile
    industry]. JPE 55:57-64 Feb 47

    Baker, J. C. Executive compensation by
    small textile companies. HBR 20:81-91
    no.1, 41

    Besse, A. The current status of wool
    textiles. HBR 20:223-32 no.2, 42

    Brainard, H. G. Price control in the cot-
    ton textile industry. SEJ 12:151-60
    Oct 45

    Cahen, A. Merchandising flow survey on
    men's clothing. [Abstract] AER/S 39:
    416-18 May 49

    -- Measuring the merchandise flow of men's
    clothing. JM 14:67-71 Jul 49

    Cohn, F. M. Educational Department,
    ILGWU. ILRR 1:704-08 Jul 48

    Douty, H. M. Minimum wage regulations
    in the seamless hosiery industry.
    SEJ 8:176-90 Oct 41

    Held, A. Health and welfare funds in the
    needle trades. ILRR 1:247-63 Jan 48

    Hinrichs, A. F. Effects of the 25-cent
    minimum wage on employment in the
    seamless hosiery industry. JASA 35:
    13-23 Mar 40

    Wolf, R. B. Collective bargaining in small-
    scale industry: a case study [in the
    hosiery manufacturing industry]. HBR 27:
    706-14 Nov 49

    Barkin, S. The regional significance of the
AA  integration movement in the southern
    textile industry. SEJ 15:395-411 Apr 49

    Markham, J. W. Regional labor productivity
    in the textile industry. AER 33:110-15
    Mar 43

    Palmer, G. L. The mobility of weavers in
    three textile centers. QJE 55:460-87
    May 41

    Brissenden, P. F. and Keating, J. M. Union-
ASN management co-operation in millinery
    manufacturing in the New York metro-
    politan area. ILRR 2:3-32 Oct 48

    De Vyver, F. T. After the shutdown: an
ASN analysis of the job-hunting experience
    of a group of Durham hosiery workers.
    JPE 48:105-13 Feb 40

## EUROPE

    Allen, G. C. The Report of the Working
EB   Party on the Cotton Industry. MS 14,
    no.3:60-73 Sep 46

15.52 MANUFACTURING INDUSTRIES (Cont.)
15.526 TEXTILES. LEATHER. CLOTHING
(Cont.)
15.5260 GENERAL (Cont.)
EUROPE (Cont.)

EB   Anonymous. A note on the merchanting of Lancashire cotton goods. MS 15:215-22 May 47

Armitage, G. Lancashire. MS 14,no.1: 72-76 Jan 46

Balogh, T. Notes on the cotton industry. 2. The spreadover in weaving. OIS 3: 55-56 Feb 22, 41

Bowen, I. and Worswick, G. D. N. The cotton industry. OIS 2,no.8:9-11 Oct 40

Briggs, A. The framework of the wool control. OEP 8:18-45 Nov 47

Brunner, E. The origins of industrial peace: the case of the British boot and shoe industry. OEP N.S.1:247-59 Jun 49

Ellis, A. W. T. The present position of the boot and shoe industry. OIS 2,no.3: 2-4 Jun 30, 40

Jones, E. Price leadership in the rayon industry. MS 12:80-96 Oct 41

Lacey, R. W. Cotton's war effort. MS 15: 26-74 Jan 47

Lomax, K. S. Analysis of demand and supply in textiles. MS 16:46-65 Jan 48

Moos, S. Some features of British cotton exports. OIS 4:93-98 Mar 14, 42

Nawrocki, Z. The prospects of the British cotton industry. EJ 54:41-46 Apr 44

Rostas, L. Productivity of labour in the cotton industry. EJ 55:192-205 Jun-Sep 45

Silverman, H. A. The optimum firm in the boot and shoe industry. OEP 6:95-111 Apr 42

Tippett, L. H. C. The study of industrial efficiency, with special reference to the cotton industry with discussion]. JRSS 110:108-22 pt.2, 47

Wadsworth, H. E. Utility cloth and clothing scheme. REStud 16:82-101 no.2, 49

Worswick, G. D. N. Notes on the cotton industry. I. The future of the industry. OIS 3:53-55 Feb 22, 41

-- Concentration in the hosiery industry. OIS 3:97-98 Apr 5, 41

-- Concentration in the Leicester hosiery industry. OIS 3:118-23 Apr 26, 41

-- The release of labour from the cotton industry. OIS 3:135-40 May 17, 41

EBI   Beacham, A. The Ulster linen industry. Ec N.S.11:199-209 Nov 44

-- Post-war planning the Ulster linen industry. EJ 55:114-21 Apr 45

OTHER COUNTRIES

FI   Chand, M. A note on the cotton textile industry in India. IJE 30:41-54 Jul 49

Das, N. K. Prospects of cotton mill industry in Bengal. IJE 28:533-46 Apr 48

Sen, S. R. Marketing and production control in the Indian jute textile industry (1884-1943). IJE 28:483-508 Apr 48

N   Dedman, M. Integration in the Australian wool textile industry. ER 24:111-16 Jun 48

15.5261 HISTORY

EB   Armytage, W. H. G. A. J. Mundella and the hosiery industry. EHR 18:91-99 no.1-2, 48

AA   Bliss, C. A. A history of Pepperell [a cotton textile company of New England]. R. BHR 23:104-06 Jun 49

EB   Carus-Wilson, E. M. The English cloth industry in the late twelfth and early thirteenth centuries. EHR 14:32-50 no.1, 44

AA   Chen, C. H. Regional differences in costs and productivity in the American cotton manufacturing industry, 1880-1910. QJE 55:533-66 Aug 41

ASN   Creamer, D. Recruiting contract laborers for the Amoskeag mills [in New Hampshire]. JEH 1:42-56 May 41

E   Lennard, R. V. An early fulling-mill: a note. EHR 17:150 no.2, 47

EI   Lopez, R. The life of the Genoese wool-workers as revealed in thirteenth-century notarial records. BHR 16: 101-05 Dec 42

ASM   Perry, J. M. Samuel Snow, tanner and cordwainer [of North Berwick, Maine]. BHR 19:183-93 Dec 45

EB   Taylor, A. J. Concentration and specialization in the Lancashire cotton industry, 1825-1850. EHR II.1:114-22 no.2-3, 49

15.527 FOREST PRODUCTS. BUILDING MATERIALS
15.5270 GENERAL

Glesinger, E. Forest products in a world economy. AER/S 35:120-29 May 45

UNITED STATES

A   Dickerman, A. B. Wastepaper. HBR 20: 446-58 no.4, 42

Guthrie, J. A. Price regulation in the paper industry. QJE 60:194-218 Feb 46

Hanks, J. J. The paper industry in the emergency. HBR 19:151-58 no.2, 41

Hood, A. A. What's ahead in building material marketing? [Abstract] AER/S 39: 418-20 May 49

Hosmer, W. A. Business organization for effective use of forest products. HBR 26: 581-96 Sep 48

James L. M. Restrictive agreements and practices in the lumber industry, 1880-1939. SEJ 13:115-25 Oct 46

Loehr, R. C. Saving the kerf: the introduction of the band saw mill. AH 23: 168-72 Jul 49

15.52  MANUFACTURING INDUSTRIES (Cont.)
15.527  FOREST PRODUCTS. BUILDING MA-
         TERIALS (Cont.)
15.5270  GENERAL (Cont.)
    UNITED STATES (Cont.)
    Long, C. D., Jr.  News print: costs and
A    competition.  HBR 18:372-83 no.3, 40
    Maclaurin, W. R.  Wages and profits in the
         paper industry, 1929-1939.  QJE 58:
         196-228 Feb 44
    Nicols, A.  The cement case.  (Economic
         consequences of recent antitrust deci-
         sions)  AER/S 39:297-310 May 49
    Starbuck, P. L.  A report on the organiza-
         tion of the Paper Cup Company.  JB 17:
         118-25 Apr 44
    Vaile, R. S.  Federal Trade Commission v.
         Cement Institute.  JM 13:224-26 Oct 48
    Wooden, W. B.  The cement basing point
         case.  JM 13:220-22 Oct 48
    Compton, W.  The Southern Pine case.
AA    LE 16:214-16 May 40
    Eliel, P.  Industrial peace and conflict: a
         study of two Pacific Coast industries
         [pulp and paper and stevedoring].
         ILRR 2:477-501 Jul 49
    Faville, D. E.  The impact of the war on
         Pacific Coast paper distributors.  JM 8:
         133-36 Oct 43
    Folweiler, A. D.  Cotton, wood pulp, and the
         man-land ratio of the deep South.  SEJ 7:
         518-28 Apr 41
    Hicks, W. T.  Recent expansion in the
         southern pulp and paper industry.  SEJ 6:
         440-48 Apr 40
    Burtt, E. J., Jr.  After the shutdown in
ASM  Howland, Maine.  SEJ 8:80-87 Jul 41

    OTHER COUNTRIES
    Bladen, V. W.  Report on an alleged com-
C    bine in the paper board shipping con-
         tainer industry.  CJE 6:293-96 May 40
    Maclaurin, W. R.  Wages and profits in the
         paper industry, 1929-39.  QJE 58:
         196-228 Feb 44
    Bowen, I.  A new index number of building
EB   materials' prices.  OIS 8:352-58 Nov 46
    -- Building materials supply.  YB 1:1-18
         Dec 48
    Bowley, A. L.  The paper shortage: A.
         Paper and books.  OIS 3:338-40 Nov 1, 41
    Leyland, N. H.  The paper shortage: B.
         The control of paper.  OIS 3:341-42
         Nov 1, 41
    Moos, S.  The cost of building materials.
         OIS 5:241-47 Oct 30, 43
    Chand, M.  A note on the paper industry.
FI   IJE 29:59-65 Jul 48
    Hocking, D. M.  Paper industries in war-
N    time. II. The economic implications of
         newsprint rationing.  ER 17:224-30
         Dec 41

    Kelly, I. M.  Paper industries in war-time.
         I.  Rationing of paper in war-time.
         ER 17:218-24 Dec 41

15.5271  HISTORY
    Burnett, E. C.  Shingle making on the
AST  lesser waters of the Big Creek of the
         French Broad River [Tennessee].
         AH 20:225-35 Oct 46
    Dennison, H. S.  Imperfect competition:
ASM  In the Dennison Manifacturing Company
         [Framingham, Massachusetts].
         JEH/S 3:48-50 Dec 43
    Lopez, R.  The English and the manufacture
EI   of writing materials in Genoa.  EHR 10:
         132-37 Nov 40
    Sharp, P. F.  The war of the substitutes:
A    the reaction of the forest industries to
         the competition of wood substitutes.
         AH 23:274-79 Oct 49

15.528  FOOD PROCESSING. TOBACCO.
         BEVERAGES
15.5280  GENERAL
    Lockley, L. C.  Dehydrated foods.  HBR 21:
         253-58 no.2, 43
    Moos, S.  Prospects of the tobacco trade.
         OIS 3:85-91 Apr 5, 41
    -- The effect of war on the sugar industry.
         OIS 3:348-55 Nov 1, 41

    UNITED STATES
    Backman, J.  Flexibility of cheese prices.
A    JPE 48:579-82 Aug 40
    Bressler, R. G., Jr.  Research determina-
         tion of economies of scale [in the oper-
         ation of milk plants].  JFE 27:526-39
         Aug 45
    Howell, L D.  Internal trade barriers for
         margarine.  JFE 25:793-806 Nov 43
    Hyson, C. D. and Sanderson, F. H.  Monop-
         olistic discrimination in the cranberry
         industry.  QJE 59:330-69 May 45
    Mickle, W. T.  Margarine legislation.
         JFE 23:567-83 Aug 41
    Nicholls, W. H.  Market-sharing in the
         packing industry.  JFE 22:225-40 Feb 40;
         A correction.  497 May 40
    -- Price flexibility and concentration in the
         agricultural processing industries.
         JPE 48:883-88 Dec 40
    -- Imperfect competition in agricultural
         processing and distributing industries.
         CJE 10:150-64 May 44
    -- Some economic aspects of the margarine
         industry.  JPE 54:221-42 Jun 46
    Teele, S. F. and Bursk, E. C.  Marketing
         practices of food manufacturers.  HBR 22:
         358-76 no.3, 44
    Tracey, M. B.  The present status of frozen
         food marketing.  JM 13:470-80 Apr 49
    Cutshall, A.  The manufacture of food and
AA   kindred products in the lower Wabash
         Valley.  AH 18:16-22 Jan 44

15.52 MANUFACTURING INDUSTRIES (Cont.)
15.528 FOOD PROCESSING. TOBACCO.
BEVERAGES (Cont.)
15.5280 GENERAL (Cont.)
UNITED STATES (Cont.)

Hardin, C. M. Are state margarine taxes
AS   constitutionally vulnerable? JFE 25:
    677-83 Aug 43

Pabst, W. R., Jr. Interstate trade barriers
  and state oleomargarine taxes. SEJ 7:
  505-17 Apr 41

Hadary, G. The candy-consumer: how
ASI   much will he buy in the postwar period?
    [A survey in South Bend, Indiana] JB 18:
    96-100 Apr 45

OTHER COUNTRIES

Goldmann, J. Beer in wartime: dilution
EB   versus concentration. OIS 4:287-90
    Oct 31, 42

Moos, S. The tea trade in war time.
  OIS 2,no.8:5-9 Oct 40

Cova, P. The Italian tobacco industry: a
EI   state monopoly. BNL 1:157-68 Oct 47

15.5281 HISTORY

Carosso, V. P. Anaheim, California: a
ASC   nineteenth century experiment in com-
    mercial viniculture. BHR 23:78-86
    Jun 49

Cochran, T. C. The economics in a busi-
A   ness history [of the Pabst Brewing Com-
    pany]. JEH/S 5:54-65 Dec 45

Frantz, J. B. Gail Borden as a business-
A   man. BHR 22:123-33 Dec 48

Jasny, N. The breads of Ephesus and
  their prices. AH 21:190-92 Jul 47

McKee, I. Jean Paul Vignes, California's
ASC   first professional winegrower. AH 22
    176-80 Jul 48

15.529 MISCELLANEOUS MANUFACTURING
15.5290 GENERAL

Brand, C. J. Experiences of a trade asso-
A   ciation in an antitrust suit [in the ferti-
    lizer industry]. JM 7:227-33 Jan 43

Freeston, T. Johnson & Johnson training
A   program. ILRR 2:623-24 Jul 49

Geiger, T. Concentration of the stove in-
A   dustry. HBR 22:19-28 no.1, 43

Lockley, L. C. Marketing mechanical re-
A   frigerators during the emergency. JM 6:
    245-51 Jan 42

Navin, T. R. World's leading cymbal
ASM   maker: Avedis Zildjian Company [of
    North Quincy, Massachusetts]. BHR 23:
    196-206 Dec 49

Sheldon, C. L. Containers go to war.
A   HBR 22:220-26 no.2, 44

Wells, F. A. Voluntary absenteeism in the
EB   cutlery trade. REStud 9:158-80 no.2, 42

Wengert, N. The land, TVA, and the ferti-
A   lizer industry. LE 25:11-21 Feb 49

15.5291 HISTORY

Bacon, E. M. Marketing sewing machines
A   in the post-Civil War years. BHR 20:
    90-94 Jun 46

Carosso, V. P. The Waltham Watch Com-
ASM   pany [of Massachusetts]: a case history.
    BHR 23:165-87 Dec 49; Correction. 24:
    51 Mar 50

Larson, H. M. The armor business in the
E   Middle Ages. BHR 14:49-64 Oct 40

Lovett, R. W. Rundell, Bridge and Rundell:
EBE   an early company history [of London
    jewelers]. BHR 23:152-62 Sep 49

Marburg, T. F. Aspects of labor adminis-
ASC   tration in the early nineteenth century
    [Connecticut button industry]. BHR 15:
    1-10 Feb 41

-- Commission agents in the button and
ASC   brass trade a century ago. [The Scovill
    Manufacturing Co. of Connecticut]
    BHR 16:8-18 Feb 42

Taylor, R. H. The sale and application of
AA   commercial fertilizers in the south
    Atlantic states to 1900. AH 21:46-52
    Jan 47

15.53 EXTRACTIVE INDUSTRIES
15.530 GENERAL

Bain, J. S., chairman. War agency records
A   concerning petroleum and solid fuels.
    [Report of a sub-committee to the Round
    table on economic research] AER/S 37:
    667-70 May 47

Balogh, T. and Worswick, G. D. N. The
EB   battle for fuel. OIS 4:261-69 Oct 10, 42

Moos, S. Incentives to the development of
EB   mineral resources. OIS 4:302-08
    Nov 21, 42

Pabst, W. R., Jr. Unstable conditions of
A   compensation and monopoly in exhausti-
    ble resource industries. JPE 50:739-49
    Oct 42

Rezneck, S. Coal and oil in the American
A   economy. JEH/S 7:55-72 '47

Tyler, P. M. Minerals and war. HBR 19:
A   1-13 no.1, 40

Usher, A. P. The resource requirements
  of an industrial economy. JEH/S 7:
    35-46 '47

Weidenhammer, R. M. A national fuel
A   policy. Pt.I-III. [Pt.II by Weidenhammer
    and W. H. Voskuil] LE 19:127-40;
    436-51; 21:223-35 May,Nov 43, Aug 45

15.531 HISTORY

Centner, C. W. Great Britain and Chilian
DSC   mining 1830-1914. EHR 12:76-82
EB   no.1-2, 42

Clow, A. and Clow, N. L. Lord Dundonald
EBS   [manufacturer of coal tar products,
    founder of the British Tar Company].
    EHR 12:47-58 no.1-2, 42

## 15.53 EXTRACTIVE INDUSTRIES (Cont.)
### 15.531 HISTORY (Cont.)

Giddens, P. H. History looks at oil.
A    BHR 20:3-16 Feb 46

Gras, N. S. B. A new study of Rockefeller.
A    R. BHR 15:49-58 Oct 41

John, A. H. Iron and coal on a Glamorgan
EBW    estate, 1700-1740. EHR 13:93-103
no.1-2, 43

Mackie, J. Aspects of the gold rush.
N    ER 23:75-89 Jun 47

Marjolin, R. Long cycles in capital inten-
EF    sity in the French coal mining industry,
1840 to 1914. REStat 23:165-75 Nov 41

Neale, E. P. The New Zealand gold rushes.
N    ER 23:250-63 Dec 47

### 15.532 COAL MINING

Raikes, H. R. Liquid fuel from coal.
SAJE 17:32-48 Mar 49

#### UNITED STATES

Glasser, C. Union wage policy in bitumi-
A    nous coal. ILRR 1:609-23 Jul 48

Howe, R. E. The Coal Marketing Agency.
JM 10:35-41 Jul 45

Northrup, H. R. The Negro and the United
Mine Workers of America. SEJ 9:
313-26 Apr 43

Pabst, W. R., Jr. Monopolistic expectations and shifting control in the anthracite industry. REStat 22:45-52 Feb 40

Simpson, F. R. Price regulation and the
public utility concept: the Sunshine
Anthracite Coal case. LE 17:378-79
Aug 41

Smith, F. G. Handling labour grievances
in the bituminous coal industry. HBR 19:
352-63 no.3, 41

Voskuil, W. H. Coke: a key industrial
material. LE 22:339-45 Nov 46

Welfling, W. Defense activity and coke
prices. SEJ 9:134-39 Oct 42

Posey, T. E. Unemployment compensation
ASW    and the coal industry in West Virginia.
SEJ 7:347-61 Jan 41

#### OTHER COUNTRIES

Balogh, T. Problems of coal production.
EB    OIS 4:177-82 Jun 27, 42

Beacham, A. Efficiency and organisation
of the British coal industry. EJ 55:
206-16 Jun-Sep 45

-- The coalfields of Britain. R. EJ 56:
319-25 Jun 46

Burchardt, F. A. The coal prospects for
1943-44. OIS 5:166-71 Jul 17, 43

-- Coal in the fifth year of war. OIS 5:
265-71 Nov 20, 43

-- Size and productivity of coal mines in
Great Britain. OIS 6:250-55 Nov 4, 44

Court, W. H. B. Problems of the British
coal industry between the wars. EHR 15:
1-24 no.1-2, 45

Ellis, A. W. T. Trade losses and the consumer: the coal levy. OIS 2,no.8:11-13
Oct 40

-- and Halpern, D. B. War-time re-organ-
ization of the coal industry. OIS 3:189-96
Jun 28, 41

George, R. F. Statistics relating to the
coal mining industry. JRSS 112:331-37
pt.3, 49

Rhodes, E. C. Output, labour and machines
in the coal mining industry in Great
Britain. Ec N.S.12:101-10 May 45

Seers, D. The coal shortage. Pt.I-II.
OIS 9:25-36; 170-76 Feb,May 47

-- Coal developments, 1946-7. OIS 9:
341-46 Oct 47

-- A note on further coal developments.
OIS 10:168 May 48

Singer, H. W. The coal question reconsidered: effects of economy and substitution. REStud 8:166-77 Jun 41

Davies, B. H. Report of the Coal Com-
HSA    mission, 1946/47. R. SAJE 17:155-65
Jun 49

Hall, P. E. The coal industry in the Union
of South Africa. SAJE 16:229-50 Sep 48

Mauldon, F. R. E. The Australian coal in-
N    dustry. R. ER 24:238-41 Dec 48

Shaw, A. G. L. The Australian coal industry, 1929-39. ER 19:46-63 Jun 43

-- The Davidson Report on the coal industry. ER 23:98-103 Jun 47

### 15.533 OTHER MINING

Hayes, S. P., Jr. Potash prices and competition. QJE 57:31-68 Nov 42

Hellig, S. R. Returns to capital invested in
HSA    the gold mining industry in South Africa
[followed by J. E. Kerrich's comment].
SAJE 17:175-84 Jun 49

Little, E. M. The base minerals (excluding
HSA    coal) of the Union of South Africa.
SAJE 17:49-73 Mar 49

### 15.534 OIL. GAS

Bain, J. S. The economics of the Pacific
AA    Coast petroleum industry: reply to J.
A. Loftus. AER 36:148-49 Mar 46

-- Rostow's proposals for petroleum
A    policy. R. [followed by E. V. Rostow's
reply and Bain's rejoinder]. JPE 57:
55-60 Feb 49

Burns, A. R. Bain's analysis of the Pacific
AA    Coast petroleum industry. R. JPE 56:
35-53 Feb 48

Burrill, C. L. Petroleum: present and
A    future. JM 8:260-67 Jan 44

Davidson, R. D. and Wernimont, K. Tenure
ASO    arrangements in Oklahoma oil fields.
LE 19:40-58 Feb 43

Diebold, W., Jr. Oil import quotas and
A    "equal treatment." AER 30:569-73
Sep 40

## 15.53 EXTRACTIVE INDUSTRIES (Cont.)
## 15.534 OIL. GAS (Cont.)

    Dillard, D. Big inch pipe lines and the
A    monopoly competition in the petroleum
    industry. LE 20:109-22 May 44

    Enke, S. Reducing gasoline prices: British
CPB    Columbia's experiment. QJE 55:443-59
    May 41

    Forbes, G. The passing of the small oil
AA    man [in the Southwest]. SEJ 7:204-15
    Oct 40

    Haussmann, F. World oil control, past and
    future: an alternative to "International
    cartelization." SR 9:334-55 Sep 42

    Hoch, M. L. The oil strike of 1945. SEJ 15:
A    117-33 Oct 48

    Kaissouni, A. M. Oil in the Middle East.
M    EgC 39:263-94 Mar 48

    Lawrence, J. S. Profits and progress.
A    HBR 26:480-91 Jul 48

    Learned, E. P. Pricing of gasoline: a case
ASO    study [in Ohio]. HBR 26:723-56 Nov 48

    Moos, S. Oil supply in the Indian and east-
FI    ern Pacific areas. OIS 4:20-25
P    Jan 10, 42

    Poole, W. H. Report of the Royal Commis-
CPA    sion on the petroleum industry of Al-
    berta. R. CJE 8:92-108 Feb 42

    Prewitt, R. A. The operation and regulation
A    of crude oil and gasoline pipe lines.
    QJE 56:177-211 Feb 42

    Swensrud, S. A. Converting war pipe lines
A    to natural gas. HBR 22:459-74 no.4, 44

    Welcker, J. W. Fair profit? HBR 26:
A    207-15 Mar 48

## 15.54 DISTRIBUTIVE TRADES
## 15.540 GENERAL

    Alderson, W. [and others] [Measurement
    of marketing efficiency]: discussion.
    JM 5:365-73 Apr 41

    -- A formula for measuring productivity in
    distribution. JM 12:442-48 Apr 48

    Cox, R. The meaning of measurement of
    productivity in distribution. JM 12:
    433-41 Apr 48

    Jeuck, J. E. On the nature of marketing
    costs. JB 16:7-13 Jan 43

    Lazo, H. Towards economical distribution.
    JM 4:249-51 Jan 40

    Robbins, G. W. Notions about the origins
    of trading. JM 11:228-36 Jan 47

    Sevin, C. H. Some aspects of distribution
    cost analysis. JM 12:92-98 Jul 47

    Turck, F. B. Man-hours as a measurement
    of marketing efficiency. JM 12:499-500
    Apr 48

    Vaile, R. S. Productivity in distribution.
    JM 13:385-86 Jan 49

    Walker, Q. F. The nature of the distribu-
    tion cost problem. JM 11:151-58 Oct 46

## UNITED STATES

    Alexander, R. S. Wartime adventures in
A    equitable distribution short of rationing:
    [Pt.I-III]. JM 10:3-13; 135-51; 11:159-73
    Jul,Oct 45, Oct 46

    Burnham, E. A. What price volume?
    HBR 20:327-35 no.3, 42

    Cassady, R., Jr. The integrated marketing
    institution and public welfare. JM 6:
    252-66 Jan 42

    Converse, P. D. Employment and wages in
    marketing during 1941. JM 6,no.4,pt.2:
    19-20 Apr 42

    -- The total cost of marketing. JM 10:389
    Apr 46

    Engle, N. H. Measurement of economic
    and marketing efficiency. JM 5:335-49
    Apr 41

    Evely, R. W. Distribution methods and
    costs in the U.S.A. REStud 14:16-33
    no.1, 46

    Giffin, R. R. Changing output per person
    employed in trade, 1900-1940. JM 12:
    242-45 Oct 47

    MacGowan, T. G. Trends in tire distribu-
    tion. JM 10:265-69 Jan 46

    McNair, M. P. Distribution costs after the
    war. HBR 23:338-59 no.3, 45

    Nance, J. J. War and postwar adjustments
    in marketing appliances. JM 8:307-09
    Jan 44

    Parr, C. M. Why the middleman? JB 17:
    23-36 Jan 44

    Tracey, M. B. The present status of frozen
    food marketing. JM 13:470-80 Apr 49

    Vaile, R. S. Efficiency within the market-
    ing structure. JM 5:350-59 Apr 41

    Eiteman, W. J. Economic basis of prices
ASA    in Alaska. AER 34:351-56 Jun 44

    Rodgers, R. and Luedicke, H. E. Dynamic
ASN    competition. HBR 27:237-49 Mar 49

## OTHER COUNTRIES

    Foster, G. M. The folk economy of rural
DM    Mexico with special reference to mar-
    keting. JM 13:153-62 Oct 48

    Anonymous. The limitation of the home
EB    trade in consumers' goods. OIS 2,no.2:
    9-10 Jun 40

    Gillespie, S. C. and Rothschild, K. W. Mi-
    gration and the distributive trades.
    REStud 13:81-83 no.2, 46

    De Swardt, S. J. Municipal markets: their
HSA    function and future. SAJE 16:182-93
    Jun 48

    Mabin, H. S. The Second Report of the
    Distribution Costs Commission. R.
    [followed by C. S. Richards' reply].
    SAJE 16:168-81 Jun 48

    Van Waasdijk, T. Investigation into the
    distributive trade in blankets (Trans-
    vaal), under conditions of controlled and
    free markets (1947-1948). SAJE 16:
    342-87 Dec 48

15.54  DISTRIBUTIVE TRADES (Cont.)
15.540  GENERAL (Cont.)
    OTHER COUNTRIES (Cont.)

    Banks, S.  The effect of the war upon the
P    distribution system of the Territory of
    Hawaii.  JB 20:220-29 Oct 47

15.541  HISTORY
    Anonymous.  An early Philadelphia mer-
ASP    chant, Charles N. Buck, 1775-1851.  R.
    BHR 16:63 Jun 42
    -- A traveling merchant opens to the West
    the trade and culture of the Orient, 67
    A.D.  R.  BHR 16:80-81 Oct 42
    -- Boston's first merchant.  BHR 18:11-12
ASM    Feb 44
    Atherton, L. E.  Personal letters of a New
ASL    Orleans mercantile clerk, 1844-1845.
    BHR 17:49-56 Jun 43
    -- Itinerant merchandising in the ante-
AA    bellum South.  BHR 19:35-59 Apr 45
    Bradshaw, T. F.  Superior methods created
A    the early chain store.  BHR 17:35-43
    Apr 43
    Clark, T. D.  Imperfect competition:  In the
AA    southern retail trade after 1865.
    JEH/S 3:38-47 Dec 43
    Gras, N. S. B.  The Steinman Hardware
ASP    Company, Lancaster, Pennsylvania.
    BHR 14:14-15 Feb 40
    -- An old store still young.  [Hager and
ASP    Brother, Lancaster, Pennsylvania]
    BHR 14:33-40 Jun 40
    -- An early sedentary merchant in the
ASM    Middle West: records available for a
    study of the career of Henry Shaw [of
    St. Louis, Missouri].  BHR 18:1-9 Feb 44
    Hower, R. M.  Captain Macy [founder of
ASN    R. H. Macy & Co.].  HBR 18:472-87
    no.4, 40
    Jennings, M., sister.  Notes on Joseph
ASP    Hertzog, an early Philadelphia merchant.
    BHR 14:65-76 Nov 40
    Wohl, R. R.  An historical introduction to
EBE    entrepreneurship: II.  [The costermonger
    of London]  EEH 1,no.4:18-27 Apr 49

15.542  WHOLESALING
    Albright, J.  Changes in wholesaling, 1929-
A    1939.  JM 6:31-37 Jul 41
    Ashley, C. A.  Investigation into an alleged
CA    combine of wholesalers and shippers of
    fruit and vegetables in western Canada.
    CJE 6:288-92 May 40
    Beckman, T. N.  Significant trends in whole-
A    saling.  JM 5:218-20 Jan 41
    -- Significant current trends in wholesaling.
A    JM 6,no.4,pt.2:9-11 Apr 42
    Duddy, E. A., and Revzan, D. A.  The loca-
ASI    tion of the South Water Wholesale Fruit
    and Vegetable Market in Chicago.  Pt.I-II.
    JB 12:386-412; 13:39-55 Oct 39, Jan 40
    Engle, N. H.  Adjustment of wholesaling to
A    1941 and after.  JM 5:431-37 Apr 41

    Hovde, H. T., ed.  Wholesaling in our
A    American economy.  JM 14:145-361
    Sep 49
    Irwin, H. S.  Middlemen's accumulations
A    and expectations in marketing farm
    products.  JFE 29:848-66 Nov 47
    Johnson, H. W.  Using an income index to
A    forecast sales of service wholesale
    druggists.  JM 9:43-48 Jul 44
    Lewis, E. H.  Wholesale market patterns.
A    JM 12:317-26 Jan 48
    Livesey, C. A.  Appraising the mill supply
    distributor.  HBR 23:493-506 no.4, 45
    -- The steel warehouse distributor.
A    HBR 25:397-408 no.3, 47
    Metz, H.  The electrical distributor:  war
A    and postwar.  JM 8:310-15 Jan 44
    Nolen, H. C.  Time and duty analysis of
A    wholesalers' salesmen.  JM 4:274-84
    Jan 40
    Petersen, E.  Solving wholesalers' prob-
A    lems through trading area research
    [with discussion by W. W. Leigh].
    JM 4,no.4,pt.2:39-46 Apr 40
    Rasmussen, E. G.  Hardware wholesale
AA    trading centers and trading territories
    in nine south-eastern states.  JM 8:
    165-71 Oct 43
    Sielaff, T. J.  Postwar wholesale dry goods
A    sales and stores.  JM 10:60-62 Jul 45
    Wales, H. G.  The Kansas City wholesale
ASK    fruit and vegetable market.  JB 19:
ASM    161-75 Jul 46

15.543  RETAILING
    Beckley, D. K.  Appraising professional
    training for retailing.  JM 14:38-45
    Jul 49
    Bellamy, R.  The changing pattern of re-
    tail distribution.  OIS 8:237-60 Aug 46
    -- Size and success in retail distribution.
    OIS 8:324-39 Oct 46
    -- Private & social cost in retail distribu-
    tion.  OIS 8:345-51 Nov 46
    Chapple, E. D. and Donald, G., Jr.  An
ASM    evaluation of department store sales-
    people by the interaction chronograph.
    [A study of the Gilchrist Company in
    Boston]  JM 12:173-85 Oct 47
    Converse, P. D.  New laws of retail gravi-
    tation.  JM 14:379-84 Oct 49
    Hollander, S., Jr.  A technique for spotting
    retail outlets.  JM 6:280-81 Jan 42
    Hutchinson, K. D.  Traffic and trade corre-
    lations: a technique in store location.
    JM 5:137-42 Oct 40
    Lewis, W. A.  Competition in retail trade.
    Ec N.S:12:202-34 Nov 45

    UNITED STATES
    Alexander, R. S.  A wartime adventure in
A    business self-regulation: the retail
    declaration of policy.  JM 11:394-98
    Apr 47

15.54 DISTRIBUTIVE TRADES (Cont.)
15.543 RETAILING (Cont.)
    UNITED STATES (Cont.)

Alt, R. M. Competition among types of re-
A    tailers in selling the same commodity.
    JM 14:441-47 Oct 49

Applebaum, W. Adjustment of retailing to
    1941 conditions. JM 5:438-42 Apr 41

Bader, L. Reaction of consumers to a two-
    price system. JM 5:41-43 Jul 40

Bayard, C. C. The defective United States
    retail price structure. SEJ 11:1-19
    Jul 44

Brooks, J. B. The organization of the sell-
    ing function in a department store.
    JM 13:189-94 Oct 48

Brown, G. H. and Mancina, F. A. A note
    on the relationship between sales and
    advertising of department stores. JB 13:
    1-16 Jan 40; A correction. 205 Apr 40

Burnham, E. A. The department store in
    its community. HBR 18:455-71 no.4, 40

-- Employee productivity in department
    stores. HBR 27:480-97 Jul 49

Comish, N H. The model stock plan in
    small stores. JM 11:402-07 Apr 47

Daly, M. An analysis of the comparability
    tables of the Census of retail distribu-
    tion. JM 10:42-53 Jul 45

Dameron, K. Retailing and consumer
    movements. JM 5:385-94 Apr 41

Engel, G. C. The importance of salespeople
    in ready-to-wear stores. JM 11:282-85
    Jan 47

Hawkinson, J. R. [Retailing in '41]: discus-
    sion. JM 5:418-19 Apr 41

Iglauer, J. Department store distribution.
    JM 8:326-28 Jan 44

Knauth, O. Considerations in the setting of
    retail prices. JM 14:1-12 Jul 49

Lebow, V. The nature of postwar retail
    competition. JM 9:11-18 Jul 44

Lewis, H. F. Lost sales opportunities in
    retailing. HBR 27:53-61 Jan 49

McNair, M. P. Wartime inflation and de-
    partment stores. HBR 22:40-53 no.1, 43

Mertes, J. E. The shopping center: a new
    trend in retailing. JM 13:374-79 Jan 49

Nystrom, P. H. Significant current trends
    in retailing. JM 5:220-22; 6,no.4,pt.2:
    8-9 Jan 41, Apr 42

Phillips, C. F. Fair trade and the retail
    drug store. JM 6:47-48 Jul 41

Read, E. V. W. [Retailing in '41]: discus-
    sion. JM 5:419-22 Apr 41

Schalk, A. F., Jr. Significant merchandising
    trends of the independent tire dealer.
    JM 12:462-69 Apr 48

Thompson, M. Department store problems.
    JM 8:21-24 Jul 43

Vorce, C. H. What is the basic drug store
    pattern? JM 10:394-96 Apr 46

Wingate, J. W. Current trends in retail dis-
    tribution. JM 5:410-18 Apr 41

Kelley, P. C. Former occupations of small
ASA    scale retailers [in Arkansas]. JM 5:
    35-37 Jul 40

Bowden, W. K. and Cassady, R., Jr. De-
ASC    centralization of retail trade in the met-
    ropolitan market area [of Los Angeles].
    JM 5:270-75 Jan 41

Cassady, R., Jr. and Bowden, W. K. Shift-
    ing retail trade within the Los Angeles
    metropolitan market. JM 8:398-404
    Apr 44

Seelye, A. L. Drug prices in cities with
ASK    and without a fair trade law [Kansas
    City, Kansas and Kansas City, Missouri].
    JM 6:16-21 Jul 41

Bennett, V. W. Consumer buying habits in
ASM    a small town located between two large
    cities [in Maryland]. JM 8:405-16 Apr 44

Doherty, R. P. The movement and concen-
ASM    tration of retail trade in metropolitan
    areas. [A study of Boston] JM 5:
    395-401 Apr 41

-- Decentralization of retail trade in Bos-
    ton. JM 6:281-86 Jan 42

Seelye, A. L. Drug prices in cities with
ASM    and without a fair trade law [Kansas
    City, Kansas and Kansas City, Missouri].
    JM 6:16-21 Jul 41

Douglas, E. Measuring the general retail
ASN    trading area: a case study [of Charlotte,
    North Carolina]. Pt.I-II. JM 13:481-97;
    14:46-60 Apr,Jul 49

Green, H. W. Retail outlets in shopping
ASO    centers stop decreasing [in the Cleve-
    land metropolitan area]. JM 10:281-82
    Jan 46

Wolfe, H. D. Dispersion of consumer pur-
    chases among competing retail outlets
    [in Ohio]. JB 15:160-65 Apr 42

Comish, N. H. Retail store operating re-
ASO    sults as guides for small merchants [in
    Oregon]. JM 11:62-64 Jul 46

Heidingsfield, M. S. Why do people shop in
ASP    downtown department stores? [A survey
    in Philadelphia]. JM 13:510-12 Apr 49


OTHER COUNTRIES

Brown, W. F. Mass merchandising in Latin
D    America: Sears, Roebuck & Co. JM 13:
    73-77 Jul 48

Froehlich, W. Changes in the central
EA    European retail trade. JM 4:258-63
    Jan 40

-- Aid for the independent retail trade: a
    step toward fascism? JM 5:276-79
    Jan 41

Reisner, E. Aid for the independent retail
    trade: a step toward fascism? JM 5:
    163-66 Oct 40

Balogh, T. Concentration in retail distribu-
EB    tion. OIS 4:201-05 Jul 18, 42

Hough, J. A. Retail sales per employee.
    MS 17:49-66 Jan 49

## 15.54 DISTRIBUTIVE TRADES (Cont.)
## 15.543 RETAILING (Cont.)
### OTHER COUNTRIES (Cont.)

Madge, C. War and the small retail shop.
EB    OIS 4,suppl.2:1-8 Apr 4, 42

Nicholls, G. L. A new plan for the non-food retail trade. OIS 4:217-20 Aug 8, 42

Worswick, G. D. N. Retail sales during the war: A. Turnover and population movements. OIS 3:207-13 Jul 19, 41

-- Rational retailing in war-time. OIS 3: 287-94 Sep 20, 41

-- The Retail trade report. OIS 4:70-74 Feb 21, 42

-- Clothing shops in the United Kingdom. OIS 6:168-72 Jul 22, 44; Erratum. 192 Aug 12, 44

Ucker, P. Swiss retail trade and fascism.
ESw    JM 6:50-53 Jul 41

## 15.544 RETAIL FOOD
### UNITED STATES

Applebaum, W. A case history of sales
A    quotas [for bread in a retail grocery chain]. JM 7:200-03 Jan 43

Breimeyer, H. F. Retail value of meat consumption relative to consumers' incomes as a measure of demand for meat. JFE 31:520-24 Aug 49

Dipman, C. W. Changes in food distribution. JM 6,no.4,pt.2:48-52 Apr 42

-- Wartime changes in food distribution. JM 8:321-25 Jan 44

Gilchrist, F. W. Self-service retailing of meat. JM 13:295-304 Jan 49

Hoffman, A. C. Changing organization of agricultural markets. JFE 22:162-72 Feb 40

Morrow, A. The war's impact on milk marketing. JM 10:235-43 Jan 46

Patzig, R. E. The effect of the war on retail food outlets. JM 9:109-13 Oct 44

Tousley, R. D. Advertising fresh fruits and vegetables. Pt.I-II. HBR 22:447-58 no.4, 44; 23:79-94 no.1, 44

Zimmerman, M. M. The supermarket and the changing retail structure. JM 5: 402-09 Apr 41

-- Super market sales and profit trends: 1941-1943. JM 9:162-63 Oct 44

-- Tomorrow's super market. JM 10: 384-88 Apr 46

Cassady, R., Jr. and Grether, E. T. Locali-
AA    ty price differentials in the western retail grocery trade. HBR 21:190-206 no.2, 43; Correction. 396 no.3, 43

Coles, J. V. Student reactions to different
ASC    groups of food stores [in Berkeley, California]. JM 10:390-94 Apr 46

-- The pattern of retail food stores in a small city [Berkeley, California]. JM 13: 163-71 Oct 48

Grether, E. T. Effects of weighting and of

distributive price controls upon retail food price comparisons [in the San Francisco Bay region]. JM 6:166-70 Oct 41

-- Geographical price policies in the grocery trade, 1941: a note. JM 8:417-22 Apr 44

Pettengill, R. B. Comparitive retail grocery ceiling prices in Los Angeles. JM 8:145-49 Oct 43

Spears, R. F. Improving super market op-
ASC    erating efficiency: a case study [of Stop & Shop, Inc. in Connecticut and Massachusetts]. JM 13:218-20 Oct 48

Converse, P. D. and Spencer, C. What
ASI    housewives think of the super-market. [A survey in Champaign, Illinois]. JM 6:371-74 Apr 42

Kelly, R. A. The North-Central States Regional Potato Marketing Project controlled retail store experiment [in Chicago]. JFE 31,pt.2:626-30 Feb 49

Haas, H. M. Price differentials among gro-
ASI    cery stores in Bloomington, Indiana. JM 5:148-55 Oct 40

Spears, R. F. Improving super market op-
ASM    erating efficiency: a case study [of Stop & Shop, Inc. in Connecticut and Massachusetts]. JM 13:218-20 Oct 48

McGarry, E. D. The mortality of independ-
ASN    ent grocery stores in Buffalo and Pittsburg, 1919-1941. JM 12:14-24 Jul 47

Wolfe, H. D. Grocery prices and marketing
ASO    functions. [A study made in several cities of Ohio] JM 6:27-30 Jul 41

McGarry, E. D. The mortality of independ-
ASP    ent grocery stores in Buffalo and Pittsburg, 1919-1941. JM 12:14-24 Jul 47

Tousley, R. D. Reducing distribution costs
ASW    in the grocery field: a case study [of the Roundup Grocery Company of Spokane, Washington]. JM 12:455-61 Apr 48

### OTHER COUNTRIES

Schneider, J. B. The Peruvian food market
DSP    and the World War. JM 9:262-68 Jan 45

Schulz, T. Retail sales during the war: B.
EB    Changes in grocery sales. OIS 3:213-23 Jul 19, 41

-- Changes in the retail trade of groceries. OIS 4:57-66 Feb 21, 42

-- Sales of groceries in 1943 and 1944. OIS 7:116-23 May 19, 45

Halliday, I. G. Some notes on the distribu-
HSA    tion of meat in Durban with special reference to beef. SAJE 8:19-36 Mar 40

-- Notes on the distribution and consumption of milk in Durban. SAJE 12:101-11 Jun 44

## 15.545 CHAIN STORES

Adelman, M. A. The A & P case: a study in
A    applied economic theory. QJE 63:238-57 May 49

## 15.54 DISTRIBUTIVE TRADES (Cont.)
### 15.545 CHAIN STORES (Cont.)

A Balmer, S. L. and Dean, J. Gearing salaries of nation-wide chains to the geographical structure of wages. JB 20: 96-115 Apr 47

A Beattie. T. E. Public relations and the chains. JM 7:245-55 Jan 43

Cassady, R., Jr. The chain-independent controversy. JM 7:57-59 Jul 42

A Converse, P. D. and Beattie, T. E. Are chain stores good citizens? JM 8:172-84 Oct 43

A Engle, N. H. Chain store distribution vs. independent wholesaling. JM 14:241-52 Sep 49

A Lazo, H. Independents, chains and the public welfare. JM 6:267-73 Jan 42

A Lebhar, G. M. The chain store postwar role. JM 8:316-20 Jan 44

ASW Oakes, R. H. Price differences for identical items in chain, voluntary group, and independent stores [in a Milwaukee suburb]. JM 14:434-36 Oct 49

A Phillips, C. F. Price policies of food chains. HBR 19:377-88 no.3, 41

## 15.55 CONSTRUCTION INDUSTRY
### 15.550 GENERAL

A Anonymous. The agreement establishing a National Joint Board for the Settlement of Jurisdictional Disputes in building and construction industries. ILRR 2:411-15 Apr 49

A Bober, W. C. The construction industry after the war. HBR 20:427-36 no.4, 42

EB Bowen, I. and Ellis, A. W. T. The building and contracting industry. OEP 7:111-24 Mar 45

EB -- Incentives and output in the building and civil engineering industries. MS 15: 157-75 May 47

-- A note on G. T. Jones' "Increasing returns." YB 1:81-84 Sep 49

C Firestone, O. J. Estimate of the gross value of construction in Canada, 1940. CJE 9:219-34 May 43

N Hamilton, J. M. and Wark, J. M. Building industry statistics. ER 24:204-17 Dec 48

EB Moos, S. Building materials and building policy. OIS 5:112-17 May 15, 43

EB -- Labour costs in housing. OIS 5:225-31 Oct 9, 43

EB -- The age structure of building labour. OIS 6:39-44 Feb 26, 44

EB -- Employment and output in the building trades. OIS 8:44-50 Feb 46

A Newcomb, R. Can the construction industry carry its immediate share of postwar employment? REStat 27:117-32 Aug 45

EBE Saville, J. The measurement of real cost in the London building industry, 1923-1939. YB 1:67-80 Sep 49

N Simkin, C. G. F. Economic planning and the N.Z. Ministry of Works. ER 23: 103-07 Jun 47

A Vermilya, H. P. Building codes: administration vs. techniques. LE 17:129-37 May 41

A Wittausch, W. K. Postwar competition for mass-produced, low-cost housing. JM 8:375-81 Apr 44

A -- Marketing prefabricated houses. HBR 26: 693-712 Nov 48

### 15.551 HISTORY

A  
EB Cooney, E. W. Capital exports, and investment in building in Britain and the U.S.A. 1856-1914. Ec N.S.16:347-54 Nov 49

## 15.56 SERVICE INDUSTRIES
### 15.560 GENERAL

White, M. and Zeisel, J. Reading indices. [An analysis of This Week Magazine in four cities] JM 6:103-11 Oct 41

UNITED STATES

A Berreman, J. V. Advertising and the sale of novels. JM 7:234-40 Jan 43

Bigelow, C. L. Elements of confusion in newspaper readership study. JM 12: 337-47 Jan 48

Borden, N. H. Use of newspapers by national advertisers. HBR 24:295-305 no.3, 46

-- Selling newspaper space to national advertisers. HBR 24:438-52 no.4, 46

Britt, S. H. Research and merchandising in a modern advertising agency. JM 13: 506-10 Apr 49

Chambers, R. W. Block booking: blind selling [in the motion picture industry]. HBR 19:496-507 no.4, 41

Fiske, M. and Handel, L. Motion picture research: content and audience analysis: response analysis. JM 11:129-34; 273-80 Oct 46, Jan 47

-- and Handel, L. New techniques for studying the effectiveness of films. JM 11: 390-93 Apr 47

Hobart, D. M. Planning a Holiday [new magazine]. JM 12:47-52 Jul 47

Hughes, W. Vox pop can pilot your paper. JM 11:371-76 Apr 47

Jacobson, D. J. What's ahead for the hotel industry? HBR 24:339-55 no.3, 46

Kinter, C. V. Cyclical considerations in the marketing problem of the newspaper industry. JM 11:66-70 Jul 46

-- The newspaper in two postwar periods. JM 13:371-72 Jan 49

Kirkpatrick, C. A. An estimate of vacation travel expenditures for 1938: a challenge. JM 5:39-41 Jul 40

Reder, M. W. Service industries and the volume of employment. AER 31:512-19 Sep 41

15.56 SERVICE INDUSTRIES (Cont.)
15.560 GENERAL (Cont.)
UNITED STATES (Cont.)

Singer, R. E. Guess again. Computing
A    tourist expenditures is tricky business
     with many pitfalls. JM 5:279-80 Jan 41

Sparlin, E. E. Public ownership versus
     state purchasing: the case of printing.
     JPE 48:211-21 Apr 40

Weintraub, D. and Magdoff, H. The service
     industries in relation to employment
     trends. Em 8:289-311 Oct 40

Weld, L. D. H. Trends in advertising, 1940
     [and 1941]. JM 5:224-25; 6,no.4,pt.2:7-8
     Jan 41, Apr 42

Woolley, C. Companies never remember.
     BHR 15:62-64 Oct 41

Zeisel, H. and Harper, V. E. The advertis-
     ing value of different magazines. JM 13:
     56-61 Jul 48

Brown, W. F. and Cassady, R., Jr. Guild
AS   pricing in the service trades. [State laws
     relating chiefly to barbering] QJE 61:
     311-38 Feb 47

Kast, M. American interstate motor tour-
     ist traffic. SEJ 7:529-37 Apr 41

Dawson, A. A. P. Hollywood's labor troubles.
ASC  ILRR 1:638-47 Jul 48

Shister, J. The economics of collective
ASO  wage bargaining: a case study [of the
     Cincinnati printing industry]. JPE 51:
     338-47 Aug 43

EUROPE
Ady, P. Cinema duties, consumption and
EB   prices. OIS 6:62-64 Mar 18, 44

Halpern, D. B. Economic aspects of the
     cinema trade. OIS 3:169-75 Jun 7, 41

15.561 HISTORY
Butlin, N. G. Collective bargaining in the
N    Sydney printing industry, 1880-1900.
     ER 23:206-26 Dec 47

Phillips, G. L. Sweep for the soot O!
EB   1750-1850. EHR II.1:151-54 no.2-3, 49

Taylor, E. G. R. The surveyor. EHR 17:
EB   121-33 no.2, 47

15.6 PUBLIC UTILITIES. ELECTRICITY.
     GAS. WATER
15.60 GENERAL
Usher, A. P. The resource requirements of
     an industrial economy. JEH/S 7:35-46 '47

UNITED STATES
Dewey, R. L. and Gray, H. M. Transporta-
A    tion and public utilities: discussion.
     AER/S 38:483-87 May 48

--, chairman. Round table on transporta-
     tion and public utility problems.
     AER/S 39:424-26 May 49

Gates, J. E. Problems in administering
     war-time shortages of electric energy.
     LE 17:477-82 Nov 41

Goldin, H. H. The employee interest in
     public utility merger and abandonment
     cases. LE 24:161-74 May 48

Jones, H. F. The relation of large scale
     production to certain costs of electric
     utilities in the United States. LE 18:
     36-46 Feb 42

-- Midwest Power Conference. LE 18:
     224-25 May 42

Lewis, B. W. Public policy and the growth
     of the power industry. JEH/S 7:47-55 '47

Muller, C. Aluminum and power control.
     LE 21:108-24 May 45

Neuner, E., Jr. Wages and employment in
     the public utility industries. LE 22:
     363-80 Nov 46

Nordin, J. A. Note on a light plant's cost
     curves. Em 15:231-35 Jul 47

Ruggles, C. O., chairman. The impact of
     national defense and the war upon public
     utilities. Abstract of specialized con-
     ference discussion. AER/S 32:216-17
     Mar 42

-- Electric power and industrial develop-
     ment. HBR 22:377-92 no.3, 44

-- Electric power in industry and agricul-
     ture. HBR 23:95-114, no.1, 44

Simpson, F. R. Recent utility activities.
     LE 19:481-82 Nov 43

Troxel, C. E. Indexes of construction cost
     for public utility industries. LE 16:
     363-68 Aug 40

-- Inflation in price-regulated industries.
     JB 22:1-16 Jan 49

De Chazeau, M. G. Electric power as a
AA   regional problem. SEJ 7:494-504 Apr 41

Smith, L. Tidal power in Maine. LE 24:
ASM  239-52 Aug 48

Julian, V. Mediation of labor disputes in
ASM  Missouri public utilities. IRRA 2:255-61
     Dec 49

Hon, R. C. The Memphis Power and Light
AST  deal. SEJ 6:344-75 Jan 40

OTHER COUNTRIES
Rippy, J. F. Electrical utilities in Puerto
DW   Rico. JB 19:221-23 Oct 46

Jervis, F. R. Gas and electricity in Britain:
EB   a study in duopoly. LE 24:31-39 Feb 48

Verhulst, M. J. J. The pure theory of pro-
EF   duction applied to the French gas indus-
     try. Em 16:295-308 Oct 48

Hocking, D. M. The economics of the gas
N    industry. ER 18:31-42 Jun 42

15.601 PUBLIC REGULATION AND OWNER-
        SHIP
Gray, H. M. The passing of the public
     utility concept. LE 16:8-20 Feb 40

Smith, H. R. The rise and fall of the pub-
     lic utility concept. LE 23:117-31 May 47

15.6 PUBLIC UTILITIES. ELECTRICITY.
  GAS. WATER (Cont.)
15.601 PUBLIC REGULATION AND OWNER-
  SHIP (Cont.)
  UNITED STATES
  Bonbright, J. C. Power aspects of the St.
A  Lawrence waterway. CJE 8:176-85
  May 42
  Cooper, W. W. The yardstick for utility
  regulation. JPE 51:258-62 Jun 43
  Duffus, W. M. The place of the government
  corporation in the public utility indus-
  tries. LE 25:29-38 Feb 49
  Fisher, C. O. [and others] Recent develop-
  ments in public utility regulation: dis-
  cussion. AER/S 36:435-50 May 46
  Harbeson, R. W. Public utility regulation:
  a new chapter. HBR 20:496-507 no.4, 42
  Morehouse, E. W. The creed of a great
  public servant [Joseph B. Eastman].
  LE 20:361-64 Nov 44
  Pritchett, C. H. Administration of federal
  power projects. LE 18:379-90 Nov 42
  Raver, P. J. Discussion of William A.
  Duffus' paper. LE 25:39-46 Feb 49
  Ruggles, C. O. Public utilities. BHR 20:
  57-68 Apr 46
  Simpson, F. R. Price regulation and the
  public utility concept: the Sunshine
  Anthracite Coal case. LE 17:378-79
  Aug 41
  -- Price regulation and the public utility
  concept: Olsen v. Nebraska. LE 18:
  223 May 42
  Smith, N. L. The outlook in regulation.
  Pt.I-II. LE 16:386-92; 17:48-53 Nov 40,
  Feb 41
  Troxel, E. Incremental cost control under
  public ownership. LE 19:292-99 Aug 43
  -- Cost behavior and the accounting pattern
  of public utility regulation. JPE 57:
  413-27 Oct 49
  Murray, V. M. Grand Coulee and Bonne-
AA  ville power in the national war effort.
  LE 18:134-39 May 42
  Lewis, B. W. State regulation in depres-
AS  sion and war. (Recent developments in
  public utility legislation) AER/S 36:
  384-404 May 46
  Bigham, T. C. Comment on the Pacific Gas
ASC  and Electric case. AER 30:351-52 Jun 40
  Mayer, R. W. Supreme Court's attitude
  toward historical cost: [note on the
  Pacific Gas and Electric case]. AER 30:
  352-53 Jun 40
  Wilson, G. L. and Rose, J. R. Pacific Gas
  and Electric Case: reply. AER 30:
  827-29 Dec 40
  Stein, A. L. The Chicago gas case. LE 16:
ASI  236-41 May 40
  -- Ouster after expiration of franchise: the
  Geneseo case again. LE 17:247-48
  May 41

  Edelmann, A. T. Kentucky accepts T.V.A.
ASK  power. LE 18:481-84 Nov 42
  Kintzi, J. Coordination of the Nebraska
ASN  public power districts. LE 16:481-83
  Nov 40

  OTHER COUNTRIES
  Bonbright, J. C. Power aspects of the St.
C  Lawrence waterway. CJE 8:176-85
  May 42
  Currie, A. W. Rate control on Canadian
  public utilities. CJE 12:148-58 May 46
  Santa María, D. Chilean state electrifica-
DSC  tion. LE 21:365-70 Sep 45

15.61 HISTORY
  Passer, H. C. The electric light and the
A  gas light: innovation and continuity in
  economic history. EEH 1,no.3:1-9
  Mar 49
  Ruggles, C. O. Public utilities: [a history
A  of regulation]. BHR 20:57-68 Apr 46

15.62 DEMAND
  Anonymous. The development of the use of
HSA  electricity in South Africa. SAJE 16:
  323-41 Dec 48
  Crowley, W. J. Elasticity of residential
A  demand for electricity: a reply [followed
  by H. A. Cutler's rejoinder]. LE 17:
  499-503 Nov 41
  Cutler, H. A. The elasticity of the resi-
A  dential demand for electricity. LE 17:
  242-45 May 41
  Falck, E. Elasticity of residential demand
A  for electricity: a reply. LE 17:498
  Nov 41
  Gates, J. E. Forecasting the demand for
A  electric energy. LE 18:77-81 Feb 42
  Jones, H. F. Forecasting the demand for
A  electric energy: a reply [followed by
  J. E. Gates' rejoinder]. LE 18:228-32
  May 42
  Knaf, H. G. Socio-economic conditions and
AS  intercity variations of electric use.
  LE 18:431-46 Nov 42
  -- Interstate differences in the saturation of
AS  wired homes, mechanical refrigerators
  and electric ranges, and their causes.
  LE 22:386-92 Nov 46
  Lienau, C. C. Statistical method: forecast-
  ing electric energy demand and regulat-
  ing supply. LE 18:102-05 Feb 42
  Nordin, J. A. The demand for electricity.
  LE 23:337-41 Aug 47
  Troxel, E. Demand elasticity and control
A  of public utility earnings. AER 38:
  372-82 Jun 48

## 15.6 PUBLIC UTILITIES. ELECTRICITY. GAS. WATER (Cont.)

### 15.63 RATE LEVEL. RATE BASE. RATE OF RETURN

Bauhan, A. E. Simulated plant-record method of life analysis of utility plant for depreciation-accounting purposes. LE 24:129-36 May 48

Bonbright, J. C. Major controversies as to the criteria of reasonable public utility rates. AER/S 30,no.5:379-89 Feb 41

Carr, W. B. A new simplified approach to mathematically calculated reserves for depreciation for accounting purposes. LE 25:304-12 Aug 49

#### UNITED STATES

Adelman, M. A. Interest rates and fair
A    return. LE 24:384-95 Nov 48

Anderson, W. H. The Supreme Court and recent public utility valuation theory. LE 21:12-22 Feb 45

Barnes, I. R. Shall going value be included in the rate-base? Pt.I-II. LE 16:286-93; 430-37 Aug,Nov 40

Becker, A. P. Fixed dividends for all public utility stock. LE 21:243-49 Aug 45

Bonbright, J. C. The depreciation reserve as a measure of actual accrued depreciation (The NARUC Depreciation Report: a symposium) LE 20:98-100 May 44

-- Utility rate control reconsidered in the light of the Hope Natural Gas case. AER/S 38:465-82 May 48

Clemens, E. W. The critical issue of depreciation in public utility valuation. SEJ 9:252-61 Jan 43

Colbert, A. R. The transition to depreciation accounting. LE 16:129-36 May 40

-- The NARUC Depreciation Report: a symposium: a review of certain conclusions. LE 20:89-97 May 44

Dudley, R. G. and Evans, W. H., eds. Public utility financing 4th quarter of 1939 - 1st quarter of 1948. [Regular feature, variously edited. Reports for the 4th quarter of each year contain also an annual summary] LE 16-24 Feb 40-May 48

Ferguson, S. Further comments on the 1944 NARUC Report. LE 21:181-84 May 45

Fisher, C. O. [and others] Recent developments in public utility regulation: discussion. AER/S 36:435-50 May 46

Glaeser, M. G. The United States Supreme Court redeems itself. LE 18:146-54 May 42

Guthmann, H. G. Public utility depreciation practice. HBR 20:213-22 no.2, 42

Hart, O. Risk factors in public utility securities. JF 3,no.3:52-64 Oct 48

Jeming, J. Public utility rates on a reproduction-cost-of-service principle. LE 17:138-50 May 41

-- An actual application of the reproduction-cost-of-service principle in rate making. LE 18:188-203 May 42

Koontz, H. D. Increased gas rates based upon higher taxes. LE 16:233-35 May 40

Kosh, D. A. Uncertainty and the provision for depreciation in the public utility industries. JB 16:209-18 Oct 43

Morehouse, E. W. and Agg, T. R. On the 1944 NARUC Report. LE 21:282-86 Aug 45

-- Observations on Riggs' and Thompson's comments on Nash, Anatomy of depreciation. LE 24:79-81 Feb 48

Ready, L. S. The unsoundness of recommendation forty-two (The NARUC Depreciation Report: a symposium). LE 20:100-05 May 44

Riggs, H. E. and Thompson, C. W. Two commentaries on Anatomy of depreciation. R. LE 23:433-38 Nov 47

Riley, R. H. Is fair return appropriate for municipal utilities? LE 16:52-60 Feb 40

Ruggles, C. O. The role of rate making. HBR 18:215-30 no.2, 40

Smith, N. L. Rail and utility investments under expanding public control. HBR 18:397-409 no.4, 40

-- Rate regulation by the Federal Power Commission. AER/S 36:405-25 May 46

Stein, A. L. Rate-making by interim order. LE 16:368-71 Aug 40

Tyndall, D. G. The stabilization of investment in two public utility industries. LE 25:382-96 Nov 49

Scharff, M. R. An incentive plan of rate
ASN   adjustment [in New Hampshire]. LE 16:475-78 Nov 40

Harbeson, R. W. The "New Jersey Plan"
ASN   of rate regulation. JB 17:220-30 Oct 44

Rose, J. R. Regulation of utility valuation
ASP   in Pennsylvania: comment. AER 33:903-04 Dec 43

Thatcher, L. W. Financial and depreciation
ASU   history of the Utah Power and Light Company. Pt.I-II. LE 15:448-55; 16:89-95 Nov 39, Feb 40

Clemens, E. W. Ratemaking policies and
ASW   practices of the Public Service Commission of Wisconsin. LE 20:223-37 Aug 44

#### OTHER COUNTRIES

Currie, A. W. Rate control of public utili-
CPB   ties in British Columbia. CJE 10:381-90 Aug 44

### 15.64 RATE STRUCTURE

Behling, B. N. Differential pricing of public utility services. JM 6,no.4,pt.2:168-70 Apr 42

Bonbright, J. C. Rate-making policies of
A   federal power projects. AER/S 36:426-34 May 46

## 15.6 PUBLIC UTILITIES. ELECTRICITY. GAS. WATER (Cont.)

### 15.64 RATE STRUCTURE (Cont.)

A  Clemens, E. W. Incremental cost pricing and discriminatory pricing. LE 21: 68-71 Feb 45

ASC  Jones, H. F. In the matter of the rates and service of the New Haven Water Company. LE 19:377-79 Aug 43

EB  Lewis, W. A. The two-part tariff. Ec N.S.8:249-70 Aug 41

A  Melamerson-Vandenhaag, E. R. A rationing rate structure. LE 19:243-45 May 43

Nordin, J. A. Allocating demand costs. LE 22:163-70 May 46

Pegrum, D. F. Incremental cost pricing: a comment [followed by E. Troxel's further comment]. LE 20:58-63 Feb 44

EB  Rowson, R. B. The two-part tariff: further notes by an electrical engineer [followed by W. A. Lewis's reply]. Ec N.S.8: 392-408 Nov 41

ASO  Sickler, B. J. Bonneville resale rates pay out. LE 16:487-91 Nov 40

Troxel, E. Incremental cost determination of utility prices. LE 18:458-67 Nov 42

-- Limitations of the incremental cost patterns of pricing. LE 19:28-39 Feb 43

-- Price discrimination in space heating. LE 24:281-92 Aug 48

### 15.65 TAXATION

A  Balet, J. W. Application of the LIFO inventory method to income tax depreciation for public utilities. NTJ 1:322-29 Dec 48

ASM  Borak, A. Tax equivalents of municipal electric utilities in Minnesota. LE 17: 59-70 Feb 41

ASM  -- Tax equivalents versus taxes of municipal and private utilities in Minnesota. LE 23:381-98 Nov 47

A  Burkhead, J. V. Corporate taxes and utility assessment: a reply [followed by J. W. Martin's rejoinder]. LE 17:115-18 Feb 41

ASN  -- and Steele, D. C. Electric rates and tax burdens in Pennsylvania and New York.
ASP  NTJ 2:278-80 Sep 49

A  Freeman, H. A. Public utility taxation. LE 23:42-49 Feb 47

A  Hellerstein, J. R. Excess profits tax relief for the electric utilities under Section 722 of the Internal Revenue Code. LE 20: 149-56 May 44

A  Martin, J. W. Corporate taxes and the assessment of public utility operating property. LE 16:262-69 Aug 40

A  O'Leary, H. J. Utility rate problems arising from recent and prospective income tax legislation. LE 18:184-87 May 42

### 15.66 HOLDING COMPANIES

Anderson, W. H. Public utility holding com-

A  panies: the death sentence and the future. LE 23:244-54 Aug 47

A  Blum, R. SEC integration of holding company systems. LE 17:423-39 Nov 41

A  Hall, J. K. Financial management of gas and electric utilities by the SEC: discussion. JF 3,no.1:50-54 Feb 48

A  Kennedy, W. F. Regulation of utility servicing under the Holding Company Act of 1935. Pt.I-III. LE 17:27-38; 171-87; 257-69 Feb,May,Aug 41

A  -- Recent developments in service company regulations. LE 18:100-02 Feb 42

A  Madden, J. T. and Backman, J. Public utility holding company stocks. JB 13: 213-33 Jul 40

AA  Smith, L. The regulation of some New England holding companies. LE 25: 289-303 Aug 49

A  Troxel, E. Capital structure control of utility companies by the Securities and Exchange Commission. JB 15:225-47 Jul 42

A  -- Financial management of gas and electric utilities by the SEC: discussion. JF 3,no.1:54-58 Feb 48

A  -- Holding company integration: several comments. LE 24:86-89 Feb 48

A  Waterman, M. H. Financial management of gas and electric utilities by the Securities and Exchange Commission. JF 3, no.1:41-50 Feb 48

## 15.7 COMMUNICATION INDUSTRIES

### 15.70 GENERAL

A  Abramovitz, C. G. Some problems in the development of the communications industry. AER 35:585-606 Sep 45

C  Allen, G. H. Wartime changes in English and Canadian radio. JM 7:220-26
EB  Jan 43

A  Beville, H. M., Jr. Surveying radio listeners by use of a probability sample. JM 14:373-78 Oct 49

A  Blum, R. Exemption of small rural telephone companies from the Wage and Hour Act. LE 16:117-20 Feb 40

ASC  Cassady, R., Jr. and Williams, R. M. Radio as an advertising medium: [a study in Los Angeles]. HBR 27:62-78 Jan 49

EB  Coase, R. H. The origin of the monopoly of broadcasting in Great Britain. Ec N.S.14: 189-210 Aug 47

EB  -- Wire broadcasting in Great Britain. Ec N.S.15:194-220 Aug 48

A  Deckinger, E. L. The network radio advertiser and summer policy. JM 13:23-26 Jul 48

A  Du Mont, A. B. Television now and tomorrow. JM 9:276-79 Jan 45

ASN  Gibson, R. L. Some preferences of television audiences [in Schenectady, N.Y.]. JM 10:289-90 Jan 46

15.7  COMMUNICATION INDUSTRIES (Cont.)
15.70  GENERAL (Cont.)

Glaeser, M. G.  The Wisconsin telephone
ASW    case.  LE 16:37-46 Feb 40

Goldin, H. H.  Governmental policy and the
A      domestic telegraph industry.  JEH 7:
       53-68 May 47

Herring, J. M.  Broadcasting and the public
A      interest.  HBR 18:344-56 no.3, 40

Hirschmann, I. A.  Television in the retail
A      field.  JM 8:394-97 Apr 44

Jensen, A.  Stochastic processes applied to
       a simple problem of administrative econ-
       omy.  NTTO 12:151-55 no.37, 48

Laybourn, G. P. and Longstaff, H. P.  Cer-
A      tain correlates of attitudes toward radio
       commercials.  JM 13:447-58 Apr 49

May, G. O.  Another milestone in regulation.
       LE 23:22-28 Feb 47

Mayer, H. and Weiner, A.  The New Jersey
ASN    Telephone Company case.  ILRR 1:
       492-99 Apr 48

Nielsen, A. C.  Trends toward mechaniza-
A      tion of radio advertising.  JM 6:217-28
       Jan 42

-- Two years of commercial operation of
A      the audimeter and the Neilsen radio in-
       dex.  JM 9:239-55 Jan 45

Payne, G. H.  Postwar radio fascimile.
       JM 10:290-91 Jan 46

Plessing, H. C.  Problems of telephone econ-
       omy as seen from a statistical point of
       view.  NTTO 12:201-13 no.37, 48

Simpson, F. R.  The handset telephone and
A      monopoly price policy.  LE 17:245-47
       May 41

-- Public ownership of telephones in U.S.
A      LE 19:99-103 Feb 43

-- Cost trends in the telephone industry.
A      LE 21:286-94 Aug 45

15.71  HISTORY

Anonymous.  Business and the telephone,
A      1878, as illustrated by early directories.
       BHR 15:81-86 Dec 41

Goldin, H. H.  Governmental policy and the
A      domestic telegraph industry.  JEH 7:
       53-68 May 47

15.8  TRANSPORTATION
15.80  GENERAL

Koopmans, T. C.  Optimum utilization of
       the transportation system.  Em 17,suppl.:
       136-45 Jul 49; Errata.  19:227 Apr 51

Sveistrup, P. P.  Some problems in laying
       out a new traffic line.  NTTO 12:255-64
       no.37, 48

UNITED STATES

Ashton, H.  The time element in transpor-
A      tation.  AER/S 37:423-40 May 47

Barton, F. L.  The Interstate Commerce
       Commission considers the class-rate
       structure.  LE 17:10-16 Feb 41

-- and McGehee, R. B.  Freight forwarders.
       HBR 20:336-47 no.3, 42

Bigham, T. C.  The Transportation Act of
       1940.  SEJ 8:1-21 Jul 41

-- Regulation of minimum rates in trans-
       portation.  QJE 61:206-31 Feb 47

Cunningham, W. J.  The transportation
       problem.  HBR 25:58-73 no.1, 46

Daggett, S.  "Transportation and national
       policy."  R.  HBR 22:199-208 no.2, 44

Dewey, R. L.  The Transportation Act of
       1940.  AER 31:15-26 Mar 41

-- chairman.  Round table on transportation
       and public utility problems.  AER/S 39:
       424-26 May 49

Duncan, C. S. [and others]  The transporta-
       tion problem: discussion.  AER/S 30:
       158-63 Mar 40

Eastman, J. B.  The adjustment of rates
       between competing forms of transporta-
       tion.  AER/S 30:124-29 Mar 40

-- Public administration of transportation
       under war conditions.  AER/S 34:86-93
       Mar 44

Edwards, F. K.  Cost analysis in transpor-
       tation.  AER/S 37:441-61 May 47

Fair, M. L. [and others]  Transportation
       and public utilities problems: discussion.
       AER/S 37:478-97 May 47

Hammerberg, D. O.  Wartime problems of
       conservation of transportation [with dis-
       cussion by C. M. Hardin].  JFE 25:147-65
       Feb 43

Harbeson, R. W.  The Transportation Act
       of 1940.  LE 17:291-302 Aug 41

Hippen, J. F.  A Wall Street man and a
       western railroad: a chapter in railroad
       administration.  BHR 23:117-48 Sep 49

Homberger, L. M.  Coordination of road and
       rail transport and the organization of the
       trucking industry: a survey.  LE 17:
       216-25 May 41

Isard, W.  Transport development and
       building cycles.  QJE 57:90-112 Nov 42

Kelso, H.  Waterways versus railways.
       AER 31:537-44 Sep 41

Mater, D. H.  Wage rates and "relative
       economy and fitness" in the transporta-
       tion industry.  JB 18:183-208 Oct 45

Morgan, C. S.  Aspects of the problem of
       public aids to transportation.  AER/S 30:
       130-39 Mar 40

Phillips, E. J., Jr.  Diversion of freight
       traffic from the railroads.  LE 16:403-15
       Nov 40

Smith, H. R.  The problem of evaluating
       regulatory policy.  SEJ 12:17-29 Jul 45

Sorrell, L. C.  Transportation and national
       defense.  JB 14:235-58 Jul 41

Talmage, G. E., Jr.  Transportation for
       war.  HBR 21:336-43 no.3, 43

Virtue, G. O.  The Federal Coordinator's
       investigation of common carrier subsi-
       dies.  LE 24:340-57 Nov 48

15.8 TRANSPORTATION (Cont.)
15.80 GENERAL (Cont.)
UNITED STATES (Cont.)

A Walker, G. Road and rail: a transatlantic comparison. JPE 54:503-21 Dec 46

Wilson, G. L. Freight rates in wartime. HBR 21:230-37 no.2, 43

OTHER COUNTRIES

C Currie, A. W. The Board of Transport Commissioners as an administrative body. CJE 11:342-58 Aug 45

CA Hewetson, H. W. Transportation in the Canadian North. (Arctic survey V) CJE 11:450-66 Aug 45

D Medernach, J. A. Transportation in Latin America. JM 6,no.4,pt.2:152-55 Apr 42

EB Allen, J. E. Railway compensation examined. EJ 58:125-28 Mar 48

Buckatzsch, E. J. War transport. OIS 4: 81-86 Mar 14, 42

-- Reorganisation of inland transport. OIS 4:297-301 Nov 21, 42

Gibb, R. The weight of consignments in transport: a further comment [followed by Lord Stamp's comment]. EJ 50: 525-34 Dec 40

Stamp, J. The weight of consignments in transport. EJ 50:242-47 Jun-Sep 40

Walker, G. Road and rail: a transatlantic comparison. JPE 54:503-21 Dec 46

-- The Transport Act 1947. EJ 58:11-30 Mar 48

EBI -- Transport in Ireland. R. EJ 59:443-44 Sep 49

FI Gadgil, D. R. Rail road coordination with special reference to rates policy. IJE 26: 488-98 Jan 46

Ramanadham, V. V. Transport in transition. IJE 25:265-73 Jan 45

-- Road-rail relations. R. IJE 27:78-84 Jul 46

N Hytten, T. Some problems of Australian transport development. ER 23:5-19 Jun 47

15.81 HISTORY

A Healy, K. T. Transportation as a factor in economic growth. JEH/S 7:72-88 '47

15.82 RAILROADS
15.820 GENERAL
UNITED STATES

A Ashton, H. Railroad costs in relation to the volume of traffic. AER 30:324-32 Jun 40

Baker, G. P. The possibilities of economies by railroad consolidation and co-ordination. AER/S 30:140-57 Mar 40

Daggett, S. Railroad traffic associations and antitrust legislation. AER/S 38: 452-64 May 48

Dewey, R. L. The maintenance of railroad credit. AER/S 36:451-65 May 46

-- and Gray, H. M. Transportation and public utilities: discussion. AER/S 38: 483-87 May 48

Dougall, H. E. and Farwell, L. C. A review of railroad financing, 1920-1938. Pt.I-III. [Pt.III by Farwell alone] LE 16:207-13; 306-17; 443-54 May,Aug,Nov 40

Ellis, D. M. Railroad land grant rates, 1850-1945. LE 21:207-22 Aug 45

Smith, E. A. The Interstate Commerce Commission, the Department of Justice, and the Supreme Court. AER/S 36: 479-93 May 46

Smith, H. R. Capital and labor in the railroad industry. HBR 23:144-56 no.2, 45

Smith, N. L. Rail and utility investments under expanding public control. HBR 18: 397-409 no.4, 40

Stevens, W. H. S. Railroad reorganizations under the Bankruptcy Act. Pt.I-II. JB 15:205-24; 361-81 Jul,Oct 42

-- [and others] Postwar railroad problems: discussion. AER/S 36:494-519 May 46

Williams, E. W., Jr. Railroad traffic and costs. AER 33:360-65 Jun 43

Wilson, G. L. Railroad land-grant rates. JB 15:266-78 Jul 42

ASI Mayer, H. M. Localization of railway facilities in metropolitan centers as typified by Chicago. LE 20:299-315 Nov 44

OTHER COUNTRIES

EB Stewart, M. The new railway agreement. OIS 3:300-04 Sep 20, 41

FI Ramanadham, V. V. Railway convention and surpluses. IJE 25:72-79 Jul 44

-- Railways and industrial location. Pt.I-II. IJE 27:163-76; 28:237-43 Oct 46, Oct 47

H Dawson, W. B. Interim report by Professor S. Herbert Frankel on the Rhodesia railways, 1943. SAJE 11:287-93 Dec 43

HSA Thirlby, G. F. The Report of the Railway Line Revision Commission. (U.G. no.20, 1940) SAJE 8:175-82 Jun 40

15.821 HISTORY

A Cochran, T. C. Some social attitudes of railroad administrators at the end of the nineteenth century. BHR 17:15-21 Feb 43

A Coman, E. T., Jr. Sidelights on the investment policies of Stanford, Huntington, Hopkins, and Crocker. BHR 16:85-89 Nov 42

A Cunningham, W. J. James J. Hill's philosophy of railroad management. BHR 15: 65-72 Nov 41

EF Dunham, A. L. How the first French railways were planned. JEH 1:12-25 May 41

A Ellis, D. M. Railroad land grant rates, 1850-1945. LE 21:207-22 Aug 45

AA Hayter, E. W. The fencing of western railways. AH 19:163-67 Jul 45

## 15.82  RAILROADS (Cont.)
## 15.821  HISTORY (Cont.)

A    Jenks, L. H.  Railroads as an economic force in American development.  JEH 4: 1-20 May 44

ASM  Kirkland, E. C.  The "Railroad scheme" of Massachusetts.  JEH 5:145-71 Nov 45

A    Larson, H. M.  Some unexplored fields in American railroad history.  BHR 16: 69-79 Oct 42

A    Leonard, W. N.  The decline of railroad consolidation.  JEH 9:1-24 May 49

AA  Merk, F.  Eastern antecedents of the Grangers.  [Railroad problems along the Middle Atlantic seaboard]  AH 23:1-8 Jan 49

EB  Morgan, E. V.  Railway investment, Bank of England policy and interest rates, 1844-8.  EH 4:329-40 Feb 40

A    Overton, R. C.  Problems of writing the history of large business units with special reference to railroads.  BHR 22: 22-35 Feb 48

ASV  Turner, C. W.  Railroad service to Virginia farmers, 1828-1860.  AH 22:239-48 Oct 48

## 15.823  RATE LEVEL.  RATE BASE.  RATE OF RETURN

A    Williams, E. W., Jr.  Railroad rate levels and earning power in an era of competitive transport.  LE 25:405-13 Nov 49

## 15.824  RATE STRUCTURE

Spal, S. G.  Agreed charges in railway freight rates abroad.  JB 16:100-06 Apr 43

### UNITED STATES

A    Barton, F. L.  Uniform freight classification and the Interstate Commerce Commission.  LE 18:312-22 Aug 42

-- Another step towards uniform freight classification.  LE 22:22-34 Feb 46

Carter, J. P.  Recent developments in railroad freight rates.  SEJ 15:379-94 Apr 49

Dewey, R. L.  Interterritorial freight rate differences in relation to the regionalization of industry.  JFE 27:433-52 May 45

Hultgren, T.  Divisions of freight rates and the interterritorial rate problem.  JPE 50:99-116 Feb 42

Locklin, D. P.  Reorganization of the railroad rate structure.  AER/S 36:466-78 May 46

Smith, E. A.  A new price policy for the railroads:  quantity or multiple-car rates.  LE 16:230-33 May 40

Wilson, G. L. and Rose, J. R.  "Out-of-pocket" cost in railroad freight rates.  QJE 60:546-60 Aug 46

AA  Barton, F. L.  Recent developments concerning the South's freight-rate problem.  SEJ 6:461-78 Apr 40

Buchanan, J. M.  Regional implications of marginal cost rate making.  SEJ 16: 53-61 Jul 49

Goff, J. H.  The interterritorial freight-rate problem and the South.  SEJ 6: 449-60 Apr 40

Heath, M. S.  The uniform class rate decision and its implications for southern economic development.  SEJ 12:213-37 Jan 46

Roberts, M.  Economic aspects of southern grain rates.  SEJ 16:44-52 Jul 49

Sullivan, R.  The southern passenger fare case.  SEJ 13:126-31 Oct 46

### OTHER COUNTRIES

C    Currie, A. W.  Freight rates and regionalism.  CJE 14:427-40 Nov 48

McDougall, J. L.  On some appendices to the Rowell-Sirois report: X.  Railway freight rates in Canada.  CJE 7:266-67 May 41

Moffat, R. E.  Some aspects of recent freight rate discussions.  CJE 14:441-52 Nov 48

FI   Balakrishna, R.  Transport rates and industrial distribution.  IJE 26:430-40 Jan 46

Gopal, M. H.  A new basis for railway rates: the social benefit of service principle.  IJE 26:441-51 Jan 46

Malhotra, P. C.  An integrated railway rate policy.  IJE 26:517-24 Jan 46

Ramanadham, V. V.  New era in railway rates.  IJE 26:420-29 Jan 46

HSA Threlfell, R. L.  Review of Board of Trade and Industries Report no. 285 and Railway Administration White Paper of May 28, 1946.  SAJE 14:310-17 Dec 46

Timmerman, W. A.  Reply to Mr. Threlfell's review of the Board of Trade & Industries' Report, No. 285.  SAJE 16:106-07 Mar 48

## 15.825  TAXATION

A    Jacoby, N. H.  The rate of capitalizing railroad earnings to establish a valuation for property taxation.  JB 13:158-71 Apr 40

A    Lynch, E. S.  Railroad taxation and abandonments.  HBR 18:496-503 no.4, 40

AA  Martin, J. W. and Pardue, B. L.  Comparative tax loads on railroads in nine southern states.  NTJ 1:25-30 Mar 48

## 15.826  LABOR

C    McDougall, J. L.  The distribution of income among wage workers in railway employment, 1939-47.  CJE 13:248-55 May 47

FI   Mallik, A. N.  Labour problems and labour legislation in India.  (With special reference to the railway industry)  IJE 20: 663-93 Apr 40

**15.82  RAILROADS (Cont.)**
**15.826  LABOR (Cont.)**

Mater, D. H.  The development and opera-
A   tion of the railroad seniority system.
    Pt.I-II.  JB 13:387-419; 14:36-67 Oct 40,
    Jan 41
    -- A statistical study of the effect of senior-
A   ity upon employee efficiency.  JB 14:
    169-204 Apr 41
    -- Effects of seniority upon the welfare of
A   the employee, the employer, and society.
    JB 14:384-418 Oct 41
Northrup, H. R.  The appropriate bargaining
A   unit question under the Railway Labor
    Act.  QJE 60:250-69 Feb 46
    -- The Railway Labor act and railway labor
A   disputes in wartime.  AER 36:324-43
    Jun 46
    -- Emergency disputes under the Railway
A   Labor Act.  IRRA 1:78-88 Dec 48

**15.83  WATER TRANSPORTATION**
**15.830  GENERAL**

Diebold, W., Jr.  Shipping in the immediate
    postwar years.  JPE 53:15-36 Mar 45
Lachmann, K.  The shipping problem at the
    end of the war.  SR 10:52-75 Feb 43
Lewis, W. A.  The inter-relations of ship-
    ping freights.  Ec N.S.8:52-76 Feb 41
Perry, H. S.  Ocean shipping.  HBR 19:
    438-50 no.4, 41
Sutton, C. T.  An enquiry into the assessing
    of salvage awards [with discussion].
    JRSS 108:41-92 pt.1-2, 45

UNITED STATES

Beckett, G.  Commerce on the Great Lakes
A   system.  JM 8:426-29 Apr 44
Deimel, H. L., Jr.  United States shipping
    policy and international economic rela-
    tions.  AER/S 36:547-60 May 46
Hutchins, J. G. B.  The declining American
    maritime industries: an unsolved prob-
    lem, 1860-1940.  JEH/S 6:103-22 '46
Kelso, H.  Inland waterway carriers.  LE 18:
    58-66 Feb 42
Lawler, P. F.  Crisis in the domestic ship-
    ping industry.  HBR 24:258-76 no.2, 46
Marx, D., Jr.  The determination of postwar
    ocean freight rates.  AER/S 36:561-74
    May 46
    -- The Merchant Ship Sales Act of 1946.
    JB 21:12-28 Jan 48
    -- Current American ship-operating sub-
    sidies.  JB 21:239-59 Oct 48
Perry, H. S.  Ocean rate regulation, World
    War II.  HBR 21:238-52 no.2, 43
    -- The wartime merchant fleet and post-
    war shipping requirements.  AER/S 36:
    520-46 May 46
Stein, A. L.  Federal regulation of water
    carriers.  LE 16:478-81 Nov 40

Sullivan, R.  The disposition of the United
    States Merchant Marine.  SEJ 11:369-75
    Apr 45
Wilson, G. L. and Kramer, R. L.  Postwar
    shipping policy: discussion.  AER/S 36:
    575-78 May 46
Eliel, P.  Labor peace in Pacific ports.
AA   HBR 19:429-37 no.4, 41
    -- Industrial peace and conflict: a study of
    two Pacific Coast industries [pulp and
    paper and stevedoring].  ILRR 2:
    477-501 Jul 49

OTHER COUNTRIES

Beckett, G.  Commerce on the Great Lakes
C   system.  JM 8:426-29 Apr 44
Balogh, T.  The shipping balance.  OIS 5:
EB   25-31 Jan 30, 43
Buckatzsch, E. J.  The canals.  OIS 3:71-74
    Mar 15, 41
Burchardt, F.  Shipping: the bottleneck.
    OIS 4:193-97 Jul 18, 42
Kendall, M. G.  Losses of U.K. merchant
    ships in World War II.  Ec N.S.15:289-93
    Nov 48
    -- United Kingdom merchant shipping sta-
    tistics.  JRSS 111:133-44 pt.2, 48
Macgregor, D. H.  Aspects of the shipping
    question.  OIS 2,no.11:7-10 Dec 40
Moos, S.  The shipping situation.  OIS 3:
    74-76 Mar 15, 41
Roberts, R. O.  Comparative shipping and
    shipbuilding costs.  Ec N.S.14:296-309
    Nov 47
Hamburger, E.  A peculiar pattern of the
EG   fifth column: the organization of the
    German seamen.  SR 9:495-509 Nov 42
Einarsen, J.  Replacement in the shipping
ESN   industry [of Norway].  REStat 28:225-30
    Nov 46
Paulson, E. W.  Relation of operating costs
    to tonnage of ships in ocean transport.
    NTTO 12:187-92 no.37, 48
Sawa, S.  Japanese and British vessels in
FC   Chinese waters [Pt.I-II].  Kyo 18,no.1:
    18-33; no.3:62-70 Jan,Jul 43
Natesan, L. A.  Shipping in relation to com-
FI   mercial policy.  IJE 28:55-60 Jul 47
Richards, C. S.  Shipping services of the
HSA   Union government and the possibilities
    of their development.  SAJE 11:269-78
    Dec 43

**15.831  HISTORY**

Aitken, H. G. J.  William Hamilton Merritt:
C   a study in Canadian entrepreneurship.
    EEH 2:1-23 Nov 49
Albion, R. G.  Early nineteenth-century
A   shipowning; a chapter in business enter-
    prise.  JEH 1:1-11 May 41
Anonymous.  A note on marine insurance in
ASM   Salem.  BHR 14:30-32 Apr 40

## 15.83 WATER TRANSPORTATION (Cont.)
## 15.831 HISTORY (Cont.)

Hadfield, E. C. R. Canals between the
EB   English and the Bristol channels.
    EHR 12:59-67 no.1-2, 42

-- The Thames navigation and the canals,
EB   1770-1830. EHR 14:172-79 no.2, 44

Hunter, L. C. The invention of the western
AA   steamboat. JEH 3:201-20 Nov 43

Hutchins, J. G. B. The declining American
A   maritime industries: an unsolved prob-
    lem, 1860-1940. JEH/S 6:103-22 '46

Rae, J. B. Federal land grants in aid of
A   canals. JEH 4:167-77 Nov 44

Redlich, F. Some remarks on the business
ASN   of a New York ship chandler in the 1810's.
    BHR 16:92-98 Nov 42

-- William Jones and his unsuccessful
A   steamboat venture of 1819. BHR 21:
    125-36 Nov 47

Rowland, B. and Snedeker, G. B. The United
A   States Court of Claims and French spolia-
    tion records. BHR 18:20-27 Apr 44

Shackell, R. S. A short historical note on
    the marine policy. SAJE 17:306-19
    Sep 49

## 15.84 AIR TRANSPORTATION
## 15.840 GENERAL

Beckett, G. Foreign trade by air. JM 12:
A   505-06 Apr 48

Bollinger, L. L. Private versus public
A   management of airports. HBR 24:518-34
    no.4, 46

Constantin, J. A. Multilateralism in inter-
    national aviation. SEJ 16:197-209 Oct 49

Crane, J. B. The economics of air trans-
A   portation. HBR 22:495-508 no.4, 44

Currie, A. W. Some economic aspects of
C   air transport. CJE 7:13-24 Feb 41

David, P. T. Aviation in the postwar world:
    discussion. AER/S 35:249-52 May 45

Frederick, J. H. and Lewis, A. D. Air
A   routes and public policy. HBR 19:482-95
    no.4, 41

-- How air transportation may affect mar-
A   keting and product development. JM 8:
    274-80 Jan 44

-- Some problems of selling air travel.
A   JM 9:144-50 Oct 44

Hackford, R. R. Our international aviation
A   policy. HBR 25:483-500 no.4, 47

Harding, W. B. Air transportation rates.
A   HBR 18:337-43 no.3, 40

Healy, K. T. Workable competition in air
A/EB transportation. AER/S 35:229-42 May 45

Hubbard, J. B. World transport aviation.
    HBR 22:509-15 no.4, 44

Isard, C. and Isard, W. Economic impli-
    cations of aircraft. QJE 59:145-69 Feb 45

Lachmann, K. War and peace economics of
    aviation. SR 7:468-79 Nov 40

Leonard, W. N. Some problems of postwar

A   air transportation. AER/S 37:462-77
    May 47

Northrup, H. R. Collective bargaining by
A   air line pilots. QJE 61:533-76 Aug 47

Wright, Q. The international regulation of
    the air. AER/S 35:243-48 May 45

## 15.85 ROAD TRANSPORTATION. HIGHWAYS
## 15.850 GENERAL

Cohen, M. A. and Lieberman, M. Collective
A   bargaining in the motor freight industry.
    ILRR 3:17-32 Oct 49

George, J. J. and Boldt, J. R., Jr. Certifi-
A   cation of motor common carriers by the
    Interstate Commerce Commission.
    Pt.I-II. LE 17:82-91; 196-206 Feb,May 41

Laight, J. C. Competition in road motor
HSA   transportation. SAJE 16:24-34 Mar 48

Morrison, H. Rate policy of Interstate
A   Commerce Commission for back-hauls
    of trucks: pricing and joint cost. LE 19:
    329-38 Aug 43

Nelson, J. C. Economies of large-scale
A   operation in the trucking industry.
    LE 17:112-15 Feb 41

-- Trends in federal regulation of motor
A   carriers. LE 18:366-73 Aug 42

Ramanadham, V. V. Road-owners and
FI   road-hauliers. IJE 25:520-32 Apr 45

Spurr, W. A. The case for the common
A   carrier in trucking. LE 24:253-63
    Aug 48

Zettel, R. M. Taxation for highways in
ASC   California. NTJ 1:207-25 Sep 48

## 15.851 HISTORY

Teiser, R. and Harroun, C. Origin of Wells,
A   Fargo & Company, 1841-1852. BHR 22:
    70-83 Jun 48

-- and Harroun, C. Wells, Fargo & Com-
ASC   pany: the first half year [in California].
    BHR 23:87-95 Jun 49

## 15.86 URBAN TRANSPORTATION
## 15.860 GENERAL

Blankenship, A. B. The movement of
    people: a field for market research.
    JM 13:44-51 Jul 48

Carroll, J. D., Jr. Some aspects of the
A   home-work relationships of industrial
    workers. LE 25:414-22 Nov 49

Cochrane, D. Travelling to work. ER 22:
N   199-218 Dec 46

Laight, J. C. Municipal passenger transport
EB   costs and revenue: United Kingdom and
HSA   South Africa 1938/9-1945/6. SAJE 17:
    443-56 Dec 49

McConnell, J. W. and Lampert, B. P.
ASN   Employee adjustment to technological
    displacement: the Fifth Avenue Coach
    Company case. ILRR 2:219-26 Jan 49

Meyers, F. Organization and collective
AA   bargaining in the local mass transpor-

## 15.86 URBAN TRANSPORTATION (Cont.)
## 15.860 GENERAL (Cont.)
Meyers, F. (cont.)
    tation industry in the Southeast. SEJ 15:
A    425-40 Apr 49

Simpson, F. R. The war's impact on urban
A    transit systems. HBR 23:460-68 no.4, 45

Sleeman, J. F. Municipal transport costs
EB    and revenue: 1938-9 and 1945-6.
    MS 16:289-301 Sep 48

Yates, S. R. Design for Chicago transit:
ASI    London style. LE 17:320-32 Aug 41

## 15.9 ATOMIC INDUSTRIES
Dembitz, L. N. [and others] The social
    and economic significance of atomic
    energy: discussion. AER/S 37:109-17
    May 47

Isard, W. Some economic implications of
    atomic energy. QJE 62:202-28 Feb 48

-- and Lansing, J. B. Comparisons of power
A    cost for atomic and conventional steam
    stations [with An addendum on the
    Cowles Commission estimates by Isard].
    REStat 31:217-28 Aug 49

Jacobs, J. K. The development of atomic
    energy. S&S 10:292-99 no.3, 46

Menke, J. R. Nuclear fission as a source
    of power. Em 15:314-34 Oct 47

Pregel, B. Peacetime uses of atomic
    energy. SR 14:27-44 Mar 47

Schurr, S. H. Economic aspects of atomic
    energy as a source of power. AER/S 37:
    98-108 May 47

-- Atomic power in selected industries.
A    HBR 27:459-79 Jul 49

# 16. AGRICULTURE

## 16.0 GENERAL
## 16.01 AGRICULTURAL SITUATION
## 16.010 GENERAL
Ciriacy-Wantrup, S. von. The relation of
    war economics to agriculture, with par-
    ticular reference to the effects of in-
    come and price inflation and deflation.
    AER/S 30:366-82 Mar 40

Purves, C. M. Major shifts in world agri-
    culture. JFE 27:245-60 May 45

Schultz, T. W. Two conditions necessary
    for economic progress in agriculture.
    CJE 10:298-311 Aug 44

-- Reflections on poverty within agriculture
    [with discussion by E. J. Long]. JFE 31,
    pt.2:1112-17 Nov 49

### UNITED STATES
Black, J. D. and Boddy, N. The agricultural
A    situation, March, 1940. REStat 22:53-73
    May 40

-- Measures for the improvement of agri-
    culture. AER/S 30,no.5:165-76 Feb 41

-- Fundamental elements in the current
    agricultural situation. JFE 23:712-25
    Nov 41

Burroughs, R. J. Consolidated balance
    sheet and income statement for agricul-
    ture. JFE 27:463-72 May 45

Davis, J. S. American agriculture: Schultz'
    analysis and policy proposals. R.
    REStat 29:80-91 May 47

Hammerberg, D. O. Farmers in a changing
    world: the 1940 Yearbook of agriculture.
    II. R. JFE 23:451-53 May 41

Hibbard, B. H. The farmer is dependent on
    national programs. AER/S 30,no.5:
    155-64 Feb 41

Johnson, S. E. Agricultural production
    after the war. JFE 27:261-80 May 45

Kaysen, C. and Lorie, J. H. A note on
    Professor Schultz's analysis of the long
    run agricultural problem [followed by
    T. W. Schultz's comment and Kaysen
    and Lorie's rejoinder]. REStat 30:
    286-97 Nov 48

Leffler, G. V. The farmer talks back.
    LE 17:108-11 Feb 41

Link, A. S. The Federal Reserve policy and
    the agricultural depression of 1920-1921.
    AH 20:166-75 Jul 46

Norton, L. J. Farmers in a changing world;
    the 1940 Yearbook of agriculture. III. R.
    JFE 23:454-55 May 41

Nourse, E. G. Agriculture in a stabilized
    economy. JFE 31,pt.2:201-12 Feb 49

Reid, M. G. Farmers in a changing world:
    the 1940 yearbook of agriculture. I. R.
    JFE 23:446-50 May 41

Schultz, T. W. Changes in economic struc-
    ture affecting American agriculture.
    JFE 28:15-27 Feb 46

-- The economic stability of American ag-
    riculture. JFE 29:809-26 Nov 47

Tolley, H. R. An appraisal of the national
    interest in the agricultural situation.
    AER/S 30,no.5:108-26 Feb 41

Wilcox, W. W. Capital in agriculture.
    QJE 58:49-64 Nov 43

-- Discussion of papers on postwar agri-
    cultural problems. JFE 28:264-66
    Feb 46

Crickman, C. W. Postwar agricultural
AA    problems in the corn belt. JFE 28:
    243-60 Feb 46

Forster, G. W. Southern agricultural econ-
    omy in the postwar era. SEJ 13:65-71
    Jul 46

Grimes, W. E. Postwar agricultural prob-
    lems in the Great Plains area. JFE 28:
    235-42 Feb 46

# 16. AGRICULTURE

## 16.01 AGRICULTURAL SITUATION (Cont.)
### 16.010 GENERAL (Cont.)

#### UNITED STATES (Cont.)

Kraenzel, C. F. New frontiers of the Great
AA  Plains. JFE 24:571-88 Aug 42

Stepp, J. M. Southern agriculture's stake
in occupational freedom. SEJ 13:46-52
Jul 46

Welch, F. J. Some economic and social
implications of agricultural adjustments
in the South [with discussion]. JFE 29:
192-208 Feb 47

#### OTHER AMERICAN COUNTRIES

Burton, G. L. The farmer and the market.
C    CJE 15:495-504 Nov 49

Witt, L. W. Changes in the agriculture of
DSB  south central Brazil. JFE 25:622-43
Aug 43

#### EUROPE

Borchert, J. R. The agriculture of England
EB  and Wales, 1939-1946. AH 22:56-62
Jan 48

Duckham, A. N. Liberty, progress, and security: fifteen centuries of British agriculture. AH 22:129-33 Jul 48

Murray, K. A. H. British agriculture: introduction. LBR 5:58-59 Jul 47

-- The outlook for British agriculture.
LBR 11:55-74 Jan 49

Nash, E. F. Changes in external factors
affecting British agriculture. LBR 8:
35-56 Apr 48

Lewis, W. A. Developing colonial agricul-
EBC  ture. TBR 2:3-21 Jun 49

Johnston, J. Irish agriculture then and
EBI  now. MS 11:105-22 Oct 40

Medici, G. The E.R.P. and the problems
EI   of Italian agriculture. BNL 1:416-26
Oct 48

Bennett, M. K. Food and agriculture in the
ER  Soviet Union, 1917-48. JPE 57:185-98
Jun 49

Harris, L. Some comparisons of socialist
and capitalist agriculture. S&S 10:
159-71 no.2, 46

Jasny, N. The plight of the collective
farms. JFE 30:304-21 May 48

Volin, L. America looks at Russian agriculture. JFE 26:46-58 Feb 44

Wellington, S. Soviet agriculture: a discussion. I. Queries [followed by L. Harris'
reply]. S&S 11:270-78 no.3, 47

#### ASIA

Agarwala, A. N. The place of agriculture
FI  vis-a-vis industry in the industrialists'
plan. IJE 25:117-23 Oct 44

-- Economic planning and agriculture.
IJE 26:61-82 Jul 45

Dubey, D. S. The place of agriculture in
the proposed plans. IJE 25:551-56 Apr 45

Ghatge, M. B. and Patel, K. S. Economics
of mixed farming in "Charotar" (Bombay
province). IJE 23:133-54 Oct 42

Lal, H. Agriculture in the Bombay plan.
IJE 26:43-60 Jul 45

Malhotra, P. C. Agricultural possibilities
in India. IJE 25:556-60 Apr 45

-- and Agarwala, A. N. Agriculture in the
industrialists' plan. IJE 25:502-10 Apr 45

Moomaw, I. W. Peasant farming in India.
JFE 24:685-94 Aug 42

Rahman, S. Can Bengal support such a
large agricultural population? IJE 27:
53-63 Jul 46

Saksena, S. P. Price level in India with
particular reference to agricultural
prices. IJE 21:798-803 Apr 41

Akhtar, S. M. Objectives of agricultural
FIP  planning for Pakistan. PEJ 1,no.1:14-23
Jul 49

Rahman, K. A. Economic reconstruction of
Pakistan with reference to agriculture.
PEJ 1,no.1:4-13 Jul 49

#### AFRICA

Mabin, H. S. Some comments on the Report
HSA  of the Reconstruction Committee of the
Department of Agriculture and Forestry.
SAJE 12:60-63 Mar 44

#### AUSTRALIA. NEW ZEALAND

Campbell, K. O. Australian agricultural
N   production in the depression. ER 20:
58-73 Jun 44

Isles, K. S. and Ramsay, A. M. Lack of
adaptability in agriculture: an economic
survey. ER 20:18-37 Jun 44

## 16.011 FOOD CROPS

Apy, P. Trends in cocoa production:
H   British West Africa. OIS 11:389-404
Dec 49

Govil, K. L. Our food: a critical study in
FI  retrospect and prospect. IJE 26:734-43
Apr 46

Hammond, R. J. British food supplies,
EB  1914-1939. EHR 16:1-14 no.1, 46

Hurt, B. R. Using agricultural census data
ASI  in a study of the chicken enterprise in
central Indiana. JFE 30:339-50 May 48

Lindberg, J. Food supply under a program
of freedom from want. SR 12:181-204
May 45

Misra, S. Food position in Orissa. IJE 26:
FI  525-34 Jan 46

Nelson, G. L. Volume of United States ex-
A   ports and imports of foods, 1909-43.
JFE 26:399-405 May 44

Neumark, S. D. World situation of fats and
oils. SAJE 15:192-203 Sep 47

Prasad, M. Decentralisation in co-opera-
FI  tive cane unions. IJE 29:55-58 Jul 48

16.011 FOOD CROPS (Cont.)

Rudra, S. K. Our food problem. IJE 24:
FI   169-78 Jan 44

Satyanarayana, M. C. Cardamom industry
FI   in India. IJE 29:385-91 Apr 49

Schultz, T. W. Food, agriculture, and trade
[with discussion]. JFE 29:1-40 Feb 47

Secrett, F. A. British horticulture: a vital
EB   industry. LBR 12:30-52 Apr 49

Sukhla, S. S. Some aspects of the Indian
FI   food problem. IJE 27:427-31 Apr 47

Tyszynski, H. Economics of the wheat
agreement. Ec N.S.16:27-39 Feb 49

Viton, A. Trends in world food economy.
JFE 29:1043-54 Nov 47

White, B. S., Jr. and Denhardt, E. T.
Chronic surpluses of agricultural commodities in the post-war period. JFE 25:
743-58 Nov 43

Williamson, W. F. The place of coffee in
A   trade with Latin America. JM 6,no.4,
D   pt.2:149-51 Apr 42

16.012 LIVESTOCK. DAIRY PRODUCTS

Cunningham, L. C. Postwar agricultural
A   problems in the dairy regions. JFE 28:
261-64 Feb 46

Rutherford, R. S. G. Fluctuations in the
N   sheep population of New South Wales,
1860-1940. ER 24:56-71 Jun 48

Walsh, R. M. Export market and price of
A   lard. JFE 25:487-94 May 43

16.013 FIBER CROPS

Ackerman, J., chairman. Adjustments in
AA   southern agriculture with special refer-
ence to cotton. [Report of the Cotton
Committee] JFE 28:341-79 Feb 46

Allen, J. S. Machines in cotton. S&S 12:
AA   240-53 no.2, 48

Blau, G. Wool in the world economy [with
discussion]. JRSS 109:179-242 pt.3, 46

Cronje, F. J. C. Wool in the South African
HSA   economy. SAJE 17:123-41 Jun 49

Duggan, I. W. Cotton, land, and people: a
AA   statement of the problem. JFE 22:188-97
Feb 40

El-Said, M. H. Seasonality of the Egyptian
ME   export trade. EgC 37:227-31 May-Dec 46

Huber, J. R. The effects of German clearing agreements and import restrictions
on cotton, 1934-1939. SEJ 6:419-39
Apr 40

Hyson, C. D. The shift toward medium
staple cotton. JFE 26:396-99 May 44

-- Maladjustments in the wool industry and
need for new policy. JFE 29:425-56
May 47

Kreider, C. The Anglo-American cotton-
A   rubber barter agreement. SEJ 7:216-24
EB   Oct 40

Lowndes, A. G. The economic condition of
N   the wool industry in Queensland. R.
ER 16:118-21 Jun 40

Murray, Sir A. R. Indian jute. LBR 5:
FI   29-42 Jul 47

Oulton, P. G. Indian cotton. LBR 1:35-40
FI   Jul 46

White, B. S., Jr. The shrinking foreign
A   market for United States cotton. QJE 54:
255-76 Feb 40

16.014 OTHER CROPS

Bauer, P. T. Some aspects of the Malayan
FM   rubber slump 1929-33. Ec N.S.11:190-98
Nov 44

-- The working of rubber regulation.
EJ 56:391-414 Sep 46

-- Malayan rubber policies. Ec N.S.14:
FM   81-107 May 47

Benham, F. The rubber industry. R.
FM   Ec N.S.16:355-68 Nov 49

Knorr, K. E. World rubber problems.
HBR 24:394-404 no.3, 46

Silcock, T. H. A note on the working of
rubber regulation [followed by P. T.
Bauer's rejoinder]. EJ 58:228-43 Jun 48

16.02 AGRICULTURAL OUTLOOK

Barlowe, R. Population pressure and food
production potentialities. LE 25:227-39
Aug 49

Black, A. G. Iranian agriculture: present
M   and prospective. JFE 30:422-42 Aug 48

Black, J. D. Coming readjustments in ag-
A   riculture: domestic phases [with discus-
sion by T. W. Schultz]. JFE 31:1-18
Feb 49

Booth, J. F. The economic problems of
C   Canadian agriculture in the war and post-
war period. CJE 8:446-59 Aug 42

Canning, J. B. Food and agriculture:
longer-run outlook and policy.
AER/S 35:405-16 May 45

Eggert, R. J. Animal fats and oils: situation and outlook. JFE 31,pt.2:331-39
Feb 49

Hurd, W. B. On some appendices to the
CA   Rowell-Sirois report: VIII Prairie popu-
lation possibilities. R. CJE 7:259-63
May 41

Jasspon, W. H. Outlook for world fats and
oils production and use. JFE 31,pt.2:
325-30 Feb 49

Lamartine Yates, P. Food and agriculture:
outlook and policy: discussion. AER/S 35:
417-18 May 45

Long, E. J. Long-time economic prospects
A   for agriculture? JFE 31:731-32 Nov 49

Mighell, R. L. [and others] Recent regional
AA   changes in farming and probable future
trends [with discussion]. JFE 24:256-84
Feb 42

Norton, L. J. Animal fats and oils: discussion. JFE 31,pt.2:339-42 Feb 49

Robinson, N. Future trends in Germany's
EG   agricultural system. JFE 26:309-26
May 44

# 16. AGRICULTURE

## 16.02 AGRICULTURAL OUTLOOK (Cont.)

AA Saunderson, M. H. Adjustments in western beef cattle production and marketing during the war and post-war periods. JFE 26:789-94 Nov 44

A Staehle, H. Relative prices and postwar markets for animal food products. QJE 59:237-79 Feb 45

AA Starch, E. The future of the Great Plains reappraised [with discussion by R. B. Tootell and G. Montgomery]. JFE 31, pt.2:917-30 Nov 49

AA Stine, O. C. Future of cotton in the economy of the South [with discussion]. JFE 23:112-37 Feb 41

A Szatrowski, Z. The consistency of U.S.D.A. estimates of possible consumption and prices of beef and pork in 1950. JFE 27: 984-89 Nov 45

EB Thompson, R. J. The future of agriculture [with discussion]. JRSS 106:32-50 pt.1, 43

## 16.03 AGRICULTURAL ECONOMICS AND RESEARCH
## 16.030 GENERAL

A Allin, B. W. The objectives and methods of agricultural economics. JFE 30:545-52 Aug 48

A Borg, W. T. Clifford V. Gregory and his writings. AH 16:116-22 Apr 42

A Edwards, E. E. Objectives for the Agricultural History Society during its second twenty-five years. AH 18:187-92 Oct 44

A Harrell, G. D. Prices paid by farmers: their use in administering wartime price control programs. JFE 25:338-50 Feb 43

Heady, E. O. Implications of particular economics in agricultural economics methodology. JFE 31,pt.2:837-50 Nov 49

Hoos, S. Implications of aggregative theories for agricultural economists. JFE 31,pt.2:851-62 Nov 49

Issawi, C. Agriculture versus industry: a reconsideration of the problem. EgC 35: 39-48 Jan-Feb 44

A Murray, W. G. Discussion of papers: research developments. JFE 28:140-43 Feb 46

Porter, H. G. The expanding scope of agricultural economics. JFE 23:138-44 Feb 41

Saloutos, T. Discussion: [agricultural economics and history]. JFE 30:555-57 Aug 48

Salter, L. A., Jr. Cross-sectional and case-grouping procedures in research analysis. JFE 24:792-805 Nov 42

Trivedi, P. M. Agricultural economy: some vital aspects. IJE 22:189-98 Oct 41

## 16.031 EDUCATION OF AGRICULTURAL ECONOMISTS

A Alsberg, C. L. Nature and scope of training for men contemplating work in the field of agricultural economics. JFE 22: 52-59 Feb 40

A Black, J. D. Training and recruitment of agricultural economic personnel: V. For public service. JFE 22:560-61 Aug 40

A Carter, R. M. Evaluation of work simplification research and teaching activities. JFE 29:225-31 Feb 47

A Conklin, H. E. A neglected point in the training of agricultural economists. JFE 29:925-37 Nov 47

Cooper, T. Training and recruitment of agricultural economic personnel: IV. A training program. JFE 22:558-59 Aug 40

Diesslin, H. G. Specialization vs. diversification in course work. JFE 31,pt.2: 540-41 Feb 49

Dowell, A. A. Some considerations in building a curriculum for agricultural economics majors. JFE 29:1319-28 Nov 47

Grimes, W. E. Personnel training and recruitment in agricultural economics [with discussion by O. B. Jesness]. JFE 22:78-83 Feb 40

Hill, F. F. Training and recruitment of agricultural economic personnel: VI. An administrator's view. JFE 22:562-66 Aug 40

Parsons, K. H. Training agricultural economists for public careers. JFE 29: 1329-40 Nov 47

A Ross, E. D. The land-grant college: a democratic adaptation. AH 15:26-36 Jan 41

A Sarle, C. F. Training and recruitment of agricultural economic personnel: VII. The government service as a career. JFE 22:567-69 Aug 40

A -- The place for enumerative surveys in research and graduate training in agricultural economics. JFE 29:237-40 Feb 47

AA Saville, R. J. Training and recruitment of agricultural economic personnel: III. The South. JFE 22:418-20 May 40

Schultz, T. W. Needed additions to the theoretical equipment of an agricultural economist. JFE 22:60-66 Feb 40

Schwartz, H. The student with an urban background and agricultural economics. JFE 22:762-65 Nov 40

Taylor, H. C. Training and recruitment of agricultural economic personnel: I. A general view. JFE 22:411-14 May 40

A Waugh, F. V. Training and recruitment of agricultural economic personnel: II. The civil servant. JFE 22:415-17 May 40

16.031 EDUCATION OF AGRICULTURAL
ECONOMISTS (Cont.)

A Wood, G. B. Training agricultural economic
majors for business careers [with discussion by O. A. Day]. JFE 29:1341-57
Nov 47

16.04 AGRICULTURAL INFORMATION AND
EDUCATION SERVICES

Black, J. D. The international food movement. AER 33:791-811 Dec 43

Broadley, Sir H. The food situation in
Europe in relation to the work of FAO.
JFE 31,pt.2:268-80 Feb 49

Dodd, N. E. The Food and Agriculture Organization of the United Nations: its history, organization, and objectives.
AH 23:81-86 Apr 49

Flexner, J. A. Food policies of the United
Nations. AER 33:812-24 Dec 43

Hobson, A. Discussion of papers on foreign
agriculture and trade problems. JFE 28:
80-83 Feb 46

Lamartine Yates, P. Food and Agriculture
Organization of the United Nations.
JFE 28:54-70 Feb 46

Whitlam, A. G. Food and Agricultural Organization of the United Nations. ER 22:
289-92 Dec 46

UNITED STATES

A Benedict, M. R. The social sciences in experiment station research. JFE 31:
253-65 May 49

Bottum, J. C. Useful techniques in an extension program in agricultural policy.
JFE 31,pt.2:687-89 Feb 49

Caparoon, C. D. and Jorgensen, E. A. Agricultural data needs in extension work.
JFE 30:282-91 May 48

Crosby, J. E. and Burch, J. W. Discussion
of papers on postwar Extension problems
in agricultural economics. JFE 28:
226-34 Feb 46

Galloway, Z. L. Useful techniques in an extension program in farm management.
JFE 31,pt.2:693-96 Feb 49

Jesness, O. B. Federal-state relationships
in agriculture. JFE 22:493-95 May 40

Malone, C. Postwar Extension problems
in farm management. JFE 28:213-26
Feb 46

Miller, L. F. Farm and home planning:
discussion [summarized]. JFE 29:189-91
Feb 47

-- Outlook and farm management. JFE 31,
pt.2:642-45 Feb 49

Ogg, W. Useful techniques in an extension
program in economic principles as applied to agriculture. JFE 31,pt.2:697-99
Feb 49

Proctor, R. E. Extension use of farm work
simplification. JFE 28:314-19 Feb 46

Stice, L. F. Useful techniques in an extension marketing program. JFE 31,pt.2:
690-92 Feb 49

Stout, W. B. Postwar Extension problems
in agricultural marketing. JFE 28:
187-98 Feb 46

Timm, T. R. An introduction to Extension
economics. JFE 31,pt.2:682-86 Feb 49

Westcott, G. W. Postwar Extension problems in general agricultural economics.
JFE 28:199-212 Feb 46

Wilson, M. L. and Dixon, H. M. Farm and
home planning: a new approach to farm
management extension work. JFE 29:
167-74 Feb 47

Young, H. N. Work simplification: review.
JFE 29:231-32 Feb 47

AA Anonymous. The history of western range
research prepared by Division of Range
Research, Forest Service, United States
Department of Agriculture. AH 18:
127-43 Jul 44

ASN Cunningham, L. C. Use of outlook in an extension program [in New York]. JFE 31,
pt.2:640-41 Feb 49

16.05 AGRICULTURAL STATISTICS

Hirsch, H. G. 1950 World census of agriculture. JFE 29:564-66 May 47

Kellett, W. G. G. International rubber statistics. JRSS 112:419-35 pt.4, 49

UNITED STATES

A Bachman, K. L. [and others] Appraisal of
the economic classification of farms.
JFE 30:680-702 Nov 48

Becker, J. A. Agricultural statistics: discussion. JFE 22:366-68 Feb 40

Benedict, M. R. [and others] Need for a new
classification of farms. JFE 26:694-708
Nov 44

Callander, W. F. and Sarle, C. F. The
Bureau of Agricultural Economics program in enumerative sampling. JFE 29:
233-36 Feb 47

Dean, J. and Wise, M. H. An appraisal of
index numbers of prices farmers pay.
JASA 36:210-18 Jun 41

Harlan, C. L. The 1945 Census enumeration of livestock on farms. JFE 29:
691-710 Aug 47

Houseman, E. E. The sample design for a
national farm survey by the Bureau of
Agricultural Economics. JFE 29:241-45
Feb 47

Jasny, N. Proposal for revision of Agricultural statistics. JFE 24:402-19 May 42

Jenkins, W. B. Agricultural census of 1940.
JFE 22:350-58 Feb 40

Jessen, R. J. The master sample project
and its use in agricultural economics.
JFE 29:531-40 May 47

Kimball, E. S. Characteristics of U.S. poultry statistics. JFE 22:359-66 Feb 40

16.05 AGRICULTURAL STATISTICS (Cont.)
UNITED STATES (Cont.)

King, A. J. and Simpson, G. D. New devel-
A opments in agricultural sampling.
JFE 22:341-49 Feb 40

-- and McCarty, D. E. Application of
sampling to agricultural statistics with
emphasis on stratified samples. JM 5:
462-73 Apr 41

Leith, W. G. Agricultural economic data:
discussion. JFE 29:1224-28 Nov 47

Malenbaum, W. Indexes on a type-farm
basis. JFE 23:584-606 Aug 41

Peterson, A. G. Agricultural price index
numbers. JASA 42:597-604 Dec 47

Pettet, Z. R. Highlights of the 1940 census
[with discussion by T. R. Hedges].
JFE 23:266-74 Feb 41

Sarle, C. F. The possibilities and limitations of objective sampling in strengthening agricultural statistics. Em 8:45-61
Jan 40

-- and Robinson, T. C. M. Measurement of
agricultural production [with discussion
by C. Hildreth]. JFE 31:213-32 May 49

Taeuber, C. Some aspects of the statistics
program in the Department of Agriculture. JASA 42:41-45 Mar 47

Tolley, H. R. and Taeuber, C. Wartime
developments in agricultural statistics.
JASA 39:411-27 Dec 44

Clauson, M. Suggestions for a sample cen-
AA sus of agriculture in the West. JFE 22:
633-37 Aug 40

Benson, A. P. State frontiers in agricul-
AS tural statistics [with discussion by R. K.
Smith]. JFE 31,pt.2:293-308 Feb 49

Waite, W. C. State index numbers of agricultural prices. JFE 29:1250-56 Nov 47

Wilcox, E. C. and Ebling, W. H. Presentation of agricultural data in the states
[with discussion by L. M. Carl]. JFE 31,
pt.2:309-24 Feb 49

King, F. P. Developing a technique for de-
ASG termining types of farming [in Georgia].
JFE 30:350-57 May 48

Hopkins, J. A. An experiment on the accu-
ASI racy of farm survey data [in Iowa].
JFE 23:492-96 May 41

OTHER COUNTRIES

Sant, P. T. and Vickery, R. E. The food and
EG agricultural statistics of the Reich Food
Administration. AH 21:177-85 Jul 47

Vickery, R. E. and Sant, P. T. Agricultural
statistics in Germany. JFE 28:1061-69
Nov 46

Anis, M. Value of agriculture products and
ME other commodities pertaining to agriculture for the years 1937-1942. EgC 36:
357-68 Mar 45

16.06 FARMERS' ORGANIZATIONS

Davis, J. H. The International Federation
of Agricultural Producers. JFE 29:
1101-06 Nov 47

Furman, A. F. and Ball, E. P. Operating a
ASC grazing association [in North Weld
County, Colorado]. LE 19:94-98 Feb 43

Goss, A. S. Legislative program of the
A National Grange. JFE 29:52-63 Feb 47

Halvorson, L. C. Problems of effective
A presentation of agricultural economic
data to the membership of farm organizations. JFE 29:1214-24 Nov 47

Herrmann, L. F. The role of the farm or-
A ganization economist in the formulation
of farm organization policy. JFE 29:
1203-08 Nov 47

Ogg, W. R. Postwar agricultural program
A [of the American Farm Bureau Federa-
tion]. JFE 29:64-76 Feb 47

Parsons, K. H. Institutional changes af-
A fecting the agricultural outlook; the agricultural perspective. JFE 31,pt.2:
1121-31 Nov 49

Saloutos, T. The expansion and decline of
AA the Nonpartisan League in the western
Middle West, 1917-1921. AH 20:235-52
Oct 46

Taylor, H. C. The farmer in the groupistic
A regime. LE 16:253-61 Aug 40

16.1 HISTORY

Fussell, G. E. History and agricultural
science. AH 19:126-27 Apr 45

Glover, W. H. Discussion: agricultural
economics and history. JFE 30:553-55
Aug 48

Gray, S. and Wyckoff, V. J. The international tobacco trade in the seventeenth
century. SEJ 7:1-26 Jul 40

Honigsheim, P. Max Weber as historian of
agriculture and rural life. AH 23:
179-213 Jul 49

Loehr, R. C. Agriculture and history.
JFE 30:537-44 Aug 48

Ross, E. D. and Tontz, R. L. The term
"agricultural revolution" as used by
economic historians. AH 22:32-38
Jan 48

UNITED STATES

Campbell, J. P. Action programs in educa-
A tion. AH 15:68-71 Apr 41

Carman, H. J. Jesse Buel, early nineteenth-
century agricultural reformer. AH 17:
1-13 Jan 43

Danhof, C. H. American evaluations of
European agriculture. JEH/S 9:61-71 '49

Demaree, A. L. The farm journals, their
editors, and their public, 1830-1860.
AH 15:182-88 Oct 41

Duncan, B. Diplomatic support of the American rice trade, 1835-1845. AH 23:92-96
Apr 49

16.1 HISTORY (Cont.)
UNITED STATES (Cont.)

A  Edwards, E. E.  Europe's contribution to the American dairy industry.  JEH/S 9: 72-84 '49

Grapp, H. F.  The early impact of Japan upon American agriculture.  AH 23: 110-16 Apr 49

Harding, T. S.  Henry L. Ellsworth, Commissioner of patents.  JFE 22:621-27 Aug 40

Lee, G. A.  The general records of the United States Department of Agriculture in the National Archives.  AH 19:242-49 Oct 45

Lemmer, G. F.  The agricultural program of a leading farm periodical, Colman's rural world.  AH 23:245-54 Oct 49

Loehr, R. C.  American husbandry; a commentary apropos of the Carman edition.  AH 14:104-09 Jul 40

Malin, J. C.  Mobility and history: reflections on the agricultural policies of the United States in relation to a mechanized world.  AH 17:177-91 Oct 43

Peterson, A. G.  Agriculture in the United States, 1839 and 1939.  JFE 22:98-110 Feb 40

-- The Agricultural History Society's first quarter century.  AH 19:193-203 Oct 45

Ross, E. D.  Agriculture in our economic history.  AH 22:65-69 Apr 48

Russ, W. A., Jr.  Godkin looks at western agrarianism: a case study.  AH 19: 233-42 Oct 45

Schmidt, L. B.  The history of American agriculture as a field of research.  AH 14: 117-26 Jul 40

Taylor, H. C.  Early history of agricultural economics.  JFE 22:84-97 Feb 40

Tucker, W. P.  Populism up-to-date: the story of the Farmers' Union.  AH 21: 198-208 Oct 47

Warner, D. F.  The Farmers' Alliance and the Farmers' Union: an American-Canadian parallelism.  AH 23:9-19 Jan 49

Woodward, C. R.  Woodrow Wilson's agricultural philosophy.  AH 14:129-42 Oct 40

AA  Atherton, L. E.  Western foodstuffs in the Army provisions trade.  AH 14:161-69 Oct 40

Bahmer, R. H.  The American Society of Equity.  AH 14:33-63 Jan 40

Bonner, J. C.  The plantation overseer and southern nationalism as revealed in the career of Garland D. Harmon.  AH 19: 1-11 Jan 45

-- Advancing trends in southern agriculture, 1840-1860.  AH 22:248-59 Oct 48

Brayer, H. O.  The influence of British capital on the western range-cattle industry.  JEH/S 9:85-98 '49

Hicks, J. D.  The western Middle West, 1900-1914.  AH 20:65-77 Apr 46

Jorgenson, L. P.  Agricultural expansion into the semiarid lands of the west north central states during the first World War.  AH 23:30-40 Jan 49

Kahn, H.  Records in the National Archives relating to the range cattle industry, 1865-1895.  AH 20:187-90 Jul 46

Kemmerer, D. L.  The pre-Civil War South's leading crop, corn.  AH 23: 236-39 Oct 49

Kollmorgen, W. M.  Immigrant settlements in southern agriculture: a commentary on the significance of cultural islands in agricultural history.  AH 19:69-78 Apr 45

Lemmer, G. F.  The spread of improved cattle through the eastern United States to 1850.  AH 21:79-93 Apr 47

Malin, J. C.  The agricultural regionalism of the Trans-Mississippi West as delineated by Cyrus Thomas.  AH 21: 208-17 Oct 47

Oliphant, J. O.  The eastward movement of cattle from the Oregon Country.  AH 20: 19-43 Jan 46

Saloutos, T.  The spring-wheat farmer in a maturing economy 1870-1920.  JEH 6: 173-90 Nov 46

ASA  Hall, A. R.  Ante-bellum Alabama agriculture.  R.  AH 16:127-28 Apr 42

ASC  Carosso, V. P.  Anaheim, California: a nineteenth century experiment in commercial viniculture.  BHR 23:78-86 Jun 49

Jones, W. O.  A California case study in location theory: the globe artichoke on the Moro Cojo.  JFE 31:538-44 Aug 49

Parsons, J. J.  Hops in early California agriculture.  AH 14:110-16 Jul 40

Reed, H. S.  Major trends in California agriculture.  AH 20:252-55 Oct 46

ASC  Dunbar, R. G.  Agricultural adjustments in eastern Colorado in the eighteen-nineties.  AH 18:41-52 Jan 44

ASD  Bausman, R. O. and Munroe, J. A.  James Tilton's notes on the agriculture of Delaware in 1788.  AH 20:176-87 Jul 46

ASG  Range, W.  The agricultural revolution in royal Georgia, 1752-1775.  AH 21:250-55 Oct 47

ASI  Destler, C. M.  Agricultural readjustment and agrarian unrest in Illinois, 1880-1896.  AH 21:104-16 Apr 47

ASI  Throne, M.  Southern Iowa agriculture, 1833-1890: the progress from subsistence to commercial corn-belt farming.  AH 23: 124-30 Apr 49

ASM  Glazer, S.  The early silk industry in Michigan.  AH 18:92-96 Apr 44

ASM  Lemmer, G. F.  The early agricultural fairs of Missouri.  AH 17:145-52 Jul 43

# 16. AGRICULTURE

## 16.1 HISTORY (Cont.)
### UNITED STATES (Cont.)

Mosk, S. A. The influence of tradition on
ASN agriculture in New Mexico. JEH/S 2:
34-51 Dec 42

Lord, C. The Farmers' Museum: the
ASN museum of the New York Historical
Association at Cooperstown. AH 17:
167-71 Jul 43

Saloutos, T. The rise of the Nonpartisan
ASN League in North Dakota, 1915-1917.
AH 20:43-61 Jan 46

Duruz, W. P. Notes on the early history of
ASO horticulture in Oregon: with special
reference to fruit-tree nurseries.
AH 15:84-97 Apr 41

Hawley, N. R. The old rice plantations in
ASS and around the Santee Experimental
Forest [in South Carolina]. AH 23:86-91
Apr 49

Schell, H. S. Adjustment problems in South
ASS Dakota. AH 14:65-74 Apr 40

True, R. H. The Virginia Board of Agricul-
ASV ture, 1841-1843. AH 14:97-103 Jul 40

Saloutos, T. The Wisconsin Society of
ASW Equity. AH 14:78-95 Apr 40

-- The decline of the Wisconsin Society of
Equity. AH 15:137-50 Jul 41

Schafer, J. The Wisconsin domesday book;
a method of research for agricultural
historians. AH 14:23-32 Jan 40

Thompson, D. O. and Glover, W. H. A
pioneer adventure in agricultural extension: a contribution from the Wisconsin
cut-over. AH 22:124-28 Apr 48

Jackson, W. T. The Wyoming Stock
ASW Growers' Association: its years of tem-
porary decline, 1886-1890. AH 22:260-70
Oct 48

### OTHER AMERICAN COUNTRIES

Fowke, V. C. An introduction to Canadian
C agricultural history. CJE 8:56-68
Feb 42

-- --- [idem] AH 16:79-90 Apr 42

Jones, R. L. The Canadian agricultural
tariff of 1843. CJE 7:528-37 Nov 41

Morton, W. L. The social philosophy of
Henry Wise Wood, the Canadian agrarian
leader. AH 22:114-23 Apr 48

Warner, D. F. The Farmers' Alliance and
the Farmers' Union: an American-
Canadian parallelism. AH 23:9-19 Jan 49

Jones, R. L. French-Canadian agriculture
CA in the St. Lawrence Valley, 1815-1850.
AH 16:137-48 Jul 42

-- The agricultural development of Lower
Canada, 1850-1867. AH 19:212-24 Oct 45

Ormsby, M. A. Agricultural development in
CPB British Columbia. AH 19:11-20 Jan 45

Bogue, A. The progress of the cattle indus-
CPO try in Ontario during the eighteen eighties.
AH 21:163-68 Jul 47

Weeks, D. The agrarian system of the
D Spanish American colonies. LE 23:
153-68 May 47

Mendez Nadal, D. and Alberts, H. W. The
DWP early history of livestock and pastures
in Puerto Rico. AH 21:61-64 Jan 47

### EUROPE

Mauri, A. The development of agricultural
E economics in Europe prior to 1925: excerpts from Angelo Mauri's "I nuovi
sviluppi dell' economia agraria." [Trans-
lated by C. Longobardi] AH 21:169-77
Jul 47

Coletta, P. E. Philip Pusey, English
EB country squire. AH 18:83-91 Apr 44

Duckham, A. N. Liberty, progress, and
security: fifteen centuries of British
agriculture. AH 22:129-33 Jul 48

Fussell, G. E. and Goodman, C. Crop
husbandry in eighteenth century England.
Pt.I-II. AH 15:202-16; 16:41-63 Oct 41,
Jan 42

-- My impressions of Arthur Young.
AH 17:135-44 Jul 43

-- "A real farmer" of eighteenth-century
England and his book, The modern
farmers guide. AH 17:211-15 Oct 43

-- The collection of agricultural statistics
in Great Britain: its origin and evolution. AH 18:161-67 Oct 44

-- English agriculture from Cobbett to
Caird (1830-80). EHR 15:79-85
no.1-2, 45

-- The farming writers of eighteenth-century England. AH 21:1-8 Jan 47

-- Home counties farming, 1840-80. EJ 57:
321-45 Sep 47

-- My impressions of William Marshall.
AH 23:57-61 Jan 49

Gazley, J. G. Arthur Young and the Society
of Arts. JEH 1:129-52 Nov 41

Harvey, N. The coming of the Swede to
Great Britain. AH 23:286-88 Oct 49

Higgins, B. H. Agriculture and war: a
comparison of agricultural conditions in
the Napoleonic and World War periods.
AH 14:1-12 Jan 40

Issawi, C. Interactions of industry and
agriculture in Great Britain since the
industrial revolution. EgC 35:243-67
Mar-Apr 44

Kendall, M. G. Oscillatory movements in
English agriculture [with discussion].
JRSS 106:91-124 pt.2, 43

Russell, Sir E. J. Rothamsted and its experiment station. AH 16:161-83 Oct 42

Woodcock, F. The price of provisions and
some social consequences in Worcestershire in the eighteenth and nineteenth
centuries. JRSS 106:268-72 pt.3, 43

Flaningam, M. L. ed. & tr. The French
EF agricultural questionnaire of 1814: The

16.1  HISTORY (Cont.)
   EUROPE (Cont.)
     Flaningam, M. L. (Cont.)
       circular letter of Becquey, The model
       agricultural questionnaire, and The reply
       for the Arrondissement of Lisieux.
       AH 23:61-75 Jan 49
     Pundt, A. G.  French agriculture and the
       industrial crisis of 1788.  JPE 49:849-74
       Dec 41
     Timoshenko, V. P.  The agrarian policies of
ER     Russia and the wars.  AH 17:192-210
       Oct 43

   ASIA
     Anderson, G. W.  Agriculture in the un-
FA    drained basin of Asia [Turkestan].
       AH 22:233-38 Oct 48
     Maverick, L. A.  Hsü Kuang-ch'i, a Chinese
FC    authority on agriculture.  AH 14:143-60
       Oct 40
     Thomas, P. J.  The prices of food grains in
FI     Madras in the 19th century.  IJE 21:
       559-68 Apr 41
     Grapp, H. F.  The early impact of Japan
FJ     upon American agriculture.  AH 23:
       110-16 Apr 49

   AUSTRALIA.  NEW ZEALAND
     Rutherford, R. S. G.  Fluctuations in the
N     sheep population of New South Wales,
       1860-1940.  ER 24:56-71 Jun 48

16.2  AGRICULTURAL SUPPLY AND DEMAND
   ANALYSIS
16.20  GENERAL
     Haavelmo, T.  Quantitative research in
       agricultural economics: the interdepend-
       ence between agriculture and the national
       economy.  JFE 29:910-24 Nov 47
     Johnson, D. G.  The use of econometric
       models in the study of agricultural
       policy.  JFE 30:117-30 Feb 48

16.22  AGRICULTURAL PRODUCTIVITY AND
   TECHNOLOGICAL CHANGE
     Heady, E. O.  Basic economic and welfare
       aspects of farm technological advance.
       JFE 31:293-316 May 49
     Hirsch, H. G.  Crop yield index numbers.
       JFE 25:583-98 Aug 43
     McNall, P. E.  Farm buildings as evidence
       of productivity of crop land.  LE 17:
       165-70 May 41
     Pine, W. H.  Measuring the economic pro-
       ductivity of land.  JFE 30:777-83 Nov 48
     Working, E. J.  Crop-yield index numbers.
       JFE 22:701-13 Nov 40
     -- Crop yield index numbers: some com-
       ments on Hirsch's views.  JFE 25:874-81
       Nov 43

UNITED STATES
   Barton, G. T.  Increased productivity of
A     the farm worker.  ILRR 1:264-82 Jan 48
   -- Effects of technological changes on cost
     reduction in agriculture: recent and
     prospective changes.  JFE 31,pt.2:442-44
     Feb 49
   Benedict, M. R.  Schisms in agricultural
     policy: agriculture as a commercial in-
     dustry comparable to other branches of
     the economy.  JFE 24:476-96 May 42
   Brewster, J. M.  Farm technological ad-
     vance and total population growth.
     JFE 27:509-25 Aug 45
   Ellickson, J. C. and Brewster, J. M.  Tech-
     nological advance and the structure of
     American agriculture.  JFE 29:827-47
     Nov 47
   Fulmer, J. L.  Relationship of the cycle in
     yields of cotton and apples to solar and
     sky radiation.  QJE 56:385-405 May 42
   Heady, E. O.  Changes in income distribu-
     tion in agriculture with special reference
     to technological progress.  JFE 26:
     435-47 Aug 44
   Heisig, C. P., chairman.  Economic impli-
     cations of technological developments in
     agricultural production.  Report of a sub-
     committee.  JFE 29:299-309 Feb 47
   Hopkins, J. A.  The scale of agricultural
     production: some corrections [followed
     by J. D. Black's rejoinder].  QJE 54:
     314-17 Feb 40
   Jasny, N.  Labor productivity in agricul-
     ture in USSR and USA.  JFE 27:419-32
     May 45
   Landstrom, K. S.  Comment on "How effi-
     cient is American agriculture?"  JFE 30:
     364-68 May 48
   Schickele, R.  Obstacles to agricultural
     production expansion.  JFE 24:447-62
     May 42
   Schultz, T. W.  How efficient is American
     agriculture.  JFE 29:644-58 Aug 47
   Wilcox, W. W.  The efficiency and stability
     of American agriculture.  JFE 30:411-21
     Aug 48
   Clawson, M.  Sequence in variation of
AA    annual precipitation in the western
     United States.  LE 23:271-87 Aug 47
   -- Range forage conditions in relation to
     annual precipitation [in western U.S.].
     LE 24:264-80 Aug 48
   DeGraff, H.  Effects of technological changes
     on northeastern agriculture.  JFE 31,
     pt.2:445-47 Feb 49
   Elkinton, C. M.  Effects of selected changes
     in technology on western agriculture.
     JFE 31,pt.2:451-53 Feb 49
   Forster, G. W.  Impact of technology on
     southern agriculture.  JFE 29:520-30
     May 47

## 16.22 AGRICULTURAL PRODUCTIVITY AND TECHNOLOGICAL CHANGE (Cont.)
### UNITED STATES (Cont.)

AA   Sayre, C. R. Technology and the cost structure on southern farms. JFE 31, pt.2:454-57 Feb 49

Wills, J. E. Effects of technological changes on cost reduction in agriculture: effects in the Midwest. JFE 31,pt.2:448-50 Feb 49

### OTHER COUNTRIES

CP   Sanderson, F. H. The new wheat condition figures, based on weather factors, for the Prairie Provinces [followed by C. F. Wilson's reply]. JASA 37:473-88 Dec 42

-- --- Rejoinder [followed by C. F. Wilson's further reply and Sanderson's concluding remarks]. JASA 39:97-101 Mar 44

E   Dániel, A. Regional differences of productivity in European agriculture. REStud 12:50-70 no.1, 44

EB   Kendall, M. G. Oscillatory movements in English agriculture [with discussion]. JRSS 106:91-124 pt.2, 43

ER   Jasny, N. Labor productivity in agriculture in USSR and USA. JFE 27:419-32 May 45

FC   Tsou, P. W. Modernization of Chinese agriculture. JFE 28:773-90 Aug 46

## 16.23 DEMAND ANALYSIS

A   Abrahamsen, M. Determining consumer preferences for sweet potatoes: methods and results. JFE 31,pt.2:635-39 Feb 49

A   Bitting, H. W. National consumer preference study for potatoes. JFE 31,pt.2:620-25 Feb 49

A   Black, J. D. The income elasticity of milk. JFE 28:845-48 Aug 46

Clawson, M. Demand interrelations for selected agricultural products. QJE 57: 265-302 Feb 43

A   -- Cattle-hog price and beef-pork consumption ratios. JFE 28:848-52 Aug 46

A   Erdman, H. E. Factors in the current expansion of the demand for food. JM 6,no.4,pt.2:22-28 Apr 42

A   Girshick, M. A. and Haavelmo, T. Statistical analysis of the demand for food: examples of simultaneous estimation of structural equations. Em 15:79-110 Apr 47

Haavelmo, T. Quantitative research in agricultural economics: the interdependence between agriculture and the national economy. JFE 29:910-24 Nov 47

ASI   Hadary, G. Relation of chocolate milk to total fluid milk consumption of factory workers. [A Chicago survey] JB 16: 70-73 Jan 43

ASI   -- Relation of chocolate milk to total fluid milk consumption of urban families [in Indiana]. JB 16:115-23 Apr 43

A   -- The relationship of chocolate milk to total fluid milk consumption. JFE 27: 210-13 Feb 45

Hoos, S. An investigation on complementarity relations between fresh fruits. JFE 23:421-33 May 41

-- --- A rejoinder. JFE 24:528-29 May 42

Kozlik, A. An investigation on complimentarity relations between fresh fruits: a reply. JFE 23:654-56 Aug 41

ASL   Mehren, G. L. and Erdman, H. E. An approach to the determination of intraseasonal shifting of demand [for Louisiana strawberries]. JFE 28:587-96 May 46

Nordin, J. A. Statistical issues in price research. JFE 31,pt.2:1089-95 Nov 49

A   Patzig, R. E. and Hadary, G. Relationship of income to milk consumption. JFE 27: 204-10 Feb 45

Szatrowski, Z. Time series correlated with the beef-pork consumption ratio. Em 13: 60-78 Jan 45

## 16.24 SUPPLY ANALYSIS

A   Barton, G. T. and Cooper, M. R. Relation of agricultural production to inputs. REStat 30:117-26 May 48

EB   Lomax, K. S. An agricultural production function for the United Kingdom, 1924 to 1947. MS 17:146-62 May 49

A   Mighell, R. L. and Allen, R. H. Supply schedules; "long-time" and "short-time." JFE 22:544-57 Aug 40

Tintner, G. A note on the derivation of production functions from farm records. Em 12:26-34 Jan 44

Waite, W. C. and Cox, R. W. The influence of prices on agricultural production. JFE 26:382-88 May 44

Walsh, R. M. Response to price in production of cotton and cottonseed. JFE 26: 359-72 May 44

## 16.25 PRICE ANALYSIS

Alcorn, G. Using price research. JFE 31, pt.2:1096-98 Nov 49

A   Anderson, R. L. Use of variance components in the analysis of hog prices in two markets. JASA 42:612-34 Dec 47

A   Armstrong, C. Farm prices and industrial wages. JFE 28:1041-48 Nov 46

A   Barton, F. L. Length of haul and farm commodity prices. JFE 23:434-45 May 41

FI   Bose, S. R. A study in Bihar rural prices. IJE 23:167-74 Oct 42

Bottum, J. C. Making price research useful. JFE 31,pt.2:1099-1101 Nov 49

A   Clark, C. M. Seasonal patterns in tobacco prices. JFE 23:339-54 Feb 41

A   Clement, S. L. Tobacco prices: discussion. JFE 23:356-61 Feb 41

## 16.25  PRICE ANALYSIS (Cont.)

Cochrane, W. W.  Farm price gyrations: an
A   aggregative hypothesis.  JFE 29:383-408
May 47

Cron, L. E.  An application of analysis of
covariance to price-quality relationships
of eggs.  JFE 22:440-45 May 40

Davis, J. S.  Food prices. (Ten economists
A   on the inflation).  REStat 30:8-10 Feb 48

Ezekiel, M.  Price analyses, wars, and depressions.  JFE 22:673-79 Nov 40

Fox, K. A.  Needed new directions in agricultural price analysis.  JFE 31,pt.2:
1080-88 Nov 49

Lindsay, J.  Sydney wholesale fruit and
N   vegetable prices.  ER 21:174-81 Dec 45

Nicholls, W. H.  Reorientation of agricul-
A   tural marketing and price research.
JFE 30:43-54 Feb 48

Pearson, F. A. and Paarlberg, D.  Sixty
A   million jobs and six million farmers.
JFE 28:28-41 Feb 46

Qureshi, A. I.  Price movements of some
FI   important agricultural commodities in
Hyderabad.  IJE 21:551-58 Apr 41

Row, B. G.  Price-level of tobacco in the
FI   Guntur area.  IJE 21:526-35 Apr 41

Srinivasamurthy, A. P. and Krishnamurthy,
FI   G. N.  The trend of agricultural prices
in Mysore during the decennium 1928-
1937.  IJE 21:536-50 Apr 41

Viswanathan, T. V.  Statistical study of the
FI   prices of foodgrains in the Madras
Presidency.  IJE 30:19-29 Jul 49

Walsh, R. M.  Statistics and research in the
field of price analysis [with discussion
by H. Halvorson].  JFE 31,pt.2:714-24
Feb 49

Wells, O. V.  Significance of the "general
A   price level" and related influences to
American agriculture [followed by J.W.
Tapp's and F. F. Hill's further com-
ments].  JFE 31,pt.2:779-99 Nov 49

## 16.26  FORECASTING

Christensen, R. P.  Food production: discussion.  JFE 31,pt.2:265-67 Feb 49

Clawson, M.; Heisig, C. P. and Hurd, E. B.
A   Long-term forecasting of fruit and nut
production.  JFE 23:550-66 Aug 41

Eggert, R. J. and Seltzer, R. E.  Accuracy of
ASK  livestock price forecasts at Kansas State
College.  JFE 31:342-45 May 49

Hathaway, D. E. and Cravens, M. E., Jr.
ASM  Quality factors affecting the price of
peaches on the Benton Harbor Market.
JFE 31,pt.2:631-34 Feb 49

Johnson, D. G.  Food production: discussion.
JFE 31,pt.2:262-65 Feb 49

Johnson, H. A. and Paarlberg, D.  A method
ASI  of predicting numbers of hens and pullets
on Indiana farms January 1.  JFE 30:
756-61 Nov 48

Kellogg, C. E.  Food production potentialities and problems.  JFE 31,pt.2:251-62
Feb 49

Parsons, K.  The problem-solution basis of
forward pricing.  R.  LE 25:423-27
Nov 49

Shaul, J. R. H.  Maize forecasts in Mazoe
H   District of Southern Rhodesia, 1920-42.
SAJE 11:294-96 Dec 43

Wilcoxen, L. C.  The market forecasting
A   significance of market movements.
JASA 37:343-51 Sep 42

## 16.3  FARM POPULATION.  LABOR FORCE.
## INCOME

### 16.30  GENERAL

Hopkins, J. A.  Changing structure of agri-
A   culture and its impacts on labor.
JFE 23:89-104 Feb 41

Khan, A. A.  Problems of "rural labour and
FIP  wages" in the West Punjab.  PEJ 1,no.1:
40-61 Jul 49

Robinson, T. C. M. and Wallrabenstein, P.
A   P.  Estimates of agricultural employ-
ment and wage rates.  JFE 31:233-52
May 49

Saville, R. J.  Changing structure of agri-
A   culture: discussion.  JFE 23:109-11
Feb 41

Vance, R. B.  How can the southern popula-
AA  tion find gainful employment?  JFE 22:
198-205 Feb 40

Wilcox, W. W.  High farm income and effi-
A   cient resource use.  JFE 31:555-57
Aug 49

### 16.31  HISTORY

Cox, L. F.  The American agricultural wage
A   earner, 1865-1900: the emergence of a
modern labor problem.  AH 22:95-114
Apr 48

Lennard, R.  The agrarian life of the Middle
E   Ages.  R.  EJ 52:45-53 Apr 42

Russel, R. R.  The effects of slavery upon
AA  nonslaveholders in the ante bellum South.
AH 15:112-26 Apr 41

Watson, J. A. S.  Land ownership, farm
EB  tenancy, and farm labor in Britain.
AH 17:73-80 Apr 43

### 16.32  POPULATION.  EMPLOYMENT.  LABOR
### FORCE

Morin, A. J.  A note on bilateral monopoly,
with special reference to seasonal agricultural labor.  JFE 31:101-15 Feb 49

Nelson, L.  The work of the Permanent
Agricultural Committee of the Interna-
tional Labour Office.  JFE 31:524-28
Aug 49

### UNITED STATES

Brewster, J. M.  Farm technological ad-
A   vance and total population growth.  JFE 27:
509-25 Aug 45

# 16. AGRICULTURE

## 16.32 POPULATION. EMPLOYMENT. LABOR FORCE. (Cont.)

### UNITED STATES (Cont.)

A    Corson, J. J. Agricultural workers and social insurance. JFE 24:285-95 Feb 42

Goldschmidt, W. R. Employment categories in American agriculture. JFE 29:554-64 May 47

Hannah, H. W. Agricultural labor and the Fair Labor Standards Act of 1938. JFE 22:421-29 May 40

Harrison, F. L. The Joads in peace and war. S&S 6:97-110 no.2, 42

Hendricks, W. A. Farm employment levels in relation to supply and demand as per cent of normal. JASA 42:271-81 Jun 47

Hill, G. W. and Marshall, D. G. Reproduction and replacement of farm population and agricultural policy. JFE 29:457-74 May 47

Johnson, D. G. Mobility as a field of economic research. SEJ 15:152-61 Oct 48

Murray, W. G. [Farm labor regulation]: discussion. JFE 24:313-14 Feb 42

Nesius, E. J. How farmers are meeting the scarcity of labor. JFE 25:305-08 Feb 43

Northrup, H. R. The Tobacco Workers International Union. QJE 56:606-26 Aug 42

Palmer, S. W. Agriculture and the labor reserve. S&S 4:388-401 no.4, 40

Parsons, K. H. Farmers and organized labor. JFE 25:367-83 May 43

Schwartz, H. Organizational problems of agricultural labor unions. JFE 23:456-66 May 41

-- Recent developments among farm labor unions. JFE 23:833-42 Nov 41

-- Farm labor adjustments after World War I. JFE 25:269-77 Feb 43

Smith, R. J. Fuller annual employment of farm labor. JFE 26:514-28 Aug 44

Warren, E. L. Hired farm labor under minimum wage and maximum hours regulation. JFE 24:296-313 Feb 42

AA    Aull, G. H. Employment prospects in southern agriculture. SEJ 13:378-85 Apr 47

McEntire, D. Migration and resettlement in the far western states. JFE 23:478-82 May 41

Poli, A. and Engstrand, W. M. Japanese agriculture on the Pacific Coast. LE 21:352-64 Sep 45

ASC    Lenhart, M. W. Analyzing labor requirements for California's major seasonal crop operations. JFE 27:963-75 Nov 45

ASL    Boonstra, C. A. Note on part-time farming [in Louisiana]. JFE 23:893-95 Nov 41

Harrison, R. W. and Kollmorgen, W. M. The place of French-speaking farmers of southern Louisiana in future land development and reclamation projects. LE 22:223-31 Aug 46

### OTHER COUNTRIES

C    Haythorne, G. V. Canadian agricultural manpower problems. JFE 31,pt.2:385-91 Feb 49

DSM    Douglas, D. W. Land and labor in Mexico. S&S 4:127-52 no.2, 40

EB    Benedict, M. R. The British program for farm labor as a contribution to American thinking on the subject. JFE 22:714-28 Nov 40

EG    Eckstein, A. Collective bargaining in German agriculture under the Weimar Republic, 1918-1933. JFE 25:458-76 May 43

FA    Yagi, Y. The problem of agricultural labour-power in the South. Kyo 18,no.1:1-17 Jan 43

FI    Dutt, K. and Das, A. C. Problem of agricultural labour in India. IJE 28:155-61 Jul 47

Ghosh, A. Agricultural labour in Bengal. IJE 28:425-42 Jan 48

Gupta, S. The agricultural labourer in Bengal. IJE 26:133-36 Jul 45

Husain, A. Some aspects of agricultural labour in Hyderabad. IJE 20:695-707 Apr 40

Jagannadham, V. Social protection for agricultural labourers. IJE 28:121-30 Jul 47

Kibe, S. M. V. Problems of agricultural labour. IJE 28:175-77 Jul 47

Malhotra, P. C. Agricultural labour in India. IJE 28:137-41 Jul 47

Misra, B. Agricultural labour in Orissa. IJE 28:443-49 Jan 48

Misra, S. Agricultural labour in U.P. IJE 28:187-95 Jul 47

Mukherjee, K. Problems of agricultural labour in India. IJE 28:163-74 Jul 47

Mukhopadhyaya, S. N. Recruitment of labour in tea plantations in India as an outlet for landless agriculturists. IJE 28:197-206 Jul 47

Rajalakshman, D. V. Agricultural labour in India. IJE 28:143-53 Jul 47

Ramakrishnan, K. C. Labour in agriculture: supply and demand. IJE 28:417-24 Jan 48

Row, B. G. Agricultural labour in Andhra Desa: some aspects. IJE 28:179-86 Jul 47

FP    Crippen, H. R. Philippine agrarian unrest: historical backgrounds. S&S 10:337-60 no.4, 46

HSA    Smith, R. H. Native farm labour in Natal. SAJE 9:154-75 Jun 41

## 16.33 MIGRATORY WORKERS

A    Ducoff, L. J. Migratory farm workers in the United States. JFE 29:711-22 Aug 47

16.3 FARM POPULATION. LABOR FORCE.
INCOME (Cont.)

16.34 INCOME. WAGES. BUDGETS. COST
AND STANDARD OF LIVING
UNITED STATES

Baughman, E. T. A note on minimum wages
A  and agricultural welfare. JFE 28:
1048-61 Nov 46

Benedict, M. R. and Adams, R. L. Methods
of wage determination in agriculture.
JFE 23:71-88 Feb 41

Black, J. D. The relation of wages to net
farm income, 1929-42 and 1939-42.
JFE 26:572-78 Aug 44

-- and MacDonald, A. Cost of living on
farms and prices paid by farmers.
JASA 39:377-86 Sep 44

-- National income and farm income.
JFE 28:560-62 May 46

Cawl, F. R. Recent changes in farm economic levels. JM 7:360-66 Apr 43

Clawson, M. and Black, J. D. Agricultural
income and the export market: 1910-
1940. JFE 24:761-71 Nov 42

Cochrane, W. W. Farm family budgets: a
moving picture. REStat 29:189-98
Aug 47; Erratum. 30:80 Feb 48

Ducoff, L. J. and Bancroft, G. Experiment
in the measurement of unpaid family
labor in agriculture. JASA 40:205-13
Jun 45

Fisher, L. H. What is a minimum adequate
farm income? JFE 25:662-70 Aug 43

Furbush, F. Farm family income and expenditures. JM 4:264-67 Jan 40

Grove, E. W. and Koffsky, N. M. Measuring
the incomes of farm people. JFE 31,
pt.2:1102-11 Nov 49

Heady, E. O. Changes in income distribution in agriculture with special reference to technological progress. JFE 26:
435-47 Aug 44

Johnson, D. G. Allocation of agricultural
income. JFE 30:724-49 Nov 48

Kaufman, J. J. Economics of minimum
wages in relation to the agricultural labor
market. JFE 31:716-25 Nov 49

Koffsky, N. Some statistical problems involved in types of farm income, by size.
JFE 29:1257-66 Nov 47

Montgomery, D. Labor's aims and what
they mean to agriculture. JFE 31,pt.2:
1141-47 Nov 49

Mulliken, O. E. Wage determination in agriculture: discussion. JFE 23:104-09
Feb 41

Schultz, T. W. Reflections on poverty
within agriculture [with discussion by E.
J. Long]. JFE 31,pt.2:1112-17 Nov 49

Southworth, H. M. Poverty within agriculture: discussion. JFE 31,pt.2:1117-18
Nov 49

White, J. W. Poverty within agriculture:
discussion. JFE 31,pt.2:1118-20 Nov 49

Wilson, M. L. Problem of poverty in agriculture [with discussion by J. I. Falconer and D. Sanderson]. JFE 22:10-33
Feb 40

Braunhut, H. J. Farm labor wage rates in
AA  the South, 1909-1948. SEJ 16:189-96
Oct 49

OTHER COUNTRIES

Burton, G. L. Agriculture's share of the
C  national income: a comment. CJE 10:
206-09 May 44

Hope, E. C. Agriculture's share of the
national income. CJE 9:384-93 Aug 43

Skeoch, L. A. Agriculture's share of the
national income further considered.
CJE 10:210-12 May 44

Coates, G. Agricultural profit-sharing in
DW  Puerto Rico. LE 24:309-11 Aug 48

Kraev, M. The collective farm labour-day.
ER  Pt.I-II. SovS 1:166-71; 261-68 Oct 49,
Jan 50

Dash, S. C. Minimum wages for agricul-
FI  tural labour. IJE 28:131-35 Jul 47

Lal, R. B. and Mathen, K. K. A note on
conditions of living of agricultural
labour and certain other rural groups in
West Bengal. IJE 28:403-16 Jan 48

Misra, S. Agricultural wages in relation to
rural cost of living [in the United
Provinces]. IJE 29:75-80 Jul 48

16.4 FARM MANAGEMENT
16.40 GENERAL

Morse, T. D. Use of economics in farming.
JFE 31,pt.2:863-69 Nov 49

Reiss, F. J. Measuring the management
factor. JFE 31,pt.2:1065-72 Nov 49

Sarle, C. F. The role of sampling in farm-
management research. JFE 29:1229-40
Nov 47

Smith, R. J. Economic functions and units
in farm organization. JFE 28:534-42
May 46

Starch, E. A. Supervised farming. JFE 22:
259-63 Feb 40

UNITED STATES

Black, J. D. Dr. Schultz on farm manage-
A  ment research. JFE 22:570-80 Aug 40

Case, H. C. M. Farm management
research: discussion. JFE 22:111-18
Feb 40

Forster, G. W. Farm management
research: Discussion. JFE 22:123-26
Feb 40

-- Contribution of farm management research to attainment of production goals.
JFE 25:110-19 Feb 43

Goodsell, W. D.; Jessen, R. J. and Wilcox,
W. W. Procedures which increase the

16. AGRICULTURE

16.4 FARM MANAGEMENT (Cont.)
16.40 GENERAL (Cont.)
    UNITED STATES (Cont.)
    Goodsell, W. D.; Jessen, R. J. and Wilcox,
      W. W. (Cont.)
A    usefulness of farm management research.
      JFE 22:753-61 Nov 40
    Hardin, L. S. Computation and use of output
      units in farm business analysis. JFE 26:
      779-84 Nov 44
    Heisig, C. P. Farm management research:
      discussion. JFE 31,pt.2:1078-79 Nov 49
    Hill, E. B. Comments on sampling to in-
      crease the usefulness of farm manage-
      ment research. JFE 23:499-501 May 41
    Hodges, J. A. Forty years of farm manage-
      ment research. JFE 24:392-401 May 42
    Homeyer, P. G. and Heady, E. O. The role
      of modern statistics in analyzing farm
      management data. JFE 29:1241-49
      Nov 47
    Hopkin, J. A. Multivariate analysis of
      farm and ranch management data.
      JFE 31,pt.2:1073-78 Nov 49
    Johnson, O. R. The family farm. JFE 26:
      529-48 Aug 44
    Johnson, S. E. and Rush, D. R. Orientation
      of farm-management research to low-
      income farms [with discussion]. JFE 23:
      218-45 Feb 41
    Kellogg, C. E. The natural sciences and
      farm planning. JFE 29:183-89 Feb 47
    Kifer, R. S. Farm management research:
      discussion. JFE 22:130-37 Feb 40
    Miller, L. F. Farm and home planning:
      discussion [summarized]. JFE 29:
      189-91 Feb 47
    Mumford, D. C. Farm management re-
      search: discussion. JFE 22:126-30
      Feb 40
    Pond, G. A. Farm management as an art:
      discussion. JFE 31,pt.2:887-88 Nov 49
    Salter, L. A., Jr. and Diehl, L. F. Part-
      time farming research. JFE 22:581-600
      Aug 40
    Shultis, A. Farm management as an art:
      discussion. JFE 31,pt.2:889-90 Nov 49
    Soth, L. Economics for the farmer.
      JFE 31,pt.2:880-87 Nov 49
    Warren, S. W. Firm and farm management
      research: discussion. JFE 22:118-23
      Feb 40
    -- Forty years of farm management surveys.
      JFE 27:18-23 Feb 45
    Westcott, G. W. Research needed in eco-
      nomics for farm and home planning.
      JFE 29:175-82 Feb 47
    Woodworth, H. Farm management research
AA   needs in New England. JFE 26:503-13
      Aug 44
    Mosher, M. L. Thirty years of farm finan-
ASI  cial and production records in Illinois.
      JFE 27:24-37 Feb 45

    Bredvold, M. Farmers' sources of infor-
ASI  mation [in Iowa]. JM 14:79-83 Jul 49
    Vanvig, A. and Nodland, T. The effect of a
ASM reduction in farm prices on farm earn-
      ings: [a Minnesota survey]. JFE 31:
      544-48 Aug 49
    Osgood, O. T. Results of two sampling
ASM methods used in farm management re-
      search [in Mississippi]. JFE 31:157-68
      Feb 49
    Burch, J. W. The Missouri plan (balanced
ASM farming). JFE 31,pt.2:870-79 Nov 49
    Cunningham, L. C. and Warren, S. W.
ASN Sampling methods in use in some of the
      farm management research at Cornell.
      JFE 29:1267-70 Nov 47
    Hurd, T. N. Farmer-worker relationships
      [in New York State]. JFE 31,pt.2:
      378-81 Feb 49

    OTHER COUNTRIES
    Menzies-Kitchin, A. W. and Chapman, W.
EB  D. War-time changes in the organisa-
      tion of two groups of eastern counties
      farms. EJ 56:57-85 Mar 46
    Yagi, Y. Two forms of agricultural man-
FA  agement in the Tropics. Kyo 17,no.3:
      20-35 Jul 42
    Singh, S. A. A statistical analysis of fac-
FI   tors affecting gross return of some
      farms in the Punjab. IJE 20:321-42
      Jan 40

16.41 HISTORY
    Thompson, E. T. The climatic theory of
      the plantation. AH 15:49-60 Jan 41

    UNITED STATES
    Danhof, C. H. Farm-making costs and the
A    "safety valve": 1850-60. JPE 49:317-59
      Jun 41
    -- The fencing problem in the eighteen-
      fifties. AH 18:168-86 Oct 44
    Flick, H. M. Elkanah Watson's activities
      on behalf of agriculture. AH 21:193-98
      Oct 47
    Hargreaves, M. W. M. Dry farming alias
      scientific farming. AH 22:39-56 Jan 48
    Bonner, J. C. The Angora goat: a footnote
AA  in southern agricultural history. AH 21:
      42-46 Jan 47
    Hall, A. R. Terracing in the southern
      Piedmont. AH 23:96-109 Apr 49
    Oliphant, J. O. The cattle herds and
      ranches of the Oregon Country, 1860-
      1890. AH 21:217-38 Oct 47
    -- and Kingston, C. S., editors. William
      Emsley Jackson's diary of a cattle drive
      from La Grande, Oregon, to Cheyenne,
      Wyoming, in 1876. AH 23:260-73 Oct 49
    Smith, R. W. Was slavery unprofitable in
      the ante-bellum South? AH 20:62-64
      Jan 46

16.4 FARM MANAGEMENT (Cont.)
16.41 HISTORY (Cont.)
UNITED STATES (Cont.)

Taylor, R. H. The sale and application of
AA commercial fertilizers in the south
Atlantic states to 1900. AH 21:46-52
Jan 47

Jordan, W. T. The management rules of an
ASA Alabama black belt plantation, 1848-1862.
AH 18:53-64 Jan 44

-- The Elisha F. King family planters of the
Alabama black belt. AH 19:152-62 Jul 45

McKee, I. Jean Paul Vignes, California's
ASC first professional winegrower. AH 22:
176-80 Jul 48

Hoyt, W. D., Jr. Two Maryland farm
ASM leases. AH 21:185-87 Jul 47

Osborn, G. C., ed. Plantation letters of a
ASM southern statesman: John Sharp Williams
and Cedar Grove [Mississippi]. AH 21:
117-26 Apr 47

Paine, C. S., ed. The diaries of a Nebraska
ASN farmer, 1876-1877. AH 22:1-31 Jan 48

Anonymous. A New York farmer's capital
ASN investment in the 1840's. BHR 20:22-24
Feb 46

Burnett, E. C. Hog raising and hog driving
AST in the region of the French Broad River
[Tennessee]. AH 20:86-103 Apr 46

Spencer, J. E. The development of agricul-
ASU tural villages in southern Utah. AH 14:
181-89 Oct 40

OTHER COUNTRIES

Clark, G. Forest clearance and prehistoric
E farming. EHR 17:45-51 no.1, 47

Buttress, F. A. and Dennis, R. W. G. The
EB early history of cereal seed treatment
in England. AH 21:93-103 Apr 47

Fussell, G. E. The dawn of high farming
in England: land reclamation in early
Victorian days. AH 22:83-95 Apr 48

Oschinsky, D. Medieval treatises on estate
accounting. EHR 17:52-61 no.1, 47

Debien, G. Land clearings and artificial
EF meadows in eighteenth-century Poitou.
AH 19:133-37 Jul 45

16.42 RESOURCE COMBINATION AND ALLO-
CATION
16.420 GENERAL

Brewster, J. M. and Parsons, H. L. Can
A prices allocate resources in American
agriculture? JFE 28:938-60 Nov 46

Ciriacy-Wantrup, S. v. Economics of joint
costs in agriculture. JFE 23:771-818
Nov 41

Collier, G. W. Common errors in evaluating farm practices. JFE 23:877-84
Nov 41

Dowell, A. A. and Winters, L. M. Economic
aspects of artificial insemination of commercial dairy cows. JFE 24:665-76
Aug 42

Engene, S. A. New light on factor analysis.
JFE 25:477-86 May 43

-- Sampling procedures used in study of
A haymaking methods. JFE 29:1271-74
Nov 47

Fellows, I. F. Developing and applying
production functions in farm management. JFE 31,pt.2:1058-64 Nov 49

Forster, G. W. Some defects in the analysis of farm management data. JFE 26:
775-79 Nov 44

Heady, E. O. Production functions from a
ASI random sample of farms [in Iowa].
JFE 28:989-1004 Nov 46

-- Elementary models in farm production
economics research. JFE 30:201-25
May 48

Johnson, S. E. Effects of changes in output
A on farmers' costs and returns. JFE 27:
176-85 Feb 45

Kozlik, A. Shape of total revenue curves.
JFE 23:843-54 Nov 41

Miller, L. F. and Preston, H. J. Relation
of feed, labor, and other costs to butterfat test. JFE 30:566-73 Aug 48

Rowley, S. The relation between farm in-
N comes and farm costs expressed in
equations. ER 23:58-65 Jun 47

Rutherford, R. S. G. Quality milk. OIS 6:
EB 161-68 Jul 22, 44

Savage, Z. Estimating the value of citrus
fruit as it develops. JFE 29:959-66
Nov 47

Tintner, G. and Brownlee, O. H. Produc-
ASI tion functions derived from farm records
[in Iowa]. JFE 26:566-71 Aug 44; A
correction. 35:123 Feb 53

Wilcox, W. W. Research in economics of
A farm production. JFE 29:632-43 Aug 47

-- and Rauchenstein, E. The effect of size
A of herd on milk production costs. JFE 30:
713-23 Nov 48

16.421 LAND. WATER. FERTILIZER

Bauer, P. T. The economics of planting
FM density in rubber growing. Ec N.S.13:
131-35 May 46

Heady, E. O. The economics of rotations
A with farm and production policy applications. JFE 30:645-64 Nov 48

Ibach, D. B. Recovering the investment in
A limestone, with particular reference to
reimbursement of vacating tenants.
JFE 31:116-30 Feb 49

Jasny, N. USSR: law on measures to ensure
ER high and stable yields in the Steppe and
Forest-Steppe regions. LE 25:351-58
Nov 49

Joss, A. Benefits from irrigation under
AA subhumid conditions [in Willamette Valley,
Oregon and the eastern part of the
Missouri River Basin]. JFE 28:543-59
May 46

# 16. AGRICULTURE

## 16.4 FARM MANAGEMENT (Cont.)
## 16.42 RESOURCE COMBINATION AND ALLO-CATION (Cont.)
## 16.421 LAND. WATER. FERTILIZER (Cont.)

Marsh, J. F. The use of "adjusted condition" for estimating yield per acre. JFE 29:514-46 May 47

Mendum, S. W. A device for analyzing yields: short cut to yield-curve problems. JFE 30:357-64 May 48

## 16.422 LABOR

A    Bachman, K. L. Capital-labor substitution in cotton farming. JFE 31,pt.2:370-73 Feb 49

Bierly, I. R. and Hoff, P. R. Work simplification: a joint problem for management, engineering, and commodity specialists. JFE 29:219-24 Feb 47

Blum, L. Job analysis in agriculture. JFE 27:195-204 Feb 45

Bookhout, B. R. Haymaking job analysis. JFE 29:761-67 Aug 47

Carter, R. M. Job analysis of chores on dairy farms. JFE 25:671-77 Aug 43

Engene, S. A. Review of papers on farm work simplification. JFE 28:337-40 Feb 46

Hardin, L. S. and Carter, R. M. An analysis of work simplification research methods and results. JFE 28:320-30 Feb 46

-- The functional approach to effective farm labor utilization. JFE 31,pt.2:382-84 Feb 49

AA    Janssen, M. An analysis of the economy of use of farm labor in the corn belt. JFE 31,pt.2:374-77 Feb 49

Scoville, O. J. Synthesis of labor inputs for hogs from time-study data. JFE 31: 549-55 Aug 49

Young, E. C. Farm work simplification studies. JFE 26:232-39 Feb 44

-- and Bierly, I. R. The future of farm work simplification research. JFE 28: 331-37 Feb 46

## 16.423 FEEDS AND FORAGE

Atkinson, L. J. The marginal feed cost of pork and lard. JFE 27:375-87 May 45

Breimyer, H. F. The efficiency of feeding livestock. JFE 25:599-621 Aug 43

Hansen, P. L. Input-output relationships in egg production. JFE 31:687-96 Nov 49

Herrmann, L. F. Diminishing returns in feeding commercial dairy herds. JFE 25: 397-409 May 43

Jensen, E. Determining input-output relationships in milk production. JFE 22: 249-58 Feb 40

Menze, R. E. An economic analysis of length of feeding period in the production of hogs. JFE 24:518-23 May 42

Nelson, A. G. Input-output relationships in fattening cattle. JFE 28:495-514 May 46

ASA    Tontz, R. L. and Harrington, A. H. Significance of hog-feed price ratios, Alabama. JFE 28:835-45 Aug 46

## 16.424 MACHINERY AND BUILDINGS

AA    Allen, J. S. Machines in cotton. S&S 12: 240-53 no.2, 48

AA    Melman, S. An industrial revolution in the cotton South. EHR II.2:59-72 no.1, 49

AA    Welch, F. J. and Miley, D. G. Mechanization of the cotton harvest. JFE 27: 928-46 Nov 45

## 16.43 RESOURCE USE UNDER UNCERTAINTY

Boulding, K. E. and Norton, L. J. The theory and measurement of price expectations: discussion. AER/S 39:167-70 May 49

ASI    Brownlee, O. H. and Gainer, W. Farmers' price anticipations and the role of uncertainty in farm planning [a study of corn and soybeans in Iowa]. JFE 31: 266-75 May 49

AA    Christensen, R. P. Expectation and performance related to conservation and production adjustments in the Midwest dairy region. JFE 23:632-45 Aug 41

A    Halcrow, H. G. Problem of farm business survival: discussion. JFE 31,pt.2:951-53 Nov 49

Horton, D. C. Adaptation of the farm capital structure to uncertainty. JFE 31: 76-100 Feb 49

A    -- and Barber, E. L. The problem of farm business survival in areas of highly variable rainfall. JFE 31,pt.2:944-50 Nov 49

A    Johnson, G. L. Problem of farm business survival: discussion. JFE 31,pt.2: 953-54 Nov 49

A    Kling, W. Determination of relative risks involved in growing truck crops. JFE 24: 694-98 Aug 42

Peries, H. E. A simple dynamical problem. IJE 24:218-20 Jan 44

A    Schickele, R. Farm business survival under extreme weather risks. JFE 31,pt.2: 931-43 Nov 49

ASI    Schultz, T. W. and Brownlee, O. H. Two trials to determine expectation models applicable to agriculture [in Iowa]. QJE 56:487-96 May 42

A    -- Spot and future prices as production guides. AER/S 39:135-49 May 49

## 16.44 FARM SIZE

Cavert, W. L. Comment on "The scale of operations in agriculture" [followed by R. W. Rudd and D. L. MacFarlane's rejoinder]. JFE 24:889-91 Nov 42

16.44 FARM SIZE (Cont.)

Hopkins, J. A.  The scale of agricultural production: some corrections [followed by J. D. Black's rejoinder].  QJE 54: 314-17 Feb 40

ASN  Kristjanson, B. H. and Schaffner, L. W. North Dakota farm size trends: an evaluation.  JFE 31,pt.2:588-91 Feb 49

A  Long, E. J.  Returns to scale in family farming: is the case overstated? JPE 57:543-46 Dec 49

May, C. O.  The influence of managerial ability and size of farm on the efficiency of agricultural production.  JFE 25: 105-09 Feb 43

AA  Meenen, H. J.  Size of farms [in the South]. JFE 31,pt.2:599-601 Feb 49

AA  Miley, D. G.  The size of farm in the South. JFE 31,pt.2:582-87 Feb 49

A  Oser, J.  Productivity of agricultural workers by size of enterprise and by regions.  JFE 30:764-70 Nov 48

Rudd, R. W. and MacFarlane, D. L.  The scale of operations in agriculture. JFE 24:420-33 May 42

A  Scoville, O. J.  Measuring the family farm. JFE 29:506-19 May 47

Skovgaard, K.  Utilisation of productive capacity and the problem of intensity in agriculture.  NTTO 12:247-54 no. 37, 48

Stigler, G. J.  Labor productivity and size of farm: a statistical pitfall.  JFE 28: 821-25 Aug 46

AA  Warren, S. W.  Size of farm in the Northeast.  JFE 31,pt.2:596-98 Feb 49

ASW  Wilcox, W. W.  The economy of small farms in Wisconsin.  JFE 28:458-75 May 46

A  Wright, K. T.  Should all farms be large? JFE 31,pt.2:592-95 Feb 49

16.45 ACCOUNTING.  COST ANALYSIS

FM  Bauer, P. T.  Rubber production costs during the great depression.  EJ 53:361-69 Dec 43

FM  -- Notes on cost.  Ec N.S.12:90-100 May 45

A  Boss, A.  Forty years of farm cost accounting records.  JFE 27:1-17 Feb 45

N  Grogan, F. O.  Production costs on four West Australian wheat farms.  ER 16: 236-44 Dec 40

Jolly, A. L.  A new system of farm accounting.  JFE 30:500-17 Aug 48

Jones, R. W.  Production costs as criteria of resource allocation and policy. JFE 30:443-66 Aug 48

Ranney, W. P.  Discussion: "A new system of farm accounting."  JFE 31:153-56 Feb 49

Schultz, T. W.  Effects of employment upon factor costs in agriculture.  JFE 29: 1122-32 Nov 47

16.46 FINANCE.  CREDIT
UNITED STATES

A  Aull, G. H.  Research needs in land tenure and farm finance.  LE 23:255-60 Aug 47

Banfield, E. C.  Ten years of the farm tenant purchase program.  JFE 31: 469-86 Aug 49

Benner, C. L.  Financing agriculture: discussion.  JFE 22:158-61 Feb 40

Black, A. G.  Some current problems in agricultural credit.  JFE 23:37-51 Feb 41

-- Wartime developments in farm credit and their postwar implications [with discussion by O. R. Johnson].  JFE 26: 124-43 Feb 44

Black, J. D.  Tailored credit for land improvements.  JFE 28:596-604 May 46

Botts, R. R.  Use of the annuity principle in transferring the farm from father to son. JFE 29:409-24 May 47

Brinser, A. and Wheeler, R. G.  Farm planning as a basis for extending agricultural credit.  JFE 30:243-58 May 48

Burroughs, R. J.  Mortgage insurance for farm housing.  JFE 27:676-82 Aug 45

Butz, E. L.  Postwar agricultural credit problems and suggested adjustments. JFE 27:281-96 May 45

Cavert, W. L.  Research work in minimum financial requirements and some related considerations for beginning farming. JFE 28:126-33 Feb 46

Heady, E. O.  Economics of farm leasing systems.  JFE 29:659-78 Aug 47

Hill, F. F.  Financing agriculture: discussion.  JFE 22:154-57 Feb 40

-- Research developments in farm finance. JFE 28:114-25 Feb 46

Horton, D. C. and Larsen, H. C.  Agricultural finance guides in wartime.  LE 19: 59-68 Feb 43

-- Methods of financing related to asset characteristics of farms [with discussion by G. W. Forster].  JFE 29:1158-80 Nov 47

Ibach, D. B.  Recovering the investment in limestone, with particular reference to reimbursement of vacating tenants. JFE 31:116-30 Feb 49

McNall, P. E. and Mitchell, D. R.  What is the basis of farm financial progress? JFE 31:529-38 Aug 49

Miller, L. F.  Farmers' investments: a neglected field.  JFE 26:391-96 May 44

Murray, W. G.  How should agriculture be financed?  JFE 22:138-47 Feb 40

Norton, L. J. [and others]  Agricultural credit: discussion.  JFE 23:62-70 Feb 41

-- The land market and farm mortgage debts, 1917-1921.  JFE 24:168-77 Feb 42

Pond, G. A. and Cavert, W. L.  How long does it take to pay for a farm starting

# 16. AGRICULTURE

16.4 FARM MANAGEMENT (Cont.)
16.46 FINANCE. CREDIT (Cont.)
UNITED STATES (Cont.)
Pond, G. A. and Cavert, W. L. (Cont.)
A   with heavy debts? JFE 26:685-93
Nov 44

Selby, H. E. A method of determining
feasible irrigation payments. JFE 24:
637-46 Aug 42

Torgerson, H. W. Agricultural finance in
the United States. Pt.I-II. LE 16:
196-206; 318-24 May, Aug 40

Young, E. C. The function of credit in
modern agriculture. JFE 23:52-62
Feb 41

Beck, P. G. and Jensen, J. C. Contributions
AA  of Farm Security Administration borrowers to agricultural production goals:
the corn-belt states. JFE 25:101-04
Feb 43

Fulmer, J. L. Relation of method of ac-
quiring farm to production factors in
cotton farming. JFE 31:337-42 May 49

Miller, L. F. Farmers' assets outside
ASP  their business. [A Pennsylvania survey]
JFE 31:143-53 Feb 49

Burkett, W. K. Some problems in deflating
ASW  farmers' debt paying performances.
[A study in Wisconsin] JFE 30:750-55
Nov 48


OTHER COUNTRIES
Cronkite, F. C. The Judicial Committee
C  and the farm debt problem. CJE 9:
557-64 Nov 43

Qureshi, A. I. The unit of farming and
EA  credit [in some European countries].
IJE 21:198-203 Oct 40

Kendall, M. G. The financing of British
EB  agriculture [with discussion]. JRSS 104:
111-42 pt.2, 41

Desai, M. B. War and rural indebtedness
FI  in Gujarat. IJE 26:101-11 Jul 45

Ghate, B. G. A scheme for the survey of
rural indebtedness in India. IJE 21:
13-29 Jul 40

Iyengar, S. K. Survey of rural indebtedness
in India: a comment. IJE 21:335-41
Jan 41

Mukerjee, K. M. The problems of agricultural indebtedness in Bengal. IJE 29:
375-84 Apr 49

Patel, S. K. J. An inquiry into the effect of
war-time prices on agricultural indebtedness. IJE 25:561-65 Apr 45

Rao, A. Loans and their classification.
IJE 22:615-23 Jan 42

Singh, V. B. The nature of rent in India.
IJE 30:77-78 Jul 49

Uqaili, N. Agricultural finance in Sind.
FIP  PEJ 1,no.2:25-31 Oct 49

Goerke, H. F. Indebtedness on marginal
N  wheat farms in Western Australia.
ER 19:77-82 Jun 43

Hannah, H. W. Family interest in the
ownership of farm land. JFE 23:895-99
Nov 41

16.5 AGRICULTURAL MARKETING
16.50 GENERAL
Abrahamsen, M. A. Marketing research
A  in agriculture. SEJ 15:80-85 Jul 48

Banfield, E. C. Planning under the Re-
A  search and Marketing Act of 1946: a
study in the sociology of knowledge.
JFE 31:48-75 Feb 49

Bjorka, K. Regional research in agricul-
A  tural marketing. JFE 27:121-37 Feb 45

Bressler, R. G., Jr. Agricultural marketing research [with discussion].
JFE 31,pt.2:553-66 Feb 49

Brownlee, O. H. Marketing research and
A  welfare economics. JFE 30:55-68
Feb 48

-- Agricultural marketing research at the
University of Chicago. JFE 31,pt.2:
1213-24 Nov 49

Brunk, M. E. The application of work
simplification techniques to marketing
research. JFE 29:209-18 Feb 47

Crockett, S. L. Some probable effects of
A  taxation on farmers' marketing practices. JFE 31:725-30 Nov 49

Erdman, H. E. Some current develop-
A  ments in agricultural marketing. Pt.I-II.
JM 5:213-15; 6,no.4,pt.2:13-14 Jan 41,
Apr 42

Gillett, R. L. and Bond, M. C. Data needs
A  for agricultural research and marketing.
JFE 30:271-81 May 48

Hauck, C. W. Team work in marketing re-
ASO  search. [An experiment in Columbus,
Ohio] JFE 29:1395-1405 Nov 47

Hedlund, G. W. Review of papers on re-
A  search and educational programs in
marketing. JFE 28:181-86 Feb 46

Hoecker, R. W. Collaboration between
A  marketing economists, engineers, and
other specialists. JFE 29:1406-12
Nov 47

Hoffman, A. C. Changing organization of
A  agricultural markets. JFE 22:162-72
Feb 40

Meyer, E. A. Developments under the
A  Research and Marketing Act of 1946:
finance, administrative organization,
procedure and policy. JFE 29:1378-82
Nov 47

Nicholls, W. H. Reorientation of agricul-
A  tural marketing and price research.
JFE 30:43-54 Feb 48

Qureshi, A. I. Marketing of agricultural
produce. IJE 20:343-70 Jan 40

Rowe, H. B. Economic significance of
A  changes in market organization. JFE 22:
173-85 Feb 40

16.5  AGRICULTURAL MARKETING (Cont.)
16.50  GENERAL (Cont.)

Shepherd, G.  Decentralization in agricul-
A   tural marketing: causes and conse-
   quences. JM 6:341-48 Apr 42
-- The field of agricultural marketing re-
A   search: objectives, definition, content,
   criteria. JFE 31:444-55 Aug 49
Smith, T. R.  Internal marketing of New
N   Zealand primary products. ER 19:
   171-84 Dec 43
Spencer, L.  Marketing research under the
A   Research and Marketing Act of 1946.
   [Summary of round table discussion]
   JFE 29:292-98 Feb 47
Stitts, T. G.  Organization of agricultural
A   markets: discussion. JFE 22:185-87
   Feb 40
Stout, W. B.  Marketing research contem-
AS  plated by the state experiment stations
   under the Research and Marketing Act
   of 1946. JFE 29:1385-88 Nov 47
Thomsen, F. L.  A critical examination of
A   marketing research. JFE 27:947-62
   Nov 45
--, chairman. Technological developments
A   in agricultural marketing. Report of a
   subcommittee. JFE 29:310-19 Feb 47
Trelogan, H. C.  Federal projects submitted
A   under the Research and Marketing Act of
   1946. JFE 29:1383-84 Nov 47
Whetham, E. H.  War-time changes in agri-
EB  cultural marketing. LBR 7:33-46 Jan 48
White, B. S.  Selecting marketing projects:
A   discussion. JFE 31,pt.2:1224-27 Nov 49
Wolf, A. F.  Measuring the effect of agri-
A   cultural advertising. JFE 26:327-47
   May 44

16.51  HISTORY

Beyer, R. C.  The marketing history of
DSC  Colombian coffee. AH 23:279-85 Oct 49
Fussell, G. E.  The traffic in farm produce
EB  in seventeenth-century England. AH 20:
   77-86 Apr 46
Guthrie, C. L.  A seventeenth century "ever-
DM  normal granary": the alhóndiga of
   colonial Mexico City. AH 15:37-43
   Jan 41
Turner, C. W.  Railroad service to Virginia
ASV  farmers, 1828-1860. AH 22:239-48
   Oct 48

16.52  COMMODITY EXCHANGES

Dow, J. C. R.  The inaccuracy of expecta-
EBE  tions. A statistical study of the Liver-
   pool cotton futures market, 1921-22,
   1937-38. Ec N.S.8:162-75 May 41
Hoos, S.  Futures trading in perishable ag-
A   ricultural commodities. JM 6:358-65
   Apr 42
Jones, F. M.  The decline of Chicago as a
A   grain futures market. JM 12:61-65
   Jul 47

Mehl, P.  Trading in wheat and corn
A   futures in relation to price movements.
   JFE 22:601-12 Aug 40
Vaile, R. S.  Cash and future prices of
A   corn. JM 9:53-54 Jul 44
-- Speculation and the price of grain.
   JM 12:497-98 Apr 48
-- Inverse carrying charges in futures
   markets. JFE 30:574-75 Aug 48
Vance, L. L.  Grain market forces in the
   light of inverse carrying charges.
   JFE 28:1036-40 Nov 46
Working, H.  Theory of the inverse carry-
   ing charge in futures markets. JFE 30:
   1-28 Feb 48
-- Professor Vaile and the theory of in-
   verse carrying charges. JFE 31:168-72
   Feb 49

16.53  MARKETING MARGINS

Irwin, H. S.  Middlemen's accumulations
A   and expectations in marketing farm
   products. JFE 29:848-66 Nov 47

16.54  SPECIFIC MARKETS AND MARKET
   CONTROL
16.540  GENERAL

Allwright, W. J. S.  Aspects of "controlled"
HSA  marketing in the Union: comments on the
   review article by L. H. Samuels [follow-
   ed by Samuels' rejoinder, Allwright's
   comment on the rejoinder and Samuels'
   further comment]. SAJE 15:206-19
   Sep 47
Bauer, P. T.  A review of the agricultural
EB  marketing schemes. Ec N.S.15:132-50
   May 48
Farrell, M. W.  Experience with provin-
CP  cial marketing schemes in Canada.
   JFE 31:610-26 Nov 49
Leslie, R. Gif fredome failye. R. [Agri-
HSA  cultural marketing control] SAJE 15:
   116-23 Jun 47
Mehren, G. L.  Elementary economic
   theory of marketing control. JFE 31,
   pt.2:1247-54 Nov 49
Samuels, L. H.  Aspects of "controlled"
HSA  marketing in the Union. R. SAJE 15:
   47-59 Mar 47
Schneider, J. B.  Agricultural marketing
ASC  control programs in California. JM 6:
   366-70 Apr 42
Taylor, G. R.  State laws which limit com-
AS  petition in agricultural products.
   JFE 22:241-48 Feb 40
Waugh, F. V.  State protectionism as a
AS  menace to a sound agricultural program.
   JM 4,no.4,pt.2:5-10 Apr 40
-- Agricultural marketing programs after
A   the war. JFE 27:297-302 May 45

# 16. AGRICULTURE

## 16.54 SPECIFIC MARKETS AND MARKET CONTROL (Cont.)
### 16.541 MILK AND DAIRY
#### UNITED STATES

Bartlett, R. W. Principles for pricing
A    market milk. JFE 31,pt.2:438-41 Feb 49

Bressler, R. G., Jr. Transportation and country assembly of milk. JFE 22: 220-24 Feb 40

Case, E. The dairyman's plight. HBR 20: 233-43 no.2, 42

Dow, G. F. Regional and interregional co-operation in dairy marketing. JFE 29: 1389-94 Nov 47

Freiberg, A. M. Milk delivery: necessity or luxury? HBR 20:116-23 no.1, 41

Froker, R. K., chairman. Dairy marketing research round-table meeting. JFE 29: 283-91 Feb 47

Hadary, G. Effectiveness of price control in the dairy industry. JB 19:76-81 Apr 46

Johnson, S. Formula pricing class I milk under market orders. JFE 31,pt.2: 428-33 Feb 49

Lent, F. B. Milk control: discussion. JFE 24:336-39 Feb 42

MacLeod, A. Important considerations in determining a fair price for fluid milk. JFE 24:315-19 Feb 42

-- Research and educational programs in the marketing of milk and dairy products. JFE 28:144-57 Feb 46

Morrow, A. The war's impact on milk marketing. JM 10:235-43 Jan 46

Mortenson, W. P. Legal possibilities and limitations of milk distribution as a public utility. Pt.I-II. LE 15:438-47; 16:61-71 Nov 39, Feb 40

Pierce, C. W. Pricing class I milk under federal orders. JFE 31,pt.2:434-37 Feb 49

Steck, L. J. Research in milk marketing. R. JFE 27:453-62 May 45

Vial, E. E. Some examples of differential pricing of milk. JM 6,no.4,pt.2:171-73 Apr 42

Welden, W. C. Formula pricing of class I milk under market orders. JFE 31,pt.2: 420-27 Feb 49

McBride, C. G. The effect of milk control
AA    programs on cooperatives [in the West]. JFE 24:320-25 Feb 42

Smith, W. J. J. Milk price differentials in the Southeast. JFE 28:742-55 Aug 46

Naden, K. D. Price policy of the Challenge
ASC   Cream & Butter Association [of California]. [Pt.I-II] JM 13:459-69; 14:27-37 Apr,Jul 49

Bressler, R. G., Jr. and MacLeod, A.
ASC   Connecticut studies milk delivery. JM 12:211-19 Oct 47

Hammerberg, D. O. Allocation of milk supplies among contiguous markets [in Connecticut]. JFE 22:215-19 Feb 40

Waugh, F. V. Connecticut's research in milk marketing: another opinion. JFE 27:707-09 Aug 45

Cladakis, N. J. and Pollard, A. J. Some
ASI   economic problems encountered in milk control administration [in New York and Chicago]. JFE 24:326-32 Feb 42

Hadary, G. Effect of method of distribution
ASI   on milk consumption [in Indiana]. JM 9: 354-58 Apr 45

Cladakis, N. J. and Pollard, A. J. Some
ASN   economic problems encountered in milk control administration [in New York and Chicago]. JFE 24:326-32 Feb 42

Young, E. C. and Bergfeld, A. J. Methods employed in an analysis of the spread between farm and consumer milk prices in New York City. JFE 31,pt.2: 1194-1202 Nov 49

#### OTHER COUNTRIES

Nadeau, J. P. Milk control in Canada.
C    JFE 24:333-36 Feb 42

Chantler, P. Six years of controlled milk
EB   prices. MS 11:123-41 Oct 40

Halliday, I. G. Notes on the distribution
HSA  and consumption of milk in Durban. SAJE 12:101-11 Jun 44

Finch, C. D. Economic problems of con-
N    trol in the milk industry. ER 21:79-88 Jun 45

Rodwell, R. R. Public control of town milk supply in New Zealand. ER 22: 261-71 Dec 46

### 16.542 FRUITS. VEGETABLES. NUTS

Ashley, C. A. Investigation into an alleged
CA   combine of wholesalers and shippers of fruit and vegetables in western Canada. CJE 6:288-92 May 40

Ellison, J. W. Marketing problems of
AA   northwestern apples, 1929-1940. AH 16: 103-15 Apr 42

Genung, J. H. Some things we do not know
A    about the marketing of perishable agricultural commodities. JM 5:162-63 Oct 40

Hamilton, H. G. Integration of marketing
ASF  and production services by Florida citrus associations. JFE 29:495-505 May 47

-- Florida Citrus Agreement. JFE 31,pt.2:
ASF  1237-43 Nov 49

Kelly, R. A. The North-Central States
AA   Regional Potato Marketing Project controlled retail store experiment [in Chicago]. JFE 31,pt.2:626-30 Feb 49

Mehren, G. L. Consumer packaging of
ASC  fruits and vegetables in California. JM 12:327-36 Jan 48

16.542 FRUITS. VEGETABLES. NUTS (Cont.)

Merchant, C. S.  Maine potato marketing
ASM     agreement and order.  JFE 31,pt.2:
        1244-46 Nov 49

Smith, S. R.  Current status of marketing
A       agreements for fruits and vegetables.
        JFE 31,pt.2:1228-36 Nov 49

Stokdyk, E. A.  Supreme Court upholds
ASC     state proration [in California].  JFE 25:
        504-06 May 43

Tousley, R. D.  Advertising fresh fruits
A       and vegetables.  Pt.I-II.  HBR 22:447-58
        no.4, 44; 23:79-94 no.1, 44

Wales, H. G. The Kansas City wholesale
ASK     fruit and vegetable market.  JB 19:
ASM     161-75 Jul 46

Wellman, H. R. and Mehren, G. L.  Some
A       considerations of research in marketing
        horticultural products.  JFE 28:170-81
        Feb 46

16.543 COTTON. WOOL

Abrahamsen, M. A.  Cotton mechanization:
A       its probable influence on marketing.
        JFE 31,pt.2:410-14 Feb 49

Ballinger, R. A.  Quality-price differentials
A       in cotton marketing: discussion.
        JFE 23:354-56 Feb 41

Cronjé, F. J. C.  The influence of raw wool
        prices on wool consumption.  SAJE 15:
        147-48 Jun 47

Faught, W. A. and Miley, D. G.  Develop-
A       ment of regional cotton marketing re-
        search.  JFE 31,pt.2:1207-12 Nov 49

Fetter, F. W.  Some neglected aspects of
A       the wool duty.  JFE 23:399-420 May 41

Horne, M. K., Jr.  The final consumption
        of cotton.  SEJ 9:302-12 Apr 43

Howell, L. D.  Quality-price differentials
A       in cotton marketing.  JFE 23:329-38
        Feb 41

Liao, T. C. The rape markets on the
FC      Chengtu Plain.  JFE 28:1016-24 Nov 46

McMillan, R. B.  Organized marketing of
N       wool.  ER 25,suppl.:59-72 Aug 49

Paulson, W. E.  Price-quality relations in
AST     the cotton market of Victoria, Texas.
        JFE 23:496-99 May 41

-- Research in cotton marketing.  JFE 31,
A       pt.2:415-19 Feb 49

Singhal, A. S.  A note on conditions of cot-
FI      ton marketing at Hathras in 1944.
        IJE 26:124-33 Jul 45

Wallace, K. J.  Australian Wool Realiza-
N       tion Commission wool price index.
        ER 25,(no.49):31-45 Dec 49

Wright, J. W.  The competitive outlook for
A       cotton.  JM 10:258-64 Jan 46

16.544 LIVESTOCK. POULTRY. EGGS

Bauer, P. T. The failure of the pigs mar-
EB      keting scheme.  MS 12:35-45 Apr 41

Dowell, A. A. and Engelman, G.  Research
A       into the problems involved in marketing
        slaughter livestock by carcass weight
        and grade [with discussion].  JFE 31,
        pt.2:343-69 Feb 49

Engelman, G.  Carcass grade and weight
A       studies in marketing livestock.  JFE 29:
        1424-28 Nov 47

Erdman, H. E. and Alcorn, G. B.  The
ASC     price-making process in the Los Angeles
        egg market.  JM 6:349-57 Apr 42

Miller, H. I.  Developments in poultry
A       marketing research.  JFE 29:1413-16
        Nov 47

-- The midwestern egg project.  JFE 31,
AA      pt.2:1203-06 Nov 49

Phillips, C. D.  Research and educational
A       programs in the marketing of livestock.
        JFE 28:158-69 Feb 46

16.545 GRAINS. CEREALS

Britnell, G. E. and Fowke, V. C.  Develop-
C       ment of wheat marketing policy in
        Canada.  JFE 31:627-42 Nov 49

Burton, G. L.  The proposal to market
C       coarse grains through the Canadian
        Wheat Board.  JFE 31:643-55 Nov 49

Larson, A. L.  Research in grain market-
        ing.  JFE 29:1417-23 Nov 47

Qureshi, A. I.  Some observations on the
FI      marketing of wheat.  IJE 21:167-74
        Oct 40

16.546 OTHER MARKETS

Converse, P. D.  Tobacco auctions
A       evaluated.  JB 16:147-59 Jul 43

Salera, V.  Australian sugar: a case study
N       in controlled marketing.  JM 6:286-90
        Jan 42

16.55 TRANSPORTATION

Barton, F. L.  Length of haul and farm
A       commodity prices.  JFE 23:434-45
        May 41

16.6 AGRICULTURAL COOPERATIVES
16.60 GENERAL

Davis, J. H.  Review of papers on agricul-
        tural cooperation.  JFE 29:128-29
        Feb 47

Erdman, H. E. Thought on cooperatives:
        discussion.  JFE 31,pt.2:915-16 Nov 49

Koller, E. F.  Cooperatives in a capitalis-
        tic economy.  JFE 29:1133-44 Nov 47

Paulson, W. E.  Contribution of coopera-
        tion to the problem of distribution.
        JFE 22:740-52 Nov 40

Robotka, F.  A theory of cooperation.
        JFE 29:94-114 Feb 47

Stern, J. K.  Unsettled questions relating
        to agricultural cooperation [with discus-
        sion by F. Robotka].  JFE 31,pt.2:
        567-76 Feb 49

# 16. AGRICULTURE

## 16.6 AGRICULTURAL COOPERATIVES (Cont.)
## 16.60 GENERAL (Cont.)

Ulrey, O. Unsettled questions relating to cooperatives and cooperation. JFE 31, pt.2:577-79 Feb 49

### UNITED STATES

A   Abrahamsen, M. A. Cooperative relationships and business performance. JFE 26:292-308 May 44

-- Farmers regional purchasing cooperatives look to research. JFE 27:694-700 Aug 45

--Cooperatives in a sound farm economy: discussion. JFE 29:1151-54 Nov 47

-- The establishment of business research programs, with special reference to farmers' regional purchasing associations. JM 12:348-61 Jan 48

Bradley, W. L. Cooperatives in a sound farm economy: discussion. JFE 29:1154-57 Nov 47

Davis, J. H. The place of cooperatives in a sound farm economy. JFE 29:1145-51 Nov 47

Dow, G. F. Regional and interregional cooperation in dairy marketing. JFE 29:1389-94 Nov 47

Hedges, H. Research developments in cooperative marketing. JFE 28:134-40 Feb 46

-- Integrating economic and legal thought relating to agricultural cooperation. JFE 31,pt.2:908-15 Nov 49

Hirsch, W. Z. The status and possibilities of rural producing cooperatives. JFE 31:697-707 Nov 49

Jensen, A. L. Integrating economic and legal thought on agricultural cooperatives. JFE 31,pt.2:891-907 Nov 49

King, J. J. Comments on "Trends in agricultural cooperation." JFE 25:506-09 May 43

Lent, F. B. Milk control: discussion. JFE 24:336-39 Feb 42

Millard, J. W. Co-operative advertising of food products. JM 6,no.4,pt.2:37-41 Apr 42

Miller, R. W. and Jensen, A. L. Failures of farmers' cooperatives. HBR 25:213-26 no.2, 47

Perregaux, E. A. The future of farm cooperatives in the United States. JFE 29:115-27 Feb 47

Rupple, G. W. Membership and public relations in agricultural cooperatives. JFE 31,pt.2:580-81 Feb 49

Selby, H. W. Farmers' cooperatives as competitors. HBR 24:215-27 no.2, 46

Stokdyk, E. A. Trends in agricultural cooperation. JFE 24:857-65 Nov 42

AA   McBride, C. G. The effect of milk control programs on cooperatives [in the West]. JFE 24:320-25 Feb 42

ASC   Naden, K. D. Price policy of the Challenge Cream & Butter Association [of California]. Pt.I-II. JM 13:459-69; 14:27-37 Apr,Jul 49

Trynin, B. Cooperative marketing: good and bad [in California]. JM 4:252-57 Jan 40

### ASIA

FC   Hsu, Y. Y. Cooperative economy in Yenan. S&S 10:17-40 no.1, 46

FI   Anonymous. Co-operative movement in Assam. (A note from the Registrar of Co-operative Societies, Assam) IJE 21:319-23 Jan 41

Ataullah, S. Punjab cooperation during a decade of depression. IJE 22:504-14 Jan 42

Balakrishna, R. Co-operative rural credit in Mysore. IJE 22:471-84 Jan 42

Beri, S. G. Co-operative multi-purpose society. IJE 22:515-31 Jan 42

Bhathera, S. S. The organisation of rural welfare. IJE 22:807-19 Jan 42

Butani, D. H. The co-operative movement in Sind. IJE 22:461-70 Jan 42

Driver, P. N. Rural co-operation in the Bombay Presidency. IJE 22:585-98 Jan 42

D'Souza, V. L. Multi-purpose society. IJE 22:546-53 Jan 42

Ghosh, H. Rural co-operation: its scope in India. IJE 22:450-60 Jan 42

Gopalaswamy, S. The capital resources of agricultural co-operative societies in Mysore. IJE 22:532-45 Jan 42

Iyengar, S. K. Rural co-operation and national planning in India. IJE 22:400-35 Jan 42

Kogekar, S. V. Rural co-operation: the old approach and the new. IJE 27:291-97 Jan 47

Mehta, V. L. Rural co-operation in India: its deficiencies. IJE 22:599-614 Jan 42

Misra, S. Co-operative agricultural credit in Orissa. IJE 22:724-38 Jan 42

Mukerji, K. Debt conciliation: a phase in the co-operative movement in Bengal (1940-43). IJE 28:563-69 Apr 48

Pillai, V. R. Some aspects of rural co-operation in Travancore. IJE 22:485-503 Jan 42

Prasad, M. Decentralisation in co-operative cane unions. IJE 29:55-58 Jul 48

Qureshi, A. I. Co-operation in theory and practice. IJE 22:436-49 Jan 42

Ramakrishnan, K. C. Revision of the Raiffeisen system [in Madras]. IJE 22:778-87 Jan 42

Row, B. G. Rural co-operation in Madras: some aspects. IJE 22:739-52 Jan 42

Saksena, S. P. Replanning of the co-operative movement in India. IJE 22:554-61 Jan 42

16.6 AGRICULTURAL COOPERATIVES (Cont.)
16.60 GENERAL (Cont.)
    ASIA (Cont.)
    Samad, S. A. Social security with special
FI    reference to India. IJE 25:331-43 Jan 45
    Santhanam, S. S. Rural co-operation in
        Madras. IJE 22:788-806 Jan 42
    Sriram, P. Resuscitation of rural credit
        societies in Madras. IJE 22:562-84
        Jan 42
    Trivedi, P. M. Rural co-operation in India:
        a study in the theory and practice of
        agricultural credit co-operation. IJE 22:
        753-77 Jan 42
    Khan, K. M. B. A. Co-operation in Pakistan:
FIP    multi-purposes societies (with special
        reference to West Punjab). PEJ 1, no.1:
        78-95 Jul 49

AFRICA
    Franklin, N. N. Co-operative credit in the
HSA    Transkeian Territories. SAJE 10:95-120
        Jun 42

    MIDDLE EAST
    Amer, A. Agricultural and co-operative
ME    credit in Egypt. EgC 39:345-48 Mar 48

16.7 GOVERNMENT PROGRAMS AND POLICIES
16.70 GENERAL
    Boulding, K. E. Economic analysis and ag-
        ricultural policy. CJE 13:436-46 Aug 47
    Johnson, D. G. The use of econometric
        models in the study of agricultural
        policy. JFE 30:117-30 Feb 48
    Renne, R. R. On agricultural policy. R.
        JFE 22:484-92 May 40

    UNITED STATES
    Benedict, M. R. Schisms in agricultural
A    policy: agriculture as a commercial in-
        dustry comparable to other branches of
        the economy. JFE 24:476-96 May 42
    Black, J. D. Land-Grant College Post-war
        agricultural policy. R. JFE 27:168-75
        Feb 45
    -- Professor Schultz and C.E.D. on agri-
        cultural policy in 1945. R. JFE 28:
        669-86 Aug 46
    Canning, J. B. Schisms in agricultural
        policy: rescue programs and managed
        agricultural progress. JFE 24:496-511
        May 42
    Clark, N. Agricultural legislation: an ap-
        praisal of current trends and problems
        ahead. JFE 29:84-93 Feb 47
    Commons, J. R. Legislative and adminis-
        trative reasoning in economics. JFE 24:
        369-91 May 42
    Davis, C. C. Place of farmers, economists
        and administrators in developing agri-
        cultural policy. JFE 22:1-9 Feb 40

Ezekiel, M. Schisms in agricultural policy:
    the shift in agricultural policy toward
    human welfare. JFE 24:463-76 May 42
Hammar, C. H. Agriculture in an expan-
    sionist economy. JFE 25:36-51 Feb 43
-- A post war program for American agri-
    culture. JFE 26:549-62 Aug 44
Hardin, C. M. Programmatic research and
    agricultural policy. JFE 29:359-82
    May 47
Horton, D. C. and Shepard, E. F. Federal
    aid to agriculture since World War I.
    AH 19:114-20 Apr 45
Jesness, O. B. Postwar agricultural policy:
    pressure vs. general welfare. JFE 28:
    1-14 Feb 46
--, chairman. Agricultural policy. [Panel
    discussion] JFE 31,pt.2:213-26 Feb 49
Johnson, N. W. Wartime experience in
    production adjustment research and
    future possibilities [with discussion].
    JFE 27:903-27 Nov 45
Johnson, S. E. Adapting agricultural pro-
    grams for war needs. JFE 24:1-16
    Feb 42
Kulsrud, C. J. The archival records of the
    Agricultural Adjustment Program.
    AH 22:197-204 Jul 48
Liss, S. Farm habilitation perspectives in
    the postwar period. JFE 29:723-44
    Aug 47
Parsons, K. H. Institutional changes affect-
    ing the agricultural outlook: the agricul-
    tural perspective. JFE 31,pt.2:1121-31
    Nov 49
Reed, J. J. Techniques for achieving agri-
    cultural goals for 1943 [with discussion
    by L. J. Norton]. JFE 25:84-94 Feb 43
Renne, R. R. [and others] Programs for
    post war: discussion. JFE 24:26-34
    Feb 42
Schultz, T. W. Economic effects of agri-
    cultural programs. AER/S 30,no.5:
    127-54 Feb 41
-- Schisms in agricultural policy: discus-
    sion. JFE 24:511-14 May 42
-- Postwar agricultural policy: a review of
    the Land-Grant Colleges Report. LE 21:
    95-107 May 45
-- Production and welfare objectives for
    American agriculture. JFE 28:444-57
    May 46
-- A note on the Davis review of "Agricul-
    ture in an unstable economy." REStat 29:
    92-94 May 47
Shepard, E. F. Costs of federal agricultural
    activities: their meaning and classifica-
    tion for purposes of economic analysis.
    JFE 27:540-52 Aug 45
Smith, T. L. and Roberts, R. W. Sources
    and distribution of the farm population
    in relation to farm benefit payments.
    JFE 23:607-18 Aug 41

# 16. AGRICULTURE

## 16.7 GOVERNMENT PROGRAMS AND POLICIES (Cont.)
### 16.70 GENERAL (Cont.)
#### UNITED STATES (Cont.)

Tugwell, R. G.  A planner's view of agriculture's future.  JFE 31:29-47 Feb 49

A

Wells, O. V.  Agricultural legislation: an appraisal of current trends and problems ahead.  JFE 29:41-51 Feb 47

Wolfe, A. B.  Schisms in agricultural policy: discussion.  JFE 24:514-17 May 42

Young, E. C. and Bottum, J. C.  Agricultural programs for the post-war period. JFE 24:17-26 Feb 42

AA

Hoover, C. B.  What changes in national policy does the South need? [with discussion by F. P. Miller]  JFE 22:206-14 Feb 40

#### OTHER COUNTRIES

Miller, J. W.  Pre-war Nazi agrarian policy.

EG

AH 15:175-81 Oct 41

Wunderlich, F.  The National Socialist agrarian program.  SR 13:33-50 Mar 46

FI

Bhan, R.  The Indian food problem.  IJE 26: 744-47 Apr 46

Dubey, D. S.  The Indian food problem. IJE 26:647-50 Apr 46

Gupta, D. L.  Future of food control in India.  IJE 26:571-78 Jan 46

Prasad, P. S. N.  Towards equilibrium in Indian agriculture: some suggestions for a post-war policy.  IJE 24:135-44 Oct 43

Qureshi, A. I.  Some thoughts on the Indian food problem.  IJE 26:359-69 Jan 46

Rao, R. V.  The Indian food problem. IJE 26:370-76 Jan 46

Row, B. G.  The Indian food problem. IJE 26:377-87 Jan 46

Sundara Rajan, V.  "Food planning in India." IJE 26:565-70 Jan 46

N

Campbell, K. O.  Production goals for primary products: some aspects of their formulation and function.  ER 22:83-98 Jun 46

### 16.71 HISTORY

A

Edwards, E. E.  Agricultural history and the Department of Agriculture.  AH 16:129-36 Jul 42

C

Fowke, V. C.  Royal Commissions and Canadian agricultural policy.  CJE 14: 163-75 May 48

AA

Hamilton, W. B.  Early cotton regulation in the lower Mississippi Valley.  AH 15: 20-25 Jan 41

EG

Rosenberg, H.  The economic impact of imperial Germany: agricultural policy. JEH/S 3:101-07 Dec 43

A

Ross, E. D.  The United States Department of Agriculture during the commissionership: a study in politics, administration, and technology, 1862-1889.  AH 20:129-43 Jul 46

EB
EG

Salter, L. A., Jr.  The challenge of Agrarpolitik.  R. LE 20:252-55 Aug 44

## 16.72  PRICE AND INCOME POLICIES
### 16.720  GENERAL

Black, J. D.  Provision for nutrition in the formulation of agricultural programs. JFE 30:703-12 Nov 48

#### UNITED STATES

A

Brownlee, O. H.  Some effects of compensatory payments [with discussion].  JFE 29: 256-60 Feb 47

Case, H. C. M.  The Agricultural Act of 1948.  JFE 31,pt.2:227-36 Feb 49

Church, L. F.  The effect of crop loans on corn prices.  JB 18:121-39 Jul 45

Cochrane, W. W.  Income payments as a substitute for support prices.  JFE 28: 1024-29 Nov 46

-- and Masucci, R. H.  Price-income effects of a food allotment program.  JFE 29: 752-60 Aug 47

Eggert, R. J.  Advantages and disadvantages of direct payments: with special emphasis on marketing considerations. JFE 29:250-55 Feb 47

Gold, N. L. [and others]  Agricultural surpluses: discussion.  JFE 22:334-40 Feb 40

Harper, F. A.  The importance of storage costs in accumulating food stocks. JFE 26:794-800 Nov 44

Heisig, C. P.  Income stability in high-risk farming areas.  JFE 28:961-72 Nov 46

Paarlberg, D.  Parity and progress. JFE 25:419-32 May 43

Parsons, K. H.  Social conflicts and agricultural programs.  JFE 23:743-64 Nov 41

Schickele, R.  The National Food Allotment Program.  JFE 28:515-33 May 46

Shepherd, G.  A rational system of agricultural price and income controls.  JFE 28: 756-72 Aug 46

-- A farm income stabilization program could be self-financing.  JFE 30:142-50 Feb 48

-- The objectives, effects and costs of feed grain storage [with discussion by R. Welborn].  JFE 31,pt.2:998-1009 Nov 49

AA

Halcrow, H. G. and Huffman, R. E.  Great Plains agriculture and Brannan's farm program.  JFE 31:497-508 Aug 49

Harrison, R. W.  A philosophy of agricultural adjustment with particular reference to the Southeast.  JFE 26:448-60 Aug 44

Hendrix, W. E.  The Brannan Plan and farm adjustment opportunities in the cotton South.  JFE 31:487-96 Aug 49

16.7 GOVERNMENT PROGRAMS AND POLI-
CIES (Cont.)
16.72 PRICE AND INCOME POLICIES (Cont.)
16.720 GENERAL (Cont.)
OTHER COUNTRIES
Britnell, G. E. Dominion legislation affect-
C    ing western agriculture, 1939. CJE 6:
275-82 May 40
Burton, G. L. The farmer and the market.
CJE 15:495-504 Nov 49
Black, J. D. Notes on developments in ag-
EB    ricultural policy and program in the
United Kingdom. JFE 28:1005-15 Nov 46
Drummond, W. M. An appraisal of rural
planning in the United Kingdom. JFE 29:
1089-1100 Nov 47
Johnson, V. W. The English Agricultural
Act, 1947. LE 24:178-81 May 48
Chao, P. C. The agricultural economics
FC    program of China. JFE 27:615-19 Aug 45
Tinley, J. M. and Mirkowich, B. M. Control
HSA   in the sugar-cane industry of South Africa.
JFE 23:537-49 Aug 41
Rosenberg, W. A note on state regulation of
N    farm incomes in New Zealand. OIS 11:
85-99 Apr 49

16.721 PRICE SUPPORTS AND STABILIZATION
POLICIES
Drummond, W. M. Objectives and methods
of government pricing of farm products.
JFE 30:665-79 Nov 48

UNITED STATES
Aandahl, A. R. A postwar forward pricing
A    plan for agriculture. JFE 27:476-82
May 45
Anonymous. Agricultural economists' views
on farm price policy. [Survey by the
Committee on Parity Concept, A.F.E.A.]
JFE 28:604-07 May 46
Barr, G. W. [and others] A price policy for
agriculture, consistent with economic
progress, that will promote adequate and
more stable income from farming.
[Honorable mention papers by Barr, M.
K. Bennett, G. P. Boals, K. Brandt, W.
W. Cochrane, R. J. Eggert, P. A. Eke,
C. C. Farrington, R. K. Froker, C. D.
Hyson, A. L. Larson, J. G. Maddox, R.
Schickele, G. Shepherd, and L. H. Simerl]
JFE 27:785-902 Nov 45
Black, J. D. Agricultural price policy,
January 1943 [with discussion]. JFE 25:
1-18 Feb 43
-- Guideposts in the development of a mar-
keting program. JFE 29:616-31 Aug 47
Borg, W. T. Food Administration experience
with hogs, 1917-19. JFE 25:444-57
May 43
Brandt, K., chairman. Outline of a price
policy for American agriculture for the
postwar period. Report of the Committee
on Parity Concepts. JFE 28:380-97 Feb 46

Brownlee, O. H. Some considerations on
forward prices. JFE 25:495-504 May 43
Cowden, T. K. Current trends in agricultural
policy. JFE 31,pt.2:800-05 Nov 49
Farnsworth, H. C. [Agricultural price sup-
ports]: discussion. AER/S 36:827-31
May 46
Froker, R. K. Discussion of price policy
winning papers. JFE 28:290-93 Feb 46
Hadary, G. An evaluation of the wartime
farm price-support programs. JB 18:
219-21 Oct 45
Hardin, C. M. The tobacco program: exception or portent? JFE 28:920-37
Nov 46
Hurlburt, V. L. Some aspects of administrative pricing as related to land economics research. LE 20:123-32 May 44
Johnson, D. G. Contribution of price policy
to the income and resource problems in
agriculture. JFE 26:631-64 Nov 44
-- A price policy for agriculture, consistent
with economic progress, that will promote adequate and more stable income
from farming. (The second award paper)
JFE 27:761-72 Nov 45
Klaasen, A. J. Department of Agriculture
on food prices. JM 13:386-87 Jan 49
Nicholls, W. H. A price policy for agriculture, consistent with economic progress,
that will promote adequate and more
stable income from farming. (The first
award paper) JFE 27:743-60 Nov 45
-- and Johnson, D. G. The farm price policy
awards, 1945: a topical digest of the winning essays. JFE 28:267-83 Feb 46
Pendleton, W. C. American sugar policy,
1948 version. JFE 30:226-42 May 48
Peterson, A. G. The politics of parity. R.
AH 16:193-94 Oct 42
Reynolds, L. G. Industrial wage policies
and farm price parity [with discussion
by J. D. Black]. JFE 25:52-64 Feb 43
Ruderman, A. P. Agricultural prices and
national income. JFE 28:571-75 May 46
Schickele, R. National food policy and sur-
plus agricultural production. JFE 29:
867-88 Nov 47
Shepherd, G. Stabilization operations of the
Commodity Credit Corporation. JFE 24:
589-610 Aug 42
-- Bases for controlling agricultural prices.
JFE 24:743-60 Nov 42
-- Controlling hog prices during the transi-
tion from war to peace. JFE 25:777-92
Nov 43
-- Changing emphases in agricultural price
control programs. JFE 26:476-502
Aug 44
Simerl, L. H. Discussion of price policy
award papers. JFE 28:284-89 Feb 46
-- Farm attitudes and methods of support-
ing prices. JFE 29:246-49 Feb 47

## 16. AGRICULTURE

### 16.7 GOVERNMENT PROGRAMS AND POLICIES (Cont.)

#### 16.721 PRICE SUPPORTS AND STABILIZATION POLICIES (Cont.)

##### UNITED STATES (Cont.)

A Stine, O. C. Parity prices. JFE 28:301-05 Feb 46

Waite, W. C. A quantitative comparison of agricultural price plans. JFE 28:575-87 May 46

Waugh, F. V. A price policy for agriculture, consistent with economic progress that will promote adequate and more stable income from farming. (The third award paper) JFE 27:773-84 Nov 45

Wellman, H. R. and Mehren, G. L. Some theoretical aspects of agricultural parity price policies and national employment. JFE 28:563-71 May 46

--, chairman. On the redefinition of parity price and parity income. Report of a committee [followed by two comments]. JFE 29:1358-77 Nov 47

Wells, O. V. Agricultural prices following World War II. JFE 26:725-36 Nov 44

Wilcox, W. W. Comments on agricultural policy. JFE 31,pt.2:806-13 Nov 49

Working, E. J. Work of the Committee on Agricultural Price Supports and Their Consequences. AER/S 35:419-21 May 45

-- Report of ad hoc Committee on Agricultural Price Supports. AER/S 36:817-26 May 46

Wright, K. T. Basic weaknesses of the parity price formula for a period of extensive adjustments in agriculture. JFE 28: 294-300 Feb 46

AA Johnson, D. G. High level support prices and corn belt agriculture. JFE 31:509-19 Aug 49

Taylor, C. T. Some economic consequences of federal aid and subsidies to southern agriculture. SEJ 14:62-72 Jul 47

##### OTHER COUNTRIES

C Britnell, G. E. and Fowke, V. C. Development of wheat marketing policy in Canada. JFE 31:627-42 Nov 49

Drummond, W. M. Canadian agricultural price problems and policies: a commentary. JFE 31:581-93 Nov 49

Fowke, V. C. Dominion aids to wheat marketing, 1929-39. CJE 6:390-402 Aug 40

Skeoch, L. A. Changes in Canadian wheat policy. CJE 9:565-69 Nov 43

Stewart, A. Stabilization of the income of the primary producer. CJE 11:359-72 Aug 45

Turner, A. H. Federal marketing and price support legislation in Canada. JFE 31: 594-609 Nov 49

EB Rutherford, R. S. G. Guaranteed prices and the farmers. OIS 6:17-23 Feb 5, 44

FI Banavalikar, A. S. Stabilisation of agricultural prices. IJE 27:417-19 Apr 47

Malhotra, P. C. A policy of stabilization of agricultural prices. IJE 26:112-16 Jul 45

HSA Hutt, W. H. [and others] Economists' protest. The operation of the Wheat Marketing Scheme, 1938-1939. Memorandum of objections. SAJE 8:37-50 Mar 40

Tinley, J. M. Control of agriculture in South Africa. SAJE 8:243-63 Sep 40

N Bergstrom, A. R. The guaranteed price for dairy products: New Zealand. ER 25, (no.49):91-97 Dec 49

Crawford, J. G. Cost of production surveys in relation to price fixing of primary products. ER 25,suppl.:29-58 Aug 49

#### 16.722 PRODUCTION CONTROLS AND ADJUSTMENT

FM Bauer, P. T. The working of rubber regulation. EJ 56:391-414 Sep 46

A Clark, N. Production policies for a permanent and profitable agriculture. LE 23:169-79 May 47

Enke, S. Regulating output via multiple prices. JFE 24:883-89 Nov 42

A Heady, E. O. The economics of rotations with farm and production policy applications. JFE 30:645-64 Nov 48

A Jesness, O. B. Distribution of farm benefit payments. JFE 23:873-77 Nov 41

AA Jones, P. E. Postwar adjustments in cotton production in the southeastern United States. LE 21:339-51 Sep 45

AA Mason, J. E. Cotton allotments in the Mississippi delta new-ground area. LE 18: 447-57 Nov 42

A -- Acreage allotments and land prices. LE 22:176-81 May 46

A Mehren, G. L. Some economic aspects of agricultural control. JFE 30:29-42 Feb 48

FM Silcock, T. H. A note on the working of rubber regulation [followed by P. T. Bauer's rejoinder]. EJ 58:228-43 Jun 48

#### 16.723 SURPLUS DISPOSAL

Condliffe, J. B. The disposal of agricultural surpluses. JFE 24:434-46 May 42

Doane, D. H. Vertical farm diversification. JFE 26:373-78 May 44

A Hoffman, A. C. Agricultural surplus programs. JM 6,no.4,pt.2:174-76 Apr 42

A Howell, L. D. Cotton surplus disposal programs. JFE 26:273-91 May 44

Johnson, D. G. The high cost of food: a suggested solution. JPE 56:54-57 Feb 48

Nelson, R. S. Export subsidies and agricultural income. JFE 23:619-31 Aug 41

A Schultz, T. W. Supporting agricultural prices by concealed dumping. JPE 56: 157-60 Apr 48

A Thomsen, F. L. Export-dumping plans. JFE 22:446-59 May 40

16.7 GOVERNMENT PROGRAMS AND POLI-
CIES (Cont.)

16.723 SURPLUS DISPOSAL (Cont.)

Waugh, F. V. Programs for using agricultural surpluses to reduce malnutrition and
to benefit farmers. JFE 22:324-34 Feb 40

A -- Food consumption programs as a part of
a farm program. JFE 26:784-88 Nov 44

A -- What shall we do with surplus foods?
JM 10:253-57 Jan 46

A Wells, O. V. Agricultural surpluses and
nutritional deficits: a statement of the
problem and some factors affecting its
solution. JFE 22:317-23 Feb 40

16.73 INTERNATIONAL ASPECTS OF DOMES-
TIC AGRICULTURAL POLICIES

A Gordon, M. S. International aspects of
American agricultural policy. AER 36:
596-612 Sep 46

A Johnson, D. G. Reconciling agricultural
and foreign trade policies. JPE 55:
567-71 Dec 47

16.74 AGRICULTURAL INSURANCE

Botts, R. R. Development of "normal" citrus
fruit yields by tree ages for use in a yield
insurance plan. JFE 23:867-72 Nov 41

A Clendenin, J. C. Crop insurance: an experiment in farm-income stabilization.
LE 16:277-85 Aug 40

Halcrow, H. G. Actuarial structures for
crop insurance. JFE 31:418-43 Aug 49

A Heisig, C. P. Income stability in high-risk
farming areas. JFE 28:961-72 Nov 46

A McCarty, D. E. Wheat yield insurance.
JFE 23:664-67 Aug 41

A Pengra, R. F. Crop production in the semiarid regions an insurable risk. JFE 29:
567-70 May 47

A Sanderson, F. H. A specific-risk scheme
for wheat crop insurance. JFE 25:
759-76 Nov 43

Wrather, S. E. Adaptation of crop insurance
to tobacco. JFE 25:410-18 May 43

16.75 TAXATION

A Barber, E. L. Modifying the federal income
tax to promote greater stability of farm
income. JFE 30:331-39 May 48

A Crockett, S. L. Some probable effects of
taxation on farmers' marketing practices. JFE 31:725-30 Nov 49

A Dowell, A. A. and Toben, G. E. Some economic effects of graduated income tax
rates on investors in farm capital.
JFE 26:348-58 May 44

Galletti, R. Taxation and agricultural policy.
IJE 22:68-86 Jul 41

A Haygood, T. F. How would a federal sales
tax affect farmers? JFE 27:649-63 Aug 45

A -- Analyzing the tax load of agriculture
[with discussion]. JFE 31,pt.2:668-81
Feb 49

FI Sengupta, S. The proposed agricultural income tax in Bengal. IJE 24:212-18 Jan 44

A Waugh, F. V. Excise taxes and economic
stability. JFE 30:399-410 Aug 48

FI Zacharias, C. W. B. Reform of land revenue
with special reference to Madras.
IJE 27:237-44 Oct 46

16.76 ADMINISTRATION

A Black, J. D. The Bureau of Agricultural
Economics: the years in between.
JFE 29:1027-42 Nov 47

A Hardin, C. M. The Bureau of Agricultural
Economics under fire: a study in valuation conflicts. JFE 28:635-68 Aug 46

A Jesness, O. B. Federal-state relationships
in agriculture. JFE 22:493-95 May 40

A Soth, L. Mr. Hoover's Department of Agriculture. JFE 31:201-12 May 49

A Tenny, L. S. The Bureau of Agricultural
Economics: the early years. JFE 29:
1017-26 Nov 47

# 17. NATURAL RESOURCES. LAND ECONOMICS

17.0 GENERAL

C Allcut, E. A. A fuel policy for Canada.
CJE 11:26-34 Feb 45

Ciriacy-Wantrup, S. von [and others]
Natural resources and international
policy: discussion. AER/S 35:130-36
May 45

ER Cressey, G. B. USSR: the geographic base
for agricultural planning. LE 25:334-36
Nov 49

Kotok, E. I. International policy on renewable natural resources. AER/S 35:
110-19 May 45

A Lamb, G. A. Post-war statistical planning
in the Department of the Interior.
JASA 42:37-41 Mar 47

Salisbury, J., Jr. and Salter, L. A., Jr.
Subsurface resources and surface land
economics. Pt.I-II. LE 17:270-79;
385-93 Aug, Nov 41

A Williamson, H. F. Prophecies of scarcity
or exhaustion of natural resources in the
United States. AER/S 35:97-109 May 45

17.1 HISTORY

ASW Wagar, J. V. K. Yellowstone's conception
rethought. LE 20:55-58 Feb 44

# 17. NATURAL RESOURCES, ETC.

## 17.2 CONSERVATION
### 17.20 GENERAL

Bunce, A. C.  Time preference and conservation.  JFE 22:533-43 Aug 40

-- Public policy and action for conservation.  JFE 24:97-108 Feb 42

Christensen, R. P.  Expectation and performance related to conservation and production adjustments in the midwest dairy region.  JFE 23:632-45 Aug 41  AA

Ciriacy-Wantrup, S. von.  Private enterprise and conservation.  JFE 24:75-96 Feb 42

-- Taxation and the conservation of resources.  QJE 58:157-95 Feb 44

-- Administrative coordination of conservation policy.  LE 22:48-58 Feb 46  A

-- Resource conservation and economic stability.  QJE 60:412-52 May 46

Frank, B.  Some aspects of the evaluation of watershed flood control projects.  LE 18: 391-411 Nov 42  A

Hammar, C. H.  Society and conservation.  JFE 24:109-23 Feb 42

Hsiang, C. Y.  A philosophy of permanent conservation.  LE 17:239-41 May 41  FC

Johnson, N. W.  Conservation: an objective or an ideal?  JFE 23:819-32 Nov 41  A

Moody, R. E.  Mr. Bunce on time preference and conservation [followed by A. C. Bunce's rejoinder and Moody's reply].  JFE 23:646-53 Aug 41

Nelson, A. Z.  Watershed management requires economic studies.  LE 18:90-91 Feb 42

Regan, M. M. and Weitzell, E. C.  Economic evaluation of soil and water conservation measures and programs.  JFE 29: 1275-94 Nov 47  A

Watkins, M. W.  Scarce raw materials: an analysis and a proposal.  AER 34:227-60 Jun 44

Wengert, N.  The land, TVA, and the fertilizer industry.  LE 25:11-21 Feb 49  A

Wooten, H. H.  The agricultural flood control program.  R.  LE 22:35-47 Feb 46  A

## 17.3 LAND ECONOMICS
### 17.30 GENERAL

Bausman, R. O.  Merits and limitations of some of the measures of land classes.  JFE 23:899-903 Nov 41

Black, J. D.  Notes on "poor land," and "submarginal land" [in two Illinois counties].  JFE 27:345-74 May 45  ASI

Bodfish, M.  Translating research into progress through the Journal of land and public utility economics.  LE 18:82-84 Feb 42

Boonstra, C. A. and Campbell, J. R.  Land classification, land-use areas, and farm management research [in Lincoln Parish, Louisiana].  JFE 23:657-64 Aug 41  ASL

Conklin, H. E.  Some new directions of land economic research in the Northeast.  JFE 31,pt.2:1043-57 Nov 49  AA

Dykstra, C. A.  A quarter century of land economics.  LE 18:1-3 Feb 42  A

Elvove, J. T.  The Florida Everglades: a region of new settlement.  LE 19:464-69 Nov 43  ASF

Gilman, V.  Land economics research: discussion.  JFE 31,pt.2:1055-57 Nov 49  A

Gray, L. C. and Regan, M.  Needed points of development and reorientation in land economic theory [with summary of discussions].  JFE 22:34-51 Feb 40

Green, H. W.  Origin and development of a continuous real property inventory.  LE 16:325-34 Aug 40  A

Harrison, R. W.  Land improvement vs. land settlement for the Southeast.  SEJ 12:30-38 Jul 45  AA

-- Land economic research in the alluvial valley of the lower Mississippi River.  JFE 29:593-615 Aug 47  AA

Henderson, S.  An experiment in forest-farm resettlement [in northern Wisconsin].  LE 22:10-21 Feb 46  ASW

Hurlburt, V. L.  Some aspects of administrative pricing as related to land economics research.  LE 20:123-32 May 44  A

-- Forage land requirements in the northeast region.  LE 21:144-53 May 45  AA

Johnson, V. W.  Land economics in transition.  LE 18:85-87 Feb 42  A

-- Twenty-five years of progress: Division of Land Economics.  LE 21:54-64 Feb 45  A

-- Land economics research.  LE 25:155-64 May 49

Kellogg, C. E.  Contributions of soil science and agronomy to rural land classification.  JFE 22:729-39 Nov 40

Kelso, M. M.  New directions for land economics research: West.  JFE 31,pt.2: 1035-42 Nov 49  AA

Landstrom, K. S.  Should non-farm agricultural land be included in the Census of agriculture?  LE 22:295-96 Aug 46  A

MacFarlane, D. L.  A quantitative test of the significance of land-use areas [in Grant County, Kentucky].  LE 18:293-98 Aug 42  ASK

Musbach, W. F. and Johnson, V. W.  National Resources Board on land classification.  LE 17:489-93 Nov 41  A

Nuttonson, M. Y.  USSR; some physical and agricultural characteristics of the drought area and its climatic analogues in the United States.  LE 25:346-51 Nov 49  ER

Pine, W. H.  Measuring the economic productivity of land.  JFE 30:777-83 Nov 48

Rowlands, D. T., chairman.  Objectives in applied land economics curricula.  Abstract of specialized conference discussion.  AER/S 32:233 Mar 42

Salter, L. A., Jr.  The content of land economics and research methods adapted to its needs [with discussion].  JFE 24: 226-55 Feb 42

17.3  LAND ECONOMICS (Cont.)
17.30  GENERAL (Cont.)
    Salter, L. A., Jr. (Cont.)
    -- Farm property and agricultural policy.
       JPE 51:13-22 Feb 43
    -- Global war and peace, and land econmics.
       LE 19:391-96 Nov 43
    Solem, M.  Effect of land purchase by FSA
AA   standard loan borrowers on agricultural
       production in northern Great Plains.
       LE 19:231-33 May 43
    Stewart, C. L.  Extended functions for in-
A    stitutional landowners.  LE 16:357-62
       Aug 40
    Upchurch, M. L.  Land economics research:
A    discussion.  JFE 31,pt.2:1054-55 Nov 49
    Wehrwein, G. S.  Institutional economics in
       land economic theory [with discussion by
       J. Ise].  JFE 23:161-72 Feb 41

17.301  GOVERNMENT POLICY
    Bennett, J. B.  A desirable wartime land
A    policy.  JFE 25:166-75 Feb 43
    Brunk, M. E.  Attacking low-income prob-
ASN  lems in rural areas of New York State.
       LE 17:493-97 Nov 41
    Coleman, W. J.  Progress in Arkansas land
ASA  policy.  LE 18:87-90 Feb 42
    Crippen, H. R.  Philippine agrarian unrest:
FP   historical backgrounds.  S&S 10:337-60
       no.4, 46
    Gadgil, D. R.  Social legislation and plans
FI    of improvement.  IJE 27:287-90 Jan 47
    Gorrie, R. M.  National land policy for the
FIP  West Punjab.  PEJ 1,no.1:29-32 Jul 49
    Kelso, M. M.  Current issues in federal
AA   land management in the western United
       States [with discussion].  JFE 29:
       1295-1318 Nov 47
    Raup, P. M.  An example of county land
ASW  management: Lincoln County, Wisconsin.
       LE 17:233-38 May 41
    Salter, L. A., Jr.  Social security: a new
A    consideration in submarginal land policy.
       LE 16:468-70 Nov 40
    -- Do we need a new land policy?  LE 22:
A    309-20 Nov 46
    Schwarz, S. M.  USSR: the shelterbelt pro-
ER   gram in its relation to other drought
       control projects.  LE 25:360-62 Nov 49
    Stokes, W. S.  The land laws of Honduras.
DC   AH 21:148-54 Jul 47

17.31  HISTORY
    Gruber, J. W.  Irrigation and land use in
       ancient Mesopotamia.  AH 22:69-77
       Apr 48
    Lee, S. C.  The theory of the agricultural
       ladder.  AH 21:53-61 Jan 47

    UNITED STATES
    Billington, R. A.  The origin of the land
A    speculator as a frontier type.  AH 19:
       204-12 Oct 45

    Cox, L. F.  Tenancy in the United States,
       1865-1900; a consideration of the validity
       of the agricultural ladder hypothesis.
       AH 18:97-105 Jul 44
    Freund, R.  Military bounty lands and the
       origins of the public domain.  AH 20:
       8-18 Jan 46
    -- John Adams and Thomas Jefferson on
       the nature of landholding in America.
       LE 24:107-19 May 48
    Mood, F.  The concept of the frontier, 1871-
       1898: comments on a select list of
       source documents.  AH 19:24-30 Jan 45
    Peffer, E. L.  Which public domain do you
       mean?  AH 23:140-46 Apr 49
    Shannon, F. A.  A post mortem on the labor-
       safety-valve theory.  AH 19:31-37 Jan 45
    Anderson, R. H.  Advancing across the
AA   eastern Mississippi Valley.  AH 17:
       97-104 Apr 43
    Dick, E.  Going beyond the ninety-fifth
       meridian.  AH 17:105-12 Apr 43
    Gates, P. W.  Land policy and tenancy in
       the prairie states.  JEH 1:60-82 May 41
    Hall, A. R.  Terracing in the southern
       Piedmont.  AH 23:96-109 Apr 49
    Loehr, R. C.  Moving back from the Atlantic
       seaboard.  AH 17:90-96 Apr 43
    Mosk, S. A.  Land policy and stock raising
       in the western United States.  AH 17:
       14-30 Jan 43
    Taylor, R. H.  Post-bellum southern rental
       contracts.  AH 17:121-28 Apr 43
    Dunbar, R. G.  Water conflicts and controls
ASC  in Colorado.  AH 22:180-86 Jul 48
    Dovell, J. E.  The Everglades, a Florida
ASF  frontier.  AH 22:187-97 Jul 48
    Mowat, C. L.  The land policy in British
       East Florida.  AH 14:75-77 Apr 40
    Reynolds, A. R.  The Kinkaid Act and its
ASN  effects on western Nebraska.  AH 23:
       20-29 Jan 49
    -- Land frauds and illegal fencing in western
       Nebraska.  AH 23:173-79 Jul 49
    Alexander, A. J.  Prelude to the antirent
ASN  war of 1845 in Delaware County, New
       York.  AH 20:104-07 Apr 46
    Ellis, D. M.  Land tenure and tenancy in the
       Hudson Valley, 1790-1860.  AH 18:75-82
       Apr 44
    Nesbitt, W. A. and Netboy, A.  The history
ASN  of settlement and land use in the Bent
       Creek Forest [North Carolina].  AH 20:
       121-27 Apr 46
    Forbes, G.  Oklahoma oil and Indiana land
ASO  tenure.  AH 15:189-94 Oct 41
    Cleworth, M. M.  Artesian-well irrigation:
ASS  its history in Brown County, South
       Dakota, 1889-1900.  AH 15:195-201 Oct 41

    OTHER AMERICAN COUNTRIES
    Weeks, D.  European antecedents of land
D    tenures and agrarian organization of
       Hispanic America.  LE 23:60-75 Feb 47

17. NATURAL RESOURCES, ETC.

17.3 LAND ECONOMICS (Cont.)
17.31 HISTORY (Cont.)
OTHER AMERICAN COUNTRIES (Cont.)
Stokes, W. S.  The land laws of Honduras.
DC  AH 21:148-54 Jul 47

EUROPE
Beresford, M. W.  Lot acres.  EHR 13:
EB  74-79 no.1-2, 43
-- Commissioners of enclosure.  EHR 16:
130-40 no.2, 46
-- Ridge and furrow and the open fields.
EHR II.1:34-45 no.1, 48
Chambers, J. D.  Enclosure and the small
landowner.  EHR 10:118-27 Nov 40
Dodwell, B.  The free tenantry of the
Hundred Rolls.  EHR 14:163-71 no.2, 44
Fussell, G. E.  The dawn of high farming
in England:  land reclamation in early
Victorian days.  AH 22:83-95 Apr 48
Habakkuk, H. J.  English landownership,
1680-1740.  EHR 10:2-17 Feb 40
Hill, C.  Professor Lavrovsky's study of a
seventeenth-century manor.  EHR 16:
125-29 no.2, 46
-- Land in the English revolution.  S&S 13:
22-49 no.1, 48-49
Hosford, W. H.  Some Lincolnshire enclo-
sure documents.  EHR II.2:73-79 no.1, 49
Hoskins, W. G.  The reclamation of the
waste in Devon, 1550-1800.  EHR 13:
80-92 no.1-2, 43
Lennard, R.  The economic position of the
Domesday villani.  EJ 56:244-64 Jun 46
-- The economic position of the Domesday
sokemen.  EJ 57:179-95 Jun 47
Mosse, G. L.  The Anti-League:  1844-1846.
EHR 17:134-42 no.2, 47
Neilson, N.  Early English woodland and
waste.  JEH 2:54-62 May 42
Singer, H. W.  An index of urban land rents
and house rents in England and Wales
1845-1913.  Em 9:221-30 Jul-Oct 41
Smith, R. A. L.  Marsh enbankment and sea
defence in medieval Kent.  EHR 10:29-37
Feb 40
Take, W. E.  Members of Parliament and the
proceedings upon enclosure bills.
EHR 12:68-75 no.1-2, 42
-- The Commons' journals as sources of information concerning the eighteenth-
century enclosure movement.  EJ 54:
75-95 Apr 44
-- Opposition to parliamentary enclosure
in eighteenth-century England.  AH 19:
137-42 Jul 45
-- Members of Parliament and their personal relations to enclosure:  a study with
special reference to Oxfordshire enclosures, 1757-1843.  AH 23:213-20
Jul 49
Taylor, E. G. R.  The surveyor.  EHR 17:
121-33 no.2, 47

Watson, J. A. S.  Land ownership, farm
tenancy, and farm labor in Britain.
AH 17:73-80 Apr 43
Geddes, A.  Conjoint-tenants and tacksmen
EBS  in the Isle of Lewis, 1715-26.  EHR II.1:
54-60 no.1, 48
Blum, J.  Land tenure in the Austrian
ECA  Monarchy before 1848.  AH 19:87-98
Apr 45
Timoshenko, V. P.  The agrarian policies
ER  of Russia and the wars.  AH 17:192-210
Oct 43
Volin, L.  The Russian peasant and serf-
dom.  AH 17:41-61 Jan 43
Weinstein, H. R.  Land hunger and national-
ism in the Ukraine, 1905-1917.  JEH 2:
24-35 May 42
Freund, R.  Squandering the public domain
ES  in Sweden:  1820-1870.  LE 22:119-30
May 46
Pettersson, V. I.  Ancient and modern
Swedish land tenure policy.  JFE 30:
322-31 May 48

ASIA
Misra, B. R.  Proprietary tenures in Oudh:
FI  a historical survey.  IJE 20:371-90
Jan 40
Qureshi, A. I. Land tenures in Hyderabad:
an historical survey.  IJE 27:177-85
Oct 46
Ike, N.  Taxation and landownership in the
FJ  westernization of Japan.  JEH 7:160-82
Nov 47

AFRICA
Robertson, H. M.  A further note on early
HSA  land tenure at the Cape.  SAJE 12:144-46
Jun 44

AUSTRALIA.  NEW ZEALAND
Clark, A. H.  The historical explanation of
N  land use in New Zealand.  JEH 5:215-30
Nov 45
Fitzpatrick, B.  The big man's frontier and
Australian farming.  AH 21:8-12 Jan 47

17.32 CONSERVATION
Black, J. D.  Tailored credit for land im-
provements.  JFE 28:596-604 May 46
Bunce, A. C.  War and soil conservation.
A  LE 18:121-33 May 42
Campbell, K. O.  The development of soil
N  conservation programmes in Australia.
LE 24:63-78 Feb 48
Ciriacy-Wantrup, S. V.  Capital returns
from soil-conservation practices [with
discussion].  JFE 29:1181-1202 Nov 47
Collier, G. W.  Problems in physical evalu-
ation of soil conservation benefits.
JFE 24:124-38 Feb 42
-- Procedures of studying returns from
conservation farming.  JFE 27:686-94
Aug 45

## 17.3 LAND ECONOMICS (Cont.)
## 17.32 CONSERVATION (Cont.)

A Crickman, C. W. Interregional economic and social aspects of an objective evaluation of soil conservation. JFE 31,pt.2: 660-63 Feb 49

Forster, G. W. [Soil conservation benefits]: discussion. JFE 24:151-53 Feb 42

A Hardin, C. M. Current proposals for the organization of conservation and land-use programs in agriculture, the United States. JFE 30:619-44 Nov 48

A Heady, E. O. Cooperating in objective soil conservation research. JFE 31,pt.2: 664-67 Feb 49

James, H. B. What John Smith needs to know about the benefits and costs of soil conservation. JFE 31,pt.2:651-54 Feb 49

ER Jasny, N. USSR: law on measures to ensure high and stable yields in the Steppe and Forest-Steppe regions. LE 25:351-58 Nov 49

Johnson, N. W. Needed developments in the evaluation of soil conservation benefits. JFE 24:139-51 Feb 42

A Johnson, V. W. Conservation aspects of land programs. LE 24:303-09 Aug 48

Jordan, G. L. [Soil conservation benefits]: discussion. JFE 24:153-56 Feb 42

ER Krimgold, D. B. USSR: conservation plan for the Steppe and Timber-Steppe regions. LE 25:336-46 Nov 49

Lange, G. A neglected point in the economics of soil conservation [followed by A. C. Bunce and W. W. Wilcox's reply]. JFE 23:467-77 May 41

A McNall, P. E. Economic phases in soil erosion control. JFE 22:613-20 Aug 40

A -- Limiting factors in erosion control demonstrations. LE 21:383-86 Sep 45

Mukherjee, B. The economics of soil erosion and its influence on national life. IJE 21:148-57 Oct 40

-- The control of soil erosion in the West and its lessons for India. IJE 21:269-84 Jan 41

ASI Musser, R. H. A farm-city plan for erosion control [in the upper Sagamon Valley, Illinois]. LE 18:323-27 Aug 42

A Nelson, A. Z. Conservation expenditures on federal lands. JFE 24:611-20 Aug 42

A Osgood, O. T. Some observations on the relation of farm land tenure to soil erosion and depletion. LE 17:410-22 Nov 41

A Sauer, E. L. Methods of evaluating soil conservation measures. JFE 31,pt.2:655-59 Feb 49

AA Saunderson, M. H. Some economic aspects of western range-land conservation. LE 16:222-26 May 40

AA -- Western range land use and conservation problems [with discussion]. JFE 31,pt.2: 985-97 Nov 49

AA Sears, A. B. The desert threat in the southern Great Plains: the historical implications of soil erosion. AH 15: 1-11 Jan 41

Taylor, M. C. An evaluation of "Evaluating soil conservation" [followed by E. C. Weitzell's rejoinder]. JFE 29:966-76 Nov 47

A Weitzell, E. C. Economics of soil conservation. Pt.I-II. LE 19:339-53; 20:330-43 Aug 43, Nov 44

-- Evaluating soil conservation. JFE 29: 475-94 May 47

## 17.33 RECLAMATION. IRRIGATION

AA Barr, G. W. Irrigation in the West: discussion. JFE 31,pt.2:982-93 Nov 49

EN Black, J. D.; Becker, J. A. and Taeuber, C. The reclamation of flooded areas of Holland. JFE 28:1070-75 Nov 46

AA Butz, E. L. Irrigation in the West: discussion. JFE 31,pt.2:983-84 Nov 49

A Clawson, M. Post-war irrigation developments and the national and regional agricultural economy. JFE 27:138-52 Feb 45

A Fuhriman, W. U. Federal aid to irrigation development. JFE 31,pt.2:965-75 Nov 49

ASC Fuller, V. Acreage limitation in federal irrigation projects with particular reference to the Central Valley Project of California. JFE 31,pt.2:976-82 Nov 49

ASL Harrison, R. W. and Kollmorgen, W. M. The place of French-speaking farmers of southern Louisiana in future land development and reclamation projects. LE 22:223-31 Aug 46

ASL -- and Kollmorgen, W. M. Past and prospective drainage reclamations in the coastal marshlands of the Mississippi River delta [Louisiana]. LE 23:297-320 Aug 47

ASL -- Louisiana's state-sponsored drainage program. SEJ 14:387-403 Apr 48

AA Huffman, R. E. War and post-war problems of irrigation planning in the northern plains. LE 19:452-63 Nov 43

A Johnson, V. W. and Walker, H., Jr. Centralization and coordination of police power for land-control measures. LE 17:17-26 Feb 41

A Joss, A. Repayment experience on federal reclamation projects. JFE 27:153-67 Feb 45

AA Kimmel, R. I. Unit reorganization program for the southern Great Plains. JFE 22: 264-69 Feb 40

AA Paschal, J. L. and Slagsvold, P. L. Irrigation development and area adjustment in the Great Plains. JFE 25:433-43 May 43

A Selby, H. E. Indirect benefits from irrigation development. LE 20:45-51 Feb 44

A -- Factors affecting value of land and water in irrigated land. LE 21:250-58 Aug 45

17. NATURAL RESOURCES, ETC.

17.3  LAND ECONOMICS (Cont.)
17.33  RECLAMATION.  IRRIGATION (Cont.)
Selby, H. E. (Cont.)
-- The importance of irrigation in the economy of the West. JFE 31,pt.2:955-64 Nov 49 — AA

Stephan, L. L. Historico-economic aspects of drainage in the Florida Everglades. SEJ 10:197-211 Jan 44 — ASF

Timmons, J. F. Institutional obstacles to land improvement. LE 22:140-50 May 46 — A

Upchurch, M. L. Grazing development in western Oregon: an experiment in cooperative land development and control. LE 17:313-19 Aug 41 — ASO

White, G. F. State regulation of flood-plain use. LE 16:352-57 Aug 40 — AS

17.34  OWNERSHIP AND TENURE
17.340  GENERAL
Duncan, O. D. Hypotheses in land tenure research. JFE 25:860-68 Nov 43

Hoffsommer, H. Progress of tenure groups. JFE 23:208-16 Feb 41

Kelso, M. M. Needed research in farm tenancy. JFE 23:291-304 Feb 41

Schickele, R. Effect of tenure systems on agricultural efficiency. JFE 23:185-207 Feb 41

Wunderlich, F. The National Socialist conception of landed property. SR 12:60-76 Feb 45

UNITED STATES
Ackerman, J. Status and appraisal of research in farm tenancy. JFE 23:277-90 Feb 41 — A

Barlowe, R. Homestead tax exemption: a tenure improvement measure? LE 23:360-70 Nov 47

Brandt, K. Farm tenancy research: discussion. JFE 23:304-10 Feb 41

Brannen, C. O. Legal aspects of land tenure: discussion. JFE 23:216-17 Feb 41

Gibson, W. L., Jr. and Walrath, A. J. Inheritance of farm property. JFE 29:938-51 Nov 47

Hammar, C. H. The land tenure ideal. LE 19:69-84 Feb 43

Hannah, H. W. Family interest in the ownership of farm land. JFE 23:895-99 Nov 41

Harris, M. Legal aspects of land tenure. JFE 23:173-84 Feb 41

Henderson, S. A plan for transferring the farm from father to son. LE 24:82-85 Feb 48

Osgood, O. T. Some observations on the relation of farm land tenure to soil erosion and depletion. LE 17:410-22 Nov 41

Parsons, K. H. Research in the succession of farms: a comment on methodology. LE 24:293-302 Aug 48

Rochester, A. On the nature of rent. S&S 4:57-69 no.1, 40

Schickele, R. War-time adjustments in farm tenure. LE 18:163-68 May 42

Tharp, M. M. A reappraisal of farm tenure research. LE 24:315-30 Nov 48

Timmons, J. F. Land tenure policy goals. LE 19:165-79 May 43

-- Farm ownership in the United States; an appraisal of the present situation and emerging problems. JFE 30:78-100 Feb 48

Wehrwein, G. S. Changes in farms and farm tenure, 1935-1940. LE 17:372-74 Aug 41

Case, H. C. M., chairman. The Committee on Land Tenure in the Corn Belt. JFE 22:628-33 Aug 40 — AA

Loomer, C. W. Problems of range land tenure [in the Great Plains]. LE 18:214-17 May 42

Penn, R. J. Tenure situation in the north central region: 1940-1944. LE 19:370-76 Aug 43

Upchurch, M. L. The partido system [in the Southwest]. LE 18:218-19 May 42

Blackburn, D. W. Common grazing in the shortleaf pine-loblolly pine-hardwoods portion of south Arkansas. JFE 29:546-53 May 47 — ASA

Sullam, V. B. The Iowa statutory provisions for automatic lease renewal. JFE 24:677-84 Aug 42 — ASI

McMillan, R. T. Characteristics of former and present farm owners. [A survey of four counties in Oklahoma] LE 20:52-55 Feb 44 — ASO

-- Are tenure differences due to tenure? [Data from three surveys in Oklahoma] JFE 28:1029-36 Nov 46

Long, E. J. The Severson community: a glimpse of northern Wisconsin in process. LE 25:193-208 May 49 — ASW

OTHER AMERICAN COUNTRIES
Weeks, D. Land tenure in Bolivia. LE 23:321-36 Aug 47 — DSB

Smith, T. L. Land tenure in Brazil. LE 20:194-201 Aug 44 — DSB

Nelson, L. The evolution of the Cuban land system. LE 25:365-81 Nov 49 — DW

EUROPE
Ritchie, J. M. Some relationships of landlord and tenant. EJ 54:366-74 Dec 44 — EB

Inman, B. T. Farm inheritance practices in Austria. LE 23:288-96 Aug 47 — ECA

ASIA
Lee, S. C. The heart of China's problem, the land tenure system. JFE 30:259-70 May 48 — FC

Bakshi, S. C. Land systems in India and agricultural prosperity. IJE 27:245-49 Oct 46 — FI

17.3  LAND ECONOMICS (Cont.)
17.34  OWNERSHIP AND TENURE (Cont.)
17.340  GENERAL (Cont.)
ASIA (Cont.)
Dash, S. R. C.  Land system in Orissa.
FI  IJE 27:205-12 Oct 46
Jagannadham, V.  Land systems in India:
with special reference to the Permanent
Settlement.  IJE 27:186-93 Oct 46
Mathur, P. N.  Landlordism in India.
IJE 27:194-98 Oct 46
Misra, B.  Land tenure in the district of
Sambalpur (Orissa).  IJE 27:199-204
Oct 46
Natarajan, B.  Economic ideas behind the
Permanent Settlement.  IJE 22:708-23
Jan 42
Sharma, S. V. S.  Tenancy systems and im-
provement of agriculture.  IJE 27:213-20
Oct 46
Sitaramayya, M.  The land systems of the
Madras Presidency with special refer-
ence to inam tenures.  IJE 27:221-31
Oct 46
Srivastava, D. P.  Land system of a district
in North Bihar.  IJE 27:232-36 Oct 46
Thomas, P. J.  The zamindari problem in
Madras.  IJE 21:1-12 Jul 40
Singer, K.  Landlords and tenant farmers of
FJ  Japan.  ER 23:238-49 Dec 47

17.341  LAND TENURE REFORM
Brandt, K.  Toward a more adequate
A  approach to the farm tenure program.
JFE 24:206-25 Feb 42
Chia, F.  Mr. Hewes, Jr., on land tenure in
FJ  Japan: a reply.  LE 25:433-34 Nov 49
Descartes, S. L.  Land reform in Puerto
DW  Rico.  LE 19:397-417 Nov 43
Douglas, D. W.  Land and labor in Mexico.
DSM  S&S 4:127-52 no.2, 40
Eckstein, A.  Land reform and the trans-
EH  formation of agriculture in Hungary.
JFE 31:456-68 Aug 49
Fernandez, R.  Land tenure in Mexico.
DM  JFE 25:219-34 Feb 43
Goldmann, J.  Agrarian reform in eastern
EA  Europe.  OIS 7:160-64 Jun 30, 45
Guleri, J.  Abolition of zamindari.  IJE 27:
FI  513-16 Apr 47
Gupta, S.  The share-cropper & the Tabhaga
FI  Bill of Bengal.  IJE 28:297-301 Oct 47
Hewes, L. I., Jr.  On the current readjust-
FJ  ment of land tenure in Japan.  LE 25:
246-59 Aug 49
Jain, T. C.  Future of land system in the
FI  Punjab.  IJE 27:517-22 Apr 47
Medici, G.  Italy and land reform.  LE 21:
EI  2-11 Feb 45
Mitchell, C.  Korean farm tenant purchase
FK  program.  LE 24:402-05 Nov 48
Moody, V. A.  Europe's recurrent land
E  problem.  AH 22:220-32 Oct 48

Pronin, D. T.  Land reform in Poland:
EP  1920-1945.  LE 25:133-45 May 49
Schultz, T. W.  Capital rationing, uncer-
A  tainty, and farm-tenancy reform.  JPE 48:
309-24 Jun 40

17.342  GOVERNMENT ACQUISITION, OWNER-
SHIP, AND ADMINISTRATION
17.3420  GENERAL
Briggs, H. R. and McGinley, A. R.  Public
A  land acquisition in law and practice.
LE 17:452-59 Nov 41
Hurd, W. B.  Postwar agricultural settle-
C  ment possibilities in Canada.  JFE 27:
388-404 May 45
Johnson, V. W.  Status of federal lands.
A  JFE 29:745-52 Aug 47
Jones, P. E.; Mason, J. E. and Elvove, J. T.
ASL  New settlement in the delta of the lower
Mississippi Valley.  [A study in north-
eastern Louisiana]  LE 17:465-76 Nov 41
Lee, A. T. M.  The problem of post-war
A  land settlement and agricultural produc-
tion.  JFE 26:461-75 Aug 44
-- Farms and homes from surplus military
A  lands.  LE 21:331-38 Sep 45
-- Land acquisition program of the War and
A  Navy Departments, World War II.
JFE 29:889-909 Nov 47
Mason, J. E. and Bertrand, A. L.  Tenure
ASL  status of new-ground settlers in Louisiana.
LE 19:233-38 May 43
Poli, A.  What has happened to Durham and
ASC  Delhi [California]?  LE 22:182-90 May 46
Schulman, S.  Legal aspects of municipal
A  land ownership.  LE 16:216-18 May 40
Steele, H. A.  Postwar land settlement op-
AA  portunities in the northern Great Plains.
JFE 27:405-18 May 45
Taylor, M. H.  Selective selling and leasing
ASN  of county land in North Dakota.  LE 19:
238-42 May 43
Wilson, A. D.  Settler relocation: a prog-
ASM  ress report on the "Minnesota plan."
LE 17:102-03 Feb 41

17.3421  VETERANS' SETTLEMENT
England, R.  Soldier settlement: revising
A  the oldest rehabilitation prospectus.
LE 20:285-98 Nov 44
Griffith, D. T.  Land settlement proposals
A  for veterans, World Wars I and II.
LE 21:73-77 Feb 45
Marshall, D. G.  Soldier settlement in agri-
ASW  culture [in Wisconsin].  LE 20:270-78
Aug 44
-- Soldier settlement in the British Empire.
EBC  LE 22:259-65 Aug 46
Tough, R. and Weintraub, R. G.  Farms
A  and homes for veterans.  LE 20:371-73
Nov 44
Wooten, H. H.  Farming opportunities for
A  veterans.  LE 21:259-67 Aug 45

# 17. NATURAL RESOURCES, ETC.

## 17.3 LAND ECONOMICS (Cont.)
## 17.35 UTILIZATION
### 17.350 GENERAL

Bausman, R. O. Social aspects of land
ASD   use in Delaware. JFE 22:637-40
Aug 40

Bertrand, A. L. A dilemma of land use
ASL   [in Louisiana]. LE 18:220-22 May 42

Clawson, M. Trends in major cropland
A   use in the United States, 1909-1941.
JFE 27:472-76 May 45

Craig, G. H. War developments in land
AA   utilization and policy in the northern
Plains [with discussion by V. L. Hurl-
burt]. JFE 25:176-89 Feb 43

Galletti, R. Making sense of land utilization figures. IJE 25:465-91 Apr 45

Gibson, W. L., Jr. Industrialization and
ASV   rural land utilization [in Virginia].
SEJ 11:353-59 Apr 45

Hall, K. S.; Mayer, H. M. and Wrigley, R.
ASI   L., Jr. Mapping Chicago's industrial
and commercial land use. LE 20:
365-70 Nov 44

Hsiang, C. Y. Land utilization in China: a
FC   critique of methodology. LE 16:226-29
May 40

Huffman, R. E. and Paschal, J. L. Inte-
AA   grating the use of irrigated and grazing
land in the northern Great Plains.
LE 18:17-27 Feb 42

Hurlburt, V. L. Long-time adjustments in
AA   forage land utilization in the northeast
region. JFE 28:476-94 May 46

Jones, W. O. A California case study in
ASC   location theory: the globe artichoke on
the Moro Cojo. JFE 31:538-44 Aug 49

Lee, S. C. Pattern of land utilization and
FC   possible expansion of cultivated area in
China. LE 23:142-52 May 47

Minaw, F. Radio-geophysical prospection
ME   for desert underground water and the
utilisation of Egyptian deserts. EgC 39:
1-9 Jan-Feb 48

Robinson, A. The Scott and Uthwatt reports
EB   on land utilisation. R. EJ 53:28-38
Apr 43

Sitterley, J. H. Some factors affecting the
ASO   rate of retirement of farms in the submarginal land area of Ohio. JFE 26:
737-53 Nov 44

-- Farm abandonment in southeastern
ASO   Ohio. LE 21:34-44 Feb 45

T[hompson], R. J. Land utilization in rural
EB   areas. R. JRSS 105:218-19 pt.3, 42

Tough, R. and Weintraub, R. G. The United
ASN   Nations and changing land use in a
metropolis [New York City]. LE 24:
186-90 May 48

Wehrwein, G. S. and Johnson, H. A. A
ASM   recreation livelihood area [in Michigan
ASW   and Wisconsin]. LE 19:193-206 May 43

## 17.351 LAND USE POLICY

Crawford, J. G. and Lange, G. County
AS   planning for land-use adjustment.
JFE 22:473-83 May 40

Hall, O. J. Policy for use of state-owned
ASA   land in Arkansas. LE 16:470-74 Nov 40

Hardin, C. M. Political and other proc-
AA   esses in formulating and implementing
land use policies in the river basins.
JFE 31,pt.2:392-400 Feb 49

Harrison, R. W. The role of the agricul-
AA   tural economists in the formulation of
land use policies in river basins.
JFE 31,pt.2:405-09 Feb 49

Huffman, R. E. County land as a factor in
ASN   adjusting the agriculture of western
North Dakota. LE 18:495-99 Nov 42

Jebens, A. B. State rural land use legis-
AS   lation in 1941. LE 18:328-38 Aug 42

Lee, A. T. M. Use of military land for
A   agriculture during World War II.
LE 23:349-59 Nov 47

Steele, H. A. Physical, economic, and
AA   social factors in formulation of land use
policies in river basins. JFE 31,pt.2:
401-04 Feb 49

Walker, H., Jr. Police power for counties.
AS   LE 17:367-72 Aug 41

-- Rural land-use legislation in the states:
AS   the war years. LE 22:232-58 Aug 46

Wernimont, K. State rural land use legis-
AS   lation in 1939 [and 1940]. LE 16:110-16;
17:103-08 Feb 40, Feb 41

## 17.36 LAND MARKET AND VALUES

Ibach, D. B. Role of soil depletion in land
valuation. JFE 22:460-72 May 40

Livers, J. J. and Craig, G. H. Role of soil
depletion in land valuation. JFE 22:
773-76 Nov 40

Young, E. C. Use of the normal value concept as a stabilizing influence in agriculture. JFE 22:148-54 Feb 40

### UNITED STATES

Baker, J. A. The graduated farm land
A   transfer stamp tax. LE 16:21-29 Feb 40

Benner, C. L. Financing agriculture: discussion. JFE 22:158-61 Feb 40

Brandt, K. A public farm land appraisal
service, its desirability and practicability. JFE 27:620-33 Aug 45

Engberg, R. C. Federal credit agencies as
an influence upon land values. JFE 29:
150-62 Feb 47

George, J. P. Correlation analysis of
farm land values. JFE 23:668-71 Aug 41

Hammar, C. H. A reaction to land value
control proposals. JFE 25:822-34
Nov 43

Larsen, H. C. Relationship of land values
to warranted values, 1910-48. JFE 30:
579-88 Aug 48

## 17.36 LAND MARKET AND VALUES (Cont.)
### UNITED STATES (Cont.)

Lewis, A. B.  Relation of income to farm
A    capital: further discussion of questions
raised by Professor Norton.  JFE 24:
523-28 May 42

McNall, P. E.  Reflections on farm valuation.  LE 21:71-73 Feb 45

Mason, J. E.  Acreage allotments and land
prices.  LE 22:176-81 May 46

Murray, W. G.  Land market regulations.
JFE 25:203-18 Feb 43

-- Implications of land value control [with
discussion].  JFE 26:240-57 Feb 44

Norton, L. J.  Lewis on relation of income
to farm capital.  JFE 23:888-93 Nov 41

-- The land market and farm mortgage
debts, 1917-1921.  JFE 24:168-77 Feb 42

Nowell, R. I.  The farm land boom.
JFE 29:130-49 Feb 47

Nybroten, N.  Estimating cash considerations in real estate transfers from internal revenue stamps.  JFE 30:558-61
Aug 48

Regan, M. M.  The farm real estate market
in war time.  LE 18:140-45 May 42

-- and Clarenbach, F. A.  Emergency
control in the farm real estate market.
JFE 24:866-82 Nov 42

-- and Clarenbach, F. A.  Land market
developments and the war.  JFE 25:
190-202 Feb 43

-- and Clarenbach, F. A.  Postwar farm
land values?  LE 21:236-42 Aug 45

Selby, H. E.  Factors affecting value of
land and water in irrigated land.  LE 21:
250-58 Aug 45

Tetreau, E. D.  The location of heirs and
the value of their inheritances: farm
and city estates.  LE 16:416-29 Nov 40

Unwin, Sir R.  Land values in relation to
planning and housing in the United
States.  LE 17:1-9 Feb 41.  Reprinted,
LE 27:280-86 Aug 51

Wall, N. J.  Review of papers by R. I.
Nowell and R. C. Engberg.  JFE 29:
163-66 Feb 47

Walter, G. H.  Non-agricultural factors in
land prices.  LE 22:173-76 May 46

Roth, A., Jr.  Needed: a method of western
AA    mountain land valuation.  LE 24:181-85
May 48

Young, D.  Farm land values in the Southeast.  LE 22:213-22 Aug 46

Cave, R. C.  Distribution of property in
ASC  two California counties, 1907 and 1935,
based on probate records.  AER 30:
818-22 Dec 40

Aschman, F. T.  Dead land: chronically
ASI   tax delinquent lands in Cook County,
Illinois.  LE 25:240-45 Aug 49

Lundy, G.  Farm real estate values in
ASS   South Dakota and the BAE index of

estimated value per acre of farm real
estate.  JFE 27:980-84 Nov 45

### OTHER COUNTRIES

Medici, G.  Some considerations on the
E    land market in Europe.  LE 22:171-73
May 46

Ward, R. L.  A note on Cape Town's draft
HSA  rating ordinance.  SAJE 11:69-75
Mar 43

-- The "Uthwatt" report in its relation to
site value rating in the Transvaal.
SAJE 11:279-81 Dec 43

Wise, H. L.  Stabilization of land values in
N    New Zealand.  ER 19:225-30 Dec 43

## 17.4 FORESTS
## 17.40 GENERAL

Bulik, J. J.  USSR: the fifteen-year af-
ER  forestation plan.  LE 25:358-60 Nov 49

Duncan, J. S.  The effect of the N.R.A.
A    Lumber Code on forest policy.  JPE 49:
91-102 Feb 41

Folweiler, A. D.  The political economy of
A    forest conservation in the United States.
LE 20:202-16 Aug 44

Ghosh, R. C.  Forest policy for Bengal.
FI   IJE 28:509-32 Apr 48

Grøn, A. H. and Jørgensen, F.  Calculation
of sylvicultural balance-numbers.
NTTO 12:123-31 no.37, 48

Hasel, A. A. and Poli, A.  A new approach
A    to forest ownership surveys.  LE 25:
1-10 Feb 49

Helburn, N.  The case for national forest
AA  roads [in the Northwest].  LE 23:371-80
Nov 47

Henderson, S.  An experiment in forest-
ASW  farm resettlement [in northern Wiscon-
sin].  LE 22:10-21 Feb 46

Lee, A. T. M.  District court upholds
ASM  constitutionality of Maryland forest
conservation law.  JFE 30:150-56 Feb 48

Lower, A. R. M.  Report of the Ontario
CPO  Royal Commission on Forestry.  R.
CJE 14:507-10 Nov 48

Mahajan, Y. S.  Forest resources and
FI   possibilities of their exploitation in
Union Karnatak.  IJE 29:351-64 Apr 49

Marquis, R. W.  Severance taxes on forest
A    products and their relation to forestry.
LE 25:315-19 Aug 49

Rozman, D.  Massachusetts forest tax law.
ASM  LE 18:363-65 Aug 42

Sharp, P. F.  The tree farm movement: its
A    origin and development.  AH 23:41-45
Jan 49

Stoddard, C. H.  Future of private forest
AA  land ownership in the northern Lake
states.  LE 18:267-83 Aug 42

-- Folweiler's Political economy of
A    forestry.  R.  LE 21:65-68 Feb 45

17. NATURAL RESOURCES, ETC.

17.4 FORESTS (Cont.)
17.40 GENERAL (Cont.)
Weitzell, E. C. Maryland's forest conser-
ASM vation law. LE 19:479-80 Nov 43
Zivnuska, J. A. Some aspects of the eco-
nomic theory of forestry. LE 25:165-72
May 49

17.41 HISTORY
Kane, L. Federal protection of public
AA timber in the upper Great Lake states.
AH 23:135-39 Apr 49
Lennard, R. The destruction of woodland
EB in the eastern counties under William
the Conqueror. EHR 15:36-43
no.1-2, 45
-- The destruction of woodland in the
EB eastern counties, 1066-1086. [Note]
EHR II.1:144 no.2-3, 49
Rector, W. G. From woods to sawmill:
A transportation problems in logging.
AH 23:239-44 Oct 49
Sharp, P. F. The war of the substitutes:
A the reaction of the forest industries to
the competition of wood substitutes.
AH 23:274-79 Oct 49

17.5 FISHERIES
17.50 GENERAL
Usher, A. P. The influence of the cod
A fishery upon the history of the North
C American seaboard. R. CJE 6:591-99
Nov 40

17.51 HISTORY
Forman, S. The New Bridge Oyster Com-
ASN pany, 1863-1868 [Long Island, N.Y.].
BHR 16:53-61 Jun 42

17.6 WATER RESOURCES
17.60 GENERAL
Glaesar, M. G. The Mexican Water
AA Treaty: Pt.I-II. LE 22:1-9, 352-62
DM Feb,Nov 46

17.7 MINERALS
17.70 GENERAL
Blumenfeld, H. Addendum: on Russia's
ER mineral resources. LE 23:439 Nov 47
Davidson, R. D. and Wernimont, K. Ten-
ASO ure arrangements in Oklahoma oil
fields. LE 19:40-58 Feb 43
Husain, M. K. A. The mineral wealth of
FIP western Pakistan. PEJ 1,no.2:51-54
Oct 49
Pratt, W. E. The earth's petroleum re-
sources. JB 17:129-45 Jul 44
Salisbury, J., Jr. and Salter, L. A., Jr.
Subsurface resources and surface land
economics. Pt.I-II. LE 17:270-79;
385-93 Aug,Nov 41
Voskuil, W. H. Postwar Russia and her
ER mineral deposits. LE 23:199-213
May 47
-- Multiple fuel needs of the American
A economy. LE 24:370-83 Nov 48

# 18. POPULATION

18.0 GENERAL
Adler, H. A. Absolute or relative rate of
decline in population growth? QJE 59:
626-34 Aug 45
Barlowe, R. Population pressure and food
production potentialities. LE 25:
227-39 Aug 49
Baykov, A. A note on the trend of popula-
ER tion and the labour problems of the
U.S.S.R. JRSS 106:349-59 pt.4, 43
Bladen, V. W. On population. R. CJE 8:
273-88 May 42
Bonné, A. Movement of population and
M economic expansion in the Middle East.
EgC 33:319-35 Apr 42
Duncombe, H. L., Jr. Population changes
A and their effects. HBR 20:437-45
no.4, 42
Galbraith, V. L. and Thomas, D. S. Birth
A rates and the interwar business cycles.
JASA 36:465-76 Dec 41
Gini, C. A coordination of the different
population theories. RIIS 11:35-66
no.1-2, 43

Gottlieb, M. The theory of optimum popu-
lation for a closed economy. JPE 53:
289-316 Dec 45
Hansen, A. H., chairman. Round table on
A population problems. AER/S 30:383-98
Mar 40
Harrod, R. F. The population problem: a
EB rejoinder. MS 11:47-58 Apr 40
Lee, S. C. Population problems in the
Pacific. R. LE 22:381-85 Nov 46
Lindberg, J. Food supply under a program
of freedom from want. SR 12:181-204
May 45
Neale, E. P. Some population maladjust-
N ments in New Zealand. ER 23:66-74
Jun 47
Pedersen, J. Interest rates, employment
and changes in population. Kyk 2:1-16
fasc.1, 48
Ross, R. Some new emphases on popula-
HSA tion analysis. SAJE 17:166-74 Jun 49
Spengler, J. J. Population movements and
A economic equilibrium in the United
States. JPE 48:153-82 Apr 40

18.0  GENERAL (Cont.)
Spengler, J. J. (Cont.)
-- Pareto on population. Pt.I-II.  QJE 58:
571-601; 59:107-33 Aug,Nov 44
-- Malthus's total population theory: a
restatement and reappraisal. Pt.I-II.
CJE 11:83-110; 234-64 Feb,May 45
-- Aspects of the economics of population
growth. Pt.I-II. SEJ 14:123-47; 233-65
Oct 47, Jan 48
Sweezy, A. R. Population growth and in-
vestment opportunity. QJE 55:64-79
Nov 40
Whelpton, P. K. Mr. Gottlieb on optimum
population: an objection [followed by
M. Gottlieb's reply]. JPE 54:368-69
Aug 46

18.1  HISTORY
Aldridge, A. O. Franklin as demographer.
A     JEH 9:25-44 May 49
Cairncross, A. K. Internal migration in
EB    Victorian England. MS 17:67-87 Jan 49
Connell, K. H. The population of Ireland
EBI   in the eighteenth century. EHR 16:
111-24 no.2, 46
Helleiner, K. F. Population movement and
E     agrarian depression in the later Middle
Ages. CJE 15:368-77 Aug 49
Hoover, E. M., Jr. Interstate redistribu-
A     tion of population, 1850-1940. JEH 1:
199-205 Nov 41
Johnson, H. B. Factors influencing the
ASM   distribution of the German pioneer popu-
lation in Minnesota. AH 19:39-57 Jan 45
Kolehmainen, J. I. Finland's agrarian
ECF   structure and overseas migration.
AH 15:44-48 Jan 41
-- Finnish overseas emigration from
R     Arctic Norway and Russia. AH 19:
224-32 Oct 45
Mood, F. A British statistician of 1854
A     analyzes the westward movement in the
United States. AH 19:142-51 Jul 45
Rasmussen, W. D. Agricultural coloniza-
DSV   tion and immigration in Venezuela,
1810-1860. AH 21:155-62 Jul 47
Robertson, H. M. The 1849 settlers in
HSA   Natal. Pt.I-II. SAJE 17:274-88; 416-42
Sep,Dec 49
Taeuber, C. Rural-urban migration.
A     AH 15:151-60 Jul 41

18.2  POLICY
Husain, A. F. A. Industrialisation and the
FI    problem of population. IJE 30:55-59
FIP   Jul 49
Minaw, F. Radio-geophysical prospection
ME    for desert underground water and the
utilisation of Egyptian deserts. EgC 39:
1-9 Jan-Feb 48
Ross, R. Population policy in Great
EB    Britain. R. SAJE 17:320-28 Sep 49

Sovani, N. V. Population planning in India.
FI    IJE 27:299-316 Jan 47; Errata. 432
Apr 47
Thomas, B. Migration and the British
EBC   Commonwealth. EI 1:1147-56 Nov 48
Tobbe, W. Governmental measures to
encourage large families. RSE 4:54-76
Jan 46

18.3  SIZE AND COMPOSITION
Christensen, R. P. Food production: discussion. JFE 31,pt.2:265-67 Feb 49
Forsyth, W. D. Population growth: some
comparisons. ER 17:248-52 Dec 41
Johnson, D. G. Food production: discussion. JFE 31,pt.2:262-65 Feb 49
Taeuber, C. and Taeuber, I. B. World
population trends. (Food supply problems) JFE 31,pt.2:237-50 Feb 49

UNITED STATES
Davis, J. S. Our amazing population up-
A     surge. JFE 31,pt.2:765-78 Nov 49
Lotka, A. J. and Spiegelman, M. The trend
of the birth rate by age of mother and
order of birth. JASA 35:595-601 Dec 40

OTHER COUNTRIES
Hughes, E. C. and McDonald, M. L. French
CPQ   and English in the economic structure
of Montreal. CJE 7:493-505 Nov 41
Grebenik, E. The quantitative aspect of the
EB    British population problem: a survey.
REStud 10:43-52 no.1, 42
Hyrenius, H. The relation between birth
ES    rates and economic activity in Sweden
1920-1944. OIS 8:14-21 Jan 46
Agarwal, A. N. Population of India and its
FI    future trend. IJE 27:389-99 Apr 47
Krishnaswami, G. V. Some aspects of the
tendency of population in India. IJE 30:
69-75 Jul 49
Nagabhushanam, K. Population of prov-
inces. IJE 29:393-97 Apr 49
Rao, G. R. Seasonal variation of births.
IJE 21:192-98 Oct 40
Sarkar, B. K. The population trend in
India with reference to food and nutri-
tion. IJE 20:271-302 Jan 40
Sen Gupta, D. N. The problem of estimat-
ing population of India during intercen-
sal years. IJE 21:80-87 Jul 40;
Erratum. 341 Jan 41
Shaul, J. R. H. Southern Rhodesian life
H     tables no.1 (European). SAJE 9:335-47
Dec 41
Houghton, D. H. Population structure of a
HSA   Ciskei Native Reserve. SAJE 17:341-48
Sep 49
Ross, R. Some new emphases in popula-
tion analysis. SAJE 17:166-74 Jun 49
Sadie, J. L. European population move-
ments in S.A. during World War II.
SAJE 16:51-69 Mar 48

## 18. POPULATION

18.3 SIZE AND COMPOSITION (Cont.)
OTHER COUNTRIES (Cont.)

Abdel-Rahman, A. G. The Egyptian nation-
ME   al life tables no.2. EgC 37:207-25
May-Dec 46

Bruns, G. R. Wartime fertility and the
N   future population of Australia. ER 19:
185-202 Dec 43

Clark, C. and Dyne, R. E. Applications
and extensions of the Karmel formula
for reproductivity. ER 22:23-39 Jun 46

Karmel, P. H. Fertility and marriages,
Australia 1933-42. ER 20:74-80 Jun 44

-- Population replacement: Australia,
1947. ER 25,(no.49):83-88 Dec 49

18.4 GEOGRAPHICAL DISTRIBUTION.
MIGRATION

Bowley, A. L. Rural population in England
EB   and Wales, 1911 and 1931. Ec N.S.13:
97-118 May 46

Cosmo, G. Unemployment and emigration
EI   in Italy in the light of the E.R.P. and
O.E.E.C. BNL 1:434-40 Oct 48

Gentilli, J. Australian rural population
N   changes. ER 25,(no.48):37-47 Jun 49

Hawley, A. H. and Bogue, D. J. Recent
A   shifts in population: the drift toward
the metropolitan district, 1930-40.
REStat 24:143-48 Aug 42

Hoover, E. M., Jr. Interstate redistribu-
A   tion of population, 1850-1940. JEH 1:
199-205 Nov 41

Lively, C. E. Adjustment of population to
ASM   rural resources in Missouri. LE 18:
67-76 Feb 42

Shryock, H. S., Jr. Internal migration and
A   the war. JASA 38:16-30 Mar 43

Simon, H. A. Effects of increased productivity upon the ratio of urban to rural
population. Em 15:31-42 Jan 47

Tetreau, E. D. The location of heirs and
ASA   the value of their inheritances: farm
ASO   and city estates [in Arizona and Ohio].
LE 16:416-29 Nov 40

18.5 CENSUS. REGISTRATION

Bailey, W. L. Avoiding "census jitters."
A   LE 16:349-51 Aug 40

Neale, E. P. The 1936 Maori census.
N   ER 16:275-80 Dec 40

-- The 1945 New Zealand census. ER 22:
N   136-41 Jun 46

Ngcobo, S. B. A note on the registration
HSA   of births and deaths among Natives.
SAJE 16:98-105 Mar 48

Proudfoot, M. J. New inquiries for the
A   Census of 1940. LE 16:102-04 Feb 40

# 19. LABOR ECONOMICS

19.0 GENERAL

Braunthal, A. Von Mises on The tragedy
E   of European labor: comment. AER 34:
121-23 Mar 44

Brown, E. H. P. Prospects of labour.
Ec N.S.16:1-10 Feb 49

Carroll, J. D., Jr. Some aspects of the
A   home-work relationships of industrial
workers. LE 25:414-22 Nov 49

Daugherty, C. R. The field of labor economics. R. AER 35:652-57 Sep 45

Elliott, R. L. The Canadian labour press
C   from 1867: a chronological annotated
directory. CJE 14:220-45 May 48;
A correction. 515 Nov 48

Hinrichs, A. F. Developments in labor
A   market and price statistics in 1945 and
1946. JASA 42:31-37 Mar 47

Logan, H. A. Economics of labour. R.
CJE 9:82-91 Feb 43

Rudra, S. K. Some aspects of the Indian
FI   labour problem. IJE 20:649-62 Apr 40

Srikantan, K. S. Indebtedness of the mill
FI   worker. IJE 21:184-92 Oct 40

19.01 LABOR PRODUCTIVITY

Arndt, H. W. Productivity in manufacturing
A   and real income per head in Great Brit-

EB   ain and the United States. OEP 8:
65-80 Nov 47

Backman, J. and Gainsbrugh, M. R.
Productivity and living standards.
ILRR 2:163-94 Jan 49

Barna, T. Note on the productivity of
labour: its concept and measurement.
OIS 8:205-16 Jul 46

Burnham, E. A. Employee productivity in
A   department stores. HBR 27:480-97
Jul 49

Dalton, M. Worker response and social
A   background. JPE 55:323-32 Aug 47

Dennison, S. R. Industrial productivity.
LBR 11:37-54 Jan 49

Evans, W. D. Productivity and human re-
A   lations. AER/S 37:412-20 May 47

Gaffey, J. D. Labor productivity in tire
A   manufacturing: a reply to L. G.
Reynolds. AER 31:837-38 Dec 41

Giffin, R. R. Changing output per person
A   employed in trade, 1900-1940. JM 12:
242-45 Oct 47

Henderson, P. D. Some comparisons of
EB   pre-war and post-war productivity.
OIS 9:347-51 Oct 47

Hirsch, J. Productivity in war and peace.
AER/S 37:397-411 May 47

## 19.01 LABOR PRODUCTIVITY (Cont.)

EG — Kuczynski, J. Productivity and exploitation under German capitalism. S&S 9:55-66 no.1, 45

A/EB — -- Productivity and exploitation under capitalism. S&S 10:148-58 no.2, 46

AA — Lester, R. A. Effectiveness of factory labor: South-North comparisons. JPE 54:60-75 Feb 46

AA — Markham, J. W. Regional labor productivity in the textile industry. AER 33:110-15 Mar 43

Read, T. T. World's output of work. AER 35: 143-45 Mar 45; Correction. 676 Sep 45

Rostas, L. Industrial production, productivity and distribution in Britain, Germany and the United States. EJ 53:39-54 Apr 43

EB — Singer, H. W. and Leser, C. E. V. Industrial productivity in England and Scotland [with discussion]. JRSS 111:309-30 pt.4, 48

## 19.1 HISTORY

A — Danhof, C. H. Economic validity of the safety-valve doctrine. JEH/S 1:96-106 Dec 41

EF — Dunham, A. L. Industrial life and labor in France 1815-1848. JEH 3:117-51 Nov 43

EF — -- Unrest in France in 1848. JEH/S 8: 74-84 '48

C — Elliott, R. L. The Canadian labour press from 1867: a chronological annotated directory. CJE 14:220-45 May 48; A correction. 515 Nov 48

A — Rayback, J. G. The American workingman and the antislavery crusade. JEH 3: 152-63 Nov 43

EB — Rostow, W. W. Business cycles, harvests, and politics: 1790-1850. JEH 1:206-21 Nov 41

EA — Turner, R. E. Economic discontent in medieval western Europe. JEH/S 8: 85-100 '48

Wolman, L. Labor policy and economic history. JEH/S 5:86-92 Dec 45

## 19.2 LABOR SUPPLY. LABOR MARKET
## 19.20 GENERAL

ER — Baykov, A. A note on the trend of population and the labour problems of the U.S.S.R. JRSS 106:349-59 pt.4, 43

A — Burchardt, F. A. Manpower in the reconversion period in U.S.A. and U.K.
EB — OIS 7:303-05 Dec 15, 45

A — Heflebower, R. B. The effects of the war on the structure of commodity and labor markets. AER/S 36:52-64 May 46

Kerr, C. Labor markets: their character and consequences. IRRA 2:69-84 Dec 49

A — McPherson, W. H., chairman. Problems of labor market research. Abstract of specialized conference discussion. AER/S 32: 213-14 Mar 42

N — Mauldon, F. R. E. Seasonal variations in labour requirements in Australian industries. ER 17:81-96 Jun 41

A — Myers, H. B. Dynamics of labor supply. JASA 36:175-84 Jun 41

Pierson, F. C. [and others] Can capitalism dispense with free labor markets? Discussion. IRRA 2:100-14 Dec 49

HSA — Smith, R. H. and Byron, F. A. The expansion of industry and the supply of labour. SAJE 9:251-64 Sep 41

## 19.201 OCCUPATIONAL CLASSIFICATION

A — Edwards, A. M. Occupation and industry statistics. JASA 36:387-92 Sep 41

A — Fels, B. and Whelpton, P. K. An industrial classification for reports from individuals. JASA 35:74-85 Mar 40

A — Hobart, D. M. Occupational classification for market research. JM 7:367-73 Apr 43

A — Palmer, G. L. Some considerations involved in appraising the adequacy of occupational statistics. JASA 36:61-70 Mar 41

A — Sogge, T. M. Industrial classes in the United States in 1940. JASA 39:516-18 Dec 44

FI — Sovani, N. V. A critique [of B. G. Ghate's Changes in the occupational distribution of the population]. IJE 23:46-58 Jul 42

## 19.202 EMPLOYMENT. UNEMPLOYMENT

Long, C. D. The concept of unemployment. QJE 57:1-30 Nov 42

### UNITED STATES

A — Bakke, E. W. The economists and unemployment. AER/S 30,no.5:294-300 Feb 41

Bancroft, G. and Welch, E. H. Recent experience with problems of labor force measurement. JASA 41:303-12 Sep 46

Carson, D. Accessions to and separations from the labor force: concepts for analyzing certain types of labor problems. JPE 49:882-94 Dec 41

Dawson, H. P., Jr. Expanding local postwar employment data to produce state estimates. JASA 40:197-204 Jun 45

Ducoff, L. J. and Hagood, M. J. Objectives, uses and types of labor force data in relation to economic policy. JASA 41: 293-302 Sep 46

Eckler, A. R. Employment and income statistics. JASA 36:381-86 Sep 41

-- The revised census series of current employment estimates. JASA 40:187-96 Jun 45

Frankel, L. R. and Stock, J. S. On the sample survey of unemployment. JASA 37:77-80 Mar 42

# 19. LABOR ECONOMICS

## 19.2 LABOR SUPPLY. LABOR MARKET (Cont.)
## 19.202 EMPLOYMENT. UNEMPLOYMENT (Cont.)
### UNITED STATES (Cont.)

A  Humphrey, D. D. Alleged "additional workers" in the measurement of unemployment. <u>R</u>. JPE 48:412-19 Jun 40

Joy, A. The meaning of unemployment statistics. JASA 36:167-74 Jun 41

Livingston, S. M. The measurement of postwar labor supply and its capacity to produce. JASA 40:20-28 Mar 45

Nixon, R. A. <u>and</u> Samuelson, P. A. Estimates of unemployment in the United States. REStat 22:101-11 Aug 40

Reede, A. H. Adequacy of employment statistics. JASA 36:71-80 Mar 41

Spengler, J. J. Some effects of changes in the age composition of the labor force. SEJ 8:157-75 Oct 41

Stewart, C. <u>and</u> Wood, L. Employment statistics in the planning of a full-employment program. JASA 41:313-21 Sep 46

Stone, R. Employment in U.S. manufacturing. <u>R</u>. EJ 54:246-52 Jun-Sep 44

Webbink, P. Unemployment in the United States, 1930-40. AER/S 30,no.5:248-72 Feb 41

Weintraub, D. <u>and</u> Magdoff, H. The service industries in relation to employment trends. Em 8:289-311 Oct 40

Woytinsky, W. S. Additional workers on the labor market in depressions: a reply to Mr. Humphrey. JPE 48:735-39 Oct 40

-- Controversial aspects of unemployment estimates in the United States. REStat 23:68-77 May 41

AA  Gittler, J. B. <u>and</u> Giffin, R. R. Changing patterns of employment in five southeastern states, 1930-1940. SEJ 11:169-82 Oct 44

Vance, R. B. <u>and</u> Danilevsky, N. Population and the pattern of unemployment in the Southeast, 1930-1937. SEJ 7:187-203 Oct 40

### OTHER COUNTRIES

EB  Åkerman, G. Unemployment and unemployment policy in England. Kyk 3:23-35 fasc.1, 49

Allen, R. G. D. The unemployment situation at the outbreak of war [with discussion]. JRSS 103:191-217 pt.2, 40

Frankel, H. The industrial distribution of the population in Great Britain in July, 1939 [with discussion]. JRSS 108:392-430 pt.3-4, 45

Leser, C. E. V. Changes in level and diversity of employment in regions of Great Britain, 1939-47. EJ 59:326-42 Sep 49

Moos, S. The age structure of building labour. OIS 6:39-44 Feb 26,44

-- Employment and output in the building trades. OIS 8:44-50 Feb 46

FI  Nair, A. N. K. Some problems relating to employment and unemployment statistics in India. IJE 28:245-59 Oct 47

N  Butlin, N. G. An index of engineering unemployment, 1852-1943. ER 22:241-60 Dec 46

## 19.21 HISTORY

AA  Bonner, J. C. The plantation overseer and southern nationalism; as revealed in the career of Garland D. Harmon. AH 19:1-11 Jan 45

EBE  Buckatzsch, E. J. Occupations in the parish registers of Sheffield, 1655-1719. EHR II.1:145-50 no.2-3, 49

N  Butlin, N. G. An index of engineering unemployment, 1852-1943. ER 22:241-60 Dec 46

ASN  Creamer, D. Recruiting contract laborers for the Amoskeag mills [in New Hampshire]. JEH 1:42-56 May 41

EB  Dessauer, M. Unemployment records, 1848-59. EHR 10:38-43 Feb 40

-- Monthly unemployment records 1854-1892. Ec N.S.7:322-26 Aug 40

FI  Halliday, I. G. Natal and indentured Indian immigration. SAJE 8:51-59 Mar 40
HSA

A  Shannon, F. A. A post mortem on the labor-safety-valve theory. AH 19:31-37 Jan 45

ASL  Sitterson, J. C. The transition from slave to free economy on the William J. Minor plantations [in Louisiana]. AH 17:216-24 Oct 43

A  Smith, A. E. Indentured servants: new light on some of the America's "first" families. JEH 2:40-53 May 42

AA  Smith, R. W. Was slavery unprofitable in the ante-bellum South? AH 20:62-64 Jan 46

FC  Wilbur, C. M. Industrial slavery in China during the former Han Dynasty (206 B.C.-A.D. 25). JEH 3:56-69 May 43

## 19.22 COMPONENTS OF THE LABOR FORCE
## 19.221 WOMEN. CHILDREN

A  Anderson, M. The postwar role of American women. AER/S 34:237-44 Mar 44

EB  Collet, C. E. The present position of women in industry. JRSS 105:122-24 pt.2, 42

EB  Godson, R. Juvenile labour supply. OIS 11:21-34 Feb-Mar 49

EB  -- The regional distribution of juvenile labour. OIS 11:269-78 Sep 49

EB  -- The industrial distribution of juvenile labour. OIS 11:337-56 Nov 49

A  Greathouse, R. S. The effect of constitutional equality on working women. AER/S 34:227-36 Mar 44

ER  Grunfeld, J. Women's work in Russia's planned economy. SR 9:22-45 Feb 42

19.22 COMPONENTS OF THE LABOR FORCE
(Cont.)
19.221 WOMEN. CHILDREN (Cont.)
Parrish, J. B. Women in the nation's labor
A market. QJE 54:527-34 May 40

19.222 OLDER WORKERS
McFarland, R. A. The older worker in in-
A dustry. HBR 21:505-20 no.4, 43
-- Physically handicapped workers.
A HBR 23:1-31 no.1, 44

19.223 RACIAL, ETHNIC, AND SOCIAL
GROUPS
Bailer, L. H. The Negro automobile
A worker. JPE 51:415-28 Oct 43
Burrows, H. R. An approach to the Indian
HSA problem in South Africa. SAJE 15:
157-77 Sep 47
Northrup, H. R. Negroes in a war industry:
A the case of shipbuilding. JB 16:160-72
Jul 43
Parkinson, R. Fair employment practices
A legislation. HBR 26:115-28 Jan 48
Powell, D. M. The Negro worker in Chicago
ASI industry. JB 20:21-32 Jan 47
Van der Horst, S. T. Native urban employ-
HSA ment: a study of Johannesburg employ-
ment records. 1936-1944. R. SAJE 16:
251-59 Sep 48
Weaver, R. C. Negro employment in the
A aircraft industry. QJE 59:597-625
Aug 45

19.225 SLAVE LABOR. FORCED LABOR
Fisher, P. Reparation labor: a preliminary
analysis. QJE 60:313-39 May 46
Ross, R. G. Commission of Inquiry into
Slave Labor. ILRR 2:619-20 Jul 49

19.23 LABOR TURNOVER. MOBILITY
Agarwala, A. N. Social security and occu-
EB pational distribution of labour in post-
war period. R. IJE 25:358-62 Jan 45
Amos, J. L. Vocational rehabilitation dur-
ing and after the war. CJE 9:164-74
May 43
Burtt, E. J., Jr. After the shutdown in
ASM Howland, Maine. SEJ 8:80-87 Jul 41
Carson, D. Occupational mobility and oc-
A cupational outlook. SEJ 14:411-19
Apr 48
Crosland, C. A. R. The movement of
EB labour in 1948. Pt.I-II. OIS 11:117-26;
194-212 May,Jul-Aug 49
Daniel, G. H. Some factors affecting the
EB movement of labour. OEP 3:144-79
Feb 40
De Vyver, F. T. After the shutdown: an
ASN analysis of the job-hunting experience
of a group of Durham hosiery workers
[Durham, North Carolina]. JPE 48:
105-13 Feb 40

Freedman, R. and Hawley, A. H. Unem-
A ployment and migration in the depres-
sion (1930-1935). JASA 43:260-72
Jun 49
Gillespie, S. C. and Rothschild, K. W.
EB Migration and the distributive trades.
REStud 13:81-83 no.2, 46
Jaffe, A. J. and Wolfbein, S. L. Internal
A migration and full employment in the
U.S. JASA 40:351-63 Sep 45
James, R. Human waste: an analysis of
EB labour turnover in industry. EJ 59:
118-23 Mar 49
Maclaurin, W. R. and Myers, C. A. Wages
and the movement of factory labor.
QJE 57:241-64 Feb 43
Makower, H., Marschak, J. and Robinson,
EB H. W. Studies in mobility of labor:
analysis for Great Britain. Pt.I-II.
OEP 2:70-97; 4:39-62 May 39, Sep 40
Palmer, G. L. The mobility of weavers in
AA three textile centers. QJE 55:460-87
May 41
Schmukler, S. The industrial alternative
ASW for farmers [in Wisconsin]. JFE 30:
156-61 Feb 48
Slichter, S. H. The impact of social secur-
A ity legislation upon mobility and enter-
prise. AER/S 30:44-60 Mar 40
Tucker, R. S. The frontier as an outlet for
A surplus labor. SEJ 7:158-86 Oct 40
Wright, W. Impact of the war on technical
A training and occupational mobility.
AER/S 33:238-48 Mar 43

19.24 RECRUITING AND TRAINING
Whitehill, A. M., Jr. Location of potential
A labor reserves from published data.
SEJ 13:257-62 Jan 47

19.3 WAGES AND HOURS
19.30 GENERAL
Ainsworth, R. B. Earnings and working
EB hours of manual wage-earners in the
United Kingdom in October, 1938 [with
discussion]. JRSS 112:35-66 pt.1, 49
Lester, R. A. Effects of the war on wages
A and hours. AER/S 33:218-37 Mar 43
Miller, G. W. Wages and hours in con-
A sumers' cooperatives in Great Britain
EB and the United States. QJE 55:294-305
Feb 41
Nicholson, J. L. Earnings and hours of
EB labour. OIS 6:107-13 May 20, 44

19.301 WAGES AND PRODUCTIVITY
Davis, J. C. and Hitch, T. K. Wages and
productivity. REStat 31:292-98 Nov 49
Ezekiel, M. Productivity, wage rates, and
A employment. AER 30:507-23 Sep 40
Harris, S. E. [Productivity and wages]: in-
troduction. REStat 31:292 Nov 49

# 19. LABOR ECONOMICS

## 19.301 WAGES AND PRODUCTIVITY (Cont.)

Kerr, C. The short-run behavior of physical productivity and average hourly earnings. REStat 31:299-309 Nov 49

A Lester, R. A. Note on wages and labor costs. SEJ 10:235-38 Jan 44

## 19.31 HISTORY

EB Jefferys, M. and Jefferys, J. B. The wages, hours and trade customs of the skilled engineer in 1861. EHR 17:27-44 no.1, 47

A Lebergott, S. Earnings of nonfarm employees in the U.S., 1890-1946. JASA 43: 74-93 Mar 48

FI Srikantan, K. S. Labour in ancient India. IJE 20:639-43 Apr 40

## 19.32 WAGE LEVELS

A Balderston, C. C. The wage-setting dilemma. HBR 20:402-05 no.4, 42

A -- Balance in wage setting. HBR 24:51-56 no.1, 45

EB Bowley, A. L. Earnings, 1938 and 1940. OIS 2,no.11:14-15 Dec 40

EB Brown, E. H. P. Real wages: a note. EJ 58:599-600 Dec 48

EB Campion, H. Changes in wage rates and earnings in 1939-1940. Report of an enquiry conducted by the National Institute of Economic and Social Research. EJ 50:189-94 Jun-Sep 40

Dunlop, J. T. Real and money wage rates: a reply. QJE 55:683-91 Aug 41

A Furth, J. H. Earnings and employment in the business cycle. REStat 24:136-42 Aug 42

A Garvy, G. and Lewis, R. E. New indexes of hourly and weekly earnings compiled by the Federal Reserve Bank of New York. JASA 42:256-70 Jun 47

FI Ghosh, D. Wage and the Indian cost of living index numbers. IJE 26:226-42 Oct 45

A Hilderbrand, G. H., Jr. The Nathan Report and its critics. AER 37:386-91 Jun 47

A Lebergott, S. Earnings of nonfarm employees in the U.S., 1890-1946. JASA 43: 74-93 Mar 48

EB Marley, J. G. and Campion, H. Changes in salaries in Great Britain, 1924-1939. JRSS 103:524-33 pt.4, 40

A Reynolds, L. G. Industrial wage policies and farm price parity [with discussion by J. D. Black]. JFE 25:52-64 Feb 43

Ruggles, R. The relative movements of real and money wage rates. QJE 55: 130-49 Nov 40

-- --- Rejoinder. QJE 55:697-700 Aug 41

Shister, J. A note on cyclical wage rigidity. AER 34:111-16 Mar 44

A Siegel, I. H. Hourly earnings and unit labor cost in manufacturing. JASA 35:455-60 Sep 40

Tarshis, L. Real and money wage rates: further comment [followed by R. F. Ruggles' rejoinder]. QJE 55:691-700 Aug 41

## 19.33 WAGE DIFFERENTIALS. WAGE STRUCTURES

### 19.330 GENERAL

A Kidner, F. L. The variation in wage ratios: comment. QJE 55:314-18 Feb 41

A Lebergott, S. Wage structures. REStat 29: 274-85 Nov 47

A Lester, R. A. Wage diversity and its theoretical implications. REStat 28: 152-59 Aug 46

A Myers, C. A. Approaches and problems in wage research. AER/S 37:367-74 May 47

A Parrish, J. B. Impact of World War II on internal wage rate structures. SEJ 15: 134-51 Oct 48

A Perlman, J. Extent and causes of differences in hourly earnings. JASA 35: 1-12 Mar 40

A Reynolds, L. G. Wage differences in local labor markets. AER 36:366-75 Jun 46

A Roberts, D. R. The distribution of private, non-agricultural employees in the United States by straight-time hourly wage rates. JASA 39:469-78 Dec 44

Staehle, H. Ability, wages, and income. REStat 25:77-87 Feb 43

A Thorndike, E. L. The variation in wage-ratios. QJE 54:369-83 May 40

HSA Van der Horst, S. T. The Industrial Council System and the community. SAJE 16:274-85 Sep 48

### 19.331 OCCUPATIONAL

EB Bowley, A. L. Relative wages and earnings in different occupations. Pt.I-II. OIS 3: 383-89; 4:1-4 Dec 13, 41, Jan 10, 42; Erratum. 55 Jan 31, 42

C McDougall, J. L. The distribution of income among wage workers in railway employment, 1939-47. CJE 13:248-55 May 47

A Maclaurin, W. R. Wages and profits in the paper industry, 1929-1939. QJE 58: 196-228 Feb 44

A Mater, D. H. Wage rates and "relative economy and fitness" in the transportation industry. JB 18:183-208 Oct 45

A Neuner, E., Jr. Wages and employment in the public utility industries. LE 22: 363-80 Nov 46

### 19.332 INDUSTRIAL

A Backman, J. Hourly wage dispersion. AER 37:918-26 Dec 47

ER Bergson, A. Distribution of the earnings bill among industrial workers in the Soviet Union, March, 1928; October, 1934. JPE 50:227-49 Apr 42

## 19.33 WAGE DIFFERENTIALS. WAGE STRUCTURES (Cont.)

### 19.333 GEOGRAPHICAL

A Balmer, S. L. and Dean, J. Gearing salaries of nation-wide chains to the geographical structure of wages. JB 20: 96-115 Apr 47

AA Lester, R. A. Trends in southern wage differentials since 1890. SEJ 11:317-44 Apr 45

AA -- Diversity in north-south wage differentials and in wage rates within the South. SEJ 12:238-62 Jan 46

AA -- Southern wage differentials: developments, analysis, and implications. SEJ 13:386-94 Apr 47

A Myers, R. J. Wartime changes in urban wage relationships. JASA 40:175-86 Jun 45

AA Roberts, D. R. A limitation upon the differential wage doctrine. QJE 57:314-22 Feb 43

AA Sufrin, S. C.; Swinyard, A. W. and Stephenson, F. M. The North-South differential: a different view. SEJ 15:184-90 Oct 48

A Van Sickle, J. V. Geographical aspects of a minimum wage. HBR 24:277-94 no.3, 46

### 19.334 AGE. SEX

Brown, E. H. P. Equal pay for equal work. EJ 59:384-98 Sep 49

A Fisher, M. J. Equal pay for equal work legislation. ILRR 2:50-57 Oct 48

### 19.35 LEGISLATION AND REGULATION

A Baughman, E. T. A note on minimum wages and agricultural welfare. JFE 28: 1048-61 Nov 46

Blum, F. H. Marginalism and economic policy: a comment. AER 37:645-52 Sep 47

A Blum, R. Exemption of small rural telephone companies from the Wage and Hour Act. LE 16:117-20 Feb 40

A Boles, W. E., Jr. Some aspects of the Fair Labor Standards Act. SEJ 6:498-511 Apr 40

A Douty, H. M. Minimum wage regulations in the seamless hosiery industry. SEJ 8: 176-90 Oct 41

A Hinrichs, A. F. Effects of the 25-cent minimum wage on employment in the seamless hosiery industry. JASA 35: 13-23 Mar 40

A Kaplan, D. Postwar labor problems: discussion. AER/S 34:195-98 Mar 44

A McCabe, D. A. Postwar labor problems: discussion. AER/S 34:193-95 Mar 44

AA Moloney, J. F. Some effects of the federal Fair Labor Standards Act upon southern industry. SEJ 9:15-23 Jul 42

A Pierson, F. The determination of minimum wage rates. AER 30:72-81 Mar 40

A Richter, I. Four years of the Fair Labor Standards Act of 1938: some problems of enforcement. JPE 51:95-111 Apr 43

FI Saksena, S. P. Applicability of the principle of minimum living wage in India. IJE 20:719-28 Apr 40

FI Seth, B. R. Minimum wage legislation. IJE 20:709-17 Apr 40

HSA Smith, R. H. Some reflections on the economics of wage fixation in South Africa. SAJE 8:91-116 Jun 40

A Stigler, G. J. The economics of minimum wage legislation. AER 36:358-65 Jun 46

A Taylor, G. W. Wage regulation in postwar America. AER/S 34:181-92 Mar 44

AA Van Sickle, J. V. Regional aspects of the problem of full employment at fair wages. SEJ 13:36-45 Jul 46

A -- Geographical aspects of a minimum wage. HBR 24:277-94 no.3, 46

A Weiss, H. Economic coverage of the Fair Labor Standards Act. QJE 58:460-81 May 44

N Wilson, J. S. G. The Western Australian basic wage, 1926-42. ER 19:83-93 Jun 43

## 19.4 TRADE UNION ORGANIZATION

### 19.40 GENERAL

Bernays, E. L. An educational program for unions. ILRR 1:103-09 Oct 47

Forsey, E. Trade union policy under full employment. CJE 12:343-55 Aug 46

Sturmthal, A. National patterns of union behavior. JPE 56:515-26 Dec 48

#### UNITED STATES

Barbash, J. Ideology and the unions.
A AER 33:868-76 Dec 43

Braunthal, A. American labor unions and the war. SR 9:293-314 Sep 42

Daugherty, C. R. Union policies and leadership in postwar America. AER/S 34: 166-80 Mar 44

Fenton, F. P. Labor's objectives. HBR 25: 463-72 no.4, 47

Kaplan, D. Postwar labor problems: discussion. AER/S 34:195-98 Mar 44

Klemm, M. The rise of independent unionism and the decline of labor oligopoly. AER 34:76-86 Mar 44

Littler, R. A code of union conduct. HBR 20:10-20 no.1, 41

Parsons, K. H. Farmers and organized labor. JFE 25:367-83 May 43

Roper, E. The public looks at labor unions. HBR 21:425-31 no.4, 43

Taft, P. The Association of Catholic Trade Unionists. ILRR 2:210-18 Jan 49

AA DeVyver, F. T. The present status of labor unions in the South, 1948. SEJ 16:1-22 Jul 49

# 19. LABOR ECONOMICS

## 19.4 TRADE UNION ORGANIZATION (Cont.)
### 19.40 GENERAL (Cont.)
OTHER COUNTRIES

EB   Halpern, D. B. The trade union movement since the outbreak of war. OIS 5:232-39 Oct 9, 43

EG   Liss, S. Revival of free labor organizations in the United States occupation zone in Germany: a preview. SEJ 13:247-56 Jan 47

FC   Epstein, I. Main directions in Chinese labor. S&S 13:313-26 no.4, 49

N   Glickman, D. L. The labor movements in Australia and New Zealand. SR 16: 199-221 Jun 49

### 19.401 THEORY
Davis, H. B. The theory of union growth. QJE 55:611-37 Aug 41

### 19.402 INTERNATIONAL LABOR MOVEMENT
Hexner, E. World industrial committees. SEJ 12:348-56 Apr 46

Sturmthal, A. The crisis of the WFTU. ILRR 1:624-38 Jul 48

### 19.403 POLITICAL ASPECTS
A   Barbash, J. Unions, government, and politics. ILRR 1:66-79 Oct 47

A   Bernstein, I. Labor and the recovery program, 1933. QJE 60:270-88 Feb 46

A   Braunthal, A. American labor in politics. SR 12:1-21 Feb 45

EB   Cole, M. British trade unions and the Labour government. ILRR 1:573-79 Jul 48

ECA   Gulick, C. A., Jr. <u>and</u> Gerschenkron, A. Errors and traditions: remarks on Ernst Karl Winter's article, "The rise and fall of Austrian labor." SR 7:45-60 Feb 40

EG   Hamburger, E. A peculiar pattern of the fifth column: the organization of the German seamen. SR 9:495-509 Nov 42

EG   Kelly, M. A. Communists in German labor organizations. JPE 57:213-26 Jun 49

A   Meyer, J. Trade union plans for post-war reconstruction in the United States. SR 11:491-505 Nov 44

A   Morse, D. A. Labor and American foreign policy. ILRR 1:18-28 Oct 47

A   Richberg, D. R. Where is organized labor going? HBR 27:405-11 Jul 49

A   Taft, P. Attempts to "radicalize" the labor movement. ILRR 1:580-92 Jul 48

### 19.404 INTER-UNION RELATIONS
A   Anonymous. The agreement establishing a National Joint Board for the Settlement of Jurisdictional Disputes in building and construction industries. ILRR 2:411-15 Apr 49

A   Fisher, P. The settlement of work jurisdictional disputes by governmental agencies. ILRR 2:335-59 Apr 49

### 19.41 HISTORY
A   Carman, H. J. Terence Vincent Powderly: an appraisal. JEH 1:83-87 May 41

EBS   Chapman, D. The New Shipwright Building Company of Dundee, 1826 to 1831. EHR 10:148-51 Nov 40

A   Foner, P. S. Labor and the Copperheads. S&S 8:223-42 no.3, 44

EB   Hobsbawm, E. J. General labour unions in Britain, 1889-1914. EHR II.1:123-42 no.2-3, 49

EB   -- Trends in the British labor movement since 1850. S&S 13:289-312 no.4, 49

AA   Meyers, F. The Knights of Labor in the South. [1878-1893] SEJ 6:479-87 Apr 40

EB   Morris, M. Chartism and the British working-class movement. S&S 12: 400-17 no.4, 48

A   Peterson, J. The trade unions and the Populist party. S&S 8:143-60 no.2, 44

### 19.42 MEMBERSHIP. ORGANIZING ACTIVITIES
A   Northrup, H. R. The Negro and the United Mine Workers of America. SEJ 9:313-26 Apr 43

A   -- Organized labor and Negro workers. JPE 51:206-21 Jun 43; Errata. 51:550 Dec 43

ASA   -- The Negro and unionism in the Birmingham, Ala., iron and steel industry. SEJ 10:27-40 Jul 43

A   Summers, C. W. Admission policies of labor unions. QJE 61:66-107 Nov 46

A   Taft, P. Dues and initiation fees in labor unions. QJE 60:219-32 Feb 46

A   Weaver, R. C. Recent events in Negro union relationships. JPE 52:234-49 Sep 44

### 19.43 STRUCTURE. ORGANIZATION. ADMINISTRATION
A   Aaron, B. Protecting civil liberties of members within trade unions. IRRA 2: 28-41 Dec 49

C   Andras, A. The government of a central labour body. CJE 13:572-80 Nov 47

A   Barkin, S. Statistical procedures in union administration. ILRR 2:406-10 Apr 49

A   Brinker, P. A. Functions of national unions as contrasted with their locals. SEJ 16: 23-34 Jul 49

A   Northrup, H. R. [and others] Postwar labor relations: discussion. AER/S 36:370-83 May 46

A   Pierson, F. C. The government of trade unions. ILRR 1:593-608 Jul 48

A   Rottenberg, S. Intra-union disputes over job control. QJE 61:619-39 Aug 47

19.4  TRADE UNION ORGANIZATION (Cont.)
19.43  STRUCTURE. ORGANIZATION. AD-
MINISTRATION (Cont.)

Shister, J.  Trade-union government: a
A   formal analysis. QJE 60:78-112 Nov 45
Taft, P.  Opposition to union officers in
A   elections. QJE 58:246-64 Feb 44
-- Judicial procedure in labor unions.
A   QJE 59:370-85 May 45
-- Democracy in trade unions. AER/S 36:
A   359-69 May 46
-- Understanding union administration.
A   HBR 24:245-57 no.2, 46
-- The constitutional power of the chief
A   officer in American labor unions.
   QJE 62:459-71 May 48
-- Status of members in unions during ap-
A   peal from a penalty imposed by the local
   union. QJE 62:610-16 Aug 48
Troxell, J. P.  Protecting members' rights
A   within the union. AER/S 32:460-75
   Mar 42
Witney, F.  Union-shop and strike-vote
A   elections: a legislative fallacy.
   ILRR 2:247-50 Jan 49
Worker, J. pseud.  My union: an inside
A   story. HBR 26:108-14 Jan 48

19.44  UNION SECURITY

Hogan, J. A.  The meaning of the union
A   shop elections. ILRR 2:319-34 Apr 49
Jansen, G. F.  The closed shop is not a
A   closed issue. ILRR 2:546-57 Jul 49
McNatt, E. B.  Toward a national wartime
A   labor policy: the union-security issue.
   JB 16:64-69 Jan 43
Spielmans, J. V.  The dilemma of the closed
A   shop. JPE 51:113-34 Apr 43
-- Union security and the right to work.
A   JPE 57:537-42 Dec 49
Toner, J. L.  The closed shop and the Taft
A   Act. JPE 56:258-62 Jun 48
Vladeck, S. C.  On the sovereignty of labor
A   unions. ILRR 1:480-85 Apr 48
Witney, F.  Union-shop and strike-vote
A   elections: a legislative fallacy.
   ILRR 2:247-50 Jan 49

19.45  LABOR LEADERS

Ginzberg, E.  American labor leaders:
A   time in office. ILRR 1:283-93 Jan 48
Selekman, B. M.  Wanted: mature labor
A   leaders. HBR 24:405-26 no.4, 46

19.46  FINANCES

Belfer, N.  Financial resources of trade-
A   unions. JPE 57:157-61 Apr 49
Kozmetsky, G.  Unions' financial reporting.
A   HBR 27:13-23 Jan 49
Sexton, R. H. and Heneman, H. G., Jr.
A   Selected annotated bibliography on union
   accounting and financial reports.
   ILRR 2:116-20 Oct 48

19.47  EDUCATIONAL PROGRAMS OF UNIONS

Cohn, F. M.  Educational Department,
A   ILGWU. ILRR 1:704-08 Jul 48
Friedlander, E.  Education in the workers'
ASN  schools of New York City. SR 7:92-101
   Feb 40
Kallen, H. M.  The American worker and
A   his education. SR 11:100-11 Feb 44
Morse, W.  Labor Extension Bill (1948).
A   ILRR 1:657-63 Jul 48
Stein, R. M.  Workers' education: today's
A   challenge. HBR 18:207-14 no.2, 40

19.48  INDIVIDUAL UNIONS

Northrup, H. R.  The Tobacco Workers
A   International Union. QJE 56:606-26
   Aug 42

19.5  INDUSTRIAL RELATIONS.  COLLECTIVE
BARGAINING
19.50  GENERAL

Harbison, F. H.  Some reflections on a
   theory of labor-management relations.
   JPE 54:1-16 Feb 46
Hare, A. E. C.  Industrial relations and
   economic theory. ER 19:11-22 Jun 43
Tead, O.  Advancing the public interest in
   labor relations. ILRR 2:391-402 Apr 49

UNITED STATES

Bowden, G. T.  The adaptive capacity of
A   workers. HBR 25:527-42 no.4, 47
Bunting, E.  Industrial relations move
   ahead. ILRR 1:231-46 Jan 48
Fox, J. B.  Labor's response to man-
   agement. HBR 21:95-99 no.1, 42
Johnson, R. W.  Human relations in modern
   business. HBR 27:521-41 Sep 49
Leiserson, W. M.  Public policy in labor
   relations. AER/S 36:336-46 May 46
Nielson, V. C.  Preparing for postwar
   personnel relations. HBR 22:239-48
   no.2, 44
Northrup, H. R. [and others]  Postwar labor
   relations: discussion. AER/S 36:370-83
   May 46
-- Industrial relations with professional
   workers. HBR 26:543-59 Sep 48
Robbins, E. C.  Management-labor cooperation. HBR 21:415-24 no.4, 43
Selekman, B. M.  Conflict and cooperation
   in labor relations. HBR 25:318-38
   no.3, 47
-- Varieties of labor relations. HBR 27:
   175-99 Mar 49
-- and Selekman, S. K.  Productivity; and
   labor relations. HBR 27:373-92 May 49
Shreve, E. O.  Objective: industrial peace.
   ILRR 1:431-42 Apr 48
Slichter, S. H.  The social control of industrial relations. IRRA 2:2-12 Dec 49
Witte, E. E.  Where we are in industrial
   relations. IRRA 1:6-20 Dec 48

19. LABOR ECONOMICS

19.5 INDUSTRIAL RELATIONS. COLLECTIVE
  BARGAINING (Cont.)
19.50 GENERAL (Cont.)
  UNITED STATES (Cont.)
  Slichter, S. H. [and others] Report to the
ASM  Governor of Massachusetts on labor-
  management relations. [Selections from
  the Report of the Governor's Labor-
  Management Committee] ILRR 1:110-28
  Oct 47
  Bigelow, J. O. Is an industrial relations
ASN  consultant engaged in unauthorized
  practice of law? [A New Jersey case]
  ILRR 1:130-34 Oct 47
  Heher, H. Industrial relations consultants
  are not engaged in unauthorized practice
  of law: a court opinion. ILRR 2:253-54
  Jan 49
  Gross, J. Charter of Toledo Labor-Manage-
ASO  ment-Citizens Committee. Introductory
  note [and text of the Charter]. ILRR 1:
  500-05 Apr 48

  OTHER COUNTRIES
  Stokes, R. S. A shipyard from within.
EB  MS 17:88-96 Jan 49
  Galenson, W. Some aspects of industrial
ESD  relations in Denmark. IRRA 2:230-41
  Dec 49
  Agarwal, A. N. Industrial relations in
FI  India. IJE 29:67-74 Jul 48
  Ali, H. Industrial relations in India with
  special reference to Hyderabad. IJE 29:
  295-300 Jan 49
  Ayyar, K. L. V. Industrial relations in
  India. IJE 29:289-93 Jan 49
  Bhattacharya, S. and Chaturvedi, H. K.
  Industrial relations in India. IJE 29:
  277-88 Jan 49
  Mahajan, Y. S. Industrial relations in India.
  IJE 29:205-14 Oct 48
  Malhotra, P. C. Industrial relations: an
  analysis of the fundamental issues in-
  volved. IJE 29:199-204 Oct 48
  Misra, H. K. Industrial relations in India.
  IJE 29:227-33 Oct 48
  Rao, R. V. Industrial relations in India.
  IJE 29:215-21 Oct 48
  Reddy, G. R. The road to industrial peace.
  IJE 30:31-40 Jul 49
  Rudra, S. K. Peace in industry. IJE 29:
  37-43 Jul 48
  Sayanna, V. V. Industrial relations in India.
  IJE 29:235-42 Oct 48

19.51 HISTORY
  Armytage, W. H. G. A. J. Mundella and the
EB  hosiery industry. EHR 18:91-99 no.1-2,
  48
  Butlin, N. G. Collective bargaining in the
N  Sydney printing industry, 1880-1900.
  ER 23:206-26 Dec 47

  Larson, H. M. An early industrial capi-
ASC  talist's labor policy and management.
  [Samuel Watkinson Collins of Connecti-
  cut]. BHR 18:132-41 Nov 44
  Marburg, T. F. Aspects of labor adminis-
ASC  tration in the early nineteenth century
  [Connecticut button industry]. BHR 15:
  1-10 Feb 41

19.52 RESEARCH. EDUCATION
  Blum, F. H. Action research and industrial
A  relations. IRRA 2:248-54 Dec 49
  Bradley, P. Industrial relations and the
A  curriculum. SR 12:433-55 Nov 45
  Cornelius Justin, brother. The study of
A  industrial and labor relations in
  Catholic colleges. ILRR 3:70-75 Oct 49
  Derber, M. The role of various disciplines
  in industrial relations research: discus-
  sion. IRRA 1:232-33 Dec 48
  Feinsinger, N. P. The contribution of the
  law to industrial relations research.
  IRRA 1:223-28 Dec 48
  Harbison, F. H. A plan for fundamental
A  research in labor relations. AER/S 37:
  375-83 May 47
  Hart, C. W. M. Industrial relations re-
CPO  search and social theory [from a socio-
  logical study of the city of Windsor,
  Ontario]. CJE 15:53-73 Feb 49
  Jehring, J. J. Audio-visual materials in
A  industrial and labor relations. [List of
  currently available materials] ILRR 3:
  80-98 Oct 49
  Kornhauser, A. The contribution of psy-
  chology to industrial relations research.
  IRRA 1:172-88 Dec 48
  Leiserson, A. The role of political science
  in industrial relations research. IRRA 1:
  189-98 Dec 48
  Luckman, C. A round table fund for labor-
A  management education. ILRR 1:128-30
  Oct 47
  McPherson, W. H. and Derber, M. The
A  formation and development of IRRA.
  IRRA 1:2-4 Dec 48
  Mills, C. W. The contribution of sociology
A  to studies of industrial relations.
  IRRA 1:199-222 Dec 48
  Selekman, B. M. The role of various disci-
  plines in industrial relations research:
  discussion. IRRA 1:229-32 Dec 48
  Ware, C. F. Trends in university programs
A  for labor education, 1946-1948. ILRR 3:
  54-69 Oct 49
  Witte, E. E. The university and labor edu-
A  cation. ILRR 1:3-17 Oct 47

19.53 UNION-MANAGEMENT RELATIONS
  Barton, B. A. Trade unions and the entre-
A  preneurial function. EEH 1,no.6:20-28
  Jun 49

19.53 UNION-MANAGEMENT RELATIONS
(Cont.)

Bergen, H. B. Management prerogatives.
A    HBR 18:275-84 no.3, 40

Brown, D. V. Management rights and the
A    collective agreement. IRRA 1:145-55
Dec 48

Brown, L. C. The shifting distribution of
A    the rights to manage. IRRA 1:132-44
Dec 48

Chamberlain, N. The organized business
A    in America. JPE 52:97-111 Jun 44

Dale, E. Increasing productivity through
A    labor-management co-operation.
ILRR 3:33-44 Oct 49

French, C. E. [and others] Collective bar-
A    gaining and management rights: discussion. IRRA 1:156-70 Dec 48

Golden, C. S. Understanding union attitudes.
A    HBR 27:412-18 Jul 49

Kestnbaum, M. A study in management
A    prerogatives. HBR 19:88-98 no.1, 40

Littler, R. M. C. Managers must manage.
A    HBR 24:366-76 no.3, 46

Peterson, F. Management efficiency and
A    collective bargaining. ILRR 1:29-49
Oct 47

Pierson, F. C. [and others] Can capitalism
dispense with free labor markets? Discussion. IRRA 2:100-14 Dec 49

Selekman, B. M. When the union enters.
A    HBR 23:129-43 no.2, 45

Shister, J. Trade union policies and non-
market values. IRRA 2:85-99 Dec 49

Teper, L. The function of management in
A    achieving sound labor relations.
ILRR 2:558-75 Jul 49

Turnbull, J. G. The small business enter-
A    prise and the management prerogative
issue. ILRR 2:33-49 Oct 48

19.54 BARGAINING SYSTEMS

Brinker, P. A. The enforcement of collec-
A    tive bargaining. QJE 62:314-22 Feb 48

Brown, E. C. The employer unit for col-
A    lective bargaining in National Labor Re-
lations Board decisions. JPE 50:321-56
Jun 42

-- Free collective bargaining or govern-
A    ment intervention? HBR 25:190-206
no.2, 47

Chamberlain, N. The nature and scope of
A    collective bargaining. QJE 58:359-87
May 44

Gregory, C. O. Some problems of policy in
A    collective bargaining practices.
AER/S 33:174-83 Mar 43

Harris, A. L. [and others] Labor problems:
A    discussion. AER/S 33:197-206 Mar 43

Hochwald, W. Collective bargaining and
economic theory. SEJ 13:228-46 Jan 47

Lindblom, C. E. Collective bargaining and
the competitive system. CJE 11:566-77
Nov 45

Logan, H. A. Trends in collective bargaining: a study in causal analysis.
CJE 9:331-47 Aug 43

Shister, J. The theory of union bargaining
power. SEJ 10:151-59 Oct 43

-- Collective bargaining and the competitive system: a comment. CJE 12:
176-78 May 46

-- The locus of union control in collective
bargaining. QJE 60:513-45 Aug 46

Taylor, G. W., chairman. Round table on
A    collective bargaining and job security.
AER/S 30:223-29 Mar 40

19.55 COLLECTIVE AGREEMENTS

Braun, K. The dual nature of collective
A    agreements. JPE 51:451-62 Oct 43

Chamberlain, N. W. The nature of the
A    collective agreement. JB 22:92-105
Apr 49

Dogadov, V. M. Change in the nature of
ER   Soviet collective agreements. SovS 1:
79-84 Jun 49

Lens, S. Meaning of the grievance proced-
A    ure. HBR 26:713-22 Nov 48

McCabe, D. A. Problems of industry-wide
A    or regional trade agreements.
AER/S 33:163-73 Mar 43

Porter, J. M., Jr. The arbitration of indus-
A    trial disputes arising from disciplinary
action. IRRA 2:262-70 Dec 49

Selekman, B. M. Living with collective
A    bargaining. HBR 20:21-33 no.1, 41

-- Administering the union agreement.
A    HBR 23:299-313 no.3, 45

-- Handling shop grievances. HBR 23:
A    469-83 no.4, 45

19.56 EMPLOYEE PARTICIPATION IN MAN-
AGEMENT

Briefs, G. A. Sociological aspects of union-
A    management co-operation. RSE 5:59-68
Jun 47

Dubin, R. Union-management co-operation
A    and productivity. ILRR 2:195-209 Jan 49

Kennedy, P. V. Labor's participation in
A    management: ethical aspects. RSE 5:
49-58 Jun 47

Schirber, M. E. The Christian obligation
A    of employees to reach and maintain
maximum production. RSE 7,no.1:55-60
Mar 49

Shannon, R. L. The industry council plan
A    as an instrument of reconstruction.
RSE 2:87-99 Jan 44

19.57 PERSONNEL MANAGEMENT
19.570 GENERAL

Hart, C. W. M. The Hawthorne experiments.
C    CJE 9:150-63 May 43

Little, E. M. Some management responsibilities for good industrial relations.
CJE 12:356-60 Aug 46

# 19. LABOR ECONOMICS

## 19.57 PERSONNEL MANAGEMENT (Cont.)
### 19.570 GENERAL (Cont.)

Mettel, G.  Managerial adjustments to labor
A   law: an outline and bibliography.  JB 17:
186-93 Jul 44

Roethlisberger, F. J.  Human relations:
A   rare, medium, or well-done?  R.
HBR 26:89-107 Jan 48

Sabsay, N.  A machinist looks at manage-
A   ment.  HBR 22:249-55 no.2, 44

Underhill, H. F.  Pre-war personnel prac-
ASI   tices in Illinois.  JB 16:14-27 Jan 43

### 19.571 SELECTION. TESTING. TRAINING AND PROMOTION

Freeston, T.  Johnson & Johnson training
A   program.  ILRR 2:623-24 Jul 49

Livingston, J. S. and Ignatius, P. R.  Effec-
A   tive use of training films.  HBR 25:
637-51 no.4a, 47

Opdyke, W. K.  Training within industry.
A   HBR 20:348-57 no.3, 42

Shaeffer, R. E.  Merit rating as a manage-
A   ment tool.  HBR 27:693-705 Nov 49

Walker, C. L., Jr.  Education and training
A   at International Harvester.  HBR 27:
542-58 Sep 49

Ward, L. B.  Personnel testing.  HBR 26:
A   181-93 Mar 48

### 19.572 FOREMEN. SUPERVISORS

Dale, E.  The American foreman unionizes.
A   JB 19:25-30 Jan 46

Kolker, K. K.  The changing status of the
A   foreman.  BHR 22:84-105 Jun 48

Leiter, R. D.  Supervisory employees and
A   the Taft-Hartley law.  SEJ 15:311-20
Jan 49

Maier, N. R. F.  A human relations program
A   for supervision.  ILRR 1:443-64 Apr 48

Northrup, H. R.  Unionization of foremen.
A   HBR 21:496-504 no.4, 43

-- The Foreman's Association of America.
A   HBR 23:187-202 no.2, 45

Roethlisberger, F. J.  The foreman: master
A   and victim of double talk.  HBR 23:283-98
no.3, 45

### 19.573 SAFETY. HEALTH. WORKMEN'S COMPENSATION
### 19.5730 GENERAL

Goldmann, F.  Labor's attitude toward health
A   insurance.  ILRR 2:90-98 Oct 48

Hamilton, A.  Science in the Soviet Union.
ER   III. Industrial medicine.  S&S 8: 69-73
no.1, 44

McMahon, J. F.  Industrial Hygiene Founda-
A   tion.  ILRR 2:624-25 Jul 49

### 19.574 HUMAN RELATIONS. MORALE

Barloon, M. J.  Financial reports to em-
A   ployees.  HBR 20:124-31 no.1, 41

Bladen, V. W.  Economics and human relations.  CJE 14:301-11 Aug 48

Brown, E. H. P.  Morale, military and industrial.  EJ 59:40-55 Mar 49

Johnson, R. W.  An employer looks at labor-
A   management relations.  ILRR 1:486-92
Apr 48

Katz, D.  Good and bad practices in attitude
surveys in industrial relations.  IRRA 2:
212-21 Dec 49

McConnell, J.  Measurement of employee
attitudes: discussion.  IRRA 2:222-25
Dec 49

MacRury, K.  Employee morale: analyses
A   of absence records and opinion polls.
ILRR 2:237-47 Jan 49

Myers, A. H.  Laws and men in labor rela-
A   tions.  HBR 21:83-94 no.1, 42

Powlison, K.  Explaining the facts to em-
A   ployees.  HBR 25:145-57 no.2, 47

Richardson, F. L. W., Jr. and Walker, C. R.
A   Work flow and human relations.  HBR 27:
107-22 Jan 49

Sabsay, N.  From the workers' point of view.
A   HBR 25:339-47 no.3, 47

Sanford, F. H.  Measurement of employee
attitudes: discussion.  IRRA 2:225-27
Dec 49

Tiffin, J.  The uses and potentialities of attitude surveys in industrial relations.
IRRA 2:204-11 Dec 49

Vicary, J. M.  Labor, management, and food.
A   HBR 26:305-12 May 48

Walker, R. G.  The misinformed employee.
A   HBR 26:267-81 May 48

Wells, F. A.  Voluntary absenteeism in the
EB   cutlery trade.  REStud 9:158-80 no.2, 42

## 19.58 CASE STUDIES

Brissenden, P. F. and Keating, J. M.
ASN   Union-management co-operation in
millinery manufacturing in the New York
metropolitan area.  ILRR 2:3-32 Oct 48

Cohen, M. A. and Lieberman, M.  Collective
A   bargaining in the motor freight industry.
ILRR 3:17-32 Oct 49

Dawson, A. A. P.  Hollywood's labor
ASC   troubles.  ILRR 1:638-47 Jul 48

Dymond, W. R.  Union-management co-op-
CPO   eration at the Toronto factory of Lever
Brothers Limited.  CJE 13:26-67 Feb 47

Eliel, P.  Labor peace in Pacific ports.
AA   HBR 19:429-37 no.4, 41

-- Industrial peace and conflict: a study of
AA   two Pacific Coast industries.  ILRR 2:
477-501 Jul 49

Lovett, R. W.  The Thompson Products
A   collection [on the company's labor rela-
tions].  BHR 23:191-95 Dec 49

Meyers, F.  Organization and collective
AA   bargaining in the local mass transportation industry in the Southeast.  SEJ 15:
425-40 Apr 49

## 19.5 INDUSTRIAL RELATIONS. COLLECTIVE BARGAINING (Cont.)

### 19.58 CASE STUDIES (Cont.)

A    Northrup, H. R. Collective bargaining by air line pilots. QJE 61:533-76 Aug 47

A    Reder, M. W. The significance of the 1948 General Motors agreement [in regard to the cost-of-living sliding scale]. REStat 31:7-14 Feb 49

A    Ross, A. M. The General Motors wage agreement of 1948. REStat 31:1-7 Feb 49

A    Ruttenberg, H. J. The fruits of industrial peace. HBR 18:285-94 no.3, 40

ASO    Shister, J. The economics of collective wage bargaining: a case study [of the Cincinnati printing industry]. JPE 51:338-47 Aug 43

A    Smith, F. G. Handling labor grievances in the bituminous coal industry. HBR 19:352-63 no.3, 41

A    Winters, R. A. Aspects of joint bargaining in the rubber industry. ILRR 3:3-16 Oct 49

## 19.59 SELECTED ISSUES

### 19.591 IMPACT OF COLLECTIVE BARGAINING

A    Edwards, C. D. Public policy toward restraints of trade by labor unions: an economic appraisal. AER/S 32:432-48 Mar 42

A    Lester, R. A. Reflections on the "labor monopoly" issue. JPE 55:513-36 Dec 47

A    Lindblom, C. E. The union as a monopoly. QJE 62:671-97 Nov 48

A    Littler, R. M. C. The public interest in the terms of collective bargains. AER/S 35:209-25 May 45

A    McNatt, E. B. Labor and the antitrust laws: the Apex decision. JPE 49:555-74 Jun 41

A    Montgomery, D. Labor's aims and what they mean to agriculture. JFE 31,pt.2:1141-47 Nov 49

A    Prince, D. C. Labor's interest: a management view. ILRR 1:50-59 Oct 47

EB    Richardson, J. H. Wage policy in full employment [comment, followed by H. W. Singer's rejoinder]. EJ 58:421-25 Sep 48

A    Robbins, J. J. Organized labor and the public interest: discussion. AER/S 35:226-28 May 45

Simons, H. C. Some reflections on syndicalism. JPE 52:1-25 Mar 44

EB    Singer, H. W. Wage policy in full employment. EJ 57:438-55 Dec 47

A    Speier, H. [and others] Economic power blocs and American capitalism: discussion. IRRA 2:192-202 Dec 49

A    Spengler, J. J. Power blocs and the formation and content of economic decision. IRRA 2:174-91 Dec 49

A    Witte, E. E. A critique of Mr. Arnold's proposed antilabor amendments to the antitrust laws. AER/S 32:449-59 Mar 42

ASM    Wolf, R. B. Collective bargaining in small-scale industry: a case study [in hosiery manufacture in Massachusetts]. HBR 27:706-14 Nov 49

## 19.592 WAGE AND EMPLOYMENT POLICIES

A    Backman, J. The budget approach to wage adjustments: a case study [in the textile industry]. JPE 55:57-64 Feb 47

A    Barkin, S. Wage policies of industrial unions. HBR 19:342-51 no.3, 41

A    Dunlop, J. T. Wage policies of trade unions. AER/S 32:290-301 Mar 42

A    Enke, S. Mr. Ross on wage policy. SEJ 15:337-39 Jan 49

A    Fisher, W. E. Union wage and hour policies and employment. [Abstract] AER/S 30:227-29 Mar 40

A    -- Union wage and hour policies and employment AER 30:290-99 Jun 40

A    Glasser, C. Union wage policy in bituminous coal. ILRR 1:609-23 Jul 48

A    Lindblom, C. E. The income goals of unionism. SEJ 14:420-32 Apr 48

Ross, A. M. The trade union as a wage-fixing institution. AER 37:566-88 Sep 47

-- The dynamics of wage determination under collective bargaining. AER 37:793-822 Dec 47

A    -- What is responsible wage policy? SEJ 14:266-84 Jan 48

Shister, J. The theory of union wage rigidity. QJE 57:522-42 Aug 43

## 19.593 SYSTEMS OF WAGE PAYMENTS. INCENTIVES

A    Barkin, S. Labor's attitude toward wage incentive plans. ILRR 1:553-72 Jul 48

EB    Bowen, I. Incentives and output in the building and civil engineering industries. MS 15:157-75 May 47

EB    Nicholson, J. L. Wages and cost of living sliding-scales. OIS 6:189-91 Aug 12, 44

Shackle, G. L. S. Some theoretical aspects of payment by results. EI 2:841-53 Nov 49

## 19.594 GUARANTEED ANNUAL WAGE. DISMISSAL COMPENSATION

Campbell, R. R. Annual wage guarantee plans. AER 35:870-90 Dec 45

-- Recent analyses of annual wage guarantees. QJE 62:542-61 Aug 48

A    Feldman, H. The annual wage: where are we? R. AER 37:823-47 Dec 47

Hochwald, W. Guaranteed wages. AER 37:303-19 Jun 47

A    Kidd, C. V. The Latimer report. 2. Relationship of guaranteed wages to unemployment compensation. ILRR 1:470-80 Apr 48

# 19. LABOR ECONOMICS

## 19.5 INDUSTRIAL RELATIONS. COLLECTIVE BARGAINING (Cont.)

### 19.594 GUARANTEED ANNUAL WAGE. DISMISSAL COMPENSATION (Cont.)

Leontief, W. The pure theory of the guaranteed annual wage contract. JPE 54: 76-79 Feb 46

A Meyer, J. The Latimer report. I. Some general observations. ILRR 1:465-70 Apr 48

Ross, H. F. Some aspects of the problem of guaranteed wages and employment. CJE 13:545-62 Nov 47

A Schmidt, E. P. Annual wage and income-security plans. JB 14:127-49 Apr 41

A Snider, J. L. Management's approach to the annual wage. HBR 24:326-38 no.3, 46

A Witte, E. E. Steadying the worker's income. HBR 24:306-25 no.3, 46

### 19.595 PROFIT-SHARING

Datta, H. K. Profit-sharing, the incentive.
FI IJE 29:223-26 Oct 48

A Rowe, R. L. Profit-sharing plans in industry. HBR 27:559-84 Sep 49

A Scanlon, J. N. Profit sharing under collective bargaining: three case studies. ILRR 2:58-75 Oct 48

A Simons, G. Economic and legal aspects of profit-sharing plans. ILRR 2:76-89 Oct 48

### 19.596 PENSIONS. FRINGE BENEFITS

A Ball, R. M. Pension plans under collective bargaining: an evaluation of their social utility. IRRA 2:127-37 Dec 49

A Barkin, S. What shall we have: retirement benefit or superannuation plans? IRRA 2: 138-47 Dec 49

A Becker, H. Labor's approach to the retirement problem. IRRA 2:116-26 Dec 49

A Gitlow, A. L. Political aspects of union welfare funds. ILRR 3:75-79 Oct 49

A Held, A. Health and welfare funds in the needle trades. ILRR 1:247-63 Jan 48

A Jensen, V. H. Pensions and retirement plans as a subject of collective bargaining. ILRR 2:227-36 Jan 49

A Rosenthal, R. J. Union-management welfare plans. QJE 62:64-94 Nov 47

A Simons, G. Payroll flexibility through employee trusts. HBR 26:441-53 Jul 48

### 19.597 TECHNOLOGICAL CHANGE AND INNOVATION

A Barkin, S. Handling work assignment changes. HBR 25:473-82 no.4, 47

ASN McConnell, J. W. and Lampert, B. P. Employee adjustment to technological displacement: the Fifth Avenue Coach Company case. ILRR 2:219-26 Jan 49

ER Rao, K. V. Economics of Stakhanovism. IJE 24:149-54 Oct 43

A Selekman, B. M. Resistance to shop changes. HBR 24:119-32 no.1, 45

A Weintraub, D. and Ober, H. Union policies relating to technological developments. [Abstract] AER/S 30:225-27 Mar 40

### 19.598 JOB STANDARDS AND EVALUATION. WORK RULES

Cook, S. and James, R. Job specification and a fair wage. EJ 57:387-93 Sep 47

A Gomberg, W. Union interest in engineering techniques. HBR 24:356-65 no.3, 46

-- Measuring the fatigue factor. ILRR 1: 80-93 Oct 47

Littauer, S. B. and Abruzzi, A. Experimental criteria for evaluating workers and operations. ILRR 2:502-26 Jul 49

A Meyer, J. Hierarchy and stratification of the shop. SR 14:168-90 Jun 47

A Percival, A. J. and Gross, G. B. Job evaluation: a case history. HBR 24: 466-97 no.4, 46

A Randle, C. W. Restrictive practices of unionism. SEJ 15:171-83 Oct 48

Vaswani, M. H. Scientific management and rationalisation. IJE 27:401-07 Apr 47

### 19.599 SENIORITY

A Harbison, F. H. The seniority problem in mass production industries. [Abstract] AER/S 30:223-25 Mar 40

-- Seniority in mass-production industries.
A JPE 48:851-64 Dec 40

A Mater, D. H. The development and operation of the railroad seniority system. Pt.I-II. JB 13:387-419; 14:36-67 Oct 40, Jan 41

-- A statistical study of the effect of seniority upon employee efficiency. JB 14:169-204 Apr 41

-- Effects of seniority upon the welfare of the employee, the employer, and society. JB 14:384-418 Oct 41

## 19.6 STRIKES. DISPUTES. METHODS OF SETTLEMENT

### 19.60 GENERAL

Daugherty, C. R. The allowable area of industrial conflict. IRRA 2:42-45 Dec 49

Forchheimer, K. Some international aspects of the strike movement. Pt.I-II. OIS 10:9-24; 294-304 Jan,Sep 48

Gagliardo, D. Strikes in a democracy. AER 31:47-55 Mar 41

### UNITED STATES

Heimann, E. On strikes and wages. SR 15:
A 82-98 Mar 48

Jurkat, E. H. and Jurkat, D. B. Economic function of strikes. ILRR 2:527-45 Jul 49

Phelps, O. W. Public policy in labor disputes: the crisis of 1946. JPE 55: 189-211 Jun 47

## 19.6 STRIKES. DISPUTES. METHODS OF SETTLEMENT (Cont.)
### 19.60 GENERAL (Cont.)
#### UNITED STATES (Cont.)

Spielmans, J. V.  Strikes under the Wagner
A    Act.  JPE 49:722-31 Oct 41
-- On strike analysis.  JPE 50:750-60 Oct 42
-- Strike profiles.  JPE 52:319-39 Dec 44

Yoder, D.  Economic changes and industrial unrest in the United States.  JPE 48: 222-37 Apr 40

#### OTHER COUNTRIES

Gomberg, E. L.  Strikes and lock-outs in
EB    Great Britain.  QJE 59:92-106 Nov 44

Knowles, K. G. J. C.  Strikes & their changing economic context.  OIS 9:285b-306 Sep 47

Forchheimer, K.  Some international as-
ES    pects of strikes; the effectiveness of large and of long strikes, with special reference to Sweden.  OIS 11:279-86 Sep 49

Bhatia, A. C.  Labour unrest in India.
FI    IJE 20:617-29 Apr 40

Jagannadham, V.  Industrial disputes in India.  IJE 29:185-97 Oct 48

Lokanathan, P. S.  Industrial disputes and legislation.  IJE 20:737-47 Apr 40

Narayanaswamy, B. V.  Industrial disputes and their settlement.  IJE 20:729-35 Apr 40

Qadir, M. A.  Post-war labour disputes in Hyderabad and their settlement.  IJE 29: 271-75 Jan 49

Rohatgi, B. N.  Labour problems and labour legislation in India.  IJE 20: 611-16 Apr 40

Kahn, E.  The right to strike in South Africa:
HSA    an historical analysis.  SAJE 11:24-47 Mar 43

### 19.62 EMERGENCY DISPUTES

Kennedy, T.  The handling of emergency
ASN    disputes [in New Jersey].  IRRA 2:14-27 Dec 49

Marceau, L. and Musgrave, R. A.  Strikes
A    in essential industries: a way out. HBR 27:286-92 May 49

Mayer, H. [and others]  Disputes that create
A    a public emergency: discussion.  IRRA 1: 89-97 Dec 48

Northrup, H. R.  Emergency disputes under
A    the Railway Labor Act.  IRRA 1:78-88 Dec 48

Rossiter, C. L.  Labor and the public inter-
A    est: discussion.  IRRA 2:46-49 Dec 49

### 19.63 MEDIATION AND ARBITRATION

Chalmers, W. E.  The conciliation process. ILRR 1:337-50 Apr 48

Hosea, H. R.  [Principles of arbitration in wage rate disputes: comment, followed by Robert Satter's reply].  ILRR 2: 112-15 Oct 48

Satter, R.  Principles of arbitration in wage rate disputes.  ILRR 1:363-85 Apr 48

Warren, E. L. and Bernstein, I.  The mediation process.  SEJ 15:441-57 Apr 49

#### UNITED STATES

Ackerman, J.  The problem of jurisdiction
A    of national and state labor relations boards.  ILRR 2:360-71 Apr 49

Bernstein, I.  Recent legislative developments affecting mediation and arbitration.  ILRR 1:406-20 Apr 48

Davey, H. W.  Hazards in labor arbitration. ILRR 1:386-405 Apr 48

Lewis, W. A.  Arbitrating a wildcat strike. HBR 27:498-504 Jul 49

Taylor, G. W.  Is compulsory arbitration inevitable?  IRRA 1:64-77 Dec 48

Warren, E. L.  The Conciliation Service: V-J day to Taft-Hartley.  ILRR 1: 351-62 Apr 48

Arenwald, W. P.  Mediation, arbitration,
ASN    and investigation of industrial disputes in New York State, 1937-40.  JPE 49: 59-89 Feb 41

#### OTHER COUNTRIES

Flexner, J. A.  Arbitration of labor disputes
EB    in Great Britain.  ILRR 1:421-30 Apr 48

Adams, J. C.  The adjudication of collective
EI    labor disputes in Italy.  QJE 56:456-74 May 42

Kumar, C. B.  A note on the working of the
FI    Bombay Industrial Disputes Act.  IJE 22: 92-96 Jul 41

Pardasani, N. H.  The Bombay Industrial Disputes Act, 1938.  IJE 21:49-66 Jul 40
-- --- [Reply to C. B. Kumar]  IJE 23: 85-86 Jul 42

Foenander, O. de R.  The Commonwealth
N    Court of Conciliation and Arbitration: a brief survey.  QJE 63:408-29 Aug 49

Ross, L.  Conciliation and arbitration in Australia and New Zealand.  Pt.I. Recent developments in Australian industrial relations.  ILRR 2:98-105 Oct 48

Sawer, G.  Conciliation and arbitration of industrial disputes.  ER 23:266-71 Dec 47

Tuck, W. R.  The Court of Arbitration in New Zealand.  ER 17:46-56 Jun 41

Weisz, M.  Conciliation and arbitration in Australia and New Zealand.  Pt.II. An analysis of results.  ILRR 2:105-12 Oct 48

# 19. LABOR ECONOMICS

19.6 STRIKES. DISPUTES. METHODS OF
  SETTLEMENT (Cont.)
19.64 CASE STUDIES
  UNITED STATES
    Hoch, M. L. The oil strike of 1945. SEJ 15:
A   117-33 Oct 48
    Mayer, H. and Weiner, A. The New Jersey
ASN   Telephone Company case. ILRR 1:
      492-99 Apr 48

19.7 LABOR LEGISLATION AND REGULATION.
  PUBLIC EMPLOYEES
19.70 GENERAL
    Dobb, M. H. The International Labour Con-
      ference. R. EJ 54:261-65 Jun-Sep 44
    Van Sickle, J. V. The International Labor
      Office: an appraisal. SEJ 12:357-64
      Apr 46

  UNITED STATES
    Abt, J. J. [and others] Trade unions and the
A   law: discussion. AER/S 32:476-89
      Mar 42
    Anrod, C. W. Philosophy and analysis of
      recent union-control legislation [with
      discussion by Sister M. Thomasine].
      RSE 6:52-84 May 48
    Brinker, P. A. The Taft-Hartley Act in op-
      eration. SEJ 16:147-60 Oct 49
    Brown, E. C. Re: "NLRB in retrospect"
      [followed by J. and L. Cohen's reply].
      ILRR 2:251-52 Jan 49
    Chamberlain, N. W. Obligations upon the
      union under the National Labor Relations
      Act. AER 37:170-77 Mar 47
    Cohen, J. and Cohen, L. The National Labor
      Relations Board in retrospect. ILRR 1:
      648-56 Jul 48
    Levy, B. H. Collective bargaining under the
      Taft-Hartley Act. HBR 26:468-79 Jul 48
    McNatt, E. B. Recent Supreme Court inter-
      pretations of labor law (1940-41). JB 14:
      356-71 Oct 41
    -- The "appropriate bargaining unit" prob-
      lem. QJE 56:93-107 Nov 41
    Masse, B. L. Moral aspects of the Taft-
      Hartley Act [with discussion by L. C.
      Bajork]. RSE 6:29-51 May 48
    Meyer, J. Labor under the Taft-Hartley
      Act. SR 15:194-210 Jun 48
    Powers, R. The Labor-Management Rela-
      tions Act of 1947: a topical digest.
      SEJ 15:67-79 Jul 48
    Slichter, S. H. The Taft-Hartley Act.
      QJE 63:1-31 Feb 49
    Spielmans, J. V. Measurements of the ef-
      fectiveness of the National Labor Rela-
      tions Act. AER 30:803-13 Dec 40
    Sutherland, A. E., Jr. The constitutionality
      of the Taft-Hartley law. ILRR 1:177-205
      Jan 48
    Witney, F. The appropriate bargaining unit
      controversy. SEJ 16:170-88 Oct 49

    Witte, E. E. Labor-management relations
      under the Taft-Hartley Act. HBR 25:
      554-75 no.4a, 47
    -- An appraisal of the Taft-Hartley Act.
      AER/S 38:368-82 May 48
    -- The Taft-Hartley Act in operation: a
      brief appraisal. ILRR 2:403-06 Apr 49
    Zingler, E. K. The National Labor Rela-
      tions Board and the federal courts.
      SEJ 7:538-55 Apr 41
    Cutler, A. T. Labor legislation in thirteen
AS   southern states. SEJ 7:297-316 Jan 41
    Doan, M. C. State labor relations acts.
      QJE 56:507-59 Aug 42
    Slichter, S. H. [and others] Report to the
ASM   Governor of Massachusetts on labor-man-
      agement relations. [Selections from the Re-
      port of the Governor's Labor-Management
      Committee]. ILRR 1:110-28 Oct 47
    Stieber, J. Minnesota Labor Relations Act:
ASM   an opinion survey. HBR 27:665-77
      Nov 49
    Killingsworth, C. C. Public regulation of
ASW   labor relations: the Wisconsin experi-
      ment. AER 33:247-63 Jun 43

  OTHER COUNTRIES
    Logan, H. A. The state and collective bar-
C    gaining. CJE 10:476-88 Nov 44
    Midanik, S. Problems of legislation relat-
      ing to collective bargaining [with discus-
      sion by M. Mackintosh]. CJE 9:348-56
      Aug 43
    Underhill, H. F. Recent Canadian labor re-
      lations legislation. JPE 48:357-73 Jun 40
    Horne, G. R. On some appendices to the
CPQ   Rowell-Sirois report: VII. Labour legis-
      lation and social services in the Province
      of Quebec. CJE 7:249-59 May 41
    Routh, G. G. C. State intervention in the
EB   regulation of wages and working condi-
      tions in Great Britain and South Africa.
      SAJE 17:289-305 Sep 49
    Wilson, Sir D. Factory inspection: a thirty-
      five years retrospect [with dis-
      cussion]. JRSS 104:209-34 pt.3, 41
    Qadir, M. A. Factory legislation and ad-
FI   ministration in Hyderabad. IJE 20:
      599-609 Apr 40
    Routh, G. G. C. State intervention in the
HSA   regulation of wages and working condi-
      tions in Great Britain and South Africa.
      SAJE 17:289-305 Sep 49
    Oxnam, D. W. New Zealand's Industrial
N    Relations Act 1949. ER 25,(no.49):88-90
      Dec 49

19.71 HISTORY
    Forsey, E. A note on the Dominion factory
C    bills of the eighteen-eighties. CJE 13:
      580-83 Nov 47
    Walker, K. O. The classical economists and
EB   the factory acts. JEH 1:168-77 Nov 41

19.7 LABOR LEGISLATION AND REGULATION.
PUBLIC EMPLOYEES (Cont.)

19.71 HISTORY (Cont.)

EB    Wilson, Sir D. Factory inspection: a thirty-five years retrospect [with discussion]. JRSS 104:209-34 pt.3, 41

19.72 GOVERNMENT LABOR. PUBLIC EMPLOYEES

Anantachar, V. S. The economics of public salaries: a criticism [followed by M. H. Gopal's rejoinder]. IJE 28:281-90 Oct 47

A    Burns, A. E. and Kerr, P. Recent changes in work-relief wage policy. AER 31: 56-66 Mar 41

AA    Clapp, G. R. Problems of union relations in public agencies [illustrated by the case of TVA]. AER/S 33:184-96 Mar 43

A    Culliton, J. W. Note on turnover in government personnel. HBR 24:512-17 no.4, 46

A    Kaplan, H. E. Concepts of public employee relations. ILRR 1:206-30 Jan 48

A    Mire, J. Collective bargaining in the public service. AER/S 36:347-58 May 46

19.73 LABOR ON GOVERNMENT CONTRACTS

A    Cooley, R. E. Labor relations problems of a federal government procurement agency. IRRA 2:242-47 Dec 49

A    Denison, E. F. The influence of the Walsh-Healey Public Contracts Act upon labor conditions. JPE 49:225-46 Apr 41

19.74 LABOR IN REGULATED INDUSTRIES

ASM    Julian, V. Mediation of labor disputes in Missouri public utilities. IRRA 2: 255-61 Dec 49

FI    Mallik, A. N. Labour problems and labour legislation in India. (With special reference to the railway industry) IJE 20: 663-93 Apr 40

A    Northrup, H. R. The appropriate bargaining unit question under the Railway Labor Act. QJE 60:250-69 Feb 46

# 20. CONSUMER ECONOMICS

20.0 GENERAL

Anshen, M. The rediscovery of the consumer. JM 5:248-53 Jan 41

Atkins, W. E. "Economics for consumers" by Gordon and "Income and consumption" by Vaile and Canoyer. R. [with discussion by L. Gordon and R. Vaile]. JM 4, no.4,pt.2:138-50 Apr 40

Beckman, T. N., chairman. Round table on recent books on consumption. [Note] AER/S 30:399 Mar 40

Brady, D. S. and Williams, F. M. Advances in the techniques of measuring and estimating consumer expenditures. JFE 27: 315-44 May 45

A    Dameron, K. Advertising and the consumer movement. JM 5:234-47 Jan 41

A    -- Retailing and consumer movements. JM 5:385-94 Apr 41

A    -- Consumer trends in 1941. JM 6,no.4, pt.2:11-12 Apr 42

A    -- Consumer meeting agenda: a study in consumer interests. JB 21:98-119 Apr 48

A    Grieg, G. Some varieties of consumer behavior described in the decisions of the Federal Trade Commission. JB 20: 191-200 Oct 47

A    Hotchkiss, G. B. Consumer economists in glass houses. JM 5:228-33 Jan 41

Kyrk, H. "The consumer and the economic order" by Waite and Cassady, "Consumption in our society" by Hoyt. R. [with discussion by E. Hoyt and R. Cassady, Jr.] JM 4,no.4,pt.2:111-23 Apr 40

A    Marshall, A. R. College courses in consumption economics. JM 5:26-34 Jul 40

Matherly, W. J. The development of consumer economics. SEJ 9:53-61 Jul 42

N    Mauldon, F. R. E. The consumer in a planned economy. ER 25,(no.48):1-17 Jun 49

N    Mountain, G. R. The position of the Australian consumer. ER 25,suppl.:123-39 Aug 49

Widener, H. W. Marketing rewritten from the consumer's point of view. R. [with discussion by J. Coles and M. Reid]. JM 4,no.4,pt.2:124-37 Apr 40

20.1 HISTORY

EB    Ashton, T. S. The standard of life of the workers in England 1790-1830. JEH/S 9:19-38 '49

FI    Sarkar, B. K. The population trend in India with reference to food and nutrition. IJE 20:271-302 Jan 40

EB    Tinbergen, J. Does consumption lag behind incomes? [Analysis of data, U.K., 1870-1910] REStat 24:1-8 Feb 42

20.2 EMPIRICAL STUDIES

20.20 GENERAL

Davis, J. S. Consumption level; consumption standard; plane of living; standard of living. JM 6:164-66 Oct 41

-- Standards and content of living. AER 35: 1-15 Mar 45

Gardner, E. H. Consumer goods classification. JM 9:275-76 Jan 45

# 20. CONSUMER ECONOMICS

## 20.2 EMPIRICAL STUDIES (Cont.)
## 20.20 GENERAL (Cont.)

Koslik, A. Concepts of plane, standard, level and satisfaction of consumption and of living. JM 9:55-57 Jul 44

### UNITED STATES

Backman, J. The budget approach to wage
A    adjustments: a case study. JPE 55: 57-64 Feb 47

Cave, R. C. Variations in expenditures where families of wage earners and clerical workers are classified by economic level. JASA 38:445-52 Dec 43

Clark, J. M. Note on income redistribution and investment. AER 37:931 Dec 47

Cochrane, W. W. Farm family budgets: a moving picture. REStat 29:189-98 Aug 47; Erratum. 30:80 Feb 48

Drager, W. Retail trade and income by states. JM 9:364-72 Apr 45

Garfield, F. R. Measuring and forecasting consumption. JASA 41:322-33 Sep 46

Gilboy, E. W. Income-expenditure relations. REStat 22:115-21 Aug 40

Goodman, R. Sampling for the 1947 Survey of consumer finances. JASA 42:439-48 Sep 47

Hollander, E. D. Price indexes and consumer expenditure studies. JM 13: 373-74 Jan 49

Howenstine, E. J., Jr. The high-cost-of-living problem after World War I. SEJ 10:222-34 Jan 44

Lubell, H. Effects of redistribution of income on consumers' expenditures. AER 37:157-70 Mar 47; A correction. 930 Dec 47

O'Leary, J. J. Consumption as a factor in postwar employment. AER/S 35:37-55 May 45

Ostrander, F. T. The Mitchell Committee's report on the cost-of-living index: comments. AER 34:849-56 Dec 44

Sayre, R. A. Cost of living indexes. JASA 36:191-200 Jun 41

Thorndike, E. L. and Woodyard, E. The cost of living in cities in relation to their size and latitude. JASA 38:238-41 Jun 43

Walker, K. F. The American city worker's standard of living: a note on technique and content. ER 24:250-53 Dec 48

Wallis, W. A. The temporal stability of consumption patterns. REStat 24:177-83 Nov 42

Wickens, A. J. What the cost-of-living index is. JB 17:146-61 Jul 44

Woodbury, R. M. Economic consumption scales and their uses. JASA 39:455-68 Dec 44

Woofter, T. J., Jr. A method of analysis of family composition and income. JASA 39: 488-96 Dec 44

Worchester, D. A., Jr. Postwar markets for consumer goods. JM 9:234-38 Jan 45

Working, H. Statistical laws of family expenditure. JASA 38:43-56 Mar 43

### OTHER AMERICAN COUNTRIES

MacGregor, D. C. Studies of the cost of
C    living in Canada. CJE 7:545-58 Nov 41

Stocking, S. B. Recent trends in consumption. CJE 7:371-81 Aug 41

### EUROPE

Forcheimer, K. Europe's average standard
E    of living. OIS 8:108-11 Apr 46

Anonymous. Cost of living of the working
EB    classes. JRSS 104:53-58 pt.1, 41

Barna, T. Indirect taxes, subsidies and the cost-of-living index. REStud 10:53-61 no.1, 42

Bowley, A. L. Working-class budgets,
EB    May 1940. OIS 2,no.5:8-11 Aug 10, 40

-- and Schulz, T. Working-class budgets: analysis of expenditure. OIS 2,no.9: 4-9 Nov 2, 40; Errata. 2,no.10:18 Nov 23, 40

-- and Schulz, T. Working class budgets: October 1940; a comparison with May. OIS 2,no.11:1-7 Dec 40; Errata. 3,no.1: 16 Jan 11, 41

-- Working-class expenditure. EJ 50: 517-24 Dec 40

-- Earnings and prices, 1904, 1914, 1937-8. REStud 8:129-42 Jun 41

-- Working-class budgets and the cost of living index I. Index of expenditure. OIS 3,suppl.1:1-3 Aug 30, 41

Massey, P. The expenditure of 1,360 British middle-class households in 1938-39 [with discussion]. JRSS 105:159-96 pt.3, 42

Nicholson, J. L. The cost of living index. OIS 3:31-32 Feb 1, 41

-- The Ministry of Labour budget inquiry. I. The cost of living index. OIS 3:45-46 Feb 22, 41

-- Variations in working class family expenditure [with discussion]. JRSS 112: 359-418 pt.4, 49

Schulz, T. Budgets of old age pensioners and households on public assistance. OIS 3:76-79 Mar 15, 41

-- Working-class budgets and the cost of living index: II. Working class budgets, June 1941. OIS 3,suppl.1:3-12 Aug 30, 41; Erratum. 3:310 Sep 20, 41

-- Working class budgets: June 1942; a comparison with June 1941. OIS 4, suppl.3:1-12 Oct 10, 42

-- Working class income and household expenditure; June, 1944. OIS 7:17-30 Feb 3, 45

20.2 EMPIRICAL STUDIES (Cont.)
20.20 GENERAL (Cont.)
EUROPE (Cont.)
Schulz, T. (Cont.)

EB
-- Income and household expenditure of working-class families with children. Pt.I-II. OIS 8:29-43; 61-80 Feb,Mar 46

-- Working class income & household expenditure. OIS 9:133-69 May 47; Erratum. 195 Jun 47

-- Family expenditure in 1947. Pt.I-II. OIS 10:353-72; 401-23 Nov,Dec 48

Seers, D. The working-class share in pre-war consumption. OIS 10:181-94 Jun 48

-- The cost of living, 1938-1948. OIS 11: 127-38 May 49

Daniel, G. H. The cost of living in Bristol.
EBE    OIS 3:324-29 Oct 11, 41

Schulz, T. Liverpool family budgets. OIS 3: 364-70 Nov 22, 41

Tagliacarne, G. Cost of living, salaries,
EI    consumption and the situation of the Italian middle classes. BNL 1:75-85 Jul 47

Friedmann, C. A. A critique of Professor
ER    Hutt's "Two studies in the statistics of Russia" [followed by W. H. Hutt's reply]. SAJE 13:332-63 Dec 45

Hutt, W. H. Two studies in the statistics of Russia [Pt.2. Soviet standards of living before the war]. SAJE 13:18-42 Mar 45

ASIA
Desai, R. C. Consumer expenditure in
FI    India, 1931-2 to 1940-1 [with discussion]. JRSS 111:261-307 pt.4, 48

Farooq, A. Standard of living in the N.-W. F. Province. IJE 23:185-92 Oct 42

Lal, R. B. and Mathen, K. K. A note on conditions of living of agricultural labour and certain other rural groups in West Bengal. IJE 28:403-16 Jan 48

Rudra, S. K. Our food problem. IJE 24: 169-78 Jan 44

AFRICA
[Anonymous] Native budgets in Johannes-
HSA    burg. A sample investigation [made by the Johannesburg Political Economy Club]. SAJE 8:129-35 Jun 40

Naidoo, V. S. Survey of the income and expenditure of Indian employees of the Durban Corporation, living at the Magazine Barracks, Durban. SAJE 14: 40-62 Mar 46

Sykes, P. C. An analysis of income and expenditure of a sample of Indian families in the Clairwood area of Durban. SAJE 9: 45-65 Mar 41; Errata. 207 Jun 41

20.21 SAVING
Katona, G. Analysis of dissaving. AER 39: 673-88 Jun 49

UNITED STATES
Balogh, T. Savings, the business cycle and
A    the trend. OIS 7:114-15 May 19, 45

Clark, C. Post-war savings in the U.S.A. OIS 7:97-103 May 19, 45

Ezekiel, M. Statistical investigations of saving, consumption, and investment. Pt.I-II. AER 32:22-49; 272-307 Mar, Jun 42

Friend, I. Ezekiel's analysis of saving, consumption, and investment. AER 32: 829-35 Dec 42

Fulcher, G. S. Annual saving and underspending of individuals, 1926-37. REStat 23:28-42 Feb 41

-- Saving of individuals in relation to income. AER 32:835-40 Dec 42

-- Life insurance saving of American families. REStat 26:93-94 May 44

Geren, P. The contribution of life insurance to the savings stream. JPE 51: 33-51 Feb 43

Hyson, C. D. Notes on savings in relation to potential markets. AER 36:891-901 Dec 46

Mendershausen, H. Differences in family savings between cities of different size and location, whites and Negroes. REStat 22:122-37 Aug 40

Modigliani, F. Fluctuations in the saving ratio: a problem in economic forecasting. SR 14:413-20 Dec 47

Schechter, H. B. Notes on consumer spendings and savings. AER 37:931-33 Dec 47

Steindl, J. Long-run changes in the propensity to save: a reply. OIS 7:103-13 May 19, 45

Tucker, R. S. Estimates of savings of American families. REStat 24:9-21 Feb 42

Vance, L. L. The interpretation of consumer dis-saving. JM 11:243-49 Jan 47

Freeman, R. C. and Bane, L. Saving and
ASI    spending patterns of the same rural families over a 10-year period, 1933-42 [in Illinois]. AER 34:344-50 Jun 44

EUROPE
Bray, J. F. L. Small savings. EJ 50:
EB    195-206 Jun-Sep 40

Durant, H. and Goldmann, J. The distribution of working-class savings. OIS 7: 1-7 Jan 13, 45

Kalecki, M. Notes on finance: "small savings." OIS 3:51-53 Feb 22, 41

-- The fall in 'small' savings. OIS 4:290-93 Oct 31, 42; Erratum 5:22 Jan 9, 43

-- The problem of 'small' savings. OIS 5: 260-65 Nov 20, 43

Radice, E. A. Consumption, savings, and war finance. OEP 4:1-14 Sep 40

Singer, H. W. How widespread are national savings? A critique of the Madge enquiry. MS 13:61-79 Aug 44

# 20.  CONSUMER ECONOMICS

20.21  SAVING (Cont.)
  EUROPE (Cont.)
  Madge, C.  The propensity to save in
EBE  Blackburn and Bristol.  EJ 50:410-48
  Dec 40
  -- and Rothbarth, E.  Saving and spending in
  Leeds; a reply to Dr. Singer's criticisms.
  MS 13:80-88 Aug 44

20.22  FOOD CONSUMPTION
  Bennett, M. K.  Essential food requirements
  in wartime.  JFE 25:835-47 Nov 43
  Black, J. D.  Provision for nutrition in the
  formulation of agricultural programs.
  JFE 30:703-12 Nov 48
  Elliott, F. F.  Redirecting world agricul-
  tural production and trade toward better
  nutrition.  JFE 26:10-30 Feb 44
  Howe, C. B.  Food consumption at the
  national level.  JFE 28:791-803 Aug 46
  Lindberg, J.  Food supply under a program
  of freedom from want.  SR 12:181-204
  May 45
  Potgieter, M.  Comments on "The cost of
  subsistence" by George J. Stigler.
  JFE 29:767-72 Aug 47
  Stigler, G. J.  The cost of subsistence.
  JFE 27:303-14 May 45

  UNITED STATES
  Brady, D. S. and Barber, H. A.  The pattern
A  of food expenditures.  REStat 30:198-206
  Aug 48
  Canning, J. B.  Food and agriculture:
  longer-run outlook and policy.  AER/S 35:
  405-16 May 45
  Cawl, F. R.  The continuing panel technique.
  JM 8:45-50 Jul 43
  Farnsworth, H. C.  Food consumption in re-
  lation to farm production and income.
  (A U.S. food and nutrition program)
  JFE 29:329-33 Feb 47
  Fulmer, J. L.  Trends in the per capita
  consumption of foods in the United States
  since 1920.  SEJ 14:404-10 Apr 48
  Gold, N. L. and Enlow, M.  The demand for
  food by low income families.  QJE 57:
  596-629 Aug 43
  Hadary, G.  The relationship of chocolate
  milk to total fluid milk consumption.
  JFE 27:210-13 Feb 45
  Hinrichs, A. F.  Developments in labor
  market and price statistics in 1945 and
  1946.  JASA 42:31-37 Mar 47
  Kling, W.  A nutritional guide to wartime
  use of agricultural resources.  JFE 25:
  683-91 Aug 43
  Maynard, L. A.  Deficiencies in the United
  States diet, and means of meeting them.
  JFE 29:320-23 Feb 47
  Patzig, R. E. and Hadary, G.  Relationship
  of income to milk consumption.  JFE 27:
  204-10 Feb 45

  Phipard, E. F. and Reid, M. G.  Low-cost
  adequate diets.  JFE 30:161-67 Feb 48
  Reid, M. G.  Nutritional aspects and farm
  family needs in a food and nutrition
  policy.  JFE 29:333-36 Feb 47
  Schickele, R.  Programs for maintaining
  food demand.  (A U.S. food and nutrition
  program)  JFE 29:325-28 Feb 47
  Southworth, H. M.  Levels of food consumption, past and prospective.  (A U.S. food
  and nutrition program)  JFE 29:323-25
  Feb 47
  Wells, O. V.  Agricultural surpluses and
  nutritional deficits; a statement of the
  problem and some factors affecting its
  solution.  JFE 22:317-23 Feb 40
  Williamson, L. and Williamson, P.  What
  we eat.  JFE 24:698-703 Aug 42
  Hadary, G.  Relation of chocolate milk to
ASI  total fluid milk consumption of factory
  workers.  [A Chicago survey]  JB 16:
  70-73 Jan 43
  -- Relation of chocolate milk to total fuild
ASI  milk consumption of urban families [in
  Indiana].  JB 16:115-23 Apr 43
  -- Effect of method of distribution on milk
  consumption [in Indiana].  JM 9:354-58
  Apr 45

  OTHER COUNTRIES
  Hopper, W. C.  Income and food consump-
C  tion.  CJE 9:487-506 Nov 43
  Mandelbaum, K.  Food consumption in
EA  north-western and western Europe,
  1943-4 & 1945.  OIS 7:287-89 Nov 24, 45
  Bowley, A. L. and Schulz, T.  Working class
EB  budgets: analysis of dietary.  OIS 2,no.6:
  5-10 Aug 31, 40
  -- A human needs diet in war time.  A.
  Purpose and method.  OIS 4:313-14
  Dec 12, 42
  -- Contract and retail food prices.  OIS 5:
  189-93 Aug 28, 43
  Rutherford, R. S. G.  The consumption and
  rationing of butter and margarine.
  OEP 3:131-43 Feb 40
  -- and Rutherford, M. E. E.  The consump-
  tion and rationing of meat and cheese.
  OEP 5:74-87 Jun 41
  -- The protein situation.  OIS 3:263-68
  Aug 30, 41
  -- Protein allocations.  OIS 5:49-51
  Feb 20, 43
  Schulz, T.  Working class budgets in Octo-
  ber: analysis of dietary.  OIS 3:25-31
  Feb 1, 41
  -- The Ministry of Labour budget inquiry.
  2. Standards of nutrition in 1918 and
  1937-8.  OIS 3:46-48 Feb 22, 41
  -- A "human needs" diet in war-time
  [March 1941 to November 1942].  OIS 3:
  92-97; 393-98; 4:148-50; 314-19 Apr 5,
  Dec 13, 41, May 16, Dec 12, 42.  Erratum.
  4:28 Jan 10, 42

20.22 FOOD CONSUMPTION (Cont.)
OTHER COUNTRIES (Cont.)
Schulz, T. (Cont.)
-- Expenditure on food and nutrition.
EB    OIS 5:41-49 Feb 20, 43; Errata. 72
Mar 13, 43
-- The trend of consumption in 1942: an
analysis of sales of groceries. OIS 5:
89-95 Apr 24, 43
-- A minimum diet in April 1943. OIS 5:
117-20 May 15, 43
-- 'Human needs' cost of living for a single
person. OIS 5:143-48 Jun 26, 43
-- A "human needs" diet in November 1943.
OIS 5:273-77 Dec 11, 43
-- Consumption of groceries: a survey of
sales of grocery shops in 1942 and 1943.
OIS 6:49-57 Mar 18, 44; Erratum. 80
Apr 8, 44
-- The cost of a 'human needs' diet.
OIS 6:94-98 Apr 29, 44
-- Family diets at low cost, November 1944.
OIS 6:297-304 Dec 4, 44
-- Food expenditure and nutrition: working
class budgets, June 1944. OIS 7:37-55
Feb 24, 45
-- Inexpensive family diets: April 1945.
OIS 7:129-37 Jun 9, 45
-- Proper nutrition at low cost: outlines of
an inexpensive family diet in November
1945. OIS 7:291-302 Dec 15, 45; Erratum.
8:54 Feb 46
-- Grocery sales and rationing. OIS 8:
97-107 Apr 46
-- Low cost family diets and individual
nutrition. OIS 8:178-89 Jun 46
-- Rationing and nutrition: inexpensive
family diets in November, 1946. OIS 8:
375-87 Dec 46
-- Feeding a family. OIS 9:183-95 Jun 47
-- Consumption of groceries and rationing
[1946]. OIS 9:261-73 Aug 47
-- Food and energy: some nutritional aspects of rationing. OIS 10:53-66 Feb 48
-- Consumption of groceries [1947]. OIS 10:
105-16 Apr 48
-- A family diet of low cost. OIS 10:129-39
May 48

-- Nutrition at low cost: inexpensive diets
for five persons in Nov., 1948. OIS 11:
9-17 Jan 49
-- A 'human needs' diet [May, 1949]. OIS 11:
149-62 Jun 49
-- Human needs diets from 1936 to 1949.
OIS 11:307-25 Oct 49; Erratum. 371
Nov 49
-- A 'human needs' diet in November 1949.
OIS 11:382-88 Dec 49
Mitra, K. Trend of dietary habits and anal-
FI    ysis of food budget in working class
families of Bihar. IJE 22:144-63 Oct 41
Schneer, R. Famine in Bengal: 1943.
S&S 11:168-79 no.2, 47
Sukhla, S. S. Some aspects of the Indian
food problem. IJE 27:427-31 Apr 47
Upadhyaya, P. K. What farmers eat in
Oudh. IJE 26:641-46 Apr 46
Khan, M. M. Economic planning for na-
FIP    tional nutrition. PEJ 1,no.1:24-28 Jul 49
Batson, E. A contribution to the study of
HSA    the relative roles of income levels and
purchasing habits in the determination
of sub-standard food consumption.
SAJE 11:106-20 Jun 43
Malherbe, M. A study of some Indian
family diets in Durban. SAJE 9:22-44
Mar 41

20.23 CONSUMPTION OF OTHER INDIVIDUAL
GOODS OR SERVICES
Elsas, M. J. Rent subsidies on a national
EB    basis. REStud 11:77-85 no.2, 44
Goldmann, J. Expenditure on rent. OIS 6:
EB    173-77 Aug 12, 44
Knaf, H. G. Interstate differences in the
A    saturation of wired homes, mechanical
refrigerators and electric ranges, and
their causes. LE 22:386-92 Nov 46
Maisel, S. J. Have we underestimated in-
A    creases in rents and shelter expendi-
tures? JPE 57:106-17 Apr 49
Mendelsohn, R. Rents and incomes.
N    ER 20:91-94 Jun 44
Ross, K. H. Working class clothing con-
EB    sumption, 1937-1938. JRSS 111:145-60
pt.2, 48

# 21. HEALTH. EDUCATION. WELFARE

21.0 GENERAL
Batheja, H. R. [and others] Discussion on
FI    social security. IJE 25:634-41 Apr 45
Michalup, E. The social insurance move-
ment [followed by R. C. White's reply].
JASA 39:519-20 Dec 44
Nakagawa, Y. The development of social
FJ    policy in Japan. Kyo 17,no.1:14-30 Jan 42
White, R. C. The social insurance move-
ment. JASA 38:358-64 Sep 43

Witte, E. E. 1944-1945 programs for post-
war social security and medical care.
REStat 27:171-88 Nov 45
Wunderlich, F. Social insurance versus
poor relief. SR 14:75-94 Mar 47

21.1 HISTORY
Carslaw, H. S. The Australian Social
N    Services Contribution and Income Tax
Acts, 1946 and 1947. ER 22:219-27;
23:177-85 Dec 46, Dec 47

21. HEALTH. EDUCATION. WELFARE

21.1 HISTORY (Cont.)

Deutsch, A. American labor and social work. S&S 8:289-304 no.4, 44

ASC Dunbar, R. G. Agricultural adjustments in eastern Colorado in the eighteen-nineties. AH 18:41-52 Jan 44

EB Levy, H. The economic history of sickness and medical benefit before the Puritan revolution. EHR 13:42-57 no.1-2, 43

EB -- The economic history of sickness and medical benefit since the Puritan revolution. EHR 14:135-60 no.2, 44

EB Morgan, J. S. The break-up of the poor law in Britain 1907-47: an historical footnote. CJE 14:209-19 May 48

A Selekman, B. M. and Selekman, S. K. Mathew Carey. HBR 19:326-41 no.3, 41

21.2 CONTRIBUTORY PUBLIC INSURANCE. SOCIAL SECURITY

21.20 GENERAL

Wunderlich, F. New trends in social insurance. SR 16:31-44 Mar 49

UNITED STATES

A Aaronson, F. M. Benefits and beneficiaries under social insurance and related programs. JASA 39:183-96 Jun 44

Bakke, E. W. and Schmidt, E. P. Social security: discussion. AER/S 34:222-26 Mar 44

Beveridge, Sir W. Social security: some trans-Atlantic comparisons [with discussion]. JRSS 106:305-32 pt.4, 43

Brown, J. D. Economic problems in the provision of security against life hazards of workers. AER/S 30:61-67 Mar 40

--, chairman. Round table on economic issues in social security policy. AER/S 30:78-79 Mar 40

-- Concepts in Old-Age and Survivors' Insurance. IRRA 1:100-06 Dec 48

Buckley, L. F. Ethical aspects of social insurance. RSE 6:1-28 May 48

Burns, E. M. Social insurance in evolution. AER/S 34:199-211 Mar 44

-- Social security developments in the United States. MS 15:198-214 May 47

Cohen, W. J. Developments in social security: discussion. IRRA 1:121-26 Dec 48

Corson, J. J. Agricultural workers and social insurance. JFE 24:285-95 Feb 42

Cruikshank, N. H. Developments in social security: discussion. IRRA 1:126-29 Dec 48

Falk, I. S. and Cohen, W. J. Social security for farm people. JFE 28:84-96 Feb 46

Hohaus, R. A. Actuarial problems in social insurance. JASA 35:37-46 Mar 40

Klein, L. R. The cost of a "Beveridge Plan" in the United States. QJE 58: 423-37 May 44

Lutz, H. L. [and others] Social security in a stable prosperity: discussion. AER/S 37:351-66 May 47

Meriam, L. Social security in an unstable world. AER/S 37:335-44 May 47

Parsons, K. H. Social security for farm people. JFE 28:97-110 Feb 46

Salter, L. A., Jr. Social security: a new consideration in submarginal land policy. LE 16:468-70 Nov 40

Slichter, S. H. The impact of social security legislation upon mobility and enterprise. AER/S 30:44-60 Mar 40

Sollenberger, I. J. Estimated cost of Old-Age and Survivors Insurance. QJE 59: 427-50 May 45

Stancliffe, B. N. "The American Beveridge." MS 15:176-97 May 47

Sweezy, A. Social security and national prosperity. S&S 8:193-204 no.3, 44

Wall, N. J. Discussion of papers on social security for farm people. JFE 28:110-13 Feb 46

Witte, E. E. What's ahead in social security. HBR 19:311-25 no.3, 41

-- American post-war social security proposals. AER 33:825-38 Dec 43

-- What to expect of social security. AER/S 34:212-21 Mar 44

OTHER AMERICAN COUNTRIES

C Cassidy, H. M. Social security developments in Canada. IRRA 1:107-20 Dec 48

Jaffary, S. K. Social security: the Beveridge and Marsh Reports. R. CJE 9: 571-92 Nov 43

CA Angers, F. A. French Canada and social security. CJE 10:355-64 Aug 44

CPQ Horne, G. R. On some appendices to the Rowell-Sirois report: VII. Labour legislation and social services in the Province of Quebec. CJE 7:249-59 May 41

EUROPE

E Dobretsberger, J. Experiences in social insurance in Europe. EgC 34:57-75 Jan-Feb 43

EB Beveridge, Sir W. Social security: some trans-Atlantic comparisons [with discussion]. JRSS 106:305-32 pt.4, 43

Burns, E. M. The Beveridge report. AER 33:512-33 Sep 43

Gibbon, Sir G. The Beveridge report. R. JRSS 105:336-50 pt.4, 42

Jaffary, S. K. Social security: the Beveridge and Marsh Reports. R. CJE 9: 571-92 Nov 43

Kaldor, N. The Beveridge report. II. The financial burden. EJ 53:10-27 Apr 43

Nicholson, J. L. The benefits and costs of the Beveridge plan. OIS 5, suppl.4: 7-18 Feb 20, 43

-- The Government's plans for social insurance. OIS 6:241-49 Nov 4, 44

## 21.2 CONTRIBUTORY PUBLIC INSURANCE. SOCIAL SECURITY (Cont.)

### 21.20 GENERAL (Cont.)

#### EUROPE (Cont.)

Owen, A. D. K. The Beveridge report. I. Its proposals. EJ 53:1-9 Apr 43

Stewart, M. C. Industrial assurance.
EB   OIS 5, suppl. 4:18-24 Feb 20, 43

Wunderlich, F. The Beveridge plan. SR 10: 233-45 May 43

Agarwala, A. N. Social insurance in Nazi
EG   Germany. R. IJE 25:362-66 Jan 45

#### ASIA

Agarwala, A. N. The social security move-
FI   ment in India. EJ 56:568-82 Dec 46

Iyengar, S. K. The problem of social security in India. IJE 25:315-24 Jan 45

Jagannadham, V. Social protection for agricultural labourers. IJE 28:121-30 Jul 47

Malkani, H. C. Social security with special reference to India. IJE 25:343-47 Jan 45

Misra, S. Can India adopt Beveridge? IJE 25:324-30 Jan 45

Rao, R. V. Social security with special reference to India. IJE 25:348-53 Jan 45

Samad, S. A. Social security with special reference to India. IJE 25:331-43 Jan 45

Sarien, R. G. Social insurance planning in India. R. IJE 25:354-58 Jan 45

#### AFRICA

Batson, E. Some points of comparison
H   between the social security proposals for the Union and for Southern Rhodesia. SAJE 13:43-51 Mar 45

-- The distribution of benefits in the social
HSA security proposals. SAJE 12:279-302 Dec 44

-- Some points of comparison between the social security proposals for the Union and for Southern Rhodesia. SAJE 13: 43-51 Mar 45

Burrows, H. R. [and others] Social security. SAJE 10:193-247 Sep 42

Franklin, N. N. A note on the Report of the Select Committee on Social Security. SAJE 12:316-18 Dec 44

Kahn, E. The Report of the Social Security Committee: some reflections. SAJE 12: 63-66 Mar 44

#### AUSTRALIA. NEW ZEALAND

Buckton, E. G. Philosophy behind New
N   Zealand's social policy. RSE 3:55-63 Dec 44

Kewley, T. H. The Commonwealth social security reports. R. ER 18:223-26 Dec 42

### 21.21 METHODS OF FINANCING

Arnold, S. Forward shifting of a payroll

tax under monopolistic competition. QJE 61:267-84 Feb 47

Booker, H. S. Lady Rhys Williams' pro-
EB   posals for the amalgamation of direct taxation with social insurance. EJ 56: 230-43 Jun 46

Hicks, J. R. and Hicks, U. K. The Bever-
EB   idge plan and local government finance. REStud 11:1-19 no.1, 43

Kalecki, M. Economic implications of the
EB   Beveridge plan. OIS 5, suppl. 4:2-7 Feb 20, 43

Macy, C. W. Social security taxes in the
A   war finance program. JPE 51:135-47 Apr 43

Mushkin, S. J. and Scitovzky, A. A formula
A   for social insurance financing. AER 35: 646-52 Sep 45

Peacock, A. T. The national insurance
EB   funds. Ec N.S.16:228-42 Aug 49

Robinson, G. B. The old-age reserve fund
A   is not "illusory." QJE 60:136-53 Nov 45

Rosenson, A. M. Monetary effects of war-
A   time social security taxes. JPE 50: 881-900 Dec 42

Swan, E. J. Financing social security.
A   AER/S 37:345-50 May 47

Underhill, H. F. The incidence of payroll taxes. QJE 57:160-62 Nov 42

### 21.3 NON-CONTRIBUTORY WELFARE PROGRAMS

### 21.30 GENERAL

Dowsett, W. T. Child endowment and in-
N   come tax exemptions. ER 17:239-47 Dec 41

Jones, J. H. [and others] Cost of living
EB   subsidies: discussion. JRSS 111:99-111 pt.2, 48

Somers, H. M. Adequacy of data in the
A   field of public aid. JASA 36:81-90 Mar 41

Tout, H. A statistical note on family allow-
EB   ances. EJ 50:51-59 Mar 40

### 21.31 FOOD SUBSIDIES

Balogh, T. The abolition of food subsidies.
EB   OIS 10:332-40 Oct 48

Elmhirst, L. K. American foreign food
A   policy: discussion. JFE 31,pt.2:290-92 Feb 49

Gold, N. L. [and others] Agricultural sur-
A   pluses: discussion. JFE 22:334-40 Feb 40

Herman, S. The food stamp plan: a study
A   in law and economics. Pt.I-II. JB 13: 331-59; 14:11-35 Oct 40, Jan 41

-- The food stamp plan: termination.
A   JB 16:173-94 Jul 43

Kahle, H. S. Notes on "The economies of public measures to subsidize food consumption," with an extension of the economic principles outlined to individual commodities. JFE 27:683-86 Aug 45

# 21. HEALTH. EDUCATION. WELFARE

## 21.31 FOOD SUBSIDIES (Cont.)

A Kozlik, A. Some aspects of the food stamp plan as applied to consumption of fats. JFE 23:483-92 May 41

A Moos, S. The two-stamp-plan, a new method of distribution. OIS 3:246-52 Aug 9, 41

EB Pigou, A. C. The food subsidies. EJ 58: 202-09 Jun 48

A Rowe, H. B. Issues in American foreign food policy. JFE 31,pt.2:281-90 Feb 49

A Schickele, R. The National Food Allotment Program. JFE 28:515-33 May 46

A -- National food policy and surplus agricultural production. JFE 29:867-88 Nov 47

A Southworth, H. M. The economics of public measures to subsidize food consumption. JFE 27:38-66 Feb 45

A Waugh, F. V. Programs for using agricultural surpluses to reduce malnutrition and to benefit farmers. JFE 22:324-34 Feb 40

A -- Food consumption programs as a part of a farm program. JFE 26:784-88 Nov 44

A -- What shall we do with surplus foods? JM 10:253-57 Jan 46

Wilson, M. L. Nutritional science and agricultural policy. JFE 24:188-205 Feb 42

## 21.4 OLD AGE ECONOMICS AND ASSISTANCE

A Andrews, D. K. Old-age security for the American farm population. JFE 27: 634-48 Aug 45

A Ball, R. M. Pension plans under collective bargaining: an evaluation of their social utility. IRRA 2:127-37 Dec 49

A Barkin, S. What shall we have: retirement benefit or superannuation plans? IRRA 2: 138-47 Dec 49

A Becker, H. Labor's approach to the retirement problem. IRRA 2:116-26 Dec 49

HSA Burrows, H. R. and De Vos, P. J. Old age pensions. SAJE 11:87-105 Jun 43

A Jenson, V. H. Pensions and retirement plans as a subject of collective bargaining. ILRR 2:227-36 Jan 49

## 21.5 VETERANS' BENEFITS

HSA Pollak, H. P. State and private provisions for soldiers' dependants. SAJE 8:446-74 Dec 40

A Siegel, I. H. and Taylor, M. F. W. Public expenditures for veterans' assistance. JPE 56:527-32 Dec 48

## 21.6 UNEMPLOYMENT ASSISTANCE

A Burns, A. E. and Kerr, P. Recent changes in work-relief wage policy. AER 31: 56-66 Mar 41

Burns, E. M. Economic problems in the provision of security against employment hazards. AER/S 30:68-77 Mar 40

AA Curtis, W. R. Unemployment compensation experience in the South. SEJ 7: 51-72 Jul 40

AA -- The development of unemployment insurance in the South. SEJ 15:43-53 Jul 48

ASN De Vyver, F. T. After the shutdown: an analysis of the job-hunting experience of a group of Durham hosiery workers. [Durham, North Carolina] JPE 48: 105-13 Feb 40

A Kidd, C. V. The Latimer report. 2. Relationship of guaranteed wages to unemployment compensation. ILRR 1:470-80 Apr 48

Langer, H. C., Jr. Maintaining full employment. AER 33:888-92 Dec 43

ASW Myers, C. A. Experience rating in Wisconsin in 1940. AER 30:835-37 Dec 40

A -- and Maclaurin, W. R. After unemployment benefits are exhausted. QJE 56: 231-55 Feb 42

A -- Experience rating in unemployment compensation. AER 35:337-54 Jun 45

ASW Posey, T. E. Unemployment compensation and the coal industry in West Virginia. SEJ 7:347-61 Jan 41

EG Rohrlich, G. F. Equalization schemes in German unemployment compensation. QJE 58:482-97 May 44

A Schmidt, E. P. Public utilities and unemployment compensation. LE 18:97-100 Feb 42

AS Shilland, P. D. Wages, income, and compensation under unemployment insurance. ILRR 3:45-53 Oct 49

A Webbink, P. Unemployment in the United States, 1930-40. AER/S 30,no.5:248-72 Feb 41

A Yntema, D. B. Changing seasonal fluctuations in the amounts of public and private assistance and earnings on CWA and WPA projects in 116 urban areas, 1929-38. JASA 35:644-52 Dec 40

## 21.7 MEDICAL ECONOMICS

A Allen, L. Medical needs of the war industry areas. S&S 8:28-39 no.1, 44

A Bjorn, W. Low-cost hospitalization protection. HBR 22:256-64 no.2, 44

EB Buckatzsch, E. J. Reform of the health services. OIS 6:68-73 Apr 8, 44

ASC Dodd, P. A. A method of making actuarial estimates for a compulsory health insurance system. [California data] JASA 41:58-69 Mar 46

A Goldmann, F. Labor's attitude toward health insurance. ILRR 2:90-98 Oct 48

A/C Gray, K. G. Canadian and American health insurance plans. CJE 12:505-09 Nov 46

Hall, O. The informal organization of the medical profession. CJE 12:30-44 Feb 46

## 21.7 MEDICAL ECONOMICS (Cont.)

Hamilton, A. Science in the Soviet Union.
ER   III. Industrial medicine. S&S 8:69-73 no.1, 44

Kuh, C. The Permanente Health Plan [in
ASC   California]. ILRR 2:309-11 Jan 49

Miller, M. D. Statistical problems in de-
A   veloping voluntary medical expense insurance plans. JASA 43:290-98 Jun 48

Myers, R. J. A critique of "A method of
A   making actuarial estimates for a compulsory health insurance system." JASA 42:123-27 Mar 47

Prindle, H. F. Sampling medical service
A   charges: a new application of sampling method. JFE 31:357-60 May 49

Richter, L. The effect of health insurance
C   on the demand for health services. CJE 10:179-205 May 44

Stern, B. J. Income and health. S&S 5: 193-206 no.3, 41

Stillman, C. W. Rural health and the Tru-
A   man Plan. JFE 31:391-408 Aug 49

Whitte, E. E. 1944-1945 programs for
A   postwar social security and medical care. REStat 27:171-88 Nov 45

## 21.8 ECONOMICS OF EDUCATION

Hall, J. P. Current tendencies in college
A   investments. JF 4:129-39 Jun 49

Taylor, J. G. College revenue bonds to
A   finance self-supporting projects. JF 4: 328-41 Dec 49

# 22. REGIONAL PLANNING AND DEVELOPMENT. HOUSING

## 22.0 GENERAL

Bland, J. [The education of planners] At
C   McGill University. LE 21:315-16 Sep 45

Dillenback, L. C. and Steadman, R. F. [The
ASN   education of planners] At Syracuse University. LE 21:317-19 Sep 45

Gaus, J. M. The education of planners: a
A   commentary on some current projects. LE 21:307-09 Sep 45

Greeley, R. B. [The education of planners]
ASM   At Massachusetts Institute of Technology. LE 21:313-15 Sep 45

House, R. B. [The education of planners]
ASN   At the University of North Carolina. LE 21:316-17 Sep 45

Perkins, G. H. [The education of planners]
ASM   At Harvard University. LE 21:311-13 Sep 45

Ratcliff, R. U. [The education of planners]
ASW   At the University of Wisconsin. LE 21: 320-21 Sep 45

Tilton, L. D. [The education of planners]
ASC   At the University of California, Berkeley. LE 21:309-11 Sep 45

Van Hise, C. R. Science and pragmatics in the education of planners. [Reprinted from Science magazine, v.16, Aug. 29, 1902] LE 24:209-20 Aug 48

Woodbury, C. Richard T. Ely and the be-
ASW   ginnings of research in urban land and housing economics [at the University of Wisconsin]. LE 25:55-66 Feb 49

## 22.1 HISTORY

Glazer, S. The rural community in the
ASM   urban age: the changes in Michigan since 1900. AH 23:130-34 Apr 49

Herbert, P. A. The story of Rileyville,
ASN   New Jersey. AH 16:1-8 Jan 42

Hovde, B. J. Critique: "American versus
A   German city planning." LE 23:239-43
EG   Aug 47

Kiley, J. C. Changes in realty values in the
ASM   nineteenth and twentieth centuries [in Boston]. BHR 15:33-41 Jun 41

Singer, H. W. An index of urban land rents
EB   and house rents in England and Wales 1845-1913. Em 9:221-30 Jul-Oct 41

Stephenson, W. H. Ante-bellum New Orleans
ASL   as an agricultural focus. AH 15:161-74 Oct 41

Wagner, M. American versus German city
A   planning. LE 22:321-38 Nov 46
EG

## 22.2 REGIONAL ECONOMICS
## 22.20 GENERAL

De Chazeau, M. G. Electric power as a
A   regional problem. SEJ 7:494-504 Apr 41

Hesseltine, W. B. Regions, classes and
A   sections in American history. LE 20: 35-44 Feb 44

Neisser, H. Economic possibilities in the
AA   [Rocky] mountain regions. SR 12:456-63 Nov 45

Vining, R. Location of industry and re-
A   gional patterns of business-cycle behavior. Em 14:37-68 Jan 46

Weeks, D. Objectives of area analysis in
ASC   the northern Sierra Nevada. LE 19: 153-64 May 43

## 22.21 THEORY

Daly, M. C. An approximation to a geographical multiplier. EJ 50:248-58 Jun-Sep 40

Garvy, G. [and others] Interregional variations in economic fluctuations: discussion. AER/S 39:120-34 May 49

## 22. REGIONAL PLANNING, ETC.

### 22.2 REGIONAL ECONOMICS (Cont.)
#### 22.21 THEORY (Cont.)

Hubert, G. A.  A framework for the study of peripheral economic areas. JFE 28: 804-20 Aug 46

Killmorgen, W. M.  Crucial deficiencies of regionalism. AER/S 35:377-89 May 45

Neff, P.  Interregional cyclical differentials: causes, measurement, and significance. AER/S 39:105-19 May 49

Van Sickle, J. V.  Regionalism: a tool of economic analysis. AER/S 35:355-67 May 45

Vining, R.  The region as a concept in business-cycle analysis. Em 14:201-18 Jul 46

-- Measuring state and regional business cycles. R. JPE 55:346-51 Aug 47

-- The region as an economic entity and certain variations to be observed in the study of systems of regions. AER/S 39: 89-104 May 49

Wolcott, L.  Regionalism: policital implement. AER/S 35:368-76 May 45

#### 22.22 INTERREGIONAL RELATIONS

Haroldson, W. C.  Comments on regional
AA  dependency. JFE 25:701-04 Aug 43

Hartland, P.  Interregional payments compared with international payments. QJE 63:392-407 Aug 49

Henderson, J. S.  Regional differentials in
A  interest rates. SEJ 11:113-32 Oct 44

Spengler, J. J.  Regional differences and
A  the future of manufacturing in America. SEJ 7:475-93 Apr 41

Vining, R.  Regional variation in cyclical
A  fluctuation viewed as a frequency distribution. Em 13:183-213 Jul 45

Waite, W. C.  Indexes of the terms of trade
AA  between areas in the United States. REStat 24:22-30 Feb 42

#### 22.23 INDUSTRIAL DISPERSION AND DIVERSIFICATION

Balogh, T.  The distribution of industry:
EB  the reform of the control of industrial location. OIS 11:107-09 Apr 49

Barlow, Sir M. [and others] Discussion on
EB  the Report of the Royal Commission on the Distribution of the Industrial Population. JRSS 103:330-43 pt.3, 40

Dennison, S. R.  The distribution of the in-
EB  dustrial population. R. EJ 50:342-47 Jun-Sep 40

Florence, P. S.  The selection of industries
EB  suitable for dispersion into rural areas [with discussion]. JRSS 107:93-116 pt.2, 44

Fogarty, M. P.  The complications of loca-
EB  tion. MS 15:251-83 Sep 47

Greene, L. S.  Industrial location and recon-
EB  struction in Great Britain. LE 17:333-43 Aug 41

Jones, J. H.  The Report of the Royal Com-
EB  mission on the Distribution of the Industrial Population. JRSS 103:323-30 pt.3, 40

Logsdon, C. S.  Some comments upon the
AS  effectiveness of state and local area development programs. SEJ 15:303-10 Jan 49

Shenfield, A. and Florence, P. S.  The econ-
EBE  omies and diseconomies of industrial concentration: the wartime experience of Coventry. REStud 12:79-99 no.2, 45

Spence-Sales, H.  Physical planning in the
EB  region: British endeavours. CJE 13: 507-13 Nov 47

Sykes, J.  Some results of the Distribution
EB  of Industry Act, 1945. MS 17:36-48 Jan 49

-- The development areas. MS 17:128-45 May 49

-- Postwar distribution of industry in
EB  Great Britain. JB 22:188-99 Jul 49

### 22.3  URBAN-METROPOLITAN STUDIES
#### 22.30  GENERAL

Andrews, R. B.  Elements in the urban-
A  fringe pattern. LE 18:169-83 May 42

-- Urban fringe studies of two Wisconsin
ASW  cities: a summary. LE 21:375-82 Sep 45

Bailey, W. L.  Appraising urban communi-
A  ties: techniques and objectives. LE 16: 1-7 Feb 40

Bauer, C.  Garden cities and the metropo-
A  lis: a reply [followed by L. Mumford's
EB  reply and L. Rodwin's rejoinder]. LE 22: 65-77 Feb 46

Bird, F. L.  The financial problems of
A  cities. AER/S 32:323-30 Mar 42

Blumenfeld, H.  On the concentric-circle theory of urban growth. LE 25:209-12 May 49

Chute, C. F. [and others] Economic prob-
A  lems of American cities: discussion. AER/S 32:341-48 Mar 42

Clark, C.  The economic functions of a city in relation to its size. Em 13:97-113 Apr 45

Copp, G. F.  Metropolitan districts: their
A  areal relationships. LE 25:213-15 May 49

Dickinson, R. E.  The scope and status of urban geography: an assessment. LE 24: 221-38 Aug 48

Diehl, L. F.  Major aspects of urbanization
ASP  in the Philadelphia metropolitan area. LE 19:316-28 Aug 43

Held, H.  New York City in the postwar
ASN  period. HBR 21:455-71 no.4, 43

Hoyt, H.  Urban decentralization. LE 16: 270-76 Aug 40

-- Economic background of cities. LE 17:
A  188-95 May 41

## 22. REGIONAL PLANNING, ETC.

22.3 URBAN-METROPOLITAN STUDIES (Cont.)
22.33 INDUSTRIAL AND SHOPPING CENTERS
(Cont.)

Cochrane, D. Travelling to work [in Mel-
N    bourne]. ER 22:199-218 Dec 46
Doherty, R. P. The movement and concen-
ASM  tration of retail trade in metropolitan
     areas. [A study of the Boston market
     area.] JM 5:395-401 Apr 41
     -- Decentralization of retail trade in Bos-
ASM  ton. JM 6:281-86 Jan 42
Goldsen, J. M. and Curtis, A. Montclair
ASN  [New Jersey] studies the shopping ex-
     periences and attitudes of its residents.
     JM 10:165-70 Oct 45
Green, H. W. Retail outlets in shopping
ASO  centers stop decreasing [in Cleveland,
     Ohio]. JM 10:281-82 Jan 46
Lillibridge, R. M. Shopping centers in
A    urban redevelopment. LE 24:137-60
     May 48
Mayer, H. M. Patterns and recent trends
ASI  of Chicago's outlying business centers.
     LE 18:4-16 Feb 42
Mertes, J. E. The shopping center: a new
A    trend in retailing. JM 13:374-79 Jan 49
Wood, R. The community goes into busi-
A    ness. HBR 26:144-55 Mar 48
Wrigley, R. L., Jr. Organized industrial
ASI  districts: with special reference to the
     Chicago area. LE 23:180-98 May 47

22.4 RURAL STUDIES
22.40 GENERAL

Allin, B. W. County planning project: a coop-
A    erative approach to agricultural planning
     [with discussion]. JFE 22:292-316 Feb 40
Banfield, E. C., Jr. Rural rehabilitation in
ASU  Washington County, Utah. LE 23:261-70
     Aug 47
Bhathera, S. S. The organisation of rural
FI   welfare. IJE 22:807-19 Jan 42
Crawford, J. G. and Lange, G. County
A    planning for land-use adjustment.
     JFE 22:473-83 May 40
Dovell, J. E. The Everglades, a Florida
ASF  frontier. AH 22:187-97 Jul 48
Duckham, A. N. and Young, J. A. Rural
EB   planning in the United Kingdom. JFE 29:
     1075-88 Nov 47
Glazer, S. The rural community in the
ASM  urban age: the changes in Michigan
     since 1900. AH 23:130-34 Apr 49
Gross, N. C. A post mortem on county
A    planning. JFE 25:644-61 Aug 43
Hammar, C. H. Regulation or development
ASM  for the Missouri Ozarks. LE 16:159-67
     May 40
Iyengar, D. K. Rural drive in Mysore.
FI   IJE 27:72-77 Jul 46
Johnson, V. W.; Timmons, J. F. and
A    Howenstine, E. J., Jr. Rural public
     works. Pt.I-II. LE 23:12-21; 132-41
     Feb,May 47

Macgregor, D. H. The Scott committee re-
EB   port. R. Ec N.S.10:1-11 Feb 43
Mathur, A. P. Economic inquiry of village
FI   Nigohan, District Rae Bareli. IJE 17:
     201-12 Oct 36
Paschal, J. L. and Slagsvold, P. L. Irriga-
AA   tion development and area adjustment in
     the Great Plains. JFE 25:433-43 May 43
Ritchie, A. B. The first four reports of the
N    Rural Reconstruction Commission. R.
     ER 21:165-73 Dec 45

22.41 ZONING

Albers, J. M. Progress in county zoning:
ASW  Marathon County, Wisconsin. LE 16:
     393-402 Nov 40
Diehl, L. F. Ordnance causes ordinance in
ASP  Crawford County, Pennsylvania. LE 18:
     357-63 Aug 42
Erdmann, A. G. The rural zoning ordinance
ASI  of Cook County. LE 16:438-42 Nov 40
Hurlburt, V. Rural zoning for Missouri?
ASM  LE 16:151-58 May 40
Joss, A. Some possible limitations of
ASN  zoning ordinances as devices for con-
     trolling land settlement [in Otsego County,
     N.Y.]. LE 21:154-59 May 45
Kingery, R. Cook County amends rural
ASI  subdivision regulations. LE 16:218-19
     May 40
Musbach, W. F. and Williams, M. C. Rural
ASM  zoning in Minnesota. LE 16:105-09
     Feb 40
Wehrwein, G. S. The administration of
ASW  rural zoning [in Wisconsin]. LE 19:
     264-91 Aug 43

22.5 HOUSING
22.50 GENERAL

Guénault, P. H. and Randall, R. J. An intro-
     duction to the housing problem. SAJE 8:
     145-61 Jun 40
Kingsbury, L. M. What is housing eco-
     nomics? LE 17:354-57 Aug 41

UNITED STATES

Adams, F. J., chairman. The neighborhood
A    concept in theory and application. Panel
     I. [Symposium: Frontiers of housing re-
     search] LE 25:67-88 Feb 49
Darling, P. A short-cut method for evalu-
     ating housing quality. LE 25:184-92
     May 49
Dean, J. P. The orientation of housing re-
     search [followed by R. U. Ratcliff's re-
     joinder]. LE 23:76-81 Feb 47
Farrier, C. W., chairman. Relationships
     of technological and social research in
     housing. Panel II. [Symposium:
     Frontiers of housing research] LE 25:
     89-102 Feb 49
Feldstein, M. J. and Bryant, L. C. Organ-
     ization of occupancy as an approach to

22.5 HOUSING (Cont.)
22.50 GENERAL (Cont.)
UNITED STATES (Cont.)

Feldstein, M. J. and Bryant, L. C. (Cont.) real estate management. LE 17:460-64 Nov 41

A   Hoyt, H. The effect of cyclical fluctuations upon real estate finance. JF 2,no.1: 51-64 Apr 47

Laronge, J. The subdivider of today and tomorrow. LE 18:423-30 Nov 42

Meadows, P. Housing the American family. JB 21:80-91 Apr 48

Schiff, E. Family size and residential construction. AER 36:97-112 Mar 46

Weaver, R. C. Race restrictive housing covenants. LE 20:183-95 Aug 44

Weimer, A. M. Housing problems: discussion. AER/S 37:524-26 May 47

ASC  Solow, A. A. Measuring the quality of urban housing environment: a new appraisal technique [used in New Haven, Connecticut]. LE 22:282-93 Aug 46

ASI  Mayer, H. M. Applications of residential data from the Chicago Land Use Survey. LE 19:85-87 Feb 43

ASN  Lee, A. T. M. and Hauck, J. F. Excessive land subdivision in the New Jersey pine area. LE 19:207-21 May 43

ASN  Dean, J. P. Only Caucasian: a study of race covenants [in Queens, Nassau and Westchester counties, N.Y.]. LE 23: 428-32 Nov 47

ASP  Cottam, H. R. Housing scales for rural Pennsylvania. JASA 38:406-16 Dec 43

OTHER COUNTRIES

DSC  Alexander, R. J. Housing in Chile. LE 25: 146-54 May 49

EB  Moos, S. Economic problems of pre-fabrication. OIS 6:202-08 Sep 2, 44

EF  Bertheim, C. S. Housing in France. LE 24: 49-62 Feb 48

EI  Alberti, S. The housing problem in Italy. BNL 1:441-52 Oct 48

Schiavi, A. People's dwelling houses in Italy. BNL 2:243-45 Oct-Dec 49

HSA  Burrows, H. R. Some basic problems in housing research. SAJE 16:1-23 Mar 48

N  Mendelsohn, R. and Hamilton, J. M. The Australian Housing Cost Index. ER 24: 87-100 Jun 48

22.51 DEMAND AND SUPPLY

A  Blumenfeld, H. A neglected factor in estimating housing demand. LE 20:264-70 Aug 44

ASP  -- Correlation between value of dwelling units and altitude [in the Philadelphia Metropolitan District]. LE 24:396-402 Nov 48

A  Bridewell, D. A. The draft and real estate transactions. LE 16:459-63 Nov 40

A  Brunsman, H. G. The housing census of 1940. JASA 36:393-400 Sep 41

A  -- and Lowery, D. Facts from the 1940 Census of housing. LE 19:89-93 Feb 43

A  -- Observations on the provision and use of data from the 1940 housing census. AER/S 37:498-507 May 47

A  Demerath, N., chairman. Housing needs and housing standards. Panel IV. [Symposium: Frontiers of housing research] LE 25:116-32 Feb 49

A  Fisher, E. M., chairman. Measuring effective demand in the housing market. Panel III. [Symposium: Frontiers of housing research] LE 25:103-15 Feb 49

ASI  Foley, D. L. An index of housing in Chicago. LE 18:209-13 May 42

A  Howard, G. E. Filtering down and the elimination of substandard housing: a reply. LE 22:294 Aug 46

ASF  Hoyt, H. Economic and housing survey of the Orlando, Florida metropolitan region. LE 23:219-27 May 47

A  Hubbard, J. B. Residential real estate. R. QJE 56:130-33 Nov 41

ASW  Keyes, S. Converted residences and the supply of housing [in Madison, Wisconsin]. LE 16:47-51 Feb 40

A  Maisel, S. J. Variables commonly ignored in housing demand analysis. LE 25: 260-74 Aug 49

EB  Moos, S. Estimates of housing needs. OIS 7:218-26 Sep 22, 45; Corrigenda. 290 Nov 24, 45

A  Pease, R. H. Today's real estate market. HBR 26:385-97 Jul 48

N  Prest, W. The present number of dwellings in Melbourne. ER 19:230-37 Dec 43

A  Ratcliff, R. U. Notes on the recent decline in home ownership. LE 20:373-77 Nov 44

A  -- Filtering down and the elimination of substandard housing. LE 21:322-30 Sep 45

A  Richmond, K. C. Some basic facts from the Census of housing. JM 9:159-61 Oct 44

ASW  Riemer, S. and Riley, M. Trailer communities on a university campus. [A Wisconsin survey] LE 23:81-83 Feb 47

A  Rosenbaum, D. The housing needs of the nonwhite population in nonfarm areas. LE 24:331-39 Nov 48

A  Wittausch, W. K. Used homes in the low-cost housing market. LE 18:350-56 Aug 42

22.52 RENTALS

ASW  Andrews, R. B. Low rent residential areas in a high rent city [Madison, Wisconsin]. LE 17:229-32 May 41

A  Bloomberg, L. N. Rent control and the housing shortage. LE 23:214-18 May 47

EB  Burchardt, F. A. Working-class housing at economic rents. OIS 7:91-96 Apr 7, 45

## 22. REGIONAL PLANNING, ETC.

22.5 HOUSING (Cont.)
22.52 RENTALS (Cont.)

Ellis, A. W. T. Rents, rates and incomes
EBE   in Bristol. REStud 11:99-108 no.2, 44

Elsas, M. J. Rent subsidies on a national
EB   basis [in Great Britain]. REStud 11:
    77-85 no.2, 44

Fogarty, M. P. The incidence of rates on
EBE   houses [in Birmingham, England].
    REStud 10:81-105 no.2, 43

Marsh, L. C. The economics of low-rent
C   housing. CJE 15:14-33 Feb 49

Prest, W. Rents in Melbourne. ER 21:
N   37-54 Jun 45

Robinson, C. Relationship between condi-
A   tion of dwellings and rentals, by race.
    LE 22:296-302 Aug 46

Woll, M. The need for better rental data.
A   LE 17:226-28 May 41

22.53 GOVERNMENT POLICY

Abrams, C. The subsidy and housing.
A   LE 22:131-39 May 46

Ashley, E. E., 3rd. Government housing
A   activities. HBR 19:230-42 no.2, 41

Bowley, M. Local rates and housing sub-
EB   sidies. REStud 8:33-43 Oct 40

-- Local authorities and housing subsidies
EB   since 1919. MS 12:57-79 Oct 41

Bronfenbrenner, J. An incentive tax pro-
A   posal for alleviation of the housing
    shortage. NTJ 1:51-61 Mar 48

Burroughs, R. J. Toward a farm housing
A   policy. LE 24:1-22 Feb 48

Colean, M. L. Housing problems: discus-
A   sion. AER/S 37:527-28 May 47

Dickson, H. Sweden plans its housing
ES   policy. LE 23:417-27 Nov 47

Downing, R. I. Housing and public policy.
N   ER 24:72-86 Jun 48

Fox, A. B. The local housing authority and
A   the municipal government. LE 17:
    280-90 Aug 41

Keyes, S. Some considerations in the eco-
ASI   nomic possibilities of slum clearance.
    [A case study of Danville, Illinois]
    LE 18:204-09 May 42

Levine, D. D. The case for tax exemption
A   of public housing. LE 17:98-101 Feb 41

Mendelsohn, R. Australian housing policy:
N   war and post-war. ER 17:57-67 Jun 41

Nelson, R. S. Federal aid for urban land
A   acquisition. LE 21:125-35 May 45

Nesbitt, G. B. Relocating Negroes from
A   urban slum clearance sites. LE 25:
    275-88 Aug 49

Nurnberg, M. Effect of business fluctua-
A   tions upon public housing finance.
    LE 19:180-92 May 43

Strunk, N. Low-cost housing under the
A   USHA experiment. LE 16:96-99 Feb 40

Tough, R. and Weintraub, R. G. Farms
A   and homes for veterans. LE 20:371-73
    Nov 44

-- and Weintraub, R. G. Socialization in
A   housing, Great Britain and the United
EB   States. LE 22:273-81 Aug 46

Woodbury, C. Objectives and accomplish-
A   ments of the veterans' emergency hous-
    ing program. AER/S 37:508-23 May 47

-- Housing in the redevelopment of Ameri-
A   can cities. LE 25:397-404 Nov 49

# 23. UNCLASSIFIED

Goodman, A. B. Westward movement of
    local government. LE 20:20-34 Feb 44

Innis, H. A. The newspaper in economic
    development. JEH/S 2:1-33 Dec 42

Lundberg, G. A. Communication [on review
    of Can science save us?] SEJ 14:321
    Jan 48

Ratchford, B. U. Certain bases of power
    politics. SEJ 11:20-33 Jul 44

# AUTHOR INDEX

AANDAHL, ANDREW R.
A postwar forward pricing plan for agriculture. JFE 27:476-82 May 45

AARON, BENJAMIN
Protecting civil liberties of members within trade unions. IRRA 2:28-41 Dec 49

AARONSON, FRANKLIN M.
Benefits and beneficiaries under social insurance and related programs. JASA 39: 183-96 Jun 44

ABBOTT, CHARLES CORTEZ
and Zuckert, E. M. Venture capital and taxation. QJE 55:667-82 Aug 41
The availability of new equity capital. AER/S 32:129-40 Mar 42
chairman. The changing outlook for investment banking: [abstract of discussion]. AER/S 32:212 Mar 42
Government and private enterprise: discussion. AER/S 33:39-41 Mar 43
Working capital during the transition. HBR 22:291-98 no.3, 44
Administration of fiscal policy. HBR 23: 46-64 no.1, 44
Management of the federal debt. HBR 24: 96-108 no.1, 45
Governmental activity in the financial field. BHR 20:51-56 Apr 46
Sources of business funds: selected statistics, 1930-44. REStat 28:135-45 Aug 46
Small business: a community problem. HBR 24:183-96 no.2, 46
The commercial banks and the public debt. AER/S 37:265-76 May 47
Public debt: history: discussion. AER/S 37:154-56 May 47
Economic penetration and power politics. HBR 26:410-24 Jul 48
Economic defense of the United States. HBR 26:613-26 Sep 48
Government debt and private investment policy. REStat 31:21-25 Feb 49
Notes on Federal Reserve policy, August, 1945-June, 1948. JF 4:101-10 Jun 49

ABDEL HAMID NAZMY, A.
see Nazmy, A. Abdel Hamid

ABDEL-RAHMAN, AHMAD GAD
The Egyptian national life tables no.2. EgC 37:207-25 May-Dec 46

ABDELLATIF AMER
see Amer, Abdellatif

ABELL, A. S.
Rural municipal difficulties in Alberta. CJE 6:555-61 Nov 40

ABID HUSAIN, M. K.
see Husain, M. K. Abid

ABRAHAM, WILLIAM ISRAEL
The comparability of national income statistics of English-speaking countries. REStat 30:207-14 Aug 48

ABRAHAMSEN, MARTIN A.
Cooperative relationships and business performance. JFE 26:292-308 May 44

Farmers regional purchasing cooperatives look to research. JFE 27:694-700 Aug 45
Cooperatives in a sound farm economy: discussion. JFE 29:1151-54 Nov 47
The establishment of business research programs, with special reference to farmers' regional purchasing associations. JM 12: 348-61 Jan 48
Marketing research in agriculture. SEJ 15: 80-85 Jul 48
Cotton mechanization: its probable influence on marketing. JFE 31,pt.2:410-14 Feb 49
Determining consumer preferences for sweet potatoes: methods and results. JFE 31, pt.2:635-39 Feb 49

ABRAMOVITZ, CARRIE GLASSER
Some problems in the development of the communications industry. AER 35: 585-606 Sep 45
Union wage policy in bituminous coal. ILRR 1:609-23 Jul 48

ABRAMOVITZ, MOSES
Savings and investment: profits vs prosperity? AER/S 32,no.2:53-88 Jun 42

ABRAMS, CHARLES
The subsidy and housing. LE 22:131-39 May 46

ABRAMSON, ADOLPH GRAUDAN
Opportunities of the economist in an industrial company. HBR 20:389-90 no.3, 42
Industrial adjustment at the end of the war: discussion. AER/S 33:137 Mar 43
The problem of full employment. HBR 22: 337-45 no.3, 44
Price policies. SEJ 12:39-47 Jul 45
Fellowships in industry. AER 38:142-44 Mar 48

ABRAMSON, VICTOR
and Phillips, C. F. The rationing of consumer goods. JB 15:1-20 Jan 42
Price freezing under the Office of Price Administration. AER 32:760-74 Dec 42
and Phillips, C. F. Retail price control. HBR 20:184-98 no.2, 42
[and others] New frontiers in economic thought: discussion. AER/S 36:139-53 May 46

ABRUZZI, ADAM and Littauer, S. B.
Experimental criteria for evaluating workers and operations. ILRR 2:502-26 Jul 49

ABT, JOHN J. [and others]
Trade unions and the law: discussion. AER/S 32:476-89 Mar 42

ACKERMAN, JEROME
The problem of jurisdiction of national and state labor relations boards. ILRR 2: 360-71 Apr 49

ACKERMAN, JOSEPH
Status and appraisal of research in farm tenancy. JFE 23:277-90 Feb 41
chairman. Adjustments in southern agriculture with special reference to cotton. [Report of the Cotton Committee] JFE 28: 341-79 Feb 46

ACKLEY, GARDNER
Spatial competition in a discontinuous market. QJE 56:212-30 Feb 42
Inflation and equality: comment. AER 39: 960-66 Sep 49

ADAM, WALTER
Some factors in Indian economic development. IJE 29:17-26 Jul 48

ADAMS, FREDERICK J., chairman
The neighborhood concept in theory and application. Panel I. [Symposium: Frontiers of housing research] LE 25:67-88 Feb 49

ADAMS, JOHN CLARKE
The adjudication of collective labor disputes in Italy. QJE 56:456-74 May 42

ADAMS, QUINCY
Marketing aspects of postwar small business. JM 9:350-53 Apr 45
Notes on business population data. JM 10: 173-75 Oct 45

ADAMS, RICHARD LABAN and Benedict, M. R.
Methods of wage determination in agriculture. JFE 23:71-88 Feb 41

ADAMS, WALTER
Accounting practices and the business cycle. JB 22:119-33 Apr 49
A political force in Indian economic development. IJE 30:1-18 Jul 49

ADAMSON, WENDELL MAVITY
Measurement of income in small geographic areas. SEJ 8:479-92 Apr 42

ADARKAR, BHALCHANDRA PUNDLIK
Interpersonal comparisons of utility. IJE 20:513-30 Apr 40
and Ghosh, D. Mr. Keynes's theory of interest. IJE 21:285-300 Jan 41
Fiscal policy muddles: a reply. IJE 23: 115-32 Oct 42

ADARKAR, BHASKAR NAMDEO
A simplified version of the trade cycle theory. Pt.I-II. IJE 21:250-68; 22:38-67 Jan, Jul 41
[The investment multiplier.] Reply. IJE 23: 83-84 Jul 42

ADELMAN, MORRIS ALBERT
"Equilibrium in multi-process industries": further comments. QJE 60:464-68 May 46
Correlations and forecasting. AER 36: 645-50 Sep 46
Interest rates and fair return. LE 24:384-95 Nov 48
The A & P case: a study in applied economic theory. QJE 63:238-57 May 49
The economic consequences of some recent antitrust decisions: the A & P case. AER/S 39:280-83 May 49
The large firm and its suppliers. REStat 31: 113-18 May 49

ADISESHIAH, M. S.
[and others] Currency expansion during the war: discussion. IJE 24:545-60 Apr 44
International economic co-operation and an international standard. IJE 25:290-300 Jan 45

[and others] Discussion on economic planning. IJE 25:641-57 Apr 45
Some aspects of post-war Indian currency. IJE 26:452-71 Jan 46

ADLER, HANS ARNOLD
Absolute or relative rate of decline in population growth? QJE 59:626-34 Aug 45
The post-war reorganization of the German banking system. QJE 63:322-41 Aug 49

ADLER, JOHN HANS
United States import demand during the inter-war period. AER 35:418-30 Jun 45
The postwar demand for United States exports. REStat 28:23-33 Feb 46

ADY, PETER HONORINE
Utility goods. OIS 4:281-87 Oct 31, 42
Some economic problems of the Middle East. OIS 5:14-20 Jan 9, 43
The U.K.C.C. in the Middle East. OIS 5: 97-103 Apr 24, 43
Rents and rent restriction. OIS 5:248-54 Oct 30, 43
Colonial industrialisation and British employment. REStud 11:42-51 no.1, 43
Inflation in India. OIS 6:9-16 Jan 15, 44
Cinema duties, consumption and prices. OIS 6:62-64 Mar 18, 44
The statistical background of clothes rationing, 1941-44. Pt.I-III. OIS 6:209-19; 225-31; 256-64 Sep 23, Oct 14, Nov 4, 44
Bulk purchasing and the colonial producer. OIS 9:321-40 Oct 47
Trends in cocoa production, British West Africa. OIS 11:389-404 Dec 49

AGARWAL, AMAR NATH
The case for cottage industries in planned economy. IJE 25:545-51 Apr 45
Population of India and its future trend. IJE 27:389-99 Apr 47
Industrial relations in India. IJE 29:67-74 Jul 48

AGARWAL, SHRIMAN NARAYAN
Gandhian economics. IJE 23:193-99 Oct 42

AGARWALA, AMAR NARAIN
The need for the study of insurance finance. IJE 21:204-06 Oct 40
Recent economic literature. IJE 23:373-87 Apr 43
Economic conditions in Baroda and Hyderabad states. IJE 25:83-89 Jul 44
A letter from J. E. Cairnes to W. S. Jevons. IJE 25:80-82 Jul 44
The place of agriculture vis-a-vis industry in the industrialists' plan. IJE 25:117-23 Oct 44
Social insurance in Nazi Germany. R. IJE 25:362-66 Jan 45
Social security and occupational distribution of labour in post-war period. R. IJE 25: 358-62 Jan 45
and Malhotra, P. C. Agriculture in the industrialists' plan. IJE 25:502-10 Apr 45
Economic planning and agriculture. IJE 26: 61-82 Jul 45

AGARWALA, AMAR NARAIN (Cont.)
The social security movement in India.
EJ 56:568-82 Dec 46
AGARWALA, SHRI NARAYAN
India and international currency plans. R.
IJE 25:372-74 Jan 45
A critique of the Gandhian plan. R. IJE 26:
262-70 Oct 45
A religious interpretation of economics.
IJE 26:299-302 Oct 45
The Gandhian plan: reply. IJE 27:69-71
Jul 46
AGG, THOMAS RADFORD
On the 1944 NARUC Report. LE 21:284-86
Aug 45
AGGARWALA, KRISHAN CHANDRA
Marshall's concept of quasi-rent. IJE 28:
555-61 Apr 48
AGNEW, HUGH E.
The history of the American Marketing
Association. JM 5:374-79 Apr 41
AHMAD GAD ABDEL-RAHMAN
see Abdel-Rahman, Ahmad Gad
AHMED, S.
State Bank of Pakistan: its constitution and
functions. PEJ 1,no.1:102-08 Jul 49
AIKENHEAD, J. T. E.
Practical problems of the retail price ceil-
ing: I. Problems of the administrator.
CJE 8:433-40 Aug 42
AINSWORTH, RALPH BOWER
Earnings and working hours of manual wage-
earners in the United Kingdom in October,
1938. JRSS 112:35-58 pt.1, 49
AIREY, C. R. The scope of price regulation.
ER 16:121-22 Jun 40
--- A reply. ER 16:280-81 Dec 40
AITKEN, HUGH GEORGE JEFFREY
The analysis of decisions. EEH 1,no.2:17-23
Feb 49
Parameters: a reply. EEH 1,no.3:23-24
Mar 49
Taussig and Joslyn on business leaders. R.
EEH 1,no.3:29-32 Mar 49
The problem of entrepreneurial freedom.
EEH 1,no.4:1-8 Apr 49
The religious sanction. EEH 1,no.4:29-30
Apr 49
A note on partial analyses. EEH 1,no.6:30
Jun 49
William Hamilton Merritt: a study in
Canadian entrepreneurship. EEH 2:1-23
Nov 49
ÅKERMAN, GUSTAV
Unemployment and unemployment policy in
England. Kyk 3:23-35 fasc.1, 49
ÅKERMAN, JOHAN
Political economic cycles. Kyk 1:107-17
fasc.2, 47
Discontinuities of employment cycles.
NTTO 12:9-12 no.37, 48
Structural limits in economic development.
DeEc 97:785-98 Nov 49

AKHTAR, SARDAR MOHAMMAD
Objectives of agricultural planning for
Pakistan. PEJ 1,no.1:14-23 Jul 49
Pakistan's provincial finance: West Punjab.
PEJ 1,no.2:1-11 Oct 49
ALA'I, HESHMAT
The liquidity crisis abroad. AER 37:908-10
Dec 47
ALAM, MAHBUB
Insurance in U.S.S.R. PEJ 1,no.2:48-50
Oct 49
ALBERS, J. M.
Progress in county zoning: Marathon
County, Wisconsin. LE 16:393-402 Nov 40
ALBERTI, SALVATORE
The housing problem in Italy. BNL 1:441-52
Oct 48
ALBERTS, HUGO W. and Mendez Nadal, D.
The early history of livestock and pastures
in Puerto Rico. AH 21:61-64 Jan 47
ALBION, ROBERT G.
Early nineteenth-century shipowning: a
chapter in business enterprise. JEH 1:
1-11 May 41
ALBRIGHT, JOHN
[Measurement of marketing efficiency]: dis-
cussion. JM 5:370-71 Apr 41
Changes in wholesaling, 1929-1939. JM 6:
31-37 Jul 41
ALCORN, GEORGE BENNETT
and Erdman, H. E. The price-making
process in the Los Angeles egg market.
JM 6:349-57 Apr 42
Using price research. JFE 31,pt.2:1096-98
Nov 49
ALDERSON, WROE
[and others] [Measurement of marketing
efficiency]: discussion. JM 5:365-73
Apr 41
Marketing classification of families. JM 6:
143-46 Oct 41
chairman. Report of sub-committee on dol-
lar classification of incomes. JM 6:
383-86 Apr 42
The marketing viewpoint in national economic
planning. JM 7:326-32 Apr 43
A formula for measuring productivity in dis-
tribution. JM 12:442-48 Apr 48
and Cox, R. Towards a theory of marketing.
JM 13:137-52 Oct 48
ALDRICH, WINTHROP WILLIAMS
The International Chamber of Commerce and
the Economic and Social Council. EI 1:
233-35 Jan 48
The management of the public debt. JF 4:
1-12 Mar 49
ALDRIDGE, ALFRED OWEN
Franklin as demographer. JEH 9:25-44
May 49
ALEXANDER, ARTHUR J.
Prelude to the antirent war of 1845 in
Delaware County, New York. AH 20:
104-07 Apr 46

ALEXANDER, RALPH SAMUEL
Wartime adventures in equitable distribution
short of rationing. [Pt.I-III] JM 10:3-13;
135-51; 11:159-73 Jul,Oct 45, Oct 46
A wartime adventure in business self-regula-
tion: the retail declaration of policy.
JM 11:394-98 Apr 47
Some aspects of sex differences in relation to
marketing. JM 12:158-72 Oct 47
chairman. Report of the Definitions Com-
mittee. JM 13:202-17 Oct 48
ALEXANDER, ROBERT JACKSON
Housing in Chile. LE 25:146-54 May 49
ALEXANDER, SIDNEY STUART
Mr. Keynes and Mr. Marx. REStud 7:123-35
Feb 40
The accelerator as a generator of steady
growth. QJE 63:174-97 May 49
The effect of size of manufacturing corpora-
tion on the distribution of the rate of re-
turn. REStat 31:229-35 Aug 49
ALGER, PHILIP LANGDON
The importance of the statistical viewpoint
in high production manufacturing. JASA 36:
50-52 Mar 41
ALI, ANWAR
Pakistan budgets: general and provincial.
PEJ 1,no.1:117-25 Jul 49
ALI, CH. IZZAT
Co-operative multipurpose societies.
PEJ 1,no.2:38-41 Oct 49
ALI, HAMID
Industrial relations in India with special
reference to Hyderabad. IJE 29:295-300
Jan 49
ALLBAUGH, LELAND G.
Working with farmers to achieve
maximum production. JFE 26:
214-29 Feb 44
ALLCUT, EDGAR ALFRED
A fuel policy for Canada. CJE 11:26-34
Feb 45
ALLEN, CLARK LEE
Rayon staple fiber: its past and its prospects.
SEJ 13:146-57 Oct 46
ALLEN, EDWARD DOUGLAS
Treasury tax policies in 1943. AER 34:
707-33 Dec 44
ALLEN, GEORGE CYRIL
An aspect of industrial reorganisation.
EJ 55:179-91 Jun-Sep 45
The Report of the Working Party on the
Cotton Industry. MS 14,no.3:60-73 Sep 46
ALLEN, GEORGE HOWARD
Wartime changes in English and Canadian
radio. JM 7:220-26 Jan 43
ALLEN, HARRY KENNETH
Illinois Commission studies tax problems.
NTJ 2:259-71 Sep 49
ALLEN, JAMES S.
Machines in cotton. S&S 12:240-53 no.2, 48
ALLEN, JOHN ERNEST
A fairer income tax. EJ 50:475-81 Dec 40

An alternative to the last two budgets. EJ 51:
498-502 Dec 41
Railway compensation examined. EJ 58:
125-28 Mar 48
ALLEN, LINCOLN
Medical needs of the war industry areas.
S&S 8:28-39 no.1, 44
ALLEN, ROY GEORGE DOUGLAS
The unemployment situation at the outbreak
of war. JRSS 103:191-207 pt.2, 40
International programming of the distribu-
tion of resources. II. Statistics and com-
bined planning. JASA 39:286-90 Sep 44
Post-war economic policy in the U.S. EJ 55:
28-46 Apr 45
Mutual aid between the U.S. and the British
Empire, 1941-45. JRSS 109:243-71
pt.3, 46
The mathematical foundations of economic
theory. QJE 63:111-27 Feb 49
Wholesale prices, 1938-48. EJ 59:137-53
Jun 49
The economic theory of index numbers.
Ec N.S.16:197-203 Aug 49
ALLEN, RUTILLUS HARRISON
and Mighell, R. L. Supply schedules, "long-
time" and "short-time." JFE 22:544-57
Aug 40
and MacFarlane, D. L. Trade reciprocity
and agriculture: discussion. JFE 24:
822-25 Nov 42
ALLIN, BUSHROD WARREN
County planning project; a cooperative ap-
proach to agricultural planning. JFE 22:
292-301 Feb 40
The objectives and methods of agricultural
economics. JFE 30:545-52 Aug 48
Theory: definition and purpose. JFE 31:
409-17 Aug 49
ALLWRIGHT, WINSTON J. S.
Aspects of "controlled" marketing in the
Union: comments on the review article by
L. H. Samuels. SAJE 15:206-17 Sep 47
ALSBERG, CARL LUCAS
Nature and scope of training for men con-
templating work in the field of agricul-
tural economics. JFE 22:52-59 Feb 40
ALT, FRANZ L.
Distributed lags. Em 10:113-28 Apr 42
ALT, RICHARD MELTON
Statistical measurement of price flexibility.
QJE 56:497-502 May 42
The internal organization of the firm and
price formation: an illustrative case.
QJE 63:92-110 Feb 49
Competition among types of retailers in
selling the same commodity. JM 14:
441-47 Oct 49
ALTER, GERALD MILTON [and others]
Present issues of the Latin-American econ-
omy: discussion. AER/S 39:406-14
May 49

ALTMAN, OSCAR LOUIS
  Private investment, full employment, and
      public funds. AER/S 30,no.5:228-36
      Feb 41
ALTSCHAFFER, J. H. RICHTER-
see Richter-Altschaffer, J. H.
ALVI, HAMZA A.
  Pakistan's system of payments. PEJ 1,no.1:
      126-37 Jul 49
ALVORD, BEN F.
  The place of lectures, recitations and labo-
      ratory work in presenting subject matter
      in introductory marketing. JFE 31,pt.2:
      729-31 Feb 49
AMER, ABDELLATIF
  Agricultural and co-operative credit in
      Egypt. EgC 39:345-48 Mar 48
AMES, EDWARD
  A method for estimating the size distribution
      of a given aggregate income. REStat 24:
      184-89 Nov 42
  and Ferguson, A. R. Technological change
      and the equilibrium level of the national
      income. QJE 62:441-58 May 48
  A theoretical and statistical dilemma; the
      contributions of Burns, Mitchell, and
      Frickey to business-cycle theory. Em 16:
      347-69 Oct 48
AMOROSO, LUIGI
  The transformation of value in the produc-
      tive process. Em 8:1-11 Jan 40
  Prices and money. Em 17,suppl.:334-40
      Jul 49; Errata. 19:227 Apr 51
AMOS, J. L.
  Vocational rehabilitation during and after the
      war. CJE 9:164-74 May 43
ANANTACHAR, V. S.
  Forces behind Pareto's law. IJE 26:302-05
      Oct 45
  The economics of public salaries: a criti-
      cism. IJE 28:281-86 Oct 47
  The determinateness of the utility function.
      IJE 28:577-79 Apr 48
  Utility and its place in economics. IJE 29:
      1-15 Jul 48
ANANTARAM, K.
  Ranade, the economist. IJE 22:387-93 Jan 42
  The future of industrial location. IJE 27:
      157-62 Oct 46
  Limitations of cheap money policy. IJE 28:
      383-87 Jan 48
  The future of international investment.
      IJE 29:171-78 Oct 48
  Pathology of India's balance of payments.
      IJE 30:115-21 Oct 49
ANDERSON, BENJAMIN M., Jr.
  Governmental economic planning. AER/S 30:
      247-62 Mar 40
ANDERSON, CLAY JEFFERSON
  The development of the pump-priming theory.
      JPE 52:144-59 Jun 44
  The compensatory theory of public works
      expenditure. JPE 53:258-74 Sep 45

ANDERSON, DON SHERMAN
  Programs for post war: discussion. JFE 24:
      32-34 Feb 42
  United States foreign trade policy: discus-
      sion. JFE 31,pt.2:516-18 Feb 49
ANDERSON, EDWARD HUTCHINGS
  The meaning of scientific management.
      HBR 27:678-92 Nov 49
ANDERSON, GEORGE W.
  Agriculture in the undrained basin of Asia.
      AH 22:233-38 Oct 48
ANDERSON, JOHN T.
  The relation of market research to post-war
      planning. JM 7:115-24 Oct 42
ANDERSON, KARL LEOPOLD
  The pricing of copper and copper alloy scrap
      and of brass and bronze ingot. AER/S 33:
      295-302 Mar 43
  Terms of sale. JM 11:250-57 Jan 47
ANDERSON, MARY
  The postwar role of American women.
      AER/S 34:237-44 Mar 44
ANDERSON, MONTGOMERY D.
  Dynamic theory of employment. SEJ 7:37-50
      Jul 40
  Employment, investment, and the multiplier.
      Em 8:240-52 Jul 40
  Investment and the valuation of capital.
      Em 10:159-68 Apr 42
  A formula for total savings. QJE 58:106-19
      Nov 43
ANDERSON, RICHARD LOREE
  Use of variance components in the analysis
      of hog prices in two markets. JASA 42:
      612-34 Dec 47
ANDERSON, ROGER V.
  Policy for full employment. R. CJE 12:
      192-203 May 46
ANDERSON, RUSSELL H.
  Advancing across the eastern Mississippi
      Valley. AH 17:97-104 Apr 43
ANDERSON, THEODORE WILBUR
  A note on a maximum-likelihood estimate.
      Em 15:241-44 Jul 47
ANDERSON, THOMAS JOEL, Jr.
  Note on "The rise of monopoly." AER 30:
      118-20 Mar 40
  Competition and monopoly in land markets.
      AER 31:341-43 Jun 41
ANDERSON, WILLIAM
  Political science, economics, and public
      policy. AER/S 34:77-85 Mar 44
  [Economic research and tax policy]: discus-
      sion. AER/S 34,no.2:22-24 Jun 44
ANDERSON, WILLIAM HARRY
  The Supreme Court and recent public utility
      valuation theory. LE 21:12-22 Feb 45
  Public utility holding companies: the death
      sentence and the future. LE 23:244-54
      Aug 47
ANDERSON, WILLIAM N.
  Western range land use: discussion.
      JFE 31,pt.2:994-96 Nov 49

ANDRAS, A.
  The government of a central labour body.
    CJE 13:572-80 Nov 47
ANDREWS, DANIEL KEITH
  Old-age security for the American farm
    population. JFE 27:634-48 Aug 45
ANDREWS, JAMES B.
  Production adjustment research: discussion.
    JFE 27:924-27 Nov 45
ANDREWS, LEE
  The interviewer problem in market research.
    JM 13:522-24 Apr 49
ANDREWS, PHILIP WALTER SAWFORD
  A further inquiry into the effects of rates of
    interest. OEP 3:32-73 Feb 40
  Food rationing and the present emergency.
    OIS 2,no.4:2-7 Jul 40
  Development-projects in Great Britain during
    the war. OIS 3:22-25 Feb 1, 41
  Food policy. OIS 3:48-51 Feb 22, 41
  A survey of industrial development in Great
    Britain planned since the commencement
    of the war. OEP 5:55-71 Jun 41
  A reconsideration of the theory of the in-
    dividual business. OEP N.S.1:54-89
    Jan 49
ANDREWS, RICHARD B.
  Low rent residential areas in a high rent
    city. LE 17:229-32 May 41
  Elements in the urban-fringe pattern. LE 18:
    169-83 May 42
  Urban fringe studies of two Wisconsin cities:
    a summary. LE 21:375-82 Sep 45
ANDREWS, WILLIAM HALSTEAD, Jr. and
  Marschak, J.
  Random simultaneous equations and the
    theory of production. Em 12:143-205
    Jul-Oct 44; Errata. 13:91 Jan 45
ANGEHRN, OTTO
  The Swiss economy in the transition period.
    OIS 8:51-54 Feb 46
ANGEL, ARTHUR D.
  Wanted: one responsible administration for
    the Greater Central Valley Project of
    California. LE 21:136-43 May 45
  Who will pay for the Central Valley Project
    of California? LE 22:266-72 Aug 46
  --- That temporary contract: a rejoinder.
    LE 23:88-90 Feb 47
  British use of public corporations. SR 14:
    321-31 Sep 47
ANGELL, JAMES WATERHOUSE
  chairman. Round table on bank deposits and
    the business cycle. AER/S 30:80-82
    Mar 40
  Defense financing and inflation: some com-
    ments on Professor Hansen's article:
    Taxation, inflation and the defense pro-
    gram. REStat 23:78-82 May 41
  Keynes and economic analysis today. R.
    REStat 30:259-64 Nov 48
  Current research in business cycles: dis-
    cussion. AER/S 39:73-77 May 49

ANGERS, FRANÇOIS ALBERT
  French Canada and social security. CJE 10:
    355-64 Aug 44
ANIS, MAHMOUD
  Value of agriculture products and other com-
    modities pertaining to agriculture for the
    years 1937-1942. EgC 36:357-68 Mar 45
ANJARIA, JASHWANTRAI JAYANTILAL
  The problem of valuation in a socialist state.
    IJE 21:361-82 Apr 41
  The Gandhian approach to Indian economics.
    IJE 22:357-66 Jan 42
ANNA, FRANCESCO COPPOLA D'
  see Coppola d'Anna, Francesco
ANROD, CHARLES W.
  [and others] Postwar labor relations: dis-
    cussion. AER/S 36:370-83 May 46
  Philosophy and analysis of recent union-
    control legislation. RSE 6:52-80 May 48
ANSHEN, MELVIN
  The rediscovery of the consumer. JM 5:
    248-53 Jan 41
ANSTEY, VERA
  Social accounting in India. IJE 27:271-77
    Jan 47
ANTHONY, ROBERT NEWTON
  Effect of size on efficiency. HBR 20:290-306
    no.3, 42
ANWAR ALI
  see Ali, Anwar
ANWAR-UL-HASAN
  see Hasan, Anwarul
AOYAMA, HIDEO
  A critical note on D. H. Robertson's theory
    of savings and investment. Pt.I-II.
    Kyo 16,no.1:49-73; no.2:64-81 Jan,Apr 41
  On the extension of the concept of a com-
    modity: a note on Hicks' theory of the
    "group of commodities." Kyo 18,no.2:
    48-68 Apr 43
APEL, HANS
  Self-liquidating wages. SR 10:301-11 Sep 43
  Marginal cost constancy and its implications.
    AER 38:870-85 Dec 48
APPELBAUM, WILLIAM
  Adjustment of retailing to 1941 conditions.
    JM 5:438-42 Apr 41
  A case history of sales quotas. JM 7:200-03
    Jan 43
  The Journal of marketing: the first ten
    years. JM 11:355-63 Apr 47
ARANT, WILLARD DAVID
  Wartime meat policies. JFE 28:903-19 Nov 46
ARENWALD, WALTER P.
  Mediation, arbitration, and investigation of
    industrial disputes in New York State,
    1937-40. JPE 49:59-89 Feb 41
ARMITAGE, GODFREY
  Lancashire. MS 14,no.1:72-76 Jan 46
ARMSTRONG, CLARENCE
  Farm prices and industrial wages. JFE 28:
    1041-48 Nov 46

ARMSTRONG, FLOYD E.
Carroll W. Doten, 1871-1942. [obit.]
JASA 37:543 Dec 42

ARMSTRONG, KENNETH P.
Effect of federal ownership of real estate
upon local self-government in the District
of Columbia. NTJ 2:343-48 Dec 49

ARMSTRONG, WALLACE EDWIN
Uncertainty and the utility function. EJ 58:
1-10 Mar 48

ARMYTAGE, W. H. G.
A. J. Mundella and the hosiery industry.
EHR 18:91-99 no.1-2, 48

ARNDT, ERNST HEINRICH DANIEL
The proposed new banking legislation.
SAJE 9:274-311 Sep 41
The building society movement in the Union.
SAJE 11:185-97 Sep 43
The Union Banking Act, 1942. SAJE 11:
235-57 Dec 43
Pre-Union building society legislation.
SAJE 16:133-56 Jun 48
Building societies in South Africa. SAJE 17:
503-10 Dec 49

ARNDT, HEINZ WOLFGANG
The monetary theory of deficit spending: a
comment on Dr. Clark Warburton's
article. REStat 28:90-92 May 46
Productivity in manufacturing and real in-
come per head in Great Britain and the
United States. OEP 8:65-80 Nov 47
The International Monetary Fund and the
treatment of cyclical balance of payments
disequilibria. ER 23:186-97 Dec 47
The concept of liquidity in international
monetary theory. REStud 15:20-26
no.1, 47
Savings in a state with a stationary popula-
tion: comment. QJE 62:623-28 Aug 48
Public finance and the national income.
ER 24:243-45 Dec 48
A pioneer of national income estimates.
EJ 59:616-25 Dec 49
Recent discussion of Keynes' theory of wages.
R. ER 25,(no.49):77-83 Dec 49

ARNOLD, PAULINE
Woman's role in market research. JM 12:
87-91 Jul 47

ARNOLD, SAM
Forward shifting of a payroll tax under
monopolistic competition. QJE 61:267-84
Feb 47

ARNOLD, THURMAN
and Livingston, J. S. Antitrust war policy
and full production. HBR 20:265-76
no.3, 42
Must 1929 repeat itself? HBR 26:32-45
Jan 48
The effectiveness of the federal antitrust
laws: a symposium. AER 39:690 Jun 49

ARPKE, FREDERICK
Land-use control in the urban fringe of
Portland, Oregon. LE 18:468-80 Nov 42

ARROW, KENNETH JOSEPH; Blackwell, D. and
Girshick, M. A.
Bayes and minimax solutions of sequential
decision problems. Em 17:213-44
Jul-Oct 49

ARTHUR, HENRY BRADFORD [and others]
Does large-scale enterprise lower costs?
Discussion. AER/S 38:165-71 May 48

ASCHER, CHARLES S.
New York City revises its zoning ordinance.
LE 16:345-49 Aug 40

ASCHER, LEONARD
A statistical analysis of recent changes in
commodity prices at wholesale. JASA 39:
35-41 Mar 44

ASCHMAN, FREDERICK T.
Dead land: chronically tax delinquent lands
in Cook County, Illinois. LE 25:240-45
Aug 49

ASHLEY, CHARLES ALLAN
Investigation into an alleged combine of
wholesalers and shippers of fruit and
vegetables in western Canada. CJE 6:
288-92 May 40
Jacques Olivier Clerc, 1917-1944. [obit.]
CJE 11:268-69 May 45

ASHLEY, EDWARD EVERETT, 3rd
Government housing activities. HBR 19:
230-42 no.2, 41

ASHLEY, PERCY
An experiment in tariff making. MS 11:1-35
Apr 40

ASHTON, HERBERT
Railroad costs in relation to the volume of
traffic. AER 30:324-32 Jun 40
The time element in transportation.
AER/S 37:423-40 May 47

ASHTON, THOMAS SOUTHCLIFFE
The bill of exchange and private banks in
Lancashire, 1790-1830. EHR 15:25-35
no.1-2, 45
The relation of economic history to economic
theory. Ec N.S.13:81-96 May 46
Some statistics of the industrial revolution
in Britain. MS 16:214-34 May 48
The standard of life of the workers in Eng-
land 1790-1830. JEH/S 9:19-38 '49

ATAULLAH, SHAIK
Punjab cooperation during a decade of de-
pression. IJE 22:504-14 Jan 42
A fourteenth century experiment in price
control. IJE 24:340-47 Apr 44
Need for war time control of food stuffs in
India. IJE 24:330-39 Apr 44

ATHERTON, LEWIS E.
Western foodstuffs in the Army provisions
trade. AH 14:161-69 Oct 40
Personal letters of a New Orleans mercantile
clerk, 1844-1845. BHR 17:49-56 Jun 43
Itinerant merchandising in the ante-bellum
South. BHR 19:35-59 Apr 45
Predecessors of the commercial drummer in
the old South. BHR 21:17-24 Feb 47

ATKINS, DAVID
    A dimensional national economy: a reply.
        JPE 52:267-69 Sep 44
ATKINS, WILLARD E.
    "Economics for consumers" by Gordon and
        "Income and consumption" by Vaile and
        Canoyer. R. JM 4,no.4,pt.2:138-46 Apr 40
ATKINSON, F. J.
    Saving and investment in a socialist state.
        REStud 15:78-83 no.2, 48
ATKINSON, LUTHER JAY
    The marginal feed cost of pork and lard.
        JFE 27:375-87 May 45
    Recent developments in economic thinking.
        JFE 29:261-77 Feb 47
ATWOOD, PAUL W.
    Marketing research as a tool of management
        in industrial goods problems. JM 12:
        295-304 Jan 48
AUBREY, HENRY G.
    Deliberate industrialization. SR 16:158-82
        Jun 49
AUKRUST, ODD
    International accounting. NTTO 12:13-22
        no.37, 48
    On the theory of social accounting. REStud 16:
        170-88 no.3, 49
AULL, GEORGE HUBERT
    Future of cotton in the South: discussion.
        JFE 23:121-24 Feb 41
    Programs for post war: discussion. JFE 24:
        29-32 Feb 42
    Employment prospects in southern agricul-
        ture. SEJ 13:378-85 Apr 47
    Research needs in land tenure and farm
        finance. LE 23:255-60 Aug 47
AUSTIN, ROBERT CARTER
    Effects of unionization in monopolistic com-
        petition on the southern worker. SEJ 16:
        81-84 Jul 49
AVISON, T. L.
    The Canadian Foreign Exchange Control
        Board. CJE 6:56-60 Feb 40
AYDELOTTE, WILLIAM O.
    The England of Marx and Mill as reflected in
        fiction. JEH/S 8:42-58 '48
AYLESWORTH, PHILLIP F.
    Farm-management research: discussion.
        JFE 23:239-45 Feb 41
AYRES, CLARENCE EDWIN
    Capitalism in retrospect. SEJ 9:293-301
        Apr 43
    Addendum to The theory of economic prog-
        ress. AER 35:937-40 Dec 45
    The impact of the great depression on eco-
        nomic thinking. AER/S 36:112-25 May 46
AYYANGAR, A. A. KRISHNASWAMI
    see Krishnaswami Ayyangar, A. A.
AYYAR, K. L. VENKATACHALAM
    Industrial relations in India. IJE 29:289-93
        Jan 49
AYZENSHTADT, A.
    The learned handmaidens of American capi-

tal. A survey of literature. [Translated
    by E. V. Domar] AER 39:930-45 Sep 49
AZIZ FAROOQ
    see Farooq, Aziz
BACH, GEORGE LELAND
    Rearmament, recovery and monetary policy.
        AER 31:27-41 Mar 41
    and Musgrave, R. A. A stable purchasing
        power bond. AER 31:823-25 Dec 41
    War financing and the distribution of income.
        AER 32:352-54 Jun 42
    Monetary-fiscal policy, debt policy, and the
        price level. AER/S 37:228-42 May 47
    Monetary-fiscal policy reconsidered. JPE 57:
        383-94 Oct 49
    Bank supervision, monetary policy, and
        governmental reorganization. JF 4:
        269-85 Dec 49
    The Federal Reserve and monetary policy
        formation. AER 39:1173-91 Dec 49
BACHMAN, KENNETH LEROY
    [and others] Recent regional changes in
        farming and probable future trends.
        JFE 24:256-84 Feb 42
    [and others] Appraisal of the economic
        classification of farms. JFE 30:680-702
        Nov 48
    Capital-labor substitution in cotton farming.
        JFE 31,pt.2:370-73 Feb 49
BACKMAN, JULES
    The causes of price inflexibility. QJE 54:
        474-89 May 40
    and Madden, J. T. Public utility holding
        company common stocks. JB 13:213-33
        Jul 40
    Flexibility of cheese prices. JPE 48:579-82
        Aug 40
    and Fishman, L. British war-time control
        of copper, lead, and zinc. QJE 55:210-38
        Feb 41
    and Fishman, L. British war time control of
        aluminum. QJE 56:18-48 Nov 41
    Price control: discussion. AER/S 33:272-76
        Mar 43
    The budget approach to wage adjustments: a
        case study. JPE 55:57-64 Feb 47
    Hourly wage dispersion. AER 37:918-26
        Dec 47
    Price inflexibility, war and postwar. JPE 56:
        428-37 Oct 48
    and Gainsbrugh, M. R. Productivity and liv-
        ing standards. ILRR 2:163-94 Jan 49
BACON, EDMUND N.
    A diagnosis and suggested treatment of an
        urban community's land problem. LE 16:
        72-88 Feb 40
BACON, ELIZABETH M.
    Marketing sewing machines in the post-Civil
        War years. BHR 20:90-94 Jun 46
BACON, LOIS BIGELOW
    European recovery and the American farmer:
        discussion. JFE 31,pt.2:533-36 Feb 49

BADER, LOUIS
   Reaction of consumers to a two-price system.
      JM 5:41-43 Jul 40
   and Hotchkiss, G. B. Attitudes of teachers of
      marketing toward consumer grade labeling.
      JM 6:274-79 Jan 42
BAER, WERNER
   Equality and prosperity. SR 10:118-22
      Feb 43
BAERWALD, FRIEDERICH
   The economics of control. RSE 34-48 Jun 47
BAGER, RACHEL
   A comparison of the respective conditions on
      which social and private building enter-
      prises may be granted government loans.
      NTTO 12:23-30 no.37, 48
BAHMER, ROBERT H.
   The American Society of Equity. AH 14:
      33-63 Jan 40
BAILER, LLOYD HARDING
   The Negro automobile worker. JPE 51:
      415-28 Oct 43
BAILEY, GEORGE D.
   Problems in reporting corporation income.
      HBR 26:513-26 Sep 48
   Concepts of income. HBR 26:680-92 Nov 48
BAILEY, KENNETH HAMILTON
   The uniform income tax plan (1942). ER 20:
      170-88 Dec 44
BAILEY, WILLIAM L.
   Appraising urban communities: techniques
      and objectives. LE 16:1-7 Feb 40
   Avoiding "census jitters." LE 16:349-51
      Aug 40
BAIN, JOE STATEN
   The Sherman Act and "The bottlenecks of
      business." R. JM 5:254-58 Jan 41
   The profit rate as a measure of monopoly
      power. QJE 55:271-93 Feb 41
   Market classifications in modern price
      theory. QJE 56:560-74 Aug 42
   Measurements of the degree of monopoly: a
      note. Ec N.S.10:66-68 Feb 43
   The normative problem in industrial regula-
      tion. AER/S 33:54-70 Mar 43
   The economics of the Pacific Coast petroleum
      industry: reply to J. A. Loftus. AER 36:
      148-49 Mar 46
   chairman. War agency records concerning
      petroleum and solid fuels. [Report of a
      subcommittee] AER/S 37:667-70 May 47
   Output quotas in imperfect cartels. QJE 62:
      617-22 Aug 48
   Rostow's proposals for petroleum policy. R.
      JPE 57:55-60 Feb 49
   Pricing in monopoly and oligopoly. AER 39:
      448-64 Mar 49
BAJORK, LEONARD C.
   [Moral aspects of the Taft-Hartley Act]: dis-
      cussion. RSE 6:47-51 May 48
BAKAY, ARCHIE J. and Myers, J. H.
   Influence of stock split-ups on market price.
      HBR 26:251-55 Mar 48

BAKER, GEORGE PIERCE
   The possibilities of economies by railroad
      consolidation and co-ordination.
      AER/S 30:140-57 Mar 40
BAKER, JOHN AUSTIN
   The graduated farm land transfer stamp tax.
      LE 16:21-29 Feb 40
   Toward a theory of land income. LE 21:
      160-66 May 45
BAKER, JOHN CALHOUN
   Pensions for executives. HBR 18:309-21
      no.3, 40
   Stock options for executives. HBR 19:106-22
      no.1, 40
   Executive compensation by small textile
      companies. HBR 20:81-91 no.1, 41
   Limiting executive salaries in wartime.
      HBR 21:50-59 no.1, 42
   A "just gauge" for executive compensation.
      HBR 22:75-87 no.1, 43
   Payments to senior corporation executives.
      QJE 59:170-84 Feb 45
BAKER, JOHN GORDON
   The universal discount as a means of eco-
      nomic stabilization. Em 16:155-84 Apr 48
BAKER, OLIVER EDWIN
   Present-day population trends and American
      agriculture. [Abstract] AER/S 30:386-93
      Mar 40
BAKKE, EDWARD WIGHT
   The economists and unemployment.
      AER/S 30,no.5:294-300 Feb 41
   Social security: discussion. AER/S 34:
      222-24 Mar 44
BAKSHI, S. C.
   Land systems in India and agricultural
      prosperity. IJE 27:245-49 Oct 46
BALAKRISHNA, RAMACHANDRA
   Rate structure of public utilities in a social-
      ist state. IJE 21:383-94 Apr 41
   Co-operative rural credit in Mysore. IJE 22:
      471-84 Jan 42
   Monopolistic influences in capitalistic econ-
      omy. IJE 24:368-73 Apr 44
   Transport rates and industrial distribution.
      IJE 26:430-40 Jan 46
   Limitations of the deductive theories of in-
      dustrial location. IJE 27:117-21 Oct 46
   India in a world trading system. IJE 28:1-8
      Jul 47
   Role of tariffs in economic expansion. IJE 28:
      207-22 Oct 47
   Budgetary scope for planning in Madras.
      IJE 29:109-16 Oct 48
   Public enterprise in a mixed economy.
      IJE 30:167-74 Oct 49
BALCOM, MARGARET N. and Maxwell, J. A.
   Gasoline rationing in the United States.
      Pt.I-II. QJE 60:561-87; 61:125-55
      Aug,Nov 46
BALDERSTON, C. CANBY
   The wage-setting dilemma. HBR 20:402-05
      no.4, 42

BALDERSTON, C. CANBY (Cont.)
Balance in wage setting. HBR 24:51-56
no.1, 45
BALDWIN, ROBERT EDWARD
Equilibrium in international trade: a dia-
grammatic analysis. QJE 62:748-62
Nov 48
BALDWIN, WILLIAM H.
The McKesson & Robbins reorganization.
HBR 20:473-82 no.4, 42
BALET, J. W.
Application of the LIFO inventory method to
income tax depreciation for public utilities.
NTJ 1:322-29 Dec 48
BALL, ELMER P. and Furman, A. F.
Operating a grazing association. LE 19:
94-98 Feb 43
BALL, ROBERT M.
Pension plans under collective bargaining:
an evaluation of their social utility.
IRRA 2:127-37 Dec 49
BALLAINE, FRANCIS K.
Businessmen and the community forum.
HBR 25:372-84 no.3, 47
BALLAINE, WESLEY CHARLES
How government purchasing procedures
strengthen monopoly elements. JPE 51:
538-46 Dec 43
New England mutual savings bank laws as
interstate barriers to the flow of capital.
AER 35:155-59 Mar 45
BALLANTINE, ARTHUR ATWOOD
The corporation and the income tax. HBR 22:
277-90 no.3, 44
The Supreme Court and business planning.
HBR 24:151-65 no.2, 46
When all the banks closed. HBR 26:129-43
Mar 48
Psychological bases for tax liability.
HBR 27:200-08 Mar 49
BALLANTYNE, MURRAY
The late Egbert Munzer: a tribute. CJE 15:
409-11 Aug 49
BALLINGER, ROY ARTHUR
Quality-price differentials in cotton market-
ing: discussion. JFE 23:354-56 Feb 41
BALLS, HERBERT R.
The development of government expenditure
control: the issue and audit phases.
CJE 10:464-75 Nov 44
BALMER, STANLEY L. and Dean, J.
Gearing salaries of nation-wide chains to the
geographical structure of wages. JB 20:
96-115 Apr 47
BALOGH, THOMAS
Foreign exchange and export trade policy.
EJ 50:1-26 Mar 40
The drift towards a rational foreign exchange
policy: an example of economic war or-
ganisation in Britain. Ec N.S.7:248-79
Aug 40
The new Order in foreign exchange control.
OIS 2,no.5:12-14 Aug 10, 40

Compensation for war-damage. OIS 2,no.7:
18-20 Sep 40
The economic effort. OIS 2,no.9:1-4
Nov 2, 40
Economic mobilization. OIS 2,no.10:5-8
Nov 23, 40
The new bill for war damage compensation.
OIS 2,no.11:16-18 Dec 40
Notes on the cotton industry. 2. The spread-
over in weaving. OIS 3:55-56 Feb 22, 41
and Burchardt, F. Concentration in the
'non-essential' industries. OIS 3:68-71
Mar 15, 41
The role of compensation in the war-
economic system. OIS 3:99-103 Apr 5, 41
The budget and economic mobilization.
OIS 3:113-18 Apr 26, 41
and Mandelbaum, K. Manpower policy in
Germany. OIS 3:279-81 Aug 30, 41
Money incentive and the production drive.
OIS 3:311-14 Oct 11, 41
Problems of coal production. OIS 4:177-82
Jun 27, 42
Concentration in retail distribution. OIS 4:
201-05 Jul 18, 42
Compensation in practice. OIS 4:231-35
Aug 29, 42
and Worswick, G. D. N. The battle for fuel.
OIS 4:261-69 Oct 10, 42
The shipping balance. OIS 5:25-31 Jan 30, 43
The foreign balance and full employment.
OIS 5,suppl.5:33-39 Aug 7, 43
Control over property. OIS 5:196-99
Aug 28, 43
The new plan for an international investment
board. OIS 5:254-56 Oct 30, 43
Compensation and public boards. OIS 5:
277-80 Dec 11, 43
The finance of scientific & applied research.
OIS 6:1-7 Jan 15, 44
The unimportance of a capital levy. OIS 6:
44-48 Feb 26, 44
Fixing exchange rates in war. OIS 6:73-76
Apr 8, 44
and Schumacher, E. F. An international
monetary fund. OIS 6:81-93 Apr 29, 44
The budget. B. The budget proposals and
technical progress. OIS 6:104-07
May 20, 44
The League of Nations on post-war foreign
trade problems. R. EJ 54:256-61
Jun-Sep 44
The importance of multilateral trade for
Britain. OIS 6:183-88 Aug 12, 44
A note on the economics of retaliation.
REStud 11:86-90 no.2, 44
Some theoretical problems of post-war
foreign investment policy. OEP 7:93-110
Mar 45
The economic problems of France. OIS 7:
61-78 Apr 7, 45
Savings, the business cycle and the trend.
OIS 7:114-15 May 19, 45

BARBER, HELEN A. and Brady, D. S.
    The pattern of food expenditures. REStat 30:
        198-206 Aug 48
BARBOUR, VIOLET
    Rigidities affecting business in the sixteenth
        and seventeenth centuries. AER/S 30:
        290-97 Mar 40
BAREAU, PAUL
    Reconstruction in the low countries. LBR 3:
        33-48 Jan 47
    The economic regeneration of France.
        LBR 4:11-25 Apr 47
BARFOD, BØRGE
    Polysony, polypoly. NTTO 12:31-39 no.37, 48
BARKER, JAMES M.
    Surveying the boundary line between govern-
        ment and private enterprise in the field
        of business. AER/S 33:1-18 Mar 43
BARKIN, SOLOMON
    Wage policies of industrial unions. HBR 19:
        342-51 no.3, 41
    [and others] The determination of wages:
        discussion. AER/S 32:302-06 Mar 42
    Handling work assignment changes. HBR 25:
        473-82 no.4, 47
    Labor's attitude toward wage incentive plans.
        ILRR 1:553-72 Jul 48
    The regional significance of the integration
        movement in the southern textile industry.
        SEJ 15:395-411 Apr 49
    Statistical procedures in union administra-
        tion. ILRR 2:406-10 Apr 49
    What shall we have: retirement benefit or
        superannuation plans? IRRA 2:138-47
        Dec 49
BARLOON, MARVIN JOHN
    Financial reports to employees. HBR 20:
        124-31 no.1, 41
    The question of steel capacity. HBR 27:
        209-36 Mar 49
BARLOW, FRANK D., Jr.
    Agriculture in the South: review. JFE 29:
        199-201 Feb 47
BARLOW, Sir MONTAGUE [and others)
    Discussion on the Report of the Royal Com-
        mission on the Distribution of the Indus-
        trial Population. JRSS 103:330-43 pt.3, 40
BARLOWE, RALEIGH
    Homestead tax exemption: a tenure improve-
        ment measure? LE 23:360-70 Nov 47
    Population pressure and food production
        potentialities. LE 25:227-39 Aug 49
BARNA, TIBOR
    The burden of death duties in terms of an
        annual tax. REStud 9:28-39 Nov 41
    Valuation of stocks and the national income.
        Ec N.S.9:349-58 Nov 42
    Indirect taxes, subsidies and the cost-of-
        living index. REStud 10:53-61 no.1, 42
    and Kaldor, N. The 1943 White Paper on
        national income and expenditure. EJ 53:
        259-74 Jun-Sep 43
    Note on the productivity of labour: its con-

cept and measurement. OIS 8:205-16
    Jul 46
The British demand for imports: a comment.
    EJ 56:662-65 Dec 46
Rebuilding London: a survey in Stepney,
    1946. REStud 13:84-108 no.2, 46
The British purchase tax. PF 1:234-42
    no.3, 46
The French national accounts. OIS 10:73-83
    Mar 48
Those 'frightfully high' profits. OIS 11:
    213-27 Jul-Aug 49
BARNARD, CHESTER IRVING
    Comments on the job of the executive.
        HBR 18:295-308 no.3, 40
    Education for executives. JB 18:175-82
        Oct 45
BARNES, IRSTON ROBERTS
    Shall going value be included in the rate-
        base? Pt.I-II. LE 16:286-93; 430-37
        Aug-Nov 40
    [and others] Postwar railroad problems:
        discussion. AER/S 36:494-519 May 46
BARNES, LEO
    How sound were private postwar forecasts?
        JPE 56:161-65 Apr 48
BARR, GEORGE W.
    A price policy for agriculture, consistent
        with economic progress, that will pro-
        mote adequate and more stable income
        from farming. JFE 27:785-89 Nov 45
    Irrigation in the West: discussion. JFE 31,
        pt.2:982-83 Nov 49
BARTELS, ROBERT D. W.
    Marketing principles. JM 9:151-57 Oct 44
BARTLETT, MAURICE STEVENSON
    A note on the statistical estimation of supply
        and demand relations from time series.
        Em 16:323-29 Oct 48
BARTLETT, ROLAND WILLEY
    Principles for pricing market milk. JFE 31,
        pt.2:438-41 Feb 49
BARTON, BRIAN A.
    Trade unions and the entrepreneurial func-
        tion. EEH 1,no.6:20-28 Jun 49
BARTON, FRANK L.
    Recent developments concerning the South's
        freight-rate problem. SEJ 6:461-78
        Apr 40
    The Interstate Commerce Commission con-
        siders the class-rate structure. LE 17:
        10-16 Feb 41
    Length of haul and farm commodity prices.
        JFE 23:434-45 May 41
    Uniform freight classification and the Inter-
        state Commerce Commission. LE 18:
        312-22 Aug 42
    The freight-rate structure and the distribu-
        tion of defense contracts. SEJ 9:122-33
        Oct 42
    and McGehee, R. B. Freight forwarders.
        HBR 20:336-47 no.3, 42
    Another step towards uniform freight classi-
        fication. LE 22:22-34 Feb 46

BARTON, GLEN THOMAS
Increased productivity of the farm worker.
ILRR 1:264-82 Jan 48
and Cooper, M. R. Relation of agricultural
production to inputs. REStat 30:117-26
May 48
Effects of technological changes on cost re-
duction in agriculture: recent and prospec-
tive changes. JFE 31,pt.2:442-44 Feb 49
BARTON, SAMUEL G.
The consumption pattern of different eco-
nomic groups under war changes. JM 8:
50-53 Jul 43
A working system for the socio-economic
classification of a national sample of
families. JM 11:364-66 Apr 47
BARUCH, BERNARD MANNES
Priorities: the synchronizing force.
HBR 19:261-70 no.3, 41
BASCH, ANTONIN
The new economic warfare: a reply. AER 32:
558-60 Sep 42
European economic regionalism. AER/S 33:
408-19 Mar 43
BASSIE, V. LEWIS
Consumers' expenditures in war and transi-
tion. REStat 28:117-30 Aug 46
Woytinsky on consumption and savings.
REStat 30:298-300 Nov 48
BASU, SAROJ KUMAR
Some aspects of cheap money policy. IJE 28:
371-75 Jan 48
BATES, GEORGE EUGENE
The board of directors. HBR 19:72-87
no.1, 40
chairman. Economic aspects of reorganiza-
tion under the Chandler Act. [Abstract of
specialized conference discussion]
AER/S 32:230-31 Mar 42
and Zuckert, E. M. Directors' indemnity:
corporate policy or public policy?
HBR 20:244-64 no.2, 42
Twenty years [of the Harvard business re-
view]. HBR 21:1-4 no.1, 42
BATES, STEWART
The price system and the war economy.
CJE 7:324-37 Aug 41
Government forecasting in Canada. CJE 12:
361-78 Aug 46
Lothar Richter (1894-1948). [obit.] CJE 15:
543-44 Nov 49
BATHEJA, H. R.
The ends and machinery of international eco-
nomic co-operation. IJE 25:306-15 Jan 45
[and others] Discussion on social security.
IJE 25:634-41 Apr 45
BATSON, EDWARD
A contribution to the study of the relative
roles of income levels and purchasing
habits in the determination of sub-standard
food consumption. SAJE 11:106-20 Jun 43
The use of random sampling in sociographical research. SAJE 12:46-56 Mar 44

The distribution of benefits in the social se-
curity proposals. SAJE 12:279-302
Dec 44
Some points of comparison between the social
security proposals for the Union and for
Southern Rhodesia. SAJE 13:43-51 Mar 45
BATT, WILLIAM L.
International programming of the distribution
of resources: I. The problem of combined
planning. JASA 39:281-85 Sep 44
BATTERA, PIETRO
Index numbers of industrial production and
capitalisation in Italy. BNL 2:118-23
Apr-Jun 49
BAUDIN, LOUIS
An outline of economic conditions in France
under the German occupation. EJ 55:
326-45 Dec 45
BAUER, CATHERINE
Garden cities and the metropolis: a reply.
LE 22:65-66 Feb 46
BAUER, PÈTER TAMÀS
Rubber and foreign exchange. EJ 50:231-41
Jun-Sep 40
The failure of the pigs marketing scheme.
MS 12:35-45 Apr 41
A note on monopoly. Ec N.S.8:194-202
May 41
Rubber production costs during the great
depression. EJ 53:361-69 Dec 43
Some aspects of the Malayan rubber slump
1929-33. Ec N.S.11:190-98 Nov 44
Notes on cost. Ec N.S.12:90-100 May 45
The economics of planting density in rubber
growing. Ec N.S.13:131-35 May 46
Future competition between natural and
synthetic rubber. MS 14,no.2:40-64
May 46
The working of rubber regulation. EJ 56:
391-414 Sep 46
Malayan rubber policies. Ec N.S.14:81-107
May 47
Lord Beveridge on full employment. R.
Kyk 1:166-76 fasc.2, 47
A review of the agricultural marketing
schemes. Ec N.S.15:132-50 May 48
[The working of rubber regulation.] A re-
joinder. EJ 58:236-43 Jun 48
BAUGHMAN, ERNEST T.
A note on minimum wages and agricultural
welfare. JFE 28:1048-61 Nov 46
BAUGHN, WILLIAM HUBERT
Capital formation and entrepreneurship in the
South. SEJ 16:161-69 Oct 49
BAUHAN, ALEX E.
Simulated plant-record method of life analy-
sis of utility plant for depreciation-
accounting purposes. LE 24:129-36
May 48
BAUMGART, GUENTHER
Weekly index numbers, measuring business
activity. JB 13:234-52 Jul 40

BAUMOL, WILLIAM JACK
Community indifference. REStud 14:44-48
no.1, 46
Notes on the theory of government procure-
ment. Ec N.S.14:1-18 Feb 47
Mathematics for economists. R. Ec N.S.14:
310-13 Nov 47
Notes on some dynamic models. EJ 58:
506-21 Dec 48
Relaying the foundations. R. Ec N.S.16:
159-68 May 49
and Graaff, J. de V. Three notes on "Expec-
tation in economics." II. R. Ec N.S.16:
338-42 Nov 49
Formalisation of Mr. Harrod's model.
EJ 59:625-29 Dec 49
BAUSMAN, ROBERT O.
Social aspects of land use in Delaware.
JFE 22:637-40 Aug 40
Merits and limitations of some of the meas-
ures of land classes. JFE 23:899-903
Nov 41
and Munroe, J. A. James Tilton's notes on
the agriculture of Delaware in 1788.
AH 20:176-87 Jul 46
BAYARD, C. C.
The defective United States retail price
structure. SEJ 11:1-19 Jul 44
BAYKOV, ALEXANDER
Development of industrial production in the
U.S.S.R. Ec N.S.8:94-103 Feb 41
The location of heavy industry in the U.S.S.R.
OIS 3:252-56 Aug 9, 41
Remarks on the experience in the organisa-
tion of "war economy" in the U.S.S.R.
EJ 51:422-38 Dec 41
Russia's economic losses. OIS 4:245-47
Sep 19, 42
A note on the trend of population and the
labour problems of the U.S.S.R. JRSS 106:
349-59 pt.4, 43
BEACH, EARL FRANCIS
A measurement of the productive capacity of
wealth. CJE 7:538-44 Nov 41
Triffin's classification of market positions.
CJE 9:69-74 Feb 43
The use of polynomials to represent cost
functions. REStud 16:158-69 no.3, 49
BEACHAM, ARTHUR
The Ulster linen industry. Ec N.S.11:
199-209 Nov 44
Post-war planning in the Ulster linen indus-
try. EJ 55:114-21 Apr 45
Efficiency and organisation of the British
coal industry. EJ 55:206-16 Jun-Sep 45
The coalfields of Britain. R. EJ 56:319-25
Jun 46
BEALE, W. T. M., Jr.; Kennedy, M. T. and
Winn, W. J.
Commodity reserve currency: a critique.
JPE 50:579-94 Aug 42
BEALES, R. E.
Industrial classification, national and inter-
national. JRSS 112:316-30 pt.3, 49

BEAN, LOUIS HYMAN
The use of the short-cut graphic method of
multiple correlation: comment. QJE 54:
318-31 Feb 40
Postwar output in the United States at full
employment. REStat 27:202-03 Nov 45
Relation of disposable income and the busi-
ness cycle to expenditures. REStat 28:
199-207 Nov 46
Wholesale prices and industrial stock prices
during and immediately after the two
world wars. REStat 29:199-200 Aug 47
BEAN, ROBERT W.
European multilateral clearing. JPE 56:
403-15 Oct 48
BEATTIE, J. R.
Some aspects of the problem of full employ-
ment. CJE 10:328-42 Aug 44
BEATTIE, T. EUGENE
Public relations and the chains. JM 7:245-55
Jan 43
and Converse, P. D. Are chain stores good
citizens? JM 8:172-84 Oct 43
Comments on marketing in southern Italy.
JM 9:269-74 Jan 45
The American soldier as a purchaser in
southern Italy. JM 9:384-86 Apr 45
Observations on southern Italy. AH 19:120-26
Apr 45
BECK, MORRIS
British anti-inflationary tax on distributed
corporate profits. NTJ 1:275-77 Sep 48
BECK, PHILIP GARRETT and Jensen, J. C.
Contributions of Farm Security Administra-
tion borrowers to agricultural production
goals: the corn-belt states. JFE 25:
101-04 Feb 43
BECKER, ARTHUR PETER
Fixed dividends for all public utility stock.
LE 21:243-49 Aug 45
Psychological production and conservation.
QJE 63:577-83 Nov 49
BECKER, HARRY
Labor's approach to the retirement problem.
IRRA 2:116-26 Dec 49
BECKER, JOSEPH A.
Agricultural statistics: discussion. JFE 22:
366-68 Feb 40
Problems in estimating food production in
wartime. JASA 39:30-34 Mar 44
with Black, J. D. and Taeuber, C. The recla-
mation of flooded areas of Holland. JFE 28:
1070-75 Nov 46
BECKERATH, HERBERT von
Interrelations between moral and economic
factors in the postwar world. AER/S 34:
25-40 Mar 44
Economic planning in the welfare state.
WA 63:49-79 Hft.1, 49
BECKETT, GRACE
The problem of reclassification in the recip-
rocal trade agreements. JPE 48:199-209
Apr 40
Effect of the reciprocal trade agreements

BECKETT, GRACE (Cont.)
upon the foreign trade of the United States.
QJE 55:80-94 Nov 40
A statistical note on the trade agreements
program. JM 5:280-82 Jan 41
Commerce on the Great Lakes system.
JM 8:426-29 Apr 44
Comments on Alaska's trade. JM 10:291-93
Jan 46
Foreign trade by air. JM 12:505-06 Apr 48
BECKHART, BENJAMIN HAGGOTT
Monetary policies and commercial bank
portfolios. AER/S 30:17-26 Mar 40
[and others] What can Europe do for itself?
Discussion. JF 3,no.1:31-40 Feb 48
BECKLEY, DONALD K.
Appraising professional training for retailing.
JM 14:38-45 Jul 49
BECKMAN, THEODORE N.
chairman. Round table on recent books on
consumption. [Note concerning the ses-
sion] AER/S 30:399 Mar 40
Significant trends in wholesaling. JM 5:
218-20 Jan 41
Significant current trends in wholesaling.
JM 6,no.4,pt.2:9-11 Apr 42
Large versus small business after the war.
AER/S 34:94-106 Mar 44
BECKWITH, BURNHAM P.
Comments on Professor Spengler's article
"Sociological presuppositions in economic
theory." SEJ 7:398-99 Jan 41
BEECROFT, R. M.
and Walker, E. R. New developments in
Australia's war economy. ER 17:1-18
Jun 41
and Walker, E. R. Changes in the stock of
Australian money. ER 17:210-17 Dec 41
BEERS, JOHN STERLING DE
see De Beers, John Sterling
BEHLING, BURTON NEUBERT
Differential pricing of public utility services.
JM 6,no.4,pt.2:168-70 Apr 42
BEHOTEGUY, W. C.
Resale price maintenance in the tire indus-
try. JM 13:315-20 Jan 49
BEHRENDT, WALTER CURT
Off-street parking: a city planning problem.
LE 16:464-67 Nov 40
BEHRMAN, JACK N.
A reappraisal of the United Kingdom's bal-
ance of payments problem under full em-
ployment. SEJ 14:173-85 Oct 47
The short-term interest rate and the velocity
of circulation. Em 16:185-90 Apr 48;
Addendum. 370 Oct 48
BEKENSTEIN, ARTHUR L.
A theoretical analysis of consumer co-opera-
tives: the managerial problem. JPE 51:
251-57 Jun 43
BELFER, NATHAN
and Bloom, G. F. Unions and real labor in-
come. SEJ 14:290-303 Jan 48

Financial resources of trade-unions.
JPE 57:157-61 Apr 49
The theory of the automatic reabsorption of
technologically displaced labor. SEJ 16:
35-43 Jul 49
Implications of capital-saving inventions.
SR 16:353-65 Sep 49
BELL, HARRY H.
Short-run equilibrium in the balance of pay-
ments. SEJ 8:366-79 Jan 42
BELL, JAMES WASHINGTON
Dewey dinner and testimonial. AER/S 30,
no.5:v-vi Feb 41
chairman. What should be the relative
spheres of private business and govern-
ment in our postwar American economy?
Symposium by past presidents of AEA.
AER/S 34:288-309 Mar 44
The function of government in postwar
American economy: a report on an experi-
ment by an ad hoc consensus committee.
AER/S 35:422-47 May 45
Domestic and international monetary policies.
A summary of the discussion of the re-
sults of a poll. AER/S 36:214-40 May 46
Report of ad hoc Committee on Monetary
Policy. (Economic opinion and public
policy) AER/S 36:807-16 May 46
BELLAMY, R.
The changing pattern of retail distribution.
OIS 8:237-60 Aug 46
Size and success in retail distribution.
OIS 8:324-39 Oct 46
Private & social cost in retail distribution.
OIS 8:345-51 Nov 46
BELLEY, BERNARD
Toward a measure of pharmaceutical adver-
tising effectiveness. JB 16:107-14 Apr 43
BELSHAW, HORACE
New Zealand in the post-war world: recon-
struction problems of a vulnerable econ-
omy. CJE 11:388-401 Aug 45
[and others] Economic problems of foreign
areas: discussion. AER/S 36:650-60
May 46
Observations on industrialisation for higher
incomes. EJ 57:379-87 Sep 47
BENEDICT, MURRAY REED
The British program for farm labor as a
contribution to American thinking on the
subject. JFE 22:714-28 Nov 40
and Adams, R. L. Methods of wage determination in agriculture. JFE 23:71-88 Feb 41
Schisms in agricultural policy: agriculture
as a commercial industry comparable to
other branches of the economy. JFE 24:
476-96 May 42
Agriculture when war ends: discussion.
JFE 25:322-25 Feb 43
[and others] Need for a new classification
of farms. JFE 26:694-708 Nov 44
The regulation of public to private lending
agencies (in agriculture) and recent

BENEDICT, MURRAY REED (Cont.)
trends in their development. JFE 27:
88-103 Feb 45
chairman. The federally sponsored credit
services to American agriculture: sug-
gestions for improvement and coordina-
tion. A report of a research committee.
JFE 29:1429-1505 Nov 47
The social sciences in experiment station re-
search. JFE 31:253-65 May 49
BENHAM, FREDERIC
The terms of trade. Ec N.S.7:360-76 Nov 40
"The taxation of war wealth." R. Ec N.S.8:
321-24 Aug 41
Wartime control of prices. R. Ec N.S.9:
58-63 Feb 42
What is the best tax-system? Ec N.S.9:
115-26 May 42
The muddle of the thirties. Ec N.S.12:1-9
Feb 45
Full employment and international trade.
Ec N.S.13:159-68 Aug 46
The rubber industry. R. Ec N.S.16:355-68
Nov 49
BENJAMIN, HAROLD S.
The Dow theory of stock prices. SR 9:204-24
May 42
BENNER, CLAUDE LEON
Financing agriculture: discussion. JFE 22:
158-61 Feb 40
BENNETT, ARCHIBALD S.
Some aspects of preparing questionnaires.
JM 10:175-79 Oct 45
Toward a solution of the "cheater problem"
among part-time research investigators.
JM 12:470-74 Apr 48
BENNETT, JOHN B.
A desirable wartime land policy. JFE 25:
166-75 Feb 43
BENNETT, MERRILL KELLEY
Essential food requirements in wartime.
JFE 25:835-47 Nov 43
A price policy for agriculture, consistent
with economic progress, that will promote
adequate and more stable income from
farming: an insurance price system.
JFE 27:790-97 Nov 45
Food and agriculture in the Soviet Union,
1917-48. JPE 57:185-98 Jun 49
BENNETT, VICTOR W.
Consumers and the Greenbelt cooperative.
JM 6:3-10 Jul 41
Consumer buying habits in a small town
located between two large cities. JM 8:
405-16 Apr 44
BENNION, EDWARD GRAHAM
Unemployment in the theories of Schumpeter
and Keynes. AER 33:336-47 Jun 43
Is unemployment chronic? HBR 23:115-28
no.1, 44
The multiplier, the acceleration principle,
and fluctuating autonomous investment.
REStat 27:85-92 May 45

The consumption function: cyclically vari-
able? REStat 28:219-24 Nov 46
BENOIT, EMILE
Net investment, consumption and full em-
ployment. AER 34:871-79 Dec 44
Seventeen post-war plans: the Pabst post-
war employment awards. AER 35:120-27
Mar 45
Interest-free deficit financing and full em-
ployment. AER 37:397-99 Jun 47
Public works in the depression. AER 38:
134-39 Mar 48
On the meaning of full employment.
REStat 30:127-34 May 48
BENSON, ARNOLD P.
State frontiers in agricultural statistics.
JFE 31,pt.2:293-304 Feb 49
BENSON, C. B. and Kimball, B. F.
Mortality characteristics of physical prop-
erty based upon location life table and re-
use ratios. Em 13:214-24 Jul 45
BENTWICH, NORMAN DE MATTOS
From Geneva to Yalta: the foundations of
the new international order. EgC 36:
285-92 Mar 45
BERESFORD, MAURICE WARWICK
Lot acres. EHR 13:74-79 no.1-2, 43
Commissioners of enclosure. EHR 16:
130-40 no.2, 46
Ridge and furrow and the open fields.
EHR II.1:34-45 no.1, 48
BERGE, WENDELL
Monopoly and the South. SEJ 13:360-69
Apr 47
Problems of enforcement and interpretation
of the Sherman Act. AER/S 38:172-81
May 48
The effectiveness of the federal antitrust
laws: a symposium. AER 39:691 Jun 49
BERGEN, HAROLD B.
Management prerogatives. HBR 18:275-84
no.3, 40
BERGER, ALFRED VIKTOR
Consistent reflation in Egypt and the high
costs of living. EgC 38:177-85 Mar-Apr 47
Problems of a Catholic economic science.
RSE 7,no.2:39-42 Sep 49
BERGER-VOESENDORF, A.
see Berger, Alfred Victor
BERGFELD, ALBERT J. and Young, E. C.
Methods employed in an analysis of the
spread between farm and consumer milk
prices in New York City. JFE 31,pt.2:
1194-1202 Nov 49
BERGSON, ABRAM
The incidence of an income tax on saving.
QJE 56:337-41 Feb 42
Distribution of the earnings bill among in-
dustrial workers in the Soviet Union
March, 1928; October, 1934. JPE 50:
227-49 Apr 42
Prices, wages, and income theory. Em 10:
275-89 Jul-Oct 42

BERGSON, ABRAM (Cont.)
Price flexibility and the level of income.
REStat 25:2-5 Feb 43
The economy of the U.S.S.R.: discussion.
AER/S 37:643-46 May 47
A problem in Soviet statistics. REStat 29:
234-42 Nov 47
BERGSTROM, A. R.
The guaranteed price for dairy products:
New Zealand. ER 25,(no.49):91-97
Dec 49
BERI, SHRIDHAR GOVIND
Price trends during the last decade and their
effects on Indian economy. IJE 21:734-84
Apr 41
Co-operative multi-purpose society. IJE 22:
515-31 Jan 42
BERLE, ADOLF AUGUSTUS, Jr.
Government function in a stabilized economy.
AER/S 33:27-38 Mar 43
The Marshall Plan in the European struggle.
SR 15:1-21 Mar 48
BERNARDELLI, HARRO
Some comment on a dynamic theory of for-
eign exchanges. IJE 23:301-18 Apr 43
BERNAYS, EDWARD L.
An educational program for unions. ILRR 1:
103-09 Oct 47
BERNHARD, RICHARD CARLTON
Myths and illogic in popular notions about
business cycles. JPE 51:53-60 Feb 43
BERNSTEIN, EDWARD MORRIS
Exchange rates under the gold standard.
JPE 48:345-56 Jun 40
War and the pattern of business cycles.
AER 30:524-35 Sep 40
A practical international monetary policy.
AER 34:771-84 Dec 44
Scarce currencies and the International
Monetary Fund. JPE 53:1-14 Mar 45
British policy and a world economy. AER 35:
891-908 Dec 45
BERNSTEIN, IRVING
Labor and the recovery program, 1933.
QJE 60:270-88 Feb 46
Recent legislative developments affecting
mediation and arbitration. ILRR 1:406-20
Apr 48
and Warren, E. L. The mediation process.
SEJ 15:441-57 Apr 49
BERNSTEIN, PETER LEWYN
Federal Reserve policy and federal debt: a
comment. AER 39:1278-81 Dec 49
BERREMAN, JOEL V.
Advertising and the sale of novels. JM 7:
234-40 Jan 43
BERRY, THOMAS SENIOR
On measuring the cost of life insurance.
JASA 35:631-43 Dec 40
BERTHEIM, C. SIDNEY
Housing in France. LE 24:49-62 Feb 48
BERTRAND, ALVIN L.
A dilemma of land use. LE 18:220-22 May 42

and Mason, J. E. Tenure status of new-
ground settlers in Louisiana. LE 19:
233-38 May 43
BESSE, ARTHUR
The current status of wool textiles. HBR 20:
223-32 no.2, 42
BESTOR, PAUL
Agricultural credit: discussion. JFE 23:
67-70 Feb 41
BETTMAN, ALFRED
A backward step in zoning. LE 16:455-57
Nov 40
BEVERIDGE, Sir WILLIAM HENRY
The trade cycle in Britain before 1850.
OEP 3:74-109 Feb 40
--- A postcript. OEP 4:63-76 Sep 40
[Communication on Lord Keynes's elevation
to the Peerage.] EJ 52:267-68 Jun-Sep 42
Social security: some trans-Atlantic com-
parisons. JRSS 106:305-21 pt.4, 43
The Government's employment policy. EJ 54:
161-76 Jun-Sep 44
Sir Hubert Llewellyn Smith (1864-1945).
[obit.] EJ 56:143-47 Mar 46
Life, liberty, and the pursuit of happiness
(1950 model). R. REStat 28:53-59 May 46
Sidney Webb (Lord Passfield 1859-1947).
[obit.] EJ 58:428-34 Sep 48
BEVILLE, HUGH MALCOLM, Jr.
Surveying radio listeners by use of a prob-
ability sample. JM 14:373-78 Oct 49
BEYER, ROBERT CARLYLE
The marketing history of Colombian coffee.
AH 23:279-85 Oct 49
BEZANSON, ANNE
Inflation and controls, Pennsylvania, 1774-
1779. JEH/S 8:1-20 '48
BHAN, R.
The Indian food problem. IJE 26:744-47
Apr 46
BHAN, R. K.
Prices in India between the two great wars.
IJE 21:785-97 Apr 41
BHAT, ATMARAM RAOJI
Regulation of organisation and management
of Indian joint stock banks. IJE 25:510-20
Apr 45
BHATANAGAR, BRIJ GOPAL
see Bhatnagar, Brij Gopal
BHATHERA, S. S.
The organisation of rural welfare. IJE 22:
807-19 Jan 42
BHATIA, AMAR CHAND
Labour unrest in India. IJE 20:617-29
Apr 40
BHATIA, BALMOKAND
The method of study. IJE 20:505-12 Apr 40
BHATNAGAR, BRIJ GOPAL
[and others] Discussions of the scope and
method of economics. IJE 20:810-21
Apr 40
Scope of economics. IJE 20:645-47 Apr 40

BHATTACHARYA, KHAGENDRA NATH
Will India face a slump? An aspect in trans-
ition economy. IJE 25:242-47 Jan 45
Economic control in India during and after
the war. IJE 25:541-45 Apr 45
Price stabilisation. IJE 26:296-99 Oct 45
Stabilisation of prices: an aspect of the post-
war currency system in India. IJE 26:
404-09 Jan 46
Some aspects of India's commercial policy.
IJE 28:17-21 Jul 47
Budgets and planning in India. IJE 29:131-34
Oct 48
India's balance of trade: a case for devalua-
tion. IJE 30:139-47 Oct 49
BHATTACHARYA, SUKUMAR and Chaturvedi,
H. K.
Industrial relations in India. IJE 29:277-88
Jan 49
BHIDE, H. B.
Scope of economics. IJE 20:423-32 Apr 40
BHOJWANI, N. K.
The financial situation in Sind. IJE 21:
892-900 Apr 41
Post-war implications of India's sterling
credits. IJE 25:1-14 Jul 44
BIDWELL, PERCY WELLS
chairman. Round table on problems of
American commercial policy. AER/S 30:
118-23 Mar 40
Professor Litman's review of The invisible
tariff. AER 30:353 Jun 40
A postwar commercial policy for the United
States. AER/S 34:340-53 Mar 44
International Trade Organization: discussion.
AER/S 37:554-56 May 47
BIERLY, IVAN R.
and Young, E. C. The future of farm work
simplification research. JFE 28:331-37
Feb 46
and Hoff, P. R. Work simplification: a joint
problem for management, engineering, and
commodity specialists. JFE 29:219-24
Feb 47
BIGELOW, CHARLES L.
Elements of confusion in newspaper reader-
ship study. JM 12:337-47 Jan 48
BIGELOW, JOHN O.
Is an industrial relations consultant engaged
in unauthorized practice of law? ILRR 1:
130-34 Oct 47
BIGHAM, TRUMAN C.
Comment on the Pacific Gas and Electric
case. AER 30:351-52 Jun 40
The Transportation Act of 1940. SEJ 8:
1-21 Jul 41
Regulation of minimum rates in transporta-
tion. QJE 61:206-31 Feb 47
BILLINGTON, RAY ALLEN
The origin of the land speculator as a
frontier type. AH 19:204-12 Oct 45
BINDOFF, STANLEY THOMAS
Clement Armstrong and his treatises of the
Commonweal. EHR 14:64-73 no.1, 44

BIRCH, ANTHONY HAROLD
Federalism and finance. MS 17:163-85
May 49
BIRD, FREDERICK LUCIEN
The financial problems of cities. AER/S 32:
323-30 Mar 42
BISHOP, PHILIP WILLIAM
Some problems of research methods. EEH 2:
46-49 Nov 49
BISHOP, ROBERT LYLE
Consumer's surplus and cardinal utility.
QJE 57:421-49 May 43
Professor Knight and the theory of demand.
JPE 54:141-69 Apr 46
Cost discontinuities, declining costs, and
marginal analysis. AER 38:607-17 Sep 48
BISSELL, RICHARD MERVIN, Jr.
Price and wage policies and the theory of
employment. Em 8:199-239 Jul 40
Prices, costs, and investment. AER/S 30,
no.5:200-27 Feb 41
[and others] Trade unions and the law:
discussion. AER/S 32:476-89 Mar 42
BITTERMANN, HENRY JOHN
Adam Smith's empiricism and the law of
nature. Pt.I-II. JPE 48:487-520; 703-34
Aug,Oct 40
BITTING, HERBERT WAYNE
National consumer preference study for
potatoes. JFE 31,pt.2:620-25 Feb 49
BJORKA, KNUTE
Regional research in agricultural marketing.
JFE 27:121-37 Feb 45
BJORN, WALTER
Low-cost hospitalization protection. HBR 22:
256-64 no.2, 44
BLACK, ALBERT GAIN
Some current problems in agricultural credit.
JFE 23:37-51 Feb 41
Wartime developments in farm credit and
their postwar implications. JFE 26:124-38
Feb 44
Iranian agriculture, present and prospective.
JFE 30:422-42 Aug 48
BLACK, DUNCAN
On the rationale of group decision-making.
JPE 56:23-34 Feb 48
The decisions of a committee using a special
majority. Em 16:245-61 Jul 48
The elasticity of committee decisions with an
altering size of majority. Em 16:262-70
Jul 48
The elasticity of committee decisions with
alterations in the members' preference
schedules. SAJE 17:88-102 Mar 49
BLACK, JOHN DONALD
[County planning project]: discussion.
JFE 22:301-05 Feb 40
[The scale of agricultural production.]
Rejoinder. QJE 54:316-17 Feb 40
and Malenbaum, W. [The use of the short-
cut graphic method of multiple correla-
tion.] Rejoinder. QJE 54:346-58 Feb 40

BLACK, JOHN DONALD (Cont.)
and Kirkpatrick, N. B. The agricultural
situation, March 1940. REStat 22:53-73
May 40
Dr. Schultz on farm management research.
JFE 22:570-80 Aug 40
Training and recruitment of agricultural
economic personnel. V. For public service. JFE 22:560-61 Aug 40
American agriculture in the new war and
defense situation. JFE 23:28-36 Feb 41
Measures for the improvement of agriculture. AER/S 30,no.5:165-76 Feb 41
Fundamental elements in the current agricultural situation. JFE 23:712-25 Nov 41
Transitions to the post-war agricultural
economy. JFE 24:52-70 Feb 42
and Clawson, M. Agricultural income and
the export market, 1910-1940. JFE 24:
761-71 Nov 42
Agricultural price policy, January 1943.
JFE 25:1-14 Feb 43
[Industrial wage policies and farm price
parity]: discussion. JFE 25:64 Feb 43
The international food movement. AER 33:
791-811 Dec 43
The food situation, May, 1943. HBR 21:
397-414 no.4, 43
and Gibbons, C. A. The war and American
agriculture. REStat 26:1-55 Feb 44
and Tsou, S. S. International commodity arrangements. QJE 58:521-52 Aug 44
The relation of wages to net farm income,
1929-42 and 1939-42. JFE 26:572-78
Aug 44
and MacDonald, A. Cost of living on farms
and prices paid by farmers. JASA 39:
377-86 Sep 44
and Hyson, C. D. Postwar soldier settlement. QJE 59:1-35 Nov 44
Land-Grant College Post-war agricultural
policy. R. JFE 27:168-75 Feb 45
Notes on "poor land," and "submarginal
land." JFE 27:345-74 May 45
Agricultural credit policy in the United
States, 1945. JFE 27:591-614 Aug 45
National income and farm income. JFE 28:
560-62 May 46
Tailored credit for land improvements.
JFE 28:596-604 May 46
The income elasticity of milk. JFE 28:
845-48 Aug 46
Professor Schultz and C.E.D. on agricultural
policy in 1945. R. JFE 28:669-86 Aug 46
Notes on developments in agricultural policy
and program in the United Kingdom.
JFE 28:1005-15 Nov 46
with Becker, J. A. and Taeuber, C. The
reclamation of flooded areas of Holland.
JFE 28:1070-75 Nov 46
[Food, agriculture, and trade.] Review of
Professor Schultz's paper. JFE 29:
20-25 Feb 47

The future of government in the farm mort-
gage field. LE 23:1-11 Feb 47
Guideposts in the development of a market-
ing program. JFE 29:616-31 Aug 47
The Bureau of Agricultural Economics: the
years in between. JFE 29:1027-42 Nov 47
Provision for nutrition in the formulation of
agricultural programs. JFE 30:703-12
Nov 48
Coming readjustments in agriculture:
domestic phases. JFE 31:1-15 Feb 49
BLACK, R. D. COLLISON
Trinity College, Dublin, and the theory of
value, 1832-1863. Ec N.S.12:140-48
Aug 45
BLACK, ROBERT F.
Wheels for defense. HBR 19:14-20 no.1, 40
BLACKBURN, BURR
Can we avoid consumer credit indigestion?
JM 4,no.4,pt.2:100-10 Apr 40
BLACKBURN, DEAN W.
Common grazing in the shortleaf pine-
loblolly pine- hardwoods portion of south
Arkansas. JFE 29:546-53 May 47
BLACKWELL, DAVID HAROLD; Arrow,
K. J. and Girshick, M. A.
Bayes and minimax solutions of sequen-
tial decision problems. Em 17:213-44
Jul-Oct 49
BLADEN, VINCENT WHEELER
Tariff policy and employment in depression.
CJE 6:72-78 Feb 40
Report on an alleged combine in the paper
board shipping container industry.
CJE 6:293-96 May 40
The history of economic ideas. R. CJE 7:
100-08 Feb 41
Mill to Marshall: the conversion of the econ-
omists. JEH/S 1:17-29 Dec 41
On population. R. CJE 8:273-88 May 42
Sir William Flux, 1867-1942. [obit.] CJE 9:
74-75 Feb 43
The Combines Investigation Commission and
post-war reconstruction. CJE 10:343-54
Aug 44
[and others] International cartels: discus-
sion. AER/S 36:768-83 May 46
Provision for social research. R. CJE 13:
287-92 May 47
Economics and human relations. CJE 14:
301-11 Aug 48
The centenary of Marx and Mill. JEH/S 8:
32-41 '48
John Stuart Mill's Principles: a centenary
estimate. AER/S 39:1-12 May 49
BLAIR, IAN DOUGLAS
Wartime problems of English agriculture.
AH 15:12-19 Jan 41
BLAIR, JOHN MALCOLM
The relation between size and efficiency of
business. REStat 24:125-35 Aug 42
Price discrimination in steel: a reply.
AER 33:369-70 Jun 43

BLAIR, JOHN MALCOLM (Cont.)
Technology and size. AER/S 38:121-52
May 48
BLAISDELL, THOMAS C., Jr.
Industrial concentration in the war.
AER/S 33:159-61 Mar 43
BLAKEY, GLADYS CAMPBELL
see entries under Blakey, Roy Gillispie and
Blakey, G. C.
BLAKEY, ROY GILLISPIE
The federal income tax, a reply to the
review. JASA 35:698-700 Dec 40
and Blakey, G. C. The two federal revenue
acts of 1940. AER 30:724-35 Dec 40
and Blakey, G. C. The Revenue Act of 1941.
AER 31:809-22 Dec 41
chairman. Co-ordination of federal, state,
and local fiscal systems. Abstract of
specialized conference discussion.
AER/S 32:214-15 Mar 42
Post-war tax policy: discussion. AER/S 36:
275-79 May 46
--- [idem] JF 1:76-80 Aug 46
BLAND, JOHN
[The education of planners.] At McGill
University. LE 21:315-16 Sep 45
BLANKENSHIP, ALBERT BRENEMAN
The case for and against the public opinion
poll. JM 5:110-13 Oct 40
Psychological difficulties in measuring con-
sumer preference. JM 6,no.4,pt.2:66-75
Apr 42
The movement of people: a field for market
research. JM 13:44-51 Jul 48
Needed: a broader concept of marketing re-
search. JM 13:305-10 Jan 49
chairman. Questionnaire preparation and
interviewer technique. [Report of a sub-
committee] JM 14:399-433 Oct 49
BLAU, GERDA
Some aspects of the theory of futures trading.
REStud 12:1-30 no.1, 44
Wool in the world economy. JRSS 109:179-235
pt.3, 46
BLISS, CHARLES ANDRESSEN
Statistics takes a second breath. HBR 18:
510-19 no.4, 40
Our trade to South America. HBR 20:107-15
no.1, 41
and McNeill, R. B. Management control in
uniform. HBR 22:227-38 no.2, 44
The reality of inventory profits. HBR 26:
527-42 Sep 48
Some field notes on freight absorption.
HBR 26:656-70 Nov 48
A history of Pepperell. R. BHR 23:104-06
Jun 49
BLOCH, HENRI SIMON
Carl Menger: the founder of the Austrian
school. JPE 48:428-33 Jun 40
Gaëtan Pirou. [obit.] AER 37:192-93 Mar 47
BLOCH, KURT
Whither Japan? SR 8:173-88 May 41

BLOCK, HERBERT
Subcontracting in German defense industries.
SR 9:4-21 Feb 42
German methods of allocating raw materials.
SR 9:356-70 Sep 42
Industrial concentration versus small busi-
ness: the trend of Nazi policy. SR 10:
175-99 May 43
Man-power allocation in Germany. HBR 21:
259-68 no.2, 43
European transportation under German rule.
SR 11:216-41 May 44
BLODGETT, RALPH HAMILTON
chairman. Round table on problems in the
teaching of economics. AER/S 30,no.5:
416-21 Feb 41
The impact of total war. AER/S 36:126-38
May 46
BLOOM, GORDON F.
A reconsideration of the theory of exploita-
tion. QJE 55:413-42 May 41
Technical progress, costs and rent.
Ec N.S.9:40-52 Feb 42
Wage policies and wage trends in the war
boom. AER 33:892-97 Dec 43
A note on Hicks's theory of invention.
AER 36:83-96 Mar 46
and Belfer, N. Unions and real labor income.
SEJ 14:290-303 Jan 48
BLOOM, SOLOMON F.
Man of his century: a reconsideration of the
historical significance of Karl Marx.
JPE 51:494-505 Dec 43
BLOOMBERG, LAWRENCE NELSON
Rent control and the housing shortage.
LE 23:214-18 May 47
BLOOMFIELD, ARTHUR IRVING
The significance of outstanding securities in
the international movement of capital.
CJE 6:495-524 Nov 40
The mechanism of adjustment of the Ameri-
can balance of payments: 1919-1929.
QJE 57:333-77 May 43
Operations of the American exchange stabili-
zation fund. REStat 26:69-87 May 44
Postwar control of international capital
movements. AER/S 36:687-709 May 46
[and others] Domestic versus international
equilibrium: discussion. AER/S 37:
581-94 May 47
Induced investment, overcomplete inter-
national adjustment, and chronic dollar
shortage. AER 39:970-75 Sep 49
BLOOR, W. F.
Postwar rubber industry capacities and
implications. JM 10:279-81 Jan 46
BLOUGH, ROY
Economic research and tax policy.
AER/S 34,no.2:1-21 Jun 44
Federal-state fiscal relations. NTJ 1:273-74
Sep 48
Measurement problems of the excess profits
tax. NTJ 1:353-65 Dec 48

BLUHM, HILDE OPPENHEIMER-
see Oppenheimer-Bluhm, Hilde

BLUM, FRED H.
Marginalism and economic policy: a comment. AER 37:645-52 Sep 47
Action research and industrial relations. IRRA 2:248-54 Dec 49

BLUM, JEROME
Land tenure in the Austrian Monarchy before 1848. AH 19:87-98 Apr 45

BLUM, LESTER
Job analysis in agriculture. JFE 27:195-204 Feb 45
The elementary course. JFE 29:278-82 Feb 47

BLUM, ROBERT
Exemption of small rural telephone companies from the Wage and Hour Act. LE 16:117-20 Feb 4C
SEC integration of holding company systems. LE 17:423-39 Nov 41

BLUM, WALTER J.
Tax policy in a democratic society. NTJ 2: 97-109 Jun 49

BLUMENFELD, HANS
A neglected factor in estimating housing demand. LE 20:264-70 Aug 44
Addendum: on Russia's mineral resources. LE 23:439 Nov 47
Correlation between value of dwelling units and altitude. LE 24:396-402 Nov 48
On the concentric-circle theory of urban growth. LE 25:209-12 May 49

BLUMER, HERBERT
Group tension and interest organizations. IRRA 2:150-64 Dec 49

BLYTH, C. D.
Some aspects of Canada's international financial relations. CJE 12:302-12 Aug 46

BOALS, GORDON PORTER
A price policy for agriculture, consistent with economic progress, that will promote adequate and more stable income from farming. JFE 27:798-806 Nov 45

BOBER, MANDELL MORTON
Price and production policies. AER/S 32, no.2:23-52 Jun 42
Marx and economic calculation. AER 36: 344-57 Jun 46
[and others] The sociology and economics of class conflict: discussion. AER/S 39: 37-46 May 49

BOBER, WILLIAM CURT
The construction industry after the war. HBR 20:427-36 no.4, 42

BODDY, FRANCIS MURRAY [and others]
The changing structure of the American economy: discussion. AER/S 36:80-92 May 46

BODDY, NORA
see Kirkpatrick, Nora Boddy

BODE, KARL
Plan analysis and process analysis. AER 33: 348-54 Jun 43

A note on the mathematical co-incidence of the instantaneous and the serial multiplier. REStat 26:221-22 Nov 44

BODFISH, MORTON
Translating research into progress through the Journal of land and public utility economics. LE 18:82-84 Feb 42

BOEHL, A.
The reconstruction boom in Switzerland. OIS 9:18-20 Jan 47

BOGUE, ALLAN
The progress of the cattle industry in Ontario during the eighteen eighties. AH 21:163-68 Jul 47

BOGUE, DON J. and Hawley, A. H.
Recent shifts in population: the drift toward the metropolitan district, 1930-40. REStat 24:143-48 Aug 42

BOLDT, JOSEPH R., Jr. and George, J. J.
Certification of motor common carriers by the Interstate Commerce Commission. Pt.I-II. LE 17:82-91; 196-206 Feb, May 41

BOLES, WALTER E., Jr.
Some aspects of the Fair Labor Standards Act. SEJ 6:498-511 Apr 40

BOLLINGER, LYNN LOUIS
Dealing with Uncle Sam. HBR 19:211-20 no.2, 41
Is subcontracting the answer? HBR 20: 171-83 no.2, 42
and Lilley, T. Maintaining a strong aircraft industry. HBR 22:178-90 no.2, 44
Marketing personal airplanes. HBR 23: 217-28 no.2, 45
with Lilley, T. and Lombard, A. E., Jr. Preserving American air power. HBR 23: 372-92 no.3, 45
Private versus public management of airports. HBR 24:518-34 no.4, 46

BONBRIGHT, JAMES CUMMINGS
Major controversies as to the criteria of reasonable public utility rates. AER/S 30, no.5:379-89 Feb 41
Power aspects of the St. Lawrence waterway. CJE 8:176-85 May 42
The depreciation reserve as a measure of actual accrued depreciation. LE 20: 98-100 May 44
Rate-making policies of federal power projects. AER/S 36:426-34 May 46
Utility rate control reconsidered in the light of the Hope Natural Gas case. AER/S 38: 465-82 May 48

BOND, MAURICE CHESTER and Gillett, R. L.
Data needs for agricultural research and marketing. JFE 30:271-81 May 48

BONHAM, HARRY D.
The prospect for heavy industry in the South. SEJ 13:395-403 Apr 47

BONN, MORITZ, J.
Planning for peace. AER/S 30:272-80 Mar 40

BONNÉ, ALFRED
Movement of population and economic expan-

BONNÉ, ALFRED (Cont.)
    sion in the Middle East. EgC 33:319-35
        Apr 42
BONNELL, ALLEN THOMAS
    The post-war international economic order.
        SEJ 9:46-52 Jul 42
BONNEN, C. A.
    Alternatives to cotton production: discussion.
        JFE 23:124-26 Feb 41
    Food and fiber production: discussion.
        JFE 26:211-13 Feb 44
    Measuring food needs: discussion. JFE 26:
        193-95 Feb 44
BONNER, JAMES C.
    The plantation overseer and southern nation-
        alism as revealed in the career of Gar-
        land D. Harmon. AH 19:1-11 Jan 45
    The Angora goat: a footnote in southern ag-
        ricultural history. AH 21:42-46 Jan 47
    Advancing trends in southern agriculture,
        1840-1860. AH 22:248-59 Oct 48
BOOKER, HAROLD S.
    Income tax and incentive to effort.
        Ec N.S.12:243-47 Nov 45
    Lady Rhys Williams' proposals for the
        amalgamation of direct taxation with
        social insurance. R. EJ 56:230-43 Jun 46
    The distribution of income under full employ-
        ment. MS 15:75-92 Jan 47
    Have we a full employment policy?
        Ec N.S.14:37-47 Feb 47
    A note on deferred export credits. EJ 59:
        253-58 Jun 49
BOOKHOUT, BYRON REID
    Haymaking job analysis. JFE 29:761-67
        Aug 47
BOONSTRA, CLARENCE A.
    and Campbell, J. R. Land classification,
        land-use areas, and farm management
        research. JFE 23:657-64 Aug 41
    Note on part-time farming. JFE 23:893-95
        Nov 41
BOOTH, JOHN FRANKLIN
    William Allen, 1892-1941. [obit.] JFE 23:
        694-95 Aug 41
    Post-war economy: discussion. JFE 24:
        70-74 Feb 42
    The economic problems of Canadian agricul-
        ture in the war and post-war period.
        CJE 8:446-59 Aug 42
BOPP, KARL RICHARD
    Central banking at the crossroads. AER/S 34:
        260-77 Mar 44
    The Bank of England. R. CJE 11:616-27
        Nov 45
BORAK, ARTHUR MARTIN
    Tax equivalents of municipal electric utili-
        ties in Minnesota. LE 17:59-70 Feb 41
    Tax equivalents versus taxes of municipal
        and private utilities in Minnesota. LE 23:
        381-98 Nov 47
BORCHERT, JOHN R.
    The agriculture of England and Wales, 1939-
        1946. AH 22:56-62 Jan 48

BORDEN, NEIL HOPPER
    Findings of the Harvard study on the eco-
        nomic effects of advertising. JM 6,no.4,
        pt.2:89-99 Apr 42
    Use of newspapers by national advertisers.
        HBR 24:295-305 no.3, 46
    Selling newspaper space to national adver-
        tisers. HBR 24:438-52 no.4, 46
    Advertising branded parts to consumers.
        HBR 25:129-44 no.1, 46
    The new trade-mark law. HBR 25:289-305
        no.3, 47
BORDEN, SIDNEY
    Cost of living variations and the personal
        exemption from the income tax. NTJ 2:
        157-65 Jun 49
BORDERS, KARL
    The problems of determining fair rents.
        JASA 37:34-40 Mar 42
BORG, LLOYD E.
    The Minnesota poll. JM 9:381-84 Apr 45
BORG, WALTER T.
    Clifford V. Gregory and his writings.
        AH 16:116-22 Apr 42
    Food Administration experience with hogs,
        1917-19. JFE 25:444-57 May 43
BORGATTA, GINO
    Interest rate policy and reconstruction re-
        quirements. BNL 1:407-15 Oct 48
BORNEMANN, ALFRED
    Accounting profits: an institution. JPE 51:
        166-68 Apr 43
BORTON, WILLIAM M.
    Marketing research by Los Angeles indus-
        trial concerns. JM 14:450-52 Oct 49
BOSE, S. R.
    Price control. IJE 20:631-38 Apr 40
    A study in Bihar rural prices. IJE 23:167-74
        Oct 42
    Some investigations in banking, currency and
        prices. IJE 24:20-37 Jul 43
    Labour in wartime. IJE 24:179-91 Jan 44
    Price policy in war-time. IJE 24:225-38
        Apr 44
BOSLAND, CHELCIE CLAYTON
    The Investment Company Act of 1940 and its
        background. Pt.I-II. JPE 49:477-529;
        687-721 Jun,Oct 41
BOSS, ANDREW
    Forty years of farm cost accounting records.
        JFE 27:1-17 Feb 45
BOTTS, RALPH R.
    Development of "normal" citrus fruit yields
        by tree ages for use in a yield insurance
        plan. JFE 23:867-72 Nov 41
    Use of the annuity principle in transferring
        the farm from father to son. JFE 29:
        409-24 May 47
BOTTUM, JOE CARROLL
    and Young, E. C. Agricultural programs for
        the post-war period. JFE 24:17-26 Feb 42
    Stabilization of the general price level.
        JFE 29:1107-21 Nov 47

BOTTUM, JOE CARROLL (Cont.)

Useful techniques in an extension program in agricultural policy. JFE 31,pt.2:687-89 Feb 49

Making price research useful. JFE 31,pt.2: 1099-1101 Nov 49

BOULDING, KENNETH EWART

The theory of the firm in the last ten years. AER 32:791-802 Dec 42

Desirable changes in the national economy after the war. JFE 26:95-100 Feb 44

A liquidity preference theory of market prices. Ec N.S.11:55-63 May 44

The incidence of a profits tax. AER 34: 567-72 Sep 44

The consumption concept in economic theory. AER/S 35:1-14 May 45

In defense of monopoly. QJE 59:524-42 Aug 45

The concept of economic surplus. AER 35: 851-69 Dec 45; Errata. 36:393 Jun 46

[In defense of monopoly.] Reply. QJE 60: 619-21 Aug 46

A note on the theory of the black market. CJE 13:115-18 Feb 47

Economic analysis and agricultural policy. CJE 13:436-46 Aug 47

Price control in a subsequent deflation. REStat 30:15-17 Feb 48

Professor Tarshis and the state of economics. AER 38:92-102 Mar 48

[and others] Does large-scale enterprise lower costs: discussion. AER/S 38: 165-71 May 48

Samuelson's Foundations: the role of mathematics in economics. R. JPE 56: 187-99 Jun 48

[The net national product concept.] Comment on Mr. Burk's note. AER 38:899 Dec 48

[and others] The economic consequences of some recent antitrust decisions: discussion. AER/S 39:311-21 May 49

The theory and measurement of price expectations: discussion. AER/S 39:167-68 May 49

Collective bargaining and fiscal policy. IRRA 2:52-68 Dec 49

BOURNEUF, ALICE ELIZABETH

Postwar international monetary institutions. RSE 2:68-79 Jan 44

Professor Williams and the Fund. AER 34: 840-47 Dec 44

[and others] International monetary and credit arrangements: discussion. AER/S 35:289-96 May 45

Lending operations of the International Monetary Fund. REStat 28:237-47 Nov 46

BOUVIER, EMILE

Economic trends in China, and in central and western Europe. RSE 7,no.1:22-29 Mar 49

BOWDEN, GORDON TOWNLEY

The adaptive capacity of workers. HBR 25: 527-42 no.4, 47

BOWDEN, WILLIAM K.

and Cassady, R., Jr. Decentralization of retail trade in the metropolitan market area. JM 5:270-75 Jan 41

and Cassady, R., Jr. Shifting retail trade within the Los Angeles metropolitan market. JM 8:398-404 Apr 44

BOWEN, HOWARD ROTHMANN

The interpretation of voting in the allocation of economic resources. QJE 58:27-48 Nov 43

Turnover of business enterprises. JB 18: 73-77 Apr 45

Significance of recent changes in the business population. JM 10:24-34 Jul 45

The incidence of the corporation income tax: a reply. AER 36:146-47 Mar 46

The teaching of money and banking. JF 4: 231-33 Sep 49

BOWEN, IAN

Building output and the trade cycle (U.K. 1924-38). OEP 3:110-30 Feb 40

and Worswick, G. D. N. The Prices of Goods Act. Pt.I-II. OIS 2,no.6:2-5; no.7:2-7 Aug 31, Sep 21, 40

and Worswick, G. D. N. The controls and war finance. OEP 4:77-104 Sep 40

and Worswick, G. D. N. The cotton industry. OIS 2,no.8:9-11 Oct 40

and Ellis, A. W. T. The building and contracting industry. OEP 7:111-24 Mar 45

The future output of the constructional industries in the United States. EJ 56:208-29 Jun 46

A new index number of building materials' prices. OIS 8:352-59 Nov 46

Incentives and output in the building and civil engineering industries. MS 15:157-75 May 47

Building materials supply. YB 1:1-18 Dec 48

A note on G. T. Jones' "Increasing returns." YB 1:81-84 Sep 49

BOWER, MARVIN

Gearing a business for national defense. HBR 19:66-71 no.1, 40

BOWLEY, Sir ARTHUR LYON

The measurement of real income. MS 11: 59-86 Apr 40

--- [Reply to Mr. Keynes.] EJ 50:340-42 Jun-Sep 40

Working-class budgets, May 1940. OIS 2,no.5: 8-11 Aug 10, 40

and Schulz, T. Working class budgets: analysis of dietary. OIS 2,no.6:5-10 Aug 31, 40

and Schulz, T. Working-class budgets: analysis of expenditure. OIS 2,no.9:4-9 Nov 2, 40; Errata. no.10:18 Nov 23, 40

Earnings, 1938 and 1940. OIS 2,no.11:14-15 Dec 40

and Schulz, T. Working class budgets: October 1940; a comparison with May. OIS 2,no.11:1-7 Dec 40; Errata. 3,no.1:16 Jan 11, 41

BRANDT, KARL
Farm tenancy research: discussion. JFE 23:
304-10 Feb 41
Toward a more adequate approach to the
farm tenure program. JFE 24:206-25
Feb 42
The prospects of European agriculture and
their implications for the United States.
JFE 26:601-12 Nov 44
A public farm land appraisal service, its
desirability and practicability. JFE 27:
620-33 Aug 45
A price policy for agriculture, consistent
with economic progress, that will promote
adequate and more stable income from
farming. JFE 27:807-12 Nov 45
chairman. Outline of a price policy for
American agriculture for the postwar
period. Report of the Committee on
Parity Concepts. JFE 28:380-97 Feb 46
BRANDT, LOUIS KOHL
Note on corporate expansion since 1940.
AER 36:141-43 Mar 46
Mr. Floyd on Mississippi corporate fees and
taxes. SEJ 15:339-40 Jan 49
Sources of funds for corporate plant expan-
sion, 1946-1948. SEJ 15:279-88 Jan 49
BRANNEN, CLAUDE O.
Legal aspects of land tenure: discussion.
JFE 23:216-17 Feb 41
BRATT, ELMER CLARK
Timing pump-priming expenditure. AER 31:
97-98 Mar 41
Business-cycle forecasting. JB 21:1-11
Jan 48
Data needed to forecast the business cycle.
JB 21:168-79 Jul 48
The use of behavior classifications in busi-
ness-cycle forecasting. JB 22:209-24
Oct 49
BRATTER, HERBERT M.
The Committee for the Nation: a case history
in monetary propaganda. JPE 49:531-53
Jun 41
BRAUN, KURT
The dual nature of collective agreements.
JPE 51:451-62 Oct 43
BRAUNHUT, HERMAN JAY
Farm labor wage rates in the South, 1909-
1948. SEJ 16:189-96 Oct 49
BRAUNTHAL, ALFRED
American labor unions and the war. SR 9:
293-314 Sep 42
Von Mises on The tragedy of European labor:
comment. AER 34:121-23 Mar 44
American labor in politics. SR 12:1-21
Feb 45
BRAY, FRANK SEWELL
An accountant's comments on the subjective
theory of value and accounting cost.
Ec N.S.13:295-99 Nov 46
BRAY, JOHN F. L.
Small savings. EJ 50:195-206 Jun-Sep 40

BRAYER, HERBERT O.
Boom town banker: Central City, Colorado,
1880. BHR 19:67-95 Jun 45
The influence of British capital on the
western range-cattle industry. JEH/S 9:
85-98 '49
BREAK, GEORGE FARRINGTON and Rolph,
E. R.
The welfare aspects of excise taxes. JPE 57:
46-54 Feb 49
BREBNER, JOHN BARTLET
Laissez faire and state intervention in nine-
teenth-century Britain. JEH/S 8:59-73 '48
BREDVOLD, MILES
Farmers' sources of information. JM 14:
79-83 Jul 49
BREESE, GERALD
The neighborhood concept in theory and ap-
plication. LE 25:81-87 Feb 49
BREIMYER, HAROLD F.
The efficiency of feeding livestock. JFE 25:
599-621 Aug 43
Retail value of meat consumption relative to
consumers' incomes as a measure of de-
mand for meat. JFE 31:520-24 Aug 49
BREMS, HANS
The interdependence of quality variations,
selling effort and price. QJE 62:418-40
May 48
Some notes on the structure of the duopoly
problem. NTTO 12:41-74 no.37, 48
BRESCIANI-TURRONI, COSTANTINO
Economic reconstruction in Italy. LBR 7:
19-32 Jan 48
BRESSLER, RAYMOND GEORGE, Jr.
Transportation and country assembly of
milk. JFE 22:220-24 Feb 40
Research determination of economies of
scale. JFE 27:526-39 Aug 45
and MacLeod, A. Connecticut studies milk
delivery. JM 12:211-19 Oct 47
Agricultural marketing research.
JFE 31,pt.2:553-62 Feb 49
BREW, MARGARET LOUISE
A home economist looks at marketing.
JM 14:72-76 Jul 49
BREWER, A. L.
The beryllium industry: a case study in
monopolistic competition. SEJ 8:336-50
Jan 42
BREWSTER, JOHN M.
Farm technological advance and total popu-
lation growth. JFE 27:509-25 Aug 45
and Parsons, H. L. Can prices allocate re-
sources in American agriculture?
JFE 28:938-60 Nov 46
and Ellickson, J. C. Technological advance
and the structure of American agriculture.
JFE 29:827-47 Nov 47
BREYER, RALPH FREDERICK
ed. Research in marketing. [Regular fea-
ture] JM 7-13 Apr 43-Apr 49
Some preliminary problems of sample de-

BREYER, RALPH FREDERICK (Cont.)
  sign for a survey of retail trade flow.
  JM 10:343-53 Apr 46
BRIDEWELL, DAVID A.
  The draft and real estate transactions.
  LE 16:459-63 Nov 40
BRIEFS, GOETZ ANTONY
  Sociological aspects of union-management
  co-operation. RSE 5:59-68 Jun 47
  Business cycles. A methodological approach.
  ZN 12:465-74 Dec 49
BRIGGS, ASA
  The framework of the wool control. OEP 8:
  18-45 Nov 47
BRIGGS, H. R. and McGinley, A. R.
  Public land acquisition in law and practice.
  LE 17:452-59 Nov 41
BRIGHT, ARTHUR AARON, Jr.
  and MacLaurin, W. R. Economic factors in-
  fluencing the development and introduc-
  tion of the fluorescent lamp. JPE 51:
  429-50 Oct 43
  and Exter, J. War, radar, and the radio in-
  dustry. HBR 25:255-72 no.2, 47
BRINKER, PAUL ALBERT
  The enforcement of collective bargaining.
  QJE 62:314-22 Feb 48
  Functions of national unions as contrasted
  with their locals. SEJ 16:23-34 Jul 49
  The Taft-Hartley Act in operation. SEJ 16:
  147-60 Oct 49
BRINSER, AYERS and Wheeler, R. G.
  Farm planning as a basis for extending agri-
  cultural credit. JFE 30:243-58 May 48
BRINTON, CRANE
  The manipulation of economic unrest.
  JEH/S 8:21-31 '48
BRISSENDEN, PAUL FREDERICK and Keating,
  J. M.
  Union-management co-operation in millinery
  manufacturing in the New York metropoli-
  tan area. ILRR 2:3-32 Oct 48
BRITNELL, GEORGE EDWIN
  Dominion legislation affecting western agri-
  culture, 1939. CJE 6:275-82 May 40
  The war and Canadian wheat. CJE 7:397-413
  Aug 41
  and Fowke, V. C. Development of wheat mar-
  keting policy in Canada. JFE 31:627-42
  Nov 49
BRITT, STEUART HENDERSON
  Research and merchandising in a modern
  advertising agency. JM 13:506-10 Apr 49
BROADLEY, Sir HERBERT
  The food situation in Europe in relation to
  the work of FAO. JFE 31,pt.2:268-80
  Feb 49
BRODIE, HENRY
  Odd-lot trading on the New York Stock Ex-
  change and financial decentralization.
  SEJ 6:488-97 Apr 40
  and Ruggles, R. An empirical approach to
  economic intelligence in World War II.
  JASA 42:72-91 Mar 47

BRODSKY, NATHAN
  Some aspects of international relief.
  QJE 62:596-609 Aug 48
  A proposal for study of military distribu-
  tion. JM 14:88-90 Jul 49
BROGAN, DENIS WILLIAM
  The American Negro problem. R. EHR 15:
  73-78 no.1-2, 45
BROMBERG, BENJAMIN
  The financial and administrative importance
  of the Knights Hospitallers to the English
  Crown. EH 4:307-11 Feb 40
  Temple banking in Rome. EHR 10:128-31
  Nov 40
  The origin of banking: religious finance in
  Babylonia. JEH 2:77-88 May 42
BRONFENBRENNER, JEAN
  see Crockett, Jean
BRONFENBRENNER, MARTIN
  Applications of the discontinuous oligopoly
  demand curve. JPE 48:420-27 Jun 40
  The Keynesian equations and the balance of
  payments. REStud 7:180-84 Jun 40
  The introductory course: comment. AER 32:
  557-58 Sep 42
  Diminishing returns in federal taxation.
  JPE 50:699-717 Oct 42
  The role of money in equilibrium capital
  theory. Em 11:35-60 Jan 43
  Minimum wages, unemployability, and relief:
  a theoretical note. SEJ 10:52-59 Jul 43
  Production functions: Cobb-Douglas, inter-
  firm, intrafirm. Em 12:35-44 Jan 44
  Some fundamentals in liquidity theory.
  QJE 59:405-26 May 45
  The dilemma of liberal economics. JPE 54:
  334-46 Aug 46
  Sales taxation and the Mints plan. REStat 29:
  39-42 Feb 47
  Price control under imperfect competition.
  AER 37:107-20 Mar 47
  Regressus in black market demand: a reply.
  AER 37:934-36 Dec 47
  The consumption function controversy.
  SEJ 14:304-20 Jan 48
  [and others] The economic theory of im-
  perfect competition, oligopoly, and
  monopoly: discussion. AER/S 38:19-32
  May 48
  Postwar political economy: the President's
  reports. R. JPE 56:373-91 Oct 48
  Price control under imperfect competition:
  the joint production problem. CJE 15:
  210-16 May 49
  Letter to the editor [on economics curricu-
  lum]. Em 17:251-52 Jul-Oct 49
BRONSON, WESLEY H.
  Dairy marketing: discussion. JFE 29:284-88
  Feb 47
BROOK, WARNER F.
  The German TVA. LE 20:217-22 Aug 44
BROOKS, JAMES B.
  The organization of the selling function in a
  department store. JM 13:189-94 Oct 48

BROVEDANI, BRUNO
Exchange rate structure and price levels in
Italy: 1947-48. BNL 1:369-80 Jul 48

BROWDER, EARL
Centralized control of war production.
S&S 7:56-63 no.1, 43

BROWN, ALLEN STANLEY
Prospects of United Kingdom recovery.
ER 25,suppl.:3-28 Aug 49

BROWN, ARTHUR JOSEPH
Resources available for war: a comparison.
OEP 3:1-22 Feb 40
Trade balances and exchange stability.
OEP 6:57-75 Apr 42
Inflation and the flight from cash. YB 1:
33-42 Sep 49

BROWN, BONNAR
Common-stock price ratios and long-term
interest rates. JB 21:180-92 Jul 48

BROWN, DOUGLASS VINCENT
Management rights and the collective agreement. IRRA 1:145-55 Dec 48

BROWN, EDGAR CARY
A note on the new Federal Reserve Board
index of production. EJ 52:127-29 Apr 42
and Patterson, G. Accelerated depreciation:
a neglected chapter in war taxation.
QJE 57:630-45 Aug 43
Pay-as-you-go corporate taxes? AER 37:
641-45 Sep 47
Tax allowances for depreciation based on
changes in the price level. NTJ 1:311-21
Dec 48
Some evidence on business expectations.
REStat 31:236-38 Aug 49

BROWN, EDWARD E.
The International Monetary Fund: a consideration of certain objections. JB 17:
199-208 Oct 44

BROWN, EMILY CLARK
The employer unit for collective bargaining
in National Labor Relations Board decisions. JPE 50:321-56 Jun 42
Free collective bargaining or government
intervention? HBR 25:190-206 no.2, 47
Re: "NLRB in retrospect." ILRR 2:251-52
Jan 49
[and others] Harry Alvin Millis 1873-1948.
[obit.] AER 39:742-50 Jun 49

BROWN, ERNEST HENRY PHELPS
Real wages: a note. EJ 58:599-600 Dec 48
Prospects of labour. Ec N.S.16:1-10 Feb 49
Morale, military and industrial. EJ 59:40-55
Mar 49
Equal pay for equal work. EJ 59:384-98
Sep 49

BROWN, GEORGE H.
A note on federal taxation of chain stores.
JB 13:74-86 Jan 40
and Mancina, F. A. A note on the relationship between sales and advertising of department stores. JB 13:1-16 Jan 40; A
correction. 205 Apr 40

and Hadary, G. Beverage preference of industrial workers; a study in consumer
preference ratings. JB 17:111-17 Apr 44
A comparison of sampling methods. JM 11:
331-37 Apr 47

BROWN, H. P.
The composition of personal income.
ER 25,(no.48):18-36 Jun 49
Some aspects of social accounting: interest
and banks. ER 25,suppl.:73-92 Aug 49

BROWN, HARRY GUNNISON
chairman. Round table on the incidence of
taxation. AER/S 30:241-46 Mar 40
Objections to the 100 per cent reserve plan.
AER 30:309-14 Jun 40
Economic rent: in what sense a surplus?
AER 31:833-35 Dec 41

BROWN, JAMES DOUGLAS
Economic problems in the provision of security against life hazards of workers.
AER/S 30:61-67 Mar 40
chairman. Round table on economic issues
in social security policy. AER/S 30:
78-79 Mar 40
Concepts in Old-Age and Survivors' Insurance. IRRA 1:100-06 Dec 48
Frank Albert Fetter 1863-1949. [obit.]
AER 39:979-81 Sep 49

BROWN, JONATHAN ALLISON
The 1937 recession in England. HBR 18:
248-60 no.2, 40

BROWN, KENNETH L.
Stephen Girard, promoter of the second Bank
of the United States. JEH 2:125-48 Nov 42

BROWN, LEO CYRIL
The shifting distribution of the rights to
manage. IRRA 1:132-44 Dec 48

BROWN, LEWIS H.
Using private business agencies to achieve
public goals in the postwar world.
AER/S 33:71-81 Mar 43

BROWN, LYNDON OSMOND
Toward a profession of marketing. JM 13:
27-31 Jul 48

BROWN, PHILIP STODDARD
Prospective national income and capital
formation in the United Kingdom. AER 36:
555-77 Sep 46

BROWN, THEODORE HENRY
Business approaches to rearmament production control. JASA 36:27-35 Mar 41
Scientific sampling in business. HBR 20:
358-68 no.3, 42
The business consultant. HBR 21:183-89
no.2, 43

BROWN, WEIR MESSICK
Some effects of a minimum wage upon the
economy as a whole. AER 30:98-107
Mar 40
--- Reply to Messrs. Mikesell, Hagen and
Sufrin. AER 30:578-79 Sep 40
"Labor-saving" and "capital-saving" inno-
vations. SEJ 13:101-14 Oct 46

BROWN, WEIR MESSICK (Cont.)
Measuring physical inventories. JASA 43:
377-90 Sep 48
BROWN, WILLIAM ADAMS, Jr.
Comments on gold and the monetary system.
AER/S 30,no.5:38-51 Feb 41
Dr. Palyi on the meaning of the gold stand-
ard. JB 14:419-23 Oct 41
The repurchase provisions of the proposed
International Monetary Fund. AER 35:
111-20 Mar 45
Gold as a monetary standard, 1914-1949.
JEH/S 9:39-49 '49
BROWN, WILLIAM FRANCIS
and Cassady, R., Jr. Guild pricing in the
service trades. QJE 61:311-38 Feb 47
The Federal Trade Commission and false
advertising. Pt.I-II. JM 12:38-46;
193-201 Jul,Oct 47
Mass merchandising in Latin America:
Sears, Roebuck & Co. JM 13:73-77 Jul 48
The broader concept of marketing research.
JM 13:527-28 Apr 49
BROWNE, GERALD WILLIAM GAYLARD
The production function for South African
manufacturing industry. SAJE 11:258-68
Dec 43
Economists and government. SAJE 14:
188-201 Sep 46
A note on tariffs and subsidies. SAJE 14:
224-25 Sep 46
The Keynesian revolution in economics.
SAJE 14:237-52 Dec 46
BROWNLEE, OSWALD HARVEY
Memory errors as they affect survey data.
JFE 22:495-97 May 40
and Schultz, T. W. Two trials to determine
expectation models applicable to agricul-
ture. QJE 56:487-96 May 42
Some considerations on forward prices.
JFE 25:495-504 May 43
and Tintner, G. Production functions de-
rived from farm records. JFE 26:566-71
Aug 44; A correction. 35:123 Feb 53
Some effects of compensatory payments.
JFE 29:256-59 Feb 47
Marketing research and welfare economics.
JFE 30:55-68 Feb 48
The C.E.D. on federal tax reform. R.
JPE 56:166-72 Apr 48
[and others] Problems of timing and admin-
istering fiscal policy in prosperity and
depression: discussion. AER/S 38:443-51
May 48
and Gainer, W. Farmers' price anticipations
and the role of uncertainty in farm plan-
ning. JFE 31:266-75 May 49
Agricultural marketing research at the Uni-
versity of Chicago. JFE 31,pt.2:1213-24
Nov 49
BRUNER, NANCY
Note on the Doolittle solution. Em 15:43-44
Jan 47

BRUNK, MAX E.
Attacking low-income problems in rural
areas of New York State. LE 17:493-97
Nov 41
The application of work simplification tech-
niques to marketing research. JFE 29:
209-18 Feb 47
Agricultural marketing research: discus-
sion. JFE 31,pt.2:562-63 Feb 49
BRUNNER, ELIZABETH
The origins of industrial peace: the case of
the British boot and shoe industry.
OEP N.S.1:247-59 Jun 49
BRUNS, GORDON R.
Wartime fertility and the future population
of Australia. ER 19:185-202 Dec 43
and Merry, D. H. Full employment: the
British, Canadian and Australian White
Papers. ER 21:223-35 Dec 45
BRUNSMAN, HOWARD G.
The housing census of 1940. JASA 36:
393-400 Sep 41
and Lowery, D. Facts from the 1940 Census
of housing. LE 19:89-93 Feb 43
The sample census of congested production
areas. JASA 39:303-10 Sep 44
Observations on the provision and use of
data from the 1940 housing census.
AER/S 37:498-507 May 47
Measuring effective demand in the housing
market. LE 25:106-08 Feb 49
BRUTZKUS, JULIUS
Trade with eastern Europe, 800-1200.
EHR 13:31-41 no.1-2, 43
BRYAN, MALCOLM H.
Mercer Griffin Evans, 1901-1939. [obit.]
SEJ 6:557-60 Apr 40
BRYANT, LYLE C.
and Feldstein, M. J. Organization of occu-
pancy as an approach to real estate
management. LE 17:460-64 Nov 41
and Feldstein, M. J. Organization of occu-
pancy in critical war localities. LE 18:
339-49 Aug 42
BRYCE, ROBERT B.
Basic issues in postwar international eco-
nomic relations. AER/S 32:165-81
Mar 42
BUCHANAN, DANIEL HOUSTON
The use of economic history in the solution
of current economic problems. SEJ 13:
370-77 Apr 47
BUCHANAN, JAMES McGILL
Regional implications of marginal cost rate
making. SEJ 16:53-61 Jul 49
The pure theory of government finance: a
suggested approach. JPE 57:496-505
Dec 49
BUCHANAN, NORMAN SHARPE
Toward a theory of fluctuations in business
profits. AER 31:731-53 Dec 41
Anticipations and industrial investment de-
cisions. AER/S 32:141-55 Mar 42

BUCHANAN, NORMAN SHARPE (Cont.)
Advertising expenditures: a suggested treatment. JPE 50:537-57 Aug 42
International investment: some post-war problems and issues. CJE 10:139-49 May 44
Deliberate industrialisation for higher incomes. EJ 56:533-53 Dec 46

BUCK, HART
Means of payment and prices in Canada, 1900-46. CJE 13:197-207 May 47

BUCKATZSCH, ERICH JOHN
Aircraft from North America. OIS 2,no.5: 14-15 Aug 10, 40
War material from the U.S.A. OIS 2,no.10: 8-11 Nov 23, 40
The canals. OIS 3:71-74 Mar 15, 41
and Moos, S. The Balkan war and the blockade of Germany. OIS 3:141-44 May 17, 41
War transport. OIS 4:81-86 Mar 14, 42
Reorganisation of inland transport. OIS 4: 297-301 Nov 21, 42
Reform of the health services. OIS 6:68-73 Apr 8, 44
An index of social conditions in the county boroughs in 1931. OIS 8:365-74 Dec 46
Occupations in the parish registers of Sheffield, 1655-1719. EHR II.1:145-50 no.2-3, 49

BUCKLEY, LOUIS FRANCIS
Ethical aspects of social insurance. RSE 6: 1-28 May 48

BUCKTON, E. G.
Philosophy behind New Zealand's social policy. RSE 3:55-63 Dec 44

BUDD, RALPH
[The corporation and the historian.] Comment. JEH/S 4:38-42 Dec 44

BUEHLER, ALFRED GRETHER
Production taxes. HBR 19:458-69 no.4, 41
Compulsory loans in war financing. HBR 21: 115-23 no.1, 42
The taxation of small business. AER/S 36: 250-64 May 46
--- [idem] JF 1:61-75 Aug 46
chairman. Improving the property tax: New England Tax Conference. NTJ 1:369-72 Dec 48

BULIK, JOSEPH J.
USSR: the fifteen-year afforestation plan. LE 25:358-60 Nov 49

BUNCE, ARTHUR C.
Time preference and conservation. JFE 22: 533-43 Aug 40
and Wilcox, W. W. Neglected point in the economics of the soil: a reply. JFE 23: 475-77 May 41
[Time preference and conservation.] A rejoinder. JFE 23:649-51 Aug 41
Public policy and action for conservation. JFE 24:97-108 Feb 42
War and soil conservation. LE 18:121-33 May 42

BUNN, MARGARET
Mass Observation: a comment on People in production. R. MS 13:24-37 Oct 43

BUNTING, EARL
Industrial relations move ahead. ILRR 1: 231-46 Jan 48

BURCH, J. W.
and Crosby, J. E. Discussion of papers on postwar Extension problems in agricultural economics. JFE 28:226-34 Feb 46
The Missouri plan (balanced farming). JFE 31,pt.2:870-79 Nov 49

BURCHARDT, FRITZ ADOLF
and Balogh, T. Concentration in the 'non-essential' industries. OIS 3:68-71 Mar 15, 41
and Worswick, G. D. N. Point rationing. OIS 3:183-89 Jun 28, 41
The White Paper on industrial and labour policy. OIS 3:235-42 Aug 9, 41
The Trade Union Congress and inflation. OIS 3:298-300 Sep 20, 41
Output and employment policy. OIS 4:29-40 Jan 10, 42
German price policy. OIS 4:117-21 Apr 4, 42
Shipping, the bottleneck. OIS 4:193-97 Jul 18, 42
Allied control for Allied supplies: the case of shipping. OIS 4:252-58 Sep 19, 42
The coal prospects for 1943-44. OIS 5: 166-71 Jul 17, 43
Coal in the fifth year of war. OIS 5:265-71 Nov 20, 43
Size and productivity of coal mines in Great Britain. OIS 6:250-55 Nov 4, 44
Sales and stocks of non-food goods 1944. OIS 7:13-16 Jan 13, 45
Working-class housing at economic rents. OIS 7:91-96 Apr 7, 45
and Balogh, T. Taxation in the transition period. OIS 7:165-73 Jul 21, 45
Reparations and reconstruction. OIS 7: 199-212 Sep 1, 45
Manpower in the reconversion period in U.S.A. and U.K. OIS 7:303-05 Dec 15, 45
and Worswick, G. D. N. Britain in transition: output and financial policy. OIS 9: 74-103 Mar,Apr 47
and Martin, K. Western Germany and reconstruction. OIS 9:405-16 Dec 47
Cuts in capital expenditure. R. OIS 10:1-8 Jan 48

BURD, HENRY A.
Mortality of men's apparel stores in Seattle, 1929-1939. JM 6:22-26 Jul 41
"Cost" under the Unfair Practices Act. JM 7:146-51 Oct 42

BURDEN, WILLIAM ARMISTEAD MOALE
Postwar status of the aircraft industry. HBR 23:211-16 no.2, 45

BURGESS, EDWIN H. [and others]
Postwar railroad problems: discussion. AER/S 36:494-519 May 46

BURGESS, ROBERT WILBUR
[A dimensional national economy.] A re-
joinder. JPE 52:270 Sep 44
Do we need a "bureau of standards" for
statistics? JM 11:281-82 Jan 47
BURGESS, WARREN RANDOLPH
Carl Snyder: an appreciation. JASA 41:
244-46 Jun 46
Leonard P. Ayres: an appreciation. JASA 42:
128-33 Mar 47
BURGOYNE, JOHN, Jr.
Conducting sales tests. JM 9:158-59 Oct 44
BURK, MONROE
Mr. Boulding's criticism of the net national
product concept. AER 38:897-98 Dec 48
BURKETT, W. K.
Some problems in deflating farmers' debt
paying performances. JFE 30:750-55
Nov 48
BURKHEAD, JESSE VERLYN
Corporate taxes and utility assessment: a
reply. LE 17:115-17 Feb 41
Property tax as a burden on shelter. LE 20:
255-63 Aug 44
Full employment and interest-free borrow-
ing. SEJ 14:1-13 Jul 47
and Steele, D. C. Electric rates and tax
burdens in Pennsylvania and New York.
NTJ 2:278-80 Sep 49
The outlook for federal budget-making.
NTJ 2:289-99 Dec 49
BURLEY, ORIN EVERETT
[Price control]: discussion. JM 8:302-06
Jan 44
BURN, DUNCAN LYALL
Recent trends in the history of the steel in-
dustry. EHR 17:95-102 no.2, 47
BURNETT, EDMUND CODY
Hog raising and hog driving in the region of
the French Broad River. AH 20:86-103
Apr 46
Shingle making on the lesser waters of the
Big Creek of the French Broad River.
AH 20:225-35 Oct 46
BURNHAM, ELIZABETH ABBOTT
The department store in its community.
HBR 18:455-71 no.4, 40
What price volume? HBR 20:327-35 no.3, 42
Employee productivity in department stores.
HBR 27:480-97 Jul 49
BURNS, ARTHUR EDWARD and Kerr, P.
Recent changes in work-relief wage policy.
AER 31:56-66 Mar 41
BURNS, ARTHUR FRANK
Frickey on the decomposition of time series.
R. REStat 26:136-47 Aug 44
Keynesian economics once again. REStat 29:
252-68 Nov 47
Current research in business cycles: discus-
sion. AER/S 39:77-83 May 49
BURNS, ARTHUR ROBERT
Concentration of production. HBR 21:277-90
no.3, 43

Bain's analysis of the Pacific Coast petrole-
um industry. R. JPE 56:35-53 Feb 48
The effectiveness of the federal antitrust
laws: a symposium. AER 39:691-95
Jun 49
BURNS, EVELINE MABEL
Economic problems in the provision of se-
curity against employment hazards.
AER/S 30:68-77 Mar 40
The Beveridge report. AER 33:512-33
Sep 43
Social insurance in evolution. AER/S 34:
199-211 Mar 44
and Spengler, J. J. The proposed publica-
tion of a periodic review of economics.
[Précis of the round table discussion]
AER/S 36:784-88 May 46
Social security developments in the United
States. MS 15:198-214 May 47
BURR, SUSAN S.
[and others] The public debt: effects on in-
stitutions and income: discussion.
AER/S 37:192-204 May 47
Problems in providing adequate statistics
on business profits. JASA 42:432-38
Sep 47
BURRILL, C. L.
Petroleum: present and future. JM 8:
260-67 Jan 44
BURROUGHS, ROY JUDSON
Consolidated balance sheet and income state-
ment for agriculture. JFE 27:463-72
May 45
Mortgage insurance for farm housing.
JFE 27:676-82 Aug 45
Toward a farm housing policy. LE 24:1-22
Feb 48
BURROWS, DON S.
A program approach to federal budgeting.
HBR 27:272-85 May 49
BURROWS, HARRY RAYMOND
[Financial policy of municipalities towards
Natives.] A comment. SAJE 8:279-81
Sep 40
with Halliday, I. G. and Smith, R. H. Price
control in war-time. SAJE 8:400-30
Dec 40
[and others] Social security. SAJE 10:
193-247 Sep 42
Fundamentals of economic policy in the
Union: a comment. SAJE 10:307-09
Dec 42
and De Vos, P. J. Old age pensions.
SAJE 11:87-105 Jun 43
"Plan for reconstruction." R. SAJE 12:
1-12 Mar 44
An approach to the Indian problem in South
Africa. SAJE 15:157-77 Sep 47
Some basic problems in housing research.
SAJE 16:1-23 Mar 48
BURSK, EDWARD COLLINS
and Teele, S. F. Marketing practices of food
manufacturers. HBR 22:358-76 no.3, 44

BURSK, EDWARD COLLINS (Cont.)
  Low-pressure selling. HBR 25:227-42
    no.2, 47
  Selling the idea of free enterprise. HBR 26:
    372-84 May 48
  and Clark, D. T. Reading habits of business
    executives. HBR 27:330-45 May 49
BURTLE, JAMES L. and Liepe, W.
  Devaluation and the cost of living in the
    United Kingdom. REStud 17:1-28
    no.1, 49
BURTON, GORDON LLOYD
  Agriculture's share of the national income:
    a comment. CJE 10:206-09 May 44
  The farmer and the market. CJE 15:495-504
    Nov 49
  The proposal to market coarse grains
    through the Canadian Wheat Board.
    JFE 31:643-55 Nov 49
BURTON, HERBERT
  The Australian war economy, May, 1943-
    May, 1945. ER 19:149-61; 20:1-17;
    189-205; 21:1-22 Dec 43, Jun,Dec 44,
    Jun 45
  The transition to a peace economy: the
    Australian economy, May-October, 1945.
    ER 21:149-64 Dec 45
BURTT, EVERETT JOHNSON, Jr.
  After the shutdown in Howland, Maine.
    SEJ 8:80-87 Jul 41
BUSSCHAU, WILLIAM JOHN
  The expansion of manufacturing industry in
    the Union. R. SAJE 13:215-31 Sep 45
  The hardships of Britain: Mr. Harrod's
    ideas. SAJE 15:248-55 Dec 47
  The case for increasing the price of gold in
    terms of all currencies. SAJE 17:1-22
    Mar 49
BUTANI, D. H.
  A socio-economic survey of Pano Akil
    Taulaka. IJE 21:328-35 Jan 41
  The problem of value in a socialist state.
    IJE 21:395-419 Apr 41
  The co-operative movement in Sind. IJE 22:
    461-70 Jan 42
  The quality and perspective of Indian eco-
    nomic thought. IJE 22:280-89 Jan 42
BUTLER, RALPH
  Growth patterns for new specialty products:
    a case study. JM 11:27-34 Jul 46
BUTLIN, NOEL G.
  An index of engineering unemployment,
    1852-1943. ER 22:241-60 Dec 46
  Collective bargaining in the Sydney printing
    industry, 1880-1900. ER 23:206-26 Dec 47
BUTLIN, SYDNEY JAMES
  The political economy of war. R. ER 16:
    96-108 Jun 40
  Arthur Duckworth. [obit.] EJ 54:443-45
    Dec 44
  The Australian Economic Association, 1887-
    1898. ER 23:20-31 Jun 47

BUTTERS, JOHN KEITH
  Tax revisions for reconversion needs.
    HBR 22:299-315 no.3, 44
  An appraisal of postwar tax plans. HBR 23:
    253-64 no.2, 45
  Taxation and new product development.
    HBR 23:451-59 no.4, 45
  Research project: effect of federal taxes on
    business. NTJ 1:91-92 Mar 48
  Management considerations on Lifo. HBR 27:
    308-29 May 49
  Federal income taxation and external vs.
    internal financing. JF 4:197-205 Sep 49
BUTTRESS, F. A. and Dennis, R. W. G.
  The early history of cereal seed treatment
    in England. AH 21:93-103 Apr 47
BUTZ, EARL L.
  Postwar agricultural credit problems and
    suggested adjustments. JFE 27:281-96
    May 45
  Irrigation in the West: discussion.
    JFE 31,pt.2:983-84 Nov 49
BYE, RAYMOND TAYLOR
  chairman. Round table on problems in the
    teaching of economics. AER/S 30:106-11
    Mar 40
  [and others] Economic adjustments after
    wars: discussion. AER/S 32:31-36
    Mar 42
  Some criteria of social economy. AER/S 34:
    1-8 Mar 44
BYRON, F. A. and Smith, R. H.
  The expansion of industry and the supply of
    labour. SAJE 9:251-64 Sep 41
CAHEN, ALFRED
  Merchandising flow survey on men's cloth-
    ing. [Abstract] AER/S 39:416-18 May 49
  Measuring the merchandise flow of men's
    clothing. JM 14:67-71 Jul 49
CAIRNCROSS, ALEXANDER KIRKLAND
  League of Nations studies of transition
    problems. R. EJ 54:252-56 Jun-Sep 44
  Internal migration in Victorian England.
    MS 17:67-87 Jan 49
CALKINS, FRANCIS JOSEPH
  Corporate reorganization under chapter X:
    a post-mortem. JF 3,no.2:19-28 Jun 48
  Federal income taxation and external vs.
    internal financing: discussion. JF 4:
    205-07 Sep 49
  University courses in finance. JF 4:244-65
    Sep 49
CALKINS, ROBERT D.
  Business education after the war. JB 18:
    1-8 Jan 45
  A challenge to business education. HBR 23:
    174-86 no.2, 45
  Objectives of business education. HBR 25:
    46-57 no.1, 46
CALLANDER, WILLIAM F. and Sarle, C. F.
  The Bureau of Agricultural Economics pro-
    gram in enumerative sampling. JFE 29:
    233-36 Feb 47

CALLARD, K. B.
  To plan or not to plan: the debate continues.
    R.  CJE 15:416-20 Aug 49
CALSOYAS, CHRIS DEMOSTHENES
  Commodity currency and commodity storage.
    AER 38:341-52 Jun 48
CAMPBELL, GEORGE CLYDE
  Problems with sampling procedures for re-
    serve valuations. JASA 43:413-27 Sep 48
CAMPBELL, J. PHIL
  Action programs in education.  AH 15:68-71
    Apr 41
CAMPBELL, JOE R. and Boonstra, C. A.
  Land classification, land-use areas, and farm
    management research. JFE 23:657-64
    Aug 41
CAMPBELL, KEITH OLIVER
  Australian agricultural production in the de-
    pression. ER 20:58-73 Jun 44
  Production goals for primary products: some
    aspects of their formulation and function.
    ER 22:83-98 Jun 46
  The development of soil conservation pro-
    grammes in Australia. LE 24:63-78
    Feb 48
CAMPBELL, RITA RICARDO
  Annual wage guarantee plans. AER 35:
    870-90 Dec 45
  Recent analyses of annual wage guarantees.
    QJE 62:542-61 Aug 48
CAMPION, HARRY
  Changes in wage rates and earnings in 1939-
    1940. EJ 50:189-94 Jun-Sep 40
  and Marley, J. G. Changes in salaries in
    Great Britain, 1924-1939. JRSS 103:
    524-33 pt.4, 40
CANNING, JOHN B.
  Foods for defense. JFE 23:697-711 Nov 41
  Schisms in agricultural policy: rescue pro-
    grams and managed agricultural progress.
    JFE 24:496-511 May 42
  The demand for agricultural commodities in
    the period of transition from war to peace.
    JFE 26:709-24 Nov 44
  Food and agriculture: longer-run outlook and
    policy. AER/S 35:405-16 May 45
CANOYER, HELEN G.
  National brand advertising and monopolistic
    competition. JM 7:152-57 Oct 42
  A study of consumer cooperative associa-
    tions in the north central states. JM 9:
    373-80 Apr 45
CAPAROON, CLARENCE D. and Jorgensen,
    E. A.
  Agricultural data needs in extension work.
    JFE 30:282-91 May 48
CAPLAN, BENJAMIN
  The premature abandonment of machinery.
    REStud 7:113-22 Feb 40
  Reinvestment and the rate of interest.
    AER 30:561-68 Sep 40
  Some Swedish stepping stones in economic
    theory: a comment. CJE 7:559-62 Nov 41

CAPRON, WILLIAM MOSHER and Isard, W.
  The future locational pattern of iron and
    steel production in the United States.
    JPE 57:118-33 Apr 49
CARL, LESLIE M.
  Agricultural data in the states: discussion.
    JFE 31,pt.2:322-24 Feb 49
CARLSON, VALDEMAR
  A plea for new texts in beginning economics.
    AER 31:102-03 Mar 41
  Democratizing money. JF 2,no.2:68-71
    Oct 47
CARMAN, HARRY J.
  Terence Vincent Powderly: an appraisal.
    JEH 1:83-87 May 41
  Jesse Buel, early nineteenth-century agri-
    cultural reformer. AH 17:1-13 Jan 43
CAROSSO, VINCENT P.
  Anaheim, California: a nineteenth century
    experiment in commercial viniculture.
    BHR 23:78-86 Jun 49
  The Waltham Watch Company: a case his-
    tory.  BHR 23:165-87 Dec 49; Correction.
    24:51 Mar 50
CARR, H. J.
  John Francis Bray. Ec N.S.7:397-415
    Nov 40
CARR, HOBART CECIL
  The problem of bank-held government debt.
    AER 36:833-42 Dec 46
CARR, WALLACE B.
  A new simplified approach to mathematically
    calculated reserves for depreciation for
    accounting purposes. LE 25:304-12
    Aug 49
CARR-SAUNDERS, Sir ALEXANDER MORRIS
  Robert René Kuczynski (1876-1947). [obit.]
    EJ 58:434-38 Sep 48
CARROLL, JOHN MURRAY
  The distribution of efficiency savings.
    QJE 55:517-20 May 41
CARROLL, JOSEPH DOUGLAS, Jr.
  Some aspects of the home-work relationships
    of industrial workers. LE 25:414-22
    Nov 49
CARSLAW, HORATIO SCOTT
  Federal and state income tax. ER 17:19-30
    Jun 41
  The uniform income tax in Australia. ER 18:
    158-67 Dec 42
  Australian income tax, 1943. ER 19:1-10
    Jun 43
  Australian income tax, 1945. ER 22:40-49
    Jun 46
  The Australian Social Services Contribution
    and Income Tax Acts, 1946 and 1947.
    ER 22:219-27 Dec 46; 23:177-85 Dec 47
CARSON, DANIEL
  Incomparabilities in "Census of manufactures"
    data. AER 31:559-60 Sep 41
  Accessions to and separations from the labor
    force: concepts for analyzing certain types
    of labor problems. JPE 49:882-94 Dec 41

CARSON, DANIEL (Cont.)
Occupational mobility and occupational out-
look. SEJ 14:411-19 Apr 48
CARSON, JAMES S.
The commercial and economic background of
marketing in Latin America. JM 6,no.4,
pt.2:137-41 Apr 42
CARSTEN, FRANCIS LUDWIG
Slavs in north-eastern Germany. EHR 11:
61-76 no.1, 41
CARTER, CHARLES FREDERICK
and Chang, T. C. A further note on the
British balance of payments. Ec N.S.13:
183-89 Aug 46
The structure of the British budget 1947.
PF 2:336-47 no.4, 47
The dual-currency problem. EJ 58:586-94
Dec 48
The British budget, April 1948. PF 3:231-34
no.3, 48
British public finance and the progress of
inflation. PF 4:28-48 no.1, 49
Problems of British public finance in 1949.
PF 4:313-20 no.4, 49
CARTER, HARVEY L.
Rural Indiana in transition, 1850-1860.
AH 20:107-21 Apr 46
CARTER, JOHN PHILIP
The prospect for economic growth: comment.
AER 37:926-30 Dec 47
Recent developments in railroad freight rates.
SEJ 15:379-94 Apr 49
CARTER, ROBERT M.
Job analysis of chores on dairy farms.
JFE 25:671-77 Aug 43
and Hardin, L. S. An analysis of work simp-
lification research methods and results.
JFE 28:320-30 Feb 46
Evaluation of work simplification research
and teaching activities. JFE 29:225-31
Feb 47
CARTER, WILLIAM D.
Mutual investment funds. HBR 27:715-40
Nov 49
CARTWRIGHT, PHILIP WINDSOR
Public attitudes toward sources of state tax
revenues. NTJ 2:368-71 Dec 49
CARUS-WILSON, ELEANOR MARY
An industrial revolution of the thirteenth
century. EHR 11:39-60 no.1, 41
The English cloth industry in the late twelfth
and early thirteenth centuries. EHR 14:
32-50 no.1, 44
CARY, WILLIAM L.
Sale and lease-back of corporate property.
HBR 27:151-64 Mar 49
CASE, EVERETT
The dairyman's plight. HBR 20:233-43
no.2, 42
CASE, HAROLD CLAYTON M.
Farm management research: discussion.
JFE 22:111-18 Feb 40

chairman. The Committee on Land Tenure
in the Corn Belt. JFE 22:628-33 Aug 40
Problems of achieving maximum food and
fiber production in the Mississippi Valley.
JFE 26:197-209 Feb 44
The Agricultural Act of 1948. JFE 31,pt.2:
227-36 Feb 49
CASSADY, RALPH, Jr.
["The consumer and the economic order"]:
discussion. JM 4,no.4,pt.2:119-23 Apr 40
Trade barriers within the United States.
HBR 18:231-47 no.2, 40
and Bowden, W. K. Decentralization of retail
trade in the metropolitan market area.
JM 5:270-75 Jan 41
Municipal trade barriers. HBR 19:364-76
no.3, 41
The integrated marketing institution and
public welfare. JM 6:252-66 Jan 42
[Consumer preference studies]: discussion.
JM 6,no.4,pt.2:87-88 Apr 42
The chain-independent controversy. JM 7:
57-59 Jul 42
and Grether, E. T. Locality price differentials in the western retail grocery trade.
HBR 21:190-206 no.2, 43; Correction.
396 no.3, 43
and Bowden, W. K. Shifting retail trade
within the Los Angeles metropolitan
market. JM 8:398-404 Apr 44
Statistical sampling techniques and marketing
research. JM 9:317-41 Apr 45
Some economic aspects of price discrimination under non-perfect market conditions.
JM 11:7-20 Jul 46
Techniques and purposes of price discrimination. JM 11:135-50 Oct 46
Legal aspects of price discrimination:
federal law. JM 11:258-72 Jan 47
and Brown, W. F. Guild pricing in the service trades. QJE 61:311-38 Feb 47
Legal aspects of price discrimination: state
law. JM 11:377-89 Apr 47
and Williams, R. M. Radio as an advertising
medium. HBR 27:62-78 Jan 49
CASSIDY, HARRY M.
Social security developments in Canada.
IRRA 1:107-20 Dec 48
CATLIN, JOHN B.
Opportunities for statisticians in industry.
JASA 40:75-79 Mar 45
CAVE, C. P. HADDON-
see Haddon-Cave, C. P.
CAVE, ROY CLINTON
Distribution of property in two California
counties, 1907 and 1935, based on probate
records. AER 30:818-22 Dec 40
Variations in expenditures where families of
wage earners and clerical workers are
classified by economic level. JASA 38:
445-52 Dec 43
CAVERT, WILLIAM LANE
Comment on "The scale of operations in

CAVERT, WILLIAM LANE (Cont.)
agriculture." JFE 24:889-90 Nov 42
and Pond, G. A. How long does it take to pay
for a farm starting with heavy debts?
JFE 26:685-93 Nov 44
Research work in minimum financial requirements and some related considerations for
beginning farming. JFE 28:126-33 Feb 46

CAVIN, JAMES PIERCE
Aspects of wartime consumption. AER/S 35:
15-36 May 45
Agricultural micro-economic studies: discussion. JFE 30:139-41 Feb 48

CAWL, FRANKLIN R.
Recent changes in farm economic levels.
JM 7:360-66 Apr 43
The continuing panel technique. JM 8:45-50
Jul 43

CEDERWALL, GUSTAV
Post-war development of Sweden's foreign
trade. OIS 9:307-14 Sep 47
An economic survey for Sweden. OIS 10:
245-54 Jul-Aug 48
and Ohlsson, I. Sweden's economy 1946-
1949. OIS 11:53-58 Feb-Mar 49

CENTNER, CHARLES WILLIAM
Great Britain and Chilian mining 1830-1914.
EHR 12:76-82 no.1-2, 42

CERIANI, LUIGI
Survey of the Italian monetary situation.
BNL 1:121-34 Jul 47

CHAIT, B.
Les fluctuations économiques et l'interdépendance des marchés: a reply. JPE 48:
740-44 Oct 40

CHALMERS, HENRY
[Economic regionalism and multilateral
trade]: discussion. AER/S 33:448-54
Mar 43

CHALMERS, WILLIAM ELLISON
The conciliation process. ILRR 1:337-50
Apr 48

CHALONER, WILLIAM HENRY
Further light on the invention of the process
for smelting iron ore with coke. EHR II.2:
185-87 no.2, 49

CHAMBERLAIN, NEIL WOLVERTON
The nature and scope of collective bargaining.
QJE 58:359-87 May 44
The organized business in America. JPE 52:
97-111 Jun 44
Professor Hansen's fiscal policy and the
debt. AER 35:400-07 Jun 45
Obligations upon the union under the National
Labor Relations Act. AER 37:170-77
Mar 47
The nature of the collective agreement.
JB 22:92-105 Apr 49
[and others] Economic power blocs and
American capitalism: discussion.
IRRA 2:192-202 Dec 49

CHAMBERLAIN, S. D.
The use of "aptitude tests" in sales management. JM 8:159-64 Oct 43

CHAMBERLIN, EDWARD HASTINGS
Advertising costs and equilibrium: a cor-
rection. REStud 12:16-20 no.2, 45
[and others] New frontiers in economic
thought: discussion. AER/S 36:139-53
May 46
Proportionality, divisibility and economies
of scale. QJE 62:229-62 Feb 48
An experimental imperfect market. JPE 56:
95-108 Apr 48
A supplementary bibliography on monopolis-
tic competition. QJE 62:629-38 Aug 48
[Proportionality, divisibility, and economies
of scale]: Reply. QJE 63:137-43 Feb 49
[Various views on the monopoly problem.]
Some final comments. REStat 31:123-29
May 49

CHAMBERS, JONATHAN DAVID
Enclosure and the small landowner. EHR 10:
118-27 Nov 40

CHAMBERS, R. D. and Rose-Innes, N.
Report of the Provincial Financial Resources
Committee. R. SAJE 12:263-78 Dec 44

CHAMBERS, ROBERT W.
Block booking: blind selling. HBR 19:
496-507 no.4, 41

CHAMBERS, STANLEY PAUL
Taxation and incentives. LBR 8:1-12 Apr 48
Taxation and the supply of capital for indus-
try. LBR 11:1-20 Jan 49

CHAMPERNOWNE, DAVID GAWEN
with Stone, R. and Meade, J. E. The preci-
sion of national income estimates.
REStud 9:111-25 no.2, 42
and Kaldor, N. Erwin Rothbarth. [obit.]
EJ 55:130-32 Apr 45
A note on J. v. Neumann's article on "A
model of economic equilibrium."
REStud 13:10-18 no.1, 45
The national income and expenditure of the
United Kingdom 1938-1945. OIS 8:130-45
May 46
Critique of the Economic survey. R. OIS 9:
57-73 Mar-Apr 47

CHAND, GYAN
The exchange stabilization funds: their func-
tion and future. IJE 20:535-43 Apr 40
Value and socialism. IJE 21:703-15 Apr 41
Local terminal taxation. IJE 22:624-36
Jan 42
Capitalism in flux: recent changes in the
structure of capitalism. IJE 24:374-86
Apr 44
Shadows of the peace. IJE 25:254-61 Jan 45
The inheritance tax in India. IJE 25:436-50
Apr 45
The post-war monetary issues in India.
IJE 26:472-87 Jan 46

CHAND, MAHESH
Scope and method of economics. IJE 20:
531-34 Apr 40
A note on the paper industry. IJE 29:59-65
Jul 48

CHAND, MAHESH (Cont.)
A note on the cotton textile industry in India.
IJE 30:41-54 Jul 49

CHANDLER, LESTER VERNON
In reply to Mr. Hicks. SEJ 7:556-57 Apr 41
[and others] A consideration of the economic
and monetary theories of J. M. Keynes:
discussion. AER/S 38:291-98 May 48
Federal Reserve policy and the federal debt.
AER 39:405-29 Mar 49

CHANG, TSE-CHUN
The British demand for imports in the inter-
war period. EJ 56:188-207 Jun 46
and Carter, C. F. A further note on the
British balance of payments. Ec N.S.13:
183-89 Aug 46
The British demand for imports: a reply.
EJ 56:665-66 Dec 46
International comparison of demand for
imports. REStud 13:53-67 no.2, 46
A note on exports and national income in
Canada. CJE 13:276-80 May 47
The British balance of payments, 1924-1938.
EJ 57:475-503 Dec 47
A statistical note on world demand for ex-
ports. REStat 30:106-16 May 48

CHANTLER, PHILIP
Six years of controlled milk prices. MS 11:
123-41 Oct 40

CHAO, PAO-CHUAN
The agricultural economics program of China.
JFE 27:615-19 Aug 45

CHAPMAN, DENNIS
The New Shipwright Building Company of
Dundee, 1826 to 1831. EHR 10:148-51
Nov 40

CHAPMAN, Sir SYDNEY JOHN
Sir Alfred Flux. [obit.] EJ 52:400-03 Dec 42
The profit motive and the economic incen-
tive. EJ 56:51-56 Mar 46

CHAPMAN, W. D. and Menzies-Kitchin, A. W.
War-time changes in the organisation of two
groups of eastern counties farms. EJ 56:
57-85 Mar 46

CHAPPLE, ELIOT DISMORE
and Donald, G., Jr. A method of evaluating
supervisory personnel. HBR 24:197-214
no.2, 46
and Donald, G., Jr. An evaluation of department store salespoeple by the interaction
chronograph. JM 12:173-85 Oct 47

CHATTERJEE, ATUL
Jahangir Cooverjee Coyajee. [obit.] EJ 53:
453-56 Dec 43

CHATTERJI, RABINDRA NATH
Essentials of a short-term commercial
policy for India. IJE 28:9-15 Jul 47

CHATTERJI, RABINDRANATH
Food rationing in India. IJE 26:622-30
Apr 46

CHATTERS, CARL H.
War-time problems of local government: II.
The effect of war on municipal finance.
CJE 9:405-07 Aug 43

The economic classification of cities and
its fiscal implications. NTJ 1:111-17
Jun 48

CHATURVEDI, H. K. and Bhattacharya, S.
Industrial relations in India. IJE 29:277-88
Jan 49

CHAUDHARI, S. C.
Business forecasting. IJE 25:160-64 Oct 44

CHAWNER, LOWELL J.
[and others] Effects of the war and defense
program upon economic conditions and
institutions: discussion. AER/S 32:
382-90 Mar 42
Some recent changes in industrial markets.
JM 6,no.4,pt.2:53-65 Apr 42

CHAZEAU, MELVIN GARDNER DE
see De Chazeau, Melvin Gardner

CHECKLAND, SYDNEY GEORGE
The Birmingham economists, 1815-1850.
EHR II.1:1-19 no.1, 48
The propagation of Ricardian economics in
England. Ec N.S.16:40-52 Feb 49

CHEEK, BRUCE M.
Economic theory and industrial pricing.
ER 25,suppl.:140-57 Aug 49

CHEN, CHEN-HAN
Regional differences in costs and productivity in the American cotton manufacturing industry, 1880-1910. QJE 55:
533-66 Aug 41

CHENAULT, LAWRENCE ROYCE
A note on business concepts and economic
theory. AER 31:98-101 Mar 41
Buchanan's theory of fluctuations in business
profits. AER 32:840-42 Dec 42

CHENERY, HOLLIS BURNLEY
Engineering production functions. QJE 63:
507-31 Nov 49

CHERINGTON, PAUL TERRY
The uses of the Census of business. [Sum-
mary of a discussion] JASA 35:107-15
Mar 40
Current progress in market research.
JM 5:225-27 Jan 41
Trends in marketing research. JM 6,no.4,
pt.2:17-18 Apr 42

CHERRINGTON, HOMER VIRGIL
National Association of Securities Dealers.
HBR 27:741-59 Nov 49

CHERRY, ROBERT G.
Analyzing the tax load of agriculture: discussion. JFE 31,pt.2:678-80 Feb 49

CHESKIN, LOUIS and Ward, L. B.
Indirect approach to market reactions.
HBR 26:572-80 Sep 48

CHEW, ARTHUR P.
Nationalistic trends in agricultural policy.
JFE 26:59-76 Feb 44
Postwar planning and the rural-urban bal-
ance. JFE 27:664-75 Aug 45

CHIA, FRANKLIN
Mr. Hewes, Jr., on land tenure in Japan: a
reply. LE 25:433-34 Nov 49

CHING-YUEN HSIANG
  see Hsiang, Ching-Yuen
CHIPMAN, JOHN S.
  The generalized bi-system multiplier.
    CJE 15:176-89 May 49
CHOPRA, VINAI KUMAR
  The scope of economics. IJE 20:459-73
    Apr 40
CHOSSUDOWSKY, E. M.
  Rationing in the U.S.S.R. REStud 8:143-65
    Jun 41
  De-rationing in the U.S.S.R. REStud 9:1-27
    Nov 41
CHOWDHURY, R. C.
  Nationalisation. IJE 27:373-87 Apr 47
CHRISTENSEN, RAYMOND P.
  Expectation and performance related to con-
    servation and production adjustments in
    the midwest dairy region. JFE 23:632-45
    Aug 41
  and Mighell, R. L. Measuring maximum con-
    tribution to food needs by producing areas.
    JFE 26:181-93 Feb 44
  Food production: discussion. JFE 31,pt.2:
    265-67 Feb 49
CHRISTENSON, CARROLL LAWRENCE
  Note on national income measurement; a
    supplement to Professor Whittaker on
    "Wealth and welfare." AER 31:107-08
    Mar 41
  Economic implications of renegotiation of
    government contracts. JPE 52:48-73
    Mar 44
CHURCH, DONALD E.
  The consumer market for canned vegetables,
    fruits, and juices. JM 11:44-54 Jul 46
CHURCH, LeROY F.
  The effect of crop loans on corn prices.
    JB 18:121-39 Jul 45
CHUTE, CHARLTON F. [and others]
  Economic problems of American cities:
    discussion. AER/S 32:341-48 Mar 42
CIANO, J. L. D.
  The pre-war "black" market for foreign bank
    notes. Ec N.S.8:378-91 Nov 41
CIPOLLA, CARLO M.
  The trends in Italian economic history in the
    later Middle Ages. EHR II.2:181-84
    no.2, 49
CIRIACY-WANTRUP, SIEGFRIED von
  The relation of war economics to agriculture,
    with particular reference to the effects of
    income and price inflation and deflation.
    AER/S 30:366-82 Mar 40
  Economics of joint costs in agriculture.
    JFE 23:771-818 Nov 41
  Private enterprise and conservation. JFE 24:
    75-96 Feb 42
  A discussion of "Food production policies in
    wartime" by Sherman E. Johnson. JFE 25:
    869-74 Nov 43
  Taxation and the conservation of resources.
    QJE 58:157-95 Feb 44

[and others] Natural resources and inter-
    national policy: discussion. AER/S 35:
    130-36 May 45
  Administrative coordination of conservation
    policy. LE 22:48-58 Feb 46
  Resource conservation and economic sta-
    bility. QJE 60:412-52 May 46
  Capital returns from soil-conservation
    practices. JFE 29:1181-96 Nov 47
CIRVANTE, V. R.
  Post-war planning and budgetary policy in
    India. IJE 29:147-54 Oct 48
CLADAKIS, N. J. and Pollard, A. J.
  Some economic problems encountered in
    milk control administration. JFE 24:
    326-32 Feb 42
CLAGUE, EWAN [and others]
  Social security in a stable prosperity: dis-
    cussion. AER/S 37:351-66 May 47
CLAPHAM, Sir JOHN HAROLD
  William Robert Scott (born August 31, 1868.
    Died April 10, 1940). [obit.] EJ 50:
    347-51 Jun-Sep 40
  Charles Louis, Elector Palatine, 1617-1680:
    an early experiment in liberalism.
    Ec N.S.7:381-96 Nov 40
  Eileen Power, 1889-1940. [obit.] Ec N.S.7:
    351-59 Nov 40
  The private business of the Bank of England,
    1744-1800. EHR 11:77-89 no.1, 41
  Imperial economics. R. EHR 14:84-88
    no.1, 44
CLAPP, GORDON R.
  Problems of union relations in public
    agencies. AER/S 33:184-96 Mar 43
CLARENBACH, FRED A.
  and Regan, M. M. Emergency control in the
    farm real estate market. JFE 24:866-82
    Nov 42
  and Regan, M. M. Land market develop-
    ments and the war. JFE 25:190-202
    Feb 43
  and Regan, M. M. Postwar farm land values?
    LE 21:236-42 Aug 45
CLARK, ANDREW H.
  The historical explanation of land use in New
    Zealand. JEH 5:215-30 Nov 45
CLARK, CARL M.
  Seasonal patterns in tobacco prices. JFE 23:
    339-54 Feb 41
  Impact of war on marketing: discussion.
    JFE 25:142-46 Feb 43
CLARK, COLIN
  [Economic progress.] Note by author.
    ER 16:269 Dec 40
  The economic functions of a city in relation
    to its size. Em 13:97-113 Apr 45
  Post-war savings in the U.S.A. OIS 7:97-103
    May 19, 45
  Public finance and changes in the value of
    money. EJ 55:371-89 Dec 45
  and Dyne, R. E. Applications and extensions
    of the Karmel formula for reproductivity.
    ER 22:23-39 Jun 46

CLARK, COLIN (Cont.)
Russian income and production statistics.
REStat 29:215-17 Nov 47
The fruits of economic progress. EI 1:
239-46 Jan 48
A system of equations explaining the United
States trade cycle, 1921 to 1941. Em 17:
93-124 Apr 49
The value of the pound. EJ 59:198-207 Jun 49
Theory of economic growth. Em 17,suppl.:
112-14 Jul 49

CLARK, DONALD T. and Bursk, E. C.
Reading habits of business executives.
HBR 27:330-45 May 49

CLARK, EUGENE and Fishman, L.
Appraisal of methods for estimating the size
distribution of a given aggregate income.
REStat 29:43-46 Feb 47

CLARK, GRAHAME
Forest clearance and prehistoric farming.
EHR 17:45-51 no.1, 47

CLARK, JOHN DAVIDSON
Can government influence business stability?
JF 2,no.1:65-75 Apr 47

CLARK, JOHN MAURICE
Toward a concept of workable competition.
AER 30:241-56 Jun 40
Further remarks on defense financing and
inflation. REStat 23:107-12 Aug 41
The relation of government to the economy
of the future. JPE 49:797-816 Dec 41
Economic adjustments after wars: the
theoretical issues. AER/S 32:1-12 Mar 42
Relations of history and theory. (Symposium
on profits and the entrepreneur) JEH/S 2:
132-42 Dec 42
Imperfect competition theory and basing-
point problems. AER 33:283-300 Jun 43
--- Rejoinder. AER 33:616-19 Sep 43
Educational functions of economics after the
war. AER/S 34:58-67 Mar 44
General aspects of price control and ration-
ing in the transition period. AER/S 35:
152-62 May 45
Hansen's "Three methods of expansion
through fiscal policy": comment. AER 35:
926-28 Dec 45
Realism and relevance in the theory of de-
mand. JPE 54:347-53 Aug 46
Mathematical economists and others: a plea
for communicability. Em 15:75-78 Apr 47
Some current cleavages among economists.
AER/S 37:1-11 May 47
Note on income redistribution and investment.
AER 37:931 Dec 47
Law and economics of basing points. AER 39:
430-47 Mar 49
Machlup on the basing-point system. R.
QJE 63:315-21 Aug 49

CLARK, LINCOLN
The cooperative one-half of one per cent.
QJE 56:321-31 Feb 42
Credit unions in the United States. JB 16:
235-46 Oct 43

The credit-union legal framework. JB 17:
51-66 Jan 44

CLARK, NOBLE
An appreciation of Leonard A. Salter, Jr.
LE 22:302-03 Aug 46
Agricultural legislation: an appraisal of
current trends and problems ahead.
JFE 29:84-93 Feb 47
Production policies for a permanent and
profitable agriculture. LE 23:169-79
May 47

CLARK, ROBERT MILLS
The municipal business tax in Canada.
CJE 14:491-501 Nov 48
Report of the Commission to Investigate
Taxation in the City of Fredericton.
CJE 14:510-11 Nov 48

CLARK, ROBERT W.
Investment Bankers Association training
courses. JF 1:91-92 Aug 46

CLARK, SAMUEL DELBERT
Economic expansion and the moral order.
CJE 6:203-25 May 40
The religious sect in Canadian economic
development. CJE 12:439-53 Nov 46
The religious factor in Canadian economic
development. JEH/S 7:89-103 '47

CLARK, THOMAS DIONYSIOUS
Imperfect competition: In the southern
retail trade after 1865. JEH/S 3:38-47
Dec 43
Records of little businesses as sources of
social and economic history. BHR 19:
151-58 Nov 45

CLARK, TOM C.
New basing point problems. HBR 24:109-18
no.1, 45

CLARKSON, ELEANOR P.
Some suggestions for field research supervisors. JM 13:321-29 Jan 49

CLAUSON, GERARD LESLIE MAKINS
The British colonial currency system.
EJ 54:1-25 Apr 44

CLAWSON, MARION
Suggestions for a sample census of agriculture in the West. JFE 22:633-37 Aug 40
with Heisig, C. P. and Hurd, E. B. Long-
term forecasting of fruit and nut production. JFE 23:550-66 Aug 41
and Black, J. D. Agricultural income and the
export market: 1910-1940. JFE 24:
761-71 Nov 42
Demand interrelations for selected agricultural products. QJE 57:265-302 Feb 43
Post-war irrigation developments and the
national and regional agricultural economy.
JFE 27:138-52 Feb 45
Trends in major cropland use in the United
States, 1909-1941. JFE 27:472-76 May 45
Cattle-hog price and beef-pork consumption
ratios. JFE 28:848-52 Aug 46
Sequence in variation of annual precipitation
in the western United States. LE 23:271-87
Aug 47

CLAWSON, MARION (Cont.)
Range forage conditions in relation to annual precipitation. LE 24:264-80 Aug 48

CLAY, Sir HENRY
The place of exports in British industry after the war. EJ 52:145-53 Jun-Sep 42
The economic outlook of the United Kingdom. AER/S 37:12-20 May 47

CLEMEN, RUDOLF ALEXANDER
The growth of rigidity in business: discussion. AER/S 30:314-15 Mar 40

CLEMENCE, RICHARD and Doody, F. S.
Modern economics and the introductory course. AER 32:334-47 Jun 42

CLEMENS, ELI WINSTON
Price discrimination in decreasing cost industries. AER 31:794-802 Dec 41
The critical issue of depreciation in public utility valuation. SEJ 9:252-61 Jan 43
Ratemaking policies and practices of the Public Service Commission of Wisconsin. LE 20:223-37 Aug 44
Incremental cost pricing and discriminatory pricing. LE 21:68-71 Feb 45
The marginal revenue curve under price discrimination. AER 38:388-90 Jun 48

CLEMENT, SELDEN L.
Tobacco prices: discussion. JFE 23:356-61 Feb 41

CLENDENIN, JOHN C.
Crop insurance: an experiment in farm-income stabilization. LE 16:277-85 Aug 40

CLERC, JACQUES OLIVIER
Walras and Pareto: their approach to applied economics and social economics. CJE 8:584-94 Nov 42

CLEVELAND, ALFRED SAXTON
NAM: spokesman for industry? HBR 26:353-71 May 48

CLEWORTH, MARC MALVERN
Artesian-well irrigation: its history in Brown County, South Dakota, 1889-1900. AH 15:195-201 Oct 41

CLOUGH, SHEPARD BANCROFT
The economic history of a young corporation [the Economic History Association]. JEH/S 1:110-11 Dec 41
The crisis in French economy at the beginning of the Revolution. R. JEH 6:191-96 Nov 46
Retardative factors in French economic development in the nineteenth and twentieth centuries. JEH/S 6:91-102 '46

CLOW, ARCHIBALD
and Clow, N. L. Lord Dundonald. EHR 12:47-58 no.1-2, 42
and Clow, N. L. Vitriol in the industrial revolution. EHR 15:44-55 no.1-2, 45

CLOW, NAN L.
see entries under Clow, Archibald and Clow, N. L.

COALE, ANSLEY JOHNSON
The problem of reducing vulnerability to atomic bombs. AER/S 37:87-97 May 47

COASE, RONALD HARRY
and Fowler, R. F. The analysis of producers' expectations. Ec N.S.7:280-92 Aug 40
Price and output policy of state enterprise: a comment. EJ 55:112-13 Apr 45
The marginal cost controversy. Ec N.S.13:169-82 Aug 46
Monopoly pricing with interrelated costs and demands. Ec N.S.13:278-94 Nov 46
The economics of uniform pricing systems. MS 15:139-56 May 47
The marginal cost controversy: some further comments. Ec N.S.14:150-53 May 47
The origin of the monopoly of broadcasting in Great Britain. Ec N.S.14:189-210 Aug 47
Wire broadcasting in Great Britain. Ec N.S.15:194-220 Aug 48

COATES, GLENN
Agricultural profit-sharing in Puerto Rico. LE 24:309-11 Aug 48

C[OATS], R[OBERT] H[AMILTON]
Simon James McLean, 1871-1946. [obit.] CJE 13:121-22 Feb 47

COBB, CHARLES W.
A regression. Em 11:265-67 Jul-Oct 43
Employment and relative inflation in Massachusetts. Em 12:130-38 Apr 44
Price and volume. Em 13:273-74 Jul 45

COCHRAN, THOMAS CHILDS
Some social attitudes of railroad administrators at the end of the nineteenth century. BHR 17:15-21 Feb 43
Historical aspects of imperfect competition: theory and history. JEH/S 3:27-32 Dec 43
New York City business records: a plan for their preservation. BHR 18:59-62 Jun 44
The New York Committee on Business Records. JEH 5:60-64 May 45
The economics in a business history. JEH/S 5:54-65 Dec 45
The empirical approach. EEH 1,no.3:24-25 Mar 49
The legend of the robber barons. EEH 1,no.5:1-7 May 49

COCHRANE, DONALD
Travelling to work. ER 22:199-218 Dec 46
Measurement of economic relationships. ER 25,(no.49):7-23 Dec 49

COCHRANE, WILLARD WESLEY
A price policy for agriculture, consistent with economic progress, that will promote adequate and more stable income from farming. JFE 27:813-20 Nov 45
Income payments as a substitute for support prices. JFE 28:1024-29 Nov 46
Farm price gyrations: an aggregative hypothesis. JFE 29:383-408 May 47

COCHRANE, WILLARD WESLEY (Cont.)
Farm family budgets: a moving picture.
REStat 29:189-98 Aug 47; Erratum. 30:80
Feb 48
and Masucci, R. H. Price-income effects of
a food allotment program. JFE 29:752-60
Aug 47

COCKFIELD, F. A.
The distribution of incomes. Ec N.S:14:
254-82 Nov 47

COHEN, JULIUS and Cohen, L.
The National Labor Relations Board in ret-
rospect. ILRR 1:648-56 Jul 48
--- Reply. ILRR 2:251-52 Jan 49

COHEN, LILLIAN
see Cohen, Julius and Cohen, L.

COHEN, MARTIN A. and Lieberman, M.
Collective bargaining in the motor freight
industry. ILRR 3:17-32 Oct 49

COHEN, RUTH LOUISA
The new British law on monopoly. AER 39:
485-90 Mar 49

COHEN, WILBUR JOSEPH
and Falk, I. S. Social security for farm
people. JFE 28:84-96 Feb 46
Developments in social security: discussion.
IRRA 1:121-26 Dec 48

COHN, FANNIA MARY
Educational Department, ILGWU. ILRR 1:
704-08 Jul 48

COHN, SAMUEL MAURICE
Keynesian economics: the propensity to con-
sume and the multiplier: discussion.
AER/S 38:308-10 May 48

COKE, J.
Farm labour situation in Canada. JFE 25:
287-94 Feb 43

COLBERG, MARSHALL RUDOLPH
Monopoly prices under joint costs: fixed
proportions. JPE 48:103-10 Feb 41

COLBERT, ASEL R.
The transition to depreciation accounting.
LE 16:129-36 May 40
The NARUC Depreciation report: a sympo-
sium: a review of certain conclusions.
LE 20:89-97 May 44

COLE, ARTHUR HARRISON
with Schumpeter, J. A. and Mason, E. S.
Frank William Taussig. [obit.] QJE 55:
337-63 May 41
Entrepreneurship as an area of research.
JEH/S 2:118-26 Dec 42
A report on research in economic history.
JEH 4:49-72 May 44
Business manuscripts: a pressing problem.
The accumulated development of unsolved
problems. JEH 5:43-59 May 45
Business history and economic history.
JEH/S 5:45-53 Dec 45
Business and the stream of social thought.
HBR 23:203-10 no.2, 45
An approach to the study of entrepreneurship:
a tribute to Edwin F. Gay. JEH/S 6:
1-15 '46

The evolving perspective of businessmen.
HBR 27:123-28 Jan 49
Dales' "Approaches." EEH 1,no.2:24 Feb 49

COLE, GEORGE DOUGLAS HOWARD
J. A. Hobson (1858-1940). [obit.] EJ 50:
351-60 Jun-Sep 40
Beatrice Webb as an economist. EJ 53:
422-37 Dec 43

COLE, MARGARET ISABEL POSTGATE
British trade unions and the labour government. ILRR 1:573-79 Jul 48

COLEAN, MILES L.
Housing problems: discussion. AER/S 37:
527-28 May 47

COLEMAN, GEORGE W.
The effect of interest rate increases on the
banking system. AER 35:671-73 Sep 45

COLEMAN, RAYMOND
Government bonds and the balanced budget.
HBR 20:75-80 no.1, 41

COLEMAN, WILLIAM J.
Progress in Arkansas land policy. LE 18:
87-90 Feb 42

COLES, JESSIE VEE
[Marketing rewritten from the consumer's
point of view]: discussion. JM 4,no.4,pt.2:
132-34 Apr 40
and Erdman, H. E. Some aspects of the arguments against grade labeling. JM 9:
256-61 Jan 45
Student reactions to different groups of food
stores. JM 10:390-94 Apr 46
The pattern of retail food stores in a small
city. JM 13:163-71 Oct 48

COLETTA, PAOLA E.
Philip Pusey, English country squire.
AH 18:83-91 Apr 44

COLLET, CLARA ELIZABETH
Henry Higgs (March 4, 1864-May 21, 1940).
[obit.] EJ 50:546-55, 558-61 Dec 40
The present position of women in industry.
JRSS 105:122-24 pt.2, 42
Charles Booth, the Denison Club and H.
Llewellyn Smith. JRSS 108:482-85
pt.3-4, 45

COLLEY, RUSSELL H.
Some practical applications of precision
sampling. JM 14:437-41 Oct 49

COLLIER, GEORGE W.
Common errors in evaluating farm practices.
JFE 23:877-84 Nov 41
Problems in physical evaluation of soil con-
servation benefits. JFE 24:124-38 Feb 42
Procedures of studying returns from con-
servation farming. JFE 27:686-94 Aug 45

COLLINS, WILLIAM T.; Walker, Q. F. and
Higgins, D. E.
The effects of federal revenue acts of 1938,
1939, and 1940 on the realization of gains
and losses on securities. JASA 35:602-14
Dec 40; A correction. 36:122 Mar 41
--- Rejoinder. JASA 36:433-35 Sep 41

COLM, GERHARD
Comments on W. I. King: "Are we suffering from economic maturity?" JPE 48: 114-18 Feb 40
Full employment through tax policy? SR 7: 447-67 Nov 40
[Revising the postwar federal tax system]: discussion. AER/S 34,no.2:39-41 Jun 44
Fiscal problems of transition and peace: discussion. AER/S 35:352-53 May 45
From estimates of national income to projections of the nation's budget. SR 12:350-69 Sep 45
[and others] Social security in a stable prosperity: discussion. AER/S 37:351-66 May 47
On the road to economic stabilization. SR 15: 265-76 Sep 48
Why public finance? NTJ 1:193-206 Sep 48
The government budget and the nation's economic budget. PF 3:5-14 no.1, 48

COMAN, EDWIN T., Jr.
Sidelights on the investment policies of Stanford, Huntington, Hopkins, and Crocker. BHR 16:85-89 Nov 42
The status of business history at the Stanford Graduate School of Business. BHR 20: 17-21 Feb 46

COMER, GEORGE P.
The outlook for effective competition. AER/S 36:154-71 May 46

COMISH, NEWEL HOWLAND
Retail store operating results as guides for small merchants. JM 11:62-64 Jul 46
The model stock plan in small stores. JM 11:402-07 Apr 47

COMMONS, JOHN ROGERS
Legislative and administrative reasoning in economics. JFE 24:369-91 May 42

COMPTON, WILSON
The Southern Pine case. LE 16:214-16 May 40

CONAN, ARTHUR ROBERT
Notes on some balance of payments figures. OIS 9:196-206 Jun 47

CONANT, JAMES BRYANT
The place of research in our national life. HBR 26:46-57 Jan 48

CONDLIFFE, JOHN BELL
The disposal of agricultural surpluses. JFE 24:434-46 May 42
War and economics. JPE 51:157-65 Apr 43
Economic power as an instrument of national policy. AER/S 34:305-14 Mar 44
Exchange stabilization and international trade. REStat 26:166-69 Nov 44
The foreign loan policy of the United States. EI 1:568-83 May 48
John H. Chapman. [obit.] ER 25,(no.48): 92-93 Jun 49

CONDRON, H. DAVID
The Knapheide Wagon Company 1848-1943. JEH 3:32-41 May 43

CONKLIN, HOWARD E.
The rural-urban economy of the Elmira-Corning region. LE 20:1-19 Feb 44
A neglected point in the training of agricultural economists. JFE 29:925-37 Nov 47
Some new directions of land economic research in the Northeast. JFE 31,pt.2: 1043-57 Nov 49

CONNELL, KENNETH HUGH
The population of Ireland in the eighteenth century. EHR 16:111-24 no.2, 46

CONNOR, WILLIAM S. and Cowden, D. J.
The use of statistical methods for economic control of quality in industry. SEJ 12: 115-29 Oct 45

CONSTANTIN, JAMES A.
Multilateralism in international aviation. SEJ 16:197-209 Oct 49

CONSTANTINE, EARL
Trade associations and government statistics. JASA 42:20-22 Mar 47

CONVERSE, PAUL DULANEY
and Spencer, C. What housewives think of the super-market. JM 6:371-74 Apr 42
Tobacco auctions evaluated. JB 16:147-59 Jul 43
and Beattie, T. E. Are chain stores good citizens? JM 8:172-84 Oct 43
The development of the science of marketing: an exploratory survey. JM 10:14-23 Jul 45
Fred Clark's bibliography as of the early 1920's. JM 10:54-57 Jul 45
The total cost of marketing. JM 10:389 Apr 46
New laws of retail gravitation. JM 14: 379-84 Oct 49

COOK, STANLEY and James, R.
Job specification and a fair wage. EJ 57: 387-93 Sep 47

COOKE, D. H. and Keirstead, B. S.
Dynamic theory of rents. CJE 12:168-72 May 46

COOKE, GILBERT WILLIAM
Savings deposits in mutual and nonmutual banks, 1911-40. JB 16:195-203 Jul 43

COOKE, HELEN J. MELLON
Significance of bank capital ratios. JPE 57: 75-77 Feb 49

COOLEY, RUSSELL E.
Labor relations problems of a federal government procurement agency. IRRA 2: 242-47 Dec 49

COOLSEN, FRANK GORDON
Pioneers in the development of advertising. JM 12:80-86 Jul 47

COONEY, E. W.
Capital exports, and investment in building in Britain and the U.S.A. 1856-1914. Ec N.S.16:347-54 Nov 49

COONLEY, HOWARD
How big should a business be? JM 5:102-09 Oct 40

COOPER, GERSHON
The role of econometric models in economic
research. JFE 30:101-16 Feb 48
COOPER, MARTIN REESE and Barton, G. T.
Relation of agricultural production to inputs.
REStat 30:117-26 May 48
COOPER, MAURICE ROYCE
Agriculture in the South: review. JFE 29:
203-05 Feb 47
COOPER, THOMAS
Training and recruitment of agricultural
economic personnel: IV. A training pro-
gram. JFE 22:558-59 Aug 40
COOPER, WILLIAM WAGER
The yardstick for utility regulation. JPE 51:
258-62 Jun 43
Theory of the firm: some suggestions for
revision. AER 39:1204-22 Dec 49
COPE, SYDNEY RAYMOND
The Goldsmids and the development of the
London money market during the Napole-
onic wars. Ec N.S.9:180-206 May 42
The original security bank. Ec N.S.13:50-55
Feb 46
COPELAND, MELVIN THOMAS
The job of an executive. HBR 18:148-60
no.2, 40
Price trends of industrial chemicals.
HBR 18:437-47 no.4, 40
COPELAND, MORRIS ALBERT
[and others] Round table on population prob-
lems. [Summaries of discussion]
AER/S 30:393-98 Mar 40
Competing products and monopolistic compe-
tition. QJE 55:1-35 Nov 40
Economic research in the federal govern-
ment. AER 31:526-36 Sep 41
A social appraisal of differential pricing.
JM 6,no.4,pt.2:177-84 Apr 42
The defense effort and the national income
response pattern. JPE 50:415-26 Jun 42
The capital budget and the war effort.
AER 33:38-49 Mar 43
How achieve full and stable employment.
AER/S 34:134-47 Mar 44
Business stabilization by agreement. AER 34:
328-39 Jun 44
Interdepartmental courses in the social sci-
ences: discussion. AER/S 35:148-49
May 45
with Jacobson, J. and Lasken, H. The WPB
index of war production. JASA 40:145-59
Jun 45
The social and economic determinants of the
distribution of income in the United States.
AER 37:56-75 Mar 47
Tracing money flows through the United
States economy. AER/S 37:31-49 May 47
Keynesian economics: savings, investment,
and wage rates: discussion. AER/S 38:
351-53 May 48
COPLAND, Sir DOUGLAS BERRY
America's economic leadership. HBR 23:
415-19 no.4, 45

Professor Jewkes and the alternative to
planning. R. ER 24:191-203 Dec 48
Balance of production in the Australian
post-war economy. ER 25,(no.49):1-6
Dec 49
COPP, GEORGE FREDERIC
Metropolitan districts: their areal relation-
ships. LE 25:213-15 May 49
COPPOCK, JOSEPH DAVID
Indifference curve analysis applied to the
food stamp plan. AER 35:99-110 Mar 45
COPPOLA D'ANNA, FRANCESCO
False aims in the I.T.O. draft charter.
BNL 1:143-48 Oct 47
Italian joint stock companies from 1938 to
1948. BNL 2:159-71 Jul-Sep 49
CORDELL, WARREN N.
The commercial use of probability samples.
JM 14:447-49 Oct 49
CORNELIUS JUSTIN, brother
The study of industrial and labor relations in
Catholic colleges. ILRR 3:70-75 Oct 49
CORNELL, FRANCIS G.
Grant-in-aid apportionment formulas.
JASA 42:92-104 Mar 47
CORNFIELD, JEROME
On certain biases in samples of human popu-
lations. JASA 37:63-68 Mar 42
CORSON, JOHN JAY
Agricultural workers and social insurance.
JFE 24:285-95 Feb 42
COSCIANI, CESARE
Italian tax policy. BNL 1:86-99 Jul 47
A critical examination of the Italian tax sys-
tem. BNL 1:311-20 Apr 48
COSMO, GIANDOMENICO
Unemployment and emigration in Italy in the
light of the E.R.P. and O.E.E.C. BNL 1:
434-40 Oct 48
Balance-sheet of the first year of the ERP
in Italy. BNL 2:111-17 Apr-Jun 49
COTTAM, HOWARD R.
Housing scales for rural Pennsylvania.
JASA 38:406-16 Dec 43
COTTLE, CHARLES SIDNEY
Factors to be considered in appraising
formula plans. SEJ 16:62-79 Jul 49
COURT, LOUIS M.
Entrepreneurial and consumer demand
theories for commodity spectra. Pt.I-II.
Em 9:135-62; 241-97 Apr, Jul-Oct 41
Invariable classical stability of entrepren-
eurial demand and supply functions.
QJE 56:134-44 Nov 41
and Lewis, H. G. Production cost indices.
REStud 10:28-42 no.1, 42
COURT, WILLIAM HENRY BASSANO
Problems of the British coal industry be-
tween the wars. EHR 15:1-24 no.1-2, 45
COURTAULD, SAMUEL
An industrialist's reflections on the future
relations of government and industry.
EJ 52:1-17 Apr 42

COURTNEY, CHARLES JAMES
How many jobs must we provide for a bal-
anced postwar economy? RSE 3:34-42
Dec 44

COUTANT, FRANK R.
Marketing's part in getting back to sound
prosperity. JM 11:285-87 Jan 47

COVA, PIETRO
The Italian tobacco industry: a state monopoly. BNL 1:157-68 Oct 47

COVER, JOHN HIGSON
[International financial relations after the
war]: discussion. AER/S 33:390-92
Mar 43

COWAN, DONALD ROSS GRANT
Trends in industrial marketing. JM 6,no.4,
pt.2:12-13 Apr 42
Commercial research for post war activities.
JM 7:49-56 Jul 42
Requisites of a successful sales program.
JM 10:244-52 Jan 46

COWDEN, DUDLEY JOHNSTONE and Connor,
W. S.
The use of statistical methods for economic
control of quality in industry. SEJ 12:
115-29 Oct 45

COWDEN, THOMAS KYLE
Current trends in agricultural policy.
JFE 31,pt.2:800-05 Nov 49

COWLES, ALFRED
Stock market forecasting. Em 12:206-14
Jul-Oct 44

COWLES, WILLARD BUNCE
Recovery in American claims abroad.
HBR 25:92-110 no.1, 46

COX, GARFIELD V.
The American economy in the interwar
period: discussion. AER/S 36:28-32
May 46
Free enterprise vs. authoritarian planning.
JB 20:59-66 Apr 47

COX, LAWANDA FENLASON
Tenancy in the United States, 1865-1900: a
consideration of the validity of the agricultural ladder hypothesis. AH 18:97-105
Jul 44
The American agricultural wage earner,
1865-1900: the emergence of a modern
labor problem. AH 22:95-114 Apr 48

COX, REAVIS
Non-price competition and the measurement
of prices. JM 10:370-83 Apr 46
The meaning and measurement of productivity
in distribution. JM 12:433-41 Apr 48
and Alderson, W. Towards a theory of mar-
keting. JM 13:137-52 Oct 48
[Commodity marketing: going where?]
General synthesis. AER/S 39:421-23
May 49

COX, REX W. and Waite, W. C.
The influence of prices on agricultural production. JFE 26:382-88 May 44

COYAJEE, Sir JEHANGIR COOVERJEE
Ranade's work as an economist. IJE 22:
307-30 Jan 42

CRAGG, ALLISTON
Streamlined shopping credit. JB 15:21-29
Jan 42

CRAIG, GLENN H.
and Livers, J. J. Role of soil depletion in
land valuation. JFE 22:773-76 Nov 40
War developments in land utilization and
policy in the northern Plains. JFE 25:
176-87 Feb 43

CRAIG, JAMES IRELAND
The general rise of prices in Egypt.
EgC 32:1-56 Jan-Feb 41
Money and prices in Egypt (preliminary
note). EgC 34:327-33 Apr-May 43
The definition of "inflation." EgC 36:35-46
Jan-Feb 45
Industry and statistics. EgC 39:39-43
Jan-Feb 48

CRAIG, Sir JOHN HERBERT McCUTCHEON
and Shirras, G. F.
Sir Isaac Newton and the currency. EJ 55:
217-41 Jun-Sep 45

CRAINE, LYLE E.
Chain store taxes as revenue measures.
NTJ 2:280-83 Sep 49

CRANE, JOHN B.
The economics of air transportation.
HBR 22:495-508 no.4, 44

CRANE, RONALD SALMON
Montesquieu and British thought. R.
JPE 49:592-600 Jun 41

CRANFILL, SAMUEL ELLIOTT
Recent contributions of John R. Commons
to economic thought. SEJ 7:63-79
Jul 40

CRAVENS, MELELLUS EUGENE and Hathaway,
D. E.
Quality factors affecting the price of peaches
on the Benton Harbor market. JFE 31,
pt.2:631-34 Feb 49

CRAWFORD, JOHN GRENFELL
and Lange, G. County planning for land-use
adjustment. JFE 22:473-83 May 40
Cost of production surveys in relation to
price fixing of primary products. ER 25,
suppl.:29-58 Aug 49

CREAMER, DANIEL
Recruiting contract laborers for the Amoskeag mills. JEH 1:42-56 May 41

CRESSEY, GEORGE B.
USSR: the geographic base for agricultural
planning. LE 25:334-36 Nov 49

CRICK, WILFRED FRANK
What's the use of economists? SAJE 14:
17-21 Mar 46
Free trade and planned economy. SAJE 15:
40-46 Mar 47

CRICKMAN, CHLORUS WILLIAM
[and others] Recent regional changes in
farming and probable future trends.
JFE 24:256-79 Feb 42

CRICKMAN, CHLORUS WILLIAM (Cont.)
Postwar agricultural problems in the corn
belt. JFE 28:243-60 Feb 46
Interregional economic and social aspects of
an objective evaluation of soil conserva-
tion. JFE 31,pt.2:660-63 Feb 49
CRIPPEN, HARLAN R.
Conflicting trends in the Populist movement.
S&S 6:133-49 no.2, 42
Workers and jobs in wartime Britain.
S&S 6:208-26 no.3, 42
Philippine agrarian unrest: historical back-
grounds. S&S 10:337-60 no.4, 46
CROCKETT, JEAN
An incentive tax proposal for alleviation of
the housing shortage. NTJ 1:51-61
Mar 48
CROCKETT, SAMUEL L.
Some probable effects of taxation on farmers'
marketing practices. JFE 31:725-30
Nov 49
CRON, LAWRENCE E.
An application of analysis of covariance to
price-quality relationships of eggs.
JFE 22:440-45 May 40
CRONIN, JOHN FRANCIS
Implementing the social encyclicals in
American economic life. RSE 5:1-18
Jun 47
The place of economics in liberal arts col-
leges and seminaries. RSE 7,no.1:1-7
Mar 49
CRONJÉ, F. J. C.
The influence of raw wool prices on wool
consumption. SAJE 15:147-48 Jun 47
Wool in the South African economy. SAJE 17:
123-41 Jun 49
CRONKITE, FREDERICK C.
The Judicial Committee and the farm debt
problem. CJE 9:557-64 Nov 43
CROOME, HONOR
Liberty, equality and full employment.
LBR 13:14-32 Jul 49
CROSBY, JAMES E. and Burch, J. W.
Discussion of papers on postwar extension
problems in agricultural economics.
JFE 28:226-34 Feb 46
CROSLAND, CHARLES ANTHONY RAVEN
The movement of labour in 1948. Pt.I-II.
OIS 11:117-26; 194-212 May, Jul-Aug 49
CROSS, IRA BROWN
A note on the use of the word "currency."
JPE 52:362-63 Dec 44
CROSS, JAMES SHORTEN
The volume and significance of mercantile
credit. JM 14:391-98 Oct 49
CROSSLAND, C. A. R.
see Crosland, Charles Anthony Raven
CROSSLEY, ARCHIBALD M.
Theory and application of representative
sampling as applied to marketing. JM 5:
456-61 Apr 41
chairman. Report of sub-committee on de-

scriptive classification of income levels.
JM 6:379-82 Apr 42
The effect of the war on income changes.
JM 7:355-59 Apr 43
The impact of war on American families.
JM 8:41-45 Jul 43
CROTEAU, JOHN TOUGAS
The credit union: legal form versus eco-
nomic function. RSE 7,no.2:10-28 Sep 49
CROWDER, WALTER FREDERICK
and Thorp, W. L. Concentration and product
characteristics as factors in price-
quantity behavior. AER/S 30,no.5:
390-408 Feb 41
Market outlook for machines and equipment.
[Abstract] AER/S 39:420-21 May 49
CROWLEY, N. G. and Haddon-Cave, C. P.
The regulation and expansion of world trade
and employment. ER 23:32-48 Jun 47
CROWLEY, W. J.
Elasticity of residential demand for elec-
tricity: a reply. LE 17:499-501 Nov 41
CROWTHER, GEOFFREY [and others]
International economic relations: discus-
sion. AER/S 33:332-35 Mar 43
CRUIKSHANK, NELSON H.
Developments in social security: discus-
sion. IRRA 1:126-29 Dec 48
CRUM, WILLIAM LEONARD
The current improvement in business profits.
REStat 22:157-60 Nov 40
Postwar federal expenditures and their im-
plications for tax policy. AER/S 35:
329-40 May 45
CRUMBAKER, CALVIN
Note on concentration of economic power.
R. JPE 50:934-44 Dec 42
CRUMP, NORMAN
[and others] Post-war international mone-
tary plans. JRSS 106:201-13 pt.3, 43
Britain's new post-war economic guide.
JASA 41:171-72 Jun 46
CULE, J. E.
Finance and industry in the eighteenth cen-
tury: the firm of Boulton and Watt. EH 4:
319-25 Feb 40
CULLITON, JAMES WILLIAM
Massachusetts prepares for tomorrow.
HBR 21:298-308 no.3, 43
Note on turnover in government personnel.
HBR 24:512-17 no.4, 46
The management challenge of marketing
costs. HBR 26:74-88 Jan 48
Business and religion. HBR 27:265-71
May 49
CUMMINGS, RICHARD O.
American interest in world agriculture,
1861-1865. AH 23:116-23 Apr 49
CUNNINGHAM, LOWELL CLEM
Regional changes in farming: discussion.
JFE 24:283-84 Feb 42
Postwar agricultural problems in the dairy
regions. JFE 28:261-64 Feb 46

CUNNINGHAM, LOWELL CLEM (Cont.)
and Warren, S. W. Sampling methods in use
in some of the farm management research
at Cornell. JFE 29:1267-70 Nov 47
Use of outlook in an extension program.
JFE 31,pt.2:640-41 Feb 49

CUNNINGHAM, ROSS M.
Locating and appraising product ideas.
JM 7:41-48 Jul 42

CUNNINGHAM, WILLIAM JAMES
James J. Hill's philosophy of railroad management. BHR 15:65-72 Nov 41
The transportation problem. HBR 25:58-73
no.1, 46

CURRIE, ARCHIBALD WILLIAM
Some economic aspects of air transport.
CJE 7:13-24 Feb 41
Rate control of public utilities in British
Columbia. CJE 10:381-90 Aug 44
The Board of Transport Commissioners as
an administrative body. CJE 11:342-58
Aug 45
Rate control on Canadian public utilities.
CJE 12:148-58 May 46
Freight rates and regionalism. CJE 14:
427-40 Nov 48

CURTIS, ALBERTA and Goldsen, J. M.
Montclair studies the shopping experiences
and attitudes of its residents. JM 10:
165-70 Oct 45

CURTIS, WILLIAM RANDOLPH
Unemployment compensation experience in
the South. SEJ 7:51-72 Jul 40
The development of unemployment insurance
in the South. SEJ 15:43-53 Jul 48

CURTISS, WILLIAM MARSHALL
Farm labor and food production. JFE 25:
301-04 Feb 43

CUSACK, MARY THOMASINE, sister
[Philosophy and analysis of recent union-
control legislation]: discussion. RSE 6:
80-84 May 48

CUTLER, ADDISON THAYER
War economics and the American people.
S&S 4:165-82 no.3, 40
Labor legislation in thirteen southern states.
SEJ 7:297-316 Jan 41

CUTLER, HOWARD ARMSTRONG
The elasticity of the residential demand for
electricity. LE 17:242-45 May 41
Elasticity of residential demand for electricity: a rejoinder. LE 17:501-03 Nov 41

CUTSHALL, ALDEN
The manufacture of food and kindred products in the lower Wabash Valley. AH 18:
16-22 Jan 44

DACEY, WILLIAM MANNING
The 1944 White Paper on national income
and expenditure. EJ 54:177-88 Jun-Sep 44
Inflation and its aftermath. LBR 1:24-34
Jul 46
The cheap money technique. LBR 3:49-63
Jan 47

Inflation under controls. LBR 4,suppl.:2-8
Apr 47
National income in the transition. LBR 5:
43-57 Jul 47
The budget, overseas borrowing and domes-
tic investment. LBR 9:34-51 Jul 48

DAGGETT, STUART
"Transportation and national policy." R.
HBR 22:199-208 no.2, 44
Railroad traffic associations and antitrust
legislation. AER/S 38:452-64 May 48

DALAL, K. N.
Cheap money. IJE 28:377-82 Jan 48

DALAL, KANTILAL LALLUBHAI
Measurement of the "burden" of the public
debt. IJE 29:135-46 Oct 48

DALE, ERNEST
The American foreman unionizes. JB 19:
25-30 Jan 46
Increasing productivity through labor-man-
agement co-operation. ILRR 3:33-44
Oct 49

DALES, JOHN H.
Approaches to entrepreneurial history.
EEH 1,no.1:10-14 Jan 49

DALTON, MELVILLE
Worker response and social background.
JPE 55:323-32 Aug 47

DALY, FREDERICK ST. LEGER
The scope and method of economics.
CJE 11:165-76 May 45

DALY, MICHAEL C.
Regional differences in rates and rateable
values in England and Wales, 1921-1936.
QJE 54:624-54 Aug 40
An approximation to a geographical multiplier. EJ 50:248-58 Jun-Sep 40
The effect of overhead costs upon the structure of the American economy. SEJ 8:
22-39 Jul 41
An analysis of the comparability tables of
the Census of retail distribution. JM 10:
42-53 Jul 45

DALY, PATRICIA
with Olson, E. and Douglas, P. H. The
production function for manufacturing in
the United States, 1904. JPE 51:61-65
Feb 43
and Douglas, P. H. The production function
for Canadian manufactures. JASA 38:
178-86 Jun 43

DAMERON, KENNETH
Advertising and the consumer movement.
JM 5:234-47 Jan 41
Retailing and consumer movements. JM 5:
385-94 Apr 41
Consumer trends in 1941. JM 6,no.4,pt.2:
11-12 Apr 42
Information in advertising. HBR 20:482-95
no.4, 42
Labeling terminology. JB 18:157-66 Jul 45
Consumer meeting agenda: a study in con-
sumer interests. JB 21:98-119 Apr 48

DANHOF, CLARENCE H.
 Farm-making costs and the "safety valve":
  1850-60. JPE 49:317-59 Jun 41
 Economic validity of the safety-valve doc-
  trine. JEH/S 1:96-106 Dec 41
 The fencing problem in the eighteen-fifties.
  AH 18:168-86 Oct 44
 American evaluations of European agricul-
  ture. JEH/S 9:61-71 '49
DANIEL, ARNOLD
 Regional differences of productivity in
  European agriculture. REStud 12:50-70
  no.1, 44
DANIEL, GORONWY H.
 Some factors affecting the movement of
  labour. OEP 3:144-79 Feb 40
 War-time consumption of food. OIS 2,no.3:
  5-6 Jun 30, 40
 War-time release of labour from consump-
  tion-goods industries. OIS 2,no.4:7-9
  Jul 40
 War-time food requirements of the United
  Kingdom. OIS 2,no.5:6-7 Aug 10, 40
 The cost of living in Bristol. OIS 3:324-29
  Oct 11, 41
DANIEL, J. LELAND
 Interest rates: long-term vs. short-term.
  Em 8:272-78 Jul 40
DANILEVSKY, NADIA and Vance, R. B.
 Population and the pattern of unemployment
  in the Southeast, 1930-1937. SEJ 7:
  187-203 Oct 40
D'ANNA, FRANCESCO COPPOLA
 see Coppola d'Anna, Francesco
DANTZIG, GEORGE B. and Wood, M.
 Programming of interdependent activities.
  Pt.I-II. [Pt.II by Dantzig alone] Em 17:
  193-99; 200-11 Jul-Oct 49
DARLING, PHILIP
 A short-cut method for evaluating housing
  quality. LE 25:184-92 May 49
DAS, ANUKUL CHANDRA and Dutt, K.
 Problem of agricultural labour in India.
  IJE 28:155-61 Jul 47
DAS, NISHITH KUMAR
 Prospects of cotton mill industry in Bengal.
  IJE 28:533-46 Apr 48
DASGUPTA, AMIYA KUMAR
 The elasticity of reciprocal demand and
  terms of international trade. IJE 22:
  164-76 Oct 41
 The Indian fiscal policy. R. IJE 23:101-14
  Oct 42
DASH, S. C.
 Minimum wages for agricultural labour.
  IJE 28:131-35 Jul 47
DASH, SHREE RAM CHANDRA
 Land system in Orissa. IJE 27:205-12 Oct 46
DATEY, C. D.
 Municipal taxation in C.P. & Berar. IJE 22:
  658-66 Jan 42
DATTA, ANIL
 International equilibrium in a complementary
  economy. IJE 23:221-56 Jan 43

DATTA, BHABATOSH
 The continuity-assumption in economic
  analysis. IJE 20:779-86 Apr 40
 The background of Ranade's economics.
  IJE 22:261-75 Jan 42
DATTA, H. K.
 Profit-sharing, the incentive. IJE 29:223-26
  Oct 48
DAUER, ERNST AUGUST
 Radical changes in industrial banks.
  HBR 25:609-24 no.4a, 47
DAUGHERTY, CARROLL ROOP
 Union policies and leadership in postwar
  America. AER/S 34:166-80 Mar 44
 The field of labor economics. R. AER 35:
  652-57 Sep 45
 The allowable area of industrial conflict.
  IRRA 2:42-45 Dec 49
DAUGHERTY, MARION ROBERTS
 The currency-banking controversy. Pt.I-II.
  SEJ 9:140-55; 241-51 Oct 42, Jan 43
DAVENPORT, DONALD HILLS
 War demands on the labor supply. HBR 19:
  451-57 no.4, 41
 Estimating labor requirements. JASA 37:
  48-53 Mar 42
 and Hitchcock, D. Swords and plowshares.
  HBR 20:307-14 no.3, 42
DAVENPORT, RUSSELL
 How big should a business be? JM 5:97-102
  Oct 40
DAVEY, HAROLD WILLIAM
 Hazards in labor arbitration. ILRR 1:
  386-405 Apr 48
DAVID, PAUL THEODORE
 Aviation in the postwar world: discussion.
  AER/S 35:249-52 May 45
DAVIDSON, JAMES WIGHTMAN
 The history of empire. R. EHR 16:68-73
  no.1, 46
DAVIDSON, ROBERT DONALD and Wernimont,
  K.
 Tenure arrangements in Oklahoma oil fields.
  LE 19:40-58 Feb 43
DAVIES, BRINSLEY H.
 Report of the Coal Commission, 1946/47. R.
  SAJE 17:155-65 Jun 49
DAVIES, EDGAR J.
 The Louisiana Property Tax Relief Fund: a
  source of financial assistance for local
  governments. NTJ 1:270-72 Sep 48
DAVIES, GEORGE REGINALD
 Pricing and price levels. Em 14:219-26
  Jul 46
DAVIS, ARTHUR K.
 Sociological elements in Veblen's economic
  theory. JPE 53:132-49 Jun 45
DAVIS, CHESTER CHARLES
 Place of farmers, economists and administra-
  tors in developing agricultural policy.
  JFE 22:1-9 Feb 40
DAVIS, HORACE BANCROFT
 The theory of union growth. QJE 55:611-37
  Aug 41

DAVIS, JOHN CORDON and Hitch, T. K.
Wages and productivity. REStat 31:292-98
Nov 49

DAVIS, JOHN HERBERT
Review of papers on agricultural coopera-
tion. JFE 29:128-29 Feb 47
The International Federation of Agricultural
Producers. JFE 29:1101-06 Nov 47
The place of cooperatives in a sound farm
economy. JFE 29:1145-51 Nov 47

DAVIS, JOSEPH STANCLIFFE
A desirable foreign trade policy for American agriculture. JFE 22:430-39 May 40
Consumption level; consumption standard;
plane of living; standard of living. JM 6:
164-66 Oct 41
Food in a world at war. HBR 19:133-42
no.2, 41
chairman. The history of American corporations: abstract of specialized conference discussion. AER/S 32:211-12
Mar 42
International commodity agreements in the
postwar world. AER/S 32:391-403
Mar 42
The world's food position and outlook.
HBR 21:43-49 no.1, 42
chairman. Round table on international commodity agreements. AER/S 33:466-72
Mar 43
Standards and content of living. AER 35:
1-15 Mar 45
Experience under intergovernmental commodity agreements, 1902-45. JPE 54:
193-220 Jun 46
American agriculture: Schultz' analysis and
policy proposals. R. REStat 29:80-91
May 47
Food prices. (Ten economists on the infla-
tion) REStat 30:8-10 Feb 48
Our amazing population upsurge. JFE 31,
pt.2:765-78 Nov 49

DAVIS, SHELBY CULLOM
Coordinating production for war. JASA 38:
417-24 Dec 43

DAVIS, WILLIAM H.
Our national patent policy. AER/S 38:235-44
May 48

DAWSON, ANTHONY A. P.
Holywood's labor troubles. ILRR 1:638-47
Jul 48

DAWSON, HARRIS P., Jr.
Expanding local postwar employment data to
produce state estimates. JASA 40:
197-204 Jun 45

DAWSON, W. B.
Interim Report by Professor S. Herbert
Frankel on the Rhodesia Railways, 1943.
SAJE 11:287-93 Dec 43

D[AY], J[OHN] P[ERCIVAL]
Professor Leacock at McGill. [obit.]
CJE 10:226-30 May 44

DAY, OSCAR A.
Training agricultural economic majors:
discussion. JFE 29:1354-57 Nov 47

DEAN, JOEL
Statistical cost curves in various industries.
[Abstract] AER/S 30:400-01 Mar 40
and Wise, M. H. An appraisal of index numbers of prices farmers pay. JASA 36:
210-18 Jun 41
Direct control of machinery prices. HBR 20:
277-89 no.3, 42
and Balmer, S. L. Gearing salaries of
nation-wide chains to the geographical
structure of wages. JB 20:96-115 Apr 47
Cost structures of enterprises and break-
even charts. AER/S 38:153-64 May 48
Cost forecasting and price policy. JM 13:
279-88 Jan 49

DEAN, JOHN P.
The orientation of housing research. LE 23:
76-80 Feb 47
Only Caucasian: a study of race covenants.
LE 23:428-32 Nov 47

DE BEERS, JOHN STERLING
Tariff aspects of a federal union. QJE 56:
49-92 Nov 41
Some aspects of Latin America's trade and
balance of payments. AER/S 39:384-95
May 49

DEBIEN, GABRIEL
Land clearings and artificial meadows in
eighteenth-century Poitou. AH 19:133-37
Jul 45
Marc Bloch and rural history. [Translated
by H. E. Hart] AH 21:187-89 Jul 47

DE CHAZEAU, MELVIN GARDNER
Round table on preserving competition versus
regulating monopoly. [Summary of
remarks] AER/S 30:213-15 Mar 40
Electric power as a regional problem.
SEJ 7:494-504 Apr 41
Employment policy and organization of industry after the war. AER 35:629-39 Sep 45
[and others] [Wage-price relations at high
level employment]: discussion. AER/S 37:
254-64 May 47

DECKINGER, E. L.
The network radio advertiser and summer
policy. JM 13:23-26 Jul 48

DEDMAN, M.
Integration in the Australian wool textile industry. ER 24:111-16 Jun 48

DE GRAAF, ANDRIES
see Graaf, Andries de

DeGRAFF, HERRELL
Effects of technological changes on north-
eastern agriculture. JFE 31,pt.2:445-47
Feb 49

DE HAAS, JACOB ANTON
World trade faces a new order. HBR 19:
243-47 no.2, 41
Buying Latin American loyalty. HBR 19:
298-310 no.3, 41

DE HAAS, JACOB ANTON (Cont.)
The democratic new order. HBR 19:470-81
no.4, 41
The future of world trade. HBR 21:100-08
no.1, 42
Economic peace through private agreements.
HBR 22:139-54 no.2, 44

DEIBLER, FREDERICK SHIPP
Horace Secrist, 1881-1943. [obit.] JASA 38:
365-66 Sep 43

DEIMEL, HENRY L., Jr.
United States shipping policy and international economic relations. AER/S 36:
547-60 May 46

DE JONGH, THEUNIS WILLEM
Monetary and banking factors and the busi-
ness cycle in the Union. SAJE 9:138-53
Jun 41

DE KOCK, MICHIEL HENDRIK
World monetary policy after the present war.
SAJE 9:113-37 Jun 41
The concepts of money, capital and credit.
SAJE 12:13-27 Mar 44
International Bank for Reconstruction and
Development. SAJE 12:223-32 Sep 44

DELAPLANE, WALTER HAROLD
The war and an agricultural economy: the
case of Colombia. SEJ 9:33-45 Jul 42

DEMAREE, ALBERT LOWTHER
The farm journals, their editors, and their
public, 1830-1860. AH 15:182-88 Oct 41

DEMARS, VERNON
Relationships of technological and social research in housing. LE 25:94-96 Feb 49

DEMBITZ, LEWIS N. [and others]
The social and economic significance of
atomic energy: discussion. AER/S 37:
109-17 May 47

DEMERATH, NICHOLAS, chairman
Housing needs and housing standards.
Panel IV. [Symposium: Frontiers of
housing research] LE 25:116-32 Feb 49

DEMING, WILLIAM EDWARDS
and Simmons, W. On the design of a sample
for dealers' inventories. JASA 41:16-33
Mar 46
Some criteria for judging the quality of surveys. JM 12:145-57 Oct 47

DEMPSEY, BERNARD WILLIAM
Economics implicit in the social encyclicals.
RSE 1:12-18 Dec 42
Ability to pay. [Presidential address] RSE 4:
1-13 Jan 46
"Ability to pay." [Based on the presidential
address before the Catholic Economic
Association] QJE 60:351-64 May 46
The roots of business responsibility. HBR 27:
393-404 Jul 49

DENHARDT, EDITH TILTON and White, B. S.,
Jr.
Chronic surpluses of agricultural commodities in the post-war period. JFE 25:
743-58 Nov 43

DENIS, HENRI
A note on the theory of tariffs. REStud 12:
110-13 no.2, 45

DENISON, EDWARD FULTON
The influence of the Walsh-Healey Public
Contracts Act upon labor conditions.
JPE 49:225-46 Apr 41
[and others] Objectives of national income
measurement: a reply to Professor
Kuznets. REStat 30:179-95 Aug 48

DENNIS, RICHARD WILLIAM GEORGE and
Buttress, F. A.
The early history of cereal seed treatment
in England. AH 21:93-103 Apr 47

DENNIS, SAMUEL J.
Housing in relation to national defense.
JASA 36:36-44 Mar 41

DENNISON, HENRY S.
[Imperfect competition.] In the Dennison
Manufacturing Company. JEH/S 3:48-50
Dec 43

DENNISON, STANLEY RAYMOND
The distribution of the industrial population.
R. EJ 50:342-47 Jun-Sep 40
Industrial productivity. LBR 11:37-54
Jan 49

DERBER, MILTON
Gasoline rationing policy and practice in
Canada and the United States. JM 8:
137-44 Oct 43
"The War Labor Board: an experiment in
wage stabilization": comment. AER 34:
572-75 Sep 44
and McPherson, W. H. The formation and
development of IRRA. IRRA 1:2-4 Dec 48
The role of various disciplines in industrial
relations research: discussion. IRRA 1:
232-33 Dec 48

DE RIDDER, VICTOR ALBERT
see Ridder, Victor Albert de

DERKSEN, JOHANNES BERNARDUS DIRK
Long cycles in residential building: an explanation. Em 8:97-116 Apr 40
and Idenburg, P. J. Methods of evaluation of
the national income of the Netherlands,
1921-1938. RIIS 8:13-30 no.1-2, 40
and Tinbergen, J. Recent experiments in
social accounting: flexible and dynamic
budgets. Em 17,suppl.:195-203 Jul 49

DE ROOVER, FLORENCE EDLER
The business records of an early Genoese
notary, 1190-1192. BHR 14:41-46 Jun 40
Partnership accounts in twelfth century
Genoa. BHR 15:87-92 Dec 41
Francesco Sassetti and the downfall of the
Medici banking house. BHR 17:65-80
Oct 43
Concerning the ancestry of the dollar sign.
BHR 19:63-64 Apr 45
Early examples of marine insurance. JEH 5:
172-200 Nov 45

DE ROOVER, RAYMOND ADRIEN
[Capitalism: concepts and history]: discussion. BHR 16:34-39 Apr 42

DE ROOVER, RAYMOND ADRIEN (Cont.)
  Money, banking, and credit in medieval
    Bruges. JEH/S 2:52-65 Dec 42
  What is dry exchange? A contribution to the
    study of English mercantilism. JPE 52:
    250-66 Sep 44
  The Medici bank: organization and manage-
    ment. JEH 6:24-52 May 46
  The three golden balls of the pawnbrokers.
    BHR 20:117-24 Oct 46
  The Medici Bank: financial and commercial
    operations. JEH 6:153-72 Nov 46
  The decline of the Medici Bank. JEH 7:
    69-82 May 47
DESAI, MAGANLAL BHAGWANJI
  War and rural indebtedness in Gujarat.
    IJE 26:101-11 Jul 45
DESAI, RAJANIKANT CHHAGANLAL
  Consumer expenditure in India, 1931-2 to
    1940-1. JRSS 111:261-98 pt.4, 48
DESCARTES, SOL LUIS
  Land reform in Puerto Rico. LE 19:397-417
    Nov 43
DE SCITOVSZKY, TIBOR
  see Scitovsky, Tibor
DESSAUER, MARIE
  Unemployment records, 1848-59. EHR 10:
    38-43 Feb 40
  Monthly unemployment records 1854-1892.
    Ec N.S.7:322-26 Aug 40
DESTLER, CHESTER McARTHUR
  Entrepreneurial leadership among the
    "robber barons": a trial balance.
    JEH/S 6:28-49 '46
  Agricultural readjustment and agrarian un-
    rest in Illinois, 1880-1896. AH 21:104-16
    Apr 47
DE SWARDT, STEPHANUS JANSEN
  Johannes Friedrich Wilhelm Grosskopf
    1885-1948. [obit.] SAJE 16:219-20
    Jun 48
  Municipal markets: their function and future.
    SAJE 16:182-93 Jun 48
DeTURO, PATRICK J. and Dewey, A. E. H.
  Economic problem of the Southeast. HBR 27:
    34-52 Jan 49
DEUTSCH, ALBERT
  American labor and social work. S&S 8:
    289-304 no.4, 44
DEUTSCH, JOHN J.
  War finance and the Canadian economy,
    1914-20. CJE 6:525-42 Nov 40
DEUTSCH, KARL WOLFGANG
  Medieval unity and the economic conditions
    for an international civilization. CJE 10:
    18-35 Feb 44
  A note on the history of entrepreneurship,
    innovation and decision-making. EEH 1,
    no.5:8-16 May 49
DE VEGH, IMRE
  Savings, investment, and consumption.
    AER/S 30,no.5:237-47 Feb 41
  Imports and income in the United States and
    Canada. REStat 23:130-46 Aug 41

  The International Clearing Union. AER 33:
    534-56 Sep 43
  Peace aims, capital requirements, and inter-
    national lending. AER/S 35:253-61 May 45
DEVONS, ELY
  The Soviet economic system. R. MS 14,
    no.3:54-59 Sep 46
  The progress of reconversion. MS 15:1-25
    Jan 47
  and Jewkes, J. The Economic survey for
    1947. R. LBR 4:1-10 Apr 47
  The British four year plan? MS 16:94-127
    Jan 48
  Economic planning in war and peace. MS 16:
    1-28 Jan 48
  The Economic survey for 1949. R. MS 17:
    111-27 May 49
DE VOS, P. J.
  [and others] Social security. SAJE 10:
    193-247 Sep 42
  and Burrows, H. R. Old age pensions.
    SAJE 11:87-105 Jun 43
DE VYVER, FRANK TRAVER
  After the shutdown; an analysis of the job-
    hunting experience of a group of Durham
    hosiery workers. JPE 48:105-13 Feb 40
  The present status of labor unions in the
    South, 1948. SEJ 16:1-22 Jul 49
DEWEY, ANNE ELIZABETH HULSE and
  DeTuro, P. J.
  Economic problem of the Southeast. HBR 27:
    34-52 Jan 49
DEWEY, DAVIS RICH
  Dewey dinner and testimonial. Remarks of
    Davis Rich Dewey at testimonial dinner.
    AER/S 30,no.5:vii-xi Feb 41
DEWEY, DONALD JEFFERSON
  Notes on the analysis of socialism as a
    vocational problem. MS 16:269-88 Sep 48
  Occupational choice in a collectivist economy.
    JPE 56:465-79 Dec 48
DEWEY, RALPH LAWRENCE
  The Transportation act of 1940. AER 31:
    15-26 Mar 41
  Interterritorial freight rate differences in
    relation to the regionalization of industry.
    JFE 27:433-52 May 45
  The maintenance of railroad credit.
    AER/S 36:451-65 May 46
  Transportation and public utilities: discus-
    sion. AER/S 38:483-85 May 48
  chairman. Round table on transportation and
    public utility problems. AER/S 39:424-26
    May 49
DEWHURST, JAMES FREDERIC
  Economic claims of government and of
    private enterprise: discussion. AER/S 33:
    105-07 Mar 43
DE WOLFF, PIETER
  see Wolff, Pieter de
DEY, HIRENDRA LAL
  Socialist economy and the problem of pricing.
    IJE 21:723-30 Apr 41

DEY, HIRENDRA LAL (Cont.)
International Monetary Fund. Pt.I-II.
IJE 25:173-78; 413-22 Oct 44, Apr 45
DHAR, BIMALENDU
Cheap money policy. IJE 28:95-103 Jul 47
DIAZ, J. GALLEGO-
see Gallego-Diaz, J.
DICE, CHARLES AMOS
and Schaffner, P. A reply to Mr. Villard.
AER 30:113 Mar 40
and Schaffner, P. Offset checks: further
reply. AER 30:825-27 Dec 40
DICHTER, ERNEST
Psychology in market research. HBR 25:
432-43 no.4, 47
A psychological view of advertising effec-
tiveness. JM 14:61-66 Jul 49
DICK, EVERETT
Going beyond the ninety-fifth meridian.
AH 17:105-12 Apr 43
DICKERMAN, ALLEN BRIGGS
Wastepaper. HBR 20:446-58 no.4, 42
DICKINSON, FRANK GREENE
An aftercost of the World War to the United
States. AER/S 30:326-39 Mar 40
DICKINSON, ROBERT E.
The scope and status of urban geography:
an assessment. LE 24:221-38 Aug 48
DICKINSON, ZENAS CLARK
Incentive problems in regulated capitalism.
AER/S 34:151-62 Mar 44
DICKSON, HARALD
Sweden plans its housing policy. LE 23:
417-27 Nov 47
A note on business planning and interest
rates. NTTO 12:75-81 no.37, 48
DICKSON, MAXCY R.
The Food Administration-educator. AH 16:
91-96 Apr 42
DIEBOLD, WILLIAM, Jr.
Oil import quotas and "equal treatment."
AER 30:569-73 Sep 40
Shipping in the immediate postwar years.
JPE 53:15-36 Mar 45
DIEHL, LARRY F.
and Salter, L. A., Jr. Part-time farming
research. JFE 22:581-600 Aug 40
Ordnance causes ordinance in Crawford
County, Pennsylvania. LE 18:357-63
Aug 42
Major aspects of urbanization in the Phila-
delphia metropolitan area. LE 19:316-28
Aug 43
DIENNER, JOHN A. [and others]
Patent policy: discussion. AER/S 38:245-60
May 48
DIESSLIN, HOWARD GUSTAF
Specialization vs. diversification in course
work. JFE 31,pt.2:540-41 Feb 49
DILLARD, DUDLEY
Keynes and Proudhon. JEH 2:63-76 May 42
Silvio Gesell's monetary theory of social
reform. AER 32:348-52 Jun 42

Big inch pipe lines and the monopoly competition in the petroleum industry. LE 20:
109-22 May 44
A note on methodology in modern economic
theory. AER 34:856-62 Dec 44
The status of the labor theory of value.
SEJ 11:345-52 Apr 45
Pragmatism and economic theory: rebuttal.
AER 35:665-67 Sep 45
The pragmatic basis of Keynes's political
economy. JEH 6:121-52 Nov 46
[and others] The role of monopoly in the
colonial trade and expansion of Europe:
discussion. AER/S 38:63-71 May 48
The Keynesian revolution and economic de-
velopment. R. JEH 8:171-77 Nov 48
DILLENBACK, L. C. and Steadman, R. F.
[The education of planners.] At Syracuse
University. LE 21:317-19 Sep 45
DINGWALL, JAMES
Equilibrium and process analysis in the
traditional theory of the firm. CJE 10:
448-63 Nov 44
DIPMAN, CARL W.
Changes in food distribution. JM 6,no.4,pt.2:
48-52 Apr 42
Wartime changes in food distribution. JM 8:
321-25 Jan 44
DIRECTOR, AARON
Does inflation change the economic effects of
war? AER/S 30:351-61 Mar 40
DIRKS, FREDERICK CARL
The rising liquidity of manufacturing com-
panies and its implications for financing
postwar conversion. JASA 39:207-17
Jun 44
DIRKSEN, CHARLES J. and Forman, L. W.
Opportunities in marketing research. JM 13:
37-43 Jul 48
DIRKSEN, CLETUS F.
The Catholic philosopher and the Catholic
economist. RSE 4:14-20 Jan 46
DIVINE, THOMAS FRANCIS
On yoking the economic forces to the social
car. RSE 1:6-11 Dec 42
The derivation of the Marshallian curve
from the Paretian indifference curves.
AER 33:125-29 Mar 43
On the place of "profit" in a capitalistic
economy. RSE 2:57-67 Jan 44
The nature of economic science and its re-
lation to social philosophy. RSE 6:106-17
May 48
DIXON, HARRISON MORTON and Wilson, M. L.
Farm and home planning: a new approach to
farm management extension work.
JFE 29:167-74 Feb 47
DIXON, ROBERT G.
Tripartitism in the National War Labor
Board. ILRR 2:372-90 Apr 49
DOAN, MASON COLLINS
State labor relations acts. QJE 56:507-59
Aug 42

DOANE, DUANE HOWARD
Vertical farm diversification. JFE 26:
373-78 May 44

DOBB, MAURICE HERBERT
"Vulgar economics" and "vulgar Marxism":
a reply. JPE 48:251-58 Apr 40
Economic planning in the Soviet Union.
S&S 6:305-14 no.4, 42
The International Labour Conference. R.
EJ 54:261-65 Jun-Sep 44
Aspects of Nazi economic policy. S&S 8:
97-103 no.2, 44
Post-war economic prospects in the U.S.S.R.
OIS 8:190-98 Jun 46
A comment on Soviet statistics. REStat 30:
34-38 Feb 48
Comment on Soviet economic statistics.
SovS 1:18-27 Jun 49

DOBLIN, ERNEST M.
Some aspects of price flexibility. REStat 22:
183-89 Nov 40
and Stolper, G. The new Federal Reserve
Board index of production. EJ 51:47-55
Apr 41
The German "profit stop" of 1941. SR 9:
371-78 Sep 42

DOBRETSBERGER, JOSEF
Experiences in social insurance in Europe.
EgC 34:57-75 Jan-Feb 43
Misunderstandings about full-employment.
EgC 36:129-55 Jan-Feb 45
A critical review of the discussions on full-
employment. Kyk 1:19-25 fasc.1, 47

DOBROVOLSKY, SERGEI P.
Corporate retained earnings and cyclical
fluctuations. AER 35:559-74 Sep 45
The effect of replacement investment on
national income and employment. JPE 55:
352-58 Aug 47
Business income taxation and asset expansion. JF 4:183-93 Sep 49

DODD, EDWARD L.
The problem of assigning a length to the
cycle to be found in a simple moving
average and in a double moving average
of chance data. Em 9:25-37 Jan 41
Certain tests for randomness applied to data
grouped into small sets. Em 10:249-57
Jul-Oct 42

DODD, NORRIS E.
The Food and Agriculture Organization of the
United Nations: its history, organization,
and objectives. AH 23:81-86 Apr 49

DODD, PAUL ALBERT
A method of making actuarial estimates for
a compulsory health insurance system.
JASA 41:58-69 Mar 46

DODWELL, BARBARA
The free tenantry of the Hundred Rolls.
EHR 14:163-71 no.2, 44

DOGADOV, VASILĬĬ MIKHAĬLOVICH
Change in the nature of Soviet collective
agreements. SovS 1:79-84 Jun 49

DOHERTY, RICHARD P.
The movement and concentration of retail
trade in metropolitan areas. JM 5:
395-401 Apr 41
Decentralization of retail trade in Boston.
JM 6:281-86 Jan 42

DOLLEY, JAMES CLAY
Ability of the banking system to absorb government bonds. JPE 51:23-31 Feb 43

DOMAR, EVSEY DAVID
and Musgrave, R. A. Proportional income
taxation and risk-taking. QJE 58:388-422
May 44
The "burden of the debt" and the national
income. AER 34:798-827 Dec 44
--- A rejoinder. AER 35:414-18 Jun 45
Capital expansion, rate of growth, and em-
ployment. Em 14:137-47 Apr 46
Expansion and employment. AER 37:34-55
Mar 47
The problem of capital accumulation.
AER 38:777-94 Dec 48
Capital accumulation and the end of pros-
perity. Em 17,suppl.:307-12 Jul 49
[The problem of capital accumulation]:
rejoinder. AER 39:1170-72 Dec 49

DONALD, GORDON, Jr.
and Chapple, E. D. A method for evaluating
supervisory personnel. HBR 24:197-214
no.2, 46
and Chapple, E. D. An evaluation of department store salespeople by the interaction
chronograph. JM 12:173-85 Oct 47

DONHAM, RICHARD
Management consultants deal with people.
HBR 19:33-41 no.1, 40

DONNAHOE, ALAN S.
Presenting seasonal variation to the busi-
ness executive. JASA 41:468-71 Dec 46
Measuring state tax burden. JPE 55:234-44
Jun 47

DONOGHUE, MANSUETUS
Economics a living subject. RSE 6:101-05
May 48

DOODY, FRANCIS STEPHEN
and Clemence, R. Modern economics and the
introductory course. AER 32:334-47
Jun 42
Keynesian policies and Christian social
teaching. RSE 7,no.2:1-9 Sep 49

DORFMAN, JOSEPH
Wesley C. Mitchell (1874-1948). EJ 59:
448-58 Sep 49

DORRANCE, GRAEME S.
The income terms of trade. REStud 16:
50-56 no.1, 48

DOUGALL, HERBERT EDWARD
The transportation problem: discussion.
AER/S 30:161-63 Mar 40
and Farwell, L. C. A review of railroad
financing, 1920-1938 Pt.I-III. [Pt.III by
Farwell alone] LE 16:207-13; 306-17;
443-54 May,Aug,Nov 40

DOUGLAS, DOROTHY WOLFF
    Land and labor in Mexico.  S&S 4:127-52
        no.2, 40
DOUGLAS, EDNA
    Protection offered to consumers by the North
        Carolina state government.  JM 7:32-40
        Jul 42
    Measuring the general retail trading area:
        a case study.  Pt.I-II.  JM 13:481-97;
        14:46-60 Apr,Jul 49
DOUGLAS, MONTEATH
    Limitations of the financial factor in a war
        economy.  CJE 8:351-63 Aug 42
DOUGLAS, PAUL HOWARD
    and Gunn, G. T.  Further measurements of
        marginal productivity.  QJE 54:399-428
        May 40
    and Gunn, G. T.  The production function for
        American manufacturing in 1919.  AER 31:
        67-80 Mar 41
    and Gunn, G. T.  A reply to Dr. Menders-
        hausen's criticism.   AER 31:564-67
        Sep 41
    and Gunn, G. T.  The production function for
        Australian manufacturing.  QJE 56:108-29
        Nov 41
    and Gunn, G. T.  The production function for
        American manufacturing for 1914.  JPE 50:
        595-602 Aug 42
    with Daly, P. and Olson, E.  The production
        function for manufacturing in the United
        States, 1904.  JPE 51:61-65 Feb 43
    and Daily, P.  The production function for
        Canadian manufactures.  JASA 38:178-86
        Jun 43
    [Irving Fisher. obit.]  AER 37:661-63 Sep 47
    Are there laws of production?  AER 38:1-41
        Mar 48
    [and others]  Harry Alvin Millis 1873-1948.
        [obit.]  AER 39:742-50 Jun 49
DOUTY, HARRY MORTIMER
    Minimum wage regulations in the seamless
        hosiery industry.  SEJ 8:176-90 Oct 41
DOVELL, JUNIUS E.
    The Everglades, a Florida frontier.  AH 22:
        187-97 Jul 48
DOW, GEORGE F.
    Regional and interregional cooperation in
        dairy marketing.  JFE 29:1389-94 Nov 47
DOW, J. C. R.
    A symposium on the theory of the forward
        market. II. Addenda to Mr. Kaldor's
        note.  REStud 7:201-02 Jun 40
    A theoretical account of futures markets.
        REStud 7:185-95 Jun 40
    The inaccuracy of expectations.  A statistical
        study of the Liverpool cotton futures mar-
        ket, 1921-22, 1937-38.  Ec N.S.8:162-75
        May 41
DOWDELL, ERIC GEORGE
    The multiplier.  OEP 4:23-38 Sep 40
    The concerted regulation of price and output.
        EJ 58:210-27 Jun 48

Oligopoly and imperfect competition.
    OEP N.S.1:217-26 Jun 49
DOWELL, AUSTIN ALLYN
    and Winters, L. M.  Economic aspects of
        artificial insemination of commercial
        dairy cows.  JFE 24:665-76 Aug 42
    Wartime transportation of farm products.
        JFE 26:159-77 Feb 44
    and Toben, G. E.  Some economic effects of
        graduated income tax rates on investors
        in farm capital.  JFE 26:348-58 May 44
    Some considerations in building a curric-
        ulum for agricultural economics majors.
        JFE 29:1319-28 Nov 47
    and Engelman, G.  Research into the prob-
        lems involved in marketing slaughter
        livestock by carcass weight and grade.
        JFE 31,pt.2:343-61 Feb 49
DOWLING, ELEANOR
    The business of government.  S&S 9:193-213
        no.3, 45
DOWLING, LYLE
    Comments on inflation.  S&S 7:52-55 no.1, 43
DOWNING, RICHARD IVAN
    The costs and achievements of price stabili-
        zation.  ER 20:38-57 Jun 44
    Prices in wartime.  ER 20:206-14 Dec 44
    Housing and public policy.  ER 24:72-86
        Jun 48
DOWNS, JAMES C., Jr.
    Rent control.  LE 17:406-09 Nov 41
    Measuring effective demand in the housing
        market.  LE 25:105-06 Feb 49
DOWSETT, WILFRED T.
    Child endowment and income tax exempt-
        tions.  ER 17:239-47 Dec 41
    Delayed action inflation.  ER 19:64-70
        Jun 43
    The tax lag myth.  ER 20:214-17 Dec 44
    A note on minimum standards for rationed
        necessities.  ER 21:89-94 Jun 45
DRAGER, WILLIAM
    The interpretation of ratios used in cost
        analyses.  JM 8:424-25 Apr 44
    Retail trade and income by states.  JM 9:
        364-72 Apr 45
DRIVER, PESHOTAN NASSERWANJI
    Rural co-operation in the Bombay Presidency.
        IJE 22:585-98 Jan 42
DRUMMOND, WILLIAM MALCOLM
    An appraisal of rural planning in the United
        Kingdom.  JFE 29:1089-1100 Nov 47
    Objectives and methods of government pric-
        ing of farm products.  JFE 30:665-79 Nov 48
    Canadian agricultural price problems and
        policies: a commentary.  JFE 31:581-93
        Nov 49
D'SOUZA, VITUS LAWRENCE
    Exchange equalisation.  IJE 20:545-55 Apr 40
    Economic valuation in a socialist state.
        IJE 21:420-34 Apr 41
    Multi-purpose society.  IJE 22:546-53 Jan 42

DUBEY, DAYA SHANKAR
  The place of agriculture in the proposed
    plans. IJE 25:551-56 Apr 45
  The Indian food problem. IJE 26:647-50
    Apr 46
DUBIN, ROBERT
  Union-management co-operation and pro-
    ductivity. ILRR 2:195-209 Jan 49
DUBS, HOMER H.
  An ancient Chinese stock of gold. JEH 2:
    36-39 May 42
DUCKHAM, ALEC NARRAWAY
  and Young, J. A. Rural planning in the
    United Kingdom. JFE 29:1075-88 Nov 47
  Liberty, progress, and security: fifteen
    centuries of British agriculture. AH 22:
    129-33 Jul 48
DUCOFF, LOUIS J.
  and Bancroft, G. Experiment in the measure-
    ment of unpaid family labor in agriculture.
    JASA 40:205-13 Jun 45
  and Hagood, M. J. Objectives, uses and types
    of labor force data in relation to economic
    policy. JASA 41:293-302 Sep 46
  Migratory farm workers in the United
    States. JFE 29:711-22 Aug 47
DUDDY, EDWARD A.
  and Revzan, D. A. The location of the South
    Water Wholesale Fruit and Vegetable
    Market in Chicago. Pt.I-II. JB 12:
    386-412; 13:39-55 Oct 39, Jan 40
  The moral implications of business as a
    profession. JB 18:63-72 Apr 45
DUDLEY, ROBERT G. and Evans, W. H.
  Public utility financing 4th quarter of 1939 -
    1st quarter of 1948. [Regular feature,
    variously edited] LE 16-24 Feb 40-May 48
DUE, JOHN FITZGERALD
  Ad valorem and specific taxes. QJE 54:
    679-85 Aug 40
  The incidence of chain store taxes. JM 5:
    128-36 Oct 40
  A theory of retail price determination.
    SEJ 7:380-97 Jan 41
  A general sales tax and the level of employ-
    ment: a reconsideration. NTJ 2:122-30
    Jun 49
DUFFUS, WILLIAM McGLASHAN
  The place of the government corporation in
    the public utility industries. LE 25:29-38
    Feb 49
DUGGAN, IVY WILLIAM
  Cotton, land, and people: a statement of the
    problem. JFE 22:188-97 Feb 40
DULAN, HAROLD ANDREW
  Common-stock investment as an inflation
    hedge, 1939-46. JB 21:230-38 Oct 48
DULLES, ELEANOR LANSING
  War and investment opportunities: an
    historical analysis. AER/S 32:112-28
    Mar 42
DU MONT, ALLEN B.
  Television now and tomorrow. JM 9:276-79
    Jan 45

DUNAYEVSKAYA, RAYA
  A new revision of Marxian economics.
    AER 34:531-37 Sep 44
  Revision or reaffirmation of Marxism?
    A rejoinder. AER 35:660-64 Sep 45
DUNBAR, ROBERT G.
  Agricultural adjustments in eastern Colorado
    in the eighteen-nineties. AH 18:41-52
    Jan 44
  Water conflicts and controls in Colorado.
    AH 22:180-86 Jul 48
DUNCAN, ACHESON JOHNSTON
  Monopoly adjustments to shifts in demand.
    Em 10:75-79 Jan 42
  "Free money" of large manufacturing corpo-
    rations and the rate of interest. Em 14:
    251-53 Jul 46
  South African capital imports, 1893-8.
    CJE 14:20-45 Feb 48
DUNCAN, BINGHAM
  Diplomatic support of the American rice
    trade, 1835-1845. AH 23:92-96 Apr 49
DUNCAN, CARSON SAMUEL
  The transportation problem: discussion.
    AER/S 30:158-61 Mar 40
DUNCAN, DELBERT JOHNSTON
  What motivates business buyers? HBR 18:
    448-54 no.4, 40
DUNCAN, GEORGE ALEXANDER
  The first year of war: its economic effects
    on twenty-six counties of Ireland. EJ 51:
    389-99 Dec 41
  The foreign trade of the Irish Free State,
    1924-47. EI 1:584-92 May 48
DUNCAN, JULIAN SMITH
  The effect of the N.R.A. Lumber Code on
    forest policy. JPE 49:91-102 Feb 41
DUNCAN, OTIS DURANT
  Hypotheses in land tenure research.
    JFE 25:860-68 Nov 43
DUNCOMBE, HENRY LYON, Jr.
  Population changes and their effects.
    HBR 20:437-45 no.4, 42
DUNHAM, ARTHUR LOUIS
  How the first French railways were planned.
    JEH 1:12-25 May 41
  Industrial life and labor in France 1815-1848.
    JEH 3:117-51 Nov 43
  Unrest in France in 1848. JEH/S 8:74-84 '48
DUNKMAN, WILLIAM EDWARD
  Postwar commercial bank lending policies.
    JF 4:87-100 Jun 49
  The teaching of money and banking.
    JF 4:234-37 Sep 49
DUNLOP, JOHN THOMAS
  Real and money wage rates: a reply.
    QJE 55:683-91 Aug 41
  and Higgins, B. "Bargaining power" and
    market structures. JPE 50:1-26 Feb 42
  Wage policies of trade unions. AER/S 32:
    290-301 Mar 42
  Wage-price relations at high level employ-
    ment. AER/S 37:243-53 May 47

DUNLOP, JOHN THOMAS (Cont.)
A review of wage-price policy. REStat 29:
154-60 Aug 47
The demand and supply functions for labor.
AER/S 38:340-50 May 48
[and others] Collective bargaining, wages
and the price level: discussion. IRRA 1:
51-61 Dec 48
DUNN, HALBERT L.
Raymond Pearl, 1879-1940. [obit.] JASA 36:
120-21 Mar 41
DUNN, WILLIAM CLYDE
Adam Smith and Edmund Burke: comple-
mentary contemporaries. SEJ 7:330-46
Jan 41
DUPRIEZ, LEON H.
Postwar exchange-rate parities: comment.
QJE 60:299-308 Feb 46
DURAND, DAVID
A simple method for estimating the size dis-
tribution of a given aggregate income.
REStat 25:227-30 Aug 43
An appraisal of the errors involved in esti-
mating the size distribution of a given
aggregate income. REStat 30:63-68
Feb 48
DURAND, EDWARD DANA
A. Manuel Fox, 1889-1942. [obit.] JASA 38:
105-06 Mar 43
Dr. Victor Selden Clark. [obit.] JASA 41:
390-92 Sep 46
Tribute to Walter F. Willcox. JASA 42:5-7
Mar 47
DURAND, JOHN DANA and Mautz, W. H.
Population and war labor supply. JASA 38:
31-42 Mar 43
DURANT, HENRY and Goldmann, J.
The distribution of working-class savings.
OIS 7:1-7 Jan 13, 45
DURBIN, EVAN FRANK MOTTRAM
Professor Hayek on economic planning and
political liberty. R. EJ 55:357-70 Dec 45
DURR, CLIFFORD J.
The postwar relationship between govern-
ment and business. AER/S 33:45-53
Mar 43
DURUZ, WILLIS PIERRE
Notes on the early history of horticulture in
Oregon; with special reference to fruit-
tree nurseries. AH 15:84-97 Apr 41
DUTT, KALYAN and Das, A. C.
Problem of agricultural labour in India.
IJE 28:155-61 Jul 47
DYKSTRA, CLARENCE A.
A quarter century of land economics. LE 18:
1-3 Feb 42
DYMOND, WILLIAM RICHARD
Union-management co-operation at the
Toronto factory of Lever Brothers
Limited. CJE 13:26-67 Feb 47
DYNE, R. E. and Clark, C.
Applications and extensions of the Karmel
formula for reproductivity. ER 22:23-39
Jun 46

EARLEY, JAMES STAINFORTH [and others]
Problems of the ITO: discussion. AER/S 39:
269-79 May 49
EAST, ROBERT A.
The business entrepreneur in a changing
colonial economy, 1763-1795. JEH/S 6:
16-27 '46
EAST, WILLIAM GORDON
The economic history of U.S.S.R. R.
EHR 16:141-44 no.2, 46
EASTERBROOK, WILLIAM THOMAS
The climate of enterprise. AER/S 39:
322-35 May 49
Political economy and enterprise. CJE 15:
322-33 Aug 49
EASTHAM, JACK KENNETH
Compensation terms for nationalised indus-
try. MS 16:29-45 Jan 48
EASTMAN, JOSEPH BARTLETT
The adjustment of rates between competing
forms of transportation. AER/S 30:124-29
Mar 40
Public administration of transportation
under war conditions. AER/S 34:86-93
Mar 44
EBENSTEIN, WILLIAM
Land and politics: Eastern Europe and
South America. R. LE 22:59-65 Feb 46
EBERLING, ERNEST J.
Old age and survivors' insurance and old age
assistance in the South. SEJ 15:54-66
Jul 48
EBERSOLE, JOHN FRANKLIN
Protecting bank bond investments. HBR 18:
410-16 no.4, 40
Banks can make more postwar jobs. HBR 22:
1-9 no.1, 43
Government can help banks make more jobs.
HBR 22:167-77 no.2, 44
EBLING, WALTER HENRY and Wilcox, E. C.
Presentation of agricultural data in the
states. JFE 31,pt.2:309-22 Feb 49
ECKLER, ALBERT ROSS
Employment and income statistics. JASA 36:
381-86 Sep 41
and Staudt, E. P. Marketing and sampling
uses of population and housing data.
JASA 38:87-92 Mar 43
The revised census series of current em-
ployment estimates. JASA 40:187-96
Jun 45
ECKSTEIN, ALEXANDER
Collective bargaining in German agriculture
under the Weimar Republic, 1918-1933.
JFE 25:458-76 May 43
Land reform and the transformation of ag-
riculture in Hungary. JFE 31:456-68
Aug 49
EDELBERG, VICTOR
Flexibility of the yield of taxation: some
econometric investigations. JRSS 103:
153-79 pt.2, 40

EDELMANN, ALEX T.
  Kentucky accepts T.V.A. power. LE 18:
    481-84 Nov 42
EDMINSTER, LYNN RAMSAY
  International trade and postwar reconstruc-
    tion. AER/S 33:301-21 Mar 43
EDMUNDS, STAHRL
  The limits of the market for ordinary life
    insurance. JM 11:117-28 Oct 46
  Outlets for life insurance investment.
    HBR 25:409-31 no.4, 47
EDSALL, RICHARD L.
  A method of measuring effectiveness of
    business and trade paper advertising.
    JM 7:208-09 Jan 43
EDWARDS, ALBA M.
  Occupation and industry statistics. JASA 36:
    387-92 Sep 41
EDWARDS, CORWIN D.
  Can the antitrust laws preserve competition?
    AER/S 30:164-79 Mar 40
  Appraisal of "fair trade" and "unfair prac-
    tices" acts. JM 5:3-15 Jul 40
  Public policy toward restraints of trade by
    labor unions: an economic appraisal.
    AER/S 32:432-48 Mar 42
  Antitrust policy toward advertising. JM 6,
    no.4,pt.2:106-11 Apr 42
  Types of differential pricing. JM 6,no.4,pt.2:
    156-67 Apr 42
  International cartels as obstacles to inter-
    national trade. AER/S 34:330-39 Mar 44
  An appraisal of the antitrust laws.
    AER/S 36:172-89 May 46
  chairman. Report of the Subcommittee on
    Concensus and recommendations as to
    Association policy. AER/S 36:832-41
    May 46
  [and others] Wage-price relations at high
    level employment: discussion. AER/S 37:
    254-64 May 47
  [and others] The Sherman Act and the en-
    forcement of competition: discussion.
    AER/S 38:203-14 May 48
  The effect of recent basing point decisions
    upon business practices. AER 38:828-42
    Dec 48
  [and others] The economic consequences of
    some recent antitrust decisions: discus-
    sion. AER/S 39:311-21 May 49
EDWARDS, EVERETT EUGENE
  Agricultural history and the Department of
    Agriculture. AH 16:129-36 Jul 42
  Objectives for the Agricultural History
    Society during its second twenty-five
    years. AH 18:187-92 Oct 44
  Europe's contribution to the American dairy
    industry. JEH/S 9:72-84 '49
EDWARDS, FORD K.
  Cost analysis in transportation. AER/S 37:
    441-61 May 47
EDWARDS, GEORGE WILLIAM
  [and others] Capital expansion, employment,

and economic stability: a reply to H. H.
    Villard. AER 31:110-12 Mar 41
  The myth of the security affiliate. JASA 37:
    225-32 Jun 42
EDWARDS, GERTRUD GREIG
  Some varieties of consumer behavior de-
    scribed in the decisions of the Federal
    Trade Commission. JB 20:191-200
    Oct 47
EFROYMSON, CLARENCE WALTER
  A note on kinked demand curves. AER 33:
    98-109 Mar 43
EGGERT, ROBERT JOHN
  A price policy for agriculture consistent
    with economic progress that will promote
    adequate and more stable income from
    farming. JFE 27:821-28 Nov 45
  Advantages and disadvantages of direct pay-
    ments with special emphasis on market-
    ing considerations. JFE 29:250-55 Feb 47
  Parity price and parity income: a modifying
    comment. JFE 29:1376-77 Nov 47
  Animal fats and oils: situation and outlook.
    JFE 31,pt.2:331-39 Feb 49
  and Seltzer, R. E. Accuracy of livestock
    price forecasts at Kansas State College.
    JFE 31:342-45 May 49
EGLE, WALTER PAUL
  [and others] Economic adjustments after
    wars: discussion. AER/S 32:31-36 Mar 42
  Money as numéraire. AER/S 37:325-31
    May 47
EICHELGRUN, G.
  Income-tax in British colonies. EJ 58:
    128-32 Mar 48
EINARSEN, JOHAN
  Replacement in the shipping industry.
    REStat 28:225-30 Nov 46
EINAUDI, LUIGI
  Achille Loria (1857-1943). [obit.] EJ 56:
    147-50 Mar 46
  Umberto Ricci. [obit.] AER 36:666-68
    Sep 46
  Greatness and decline of planned economy
    in the Hellenistic world. R. [Translated
    by R. H. F. Dalton] Pt.I-II. Kyk 2:193-210;
    289-316 fasc.3,4, 48
EINAUDI, MARIO
  Nationalization in France and Italy. SR 15:
    22-43 Mar 48
EINZIG, PAUL
  Hitler's "new order" in theory and practice.
    EJ 51:1-18 Apr 41
  A plan for Germany's economic disarmament.
    EJ 52:176-85 Jun-Sep 42
EITEMAN, WILFORD JOHN
  Comment on "Offset checks as a component
    of the money supply" by Mr. Villard.
    AER 30:114-15 Mar 40
  Security regulation and the volume of new
    issues. SEJ 7:27-36 Jul 40
  Effect of franchise taxes upon corporate lo-
    cation. SEJ 9:234-40 Jan 43

EITEMAN, WILFORD JOHN (Cont.)
Economic basis of prices in Alaska. AER 34:
351-56 Jun 44
The equilibrium of the firm in multi-process
industries. QJE 59:280-86 Feb 45
Factors determining the location of the least
cost point. AER 37:910-18 Dec 47
The least cost point, capacity, and marginal
analysis: a rejoinder. AER 38:899-904
Dec 48
Current investment tendencies: discussion.
JF 4:176-79 Jun 49

EKE, PAUL A.
A price policy for agriculture, consistent
with economic progress that will promote
adequate and more stable income from
farming. JFE 27:829-36 Nov 45

EKKER, MARTIN HENDRIK
A scheme of international compensation:
postscript. Em 17:150-53 Apr 49

ELDER, ROBERT FAIRCHILD
What sales management expects from research. JM 13:52-55 Jul 48

EL FALAKI, MAHMOUD SALEH
Post-war planning of currency and the mone-
tary market in Egypt. EgC 35:187-204
Jan-Feb 44
The Bretton Woods' international finance
program. EgC 36:157-201 Jan-Feb 45
Egypt and the organisation of the inter-
national finance to-day. EgC 38:101-14
Jan-Feb 47

EL-GRITLY, A. A. I.
The structure of modern industry in Egypt.
EgC 38:363-582 Nov-Dec 47

ELIEL, PAUL
Labor peace in Pacific ports. HBR 19:
429-37 no.4, 41
Industrial peace and conflict: a study of two
Pacific Coast industries. ILRR 2:477-501
Jul 49

ELKINTON, CHARLES M.
A study of student values and inconsistent
reasoning. AER 31:557-59 Sep 41
Effects of selected changes in technology on
western agriculture. JFE 31,pt.2:451-53
Feb 49
Foreign trade problems: further comment.
JFE 31,pt.2:832-36 Nov 49

ELLICKSON, JOHN C.
and Brewster, J. M. Technological advance
and the structure of American agriculture.
JFE 29:827-47 Nov 47
[and others] Appraisal of the economic
classification of farms. JFE 30:680-702
Nov 48

ELLIOTT, FOSTER FLOYD
Agriculture when the war ends. JFE 25:
309-22 Feb 43
Redirecting world agricultural production
and trade toward better nutrition. JFE 26:
10-30 Feb 44
[and others] Need for a new classification of
farms. JFE 26:694-708 Nov 44

A proposed world trade board for expanding
international trade. JFE 27:571-90
Aug 45

ELLIOTT, GEORGE ALEXANDER
The relation of protective duties to domestic production. CJE 6:296-98 May 40
On some appendices to the Rowell-Sirois
report. V. Dominion monetary policy,
1929-1934. CJE 7:88-91 Feb 41
Price ceilings and international trade theory.
CJE 8:186-96 May 42
The significance of the general theory of employment, interest, and money. CJE 13:
372-78 Aug 47

ELLIOTT, ROBBINS L.
The Canadian labour press from 1867: a
chronological annotated directory.
CJE 14:220-45 May 48; A correction.
515 Nov 48

ELLIS, A. W. T.
The present position of the boot and shoe
industry. OIS 2,no.3:2-4 Jun 30, 40
Trade losses and the consumer: the coal
levy. OIS 2,no.8:11-13 Oct 40
and Halpern, D. B. War-time re-organiza-
tion of the coal industry. OIS 3:189-96
Jun 28, 41
Rents, rates and incomes in Bristol.
REStud 11:99-108 no.2, 44
and Bowen, I. The building and contracting
industry. OEP 7:111-24 Mar 45

ELLIS, DAVID MALDWYN
Land tenure and tenancy in the Hudson
Valley, 1790-1860. AH 18:75-82 Apr 44
Railroad land grant rates, 1850-1945.
LE 21:207-22 Aug 45

ELLIS, HOWARD SYLVESTER
Monetary policy and investment. AER/S 30:
27-38 Mar 40
Exchange control in Germany. QJE 54,no.4,
pt.2:1-220 Aug 40
and Fellner, W. Hicks and the time-period
controversy. JPE 48:563-78 Aug 40
Frank William Taussig, 1859-1940. [obit.]
AER 31:209-11 Mar 41
The problem of exchange systems in the
postwar world. AER/S 32:195-205 Mar 42
and Fellner, W. External economies and
diseconomies. AER 33:493-511 Sep 43
Can national and international monetary
policies be reconciled? AER/S 34:385-95
Mar 44
Gustav Cassel 1866-1945. [obit.] AER 35:
508-10 Jun 45
Competition and welfare. CJE 11:554-65
Nov 45
Postwar economic policies. R. REStat 28:
34-39 Feb 46
Comments on the Mints and Hansen papers.
(A symposium on fiscal and monetary
policy) Restat 28:74-77 May 46
The changing character of money: summary
and comments. AER/S 37:332-34 May 47

ELLIS, HOWARD SYLVESTER (Cont.)
  [and others] Domestic versus international
    equilibrium: discussion. AER/S 37:581-94
    May 47
  Exchange control and discrimination.
    AER 37:877-88 Dec 47
  The dollar shortage in theory and fact.
    CJE 14:358-72 Aug 48
  The state of the "new economics." AER 39:
    465-77 Mar 49
  Research as seen in a survey of contempo-
    rary economics. AER/S 39:427-39 May 49
  The January 1949 economic report of the
    President: appraisal. REStat 31:174-76
    Aug 49
ELLISON, JOSEPH WALDO
  Marketing problems of northwestern apples,
    1929-1940. AH 16:103-15 Apr 42
ELLSWORTH, PAUL THEODORE
  A comparison of international trade theories.
    AER 30:285-89 Jun 40
  An economic foreign policy for America.
    AER/S 30,no.5:301-19 Feb 41
  The Havana Charter: comment. AER 39:
    1268-73 Dec 49
ELMHIRST, LEONARD K.
  American foreign food policy: discussion.
    JFE 31,pt.2:290-92 Feb 49
EL-SAID, MOHAMED HOSNY
  Seasonality of the Egyptian export trade.
    EgC 37:227-31 May-Dec 46
ELSAS, MORITZ JOHN
  War and housing. EJ 50:42-50 Mar 40
  Rent subsidies on a national basis. REStud 11:
    77-85 no.2, 44
ELVOVE, JOSEPH TEVYA
  with Jones, P. E. and Mason, J. E. New
    settlement in the delta of the lower
    Mississippi Valley. LE 17:465-76 Nov 41
  The Florida Everglades: a region of new
    settlement. LE 19:464-69 Nov 43
EMSPAK, JULIUS
  Labor-management war production councils.
    S&S 7:88-96 no.1, 43
ENGBERG, RUSSELL C.
  Federal credit agencies as an influence
    upon land values. JFE 29:150-62 Feb 47
  Risks in agricultural lending. JFE 31,pt.2:
    602-11 Feb 49
ENGEL, GEORGE C.
  The importance of salespeople in ready-to-
    wear stores. JM 11:282-85 Jan 47
ENGELMAN, GERALD
  Carcass grade and weight studies in market-
    ing livestock. JFE 29:1424-28 Nov 47
  and Dowell, A. A. Research into the prob-
    lems involved in marketing slaughter live-
    stock by carcass weight and grade.
    JFE 31,pt.2:343-61 Feb 49
ENGENE, SELMER A.
  New light on factor analysis. JFE 25:477-86
    May 43
  Review of papers on farm work simplifica-
    tion. JFE 28:337-40 Feb 46

Sampling procedures used in study of hay-
    making methods. JFE 29:1271-74 Nov 47
ENGLAND, ROBERT
  Soldier settlement: revising the oldest re-
    habilitation prospectus. LE 20:285-98
    Nov 44
ENGLAND, WILLIAM H.
  The Federal Trade Commission's corpora-
    tion reports. JASA 42:22-24 Mar 47
ENGLE, NATHANAEL HOWARD
  Gaps in marketing research. JM 4:345-53
    Apr 40
  Adjustment of wholesaling to 1941 and after.
    JM 5:431-37 Apr 41
  Measurement of economic and marketing ef-
    ficiency. JM 5:335-49 Apr 41
  The Pacific Northwest light metals industry.
    JM 8:253-59 Jan 44
  Wages, prices, and profits. JB 20:121-30
    Jul 47
  Chain store distribution vs. independent
    wholesaling. JM 14:241-52 Sep 49
ENGLUND, ERIC
  Gustav Cassel's Autobiography. R. QJE 57:
    466-93 May 43
ENGQUIST, ERNEST JOHN, Jr. and Miller, W. S.
  Measuring retailers' inventories. JM 9:
    49-52 Jul 44
ENGSTRAND, WARREN M. and Poli, A.
  Japanese agriculture on the Pacific Coast.
    LE 21:352-64 Sep 45
ENKE, STEPHEN
  Reducing gasoline prices: British Columbia's
    experiment. QJE 55:443-59 May 41
  Profit maximization under monopolistic
    competition. AER 31:317-26 Jun 41
  Space and value. QJE 56:627-37 Aug 42
  Regulating output via multiple prices.
    JFE 24:883-89 Nov 42
  Price control and rationing. AER 32:842-43
    Dec 42
  The monopsony case for tariffs. QJE 58:
    229-45 Feb 44
  Consumer cooperatives and economic effi-
    ciency. AER 35:148-55 Mar 45
  Monopolistic output and international trade.
    QJE 60:233-49 Feb 46
  Mr. Ross on wage policy. SEJ 15:337-39
    Jan 49
  Resource malallocation within firms.
    QJE 63:572-76 Nov 49
ENLOW, MAXINE and Gold, N. L.
  The demand for food by low income families.
    QJE 57:596-629 Aug 43
ENSLEY, GROVER WILLIAM
  A budget for the nation. SR 10:280-300 Sep 43
  and Goode, R. Mr. Warburton on the gap.
    AER 33:897-99 Dec 43
  Suggested lines of economic research needed
    to carry out objectives of the Employment
    Act. AER/S 39:453-63 May 49
EPSTEIN, ISRAEL
  Main directions in Chinese labor. S&S 13:
    313-26 no.4, 49

EPSTEIN, MORDECAI
see Epstein, Mortimer
EPSTEIN, MORTIMER
Werner Sombart (January 19, 1863-May 13,
1941). [obit.] EJ 51:523-26 Dec 41
EPSTEIN, RALPH CECIL
Price dispersion and aggregative analysis.
AER 37:402-07 Jun 47
ERDMAN, HENRY ERNEST
Some current developments in agricultural
marketing. Pt.I-II. JM 5:213-15; 6,no.4,
pt.2: 13-14 Jan 41, Apr 42
Factors in the current expansion of the demand for food. JM 6,no.4,pt.2:22-28
Apr 42
and Alcorn, G. B. The price-making process
in the Los Angeles egg market. JM 6:
349-57 Apr 42
Interpretation of variations in cost data for
a group of individual firms. JFE 26:
388-91 May 44
and Coles, J. V. Some aspects of the arguments against grade labeling. JM 9:
256-61 Jan 45
and Mehren, G. L. An approach to the determination of intraseasonal shifting of
demand. JFE 28:587-96 May 46
Thought on cooperatives: discussion.
JFE 31,pt.2:915-16 Nov 49
ERDMANN, ARTHUR G.
The rural zoning ordinance  of Cook County.
LE 16:438-42 Nov 40
EUCKEN, WALTER
Heinrich von Stackelberg (1905-1946). [obit.]
EJ 58:132-35 Mar 48
On the theory of the centrally administered
economy: an analysis of the German ex-
periment. (Translated by T. W. Hutchi-
son) Pt.I-II. Ec N.S.15:79-100; 173-93
May,Aug 48
EVANS, GEORGE HEBERTON, Jr.
Business incorporations: their nature and
significance. JEH/S 1:67-85 Dec 41
[and others] The determinants of investment
decision: discussion. AER/S 32:156-64
Mar 42
A theory of entrepreneurship. JEH/S 2:
142-46 Dec 42
The entrepreneur and economic theory: a
historical and analytical approach.
AER/S 39:336-48 May 49
EVANS, JAMES G. [and others]
Round table on population problems: [discus-
sion]. AER/S 30:393-98 Mar 40
EVANS, JOHN W.
United States foreign trade policy: a practical
approach. JFE 31,pt.2:504-16 Feb 49
EVANS, M. J.
Case study in industrial marketing. JM 5:
443-45 Apr 41
EVANS, WALTER HARRISON and Dudley, R. G.
Public utility financing 4th quarter of 1939 -
1st quarter of 1948. [Regular feature,

variously edited.] LE 16-24 Feb 40-
May 48
EVANS, WILMOTH DUANE
and Siegel, I. H. The meaning of productivity
indexes. JASA 37:103-11 Mar 42
Productivity and human relations. AER/S 37:
412-20 May 47
Recent productivity trends and their implica-
tions. JASA 42:211-23 Jun 47
EVELY, RICHARD WILLIAM
Distribution methods and costs in the U.S.A.
REStud 14:16-33 no.1, 46
EVINITSKY, ALFRED
Value theory and socialism. S&S 9:260-63
no.3, 45
EXTER, JOHN and Bright, A. A., Jr.
War, radar, and the radio industry.
HBR 25:255-72 no.2, 47
EZEKIEL, MORDECAI
[The use of the short-cut graphic method of
multiple correlation.] Further comment.
QJE 54:331-46 Feb 40
Productivity, wage rates, and employment.
AER 30:507-23 Sep 40
A check on a multiple correlation result.
JFE 22:766-68 Nov 40
Price analyses, wars, and depressions.
JFE 22:673-79 Nov 40
and Wylie, K. H. The cost curve for steel
production. JPE 48:777-821 Dec 40
and Wylie, K. H. Cost functions for the
steel industry. JASA 36:91-99 Mar 41
Statistical investigations of saving, con-
sumption, and investment. Pt.I-II.
AER 32:22-49; 272-307 Mar,Jun 42
Schisms in agricultural policy: the shift in
agricultural policy toward human welfare.
JFE 24:463-76 May 42
The statistical determination of the investment schedule. Em 12:89-90 Jan 44
Desirable changes in the national economy
for the postwar period. JFE 26:101-09
Feb 44
Is government intervention or planning consistent with antitrust policy? AER/S 36:
190-204 May 46
[and others] Wage-price relations at high
level employment: discussion. AER/S 37:
254-64 May 47
FABRA RIBAS, ANTONIO
The Catholics of the Americas and cooperation. RSE 7,no.1:30-54 Mar 49
FABRICANT, SOLOMON
[Capital expansion, employment and economic
stability.] Rejoinder. JASA 35:703-06
Dec 40
[and others] Input-output analysis and its
use in peace and war economies: discussion. AER/S 39:226-40 May 49
FAGAN, ELMER DANIEL
Tax shifting in the market period. AER 32:
72-86 Mar 42; Correction. 356 Jun 42

FAGERHOLT, G. and Hald, A.
A few remarks on the application of statistical methods in industry. NTTO 12:83-88
no.37, 48

FAIN, JOHN TYREE
Ruskin and the orthodox political economists.
SEJ 10:1-13 Jul 43

FAINSOD, MERLE
and Thompson, W. The OPA economy for
victory program. JM 7:319-24 Apr 43
Political and administrative aspects of price
control in the war-peace transition.
AER/S 35:175-85 May 45
Economic interests and the political process.
IRRA 2:165-73 Dec 49

FAIR, MARVIN LUKE [and others]
Transportation and public utilities problems:
discussion. AER 37:478-97 May 47

FAIRCHILD, FRED ROGERS
The federal financial system. AER 31:280-97
Jun 41

FAIRCHILD, MILDRED
Women in war industry. S&S 7:14-23 no.1, 43

FALAKI, MAHMOUD SALEH EL
see El Falaki, Mahmoud Saleh

FALCK, EDWARD
Elasticity of residential demand for electricity: a reply. LE 17:498 Nov 41

FALCONER, JOHN IRONSIDE
[Problem of poverty in agriculture]: discussion. JFE 22:29-31 Feb 40

FALK, ISIDORE SYDNEY and Cohen, W. J.
Social security for farm people. JFE 28:
84-96 Feb 46

FANG, HSIEN-T'ING
Economic reconstruction in wartime China.
HBR 20:415-26 no.4, 42

FARIOLETTI, MARIUS
The 1948 audit control program for federal
individual income tax returns. NTJ 2:
142-50 Jun 49

FARNSWORTH, HELEN CHERINGTON
[Agricultural price supports]: discussion.
AER/S 36:827-31 May 46
[Food, agriculture, and trade.] Review of
Professor Schultz's paper. JFE 29:37-40
Feb 47
Food consumption in relation to farm produc-
tion and income. JFE 29:329-33 Feb 47
The European recovery program and the
American farmer. JFE 31,pt.2:519-33
Feb 49

FAROOQ, AZIZ
Standard of living in the N.-W.F. Province.
IJE 23:185-92 Oct 42

FARRELL, MARVIN WILLIAM
Experience with provincial marketing
schemes in Canada. JFE 31:610-26
Nov 49

FARRIER, CLARENCE W., chairman
Relationships of technological and social research in housing. Panel II. LE 25:
89-102 Feb 49

FARRINGTON, CARL C.
A price policy for agriculture, consistent
with economic progress, that will promote adequate and more stable income
from farming. JFE 27:837-43 Nov 45

FARWELL, LORING CHAPMAN and Dougall,
H. E.
A review of railroad financing, 1920-1938.
Pt.I-III. LE 16:207-13; 306-17; 433-54
May,Aug,Nov 40

FASIANI, MAURO
Tax distribution and Pareto's law in a re-
cent theoretical study. R. EI 2:469-91
Mar 49

FAUGHT, WILLIAM A. and Miley, D. G.
Development of regional cotton marketing
research. JFE 31,pt.2:1207-12 Nov 49

FAVILLE, DAVID E.
The impact of the war on Pacific Coast
paper distributors. JM 8:133-36 Oct 43

FAY, CHARLES RYLE
The growth of the new empire, 1783-1870.
R. EJ 51:80-91 Apr 41
Professor John Hilton (1880-1943). [obit.]
EJ 53:449-50 Dec 43

FEDERICI, LUIGI
Six months of Italian economic policy.
BNL 1:246-59 Jan 48
Causes of the decline in the stock exchange
in Italy. BNL 2:211-24 Oct-Dec 49

FEILER, ARTHUR
Conscription of capital. SR 8:1-23 Feb 41
Economic impacts of the war. SR 8:297-309
Sep 41
"Full employment of resources" and war
economy. SR 9:141-45 Feb 42

FEINSINGER, NATHAN P.
The contribution of the law to industrial relations research. IRRA 1:223-28 Dec 48

FELDMAN, EDWARD S.
Exemption of house furnishings from property taxation. NTJ 2:334-42 Dec 49

FELDMAN, GEORGE J.
Anti-trust paradoxes. JM 6:147-51 Oct 41

FELDMAN, HERMAN
The annual wage: where are we? R.
AER 37:823-47 Dec 47

FELDSTEIN, MARC J.
and Bryant, L. C. Organization of occupancy
as an approach to real estate management.
LE 17:460-64 Nov 41
and Bryant, L. C. Organization of occupancy
in critical war localities. LE 18:339-49
Aug 42

FELLNER, WILLIAM JOHN
and Ellis, H. S. Hicks and the time-period
controversy. JPE 48:563-78 Aug 40
and Somers, H. M. Alternative monetary approaches to interest theory. REStat 23:
43-48 Feb 41
The technological argument of the stagnation
thesis. QJE 55:638-51 Aug 41
War finance and inflation. AER 32:235-54
Jun 42

FELLNER, WILLIAM JOHN (Cont.)
Monetary policies and hoarding in periods
of stagnation. JPE 51:191-205 Jun 43
and Ellis, H. S. External economies and dis-
economies. AER 33:493-511 Sep 43
Period analysis and timeless equilibrium.
QJE 58:315-22 Feb 44
and Somers, H. M. Comment on Dr. Lerner's
note [on interest theory]. REStat 26:92
May 44
The commercial policy implications of the
Fund and Bank. AER/S 35:262-71 May 45
[and others] The problem of "full employ-
ment": discussion. AER/S 36:319-35
May 46
Postscript on war inflation: a lesson from
World War II. AER 37:76-91 Mar 47
Hansen on full-employment policies. R.
JPE 55:254-56 Jun 47
Prices and wages under bilateral monopoly.
QJE 61:503-32 Aug 47
Monetary policy and the elasticity of liquidity
functions. REStat 30:42-44 Feb 48
Average-cost pricing and the theory of un-
certainty. JPE 56:249-52 Jun 48
and Somers, H. M. Note on "stocks" and
"flows" in monetary interest theory.
REStat 31:145-46 May 49
FELLOWS, IRVING F.
Developing and applying production functions
in farm management. JFE 31,pt.2:1058-64
Nov 49
FELS, BRUNO and Whelpton, P. K.
An industrial classification for reports from
individuals. JASA 35:74-85 Mar 40
FELS, RENDIGS
Regional multilateral clearing. JPE 56:
342-43 Aug 48
The long-wave depression, 1873-97.
REStat 31:69-73 Feb 49
Free trade and southern progress. SEJ 16:
84-86 Jul 49
Warburton vs Hansen and Keynes. AER 39:
923-29 Sep 49
Gold and international equilibrium. AER 39:
1281-83 Dec 49
FENTON, FRANK P.
Labor's objectives. HBR 25:463-72 no.4, 47
FERBER, ROBERT
The disproportionate method of market
sampling. JB 19:67-75 Apr 46
Weekly versus monthly consumer purchase
panels. JM 13:223-24 Oct 48
FERGER, WIRTH FITCH
The measurement of tax shifting: economics
and law. QJE 54:429-54 May 40
Historical note on the purchasing power con-
cept, and index numbers. JASA 41:53-57
Mar 46
The role of economics in federal tax admin-
istration. NTJ 1:97-110 Jun 48
FERGUSON, ALLEN RICHMOND and Ames. E.
Technological change and the equilibrium

level of the national income. QJE 62:
441-58 May 48
FERGUSON, ELI
Risks in agricultural lending: discussion.
JFE 31,pt.2:613-19 Feb 49
FERGUSON, SAMUEL
Further comments on the 1944 NARUC
Report. LE 21:181-84 May 45
FERGUSSON, DONALD A.
The Industrial Development Bank of Canada.
JB 21:214-29 Oct 48
FERNANDEZ, RAMON
Land tenure in Mexico. JFE 25:219-34
Feb 43
FETTER, FRANK ALBERT
The pricing of steel in South Africa. R.
SAJE 9:235-50 Sep 41
Lauderdale's oversaving theory. AER 35:
263-83 Jun 45
[and others] Edwin Walter Kemmerer
1875-1945. [obit.] AER 36:219-21 Mar 46
Exit basing point pricing. AER 38:815-27
Dec 48
The effectiveness of the federal antitrust
laws: a symposium. AER 39:695-96
Jun 49
FETTER, FRANK WHITSON
Some neglected aspects of the wool duty.
JFE 23:399-420 May 41
The economists' tariff protest of 1930.
AER 32:355-56 Jun 42
The life and writings of John Wheatley.
JPE 50:357-76 Jun 42
The Bullion report [of 1810] reëxamined.
QJE 56:655-65 Aug 42
The need for postwar foreign lending.
AER/S 33:342-46 Mar 43
History of public debt in Latin America.
AER/S 37:142-50 May 47
The economic reports of the President and
the problem of inflation. R. QJE 63:
273-81 May 49
FEUER, LEWIS S.
The economic factor in history. S&S 4:
168-92 no.2, 40
FIELD, HAROLD
A note on exchange stability. REStud 15:
46-49 no.1, 47
FIELDS, R. H.
Lord Keynes's theory of wages. ER 22:
284-89 Dec 46
F[ILLEY], H[ORACE] C[LYDE]
Lewis F. Garey, 1886-1941. [obit.] JFE 23:
936-37 Nov 41
FINCH, C. D.
Economic problems of control in the milk
industry. ER 21:79-88 Jun 45
FINER, HERMAN
Post-war reconstruction in Great Britain.
CJE 8:493-513 Nov 42
FINKELSTEIN, ISAIAH; Gayer, A. D. and
Jacobson, A.
British share prices, 1811-1850. REStat 22:
78-93 May 40

FIRESTONE, O. J.
Estimate of the gross value of construction
in Canada, 1940. CJE 9:219-34 May 43
FIRTH, GERALD GILL
A note on supply. ER 16:111-14 Jun 40
Article seven: a programme for prosperity?
ER 18:1-15 Jun 42
FISCHOFF, EPHRAIM
The Protestant ethic and the spirit of capi-
talism. SR 11:53-77 Feb 44
FISHER, ALLAN GEORGE BERNARD
A liberal new order. R. Ec N.S.10:176-87
May 43
Some essential factors in the evolution of
international trade. MS 13:1-23 Oct 43
"Full employment" and income inequality.
EJ 56:18-26 Mar 46
Tertiary production as a postwar inter-
national economic problem. REStat 28:
146-51 Aug 46
Nicholas Mirkovich (1915-1944). [obit.]
EJ 56:510-11 Sep 46
Less stabilisation: more stability. Kyk 1:
1-18 fasc.1, 47
FISHER, CLYDE OLIN [and others]
Recent developments in public utility regu-
lation: discussion. AER/S 36:435-50
May 46
FISHER, ERNEST McKINLEY
Economic aspects of zoning, blighted areas,
and rehabilitation laws. AER/S 32:331-40
Mar 42
chairman. Measuring effective demand in
the housing market. Panel III. LE 25:
103-15 Feb 49
FISHER, FREDERICK JACK
Commercial trends and policy in sixteenth-
century England. EHR 10:95-117 Nov 40
FISHER, IRVING
Mathematical method in the social sciences.
Em 9:185-97 Jul-Oct 41
Rebuttal to Professor Crum and Mr. Mus-
grave. [The double taxation of saving]
AER 32:111-17 Mar 42
Paradoxes in taxing savings. Em 10:147-58
Apr 42
Income-tax revision: reply. Em 11:88-94
Jan 43
[Tribute to Irving Fisher.] Response.
JASA 42:4-5 Mar 47
--- [idem] Em 15:73-74 Apr 47
FISHER, LLOYD H.
What is a minimum adequate farm income?
JFE 25:662-70 Aug 43
FISHER, MARGUERITE J.
Equal pay for equal work legislation.
ILRR 2:50-57 Oct 48
FISHER, PAUL
The National War Labor Board and postwar
industrial relations. QJE 59:483-523
Aug 45
Reparation labor: a preliminary analysis.
QJE 60:313-39 May 46

The settlement of work jurisdictional disputes by governmental agencies. ILRR 2:
335-59 Apr 49
[and others] Can capitalism dispense with
free labor markets? Discussion.
IRRA 2:100-14 Dec 49
FISHER, WALDO EMANUEL
Union wage and hour policies and employment. [Abstract] AER/S 30:227-29
Mar 40
Union wage and hour policies and employment. AER 30:290-99 Jun 40
FISHMAN, LEO
and Backman, J. British war-time control
of copper, lead, and zinc. QJE 55:210-38
Feb 41
and Backman, J. British war time control
of aluminum. QJE 56:18-48 Nov 41
Wartime control of tin in Great Britain,
1939-41. JPE 54:413-35 Oct 46
and Clark, E. Appraisal of methods for
estimating the size distribution of a given
aggregate income. REStat 29:43-46
Feb 47
FISK, GEORGE
Methods of handling certain field research
problems. JM 12:382-84 Jan 48
FISKE, MARJORIE
and Handel, L. Motion picture research:
content and audience analysis; response
analysis. JM 11:129-34; 273-80 Oct 46,
Jan 47
and Handel, L. New techniques for studying
the effectiveness of films. JM 11:390-93
Apr 47
FITE, GILBERT C.
South Dakota's rural credit system: a
venture in state socialism, 1917-1946.
AH 21:239-49 Oct 47
FitzGERALD, DENNIS ALFRED
Coming readjustments in agriculture; the
international phase. JFE 31:19-28 Feb 49
FITZPATRICK, BRIAN
The big man's frontier and Australian farm-
ing. AH 21:8-12 Jan 47
FITZPATRICK, F. STUART
Defense housing. LE 16:344-45 Aug 40
FLANDERS, RALPH EDWARD
[Revising the postwar federal tax system]:
discussion. AER/S 34,no.2:41-43 Jun 44
The moral dilemma of an industrialist.
HBR 23:433-41 no.4, 45
Economics collides with ethics. AER/S 38:
357-67 May 48
FLANINGAM, MILETUS L. ed. & tr.
The French agricultural questionnaire of
1814: The circular letter of Becquey, The
model agricultural questionnaire, and The
reply for the Arrondissement of Lisieux.
AH 23:61-75 Jan 49
FLEMING, JOHM MARCUS
Price and output policy of state enterprise:
comment. EJ 54:328-37 Dec 44

FLEMING, JOHM MARCUS (Cont.)
A new synthesis of welfare economics. R.
MS 14,no.3:1-18 Sep 46

FLEMMING, CECILE WHITE
see Flemming, Edwin G. and Flemming,
C. W.

FLEMMING, EDWIN G. and Flemming, C. W.
Test-selected salesmen. JM 10:336-42
Apr 46

FLEXNER, JEAN ATHERTON
Food policies of the United Nations. AER 33:
812-24 Dec 43
Arbitration of labor disputes in Great
Britain. ILRR 1:421-30 Apr 48

FLICK, HUGH M.
Elkanah Watson's activities on behalf of
agriculture. AH 21:193-98 Oct 47

FLOOD, MERRILL M.
Recursive methods in business-cycle analysis. Em 8:333-53 Oct 40

FLORENCE, PHILIP SARGANT
and Wensley, A. J. Recent industrial concentration, especially in the Midlands.
REStud 7:139-58 Jun 40
and Shenfield, A. Labour for the war industries: the experience of Coventry.
REStud 12:31-49 no.1, 44
The selection of industries suitable for dispersion into rural areas. JRSS 107:
93-107 pt.2, 44
and Shenfield, A. The economies and diseconomies of industrial concentration:
the wartime experience of Coventry.
REStud 12:79-99 no.2, 45
The statistical analysis of joint stock company control. JRSS 110:2-19 pt.1, 47

FLOYD, JOE SUMMERS
The changing impact of national banking
costs, 1921-43. SEJ 12:365-75 Apr 46

FOENANDER, ORWELL DE RUYTER
The Commonwealth Court of Conciliation
and Arbitration: a brief survey. QJE 63:
408-29 Aug 49

FOG, BJARKE
Dynamic price problems under monopolistic competition. NTTO 11:257-70 no.36, 47
Price theory and reality. NTTO 12:89-94
no.37, 48

FOGARTY, MICHAEL PATRICK
The incidence of rates on houses.
REStud 10:81-105 no.2, 43
The complications of location. MS 15:251-83
Sep 47

FOH-SHEN WANG
see Wang, Foh-Shen

FOLEY, DONALD L.
An index of housing in Chicago. LE 18:
209-13 May 42

FOLK, GEORGE E. [and others]
Patent policy: discussion. AER/S 38:
245-60 May 48

FOLWEILER, ALFRED DAVID
Cotton, wood pulp, and the man-land ratio of
the deep South. SEJ 7:518-28 Apr 41

The political economy of forest conservation in the United States. LE 20:202-16
Aug 44

FONER, PHILIP S.
Labor and the Copperheads. S&S 8:223-42
no.3, 44

FONG, H. D.
see Fang, Hsien-t'ing

FOOTE, RICHARD J.
Wartime dairy policies. JFE 29:679-90
Aug 47

FORBES, GERALD
The passing of the small oil man. SEJ 7:
204-15 Oct 40
Oklahoma oil and Indian land tenure.
AH 15:189-94 Oct 41

FORCHHEIMER, KARL
The 'short cycle' in its international aspects.
OEP 7:1-20 Mar 45
War-time changes in industrial employment:
a comparison between the two world wars.
OIS 7:269-78 Nov 24, 45
Europe's average standard of living. OIS 8:
108-11 Apr 46
The role of relative wage differences in inter-
national trade. QJE 62:1-30 Nov 47
Some international aspects of the strike
movement. Pt.I-II. OIS 10:9-24; 294-304
Jan,Sep 48
Some international aspects of strikes: the
effectiveness of large and of long strikes,
with special reference to Sweden. OIS 11:
279-86 Sep 49

FORGE, F. WALDO
The taxation of industry. TBR 4:24-33
Dec 49

FORMAN, LEWIS W. and Dirksen, C. J.
Opportunities in marketing research.
JM 13:37-43 Jul 48

FORMAN, SIDNEY
The New Bridge Oyster Company, 1863-1868.
BHR 16:53-61 Jun 42

FORSEY, EUGENE
Trade union policy under full employment.
CJE 12:343-55 Aug 46
A note on the Dominion factory bills of the
eighteen-eighties. CJE 13:580-83 Nov 47

FORSTER, GARNET WOLSEY
Farm management research: discussion.
JFE 22:123-26 Feb 40
Farm-management research: discussion.
JFE 23:236-37 Feb 41
[Soil conservation benefits]: discussion.
JFE 24:151-53 Feb 42
Contribution of farm management research
to attainment of production goals. JFE 25:
110-19 Feb 43
Some defects in the analysis of farm manage-
ment data. JFE 26:775-79 Nov 44
Southern agricultural economy in the postwar
era. SEJ 13:65-71 Jul 46
Impact of technology on southern agriculture.
JFE 29:520-30 May 47

FORSTER, GARNET WOLSEY (Cont.)
[Methods of financing related to asset char-
acteristics of farms]: discussion.
JFE 29:1180 Nov 47

FORSYTH, WILLIAM DOUGLASS
Population growth: some comparisons. ER 17:
248-52 Dec 41

FORT, DONALD M.
A theory of general short-run equilibrium.
Em 13:293-310 Oct 45

FOSSATI, ERALDO
Vilfredo Pareto and John Maynard Keynes:
one or two economic systems? Met 1:
126-30 Oct 49

FOSTER, GEORGE M.
The folk economy of rural Mexico with
special reference to marketing. JM 13:
153-62 Oct 48

FOSTER, WILLIAM TRUFANT
Consumer credit charges after the war.
JB 17:16-22 Jan 44

FOURNIER, LESLIE THOMAS [and others]
Recent developments in public utility regula-
tion: discussion. AER/S 36:435-50
May 46

FOWKE, VERNON CLIFFORD
Dominion aids to wheat marketing, 1929-39.
CJE 6:390-402 Aug 40
On some appendices to the Rowell-Sirois
report. II. The economic background.
CJE 7:73-78 Feb 41
An introduction to Canadian agricultural
history. CJE 8:56-68 Feb 42
--- [idem] AH 16:79-90 Apr 42
Economic effects of the war on the prairie
economy. CJE 11:373-87 Aug 45
Royal Commissions and Canadian agricultural
policy. CJE 14:163-75 May 48
and Britnell, G. E. Development of wheat
marketing policy in Canada. JFE 31:
627-42 Nov 49

FOWLER, RONALD FREDERICK and Coase,
R. H.
The analysis of producers' expectations.
Ec N.S.7:280-92 Aug 40

FOX, ANNETTE BAKER
The local housing authority and the municipal government. LE 17:280-90 Aug 41

FOX, HAROLD G.
Patents in relation to monopoly. CJE 12:
328-42 Aug 46
--- A rejoinder. CJE 13:68-80 Feb 47

FOX, JOHN BAYLEY
Labor's response to management. HBR 21:
95-99 no.1, 42

FOX, KARL AUGUST
Needed new directions in agricultural price
analysis. JFE 31,pt.2:1080-88 Nov 49

FRANCHINI-STAPPO, ALESSANDRO
Components and significance of the circular
velocity of money. [Translated by O. R.
Agresti] EI 2:236-49 Feb 49

FRANCISCO, L. MERCER
The talking picture: an example of the
machine method applied to selling. JM 9:
119-23 Oct 44

FRANK, BERNARD
Some aspects of the evaluation of watershed
flood control projects. LE 18:391-411
Nov 42

FRANK, MARJI
Measurement and elimination of confusion
elements in recognition surveys. JM 12:
362-64 Jan 48

FRANKEL, H.
Quantitative and qualitative full employment.
OIS 3:342-46 Nov 1, 41; Erratum. 381
Nov 22, 41
The employment of married women. OIS 4:
183-85 Jun 27, 42
Industrialisation of agricultural countries
and the possibilities of a new international
division of labour. EJ 53:188-201
Jun-Sep 43
The industrial distribution of the population
of Great Britain in July, 1939. JRSS 108:
392-422 pt.3-4, 45
Reconstruction in Europe. R. OIS 9:44-50
Feb 47

FRANKEL, LESTER R. and Stock, R. S.
On the sample survey of unemployment.
JASA 37:77-80 Mar 42

FRANKEL, SALLY HERBERT
and Newmark, S. D. Note on the national income of the Union of South Africa.
1927/28, 1932/33, 1934/35. SAJE 8:
78-80 Mar 40
Consumption, investment and war expenditure in relation to the South African
national income [1938/39-1944/45].
SAJE 9:445-48; 11:75-77; 12:147-49;
13:132-35; 14:220-23 Dec 41, Mar 43,
Jun 44, Jun 45, Sep 46
World economic solidarity. SAJE 10:169-92
Sep 42
and Herzfeld, H. European income distribution in the Union of South Africa and the
effect thereon of income taxation.
SAJE 11:121-36 Jun 43
World economic welfare. SAJE 11:165-84
Sep 43; Errata. 296 Dec 43
and Herzfeld, H. An analysis of the growth
of the national income of the Union in the
period of prosperity before the war.
SAJE 12:112-38 Jun 44
Whither South Africa? An economic approach.
SAJE 15:27-39 Mar 47
Expenditure in relation to national income.
SAJE 15:276-79 Dec 47

FRANKLIN, NORTON NORRIS
and Yamey, B. S. An enquiry into some
effects of a wage determination in Grahamstown. SAJE 9:416-22 Dec 41
Economic welfare and the development of the
Native Reserves. SAJE 10:1-15 Mar 42

FRANKLIN, NORTON NORRIS (Cont.)
  Co-operative credit in the Transkeian terri-
    tories. SAJE 10:95-120 Jun 42
  A note on the report of the Select Committee
    on Social Security. SAJE 12:316-18 Dec 44
FRANTZ, JOE B.
  Gail Borden as a businessman. BHR 22:
    123-33 Dec 48
FRANZEN, RAYMOND
  and Teilhet, D. A method for measuring
    product acceptance. JM 5:156-61 Oct 40
  Inequalities which affect scores of advertise-
    ments. JM 6,no.4,pt.2:128-32 Apr 42
FRANZSEN, D. G.
  The secular stagnation-thesis and the prob-
    lem of economic stability. SAJE 10:
    282-94 Dec 42
  Methodological issues in the theory of price
    flexibility. SAJE 15:87-115 Jun 47
  Some methodological problems raised by the
    calculation of the Union's national income,
    by income type. SAJE 16:157-67 Jun 48
FRED, EDWIN B.
  In memoriam to Leonard A. Salter, Jr.
    [obit.] LE 22:117-18 May 46
FREDERICK, JOHN HUTCHINSON
  and Lewis, A. D. Air routes and public
    policy. HBR 19:482-95 no.4, 41
  How air transportation may affect marketing
    and product development. JM 8:274-80
    Jan 44
  Some problems of selling air travel. JM 9:
    144-50 Oct 44
FREEDMAN, RONALD and Hawley, A. H.
  Unemployment and migration in the depres-
    sion (1930-1935). JASA 43:260-72 Jun 49
FREELAND, WILLARD E.
  Scientific management in marketing.
    JM 4,no.4, pt.2:31-38 Apr 40
FREEMAN, HARROP A.
  Public utility taxation. LE 23:42-49 Feb 47
FREEMAN, RUTH CRAWFORD and Bane, L.
  Saving and spending patterns of the same
    rural families over a 10-year period,
    1933-42. AER 34:344-50 Jun 44
FREER, ROBERT E.
  Informative and nondeceptive advertising.
    JM 13:358-63 Jan 49
FREESTON, THOMAS
  Johnson & Johnson training program.
    ILRR 2:623-24 Jul 49
FREIBERG, ALBERT MAURICE
  Milk delivery: necessity or luxury? HBR 20:
    116-23 no.1, 41
FRENCH, CARROLL E. [and others]
  Collective bargaining and management rights:
    discussion. IRRA 1:156-70 Dec 48
FREUND, RUDOLF
  Turner's theory of social evolution. AH 19:
    78-87 Apr 45
  Military bounty lands and the origins of the
    public domain. AH 20:8-18 Jan 46
  Squandering the public domain in Sweden:
    1820-1870. LE 22:119-30 May 46

  John Adams and Thomas Jefferson on the
    nature of landholding in America. LE 24:
    107-19 May 48
  Methods of financing the European Recovery
    Program. SEJ 15:267-78 Jan 49
FRIDAY, FRANK ADZLEY
  United Kingdom export target. OIS 8:168-77
    Jun 46
FRIEDIN, JESSE
  The National War Labor Board: an achieve-
    ment in tri-partite administration. S&S 7:
    80-87 no.1, 43
FRIEDLAENDER, HEINRICH E.
  The story of the nitrogen process in France:
    an experiment in post-war planning.
    JB 16:247-52 Oct 43
FRIEDLANDER, ETTA
  Education in the workers' schools of New
    York City. SR 7:92-101 Feb 40
FRIEDMAN, LEE M.
  The drummer in early American merchan-
    dise distribution. BHR 21:39-44 Apr 47
  The first chamber of commerce in the
    United States. BHR 21:137-43 Nov 47
FRIEDMAN, MILTON
  The spendings tax as a wartime fiscal
    measure. AER 33:50-62 Mar 43
  Lange on price flexibility and employment:
    a methodological criticism. AER 36:
    613-31 Sep 46
  Lerner on The economics of control. R.
    JPE 55:405-16 Oct 47
  A monetary and fiscal framework for eco-
    nomic stability. AER 38:245-64 Jun 48
  and Savage, L. J. The utility analysis of
    choices involving risk. JPE 56:279-304
    Aug 48
  [and others] Liquidity and uncertainty:
    discussion. AER/S 39:196-210 May 49
  [Professor Friedman's proposal.] Rejoinder.
    AER 39:949-55 Sep 49
  The Marshallian demand curve. JPE 57:
    463-95 Dec 49
FRIEDMANN, C. A.
  A critique of Professor Hutt's "Two studies
    in the statistics of Russia." SAJE 13:
    332-43 Dec 45
FRIEND, IRWIN
  Ezekiel's analysis of saving, consumption,
    and investment. AER 32:829-35 Dec 42
  Relationship between consumers' expendi-
    tures, savings, and disposable income.
    REStat 28:208-15 Nov 46
  Consumption-saving function: comments.
    REStat 30:301-03 Nov 48
  and Jacobs, W. Input-output analysis and its
    use in peace and war economies: discus-
    sion. AER/S 39:228-32 May 49
FRISCH, RAGNAR
  The responsibility of the econometrician.
    Em 14:1-4 Jan 46
  Tribute to Irving Fisher. JASA 42:2-4
    Mar 47
  --- [idem.] Em 15:71-73 Apr 47

FRISCH, RAGNAR (Cont.)
> On the need for forecasting a multilateral
> balance of payments. AER 37:535-51
> Sep 47
>
> Repercussion studies at Oslo. AER 38:
> 367-72 Jun 48
>
> Outline of a system of multicompensatory
> trade. REStat 30:265-71 Nov 48
>
> Overdeterminateness and optimum equilib-
> rium. NTTO 12:95-105 no.37, 48
>
> On the zeros of homogeneous functions.
> Em 17:28-29 Jan 49
>
> Prolegomena to a pressure-analysis of
> economic phenomena. Met 1:135-60
> Dec 49

FROEHLICH, WALTER
> Changes in the central European retail trade.
> JM 4:258-63 Jan 40
>
> Aid for the independent retail trade: a step
> toward fascism? JM 5:276-79 Jan 41
>
> International economic problems of a post-
> war world. RSE 1:31-53 Dec 42
>
> [How many jobs must we provide for a bal-
> anced postwar economy?] Discussion.
> RSE 3:42-44 Dec 44
>
> The role of income determination in reinvest-
> ment and investment. AER 38:78-91
> Mar 48

FROKER, RUDOLPH K.
> A price policy for agriculture, consistent
> with economic progress, that will promote
> adequate and more stable income from
> farming. JFE 27:844-51 Nov 45
>
> Discussion of price policy winning papers.
> JFE 28:290-93 Feb 46
>
> chairman. Dairy marketing research round-
> table meeting. JFE 29:283-91 Feb 47

FROMAN, LEWIS ACRELIUS
> Graduate students in economics, 1904-1940.
> AER 32:817-26 Dec 42
>
> The adequacy of bank equities. JF 2,no.2:
> 22-30 Oct 47

FROMMER, JOSEPH C.
> A price formula for multiple-commodity
> monetary reserve. Em 13:153-60 Apr 45

FROTHINGHAM, ROY S., chairman
> Preparation and presentation of the research
> report. JM 13:62-72 Jul 48

FRY, RICHARD
> The British business man: 1900-1949.
> EEH 2:35-43 Nov 49

FUHRIMAN, WALTER U.
> Federal aid to irrigation development.
> JFE 31,pt.2:965-75 Nov 49

FULCHER, GORDON SCOTT
> Annual saving and underspending of individu-
> als, 1926-37. REStat 23:28-42 Feb 41
>
> Saving of individuals in relation to income.
> AER 32:835-40 Dec 42
>
> Life insurance saving of American families.
> REStat 26:93-94 May 44

FULLBROOK, EARL STANFIELD
> The functional concept in marketing. JM 4:
> 229-37 Jan 40

FULLER, VARDEN
> Acreage limitation in federal irrigation
> projects with particular reference to the
> Central Valley Project of California.
> JFE 31,pt.2:976-82 Nov 49

FULMER, JOHN LEONARD
> Relationship of the cycle in yields of cotton
> and apples to solar and sky radiation.
> QJE 56:385-405 May 42
>
> Trends in the per capita consumption of
> foods in the United States since 1920.
> SEJ 14:404-10 Apr 48
>
> Relation of method of acquiring farm to
> production factors in cotton farming.
> JFE 31:337-42 May 49

FURBER, HOLDEN
> The United Company of Merchants of Eng-
> land Trading to the East Indies, 1783-96.
> EHR 10:138-47 Nov 40

FURBUSH, FRANK
> Farm family income and expenditures.
> JM 4:264-67 Jan 40

FURMAN, ALAN F. and Ball, E. P.
> Operating a grazing association. LE 19:
> 94-98 Feb 43

FURTH, JOSEF HERBERT
> Trade barriers in central Europe. JM 4,
> no.4,pt.2:25-30 Apr 40
>
> Earnings and employment in the business
> cycle. REStat 24:136-42 Aug 42
>
> Short-run escape clauses of the Havana
> Charter. AER/S 39:252-60 May 49

FUSSELL, GEORGE EDWIN
> and Goodman, C. Crop husbandry in eight-
> eenth century England. Pt.I-II. AH 15:
> 202-16; 16:41-63 Oct 41, Jan 42
>
> My impressions of Arthur Young. AH 17:
> 135-44 Jul 43
>
> "A real farmer" of eighteenth-century Eng-
> land and his book, The modern farmers
> guide. AH 17:211-15 Oct 43
>
> The collection of agricultural statistics in
> Great Britain: its origin and evolution.
> AH 18:161-67 Oct 44
>
> History and agricultural science. AH 19:
> 126-27 Apr 45
>
> English agriculture from Cobbett to Caird
> (1830-80). EHR 15:79-85 no.1-2, 45
>
> The traffic in farm produce in seventeenth-
> century England. AH 20:77-86 Apr 46
>
> The farming writers of eighteenth-century
> England. AH 21:1-8 Jan 47
>
> Home counties farming, 1840-80. EJ 57:
> 321-45 Sep 47
>
> The dawn of high farming in England: land
> reclamation in early Victorian days.
> AH 22:83-95 Apr 48
>
> My impressions of William Marshall. AH 23:
> 57-61 Jan 49

GAATHON, ARIEH LUDWIG
National income and outlay with reference to
savings, capital movements and investment. SAJE 12:28-45 Mar 44

GADGIL, DHANANJAYA RAMCHANDRA
Rail road coordination with special reference
to rates policy. IJE 26:488-98 Jan 46
Social legislation and plans of improvement.
IJE 27:287-90 Jan 47

GADRE, R. N.
The effects of war on the agricultural pro-
duction and crop planning in the C.P. &
Berar. IJE 28:269-80 Oct 47

GAEV, V.
Plans for full employment after the war.
S&S 9:67-76 no.1, 45

GAFFEY, JOHN DEAN
Labor productivity in tire manufacturing: a
reply to L. G. Reynolds. AER 31:837-38
Dec 41

GAGE, DANIEL DUDLEY
Wartime experiment in federal rent control.
LE 23:50-59 Feb 47

GAGLIARDO, DOMENICO
Strikes in a democracy. AER 31:47-55
Mar 41

GAINER, WALTER and Brownlee, O. H.
Farmers' price anticipations and the role of
uncertainty in farm planning. JFE 31:
266-75 May 49

GAINSBRUGH, MARTIN R. and Backman, J.
Productivity and living standards. ILRR 2:
163-94 Jan 49

GALBRAITH, JOHN KENNETH
Defense financing and inflation: some com-
ments on Professor Hansen's article: The
selection and timing of inflation controls.
REStat 23:82-85 May 41
Price control: some lessons from the first
phase. AER/S 33:251-59 Mar 43
[and others] New frontiers in economic
thought: discussion. AER/S 36:139-53
May 46
Reflections on price control. QJE 60:475-89
Aug 46
and Baran, P. A. Professor Despres on
"Effects of strategic bombing on the
German war economy." REStat 29:132-34
May 47
The disequilibrium system. AER 37:287-302
Jun 47
[and others] Problems of timing and admin-
istering fiscal policy in prosperity and
depression: discussion. AER/S 38:443-51
May 48
Appraisal of marketing research. [Abstract]
AER/S 39:415-16 May 49

GALBRAITH, VIRGINIA LEE and Thomas, D. S.
Birth rates and the interwar business cycles.
JASA 36:465-76 Dec 41

GALBREATH, CHARLES EDWARD and Mikesell,
R. F.
Subsidies and price control. AER 32:524-37
Sep 42

GALENSON, WALTER
Some aspects of industrial relations in Denmark. IRRA 2:230-41 Dec 49

GALLEGO-DIAZ, J.
A note on the arc elasticity of demand.
REStud 12:114-15 no.2, 45

GALLETTI, R.
Taxation and agricultural policy. IJE 22:
68-86 Jul 41
Pure economics and social engineering.
IJE 23:319-63 Apr 43
Making sense of land utilization figures.
IJE 25:465-91 Apr 45

GALLOWAY, ZACHARY L.
Useful techniques in an extension program
in farm management. JFE 31,pt.2:693-96
Feb 49

GAMBINO, AMEDEO
Recent developments in banking activity in
Italy. BNL 1:109-20 Jul 47

GARDNER, EDWARD H.
The business view of advertising policy.
JM 6,no.4,pt.2:112-17 Apr 42
Consumer goods classification. JM 9:275-76
Jan 45

GARDNER, WALTER RICHMOND
The future international position of the
United States as affected by the Fund and
Bank. AER/S 35:272-88 May 45

GARFIELD, FRANK RICHARDSON
Measurement of industrial production since
1939. JASA 39:439-54 Dec 44
Measuring and forecasting consumption.
JASA 41:322-33 Sep 46
Transition forecasts in review. AER/S 37:
71-80 May 47

GARLAND, JOHN MANSON
Some aspects of full employment. Pt.I-II.
ER 20:152-69; 21:23-36 Dec 44, Jun 45

GARMANY, J. W.
South Africa and the Sterling Area. SAJE 17:
480-91 Dec 49

GARNER, SAMUEL PAUL
Application of burden in wartime industries.
SEJ 11:360-68 Apr 45

GARNSEY, MORRIS EUGENE
Postwar exchange-rate parities. QJE 60:
113-35 Nov 45
--- Reply. QJE 60:624-30 Aug 46

GARVER, FREDERIC BENJAMIN
Government and private enterprise: discus-
sion. AER/S 33:82-83 Mar 43
Cartels, combinations and the public interest.
JFE 26:613-30 Nov 44

GARVY, GEORGE
Kondratieff's theory of long cycles.
REStat 25:203-20 Aug 43
Dr. Rhodes' analysis of the distribution of
single incomes in the United States.
Ec N.S.11:104-05 May 44
Rivals and interlopers in the history of the
New York security market. JPE 52:
128-43 Jun 44

GARVY, GEORGE (Cont.)
and Lewis, R. E.  New indexes of hourly and
weekly earnings compiled by the Federal
Reserve Bank of New York.  JASA 42:
256-70 Jun 47

Keynesian economics: the propensity to
consume and the multiplier: discussion.
AER/S 38:306-08 May 48

The role of dissaving in economic analysis.
JPE 56:416-27 Oct 48

[and others]  Interregional variations in economic fluctuations: discussion.
AER/S 39:120-34 May 49

GASTON, HERBERT E.
The government as a business: a consideration of budget problems in relation to the
general welfare.  SR 7:434-46 Nov 40

GASTON, THOMAS L.
A conservationist's appraisal of the Missouri
development program.  JFE 31,pt.2:
1024-29 Nov 49

GATES, JAMES EDWARD
Problems in administering war-time short-
ages of electric energy.  LE 17:477-82
Nov 41

Forecasting the demand for electric energy.
LE 18:77-81 Feb 42

--- A rejoinder.  LE 18:230-32 May 42

GATES, PAUL WALLACE
Land policy and tenancy in the prairie states.
JEH 1:60-82 May 41

GAUMNITZ, EDWIN WILLIAM
Agricultural marketing research: discussion.
JFE 31,pt.2:565-66 Feb 49

GAUS, JOHN M.
The education of planners: a commentary on
some current projects.  LE 21:307-09
Sep 45

GAY, EDWIN FRANCIS
The tasks of economic history.  JEH/S 1:
9-16 Dec 41

GAY, LEON S.
A new approach to local business history.
BHR 21:3-9 Feb 47

GAYER, ARTHUR DAVID; Jacobson, A. and
Finkelstein, I.
British share prices, 1811-1850. REStat 22:
78-93 May 40

GAZLEY, JOHN G.
Arthur Young and the Society of Arts. JEH 1:
129-52 Nov 41

GEARY, ROBERT CHARLES
The concept of net volume of output, with
special reference to Irish data. JRSS 107:
251-59 pt.3-4, 44

--- Rejoinder to Messrs. Leak and Maizels.
JRSS 107:290-92 pt.3-4, 44

Determination of linear relations between
systematic parts of variables with errors
of observation the variances of which are
unknown. Em 17:30-58 Jan 49

GEDDES, ARTHUR
Conjoint-tenants and tacksmen in the Isle of

Lewis, 1715-26.  EHR II.1:54-60 no.1, 48

GEHRELS, FRANZ
Inflationary effects of a balanced budget
under full employment.  AER 39:1276-78
Dec 49

GEIGER, THEODORE
Concentration of the stove industry.  HBR 22:
19-28 no.1, 43

GEIRINGER, HILDA
A new explanation of nonnormal dispersion
in the Lexis theory.  Em 10:53-60 Jan 42

GELTING, JØRGEN
On redistribution of income.  NTTO 12:
107-09 no.37, 48

GENTILLI, JOSEPH
Australian rural population changes.
ER 25,(no.48):37-47 Jun 49

GENUNG, J. H.
Some things we do not know about the marketing of perishable agricultural commodities.  JM 5:162-63 Oct 40

GEORGE, CECIL OSWALD
British public finance in peace and war.
JRSS 104:235-65 pt.3, 41

GEORGE, EDWIN BLACK
and Landry, R. J.  Policy suggestions,
January 1947-June 1948.  REStat 29:
24-28 Feb 47

[and others]  The economic consequences of
some recent antitrust decisions: discussion.  AER/S 39:311-21 May 49

GEORGE, HARRY B., Jr.
Buying perishables for the armed forces.
HBR 22:209-19 no.2, 44

GEORGE, JAMES P.
Correlation analysis of farm land values.
JFE 23:668-71 Aug 41

GEORGE, JOHN J. and Boldt, J. R., Jr.
Certification of motor common carriers by
the Interstate Commerce Commission.
Pt.I-II.  LE 17:82-91; 196-206 Feb, May 41

GEORGE, RONALD F.
James William Verdier, O.B.E. [obit.]
JRSS 111:376 pt.4, 48

Conrad Alexander Verrijn Stuart. [obit.]
JRSS 112:346 pt.3, 49

Statistics relating to the coal mining industry.  JRSS 112:331-37 pt.3, 49

GEORGESCU-ROEGEN, NICHOLAS
Further contribution to the scatter analysis.
Em 17,suppl.:39-42 Jul 49

GEREN, PAUL
The contribution of life insurance to the
savings stream.  JPE 51:33-51 Feb 43

The role of velocity of circulation in the
present rise of prices.  IJE 24:99-116
Oct 43

GERRISH, CATHERINE RUGGLES
Treasury tax studies.  Pt.I-II.  NTJ 1:144-53;
250-60 Jun, Sep 48

GERSCHENKRON, ALEXANDER
and Gulick, C. A., Jr.  Errors and traditions:
remarks on Ernst Karl Winter's article,

GERSCHENKRON, ALEXANDER (Cont.)
"The rise and fall of Austrian labor."
SR 7:45-60 Feb 40
International Trade Organization: discussion.
AER/S 37:556-59 May 47
Russia and the International Trade Organiza-
tion. AER/S 37:624-42 May 47
The Soviet indices of industrial production.
REStat 29:217-26 Nov 47
The rate of industrial growth in Russia since
1885. JEH/S 7:144-74 '47
GETTELL, RICHARD GLENN
Changing competitive conditions in the mar-
keting of tires. JM 6:112-23 Oct 41
Rationing: a pragmatic problem for econo-
mists. AER/S 33:260-71 Mar 43
GHATE, BHALCHANDRA G.
A scheme for the survey of rural indebted-
ness in India. IJE 21:13-29 Jul 40
GHATGE, M. B. and Patel, K. S.
Economics of mixed farming in "Charotar"
(Bombay Province). IJE 23:133-54 Oct 42
GHENT, M. DAL
Selection and training of commercial re-
search analysts. JM 14:22-26 Jul 49
GHISELLI, EDWIN E.
Some further points on public opinion polls.
JM 5:115-19 Oct 40
GHOSH, AMBICA
Agricultural labour in Bengal. IJE 28:425-42
Jan 48
GHOSH, D. and Adarkar, B. P.
Mr. Keynes's theory of interest. IJE 21:
285-300 Jan 41
GHOSH, DEBABRATA
Wage and the Indian cost of living index
numbers. IJE 26:226-42 Oct 45
GHOSH, HARICHARAN
Review of finances in Bengal (1937-41).
IJE 21:569-93 Apr 41
Rural co-operation: its scope in India.
IJE 22:450-60 Jan 42
The rationale of salt tax in India. IJE 27:
493-501 Apr 47
GHOSH, MOHIT KUMAR
Inflation: a possible remedy. IJE 23:
371-72 Apr 43
Control of inflation. IJE 24:73-75 Jul 43
GHOSH, RAMESH CHANDRA
Forest policy for Bengal. IJE 28:509-32
Apr 48
GIBB, GEORGE SWEET
The pre-industrial revolution in America: a
field for local research. BHR 20:103-16
Oct 46
Three early railroad equipment contracts.
BHR 21:10-17 Feb 47
GIBB, ROGER
The weight of consignments in transport: a
further comment. EJ 50:525-32 Dec 40
GIBBON, Sir GWILYM
The Beveridge Report. R. JRSS 105:336-40
pt.4, 42

GIBBONS, CHARLES A. and Black, J. D.
The war and American agriculture.
REStat 26:1-55 Feb 44
GIBLIN, LYNDHURST FALKINER
Economic progress. R. ER 16:262-69
Dec 40
"Estimates of national income and public
authority income and expenditure," pre-
sented by the Right Hon. J. B. Chifley
for the information of honourable mem-
bers on the occasion of the budget,
1945-46. R. ER 21:254-56 Dec 45
John Maynard Keynes. (Some personal notes)
ER 22:1-3 Jun 46
The Record and its editors (1925-1946).
ER 23:1-4 Jun 47
GIBSON, JAMES DOUGLAS
The Canadian balance of international pay-
ments: a study of methods and results.
CJE 6:282-88 May 40
Business prospects in Canada. CJE 15:
394-401 Aug 49
GIBSON, ROBERT L.
Some preferences of television audiences.
JM 10:289-90 Jan 46
GIBSON, WILLIAM LLOYD, Jr.
Industrialization and rural land utilization.
SEJ 11:353-59 Apr 45
and Walrath, A. J. Inheritance of farm
property. JFE 29:938-51 Nov 47
GIDDENS, PAUL HENRY
History looks at oil. BHR 20:3-16 Feb 46
GIDEONSE, HARRY DAVID
The relation of American foreign-trade
policy to New Deal domestic policy.
AER 30:87-97 Mar 40
GIFFIN, ROSCOE RAYMOND
and Gittler, J. B. Changing patterns of em-
ployment in five southeastern states,
1930-1940. SEJ 11:169-82 Oct 44
Changing output per person employed in
trade, 1900-1940. JM 12:242-45 Oct 47
GILBERT, DONALD WOOD
[The incidence of sales taxes.] Rejoinder.
QJE 54:686-93 Aug 40
Cycles in municipal finance. REStat 22:
190-202 Nov 40
Taxation and economic stability. QJE 56:
406-29 May 42
GILBERT, HORACE NATHANIEL
The emergency in aircraft manufacture.
HBR 19:508-19 no.4, 41
The expansion of shipbuilding. HBR 20:
156-70 no.2, 42
From industrial mobilization to war pro-
duction. HBR 21:124-36 no.1, 42
GILBERT, JOHN CANNON
Anglo-French financial co-operation during
the war, 1914-18. REStud 7:159-68 Jun 40
Professor Polanyi's Full employment and
free trade. R. MS 14,no.2:85-97 May 46
GILBERT, MILTON
Measuring national income as affected by the
war. JASA 37:186-98 Jun 42

GILBERT, MILTON (Cont.)
U.S. national income statistics. EJ 53:76-82
Apr 43
National product, war and prewar: some
comments on Professor Kuznets' study.
REStat 26:109-18 Aug 44
Expanding civilian production and employment after the war: discussion. AER/S 35:
90-93 May 45
and Jaszi, G. The 1945 White Paper on national income and expenditure. R. EJ 55:
444-54 Dec 45
[and others] Objectives of national income
measurement: a reply to Professor Kuznets. REStat 30:179-95 Aug 48
[and others] Measurement of national
income: discussion. Em 17,suppl.:255-72
Jul 49

GILBERT, RICHARD VINCENT and Perlo, V.
The investment-factor method of forecast-
ing business activity. Em 10:311-16
Jul-Oct 42; A correction. 11:94 Jan 43

GILBOY, ELIZABETH WATERMAN
Income-expenditure relations. REStat 22:
115-21 Aug 40
Changes in consumption expenditures and the
defense program. REStat 23:155-64
Nov 41

GILCHRIST, FRANKLIN W.
Self-service retailing of meat. JM 13:
295-304 Jan 49

GILFILLAN, SEABURY COLUM
Invention as a factor in economic history.
JEH/S 5:66-85 Dec 45

GILLES, ROBERT C.
International comparison of wholesale prices.
REStat 22:150-56 Aug 40

GILLESPIE, SARAH C. and Rothschild, K. W.
Migration and the distributive trades.
REStud 13:81-83 no.2, 46

GILLETT, ROY LEWIS and Bond, M. C.
Data needs for agricultural research and
marketing. JFE 30:271-81 May 48

GILLIATT, NEAL
Marketing implications in the OPA community pricing program. JM 9:101-08 Oct 44

GILMAN, VIRGIL
Land economics research: discussion.
JFE 31,pt.2:1055-57 Nov 49

GINI, CORRADO
A coordination of the different population
theories. RIIS 11:35-66 no.1-2, 43
On national income. BNL 1:63-74 Jul 47
Evolution of the psychology of work and of
accumulation. BNL 1:207-19 Jan 48
The content and use of estimates of the
national income. BNL 1:271-310 Apr 48
Apparent and real causes of American prosperity. BNL 1:351-64 Jul 48
Bilateral and multilateral trade. BNL 2:
3-11 Jan-Mar 49
Savings, technical progress and unemployment. [Translated by O. R. Agresti] EI 2:
187-205 Feb 49

The valuation of commodities for direct
consumption. BNL 2:108-10 Apr-Jun 49
National income estimates. RIIS 17:119-28
no.3-4, 49

GINZBERG, ELI
The conference on science, philosophy and
religion in their relation to the democratic
way of life. AER 31:108-09 Mar 41
American labor leaders: time in office.
ILRR 1:283-93 Jan 48

GIRSHICK, MEYER ABRAHAM
The application of the theory of linear
hypotheses to the coefficient of elasticity
of demand. JASA 37:233-37 Jun 42
and Haavelmo, T. Statistical analysis of the
demand for food: examples of simultaneous
estimation of structural equations. Em 15:
79-110 Apr 47
with Arrow, K. J. and Blackwell, D. Bayes
and minimax solutions of sequential decision problems. Em 17:213-44 Jul-Oct 49

GITLOW, ABRAHAM LEO
Political aspects of union welfare funds.
ILRR 3:75-79 Oct 49

GITTLER, JOSEPH B. and Giffin, R. R.
Changing patterns of employment in five
southeastern states, 1930-1940. SEJ 11:
169-82 Oct 44

GIVEN, WILLIAM B., Jr.
Freedom within management. HBR 24:
427-37 no.4, 46

GLAESER, MARTIN GUSTAVE
The Wisconsin telephone case. LE 16:37-46
Feb 40
The United States Supreme Court redeems
itself. LE 18:146-54 May 42
The Mexican Water Treaty: Pt.I-II. LE 22:
1-9; 352-62 Feb,Nov 46

GLASSER, CARRIE
see Abramovitz, Carrie Glasser

GLAZER, SIDNEY
The early silk industry in Michigan. AH 18:
92-96 Apr 44
The rural community in the urban age: the
changes in Michigan since 1900. AH 23:
130-34 Apr 49

GLENDAY, ROY GONCALVES [and others]
Economic reconstruction after the war:
discussion. JRSS 105:17-35 pt.1, 42

GLESINGER, EGON
Forest products in a world economy.
AER/S 35:120-29 May 45

GLICKMAN, DAVID LLOYD
The British imperial preference system.
QJE 61:439-70 May 47
The labor movements in Australia and New
Zealand. SR 16:199-221 Jun 49

GLOERFELT-TARP, B.
The marginal productivity function and the
Walras Cassel system of equations.
NTTO 12:111-21 no.37, 48

GLOVER, JOHN DESMOND
Defense "lending": 1918 and 1941. HBR 19:
197-210 no.2, 41

GLOVER, WILBUR H.
and Thompson, D. O.  A pioneer adventure in
agricultural extension: a contribution
from the Wisconsin cut-over.  AH 22:
124-28 Apr 48
Discussion: agricultural economics and
history.  JFE 30:553-55 Aug 48
GODSON, R.
Juvenile labour supply.  OIS 11:21-34
Feb-Mar 49
The regional distribution of juvenile labour.
OIS 11:269-78 Sep 49
The industrial distribution of juvenile labour.
OIS 11:337-56 Nov 49
GOEBEL, DOROTHY BURNE
British-American rivalry in the Chilean
trade, 1817-1820.  JEH 2:190-202 Nov 42
GOERKE, H. F.
Indebtedness on marginal wheat farms in
Western Australia.  ER 19:77-82 Jun 43
GOFF, JOHN HEDGES
The interterritorial freight-rate problem
and the South.  SEJ 6:449-60 Apr 40
GOLAY, J. F.
Development projects in Great Britain in the
first half of 1941.  OIS 3:315-17 Oct 11, 41
GOLD, NORMAN LEON
Agricultural surpluses: discussion.  JFE 22:
334-36 Feb 40
and Enlow, M.  The demand for food by low
income families.  QJE 57:596-629 Aug 43
GOLDBERG, SIMON ABRAHAM
The development of national accounts in
Canada.  CJE 15:34-52 Feb 49
The concept of disposable income: a reply.
CJE 15:539-42 Nov 49
GOLDEN, CLINTON STRONG
Understanding union attitudes.  HBR 27:
412-18 Jul 49
GOLDENBERG, LEON
Savings in a state with a stationary popula-
tion.  QJE 61:40-65 Nov 46
GOLDENWEISER, EMANUEL ALEXANDER
Research and policy.  JASA 39:1-9 Mar 44
The economist and the state.  AER 37:1-12
Mar 47
[and others]  The public debt: effects on in-
stitutions and income: discussion.
AER/S 37:192-204 May 47
Federal Reserve objectives and policies:
retrospect and prospect.  AER 37:320-38
Jun 47
Pritchard on the Federal Reserve bank note:
comment.  JPE 55:359-60 Aug 47
GOLDFIELD, EDWIN DAVID
The wartime labor force in major industrial
areas.  REStat 27:133-40 Aug 45
GOLDIN, HYMAN HOWARD
Governmental policy and the domestic tele-
graph industry.  JEH 7:53-68 May 47
The employee interest in public utility
merger and abandonment cases.  LE 24:
161-74 May 48

GOLDMANN, FRANZ
Labor's attitude toward health insurance.
ILRR 2:90-98 Oct 48
GOLDMANN, JOSEF
The new building programme.  OIS 4:228-30
Aug 29, 42
Differential rationing in practice.  OIS 4:
274-76 Oct 10, 42
Beer in wartime: dilution versus concentra-
tion.  OIS 4:287-90 Oct 31, 42
The economic significance of French North
Africa.  OIS 4:308-10 Nov 21, 42
Taxation of tobacco, beer and cinema at-
tendances.  OIS 5:35-39 Jan 30, 43
Meat and wheat.  OIS 5:73-76 Apr 3, 43
and Rothschild, K. W.  Point rationing of
foodstuffs.  OIS 5:129-33 Jun 5, 43
Consumption of milk.  OIS 5:148-51 Jun 26,43
The armament industry of Czechoslovakia.
OIS 5:200-03 Aug 28, 43
Consumption and rationing in the United
States.  OIS 5:221-25 Oct 9,  43
Expenditure on rent.  OIS 6:173-77 Aug 12,44
and Durant, H.  The distribution of working-
class savings.  OIS 7:1-7 Jan 13, 45
Agrarian reform in eastern Europe.  OIS 7:
160-64 Jun 30, 45
Czechoslovak industry after nationalization.
OIS 8:88-90 Mar 46
GOLDSCHMIDT, WALTER R.
Employment categories in American agricul-
ture.  JFE 29:554-64 May 47
GOLDSEN, JOSEPH M. and Curtis, A.
Montclair studies the shopping experiences
and attitudes of its residents.  JM 10:
165-70 Oct 45
GOLDSMITH, RAYMOND W. [and others]
Input-output analysis and its use in peace
and war economies: discussion.
AER/S 39:226-40 May 49
GOLDSTEIN, MORTIMER D.
War-time aluminum statistics.  JASA 41:
34-52 Mar 46
GOMBERG, EUGENE L.
Strikes and lock-outs in Great Britain.
QJE 59:92-106 Nov 44
GOMBERG, WILLIAM
Union interest in engineering techniques.
HBR 24:356-65 no.3, 46
Measuring the fatigue factor.  ILRR 1:80-93
Oct 47
GOODALL, MERRILL R.
Land and power administration of the Central
Valley Project.  LE 18:299-311 Aug 42
River valley planning in India: the Damodar.
LE 21:371-75 Sep 45
GOODE, RICHARD
and Ensley, G. W.  Mr. Warburton on the gap.
AER 33:897-99 Dec 43
The corporate income tax and the price level.
AER 35:40-58 Mar 45
--- Rejoinder.  AER 36:147-48 Mar 46
Federal tax legislative activities in 1947.
NTJ 1:67-78 Mar 48

GOODE, RICHARD (Cont.)
  Investigation of the Bureau of Internal
    Revenue. NTJ 1:261-69 Sep 48
  Federal finances in 1948. NTJ 2:71-87
    Mar 49
  The income tax and the supply of labor.
    JPE 57:428-37 Oct 49
GOODMAN, A. BRISTOL
  and Groves, H. M. A pattern of successful
    property tax administration: the Wiscon-
    sin experience. Pt.I-III. LE 19:141-52;
    300-15; 418-35 May,Aug,Nov 43
  Westward movement of local government.
    LE 20:20-34 Feb 44
GOODMAN, CONSTANCE and Fussell, G. E.
  Crop husbandry in eighteenth century Eng-
    land. Pt.I-II. AH 15:202-16; 16:41-63
    Oct 41, Jan 42
GOODMAN, ROE
  Sampling for the 1947 Survey of consumer
    finances. JASA 42:439-48 Sep 47
GOODRICH, CARTER
  The effect of the war on the position of labor.
    AER/S 32:416-25 Mar 42
  Productivity in the American economy: dis-
    cussion. AER/S 37:421-22 May 47
  [and others] Possibilities for a realistic
    theory of entrepreneurship: discussion.
    AER/S 39:349-55 May 49
GOODSELL, WYLIE D.
  with Jessen, R. J. and Wilcox, W. W. Pro-
    cedures which increase the usefulness of
    farm management research. JFE 22:
    753-61 Nov 40
  [and others] Appraisal of the economic
    classification of farms. JFE 30:680-702
    Nov 48
GOODWIN, RICHARD MURPHY
  The supply of bank money in England and
    Wales, 1920-1938. OEP 5:1-29 Jun 41
  Keynesian and other interest theories.
    REStat 25:6-12 Feb 43
  Multiplier effects of a balanced budget: the
    implication of a lag for Mr. Haavelmo's
    analysis. Em 14:150-51 Apr 46
  Innovations and the irregularity of economic
    cycles. REStat 28:95-104 May 46
  Dynamical coupling with especial reference
    to markets having production lags. Em 15:
    181-204 Jul 47
  [and others] Liquidity and uncertainty: dis-
    cussion. AER/S 39:196-210 May 49
  The multiplier as matrix. EJ 59:537-55
    Dec 49
GOPAL, MYSORE HATTI
  The return to classicism and after. IJE 20:
    405-21 Apr 40
  The role of cost in socialist pricing. IJE 21:
    435-55 Apr 41
  Public expenditure in Mysore: a review.
    IJE 21:594-604 Apr 41
  A neglected source of local revenues.
    IJE 22:820-31 Jan 42

An enquiry into indebtedness in a Mysore
  village. IJE 23:1-23 Jul 42
The depositor and bank management. IJE 24:
  348-54 Apr 44
The role of the excess profits tax in modify-
  ing capitalism. IJE 24:387-94 Apr 44
A new basis for railway rates: the social
  benefit of service principle. IJE 26:
  441-51 Jan 46
The economics of public salaries: a rejoinder.
  IJE 28:287-90 Oct 47
Planning of production through tax adjust-
  ments. IJE 29:155-63 Oct 48
GOPALASWAMY, S.
  Non-tax revenue of Mysore. IJE 21:618-33
    Apr 41
  The capital resources of agricultural co-
    operative societies in Mysore. IJE 22:
    532-45 Jan 42
  Co-ordination and control of banking in
    Mysore. IJE 24:38-58 Jul 43
GORDON, LELAND JAMES
  ["Economics for consumers."] Discussion.
    JM 4,no.4,pt.2:146-48 Apr 40
GORDON, LINCOLN
  Government controls in war and peace.
    BHR 20:42-51 Apr 46
  An official appraisal of the war economy
    and its administration. R. REStat 29:
    183-88 Aug 47
  ERP in operation. HBR 27:129-50 Mar 49
  Libertarianism at bay. R. AER 39:976-78
    Sep 49
GORDON, MARGARET SHAUGNESSY
  [Economic regionalism and multilateral
    trade]: discussion. AER/S 33:446-48
    Mar 43
  International aspects of American agricul-
    tural policy. AER 36:596-612 Sep 46
  The character and significance of the gen-
    eral commitments that nations will make
    under the ITO Charter. AER/S 39:241-51
    May 49
GORDON, NATHAN N.
  The second session of the United Nations
    Fiscal Commission. NTJ 2:166-72 Jun 49
GORDON, ROBERT AARON
  Ownership and compensation as incentives
    to corporation executives. QJE 54:455-73
    May 40
  Period and velocity as statistical concepts.
    QJE 55:306-13 Feb 41
  Government and private enterprise: discus-
    sion. AER/S 33:83-86 Mar 43
  Economic theory in relation to the long-run
    postwar situation: discussion. AER/S 34:
    163-65 Mar 44
  International programming of the distribu-
    tion of resources. III. The Combined Raw
    Materials Board. JASA 39:291-96 Sep 44
  Keynesian economics: savings, investment,
    and wage rates: discussion. AER/S 38:
    354-56 May 48

**GORDON, ROBERT AARON (Cont.)**
Short-period price determination in theory
and practice. AER 38:265-88 Jun 48
Business cycles in the interwar period: the
"quantitative-historical" approach.
AER/S 39:47-63 May 49

**GORGAS, NELLIE**
The storage and issuance of hospital supplies.
Pt.I-II. JB 13:172-204; 275-315
Apr,Jul 40

**GORRIE, ROBERT McLAGAN**
National land policy for the West Punjab.
PEJ 1,no.1:29-32 Jul 49

**GOSS, ALBERT S.**
Legislative program of the National Grange.
JFE 29:52-63 Feb 47

**GOTTLIEB, MANUEL**
The theory of optimum population for a
closed economy. JPE 53:289-316 Dec 45

**GOVIL, KAUHAIYA LAL**
U.K.C.C. and India. R. IJE 25:376 Jan 45
Our food: a critical study in retrospect and
prospect. IJE 26:734-43 Apr 46

**GOVINDAROW, B.**
see Row, B. Govinda

**GRAAFF, ANDRIES de**
Price disparity and business cycles. Kyk 1:
358-69 fasc.4, 47

**GRAAFF, J. DE V.**
Fluctuations in income concentration; with
special reference to changes in the con-
centration of supertaxable incomes in
South Africa: July, 1915-June, 1943.
SAJE 14:22-39 Mar 46
A note on the relative merits of tariffs and
subsidies. SAJE 15:149-50 Jun 47
Towards an austerity theory of value.
SAJE 16:35-50 Mar 48
Rothbarth's "virtual price system" and the
Slutsky equation. REStud 15:91-95 no.2,48
and Baumol, W. Three notes on "Expecta-
tion in economics." II. R. Ec N.S.16:
338-42 Nov 49
On optimum tariff structures. REStud 17:
47-59 no.1, 49

**GRAGG, CHARLES INSCO**
Marketing and the defense program. JM 5:
423-30 Apr 41
Negotiated contracts. HBR 19:221-29 no.2,41
with Grimshaw, A. and Teele, S. F. Competition under rationing. HBR 20:141-55
no.2, 42
and Teele, S. F. The proposed full employment act. HBR 23:323-37 no.3, 45

**GRAHAM, BENJAMIN**
The critique of Commodity-reserve currency:
a point-by-point reply. JPE 51:66-69
Feb 43
The hours of work and full employment.
AER 35:432-35 Jun 45
Money as pure commodity. AER/S 37:304-07
May 47
National productivity: its relationship to un-
employment-in-prosperity. AER/S 37:
384-96 May 47

**GRAHAM, FRANK DUNSTONE**
Achilles' heels in monetary standards.
AER 30:16-32 Mar 40
The primary functions of money and their
consummation in monetary policy.
AER/S 30:1-16 Mar 40
100 per cent reserves: comment. AER 31:
338-40 Jun 41
Transition to a commodity reserve currency.
AER 31:520-25 Sep 41
Commodity-reserve currency: a criticism
of the critique. JPE 51:70-75 Feb 43
[and others] International economic rela-
tions: discussion. AER/S 33:332-35
Mar 43
International monetary problems: discussion.
AER/S 34:399-401 Mar 44
[and others] Political science, political
economy, and values: discussion.
AER/S 34:48-57 Mar 44
Keynes vs. Hayek on a commodity reserve
currency. EJ 54:422-29 Dec 44
[and others] Edwin Walter Kemmerer,
1875-1945. [obit.] AER 36:219-21 Mar 46
Exchange rates: bound or free? JF 4:13-27
Mar 49

**GRAJDANZEV, ANDREW JONAH**
Japan's wartime production: comment.
AER 33:905-06 Dec 43

**GRAMPP, WILLIAM DYER**
The third century of mercantilism. SEJ 10:
292-302 Apr 44
John Taylor: economist of southern
agrarianism. SEJ 11:255-68 Jan 45
A re-examination of Jeffersonian economics.
SEJ 12:263-82 Jan 46
The Italian lira, 1938-45. JPE 54:309-33
Aug 46
The political economy of Poor Richard.
JPE 55:132-41 Apr 47
Adam Smith and the economic man. JPE 56:
315-36 Aug 48
On the politics of the classical economists.
QJE 62:714-47 Nov 48

**GRAPP, HENRY F.**
The early impact of Japan upon American
agriculture. AH 23:110-16 Apr 49

**GRAS, NORMAN SCOTT BRIEN**
The Steinman Hardware Company, Lancaster,
Pennsylvania. BHR 14:14-15 Feb 40
The growth of rigidity in business during the
Middle Ages. AER/S 30:281-89 Mar 40
An old store still young. BHR 14:33-40
Jun 40
The growth of rigidities. HBR 18:322-36
no.3, 40
A new study of Rockefeller. R. BHR 15:
49-58 Oct 41
Capitalism: concepts and history. BHR 16:
21-34 Apr 42

GRAS, NORMAN SCOTT BRIEN (Cont.)

The social implications of business administration. BHR 17:2-5 Feb 43

An early sedentary merchant in the Middle West: records available for a study of the career of Henry Shaw. BHR 18:1-9 Feb 44

Religion and business. BHR 18:27-32 Apr 44

Are you writing a business history? BHR 18: 73-110 Oct 44

Shifts in public relations. BHR 19:97-148 Oct 45

J. Franklin Ebersole, 1884-1945. [obit.] BHR 19:177-78 Nov 45

Sir Andrew Freeport, a merchant of London. BHR 19:159-62 Nov 45

Historical background [of government control]. BHR 20:36-42 Apr 46

What type of business history are you writing? BHR 20:146-58 Nov 46

War and business: four century-long struggles. BHR 20:165-89 Dec 46

Edwin Francis Gay. EHR 16:60-62 no.1, 46

What is capitalism in the light of history? BHR 21:79-120 Oct 47

Behavior of business men in a changing world. BHR 23:1-65 Mar 49

Leadership, past and present. HBR 27: 419-37 Jul 49

A great Indian industrialist: Jamsetji Nusserwanji Tata, 1839-1904. BHR 23: 149-51 Sep 49

GRAUE, ERWIN

Inventions and production. REStat 25:221-23 Aug 43

GRAY, ALEXANDER

Economics: yesterday and to-morrow. EJ 59:510-30 Dec 49

GRAY, HORACE MONTGOMERY

The passing of the public utility concept. LE 16:8-20 Feb 40

[and others] The progress of concentration in industry: discussion. AER/S 38:109-20 May 48

Transportation and public utilities: discussion. AER/S 38:485-87 May 48

GRAY, KENNETH GEORGE

Canadian and American health insurance plans. CJE 12:505-09 Nov 46

GRAY, LEWIS CECIL and Regan, M.

Needed points of development and reorientation in land economic theory. JFE 22: 34-46 Feb 40

GRAY, STANLEY and Wyckoff, V. J.

The international tobacco trade in the seventeenth century. SEJ 7:1-26 Jul 40

GRAYSON, HENRY

The econometric approach: a critical analysis. JPE 56:253-57 Jun 48

GRAZZI, UMBERTO

Some aspects of the Franco-Italian Customs Union in regard to the gradual manner of its achievement. BNL 1:365-68 Jul 48

GREATHOUSE, REBEKAH SCANDRETT

The effect of constitutional equality on working women. AER/S 34:227-36 Mar 44

GREBENIK, E.

The quantitative aspect of the British population problem: a survey. REStud 10: 43-52 no.1, 42

GREBLER, LEO

The home mortgage structure in transition. HBR 18:357-71 no.3, 40

Housing policy and the building cycle. REStat 24:66-74 May 42

Stabilizing residential construction: a review of the postwar test. AER 39:898-910 Sep 49

GREELEY, ROLAND BRADFORD

[The education of planners] At Massachusetts Institute of Technology. LE 21: 313-15 Sep 45

GREEN, ARTHUR ROMNEY

The tax curve. EJ 50:469-74 Dec 40

Social reconstruction by the regulation of incomes. EJ 52:37-44 Apr 42

GREEN, CONSTANCE McLAUGHLIN

What has the business administrator contributed to society? BHR 17:22-26 Feb 43

GREEN, HOWARD WHIPPLE

Origin and development of a continuous real property inventory. LE 16:325-34 Aug 40

Retail outlets in shopping centers stop decreasing. JM 10:281-82 Jan 46

GREENBERG, ALLAN

A method for coding questionnaires in market surveys. JM 14:456-58 Oct 49

GREENE, FRED T.

Significant post-depression changes in savings and loan practices. LE 16:30-36 Feb 40

GREENE, LEE S.

Industrial location and reconstruction in Great Britain. LE 17:333-43 Aug 41

GREENWOOD, HERBERT

Reform in published accounts? SAJE 11: 137-44 Jun 43

G[REENWOOD], M[AJOR]

H. W. M. [obit.] JRSS 104:85-90 pt.1, 41

GREER, GUY

[and others] Economic problems of American cities: discussion. AER/S 32:341-48 Mar 42

City replanning and rebuilding. LE 18:284-92 Aug 42

GREGORY, CHARLES OSCAR

Some problems of policy in collective bargaining practices. AER/S 33:174-83 Mar 43

GREGORY, PAUL MICHAEL

Imperfect competition in the mortgage market. SEJ 10:275-91 Apr 44

An appraisal of mortgage advertising. HBR 23:32-45 no.1, 44

GREGORY, PAUL MICHAEL (Cont.)
The mortgage portfolio of mutual savings
banks. QJE 61:232-66 Feb 47
A theory of purposeful obsolescence. SEJ 14:
24-45 Jul 47
An economic interpretation of women's
fashions. SEJ 14:148-62 Oct 47
Fashion and monopolistic competition.
JPE 56:69-75 Feb 48
GREGORY, Sir THEODORE
The problems of the under-developed world.
LBR 10:39-56 Oct 48
GREIG, GERTRUD B.
see Edwards, Gertrud Greig
GRETHER, EWALD THEOPHILUS
chairman. Round table on price control
under "fair trade" legislation. AER/S 30:
112-17 Mar 40
Current trends affecting pricing policies.
JM 5:222-23 Jan 41
Effects of weighting and of distributive price
controls upon retail food price compari-
sons. JM 6:166-70 Oct 41
Price policy trends, 1941. JM 6,no.4,pt.2:
16-17 Apr 42
Price control and rationing under the Office
of Price Administration: a brief selective
appraisal. JM 7:300-18 Apr 43
and Cassady, R., Jr. Locality price differ-
entials in the western retail grocery trade.
HBR 21:190-206 no.2, 43; Correction. 396
no.3, 43
Long run postwar aspects of price control.
JM 8:296-301 Jan 44
Geographical price policies in the grocery
trade, 1941: a note. JM 8:417-22 Apr 44
[and others] The changing structure of the
American economy: discussion.
AER/S 36:80-92 May 46
The Federal Trade Commission versus re-
sale price maintenance. JM 12:1-13
Jul 47
The postwar market and industrialization in
California. JM 12:311-16 Jan 48
Preparedness for war and general economic
policy. AER/S 39:366-77 May 49
GRIFFITH, DONALD T.
Land settlement proposals for veterans,
World Wars I and II. LE 21:73-77 Feb 45
GRIFFITH, EDWIN CLAYBROOK
Deficit financing and the future of capitalism.
SEJ 12:130-40 Oct 45
Some aspects of the South's financial develop-
ment, 1929-1946. SEJ 15:162-70 Oct 48
GRIFFITHS, F. J.
Further comments on prices under fair
trade. JM 13:381-83 Jan 49
GRIMES, WALDO ERNEST
Personnel training and recruitment in agri-
cultural economics. JFE 22:78-80 Feb 40
Readjustments in agriculture: discussion.
JFE 26:89-91 Feb 44
Postwar agricultural problems in the Great
Plains area. JFE 28:235-42 Feb 46

GRIMES, WILLIAM H.
Distribution and the finance company.
HBR 18:199-206 no.2, 40
GRIMSHAW, AUSTIN; Gragg, C. I. and Teele,
S. F.
Competition under rationing. HBR 20:141-55
no.2, 42
GRITLY, A. A. I. EL-
see El-Gritley, A. A. I.
GRIZIOTTI, BENVENUTO
Three forms of capital levy in Italy. BNL 1:
149-56 Oct 47
GRODINSKY, JULIUS [and others]
The determinants of investment decision:
discussion. AER/S 32:156-64 Mar 42
GROGAN, F. O.
Production costs on four West Australian
wheat farms. ER 16:236-44 Dec 40
GRØN, ALFRED HOWARD and Jørgensen, F.
Calculation of sylvicultural balance-numbers.
NTTO 12:123-31 no.37, 48
GROSS, GLEN B. and Percival, A. J.
Job evaluation: a case history. HBR 24:
466-97 no.4, 46
GROSS, JEROME
Charter of Toledo Labor-Management-
Citizens Committee. Introductory note.
ILRR 1:500-05 Apr 48
GROSS, NEAL C.
A post mortem on county planning. JFE 25:
644-61 Aug 43
GROSSMAN, HENRYK
The evolutionist revolt against classical
economics. Pt.I-II. JPE 51:381-96;
506-22 Oct,Dec 43
W. Playfair, the earliest theorist of capital-
ist development. EHR 18:65-83 no.1-2,48
GROVE, ERNEST WILSON and Koffsky, N. M.
Measuring the incomes of farm people.
JFE 31,pt.2:1102-11 Nov 49
GROVES, HAROLD MARTIN
Round table on the incidence of taxation.
[Summary of discussion] AER/S 30:
244-45 Mar 40
and Goodman, A. B. A pattern of successful
property tax administration: the Wiscon-
sin experience. Pt.I-III. LE 19:141-52;
300-15; 418-35 May,Aug,Nov 43
Revising the postwar federal tax system.
AER/S 34,no.2:27-38 Jun 44
Personal versus corporate income taxes.
AER/S 36:241-49 May 46
--- [idem] JF 1:52-60 Aug 46
Income versus property taxation for state
and local governments. LE 22:346-50
Nov 46
The property tax in Canada and the United
States. Pt.I-II. LE 24:23-30; 120-28
Feb,May
Neutrality in taxation. NTJ 1:18-24 Mar 48
[and others] Fiscal policy in prosperity and
depression: discussion. AER/S 38:404-16
May 48

GROVES, HAROLD MARTIN (Cont.)
Impressions of property taxation in Aus-
tralia and New Zealand. LE 25:22-28
Feb 49
Taxation in Australia and New Zealand.
NTJ 2:1-11 Mar 49
GRUBER, JACOB W.
Irrigation and land use in ancient Meso-
potamia. AH 22:69-77 Apr 48
GRUCHY, ALLAN GARFIELD
John R. Commons' concept of twentieth-
century economics. JPE 48:823-49
Dec 40
J. M. Keynes' concept of economic science.
SEJ 15:249-66 Jan 49
GRUENBAUM, LUDWIG
see Gaathon, Arieh Ludwig
GRUNBERG, EMILE
The mobilization of capacity and resources
of small-scale enterprises in Germany.
Pt.I-II. JB 14:319-44; 15:56-89 Oct 41,
Jan 42
GRUNDFEST, HARRY
The utilization of scientists. S&S 7:24-31
no.1, 43
GRUNFEL, JUDITH
Women's work in Russia's planned economy.
SR 9:22-45 Feb 42
Mobilization of women in Germany. SR 9:
476-94 Nov 42
GRUNWALD, KURT
State and industry in the Middle East.
EgC 31:225-31 Mar 40
Industrial credit survey 1919-1939. EgC 33:
143-314 Feb-Mar 42
GUELFAT, ISAAC
Franz Oppenheimer. [obit.] EJ 55:132-37
Apr 45
GUÉNAULT, P. H.
and Randall, R. J. An introduction to the
housing problem. SAJE 8:145-61 Jun 40
Labour supply. SAJE 8:388-99 Dec 40
and Reedman, J. N. The war and the budget.
SAJE 8:364-71 Dec 40
[and others] Financing the South African war
effort. I. The inflation danger in the Union:
a comment. SAJE 9:176-83 Jun 41
GUILLEBAUD, CLAUDE WILLIAM
Hitler's new economic order for Europe.
EJ 50:449-60 Dec 40
The evolution of Marshall's Principles of
economics. EJ 52:330-49 Dec 42
GULERI, J.
Abolition of zamindari. IJE 27:513-16 Apr 47
GULICK, CHARLES ADAMS and Gerschenkron,
A.
Errors and traditions: remarks on Ernst
Karl Winter's article; "The rise and fall
of Austrian labor." SR 7:45-60 Feb 40
GUNDRY, HENRY
Some features of wartime finance and ex-
change control in the South-West African
karakul trade. SAJE 13:318-25 Dec 45

GUNN, GRACE THOMPSON
and Douglas, P. H. Further measurements
of marginal productivity. QJE 54:399-428
May 40
and Douglas, P. H. The production function
for American manufacturing in 1919.
AER 31:67-80 Mar 41
and Douglas, P. H. A reply to Dr. Mendershausen's criticism. AER 31:564-69 Sep 41
and Douglas, P. H. The production function
for Australian manufacturing. QJE 56:
108-29 Nov 41
and Douglas, P. H. The production function
for American manufacturing for 1914.
JPE 50:595-602 Aug 42
GUPTA, D. L.
Future of food control in India. IJE 26:
571-78 Jan 46
War and distribution of incomes. IJE 27:
409-15 Apr 47
GUPTA, D. N. SEN
see Sen Gupta, Debendra Nath
GUPTA, RITENDRA NATH SEN
see Sen Gupta, Ritendra Nath
GUPTA, S. SEN
see Sengupta, Sovona
GUPTA, SADHANA
The agricultural labourer in Bengal. IJE 26:
133-36 Jul 45
The share-cropper & the Tebhaga Bill of
Bengal. IJE 28:297-301 Oct 47
GURTOO, D. N.
Balance of payment of India. IJE 30:129-37
Oct 49
GUSTIN, ROSSMAN PROSPER and Holme, S. A.
An approach to postwar planning. HBR 20:
459-72 no.4, 42
GUTHEIM, FREDERIC A.
Housing needs and housing standards. LE 25:
123-27 Feb 49
GUTHMANN, HARRY GEORGE
The effect of the undistributed profits tax
upon the distribution of corporate earn-
ings: a note. Em 8:354-56 Oct 40
Public utility depreciation practice. HBR 20:
213-22 no.2, 42
Dilution and common stock financing.
HBR 23:246-52 no.2, 45
GUTHRIE, CHESTER L.
A seventeenth century "ever-normal
granary": the alhóndiga of colonial Mexico
City. AH 15:37-43 Jan 41
GUTHRIE, JOHN ALEXANDER
Price regulation in the paper industry.
QJE 60:194-218 Feb 46
GUTT, CAMILLE
Exchange rates and the International Mone-
tary Fund. REStat 30:81-90 May 48
HAAG, HERMAN M.
Transportation of farm products: discussion.
JFE 26:177-80 Feb 44
HAAS, HAROLD M.
Price differentials among grocery stores in

HAAS, HAROLD M. (Cont.)
Bloomington, Indiana. JM 5:148-55 Oct 40
HAAS, JACOB ANTON DE
see De Haas, Jacob Anton
HAAVELMO, TRYGVE
The inadequacy of testing dynamic theory by
comparing theoretical solutions and ob-
served cycles. Em 8:312-21 Oct 40
A note on the variate difference method.
Em 9:74-79 Jan 41
The effect of the rate of interest on invest-
ment: a note. REStat 23:49-52 Feb 41
The statistical implications of a system of
simultaneous equations. Em 11:1-12
Jan 43
Statistical testing of business-cycle theories.
REStat 25:13-18 Feb 43
The probability approach in econometrics.
Em 12,suppl.:1-115 Jul 44
Multiplier effects of a balanced budget.
Em 13:311-18 Oct 45
--- Reply. Em 14:156-58 Apr 46
Methods of measuring the marginal propen-
sity to consume. JASA 42:105-22 Mar 47
and Girshick, M. A. Statistical analysis of
the demand for food: examples of simul-
taneous estimation of structural equations.
Em 15:79-110 Apr 47
Family expenditures and the marginal pro-
pensity to consume. Em 15:335-41 Oct 47
Quantitative research in agricultural eco-
nomics: the interdependence between ag-
riculture and the national economy.
JFE 29:910-24 Nov 47
A note on the theory of investment.
REStud 16:78-81 no.2, 49
HABAKKUK, HROTHGAR JOHN
English landownership, 1680-1740. EHR 10:
2-17 Feb 40
HABBU, R. K.
Commercial policy of India. IJE 28:397-402
Jan 48
International economic relations. IJE 29:
179-84 Oct 48
HABER, WILLIAM
Manpower and employment problems in
transition from war to peace. REStat 26:
57-68 May 44
and Welch, E. The labor force during recon-
version. Estimated changes in employ-
ment and labor force distribution during
transition period. REStat 26:194-205
Nov 44
HABERLER, GOTTFRIED
chairman. Problems of international economic policy: abstract of specialized
conference discussion. AER/S 32:206-11
Mar 42
[and others] International economic relations: discussion. AER/S 33:332-35
Mar 43
Currency depreciation and the International
Monetary Fund. REStat 26:178-81 Nov 44

Some comments on Professor Hansen's
note. (Symposium on the International
Monetary Fund) REStat 26:191-93 Nov 44
The choice of exchange rates after the war.
AER 35:308-18 Jun 45
Some observations on the Murray Full Em-
ployment Bill. REStat 27:106-09 Aug 45
Multiplier effects of a balanced budget: some
monetary implications of Mr. Haavelmo's
paper. Em 14:148-55 Apr 46
The place of The general theory of employ-
ment, interest, and money in the history
of economic thought. REStat 28:187-94
Nov 46
[The foreign trade multiplier.] Comment.
AER 37:898-906 Dec 47
and Polak, J. J. [The foreign trade multi-
plier.] A restatement. AER 37:906-07
Dec 47
The present cyclical situation of the Ameri-
can economy in the light of business cycle
theory. EI 1:235-39 Jan 48
Causes and cures of inflation. REStat 30:
10-14 Feb 48
Some economic problems of the European
Recovery Program. AER 38:495-525
Sep 48
Comments on "National central banking and
the international economy." EI 1:1117-32
Nov 48
Current research in business cycles: discus-
sion. AER/S 39:84-88 May 49
[Professor Leontief on Lord Keynes.]
Further comment. QJE 63:569-71 Nov 49
The market for foreign exchange and the
stability of the balance of payments: a
theoretical analysis. Kyk 3:193-218
fasc.3, 49
HACKER, LOUIS MORTON
The contemporary civilization course at
Columbia College. AER/S 35:137-47
May 45
HACKFORD, ROBERT RUSSELL
Our international aviation policy. HBR 25:
483-500 no.4, 47
HADARY, GIDEON
Relation of chocolate milk to total fluid milk
consumption of factory workers. JB 16:
70-73 Jan 43
Relation of chocolate milk to total fluid milk
consumption of urban families. JB 16:
115-23 Apr 43
and Brown, G. H. Beverage preference of
industrial workers: a study in consumer
preference ratings. JB 17:111-17 Apr 44
The relationship of chocolate milk to total
fluid milk consumption. JFE 27:210-13
Feb 45
and Patzig, R. E. Relationship of income to
milk consumption. JFE 27:204-10 Feb 45
The candy-consumer: how much will he buy
in the postwar period? JB 18:96-100
Apr 45

HADARY, GIDEON (Cont.)

Effect of method of distribution on milk consumption. JM 9:354-58 Apr 45

An evaluation of the wartime farm price-support programs. JB 18:219-21 Oct 45

The use of taste response tests in market research. JM 10:152-55 Oct 45

Effectiveness of price control in the dairy industry. JB 19:76-81 Apr 46

HADDON-CAVE, C. P.

Trends in the concentration of operations of Australian secondary industries, 1923-1943. ER 21:65-78 Jun 45

and Crowley, N. G. The regulation and expansion of world trade and employment. ER 23:32-48 Jun 47

Shipping and shipbuilding. ER 23:274-76 Dec 47

HADFIELD, ELLIS CHARLES RAYMOND

Canals between the English and the Bristol channels. EHR 12:59-67 no.1-2, 42

The Thames navigation and the canals, 1770-1830. EHR 14:172-79 no.2, 44

HADLEY, ELEANOR MARTHA

Trust busting in Japan. HBR 26:425-40 Jul 48

HAENSEL, PAUL

Soviet finances. PF 1:38-51 no.1, 46

Financing World War II in the United States of America. PF 1:329-56 no.4, 46

Soviet "inflation" reform. PF 3:107-08 no.2, 48

HAGEN, EVERETT EINAR

Elasticity of demand and a minimum wage. AER 30:574-76 Sep 40

Saving, investment and technological unemployment. AER 32:553-55 Sep 42

Capital theory in a system with no agents fixed in quantity. JPE 50:837-59 Dec 42

and Kirkpatrick, N. B. The national output at full employment in 1950. AER 34:472-500 Sep 44

Postwar output in the United States at full employment. REStat 27:45-59 May 45

The Brookings and Tucker estimates: further comments. REStat 27:196-201 Nov 45

Dr. Mayer on postwar national income. JPE 54:177 Apr 46

Multiplier effects of a balanced budget: further analysis. Em 14:152-55 Apr 46

The reconversion period: reflections of a forecaster. REStat 29:95-101 May 47

The problem of timing fiscal policy. AER/S 38:417-29 May 48

The January 1949 Economic report of the President: appraisal. REStat 31:178-81 Aug 49

HAGIOS, J. ANTON

Credit terms as an element in merchandising competition. JM 4,no.4,pt.2:70-78 Apr 40

HAGOOD, MARGARET JARMAN and Ducoff, L. J.

Objectives, uses and types of labor force data in relation to economic policy. JASA 41:293-302 Sep 46

HAGSTROEM, KARL GUSTAF

The theory of depreciation: a reply. Em 9:89-92 Jan 41

HAGUE, DOUGLAS CHALMERS

Economic theory and business behavior. REStud 16:144-57 no.3, 49

HAHN, ALBERT

Capital is made at home. SR 11:242-58 May 44

Compensating reactions to compensatory spending. AER 35:28-39 Mar 45

The effects of saving on employment and consumption. JM 11:35-43 Jul 46

Wage flexibility upwards. SR 14:148-67 Jun 47

Anachronism of the liquidity preference concept. Kyk 1:203-20 fasc.3, 47

HAHN, DOROTHY

Investment repercussions: a comment. QJE 63:430-32 Aug 49

HAHN, F. H.

A note on profit and uncertainty. Ec N.S.14:211-25 Aug 47

and McLeod, A. N. Proportionality, divisibility, and economies of scale: two comments. QJE 63:128-37 Feb 49

HAHN, LUCIEN ALBERT

see Hahn, Albert

HAIGHT, F. A.

The nature and significance of fascism. SAJE 8:224-42 Sep 40

HAINES, WALTER WELLS

Keynes, White, and history. QJE 58:120-33 Nov 43

Capacity production and the least cost point. AER 38:617-24 Sep 48

--- Reply. AER 39:1287-89 Dec 49

HAJELA, PRAYAG DAS

The foreign trade policy of the new India government. IJE 28:293-96 Oct 47

HALASI, ALBERT

International monetary cooperation. SR 9:183-203 May 42

HALCROW, HAROLD G.

Analyzing the tax load of agriculture: discussion. JFE 31,pt.2:680-81 Feb 49

Actuarial structures for crop insurance. JFE 31:418-43 Aug 49

and Huffman, R. E. Great Plains agriculture and Brannan's farm program. JFE 31:497-508 Aug 49

Problem of farm business survival: discussion. JFE 31,pt.2:951-53 Nov 49

HALD, ANDERS

The decomposition of a series of observations composed of a trend, a periodic movement and a stochastic variable. NTTO 11:97-196 no.36, 47

HALD, ANDERS (Cont.)
  and Fagerholt, G.  A few remarks on the ap-
    plication of statistical methods in indus-
    try.  NTTO 12:83-88 no.37, 48
HALDANE, BERNARD
  A pattern for executive placement.  HBR 25:
    652-63 no.4a, 47
HALÉVY, ELIE
  The age of tyrannies.  [Translated by M.
    Wallas]  Ec N.S.8:77-93 Feb 41
HALEY, BERNARD FRANCIS
  The federal budget: economic consequences
    of deficit financing.  AER/S 30,no.5:67-87
    Feb 41
  The relation between cartel policy and com-
    modity agreement policy.  AER/S 36:
    717-34 May 46
HALL, ARTHUR R.
  Ante-bellum Alabama agriculture.  R.  AH 16:
    127-28 Apr 42
  Terracing in the Southern Piedmont.  AH 23:
    96-109 Apr 49
HALL, J. PARKER
  Current tendencies in college investments.
    JF 4:129-39 Jun 49
HALL, JAMES KENDALL
  Incidence of death duties.  AER 30:46-59
    Mar 40
  Excise tax incidence and the postwar econ-
    omy.  AER/S 32:83-101 Mar 42
  Financial management of gas and electric
    utilities by the SEC: discussion.  JF 3,
    no.1:50-54 Feb 48
HALL, KINGSLEY S.; Mayer, H. M. and
  Wrigley, R. L., Jr.
  Mapping Chicago's industrial and commer-
    cial land use.  LE 20:365-70 Nov 44
HALL, ORVILLE JACQUELIN
  Policy for use of state-owned land in
    Arkansas.  LE 16:470-74 Nov 40
HALL, OSWALD
  The informal organization of the medical
    profession.  CJE 12:30-44 Feb 46
HALL, P. E.
  The coal industry in the Union of South
    Africa.  SAJE 16:229-50 Sep 48
HALL, RAY OVID
  Some neglected relationships in the balance
    of payments.  AER 31:81-86 Mar 41
HALL, Sir ROBERT LOWE [and others]
  [The future of international investment]:
    discussion.  AER/S 33:355-61 Mar 43
HALLETT, RALPH H.
  Postwar shipping policy: discussion.
    AER/S 36:594-97 May 46
HALLIDAY, I. G.
  Natal and indentured Indian immigration.
    SAJE 8:51-59 Mar 40
  Some notes on the distribution of meat in
    Durban with special reference to beef.
    SAJE 8:19-36 Mar 40
  with Burrows, H. R. and Smith, R. H.  Price
    control in war-time. SAJE 8:400-30 Dec 40

[and others]  Social security.  SAJE 10:
  193-247 Sep 42
Notes on the distribution and consumption of
  milk in Durban.  SAJE 12:101-11 Jun 44
HALM, GEORGE NIKOLAUS
The International Monetary Fund.  REStat 26:
  170-75 Nov 44
HALPERN, D. B.
Economic aspects of the cinema trade.
  OIS 3:169-75 Jun 7, 41
and Ellis, A. W. T.  War-time re-organiza-
  tion of the coal industry.  OIS 3:189-96
  Jun 28, 41
The co-operative movement since the out-
  break of war.  OIS 3:318-24 Oct 11, 41;
  Erratum. 358 Nov 1, 41
The rayon industry and the war.  OIS 4:
  136-42 Apr 25, 42
The salvage of waste material.  OIS 4:235-41
  Aug 29, 42; Erratum. 260 Sep 19, 42
The trade union movement since the outbreak
  of war.  OIS 5:232-39 Oct 9, 43
The plastic industry.  OIS 6:125-30 Jun 10, 44
HALVORSON, HARLOW W.
and Waite, W. C.  Relative importance of
  changes in demand and quantity on pro-
  ducer revenues. JFE 22:776-79 Nov 40
Statistics and research in price analysis:
  discussion.  JFE 31,pt.2:722-24 Feb 49
HALVORSON, LLOYD CHESTER
Problems of effective presentation of agri-
  cultural economic data to the membership
  of farm organizations.  JFE 29:1214-24
  Nov 47
HAM, WILLIAM THOMAS
Wage stabilization in agriculture.  JFE 27:
  104-20 Feb 45
HAMBERG, DANIEL
Minimum wages and the level of employ-
  ment.  SEJ 15:321-36 Jan 49
HAMBURGER, ERNEST
A peculiar pattern of the fifth column:  the
  organization of the German seamen.
  SR 9:495-509 Nov 42
and Johnson, A.  The economic problem of
  Germany.  SR 13:135-82 Jun 46
HAMER, PHILIP M.
Round table on economic research: discus-
  sion.  AER/S 37:700 May 47
HAMILL, CHALMERS
The structure of postwar American business:
  discussion.  AER/S 34:131-33 Mar 44
HAMILTON, ALICE
Science in the Soviet Union. III.  Industrial
  medicine.  S&S 8:69-73 no.1, 44
HAMILTON, EARL J.
The growth of rigidity in business during the
  eighteenth century.  AER/S 30:298-305
  Mar 40
Profit inflation and the industrial revolution,
  1751-1800.  QJE 56:256-73 Feb 42
[and others]  The determinants of investment decision: discussion.  AER/S 32:
  156-64 Mar 42

HAMILTON, EARL, J. (Cont.)
chairman. The economic effects of war.
Abstract of specialized conference dis-
cussion. AER/S 32:227-30 Mar 42
Sir William Beveridge's price history. R.
EJ 52:54-58 Apr 42
Monetary disorder and economic decadence
in Spain, 1651-1700. JPE 51:477-93
Dec 43
Monetary problems in Spain and Spanish
America 1751-1800. JEH 4:21-48 May 44
War and inflation in Spain, 1780-1800.
QJE 59:36-77 Nov 44
Use and misuse of price history. JEH/S 4:
47-60 Dec 44
The foundation of the Bank of Spain. JPE 53:
97-114 Jun 45
The first twenty years of the Bank of Spain.
Pt.I-II. JPE 54:17-37; 116-40 Feb,Apr 46
Origin and growth of the national debt in
western Europe. AER/S 37:118-30 May 47
Edwin Francis Gay. [obit.] AER 37:410-13
Jun 47
The role of monopoly in the overseas expan-
sion and colonial trade of Europe before
1800. AER/S 38:33-53 May 48
Spanish banking schemes before 1700.
JPE 57:134-56 Apr 49
Plans for a national bank in Spain, 1701-83.
JPE 57:315-36 Aug 49
HAMILTON, HENRY GLENN
Integration of marketing and production
services by Florida citrus associations.
JFE 29:495-505 May 47
Florida Citrus Agreement. JFE 31,pt.2:
1237-43 Nov 49
HAMILTON, JOHN M.
and Mendelsohn, R. The Australian housing
cost index. ER 24:87-100 Jun 48
and Wark, J. M. Building industry statistics.
ER 24:204-17 Dec 48
HAMILTON, WALTON HALE
The control of strategic materials. AER 34:
261-79 Jun 44
The economic man affects a national role.
AER/S 36:735-44 May 46
HAMILTON, WILLIAM BASKERVILLE
Early cotton regulation in the lower Missis-
sippi Valley. AH 15:20-25 Jan 41
HAMMAR, CONRAD H.
Regulation or development for the Missouri
Ozarks. LE 16:159-67 May 40
Reconsideration of rent theory as it applies
to agricultural land. JFE 23:145-60
Feb 41
Land economics: discussion. JFE 24:247-49
Feb 42
Society and conservation. JFE 24:109-23
Feb 42
Agriculture in an expansionist economy.
JFE 25:36-51 Feb 43
The land tenure ideal. LE 19:69-84 Feb 43
A reaction to land value control proposals.
JFE 25:822-34 Nov 43

A post war program for American agricul-
ture. JFE 26:549-62 Aug 44
HAMMER, JACOB
Rostovtzeff's "Social and economic history
of the Hellenistic world." R. JEH 3:
70-81 May 43
HAMMERBERG, D. O.
Allocation of milk supplies among contigu-
ous markets. JFE 22:215-19 Feb 40
Farmers in a changing world: the 1940
Yearbook of agriculture. II. R. JFE 23:
451-53 May 41
Wartime problems of conservation of trans-
portation. JFE 25:147-63 Feb 43
HAMMOND, BRAY
Jackson, Biddle, and the Bank of the United
States. JEH 7:1-23 May 47
The Chestnut Street raid on Wall Street,
1839. QJE 61:605-18 Aug 47
Banking in the early West: monopoly, pro-
hibition, and laissez faire. JEH 8:1-25
May 48
HAMMOND, MASON
Economic stagnation in the early Roman
empire. JEH/S 6:63-90 '46
HAMMOND, RICHARD JAMES
British food supplies, 1914-1939. EHR 16:
1-14 no.1, 46
HAMMOND, SETH
Location theory and the cotton industry.
JEH/S 2:101-17 Dec 42
HANDEL, LEO
and Fiske, M. Motion picture research:
content and audience analysis; response
analysis. JM 11:129-34; 273-80 Oct 46,
Jan 47
and Fiske, M. New techniques for studying
the effectiveness of films. JM 11:390-93
Apr 47
HANDLER, A. BENJAMIN, Jr.
Housing needs and housing standards. LE 25:
117-23 Feb 49
HANDLIN, MARY FLUG and Handlin, O.
Origins of the American business corpora-
tion. JEH 5:1-23 May 45
HANDLIN, OSCAR
Laissez-faire thought in Massachusetts,
1790-1880. JEH/S 3:55-65 Dec 43
and Handlin, M. F. Origins of the American
business corporation. JEH 5:1-23 May 45
HANEY, LEWIS H.
Professor Bowman's review of Value and
distribution. AER 30:582-83 Sep 40
HANKINS, FRANK W.
Arithmetic for sales management. JM 7:
59-64 Jul 42
HANKS, JAMES JUDGE
The paper industry in the emergency.
HBR 19:151-58 no.2, 41
HANNAH, HAROLD WINFORD
Agricultural labor and the Fair Labor
Standards Act of 1938. JFE 22:421-29
May 40

HANNAH, HAROLD WINFORD (Cont.)
Family interest in the ownership of farm
land. JFE 23:895-99 Nov 41

HANSEN, ALVIN HARVEY
chairman. Round table on population problems. AER/S 30:383-98 Mar 40
Extensive expansion and population growth.
JPE 48:583-85 Aug 40
Defense financing and inflation potentialities.
REStat 23:1-7 Feb 41
and Upgren, A. R. Some aspects, near-term
and long-term, of the international posi-
tion of the United States. AER/S 30,no.5:
366-72 Feb 41
Defense financing and inflation: some addi-
tional comments on the inflation sympo-
sium. REStat 23:91-93 May 41
A general view of the institutional effects of
the war. AER/S 32:351-59 Mar 42
A brief note on "fundamental disequilibrium."
REStat 26:182-84 Nov 44
A note on fiscal policy: a clarification.
AER 35:408-10 Jun 45
Three methods of expansion through fiscal
policy. AER 35:382-87 Jun 45
A new goal of national policy: full employ-
ment. REStat 27:102-03 Aug 45
[Hansen's "Three methods of expansion
through fiscal policy."] Comment.
AER 35:928 Dec 45
Some notes on Terborgh's "The bogey of
economic maturity." REStat 28:13-17
Feb 46
Notes on Mints' paper on monetary policy.
REStat 28:69-74 May 46
Keynes and The general theory. REStat 28:
182-87 Nov 46
The first reports under the Employment
Act of 1946. REStat 29:69-74 May 47
Cost functions and full employment. AER 37:
552-65 Sep 47
Needed: a cycle policy. ILRR 1:60-65 Oct 47
Dr. Burns on Keynesian economics.
REStat 29:247-52 Nov 47
--- Brief rejoinder. REStat 29:268 Nov 47
A note on savings and investment. REStat 30:
30-33 Feb 48
[How to manage the national debt.] Comments
on the symposium. REStat 31:30-32
Feb 49
Wesley Mitchell, social scientist and social
counselor. REStat 31:245-55 Nov 49

HANSEN, HARRY LOUIS
Premium merchandising. HBR 19:185-96
no.2, 41

HANSEN, MORRIS H.
and Hauser, P. M. On sampling in market
surveys. JM 9:26-31 Jul 44
and Hurwitz, W. N. Dependable samples for
market surveys. JM 14:363-72 Oct 49

HANSEN, PETER L.
Input-output relationships in egg production.
JFE 31:687-96 Nov 49

HANSON, ERIC JOHN and Stewart, A.
Some aspects of rural municipal finance.
CJE 14:481-90 Nov 48

HARALDSON, W. C.
Welfare economics and rationing. QJE 58:
146-48 Nov 43

HARBESON, ROBERT WILLIS
The Transportation Act of 1940. LE 17:
291-302 Aug 41
Public utility regulation: a new chapter.
HBR 20:496-507 no.4, 42
The case for an introductory course in economic theory. AER 33:121-25 Mar 43
The "New Jersey Plan" of rate regulation.
JB 17:220-30 Oct 44
[and others] Postwar railroad problems:
discussion. AER/S 36:494-519 May 46
[and others] Transportation and public
utilities problems: discussion. AER/S 37:
478-97 May 47

HARBISON, FREDERICK HARRIS
The seniority problem in mass production
industries. [Abstract] AER/S 30:223-25
Mar 40
Seniority in mass-production industries.
JPE 48:851-64 Dec 40
Some reflections on a theory of labor-man-
agement relations. JPE 54:1-16 Feb 46
A plan for fundamental research in labor
relations. AER/S 37:375-83 May 47
[and others] Harry Alvin Millis 1873-1948.
[obit.] AER 39:742-50 Jun 49

HARDIN, CHARLES MEYER
Are state margarine taxes constitutionally
vulnerable? JFE 25:677-83 Aug 43
The Bureau of Agricultural Economics under
fire: a study in valuation conflicts.
JFE 28:635-68 Aug 46
The tobacco program: exception or portent?
JFE 28:920-37 Nov 46
Programmatic research and agricultural
policy. JFE 29:359-82 May 47
Current proposals for the organization of
conservation and land-use programs in
agriculture, the United States. JFE 30:
619-44 Nov 48
Political and other processes in formulating
and implementing land use policies in the
river basins. JFE 31,pt.2:392-400
Feb 49

HARDIN, CLIFFORD MORRIS
Conservation of transportation: discussion.
JFE 25:163-65 Feb 43

HARDIN, LOWELL STEWART
and Warren, S. W. Maintaining farm output
with a scarcity of production factors.
JFE 25:95-100 Feb 43
Computation and use of output units in farm
business analysis. JFE 26:779-84 Nov 44
and Carter, R. M. An analysis of work simplification research methods and results.
JFE 28:320-30 Feb 46

HARDIN, LOWELL STEWART (Cont.)
   The functional approach to effective farm
      labor utilization. JFE 31,pt.2:382-84
      Feb 49
HARDING, THOMAS SWANN
   Henry L. Ellsworth, Commissioner of
      Patents. JFE 22:621-27 Aug 40
HARDING, WILLIAM BARCLAY
   Air transportation rates. HBR 18:337-43
      no.3, 40
HARDY, CHARLES OSCAR
   chairman. Round table on the economics of
      war. AER/S 30:362-65 Mar 40
   [and others] Economic consequences of war
      since 1790: discussion. AER/S 30,no.5:
      362-65 Feb 41
   The price level and the gold problem: ret-
      rospect and prospect. AER/S 30,no.5:
      18-29 Feb 41
   War finance, price control, and industrial
      mobilization. JB 14:222-34 Jul 41
   Professor Lester's questions on gold.
      AER 31:560-62 Sep 41
   Adjustments and maladjustments in the
      United States after the first World War.
      AER/S 32:24-30 Mar 42
   Fiscal policy and the national income. R.
      AER 32:103-10 Mar 42
   Schumpeter on Capitalism, socialism, and
      democracy. R. JPE 53:348-56 Dec 45
   Economic opinion and public policy: discus-
      sion. AER/S 36:842-44 May 46
   Federal Reserve System report for 1945. R.
      HBR 25:207-12 no.2, 47
   Fiscal operations as instruments of economic
      stabilization. AER/S 38:395-403 May 48
   Liberalism in the modern state: the philoso-
      phy of Henry Simons. R. JPE 56:305-14
      Aug 48
HARE, ANTHONY EDWARD CHRISTIAN
   Industrial relations and economic theory.
      ER 19:11-22 Jun 43
HARGREAVES, ERIC LYDE
   Price control of (non-food) consumer goods.
      OEP 8:1-11 Nov 47
HARGREAVES, HERBERT WALTER
   The guaranteed security in federal finance.
      JPE 50:559-77 Aug 42
HARGREAVES, MARY WILMA M.
   Dry farming alias scientific farming.
      AH 22:39-56 Jan 48
HARICHARAN GHOSH
   see Ghosh, Haricharan
HARING, ALBERT
   [Consumer credit and retail distribution.]
      Discussion. JM 4,no.4,pt.2:110 Apr 40
HARING, CHESTER E.
   The Haring indexes of local business condi-
      tions. JM 9:217-24 Jan 45
HARLAN, CHARLES LeROY
   The 1945 census enumeration of livestock on
      farms. JFE 29:691-710 Aug 47

HAROLD, GILBERT
   The savings and loan association as a refuge
      for trust funds. JB 15:166-83 Apr 42
HAROLDSON, W. C.
   Comments on regional dependency. JFE 25:
      701-04 Aug 43
HARPER, FLOYD ARTHUR
   The importance of storage costs in accumu-
      lating food stocks. JFE 26:794-800 Nov 44
HARPER, LAWRENCE A. [and others]
   The role of monopoly in the colonial trade
      and expansion of Europe: discussion.
      AER/S 38:63-71 May 48
HARPER, VIRGINIA EPES and Zeisel, H.
   The advertising value of different magazines.
      JM 13:56-61 Jul 48
HARRELL, GEORGE D.
   Prices paid by farmers: their use in admin-
      istering wartime price control programs.
      JFE 25:338-50 Feb 43
HARRINGTON, ALBERT H. and Tontz, R. L.
   Significance of hog-feed price ratios,
      Alabama. JFE 28:835-45 Aug 46
HARRIS, ABRAM LINCOLN
   Sombart and German (national) socialism.
      JPE 50:805-35 Dec 42
   [and others] Labor problems: discussion.
      AER/S 33:197-206 Mar 43
   The scholastic revival: the economics of
      Heinrich Pesch. JPE 54:38-59 Feb 46
   [and others] New frontiers in economic
      thought: discussion. AER/S 36:139-53
      May 46
HARRIS, KENNETH SEAR
   Canada's industrial transformation. HBR 22:
      155-66 no.2, 44
HARRIS, LEM
   Some comparisons of socialist and capitalist
      agriculture. S&S 10:159-71 no.2, 46
   Soviet agriculture: a discussion. II. Reply.
      S&S 11:272-78 no.3, 47
HARRIS, MARSHALL
   Legal aspects of land tenure. JFE 23:173-84
      Feb 41
HARRIS, SEYMOUR EDWIN
   Gold and the American economy. REStat 22:
      1-12 Feb 40
   American gold policy and Allied war eco-
      nomics. EJ 50:224-30 Jun-Sep 40
   The official and unofficial markets for ster-
      ling. QJE 54:655-64 Aug 40
   External aspects of a war and a defense
      economy: the British and American cases.
      REStat 23:8-24 Feb 41
   The British White Paper on war finance and
      national income and expenditure. JPE 50:
      27-44 Feb 42
   Subsidies and inflation. AER 33:557-72
      Sep 43
   The contributions of Bretton Woods and some
      unsolved problems. REStat 26:175-77
      Nov 44

HARRIS, SEYMOUR EDWIN (Cont.)
Some aspects of the Murray Full Employ-
ment Bill. REStat 27:104-06 Aug 45
A one per cent war? AER 35:667-71 Sep 45
Dollar scarcity: some remarks inspired by
Lord Keynes' last article. EJ 57:165-78
Jun 47
Some aspects of the wage problem.
REStat 29:145-53 Aug 47
[Symposium: wage policy.] Introduction.
REStat 29:137-39 Aug 47
[Appraisals of Russian economic statistics.]
Introduction. REStat 29:213-14 Nov 47
New England's decline in the American econ-
omy. HBR 25:348-71 no.3, 47
Cost of the Marshall plan to the United
States. JF 3,no.1:1-15 Feb 48
[Ten economists on the inflation.] Introduc-
tion. REStat 30:1-3 Feb 48
[How to manage the national debt.] Introduc-
tion. REStat 31:15-17 Feb 49
The inflationary process in theory and recent
history. REStat 31:200-10 Aug 49
The January 1949 Economic report of the
President: introduction. REStat 31:165-66
Aug 49
Effectiveness and coordination of monetary,
credit, and fiscal policies. Met 1:90-104
Oct 49
[Comments on the steel report.] Introduc-
tory remarks. REStat 31:280-82 Nov 49
Devaluation of the pound sterling. HBR 27:
781-90 Nov 49
[Productivity and wages.] Introduction.
REStat 31:292 Nov 49
HARRISON, FRANK L.
The Joads in peace and war. S&S 6:97-110
no.2, 42
HARRISON, ROBERT WILLMOTT
A philosophy of agricultural adjustment with
particular reference to the Southeast.
JFE 26:448-60 Aug 44
Land improvement vs. land settlement for the
Southeast. SEJ 12:30-38 Jul 45
and Kollmorgen, W. M. The place of French-
speaking farmers of southern Louisiana in
future land development and reclamation
projects. LE 22:223-31 Aug 46
Land economic research in the alluvial valley
of the lower Mississippi River. JFE 29:
593-615 Aug 47
and Kollmorgen, W. M. Past and prospective
drainage reclamations in the coastal
marshlands of the Mississippi River delta.
LE 23:297-320 Aug 47
Louisiana's state-sponsored drainage program. SEJ 14:387-403 Apr 48
The role of the agricultural economists in the
formulation of land use policies in river
basins. JFE 31,pt.2:405-09 Feb 49
HARRISS, CLEMENT LOWELL
Revenue implications of a progressive-rate
tax on expenditures. A study of selected

aspects of Irving Fisher's proposal to
eliminate savings from the income tax
base. REStat 25:175-91 Aug 43
Federal estate taxes and philanthropic be-
quests. JPE 57:337-44 Aug 49
Wealth estimates as affected by audit of
estate tax returns. NTJ 2:316-33 Dec 49
HARROD, ROY FORBES
The population problem: a rejoinder. MS 11:
47-58 Apr 40
Full employment and security of livelihood.
EJ 53:321-42 Dec 43
and R[obinson], E. A. G. John Maynard
Keynes. [obit.] EJ 56:171 Jun 46
Professor Hayek on individualism. R.
EJ 56:435-42 Sep 46
John Maynard Keynes. REStat 28:178-82
Nov 46
A comment [on R. Triffin's National central
banking and the international economy].
REStud 14:95-97 no.2, 47
The fall in consumption. OIS 10:162-67
May 48
European Union. LBR 9:1-20 Jul 48
The fall in consumption: a rejoinder. OIS 10:
235-44; 290-93 Jul-Aug, Sept 48
Wesley Mitchell in Oxford. EJ 59:459-60
Sep 49
HARROUN, CATHERINE
and Teiser, R. Origin of Wells, Fargo &
Company, 1841-1852. BHR 22:70-83
Jun 48
and Teiser, R. Wells, Fargo & Company:
the first half year. BHR 23:87-95 Jun 49
HART, ALBERT GAILORD
Uncertainty and inducements to invest.
REStud 8:49-53 Oct 40
Peculiarities of indifference maps involving
money. REStud 8:126-28 Feb 41
Defense financing and inflation: some com-
ments on Professor Hansen's article:
Safeguards against inflation. REStat 23:
85-87 May 41
Use of flexible taxes to combat inflation.
AER 32:87-102 Mar 42
What it takes to block inflation. REStat 24:
101-13 Aug 42
Postwar effects to be expected from wartime
liquid accumulations. AER/S 35:341-51
May 45
"Model-building" and fiscal policy. AER 35:
531-58 Sep 45
Facts, issues, and policies. (The problem of
"full employment") AER/S 36:280-90
May 46
National budgets and national policy: a re-
joinder. AER 36:632-36 Sep 46
Timing and administering fiscal policy: how
to give relevant counsel. AER/S 38:430-42
May 48
Assets, liquidity, and investment. AER/S 39:
171-81 May 49

HART, CHARLES WILLIAM MERTON
The Hawthorne experiments. CJE 9:150-63 May 43
Industrial relations research and social theory. CJE 15:53-73 Feb 49

HART, JAMES K.
The management of figures. HBR 27:24-33 Jan 49

HART, LAURENCE C.
Essentials of successful marketing: a case history in manufacturer-distributor collaboration. JM 13:195-201 Oct 48

HART, ORSON HENRY
Risk factors in public utility securities. JF 3,no.3:52-64 Oct 48

HARTKEMEIER, HARRY PELLE
Seasonal variation in the volume of bills discounted. Em 12:125-29 Apr 44
The use of data collected by poorly trained enumerators. JPE 52:164-66 Jun 44

HARTLAND, PENELOPE C.
see Thunberg, Penelope Hartland

HARTLEY Sir HAROLD
British war controls: the legal framework. MS 11:163-76 Oct 40
Limiting factors in world development, or what is possible? SAJE 16:260-73 Sep 48

HARTWELL, JOHN M., Jr.
Interest rates by loan size and geographical region. JASA 42:242-45 Jun 47

HARTWIG, JOSEPH D.
Should the accountant depreciate investment buildings held by trustees under testamentary trusts? JB 18:41-55 Jan 45

HARTZ, LOUIS
Laissez-faire thought in Pennsylvania, 1776-1860. JEH/S 3:66-77 Dec 43

HARVEY, NIGEL
The coming of the Swede to Great Britain. AH 23:286-88 Oct 49

HARVIE, C. H.
A note on deferred export credits. EJ 58:425-28 Sep 48

HARVILL, RICHARD ANDERSON
The economy of the South. JPE 48:33-61 Feb 40

HARWOOD, EDWARD CROSBY
Comment on A neglected component of the money supply. AER 30:115 Mar 40
Comment on review of Cause and control of the business cycle. AER 30:832 Dec 40

HASSAN MOHAMED HUSSEIN
see Hussein, Hassan Mohamed

HASAN, ANWARUL [and others]
Discussion on transition from war to peace economy. IJE 25:629-34 Apr 45

HASAN, M. A.
The theory of rent. IJE 28:571-76 Apr 48

HASSAN, MOHAMMAD
Gandhiji's economic ideals and creed. IJE 21:131-47 Oct 40

HASEL, AUSTIN ALEXANDER and Poli, A.
A new approach to forest ownership surveys. LE 25:1-10 Feb 49

HASSAN
see Hasan

HATHAWAY, DALE ERNEST and Cravens, M. E., Jr.
Quality factors affecting the price of peaches on the Benton Harbor market. JFE 31, pt.2:631-34 Feb 49

HAUCK, CHARLES W.
Team work in marketing research. JFE 29:1395-1405 Nov 47

HAUCK, JOSEPH F. and Lee, A. T. M.
Excessive land subdivision and the New Jersey pine area. LE 19:207-21 May 43

HAUSER, PHILIP M.
and Hansen, M. H. On sampling in market surveys. JM 9:26-31 Jul 44
The statistical program of the Census Bureau. JASA 42:24-30 Mar 47

HAUSSMANN, FREDERICK
World oil control, past and future: an alternative to "international cartelization." SR 9:334-55 Sep 42

HAVENS, RALPH MURRAY
Laissez-faire theory in presidential messages during the nineteenth century. JEH/S 1:86-95 Dec 41
Reactions of the federal government to the 1837-1843 depression. SEJ 8:380-90 Jan 42
Note on effect of denazification upon property rights in Germany. SEJ 13:158-61 Oct 46

HAWES, ALEXANDER B.
Issues and policies of contract termination. AER/S 33:150-58 Mar 43

HAWKINS, DAVID
Some conditions of macroeconomic stability. Em 16:309-22 Oct 48
and Simon, H. A. Note: some conditions of macroeconomic stability. Em 17:245-48 Jul-Oct 49

HAWKINS, EDWARD RUSSELL
Marketing and the theory of monopolistic competition. JM 4:382-89 Apr 40

HAWKINS, EVERETT DAY, chairman
Technical aspects of applying a dismissal wage to defense workers. Abstract of specialized conference discussion. AER/S 32:215-16 Mar 42

HAWKINSON, JAMES R.
[Retailing in '41]: discussion. JM 5:418-19 Apr 41

HAWLEY, AMOS H.
and Bogue, D. J. Recent shifts in population: the drift toward the metropolitan district, 1930-40. REStat 24:143-48 Aug 42
and Freedman, R. Unemployment and migration in the depression (1930-1935). JASA 43:260-72 Jun 49

HAWLEY, NORMAN R.
The old rice plantations in and around the Santee experimental forest. AH 23:86-91 Apr 49

HAWTREY, RALPH GEORGE
  The trade cycle and capital intensity.
    Ec N.S.7:1-15 Feb 40
  Mr. Kaldor on the forward market. REStud 7:
    202-05 Jun 40
  Professor Hayek's Pure theory of capital.
    R. EJ 51:281-90 Jun-Sep 41
  W. A. Shaw. [obit.] EJ 53:290 Jun-Sep 43
  Competition from newcomers. Ec N.S. 10:
    219-22 Aug 43
  Livelihood and full employment. EJ 54:
    417-22 Dec 44
  The need for faith. EJ 56:351-65 Sep 46
  Sir Charles Addis (1861-1945). [obit.]
    EJ 56:507-10 Sep 46
  Lord Keynes. [obit.] JRSS 109:169 pt.2, 46
  Irving Fisher. [obit.] JRSS 110:85 pt.1, 47
  Monetary aspects of the economic situation.
    AER 38:42-55 Mar 48
  The function of exchange rates. OEP N.S.1:
    145-56 Jun 49
HAY, DENYS
  The official history of the Ministry of Muni-
    tions 1915-1919. R. EHR 14:185-90
    no.2, 44
HAYEK, FRIEDRICH AUGUST von
  Socialist calculation: the competitive solu-
    tion. Ec N.S.7:125-49 May 40
  The counter-revolution of science. Pt.I-III.
    Ec N.S.8:9-36; 119-50; 281-320 Feb,May,
    Aug 41
  Maintaining capital intact: a reply.
    Ec N.S.8:276-80 Aug 41
  The Ricardo effect. Ec N.S.9:127-52 May 42
  Scientism and the study of society. Pt.I-III.
    Ec N.S.9:267-91; 10:34-63; 11:27-39
    Aug 42, Feb 43, Feb 44
  A comment [on N. Kaldor's "Professor Hayek
    and the concertina-effect]. Ec N.S.9:
    383-85 Nov 42
  ["Scientism and the study of society": re-
    joinder.] Ec N.S.10:188-89 May 43
  A commodity reserve currency. EJ 53:
    176-84 Jun-Sep 43
  Professor Hayek's theory of interest: a
    comment. Ec N.S.10:311 Nov 43
  The geometrical representation of comple-
    mentarity. REStud 10:122-25 no.2, 43
  Richard von Strigl. [obit.] EJ 54:284-86
    Jun-Sep 44
  Time-preference and productivity: a recon-
    sideration. Ec N.S.12:22-25 Feb 45
  ed. Notes on N. W. Senior's Political econ-
    omy, by John Stuart Mill. [Edited by
    F. A. Hayek] Ec N.S.12:134-39 Aug 45
  The use of knowledge in society. AER 35:
    519-30 Sep 45
  The London School of Economics 1895-1945.
    Ec N.S.13:1-31 Feb 46
  Wesley Clair Mitchell, 1874-1948. [obit.]
    JRSS 111:254-55 pt.2, 48
HAYES, JOHN PHILIP
  A note on selling costs and the equilibrium of

the firm. REStud 12:106-09 no.2, 45
HAYES, SAMUEL PERKINS, Jr.
  Potash prices and competition. QJE 57:
    31-68 Nov 42
  Commercial surveys as an aid in the deter-
    mination of public policy: a case study.
    JM 12:475-82 Apr 48
HAYGOOD, TYLER F.
  How would a federal sales tax affect
    farmers? JFE 27:649-63 Aug 45
  Analyzing the tax load of agriculture.
    JFE 31,pt.2:668-78 Feb 49
HAYNES, ELDRIDGE
  Industrial production and marketing. JM 8:
    13-20 Jul 43
HAYS, JAMES S. and Ratzkin, J. L.
  Trade association practices and antitrust
    law. HBR 25:501-20 no.4, 47
HAYTER, EARL W.
  The western farmers and the drivewell
    patent controversy. AH 16:16-28 Jan 42
  The fencing of western railways. AH 19:
    163-67 Jul 45
HAYTHORNE, GEORGE VICKERS
  Agricultural man-power. CJE 9:366-83
    Aug 43
  Canadian agricultural manpower problems.
    JFE 31,pt.2:385-91 Feb 49
HAZARD, WILLIS HATFIELD
  The literature of life insurance. HBR 19:
    123-32 no.1, 40
  Marketing life insurance: its history in
    America. R. BHR 16:1-7 Feb 42
HEAD, NEIL C.
  The basing point cases. HBR 26:641-55
    Nov 48
HEADY, EARL O.
  Changes in income distribution in agricul-
    ture with special reference to technologi-
    cal progress. JFE 26:435-47 Aug 44
  Production functions from a random sample
    of farms. JFE 28:989-1004 Nov 46
  Economics of farm leasing systems. JFE 29:
    659-78 Aug 47
  and Homeyer, P. G. The role of modern
    statistics in analyzing farm management
    data. JFE 29:1241-49 Nov 47
  Elementary models in farm production eco-
    nomics research. JFE 30:201-25 May 48
  The economics of rotations with farm and
    production policy applications. JFE 30:
    645-64 Nov 48
  Cooperating in objective soil conservation
    research. JFE 31,pt.2:664-67 Feb 49
  Basic economic and welfare aspects of farm
    technological advance. JFE 31:293-316
    May 49
  Implications of particular economics in ag-
    ricultural economics methodology.
    JFE 31,pt.2:837-50 Nov 49
HEALY, KENT TENNEY
  Workable competition in air transportation.
    AER/S 35:229-42 May 45

HEALY, KENT TENNEY (Cont.)
Transportation as a factor in economic
growth. JEH/S 7:72-88 '47
HEATH, MILTON SYDNEY
Laissez-faire in Georgia, 1732-1860.
JEH/S 3:78-100 Dec 43
The uniform class rate decision and its im-
plications for southern economic develop-
ment. SEJ 12:213-37 Jan 46
HEATHERINGTON, DONALD FULLER [and
others]
Economic problems of foreign areas: dis-
cussion. AER/S 36:650-60 May 46
HEATON, HERBERT
Rigidity in business since the industrial
revolution. AER/S 30:306-13 Mar 40
Non-importation, 1806-1812. JEH 1:178-98
Nov 41
The early history of the Economic History
Association. JEH/S 1:107-09 Dec 41
A merchant adventurer in Brazil 1808-1818.
JEH 6:1-23 May 46
Other wests than ours. JEH/S 6:50-62 '46
The making of an economic historian.
JEH/S 9:1-18 '49
HECKSCHER, GUNNAR
Pluralist democracy: the Swedish experi-
ence. SR 15:417-61 Dec 48
HEDGES, HAROLD
Research developments in cooperative mar-
keting. JFE 28:134-40 Feb 46
Integrating economic and legal thought re-
lating to agricultural cooperation.
JFE 31,pt.2:908-15 Nov 49
HEDGES, MARION HAWTHORNE [and others]
Labor problems: discussion. AER/S 33:
197-206 Mar 43
HEDGES, TRIMBLE R.
Agricultural census: discussion. JFE 23:
271-74 Feb 41
HEDLUND, GLENN W.
Review of papers on research and educational
programs in marketing. JFE 28:181-86
Feb 46
HEER, CLARENCE
State and local finance in the postwar plans
of the South. SEJ 11:246-54 Jan 45
HEFLEBOWER, RICHARD BROOKS
The effect of dynamic forces on the elasticity
of revenue curves. QJE 55:652-66 Aug 41
The effects of the war on the structure of
commodity and labor markets. AER/S 36:
52-64 May 46
chairman. Content and research uses of
price control and rationing records.
[Report of a subcommittee] AER/S 37:
651-66 May 47
Food prices, wage rates, and inflation.
REStat 30:27-29 Feb 48
[and others] Round table on economic research: discussion. AER/S 39:464-72
May 49

HEHER, HARRY
Industrial relations consultants are not en-
gaged in unauthorized practice of law: a
court opinion. ILRR 2:253-54 Jan 49
HEICHELHEIM, FRITZ MORITZ
Professor Rostovtzeff's history of the
Hellenistic World. R. EJ 52:59-61 Apr 42
HEIDINGSFIELD, MYRON S.
Why do people shop in downtown department
stores? JM 13:510-12 Apr 49
HEILBRONER, ROBERT LOUIS
Saving and investment: dynamic aspects.
AER 32:827-28 Dec 42
HEILPERIN, MICHAEL ANGELO [and others]
[The future of international investment]:
discussion. AER/S 33:355-61 Mar 43
HEIMANN, EDUARD
Franz Oppenheimer's economic ideas.
SR 11:27-39 Feb 44
The central theme in the history of eco-
nomics. SR 11:202-15 May 44
Industrial society and democracy. SR 12:
43-59 Feb 45
Professor Hayek on German socialism.
AER 35:935-37 Dec 45
Recent literature on economic systems. R.
SR 13:103-16 Mar 46
On strikes and wages. SR 15:82-98 Mar 48
HEISIG, CARL P.
with Clawson, M. and Hurd, E. B. Long-
term forecasting of fruit and nut produc-
tion. JFE 23:550-66 Aug 41
Income stability in high-risk farming areas.
JFE 28:961-72 Nov 46
chairman. Economic implications of tech-
nological developments in agricultural
production. Report of a sub-committee.
JFE 29:299-309 Feb 47
Farm management research: discussion.
JFE 31,pt.2:1078-79 Nov 49
HELBURN, NICHOLAS
The case for national forest roads. LE 23:
371-80 Nov 47
HELBURN, STEPHEN
Location of industry. LE 19:253-63 Aug 43
HELD, ADOLPH
Health and welfare funds in the needle trades.
ILRR 1:247-63 Jan 48
HELD, HARRY
New York City in the postwar period.
HBR 21:455-71 no.4, 43
HELLEINER, KARL F.
Deposit banking in Mediterranean Europe.
CJE 12:214-18 May 46
Population movement and agrarian depres-
sion in the later Middle Ages. CJE 15:
368-77 Aug 49
HELLER, WALTER W.
Tax and monetary reform in occupied
Germany. NTJ 2:215-31 Sep 49
HELLERSTEIN, JEROME R.
Excess profits tax relief for the electric
utilities under Section 722 of the Internal
Revenue Code. LE 20:149-56 May 44

HELLIG, S. R.
Returns to capital invested in the gold mining industry in South Africa. SAJE 17:175-84 Jun 49

HENDERSON, ALEXANDER MORELL
A further note on the problem of bilateral monopoly. JPE 48:238-43 Apr 40
Consumer's surplus and the compensating variation. REStud 8:117-21 Feb 41
The pricing of public utility undertakings. MS 15:223-50 Sep 47
A note on the theory of rationing. REStud 15: 42-45 no.1, 47
A geometrical note on bulk purchase. Ec N.S.15:61-69 Feb 48
The case for indirect taxation. EJ 58: 538-53 Dec 48
Prices and profits in state enterprise. REStud 16:13-24 no.1, 48
The restriction of foreign trade. MS 17:12-35 Jan 49

HENDERSON, Sir HUBERT DOUGLAS
Marjorie Eve Robinson. [obit.] EJ 50: 161-62 Mar 40
Josiah Charles Stamp, Baron Stamp of Shortlands (June 21, 1880, to April 16, 1941). [obit.] EJ 51:338-47 Jun-Sep 41
The Anglo-American financial agreement. OIS 8:1-13 Jan 46
The implications of the Marshall speech. OIS 9:274-82 Aug 47
Cheap money and the budget. EJ 57:265-71 Sep 47
The international economy. REStud 14: 76-81 no.2, 47
The price system. EJ 58:467-82 Dec 48
The function of exchange rates. OEP N.S.1: 1-17 Jan 49
A comment [on Hawtrey's "The function of exchange rates"]. OEP N.S.1:157-58 Jun 49
A criticism of the Havana charter. AER 39: 605-17 Jun 49
The moral of the British crisis. REStat 31: 256-60 Nov 49

HENDERSON, JOHN S.
Regional differentials in interest rates. SEJ 11:113-32 Oct 44
Geometrical note on elasticity of demand. AER 36:662-63 Sep 46

HENDERSON, LEON and Nelson, D. M.
Prices, profits, and government. HBR 19: 389-404 no.4, 41

HENDERSON, PATRICK DAVID
Some comparisons of pre-war and post-war productivity. OIS 9:347-51 Oct 47
and Seers, D. The technique and progress of Czechoslovakia's two-year plan. OIS 9:357-74 Nov 47
with Seers, D. and Wallis, P. F. D. Notes on estimating national income components. OIS 11:59-70 Feb-Mar 49

HENDERSON, ROBERT D.
Company response to coupon inquiries. JM 13:368-71 Jan 49

HENDERSON, RONALD FRANK
The significance of the new issue market for the finance of industry. EJ 58:63-73 Mar 48

HENDERSON, SIDNEY
and Upchurch, M. L. Relocation of manpower and zoning. LE 19:1-17 Feb 43
An experiment in forest-farm resettlement. LE 22:10-21 Feb 46
A plan for transferring the farm from father to son. LE 24:82-85 Feb 48

HENDERSON, WILLIAM OTTO
The war economy of German East Africa, 1914-1917. EHR 13:104-10 no.1-2, 43
British economic activity in the German colonies, 1884-1914. EHR 15:56-66 no.1-2, 45
German economic penetration in the Middle East, 1870-1914. EHR 18:54-64 no.1-2, 48

HENDRICKS, WALTER A.
Farm employment levels in relation to supply and demand as per cent of normal. JASA 42:271-81 Jun 47

HENDRICKSON, CLARENCE IRVING
[Reconsideration of rent theory as it applies to agricultural land]: discussion. JFE 23: 170-71 Feb 41

HENDRIX, WILLIAM ELBERT
The Brannan Plan and farm adjustment opportunities in the cotton South. JFE 31: 487-96 Aug 49

HENEMAN, HERBERT GERHARD, Jr. and Sexton, R. H.
Selected annotated bibliography on union accounting and financial reports. ILRR 2: 116-20 Oct 48

HENGREN, RAYMOND E. and Smith, T.
Bank capital: the problem restated. JPE 55: 553-66 Dec 47

HENIG, HARRY
and Unterberger, S. H. Wage control in wartime and transition. AER 35:319-36 Jun 45
and Unterberger, S. H. Theory of wage control in the transition period. SEJ 12: 283-89 Jan 46

HENRICH, FREDERICK K.
The development of American laissez faire: a general view of the age of Washington. JEH/S 3:51-54 Dec 43

HENRIKSEN, ERIK KARL
Simultaneous operation of several machines by one person. Application of a method of probability. NTTO 12:133-40 no.37, 48

HENRY, JAMES A.
Some comments on Professor Hutt's "Full employment and the future of industry." SAJE 14:67-70 Mar 46
Some aspects of the economic development of Northern Rhodesia. SAJE 14:100-16 Jun 46

HERBERT, PAUL A.
The story of Rileyville, New Jersey. AH 16:
1-8 Jan 42
HERMAN, SAMUEL
The food stamp plan: a study in law and
economics. Pt.I-II. JB 13:331-59;
14:11-35 Oct 40, Jan 41
The food stamp plan: termination. JB 16:
173-94 Jul 43
HERMENS, FERDINAND ALOYS
Domestic postwar problems. RSE 1:23-30
Dec 42
and Wallace, G. S. Inflation and anti-infla-
tion policies in the United States, 1939-
1949. ZS 105:675-709 Hft.4, 49
HERRING, JAMES MORTON
Broadcasting and the public interest.
HBR 18:344-56 no.3, 40
HERRING, JOHN WOODBRIDGE
Trails to new America: reply to W. I. King.
AER 31:345-46 Jun 41
HERRMANN, LOUIS F.
Diminishing returns in feeding commercial
dairy herds. JFE 25:397-409 May 43
The role of the farm organization economist
in the formulation of farm organization
policy. JFE 29:1203-08 Nov 47
HERSEY, ARTHUR BAIRD
Sources and uses of corporation funds.
JASA 36:265-74 Jun 41
HERSKOVITS, MELVILLE J.
Economics and anthropology: a rejoinder.
JPE 49:269-78 Apr 41
HERZEL, WILLIAM GEORGE
State tax legislation in 1947. NTJ 1:79-90
Mar 48
HERZFELD, HANS
and Frankel, S. H. European income distri-
bution in the Union of South Africa and
the effect thereon of income taxation.
SAJE 11:121-36 Jun 43
and Frankel, S. H. An analysis of the growth
of the national income of the Union in the
period of prosperity before the war.
SAJE 12:112-38 Jun 44
HESSELTINE, WILLIAM B.
Regions, classes and sections in American
history. LE 20:35-44 Feb 44
HEUSNER, WILLIAM WILDER, chairman
Marketing research in American industry.
Pt.I-II. [Report by the Committee on
Marketing Research] JM 11:338-54;
12:25-37 Apr,Jul 47
HEWES, AMY
Revision of the elementary course. [Sum-
mary of a paper on problems in the teach-
ing of economics] AER/S 30:107-09
Mar 40
HEWES, LAURENCE I., Jr.
On the current readjustment of land tenure
in Japan. LE 25:246-59 Aug 49
HEWETSON, HENRY WELDON
Transportation in the Canadian North.
CJE 11:450-66 Aug 45

HEWETT, WILLIAM WALLACE
The use of economic principles in the teach-
ing of applied subjects. [Summary]
AER/S 30:109-10 Mar 40
The use of economic principles in the teach-
ing of applied subjects. AER 30:333-38
Jun 40
Some problems in teaching elementary eco-
nomics. AER/S 36:853-56 May 46
HEXNER, ERVIN
American participation in the International
Steel Cartel. SEJ 8:54-79 Jul 41
International cartels in the postwar world.
SEJ 10:114-35 Oct 43
The political economy of international
cartels: discussion. AER/S 35:321-24
May 45
World industrial committees. SEJ 12:
348-56 Apr 46
HEYWARD, ERIC JOHN RICHARD
H. von Stackelberg's work on duopoly.
ER 17:99-106 Jun 41
HEYWOOD, P. K.
Practical problems of the retail price ceil-
ing: II. Problems of the retailer. CJE 8:
440-45 Aug 42
HIBBARD, BENJAMIN HORACE
chairman. Max Sering. [obit.] JFE 22:409
Feb 40
The farmer is dependent on national pro-
grams. AER/S 30:no.5:155-64 Feb 41
George Simon Wehrwein. [obit.] JFE 27:
232 Feb 45
HICKS, EARL
Alexander del Mar, critic of metallism.
SEJ 6:314-32 Jan 40
HICKS, JOHN DONALD
The western Middle West, 1900-1914. AH 20:
65-77 Apr 46
HICKS, JOHN RICHARD
The valuation of the social income. Ec N.S.7:
105-24 May 40
A comment [on O. Lange's Complementarity
and interrelations of shifts in demand].
REStud 8:64-65 Oct 40
The rehabilitation of consumers' surplus.
REStud 8:108-16 Feb 41
Saving and the rate of interest in war-time.
MS 12:21-27 Apr 41
The monetary theory of D. H. Robertson. R.
Ec N.S.9:53-57 Feb 42
Maintaining capital intact: a further sugges-
tion. Ec N.S.9:174-79 May 42
Consumers' surplus and index-numbers.
REStud 9:126-37 no.2, 42
and Hicks, U. K. The Beveridge plan and
local government finance. REStud 11:
1-19 no.1, 43
The four consumer's surpluses. REStud 11:
31-41 no.1, 43
History of economic doctrine. R. EHR 13:
111-15 no.1-2, 43
[The inter-relations of shifts in demand:
comment.] REStud 12:72-75 no.1, 44

HICKS, JOHN RICHARD (Cont.)
Recent contributions to general equilibrium
economics. R. Ec N.S.12:235-42 Nov 45
The generalised theory of consumer's sur-
plus. REStud 13:68-74 no.2, 46
World recovery after war: a theoretical
analysis. EJ 57:151-64 Jun 47
The empty economy. LBR 5:1-13 Jul 47
The valuation of the social income: a com-
ment on Professor Kuznets' reflections.
Ec N.S.15:163-72 Aug 48
Mr. Harrod's dynamic theory. R. Ec N.S.16:
106-21 May 49
Devaluation and world trade. TBR 4:3-23
Dec 49
HICKS, URSULA KATHLEEN
Lags in tax collection: a neglected problem
in war finance. REStud 8:89-99 Feb 41
and Hicks, J. R. The Beveridge plan and
local government finance. REStud 11:
1-19 no.1, 43
The terminology of tax analysis. EJ 56:
38-50 Mar 46
National and local finance. EJ 56:609-22
Dec 46
The grant provisions of the local government
bill. OIS 10:33-52 Feb 48
HICKS, WILLIAM TROTTER
Recent expansion in the southern pulp and
paper industry. SEJ 6:440-48 Apr 40
HIDY, RALPH WILLARD
The organization and functions of Anglo-
American merchant bankers, 1815-1860.
JEH/S 1:53-66 Dec 41
A leaf from investment history. HBR 20:
65-74 no.1, 41
Cushioning a crisis in the London money
market. BHR 20:131-45 Nov 46
Importance of the history of the large busi-
ness unit. BHR 22:4-11 Feb 48
Problems in collaborative writing of busi-
ness history. BHR 23:67-77 Jun 49
HIGGINS, BENJAMIN HOWARD
Agriculture and war: a comparison of agri-
cultural conditions in the Napoleonic and
World War periods. AH 14:1-12 Jan 40
[A note on Mr. Higgins' "Indeterminancy in
non-perfect competition."] Reply.
AER 30:348-50 Jun 40
The incidence of sales taxes: a note on
methodology. QJE 54:665-72 Aug 40
Comments on 100 per cent money. AER 31:
91-96 Mar 41
A diagrammatic analysis of the supply of
loan funds. Em 9:231-40 Jul-Oct 41
and Dunlop, J. T. "Bargaining power" and
market structures. JPE 50:1-26 Feb 42
Post-war tax policy. Pt.I-II. CJE 9:408-28;
532-56 Aug,Nov 43
The doctrine of economic maturity. R.
AER 36:133-41 Mar 46
The economic man and economic science. R.
CJE 13:587-99 Nov 47

To save or not to save? R. CJE 14:98-107
Feb 48
[and others] Problems of timing and admin-
istering fiscal policy in prosperity and
depression: discussion. AER/S 38:
443-51 May 48
Towards a dynamic economics. R. ER 24:
173-90 Dec 48
The optimum wage rate. REStat 31:130-39
May 49
Reder on wage-price policy. CJE 15:203-06
May 49
HIGGINS, DOROTHEA E.; Walker, Q. F. and
Collins, W. T.
The effects of federal revenue acts of 1938,
1939, and 1940 on the realization of gains
and losses on securities. JASA 35:602-14
Dec 40; A correction. 36:122 Mar 41
--- Rejoinder. JASA 36:433-35 Sep 41
HIGGINS, GEORGE G.
Social action program of the National
Catholic Welfare Conference. RSE 7,no.2:
34-38 Sep 49
HILDEBRAND, GEORGE HERBERT
Monopolization and the decline of investment
opportunity. AER 33:591-601 Sep 43
The Nathan Report and its critics. AER 37:
386-91 Jun 47
HILDRETH, CLIFFORD
A note on maximization criteria. QJE 61:
156-64 Nov 46
[Measurement of agricultural production]:
discussion. JFE 31:231-32 May 49
HILGERDT, FOLKE
The case for multilateral trade. AER/S 33:
393-407 Mar 43
HILGERT, JOSEPH ROBERT
Use of sales aptitude tests. HBR 23:484-92
no.4, 45
H[ILL], A[USTIN] B[RADFORD]
Sir Duncan Wilson. [obit.] JRSS 108:245
pt.1-2, 45
HILL, CHRISTOPHER
Professor Lavrovsky's study of a seventeenth-
century manor. EHR 16:125-29 no.2, 46
Land in the English revolution. S&S 13:22-49
no.1, 48-49
HILL, ELTON BRAINARD
Comments on sampling to increase the use-
fulness of farm management research.
JFE 23:499-501 May 41
HILL, FORREST FRANK
Financing agriculture: discussion. JFE 22:
154-57 Feb 40
Training and recruitment of agricultural
economic personnel. VI. An administra-
tor's view. JFE 22:562-66 Aug 40
Research developments in farm finance.
JFE 28:114-25 Feb 46
General price level and related factors:
further comment. JFE 31,pt.2:793-99
Nov 49

HILL, GEORGE W. and Marshall, D. G.
Reproduction and replacement of farm population and agricultural policy. JFE 29:
457-74 May 47

HILL, LYMAN
Marketing and employment. JM 11:65-66
Jul 46

HILL, WALTER
Planning industry's future in Britain. HBR 22:
129-38 no.2, 44
Whither British industry? HBR 22:328-36
no.3, 44

HILLHOUSE, ALBERT MILLER [and others]
Economic problems of American cities:
discussion. AER/S 32:341-48 Mar 42

HILLMANN, H. C.
Analysis of Germany's foreign trade and the
war. Ec N.S.7:66-88 Feb 40

HILTON, RODNEY HOWARD
Peasant movements in England before 1381.
EHR II.2:117-36 no.2, 49

HIMMEL, CLAIRE and Smith, E. R.
Some major recent market changes. JM 9:
225-33 Jan 45

HINRICHS, ALBERT FORD
Effects of the 25-cent minimum wage on em-
ployment in the seamless hosiery industry.
JASA 35:13-23 Mar 40
The defence programme and labour supply
in the United States. CJE 7:414-25 Aug 41
Charles P. Neill, 1865-1942. [obit.]
JASA 38:110-11 Mar 43
Developments in labor market and price sta-
tistics in 1945 and 1946. JASA 42:31-37
Mar 47

HINSHAW, RANDALL
American prosperity and the British balance-
of-payments problem. REStat 27:1-9
Feb 45
and Metzler, L. A. World prosperity and the
British balance of payments. REStat 27:
156-70 Nov 45
Foreign investment and American employment. AER/S 36:661-71 May 46
Professor Frisch on discrimination and multilateral trade. REStat 30:271-75 Nov 48

HIPPEN, JOHN F.
A Wall Street man and a western railroad:
a chapter in railroad administration.
BHR 23:117-48 Sep 49

HIROSE, ARTHUR PIERSON
Market research as a practical help in reconversion problems. JM 9:342-49 Apr 45

HIRSCH, HANS G.
Crop yield index numbers. JFE 25:583-98
Aug 43
1950 World census of agriculture. JFE 29:
564-66 May 47

HIRSCH, JULIUS
Evaluation of our wartime price control.
JM 8:281-88 Jan 44
Facts and fantasies concerning full employ-
ment. AER/S 34:118-27 Mar 44

Productivity in war and peace. AER/S 37:
397-411 May 47

HIRSCH, WERNER ZVI
The status and possibilities of rural producing cooperatives. JFE 31:697-707 Nov 49

HIRSCHMAN, ALBERT O.
The commodity structure of world trade.
QJE 57:565-95 Aug 43
Inflation and deflation in Italy. AER 38:
598-606 Sep 48
Disinflation, discrimination, and the dollar
shortage. AER 38:886-92 Dec 48
Devaluation and the trade balance: a note.
REStat 31:50-53 Feb 49
International aspects of a recession. AER 39:
1245-53 Dec 49

HIRSCHMANN, IRA ARTHUR
Television in the retail field. JM 8:394-97
Apr 44

HIRSHLEIFER, JACK
A note on expectations. AER 36:901-03
Dec 46

HIRST, R. R.
Inflation: its impact on enterprises. ER 25,
(no.49):24-30 Dec 49

HITCH, CHARLES JOHNSTON
The controls in post-war reconstruction.
OEP 6:43-56 Apr 42
Lessons of reconversion. REStat 29:16-20
Feb 47

HITCH, THOMAS KEMPER and Davis, J. C.
Wages and productivity. REStat 31:292-98
Nov 49

HITCHCOCK, DAL and Davenport, D. H.
Swords and plowshares. HBR 20:307-14
no.3, 42

HOAGLAND, HENRY E.
Housing and national defense. LE 16:377-81
Nov 40

HOBART, DONALD M.
Probable effects of a national emergency on
marketing functions and policies. JM 4,
no.4, pt.2:59-65 Apr 40
Occupational classification for market research. JM 7:367-73 Apr 43
Planning a Holiday. JM 12:47-52 Jul 47

HOBEN, EDMOND H.
Relationships of technological and social research in housing. LE 25:99-101 Feb 49

HOBSBAWM, ERIC J.
General labour unions in Britain, 1889-1914.
EHR II.1:123-42 no.2-3, 49
Trends in the British labor movement since
1850. S&S 13:289-312 no.4, 49

HOBSON, ASHER
War adjustments for American agriculture.
JFE 22:269-78 Feb 40
Discussion of papers on foreign agriculture
and trade problems. JFE 28:80-83 Feb 46

HOCH, MYRON L.
The oil strike of 1945. SEJ 15:117-33 Oct 48

HOCHMUTH, HAROLD ROBERT
Western range land use: discussion. JFE 31,
pt.2:996-97 Nov 49

HOCHWALD, WERNER
  Collective bargaining and economic theory.
    SEJ 13:228-46 Jan 47
  Guaranteed wages. AER 37:303-19 Jun 47
HOCKING, DOUGLAS MITCHELL
  Paper industries in war-time. II. The eco-
    nomic implications of newsprint rationing.
    ER 17:224-30 Dec 41
  The economics of the gas industry. ER 18:
    31-42 Jun 42
HODGES, JULIAN ADAIR
  Regional changes in farming: discussion.
    JFE 24:276-79 Feb 42
  Forty years of farm management research.
    JFE 24:392-401 May 42
  Waldo E. Grimes. [obit.] JFE 29:797-98
    Aug 47
HODGES, T. M.
  The peopling of the hinterland and the port
    of Cardiff. EHR 17:62-72 no.1, 47
  Early banking in Cardiff. EHR 18:84-90
    no.1-2, 48
  The history of the Newport and Caerleon
    Savings Bank (1830-1888). EHR II.2:
    188-99 no.2, 49
HOECKER, RAYMOND WILLIAM
  Collaboration between marketing economists,
    engineers, and other specialists. JFE 29:
    JFE 29:1406-12 Nov 47
HOFF, PAUL R. and Bierly, I. R.
  Work simplification: a joint problem for
    management, engineering, and commodity
    specialists. JFE 29:219-24 Feb 47
HOFFENBERG, MARVIN
  Estimates of national output, distributed in-
    come, consumer spending, saving, and
    capital formation. REStat 25:101-74
    May 43; Correction. 201 Aug 43
  [and others] Input-output analysis and its
    use in peace and war economies: discus-
    sion. AER/S 39:226-40 May 49
HOFFMAN, AUSTIN CLAIR
  Changing organization of agricultural mar-
    kets. JFE 22:162-72 Feb 40
  Agricultural surplus programs. JM 6,no.4,
    pt.2:174-76 Apr 42
  and Segal, S. A. Food price control: policy
    and mechanics. JFE 25:19-33 Feb 43
  Pricing of farm products: discussion. JFE 26:
    121-23 Feb 44
  Current institutional trends in business.
    JFE 31,pt.2:1132-40 Nov 49
HOFFMAN, C. T.
  A guide to postwar planning for the manufac-
    turer. JM 9:5-10 Jul 44
HOFFMAN, MICHAEL LINDSAY
  Capital movements and international payments
    in postwar Europe. REStat 31:261-65
    Nov 49
HOFFMAN, PAUL G.
  Planning for post-war opportunity. JM 8:
    33-40 Jul 43
  Business plans for postwar expansion.
    AER/S 35:85-89 May 45

The survival of free enterprise. HBR 25:
    21-27 no.1, 46
HOFFMAN, W.
  The growth of industrial production in Great
    Britain: a quantitative study. EHR II.2:
    162-80 no.2, 49
HOFFSOMMER, HAROLD
  Progress of tenure groups. JFE 23:208-16
    Feb 41
HOGAN, JOHN ARTHUR
  The meaning of the union shop elections.
    ILRR 2:319-34 Apr 49
HOHAUS, REINHARD A.
  Actuarial problems in social insurance.
    JASA 35:37-46 Mar 40
HOLBEN, RALPH ERDMAN
  General expenditure rationing with particu-
    lar reference to the Kalecki plan. AER 32:
    513-23 Sep 42
  In defense of monopoly: comment. QJE 60:
    612-15 Aug 46
  Planned economy in Norway: comment.
    AER 39:1283-87 Dec 49
HOLDEN, ARTHUR C.
  Urban Redevelopment Corporations Act
    vetoed by New York Governor. LE 16:
    219-21 May 40
  Urban redevelopment corporations. LE 18:
    412-22 Nov 42
  Technique of urban redevelopment. Pt.I-III.
    LE 20:133-48; 238-51; 21:45-53 May,
    Aug 44, Feb 45
HOLDEN, GRENVILLE
  Rationing and exchange control in British
    war finance. QJE 54:171-200 Feb 40. A
    correction. 694-95 Aug 40
  Incidence of taxation as an analytical concept.
    AER 30:774-86 Dec 40
HOLLAND, WILLIAM LANCELOT
  Postwar political economy of the Far East
    and the Pacific. AER/S 34:356-67 Mar 44
HOLLANDER, EDWARD D.
  Price indexes and consumer expenditure
    studies. JM 13:373-74 Jan 49
HOLLANDER, SIDNEY, Jr.
  A technique for spotting retail outlets.
    JM 6:280-81 Jan 42
  A rationale for advertising expenditures.
    HBR 27:79-87 Jan 49
HOLLOWAY, J. E.
  The Bretton Woods Conference and the Inter-
    national Monetary Fund. SAJE 12:205-22
    Sep 44
HOLME, S. A. and Gustin, R. P.
  An approach to postwar planning. HBR 20:
    459-72 no.4, 42
HOLT, CHARLES CARTER
  and Samuelson, P. A. The graphic depiction
    of elasticity of demand. JPE 54:354-57
    Aug 46
  Averaging of income for tax purposes: equity
    and fiscal-policy considerations. NTJ 2:
    349-61 Dec 49

HOLTON, HILMA
Survey of the teaching of business history.
BHR 23:96-103 Jun 49
HOLZMAN, FRANKLYN DUNN
Discrimination in international trade.
AER 39:1233-44 Dec 49
HOLZMAN, ROBERT S.
Interstate tax barriers to marketing. JM 12:
72-79 Jul 47
HOMAN, PAUL THOMAS
In what areas should antitrust policy be re-
placed? AER/S 30:180-93 Mar 40
chairman. Round table on economic
research. AER/S 30,no.5:409-15 Feb 41
Economics in the war period. AER 36:
855-71 Dec 46
Research in prices, wages, and profits.
AER/S 39:440-43 May 49
HOMBERGER, LUDWIG M.
Coordination of road and rail transport and
the organization of the trucking industry.
LE 17:216-25 May 41
HOMEYER, PAUL G. and Heady, E. O.
The role of modern statistics in analyzing
farm management data. JFE 29:1241-49
Nov 47
HON, RALPH CLIFFORD
The Memphis Power and Light deal. SEJ 6:
344-75 Jan 40
The South in a war economy. SEJ 8:291-308
Jan 42
HONE, JOSEPH
Richard Cantillon, economist: biographical
note. EJ 54:96-100 Apr 44
HONIGSHEIM, PAUL
Max Weber as historian of agriculture and
rural life. AH 23:179-213 Jul 49
HONJO, EIJIRO
The economic thought in the middle period of
the Tokugawa era. Kyo 15,no.2:1-33
Apr 40
Economic thought in the latter period of the
Tokugawa era. Kyo 15,no.4:1-24 Oct 40
The development of the study of the economic
history of Japan subsequent to the Meiji
restoration. Kyo 16,no.1:18-31 Jan 41
Views in the taxation on commerce in the
closing days of Tokugawa age. Kyo 16,
no.3:1-15 Jul 41
Facts and ideas of Japan's over-sea develop-
ment prior to the Meiji restoration.
Kyo 17,no.1:1-13 Jan 42
The formation of "Japanese political econ-
omy." Kyo 17,no.2:1-19 Apr 42
The original current of "Japanese political
economy." Kyo 17,no.3:1-19 Jul 42
HOOD, ALEXANDER LAMBERT
Great Britain's economic problem. HBR 25:
625-36 no.4a, 47
HOOD, ARTHUR A.
What's ahead in building material marketing?
[Abstract] AER/S 39:418-20 May 49

HOOD, WILLIAM CLARENCE
Some aspects of the treatment of time in
economic theory. CJE 14:453-68 Nov 48
Structural changes in the Dominion person-
al income tax, 1932-49. CJE 15:220-27
May 49
HOOS, SIDNEY
An investigation on complementarity rela-
tions between fresh fruits. JFE 23:421-33
May 41
Futures trading in perishable agricultural
commodities. JM 6:358-65 Apr 42
An investigation on complementarity rela-
tions between fresh fruits: a rejoinder.
JFE 24:528-29 May 42
The determination of military subsistence
requirements. JFE 28:973-88 Nov 46
Implications of aggregative theories for ag-
ricultural economists. JFE 31,pt.2:
851-62 Nov 49
HOOVER, CALVIN BRYCE
What changes in national policy does the
South need? JFE 22:206-12 Feb 40
Economic planning and the problem of full
employment. AER/S 30:263-71 Mar 40
[and others] Economic consequences of war
since 1790: discussion. AER/S 30,no.5:
362-65 Feb 41
The future of the German economy.
AER/S 36:642-49 May 46
What can Europe do for itself? JF 3,no.1:
16-31 Feb 48
Keynes and the economic system. JPE 56:
392-402 Oct 48
[and others] Problems of the ITO: discus-
sion. AER/S 39:269-79 May 49
HOOVER, EDGAR MALONE
Interstate redistribution of population,
1850-1940. JEH 1:199-205 Nov 41
and McLaughlin, G. E. Strategic factors in
plant location. HBR 20:133-40 no.2, 42
Research in the area of productive capacity
and investment. AER/S 39:444-52 May 49
HOOVER, ETHEL DALLMEYER and Williams,
F. M.
Measuring price and quality of consumers'
goods. JM 10:354-69 Apr 46
HOPE, ERNEST CHARLES
Agriculture's share of the national income.
CJE 9:384-93 Aug 43
HOPE, RONALD
Profits in British industry from 1924 to
1935. OEP N.S.1:159-81 Jun 49
HOPKIN, JOHN A.
Multivariate analysis of farm and ranch
management data. JFE 31,pt.2:1073-78
Nov 49
HOPKINS, JOHN ABEL
The scale of agricultural production: some
corrections. QJE 54:314-16 Feb 40
Changing structure of agriculture and its
impacts on labor. JFE 23:89-104 Feb 41

HOPKINS, JOHN ABEL (Cont.)
An experiment on the accuracy of farm survey data. JFE 23:492-96 May 41
Significance of the Geneva Trade Conference to United States agriculture. JFE 29: 1055-71 Nov 47

HOPPER, WILBERT CLAYTON
Income and food consumption. CJE 9: 487-506 Nov 43

HORIE, YASUZO
The development of the domestic market in the early years of Meiji. Kyo 15,no.1: 45-59 Jan 40
An outline of economic policy in the Tokugawa period. Kyo 15,no.4:44-65 Oct 40
The encouragement of kokusan or native products in the Tokugawa period. Kyo 16, no.2:44-63 Apr 41
Clan monopoly policy in the Tokugawa period. Kyo 17,no.1:31-52 Jan 42
Development of economic policy in the closing days of the Tokugawa period. Kyo 17,no.4:48-63 Oct 42

HORNE, GILBERT RICHARD
On some appendices to the Rowell-Sirois report: VII. Labour legislation and social services in the province of Quebec. CJE 7:249-59 May 41

HORNE, McDONALD KELSO, Jr.
The final consumption of cotton. SEJ 9: 302-12 Apr 43

HORNER, F. B.
The demand equation for a raw material in empirical studies. ER 25,(no.48):85-91 Jun 49

HORNIKER, ARTHUR LEON
German contracting in occupied Europe. HBR 25:74-91 no.1, 46

HORSEFIELD, JOHN KEITH
The Bank and its treasure. Ec N.S.7:161-78 May 40
The duties of a banker. Pt.I-II. Ec N.S.8: 37-51; 11:74-85 Feb 41, May 44
Gibson and Johnson: a forgotten cause célèbre. Ec N.S.10:233-37 Aug 43
The origins of the Bank Charter Act, 1844. Ec N.S. 11:180-89 Nov 44
The cash ratio in English banks before 1800. JPE 57:70-74 Feb 49
The opinions of Horsley Palmer, Governor of the Bank of England, 1830-33. Ec N.S. 16:143-58 May 49
The bankers and the bullionists in 1819. JPE 57:442-48 Oct 49
The Bank of England as mentor. EHR II.2: 80-87 no.1, 49

HORTON, DONALD CLARE
Insurance aspects of extra-risk mortgage loans. JFE 23:855-66 Nov 41
and Larsen, H. C. Agricultural finance guides in wartime. LE 19:59-68 Feb 43
Finance and effective wartime use of agricul-

tural resources. SEJ 10:14-26 Jul 43
and Shepard, E. F. Federal aid to agriculture since World War I. AH 19:114-20 Apr 45
Methods of financing related to asset characteristics of farms. JFE 29:1158-79 Nov 47
Adaptation of the farm capital structure to uncertainty. JFE 31:76-100 Feb 49
and Barber, E. L. The problem of farm business survival in areas of highly variable rainfall. JFE 31,pt.2:944-50 Nov 49

HOSEA, HAROLD R.
[Principles of arbitration in wage rate disputes: comment.] ILRR 2:112-14 Oct 48

HOSELITZ, BERT FRANK
Socialist planning and international economic relations. AER 33:839-51 Dec 43
Professor Hayek on German socialism. I. AER 35:929-34 Dec 45
The cartel report. CJE 12:172-75 May 46
International cartel policy. JPE 55:1-27 Feb 47
Four reports on economic aid to Europe. JPE 56:109-23 Apr 48
Socialism, communism, and international trade. JPE 57:227-41 Jun 49

HOSFORD, W. H.
Some Lincolnshire enclosure documents. EHR II.2:73-79 no.1, 49

HOSKINS, WILLIAM GEORGE
The reclamation of the waste in Devon, 1550-1800. EHR 13:80-92 no.1-2, 43

HOSMER, WINDSOR ARNOLD
Funding depreciation and maintenance reserves under war conditions. HBR 21: 369-84 no.3, 43
Business organization for effective use of forest products. HBR 26:581-96 Sep 48

HOSNY EL-SAID, MOHAMED
see El Said, Mohamed Hosny

HOTCHKISS, GEORGE BURTON
Consumer economists in glass houses. JM 5: 228-33 Jan 41
and Bader, L. Attitudes of teachers of marketing toward consumer grade labeling. JM 6:274-79 Jan 42
Evaluation of the Harvard study. JM 6,no.4, pt.2:100-05 Apr 42
Some fundamental objections to mandatory A B C grades. JM 10:128-34 Oct 45

HOTELLING, HAROLD
Income-tax revision as proposed by Irving Fisher. Em 11:83-87 Jan 43

HOTELLING, SUSANNE E.
[Les fluctuations économiques et l'interdépendance des marchés]: a rejoinder. JPE 48:744-46 Oct 40

HOUGH, JOHN ASPEY
Retail sales per employee. MS 17:49-66 Jan 49

HOUGHTON, D. HOBART
Changing emphasis in public finance. SAJE 15:60-67 Mar 47

HOUGHTON, D. HOBART (Cont.)
    Population structure of a Ciskei Native Re-
        serve. SAJE 17:341-48 Sep 49
HOUGHTON, HARRISON F.
    The growth of big business. AER/S 38:72-93
        May 48
HOUSE, ROBERT BURTON
    [The education of planners.] At the Univer-
        sity of North Carolina. LE 21:316-17
        Sep 45
HOUSEMAN, EARL E.
    The sample design for a national farm sur-
        vey by the Bureau of Agricultural Eco-
        nomics. JFE 29:241-45 Feb 47
HOVDE, BRYN JAKOB
    Critique: "American versus German city
        planning." LE 23:239-43 Aug 47
    The economic and social crisis of Europe.
        SR 16:271-88 Sep 49
HOVDE, HOWARD T.
    The marketing viewpoint in planning for com-
        munity betterment. JM 7:337-41 Apr 43
    Wholesaling in our American economy.
        JM 14:145-361 Sep 49
HOWARD, FRANK A.
    Synthetic rubber. HBR 20:1-9 no.1, 41
HOWARD, GORDON E.
    Filtering down and the elimination of sub-
        standard housing: a reply. LE 22:294
        Aug 46
HOWARD, STANLEY EDWIN
    The Trust Indenture Act of 1939. LE 16:
        168-80 May 40
    and Kemmerer, E. W. Frank Albert Fetter.
        A birthday note. AER 33:230-35 Mar 43
    [and others] Edwin Walter Kemmerer
        1875-1945. [obit.] AER 36:219-21 Mar 46
HOWE, CHARLES B.
    Food consumption at the national level.
        JFE 28:791-803 Aug 46
HOWE, R. E.
    The Coal Marketing Agency. JM 10:35-41
        Jul 45
HOWELL, LEANDER D.
    Quality-price differentials in cotton market-
        ing. JFE 23:329-38 Feb 41
    Internal trade barriers for margarine.
        JFE 25:793-806 Nov 43
    Cotton surplus disposal programs. JFE 26:
        273-91 May 44
    Does the consumer benefit from price in-
        stability? QJE 59:287-95 Feb 45
HOWELL, PAUL LLOYD
    The effects of federal income taxation on the
        form of external financing by business.
        JF 4:208-22 Sep 49
HOWENSTINE, EMANUEL JAY
    The Industrial Board, precursor of the
        N.R.A.: the price-reduction movement
        after World War I. JPE 51:235-50 Jun 43
    Demobilization after the first World War.
        QJE 58:91-105 Nov 43
    The domestic retreat after World War I.
        SR 10:480-86 Nov 43

Public works program after World War I.
    JPE 51:523-37 Dec 43
The high-cost-of-living problem after World
    War I. SEJ 10:222-34 Jan 44
Why "normalcy" failed. SR 11:363-66 Sep 44
Dovetailing rural public works into employ-
    ment policy. REStat 28:165-69 Aug 46
Some principles of compensatory action.
    QJE 61:165-68 Nov 46
Public works policy in the twenties. SR 13:
    479-500 Dec 46
with Johnson, V. W. and Timmons, J. F.
    Rural public works. Pt.I-II. LE 23:12-21;
    132-41 Feb,May 47
An inventory of public construction needs.
    AER 38:353-66 Jun 48
HOWER, RALPH MERLE
    Captain Macy. HBR 18:472-87 no.4, 40
    Problems and opportunities in the field of
        business history. BHR 15:17-26 Apr 41
    chairman. The effect of managerial policy
        upon the structure of American business.
        Abstract of specialized conference dis-
        cussion. AER/S 32:226-27 Mar 42
    The effect of managerial policy upon the
        structure of American business. [Abridge-
        ment] BHR 16:42-52 Apr 42
HOYT, ELIZABETH ELLIS
    ["Consumption in our society."] Discussion.
        JM 4,no.4,pt.2:117-19 Apr 40
HOYT, HOMER
    Urban decentralization. LE 16:270-76
        Aug 40
    Economic background of cities. LE 17:
        188-95 May 41
    Rebuilding American cities after the war.
        LE 19:364-68 Aug 43
    The effect of cyclical fluctuations upon real
        estate finance. JF 2,no.1:51-64 Apr 47
    Economic and housing survey of the Orlando,
        Florida metropolitan region. LE 23:
        219-27 May 47
HOYT, WILLIAM D., Jr.
    Two Maryland farm leases. AH 21:185-87
        Jul 47
HOZUMI, FUMIO
    Ssu-ma Chien's economic outlook. Kyo 15,
        no.1:16-29 Jan 40
    A study of the character of current Chinese
        economy. Kyo 15,no.3:41-66 Jul 40
    On the monetary ideas as seen in the Records
        of economics and finance in the Sung his-
        tory. Kyo 17,no.3:36-59 Jul 42
    The Chinese ideas of money. Kyo 18,no.1:
        34-57 Jan 43
HSIANG, CHING-YUEN
    Land utilization in China. a critique of
        methodology. LE 16:226-29 May 40
    A philosophy of permanent conservation.
        LE 17:239-41 May 41
HSIEN-T'ING FANG
    see Fang, Hsien-t'ing

HSU, YUNG-YING
Cooperative economy in Yenan. S&S 10:
17-40 no.1, 46
HU, KUANG TAI
Investment in China's postwar industry.
HBR 21:309-20 no.3, 43
HUANG, ANDREW CHUNG
The inflation in China. QJE 62:562-75 Aug 48
HUBBARD, JOSEPH BRADLEY
Industrial bond and preferred stock refund-
ings, 1933-1937. REStat 22:17-44 Feb 40
Easy money: doctrine and results. HBR 19:
52-65 no.1, 40
Residential real estate. R. QJE 56:130-33
Nov 41
Nonrefunding security flotations and capital
structures. REStat 25:192-201 Aug 43
World transport aviation. HBR 22:509-15
no.4, 44
Reconversion. REStat 29:31-38 Feb 47
HUBBARD, JOSHUA CLAPP
A model of the forty-month or trade cycle.
JPE 50:197-225 Apr 42
Income creation by means of income taxation.
QJE 58:265-89 Feb 44
The proportional personal-income tax as an
instrument of income creation. EJ 59:
56-67 Mar 49
HUBER, JOHN RICHARD
The effects of German clearing agreements
and import restrictions on cotton, 1934-
1939. SEJ 6:419-39 Apr 40
HUBERT, GILES A.
A framework for the study of peripheral eco-
nomic areas. JFE 28:804-20 Aug 46
War and the trade orientation of Haiti.
SEJ 13:276-84 Jan 47
HUDSON, PHILIP GRAYDON
Principles of economics prerequisite to
courses in public finance. AER 30:582
Sep 40
The possibility of maintaining a positive rate
of physical production growth. SEJ 8:
191-200 Oct 41
HUEGY, HARVEY WILBORN
[Measurement of marketing efficiency]: dis-
cussion. JM 5:371-73 Apr 41
HUFFMAN, ROY E.
and Paschal, J. L. Integrating the use of
irrigated and grazing land in the northern
Great Plains. LE 18:17-27 Feb 42
County land as a factor in adjusting the agriculture of western North Dakota. LE 18:
495-99 Nov 42
War and post-war problems of irrigation
planning in the northern plains. LE 19:
452-63 Nov 43
and Halcrow, H. G. Great Plains agriculture and Brannan's farm program.
JFE 31:497-508 Aug 49
HUGHES, EVERETT C. and McDonald, M. L.
French and English in the economic structure
of Montreal. CJE 7:493-505 Nov 41

HUGHES, FRANCIS
Soviet invention awards. EJ 55:291-97
Jun-Sep 45
Incentive for Soviet initiative. EJ 56:415-25
Sep 46
HUGHES, GENEVIEVE E.
Postwar changes in individual income taxes:
United States, United Kingdom, and
Canada. NTJ 1:175-83 Jun 48
HUGHES, W. J.
Income tax allowances for dependents.
EJ 51:502-07 Dec 41
HUGHES, WESLEY
Vox pop can pilot your paper. JM 11:371-76
Apr 47
HULA, ERICH
The Dumbarton Oaks proposals. SR 12:
135-56 May 45
HULSE, ANN ELIZABETH
see Dewey, Anne Elizabeth Hulse
HULTGREN, THOR
Divisions of freight rates and the inter-
territorial rate problem. JPE 50:99-116
Feb 42
HUMPHREY, DON DOUGAN
Alleged "additional workers" in the measure-
ment of unemployment. R. JPE 48:
412-19 Jun 40
Price control in outline. AER 32:744-59
Dec 42
HUNSBERGER, WARREN SEABURY
[and others] Economic problems of foreign
areas: discussion. AER/S 36:650-60
May 46
Economic research of interest to the Depart-
ment of State. AER/S 37:681-89 May 47
HUNT, PEARSON
The financial policy of corporations. QJE 57:
303-13 Feb 43
HUNTER, HOLLAND
The planning of investments in the Soviet
Union. REStat 31:54-62 Feb 49
HUNTER, LOUIS CLAIR
The invention of the western steamboat.
JEH 3:201-20 Nov 43
HURD, EDGAR B.; Clawson, M. and Heisig, C. P.
Long-term forecasting of fruit and nut pro-
duction. JFE 23:550-66 Aug 41
HURD, THOMAS NORMAN
Farmer-worker relationships. JFE 31,pt.2:
378-81 Feb 49
HURD, WILLIAM BURTON
On some appendices to the Rowell-Sirois
report: VIII. Prairie population possibili-
ties. CJE 7:259-63 May 41
Postwar agricultural settlement possibilities
in Canada. JFE 27:388-404 May 45
HURLBURT, VIRGIL L.
Rural zoning for Missouri? LE 16:151-58
May 40
Wartime land policy: discussion. JFE 25:
187-89 Feb 43
Some aspects of administrative pricing as

HYSON, CHARLES DAVID (Cont.)
   adequate and more stable income from
   farming. JFE 27:852-60 Nov 45
Notes on savings in relation to potential
   markets. AER 36:891-901 Dec 46
Maladjustments in the wool industry and
   need for new policy. JFE 29:425-56
   May 47
and Neal, A. C. New England's economic
   prospects. HBR 26:156-80 Mar 48
and Hyson, W. P. Geometrical measurement
   of elasticities. AER 39:728-29 Jun 49
HYSON, W. P.
see Hyson, Charles David and Hyson, W. P.
HYTTEN, TORLEIV
   Some problems of Australian transport development. ER 23:5-19 Jun 47
IBACH, DONALD B.
   Role of soil depletion in land valuation.
   JFE 22:460-72 May 40
Recovering the investment in limestone, with
   particular reference to reimbursement of
   vacating tenants. JFE 31:116-30 Feb 49
IDENBURG, PHILIPPUS JACOBUS and
   Derksen, J. B. D.
Methods of evaluation of the national income
   of the Netherlands, 1921-1938. RIIS 8:
   13-30 no.1-2, 40
IDRIS, S. M.
   [and others] Discussion on "India and inter-
   national economic co-operation." IJE 25:
   626-29 Apr 45
A bird's eye view of Pakistan economy.
   PEJ 1,no.2:55-66 Oct 49
IGLAUER, JAY
   Department store distribution. JM 8:326-28
   Jan 44
IGNATIUS, PAUL ROBERT and Livingston, J. S.
   Effective use of training films. HBR 25:
   637-51 no.4a, 47
IHLEFELD, AUGUST
   Reducing the bank deposit insurance premium.
   HBR 27:438-48 Jul 49
IKE, NOBUTAKA
   Taxation and landownership in the westerni-
   zation of Japan. JEH 7:160-82 Nov 47
IMLAH, ALBERT H.
   Real values in British foreign trade, 1798-
   1853. JEH 8:133-52 Nov 48
IMPERATORI, MARIO
   The construction of wholesale price index
   numbers and wholesale price trend in
   Italy, May 1946-July 1949. BNL 2:172-78
   Jul-Sep 49
INCE, GODFREY H.
   Mobilisation of man-power in Great Britain
   for the second Great War. MS 14,no.1:
   17-52 Jan 46
INMAN, BUIS T.
   Farm inheritance practices in Austria.
   LE 23:288-96 Aug 47
INMAN, SAMUEL GUY
   Planning Pan-American trade. HBR 18:
   137-47 no.2, 40

INNES, N. ROSE-
   see Rose-Innes, N.
INNIS, HAROLD ADAMS
   Arthur James Glazebrook. [obit.] CJE 7:
   92-94 Feb 41
The newspaper in economic development.
   JEH/S 2:1-33 Dec 42
Decentralization and democracy. CJE 9:
   317-30 Aug 43
Stephen Butler Leacock (1869-1944). [obit.]
   CJE 10:216-26 May 44
On the economic significance of culture.
   JEH/S 4:80-97 Dec 44
Edward Johns Urwick, 1867-1945. [obit.]
   CJE 11:265-68 May 45
IRVINE, ALEXANDER GEORGE and Shaul, J.
   R. H.
The national income of Southern Rhodesia,
   1946-1948. SAJE 17:511-15 Dec 49
IRVINE, WILLIAM
   George Bernard Shaw and Karl Marx.
   JEH 6:53-72 May 46
IRVING, JOHN A.
   The evolution of the social credit movement.
   CJE 14:321-41 Aug 48
IRWIN, HAROLD SPEER
   Middlemen's accumulations and expectations
   in marketing farm products. JFE 29:
   848-66 Nov 47
ISAACS, ASHER [and others]
   Effects of the war and defense program upon
   economic conditions and institutions: dis-
   cussion. AER/S 32:426-31 Mar 42
ISAACS, NATHAN
   Price control by law. HBR 18:504-09 no.4, 40
ISAACS, REGINALD
   The neighborhood concept in theory and ap-
   plication. LE 25:73-78 Feb 49
ISARD, CAROLINE
   and Isard, W. The transport-building cycle
   in urban development: Chicago.
   REStat 25:224-26 Aug 43
   and Isard, W. Economic implications of air-
   craft. QJE 59:145-69 Feb 45
ISARD, WALTER
   A neglected cycle: the transport-building
   cycle. REStat 24:149-58 Nov 42
Transport development and building cycles.
   QJE 57:90-112 Nov 42
and Isard, C. The transport-building cycle
   in urban development: Chicago.
   REStat 25:224-26 Aug 43
and Isard, C. Economic implications of aircraft. QJE 59:145-69 Feb 45
Some economic implications of atomic energy.
   QJE 62:202-28 Feb 48
Some locational factors in the iron and steel
   industry since the early nineteenth century.
   JPE 56:203-17 Jun 48
and Capron, W. M. The future locational pattern of iron and steel production in the
   United States. JPE 57:118-33 Apr 49
[and others] Interregional variations in eco-

ISARD, WALTER (Cont.)
    nomic fluctuations: discussion. AER/S 39:
      120-34 May 49
    An addendum on the Cowles Commission
      estimates. (Comparisons of power cost
      for atomic and conventional steam sta-
      tions.) REStat 31:226-28 Aug 49
    and Lansing, J. B. Comparisons of power
      cost for atomic and conventional steam
      stations. REStat 31:217-26 Aug 49
    The general theory of location and space-
      economy. QJE 63:476-506 Nov 49
ISE, JOHN
    Monopoly elements in rent. AER 30:33-45
      Mar 40
    Institutional economics in land economic
      theory: discussion. JFE 23:171-72 Feb 41
    [and others] Natural resources and inter-
      national policy: discussion. AER/S 35:
      130-36 May 45
    The futility of trust-busting. AER/S 38:
      488-501 May 48
ISLES, KEITH SYDNEY
    Some aspects of war finance. ER 16:191-207
      Dec 40
    The building of a war economy. ER 18:58-74
      Jun 42
    Employment and equilibrium: a theoretical
      discussion. R. ER 19:212-24 Dec 43
    and Ramsay, A. M. Lack of adaptability in
      agriculture: an economic survey. ER 20:
      18-37 Jun 44
ISSAWI, CHARLES
    To what extent are the costs of a war borne
      by future generations. EgC 31:39-44
      Jan 40
    and Rosenfeld, F. Company profits in Egypt
      1929-1939. EgC 32:679-86 Nov 41
    Company profits in Egypt, 1940-1941.
      EgC 33:577-80 May-Nov 42
    Agriculture versus industry: a reconsidera-
      tion of the problem. EgC 35:39-48
      Jan-Feb 44
    Interactions of industry and agriculture in
      Great Britain since the industrial revolu-
      tion. EgC 35:243-67 Mar-Apr 44
IVERSEN, CARL
    Post-war economic problems in Denmark.
      LBR 10:22-38 Oct 48
IYENGAR, D. KRISHNA
    Rural drive in Mysore. IJE 27:72-77 Jul 46
IYENGAR, S. KESAVA
    Survey of rural indebtedness in India: a com-
      ment. IJE 21:335-41 Jan 41
    "British" & "Indian" finance. IJE 21:830-70
      Apr 41
    Rural co-operation and national planning in
      India. IJE 22:400-35 Jan 42
    The investment multiplier. IJE 23:80-82 Jul 42
    A note on the working of the departmentalisa-
      tion scheme of finances in Hyderabad State
      during eighteen years. IJE 23:24-45 Jul 42
    Central banking in Hyderabad. EJ 53:274-80
      Jun-Sep 43

    Economic control in India during the
      war. IJE 24:239-60 Apr 44
    Industrialisation and agriculture in India
      post-war planning. EJ 54:189-205
      Jun-Sep 44
    Post-war economic planning in India: bal-
      ances and weightages. IJE 25:47-55 Jul 44
    The problem of social security in India.
      IJE 25:315-24 Jan 45
    Post-war currency system in India. IJE 26:
      499-507 Jan 46
JACKSON, EDWARD FRANCIS
    and Stone, R. Economic models with special
      reference to Mr. Kaldor's system. EJ 56:
      554-67 Dec 46
    Comments on Mr. Harrod's paper. OIS 10:
      209-13 Jun 48; Erratum. 234 Jul-Aug 48
    The fall in consumption: a further note.
      OIS 10:290 Sep 48
JACKSON, WILLIAM TURRENTINE
    The Wyoming Stock Growers' Association:
      its years of temporary decline, 1886-1890.
      AH 22:260-70 Oct 48
JACOBS, JACOB LOUIS
    Systematic assessment of property for tax
      equalization. LE 17:71-81 Feb 41
    Neighborhood and property obsolescence in
      the assessment process. LE 17:344-53
      Aug 41
JACOBS, JOHN K.
    The development of atomic energy. S&S 10:
      292-99 no.3, 46
JACOBS, WALTER and Friend, I.
    Input-output analysis and its use in peace
      and war economies: discussion. AER/S 39:
      228-32 May 49
JACOBSON, ANNA
    see Schwartz, Anna Jacobson
JACOBSON, DAVID J.
    What's ahead for the hotel industry? HBR 24:
      339-55 no.3, 46
JACOBSON, JEROME; Copeland, M. A. and
    Lasken, H.
    The WPB index of war production. JASA 40:
      145-59 Jun 45
JACOBY, NEIL HERMAN
    The rate of capitalizing railroad earnings to
      establish a valuation for property taxation.
      JB 13:158-71 Apr 40
    Government loan agencies and commercial
      banking. AER/S 32:250-60 Mar 42
    The American economy during and after the
      war: a look ahead. JB 15:289-305 Oct 42
    The demand for funds by American business
      enterprises: retrospect and prospect.
      Pt.I-II. JF 3,no.3:27-38; 4:47-59 Oct 48,
      Mar 49
JAFFARY, STUART K.
    Social security: the Beveridge and Marsh
      Reports. R. CJE 9:571-92 Nov 43
JAFFE, ABRAM, J. and Wolfbein, S. L.
    Internal migration and full employment in the
      U.S. JASA 40:351-63 Sep 45

JAFFE, PHILIP J.
  Economic provincialism and American Far
    Eastern policy. S&S 5:289-309 no.4, 41
JAFFÉ, WILLIAM [and others]
  The economic theory of imperfect competi-
    tion, oligopoly, and monopoly: discussion.
    AER/S 38:19-32 May 48
JAGANNADHAM, VEDULA
  Land systems in India: with special refer-
    ence to the Permanent Settlement. IJE 27:
    186-93 Oct 46
  Social protection for agricultural labourers.
    IJE 28:121-30 Jul 47
  Industrial disputes in India. IJE 29:185-97
    Oct 48
JAIN, LAKSHMI CHANDRA
  Presidential address [before the Indian Eco-
    nomic Association]. IJE 20:797-809 Apr 40
JAIN, PRAKASH CHANDRA
  Recent monetary technique: [discussion].
    IJE 20:824-25 Apr 40
JAIN, TARA CHAND
  Future of land system in the Punjab. IJE 27:
    517-22 Apr 47
JAMES, CLIFFORD LESTER
  Industrial concentration and trade barriers.
    SEJ 14:163-72 Oct 47
JAMES, FRANCIS GODWIN
  Charity endowments as sources of local
    credit in seventeenth- and eighteenth-
    century England. JEH 8:153-70 Nov 48
JAMES, HERMAN BROOKS
  What John Smith needs to know about the
    benefits and costs of soil conservation.
    JFE 31,pt.2:651-54 Feb 49
JAMES, LEE MORTON
  Restrictive agreements and practices in the
    lumber industry, 1880-1939. SEJ 13:
    115-25 Oct 46
JAMES, ROBERT
  and Cook, S. Job specification and a fair
    wage. EJ 57:387-93 Sep 47
  Human waste: an analysis of labour turnover
    in industry. EJ 59:118-23 Mar 49
JANES, CLAUD VICTOR
  History of exchange control in Australia.
    ER 16:16-33 Jun 40
JANSEN, GEORGE F.
  The closed shop is not a closed issue.
    ILRR 2:546-57 Jul 49
JANSSEN, MELVIN
  An analysis of the economy of use of farm
    labor in the corn belt. JFE 31,pt.2:374-77
    Feb 49
JANTZEN, IVAR
  Social production theory. NTTO 12:141-50
    no.37, 48
  Laws of production and cost. Em 17,suppl.:
    58-67 Jul 49
JASNY, NAUM
  Proposal for revision of Agricultural statis-
    tics. JFE 24:402-19 May 42
  Labor productivity in agriculture in USSR
    and USA. JFE 27:419-32 May 45·

  The breads of Ephesus and their prices.
    AH 21:190-92 Jul 47
  Intricacies of Russian national-income
    indexes. JPE 55:299-322 Aug 47
  The plight of the collective farms. JFE 30:
    304-21 May 48
  USSR: law on measures to ensure high and
    stable yields in the Steppe and Forest-
    Steppe regions. LE 25:351-58 Nov 49
JASSPON, W. H.
  Outlook for world fats and oils production
    and use. JFE 31,pt.2:325-30 Feb 49
JASTRAM, ROY W.
  Economic welfare: a comment. EJ 50:
    156-57 Mar 40
  The shifting of sales taxes. QJE 54:673-78
    Aug 40
  Advertising outlays under oligopoly.
    REStat 31:106-09 May 49
  Advertising ratios planned by large-scale
    advertisers. JM 14:13-21 Jul 49
JASZI, GEORGE
  and Musgrave, R. A. Taxation of war
    wealth. R. CJE 8:260-72 May 42
  and Gilbert, M. The 1945 White Paper on
    national income and expenditure. R.
    EJ 55:444-54 Dec 45
  [and others] Objectives of national income
    measurement: a reply to Professor
    Kuznets. REStat 30:179-95 Aug 48
JEAL, E. F.
  Accounting and the price level. SAJE 17:
    105-10 Mar 49
  Dollar despotism. SAJE 17:111-13 Mar 49
JEBENS, ARTHUR B.
  State rural land use legislation in 1941.
    LE 18:328-38 Aug 42
JEFFERYS, JAMES BAVINGTON
  The denomination and character of shares,
    1855-1885. EHR 16:45-55 no.1, 46
  and Jefferys, M. The wages, hours and
    trade customs of the skilled engineer in
    1861. EHR 17:27-44 no.1, 47
JEFFERYS, MARGOT and Jefferys, J. B.
  The wages, hours and trade customs of the
    skilled engineer in 1861. EHR 17:27-44
    no.1, 47
JEHRING, JOHN JAMES
  Audio-visual materials in industrial and labor
    relations. ILRR 3:80-98 Oct 49
JEMING, JOSEPH
  Public utility rates on a reproduction-cost-of-
    service principle. LE 17:138-50 May 41
  An actual application of the reproduction-
    cost-of-service principle in rate making.
    LE 18:188-203 May 42
  Estimates of average service life and life ex-
    pectancies and the standard deviation of
    such estimates. Em 11:141-50 Apr 43
JENKINS, WARDER B.
  Agricultural census of 1940. JFE 22:350-58
    Feb 40

JENKS, LELAND HAMILTON
   Railroads as an economic force in American
   development. JEH 4:1-20 May 44
   British experience with foreign investments.
   JEH/S 4:68-79 Dec 44
   Methodological problems of typologies.
   EEH 1,no.1:3-7 Jan 49
JENNINGS, MARIETTA, sister
   Notes on Joseph Hertzog, an early Philadel-
   phia merchant. BHR 14:65-76 Nov 40
JENSEN, ADOLPH LADRU
   and Miller, R. W. Failures of farmers'
   cooperatives. HBR 25:213-26 no.2, 47
   Integrating economic and legal thought on
   agricultural cooperatives. JFE 31,pt.2:
   891-907 Nov 49
JENSEN, ARNE
   Stochastic processes applied to a simple
   problem of administrative economy.
   NTTO 12:151-55 no.37, 48
JENSEN, EINAR
   Determining input-output relationships in
   milk production. JFE 22:249-58 Feb 40
   Comparison of results of two methods of
   analysis. JFE 22:769-72 Nov 40
   Rehabilitation of agriculture in German-
   occupied Europe. JFE 26:31-45 Feb 44
JENSEN, JAMES C. and Beck, P. G.
   Contributions of Farm Security Administra-
   tion borrowers to agricultural production
   goals: the corn-belt states. JFE 25:
   101-04 Feb 43
JENSEN, VERNON HORTIN
   Pensions and retirement plans as a subject
   of collective bargaining. ILRR 2:227-36
   Jan 49
JERVIS, F. R. J.
   The handicap of Britain's early start.
   MS 15:112-22 Jan 47
   Gas and electricity in Britain: a study in
   duopoly. LE 24:31-39 Feb 48
JESNESS, OSCAR BERNARD
   Personnel training and recruitment in agri-
   cultural economics: discussion. JFE 22:
   78-80 Feb 40
   Federal-state relationships in agriculture.
   JFE 22:493-95 May 40
   Newly developing international situation and
   American agriculture. JFE 23:1-14
   Feb 41
   Distribution of farm benefit payments.
   JFE 23:873-77 Nov 41
   Postwar agricultural policy: pressure vs.
   general welfare. JFE 28:1-14 Feb 46
   and P[ond], G. A. Andrew Boss, 1867-1947.
   [obit.] JFE 29:355-57 Feb 47
   chairman. Agricultural policy. [Panel dis-
   cussion] JFE 31,pt.2:213-26 Feb 49
   Foreign trade policy: which way? JFE 31,
   pt.2:814-24 Nov 49
JESSEN, RAYMOND J.
   with Goodsell, W. D. and Wilcox, W. W.
   Procedures which increase the useful-

ness of farm management research.
   JFE 22:753-61 Nov 40
   The master sample project and its use in
   agricultural economics. JFE 29:531-40
   May 47
JEUCK, JOHN EDWARD
   Direct-mail advertising to doctors. JB 13:
   17-38 Jan 40
   On the nature of marketing costs. JB 16:
   7-13 Jan 43
JEWETT, FRANK B. [and others]
   Patent policy: discussion. AER/S 38:245-60
   May 48
JEWKES, JOHN
   Is British industry inefficient? MS 14,no.1:
   1-16 Jan 46
   Second thoughts on the British White Paper
   on employment policy. MS 14,no.2:65-84
   May 46
   Variety among the planners. MS 15:93-111
   Jan 47
   and Devons, E. The Economic survey for
   1947. R. LBR 4:1-10 Apr·47
JOHN, ARTHUR HENRY
   Iron and coal on a Glamorgan estate, 1700-
   1740. EHR 13:93-103 no.1-2, 43
JOHNSON, ALBERT REX
   Some international angles on postwar agri-
   cultural trade. JM 11:174-78 Oct 46
JOHNSON, ALVIN
   The coming peace crisis. SR 11:305-11
   Sep 44
   and Hamburger, E. The economic problem
   of Germany. SR 13:135-82 Jun 46
   The economic position of Israel. SR 15:
   395-402 Dec 48
   The theory of the nth wages round. SR 16:
   416-24 Dec 49
JOHNSON, ARNO HALLOCK
   Advertising and marketing opportunities in
   the postwar period. JM 10:113-27 Oct 45
   Market potentials, 1948. HBR 26:11-31
   Jan 48
JOHNSON, BYRON LINDBERG
   Denver adopts local sales tax. NTJ 1:184-86
   Jun 48
   Income tax deductibility: a reply. NTJ 2:
   88-89 Mar 49
JOHNSON, DAVID GALE
   Contribution of price policy to the income
   and resource problems in agriculture.
   JFE 26:631-64 Nov 44
   A price policy for agriculture, consistent
   with economic progress, that will promote
   adequate and more stable income from
   farming. (The second award paper)
   JFE 27:761-72 Nov 45
   and Nicholls, W. H. The farm price policy
   awards, 1945: a topical digest of the win-
   ning essays. JFE 28:267-83 Feb 46
   Reconciling agricultural and foreign trade
   policies. JPE 55:567-71 Dec 47
   The high cost of food: a suggested solution.
   JPE 56:54-57 Feb 48

JOHNSON, DAVID GALE (Cont.)
    The use of econometric models in the study
        of agricultural policy. JFE 30:117-30
        Feb 48
    Mobility as a field of economic research.
        SEJ 15:152-61 Oct 48
    Allocation of agricultural income. JFE 30:
        724-49 Nov 48
    Food production: discussion. JFE 31,pt.2:
        262-65 Feb 49
    High level support prices and corn belt ag-
        riculture. JFE 31:509-19 Aug 49
JOHNSON, EDGAR AUGUSTUS JEROME
    New tools for the economic historian.
        JEH/S 1:30-38 Dec 41
JOHNSON, EDWIN CHARLES
    What elements enter into a desirable resale
        policy? JFE 22:285-91 Feb 40
JOHNSON, GERALD C.
    Effective marketing begins on the design
        board. JM 13:32-36 Jul 48
JOHNSON, GLEN LEROY
    Problem of farm business survival: discus-
        sion. JFE 31:pt.2:953-54 Nov 49
JOHNSON, HARRY GORDON
    An error in Ricardo's exposition of his
        theory of rent. QJE 62:792-93 Nov 48
    Malthus on the high price of provisions.
        CJE 15:190-202 May 49
    Demand for commodities is not demand for
        labour. EJ 59:531-36 Dec 49
JOHNSON, HERBERT WEBSTER
    Using an income index to forecast sales of
        service wholesale druggists. JM 9:43-48
        Jul 44
JOHNSON, HILDEGARD BINDER
    Factors influencing the distribution of the
        German pioneer population in Minnesota.
        AH 19:39-57 Jan 45
JOHNSON, HUGH A.
    and Wehrwein, G. S. Zoning land for recrea-
        tion. LE 18:47-57 Feb 42
    and Wehrwein, G. S. A recreation livelihood
        area. LE 19:193-206 May 43
    and Paarlberg, D. A method of predicting
        numbers of hens and pullets on Indiana
        farms January 1. JFE 30:756-61 Nov 48
JOHNSON, NEIL W.
    Conservation: an objective or an ideal?
        JFE 23:819-32 Nov 41
    Needed developments in the evaluation of
        soil conservation benefits. JFE 24:139-51
        Feb 42
    with Johnson, S. E. and Tetro, R. C. Re-
        sources available for agricultural produc-
        tion in 1943. JFE 25:65-83 Feb 43
    Wartime experience in production adjust-
        ment research and future possibilities.
        JFE 27:903-23 Nov 45
JOHNSON, NORRIS OLIVER
    Federal Reserve Bank of New York indexes
        of production and trade. JASA 36:423-25
        Sep 41

JOHNSON, OLIVER R.
    Farm-management research: discussion.
        JFE 23:232-36 Feb 41
    Developments in farm credit: discussion.
        JFE 26:138-43 Feb 44
    The family farm. JFE 26:529-48 Aug 44
JOHNSON, RICHARD BUHMANN
    The cost of legal reserve life insurance.
        SEJ 8:351-65 Jan 42
JOHNSON, RICHARD NEWHALL
    Facts and trends of government control af-
        fecting consumer economy. JM 8:5-12
        Jul 43
JOHNSON, ROBERT WOOD
    Executive myopia. JB 19:63-66 Apr 46
    An employer looks at labor-management
        relations. ILRR 1:486-92 Apr 48
    Human relations in modern business. HBR 27:
        521-41 Sep 49
JOHNSON, SAMUEL YORKS
    Expediting in wartime. HBR 21:344-57
        no.3, 43
JOHNSON, SHERMAN ELLSWORTH
    and Rush, D. R. Orientation of farm-man-
        agement research to low-income farms.
        JFE 23:218-32 Feb 41
    Adapting agricultural programs for war
        needs. JFE 24:1-16 Feb 42
    with Tetro, R. C. and Johnson, N. W. Re-
        sources available for agricultural produc-
        tion in 1943. JFE 25:65-83 Feb 43
    Food production policies in wartime. JFE 25:
        545-59 Aug 43
    Effects of changes in output on farmers'
        costs and returns. JFE 27:176-85 Feb 45
    Agricultural production after the war.
        JFE 27:261-80 May 45
JOHNSON, STEWART
    Formula pricing class I milk under market
        orders. JFE 31,pt.2:428-33 Feb 49
JOHNSON, VERNON WEBSTER
    and Walker, H., Jr. Centralization and co-
        ordination of police power for land-con-
        trol measures. LE 17:17-26 Feb 41
    and Musbach, W. F. National Resources
        Board on land classification. LE 17:
        489-93 Nov 41
    Land economics in transition. LE 18:85-87
        Feb 42
    and Timmons, J. F. Public works on private
        land. JFE 26:665-84 Nov 44
    Twenty-five years of progress: Division of
        Land Economics. LE 21:54-64 Feb 45
    with Timmons, J. F. and Howenstine, E. J.,
        Jr. Rural public works. Pt.I-II. LE 23:
        12-21; 132-41 Feb,May 47
    Status of federal lands. JFE 29:745-52
        Aug 47
    The English Agricultural Act, 1947. LE 24:
        178-81 May 48
    Conservation aspects of land programs.
        LE 24:303-09 Aug 48
    Problem research. JFE 30:576-78 Aug 48

JOHNSON, VERNON WEBSTER (Cont.)
Land economics research. LE 25:155-64
May 49
JOHNSTON, BRUCE FOSTER
Japan: the race between food and population.
JFE 31:276-92 May 49
JOHNSTON, ERIC A.
Economists and the economy. JPE 52:160-63
Jun 44
JOHNSTON, JOSEPH
Irish agriculture then and now. MS 11:105-22
Oct 40
JOHNSTON, PAUL EVANS
Farm labor situation and its effect on agri-
cultural production in the corn belt.
JFE 25:278-86 Feb 43
JOLLY, A. L.
A new system of farm accounting. JFE 30:
500-17 Aug 48
JOLLY, PIERRE
Aspects of the French economy. HBR 26:
257-66 May 48
JONES, CARRIE MAUDE
Urban planning and public opinion. LE 19:
87-89 Feb 43
JONES, CLAUDE
Adam Smith's library: some additions.
EH 4:326-28 Feb 40
JONES, EDGAR
Price leadership in the rayon industry.
MS 12:80-96 Oct 41
JONES, FRED MITCHELL
A new interpretation of marketing functions.
JM 7:256-60 Jan 43
The decline of Chicago as a grain futures
market. JM 12:61-65 Jul 47
JONES, GEORGE S., Jr.
Salesmanship's responsibility for the future.
JM 8:75-78 Jul 43
JONES, HERSCHEL FEDERMAN
The relation of large scale production to
certain costs of electric utilities in the
United States. LE 18:36-46 Feb 42
Forecasting the demand for electric energy:
a reply. LE 18:228-30 May 42
Midwest Power Conference. LE 18:224-25
May 42
In the matter of the rates and service of the
New Haven Water Company. LE 19:377-79
Aug 43
JONES, HOMER
A general appraisal of present rules and
procedures [of bank supervision], 1929-39.
[Summary] AER/S 30:230-32 Mar 40
An appraisal of the rules and procedures of
bank supervision, 1929-39. JPE 48:
183-98 Apr 40
Investment prospects. JF 2,no.1:15-33 Apr 47
The optimum rate of investment, the savings
institutions, and the banks. AER/S 38:
321-39 May 48
The flow of savings. Pt.I-II. JF 3,no.3:1-26;
4:28-46 Oct 48, Mar 49

JONES, HOWARD L.
Note on square-root charts. Em 14:313-15
Oct 46
JONES, JOHN HARRY
The Report of the Royal Commission on the
Distribution of the Industrial Population.
JRSS 103:323-30 pt.3, 40
[and others] Cost of living subsidies.
JRSS 111:99-111 pt.2, 48
JONES, LAWRENCE A.
Risks in agricultural lending: discussion.
JFE 31,pt.2:611-13 Feb 49
JONES, MARTIN VINCENT
Wage-rate reductions as a stimulus to re-
covery. JB 14:68-82 Jan 41
Secular and cyclical saving propensities.
JB 17:1-15 Jan 44
JONES, PHILLIP EUGENE
with Mason, J. E. and Elvove, J. T. New
settlement in the delta of the lower
Mississippi Valley. LE 17:465-76 Nov 41
Postwar adjustments in cotton production in
the southeastern United States. LE 21:
339-51 Sep 45
JONES, ROBERT LESLIE
The Canadian agricultural tariff of 1843.
CJE 7:528-37 Nov 41
French-Canadian agriculture in the St.
Lawrence Valley, 1815-1850. AH 16:
137-48 Jul 42
The agricultural development of Lower
Canada, 1850-1867. AH 19:212-24 Oct 45
JONES, RONALD WADE
Production costs as criteria of resource
allocation and policy. JFE 30:443-66
Aug 48
JONES, WILLIAM ORVILLE
Impact of the war on United States flour
consumption. JFE 30:518-36 Aug 48
A California case study in location theory:
the globe artichoke on the Moro Cojo.
JFE 31:538-44 Aug 49
JONGH, THEUNIS WILLEM DE
see De Jongh, Theunis Willem
JORDAN, GARRET LOWELL
[Soil conservation benefits]: discussion.
JFE 24:153-56 Feb 42
JORDAN, WEYMOUTH T.
The management rules of an Alabama black
belt plantation, 1848-1862. AH 18:53-64
Jan 44
The Elisha F. King family planters of the
Alabama black belt. AH 19:152-62 Jul 45
JORGENSEN, E. A. and Caparoon, C. D.
Agricultural data needs in extension work.
JFE 30:282-91 May 48
JØRGENSEN, Frits and Grøn, A. H.
Calculation of sylvicultural balance-numbers.
NTTO 12:123-31 no.37, 48
JORGENSON, LLOYD P.
Agricultural expansion into the semiarid
lands of the west north central states dur-
ing the first World War. AH 23:30-40
Jan 49

JOSEPH, JULIUS JOSEPH
  The mobilization of man-power. S&S 7:2-13
    no.1, 43
  European recovery and United States aid.
    S&S 12:293-383 no.3, 48
  Trends in the Marshall Plan. S&S 13:1-21
    no.1, 49
JOSEPH, MARGARET F. W.
  The British White Paper on employment
    policy. AER 34:561-67 Sep 44
JOSHI, TRYAMBAK MAHADEV
  The functions of economic analysis. IJE 20:
    773-78 Apr 40
  The "depression finance" of the Bombay
    government. IJE 21:605-17 Apr 41
  A critique of "Indian economics." IJE 22:
    276-79 Jan 42
  Some economic and financial problems of the
    transition from war to peace. IJE 25:
    224-35 Jan 45
JOSS, ALEXANDER
  Repayment experience on federal reclama-
    tion projects. JFE 27:153-67 Feb 45
  Some possible limitations of zoning
    ordinances as devices for controlling land
    settlement. LE 21:154-59 May 45
  Benefits from irrigation under sub-humid
    conditions. JFE 28:543-59 May 46
JOY, ARYNESS
  see Wickens, Aryness Joy
JUCIUS, MICHAEL JAMES
  Historical development of uniform accounting.
    JB 16:219-29 Oct 43
  Uniform accounting and pricing policies.
    JB 17:37-50 Jan 44
JUDD, P. R.
  Indifference curves and the rate of interest
    on government securities. ER 17:232-39
    Dec 41
JULIAN, VANCE
  Mediation of labor disputes in Missouri
    public utilities. IRRA 2:255-61 Dec 49
JULIBER, GUSTAVE S.
  Relation between seasonal amplitudes and
    the level of production; an application to
    the production of steel ingots. JASA 36:
    485-92 Dec 41
JURKAT, DOROTHY B.
  see Jurkat, Ernest Herman and Jurkat, D. B.
JURKAT, ERNEST HERMAN and Jurkat, D. B.
  Economic function of strikes. ILRR 2:527-45
    Jul 49
JUSTIN, brother
  see Cornelius Justin, brother
KAFKA, ALEXANDER
  Professor Hicks's theory of money interest.
    AER 31:327-29 Jun 41
KAHLE, HUMBERT S.
  Notes on "The economies of public meas-
    ures to subsidize food consumption," with
    an extension of the economic principles
    outlined to individual commodities. JFE 27:
    683-86 Aug 45

KÄHLER, ALFRED
  The prospects of inflation. SR 8:156-72
    May 41
  On the economics of war finance. SR 9:
    458-75 Nov 42
  The public debt in the financial structure.
    SR 11:11-26 Feb 44
  The British devaluation. SR 16:474-88
    Dec 49
KAHN, ALFRED EDWARD
  Fundamental deficiencies of the American
    patent law. AER 30:475-91 Sep 40
  Palestine: a problem in economic evaluation.
    AER 34:538-60 Sep 44
  The British balance of payments and prob-
    lems of domestic policy. QJE 61:368-96
    May 47
  [and others] Patent policy: discussion.
    AER/S 38:245-60 May 48
  The burden of import duties: a comment.
    AER 38:857-67 Dec 48
KAHN, ELLISON
  The study of economic history in South
    Africa and the concept of the "frontier
    spirit." R. SAJE 10:36-46 Mar 42
  Whither our war-time Native policy?
    SAJE 10:126-52 Jun 42
  The right to strike in South Africa: an
    historical analysis. SAJE 11:24-47
    Mar 43
  The Report of the Social Security Committee:
    some reflections. SAJE 12:63-66 Mar 44
  Death duties in South Africa. SAJE 14:81-99
    Jun 46
  Keynes' influence on theory and public policy.
    R. SAJE 16:70-74 Mar 48
KAHN, HERMAN
  Records in the National Archives relating to
    the range cattle industry, 1865-1895.
    AH 20:187-90 Jul 46
KAHN, RICHARD FERDINAND
  Tariffs and the terms of trade. REStud 15:
    14-19 no.1, 47
  Professor Meade on planning. R. EJ 59:1-16
    Mar 49
  The International Bank for Reconstruction
    and Development. R. EJ 59:445-47 Sep 49
  A possible intra-European payments scheme.
    Ec N.S.16:293-304 Nov 49
KAISSOUNI, A. M.
  Oil in the Middle East. EgC 39:263-94
    Mar 48
KALDOR, DONALD R.
  Farm labor situation in Iowa. JFE 25:
    295-97 Feb 43
KALDOR, NICHOLAS
  [Money wage cuts in relation to unemploy-
    ment.] A comment. REStud 7:137 Feb 40
  The trade cycle and capital intensity: a reply.
    Ec N.S.7:16-22 Feb 40
  A model of the trade cycle. EJ 50:78-92
    Mar 40
  A note on the theory of the forward market.
    REStud 7:196-201 Jun 40

KALECKI, MICHAEL (Cont.)

Excess profits tax and post-war re-equipment. OIS 6:58-61 Mar 18, 44

Professor Pigou on "The classical stationary
state": a comment. EJ 54:131-32 Apr 44

The budget: A. The stabilisation policy.
OIS 6:101-04 May 20, 44

The White Paper on employment policy.
OIS 6:131-35 Jun 10, 44

The White Paper on the national income and
expenditure in the years 1938-1943.
OIS 6:137-44 Jul 1, 44

Employment in the United Kingdom during
and after the transition period. OIS 6:
265-87 Dec 4, 44

Full employment by stimulating private investment? OEP 7:83-92 Mar 45

On the Gibrat distribution. Em 13:161-70
Apr 45

The work of Erwin Rothbarth. REStud 12:
121-22 no.2, 45

A comment on "monetary policy." REStat 28:
81-84 May 46

Multilateralism and full employment.
CJE 12:322-27 Aug 46

The maintenance of full employment after
the transition period: a rejoinder to Mr.
Woytinsky's note. AER 37:391-97 Jun 47

Determinants of the increase in the cost of
living in the United States. REStat 30:
22-24 Feb 48

Further comments on the Department of
Commerce series. REStat 30:195-97
Aug 48

A new approach to the problem of business
cycles. REStud 16:57-64 no.2, 49

KALLEN, HORACE MEYER

The American worker and his education.
SR 11:100-11 Feb 44

KAMM, JACOB OSWALD

American security price movements compared to foreign security price movements.
JF 3,no.2:59-70 Jun 48

KANE, LUCILE M.

Federal protection of public timber in the
upper Great Lake States. AH 23:135-39
Apr 49

KANTOROVITZ, PAUL P.

The future of world trade: towards the International Trade Conference, 1946. EgC 36:
609-762 Dec 45

KAPLAN, DAVID

Postwar labor problems: discussion.
AER/S 34:195-98 Mar 44

KAPLAN, H. ELIOT

Concepts of public employee relations.
ILRR 1:206-30 Jan 48

KAPLAN, JACOB JULIUS

Rationing objectives and allotments, illustrated with sugar data. JFE 24:647-64
Aug 42

Some problems in rationing meats.
REStat 24:159-65 Nov 42

KAPLAN, MORTIMER

A method of analyzing the elements of foreclosure risk. JASA 37:247-55 Jun 42

KAPP, KARL WILLIAM

Rational human conduct and modern industrial society. SEJ 10:136-50 Oct 43

Teaching of economics: a new approach.
SEJ 12:376-83 Apr 46

Methods of visual presentation and the
teaching of economics. AER 37:652-54
Sep 47

KARMEL, PETER HENRY

Fertility and marriages, Australia 1933-42.
ER 20:74-80 Jun 44

The relation between Laspeyre's and
Paasche's index numbers for measuring
price changes. ER 21:261-64 Dec 45

Population replacement: Australia, 1947.
ER 25,(no.49):83-88 Dec 49

KARVE, DATTATRAYA GOPAL

Value in a socialistic state. IJE 21:456-69
Apr 41

Ranade and economic planning. IJE 22:
235-44 Jan 42

Towards progress in economics: a plea for
strengthening its foundations and broadening its scope. IJE 26:685-715 Apr 46

Free trade among nations: American proposals. IJE 27:279-85 Jan 47

The late Prof. V. G. Kale of Poona. [obit.]
IJE 27:335-37 Jan 47

KARWAL, G. D.

The scope of economics: economics and
practice. IJE 20:749-59 Apr 40

Is economics non-moral? IJE 24:75-80
Jul 43

KAST, MATTHEUS

American interstate motor tourist traffic.
SEJ 7:529-37 Apr 41

KATKOFF, VLADIMIR

Financing of agriculture in Russia. JFE 22:
640-46 Aug 40

KATONA, GEORGE

and Leavens, D. H. Price increases and uptrading: the change in advertised prices
of apparel and house furnishings. JB 17:
231-43 Oct 44

Psychological analysis of business decisions
and expectations. AER 36:44-62 Mar 46

and Likert, R. Relationship between consumer expenditures and savings: the
contribution of survey research.
REStat 28:197-99 Nov 46

Contribution of psychological data to economic analysis. JASA 42:449-59 Sep 47

Effect of income changes on the rate of saving. REStat 31:95-103 May 49

Analysis of dissaving. AER 39:673-88 Jun 49

KATZ, DANIEL

Good and bad practices in attitude surveys in
industrial relations. IRRA 2:212-21
Dec 49

KATZ, MILTON
Round table on preserving competition versus
regulating monopoly. [Summary of re-
marks] AER/S 30:215-17 Mar 40
A case study in international organization.
HBR 25:1-20 no.1, 46
KAUFMAN, JACOB J.
Farm labor during World War II. JFE 31:
131-42 Feb 49
Economics of minimum wages in relation to
the agricultural labor market. JFE 31:
716-25 Nov 49
KAUFMANN, FELIX
On the postulates of economic theory. SR 9:
379-95 Sep 42
KAYSEN, CARL
A revolution in economic theory? R.
REStud 14:1-15 no.1, 46
and Lorie, J. H. A note on Professor
Schultz's analysis of the long run agricul-
tural problem. REStat 30:286-97 Nov 48
A dynamic aspect of the monopoly problem.
REStat 31:109-13 May 49
Basing point pricing and public policy.
QJE 63:289-314 Aug 49
KAZAKÉVICH, VLADIMIR D.
The war and American finance. S&S 4:153-67
no.2, 40
The economic strength of the Soviet Union.
S&S 5:385-89 no.4, 41
KEATING, JOHN M. and Brissenden, P. F.
Union-management co-operation in millinery
manufacturing in the New York metropoli-
tan area. ILRR 2:3-32 Oct 48
KEBKER, VANT WILMOT
Operation of the Unfair Trade Practices Act
in the large cities of Kansas. JM 7:22-31
Jul 42
Will grade labeling pay? JM 8:185-88 Oct 43
KEEZER, DEXTER MERRIAM
Observations on rationing and price control
in Great Britain. AER 33:264-82 Jun 43
[and others] Postwar labor relations: discus-
sion. AER/S 36:370-83 May 46
Observations on the operations of the National
War Labor Board. AER 36:233-57 Jun 46
chairman. The effectiveness of the federal
antitrust laws: a symposium. AER 39:
689-724 Jun 49
KEFAUVER, ESTES
Needed changes in [anti-trust] legislation.
AER/S 38:182-202 May 48
KEILHAU, WILHELM
Main trends in Norway's economy. LBR 9:
21-33 Jul 48
KEIRSTEAD, BURTON SEELEY
The effects of the war on the concept of
national interest. CJE 8:197-212 May 42
Technical advance and economic equilibria.
CJE 9:55-68 Feb 43
A note on "equilibrium in process." CJE 9:
235-42 May 43
Liberty and a planned economy. R. CJE 11:
281-85 May 45

and Cooke, D. H. Dynamic theory of rents.
CJE 12:168-72 May 46
The dynamic theory of rents: a rejoinder.
CJE 13:285 May 47
and Mankiewicz, R. H. The works of
François Simiand. R. CJE 14:249-54
May 48
Economic man in relation to his natural en-
vironment. R. CJE 15:231-36 May 49
KELLETT, W. G. G.
International rubber statistics. JRSS 112:
419-35 pt.4, 49
KELLEY, DARWIN N.
The McNary-Haugen Bills, 1924-1928: an
attempt to make the tariff effective for
farm products. AH 14:170-80 Oct 40
KELLEY, PEARCE CLEMENT
Former occupations of small scale retailers.
JM 5:35-37 Jul 40
KELLOCK, JAMES
Ranade and after: a study of the development
of economic thought in India. IJE 22:
245-60 Jan 42
KELLOGG, CHARLES E.
Contributions of soil science and agronomy
to rural land classification. JFE 22:
729-39 Nov 40
The natural sciences and farm planning.
JFE 29:183-89 Feb 47
Food production potentialities and problems.
JFE 31,pt.2:251-62 Feb 49
KELLY, I. M.
Paper industries in war-time. I. Rationing
of paper in war-time. ER 17:218-24
Dec 41
KELLY, MATTHEW A.
Communists in German labor organizations.
JPE 57:213-26 Jun 49
KELLY, ROSS ANTHONY
The North-Central States Regional Potato
Marketing Project controlled retail store
experiment. JFE 31,pt.2:626-30 Feb 49
KELLY, THOMAS HERBERT
Social and economic statistics in the Union.
R. SAJE 13:304-17 Dec 45
KELLY, W. S.
Primary products prices. ER 19:162-70
Dec 43
KELSO, HAROLD
Waterways versus railways. AER 31:537-44
Sep 41
"Navigable waters" as a legal fiction. LE 17:
394-405 Nov 41
Inland waterway carriers. LE 18:58-66
Feb 42
KELSO, MAURICE M.
[Needed points of development and reorienta-
tion in land economic theory: summary of]
discussions. JFE 22:46-51 Feb 40
Needed research in farm tenancy. JFE 23:
291-304 Feb 41
Current issues in federal land management
in the western United States. JFE 29:
1295-1314 Nov 47

KELSO, MAURICE M. (Cont.)
New directions for land economics research:
West. JFE 31,pt.2:1035-42 Nov 49

KEMMERER, DONALD LORENZO
The pre-Civil War South's leading crop,
corn. AH 23:236-39 Oct 49

KEMMERER, EDWIN WALTER and Howard,
S. E.
Frank Albert Fetter. A birthday note.
AER 33:230-35 Mar 43

KEMP, ARTHUR
A terminological note on indifference curves.
SEJ 8:88-92 Jul 41
Professor Whittaker on indifference curves.
AER 31:569-70 Sep 41
Chromium: a strategic material. HBR 20:
199-212 no.2, 42

KEMP, MURRAY C.
Interest and the money supply in Keynes'
economics. ER 25,(no.49):64-73 Dec 49

KENDALL, MAURICE GEORGE
The financing of British agriculture.
JRSS 104:111-35 pt.2, 41
Oscillatory movements in English agricul-
ture. JRSS 106:91-117 pt.2, 43
Losses of U.K. merchant ships in World War
II. Ec N.S.15:289-93 Nov 48
United Kingdom merchant shipping statistics.
JRSS 111:133-44 pt.2, 48
The estimation of parameters in linear auto-
regressive time series. Em 17,suppl.:
44-56 Jul 49

KENDRICK, MYRON SLADE
Round table on the incidence of taxation.
[Summary of discussion] AER/S 30:245
Mar 40
Comment on Incidence of taxation. AER 31:
110 Mar 41

KENKEL, JOSEPH B.
Teaching economics in college. RSE 6:85-91
May 48

KENNEDY, CHARLES
Period analysis and the demand for money.
REStud 16:41-49 no.1, 48

KENNEDY, CHARLES JOHNSTON
Introducing college freshmen to business
history. BHR 22:57-63 Apr 48

KENNEDY, MAYNARD THOMAS
see Kennedy, Thomas

KENNEDY, PAUL V.
Labor's participation in management: ethical
aspects. RSE 5:49-58 Jun 47

KENNEDY, THOMAS
with Beale, W. T. M., Jr. and Winn, W. J.
Commodity reserve currency: a critique.
JPE 50:579-94 Aug 42
The handling of emergency disputes. IRRA 2:
14-27 Dec 49

KENNEDY, WILLIAM FRANCIS
Regulation of utility servicing under the
Holding Company Act of 1935. Pt.I-III.
LE 17:27-38; 171-87; 257-69 Feb,May,
Aug 41

Recent developments in service company
regulations. LE 18:100-02 Feb 42

KENNET, [EDWARD HILTON YOUNG, baron]
What did Mr. Malthus say in 1798? LBR 2:
18-24 Oct 46

KEPNER, PAUL V.
[County planning project]: discussion.
JFE 22:305-10 Feb 40

KERR, CLARK
The short-run behavior of physical produc-
tivity and average hourly earnings.
REStat 31:299-309 Nov 49
Labor markets: their character and conse-
quences. IRRA 2:69-84 Dec 49

KERR, PEYTON and Burns, A. E.
Recent changes in work-relief wage policy.
AER 31:56-66 Mar 41

KERRICH, J. E.
[Returns to capital invested in the gold
mining industry in South Africa.] Comment. SAJE 17:184 Jun 49

KERSHAW, JOSEPH ALEXANDER
Postwar Brazilian economic problems.
AER 38:328-40 Jun 48

KESAVA IYENGAR, S.
see Iyengar, S. Kesava

KESSLER, WILLIAM CONRAD
A statistical study of the New York General
Incorporation Act of 1811. JPE 48:877-82
Dec 40
Incorporation in New England: a statistical
study, 1800-1875. JEH 8:43-62 May 48

KESTNBAUM, MEYER
A study in management prerogatives.
HBR 19:88-98 no.1, 40

KETCHUM, MARSHALL DANA
Working-capital financing in a war economy.
JB 15:306-42 Oct 42
Plant financing in a war economy. JB 16:
28-50 Jan 43
The financial problem of small business.
Pt.I-II. JB 17:67-90; 162-85 Apr,Jul 44
Investment management through formula
timing plans. JB 20:156-69 Jul 47
Adjustment for the secular trend of stock
prices in formula timing plans. JB 21:
29-49 Jan 48
Can life insurance companies use formula
plans? JB 22:30-49 Jan 49
The effects of federal income taxation on the
form of external financing: discussion.
JF 4:222-26 Sep 49

KEWLEY, T. H.
The Commonwealth social security reports.
R. ER 18:223-26 Dec 42

KEYES, SCOTT
Converted residences and the supply of hous-
ing. LE 16:47-51 Feb 40
Some considerations in the economic possi-
bilities of slum clearance. LE 18:204-09
May 42

KEYFITZ, NATHAN
The sampling approach to economic data.
CJE 11:467-77 Aug 45

KEYNES, JOHN MAYNARD
  The concept of national income: a supple-
    mentary note. EJ 50:60-65 Mar 40
  [On a method of statistical business-cycle
    research.] Comment. EJ 50:154-56
    Mar 40
  [The measurement of real income: reply to
    A. L. Bowley.] EJ 50:341 Jun-Sep 40
  Henry Higgs (March 4, 1864-May 21, 1940).
    [obit.] EJ 50:555-58 Dec 40
  The Society's jubilee 1890-1940. EJ 50:
    401-09 Dec 40
  The objective of international price stability.
    EJ 53:185-87 Jun-Sep 43
  Leonard Darwin (1850-1943). [obit.] EJ 53:
    438-39 Dec 43
  Mary Paley Marshall (1850-1944). [obit.]
    EJ 54:268-84 Jun-Sep 44
  Note. [Reply to F. D. Graham] EJ 54:429-30
    Dec 44
  The balance of payments of the United States.
    EJ 56:172-87 Jun 46
KHALIL, K. F.
  Pakistan's foreign trade: analysis and pros-
    pects. PEJ 1,no.1:69-77 Jul 49
KHAN, AFTAB AHMAD
  The State Bank of Pakistan. PEJ 1,no.1:
    96-101 Jul 49
KHAN, ALI ASGHAR
  Problems of "rural labour and wages" in the
    West Punjab. PEJ 1,no.1:40-61 Jul 49
KHAN, KHAN MUHAMMAD BASHIR AHMAD
  Co-operation in Pakistan multipurposes
    societies (with special reference to West
    Punjab). PEJ 1,no.1:78-95 Jul 49
KHAN, MOHAMMAD MUSA
  Economic planning for national nutrition.
    PEJ 1,no.1:24-28 Jul 49
KHAN, MOHAMMAD YUNUS
  Review of co-operation in N.-W.F.P.
    PEJ 1,no.2:42-47 Oct 49
KIBE, M. V.
  Problems of agricultural labour. IJE 28:
    175-77 Jul 47
  Monetary policy and inflation in India: debase-
    ment of currency and its effect. IJE 30:
    197-98 Oct 49
KIDD, CHARLES V.
  The Latimer report: 2. Relationship of
    guaranteed wages to unemployment com-
    pensation. ILRR 1:470-80 Apr 48
KIDNER, FRANK LEROY
  The variation in wage ratios: comment.
    QJE 55:314-18 Feb 41
  [and others] Interregional variations in eco-
    nomic fluctuations: discussion. AER/S 39:
    120-34 May 49
KIFER, RUSSELL STANLEY
  Farm management research: discussion.
    JFE 22:130-37 Feb 40
KILDUFF, VERA REYNOLDS
  see Russell, Vera Kilduff

KILEY, JOHN C.
  Changes in realty values in the nineteenth
    and twentieth centuries. BHR 15:33-41
    Jun 41
KILLEEN, EDWARD C.
  Ethics, data for the economist. RSE 7,no.1:
    8-21 Mar 49
KILLINGSWORTH, CHARLES CLINTON
  Public regulation of labor relations: the
    Wisconsin experiment. AER 33:247-63
    Jun 43
  [and others] Can capitalism dispense with
    free labor markets? Discussion. IRRA 2:
    100-14 Dec 49
KIMBALL, BRADFORD F.
  General theory of plant account subject to
    constant mortality law of retirements.
    Em 11:61-82 Jan 43
  The failure of the unit-summation procedure
    as a group method of estimating depre-
    ciation. Em 13:225-44 Jul 45
  and Benson, C. B. Mortality characteristics
    of physical property based upon location
    life table and re-use ratios. Em 13:
    214-24 Jul 45
  A system of life tables for physical property
    based on the truncated normal distribu-
    tion. Em 15:342-60 Oct 47; Errata. 21:
    370 Apr 53
KIMBALL, ELIAS SMITH
  Characteristics of U.S. poultry statistics.
    JFE 22:359-66 Feb 40
KIMMEL, ROY I.
  Unit reorganization program for the southern
    Great Plains. JFE 22:264-69 Feb 40
KINDLEBERGER, CHARLES POOR
  Planning for foreign investment. AER/S 33:
    347-54 Mar 43
  The foreign-trade multiplier, the propensity
    to import and balance-of-payments equil-
    ibrium. AER 39:491-94 Mar 49
  [Induced investment, overcomplete inter-
    national adjustment, and chronic dollar
    shortage.] Rejoinder. AER 39:975 Sep 49
KING, ARNOLD J.
  and Simpson, G. D. New developments in ag-
    ricultural sampling. JFE 22:341-49 Feb 40
  and McCarty, D. E. Application of sampling
    to agricultural statistics with emphasis
    on stratified samples. JM 5:462-73 Apr 41
KING, FRANK P.
  Developing a technique for determining types
    of farming. JFE 30:350-57 May 48
KING, HERBERT WILLIAM HENRY
  The New Zealand budget, 1941-1942, 1942-
    1943, 1943-1944. ER 17:265-71; 18:217-22;
    19:237-40 Dec 41, Dec 42, Dec 43
  The New Zealand government finances,
    1945-46--1947-48 [i.e., 1948-49]. ER 22:
    293-98; 23:271-74; 24:254-56; 25,(no.49):
    98-99 Dec 46-Dec 49
KING, JOE JUDSON
  Comments on "Trends in agricultural coop-
    eration." JFE 25:506-09 May 43

KING, JOE JUDSON (Cont.)
  FSA group services in the Pacific Northwest.
    HBR 22:475-76 no.4, 44
KING, WILFRED THOMAS COUSINS
  The Bank of England. R. EHR 15:67-72
    no.1-2, 45
KINGERY, ROBERT
  Cook County amends rural subdivision regu-
    lations. LE 16:218-19 May 40
KINGSBURY, LAURA MABEL
  What is housing economics?  LE 17:354-57
    Aug 41
KINGSTON, CEYLON SAMUEL and Oliphant,
  J. O.
  William Emsley Jackson's diary of a cattle
    drive from La Grande, Oregon, to
    Cheyenne, Wyoming, in 1876.  AH 23:
    260-73 Oct 49
KINTER, CHARLES V.
  Cyclical considerations in the marketing
    problem of the newspaper industry.
    JM 11:66-70 Jul 46
  The newspaper in two postwar periods.
    JM 13:371-72 Jan 49
KINTZI, JACK
  Coordination of the Nebraska public power
    districts. LE 16:481-83 Nov 40
KIRCHBERGER, HANS
  An ancient experience with price control.
    JFE 24:621-36 Aug 42
KIRCHER, PAUL
  Common dollar accounting for investments.
    JB 22:242-48 Oct 49
KIRKENFELD, THOMAS
  The paradox of profit.  S&S 12:33-41 no.1, 48
KIRKLAND, EDWARD CHASE
  The "Railroad scheme" of Massachusetts.
    JEH 5:145-71 Nov 45
  The place of theory in teaching American
    economic history. JEH/S 9:99-102 '49
KIRKPATRICK, CHARLES ATKINSON
  An estimate of vacation travel expenditures
    for 1938: a challenge. JM 5:39-41 Jul 40
KIRKPATRICK, NORA BODDY
  and Black, J. D. The agricultural situation,
    March 1940. REStat 22:53-73 May 40
  and Hagen, E. E. The national output at full
    employment in 1950. AER 34:472-500
    Sep 44
KIRTY, V. S. RAMACHANDRA
  The classical theory of equilibrium and the
    monetary theory of the trade cycle.
    IJE 22:177-88 Oct 41
  The beginnings of monetary explanation of the
    trade cycle. IJE 25:491-502 Apr 45
KISSELGOFF, AVRAM
  Liquidity preference of large manufacturing
    corporations (1921-1939). Em 13:334-46
    Oct 45
  "Free money" of large manufacturing corpo-
    rations and the rate of interest: a reply.
    Em 14:254 Jul 46

KITCHIN, ALEXANDER WILLIAM MENZIES-
  see Menzies-Kitchin, Alexander William
KITTRIDGE, G. W.
  Services for sale.  JM 5:125-27 Oct 40
KLAASEN, ADRIAN J.
  Department of Agriculture on food prices.
    JM 13:386-87 Jan 49
KLAGSBRUNN, HANS A.
  Some aspects of war plant financing.
    AER/S 33:119-27 Mar 43
KLARMAN, HERBERT ELIAS
  Income tax deductibility. NTJ 1:241-49
    Sep 48
  --- A rejoinder. NTJ 2:89-90 Mar 49
KLEIN, BURTON
  Germany's preparation for war: a re-exami-
    nation. AER 38:56-77 Mar 48
KLEIN, LAWRENCE ROBERT
  The relationship between total output and
    man-hour output: comment. QJE 56:
    342-43 Feb 42
  Pitfalls in the statistical determination of
    the investment schedule. Em 11:246-58
    Jul-Oct 43
  --- A reply. Em 12:91-92 Jan 44
  The cost of a "Beveridge Plan" in the United
    States. QJE 58:423-37 May 44
  Macroeconomics and the theory of rational
    behavior. Em 14:93-108 Apr 46
  A post-mortem on transition predictions of
    national product. JPE 54:289-308 Aug 46
  Remarks on the theory of aggregation. Em 14:
    303-12 Oct 46
  Theories of effective demand and employment.
    JPE 55:108-32 Apr 47
  The use of econometric models as a guide to
    economic policy. Em 15:111-51 Apr 47
  Planned economy in Norway. AER 38:
    795-814 Dec 48
  Notes on the theory of investment. Kyk 2:
    97-117 fasc.2, 48
  A scheme of international compensation.
    Em 17:145-49 Apr 49
KLEMM, MARY
  The rise of independent unionism and the de-
    cline of labor oligopoly. AER 34:76-86
    Mar 44
KLING, WILLIAM
  Determination of relative risks involved in
    growing truck crops. JFE 24:694-98
    Aug 42
  A nutritional guide to wartime use of agricul-
    tural resources. JFE 25:683-91 Aug 43
  Food waste in distribution and use. JFE 25:
    848-59 Nov 43
KLOPSTOCK, FRED HERMAN
  Monetary reform in liberated Europe.
    AER 36:578-95 Sep 46
  Western Europe's attack on inflation.
    HBR 26:597-612 Sep 48
  Monetary reform in Western Germany.
    JPE 57:277-92 Aug 49

KLOVE, ROBERT C.
A technique for delimiting Chicago's blighted areas. LE 17:483-84 Nov 41

KNAF, HENRY G.
Socio-economic conditions and intercity variations of electric use. LE 18:431-46 Nov 42
Interstate differences in the saturation of wired homes, mechanical refrigerators and electric ranges, and their causes. LE 22:386-92 Nov 46

KNAPP, JOHN
The theory of international capital movements and its verifications. REStud 10: 115-21 no.2, 43

K[NAPP], J[OSEPH] G[RANT]
Ellis A. Stokdyk. [obit.] JFE 28:886 Aug 46

KNAUTH, OSWALD WHITMAN
Considerations in the setting of retail prices. JM 14:1-12 Jul 49

KNIGHT, BRUCE WINTON
Postwar costs of a new war. AER/S 30: 340-50 Mar 40

KNIGHT, FRANK HYNEMAN
"What is truth" in economics? R. JPE 48: 1-32 Feb 40
Professor Parsons on economic motivation. CJE 6:460-65 Aug 40
Anthropology and economics. R. JPE 49: 247-68 Apr 41
The business cycle, interest, and money: a methodological approach. REStat 23: 53-67 May 41
[The significance and basic postulates of economic theory.] A rejoinder. JPE 49: 750-53 Oct 41
Professor Mises and the theory of capital. R. Ec N.S.8:409-27 Nov 41
The role of the individual in the economic world of the future. JPE 49:817-32 Dec 41
Profit and entrepreneurial functions. JEH/S 2:126-32 Dec 42
Diminishing returns from investment. JPE 52: 26-47 Mar 44
Economics, political science, and education. AER/S 34:68-76 Mar 44
[and others] Political science, political economy, and values: discussion. AER/S 34:48-57 Mar 44
Realism and relevance in the theory of demand. JPE 52:289-318 Dec 44
Comment on Mr. Bishop's article [on the theory of demand]. JPE 54:170-76 Apr 46
Immutable law in economics: its reality and limitations. AER/S 36:93-111 May 46
Heimann's history of doctrine and current issues. R. JPE 54:363-67 Aug 46
Freedom under planning. R. JPE 54:451-54 Oct 46
Salvation by science: the gospel according to Professor Lundberg. R. JPE 55:537-52 Dec 47
Professor Heimann on religion and economics. R. JPE 56:480-97 Dec 48

Truth and relevance at bay. AER 39:1273-76 Dec 49

KNORR, KLAUS E.
Access to raw materials in the postwar world. HBR 21:385-96 no.3, 43
World rubber problems. HBR 24:394-404 no.3, 46
The functions of an International Trade Organization: possibilities and limitations. AER/S 37:542-53 May 47

KNOWLES, KENNETH GUY JACK CHARLES
Strikes & their changing economic context. OIS 9:285b-306 Sep 47

KNOX, FRANK ALBERT
Canadian war finance and the balance of payments, 1914-18. CJE 6:226-57 May 40
Some aspects of Canada's post-war export problem. CJE 10:312-27 Aug 44
The international gold standard reinterpreted. R. CJE 10:502-07 Nov 44
Canada's balance of international payments, 1940-5. CJE 13:345-62 Aug 47

KNOX, JAMES MILTON
and Mack, C. E. Disposition of government property. HBR 22:54-62 no.1, 43
Private enterprise in shipbuilding. HBR 24: 75-84 no.1, 45

KNUDSEN, LILA F.
Interdependence in a series. JASA 35:507-14 Sep 40

KOCK, KARIN
Swedish economic policy during the war. REStud 10:75-80 no.2, 43

KOCK, MICHIEL HENDRIK DE
see De Kock, Michiel Hendrik

KOEBNER, RICHARD
The concept of economic imperialism. EHR II.2:1-29 no.1, 49

KOED, HOLGER
Some aspects of the rationalization of public administration. NTTO 12:157-65 no.37, 48

KOFFSKY, NATHAN
Some statistical problems involved in types of farm income, by size. JFE 29:1257-66 Nov 47
An additional view on the consumption function. REStat 30:55-56 Feb 48
and Grove, E. W. Measuring the incomes of farm people. JFE 31,pt.2:1102-11 Nov 49

KOGEKAR, SADANAND VASUDEO
[and others] Discussion on "India and international economic co-operation." IJE 25: 626-29 Apr 45
Rural co-operation: the old approach and the new. IJE 27:291-97 Jan 47

KOJIMA, SHOTARO
Special currency system of China: a study on the "Wei Wah" system in Shanghai. Kyo 16, no.3:16-50 Jul 41
The Wei Wah system as a special credit system of China. Kyo 16,no.4:1-19 Oct 41
Financial circles in Shanghai following the outbreak of the Greater East Asia War. Kyo 18,no.2:1-26 Apr 43

KOJIMA, SHOTARO (Cont.)
   The origination and extinction of currency in
      the world of circulation. Kyo 18,no.4:
      1-18 Oct 43
KOLEHMAINEN, JOHN ILMARI
   Finland's agrarian structure and overseas
      migration. AH 15:44-48 Jan 41
   Finnish overseas emigration from arctic
      Norway and Russia. AH 19:224-32 Oct 45
KOLESNIKOFF, VLADIMIR S.
   Standard classification of industries in the
      United States. JASA 35:65-73 Mar 40
   Standard commodity classification. JASA 39:
      42-52 Mar 44
KOLKER, KENNETH K.
   The changing status of the foreman. BHR 22:
      84-105 Jun 48
KOLLER, E. FRED
   Cooperatives in a capitalistic economy.
      JFE 29:1133-44 Nov 47
KOLLMORGEN, WALTER M.
   Immigrant settlements in southern agricul-
      ture; a commentary on the significance of
      cultural islands in agricultural history.
      AH 19:69-78 Apr 45
   Crucial deficiencies of regionalism.
      AER/S 35:377-89 May 45
   and Harrison, R. W. The place of French-
      speaking farmers of southern Louisiana
      in future land development and reclama-
      tion projects. LE 22:223-31 Aug 46
   and Harrison, R. W. Past and prospective
      drainage reclamations in the coastal
      marshlands of the Mississippi River delta.
      LE 23:297-320 Aug 47
KOO, ANTHONY Y. C.
   Income elasticity of demand for imports and
      terms of trade. AER 39:966-70 Sep 49
KOONTZ, HAROLD D.
   Increased gas rates based upon higher taxes.
      LE 16:233-35 May 40
   [and others] Postwar railroad problems:
      discussion. AER/S 36:494-519 May 46
KOOPMANS, TJALLING CHARLES
   The degree of damping in business cycles.
      Em 8:79-89 Jan 40
   Distributed lags in dynamic economics.
      Em 9:128-34 Apr 41
   The logic of econometric business-cycle re-
      search. JPE 49:157-81 Apr 41
   The dynamics of inflation. REStat 24:53-65
      May 42
   --- A reply. REStat 24:190 Nov 42
   Durable consumers' goods and the prevention
      of post-war inflation. AER 33:882-88
      Dec 43
   Statistical estimation of simultaneous eco-
      nomic relations. JASA 40:448-66 Dec 45
   Measurement without theory. R. REStat 29:
      161-72 Aug 47
   Identification problems in economic model
      construction. Em 17:125-44 Apr 49
   The econometric approach to business fluc-

tuations. AER/S 39:64-72 May 49
   [and others] Input-output analysis and its
      use in peace and war economies: discus-
      sion. AER/S 39:226-40 May 49
   [Koopmans on the choice of variables to be
      studied and of methods of measurement.]
      A reply. REStat 31:86-91 May 49
   Optimum utilization of the transportation
      system. Em 17,suppl.:136-45 Jul 49;
      Errata. 19:227 Apr 51
KORICAN, OTTO H.
   Aims of our foreign investment policy.
      HBR 24:498-511 no.4, 46
KORNHAUSER, ARTHUR
   The contribution of psychology to industrial
      relations research. IRRA 1:172-88 Dec 48
KOSH, DAVID A.
   Uncertainty and the provision for deprecia-
      tion in the public utility industries. JB 16:
      209-18 Oct 43
KOTOK, EDWARD I.
   International policy on renewable natural re-
      sources. AER/S 35:110-19 May 45
KOVACS, LEO
   An instalment plan for post-war deliveries.
      EJ 51:492-98 Dec 41
KOZÁK, JAN
   Czechoslovak budget economy after the war.
      PF 3:329-46 no.4, 48
KOZLIK, ADOLF
   Conditions for demand curves whose curves
      of total revenue, consumers' surplus,
      total benefit, and compromise benefit are
      convex. Em 8:263-71 Jul 40
   Note on the terminology convex and concave.
      AER 31:103-05 Mar 41
   Some aspects of the food stamp plan as ap-
      plied to consumption of fats. JFE 23:
      483-92 May 41
   An investigation on complimentarity rela-
      tions between fresh fruits: a reply.
      JFE 23:654-56 Aug 41
   The use of per capita figures for demand
      curves. JASA 36:417-22 Sep 41
   Note on consumers' surplus. JPE 49:754-62
      Oct 41
   Shape of total revenue curves. JFE 23:843-54
      Nov 41
   Note on the integrability condition for inter-
      related demand. REStud 10:73-74 no.1, 42
   Application of the indifference curves analy-
      sis to rising demand curves. AER 33:
      129-30 Mar 43
   Concepts of plane, standard, level and satis-
      faction of consumption and of living. JM 9:
      55-57 Jul 44
KOZMETSKY, GEORGE
   Unions' financial reporting. HBR 27:13-23
      Jan 49
KRAENZEL, CARL F.
   New frontiers of the Great Plains. JFE 24:
      571-88 Aug 42

KRAEV, M.
The collective farm labour-day. Pt.I-II.
SovS 1:166-71; 261-68 Oct 49, Jan 50
KRAMER, ROLAND L. and Wilson, G. L.
Postwar shipping policy: discussion.
AER/S 36:575-78 May 46
KREIDER, CARL
The Anglo-American cotton-rubber barter
agreement. SEJ 7:216-24 Oct 40
Valuation for customs. QJE 56:157-59
Nov 41
The effect of American trade agreements on
third countries: retrospect. AER 31:
780-93 Dec 41
KREPS, THEODORE JOHN
Consumption: a vast underdeveloped eco-
nomic frontier. AER/S 30,no.5:177-99
Feb 41
Cartels, a phase of business haute politique.
AER/S 35:297-311 May 45
The effectiveness of the federal antitrust
laws: a symposium. AER 39:696-703
Jun 49
KRIGE, EILEEN JENSEN
Economics of exchange in a primitive society.
SAJE 9:1-21 Mar 41
KRIMGOLD, DEY BER
USSR: conservation plan for the Steppe and
Timber-Steppe regions. LE 25:336-46
Nov 49
KRISHNA, VASIREDDI SREE
International co-operation for controlling
trade cycles. IJE 25:301-06 Jan 45
India and the Sterling Area. IJE 26:508-16
Jan 46
KRISHNA IYENGAR, D.
see Iyengar, D. Krishna
KRISHNAMURTI, B. V.
The State under the Bombay Plan. IJE 26:
243-61 Oct 45
KRISHNAMURTHY, G. N.
and Srinivasamurthy, A. P. The trend of ag-
ricultural prices in Mysore during the
decennium 1928-1937. IJE 21:536-50
Apr 41
Finances of district boards in Mysore. IJE 22:
837-48 Jan 42
KRISHNA MURTHY, T.
Output and price in a socialist economy.
IJE 21:470-75 Apr 41
KRISHNAN, K. C. RAMA
see Ramakrishnan, K. C.
KRISHNASWAMI, ARCOT
Marshall's theory of money and interest.
IJE 22:121-43 Oct 41
Marshall's contribution to Indian economics.
IJE 22:875-97 Apr 42
Rural credit. IJE 22:908-32 Apr 42
KRISHNASWAMI, G. V.
Some aspects of the tendency of population in
India. IJE 30:69-75 Jul 49
KRISHNASWAMI AYYANGAR, A. A.
Inequalities [of incomes]. IJE 24:65-70 Jul 43

KRISTENSSON, ROBERT
The consequences of errors in accounting
due to inflation 1914-18. EH 4:371-83
Feb 40
Division of labour as an optimum problem in
organization and management. NTTO 12:
167-74 no.37, 48
KRISTJANSON, BALDUR H. and Schaffner, L. W.
North Dakota farm size trends; an evalua-
tion. JFE 31,pt.2:588-91 Feb 49
KRIZ, MIROSLAV ANTHONY
Central banks and the State today. AER 38:
565-80 Sep 48
KROST, MARTIN
The significance of American deposit move-
ments since 1929. [Summary] AER/S 30:
80-81 Mar 40
KUCZYNSKI, JURGEN
Productivity and exploitation under German
capitalism. S&S 9:55-66 no.1, 45
Productivity and exploitation under capital-
ism. S&S 10:148-58 no.2, 46
KUEHN, GEORGE W.
The novels of Thomas Deloney as source for
"climate of opinion" in sixteenth-century
economic history. JPE 48:865-75 Dec 40
KUH, CLIFFORD
The Permanente Health Plan. ILRR 2:309-11
Jan 49
KULKARNI, N. K.
Inflation and Indian monetary policy. IJE 30:
175-84 Oct 49
KULSRUD, CARL J.
The archival records of the Agricultural Ad-
justment Program. AH 22:197-204 Jul 48
KUMAR, C. B.
A note on the working of the Bombay Indus-
trial Disputes Act. IJE 22:92-96 Jul 41
KUMAR, GIRJA
A note on some problems arising out of pay-
ment of compensation. IJE 29:399-402
Apr 49
KUMAR, K.
International currency experience during the
inter-war period. R. IJE 25:374-76
Jan 45
KURIHARA, KENNETH K.
Post-war inflation and fiscal-monetary policy
in Japan. AER 36:843-54 Dec 46
Foreign investment and full employment.
JPE 55:459-64 Oct 47
Toward a new theory of monetary sovereignty.
JPE 57:162-70 Apr 49
KUZNETS, GEORGE M.
The use of econometric models in agricul-
tural micro-economic studies. JFE 30:
131-39 Feb 48
KUZNETS, SIMON
National and regional measures of income.
SEJ 6:291-313 Jan 40
Schumpeter's business cycles. AER 30:
257-71 Jun 40
Economic progress. R. MS 12:28-34 Apr 41

KUZNETS, SIMON (Cont.)

Statistics and economic history. JEH 1: 26-41 May 41

National income and taxable capacity. AER/S 32:37-75 Mar 42

[National product, war and prewar.] Reply. REStat 26:126-35 Aug 44

Measurement of economic growth. JEH/S 7: 10-34 '47

On the valuation of social income: reflections on Professor Hicks' article. Pt.I-II. Ec N.S.15:1-16; 116-31 Feb,May 48

National income: a new version. (Discussion of the new Department of Commerce income series) REStat 30:151-79 Aug 48

Wesley Clair Mitchell, 1874-1948 an appreciation. JASA 43:126-31 Mar 49

National income and industrial structure. Em 17,suppl.:205-39 Jul 49

KYRK, HAZEL

"The consumer and the economic order" by Waite and Cassady, "Consumption in our society" by Hoyt. R. JM 4,no.4,pt.2: 111-17 Apr 40

LABINI, PAOLO SYLOS

The Keynesians (a letter from America to a friend). [Translated by O. R. Agresti] BNL 2:238-42 Oct-Dec 49

LACEY, K.

Commodity stocks and the trade cycle. Ec N.S.11:12-18 Feb 44

--- A reply. Ec N.S.11:140-42 Aug 44

Some implications of the first in-first out method of stock valuation. Ec N.S.12: 26-30 Feb 45

Commodity stock values and E.P.T. EJ 55: 2-16 Apr 45

Profit measurement and the trade cycle. EJ 57:456-74 Dec 47

LACEY, R. W.

Cotton's war effort. MS 15:26-74 Jan 47

LACHMANN, KURT

The Franco-British bloc. (Economic and social developments through the European war) SR 7:229-42 May 40

War and peace economics of aviation. SR 7: 468-79 Nov 40

The Hermann Göring Works. SR 8:24-40 Feb 41

More on the Hermann Göring Works. SR 9: 396-401 Sep 42

The shipping problem at the end of the war. SR 10:52-75 Feb 43

LACHMANN, LUDWIG M.

A reconsideration of the Austrian theory of industrial fluctuations. Ec N.S.7:179-96 May 40

On the measurement of capital. Ec N.S.8: 361-77 Nov 41

The role of expectations in economics as a social science. Ec N.S.10:12-23 Feb 43

Finance capitalism? Ec N.S.11:64-73 May 44

Notes on the proposals for international currency stabilization. REStat 26:184-91 Nov 44

A note on the elasticity of expectations. Ec N.S.12:248-53 Nov 45

Complementarity and substitution in the theory of capital. Ec N.S.14:108-19 May 47

Investment repercussions. QJE 62:698-713 Nov 48

--- Reply. QJE 63:432-34 Aug 49

LACKANY, SANNY

Post-war problems. EgC 35:99-105 Jan-Feb 44

From the Middle East Monetary Conference to Bretton Woods. EgC 36:95-109 Jan-Feb 45

LADENBURG, HUBERT

Plan for a postwar world clearing bank. SR 9:510-29 Nov 42

LAFFER, KINGSLEY

Taxation reform in Australia. ER 18:168-79 Dec 42

LAIGHT, J. C.

Competition in road motor transportation. SAJE 16:24-34 Mar 48

Municipal passenger transport costs and revenue: United Kingdom and South Africa 1938/9-1945/6. SAJE 17:443-56 Dec 49

LAKE, WILFRED S.

The end of the Suffolk system. JEH 7: 183-207 Nov 47

LAL, HARBANS

Agriculture in the Bombay Plan. IJE 26: 43-60 Jul 45

LAL, R. B. and Mathen, K. K.

A note on conditions of living of agricultural labour and certain other rural groups in West Bengal. IJE 28:403-16 Jan 48

LALWANI, KASTURCHAND

The future of gold vis-a-vis currency plans. Pt.I-II. IJE 25:15-23; 103-16 Jul,Oct 44

Tax relief vs. 100% E.P.T. IJE 25:149-53 Oct 44

Reflections on future economic order: international and national. Pt.I-II. IJE 25: 450-65; 26:29-42 Apr,Jul 45

Combination as a form of business organisation in India. IJE 26:191-225 Oct 45

Cost and efficiency in Indian business. Pt.I-II. IJE 26:579-96; 27:1-20 Apr,Jul 46

Dividend policy in Indian business. IJE 28: 261-68 Oct 47

Fundamentals of economic planning in free India. IJE 29:337-50 Apr 49

LAMARTINE YATES, PAUL

Food and agriculture: outlook and policy: discussion. AER/S 35:417-18 May 45

Food and Agriculture Organization of the United Nations. JFE 28:54-70 Feb 46

[Food, agriculture, and trade.] Review of Professor Schultz's paper. JFE 29:33-36 Feb 47

LAMB, GEORGE ANTHONY
Post-war statistical planning in the Department of the Interior. JASA 42:37-41 Mar 47

LAMONTAGNE, MAURICE
Some French contributions to economic theory. CJE 13:514-32 Nov 47

LAMPERT, BERNARD P. and McConnell, J. W.
Employee adjustment to technological displacement: the Fifth Avenue Coach Company case. ILRR 2:219-26 Jan 49

LA NAUZE, JOHN ANDREW
The modern use of "economist." ER 16: 125-26 Jun 40
Jevons in Sydney. ER 17:31-45 Jun 41
Two notes on Hearn. ER 17:255-58 Dec 41
A manuscript attributed to Adam Smith. EJ 55:288-91 Jun-Sep 45
Australian tariffs and imperial control. Pt.I-II. ER 24:1-17; 218-34 Jun,Dec 48

LANDAUER, CARL
Literature on economic planning. R. SR 7: 496-508 Nov 40
Economic planning and the science of economics: comment. AER 31:825-31 Dec 41
From Marx to Menger: the recent development of Soviet economics. AER 34:340-44 Jun 44
The German reparations problem. JPE 56: 344-47 Aug 48

LANDES, DAVID SAUL
A note on cultural factors in entrepreneurship. EEH 1,no.1:8-9 Jan 49
Dales' "Approaches." EEH 1,no.4:28-29 Apr 49
French entrepreneurship and industrial growth in the nineteenth century. JEH 9: 45-61 May 49

LANDIS, JAMES M.
Economic relationships between the United States and Egypt. EgC 36:217-27 Mar 45

LANDRY, RICHARD SABOURIN
The Federal Trade Commission and "unfair competition" in foreign trade. AER 35: 575-84 Sep 45

LANDRY, ROBERT JOHN and George, E. B.
Policy suggestions, January 1947-June 1948. REStat 29:24-28 Feb 47

LANDSTROM, KARL S.
Should non-farm agricultural land be included in the Census of agriculture? LE 22:295-96 Aug 46
Comment on "How efficient is American agriculture?" JFE 30:364-68 May 48

LANDUYT, BERNARD FRANCIS
Economic upheaval in the Pacific basin. RSE 4:40-53 Jan 46

LANE, FREDERIC CHAPIN
Family partnerships and joint ventures in the Venetian Republic. JEH 4:178-96 Nov 44
Venture accounting in medieval business management. BHR 19:164-73 Nov 45

LANG, FRANK
Insurance research. JM 12:66-71 Jul 47

LANG, RICHARD OTTO
Problems of statistical control: military aspects. JASA 36:11-17 Mar 41

LANGE, GUNNAR
and Crawford, J. G. County planning for land-use adjustment. JFE 22:473-83 May 40
A neglected point in the economics of soil conservation. JFE 23:467-74 May 41

LANGE, OSKAR
Adam Krzyzanowski. [obit.] EJ 50:159-61 Mar 40
Complementarity and interrelations of shifts in demand. REStud 8:58-63 Oct 40
The foundations of welfare economics. Em 10:215-28 Jul-Oct 42
Theoretical derivation of elasticities of demand and supply: the direct method. Em 10:193-214 Jul-Oct 42
A note on innovations. REStat 25:19-25 Feb 43
The theory of the multiplier. Em 11:227-45 Jul-Oct 43
[The inter-relations of shifts in demand: comment.] REStud 12:75-78 no.1, 44
Marxian economics in the Soviet Union. AER 35:127-33 Mar 45
The scope and method of economics. REStud 13:19-32 no.1, 45
The practice of economic planning and the optimum allocation of resources. Em 17,suppl.:166-70 Jul 49

LANGER, HENRY CHARLES, Jr.
Maintaining full employment. AER 33:888-92 Dec 43

LANGSFORD, ETHELBERT LEE
Agriculture in the South: review. JFE 29: 201-03 Feb 47

LANSING, JOHN BELCHER
Comments on the economists' opinion survey. AER 36:143-46 Mar 46
and Isard, W. Comparisons of power cost for atomic and conventional steam stations. REStat 31:217-26 Aug 49

LANSTON, AUBREY G.
Crucial problem of the federal debt. HBR 24:133-50 no.2, 46

LAPIN, BERENICE B.
Occupancy of housing in war-production centers. LE 19:222-24 May 43

LARONGE, JOSEPH
The subdivider of today and tomorrow. LE 18:423-30 Nov 42

LARSEN, HARALD CHRISTIAN
and Horton, D. C. Agricultural finance guides in wartime. LE 19:59-68 Feb 43
Relationship of land values to warranted values, 1910-48. JFE 30:579-88 Aug 48

LARSON, ADLOWE LYLE
A price policy for agriculture, consistent with economic progress, that will promote ade-

LARSON, ADLOWE LYLE (Cont.)
    quate and more stable income from farm-
       ing. JFE 27:861-70 Nov 45
    The fixity gradient: a tool for fixed and vari-
       able cost analysis. JFE 28:825-34 Aug 46
    Research in grain marketing. JFE 29:
       1417-23 Nov 47
LARSON, HENRIETTA MELIA
    The armor business in the Middle Ages.
       BHR 14:49-64 Oct 40
    [Capitalism: concepts and history]: discus-
       sion. BHR 16:39-42 Apr 42
    Some unexplored fields in American rail-
       road history. BHR 16:69-79 Oct 42
    Some general considerations [on business
       administration]. BHR 17:27-31 Feb 43
    An early industrial capitalist's labor policy
       and management. BHR 18:132-41 Nov 44
    Business men as collectors. BHR 18:162-70
       Dec 44
    Danger in business history. HBR 22:316-27
       no.3, 44
    "Plutarch's lives" of trade: the first series
       of American business biographies.
       BHR 20:28-32 Feb 46
    The Business History Foundation, Inc.
       BHR 21:51-54 Jun 47
    Business history: retrospect and prospect.
       BHR 21:173-99 Dec 47
    Availability of records for research in the
       history of large business concerns.
       BHR 22:12-21 Feb 48
LARY, HAL BUCKNER
    The domestic effects of foreign investment.
       AER/S 36:672-86 May 46
LASKEN, HERMAN; Copeland, M. A. and Jacob-
    son, J.
    The WPB index of war production. JASA 40:
       145-59 Jun 45
LASSER, JACOB KAY
    State income tax simplification in Vermont.
       NTJ 1:62-66 Mar 48
LATTIMER, JOHN ERNEST
    The British bacon agreement. CJE 6:60-67
       Feb 40
    Canadian agricultural post-war planning.
       JFE 25:326-35 Feb 43
LATTIMORE, OWEN
    Inner Asian frontiers: Chinese and Russian
       margins of expansion. JEH 7:24-52
       May 47
LAUTERBACH, ALBERT
    From rationing to informed consumption.
       JB 17:209-19 Oct 44
LAWLER, P. J.
    The consumption function. ER 25,suppl.:
       93-122 Aug 49
LAWLER, PAUL FREDERICK
    Crisis in the domestic shipping industry.
       HBR 24:258-76 no.2, 46
    A note on control in small businesses.
       HBR 25:521-26 no.4, 47

LAWRENCE, JOSEPH STAGG
    Profits and progress. HBR 26:480-91
       Jul 48
LAWSON, ERIC WILFRED
    The choice of capitalization ratios in prac-
       tice. SEJ 9:335-49 Apr 43
LAYBOURN, G. P. and Longstaff, H. P.
    Certain correlates of attitudes toward radio
       commercials. JM 13:447-58 Apr 49
LAZAROFF, LOUIS [and others]
    Harry Alvin Millis 1873-1948. [obit.]
       AER 39:742-50 Jun 49
LAZERE, MONROE
    Welfare economics a misnomer. AER 30:
       346-47 Jun 40
LAZO, HECTOR
    Towards economical distribution. JM 4:
       249-51 Jan 40
    Independents, chains and the public welfare.
       JM 6:267-73 Jan 42
LEACH, CAMPBELL W.
    Excess profits taxation: II. A business man's
       view. CJE 7:363-70 Aug 41
LEAK, HECTOR
    Sir Alfred William Flux, C.B. [obit.]
       JRSS 105:144-47 pt.2, 42
    Volume of industrial production. JRSS 106:
       60-63 pt.1, 43
    and Maizels, A. [The concept of net volume
       of output, with special reference to Irish
       data.] Note on Dr. Geary's paper.
       JRSS 107:259-61 pt.3-4, 44
    and Maizels, A. The structure of British
       industry. JRSS 108:142-99 pt.1-2, 45
    Sir Percy Ashley, K.B.E., C.B. [obit.]
       JRSS 108:479-80 pt.3-4, 45
    Sedley Anthony Cudmore. [obit.] JRSS 109:
       169-70 pt.2, 46
    Statistics of the censuses of production and
       distribution. JRSS 112:67-80 pt.1, 49
LEARNED, EDMUND PHILIP
    Pricing of gasoline: a case study. HBR 26:
       723-56 Nov 48
    Problems of a new executive. HBR 27:362-72
       May 49
LEAVENS, DICKSON HAMMOND
    Rupee circulation in India. AER 31:87-90
       Mar 41
    and Katona, G. Price increases and uptrad-
       ing: the change in advertised prices of
       apparel and house furnishings. JB 17:
       231-43 Oct 44
    Bullion prices and the gold-silver ratio,
       "1929-1945." REStat 28:160-64 Aug 46
    Accuracy in the Doolittle solution. Em 15:
       45-50 Jan 47
LEAVITT, JOHN ANTON and Spero, H.
    Inflation as a post-war problem. JPE 51:
       356-60 Aug 43
LEBERGOTT, STANLEY
    Forecasting the national product. AER 35:
       59-80 Mar 45

LEBERGOTT, STANLEY (Cont.)
    Wage structures. REStat 29:274-85 Nov 47
    Earnings of nonfarm employees in the U.S.,
        1890-1946. JASA 43:74-93 Mar 48
LEBHAR, GODFREY M.
    The chain store postwar role. JM 8:316-20
        Jan 44
LEBOW, VICTOR
    The nature of postwar retail competition.
        JM 9:11-18 Jul 44
    Our changing channels of distribution. JM 13:
        12-22 Jul 48
    New outlooks for marketing. JB 22:160-68
        Jul 49
LEE, ALVIN T. M.
    and Hauck, J. F. Excessive land subdivision
        in the New Jersey pine area. LE 19:
        207-21 May 43
    The problem of post-war land settlement
        and agricultural production. JFE 26:
        461-75 Aug 44
    Farms and homes from surplus military
        lands. LE 21:331-38 Sep 45
    Land acquisition program of the War and
        Navy Departments, World War II. JFE 29:
        889-909 Nov 47
    Use of military land for agriculture during
        World War II. LE 23:349-59 Nov 47
    District court upholds constitutionality of
        Maryland forest conservation law. JFE 30:
        150-56 Feb 48
LEE, GUY A.
    The general records of the United States
        Department of Agriculture in the National
        Archives. AH 19:242-49 Oct 45
LEE, MAURICE W.
    Recent trends in chain-store tax legislation.
        JB 13:253-74 Jul 40
    Taxation, defense, and consumer purchasing
        power. JM 6:11-15 Jul 41
    Appraisal of the Pacific Northwest. HBR 26:
        282-304 May 48
LEE, SHU-CHING
    Population problems in the Pacific. R.
        LE 22:381-85 Nov 46
    The theory of the agricultural ladder.
        AH 21:53-61 Jan 47
    Pattern of land utilization and possible ex-
        pansion of cultivated area in China.
        LE 23:142-52 May 47
    The heart of China's problem, the land ten-
        ure system. JFE 30:259-70 May 48
LEEMAN, WAYNE A.
    An evaluation of organized speculation.
        SEJ 16:139-46 Oct 49
LEFFLER, GEORGE V.
    The farmer talks back. LE 17:108-11 Feb 41
LEHMANN, FRITZ
    The gold problem. SR 7:125-50 May 40
LEIGH, ARTHUR H.
    Von Thünen's theory of distribution and the
        advent of marginal analysis. JPE 54:
        481-502 Dec 46

LEIGH, WARREN W.
    [Solving wholesalers' problems through
        trading area research.] Discussion.
        JM 4,no.4,pt.2:45-46 Apr 40
LEISERSON, AVERY
    Coordination of federal budgetary and appro-
        priations procedures under the Legisla-
        tive Reorganization Act of 1946. NTJ 1:
        118-26 Jun 48
    The role of political science in industrial
        relations research. IRRA 1:189-98
        Dec 48
LEISERSON, WILLIAM MORRIS
    Public policy in labor relations. AER/S 36:
        336-46 May 46
    [and others] Harry Alvin Millis 1873-1948.
        [obit.] AER 39:742-50 Jun 49
LEITER, ROBERT D.
    Supervisory employees and the Taft-Hartley
        law. SEJ 15:311-20 Jan 49
LEITH, W. GORDON
    Agricultural economic data: discussion.
        JFE 29:1224-28 Nov 47
LELAND, SIMEON ELBRIDGE
    Management of the public debt after the war.
        AER/S 34,no.2:89-132 Jun 44
    The government, the banks and the national
        debt. JF 1:5-26 Aug 46
    chairman. Round table on economic research.
        [Report] AER/S 37:649-50 May 47
    [and others] Harry Alvin Millis 1873-1948.
        [obit.] AER 39:742-50 Jun 49
LEMMER, GEORGE F.
    The early agricultural fairs of Missouri.
        AH 17:145-52 Jul 43
    The spread of improved cattle through the
        eastern United States to 1850. AH 21:
        79-93 Apr 47
    The agricultural program of a leading farm
        periodical, Colman's rural world. AH 23:
        245-54 Oct 49
LENGYEL, SAMUEL JOSEPH
    Insurance in the international balances of
        payments. JASA 39:428-38 Dec 44
LENHART, MARGOT WAKEMAN
    Analyzing labor requirements for California's
        major seasonal crop operations. JFE 27:
        963-75 Nov 45
LENNARD, REGINALD VIVIAN
    The agrarian life of the Middle Ages. R.
        EJ 52:45-53 Apr 42
    The origin of the fiscal carucate. EHR 14:
        51-63 no.1, 44
    The destruction of woodland in the eastern
        counties under William the Conqueror.
        EHR 15:36-43 no.1-2, 45
    The economic position of the Domesday
        villani. EJ 56:244-64 Jun 46
    The economic position of the Domesday
        sokemen. EJ 57:179-95 Jun 47
    An early fulling-mill: a note. EHR 17:150
        no.2, 47

LESTER, RICHARD ALLEN (Cont.)
  Effects of the war on wages and hours.
    AER/S 33:218-37 Mar 43
  Note on wages and labor costs. SEJ 10:
    235-38 Jan 44
  Trends in southern wage differentials since
    1890. SEJ 11:317-44 Apr 45
  Diversity in North-South wage differentials
    and in wage rates within the South.
    SEJ 12:238-62 Jan 46
  Effectiveness of factory labor: South-North
    comparisons. JPE 54:60-75 Feb 46
  Shortcomings of marginal analysis for wage-
    employment problems. AER 36:63-82
    Mar 46
  Wage diversity and its theoretical implica-
    tions. REStat 28:152-59 Aug 46
  Marginalism, minimum wages, and labor
    markets. AER 37:135-48 Mar 47
  Southern wage differentials: developments,
    analysis, and implications. SEJ 13:386-94
    Apr 47
  Reflections on the "labor monopoly" issue.
    JPE 55:513-36 Dec 47
  Absence of elasticity considerations in de-
    mand to the firm. SEJ 14:285-89 Jan 48
  The influence of unionism upon earnings:
    comment. QJE 62:783-87 Nov 48
  Equilibrium of the firm. AER 39:478-84
    Mar 49
LESTOCQUOY, JEAN
  The tenth century. EHR 17:1-14 no.1, 47
LEUILLIOT, PAUL
  Recent French writings in the social and eco-
    nomic history of modern France. [Pt.I-II]
    EHR II.1:61-72; II.2:200-05 no.1, 48,
    no.2, 49; [bibliography] II.5:400-11 no.3, 53
LEUNBACH, GUSTAV
  The theory of games and economic behaviour,
    Johann v. Neumann and Oscar Morgen-
    stern. R. NTTO 12:175-78 no.37, 48
LEVI, EDWARD H.
  The effectiveness of the federal antitrust
    laws: a symposium. AER 39:703 Jun 49
LEVIN, GERSON
  Government egg programs during wartime, a
    review and appraisal. JFE 28:887-902
    Nov 46
LEVINE, DAVID D.
  The case for tax exemption of public housing.
    LE 17:98-101 Feb 41
LEVINE, LOUIS
  The impact of war on labor supply and labor
    utilization. JASA 37:54-62 Mar 42
LEVY, BERYL HAROLD
  Collective bargaining under the Taft-Hartley
    Act. HBR 26:468-79 Jul 48
LEVY, HERMANN
  The economic history of sickness and medi-
    cal benefit before the Puritan Revolution.
    EHR 13:42-57 no.1-2, 43
  The economic history of sickness and medi-
    cal benefit since the Puritan Revolution.
    EHR 14:135-60 no.2, 44

LEVY, MARION J. Jr.
  Note on some Chamberlinian solutions.
    AER 30:344-46 Jun 40
LEWIS, ARDRON B.
  Relation of income to farm capital. JFE 24:
    523-28 May 42
LEWIS, ARTHUR DEE and Frederick, J. H.
  Air routes and public policy. HBR 19:
    482-95 no.4, 41
LEWIS, BEN WILLIAM
  State regulation in depression and war.
    (Recent developments in public utility
    regulation.) AER/S 36:384-404 May 46
  Public policy and the growth of the power in-
    dustry. JEH/S 7:47-55 '47
  [and others] The Sherman Act and the en-
    forcement of competition: discussion.
    AER/S 38:203-14 May 48
  The economics of preparedness for war:
    discussion. AER/S 39:378-79 May 49
  The effectiveness of the federal antitrust
    laws: a symposium. AER 39:703-09
    Jun 49
LEWIS, CLEONA [and others]
  Capital expansion, employment, and eco-
    nomic stability: a reply to H. H. Villard.
    AER 31:110-12 Mar 41
LEWIS, EDWIN HENDERSON
  Wholesale market patterns. JM 12:317-26
    Jan 48
LEWIS, ERNEST MICHAEL ROY and Miller,
  K. W.
  Notes on the balance of payments of the
    British and French empires with non-
    sterling countries. ER 16:114-18 Jun 40
LEWIS, GEORGE M.
  Marketing slaughter livestock: discussion.
    JFE 31,pt.2:361-64 Feb 49
LEWIS, HAROLD GREGG
  The nature of the demand for steel.
    JASA 36:110-15 Mar 41
  and Court, L. M. Production cost indices.
    REStud 10:28-42 no.1, 42
  Henry Calvert Simons. [obit.] AER 36:668-69
    Sep 46
  Some observations on duopoly theory.
    AER/S 38:1-9 May 48
LEWIS, HARRIE FRANCIS
  A comparison of consumer responses to
    weekly and monthly purchase panels.
    JM 12:449-54 Apr 48; Erratum. 13:231
    Oct 48
  Lost sales opportunities in retailing. HBR 27:
    53-61 Jan 49
LEWIS, HOWARD THOMPSON
  Subcontracting: the current problem. HBR 19:
    405-18 no.4, 41
  and Livesey, C. A. Materials management in
    the airframe industry. HBR 22:477-94
    no.4, 44
  This business of procurement. HBR 24:
    377-93 no.3, 46
  Evaluating departmental efficiency. HBR 26:
    313-28 May 48

LEWIS, ROBERT EDWARD and Garvy, G.
  New indexes of hourly and weekly earnings
    complied by the Federal Reserve Bank of
    New York. JASA 42:256-70 Jun 47
LEWIS, WILLARD A.
  Arbitrating a wildcat strike. HBR 27:
    498-504 Jul 49
LEWIS, WILLIAM ARTHUR
  The inter-relations of shipping freights.
    Ec N.S.8:52-76 Feb 41
  The two-part tariff. Ec N.S.8:249-70 Aug 41
  --- A reply. Ec N.S.8:399-408 Nov 41
  Notes on the economics of loyalty. Ec N.S.9:
    333-48 Nov 42
  Competition in retail trade. Ec N.S.12:
    202-34 Nov 45
  Fixed costs. Ec N.S.13:231-58 Nov 46
  The prospect before us. MS 16:129-64
    May 48
  The British Monopolies Act. MS 17:208-17
    May 49
  Developing colonial agriculture. TBR 2:3-21
    Jun 49
  and Meyer, F. V. The effects of an overseas
    slump on the British economy. MS 17:
    233-65 Sep 49
LEYLAND, NORMAN HARRISON
  The paper shortage: B. The control of paper.
    OIS 3:341-42 Nov 1, 41
  A note on price and quality. OEP N.S.1:
    269-72 Jun 49
LI, CHOH-MING
  A note on Professor Hicks' value and capital.
    REStud 9:74-76 Nov 41
  Inflation in wartime China. REStat 27:23-33
    Feb 45
LIAO, T'AI-CH'U
  The rape markets on the Chengtu Plain.
    JFE 28:1016-24 Nov 46
  The An Lo Szu market of Chengtu: a field
    study. BHR 21:155-71 Dec 47
LICHTENSTEIN, WALTER
  Recent literature on the gold problem. R.
    JB 13:146-58 Apr 40
LIEBERMAN, MARTIN and Cohen, M. A.
  Collective bargaining in the motor freight in-
    dustry. ILRR 3:17-32 Oct 49
LIENAU, C. C.
  Statistical method: forecasting electric en-
    ergy demand and regulating supply. LE 18:
    102-05 Feb 42
LIEPE, WOLFRAM and Burtle, J. L.
  Devaluation and the cost of living in the
    United Kingdom. REStud 17:1-28 no.1, 49
LIKERT, RENSIS and Katona, G.
  Relationship between consumer expenditures
    and savings: the contribution of survey
    research. REStat 28:197-99 Nov 46
LILLEY, TOM
  and Bollinger, L. L. Maintaining a strong
    aircraft industry. HBR 22:178-90 no.2, 44
  with Bollinger, L. L. and Lombard, A. E., Jr.
    Preserving American air power. HBR 23:
    372-92 no.3, 45

LILLIBRIDGE, ROBERT M.
  Shopping centers in urban redevelopment.
    LE 24:137-60 May 48
LINDBERG, JOHN
  Food supply under a program of freedom
    from want. SR 12:181-204 May 45
LINDBLOM, CHARLES EDWARD
  Long-run considerations in employment
    stabilization and unemployment compen-
    sation. QJE 56:145-51 Nov 41
  Pay roll taxation and employment stabiliza-
    tion. QJE 57:657-58 Aug 43
  Collective bargaining and the competitive
    system. CJE 11:566-77 Nov 45
  The income goals of unionism. SEJ 14:
    420-32 Apr 48
  "Bargaining power" in price and wage de-
    termination. QJE 62:396-417 May 48
  The union as a monopoly. QJE 62:671-97
    Nov 48
LINDEMAN, JOHN
  The armaments program and national income.
    AER 31:42-46 Mar 41
LINDHOLM, RICHARD WADSWORTH
  Note on the effect of tax reduction. AER 36:
    910 Dec 46
  German finance in World War II. AER 37:
    121-34 Mar 47
LINDSAY, J.
  Sidney wholesale fruit and vegetable prices.
    ER 21:174-81 Dec 45
LINFORD, R. J. and Walker, E. R.
  War-time price control and price movements
    in an open economy: Australia 1914-20
    and 1939-40. REStat 24:75-86 May 42
L[ININGER], F[RED] F[OUSE]
  Frederick Pattison Weaver, 1882-1940.
    [obit.] JFE 22:829 Nov 40
LINK, ARTHUR S.
  The Federal Reserve policy and the agricul-
    tural depression of 1920-1921. AH 20:
    166-75 Jul 46
LINTNER, JOHN
  Our tremendous mortgage debt. HBR 27:
    88-106 Jan 49
LINVILLE, FRANCIS A.
  An agricultural policy for hemisphere de-
    fense. JFE 23:726-42 Nov 41
  Latin American aspects of post-war agricul-
    tural readjustments. JFE 24:42-51 Feb 42
LIPKOWITZ, IRVING
  The effectiveness of the federal antitrust
    laws: a symposium. AER 39:709-11
    Jun 49
LISMAN, JOHANNES HUBERTUS CORNELIUS
  Econometrics and thermodynamics: a re-
    mark on Davis' theory of budgets. Em 17:
    59-62 Jan 49
LISS, SAMUEL
  Revival of free labor organizations in the
    United States occupation zone in Germany:
    a preview. SEJ 13:247-56 Jan 47
  Farm habilitation perspectives in the postwar
    period. JFE 29:723-44 Aug 47

LITMAN, SIMON
David Kinley 1861-1944. [obit.] AER 35: 1041-44 Dec 45

LITTAUER, SEBASTIAN B. and Abruzzi, A.
Experimental criteria for evaluating workers and operations. ILRR 2:502-26 Jul 49

LITTLE, E. M.
The base minerals (excluding coal) of the Union of South Africa. SAJE 17:49-73 Mar 49

LITTLE, ELLIOTT MENZIES
Some management responsibilities for good industrial relations. CJE 12:356-60 Aug 46

LITTLE, IAN MALCOLM DAVID
A reformulation of the theory of consumer's behavior. OEP N.S.1:90-99 Jan 49
The valuation of the social income. Ec N.S.16:11-26 Feb 49
The foundations of welfare economics. OEP N.S.1:227-46 Jun 49
A note on the interpretation of index numbers. Ec N.S.16:369-70 Nov 49
Welfare and tariffs. REStud 16:65-70 no.2, 49
The economist and the state. REStud 17: 75-76 no.1, 49

LITTLER, H. G.
A pure theory of money. CJE 10:422-47 Nov 44

LITTLER, ROBERT M. C.
A code of union conduct. HBR 20:10-20 no.1, 41
The public interest in the terms of collective bargains. AER/S 35:209-25 May 45
Managers must manage. HBR 24:366-76 no.3, 46

LIU, TA-CHUNG
China's foreign exchange problems: a proposed solution. AER 31:266-79 Jun 41

LIVELY, CHARLES ELSON
Adjustment of population to rural resources in Missouri. LE 18:67-76 Feb 42

LIVERMORE, SHAW
Concentration of control now as compared with 1890. JM 4:362-69 Apr 40

LIVERS, J. J. and Craig, G. H.
Role of soil depletion in land valuation. JFE 22:773-76 Nov 40

LIVESEY, CHARLES ATKINS
and Lewis, H. T. Materials management in the airframe industry. HBR 22:477-94 no.4, 44
Appraising the mill supply distributor. HBR 23:493-506 no.4, 45
The steel warehouse distributor. HBR 25: 397-408 no.3, 47

LIVINGSTON, JULIUS STERLING
and Arnold, T. Antitrust war policy and full production. HBR 20:265-76 no.3, 42
and Ignatius, P. R. Effective use of training films. HBR 25:637-51 no.4a, 47

LIVINGSTON, S. MORRIS
The marketing viewpoint in planning for the

business enterprise. JM 7:332-36 Apr 43
Forecasting postwar demand. Em 13:15-24 Jan 45
The measurement of postwar labor supply and its capacity to produce. JASA 40: 20-28 Mar 45
[and others] Consumption economics: discussion. AER/S 35:56-66 May 45
Economic policy in the transition. REStat 29: 20-24 Feb 47

LLOYD, EDWARD MAYOW HASTINGS
Some notes on point rationing. REStat 24: 49-52 May 42
Price control and control of inflation. REStat 27:149-55 Nov 45

LLOYD, I. S.
Basic economese: new science or new language? R. SAJE 17:74-87 Mar 49
The environment of business decision: some reflections on the history of Rolls-Royce. SAJE 17:457-79 Dec 49

LOCKLEY, LAWRENCE CAMPBELL
and Watson, A. N. Some fundamental considerations in the conduct of polls. JM 5: 113-15 Oct 40
Marketing mechanical refrigerators during the emergency. JM 6:245-51 Jan 42
Trade associations as advertisers. JM 8: 189-93 Oct 43
Dehydrated foods. HBR 21:253-58 no.2, 43
Theories of pricing in marketing. JM 13: 364-66 Jan 49

LOCKLIN, DAVID PHILIP
Reorganization of the railroad rate structure. AER/S 36:466-78 May 46

LOCKWOOD, WILLIAM WIRT
Postwar trade relations in the Far East. AER/S 33:420-30 Mar 43

LODEWYCKX, AUGUSTIN
The Benelux Economic Union. ER 23:227-37 Dec 47

LOEHR, RODNEY C.
American husbandry; a commentary apropos of the Carman edition. AH 14:104-09 Jul 40
Moving back from the Atlantic seaboard. AH 17:90-96 Apr 43
Agriculture and history. JFE 30:537-44 Aug 48
Saving the kerf: the introduction of the band saw mill. AH 23:168-72 Jul 49

LOFTUS, JOHN A.
United States commercial policy. JB 21: 193-202 Jul 48
Permanent exceptions to the commercial policy provisions of the ITO Charter. AER/S 39:261-68 May 49

LOGAN, HAROLD AMOS
Economics of labour. R. CJE 9:82-91 Feb 43
Trends in collective bargaining: a study in causal analysis. CJE 9:331-47 Aug 43
The state and collective bargaining. CJE 10: 476-88 Nov 44

LOWER, ARTHUR REGINALD MARSDEN
Report of the Ontario Royal Commission on
Forestry. R. CJE 14:507-10 Nov 48
LOWERY, DAVE and Brunsman, H. G.
Facts from the 1940 Census of housing.
LE 19:89-93 Feb 43
LOWNDES, ARTHUR G.
The economic condition of the wool industry
in Queensland. R. ER 16:118-21 Jun 40
LOWRY, G. M. L.
The timing and control of a rise in the South
African price of gold. SAJE 17:202-04
Jun 49
LOWRY, ROBERT E.
Municipal subsidies to industries in Tennes-
see. SEJ 7:317-29 Jan 41
LUBAR, M. C.
Financing urban redevelopment. LE 22:
151-62 May 46
LUBELL, HAROLD
Effects of redistribution of income on con-
sumers' expenditures. AER 37:157-70
Mar 47; A correction. 930 Dec 47
LUCAS, DARRELL B.
A controlled recognition technique for meas-
uring magazine advertising audiences.
JM 6,no.4,pt.2:133-36 Apr 42
LUCK, DAVID J.
Education for marketing research. JM 14:
385-90 Oct 49
LUCKMAN, CHARLES
A round table fund for labor-management
education. ILRR 1:128-30 Oct 47
LUDEKE, HERBERT C.
A test for two methods commonly used in
reader-interest surveys. JM 10:171-73
Oct 45
LUEDICKE, H. E. and Rodgers, R.
Dynamic competition. HBR 27:237-49 Mar 49
LUKE, H. ALAN
Dairy marketing: discussion. JFE 29:288-91
Feb 47
LUNDBERG, ERIK
Readjustment problems in Sweden. OIS 8:
81-87 Mar 46
and Ohlsson, I. Models of the future national
income in Sweden. OIS 8:301-03 Sep 46
Economic prospects and the risk of inflation
in Sweden. OIS 9:37-43 Feb 47
LUNDBERG, GEORGE A.
Communication [on review of Can science
save us?]. SEJ 14:321 Jan 48
LUNDY, GABRIEL
Farm real estate values in South Dakota and
the BAE index of estimated value per acre
of farm real estate. JFE 27:980-84
Nov 45
LURIE, RICHARD
The company promotion boom in South
Africa 1933-38: an analysis of new
Johannesburg stock exchange quotations.
SAJE 9:265-73 Sep 41

LUSHER, DAVID W.
The structure of interest rates and the
Keynesian theory of interest. JPE 50:
272-79 Apr 42
LUTZ, FRIEDRICH AUGUST
The structure of interest rates. QJE 55:
36-63 Nov 40
Professor Hayek's theory of interest.
Ec N.S.10:302-10 Nov 43
History and theory in economics. R.
Ec N.S.11:210-14 Nov 44
The criterion of maximum profits in the
theory of investment. QJE 60:56-77
Nov 45
The interest rate and investment in a dynamic
economy. AER 35:811-30 Dec 45
The German currency reform and the re-
vival of the German economy. Ec N.S.16:
122-42 May 49
LUTZ, HARLEY LEIST
The Canadian Royal Commission on
Dominion-Provincial Relations. JPE 49:
111-16 Feb 41
[and others] Social security in a stable
prosperity: discussion. AER/S 37:
351-66 May 47
LUZZATTO, GINO
The depreciation of the peso and trade be-
tween Italy and Argentina. BNL 1:427-33
Oct 48
LYDALL, HAROLD FRENCH
Unemployment in an unplanned economy.
EJ 56:366-82 Sep 46
LYNCH, EDWARD STEPHEN
A note on Mr. Higgins' "Indeterminancy in
non-perfect competition." AER 30:347-48
Jun 40
Railroad taxation and abandonments.
HBR 18:496-503 no.4, 40
LYON, LEVERETT SAMUEL
The private-enterprise system confronts
emergency. JB 14:259-69 Jul 41
Economic problems of American cities.
AER/S 32:307-22 Mar 42
Government and American economic life.
JB 22:83-91 Apr 49
MABIN, H. S.
Some comments on the Report of the Recon-
struction Committee of the Department of
Agriculture and Forestry. SAJE 12:60-63
Mar 44
The Second Report of the Distribution Costs
Commission. R. SAJE 16:168-76 Jun 48
McALLISTER, BRECK P.
The effectiveness of the federal antitrust
laws: a symposium. AER 39:713-15
Jun 49
McANEAR, BEVERLY
Mr. Robert R. Livingston's reasons against
a land tax. JPE 48:63-90 Feb 40
McAVOY, B. L.
A philosopher's comment on philosophico-
economic relations. RSE 4:25-30 Jan 46

McBRIDE, CHARLES GROVER
  The effect of milk control programs on co-
    operatives. JFE 24:320-25 Feb 42
McCABE, DAVID ALOYSIUS
  [and others] Trade unions and the law: dis-
    cussion. AER/S 32:476-89 Mar 42
  Problems of industry-wide or regional trade
    agreements. AER/S 33:163-73 Mar 43
  Postwar labor problems: discussion.
    AER/S 34:193-95 Mar 44
  [and others] Edwin Walter Kemmerer 1875-
    1945. [obit.] AER 36:219-21 Mar 46
McCANN, HELEN
  The business papers of Emerson Cole.
    BHR 14:81-86 Dec 40
McCARTHY, PHILIP J.
  Employment policies and the Employment
    Act. RSE 7,no.2:29-33 Sep 49
McCARTY, DALE F.
  and King, A. J. Application of sampling to
    agricultural statistics with emphasis on
    stratified samples. JM 5:462-73 Apr 41
  Wheat yield insurance. JFE 23:664-67 Aug 41
McCLOY, JOHN J.
  Europe's hope for recovery. EI 1:551-61
    May 48
McCONNELL, JOHN W.
  and Lampert, B. P. Employee adjustment to
    technological displacement: the Fifth
    Avenue Coach Company case. ILRR 2:
    219-26 Jan 49
  [and others] The sociology and economics of
    class conflict: discussion. AER/S 29:
    37-46 May 49
  Measurement of employee attitudes: discus-
    sion. IRRA 2:222-25 Dec 49
McCRACKEN, HARLAN LINNEUS
  Economic contradictions. SEJ 13:343-59 Apr 47
  [and others] The economic theory of im-
    perfect competition, oligopoly, and monop-
    oly: discussion. AER/S 38:19-32 May 48
  The effectiveness of the federal antitrust
    laws: a symposium. AER 39:716 Jun 49
McCURRACH, D. F.
  Britain's U.S. dollar problems 1939-45.
    EJ 58:356-72 Sep 48
McDIARMID, FERGUS J.
  Life company investments and the capital
    markets. JASA 43:265-73 Jun 48
  Current trends in institutional investments.
    JF 4:119-28 Jun 49
McDIARMID, ORVILLE JOHN
  Some aspects of the Canadian automobile in-
    dustry. CJE 6:258-74 May 40
MacDONALD, ALTHEA and Black, J. D.
  Cost of living on farms and prices paid by
    farmers. JASA 39:377-86 Sep 44
McDONALD, MARGARET LILLOOET and
  Hughes, E. C.
  French and English in the economic struc-
    ture of Montreal. CJE 7:493-505 Nov 41
McDOUGALL, ARCHIBALD
  The White Paper on employment policy.
    RSE 3:18-33 Dec 44

MacDOUGALL, GEORGE DONALD ALASTAIR
  World economic survey, 1941-1942. R.
    EJ 53:280-84 Jun-Sep 43
  Britain's bargaining power. EJ 56:27-37
    Mar 46
  Britain's foreign trade problem. EJ 57:
    69-113 Mar 47
  Notes on non-discrimination. OIS 9:375-94
    Nov 47
  Britain's foreign trade problem: a reply.
    EJ 58:86-98 Mar 48
  Notes on Britain's bargaining power.
    OEP N.S.1:18-39 Jan 49
McDOUGALL, JOHN LORNE
  On some appendices to the Rowell-Sirois
    report: X. Railway freight rates in
    Canada. CJE 7:266-67 May 41
  The earning power of Canadian corporate
    capital, 1934-40. CJE 8:557-65 Nov 42
  The distribution of income among wage
    workers in railway employment, 1939-47.
    CJE 13:248-55 May 47
MACE, MYLES LaGRANGE
  Nathan Isaacs. [obit.] BHR 16:19-20 Feb 42
  and Smith, D. T. Tax uncertainties in corpo-
    rate financing. HBR 20:315-26 no.3, 42
  Management assistance for small business.
    HBR 25:587-94 no.4a, 47
McENTIRE, DAVIS
  Migration and resettlement in the far
    western states. JFE 23:478-82 May 41
McFALL, ROBERT J.
  Can we stabilize purchasing power at a high
    level? JM 8:61-74 Jul 43
McFARLAND, CARTER
  An economic evaluation of FHA's property
    improvement program. LE 23:399-416
    Nov 47
McFARLAND, ROSS ARMSTRONG
  The older worker in industry. HBR 21:
    505-20 no.4, 43
  Physically handicapped workers. HBR 23:
    1-31 no.1, 44
MacFARLANE, DAVID LIVINGSTON
  and Rudd, R. W. The scale of operations in
    agriculture. JFE 24:420-33 May 42
  --- Rejoinder. JFE 24:891 Nov 42
  A quantitative test of the significance of
    land-use areas. LE 18:293-98 Aug 42
  and Allen, R. H. Trade reciprocity and ag-
    riculture: discussion. JFE 24:822-25
    Nov 42
  Ceiling over ceiling pricing. JFE 26:800-03
    Nov 44
  The UNRRA experience in relation to devel-
    opments in food and agriculture. JFE 30:
    69-77 Feb 48
McFERRIN, JOHN BERRY
  Resources for financing industry in the South.
    SEJ 14:46-61 Jul 47
McGARRY, EDMUND DANIELS
  The mortality of independent grocery stores
    in Buffalo and Pittsburgh, 1919-1941.
    JM 12:14-24 Jul 47

MacGARVEY, CHARLES J.
Notes on Adam Smith's library and the Bonar
catalogue 1932. EJ 59:259-64 Jun 49
McGEHEE, R. BRUCE and Barton, F. L.
Freight forwarders. HBR 20:336-47 no.3, 42
MacGIBBON, DUNCAN ALEXANDER
Dr. James Bonar. [obit.] CJE 7:283-84
May 41
Robert McQueen, 1896-1941. [obit.] CJE 7:
278-81 May 41
Fiscal policy and business cycles. R.
CJE 9:77-82 Feb 43
International monetary control. CJE 11:
1-13 Feb 45
Harald Smith Patton, 1889-1945. [obit.]
CJE 11:614-15 Nov 45
The administration of the Income War Tax
Act. CJE 12:75-78 Feb 46
McGILL, VIVIAN JERAULD
Cartels and the settlement with Germany.
S&S 9:23-54 no.1, 45
McGINLEY, A. R. and Briggs, H. R.
Public land acquisition in law and practice.
LE 17:452-59 Nov 41
MacGOWAN, THOMAS GREEN
Trends in tire distribution. JM 10:265-69
Jan 46
Forecasting sales. HBR 27:760-70 Nov 49
MACGREGOR, DAVID HUTCHINSON
Aspects of the shipping question. OIS 2, no.11:
7-10 Dec 40
Marshall and his book. Ec N.S.9:313-24 Nov 42
The Scott Committee report. R. Ec N.S.10:
1-11 Feb 43
MacGREGOR, DONALD CHALMERS
Gross and net investment in Canada: tenta-
tive estimates. CJE 7:39-68 Feb 41
Studies of the cost of living in Canada.
CJE 7:545-58 Nov 41
Recent studies on national income. Pt.I-II.
R. CJE 11:115-29; 270-80 Feb, May 45
Manufacturers' expenses, net production,
and rigid costs in Canada. REStat 27:
60-73 May 45
The problem of price level in Canada.
CJE 13:157-96 May 47
McGREGOR, DOUGLAS
"Motives" as a tool of market research.
HBR 19:42-51 no.1, 40
MacGREGOR, J. J.
Britain's wartime food policy. JFE 25:
384-96 May 43
McGREW, JAMES W.
Effect of a food exemption on the incidence of
a retail sales tax. NTJ 2:362-67 Dec 49
MACHLUP, FRITZ
The theory of foreign exchanges. Pt.I-II.
Ec N.S.6:375-97; 7:23-49 Nov 39. Feb 40
Professor Hicks' statics. R. QJE 54:277-97
Feb 40
Bank deposits and the stock market in the
cycle. AER/S 30:83-91 Mar 40
Eight questions on gold: a review. AER/S 30,
no.5:30-37 Feb 41

Competition, pliopoly and profit. Pt.I-II.
Ec N.S.9:1-23; 153-73 Feb, May 42
[Differential pricing and the general welfare]:
discussion. JM 6 no.4, pt.2:184-85 Apr 42
Forced or induced saving: an exploration
into its synonyms and homonyms.
REStat 25:26-39 Feb 43
The division of labor between government
and private enterprise. AER/S 33:87-104
Mar 43
Capitalism and its future appraised by two
liberal economists. AER 33:301-20 Jun 43
[and others] International cartels: discus-
sion. AER/S 36:768-83 May 46
Marginal analysis and empirical research.
AER 36:519-54 Sep 46
Rejoinder to an antimarginalist. AER 37:
148-54 Mar 47
Misconceptions about the current inflation.
REStat 30:17-22 Feb 48; Correction. 230
Aug 48
The economics of preparedness for war:
discussion. AER/S 39:379-83 May 49
The inflationary process: comments.
REStat 31:210-12 Aug 49
The teaching of money and banking. JF 4:
227-30 Sep 49
McINTYRE, FRANCIS
The effect of the undistributed profits tax:
a reply. Em 8:357-60 Oct 40
Wholesale price indexes. JASA 36:185-90
Jun 41
McISAAC, ARCHIBALD McDONALD [and others]
Recent developments in public utility regula-
tion: discussion. AER/S 36:435-50
May 46
MacIVER, ROBERT MORRISON
History and social causation. JEH/S 3:
135-45 Dec 43
McIVOR, RUSSEL CRAIG
Canadian war-time fiscal policy, 1939-45.
CJE 14:62-93 Feb 48
MACK, CLIFTON E. and Knox, J. M.
Disposition of government property. HBR 22:
54-62 no.1, 43
MACK, RUTH PRINCE
The direction of change in income and the
consumption function. REStat 30:239-58
Nov 48
McKEAN, ROLAND NEELY
Liquidity and a national balance sheet.
JPE 57:506-22 Dec 49
McKEE, IRVING
Jean Paul Vignes, California's first profes-
sional winegrower. AH 22:176-80 Jul 48
MacKEIGAN, I. M.
Alfred Burpee Balcom, 1876-1943. [obit.]
CJE 10:79 Feb 44
Notes on "Patents in relation to monopoly."
CJE 12:470-82 Nov 46
McKENZIE, CARL H.
An experiment in the retention and preserva-
tion of corporate records. BHR 17, no.1,
suppl.:3-23 Feb 43

MACKIE, J.
  Aspects of the gold rush. ER 23:75-89
    Jun 47
McKINLEY, GORDON WELLS
  The residual item in the balance of inter-
    national payments. AER 31:308-16 Jun 41
MACKINTOSH, MARGARET
  [Problems of legislation relating to collec-
    tive bargaining]: discussion. CJE 9:
    354-56 Aug 43
MACKINTOSH, WILLIAM ARCHIBALD
  Norman McLeod Rogers, 1894-1940. [obit.]
    CJE 6:476-78 Aug 40
  Reciprocity. R. CJE 6:611-20 Nov 40
  O. D. Skelton, 1878-1941. [obit.] CJE 7:
    270-78 May 41
  The price system and the procurement of
    essential supplies. CJE 7:338-49 Aug 41
  Canadian war financing. JPE 50:481-500
    Aug 42
  Keynes as a public servant. CJE 13:379-83
    Aug 47
  Canada and the world economy in the making.
    LBR 12:12-28 Apr 49
McLAUGHLIN, GLENN EVERETT
  and Hoover, E. M., Jr. Strategic factors in
    plant location. HBR 20:133-40 no.2, 42
  Wartime expansion in industrial capacities.
    AER/S 33:108-18 Mar 43
  [and others] The changing structure of the
    American economy: discussion.
    AER/S 36:80-92 May 46
MACLAURIN, WILLIAM RUPERT
  and Myers, C. A. After unemployment bene-
    fits are exhausted. QJE 56:231-55 Feb 42
  [and others] The determination of wages:
    discussion. AER/S 32:302-06 Mar 42
  chairman. Economics of industrial research.
    Abstract of specialized conference dis-
    cussion. AER/S 32:231-32 Mar 42
  and Myers, C. A. Wages and the movement
    of factory labor. QJE 57:241-64 Feb 43
  and Bright, A. A., Jr. Economic factors in-
    fluencing the development and introduction
    of the fluorescent lamp. JPE 51:429-50
    Oct 43
  Wages and profits in the paper industry,
    1929-1939. QJE 58:196-228 Feb 44
  Federal support for scientific research.
    HBR 25:385-96 no.3, 47
  [and others] Possibilities for a realistic
    theory of entrepreneurship: discussion.
    AER/S 39:349-55 May 49
McLEAN, JOHN GODFREY
  Sale of war surpluses to speculators. HBR 23:
    229-45 no.2, 45
MacLEOD, ALAN
  Important considerations in determining a
    fair price for fluid milk. JFE 24:315-19
    Feb 42
  Research and educational programs in the
    marketing of milk and dairy products.
    JFE 28:144-57 Feb 46

  and Bressler, R. G., Jr. Connecticut studies
    milk delivery. JM 12:211-19 Oct 47
McLEOD, ALEXANDER NORMAN
  The financing of employment-maintaining
    expenditures. AER 35:640-45 Sep 45
  and Hahn, F. H. Proportionality, divisibility,
    and economies of scale: two comments.
    QJE 63:128-37 Feb 49
McLEOD, J. H.
  Regional changes in farming: discussion.
    JFE 24:279-83 Feb 42
McMAHON, JOHN F.
  Industrial Hygiene Foundation. ILRR 2:
    624-25 Jul 49
MACMILLAN, DANIEL
  Marshall's Principles of economics: a
    bibliographical note. EJ 52:290-93
    Dec 42
McMILLAN, R. B.
  Organized marketing of wool. ER 25,suppl.:
    59-72 Aug 49
McMILLAN, ROBERT T.
  Characteristics of former and present farm
    owners. LE 20:52-55 Feb 44
  Are tenure differences due to tenure?
    JFE 28:1029-36 Nov 46
McMURRY, ROBERT N.
  Psychology in selling. JM 9:114-18 Oct 44
McNAIR, MALCOLM PERRINE
  Wartime inflation and department stores.
    HBR 22:40-53 no.1, 43
  Some practical questions about the Murray
    Bill. REStat 27:113-16 Aug 45
  Distribution costs after the war. HBR 23:
    338-59 no.3, 45
  The full employment problem. HBR 24:1-21
    no.1, 45
McNALL, PRESTON ESSEX
  Economic phases in soil erosion control.
    JFE 22:613-20 Aug 40
  Farm buildings as evidence of productivity
    of crop land. LE 17:165-70 May 41
  Reflections on farm valuation. LE 21:71-73
    Feb 45
  Limiting factors in erosion control demon-
    strations. LE 21:383-86 Sep 45
  and Mitchell, D. R. What is the basis of
    farm financial progress? JFE 31:529-38
    Aug 49
McNATT, EMMETT B.
  Labor and the antitrust laws: the Apex de-
    cision. JPE 49:555-74 Jun 41
  Recent Supreme Court interpretations of
    labor law (1940-41). JB 14:356-71 Oct 41
  The "appropriate bargaining unit" problem.
    QJE 56:93-107 Nov 41
  [and others] Trade unions and the law: dis-
    cussion. AER/S 32:476-89 Mar 42
  Wage policy in the defense program. SEJ 8:
    504-12 Apr 42
  Toward a national wartime labor policy: the
    union-security issue. JB 16:64-69 Jan 43
  Toward a national wartime labor policy: the
    wage issue. JPE 51:1-11 Feb 43

McNEAL, DEAN
  The development and use of economic in-
    formation and forecasts by industry.
    JFE 31,pt.2:646-50 Feb 49
McNEILL, RUSSELL BLAIR
  and Bliss, C. A. Management control in
    uniform. HBR 22:227-38 no.2, 44
  The lease as a marketing tool. HBR 22:
    415-30 no.4, 44
MACON, HERSHAL LUTHER
  Payments in lieu of state and local taxes.
    SEJ 8:493-503 Apr 42
  War and postwar developments in state ex-
    penditures for the Southeast. SEJ 15:
    30-42 Jul 48
MACPHERSON, LOGAN GRANT
  Report of the Royal Commission on the
    Municipal Finances and Administration
    of the City of Winnipeg, 1939. CJE 6:
    68-72 Feb 40
McPHERSON, WILLIAM HESTON
  chairman. Problems of labor market re-
    search: abstract of specialized conference
    discussion. AER/S 32:213-14 Mar 42
  and Derber, M. The formation and develop-
    ment of IRRA. IRRA 1:2-4 Dec 48
McQUEEN, ROBERT
  The approach to economics. R. CJE 6:
    79-85 Feb 40
  Central banking in the Dominions. R. CJE 6:
    599-610 Nov 40
MACROSTY, HENRY WILLIAM
  The overseas trade of the United Kingdom
    1930-39. JRSS 103:451-80 pt.4, 40
MacRURY, KING
  Employee morale: analyses of absence
    records and opinion polls. ILRR 2:237-47
    Jan 49
MACY, CHARLES WARD
  Social security taxes in the war finance pro-
    gram. JPE 51:135-47 Apr 43
  Incidence or effects of the corporation income
    tax? AER 36:903-06 Dec 46
MACY, ROBERT MILLER
  Forecasting demand for U.S. Army supplies
    in wartime. JM 10:156-64 Oct 45
MADAN, BALKRISHNA
  Financial problems under provincial auton-
    omy. IJE 21:689-702 Apr 41
MADDEN, JOHN THOMAS and Backman, J.
  Public utility holding company common
    stocks. JB 13:213-33 Jul 40
MADDOX, JAMES GRAY
  A price policy for agriculture, consistent
    with economic progress, that will promote
    adequate and more stable income from
    farming. JFE 27:871-77 Nov 45
MADGE, CHARLES
  War-time saving and spending: a district
    survey. EJ 50:327-39 Jun-Sep 40
  The propensity to save in Blackburn and
    Bristol. EJ 50:410-48 Dec 40
  Public opinion and paying for the war. EJ 51:
    36-46 Apr 41

War and the small retail shop. OIS 4,suppl.
  2:1-8 Apr 4, 42
  and Rothbarth, E. Saving and spending in
    Leeds: a reply to Dr. Singer's criticisms.
    MS 13:80-88 Aug 44
MAGDOFF, HARRY and Weintraub, D.
  The service industries in relation to employ-
    ment trends. Em 8:289-311 Oct 40
MAGEE, JAMES DYSART [and others]
  Capital expansion, employment, and economic
    stability: a reply to H. H. Villard. AER 31:
    110-12 Mar 41
MAGEE, JOHN HENRY
  The future of the commercial insurance
    business. HBR 21:321-35 no.3, 43
MAHAJAN, YADAU S.
  Industrial relations in India. IJE 29:205-14
    Oct 48
  Forest resources and possibilities of their
    exploitation in Union Karnatak. IJE 29:
    351-64 Apr 49
MAHALANOBIS, PRASANTA CHANDRA
  Clara Elizabeth Collet. [obit.] JRSS 111:
    254 pt.3, 48
MAHMOUD ANIS
  see Anis, Mahmoud
MAHMOUD SALEH EL FALAKI
  see El Falaki, Mahmoud Saleh
MAIER, NORMAN R. F.
  A human relations program for supervision.
    ILRR 1:443-64 Apr 48
MAISEL, SHERMAN JOSEPH
  Have we underestimated increases in rents
    and shelter expenditures? JPE 57:106-17
    Apr 49
  Timing and flexibility of a public works pro-
    gram. REStat 31:147-52 May 49
  Variables commonly ignored in housing de-
    mand analysis. LE 25:260-74 Aug 49
MAIZELS, ALFRED
  Consumption, investment and national ex-
    penditure in wartime. Ec N.S.8:151-61
    May 41
  and Leak, H. [The concept of net volume of
    output, with special reference to Irish
    data.] Note on Dr. Geary's paper.
    JRSS 107:259-61 pt.3-4, 44
  and Leak, H. The structure of British in-
    dustry. JRSS 108:142-99 pt.1-2, 45
  The oversea trade statistics of the United
    Kingdom. JRSS 112:207-23 pt.2, 49
MAKOWER, HELEN
  with Marschak, J. and Robinson, H. W.
    Studies in mobility of labor: analysis for
    Great Britain. Pt.I-II. OEP 2:70-97;
    4:39-62 May 39, Sep 40
  Rationing and value theory. REStud 13:75-80
    no.2, 46
MALAN, G. H. T.
  An objective ordinal theory of value. SAJE 13:
    117-28 Jun 45
MALCOLM, THEODORE
  A new research tool. JM 5:38-39 Jul 40

MALEDON, WILLIAM J.
Research in retail distribution; its methods
and problems. JM 4:238-48 Jan 40
MALENBAUM, WILFRED
and Black, J. D. [The use of the short-cut
graphic method of multiple correlation.]
Rejoinder. QJE 54:346-58 Feb 40
--- Concluding remarks. QJE 54:358-64
Feb 40
The cost of distribution. QJE 55:255-70
Feb 41
Indexes on a type-farm basis. JFE 23:
584-606 Aug 41
[United States and world needs]: discussion.
JFE 29:1072-74 Nov 47
MALHERBE, MARGUERITE
A study of some Indian family diets in Durban.
SAJE 9:22-44 Mar 41
MALHOTRA, DAYA KRISHAN
Finance of local bodies in the Punjab.
IJE 22:933-45 Apr 42
Indian currency: past, present and future.
IJE 24:202-11 Jan 44
MALHOTRA, PREM CHAND
Scope of economics: a discussion of the rela-
tion between economics and ethics.
IJE 20:451-58 Apr 40
[Monetary policy of India]: discussion.
IJE 20:822-23 Apr 40
How to raise the Indian standard of living?
IJE 25:166-68 Oct 44
Transition from war to peace economy.
IJE 25:261-65 Jan 45
Agricultural possibilities in India. IJE 25:
556-60 Apr 45
and Agarwala, A. N. Agriculture in the in-
dustrialists' plan. IJE 25:502-10 Apr 45
A policy of stabilization of agricultural
prices. IJE 26:112-16 Jul 45
An integrated railway rate policy. IJE 26:
517-24 Jan 46
Reconstructing the Indian tax system: some
broad considerations. IJE 27:250-55
Oct 46
Agricultural labour in India. IJE 28:137-41
Jul 47
Industrial relations: an analysis of the funda-
mental issues involved. IJE 29:199-204
Oct 48
India's balance of payments. IJE 30:109-14
Oct 49
MALIN, JAMES C.
Mobility and history: reflections on the agri-
cultural policies of the United States in re-
lation to a mechanized world. AH 17:
177-91 Oct 43
Space and history: reflections on the closed-
space doctrines of Turner and Mackinder
and the challenge of those ideas by the air
age. Pt.I-II. AH 18:65-74; 107-26
Apr,Jul 44
The agricultural regionalism of the Trans-
Mississippi West as delineated by Cyrus
Thomas. AH 21:208-17 Oct 47

MALKANI, H. C.
Social security with special reference to
India. IJE 25:343-47 Jan 45
Post-war currency system in India. IJE 26:
388-91 Jan 46
MALLIK, A. N.
Labour problems and labour legislation in
India. (With special reference to the
railway industry.) IJE 20:663-93 Apr 40
MALLORY, JAMES RUSSELL
Disallowance and the national interest: the
Alberta social credit legislation of 1937.
CJE 14:342-57 Aug 48
MALONE, CARL
Postwar Extension problems in farm man-
agement. JFE 28:213-26 Feb 46
MALOTT, DEANE WALDO
Does futures trading influence prices?
HBR 18:177-90 no.2, 40
MANCINA, FRANK A. and Brown, G. H.
A note on the relationship between sales and
advertising of department stores. JB 13:
1-16 Jan 40; A correction. 205 Apr 40
MANCINI, GUGLIELMO
Aspects and problems of the Italian stock
market. BNL 1:321-37 Apr 48
MANCINI, MARCELLO
The Italian money market and the financing
of the Treasury. BNL 1:100-08 Jul 47
Bank credits in Italy; classified by business
branches and bank groups (1936-1946).
BNL 1:184-96 Oct 47
The banking year 1947 in Italy. BNL 1:
381-89 Jul 48
MANDELBAUM, K.
Germany's wage bill and national income in
the first year of the war. OIS 3:223-25
Jul 19, 41
and Balogh, T. Manpower policy in Germany.
OIS 3:279-81 Aug 30, 41
Food consumption in north-western and
western Europe, 1943-4 & 1945. OIS 7:
287-89 Nov 24, 45
MANES, ALFRED
Insuranble hazards. JB 14:1-10 Jan 41
Outlines of a general economic history of
insurance. JB 15:30-48 Jan 42
MANKIEWICZ, RENÉ H. and Keirstead, B. S.
The works of François Simiand. R. CJE 14:
249-54 May 48
MANN, FRITZ KARL
[and others] Problems of taxation: discus-
sion. AER/S 32:102-11 Mar 42
The dual-debt system as a method of financ-
ing government corporations. JPE 55:
39-56 Feb 47
The threefold economic function of taxation.
PF 2:5-15 no.1-2, 47
A fiscal testament of the New Deal. PF 2:
244-48 no.3, 47
Re-orientation through fiscal theory. Kyk 3:
116-29 fasc.2, 49

MANN, HENRY B.
  and Wald, A.  On the statistical treatment of
    linear stochastic difference equations.
    Em 11:173-220 Jul-Oct 43
  Nonparametric tests against trend.  Em 13:
    245-59 Jul 45
MANNE, ALAN SUSSMANN
  Some notes on the acceleration principle.
    REStat 27:93-99 May 45
MANNING, RAYMOND E.
  Depreciation in the tax laws and practices of
    the United States, Australia, Canada,
    Great Britain, New Zealand, and South
    Africa.  NTJ 1:154-74 Jun 48; Erratum.
    283 Sep 48
  Burden of state and local taxes in 18 large
    cities.  NTJ 2:173-78 Jun 49
MARBURG, THEODORE FRANCIS
  Aspects of labor administration in the early
    nineteenth century.  BHR 15:1-10 Feb 41
  Commission agents in the button and brass
    trade a century ago.  BHR 16:8-18 Feb 42
  Imperfect competition: in brass manufac-
    turing during the 1830's.  JEH/S 3:33-37
    Dec 43
  Manufacturer's drummer, 1832.  BHR 22:
    40-56 Apr 48
  Manufacturer's drummer, 1952, with com-
    ments on western and southern markets.
    BHR 22:106-14 Jun 48
MARCEAU, LeROY and Musgrave, R. A.
  Strikes in essential industries: a way out.
    HBR 27:286-92 May 49
MARCHAL, JEAN
  The state and its budget: from the budget of
    the Patrimonial state to the budget of the
    Faustian state.  PF 3:23-34 no.1, 48
MARCUS, EDWARD
  The interest-rate structure.  REStat 30:
    223-26 Aug 48
MARCUSE, SOPHIE
  An application of the control chart method to
    the testing and marketing of foods.
    JASA 40:214-22 Jun 45
MARGET, ARTHUR WILLIAM
  Monetary theory at the textbook level.
    AER 32:775-90 Dec 42
MARGOLIS, CHARLES
  Traceable response as a method of evaluat-
    ing industrial advertising: a case study.
    JM 12:202-10 Oct 47
MARGOLIS, JULIUS
  Public works and economic stability.  JPE 57:
    293-303 Aug 49
MARJOLIN, ROBERT
  Long cycles in capital intensity in the French
    coal mining industry, 1840 to 1914.
    REStat 23:165-75 Nov 41
MARKHAM, JESSE WILLIAM
  Regional labor productivity in the textile in-
    dustry.  AER 33:110-15 Mar 43
MARLEY, JOAN G.
  and Campion, H.  Changes in salaries in

Great Britain, 1924-1939.  JRSS 103:
    524-33 pt.4, 40
A statistical and economic survey of certain
    aspects of the beef producing, milk pro-
    ducing and cattle rearing industries in
    Great Britain between 1939 and 1945.
    JRSS 110:187-244 pt.3, 47
MARONI, YVES
  Discrimination under market interdepend-
    ence.  QJE 62:95-117 Nov 47
MARQUIS, RALPH WILLIAM
  Severance taxes on forest products and their
    relation to forestry.  LE 25:315-19 Aug 49
MARRAMA, VITTORIO
  Short notes on a model of the trade cycle.
    REStud 14:34-40 no.1, 46
  Some observations on Professor Lange's
    analysis.  Ec N.S.14:120-33 May 47
  Some aspects of Italian economy and the
    theory of full employment.  BNL 1:220-27
    Jan 48
MARS, J.
  The integration of the balance of payments
    into national income accounts.  YB 1:
    43-66 Sep 49
MARSCHAK, JACOB
  with Makower, H. and Robinson, H. W.
    Studies in mobility of labor: analysis for
    Great Britain.  Pt.I-II.  OEP 2:70-97;
    4:39-62 May 39, Sep 40
  Peace economics.  SR 7:280-98 Sep 40
  Lack of confidence.  SR 8:41-62 Feb 41
  A discussion of methods in economics.  R.
    JPE 49:441-48 Jun 41
  The task of economic stabilization.  SR 8:
    361-72 Sep 41
  Wicksell's two interest rates.  SR 8:469-78
    Nov 41
  Identity and stability in economics: a survey.
    Em 10:61-74 Jan 42
  Demand elasticities reviewed.  Em 11:25-34
    Jan 43
  Money illusion and demand analysis.
    REStat 25:40-48 Feb 43
  Income inequality and demand studies: a
    note.  Em 11:163-66 Apr 43
  and Andrews, W. H., Jr.  Random simultan-
    eous equations and the theory of produc-
    tion.  Em 12:143-205 Jul-Oct 44; Errata.
    13:91 Jan 45
  A cross section of business cycle discus-
    sion.  AER 35:368-81 Jun 45
  Neumann's and Morgenstern's new approach
    to static economics.  R.  JPE 54:97-115
    Apr 46
  Economic structure, path, policy, and pre-
    diction.  AER/S 37:81-84 May 47
  [and others]  The social and economic sig-
    nificance of atomic energy: discussion.
    AER/S 37:109-17 May 47
  On mathematics for economists.  R.
    REStat 29:269-73 Nov 47

MARSCHAK, JACOB (Cont.)
Role of liquidity under complete and incomplete information. AER/S 39:182-95 May 49

MARSH, DONALD BAILEY
The scope of the theory of international trade under monopolistic competition. QJE 56: 475-86 May 42
Fiscal policy and tariffs in post-war international trade. CJE 9:507-31 Nov 43

MARSH, JOHN F.
The use of "adjusted condition" for estimating yield per acre. JFE 29:541-46 May 47

MARSH, LEONARD CHARLES
The economics of low-rent housing. CJE 15: 14-33 Feb 49

MARSHALL, ALPHEUS R.
College courses in consumption economics. JM 5:26-34 Jul 40

MARSHALL, DOUGLAS G.
Soldier settlement in agriculture. LE 20: 270-78 Aug 44
Soldier settlement in the British Empire. LE 22:259-65 Aug 46
and Hill, G. W. Reproduction and replacement of farm population and agricultural policy. JFE 29:457-74 May 47

MARSHALL, HERBERT
Sedley Anthony Cudmore, 1878-1945. [obit.] JASA 41:75-76 Mar 46

MARSHALL, LEON CARROLL
Groups and their co-ordination: backgrounds of administration. JB 14:205-21 Jul 41

MARTIN, BOYCE FICKLEN
Southern industrial development. HBR 19: 159-76 no.2, 41
The cellulose South. HBR 20:43-52 no.1, 41
What business learns from war. HBR 21: 358-68 no.3, 43

MARTIN, EDWIN M.
The disposition of government financed industrial facilities in the postwar period. AER/S 33:128-36 Mar 43

MARTIN, JAMES WALTER
Corporate taxes and the assessment of public utility operating property. LE 16:262-69 Aug 40
--- A rejoinder. LE 17:117-18 Feb 41
The reorganization of revenue administration in Colorado. SEJ 8:395-97 Jan 42
Should the federal government tax state and local bond interest? SEJ 8:323-35 Jan 42
and Pardue, B. L. Comparative tax loads on railroads in nine southern states. NTJ 1: 25-30 Mar 48
State and local taxation in the Southeast and the war. SEJ 14:376-86 Apr 48
American taxation and World War II. PF 4: 112-20 no.2, 49

MARTIN, JOHN HENRY
Present status of priorities. HBR 19:271-85 no.3, 41
Administration of priorities. HBR 19:419-28 no.4, 41

Priorities and allocation. HBR 20:406-14 no.4, 42
Interim report on CMP. HBR 21:472-84 no.4, 43

MARTIN, KURT
and Burchardt, F. A. Western Germany and reconstruction. OIS 9:405-16 Dec 47
and Worswick, G. D. N. Prices and wages policy. OIS 10:84-93 Mar 48
and Thackeray, F. G. The terms of trade of selected countries, 1870-1938. OIS 10: 373-94 Nov 48
Capital movements, the terms of trade and the balance of payments. OIS 11:357-66 Nov 49

MARX, DANIEL, Jr.
The structure of interest rates: comment. QJE 56:152-56 Nov 41
The determination of postwar ocean freight rates. AER/S 36:561-74 May 46
The Merchant Ship Sales Act of 1946. JB 21: 12-28 Jan 48
Current American ship-operating subsidies. JB 21:239-59 Oct 48

MARX, WERNER
The law of diminishing marginal utility of income: an investigation of its validity. Kyk 3:254-72 fasc.3, 49

MARY THOMASINE, sister
see Cusack, Mary Thomasine, sister

MARY YOLANDE, sister
see Schulte, Mary Yolande, sister

MASON, EDWARD SAGENDORPH
chairman. Round table on preserving competition versus regulating monopoly. AER/S 30:213-18 Mar 40
with Schumpeter, J. A. and Cole, A. H. Frank William Taussig. [obit.] QJE 55: 337-63 May 41
chairman. Consensus report on the Webb-Pomerene law. AER 37:848-63 Dec 47
Some reflections on the wage-price problem. IRRA 1:22-34 Dec 48
[Various views on the monopoly problem.] Introduction. REStat 31:104-06 May 49
The effectiveness of the federal antitrust laws: a symposium. AER 39:712-13 Jun 49

MASON, JOHN EVERETT
with Jones, P. E. and Elvove, J. T. New settlement in the delta of the lower Mississippi Valley. LE 17:465-76 Nov 41
Cotton allotments in the Mississippi delta new-ground area. LE 18:447-57 Nov 42
and Bertrand, A. L. Tenure status of new-ground settlers in Louisiana. LE 19: 233-38 May 43
Constitutionality of zoning challenged in Virginia. LE 22:77-78 Feb 46
Acreage allotments and land prices. LE 22: 176-81 May 46

MASSE, BENJAMIN L.
Moral aspects of the Taft-Hartley Act. RSE 6:29-46 May 48

MASSEL, MARK S.
Reappraisal of depreciation and obsolescence. HBR 24:85-95 no.1, 45

MASSEY, PHILIP
The expenditure of 1,360 British middle-class households in 1938-39. JRSS 105: 159-85 pt. 3, 42

MASUCCI, ROBERT H. and Cochrane, W. W.
Price-income effects of a food allotment program. JFE 29:752-60 Aug 47

MATER, DAN HARRISON
The development and operation of the railroad seniority system. Pt.I-II. JB 13: 387-419; 14:32-67 Oct 40, Jan 41
A statistical study of the effect of seniority upon employee efficiency. JB 14:169-204 Apr 41
Effects of seniority upon the welfare of the employee, the employer, and society. JB 14:384-418 Oct 41
Wage rates and "relative economy and fitness" in the transportation industry. JB 18:183-208 Oct 45

MATEYO, GEORGE
Latin American consumers: some problems in reaching them by advertising. JM 6, no.4,pt.2:142-48 Apr 42

MATHEN, K. K. and Lal, R. B.
A note on conditions of living of agricultural labour and certain other rural groups in West Bengal. IJE 28:403-16 Jan 48

MATHERLY, WALTER JEFFRIES
The history of the Southern Economic Association, 1927-1939. SEJ 7:225-40 Oct 40
The development of consumer economics. SEJ 9:53-61 Jul 42
The regulation of consumer credit. SEJ 11: 34-44 Jul 44

MATHUR, P. N.
Landlordism in India. IJE 27:194-98 Oct 46

MATSUOKA, KOJI
The inflation of Chinese legal tender. Kyo 16,no.2:22-43 Apr 41
The currency system in French Indo-China. Kyo 17,no.2:44-63 Apr 42
Southern economy: its currency and financial problems. Kyo 17,no.4:27-47 Oct 42

MAULDON, FRANK RICHARD EDWARD
Seasonal variations in labour requirements in Australian industries. ER 17:81-96 Jun 41
The Australian coal industry. R. ER 24: 238-41 Dec 48
The consumer in a planned economy. ER 25,(no.48):1-17 Jun 49

MAURI, ANGELO
The development of agricultural economics in Europe prior to 1925: excerpts from Angelo Mauri's "I nuovi sviluppi dell' economia agraria." [Translated by C. Longobardi] AH 21:169-77 Jul 47

MAUTZ, WILLIAM H. and Durand, J. D.
Population and war labor supply. JASA 38: 31-42 Mar 43

MAVERICK, LEWIS ADAMS
The Chinese and the physiocrats: a supplement. EH 4:312-18 Feb 40
Demand and supply curves. QJE 54:307-13 Feb 40
Hsü Kuang-ch'i, a Chinese authority on agriculture. AH 14:143-60 Oct 40

MAXWELL, JAMES ACKLEY
The recent history of the Australian Loan Council. CJE 6:22-38 Feb 40
On some appendices to the Rowell-Sirois Report: VI. Public Finance. CJE 7: 244-49 May 41
Canadian dominion-provincial relations. QJE 55:584-610 Aug 41
The capital budget. QJE 57:450-65 May 43
and Balcom, M. N. Gasoline rationing in the United States. Pt.I-II. QJE 60:561-87; 61:125-55 Aug,Nov 46
Fiscal program of the 80th Congress. HBR 26:63-73 Jan 48

MAY, CLYDE O.
The influence of managerial ability and size of farm on the efficiency of agricultural production. JFE 25:105-09 Feb 43

MAY, GEORGE OLIVER
[The federal income tax.] Rejoinder. JASA 35:700 Dec 40
Gross income. QJE 55:521-25 May 41
Corporate structures and federal income taxation. HBR 22:10-18 no.1, 43
Another milestone in regulation. LE 23: 22-28 Feb 47

MAY, KENNETH OWNSWORTH
The aggregation problem for a one-industry model. Em 14:285-98 Oct 46
Technological change and aggregation. Em 15:51-63 Jan 47
Value and price of production: a note on Winternitz' solution. EJ 58:596-99 Dec 48
The structure of classical value theories. REStud 17:60-69 no.1, 49

MAYER, HAROLD M.
Patterns and recent trends of Chicago's outlying business centers. LE 18:4-16 Feb 42
Applications of residential data from the Chicago Land Use Survey. LE 19:85-87 Feb 43
Localization of railway facilities in metropolitan centers as typified by Chicago. LE 20:299-315 Nov 44
with Hall, K. S. and Wrigley, R. L., Jr. Mapping Chicago's industrial and commercial land use. LE 20:365-70 Nov 44

MAYER, HENRY
and Weiner, A. The New Jersey Telephone Company case. ILRR 1:492-99 Apr 48
[and others] Disputes that create a public emergency: discussion. IRRA 1:89-97 Dec 48

MAYER, JOSEPH
National product distortions: war and postwar. SEJ 12:141-50 Oct 45

MAYER, JOSEPH (Cont.)
    [and others] Postwar national income: an
    appraisal of criticisms of the Brookings
    Institution estimate. REStat 27:189-91
    Nov 45
    Deficiencies in the gross-national-product
    concept as a national measure. JPE 53:
    357-63 Dec 45
    Dr. Mayer on postwar national income: a
    reply. JPE 54:454 Oct 46
MAYER, KURT
    Small business as a social institution.
    SR 14:332-49 Sep 47
MAYER, ROBERT WALLACE
    Supreme Court's attitude toward historical
    cost. AER 30:352-53 Jun 40
MAYNARD, LEONARD AMBY
    Deficiencies in the United States diet, and
    means of meeting them. JFE 29:320-23
    Feb 47
MEADE, JAMES EDWARD
    and Stone. R. The construction of tables of
    national income, expenditure, savings and
    investment. EJ 51:216-33 Jun-Sep 41
    with Stone, R. and Champernowne, D. G. The
    precision of national income estimates.
    REStud 9:111-25 no.2, 42
    Price and output policy of state enterprise.
    EJ 54:321-28, 337-39 Dec 44
    Mr. Lerner on "The economics of control."
    R. EJ 55:47-69 Apr 45
    Bretton Woods, Havana and the United King-
    dom balance of payments. LBR 7:1-18
    Jan 48
    Planning without prices. Ec N.S.15:28-35
    Feb 48
    Financial policy and the balance of payments.
    Ec N.S.15:101-15 May 48
    National income, national expenditure and the
    balance of payments. Pt.I-II. EJ 58:
    483-505; 59:17-39 Dec 48, Mar 49
    A geometrical representation of balance of
    payments policy. Ec N.S.16:305-20 Nov 49
MEADOWS, PAUL
    Professional behavior and industrial society.
    JB 19:145-50 Jul 46
    Housing the American family. JB 21:80-91
    Apr 48
MEANS, GARDINER COIT
    Big business, administered prices, and the
    problem of full employment. JM 4:370-78
    Apr 40
    The American economy in the interwar
    period: discussion. AER/S 36:32-35
    May 46
MEDERNACH, JOSEPH A.
    Transportation in Latin America. JM 6,no.4,
    pt.2:152-55 Apr 42
MEDICI, GUISEPPE
    Italy and land reform. LE 21:2-11 Feb 45
    Some considerations on the land market in
    Europe. LE 22:171-73 May 46
    The E.R.P. and the problems of Italian agri-
    culture. BNL 1:416-26 Oct 48

MEE, JOHN F.
    [Scientific management in marketing]: dis-
    cussion. JM 4,no.4,pt.2:38 Apr 40
MEEHAN, MICHAEL JOSEPH
    Impact of defense upon industrial capacity
    and investment. JASA 37:22-33 Mar 42
    Economic dimensions of postwar readjust-
    ments. RSE 2:81-86 Jan 44
    Industry and business statistics. JASA 40:
    229-31 Jun 45
MEENEN, HENRY J.
    Size of farms. JFE 31,pt.2:599-601 Feb 49
MEHL, PAUL
    Trading in wheat and corn futures in relation
    to price movements. JFE 22:601-12
    Aug 40
MEHREN, GEORGE L.
    and Wellman, H. R. Some considerations of
    research in marketing horticultural
    products. JFE 28:170-81 Feb 46
    and Erdman, H. E. An approach to the de-
    termination of intraseasonal shifting of
    demand. JFE 28:587-96 May 46
    and Wellman, H. R. Some theoretical aspects
    of agricultural parity price policies and
    national employment. JFE 28:563-71
    May 46
    Consumer packaging of fruits and vegetables
    in California. JM 12:327-36 Jan 48
    Some economic aspects of agricultural
    control. JFE 30:29-42 Feb 48
    Elementary economic theory of marketing
    control. JFE 31,pt.2:1247-54 Nov 49
MEHTA, Sir CHUNILAL B.
    Planning and reconstruction. IJE 25:41-46
    Jul 44
MEHTA, JAMSHED KAIKHASROO
    The scope of economics. IJE 20:395-404
    Apr 40
    Diagrammatical representation of marginal,
    average and total prime and supplementary
    costs. IJE 21:74-79 Jul 40
    The negative rate of interest. IJE 21:301-06
    Jan 41
    Rent in economic theory. IJE 23:59-67 Jul 42
    The conception of market in economic theory.
    IJE 23:364-71 Apr 43
    The representative firm and its place in the
    study of dynamic economics. IJE 24:
    126-34 Oct 43
    Taxation of monopoly. IJE 25:124-29 Oct 44
    The concepts of static and dynamic equilibria
    in the general theory of value. IJE 26:
    1-10 Jul 45
    Competition and the demand curve. IJE 28:
    547-54 Apr 48
MEHTA, M. M.
    Corporate size and rate of profit. IJE 29:
    365-73 Apr 49
    Relation between size and efficiency. IJE 30:
    61-67 Jul 49
MEHTA, VAIKUNTH L.
    Rural co-operation in India: its deficiencies.
    IJE 22:599-614 Jan 42

MEIER, GERALD MARVIN
The trade matrix: a further comment on
Professor Frisch's paper. AER 38:
624-26 Sep 48
The theory of comparative costs reconsid-
ered. OEP N.S.1:199-216 Jun 49

MEINHARDT, MARIE DESSAUER-
see Dessauer, Marie

MELAMERSON-VANDENHAAG, ERNEST R.
A rationing rate structure. LE 19:243-45
May 43

MELLON, THOMAS
Selections from the autobiography of Thomas
Mellon. Pt.I-II. BHR 18:145-54; 19:12-26
Dec 44, Feb 45

MELMAN, SEYMOUR
An industrial revolution in the cotton South.
EHR II.2:59-72 no.1, 49

MELVILLE, LESLIE GALFREID
Economics of new orders. ER 18:143-57
Dec 42
Some post-war problems. ER 22:4-22 Jun 46
Where are we going? ER 22:193-98 Dec 46

MENA, RAÚL ORTIZ
see Ortiz Mena, Raúl

MENDELSOHN, RONALD
Australian housing policy: war and post-war.
ER 17:57-67 Jun 41
Rents and incomes. ER 20:91-94 Jun 44
and Hamilton, J. M. The Australian housing
cost index. ER 24:87-100 Jun 48

MENDERSHAUSEN, HORST
Differences in family savings between cities
of different size and location, whites and
Negroes. REStat 22:122-37 Aug 40
On the significance of another production
function: a comment [and rejoinder].
AER 31:563-64; 657-69 Sep 41
Concept and teaching of economics. AER 36:
376-84 Jun 46
Prices, money and the distribution of goods
in postwar Germany. AER 39:646-72
Jun 49
Future foreign financing. REStat 31:266-79
Nov 49

MENDEZ NADAL, DOLORES and Alberts, H. W.
The early history of livestock and pastures
in Puerto Rico. AH 21:61-64 Jan 47

MENDUM, SAMUEL WARREN
A device for analyzing yields: short cut to
yield-curve problems. JFE 30:357-64
May 48

MENKE, J. R.
Nuclear fission as a source of power. Em 15:
314-34 Oct 47

MENZE, ROBERT E.
An economic analysis of length of feeding
period in the production of hogs. JFE 24:
518-23 May 42

MENZIES-KITCHIN, ALEXANDER WILLIAM
and Chapman, W. D.
War-time changes in the organisation of two
groups of eastern counties farms. EJ 56:
57-85 Mar 46

MERCHANT, CHARLES S.
Maine potato marketing agreement and
order. JFE 31,pt.2:1244-46 Nov 49

MERIAM, LEWIS
Social security in an unstable world.
AER/S 37:335-44 May 47

MERIAM, RICHARD STOCKTON
The question of controls. HBR 26:454-67
Jul 48

MERING, OTTO von
Some problems of methodology in modern
economic theory. AER 34:87-97 Mar 44
Pragmatism and economic theory: a rejoinder [and a final word]. AER 35:
145-47; 667 Mar,Sep 45

MERK, FREDERICK
Eastern antecedents of the Grangers. AH 23:
1-8 Jan 49

MERLIN, SIDNEY
Trends in German economic control since
1933. QJE 57:169-207 Feb 43
The theory of economic change. QJE 59:
185-205 Feb 45

MERRIAM, MALCOLM L.
Influence of retail credit upon the continuity
of demand. JM 4,no.4,pt.2:89-99 Apr 40

MERRY, DONALD HENRY and Bruns, G. R.
Full employment: the British, Canadian and
Australian White Papers. ER 21:223-35
Dec 45

MERTES, JOHN E.
The shopping center: a new trend in retailing. JM 13:374-79 Jan 49

METTEL, GERTRUDE
Managerial adjustments to labor law: an
outline and bibliography. JB 17:186-93
Jul 44

METZ, HERBERT
The electrical distributor: war and postwar.
JM 8:310-15 Jan 44

METZLER, LLOYD APPLETON
The assumptions implied in least squares
demand techniques. REStat 22:138-49
Aug 40
The nature and stability of inventory cycles.
REStat 23:113-29 Aug 41
Underemployment equilibrium in international
trade. Em 10:97-112 Apr 42
The transfer problem reconsidered. JPE 50:
397-414 Jun 42
Effects of income redistribution. REStat 25:
49-57 Feb 43
Stability of multiple markets: the Hicks
conditions. Em 13:277-92 Oct 45
and Hinshaw, R. World prosperity and the
British balance of payments. REStat 27:
156-70 Nov 45
Business cycles and the modern theory of
employment. AER 36:278-91 Jun 46
Factors governing the length of inventory
cycles. REStat 29:1-15 Feb 47
Tariffs, the terms of trade, and the distribution of national income. JPE 57:1-29
Feb 49

METZLER, LLOYD APPLETON (Cont.)
Tariffs, international demand, and domestic prices. JPE 57:345-51 Aug 49
MEYER, E. A.
Developments under the Research and Marketing Act of 1946: finance, administrative organization, procedure and policy. JFE 29:1378-82 Nov 47
MEYER, FREDERICK VICTOR
Bulk purchases. Ec N.S.15:51-60 Feb 48
Economic change in the North-West. MS 17: 1-11 Jan 49
and Lewis, W. A. The effects of an overseas slump on the British economy. MS 17: 233-65 Sep 49
MEYER, JULIE
Trade union plans for post-war reconstruction in the United States. SR 11:491-505 Nov 44
Hierarchy and stratification of the shop. SR 14:168-90 Jun 47
The Latimer report. I. Some general observations. ILRR 1:465-70 Apr 48
Labor under the Taft-Hartley Act. SR 15: 194-210 Jun 48
MEYERS, ALBERT LEONARD
Some implications of full-employment policy. JPE 54:258-65 Jun 46
MEYERS, ERNEST S.
Some observations on the trade associations and the law. JM 12:379-81 Jan 48
MEYERS, FREDERIC
The Knights of Labor in the South. SEJ 6: 479-87 Apr 40
Organization and collective bargaining in the local mass transportation industry in the Southeast. SEJ 15:425-40 Apr 49
MÍCHALUP, ERIC
The social insurance movement. JASA 39: 519-20 Dec 44
MICHELL, HUMFREY
Economic history of the Hellenistic world. R. CJE 8:247-60 May 42
Monetary reconstruction. CJE 8:339-50 Aug 42
The impact of sudden accessions of treasure upon prices and real wages. CJE 12:1-17 Feb 46
Sedley Anthony Cudmore, 1878-1945. [obit.] CJE 12:93-94 Feb 46
The edict of Diocletian: a study of price fixing in the Roman Empire. CJE 13:1-12 Feb 47
MICKLE, W. T.
Margarine legislation. JFE 23:567-83 Aug 41
MICOLEAU, HENRI LeBREC
The economist and management. HBR 20: 380-81 no.3, 42
MIDANIK, S.
Problems of legislation relating to collective bargaining. CJE 9:348-53 Aug 43
MIGHELL, RONALD LESTER
and Allen, R. H. Supply schedules: "long-

time" and "short-time." JFE 22:544-57 Aug 40
[and others] Recent regional changes in farming and probable future trends. JFE 24:256-79 Feb 42
Effects of American-Canadian trade reciprocity on agriculture. JFE 24: 806-21 Nov 42
and Christensen, R. P. Measuring maximum contribution to food needs by producing areas. JFE 26:181-93 Feb 44
MIKESELL, RAYMOND FRECH
A note on the effects of minimum wages on the propensity to consume. AER 30:574 Sep 40
Oligopoly and the short-run demand for labor. QJE 55:161-66 Nov 40
The possibility of a positively sloped demand curve for labor. AER 30:829-32 Dec 40
and Galbreath, C. E. Subsidies and price control. AER 32:524-37 Sep 42
Financial problems of the Middle East. JPE 53:164-76 Jun 45
The key currency proposal. QJE 59:563-76 Aug 45
Gold sales as an anti-inflationary device. REStat 28:105-08 May 46
[and others] International investment: discussion. AER/S 36:710-16 May 46
United States international financial policy. CJE 12:313-21 Aug 46
The determination of postwar exchange rates. SEJ 13:263-75 Jan 47
[and others] Domestic versus international equilibrium: discussion. AER/S 37: 581-94 May 47
Quantitative and exchange restrictions under the ITO charter. AER 37:351-68 Jun 47
The role of the international monetary agreements in a world of planned economies. JPE 55:497-512 Dec 47
Regional multilateral payments arrangements. QJE 62:500-18 Aug 48
International disequilibrium and the postwar world. AER 39:618-45 Jun 49
The International Monetary Fund. JPE 57: 395-412 Oct 49
MILEY, D. GRAY
and Welch, F. J. Mechanization of the cotton harvest. JFE 27:928-46 Nov 45
The size of farm in the South. JFE 31,pt.2: 582-87 Feb 49
and Faught, W. A. Development of regional cotton marketing research. JFE 31,pt.2: 1207-12 Nov 49
MILLARD, JAMES WILLIAM
Co-operative advertising of food products. JM 6,no.4,pt.2:37-41 Apr 42
MILLER, AGNES ROMAN
China's first post-war budget. PF 2:354-62 no.4, 47

MILLER, FRANCIS P.
[What changes in national policy does the
South need?] Discussion. JFE 22:212-14
Feb 40

MILLER, GLENN W.
Wages and hours in consumers' cooperatives
in Great Britain and the United States.
QJE 55:294-305 Feb 41

MILLER, HENRY S.
Italian monetary and exchange policies under
fascism. AER 30:554-60 Sep 40

MILLER, HERMON I.
Developments in poultry marketing research.
JFE 29:1413-16 Nov 47
The midwestern egg project. JFE 31,pt.2:
1203-06 Nov 49

MILLER, J. DON, Jr.
Wages-fund theory and the popular influence
of economists. AER 30:108-12 Mar 40
The academic mind in business. JB 20:
146-55 Jul 47

M[ILLER], J[ACOB]
Some recent developments in Soviet economic
thought. SovS 1:119-27 Oct 49

MILLER, JAMES W.
Pre-war Nazi agrarian policy. AH 15:175-81
Oct 41

MILLER, JOHN PERRY
The tactics of retail price control. QJE 57:
497-521 Aug 43
Military procurement in peacetime. HBR 25:
444-62 no.4, 47

MILLER, JOSEPH L. [and others]
Disputes that create a public emergency:
discussion. IRRA 1:89-97 Dec 48

MILLER, K. W. and Lewis, E. M. R.
Notes on the balance of payments of the
British and French empires with non-
sterling countries. ER 16:114-18 Jun 40

MILLER, LEONARD F.
Farmers' investments, a neglected field.
JFE 26:391-96 May 44
Farm and home planning: discussion [sum-
marized]. JFE 29:189-91 Feb 47
and Preston, H. J. Relation of feed, labor,
and other costs to butterfat test. JFE 30:
566-73 Aug 48
Farmers' assets outside their business.
JFE 31:143-53 Feb 49
Outlook and farm management. JFE 31,pt.2:
642-45 Feb 49

MILLER, MERTON HOWARD and Musgrave,
R. A.
Built-in flexibility. AER 38:122-28 Mar 48

MILLER, MORTON D.
Statistical problems in developing voluntary
medical expense insurance plans.
JASA 43:290-98 Jun 48

MILLER, RAYMOND W. and Jensen, A. L.
Failures of farmers' cooperatives. HBR 25:
213-26 no.2, 47

MILLER, STANLEY LAWRENCE
The equity capital problem. HBR 26:671-79
Nov 48

MILLER, WILLIAM
A note on the history of business corpora-
tions in Pennsylvania, 1800-1860. QJE 55:
150-60 Nov 40
American historians and the business elite.
JEH 9:184-208 Nov 49
The problems [of research methods] resolved.
EEH 2:49-51 Nov 49

MILLER, WILSON S. and Engquist, E. J., Jr.
Measuring retailers' inventories. JM 9:
49-52 Jul 44

MILLS, CHARLES WRIGHT
The American business elite: a collective
portrait. JEH/S 5:20-44 Dec 45
The contribution of sociology to studies of
industrial relations. IRRA 1:199-222
Dec 48

MILLS, FREDERICK CECIL
Economics in a time of change. AER 31:
1-14 Mar 41
chairman. An appraisal of the U.S. Bureau
of Labor Statistics cost of living index by
a special committee. JASA 38:387-405
Dec 43
Elasticity of physical quantities and flexibility
of unit prices in the dimension of time.
JASA 41:439-67 Dec 46
The economic outlook of Friday and Edie and
Ayres. AER/S 37:50 May 47
Living costs, prices, and productivity.
REStat 30:6-8 Feb 48
Round table in commemoration of the centen-
ary of the Communist Manifesto: the
sociology and economics of class conflict:
opening remarks. AER/S 39:13-15 May 49
Wesley Clair Mitchell 1874-1948. [obit.]
AER 39:730-42 Jun 49

MILLS, MARK CARTER
Principles and practice in public finance.
AER 31:101 Mar 41
American government finance 1930-1940.
SAJE 9:361-78 Dec 41

MILLS, THOMAS J.
Notes on the productivity conference. AER 37:
187-90 Mar 47

MINAW, FARIS
Radio-geophysical prospection for desert
underground water and the utilisation of
Egyptian deserts. EgC 39:1-9 Jan-Feb 48

MINTS, LLOYD WYNN
Monetary policy. REStat 28:60-69 May 46

MIRE, JOSEPH
Collective bargaining in the public service.
AER/S 36:347-58 May 46

MIRKOWICH, BEATRICE M. and Tinley, J. M.
Control in the sugar-cane industry of South
Africa. JFE 23:537-49 Aug 41

MIRKOWICH, NICHOLAS
The place of J. B. Clark and E. R. A. Selig-
man in American economic science.
IJE 21:67-74 Jul 40
Schumpeter's theory of economic develop-
ment. AER 30:580 Sep 40

MIRKOWICH, NICHOLAS (Cont.)
  The economics of John A. Hobson. IJE 23:
    175-85 Oct 42
MISES, LUDWIG von
  "Elastic expectations" and the Austrian
    theory of the trade cycle. Ec N.S.10:
    251-52 Aug 43
MISHAN, EDWARD JOSHUA
  Realism and relevance in consumer's sur-
    plus. REStud 15:27-33 no.1, 47
MISHRA
  see Misra
MISRA, BABU RAM
  Proprietary tenures in Oudh: a historical
    survey. IJE 20:371-90 Jan 40
MISRA, BIDVADHAR
  Land tenure in the district of Sambalpur
    (Orissa). IJE 27:199-204 Oct 46
  Agricultural labour in Orissa. IJE 28:443-49
    Jan 48
  Can the government of India finance a plan at
    present? IJE 29:243-47 Jan 49
MISRA, HAREKRISHNA
  Cheap money and its place in the postwar
    economy of India. IJE 28:89-93 Jul 47
  Industrial relations in India. IJE 29:227-33
    Oct 48
MISRA, JAI KRISHNA
  Price level and balance of payments of India
    in recent years. IJE 30:123-27 Oct 49
MISRA, SADASIV
  Five years of Orissa budget. IJE 21:634-47
    Apr 41
  Co-operative agricultural credit in Orissa.
    IJE 22:724-38 Jan 42
  Can India adopt Beveridge? IJE 25:324-30
    Jan 45
  Food position in Orissa. IJE 26:525-34
    Jan 46
MISRA SHRIDHAR
  Agricultural labour in U.P. IJE 28:187-95
    Jul 47
  Agricultural wages in relation to rural cost
    of living. IJE 29:75-80 Jul 48
MITCHELL, BROADUS
  The teaching of controversial questions.
    [Summary] AER/S 30:106-07 Mar 40
  Treatment of controversial questions in the
    teaching of political economy. AER 30:
    339-43 Jun 40
MITCHELL, CHARLES CLYDE
  Korean farm tenant purchase program.
    LE 24:402-05 Nov 48
  A comment on "planning and control."
    JFE 31:708-11 Nov 49
MITCHELL, DONALD RICHARDS and McNall,
  P. E.
  What is the basis of farm financial progress?
    JFE 31:529-38 Aug 49
MITCHELL, GEORGE WILDER
  Using sales data to measure the quality of
    property tax administration. NTJ 1:
    330-40 Dec 48

MITCHELL, ROBERT BUCHANAN
  The neighborhood concept in theory and ap-
    plication. LE 25:78-81 Feb 49
MITCHELL, WESLEY CLAIR
  [and others] Economic consequences of war
    since 1790: discussion. AER/S 30,no.5:
    362-65 Feb 41
  J. Laurence Laughlin. R. JPE 49:875-81
    Dec 41
  Economics in a unified world. SR 11:1-10
    Feb 44
  [and others] Political science, political
    economy, and values: discussion.
    AER/S 34:48-57 Mar 44
  The role of money in economic history.
    JEH/S 4:61-67 Dec 44
MITNITZKY, MARK
  Some monetary aspects of government bor-
    rowing. AER 33:21-37 Mar 43
MITRA, K.
  Trend of dietary habits and analysis of food
    budget in working class families of Bihar.
    IJE 22:144-63 Oct 41
MODIGLIANI, FRANCO
  Liquidity preference and the theory of inter-
    est and money. Em 12:45-88 Jan 44
  Fluctuations in the saving ratio: a problem
    in economic forecasting. SR 14:413-20
    Dec 47
  [and others] Liquidity and uncertainty: dis-
    cussion. AER/S 196-210 May 49
MOFFAT, ROBERT E.
  Financial relations between the Australian
    Commonwealth and the Australian states.
    CJE 13:465-79 Aug 47
  Some aspects of recent freight rate discus-
    sions. CJE 14:441-52 Nov 48
MOGILNITSKY, THEODOSI ALEXIS
  [Public policy and postwar employment in
    the United States]: discussion. RSE 3:
    53-54 Dec 44
MOHAMED HOSNY EL-SAID
  see El-Said, Mohamed Hosny
MOLINARI, ALESSANDRO
  Future responsibilities of the Italian indus-
    try. BNL 1:3-9 Apr 47
  Southern Italy. BNL 2:25-47 Jan-Mar 49
MOLL, WILLIAM J.
  Survey of consumer buying intent. JM 8:
    54-58 Jul 43
MOLLAT, MICHEL
  Anglo-Norman trade in the fifteenth century.
    EHR 17:143-50 no.2, 47
MOLONEY, JOHN FREDERICK
  Some effects of the federal Fair Labor Stand-
    ards Act upon southern industry. SEJ 9:
    15-23 Jul 42
MONSON, ASTRID
  see Monson, Donald and Monson, A.
MONSON, DONALD and Monson, A.
  The development and practice of compensa-
    tion and betterment in present English
    planning law. LE 25:173-83 May 49

MONTGOMERY, ARTHUR
Gustav Cassel (1866-1945). [obit.] EJ 57: 532-42 Dec 47
Post-war economic problems in Sweden. LBR 8:20-34 Apr 48

MONTGOMERY, DONALD
Labor's aims and what they mean to agriculture. JFE 31,pt.2:1141-47 Nov 49

MONTGOMERY, GEORGE
Future of the Great Plains: discussion. JFE 31,pt.2:929-30 Nov 49

MONTGOMERY, ROYAL EWART [and others]
The determination of wages: discussion. AER/S 32:302-06 Mar 42

MOOD, FULMER
The concept of the frontier, 1871-1898: comments on a select list of source documents. AH 19:24-30 Jan 45
A British statistician of 1854 analyzes the westward movement in the United States. AH 19:142-51 Jul 45

MOODY, RICHARD E.
Mr. Bunce on time preference and conservation. JFE 23:646-53 Aug 41

MOODY, VERNIE ALTON
Europe's recurrent land problem. AH 22: 220-32 Oct 48

MOOMAW, I. W.
Peasant farming in India. JFE 24:685-94 Aug 42

MOONITZ, MAURICE
The risk of obsolescence and the importance of the rate of interest. JPE 51:348-55 Aug 43

MOORE, GEOFFREY HOYT
Industrial materials production, World Wars I and II. JASA 39:335-44 Sep 44
Accuracy of government statistics. HBR 25: 306-17 no.3, 47

MOORE, WAYNE R. and Nordin, J. A.
Bronfenbrenner on the black market. AER 37:933-34 Dec 47

MOORE, WILBERT ELLIS
Primitives and peasants in industry. SR 15: 44-81 Mar 48
Theoretical aspects of industrialization. SR 15:277-303 Sep 48

MOORE, WILLIAM HOYT
Termination of contracts and disposal of surpluses after the first World War. AER/S 33:138-49 Mar 43
State experiments in mortgage lending. JB 22:169-77 Jul 49

MOOS, S.
The tea trade in war time. OIS 2,no.8:5-9 Oct 40
The accumulation of raw material surpluses. OIS 2,no.11:11-14 Dec 40; Errata. 3:16 Jan 11, 41
International commodity control. OIS 3:7-11 Jan 11, 41
The shipping situation. OIS 3:74-76 Mar 15, 41

Prospects of the tobacco trade. OIS 3:85-91 Apr 5, 41
Yugoslavia's foreign trade during the first year of war. OIS 3:124-29 Apr 26, 41
and Buckatzsch, E. J. The Balkan war and the blockade of Germany. OIS 3:141-44 May 17, 41
The two-stamp-plan, a new method of distribution. OIS 3:246-52 Aug 9, 41
The effect of war on the sugar industry. OIS 3:348-55 Nov 1, 41
Oil supply in the Indian and eastern Pacific areas. OIS 4:20-25 Jan 10, 42
Some features of British cotton exports. OIS 4:93-98 Mar 14, 42
The aluminium revolution. OIS 4:209-14 Aug 8, 42
Incentives to the development of mineral resources. OIS 4:302-08 Nov 21, 42
Natural versus synthetic rubber. OIS 5: 51-55 Feb 20, 43; Erratum. 72 Mar 13, 43
Building materials and building policy. OIS 5:112-17 May 15, 43
Statistics of advertising. OIS 5:181-87 Aug 7, 43; Erratum. 204 Aug 28, 43
Labour costs in housing. OIS 5:225-31 Oct 9, 43
The cost of building materials. OIS 5:241-47 Oct 30, 43
Aluminium prices. OIS 5:280-83 Dec 11, 43
The age of structure of building labour. OIS 6:39-44 Feb 26, 44
The change in non-ferrous metal prices. OIS 6:117-24 Jun 10, 44
Economic problems of pre-fabrication. OIS 6:202-08 Sep 2, 44
The foreign trade of west European countries. Pt.I-II. OIS 7:7-13; 56-60 Jan 13, Feb 24, 45
Laissez-faire, planning and ethics. EJ 55: 17-27 Apr 45
Building societies and building finance. OIS 7:149-59 Jun 30, 45
Estimates of housing needs. OIS 7:218-26 Sep 22, 45; Corrigenda. 290 Nov 24, 45
Employment and output in the building trades. OIS 8:44-50 Feb 46
Price formation and price maintenance on the aluminium market. MS 16:66-93 Jan 48
The structure of the British aluminium industry. EJ 58:522-37 Dec 48

MORAZÉ, P.
The Treaty of 1860 and the industry of the Department of the North. EHR 10:18-28 Feb 40

MORDECAI, EZEKIEL and Wylie, K. H.
The cost curve for steel production. JPE 48: 777-821 Dec 40

MOREHOUSE, EDWARD WARD
The creed of a great public servant. LE 20: 361-64 Nov 44
On the 1944 NARUC Report. LE 21:282-84 Aug 45

MOREHOUSE, EDWARD WARD (Cont.)

[and others] Recent developments in public utility regulation: discussion. AER/S 36: 435-50 May 46

Observations on Riggs' and Thompson's comments on Nash, Anatomy of depreciation. LE 24:79-81 Feb 48

MORGAN, A.

The Japanese currency reform: a lesson in monetary experience. OIS 10:424-37 Dec 48

MORGAN, CHARLES STILLMAN

Aspects of the problem of public aids to transportation. AER/S 30:130-39 Mar 40

The transportation problem: discussion. AER/S 30:163 Mar 40

MORGAN, D. J.

Commentary on "Great Britain's trade policy." SR 12:370-74 Sep 45

The economy of Europe. R. Ec N.S.16: 255-62 Aug 49

The British commonwealth and European economic co-operation. EJ 59:307-25 Sep 49

MORGAN, EDWARD VICTOR

Railway investment, Bank of England policy and interest rates, 1844-8. EH 4:329-40 Feb 40

The plans for an international clearing system. Ec N.S.10:297-301 Nov 43

The joint statement by experts on the establishment of an international monetary fund. Ec N.S.11:112-18 Aug 44

The future of interest rates. EJ 54:340-51 Dec 44

Some thoughts on the nature of interest. OEP N.S.1:182-90 Jun 49

MORGAN, HENRY D.

Financing of state veterans' bonuses. NTJ 1:233-40 Sep 48

MORGAN, JAMES NEWTON

Can we measure the marginal utility of money? Em 13:129-52 Apr 45

The burden of import duties: a comment. AER 37:407-09 Jun 47

The measurement of gains and losses. QJE 62:287-308 Feb 48

Bilateral monopoly and the competitive output. QJE 63:371-91 Aug 49

MORGAN, JOHN S.

The break-up of the poor law in Britain 1907-47: an historical footnote. CJE 14: 209-19 May 48

MORGAN, LUCY

The impact of war taxation on eighty Canadian corporations. CJE 8:566-83 Nov 42

MORGAN, THEODORE

Interest, time preference, and the yield of capital. AER 35:81-98 Mar 45; Correction. 437 Jun 45

A measure of monopoly in selling. QJE 60: 461-63 May 46

MORGENSTERN, OSKAR

Unemployment: analysis of factors. AER/S 30,no.5:273-93 Feb 41

Professor Hicks on Value and capital. R. JPE 49:361-93 Jun 41

[and others] Effects of the war and defense program upon economic conditions and institutions: discussion. AER/S 32: 382-90 Mar 42

On the international spread of business cycles. JPE 51:287-309 Aug 43

Demand theory reconsidered. QJE 62: 165-201 Feb 48

Oligopoly, monopolistic competition, and the theory of games. AER/S 38:10-18 May 48

[and others] Input-output analysis and its use in peace and war economies: discussion. AER/S 39:226-40 May 49

Economics and the theory of games. Kyk 3: 294-308 fasc.4, 49

MORIN, ALEXANDER JOSEPH

A note on bilateral monopoly, with special reference to seasonal agricultural labor. JFE 31:101-15 Feb 49

MORISON, F. L.

Ohio farm labor situation. JFE 25:298-300 Feb 43

MORRIS, BRUCE ROBERT

Price control at the retail level. QJE 58: 323-24 Feb 44

MORRIS, MAX

Chartism and the British working-class movement. S&S 12:400-17 no.4, 48

MORRISON, HUNTER

Rate policy of Interstate Commerce Commission for back-hauls of trucks: pricing and joint cost. LE 19:329-38 Aug 43

MORRISON, PAUL LESLIE

Trends in investment policies of individuals. JF 4:156-76 Jun 49

MORROW, ALEXANDER

The war's impact on milk marketing. JM 10: 235-43 Jan 46

MORS, WALLACE PETER

Rate regulation in the field of consumer credit. Pt.I-II. JB 16:51-63; 124-37 Jan,Apr 43

Commercial banks and competitive trends in consumer instalment financing. JB 21: 133-67 Jul 48

MORSE, DAVID A.

Labor and American foreign policy. ILRR 1: 18-28 Oct 47

MORSE, TRUE D.

Use of economics in farming. JFE 31, pt.2:863-69 Nov 49

MORSE, WAYNE

Labor Extension Bill (1948). ILRR 1:657-63 Jul 48

MORTENSON, WILLIAM PETER

Legal possibilities and limitations of milk distribution as a public utility. Pt.I-II. LE 15:438-47; 16:61-71 Nov 39, Feb 40

MORTON, WALTER ALBERT
   A zero deposit rate. AER 30:536-53 Sep 40
   William A. Scott 1862-1944. [obit.] AER 35:
     786-87 Sep 45
MORTON, WILLIAM LEWIS
   The social philosophy of Henry Wise Wood,
     the Canadian agrarian leader. AH 22:
     114-23 Apr 48
MOSAK, JACOB LOUIS
   Some theoretical implications of the statis-
     tical analysis of demand and cost func-
     tions for steel. JASA 36:100-10 Mar 41
   Wage increases and employment. AER 31:
     330-32 Jun 41
   and Salant, W. S. Income, money and prices
     in wartime. AER 34:828-39 Dec 44
   National budgets and national policy. AER 36:
     20-43 Mar 46
   --- A final reply. AER 36:637-41 Sep 46
MOSCHELES, J.
   The South Seas in the modern world. ER 18:
     82-87 Jun 42
MOSES, LIONEL B.
   Merchandising the advertising campaign.
     JM 9:124-26 Oct 44
MOSHER, MARTIN LUTHER
   Thirty years of farm financial and produc-
     tion records in Illinois. JFE 27:24-37
     Feb 45
MOSK, SANFORD ALEXANDER
   The influence of tradition on agriculture in
     New Mexico. JEH/S 2:34-51 Dec 42
   Land policy and stock raising in the western
     United States. AH 17:14-30 Jan 43
MOSSE, GEORGE L.
   The Anti-League: 1844-1846. EHR 17:
     134-42 no.2, 47
MOSSMAN, F. H.
   Grade labeling for canned fruits and vege-
     tables. JM 7:241-44 Jan 43
MOULTON, HAROLD GLENN
   [and others] Capital expansion, employment
     and economic stability: a reply to the
     review. JASA 35:700-03 Dec 40
   --- A reply to H. H. Villard. AER 31:110-12
     Mar 41
   D. McC. Wright's character attack. AER 34:
     116-21 Mar 44
MOULTON, J. S.
   Who will pay for the Central Valley Project
     of California? A reply. LE 23:86-87
     Feb 47
MOUNTAIN, G. R.
   The position of the Australian consumer.
     ER 25,suppl.:123-39 Aug 49
MOWAT, CHARLES L.
   The land policy in British East Florida.
     AH 14:75-77 Apr 40
MUDGETT, BRUCE D.
   The cost-of-living index and Konüs' condition.
     Em 13:171-81 Apr 45
MUELLER, FRANZ H.
   The principle of solidarity in the teachings of

Father Henry Pesch, S.J. RSE 4:31-39
   Jan 46
MUHAJIR, A.
   Banking in East Pakistan. PEJ 1,no.1:112-16
     Jul 49
MUKHERJEE, B.
   The economics of soil erosion and its influ-
     ence on national life. IJE 21:148-57
     Oct 40
   The control of soil erosion in the West and
     its lessons for India. IJE 21:269-84
     Jan 41
MUKHERJEE, BANKIM CHANDRA
   Economy of the province of West Bengal and
     its relations with Pakistan. IJE 29:45-54
     Jul 48
MUKERJI, KARUNA MOY
   Problems of agricultural labour in India.
     IJE 28:163-74 Jul 47
   Debt conciliation: a phase in the co-opera-
     tive movement in Bengal (1940-43).
     IJE 28:563-69 Apr 48
   The problems of agricultural indebtedness
     in Bengal. IJE 29:375-94 Apr 49
MUKHERJEE, MONI MOHAN
   A note on trend of concentration ratio.
     IJE 28:291-92 Oct 47
MUKERJEE, RADHAKAMAL
   The sociological assumptions and norms of
     classicism. IJE 20:303-20 Jan 40
   The sociological elements in price economics.
     IJE 21:109-30 Oct 40
   Typology of contrasted economic systems: a
     clue to the methods of analysis of Indian
     economic conditions. IJE 22:290-306
     Jan 42
MUKHOPADHYAYA, S. N.
   Recruitment of labour in tea plantations in
     India as an outlet for landless agricul-
     turists. IJE 28:197-206 Jul 47
MULCAHY, RICHARD EDWARD
   The welfare economics of Heinrich Pesch.
     QJE 63:342-60 Aug 49
MULLEN, WADSWORTH H.
   Measurement of national advertising.
     HBR 27:622-45 Sep 49
MULLER, CHARLOTTE FELDMAN
   British war finance and the banks. JB 16:
     77-99 Apr 43
   Aluminum and power control. LE 21:108-24
     May 45
MULLIKEN, OTIS EMERY
   Wage determination in agriculture: discus-
     sion. JFE 23:104-09 Feb 41
MUMFORD, DWIGHT CURTIS
   Farm management research: discussion.
     JFE 22:126-30 Feb 40
MUMFORD, LEWIS
   Garden cities and the metropolis: a reply.
     LE 22:66-69 Feb 46
MUND, VERNON ARTHUR
   The "freight allowed" method of price quota-
     tion. QJE 54:232-45 Feb 40

MUSGRAVE, RICHARD ABEL (Cont.)
Debt management and inflation. REStat 31:
25-29 Feb 49
and Marceau, L. Strikes in essential industries: a way out. HBR 27:286-92 May 49
Business income taxation and asset expan-
sion: discussion. JF 4:193-96 Sep 49
MUSHKIN, SELMA J.
and Scitovzky, A. A formula for social insurance financing. AER 35:646-52 Sep 45
[and others] Social security in a stable prosperity: discussion. AER/S 37:351-66
May 47
MUSSER, RALPH H.
A farm-city plan for erosion control. LE 18:
323-27 Aug 42
MUTYALA, JAYA
International economic relations. IJE 29:
257-63 Jan 49
MYERS, AARON HOWARD
Laws and men in labor relations. HBR 21:
83-94 no.1, 42
MYERS, CHARLES ANDREW
Experience rating in Wisconsin in 1940.
AER 30:835-37 Dec 40
and Maclaurin, W. R. After unemployment
benefits are exhausted. QJE 56:231-55
Feb 42
and Maclaurin, W. R. Wages and the move-
ment of factory labor. QJE 57:241-64
Feb 43
Wartime concentration of production. JPE 51:
222-34 Jun 43
Experience rating in unemployment compen-
sation. AER 35:337-54 Jun 45
Approaches and problems in wage research.
AER/S 37:367-74 May 47
MYERS, HOWARD BARTON
Dynamics of labor supply. JASA 36:175-84
Jun 41
Defense migration and labor supply. JASA 37:
69-76 Mar 42
Corrington Calhoun Gill 1898-1946. [obit.]
JASA 41:393-94 Sep 46
MYERS, JOHN HOLMES
Tariffs and prices: a diagrammatic repre-
sentation. AER 31:553-57 Sep 41
and Bakay, A. J. Influence of stock split-ups
on market price. HBR 26:251-55 Mar 48
MYERS, ROBERT JAMES
and Ober, H. Statistics for wage stabiliza-
tion. JASA 38:425-37 Dec 43
Wartime changes in urban wage relationships.
JASA 40:175-86 Jun 45
A critique of "A method of making actuarial
estimates for a compulsory health insur-
ance system." JASA 42:123-27 Mar 47
MYINT, HLA
The welfare significance of productive labour.
REStud 11:20-30 no.1, 43
The classical view of the economic problem.
Ec N.S.13:119-30 May 46

MYRVOLL, OLE
The profit motive and the theory of partial
equilibrium of the firm. NTTO 12:179-86
no.37, 48
NADAL, DOLORES MENDEZ
see Mendez Nadal, Dolores
NADEAU, JOSEPH PETER
Milk control in Canada. JFE 24:333-36
Feb 42
NADEN, KENNETH D.
Price policy of the Challenge Cream & But-
ter Association. Pt.I-II. JM 13:459-69;
14:27-37 Apr,Jul 49
NAESS, RAGNAR D.
The outlook for incomes and spending.
AER/S 37:58-63 May 47
NAFZIGER, RALPH O.
Problems in reader-interest surveys.
JM 9:359-63 Apr 45
NAG, D. S.
The Gandhian plan: a rejoinder. IJE 27:
64-68 Jul 46
NAGABHUSHANAM, K.
Population of provinces. IJE 29:393-97
Apr 49
NAIDOO, V. SIRKARI
Survey of the income and expenditure of
Indian employees of the Durban Corpora-
tion, living at the Magazine Barracks,
Durban. SAJE 14:40-62 Mar 46
NAIDU, B. V. NARAYANASWAMY
see Narayanaswami Naidu, Bijayeti Venkata
NAIR, A. N. K.
Some problems relating to employment and
unemployment statistics in India. IJE 28:
245-59 Oct 47
NAKAGAWA, YONOSUKE
The development of social policy in Japan.
Kyo 17,no.1:14-30 Jan 42
The Greater East Asia War and the renais-
sance of the Japanese woman. Kyo 19,
no.1:1-19 Jan 44
NANCE, J. J.
War and postwar adjustments in marketing
appliances. JM 8:307-09 Jan 44
NANJUNDAIYA, K. S.
The tax system of Mysore State. IJE 21:
648-67 Apr 41
NARASIMHAM, NUTI VENKATA APPALA
Terms of trade and commercial policy.
IJE 28:39-48 Jul 47
NARAYAN PRASAD, P. S.
see Prasad, Panday Sundara Narayan
NARAYANASWAMY NAIDU, BIJAYETI VENKATA
Industrial disputes and their settlement.
IJE 20:729-35 Apr 40
Finances of the Madras Province, 1920-40.
IJE 21:881-91 Apr 41
A review of Madras local finance. IJE 22:
637-48 Jan 42
India and post-war reconstruction. IJE 24:
463-524 Apr 44

NASH, E. F.
Changes in external factors affecting British agriculture. LBR 8:35-56 Apr 48
NATARAJAN, BALASUBRAMANIAM
Economic ideas behind the Permanent Settlement. IJE 22:708-23 Jan 42
NATESAN, L. A.
Shipping in relation to commercial policy. IJE 28:55-60 Jul 47
NATHAN, OTTO
Population movements and cyclical movements. [Abstract] AER/S 30:384-86 Mar 40
Consumption in Germany during the period of rearmament. QJE 56:349-84 May 42
NATHAN, ROBERT ROY
Problems of statistical control: economic aspects. JASA 36:18-26 Mar 41
Comments of Sumner H. Slichter [on the steel report]. REStat 31:288-91 Nov 49
NAVIN, THOMAS RANDALL
Evaluating the methods of the business administrator. BHR 17:11-14 Feb 43
The Wellman-Woodman patent controversy in the cotton textile machinery industry. BHR 21:144-52 Nov 47
World's leading cymbal maker: Avedis Zildjian Company. BHR 23:196-206 Dec 49
NAWROCKI, Z.
The prospects of the British cotton industry. EJ 54:41-46 Apr 44
NAZMY, A. ABDEL HAMID
The Australian experience. EgC 35:49-53 Jan-Feb 44
The land is a bottomless sink for Egyptian capital. EgC 35:239-41 Mar-Apr 44
NEAL, ALFRED C.
The "planning approach" in public economy. QJE 54:246-54 Feb 40
Marginal cost and dynamic equilibrium of the firm. JPE 50:45-64 Feb 42
Comment on review of Industrial concentration and price inflexibility. AER 33: 622-25 Sep 43
and Hyson, C. D. New England's economic prospects. HBR 26:156-80 Mar 48
[and others] Round table on economic research: discussion. AER/S 39:464-72 May 49
NEALE, EDWARD PERCY
The 1936 Maori census. ER 16:275-80 Dec 40
Recent New Zealand data regarding the incomes of individuals. ER 17:68-80 Jun 41
New Zealand general government finances, 1944-45. ER 20:222-26 Dec 44
The New Zealand war-time prices index. ER 21:94-100 Jun 45
The growth of New Zealand's general government debt. ER 21:182-96 Dec 45
The New Zealand government finances, 1945-46. ER 21:256-61 Dec 45
The 1945 New Zealand census. ER 22:136-41 Jun 46

Some population maladjustments in New Zealand. ER 23:66-74 Jun 47
The New Zealand gold rushes. ER 23:250-63 Dec 47
The N.Z. exchange alteration of August 1948. ER 24:245-49 Dec 48
NEBOLSINE, GEORGE
The effectiveness of the federal antitrust laws: a symposium. AER 39:716-18 Jun 49
NEEDHAM, JOSEPH
The utilization of scientists in England. S&S 7:32-35 no.1, 43
NEF, JOHN ULRIC
Industrial Europe at the time of the Reformation (ca.1515-ca.1540). [Pt.I-II] JPE 49: 1-40; 183-224 Feb,Apr 41
Silver production in central Europe, 1450-1618. JPE 49:575-91 Jun 41
The responsibility of economic historians. JEH/S 1:1-8 Dec 41
War and economic progress 1540-1640. EHR 12:13-38 no.1-2, 42
The industrial revolution reconsidered. JEH 3:1-31 May 43
Wars and the rise of industrial civilization, 1640-1740. CJE 10:36-78 Feb 44
What is economic history? JEH/S 4:1-19 Dec 44
NEFF, PHILIP
Interregional cyclical differentials: causes, measurement, and significance. AER/S 39:105-19 May 49
Professor Friedman's proposal: a comment. AER 39:946-56 Sep 49
NEIFELD, MORRIS R.
and Robichaud, A. E. Lenders exchanges in the personal finance business. JM 4: 268-73 Jan 40
Consumer credit: impact of the war. JM 7: 342-44 Apr 43
NEILL, THOMAS P.
The Physiocrats' concept of economics. QJE 63:532-53 Nov 49
NEILSON, NELLIE
Early English woodland and waste. JEH 2: 54-62 May 42
NEISSER, HANS
The economics of the short run: remarks on John R. Hicks' "Value and capital." SR 7:32-44 Feb 40
A note on Pareto's theory of production. Em 8:253-62 Jul 40
The price level and the gold problem. AER/S 30,no.5:1-17 Feb 41
Capital gains and the valuation of capital and income. Em 9:198-220 Jul-Oct 41
Professor Lester's questions on gold. AER 31:562-63 Sep 41
Monetary equilibrium and the natural rate of interest. SR 8:454-68 Nov 41

NEISSER, HANS (Cont.)
"Permanent" technological unemployment: "demand for commodities is not demand for labor." AER 32:50-71 Mar 42
The concept of technological unemployment: a reply to Mr. Hagen's criticism. AER 32: 555-57 Sep 42
Theoretical aspects of rationing. QJE 57: 378-97 May 43
An international reserve bank: comments on the American and British plans. SR 10: 265-79 Sep 43
The new economics of spending: a theoretical analysis. Em 12:237-55 Jul-Oct 44
Comments on "Capital is made at home." SR 11:367-71 Sep 44
The economics of a stationary population. SR 11:470-90 Nov 44
Government net contribution and foreign balance as offset to savings. REStat 26: 216-20 Nov 44
Economic possibilities in the mountain regions. SR 12:456-63 Nov 45
Keynes as an economist. SR 13:225-35 Jun 46
The significance of foreign trade for domestic employment. SR 13:307-25 Sep 46
Concept and teaching of economics: comment. AER 36:906-08 Dec 46
Employment in 1947. SR 14:95-103 Mar 47
The nature of import propensities and the foreign trade multiplier. EI 2:573-87 Aug 49
The economic state of the nation. SR 16: 320-31 Sep 49

NEISWANGER, WILLIAM ADDISON
Price control in the machinery industries. AER/S 33:287-94 Mar 43

NELSON, AARON G.
Input-output relationships in fattening cattle. JFE 28:495-514 May 46
Capital returns from soil-conservation practices: discussion. JFE 29:1196-99 Nov 47

NELSON, ALF Z.
Watershed management requires economic studies. LE 18:90-91 Feb 42
Conservation expenditures on federal lands. JFE 24:611-20 Aug 42

NELSON, BENJAMIN N.
The usurer and the merchant prince: Italian businessmen and the ecclesiastical law of restitution, 1100-1550. JEH/S 7:104-22 '47

NELSON, DONALD M. and Henderson, L.
Prices, profits, and government. HBR 19: 389-404 no.4, 41

NELSON, G. LOIS
Volume of United States exports and imports of foods, 1909-43. JFE 26:399-405 May 44

NELSON, JAMES CECIL
Economies of large-scale operation in the trucking industry. LE 17:112-15 Feb 41
Trends in federal regulation of motor carriers. LE 18:366-72 Aug 42
[and others] Postwar railroad problems: discussion. AER/S 36:494-519 May 46
[and others] Transportation and public utility problems: discussion. AER/S 37: 478-97 May 47

NELSON, LOWRY
The work of the Permanent Agricultural Committee of the International Labour Office. JFE 31:524-28 Aug 49
The evolution of the Cuban land system. LE 25:365-81 Nov 49

NELSON, RICHARD WARD
How dead is the benefit theory? AER 30: 117-18 Mar 40

NELSON, ROGER SHERWOOD
Export subsidies and agricultural income. JFE 23:619-31 Aug 41
Federal aid for urban land acquisition. LE 21:125-35 May 45

NELSON, SAUL
Round table on preserving competition versus regulating monopoly. [Summary of remarks] AER/S 30:217-18 Mar 40
Basing-point problems: comment. AER 33: 620-22 Sep 43
Preservation of war records. AER/S 36: 793-98 May 46

NEMMERS, ERWIN ESSER
Principles of war-contract termination. JB 18:35-40 Jan 45
Economic aspects of termination of war contracts. QJE 59:386-404 May 45

NERLOVE, SAMUEL HENRY
War expansion and price inflation. JB 15: 95-130 Apr 42
Renegotiation of war contracts and the public interest. JB 17:104-10 Apr 44
Common stocks as investments for American life insurance companies: a non-academic view. Pt.I-II. JF 3,no.3:39-51; 4:60-77 Oct 48, Mar 49

NESBITT, GEORGE B.
Relocating Negroes from urban slum clearance sites. LE 25:275-88 Aug 49

NESBITT, WILLIAM A. and Netboy, A.
The history of settlement and land use in the Bent Creek Forest. AH 20:121-27 Apr 46

NESIUS, ERNEST J.
How farmers are meeting the scarcity of labor. JFE 25:305-08 Feb 43

NETBOY, ANTHONY and Nesbitt, W. A.
The history of settlement and land use in the Bent Creek Forest. AH 20:121-27 Apr 46

NETTELS, CURTIS PUTNAM
Economic consequences of war: costs of production. JEH/S 3:1-8 Dec 43

NEUMAN, ANDRZEJ MARCIN
Private profits and extra-budgetary revenue. OIS 6:178-83 Aug 12, 44
Real economies and the balance of industry. EJ 58:373-84 Sep 48

NEUMANN, JOHN VON
see Von Neumann, John

NEUMARK, SOLOMON DANIEL
and Frankel, S. H. Note on the national in-

NEUMARK, SOLOMON DANIEL (Cont.)
come of the Union of South Africa.
1927/28, 1932/33, 1934/35. SAJE 8:
78-80 Mar 40
The war and its effect on agricultural prices
and surpluses in South Africa. SAJE 8:
431-45 Dec 40
World situation of fats and oils. SAJE 15:
192-203 Sep 47
NEUNER, EDWARD, Jr.
Wages and employment in the public utility
industries. LE 22:363-80 Nov 46
NEWBURY, FRANK DAVIES
A forecast of business prospects. HBR 25:
273-88 no.3, 47
NEWCOMB, E. L.
In defense of "fair trade." JM 13:84-85
Jul 48
NEWCOMB, ROBINSON
Can the construction industry carry its im-
mediate share of postwar employment?
REStat 27:117-32 Aug 45
NEWCOMER, MABEL
Congressional tax policies in 1943. AER 34:
734-56 Dec 44
chairman. Report of the Subcommittee on the
Undergraduate Economics Curriculum and
Related Areas of Study. AER/S 36:845-47
May 46
War and postwar developments in the Ger-
man tax system. NTJ 1:1-11 Mar 48
NEWMAN, PHILIP CHARLES
Key German cartels under the Nazi regime.
QJE 62:576-95 Aug 48
NEYMAN, JERZY and Scott, E. L.
Consistent estimates based on partially con-
sistent observations. Em 16:1-32 Jan 48
NGCOBO, SELBY B.
A note on the registration of births and
deaths among Natives. SAJE 16:98-105
Mar 48
NICHOL, ARCHIBALD JAMIESON
Probability analysis in the theory of demand,
net revenue and price. JPE 49:637-61
Oct 41
Production and the probabilities of cost.
QJE 57:69-89 Nov 42
Monopoly supply and monopsony demand.
JPE 50:861-79 Dec 42
NICHOLLS, G. L.
A new plan for the non-food retail trade.
OIS 4:217-20 Aug 8, 42
NICHOLLS, WILLIAM HORD
Market-sharing in the packing industry.
JFE 22:225-40 Feb 40; A correction. 497
May 40
Price flexibility and concentration in the ag-
ricultural processing industries. JPE 48:
883-88 Dec 40
Constitutional aspects of public regulation of
business price policies. JFE 25:560-82
Aug 43
Social biases and recent theories of compe-
tition. QJE 58:1-26 Nov 43

Federal regulatory agencies and the courts.
AER 34:56-75 Mar 44
Imperfect competition in agricultural processing and distributing industries. CJE 10:
150-64 May 44
Dr. Nourse on low-price policy. R. JFE 26:
754-65 Nov 44
A price policy for agriculture, consistent
with economic progress, that will promote
adequate and more stable income from
farming. (The first award paper) JFE 27:
743-60 Nov 45
and Johnson, D. G. The farm price policy
awards, 1945: a topical digest of the win-
ning essays. JFE 28:267-83 Feb 46
Some economic aspects of the margarine
industry. JPE 54:221-42 Jun 46
Reorientation of agricultural marketing and
price research. JFE 30:43-54 Feb 48
The tobacco case of 1946. AER/S 39:284-96
May 49
NICHOLS, CHARLES K.
The statistical work of the League of Nations
in economic, financial and related fields.
JASA 37:336-42 Sep 42
NICHOLS, RUSSELL T.
Soviet production estimates. JPE 57:249-50
Jun 49
NICHOLSON, JEROME LEE
The cost of living index. OIS 3:31-32
Feb 1, 41
The Ministry of Labour budget inquiry. I.
The cost of living index. OIS 3:45-46
Feb 22, 41
Signs of inflation. OIS 3:65-67 Mar 15, 41
The trend of wages. OIS 3:242-46 Aug 9, 41
The burden of the war: A. Changes in real
incomes, 1938 to 1940. OIS 4:5-10
Jan 10, 42
Wages and income tax. OIS 4:87-89
Mar 14, 42
and Worswick, G. D. N. Consumption and
rationing. OIS 4:132-35 Apr 25, 42
The burden of the war. OIS 4:166-69
Jun 6, 42
The distribution of incomes. OIS 4:225-28
Aug 29, 42
Wages and prices. OIS 4:319-25 Dec 12, 42
Rationing and index numbers. REStud 10:
68-72 no.1, 42
Earnings of workpeople in 1938 and 1942.
OIS 5:31-35 Jan 30, 43
The benefits and costs of the Beveridge plan.
OIS 5,suppl.4:7-18 Feb 20, 43
Substitution of women for men in industry.
OIS 5:85-87 Apr 3, 43
The distribution of the war burden. OIS 5:
105-12 May 15, 43
Some new estimates of consumption. OIS 5:
162-65 Jul 17, 43
Earnings in January 1943. OIS 5:193-95
Aug 28, 43
The distribution of incomes. OIS 6:23-29
Feb 5, 44

NICHOLSON, JEROME LEE (Cont.)
Earnings and hours of labour. OIS 6:107-13
May 20, 44
The distribution of the war burden. OIS 6:
153-61 Jul 22, 44; Erratum. 192 Aug 12, 44
Wages and cost of living sliding-scales.
OIS 6:189-91 Aug 12, 44
Changes in consumption, 1938 to 1943.
OIS 6:219-24 Sep 23, 44
Wages during the war. OIS 6:232-35
Oct 14, 44
The government's plans for social insurance.
OIS 6:241-49 Nov 4, 44
Employment and national income during the
war. OIS 7:230-44 Oct 13, 45; Corrigenda.
268 Nov 3, 45
The changes in income tax. OIS 7:262-66
Nov 3, 45
Earnings, hours, and mobility of labour.
OIS 8:146-63 May 46
Variations in working class family expendi-
ture. JRSS 112:359-411 pt.4, 49
NICKERSON, CLARENCE B.
The cost element in pricing. HBR 18:417-28
no.4, 40
Liquidity of war producers. HBR 20:369-74
no.3, 42
NICOLS, ALFRED
The rehabilitation of pure competition.
QJE 62:31-63 Nov 47
The cement case. AER/S 39:297-310 May 49
The development of monopolistic competition
and the monopoly problem. REStat 31:
118-23 May 49
NIEBYL, KARL HEINRICH
The need for a concept of value in economic
theory. QJE 54:201-16 Feb 40
A reexamination of the classical theory of
inflation. AER 30:759-73 Dec 40
The cynical Mr. Keynes. S&S 4:234-39
no.3, 40
What rights should the holder of money have?
AER/S 37:299-303 May 47
NIELSEN, ARTHUR C.
Trends toward mechanization of radio adver-
tising. JM 6:217-28 Jan 42
Two years of commercial operation of the
audimeter and the Nielsen radio index.
JM 9:239-55 Jan 45
NIELSON, VIGO C.
Preparing for postwar personnel relations.
HBR 22:239-48 no.2, 44
NIMMO, J. F.
Reports of Commonwealth Parliamentary
Joint Committee on Profits. R. ER 18:
226-28 Dec 42
NIXON, RUSSELL ARTHUR and Samuelson, P. A.
Estimates of unemployment in the United
States. REStat 22:101-11 Aug 40
NODLAND, TRUMAN and Vanvig, A.
The effect of a reduction in farm prices on
farm earnings. JFE 31:544-48 Aug 49
NOGARO, BERTRAND
Hungary's recent monetary crisis and its

theoretical meaning. AER 38:526-42
Sep 48
--- Rejoinder. AER 39:960 Sep 49
NOLEN, HERMAN C.
Time and duty analysis of wholesalers'
salesmen. JM 4:274-84 Jan 40
NORDIN, JOHN A.
Spatial allocation of selling expenses. JM 7:
210-19 Jan 43
Allocating demand costs. LE 22:163-70
May 46
The marginal cost controversy: a reply.
Ec N.S.14:134-49 May 47
Note on a light plant's cost curves. Em 15:
231-35 Jul 47
The demand for electricity. LE 23:337-41
Aug 47
and Moore, W. R. Bronfenbrenner on the
black market. AER 37:933-34 Dec 47
Statistical issues in price research.
JFE 31,pt.2:1089-95 Nov 49
NORRIS, HARRY
Commodity stocks and the trade cycle: 1.
A note. Ec N.S.11:138-40 Aug 44
Notes on the relationship between economists
and accountants. EJ 54:375-83 Dec 44
Profit: accounting theory and economics.
Ec N.S.12:125-33 Aug 45
Fiscal policy and the propensity to consume:
a note. EJ 56:316-18 Jun 46
State enterprise price and output policy and
the problem of cost imputation. Ec N.S.14:
54-62 Feb 47
NORTHROP, FILMER STUART CUCKOW
The impossibility of a theoretical science of
economic dynamics. QJE 56:1-17 Nov 41
NORTHRUP, HERBERT ROOF
The Tobacco Workers International Union.
QJE 56:606-26 Aug 42
The Negro and the United Mine Workers of
America. SEJ 9:313-26 Apr 43
Organized labor and Negro workers. JPE 51:
206-21 Jun 43; Errata. 550 Dec 43
The Negro and unionism in the Birmingham,
Ala., iron and steel industry. SEJ 10:
27-40 Jul 43
Negroes in a war industry: the case of ship-
building. JB 16:160-72 Jul 43
Unionization of foremen. HBR 21:496-504
no.4, 43
The Foreman's Association of America.
HBR 23:187-202 no.2, 45
The appropriate bargaining unit question
under the Railway Labor Act. QJE 60:
250-69 Feb 46
[and others] Postwar labor relations: dis-
cussion. AER/S 36:370-83 May 46
The Railway Labor Act and railway labor
disputes in wartime. AER 36:324-43
Jun 46
Collective bargaining by air line pilots.
QJE 61:533-76 Aug 47

**NORTHRUP, HERBERT ROOF (Cont.)**
Industrial relations with professional workers. HBR 26:543-59 Sep 48
Emergency disputes under the Railway Labor Act. IRRA 1:78-88 Dec 48

**NORTON, JAMES E.**
[Teaching economics in college]: discussion. RSE 6:91-96 May 48

**NORTON, LAURENCE JOSEPH**
When and under what conditions should a mortgage on a farm be foreclosed? JFE 22:270-76 Feb 40
Agricultural credit: discussion. JFE 23: 62-65 Feb 41
Farmers in a changing world: the 1940 Yearbook of agriculture. III. R. JFE 23: 454-55 May 41
Lewis on relation of income to farm capital. JFE 23:888-93 Nov 41
The land market and farm mortgage debts, 1917-1921. JFE 24:168-77 Feb 42
Achieving agricultural goals: discussion. JFE 25:92-94 Feb 43
Animal fats and oils: discussion. JFE 31, pt.2:339-42 Feb 49
Market and marketing research in the Midwest. JFE 31:350-55 May 49
The theory and measurement of price expectations: discussion. AER/S 39:168-70 May 49

**NOURSE, EDWIN GRISWOLD**
The meaning of "price policy." QJE 55: 175-209 Feb 41
Collective bargaining and the common interest. AER 33:1-20 Mar 43
The structure of postwar American business: discussion. AER/S 34:128-31 Mar 44
Addendum: from analysis to prediction. JFE 26:766-74 Nov 44
[and others] Consumption economics: discussion. AER/S 35:56-66 May 45
Developments concerning the National Research Foundation. AER/S 36:789-92 May 46
Economics in the public service. AER/S 37: 21-30 May 47
Agriculture in a stabilized economy. JFE 31, pt.2:201-12 Feb 49

**NOVICK, DAVID**
Statistical materials collected by the War Production Board. REStat 28:131-34 Aug 46
Research opportunities in the War Production Board records. AER/S 37:690-99 May 47
and Steiner, G. A. The War Production Board's statistical reporting experience. Pt.I-VI. JASA 43:201-30; 463-74; 474-88; 575-96; 44:413-43 Jan 48-Sep 49

**NOWELL, REYNOLDS IRWIN**
The farm land boom. JFE 29:130-49 Feb 47

**NOYES, CHARLES REINOLD**
Certain problems in the empirical study of costs. AER 31:473-92 Sep 41

The prospect for economic growth. AER 37: 13-33 Mar 47
--- Rejoinder. AER 38:394-96 Jun 48

**NUGENT, ROLF**
Post-war-delivery installment sales and government controls. JM 7:350-53 Apr 43

**NURKSE, RAGNAR**
[and others] International monetary and credit arrangements: discussion. AER/S 35:289-96 May 45
International monetary policy and the search for economic stability. AER/S 37:569-80 May 47

**NURNBERG, MAX**
Housing between boom and bottlenecks. SR 8:189-212 May 41
Effect of business fluctuations upon public housing finance. LE 19:180-92 May 43

**NUSSBAUM, FREDERICK LOUIS** and Schweitzer, A.
The professors versus the people. AER 33: 906-07 Dec 43

**NUTTONSON, MICHAEL Y.**
USSR; some physical and agricultural characteristics of the drought area and its climatic analogues in the United States. LE 25:346-51 Nov 49

**NYBROTEN, NORMAN**
Estimating cash considerations in real estate transfers from internal revenue stamps. JFE 30:558-61 Aug 48
Rate of commodity disappearance and consumer preference. JFE 31:346-50 May 49

**NYMAN, CARL R.**
Visual analysis: a new method in market research. JM 8:249-52 Jan 44

**NYSTROM, PAUL HENRY**
Significant current trends in retailing. JM 5:220-22; 6,no.4,pt.2:8-9 Jan 41, Apr 42

**OAKES, EUGENE ERNEST**
The federal offset and the American death tax system. QJE 54:566-98 Aug 40
The incidence of the general income tax. AER/S 32:76-82 Mar 42

**OAKES, RALPH HATHAWAY**
Price differences for identical items in chain, voluntary group, and independent stores. JM 14:434-36 Oct 49

**OBER, HARRY**
and Weintraub, D. Union policies relating to technological developments. [Abstract] AER/S 30:225-27 Mar 40
and Myers, R. J. Statistics for wage stabilization. JASA 38:425-37 Dec 43

**O'BRIEN, GEORGE**
Rev. Professor T. A. Finlay, S.J. [obit.] EJ 50:157-59 Mar 40
J. S. Mill and J. E. Cairnes. Ec N.S.10: 273-85 Nov 43

**O'CONNELL, JOHN S.**
A study in selling sterling silver. JM 10: 64-66 Jul 45

O'DONNELL, CYRIL
   Problems in the organization of multiplant
     production control. JB 18:140-44 Jul 45
   Control of business forms. JB 19:176-82
     Jul 46
OEHLER, C. M.
   Measuring the believability of advertising
     claims. JM 9:127-31 Oct 44
OGG, W. RAYMOND
   Postwar agricultural program [of the Ameri-
     can Farm Bureau Federation]. JFE 29:
     64-76 Feb 47
OGG, WALLACE ELMER
   Useful techniques in an extension program
     in economic principles as applied to agri-
     culture. JFE 31,pt.2:697-99 Feb 49
OHLSSON, INGVAR
   and Lundberg, E. Models of the future
     national income in Sweden. OIS 8:301-03
     Sep 46
   and Cederwall, G. Sweden's economy 1946-
     1949. OIS 11:53-58 Feb-Mar 49
O'LEARY, EDMUND BERNARD
   The teaching of economics. RSE 1:54-55
     Dec 42
O'LEARY, H. J.
   Utility rate problems arising from recent
     and prospective income tax legislation.
     LE 18:184-87 May 42
O'LEARY, JAMES JOHN
   A general wage ceiling. SEJ 9:24-32 Jul 42
   Malthus and Keynes. JPE 50:901-19 Dec 42
   Should federal deposit insurance be extended?
     SEJ 10:41-51 Jul 43
   Malthus's general theory of employment and
     the post-Napoleonic depressions. JEH 3:
     185-200 Nov 43
   Consumption as a factor in postwar employ-
     ment. AER/S 35:37-55 May 45
O'LEARY, JOSEPH M.
   The teaching of economics in public high
     schools. QJE 54:502-18 May 40
O'LEARY, PAUL MARTIN
   Round table on problems in the teaching of
     economics: [discussion]. AER/S 30:
     110-11 Mar 40
   Price control and rationing in the war-peace
     transition: discussion. AER/S 35:186-88
     May 45
OLIPHANT, JAMES ORIN
   The eastward movement of cattle from the
     Oregon Country. AH 20:19-43 Jan 46
   The cattle herds and ranches of the Oregon
     Country, 1860-1890. AH 21:217-38 Oct 47
   and Kingston, C. S., editors. William Emsley
     Jackson's diary of a cattle drive from La
     Grande, Oregon, to Cheyenne, Wyoming,
     in 1876. AH 23:260-73 Oct 49
OLIVER, HENRY MADISON, Jr.
   Does wage reduction aid employment by
     lowering prices? SEJ 6:333-43 Jan 40
   The relationship between total output and
     man-hour output in American manufactur-
     ing industry. QJE 55:239-54 Feb 41

War and inflation since 1790 in England,
   France, Germany, and the United States.
   AER/S 30,no.5:344-51 Feb 41
The relationship of total output to man-hour
   output: reply. QJE 59:640-41 Aug 45
Income, region, community-size and color.
   QJE 60:588-99 Aug 46
Average cost and long-run elasticity of de-
   mand. JPE 55:212-21 Jun 47
Marginal theory and business behavior.
   AER 37:375-83 Jun 47
A note on velocity. REStat 31:153-54 May 49
Expectations, lags, and labor-saving bias.
   SEJ 16:80-81 Jul 49
The analytical value of employment-equilib-
   rium models. SEJ 16:129-38 Oct 49
OLSEN, ARDEN B.
   Mormon mercantile cooperation in Utah.
     JM 6:136-42 Oct 41
OLSON, ERNEST CHARLES
   with Daly, P. and Douglas, P. H. The pro-
     duction function for manufacturing in the
     United States, 1904. JPE 51:61-65 Feb 43
   Factors affecting international differences in
     production. AER/S 38:502-22 May 48
OLSON, JAMES CHESTER
   Is your company prepared for rough weather?
     HBR 25:595-608 no.4a, 47
O'NEIL, WALTER GEORGE
   Do high corporate taxes deter investment?
     HBR 22:443-46 no.4, 44
OPDYKE, WILLIAM K.
   Training within industry. HBR 20:348-57
     no.3, 42
OPIE, REDVERS
   The objectives of monetary policy: discus-
     sion. AER/S 30:40-42 Mar 40
   Frank William Taussig (1859-1940). [obit.]
     EJ 51:347-68 Jun-Sep 41
   A British view of postwar trade. AER/S 33:
     322-31 Mar 43
   International monetary problems: discus-
     sion. AER/S 34:396-99 Mar 44
OPPENHEIMER-BLUHM, HILDE
   Industrialization in Palestine. SR 8:438-53
     Nov 41
ORMSBY, HERBERT F.
   Postwar industrial planning on the Pacific
     Coast. JM 8:156-58 Oct 43
ORMSBY, MARGARET ANCHORETTA
   Agricultural development in British Columbia.
     AH 19:11-20 Jan 45
ORTIZ MENA, RAÚL
   Monetary problems in Mexico. JB 20:1-8
     Jan 47
OSBORN, GEORGE C. ed.
   Plantation letters of a southern statesman:
     John Sharp Williams and Cedar Grove.
     AH 21:117-26 Apr 47
OSBORNE, DAVID R.
   Sales training for the new type of selling.
     JM 8:79-82 Jul 43
   Trends in the selection and training of sales-
     men. JM 11:70-73 Jul 46

OSBORNE, R. G. and Walker, E. R.
  Federalism in Canada. ER 16:245-59 Dec 40
OSCHINSKY, D.
  Medieval treatises on estate accounting.
    EHR 17:52-61 no.1, 47
OSER, JACOB
  Productivity of agricultural workers by size
    of enterprise and by regions. JFE 30:
    764-70 Nov 48
OSGOOD, OTIS T.
  Some observations on the relation of farm
    land tenure to soil erosion and depletion.
    LE 17:410-22 Nov 41
  Results of two sampling methods used in
    farm management research. JFE 31:
    157-68 Feb 49
OSHIMA, HARRY TATSUMI
  Veblen on Japan. SR 10:487-94 Nov 43
OSTRANDER, FRANK TAYLOR
  The Mitchell Committee's report on the
    cost-of-living index: comments. AER 34:
    849-56 Dec 44
OSTROLENK, BERNARD
  A note on Mr. Silverstein's article. JB 13:
    420-23 Oct 40
OSTROVITIANOV, KONSTANTIN
  Basic laws of development of socialist econ-
    omy. S&S 9:232-51 no.3, 45
OTIS, BROOKS
  The communists and the labor theory of
    value. AER 35:134-37 Mar 45
OTSUKA, ICHIRO
  On the liquidity of industrial enterprise.
    Kyo 19,no.1:20-43 Jan 44
OTTMAN, ALLEN HATFIELD
  The economist's reports. HBR 20:388-89
    no.3, 42
OU, PAO-SAN
  Ex-ante saving and liquidity-preferences.
    REStud 11:52-56 no.1, 43
  International payments in national income.
    QJE 60:289-98 Feb 46
  and Wang, F. S. Industrial production and
    employment in pre-war China. EJ 56:
    426-34 Sep 46
  A new estimate of China's national income.
    JPE 54:547-54 Dec 46
OULTON, P. G.
  Indian cotton. LBR 1:35-40 Jul 46
OVERTON, RICHARD CLEGHORN
  Problems of writing the history of large
    business units with special reference to
    railroads. BHR 22:22-35 Feb 48
OWEN, ARTHUR DAVID KEMP
  The Beveridge report. I. Its proposals.
    EJ 53:1-9 Apr 43
OXENFELDT, ALFRED RICHARD
  Monopoly dissolution: a proposal outlined.
    AER 36:384-91 Jun 46
  and Oxenfeldt, G. E. Businessmen's informa-
    tion about profitability of local enterprises.
    JPE 55:257-61 Jun 47

OXENFELDT, GERTRUDE E.
  see Oxenfeldt, Alfred Richard and Oxenfeldt,
    G. E.
OXNAM, D. W.
  New Zealand's Industrial Relations Act 1949.
    ER 25,(no.49):88-90 Dec 49
  Some observations on changes in money and
    real incomes in Australia, 1938-39 to
    1948-49. ER 25,(no.49):46-63 Dec 49
PAARLBERG, DON
  Parity and progress. JFE 25:419-32 May 43
  and Pearson, F. A. Sixty million jobs and
    six million farmers. JFE 28:28-41 Feb 46
  and Johnson, H. A. A method of predicting
    numbers of hens and pullets on Indiana
    farms January 1. JFE 30:756-61 Nov 48
PABST, WILLIAM R., Jr.
  Monopolistic expectations and shifting con-
    trol in the anthracite industry. REStat 22:
    45-52 Feb 40
  Interstate trade barriers and state oleo-
    margarine taxes. SEJ 7:505-17 Apr 41
  Unstable conditions of competition and
    monopoly in exhaustible resource indus-
    tries. JPE 50:739-49 Oct 42
PAECHTER, HEINZ
  Recent trends in the German Command
    economy. JPE 52:217-33 Sep 44
PAGLIN, MORTON
  Fetter on Lauderdale. AER 36:391-93 Jun 46
PAINE, CLARENCE S., ed.
  The diaries of a Nebraska farmer, 1876-1877.
    AH 22:1-31 Jan 48
PAINTER, MARY S. and Musgrave, R. A.
  The impact of alternative tax structures on
    personal consumption and saving. QJE 62:
    475-99 Aug 48
PAISH, FRANK WALTER
  British floating debt policy. Ec N.S.7:225-47
    Aug 40
  Capital value and income. Ec N.S.7:416-18
    Nov 40
  Economic incentive in wartime. Ec N.S.8:
    239-48 Aug 41
  Cheap money policy. Ec N.S.14:167-79
    Aug 47
  Britain's economic problem. AER 38:118-21
    Mar 48
  The January 1949 economic report of the
    President: appraisal. REStat 31:172-74
    Aug 49
PALMER, GLADYS LOUISE
  Some considerations involved in appraising
    the adequacy of occupational statistics.
    JASA 36:61-70 Mar 41
  The mobility of weavers in three textile
    centers. QJE 55:460-87 May 41
PALMER, SANFORD W.
  Agriculture and the labor reserve. S&S 4:
    388-401 no.4, 40
PALYI, MELCHIOR
  The meaning of the gold standard. R. JB 14:
    294-314 Jul 41

PALYI, MELCHIOR (Cont.)
  England versus gold: a rejoinder to Profes-
    sor Brown. JB 14:423-26 Oct 41
  Interest rates in the managed economy.
    LE 18:28-35 Feb 42
PANDE, J. K.
  A formula for limits of variations in a
    weighted index due to a new series of
    weights. IJE 21:324-28 Jan 41
PANUCH, J. ANTHONY
  Investor protection in reorganization.
    HBR 19:21-32 no.1, 40
PAO-CHUAN CHAO
  see Chao, Pao-Chuan
PAO-SAN OU
  see Ou, Pao-San
PAPANDREOU, ANDREAS GEORGE
  Market structure and monopoly power.
    AER 39:883-97 Sep 49
PAPI, GIUSEPPE UGO
  The dilemma of the O.E.E.C. BNL 2:103-07
    Apr-Jun 49
PÂQUET, R.
  The economic recovery of Belgium. MS 17:
    202-07 May 49
PARADISO, LOUIS J.
  Significance of inventories in the current
    economic situation. JASA 43:361-76
    Sep 48
PARANJPE, V. M.
  A monetary system for India. IJE 26:544-53
    Jan 46
  Theory of location of industry. IJE 27:131-39
    Oct 46
  Cheap money policy. IJE 28:83-88 Jul 47
  Commercial policy for India. IJE 28:31-38
    Jul 47
  The dollar shortage and the international
    monetary co-operation. IJE 29:165-70
    Oct 48
  National budgets and economic planning.
    IJE 29:117-24 Oct 48
PARDASANI, N. S.
  The Bombay Industrial Disputes Act, 1938.
    IJE 21:49-66 Jul 40
  --- [Reply to C. B. Kumar.] IJE 23:85-86
    Jul 42
  Post-war currency system in India. IJE 26:
    535-43 Jan 46
PARDUE, BEULAH LEA
  and Martin, J. W. Comparative tax loads on
    railroads in nine southern states. NTJ 1:
    25-30 Mar 48
  and Reeves, H. C. Some reasons why prop-
    erty is poorly assessed for taxation.
    NTJ 1:366-68 Dec 48
PARGELLIS, STANLEY
  The corporation and the historian. JEH/S 4:
    29-37 Dec 44
PARKER, ALWYN
  Mantoux versus Keynes. R. LBR 3:1-20
    Jan 47
  Contemporary Scandinavia: historical
    foreword. LBR 8:13-19 Apr 48

  Benelux. LBR 14:32-54 Oct 49
PARKIN, NORMAN CHESTER
  Renegotiation of war contract prices. JB 17:
    91-103 Apr 44
  Marketing aspects of the renegotiation of war
    contract prices. JM 9:207-16 Jan 45
  Management statistics in war contract rene-
    gotiation. JASA 40:504-19 Dec 45
  Some economic concepts affecting the rene-
    gotiation of war contracts. JB 19:31-42
    Jan 46
  Control of war contract profits. HBR 26:
    230-50 Mar 48
PARKINSON, JOSEPH FREDERICK
  Some problems of war finance in Canada.
    CJE 6:403-23 Aug 40
PARKINSON, ROYAL
  Fair employment practices legislation.
    HBR 26:115-28 Jan 48
PARR, CHARLES McKEW
  Why the middleman? JB 17:23-36 Jan 44
PARRISH, JOHN BISHOP
  Women in the nation's labor market.
    QJE 54:527-34 May 40
  "Principles of economics prerequisite to
    courses in public finance": a rejoinder.
    AER 31:102 Mar 41
  Impact of World War II on internal wage rate
    structures. SEJ 15:134-51 Oct 48
PARRY, CORLISS LLOYD
  European insurance companies and real
    estate: with particular reference to hous-
    ing. LE 16:294-305 Aug 40
PARSONS, HOWARD LESLIE and Brewster, J. M.
  Can prices allocate resources in American
    agriculture? JFE 28:938-60 Nov 46
PARSONS, JAMES J.
  Hops in early California agriculture. AH 14:
    110-16 Jul 40
PARSONS, KENNETH HERALD
  Social conflicts and agricultural programs.
    JFE 23:743-64 Nov 41
  John R. Commons' point of view. LE 18:
    245-66 Aug 42
  Farmers and organized labor. JFE 25:
    367-83 May 43
  Social security for farm people. JFE 28:
    97-110 Feb 46
  and P[enn], R. J. Leonard A. Salter, Jr.
    [obit.] JFE 28:885 Aug 46
  Training agricultural economists for public
    careers. JFE 29:1329-40 Nov 47
  The development of Salter's conception of
    research. LE 24:175-78 May 48
  Research in the succession of farms: a com-
    ment on methodology. LE 24:293-302
    Aug 48
  Institutional changes affecting the agricul-
    tural outlook; the agricultural perspective.
    JFE 31,pt.2:1121-31 Nov 49
  The logical foundations of economic research.
    JFE 31:656-86 Nov 49
  The problem-solution basis of forward pric-
    ing. R. LE 25:423-27 Nov 49

PARSONS, TALCOTT
The motivation of economic activities.
CJE 6:187-202 May 40
--- Reply to Professor Knight. CJE 6:
466-72 Aug 40
Social classes and class conflict in the light
of recent sociological theory. AER/S 39:
16-26 May 49
PASCHAL, JAMES L.
and Huffman, R. E. Integrating the use of
irrigated and grazing land in the northern
Great Plains. LE 18:17-27 Feb 42
and Slagsvold, P. L. Irrigation development
and area adjustment in the Great Plains.
JFE 25:433-43 May 43
PASSER, HAROLD CLARENCE
Entrepreneurial history and economics.
EEH 1,no.1:21-25 Jan 49
The electric light and the gas light: innova-
tion and continuity in economic history.
EEH 1,no.3:1-9 Mar 49
E. H. Goff: an entrepreneur who failed.
EEH 1,no.5:17-25 May 49
Economic factors in entrepreneurial history.
EEH 1,no.5:29-30 May 49
PASVOLSKY, LEO
Some aspects of our foreign economic policy.
AER/S 30,no.5:320-37 Feb 41
chairman. Round table on bases of inter-
national economic relations. AER/S 33:
455-65 Mar 43; A correction. AER 33:625
Sep 43
PATCHIN, ROBERT H. [and others]
Postwar shipping policy: discussion.
AER/S 36:575-602 May 46
PATEL, K. S. and Ghatge, M. B.
Economics of mixed farming in "Charotar"
(Bombay Province). IJE 23:133-54 Oct 42
PATEL, S. K. J.
An inquiry into the effect of war-time prices
on agricultural indebtedness. IJE 25:
561-65 Apr 45
PATEL, SURENDRA J.
British economic thought and the treatment
of India as a colony. IJE 27:367-71 Apr 47
Marxism and recent economic thought.
S&S 11:52-65 no.1, 47
PATERSON, DAVID G.
Marketing slaughter livestock: discussion.
JFE 31,pt.2:364-67 Feb 49
PATINKIN, DON
Multiple-plant firms, cartels, and imperfect
competition. QJE 61:173-205 Feb 47
Note on the allocation of output. QJE 61:
651-57 Aug 47
Relative prices, Say's law, and the demand
for money. Em 16:135-54 Apr 48
Price flexibility and full employment.
AER 38:543-64 Sep 48
The indeterminacy of absolute prices in
classical economic theory. Em 17:1-27
Jan 49
Price flexibility and full employment: reply.
AER 39:726-28 Jun 49

Involuntary unemployment and the Keynesian
supply function. EJ 59:360-83 Sep 49
PATON, MARY R.
Selection of tabulation method, machine or
manual. JM 6:229-35 Jan 42
PATTERSON, ERNEST MINOR
United States in the world economy, 1940: a
summary. AER/S 30,no.5:328-43 Feb 41
PATTERSON, GARDNER
and Brown, E. C. Accelerated depreciation:
a neglected chapter in war taxation.
QJE 57:630-45 Aug 43
The Export-Import Bank. QJE 58:65-90
Nov 43
and Polk, J. The emerging pattern of
bilateralism. QJE 62:118-42 Nov 47
PATTON, HARALD SMITH
The war and North American agriculture.
CJE 7:382-96 Aug 41
Wartime wheat policy in Canada. JFE 24:
772-91 Nov 42
Canadian agricultural post-war planning:
discussion. JFE 25:335-37 Feb 43
PATTON, ROBERT DEAN [and others]
Economic consequences of war since 1790:
discussion. AER/S 30,no.5:362-65 Feb 41
PATZIG, RUDOLPH E.
The effect of the war on retail food outlets.
JM 9:109-13 Oct 44
and Hadary, G. Relationship of income to
milk consumption. JFE 27:204-10 Feb 45
PAUL, RANDOLPH EVERNGHIM
Redesigning federal taxation. HBR 19:143-50
no.2, 41
PAULSON, EILIF WOLFF
Relation of operating costs to tonnage of
ships in ocean transport. NTTO 12:
187-92 no.37, 48
PAULSON, WALTER E.
Contribution of cooperation to the problem of
distribution. JFE 22:740-52 Nov 40
Price-quality relations in the cotton market
of Victoria, Texas. JFE 23:496-99 May 41
Diagrammatic economics. JFE 28:687-722
Aug 46
Characteristics of the marginal cost curve.
JFE 30:467-99 Aug 48
Research in cotton marketing. JFE 31,pt.2:
415-19 Feb 49
PAYNE, GEORGE HENRY
Postwar radio facsimile. JM 10:290-91
Jan 46
PAYNE, HAPPER
Standardized description, a form of specifi-
cation labeling. JM 12:234-41 Oct 47
PAZOS, FELIPE
Inflation and exchange instability in Latin
America. AER/S 39:396-405 May 49
PEACOCK, ALAN TURNER
The national insurance funds. Ec N.S.16:
228-42 Aug 49
PEAK, GEORGE W.
Administration of the Montana Unfair Prac-
tices Act. JB 15:140-59 Apr 42

PEARCE, BRIAN
  Elizabethan food policy and the armed forces.
    EHR 12:39-46 no.1-2, 42
PEARSON, FRANK ASHMORE and Paarlberg,
    D.
  Sixty million jobs and six million farmers.
    JFE 28:28-41 Feb 46
PEASE, ROBERT H.
  Today's real estate market. HBR 26:385-97
    Jul 48
PEDERSEN, JØRGEN
  The control of the value of money in a free
    economy. NTTO 12:193-99 no.37, 48
  Interest rates, employment and changes in
    population. Kyk 2:1-16 fasc.1, 48
PEFFER, E. LOUISE
  Which public domain do you mean? AH 23:
    140-46 Apr 49
PEGRUM, DUDLEY FRANK
  The public corporation as a regulatory de-
    vice. LE 16:335-43 Aug 40
  Economic planning and the science of eco-
    nomics. AER 31:298-307 Jun 41
  --- Rejoinder. AER 31:831-33 Dec 41
  Economic planning in a democratic society.
    LE 19:18-27 Feb 43
  Incremental cost pricing: a comment. LE 20:
    58-60 Feb 44
  Economic contributions of the United States
    to civilization. SEJ 11:157-68 Oct 44
PELTZER, ERNST
  Industrialization of young countries and the
    change in the international division of
    labor. SR 7:299-325 Sep 40
PENDLETON, WILLIAM CLYDE
  American sugar policy: 1948 version.
    JFE 30:226-42 May 48
PENGRA, RAY F.
  Crop production in the semi-arid regions an
    insurable risk. JFE 29:567-70 May 47
PENN, RAYMOND J.
  Tenure situation in the north central region:
    1940-1944. LE 19:370-76 Aug 43
  and P[arsons], K. H. Leonard A. Salter, Jr.
    [obit.] JFE 28:885 Aug 46
  Federal land management: discussion.
    JFE 29:1315-18 Nov 47
PERCIVAL, ANDREW J. and Gross, G. B.
  Job evaluation: a case history. HBR 24:
    466-97 no.4, 46
PERIES, HERMON ERIC
  A note on the problem of a durable good.
    IJE 21:207-09 Oct 40
  Dynamical equilibrium with two alternative
    uses. IJE 22:87-91 Jul 41
  A simple dynamical problem. IJE 24:218-20
    Jan 44
  Distribution of incomes. IJE 27:90-91 Jul 46
PERKINS, GEORGE HOLMES
  [The education of planners.] At Harvard
    University. LE 21:311-13 Sep 45
  Housing needs and housing standards. LE 25:
    127-29 Feb 49

PERKINS, JOHN SHEPHARD
  Management research. HBR 18:488-95
    no.4, 40
  A critical appraisal of business statistics.
    JASA 37:220-24 Jun 42
PERLMAN, JACOB
  Extent and causes of differences in hourly
    earnings. JASA 35:1-12 Mar 40
PERLMAN, SELIG
  John Rogers Commons 1862-1945. [obit.]
    AER 35:782-86 Sep 45
PERLO, VICTOR and Gilbert, R. V.
  The investment-factor method of forecasting
    business activity. Em 10:311-16
    Jul-Oct 42; A correction. 11:94 Jan 43
PERREGAUX, EDMOND ADRIAN
  The future of farm cooperatives in the United
    States. JFE 29:115-27 Feb 47
PERRY, HOBART S.
  Ocean shipping. HBR 19:438-50 no.4, 41
  Ocean rate regulation, World War II. HBR 21:
    238-52 no.2, 43
  The wartime merchant fleet and postwar
    shipping requirements. AER/S 36:520-46
    May 46
PERRY, JOSEPHA M.
  Sketch of the life and work of Milton Prince
    Higgins, 1842-1912. BHR 18:33-54 Jun 44
  Samuel Snow, tanner and cordwainer.
    BHR 19:183-93 Dec 45
PERTINAX [pseud]
  Letter to the editor [on lack of mathematics
    in economics curriculum]. Em 17:90-92
    Jan 49
PESMAZOGLU, J. S.
  Some international aspects of British
    cyclical fluctuations, 1870-1913.
    REStud 16:117-43 no.3, 49
PETERSEN, ELMORE
  Solving wholesalers' problems through trad-
    ing area research. JM 4,no.4,pt.2:39-45
    Apr 40
PETERSEN, KAAVE
  Economic conditions in Norway. OIS 8:112-16
    Apr 46
PETERSON, ARTHUR GOODWIN
  Agriculture in the United States, 1839 and
    1939. JFE 22:98-110 Feb 40
  The politics of parity. R. AH 16:193-94
    Oct 42
  Governmental policy relating to farm
    machinery in World War I. AH 17:31-40
    Jan 43
  The Agricultural History Society's first
    quarter century. AH 19:193-203 Oct 45
  Agricultural price index numbers. JASA 42:
    597-604 Dec 47
PETERSON, FLORENCE
  Management efficiency and collective bargain-
    ing. ILRR 1:29-49 Oct 47
PETERSON, JAMES
  The trade unions and the Populist Party.
    S&S 8:143-60 no.2, 44

PETERSON, WALTER C.
The Los Angeles City sales tax administration. NTJ 2:232-46 Sep 49
PETRIE, JOSEPH RICHARDS
Business efficiency in the Canadian war effort. CJE 9:357-65 Aug 43
Wilfred Currier Keirstead, 1871-1944. [obit.] CJE 11:111-14 Feb 45
PETTENGILL, ROBERT BUNNELL
Division of the tax burden among income groups in the United States in 1936. AER 30:60-71 Mar 40
Comparative retail grocery ceiling prices in Los Angeles. JM 8:145-49 Oct 43
PETTERSSON, VILHELM IRGENS
Ancient and modern Swedish land tenure policy. JFE 30:322-31 May 48
PETTET, ZELLMER ROSWELL
Highlights of the 1940 census. JFE 23: 266-71 Feb 41
PHELPS, CLYDE WILLIAM
Monopolistic and imperfect competition in consumer loans. JM 8:382-93 Apr 44
PHELPS, DUDLEY MAYNARD
Certification marks under the Lanham Act. JM 13:498-505 Apr 49
PHELPS, KATHERINE and Strohkarck, F.
The mechanics of constructing a market area map. JM 12:493-96 Apr 48
PHELPS, ORME WHEELOCK
The Supreme Court and regulatory taxation. JB 14:99-126 Apr 41
A theory of business communication. JB 15: 343-60 Oct 42
Public policy in labor disputes: the crisis of 1946. JPE 55:189-211 Jun 47
Collective bargaining, Keynesian model. AER 38:581-97 Sep 48
PHELPS BROWN, ERNEST HENRY
see Brown, Ernest Henry Phelps
PHILIP, KJELD
A statistical measurement of the liquidity preference of private banks. REStud 16: 71-77 no.2, 49
PHILLIPS, CARROLL DAVIDSON
Research and educational programs in the marketing of livestock. JFE 28:158-69 Feb 46
PHILLIPS, CHARLES FRANKLIN
A critical analysis of recent literature dealing with marketing efficiency. JM 5: 360-65 Apr 41
Fair trade and the retail drug store. JM 6: 47-48 Jul 41
Price policies of food chains. HBR 19:377-88 no.3, 41
and Abramson, V. The rationing of consumer goods. JB 15:1-20 Jan 42
and Abramson, V. Retail price control. HBR 20:184-98 no.2, 42
Impact of shortages on marketing. HBR 21: 432-42 no.4, 43
Price control in immediate postwar economy. JM 8:289-95 Jan 44

Some observations on rationing. JB 18:9-20 Jan 45
chairman. Major areas for marketing research. [Report of three conferences] JM 11:21-26 Jul 46
PHILLIPS, EDMUND JOHN, Jr.
Diversion of freight traffic from the railroads. LE 16:403-15 Nov 40
PHILLIPS, GEORGE L.
Sweep for the soot O! 1750-1850. EHR II.1: 151-54 no.2-3, 49
PHILLIPS, JEWELL CASS
Tax exempt real estate in Philadelphia. LE 17:361-66 Aug 41
PHIPARD, ESTHER F. and Reid, M. G.
Low-cost adequate diets. JFE 30:161-67 Feb 48
PIERCE, CLARE W.
Pricing class I milk under federal orders. JFE 31,pt.2:434-37 Feb 49
PIERCE, S. D. and Plumptre, A. F. W.
Canada's relations with war-time agencies in Washington. CJE 11:402-19 Aug 45
PIERSON, FRANK COOK
The determination of minimum wage rates. AER 30:72-81 Mar 40
The government of trade unions. ILRR 1: 593-608 Jul 48
[and others] Can capitalism dispense with free labor markets? Discussion. IRRA 2: 100-14 Dec 49
PIERSON, JOHN HERMAN GROESBECK
[How achieve full and stable employment]: discussion. AER/S 34:148-50 Mar 44
The underwriting of aggregate consumer spending as a pillar of full-employment policy. AER 34:21-55 Mar 44
Expanding civilian production and employment after the war: discussion. AER/S 35: 93-96 May 45
[and others] The problem of "full employment": discussion. AER/S 36:319-35 May 46
The underwriting approach to full employment: a further explanation. REStat 31: 182-92 Aug 49
PIETRANERA, GIULIO
Considerations on the dynamics of the Italian inflation. BNL 1:20-52 Apr 47
Note about the "Survey of current inflationary and deflationary tendencies" prepared by the United Nations Department of Economic Affairs. BNL 1:260-63 Jan 48
and Zacchia, C. Recent banking developments in Italy: December 1947-September 1949. BNL 2:225-37 Oct-Dec 49
PIGOU, ARTHUR CECIL
The measurement of real income. EJ 50: 524-25 Dec 40
War finance and inflation. EJ 50:461-68 Dec 40
Newspaper reviewers, economics and mathematics. EJ 51:276-80 Jun-Sep 41

PIGOU, ARTHUR CECIL (Cont.)

Maintaining capital intact. Ec N.S.8:271-75 Aug 41

Types of war inflation. EJ 51:439-48 Dec 41; [Errata]. 52:131 Apr 42

Models of short-period equilibrium. EJ 52: 250-57 Jun-Sep 42

Comparisons of real income. Ec N.S.10: 93-98 May 43

The classical stationary state. EJ 53:343-51 Dec 43

Some considerations on stability conditions, employment and real wage rates. EJ 55: 346-56 Dec 45

1946 and 1919. LBR 1:9-23 Jul 46

Economic progress in a stable environment. Ec N.S.14:180-88 Aug 47

Central planning and Professor Robbins. Ec N.S.15:17-27 Feb 48

The food subsidies. EJ 58:202-09 Jun 48

A comment on duopoly. Ec N.S.15:254-58 Nov 48

Mill and the wages fund. EJ 59:171-80 Jun 49

PILLAI, V. R.

Some aspects of rural co-operation in Travancore. IJE 22:485-503 Jan 42

Regulation of joint-stock banking in India. IJE 24:355-60 Apr 44

Money and the nations. IJE 25:282-89 Jan 45

Post-war Indian monetary policy. IJE 26: 392-403 Jan 46

PINE, WILFRED H.

A study of farm labor in two years of war. JFE 26:563-65 Aug 44

Measuring the economic productivity of land. JFE 30:777-83 Nov 48

PINNEY, HARVEY

The institutional man. JPE 48:543-62 Aug 40

PINO, NICOLO

Comment on "A statistical note on the trade agreement program." JM 6:48-50 Jul 41

PITIGLIANI, FAUSTO R.

The development of Italian cartels under fascism. JPE 48:375-400 Jun 40

PITT, ROMAN F.

Government price fixing in Italy, 1922-1940. SEJ 8:218-37 Oct 41

PLANT, Sir ARNOLD

Monopolies and restrictive practices. LBR 10:1-21 Oct 48

Patent and copyright reform. TBR 3:3-21 Sep 49

PLESSING, H. C.

Problems of telephone economy as seen from a statistical point of view. NTTO 12: 201-13 no.37, 48

PLUMPTRE, ARTHUR FitzWALTER WYNNE

An approach to war finance. CJE 7:1-12 Feb 41

[International financial relations after the war]: discussion. AER/S 33:388-90 Mar 43

and Pierce, S. D. Canada's relations with war-time agencies in Washington. CJE 11: 402-19 Aug 45

The theory of the black market: further considerations. CJE 13:280-82 May 47

Keynes in Cambridge. [obit.] CJE 13: 366-71 Aug 47

PODUVAL, R. N.

Travancore finances during the last decade. IJE 23:68-79 Jul 42

Multiplier, "pump-priming" and "acceleration." IJE 23:271-76 Jan 43

The economic effects of taxes. IJE 24:117-25 Oct 43

Monetary policy and the trade cycle. IJE 24: 192-201 Jan 44

War-time control of foreign exchanges in India. IJE 24:261-65 Apr 44

Cheap money policy in India. IJE 28:365-69 Jan 48

Budgeting for full employment. IJE 29: 125-30 Oct 48

India's commodity balance of trade since the war. IJE 30:149-60 Oct 49

POINDEXTER, JULIUS CARL

Fallacies of interest-free deficit financing. QJE 58:438-59 May 44

--- Rejoinder. QJE 60:154-65 Nov 45

A critique of functional finance through quasi-free bank credit. AER 36:311-23 Jun 46

Some misconceptions of banking and interest theory. SEJ 13:132-45 Oct 46

Professors Pritchard and Benoit-Smullyan on bank-financed functional deficits: a reply. AER 38:391-94 Jun 48

POLAK, JACQUES JACOBUS

Rationing of purchasing power to restrict consumption. Ec N.S.8:223-38 Aug 41

Balance of payments problems of countries reconstructing with the help of foreign loans. QJE 57:208-40 Feb 43

European exchange depreciation in the early twenties. Em 11:151-62 Apr 43

On the theory of price control. REStat 27: 10-16 Feb 45

[and others] International investment: discussion. AER/S 36:710-16 May 46

Exchange depreciation and international monetary stability. REStat 29:173-82 Aug 47

The foreign trade multiplier. AER 37:889-97 Dec 47

and Haberler, G. [The foreign trade multiplier]: A restatement. AER 37:906-07 Dec 47

Balancing international trade: a comment on Professor Frisch's paper. AER 38:139-42 Mar 48

POLANYI, MICHAEL

Economics by motion symbols. REStud 8: 1-19 Oct 40

The growth of thought in society. Ec N.S.8: 428-56 Nov 41

POLANYI, MICHAEL (Cont.)
Patent reform. REStud 11:61-76 no.2, 44
Planning and spontaneous order. MS 16: 237-68 Sep 48

POLI, ADON
and Engstrand, W. M. Japanese agriculture on the Pacific Coast. LE 21:352-64 Sep 45
What has happened to Durham and Delhi? LE 22:182-90 May 46
and Hasel, A. A. A new approach to forest ownership surveys. LE 25:1-10 Feb 49

POLK, JUDD
The future of frozen foreign funds. AER 32: 255-71 Jun 42
and Patterson, G. The emerging pattern of bilateralism. QJE 62:118-42 Nov 47

POLLAK, HANSI P.
State and private provisions for soldiers' dependants. SAJE 8:446-74 Dec 40

POLLARD, ANSON J. and Cladakis, N. J.
Some economic problems encountered in milk control administration. JFE 24: 326-32 Feb 42

POLLOCK, FREDERICK
Economics of war: influence of preparedness on western European economic life. AER/S 30:317-25 Mar 40

POND, GEORGE A.
Achieving maximum production: discussion. JFE 26:229-31 Feb 44
Measuring food needs: discussion. JFE 26: 195-96 May 44
and Cavert, W. L. How long does it take to pay for a farm starting with heavy debts? JFE 26:685-93 Nov 44
Production adjustment research: discussion. JFE 27:923-24 Nov 45
and J[esness], O. B. Andrew Boss, 1867- 1947. [obit.] JFE 29:355-57 Feb 47
Farm management as an art: discussion. JFE 31,pt.2:887-88 Nov 49

POND, SHEPARD
The ducat; once an important coin in European business. BHR 14:17-19 Apr 40
The louis d'or. BHR 14:77-80 Nov 40
The Spanish dollar: the world's most famous silver coin. BHR 15:12-16 Feb 41
The Maria Theresa Thaler: a famous trade coin. BHR 15:26-31 Apr 41

POOLE, KENYON EDWARDS
The problem of simplicity in the enactment of tax legislation, 1920-40. JPE 49: 895-905 Dec 41
Problems of administration and equity under a spendings tax. AER 33:63-73 Mar 43
National economic policies and international monetary cooperation. AER 37:369-75 Jun 47

POOLE, WILLIAM HAROLD
Report of the Royal Commission on the petroleum industry of Alberta. R. CJE 8: 92-108 Feb 42

POPPER, KARL
The poverty of historicism. Pt.I-III.

Ec N.S.11:86-103; 119-37; 12:69-89 May,Aug 44, May 45

POPPLE, CHARLES STERLING
Group banking. HBR 22:191-98 no.2, 44

PORTER, HORACE G.
The expanding scope of agricultural economics. JFE 23:138-44 Feb 41
Capital returns from soil-conservation practices: discussion. JFE 29:1199-1202 Nov 47

PORTER, JAMES MELVILLE, Jr.
The arbitration of industrial disputes arising from disciplinary action. IRRA 2:262-70 Dec 49

PORTER, KENNETH WIGGINS
The business man in American folklore. BHR 18:113-30 Nov 44

POSEY, THOMAS EDWARD
Unemployment compensation and the coal industry in West Virginia. SEJ 7:347-61 Jan 41

POSNER, LOUIS S.
The lesson of guaranteed mortgage certificates. HBR 26:560-71 Sep 48

POSTAN, MICHAEL MOISSEY
Some social consequences of the Hundred Years' War. EHR 12:1-12 no.1-2, 42
Marc Bloch: an obituary note. EHR 14: 161-62 no.2, 44
The rise of a money economy. EHR 14: 123-34 no.2, 44
Early banking. R. EHR 16:63-67 no.1, 46
Sir John Clapham. [obit.] EHR 16:56-59 no.1, 46

POTGIETER, MARTHA
Comments on "The cost of subsistence" by George J. Stigler. JFE 29:767-72 Aug 47

POTTER, ALLEN
The financing of a product from producer to consumer: an important subject for research in the field of marketing. JM 10: 66-67 Jul 45

POUNDS, NORMAN JOHN GREVILL
The discovery of china clay. EHR II.1:20-33 no.1, 48

POWELL, DOROTHY M.
The Negro worker in Chicago industry. JB 20: 21-32 Jan 47

POWERS, RICHARD
The Labor-Management Relations Act of 1947: a topical digest. SEJ 15:67-79 Jul 48

POWICKE, Sir FREDERICK MAURICE
The economic motive in politics. EHR 16: 85-92 no.2, 46

POWLINSON, KEITH
Explaining the facts to employees. HBR 25: 145-57 no.2, 47

PRASAD, MAHADEO
Decentralisation in co-operative cane unions. IJE 29:55-58 Jul 48

PRASAD, PANDAY SUNDARA NARAYAN
Economics and political economy. IJE 20: 485-504 Apr 40

PRASAD, PANDAY SUNDARA NARAYAN (Cont.)
Disinterring the labour theory of value.
IJE 21:175-83 Oct 40
Towards equilibrium in Indian agriculture:
some suggestions for a post-war policy.
IJE 24:135-44 Oct 43
Market mechanism under control: its impli-
cations for economic theory. IJE 24:
395-402 Apr 44
Some ambiguities in the Bombay Plan.
IJE 25:24-40 Jul 44
PRATT, WALLACE E.
The earth's petroleum resources. JB 17:
129-45 Jul 44
PRAY, KENNETH L.
Financial status of federal corporations.
HBR 25:158-68 no.2, 47
PREGEL, BORIS
Peacetime uses of atomic energy. SR 14:
27-44 Mar 47
PREINREICH, GABRIEL A. D.
The economic life of industrial equipment.
Em 8:12-44 Jan 40
Note on the theory of depreciation. Em 9:
80-88 Jan 41
Progressive taxation and proportionate sac-
rifice. AER 38:103-17 Mar 48
The mathematical theory of the firm. EI 2:
492-508 Mar 49
PREST, ALAN RICHMOND
Notes on the history of the Giffen paradox:
comment. JPE 56:58-60 Feb 48
National income of the United Kingdom.
EJ 58:31-62 Mar 48
Some experiments in demand analysis.
REStat 31:33-49 Feb 49
PREST, WILFRED
The scope of price regulation: a comment.
ER 16:122-24 Jun 40
Taussig's Principles. R. ER 16:270-75
Dec 40
War-time controls and post-war planning.
ER 18:211-17 Dec 42
The pure theory of capital. R. ER 19:71-77
Jun 43
The present number of dwellings in Mel-
bourne. ER 19:230-37 Dec 43
Rents in Melbourne. ER 21:37-54 Jun 45
PRESTON, HOMER J. and Miller, L. F.
Relation of feed, labor, and other costs to
butterfat test. JFE 30:566-73 Aug 48
PRESTON, HOWARD HALL [and others]
Banking problems: discussion. AER/S 37:
289-98 May 47
PREWITT, ROY A.
The operation and regulation of crude oil and
gasoline pipe lines. QJE 56:177-211 Feb 42
PRIBRAM, KARL
Residual, differential, and absolute urban
ground rents and their cyclical fluctua-
tions. Em 8:62-78 Jan 40
Housing policy and the defense program.
AER 31:803-08 Dec 41

Employment stabilization through pay roll
taxation. QJE 57:142-52 Nov 42
PRICE, DON K. [and others]
Economic power blocs and American capital-
ism: discussion. IRRA 2:192-202 Dec 49
P[RICE], L[ANGFORD] L[OVELL]
James Bonar, M.A., LL.D. [obit.] JRSS 104:
91-94 pt.1, 41
PRINCE, CHARLES
The USSR's role in international finance.
HBR 25:111-28 no.1, 46
PRINCE, DAVID CHANDLER
Labor's interest: a management view.
ILRR 1:50-59 Oct 47
PRINDLE, H. F.
Sampling medical service charges: a new
application of sampling method. JFE 31:
357-60 May 49
PRITCHARD, LELAND JAMES
The effects of specific and ad valorem taxes.
QJE 58:149-52 Nov 43
The Federal Reserve bank note. JPE 55:
157-66 Apr 47
The nature of bank credit: a comment.
AER 37:399-402 Jun 47
PRITCHARD, NORRIS T.
Pricing of production credit to farmers.
JFE 30:588-91 Aug 48
PRITCHETT, CHARLES HERMAN
Administration of federal power projects.
LE 18:379-90 Nov 42
PROCHNOW, HERBERT VICTOR
Bank liquidity and the new doctrine of antici-
pated income. JF 4:298-314 Dec 49
PROCTOR, ROY E.
Extension use of farm work simplification.
JFE 28:314-19 Feb 46
PRONIN, DIMITRI T.
Land reform in Poland: 1920-1945. LE 25:
133-45 May 49
PROUDFOOT, MALCOLM JARVIS
New inquiries for the census of 1940. LE 16:
102-04 Feb 40
PRUEFER, CLIFFORD HUEBNER
The excess profits tax and defense financing.
SEJ 8:40-53 Jul 41
PRZEWORSKA, Z. M.
A market research method and its applica-
tion to war-time problems. OIS 3:370-74
Nov 22, 41
PU, SHOU SHAN
A note on macroeconomics. Em 14:299-302
Oct 46
PUFFER, CLAUDE E.
Indifference curves versus marginal utility.
AER 30:118 Mar 40
PUFFER, EVELYN H.
A great business lawyer: [Daniel Webster].
BHR 16:61-62 Jun 42
PUMPHREY, LOWELL MASON
Material in the national archives of especial
interest for economists. AER 31:344-45
Jun 41

PUMPHREY, LOWELL MASON (Cont.)
The exchange equilization account of Great
Britain, 1932-1939: exchange operations.
AER 32:803-16 Dec 42

PUNDT, ALFRED G.
French agriculture and the industrial crisis
of 1788. JPE 49:849-74 Dec 41

PURVES, C. M.
Major shifts in world agriculture. JFE 27:
245-60 May 45

QADIR, M. ABDUL
Factory legislation and administration in
Hyderabad. IJE 20:599-609 Apr 40
The economic ideas of Ibn Khaldun. IJE 22:
898-907 Apr 42
Industrial disputes during war time and their
settlement. IJE 24:266-71 Apr 44
Post-war labour disputes in Hyderabad and
their settlement. IJE 29:271-75 Jan 49

QUANTIUS, FRANCES WELLS
Sales taxes and the propensity to consume.
SEJ 11:269-73 Jan 45
The insurance of bank loans and its implica-
tions. JB 19:133-44 Jul 46

QUIGLEY, THOMAS J.
The place of economics in the common school
curriculum. RSE 7,no.2:43-47 Sep 49

QURESHI, ANWAR IQBAL
Marketing of agricultural produce. IJE 20:
343-70 Jan 40
The scope of economics. IJE 20:433-42
Apr 40
The state and economic life: a reply to some
of the criticisms. IJE 21:30-48 Jul 40
Some observations on the marketing of wheat.
IJE 21:167-74 Oct 40
The unit of farming and credit. IJE 21:
198-203 Oct 40
A note on the financial system of Hyderabad.
IJE 21:668-77 Apr 41
Price movements of some important agricul-
tural commodities in Hyderabad. IJE 21:
551-58 Apr 41
Co-operation in theory and practice. IJE 22:
436-49 Jan 42
Control of prices. IJE 24:272-80 Apr 44
Some structural changes in the post-war
world economy. IJE 24:409-17 Apr 44
The new budget of Hyderabad. IJE 25:169-72
Oct 44
International economic co-operation. IJE 25:
274-82 Jan 45
A planned economy for Hyderabad. IJE 26:
83-100 Jul 45
Some thoughts on the Indian food problem.
IJE 26:359-69 Jan 46
Land tenures in Hyderabad: an historical
survey. IJE 27:177-85 Oct 46
The future of cottage industries. PEJ 1,no.1:
62-68 Jul 49

RADFORD, R. A.
The economic organisation of a P.O.W. camp.
Ec N.S.12:189-201 Nov 45

RADICE, EDWARD ALBERT
Consumption, savings, and war finance.
OEP 4:1-14 Sep 40
The national income. (Essays in bibliogra-
phy and criticism III) EHR 14:180-84
no.2, 44

RADOMYSLER, A.
Welfare economics and economic policy. R.
Ec N.S.13:190-204 Aug 46

RAE, JOHN BELL
Federal land grants in aid of canals. JEH 4:
167-77 Nov 44

RAGHAVA RAO, G.
see Rao, G. Raghava

RAHMAN, AHMAD GAD ABDEL-
see Abdel-Rahman, Ahmad Gad

RAHMAN, KHAN ABDUL
Economic reconstruction of Pakistan with
reference to agriculture. PEJ 1,no.1:
4-13 Jul 49

RAHMAN, SHAFIQUR
Can Bengal support such a large agricultural
population? IJE 27:53-63 Jul 46

RAHMER, B. A.
Note on "The industrialisation of backward
areas." EJ 56:657-62 Dec 46

RAIKES, H. R.
Liquid fuel from coal. SAJE 17:32-48
Mar 49

RAJ, J. S.
The rôle of national wage and income struc-
tures in international trade. IJE 21:
233-49 Jan 41
A dynamic theory of the foreign exchanges.
IJE 23:155-66 Oct 42
International equilibrium in a complementary
economy. IJE 24:71-73 Jul 43
A note on the changes in prices and imports
occasioned by the imposition of a tariff.
IJE 25:154-59 Oct 44

RAJALAKSHMAN, D. V.
Cereal rationing in the Madras Presidency.
IJE 26:116-24 Jul 45
Agricultural labour in India. IJE 28:143-53
Jul 47

RAJAN, V. SUNDARA
see Sundara Rajan, V.

RAM, VANGALA SHIVA
Price control in the U.P. IJE 24:281-90
Apr 44

RAMAKRISHNA REDDY, G.
see Reddy, G. Ramakrishna

RAMAKRISHNAN, K. C.
Revision of the Raiffeisen system. IJE 22:
778-87 Jan 42
Labour in agriculture: supply and demand.
IJE 28:417-24 Jan 48

RAMAM, P. SRI
see Sriram, P.

RAMANADHAM, VENKATA VEMURI
War and road transport. IJE 24:291-99
Apr 44
Railway convention and surpluses. IJE 25:
72-79 Jul 44

RAMANADHAM, VENKATA VEMURI (Cont.)
Transport in transition. IJE 25:265-73
Jan 45
Road-owners and road-hauliers. IJE 25:
520-32 Apr 45
New era in railway rates. IJE 26:420-29
Jan 46
Road-rail relations. R. IJE 27:78-84 Jul 46
Railways and industrial location. Pt.I-II.
IJE 27:163-76; 28:237-43 Oct 46, Oct 47
RAMCHANDRA KIRTY, V. S.
see Kirty, V. S. Ramchandra
RAMSAY, A. M. and Isles, K. S.
Lack of adaptability in agriculture: an eco-
nomic survey. ER 20:18-37 Jun 44
RAMSAY, GEORGE DANIEL
Industrial laisser-faire and the policy of
Cromwell. EHR 16:93-110 no.2, 46
RAMSOWER, HARRY CLIFFORD
[County planning project]: discussion.
JFE 22:314-16 Feb 40
RAND, RAY BENEDICT
Pharmaceutical advertising to doctors.
JB 14:150-68 Apr 41
RANDALL, RICHARD JAMES
and Guénault, P. H. An introduction to the
housing problem. SAJE 8:145-61 Jun 40
Municipal enterprise. R. SAJE 8:117-28
Jun 40
[Financial policy of municipalities towards
Natives.] A reply. SAJE 8:282-93 Sep 40
War finance and the South African war budg-
ets 1941-42 and 1942-43. SAJE 9:348-60
Dec 41
Full employment in war-time. SAJE 10:
121-25 Jun 42
RANDERSON, H. R.
Import reduction and Australia's war effort.
ER 16:34-49 Jun 40
Maximum and equity in relation to the
Empire's war effort. ER 16:177-90
Dec 40
RANDLE, CLINTON WILSON
Restrictive practices of unionism. SEJ 15:
171-83 Oct 48
RANGE, WILLARD
The agricultural revolution in royal Georgia,
1752-1775. AH 21:250-55 Oct 47
RANNEY, W. P.
Discussion: "A new system of farm account-
ing." JFE 31:153-56 Feb 49
RAO, A. SESHGIRI
War and recent trends in India's foreign
trade. Pt.I-II. IJE 25:64-71; 141-48
Jul,Oct 44
RAO, APPA
Loans and their classification. IJE 22:
615-23 Jan 42
RAO, B. GOVINDA
see Row, B. Govinda
RAO, B. R. SUBBA
Recent developments in central bank tech-
nique. IJE 20:587-98 Apr 40

Determination of prices in Soviet Russia.
IJE 21:497-510 Apr 41
State in relation to local finance in Mysore.
IJE 22:649-57 Jan 42
RAO, B. SARVESWARA
Cheap money policy. IJE 28:67-74 Jul 47
Equilibrium exchange rates and the I.M.F.
IJE 29:249-56 Jan 49
RAO, CALYAMPUDI RADHAKRISHNA
Note on a problem of Ragnar Frisch. Em 15:
245-49 Jul 47; Correction. 17:212
Jul-Oct 49
RAO, G. RAGHAVA
Seasonal variation of births. IJE 21:192-98
Oct 40
RAO, K. V.
Value in a socialistic state. IJE 21:476-87
Apr 41
The scope of local finance. IJE 22:832-36
Jan 42
Economics of Stakhanovism. IJE 24:149-54
Oct 43
Economics of price control. IJE 24:300-07
Apr 44
War to peace economy in India. IJE 25:
247-53 Jan 45
RAO, R. VISWESWAR
Social security with special reference to
India. IJE 25:348-53 Jan 45
The Indian food problem. IJE 26:370-76
Jan 46
Location of industry in India. IJE 27:140-48
Oct 46
Industrial policy of India with special refer-
ence to tariffs. IJE 28:23-30 Jul 47
Industrial relations in India. IJE 29:215-21
Oct 48
Mixed economy in theory and practice, with
special reference to India. IJE 30:193-96
Oct 49
RAO, T. HANUMANTA
Structural changes in capitalistic economy:
ideas of Keynes and Karl Marx. IJE 24:
418-43 Apr 44
RAO, T. SATYANARAYANA
Easy money policy. IJE 20:557-65 Apr 40
Saving, investment and enterprise in a
socialistic state. IJE 21:488-96 Apr 41
Reorganization of local finance in India.
IJE 22:677-88 Jan 42
The control of inflation in India. IJE 24:
308-13 Apr 44
RAPP, ROBERT E.
The Hamilton National Associates, Inc.: a
case study in group banking. Pt.I-II.
SEJ 9:1-14; 105-21 Jul, Oct 42
RAPPARD, WILLIAM EMANUEL
The economic position of Switzerland.
LBR 11:21-36 Jan 49
RASMINSKY, LOUIS
Anglo-American trade prospects: a Canadian
view. EJ 55:161-78 Jun-Sep 45

RASMUSSEN, E. GUY
  Hardware wholesale trading centers and
    trading territories in nine south-eastern
    states. JM 8:165-71 Oct 43
RASMUSSEN, POUL NØRREGAARD
  Some remarks on the joint effects of simul-
    taneous relations between economic
    variables. NTTO 12:215-22 no.37, 48
RASMUSSEN, WAYNE D.
  Colonia Tovar, Venezuela. AH 17:156-66
    Jul 43
  Agricultural colonization and immigration in
    Venezuela, 1810-1860. AH 21:155-62
    Jul 47
RATCHFORD, BENJAMIN ULYSSES
  New forms of state debts. SEJ 8:459-78
    Apr 42
  The burden of a domestic debt. AER 32:
    451-67 Sep 42
  Some preliminary observations on price con-
    trol. SEJ 10:99-113 Oct 43
  Certain bases of power politics. SEJ 11:
    20-33 Jul 44
  Mr. Domar's "Burden of the debt." AER 35:
    411-14 Jun 45
  The federal excess profits tax. Pt.I-II.
    SEJ 12:1-16; 97-114 Jul,Oct 45
  History of the federal debt in the United
    States. AER/S 37:131-41 May 47
  The South's stake in international trade: past,
    present, and prospective. SEJ 14:361-75
    Apr 48
  Public finances in the southern region of the
    United States. NTJ 1:289-310 Dec 48
  The economics of public debts. PF 3:299-310
    no.4, 48
  The monetary effects of public debts. PF 4:
    5-16 no.1, 49
RATCLIFF, RICHARD UPDEGRAFF
  A land economist looks at city planning.
    LE 20:106-08 May 44
  Notes on the recent decline in home owner-
    ship. LE 20:373-77 Nov 44
  [The education of planners.] At the Univer-
    sity of Wisconsin. LE 21:320-21 Sep 45
  Filtering down and the elimination of sub-
    standard housing. LE 21:322-30 Sep 45
  The orientation of housing research: a re-
    joinder. LE 23:81 Feb 47
  Relationships of technological and social re-
    search in housing. LE 25:91-94 Feb 49
RATURI, ANAND SARAN
  Liquidity preference, price movements, and
    deposits of Indian joint stock banks.
    IJE 27:85-89 Jul 46
RATZKIN, JACK L. and Hays, J. S.
  Trade association practices and antitrust
    law. HBR 25:501-20 no.4, 47
RAUCHENSTEIN, EMIL and Wilcox, W. W.
  The effect of size of herd on milk production
    costs. JFE 30:713-23 Nov 48
RAUP, PHILIP M.
  An example of county land management:

Lincoln County, Wisconsin. LE 17:233-38
    May 41
RAVENSCROFT, A. P.
  National accounts and national income.
    Memorandum no.2 Union government
    public debt and interest. SAJE 16:296-305
    Sep 48
  Dividends on industrial shares 1947-48.
    SAJE 17:349-57 Sep 49
RAVER, PAUL JEROME
  Discussion of William A. Duffus' paper.
    [The place of the government corporation
    in the public utility industries.] LE 25:
    39-46 Feb 49
RAYBACK, JOSEPH G.
  The American workingman and the antislavery
    crusade. JEH 3:152-63 Nov 43
RAYMOND, FRED INGALLS [and others]
  The Sherman Act and the enforcement of
    competition: discussion. AER/S 38:
    203-14 May 48
READ, EATON VAN WERT
  [Retailing in '41]: discussion. JM 5:419-22
    Apr 41
READ, THOMAS T.
  World's output of work. AER 35:143-45
    Mar 45; Correction. 676 Sep 45
READY, LESTER S.
  The unsoundness of recommendation forty-
    two. (The NARUC Depreciation report:
    a symposium) LE 20:100-05 May 44
REBENSBURG, G. A.
  Market analysis: a case study. JM 9:141-43
    Oct 44
RECORD, JANE CASSELS
  The War Labor Board: an experiment in wage
    stabilization. AER 34:98-110 Mar 44
  --- Reply. AER 34:575-77 Sep 44
RECTOR, WILLIAM G.
  From woods to sawmill: transportation prob-
    lems in logging. AH 23:239-44 Oct 49
REDDY, G. RAMAKRISHNA
  The road to industrial peace. IJE 30:31-40
    Jul 49
REDER, MELVIN WARREN
  Inter-temporal relations of demand and sup-
    ply within the firm. CJE 7:25-38 Feb 41
  Monopolistic competition and the stability
    conditions. REStud 8:122-25 Feb 41
  Service industries and the volume of employ-
    ment. AER 31:512-19 Sep 41
  Welfare economics and rationing. QJE 57:
    153-59 Nov 42
  An alternative interpretation of the Cobb-
    Douglas function. Em 11:259-64 Jul-Oct 43
  Interest and employment. JPE 54:243-57
    Jun 46
  A reconsideration of the marginal produc-
    tivity theory. JPE 55:450-58 Oct 47
  The theoretical problems of a national wage-
    price policy. CJE 14:46-61 Feb 48
  [and others] A consideration of the economic
    and monetary theories of J. M. Keynes:
    discussion. AER/S 38:291-98 May 48

REDER, MELVIN WARREN (Cont.)
   Professor Samuelson on the foundations of
      economic analysis. R. CJE 14:516-30
      Nov 48
   The significance of the 1948 General Motors
      agreement. REStat 31:7-14 Feb 49
   A further comment on wage-price policy.
      CJE 15:206-10 May 49
REDLICH, FRITZ
   Some remarks on the business of a New York
      ship chandler in the 1810's. BHR 16:
      92-98 Nov 42
   The business activities of Eric Bollmann: an
      international business promoter, 1797-
      1821. Pt.I-II. BHR 17:81-91; 103-12
      Nov,Dec 43
   Bank money in the United States during the
      first half of the nineteenth century.
      SEJ 10:212-21 Jan 44
   The leaders of the German steam-engine
      industry during the first hundred years.
      JEH 4:121-48 Nov 44
   "Translating" economic policy into business
      policy: an illustration from the resump-
      tion of specie payments in 1879. BHR 20:
      190-95 Dec 46
   Rental analysis in wartime. JPE 55:245-53
      Jun 47
   William Jones and his unsuccessful steam-
      boat venture of 1819. BHR 21:125-36
      Nov 47
   Jacques Laffitte and the beginnings of invest-
      ment banking in France. BHR 22:137-61
      Dec 48
   The origin of the concepts of "entrepreneur"
      and "creative entrepreneur." EEH 1,no.2:
      1-7 Feb 49
   Banking in mediaeval Bruges. R. BHR 23:
      109-12 Jun 49
REED, EDWARD W.
   Coordination of federal and state income
      taxes. SEJ 15:458-72 Apr 49
REED, HAROLD LYLE
   Economists on industrial stagnation. JPE 48:
      244-50 Apr 40
   Principles of banking reform. AER/S 37:
      277-88 May 47
REED, HOWARD S.
   Major trends in California agriculture.
      AH 20:252-55 Oct 46
REED, J. JOE
   Techniques for achieving agricultural goals
      for 1943. JFE 25:84-92 Feb 43
REED, VERGIL D.
   Governmental activity in marketing.
      JM 6,no.4,pt.2:18-19 Apr 42
   War time facts and peace time needs.
      JASA 39:144-54 Jun 44
   Promotion and research. JM 11:367-70
      Apr 47
   chairman. Selection, training, and supervi-
      sion of field interviewers in marketing
      research. [Report of a committee]
      JM 12:365-78 Jan 48

REEDE, ARTHUR H.
   Adequacy of employment statistics. JASA 36:
      71-80 Mar 41
REEDMAN, J. N.
   Exchange policy and import control. SAJE 8:
      372-87 Dec 40
   and Guénault, P. H. The war and the budget.
      SAJE 8:364-71 Dec 40
   Gold and post-war currency standards.
      SAJE 9:379-99 Dec 41
   A note on the table of net investment in the
      Third interim report of the Industrial and
      Agricultural Requirements Commission.
      SAJE 10:82-84 Mar 42
   Public works and employment: a note on
      Professor Hutt's critique of the first Re-
      port of the Social and Economic Planning
      Council. SAJE 11:152-57 Jun 43
   Some reflections on the teaching of business
      cycle theory. R. SAJE 13:52-57 Mar 45
REEVES, H. CLYDE and Pardue, B. L.
   Some reasons why property is poorly as-
      sessed for taxation. NTJ 1:366-68 Dec 48
REGAN, MARK M.
   and Gray, L. C. Needed points of develop-
      ment and reorientation in land economic
      theory. JFE 22:34-46 Feb 40
   The farm real estate market in war time.
      LE 18:140-45 May 42
   and Clarenbach, F. A. Emergency control
      in the farm real estate market. JFE 24:
      866-82 Nov 42
   and Clarenbach, F. A. Land market develop-
      ments and the war. JFE 25:190-202 Feb 43
   and Clarenbach, F. A. Postwar farm land
      values? LE 21:236-42 Aug 45
   and Weitzell, E. C. Economic evaluation of
      soil and water conservation measures and
      programs. JFE 29:1275-94 Nov 47
REID, MARGARET GILPIN
   [Marketing rewritten from the consumer's
      point of view]: discussion. JM 4,no.4,pt.2:
      134-37 Apr 40
   Farmers in a changing world: the 1940 Year-
      book of agriculture. R. JFE 23:446-50
      May 41
   Nutritional aspects and farm family needs
      in a food and nutrition policy. JFE 29:
      333-36 Feb 47
   and Phipard, E. F. Low-cost adequate diets.
      JFE 30:161-67 Feb 48
REIERSØL, OLAV
   Confluence analysis by means of lag moments
      and other methods of confluence analysis.
      Em 9:1-24 Jan 41
REIERSON, ROY LESTER and Riddle, J. H.
   An analysis of the certificate reserve plan.
      JF 1:27-51 Aug 46
REIK, RICHARD
   Compulsory licensing of patents. AER 36:
      813-82 Dec 46
REILLY, EDWARD ERNEST
   The use of the elasticity concept in economic
      theory; with special reference to some

REILLY, EDWARD ERNEST (Cont.)
    economic effects of a commodity tax.
    CJE 6:39-55 Feb 40
REINHARDT, HEDWIG
    On the incidence of public debt. SR 12:205-26
    May 45
    The great debt redemption, 1946-1947. SR 15:
    170-93 Jun 48
REISNER, EDWIN
    Aid for the independent retail trade: a step
    toward fascism? JM 5:163-66 Oct 40
REISS, FRANKLIN JACOB
    Measuring the management factor. JFE 31,
    pt.2:1065-72 Nov 49
REITZ, JULIUS WAYNE
    War-time price control of fresh citrus fruits.
    JFE 27:553-70 Aug 45
REMER, CHARLES FREDERICK
    Economic reconstruction in the Far East.
    AER/S 36:603-12 May 46
RENIER, GUSTAV JOHANNES
    History and ourselves. Ec N.S.15:270-75
    Nov 48
RENNE, ROLAND ROGER
    On agricultural policy. R. JFE 22:484-92
    May 40
    Land economics: discussion. JFE 24:249-51
    Feb 42
    Programs for post war: discussion. JFE 24:
    26-29 Feb 42
    An economist's appraisal of the Missouri
    River development program. JFE 31,pt.2:
    1017-23 Nov 49
RENWICK, CYRIL C.
    The equilibrium of the firm in monopolistic
    and imperfect competition theories. ER 24:
    32-41 Jun 48
REUBENS, BEATRICE G.
    Unemployment in war-time Britain. QJE 59:
    206-36 Feb 45
REUBENS, EDWIN PIERCE
    Small-scale industry in Japan. QJE 61:
    577-604 Aug 47
REVZAN, DAVID ALLEN and Duddy, E. A.
    The location of the South Water Wholesale
    Fruit and Vegetable Market in Chicago.
    Pt.I-II. JB 12:386-412; 13:39-55 Oct 39,
    Jan 40
REWOLDT, STEWART HENRY
    Assignment of trade marks. JM 12:483-87
    Apr 48
REYBURN, HUGH ADAM
    Wage and price movements. SAJE 8:183-84
    Jun 40
REYNOLDS, ARTHUR RAE
    The Kinkaid Act and its effects on western
    Nebraska. AH 23:20-29 Jan 49
    Land frauds and illegal fencing in western
    Nebraska. AH 23:173-79 Jul 49
REYNOLDS, LLOYD GEORGE
    Cutthroat competition. AER 30:736-47 Dec 40
    Relations between wage rates, costs, and
    prices. AER/S 32:275-89 Mar 42

    Industrial wage policies and farm price
    parity. JFE 25:52-64 Feb 43
    [and others] Postwar labor relations: dis-
    cussion. AER/S 36:370-83 May 46
    The supply of labor to the firm. QJE 60:
    390-411 May 46
    Wage differences in local labor markets.
    AER 36:366-75 Jun 46
    Toward a short-run theory of wages.
    AER 38:289-308 Jun 48
    Wage bargaining, price changes, and employ-
    ment. IRRA 1:35-50 Dec 48
REYNOLDS, ROBERT L.
    In search of a business class in thirteenth-
    century Genoa. JEH/S 5:1-19 Dec 45
REZNECK, SAMUEL
    The influence of depression upon American
    opinion, 1857-1859. JEH 2:1-23 May 42
    Coal and oil in the American economy.
    JEH/S 7:55-72 '47
RHODES, EDMUND CECIL
    The distribution of incomes. Ec N.S.9:245-56
    Aug 42
    The distribution of incomes in the United
    States. Ec N.S.10:223-32 Aug 43
    Professor John Hilton. [obit.] JRSS 106:
    293-94 pt.3, 43
    The Pareto distribution of incomes.
    Ec N.S.11:1-11 Feb 44
    Comments on Dr. Garvy's note. Ec N.S.11:
    106 May 44
    The distribution of family incomes.
    Ec N.S.12:31-35 Feb 45
    Output, labour and machines in the coal
    mining industry in Great Britain.
    Ec N.S.12:101-10 May 45
    The distribution of earned and investment
    incomes in the United Kingdom.
    Ec N.S.16:53-65 Feb 49
RIBAS, ANTONIO FABRA
    see Fabra Ribas, Antonio
RICARDO, RITA
    see Campbell, Rita Ricardo
RICE, FRANCES R; Williams, F. M. and
    Schell, E. D.
    Cost of living indexes in wartime. JASA 37:
    415-24 Dec 42
RICE, STUART ARTHUR
    Collection of economic statistics in the
    United States. RIIS 13:62-85 no.1-4, 45
    The United Nations Statistical Commission.
    Em 14:242-50 Jul 46
RICE, WILLIAM B.
    Quality control applied to business adminis-
    tration. JASA 38:228-32 Jun 43
RICHARDS, CECIL SYDNEY
    Some economic and administrative aspects of
    South Africa's war effort. SAJE 8:325-63
    Dec 40; Errata. 9:207 Jun 41
    Fundamentals of economic policy in the
    Union. R. SAJE 10:47-72 Mar 42
    --- A reply with a comment on the question
    of rationalisation. SAJE 10:310-14 Dec 42

RICHARDS, CECIL SYDNEY (Cont.)
 Shipping services of the Union government
  and the possibilities of their development.
  SAJE 11:269-78 Dec 43
 The task before us: with special reference to
  industry. SAJE 12:157-204 Sep 44
 --- A reply. SAJE 13:64-67 Mar 45
 Note on the design for the "Pearsall Mem-
  orial Founders Medal" and new monogram
  for the Journal. SAJE 13:136 Jun 45
 Economic incentives in the post-war world.
  SAJE 13:145-69 Sep 45
 Industrial possibilities and potentialities of
  Northern Rhodesia. R. SAJE 13:203-14
  Sep 45
 [The Second Report of the Distribution Costs
  Commission.] Reply. SAJE 16:177-81
  Jun 48
 The case for increasing the price of gold in
  terms of all currencies: a comment.
  SAJE 17:23-31 Mar 49
 Some thoughts on the Union's economic out-
  look. SAJE 17:142-54 Jun 49
 The Report of the Company Law Amendment
  Enquiry Commission. R. SAJE 17:229-51
  Sep 49
RICHARDSON, FREDERICK LEOPOLD
 WILLIAM, Jr. and Walker, C. R.
 Work flow and human relations. HBR 27:
  107-22 Jan 49
RICHARDSON, JOHN HENRY
 Some remedies for post-war unemployment.
  EJ 51:449-57 Dec 41
 Consumer rationing in Great Britain. CJE 8:
  69-82 Feb 42
 Livelihood and full employment. EJ 56:
  139-43 Mar 46
 Wage policy in full employment. EJ 58:
  421-24 Sep 48
RICHBERG, DONALD RANDALL
 Where is organized labor going? HBR 27:
  405-11 Jul 49
RICHMOND, K. CECIL
 Some basic facts from the Census of housing.
  JM 9:159-61 Oct 44
RICHTER, IRVING
 Four years of the Fair Labor Standards Act
  of 1938: some problems of enforcement.
  JPE 51:95-111 Apr 43
RICHTER, LOTHAR
 The effect of health insurance on the demand
  for health services. CJE 10:179-205
  May 44
RICHTER-ALTSCHAFFER, J. H.
 War-time price control in the United King-
  dom. JFE 22:680-90 Nov 40
RIDDER, VICTOR ALBERT de
 The Belgian monetary reform. REStud 15:
  51-69 no.2, 48
 The Belgian monetary reform: an appraisal
  of the results. REStud 16:25-40 no.1, 48
RIDDLE, JESSE HALE and Reierson, R. L.
 An analysis of the certificate reserve plan.
  JF 1:27-51 Aug 46

RIEFLER, WINFIELD WILLIAM
 Government and the statistician. JASA 37:
  1-11 Mar 42
 A proposal for an international buffer-stock
  agency. JPE 54:538-46 Dec 46
RIEMER, SVEND
 and Riley, M. Trailer communities on a
  university campus. LE 23:81-83 Feb 47
 Escape into decentralization? LE 24:40-48
  Feb 48
 The neighborhood concept in theory and ap-
  plication. LE 25:69-72 Feb 49
RIEMERSMA, JELLE C.
 Calvinism and capitalism in Holland, 1550-
  1650. EEH 1,no.3:19-22 Mar 49
 Max Weber's "Protestant ethic": an example
  of historical conceptualization. EEH 1,no.6:
  11-19 Jun 49
RIENZI, EMANUELE
 The distribution of share capital of Italian
  banking companies. BNL 1:10-19 Apr 47
 The participation of foreign capital in
  Italian joint-stock companies at the out-
  break of the second World War. BNL 1:
  338-43 Apr 48
 Distribution of shareholders among Italian
  joint stock companies. BNL 1:390-95
  Jul 48
RIGGS, HENRY E. and Thompson, C. W.
 Two commentaries on Anatomy of deprecia-
  tion. R. LE 23:433-38 Nov 47
RILEY, MARGARET E. and Walker, E. R.
 Australia's war economy: developments
  from December, 1939, to May, 1940.
  ER 16:78-81 Jun 40
RILEY, MARVIN and Riemer, S.
 Trailer communities on a university campus.
  LE 23:81-83 Feb 47
RILEY, RODERICK HAMILTON
 Is fair return appropriate for municipal
  utilities? LE 16:52-60 Feb 40
RIPPY, JAMES FRED
 South America's foreign trade and hemis-
  phere defense. JB 14:89-98 Apr 41
 South American investments and hemisphere
  defense. JB 14:345-55 Oct 41
 Electrical utilities in Puerto Rico. JB 19:
  221-23 Oct 46
 German investments in Guatemala. JB 20:
  212-19 Oct 47
 German investments in Argentina. JB 21:
  50-54 Jan 48
 British investments in Latin America, 1939.
  JPE 56:63-68 Feb 48
 German investments in Latin America.
  JB 21:63-73 Apr 48
 Investments of citizens of the United States
  in Latin America. JB 22:17-29 Jan 49
RIST, CHARLES
 The measure of gold. R. SAJE 17:371-79
  Dec 49
RITCHIE, ALAN BLACKWOOD
 The first four reports of the Rural Recon-

RITCHIE, ALAN BLACKWOOD (Cont.)
struction Commission. R. ER 21:165-73
Dec 45
RITCHIE, J. MURIEL
Some relationships of landlord and tenant.
EJ 54:366-74 Dec 44
RIVEL, ROBERT BRADIN
Industrial composition of the business loans
of the Chase National Bank, 1940-47.
JB 22:50-59 Jan 49
The use of average maturity in the analysis
of commercial bank investments. JF 4:
342-47 Dec 49
RIX, MARGARET S.
Company law: 1844 and today. EJ 55:
242-60 Jun-Sep 45
ROBBINS, EDWIN CLYDE
War-time labor productivity. HBR 19:99-105
no.1, 40
Management-labor cooperation. HBR 21:
415-24 no.4, 43
ROBBINS, GEORGE W.
Notions about the origins of trading. JM 11:
228-36 Jan 47
Preparation and presentation of the research
report. JM 13:62-72 Jul 48
ROBBINS, I. D.
Management services for small business
through trade associations. HBR 26:
627-40 Sep 48
ROBBINS, JAMES J.
Organized labor and the public interest:
discussion. AER/S 35:226-28 May 45
ROBBINS, LIONEL
Economic prospects. LBR 3:21-32 Jan 47
Inquest on the crisis. LBR 6:1-27 Oct 47
The economist in the twentieth century.
Ec N.S.16:93-105 May 49
The sterling problem. LBR 14:1-31 Oct 49
ROBBINS, SIDNEY M.
and Murphy, T. E. Industrial preparedness.
HBR 26:329-52 May 48
and Murphy, T. E. Economics of scheduling
for industrial mobilization. JPE 57:30-45
Feb 49
Competitive bidding in sale of securities.
HBR 27:646-64 Sep 49
ROBERTS, DAVID RENSHAW
A limitation upon the differential wage doc-
trine. QJE 57:314-22 Feb 43
The distribution of private, non-agricultural
employees in the United States by straight-
time hourly wage rates. JASA 39:469-78
Dec 44
ROBERTS, HARRY V.
The measurement of advertising results.
JB 20:131-45 Jul 47
ROBERTS, MERRILL JOSEPH
Recent innovations in railroad freight and
passenger equipment. JB 13:56-73 Jan 40
Economic aspects of southern grain rates.
SEJ 16:44-52 Jul 49

ROBERTS, R. O.
Ricardo's theory of public debts. Ec N.S.9:
257-66 Aug 42
Thomas Chalmers on the public debt.
Ec N.S.12:111-16 May 45
Comparative shipping and shipbuilding costs.
Ec N.S.14:296-309 Nov 47
ROBERTS, RALPH W. and Smith, T. L.
Sources and distribution of the farm popula-
tion in relation to farm benefit payments.
JFE 23:607-18 Aug 41
ROBERTSON, CHARLES JOHN
Monoexport in Africa. SAJE 8:1-18 Mar 40
ROBERTSON, DENNIS HOLME
A Spanish contribution to the theory of fluc-
tuations. Ec N.S.7:50-65 Feb 40
The post-war monetary plans. EJ 53:352-60
Dec 43
The inter-relations of shifts in demand.
REStud 12:71-72 no.1, 44
The problem of exports. EJ 55:321-25
Dec 45
The economic outlook. EJ 57:421-37 Dec 47
New light on an old story. R. Ec N.S.15:
294-300 Nov 48
What has happened to the rate of interest?
TBR 1:15-31 Mar 49
Britain and European recovery. LBR 13:1-13
Jul 49
On sticking to one's last. EJ 59:505-09
Dec 49
ROBERTSON, HECTOR MENTEITH
Reflexions on Malthus and his predecessors.
SAJE 10:295-306 Dec 42
A further note on early land tenure at the
Cape. SAJE 12:144-46 Jun 44
Panaceas, past and present: the history of
some current ways of thought and plans
for economic reform. SAJE 12:251-62
Dec 44
The economic development of the Cape under
Van Riebeek. Pt.I-IV. SAJE 13:1-17;
75-90; 170-84; 245-62 Mar,Jun,Sep,Dec 45
Economic historians and their colleagues.
SAJE 14:202-11 Sep 46
Some problems in writing an official "civil"
history of the war. SAJE 16:405-14
Dec 48
The 1849 settlers in Natal. Pt.I-II. SAJE 17:
274-88; 416-42 Sep,Dec 49
ROBERTSON, ROSS MARSHALL
Mathematical economics before Cournot.
JPE 57:523-36 Dec 49
ROBICHAUD, A. E. and Neifeld, M. R.
Lenders exchanges in the personal finance
business. JM 4:268-73 Jan 40
ROBINSON, AUSTIN
see Robinson, Edward Austin Gossage
ROBINSON, CORIENNE
Relationship between condition of dwellings
and rentals, by race. LE 22:296-302
Aug 46

ROBINSON, EDWARD AUSTIN GOSSAGE
A problem in the theory of industrial loca-
tion. EJ 51:270-75 Jun-Sep 41
The Scott and Uthwatt reports on land utilisa-
tion. R. EJ 53:28-38 Apr 43
Official statistics. R. EJ 53:418-22 Dec 43
The qualifications of statisticians. EJ 54:
265-68 Jun-Sep 44
Sir William Beveridge on full employment.
R. EJ 55:70-76 Apr 45
and H[arrod], R. F. John Maynard Keynes.
[obit.] EJ 56:171 Jun 46
John Maynard Keynes (1883-1946). [obit.]
EJ 57:1-68 Mar 47
Five economic surveys. R. EJ 59:629-38
Dec 49

ROBINSON, GEORGE BUCHAN
The old-age reserve fund is not "illusory."
QJE 60:136-53 Nov 45

ROBINSON, HERBERT WILLIAM; Makower, H.
and Marschak, J.
Studies in mobility of labor: analysis for
Great Britain. Pt.I-II. OEP 2:70-97;
4:39-62 May 39, Sep 40

ROBINSON, JESSE S.
John Henry Gray 1859-1946. [obit.] AER 36:
664-66 Sep 46

ROBINSON, JOAN
Rising supply price. Ec N.S.8:1-8 Feb 41
Marx on unemployment. EJ 51:234-48
Jun-Sep 41
The international currency proposals. EJ 53:
161-75 Jun-Sep 43
The United States in the world economy. R.
EJ 54:430-37 Dec 44
The pure theory of international trade.
REStud 14:98-112 no.2, 47
Mr. Harrod's dynamics. EJ 59:68-85 Mar 49

ROBINSON, LELAND REX
Corporate earnings on share and borrowed
capital in percentages of gross income
(1918-1940). JASA 36:253-64 Jun 41

ROBINSON, NEHEMIAH
Future trends in Germany's agricultural
system. JFE 26:309-26 May 44
German foreign trade and industry after the
first World War. QJE 58:615-36 Aug 44
Problems of European reconstruction.
QJE 60:1-55 Nov 45

ROBINSON, ROLAND INWOOD
Appropriate objectives and functions of sup-
ervisory standards. [Summary]
AER/S 30:232-34 Mar 40
The capital-deposit ratio in banking supervi-
sion. JPE 49:41-57 Feb 41
The downward course of consumer credit.
JM 7:345-49 Apr 43
Money supply and liquid asset formation.
AER 36:127-33 Mar 46
Bank capital and dividend policies. HBR 26:
398-409 Jul 48
Central banks and the state: a comment.
AER 39:494-96 Mar 49

The teaching of money and banking. JF 4:
237-42 Sep 49

ROBINSON, THOMAS C. M.
and Wallrabenstein, P. P. Estimates of agricultural employment and wage rates.
JFE 31:233-52 May 49
and Sarle, C. F. Measurement of agricultural
production. JFE 31:213-30 May 49

ROBISON, SOPHIA MOSES and Tough, R.
Toward post-war planning for Yorkville.
Pt.I-IV. LE 18:485-94; 19:354-63; 470-78;
20:156-63 Nov 42, Aug,Nov 43, May 44

ROBOTKA, FRANK
A theory of cooperation. JFE 29:94-114
Feb 47
Agricultural cooperation: discussion.
JFE 31,pt.2:574-76 Feb 49

ROCHESTER, ANNA
On the nature of rent. S&S 4:57-69 no.1, 40

RODAN, PAUL N. ROSENSTEIN-
see Rosenstein-Rodan, Paul N.

RODANO, CARLO
The economic future of Europe and the ERP.
BNL 2:135-45 Jul-Sep 49

RODGERS, RAYMOND and Luedicke, H. E.
Dynamic competition. HBR 27:237-49 Mar 49

RODRIQUEZ, ALFRED
A plan for organization of small manufacturers for participation in production for
war. JB 15:49-55 Jan 42

RODWELL, H. R.
Public control of town milk supply in New
Zealand. ER 22:261-71 Dec 46

RODWIN, LLOYD
Two approaches to industrial location analy-
sis. LE 21:23-33 Feb 45
Garden cities and the metropolis. LE 21:
268-81 Aug 45
--- A rejoinder. LE 22:69-77 Feb 46

ROEGEN, NICHOLAS GEORGESCU-
see Georgescu-Roegen, Nicholas

ROETHLISBERGER, FRITZ JULES
The foreman: master and victim of double
talk. HBR 23:283-98 no.3, 45
Human relations: rare, medium, or well-
done? HBR 26:89-107 Jan 48

ROGERS, BEATRICE ALLEN
and Tucker, D. S. Davis Rich Dewey, 1858-
1942. [obit.] AER 33:236-38 Mar 43
and Tucker, D. S. Davis Rich Dewey, 1858-
1942. [obit.] JASA 38:107-09 Mar 43

ROGERS, JOHN F.
Aims and limitations of British planning.
S&S 13:97-117 no.2, 49

ROGIN, LEO
Werner Sombart and the uses of transcendentalism. AER 31:493-511 Sep 41
Marx and Engels on distribution in a socialist society. AER 35:137-43 Mar 45

ROHATGI, B. N.
Labour problems and labour legislation in
India. IJE 20:611-16 Apr 40
Some aspects of provincial finance. IJE 21:
678-88 Apr 41

**ROHRLICH, GEORGE FRIEDRICH**
Equalization schemes in German unemploy-
ment compensation. QJE 58:482-97
May 44

**ROLL, ERICH**
The social significance of recent trends in
economic theory. CJE 6:448-59 Aug 40

**ROLPH, EARL ROBERT**
Mr. Sumberg's interpretation of the Soviet
turnover tax. AER 36:661-62 Sep 46
The burden of import duties. AER 36:
788-812 Dec 46
The payment of interest on Series E bonds.
AER/S 37:318-21 May 47
The burden of import duties with fixed ex-
change rates. AER 37:604-32 Sep 47
The concept of transfers in national income
estimates. QJE 62:327-61 May 48
[The burden of import duties.] Rejoinder.
AER 38:867-69 Dec 48
and Break, G. F. The welfare aspects of ex-
cise taxes. JPE 57:46-54 Feb 49

**ROMAN, AGNES**
see Miller, Agnes Roman

**ROMANES, JOHN HYSLOP**
[Communication relating to the Muir portrait
of Adam Smith.] EJ 55:465-66 Dec 45

**RONA, F.**
Objectives and methods of exchange control
in the United Kingdom during the war and
post-war transition. Ec N.S.13:259-77
Nov 46

**ROOS, CHARLES FREDERICK**
and Von Szeliski, V. S. The determination of
interest rates. JPE 50:501-35 Aug 42
and Von Szeliski, V. S. The demand for durable goods. Em 11:97-122 Apr 43
[and others] Forecasting postwar demand:
discussion. Em 13:54-59 Jan 45
A future role for the Econometric Society in
international statistics. Em 16:127-34
Apr 48
The demand for investment goods. AER/S 38:
311-20 May 48
Business planning and statistical analysis.
Em 17,suppl.:69-70 Jul 49

**ROOSE, KENNETH DAVIS**
The recession of 1937-38. JPE 56:239-48
Jun 48

**ROOT, ALFRED R. and Welch, A. C.**
The continuing consumer study: a basic
method for the engineering of advertising.
JM 7:3-21 Jul 42

**ROOVER, FLORENCE EDLER DE**
see De Roover, Florence Edler

**ROOVER, RAYMOND DE**
see De Roover, Raymond Adrien

**ROPER, ELMO**
The public looks at labor unions. HBR 21:
425-31 no.4, 43
The public looks at business. HBR 27:165-74
Mar 49

**RÖPKE, WILHELM**
Repressed inflation. Kyk 1:242-53 fasc.3, 47

**ROSA, ROBERT VINCENT**
A multiplier analysis of armament expenditure. AER 31:249-65 Jun 41
Some small business problems indicated by
the industrial loan experience of the
Federal Reserve Bank of New York. JF 2,
no.1:91-100 Apr 47
Small business and depression. HBR 26:
58-62 Jan 48
Use of the consumption function in short run
forecasting. REStat 30:91-105 May 48
The problem of French recovery. EJ 59:
154-70 Jun 49

**ROSE, ALBERT**
Wars, innovations and long cycles: a brief
comment. AER 31:105-07 Mar 41

**ROSE, JOSEPH R.**
and Wilson, G. L. Pacific Gas and Electric
case: reply. AER 30:827-29 Dec 40
Regulation of utility valuation in Pennsylvania:
comment. AER 33:903-04 Dec 43
and Wilson, G. L. "Out-of-pocket" cost in
railroad freight rates. QJE 60:546-60
Aug 46
Business education in a university. JB 20:
183-90 Oct 47

**ROSE, WALTER JOHN**
A "made to measure" tariff. ER 21:212-22
Dec 45

**ROSE-INNES, N. and Chambers, R. D.**
Report of the Provincial Financial Resources
Committee. R. SAJE 12:263-78 Dec 44

**ROSEN, JOSEF**
On the calculation of cost-of-living index
figures. Kyk 3:325-51 fasc.4, 49

**ROSEN, MARTIN M.**
Population, growth, investment, and economic
recovery. AER 32:122-25 Mar 42
The demand for cigarettes in Austria.
SEJ 14:186-91 Oct 47

**ROSENBAUM, DOUGLAS**
The housing needs of the nonwhite population
in nonfarm areas. LE 24:331-39 Nov 48

**ROSENBAUM, E.**
Gerhart von Schulze-Gaevernitz (July 25,
1864-July 10, 1943). [obit.] EJ 53:450-53
Dec 43

**ROSENBAUM, E. M.**
War economics. A bibliographical approach.
Ec N.S.9:64-94 Feb 42

**ROSENBERG, BERNARD**
Veblen and Marx. SR 15:99-117 Mar 48

**ROSENBERG, HANS**
The economic impact of Imperial Germany:
agricultural policy. JEH/S 3:101-07
Dec 43
Political and social consequences of the Great
Depression of 1873-1896 in central Europe.
EHR 13:58-73 no.1-2, 43

**ROSENBERG, WOLFGANG**
Second report of the N.Z. National Service
Department. R. ER 20:218-21 Dec 44

ROSENBERG, WOLFGANG (Cont.)
A note on state regulation of farm incomes in New Zealand. OIS 11:85-99 Apr 49
New Zealand official estimates of national income. ER 25,(no.48):74-81 Jun 49

ROSENFELD, FÉLIX and Issawi, C.
Company profits in Egypt 1929-1939. EgC 32: 679-86 Nov 41

ROSENSON, ALEXANDER MOSES
Proposal for cushioning the transition to a peacetime economy. AER 32:117-22 Mar 42
Monetary effects of wartime social security taxes. JPE 50:881-900 Dec 42
The terms of the Anglo-American financial agreement. AER 37:178-87 Mar 47
International commodity reserve standard reconsidered. REStat 30:135-40 May 48

ROSENSTEIN-RODAN, PAUL N.
Problems of industrialisation of eastern and south-eastern Europe. EJ 53:202-11 Jun-Sep 43

ROSENTHAL, RICHARD LAURENCE
$R_x$ for smaller business. HBR 24:22-31 no.1, 45

ROSENTHAL, ROBERT J.
Union-management welfare plans. QJE 62: 64-94 Nov 47

ROSS, ARTHUR M.
The trade union as a wage-fixing institution. AER 37:566-88 Sep 47
The dynamics of wage determination under collective bargaining. AER 37:793-822 Dec 47
What is responsible wage policy? SEJ 14: 266-84 Jan 48
The influence of unionism upon earnings. QJE 62:263-86 Feb 48
--- Reply [and addendum]. QJE 62:787-91 Nov 48
The General Motors wage agreement of 1948. REStat 31:1-7 Feb 49

ROSS, EARLE D.
The land-grant college: a democratic adaptation. AH 15:26-36 Jan 41
The United States Department of Agriculture during the commissionership: a study in politics, administration, and technology, 1862-1889. AH 20:129-43 Jul 46
and Tontz, R. L. The term "agricultural revolution" as used by economic historians. AH 22:32-38 Jan 48
Agriculture in our economic history. AH 22: 65-69 Apr 48

ROSS, H. F.
Some aspects of the problem of guaranteed wages and employment. CJE 13:545-62 Nov 47

ROSS, K. H.
Working class clothing consumption, 1937-1938. JRSS 111:145-60 pt.2, 48

ROSS, LLOYD
Conciliation and arbitration in Australia and New Zealand. Pt.I. Recent developments in Australian industrial relations. ILRR 2: 98-105 Oct 48

ROSS, RALPH GILBERT
Commission of Inquiry into Slave Labor. ILRR 2:619-20 Jul 49

ROSS, RHONA
Some new emphases in population analysis. SAJE 17:166-74 Jun 49
Population policy in Great Britain. R. SAJE 17:320-28 Sep 49

ROSSITER, CLINTON L.
Labor and the public interest: discussion. IRRA 2:46-49 Dec 49

ROSSOUW, GEORGE STEFANUS HAUPTFLEISCH
The problem of imperial preference. SAJE 14: 173-87 Sep 46

ROSTAS, LÁSZLÓ
Capital levies in central Europe, 1919-24. REStud 8:20-32 Oct 40
Industrial production, productivity and distribution in Britain, Germany and the United States. EJ 53:39-54 Apr 43
Productivity of labour in the cotton industry. EJ 55:192-205 Jun-Sep 45

ROSTOW, EUGENE VICTOR
Two aspects of lend-lease economics. AER/S 33:377-81 Mar 43
[Rostow's proposals for petroleum policy.] A reply. JPE 57:60-68 Feb 49

ROSTOW, WALT WHITMAN
Explanations of the "great depression," 1873-96: an historian's view of modern monetary theory. EH 4:356-70 Feb 40
Business cycles, harvests, and politics: 1790-1850. JEH 1:206-21 Nov 41
Adjustments and maladjustments after the Napoleonic wars. AER/S 32:13-23 Mar 42
Some aspects of price control and rationing. AER 32:486-500 Sep 42
The political basis for U.S. foreign policy. LBR 6:39-49 Oct 47

ROTH, ARTHUR, Jr.
Needed: a method of western mountain land valuation. LE 24:181-85 May 48

ROTHBARTH, ERWIN
The measurement of changes in real income under conditions of rationing. REStud 8: 100-07 Feb 41
Bowley's Studies in national income. R. EJ 53:55-59 Apr 43
and Madge, C. Saving and spending in Leeds: a reply to Dr. Singer's criticisms. MS 13: 80-88 Aug 44
A note on an index number problem. REStud 11:91-98 no.2, 44
Causes of the superior efficiency of U.S.A. industry as compared with British industry. EJ 56:383-90 Sep 46

ROTHSCHILD, KURT WILSON
The degree of monopoly. Ec N.S.9:24-39 Feb 42
A note on advertising. EJ 52:112-21 Apr 42

ROTHSCHILD, KURT WILSON (Cont.)
  Advertising in war-time. OIS 4:169-75
    Jun 6, 42
  Monopsony, buying costs, and welfare ex-
    penditure. REStud 10:62-67 no.1, 42
  A further note on the degree of monopoly.
    Ec N.S.10:69-70 Feb 43
  and Goldmann, J. Point rationing of food-
    stuffs. OIS 5:129-33 Jun 5, 43
  Public expenditure in the national income:
    a note. Ec N.S.11:19-22 Feb 44
  The small nation and world trade. EJ 54:
    26-40 Apr 44
  Rationing and the consumer. OEP 7:67-82
    Mar 45
  Wages and risk-bearing. OIS 7:193-98
    Sep 1, 45
  [In defense of monopoly.] Further comment.
    QJE 60:615-18 Aug 46
  and Gillespie, S. C. Migration and the dis-
    tributive trades. REStud 13:81-83 no.2, 46
  The meaning of rationality: a note on Prof-
    essor Lange's article. REStud 14:50-52
    no.1, 46
  Price theory and oligopoly. EJ 57:299-320
    Sep 47
ROTTENBERG, SIMON
  Intra-union disputes over job control.
    QJE 61:619-39 Aug 47
ROTWEIN, EUGENE
  Post-World War I price movements and price
    policy. JPE 53:234-57 Sep 45
ROUTH, G. G. C.
  State intervention in the regulation of wages
    and working conditions in Great Britain
    and South Africa. SAJE 17:289-305 Sep 49
ROW, B. GOVINDA
  Scope and method of economics. IJE 20:
    475-83 Apr 40
  Price-level of tobacco in the Guntur area.
    IJE 21:526-35 Apr 41
  Rural co-operation in Madras: some aspects.
    IJE 22:739-52 Jan 42
  Some aspects of economic control in India
    during the war. IJE 24:314-22 Apr 44
  The Indian food problem. IJE 26:377-87
    Jan 46
  The theory of location of industries with ref-
    erence to India. IJE 27:122-30 Oct 46
  V. G. Kale: his industrial outlook. IJE 27:
    323-30 Jan 47
  Agricultural labour in Andhra Desa: some
    aspects. IJE 28:179-86 Jul 47
ROWE, HAROLD B.
  Economic significance of changes in market
    organization. JFE 22:173-85 Feb 40
  Use of wartime government records in eco-
    nomic research. AER/S 36:799-806
    May 46
  Issues in American foreign food policy.
    JFE 31,pt.2:281-90 Feb 49
ROWE, ROBERT L.
  Profit-sharing plans in industry. HBR 27:
    559-84 Sep 49

ROWLAND, BUFORD and Snedeker, G. B.
  The United States Court of Claims and
    French spoliation records. BHR 18:20-27
    Apr 44
ROWLANDS, DAVID THOMAS
  Defense housing insurance. LE 17:357-61
    Aug 41
  [and others] Economic problems of Ameri-
    can cities: discussion. AER/S 32:341-48
    Mar 42
  chairman. Objectives in applied land eco-
    nomics curricula. Abstract of specialized
    conference discussion. AER/S 32:233
    Mar 42
ROWLEY, SHEILA
  The relation between farm incomes and farm
    costs expressed in equations. ER 23:
    58-65 Jun 47
ROWNTREE, RICHARDSON HENRY
  Note on constant marginal cost. AER 31:
    335-38 Jun 41
ROWSON, R. B.
  The two-part tariff. Further notes by an
    electrical engineer. Ec N.S.8:392-98
    Nov 41
ROY, PARIMAL
  On Marshall's statics and dynamics. IJE 20:
    761-71 Apr 40
  The mercantilist view of money in relation
    to public finance. IJE 23:257-70 Jan 43
  On the nature of mercantilist tariff. IJE 24:
    1-19 Jul 43
  On the definition of mercantilism. IJE 25:
    130-40 Oct 44
  On the conception of collective wants.
    IJE 26:11-28 Jul 45
ROZMAN, DAVID
  Massachusetts forest tax law. LE 18:363-65
    Aug 42
RUBIN, H. and Klein, L. R.
  A constant-utility index of the cost of living.
    REStud 15:84-87 no.2, 48
RUDD, ROBERT W. and MacFarlane, D. L.
  The scale of operations in agriculture.
    JFE 24:420-33 May 42
  --- Rejoinder. JFE 24:891 Nov 42
RUDDOCK, ALWYN A.
  Alien hosting in Southampton in the fifteenth
    century. EHR 16:30-37 no.1, 46
  London capitalists and the decline of
    Southampton in the early Tudor period.
    EHR II.2:137-51 no.2, 49
RUDERMAN, ARMAND PETER
  Wartime food-consumption patterns and the
    cost of living. JB 17:244-49 Oct 44
  Agricultural prices and national income.
    JFE 28:571-75 May 46
RUDRA, S. K.
  Some aspects of the Indian labour problem.
    IJE 20:649-62 Apr 40
  Value in the socialist state. IJE 21:716-22
    Apr 41
  Our food problem. IJE 24:169-78 Jan 44

RUDRA, S. K. (Cont.)
Post-war Indian economic development.
IJE 25:423-35 Apr 45
Rationing of foodgrains in the U.P. during
World War II. IJE 26:716-33 Apr 46
Peace in industry. IJE 29:37-43 Jul 48

RUEFF, JACQUES
The fallacies of Lord Keynes' General theory.
QJE 61:343-67 May 47
--- Reply. QJE 62:771-82 Nov 48

RUGGLES, CLYDE ORVAL
The role of rate making. HBR 18:215-30
no.2, 40
chairman. The impact of national defense
and the war upon public utilities. Abstract
of specialized conference discussion.
AER/S 32:216-17 Mar 42
Electric power and industrial development.
HBR 22:377-92 no.3, 44
Electric power in industry and agriculture.
HBR 23:95-114 no.1, 44
Government control of business. HBR 24:
32-50 no.1, 45
Public utilities. BHR 20:57-68 Apr 46

RUGGLES, NANCY DUNLAP
The welfare basis of the marginal cost pricing principle. REStud 17:29-46 no.1, 49

RUGGLES, RICHARD
The relative movements of real and money
wage rates. QJE 55:130-49 Nov 40
The concept of linear total cost-output
regressions. AER 31:332-35 Jun 41
[Real money and wage rates.] Rejoinder.
QJE 55:697-700 Aug 41
and Brodie, H. An empirical approach to
economic intelligence in World War II.
JASA 42:72-91 Mar 47

RUIST, ERIK
Standard errors of the tilling coefficients
used in confluence analysis. Em 14:
235-41 Jul 46

RUML, BEARDSLEY
Tax policies for prosperity. AER/S 36:
265-74 May 46
--- [idem] JF 1:81-90 Aug 46

RUPPLE, GEORGE W.
Membership and public relations in agricul-
tural cooperatives. JFE 31,pt.2:580-81
Feb 49

RUSH, DONALD R. and Johnson, S. E.
Orientation of farm-management research
to low-income farms. JFE 23:218-32
Feb 41

RUSH, RICHARD H.
A case study of postwar planning by business.
JM 8:150-55 Oct 43

RUSS, WILLIAM A., Jr.
Godkin looks at western agrarianism: a
case study. AH 19:233-42 Oct 45

RUSSEL, ROBERT R.
The effects of slavery upon nonslaveholders
in the ante bellum South. AH 15:112-26
Apr 41

RUSSELL, Sir EDWARD JOHN
Rothamsted and its experiment station.
AH 16:161-83 Oct 42

RUSSELL, HORACE
Defense housing and the Lanham Bill. LE 16:
457-59 Nov 40

RUSSELL, VERA KILDUFF
Economic factors in the development of
Canadian-American trade. SEJ 8:201-17
Oct 41

RUTHERFORD, HARRY KENNETH
Industrial preparedness. JM 4,no.4,pt.2:
47-50 Apr 40

RUTHERFORD, M. E. E. and Rutherford, R.
S. G.
The consumption and rationing of meat and
cheese. OEP 5:74-87 Jun 41

RUTHERFORD, ROBERT STEWART GREGG
The consumption and rationing of butter and
margarine. OEP 3:131-43 Feb 40
and Rutherford, M. E. E. The consumption
and rationing of meat and cheese. OEP 5:
74-87 Jun 41
The protein situation. OIS 3:263-68
Aug 30, 41
Protein allocations. OIS 5:49-51 Feb 20, 43
Guaranteed prices and the farmers.
OIS 6:17-23 Feb 5, 44
Quality milk. OIS 6:161-68 Jul 22, 44
Fluctuations in the sheep population of New
South Wales, 1860-1940. ER 24:56-71
Jun 48

RUTTENBERG, HAROLD J.
The fruits of industrial peace. HBR 18:
285-94 no.3, 40

RYAN, JOHN AUGUSTINE
Two objectives for Catholic economists.
RSE 1:1-5 Dec 42
Some economic aspects of European relief
and rehabilitation. RSE 3:1-8 Dec 44

SABSAY, NAHUM
A machinist looks at management. HBR 22:
249-55 no.2, 44
From the workers' point of view. HBR 25:
339-47 no.3, 47

SADIE, J. L.
A note on the business cycle in South Africa,
1939-1940. SAJE 14:70-75 Mar 46
Public finance and the business cycle in
South Africa, 1910-1940. SAJE 14:132-60
Jun 46
European population movements in S.A. dur-
ing World War II. SAJE 16:51-69 Mar 48
Further observations on foreign exchange
rates. SAJE 16:194-201 Jun 48

SAHA, K. B.
India's balance of payments. IJE 30:101-07
Oct 49

SAHASRABUDHE, V. G.
Post-war monetary system for India.
IJE 26:554-64 Jan 46
Cheap money policy in free India. IJE 28:
75-81 Jul 47

SAHASRABUDHE, V. G. (Cont.)
  Devaluation and inflation. IJE 30:199-204
    Oct 49
SAID, MOHAMED HOSNY EL-
  see El-Said, Mohamed Hosny
SAILOR, VANCE L.
  Bank supervision and the business cycle.
    JF 3,no.3:65-77 Oct 48
SAKSENA, SHITLA PRASAD
  Applicability of the principle of minimum
    living wage in India. IJE 20:719-28 Apr 40
  Price level in India with particular refer-
    ence to agricultural prices. IJE 21:
    798-803 Apr 41
  Replanning of the co-operative movement in
    India. IJE 22:554-61 Jan 42
SALANT, WALTER S.
  The demand for money and the concept of
    income velocity. JPE 49:395-421 Jun 41
  The inflationary gap. AER 32:308-20 Jun 42
  [Economic research and tax policy]: discus-
    sion. AER/S 34,no.2:24-26 Jun 44
  and Mosak, J. L. Income, money and prices
    in wartime. AER 34:828-39 Dec 44
  [and others] Fiscal policy in prosperity and
    depression: discussion. AER/S 38:404-16
    May 48
SALEH EL FALAKI, MAHMOUD
  see El Falaki, Mahmoud Saleh
SALERA, VIRGIL
  Australian sugar: a case study in controlled
    marketing. JM 6:286-90 Jan 42
  Taxation and economic stability. QJE 57:
    323-25 Feb 43
  Aspects of the basing-point system: comment.
    AER 33:900-02 Dec 43
  Exchange-rate parities: comment [followed
    by M. E. Garnsey's reply]. QJE 60:
    622-24 Aug 46
  Mikesell on international monetary agree-
    ments and planned economies. JPE 56:
    442-46 Oct 48
SALES, H. SPENCE-
  see Spence-Sales, H.
SALIERS, EARL A.
  Depreciation inventoried. JB 13:87-88 Jan 40
SALIM, P. B. A.
  Irrigation and power development in Pakistan.
    PEJ 1,no.1:33-39 Jul 49
SALISBURY, JAMES, Jr. and Salter, L. A., Jr.
  Subsurface resources and surface land eco-
    nomics. Pt.I-II. LE 17:270-79; 385-93
    Aug,Nov 41
SALISBURY, PHILIP
  Planning sales campaigns in forty-eight
    sovereignties. JM 4,pt.2:17-24 Apr 40
  Has advertising come of age? JM 8:25-32
    Jul 43
SALOMON, ALBERT
  Adam Smith as sociologist. SR 12:22-42
    Feb 45
SALOUTOS, THEODORE
  The Wisconsin Society of Equity. AH 14:
    78-95 Apr 40

The decline of the Wisconsin Society of
  Equity. AH 15:137-50 Jul 41
The rise of the Nonpartisan League in North
  Dakota, 1915-1917. AH 20:43-61 Jan 46
The expansion and decline of the Nonpartisan
  League in the western Middle West, 1917-
  1921. AH 20:235-52 Oct 46
The spring-wheat farmer in a maturing econ-
  omy 1870-1920. JEH 6:173-90 Nov 46
The agricultural problem and nineteenth-
  century industrialism. AH 22:156-74
  Jul 48
[Agricultural economics and history]: dis-
  cussion. JFE 30:555-57 Aug 48
SALTER, LEONARD AUSTIN, Jr.
  and Diehl, L. F. Part-time farming research.
    JFE 22:581-600 Aug 40
  Social security: a new consideration in sub-
    marginal land policy. LE 16:468-70
    Nov 40
  and Salisbury, J., Jr. Subsurface resources
    and surface land economics. Pt.I-II.
    LE 17:270-79; 385-93 Aug,Nov 41
  The content of land economics and research
    methods adapted to its needs. JFE 24:
    226-47 Feb 42
  Transition in the northern Lake states. LE 18:
    92-96 Feb 42
  Cross-sectional and case-grouping proce-
    dures in research analysis. JFE 24:
    792-805 Nov 42
  Farm property and agricultural policy.
    JPE 51:13-22 Feb 43
  Global war and peace, and land economics.
    LE 19:391-96 Nov 43
  The challenge of Agrarpolitik. R. LE 20:
    252-55 Aug 44
  George S. Wehrwein, 1883-1945. [obit.]
    AER 35:511 Jun 45
  Do we need a new land policy? LE 22:309-20
    Nov 46
SALZ, ARTHUR
  Economic liberalism reinterpreted. SR 8:
    373-89 Sep 41
  [and others] Effects of the war and defense
    program upon economic conditions and
    institutions: discussion. AER/S 32:
    426-31 Mar 42
  The present position of economics.
    AER/S 34:15-24 Mar 44
SAMAD, S. A.
  The relativity of economic phenomena.
    IJE 20:443-50 Apr 40
  Social security with special reference to
    India. IJE 25:331-43 Jan 45
SAMANT, DATTATRAYA RAMKRISHNA
  The new industrial policy of the government
    of India. IJE 26:631-40 Apr 46
  Restrictive tax structure of the central gov-
    ernment. IJE 27:256-63 Oct 46
SAMUELS, L. H.
  Aspects of "controlled" marketing in the
    Union. R. SAJE 15:47-59 Mar 47

SAMUELS, L. H. (Cont.)
--- Rejoinder [and] further rejoinder.
SAJE 15:209-11; 218-19 Sep 47
SAMUELSON, PAUL ANTHONY
and Nixon, R. A. Estimates of unemploy-
ment in the United States. REStat 22:
101-11 Aug 40
The theory of pump-priming reëxamined.
AER 30:492-506 Sep 40
The stability of equilibrium: comparative
statics and dynamics. Em 9:97-120
Apr 41
Professor Pigou's Employment and equilib-
rium. R. AER 31:545-52 Sep 41
and Stolper, W. F. Protection and real wages.
REStud 9:58-73 Nov 41
A note on alternative regressions. Em 10:
80-83 Jan 42
The stability of equilibrium: linear and non-
linear systems. Em 10:1-25 Jan 42
Fiscal policy and income determination.
QJE 56:575-605 Aug 42
Dynamics, statics, and the stationary state.
REStat 25:58-68 Feb 43
A fundamental multiplier identity. Em 11:
221-26 Jul-Oct 43
Further commentary on welfare economics.
AER 33:604-07 Sep 43
The relation between Hicksian stability and
true dynamic stability. Em 12:256-57
Jul-Oct 44
The effect of interest rate increases on the
banking system. AER 35:16-27 Mar 45
The turn of the screw. AER 35:674-76 Sep 45
Lord Keynes and the General theory. Em 14:
187-200 Jul 46
and Holt, C. C. The graphic depiction of
elasticity of demand. JPE 54:354-57
Aug 46
Comparative statics and the logic of economic
maximizing. REStud 14:41-43 no.1, 46
Exact distribution of continuous variables in
sequential analysis. Em 16:191-98 Apr 48
International trade and the equalisation of
factor prices. EJ 58:163-84 Jun 48
Consumption theory in terms of revealed
preference. Ec N.S.15:243-53 Nov 48
Some implications of "linearity." REStud 15:
88-90 no.2, 48
International factor-price equalisation once
again. EJ 59:181-97 Jun 49
SANDEE, JAN
Independent applications of national accounts.
Ec N.S.16:249-54 Aug 49
SANDERS, THOMAS HENRY
British accounting practices and the profes-
sion. HBR 18:161-76 no.2, 40
Renegotiation of contract prices. HBR 21:
164-82 no.2, 43
Government by "accounting principles." R.
HBR 22:265-76 no.3, 44
The annual report: portrait of a business.
HBR 27:1-12 Jan 49

Depreciation and 1949 price levels. HBR 27:
293-307 May 49
Two concepts of accounting. HBR 27:505-20
Jul 49
SANDERSON, DWIGHT
[Problem of poverty in agriculture]: discus-
sion. JFE 22:31-33 Feb 40
SANDERSON, FRED HUGO
The new wheat condition figures, based on
weather factors, for the Prairie Prov-
inces. JASA 37:473-83 Dec 42
A specific-risk scheme for wheat crop in-
surance. JFE 25:759-76 Nov 43
The new wheat condition figures, based on
weather factors, for the Prairie Provinces: rejoinder [and concluding remarks].
JASA 39:97-101 Mar 44
and Hyson, C. D. Monopolistic discrimina-
tion in the cranberry industry. QJE 59:
330-69 May 45
SANDERSON, G. B.
A note on the theory of investment.
Ec N.S.8:176-93 May 41
SANFORD, FILLMORE H.
Measurement of employee attitudes: discus-
sion. IRRA 2:225-27 Dec 49
SANT, PAUL T.
and Vickery, R. E. Agricultural statistics
in Germany. JFE 28:1061-69 Nov 46
and Vickery, R. E. The food and agricultural
statistics of the Reich Food Administra-
tion. AH 21:177-85 Jul 47
SANTA MARÍA, DOMINGO
Chilean state electrification. LE 21:365-70
Sep 45
SANTHANAM, S. S.
Rural co-operation in Madras. IJE 22:
788-806 Jan 42
SAPORI, ARMANDO
The Medici Bank. BNL 2:195-210 Oct-Dec 49
SARACENO, PASQUALE
Public expenditure, savings and foreign
loans in the development of southern Italy.
BNL 2:146-58 Jul-Sep 49
SARDÀ, JUAN
Spanish prices in the nineteenth century.
QJE 62:143-59 Nov 47
SARIEN, R. G.
Social insurance planning in India. R.
IJE 25:354-58 Jan 45
SARKAR, BENOY KUMAR
The population trend in India with reference
to food and nutrition. IJE 20:271-302
Jan 40
SARKAR, K. C.
Public debts in the U.P. 1921-37. IJE 21:
871-80 Apr 41
SARKAR, N. K.
Subjective cost of financing industrialisation.
IJE 29:27-35 Jul 48
SARLE, CHARLES F.
The possibilities and limitations of objective
sampling in strengthening agricultural
statistics. Em 8:45-61 Jan 40

SARLE, CHARLES F. (Cont.)

Training and recruitment of agricultural economic personnel. VII. The government service as a career. JFE 22:567-69 Aug 40

and Callander, W. F. The Bureau of Agricultural Economics program in enumerative sampling. JFE 29:233-36 Feb 47

The place for enumerative surveys in research and graduate training in agricultural economics. JFE 29:237-40 Feb 47

The role of sampling in farm-management research. JFE 29:1229-40 Nov 47

and Robinson, T. C. M. Measurement of agricultural production. JFE 31:213-30 May 49

SARVESWARA RAO, B.

see Rao, B. Sarveswara

SASULY, MAX

Irving Fisher and social science. Em 15:255-78 Oct 47

SATTER, ROBERT

Principles of arbitration in wage rate disputes. ILRR 1:363-85 Apr 48

--- [Reply] ILRR 2:114-15 Oct 48

SATYANARAYANA, M. C.

Cardamom industry in India. IJE 29:385-91 Apr 49

SATYANARAYANARAO, T.

see Rao, T. Satyanarayana

SAUER, ELMER L.

Methods of evaluating soil conservation measures. JFE 31,pt.2:655-59 Feb 49

SAULNIER, RAYMOND JOSEPH

The objectives of monetary policy: discussion. AER/S 30:42-43 Mar 40

[Postwar international monetary institutions]: discussion. RSE 2:79-80 Jan 44

The transition to peace under military government. RSE 3:9-17 Dec 44

The financial research program of the National Bureau of Economic Research. JF 2,no.1:4-14 Apr 47

[and others] The public debt: effects on institutions and income: discussion. AER/S 37:192-204 May 47

Institutional changes affecting the exercise of monetary controls. RSE 5:19-34 Jun 47

Postwar monetary and credit policies: discussion. JF 4:110-14 Jun 49

SAUNDERS, ALEXANDER MORRIS CARR-

see Carr-Saunders, Sir Alexander Morris

SAUNDERS, CHRISTOPHER THOMAS

Man-power distribution 1939-1945: some international comparisons. MS 14,no.2:1-39 May 46

SAUNDERSON, MONT H.

Some economic aspects of western rangeland conservation. LE 16:222-26 May 40

Adjustments in western beef cattle production and marketing during the war and post-war periods. JFE 26:789-94 Nov 44

Western range land use and conservation problems. JFE 31,pt.2:985-94 Nov 49

SAVAGE, LEONARD JIMMIE

and Smithies, A. A dynamic problem in duopoly. Em 8:130-43 Apr 40

Samuelson's Foundations: its mathematics. R. JPE 56:200-02 Jun 48

and Friedman, M. The utility analysis of choices involving risk. JPE 56:279-304 Aug 48

SAVAGE, ZACH

Estimating the value of citrus fruit as it develops. JFE 29:959-66 Nov 47

SAVILLE, JOHN

The measurement of real cost in the London building industry, 1923-1939. YB 1:67-80 Sep 49

SAVILLE, ROSCOE JOSEPH

Training and recruitment of agricultural economic personnel: III. The South. JFE 22:418-20 May 40

Changing structure of agriculture: discussion. JFE 23:109-11 Feb 41

Food and fiber production: discussion. JFE 26:209-11 Feb 44

SAWA, SEMPEI

The organization of insurance pools in Japan. Kyo 15,no.1:60-67 Jan 40

Japanese and British vessels in Chinese waters. [Pt.I-II] Kyo 18,no.1:18-33; no.3:62-70 Jan,Jul 43

SAWER, GEOFFREY

Conciliation and arbitration of industrial disputes. ER 23:266-71 Dec 47

SAYANNA, V. V.

Industrial relations in India. IJE 29:235-42 Oct 48

SAYERS, RICHARD SIDNEY

Business men and the terms of borrowing. OEP 3:23-31 Feb 40

Central banking in the light of recent British and American experience. QJE 63:198-211 May 49

SAYRE, CHARLES R.

Agriculture in the South: review. JFE 29:205-08 Feb 47

Technology and the cost structure on southern farms. JFE 31,pt.2:454-57 Feb 49

SAYRE, ROBERT A.

Cost of living indexes. JASA 36:191-200 Jun 41

SCANLON, JOSEPH N.

Profit sharing under collective bargaining: three case studies. ILRR 2:58-75 Oct 48

SCARF, IRENE W.

Haslingden: a problem in balance. MS 17:297-316 Sep 49

SCHAARS, MARVIN A.

Daniel H. Otis. [obit.] JFE 24:555 May 42

Marketing slaughter livestock: discussion. JFE 31,pt.2:367-69 Feb 49

SCHAFER, JOSEPH

The Wisconsin domesday book: a method of research for agricultural historians. AH 14:23-32 Jan 40

SCHAFFNER, LeROY W. and Kristjanson, B. H.
North Dakota farm size trends: an evalua-
tion. JFE 31,pt.2:588-91 Feb 49
SCHAFFNER, PHILIP PETTIBONE
and Dice, C. A. A reply to Mr. Villard.
AER 30:113 Mar 40
and Dice, C. A. Offset checks: further reply.
AER 30:825-27 Dec 40
SCHALK, A. F., Jr.
Significant merchandising trends of the inde-
pendent tire dealer. JM 12:462-69 Apr 48
SCHARFF, MAURICE R.
An incentive plan of rate adjustment. LE 16:
475-78 Nov 40
SCHAUDER, H.
The economist and the engineer: an analysis
and a synthesis. SAJE 12:303-12 Dec 44
The chemical industry in South Africa before
union (1910). SAJE 14:277-87 Dec 46
SCHECHTER, HENRY B.
Notes on consumer spendings and savings.
AER 37:931-33 Dec 47
SCHEICK, W. H.
Relationships of technological and social re-
search in housing. LE 25:97-99 Feb 49
SCHELL, EMIL D.; Williams, F. M. and Rice,
F. R.
Cost of living indexes in wartime. JASA 37:
415-24 Dec 42
SCHELL, HERBERT S.
Adjustment problems in South Dakota. AH 14:
65-74 Apr 40
SCHELLING, THOMAS CROMBIE
Raise profits by raising wages? Em 14:
227-34 Jul 46
Capital growth and equilibrium. AER 37:
864-76 Dec 47
Income determination: a graphic solution.
REStat 30:227-29 Aug 48
The dynamics of price flexibility. AER 39:
911-22 Sep 49
SCHENK, WILHELM
A seventeenth-century radical. EHR 14:
74-83 no.1, 44
SCHIAVI, ALESSANDRO
People's dwelling houses in Italy. BNL 2:
243-45 Oct-Dec 49
SCHICKELE, RAINER
Effect of tenure systems on agricultural ef-
ficiency. JFE 23:185-207 Feb 41
Obstacles to agricultural production expan-
sion. JFE 24:447-62 May 42
War-time adjustments in farm tenure.
LE 18:163-68 May 42
Farm tenure under the strain of war. JFE 25:
235-44 Feb 43
A price policy for agriculture, consistent
with economic progress, that will promote
adequate and more stable income from
farming. JFE 27:878-85 Nov 45
The National Food Allotment Program.
JFE 28:515-33 May 46
Programs for maintaining food demand. (A

U.S. food and nutrition program) JFE 29:
325-28 Feb 47
National food policy and surplus agricultural
production. JFE 29:867-88 Nov 47
Farm business survival under extreme
weather risks. JFE 31,pt.2:931-43 Nov 49
SCHIFF, ERICH
Direct investments, terms of trade, and bal-
ance of payments. QJE 56:307-20 Feb 42
Dutch foreign-trade policy and the infant-
industry argument for protection. JPE 50:
280-90 Apr 42
Family size and residential construction.
AER 36:97-112 Mar 46
Employment during the transition period, in
prospect and retrospect. REStat 28:
231-36 Nov 46
SCHILLER, IRVING P.
A program for the management of business
records. BHR 21:44-48 Apr 47
SCHIRBER, MARTIN EDWARD
The Christian obligation of employees to
reach and maintain maximum production.
RSE 7,no.1:55-60 Mar 49
SCHJANDER, FREDRIK
Norwegian savings banks and the state of the
money market during and after the war.
SAJE 15:73-77 Mar 47
SCHLAUCH, MARGARET
The revolt of 1381 in England. S&S 4:414-32
no.4, 40
Scandinavia: the dilemma of the middle
way. S&S 9:97-124 no.2, 45
S[CHLESINGER], R[UDOLF]
The discussions on E. Varga's book on
capitalist war economy. SovS 1:28-40
Jun 49
SCHMALZ, CARL NELSON
Retail credit in the postwar world. HBR 22:
63-74 no.1, 43
SCHMIDT, CARL THEODORE
Concentration of joint-stock enterprise in
Italy. AER 30:82-86 Mar 40
SCHMIDT, EMERSON P.
Annual wage and income-security plans.
JB 14:127-49 Apr 41
Public utilities and unemployment compensa-
tion. LE 18:97-100 Feb 42
Private versus public debt. AER 33:119-21
Mar 43
Social security: discussion. AER/S 34:
224-26 Mar 44
Monopoly and competition: discussion.
AER/S 36:209-13 May 46
SCHMIDT, LEO ANTON
Navy accounting: a lesson in adaptation.
HBR 25:243-54 no.2, 47
SCHMIDT, LOUIS BERNARD
The history of American agriculture as a
field of research. AH 14:117-26 Jul 40
SCHMÖLDERS, GÜNTER
Jens Jessen (1896-1944). [obit.] EJ 58:
135-36 Mar 48

SCHMUKLER, SIDNEY
The industrial alternative for farmers.
JFE 30:156-61 Feb 48
SCHNEER, RICHARD
Famine in Bengal: 1943. S&S 11:168-79
no.2, 47
SCHNEIDER, ERICH
A note on the consumption function. NTTO 12:
223-27 no.37, 48
SCHNEIDER, JOHN B.
Agricultural marketing control programs in
California. JM 6:366-70 Apr 42
The Peruvian food market and the World War.
JM 9:262-68 Jan 45
SCHNIERER, F.
Economics of socialism. R. ER 17:258-62
Dec 41
SCHOENFELDT, LEE
The departmental economist. HBR 20:
386-88 no.3, 42
SCHOEPPERLE, VICTOR
Future of international investment: private
versus public foreign lending. AER/S 33:
336-41 Mar 43
SCHOUTEN, D. B. J.
Theory and practice of the capital levies in
the Netherlands. OIS 10:117-22 Apr 48
SCHREIER, FRED T.
and Wood, A. J. Motivation analysis in mar-
ket research. JM 13:172-82 Oct 48
--- Reply to criticism by Lazare Teper.
JM 14:453-56 Oct 49
SCHROCK, EDWARD M.
Matters of misconception concerning the
quality control chart. JASA 39:325-34
Sep 44
SCHUETZ, ALFRED
The problem of rationality in the social
world. Ec N.S.10:130-49 May 43
SCHULLER, GEORGE J.
Isolationism in economic method. QJE 63:
439-75 Nov 49
SCHÜLLER, RICHARD
Commercial policy between the two wars:
personal observations of a participant.
SR 10:152-74 May 43
Great Britain's trade policy. SR 11:268-84
Sep 44
--- Rejoinder. SR 12:375-77 Sep 45
Trieste. SR 13:399-409 Dec 46
Foreign trade policies of the United States
and Soviet Russia. SR 14:135-47 Jun 47
The ITO charter. SR 15:135-45 Jun 48
A free-trade area. SR 16:151-57 Jun 49
SCHULMAN, SIDNEY
Legal aspects of municipal land ownership.
LE 16:216-18 May 40
SCHULTE, MARY YOLANDE, sister
Some economic and ethical considerations
for legislation protecting the consumer.
RSE 7,no.1:73-81 Mar 49
SCHULTZ, THEODORE WILLIAM
Needed additions to the theoretical equipment

of an agricultural economist. JFE 22:
60-66 Feb 40
Capital rationing, uncertainty, and farm-
tenancy reform. JPE 48:309-24 Jun 40
Economic effects of agricultural programs.
AER/S 30,no.5:127-54 Feb 41
Schisms in agricultural policy: discussion.
JFE 24:511-14 May 42
and Brownlee, O. H. Two trials to deter-
mine expectation models applicable to ag-
riculture. QJE 56:487-96 May 42
Transition readjustments in agriculture.
JFE 26:77-88 Feb 44
Two conditions necessary for economic
progress in agriculture. CJE 10:298-311
Aug 44
Postwar agricultural policy: a review of the
Land-Grant Colleges Report. LE 21:
95-107 May 45
Changes in economic structure affecting
American agriculture. JFE 28:15-27
Feb 46
Production and welfare objectives for
American agriculture. JFE 28:444-57
May 46
Food, agriculture, and trade. JFE 29:1-19
Feb 47
A note on the Davis review of "Agriculture
in an unstable economy." REStat 29:
92-94 May 47
How efficient is American agriculture.
JFE 29:644-58 Aug 47
The economic stability of American agricul-
ture. JFE 29:809-26 Nov 47
Effects of employment upon factor costs in
agriculture. JFE 29:1122-32 Nov 47
Supporting agricultural prices by concealed
dumping. JPE 56:157-60 Apr 48
[A note on Professor Schultz's analysis of
the long run agricultural problem.] A
comment. REStat 30:295-96 Nov 48
[Coming readjustments in agriculture:
domestic phases.] Discussion of Profes-
sor John D. Black's paper. JFE 31:16-18
Feb 49
Spot and future prices as production guides.
AER/S 39:135-49 May 49
Reflections on poverty within agriculture.
JFE 31,pt.2:1112-13 Nov 49
SCHULTZ, WILLIAM J.
The credit man in marketing conferences.
JM 11:73-77 Jul 46
SCHULZ, T.
and Bowley, A. L. Working class budgets:
analysis of dietary. OIS 2,no.6:5-10
Aug 31, 40
and Bowley, A. L. Working-class budgets:
analysis of expenditure. OIS 2,no.9:4-9
Nov 2, 40; Errata. no.10:18 Nov 23, 40
and Bowley, A. L. Working class budgets:
October 1940; a comparison with May.
OIS 2,no.11:1-7 Dec 40; Errata. 3,no.1:
16 Jan 11, 41

SCHULZ, T. (Cont.)
  Working class budgets in October: analysis
    of dietary. OIS 3:25-31 Feb 1, 41
  The Ministry of Labour budget inquiry. 2.
    Standards of nutrition in 1918 and 1937-8.
    OIS 3:46-48 Feb 22, 41
  Budgets of old age pensioners and house-
    holds on public assistance. OIS 3:76-79
    Mar 15, 41
  A "human needs" diet in war-time. OIS 3:
    92-97 Apr 5, 41
  Retail sales during the war: B. Changes in
    grocery sales. OIS 3:213-23 Jul 19, 41
  Working-class budgets and the cost of living
    index. II. Working class budgets, June
    1941. OIS 3,suppl.1:3-12 Aug 30, 41;
    Erratum. 3:310 Sep 20, 41
  Liverpool family budgets. OIS 3:364-70
    Nov 22, 41
  A 'human needs' diet in war time: changes
    from March 1941 to November 1941.
    OIS 3:393-98 Dec 13, 41; Erratum. 4:28
    Jan 10, 42
  Changes in the retail trade of groceries.
    OIS 4:57-66 Feb 21, 42
  Labour and industrial output. OIS 4:89-93
    Mar 14, 42
  A 'human needs' diet in war time: changes
    from November 1941 to April 1942.
    OIS 4:148-50 May 16, 42
  Working class budgets: June 1942; a compari-
    son with June 1941. OIS 4,suppl.3:1-12
    Oct 10, 42
  A human needs diet in war time: B. Changes
    from April to November 1942. OIS 4:
    314-19 Dec 12, 42
  Expenditure on food and nutrition. OIS 5:
    41-49 Feb 20, 43; Errata. 72 Mar 13, 43
  The trend of consumption in 1942: an analy-
    sis of sales of groceries. OIS 5:89-95
    Apr 24, 43
  A minimum diet in April 1943. OIS 5:117-20
    May 15, 43
  'Human needs' cost of living for a single
    person. OIS 5:143-48 Jun 26, 43
  A "human needs" diet in November 1943.
    OIS 5:273-77 Dec 11, 43
  Working-class budgets in war time. OIS 6,
    suppl.6:4-27 Feb 5, 44
  Consumption of groceries: a survey of sales
    of grocery shops in 1942 and 1943. OIS 6:
    49-57 Mar 18, 44; Erratum. 80 Apr 8, 44
  The cost of a 'human needs' diet. OIS 6:
    94-98 Apr 29, 44
  Food consumption in the United Kingdom,
    the United States and Canada. OIS 6:
    145-50 Jul 1, 44
  Family diets at low cost, November 1944.
    OIS 6:297-304 Dec 4, 44
  Working class income and household expendi-
    ture; June, 1944. OIS 7:17-30 Feb 3, 45
  Food expenditure and nutrition; working class
    budgets, June 1944. OIS 7:37-55 Feb 24, 45

  Sales of groceries in 1943 and 1944. OIS 7:
    116-23 May 19, 45
  Inexpensive family diets: April 1945. OIS 7:
    129-37 Jun 9, 45
  Proper nutrition at low cost: outlines of an
    inexpensive family diet in November 1945.
    OIS 7:291-302 Dec 15, 45; Erratum. 8:54
    Feb 46
  Income and household expenditure of working-
    class families with children. Pt.I-II.
    OIS 8:29-43; 61-80 Feb,Mar 46
  Grocery sales and rationing. OIS 8:97-107
    Apr 46
  Low cost family diets and individual nutri-
    tion. OIS 8:178-89 Jun 46
  Rationing and nutrition: inexpensive family
    diets in November, 1946. OIS 8:375-87
    Dec 46
  Working class income & household expendi-
    ture. OIS 9:133-69 May 47; Erratum. 195
    Jun 47
  Feeding a family. OIS 9:183-95 Jun 47
  Consumption of groceries and rationing.
    OIS 9:261-73 Aug 47
  Food and energy: some nutritional aspects
    of rationing. OIS 10:53-66 Feb 48
  Consumption of groceries. OIS 10:105-16
    Apr 48
  A family diet of low cost. OIS 10:129-39
    May 48
  Family expenditure in 1947. Pt.I-II. OIS 10:
    353-72; 401-23 Nov,Dec 48
  Nutrition at low cost: inexpensive diets for
    five persons in Nov., 1948. OIS 11:9-17
    Jan 49
  A 'human needs' diet. OIS 11:149-62 Jun 49
  Human needs diets from 1936 to 1949.
    OIS 11:307-25 Oct 49; Erratum. 371
    Nov 49
  A 'human needs' diet in November 1949.
    OIS 11:382-88 Dec 49
SCHUMACHER, E. F.
  Multilateral clearing. Ec N.S.10:150-65
    May 43
  and Kalecki, M. International clearing and
    long-term lending. OIS 5,suppl.5:29-33
    Aug 7, 43
  The new currency plans. OIS 5,suppl.5:8-29
    Aug 7, 43
  and Baloch, T. An international monetary
    fund. OIS 6:81-93 Apr 29, 44
  Anglo-Egyptian currency relations. OIS 7:
    30-36 Feb 3, 45
  Tax incentives for export. OIS 7:124-28
    May 19, 45
SCHUMANN, CHRISTIAN GUSTAV WALDEMAR
  Aspects of the problem of full employment in
    South Africa. SAJE 16:115-32 Jun 48
SCHUMPETER, JOSEPH ALOIS
  with Cole, A. H. and Mason, E. S.
    Frank William Taussig. [obit.] QJE 55:
    337-63 May 41
  Alfred Marshall's principles: a semi-

SCHUMPETER, JOSEPH ALOIS (Cont.)
    centennial appraisal. AER 31:236-48
    Jun 41
    chairman. Round table on cost and demand
    functions of the individual firm.
    AER/S 32:349-50 Mar 42
    The decade of the twenties. (The American
    economy in the interwar period.)
    AER/S 36:1-10 May 46
    John Maynard Keynes 1883-1946. AER 36:
    495-518 Sep 46
    Keynes and statistics. REStat 28:194-96
    Nov 46
    The creative response in economic history.
    JEH 7:149-59 Nov 47
    Theoretical problems of economic growth.
    JEH/S 7:1-9 '47
    Irving Fisher's econometrics. Em 16:219-31
    Jul 48
    Statement on the choice of textbooks. AER 38:
    626 Sep 48
    Science and ideology. AER 39:345-59 Mar 49
    Vilfredo Pareto (1848-1923). QJE 63:147-73
    May 49
    The Communist Manifesto in sociology and
    economics. JPE 57:199-212 Jun 49
    English economists and the state-managed
    economy. R. JPE 57:371-82 Oct 49
SCHURR, SAM HAROLD
    Economic aspects of atomic energy as a
    source of power. AER/S 37:98-108
    May 47
    [and others] The social and economic signifi-
    cance of atomic energy: discussion.
    AER/S 37:109-17 May 47
    Atomic power in selected industries. HBR 27:
    459-79 Jul 49
SCHWARTZ, ANNA JACOBSON
    with Gayer, A. D. and Finkelstein, I. British
    share prices, 1811-1850. REStat 22:78-93
    May 40
    The beginning of competitive banking in
    Philadelphia, 1782-1809. JPE 55:417-31
    Oct 47
    An attempt at synthesis in American banking
    history. R. JEH 7:208-17 Nov 47
SCHWARTZ, CHARLES F. [and others]
    Objectives of national income measurement:
    a reply to Professor Kuznets. REStat 30:
    179-95 Aug 48
SCHWARTZ, DAVID S.
    Investigations of the Columbia Basin project
    and their procedural significance. LE 23:
    83-86 Feb 47
SCHWARTZ, GEORGE LEOPOLD
    The significance of fiscal statistics.
    JRSS 105:92-103 pt.2, 42
    Planning and economic privilege. (The
    notion of equity in economics) MS 14,
    no.1:53-71 Jan 46
SCHWARTZ, HARRY
    The student with an urban background and
    agricultural economics. JFE 22:762-65
    Nov 40

    Organizational problems of agricultural
    labor unions. JFE 23:456-66 May 41
    Recent developments among farm labor
    unions. JFE 23:833-42 Nov 41
    Agricultural labor in the first World War.
    JFE 24:178-87 Feb 42
    Hired farm labor in World War II. JFE 24:
    826-44 Nov 42
    Farm labor adjustments after World War I.
    JFE 25:269-77 Feb 43
    Farm labor policy, 1942-1943. JFE 25:
    691-701 Aug 43
    Recent activities of Soviet economists.
    AER 36:650-58 Sep 46
    Prices in the Soviet war economy. AER 36:
    872-82 Dec 46
    Official criticism of Soviet Economics
    Institute. AER 37:190-91 Mar 47
    Soviet economic reconversion, 1945-46.
    AER/S 37:611-23 May 47
    On the use of Soviet statistics. JASA 42:
    401-06 Sep 47
    A critique of "Appraisals of Russian eco-
    nomic statistics." REStat 30:38-41
    Feb 48
    Soviet postwar industrial production.
    JPE 56:438-41 Oct 48
SCHWARZ, SOLOMON M.
    Heads of Russian factories: a sociological
    study. SR 9:315-33 Sep 42
    The industrial enterprise in Russia. HBR 23:
    265-76 no.3, 45
    USSR: the shelterbelt program in its relation
    to other drought control projects. LE 25:
    360-62 Nov 49
SCHWEITZER, ARTHUR
    The role of foreign trade in the Nazi war
    economy. JPE 51:322-37 Aug 43
    and Nussbaum, F. L. The professors versus
    the people. AER 33:906-07 Dec 43
    Big business and the Nazi party in Germany.
    JB 19:1-24 Jan 46
    Big business and private property under the
    Nazis. JB 19:99-126 Apr 46
    Profits under Nazi planning. QJE 61:1-25
    Nov 46
    Schacht's regulation of money and capital
    markets. JF 3,no.2:1-18 Jun 48
    Must rearmament lead to regulation? JB 21:
    203-13 Oct 48
SCHWENGER, ROBERT B.
    World agricultural policies and the expansion
    of trade. JFE 27:67-87 Feb 45
    The prospect for postwar agricultural ex-
    ports from the United States. JFE 28:
    42-53 Feb 46
    [and others] International cartels: discus-
    sion. AER/S 36:768-83 May 46
    [Food, agriculture, and trade.] Review of
    Professor Schultz's paper. JFE 29:26-32
    Feb 47
SCHWIEGER, ALBERT JAMES
    Subcontracting: a device for expansion.
    HBR 22:88-92 no.1 43

SCITOVSKY, ANNE and Mushkin, S. J.
A formula for social insurance financing.
AER 35:646-52 Sep 45

SCITOVSKY, TIBOR
A study of interest and capital. Ec N.S.7:
293-317 Aug 40
Capital accumulation, employment and price
rigidity. REStud 8:69-88 Feb 41
Prices under monopoly and competition.
JPE 49:663-85 Oct 41
A note on welfare propositions in economics.
REStud 9:77-88 Nov 41
The political economy of consumers' ration-
ing. REStat 24:114-24 Aug 42
A reconsideration of the theory of tariffs.
REStud 9:89-110 no.2, 42
A note on profit maximisation and its impli-
cations. REStud 11:57-60 no.1, 43
Some consequences of the habit of judging
quality by price. REStud 12:100-05
no.2, 45

SCOON, ROBERT
Professor Robbins' definition of economics.
R. JPE 51:310-21 Aug 43

SCOTT, ELIZABETH LEONARD and Neyman, J.
Consistent estimates based on partially consistent observations. Em 16:1-32 Jan 48

SCOTT, IRA OSCAR, Jr.
Professor Leontief on Lord Keynes. QJE 63:
554-67 Nov 49

SCOTT, JAMES DACON
Advertising when consumers cannot buy.
HBR 21:207-29 no.2, 43
Advertising when buying is restricted.
HBR 21:443-54 no.4, 43

SCOTT, R. H.
"Bretton Woods." ER 23:49-57 Jun 47

SCOVILLE, ORLIN JAMES
Measuring the family farm. JFE 29:506-19
May 47
Synthesis of labor inputs for hogs from time-
study data. JFE 31:549-55 Aug 49

SCOVILLE, WARREN CANDLER
Technology and the French glass industry,
1640-1740. JEH 1:153-67 Nov 41
State policy and the French glass industry,
1640-1789. QJE 56:430-55 May 42
Large-scale production in the French plate-
glass industry, 1665-1789. JPE 50:
669-98 Oct 42
Growth of the American glass industry to
1880. [Pt.I-II] JPE 52:193-216; 340-55
Sep,Dec 44

SEARS, ALFRED B.
The desert threat in the southern Great
Plains; the historical implications of soil
erosion. AH 15:1-11 Jan 41

SECRETT, FREDERICK AUGUSTUS
British horticulture: a vital industry.
LBR 12:30-52 Apr 49

SEELYE, ALFRED L.
Drug prices in cities with and without a fair
trade law. JM 6:16-21 Jul 41

The importance of economic theory in marketing courses. JM 11:223-27 Jan 47

SEERS, DUDLEY
Social accounting. ER 22:117-32 Jun 46
The coal shortage. Pt.I-II. OIS 9:25-36;
170-76 Feb,May 47
The 1947 national income White Paper.
OIS 9:228-53 Jul 47
Coal developments, 1946-7. OIS 9:341-46
Oct 47
and Henderson, P. D. The technique and
progress of Czechoslovakia's two-year
plan. OIS 9:357-74 Nov 47
The increase in the working-class cost-of-
living since before the war. OIS 10:
140-61 May 48
A note on further coal developments. OIS 10:
168 May 48
The working-class share in pre-war con-
sumption. OIS 10:181-94 Jun 48
The increase in the middle-class cost-of-
living since before the war. OIS 10:
255-68 Jul-Aug 48
The national product before and after the
war. OIS 10:309-31 Oct 48
Is there bias in the Interim index of retail
prices? OIS 11:1-8 Jan 49
with Henderson, P. D. and Wallis, P. F. D.
Notes on estimating national income components. OIS 11:59-70 Feb-Mar 49
British industrial recovery. OIS 11:100-06
Apr 49
The cost of living, 1938-1948. OIS 11:127-38
May 49
and Wallis, P. F. D. Changes in real national
income. OIS 11:163-76 Jun 49
A note on current Marxist definitions of the
national income. OEP N.S.1:260-68 Jun 49
and Wallis, P. F. D. A national income
matrix. OIS 11:181-93 Jul-Aug 49
Income distribution in 1938 and 1947.
OIS 11:253-68 Sep 49
Quarterly estimates of the national income.
OIS 11:293-306; 373-81 Oct,Dec 49

SEGAL, S. A. and Hoffman, A. C.
Food price control: policy and mechanics.
JFE 25:19-33 Feb 43

SEGHERS, PAUL D.
Tax accounting compared with recognized
accounting principles. NTJ 1:341-52
Dec 48

SELBY, HALBERT EDGERTON
A method of determining feasible irrigation
payments. JFE 24:637-46 Aug 42
Indirect benefits from irrigation development.
LE 20:45-51 Feb 44
Factors affecting value of land and water in
irrigated land. LE 21:250-58 Aug 45
The importance of irrigation in the economy
of the West. JFE 31,pt.2:955-64 Nov 49

SELBY, HOWARD W.
Farmers' cooperatives as competitors.
HBR 24:215-27 no.2, 46

SELEKMAN, BENJAMIN MORRIS
and Selekman, S. K. Mathew Carey. HBR 19:
326-41 no.3, 41
Living with collective bargaining. HBR 20:
21-33 no.1, 41
When the union enters. HBR 23:129-43
no.2, 45
Administering the union agreement. HBR 23:
299-313 no.3, 45
Handling shop grievances. HBR 23:469-83
no.4, 45
Resistance to shop changes. HBR 24:119-32
no.1, 45
Wanted: mature managers. HBR 24:228-44
no.2, 46
Wanted: mature labor leaders. HBR 24:
405-26 no.4, 46
Conflict and cooperation in labor relations.
HBR 25:318-38 no.3, 47
The role of various disciplines in industrial
relations research: discussion. IRRA 1:
229-32 Dec 48
Varieties of labor relations. HBR 27:175-99
Mar 49
and Selekman, S. K. Productivity and labor
relations. HBR 27:373-92 May 49
SELEKMAN, SYLVIA KOPALD
and Selekman, B. M. Mathew Carey. HBR 19:
326-41 no.3, 41
and Selekman, B. M. Productivity and labor
relations. HBR 27:373-92 May 49
SELIGMAN, HAROLD LEONARD
The problem of excessive commercial bank
earnings. QJE 60:365-89 May 46
SELLERS, MARIE
Pre-testing of products by consumer juries.
JM 6,no.4,pt.2:76-80 Apr 42
SELTZER, LAWRENCE HOWARD
The problem of our excessive banking re-
serves. JASA 35:24-36 Mar 40
Direct versus fiscal and institutional factors.
AER/S 30,no.5:99-107 Feb 41
Postwar domestic monetary problems: dis-
cussion. AER/S 34:280-87 Mar 44
[Management of the public debt after the war]:
discussion. AER/S 34,no.2:134-38 Jun 44
Is a rise in interest rates desirable or in-
evitable? AER 35:831-50 Dec 45
The changed environment of monetary-bank-
ing policy. AER/S 36:65-79 May 46
[and others] The public debt: effects on in-
stitutions and income: discussion.
AER/S 37:192-204 May 47
Notes on managing the public debt. REStat 31:
17-21 Feb 49
SELTZER, RAYMOND E. and Eggert, R. J.
Accuracy of livestock price forecasts at
Kansas State College. JFE 31:342-45
May 49
SEN, KHAGENDRA N.
Economic thinking in the Indian National
Congress. IJE 22:689-707 Jan 42

SEN, MIHIR KUMAR
International economic relations. IJE 29:
265-69 Jan 49
SEN, SAMAR RANJAN
Sir James Steuart's general theory of em-
ployment, interest and money. Ec N.S.14:
19-36 Feb 47
Marketing and production control in the
Indian jute textile industry (1884-1943).
IJE 28:483-508 Apr 48
SEN GUPTA, DEBENDRA NATH
The problem of estimating population of
India during intercensal years. IJE 21:
80-87 Jul 40; Erratum. 341 Jan 41
SEN GUPTA, RITENDRA NATH
China's Indusco. IJE 23:277-81 Jan 43
India's trade with U.S.S.R. IJE 24:145-49
Oct 43
SENGUPTA, SOVONA
Banking reform in India. IJE 24:59-65 Jul 43
The proposed agricultural income tax in
Bengal. IJE 24:212-18 Jan 44
Banking reform, with special reference to
the draft bank bill proposed by the Re-
serve Bank of India. IJE 24:361-67
Apr 44
Capital requirements of the Bombay Plan for
economic development of India. IJE 25:
56-63 Jul 44
Essentials of an appropriate commercial
policy for India. IJE 28:49-54 Jul 47
SESHGIRI RAO, A.
see Rao, A. Seshgiri
SETH, BAL RAJ
Minimum wage legislation. IJE 20:709-17
Apr 40
Public revenue and expenditure in the United
Provinces 1921-41. IJE 21:804-18 Apr 41
SEVERSON, LEWIS
Some current books on the economics of
total war. R. JPE 51:169-74 Apr 43
General relief provisions of the excess
profits tax. NTJ 2:247-58 Sep 49
SEVIN, CHARLES HENRY
Some aspects of distribution cost analysis.
JM 12:92-98 Jul 47
SEXTON, ROBERT H. and Heneman, H. G., Jr.
Selected annotated bibliography on union
accounting and financial reports. ILRR 2:
116-20 Oct 48
SEYMOUR, WALTON [and others]
Recent developments in public utility regula-
tion: discussion. AER/S 36:435-50 May 46
SHACKELL, R. S.
A short historical note on the marine policy.
SAJE 17:306-19 Sep 49
SHACKLE, GEORGE LENNOX SHARMAN
The nature of the inducement to invest.
REStud 8:44-48 Oct 40
--- A reply to Professor Hart. REStud 8:
54-57 Oct 40
A means of promoting investment. EJ 51:
249-60 Jun-Sep 41

SHACKLE, GEORGE LENNOX SHARMAN
(Cont.)
A theory of investment-decisions. OEP 6:
77-94 Apr 42
The expectational dynamics of the individual.
Ec N.S.10:99-129 May 43
An analysis of speculative choice. Ec N.S.12:
10-21 Feb 45
Myrdal's analysis of monetary equilibrium.
OEP 7:47-66 Mar 45
Interest-rates and the pace of investment.
EJ 56:1-17 Mar 46
The deflative or inflative tendency of govern-
ment receipts and disbursements. OEP 8:
46-64 Nov 47
The nature of interest-rates. OEP N.S.1:
100-20 Jan 49
Some theoretical aspects of payment by re-
sults. EI 2:841-53 Nov 49
Three notes on "Expectation in economics."
III. Ec N.S.16:343-46 Nov 49
Probability and uncertainty. Met 1:161-73
Dec 49
A non-additive measure of uncertainty.
REStud 17:70-74 no.1, 49
SHAEFFER, ROBERT E.
Merit rating as a management tool. HBR 27:
693-705 Nov 49
SHAFI, S. M.
Problem of value in a socialist state.
IJE 21:731-33 Apr 41
SHAFIQ-UR-RAHMAN
see Rahman, Safiqur
SHANNON, FRED A.
A post mortem on the labor-safety-valve
theory. AH 19:31-37 Jan 45
SHANNON, HERBERT AUSTIN
The British payments and exchange control
system. QJE 63:212-37 May 49
SHANNON, ROBERT L.
The industry council plan as an instrument
of reconstruction. RSE 2:87-99 Jan 44
SHAPIRO, ELI
Experience with reductions in the small-loan
rate in Wisconsin. JB 18:209-18 Oct 45
Liquidation record of Wisconsin credit unions.
JB 19:82-98 Apr 46
The wartime experience of Wisconsin credit
unions. JB 20:201-11 Oct 47
SHAPIRO, SOLOMON
The distribution of deposits and currency in
the United States, 1929-1939. JASA 38:
438-44 Dec 43
SHARFMAN, ISAIAH LEO
Law and economics. AER 36:1-19 Mar 46
SHARIF, MOHAMMAD RAIHAN
The role of co-operation in Pakistan.
PEJ 1,no.2:32-37 Oct 49
SHARMA, S. V. S.
Tenancy systems and improvement of agri-
culture. IJE 27:213-20 Oct 46
SHARP, MITCHELL W.
Allied wheat buying in relationship to

Canadian marketing policy, 1914-18.
CJE 6:372-89 Aug 40
SHARP, PAUL F.
The American farmer and the "last best
West." AH 21:65-75 Apr 47
The tree farm movement: its origin and
development. AH 23:41-45 Jan 49
The war of the substitutes: the reaction of
the forest industries to the competition
of wood substitutes. AH 23:274-79 Oct 49
SHARPE, GAIL E.
Federal financing in the United States, 1941-
1946. SAJE 15:1-26 Mar 47
SHAUL, JOHN R. H.
Southern Rhodesian life tables no.1 (Euro-
pean). SAJE 9:335-47 Dec 41
Maize forecasts in Mazoe district of Southern
Rhodesia, 1920-42. SAJE 11:294-96
Dec 43
and Irvine, A. G. The national income of
Southern Rhodesia, 1946-1948. SAJE 17:
511-15 Dec 49
SHAVELL, HENRY
Postwar taxation in Japan. JPE 56:124-37
Apr 48
Taxation reform in occupied Japan. NTJ 1:
127-43 Jun 48
SHAW, ALAN GEORGE LEWERS
The Australian coal industry, 1929-39.
ER 19:46-63 Jun 43
The Davidson report on the coal industry.
ER 23:98-103 Jun 47
SHAW, EDWARD STONE
Elements of a theory of inventory. JPE 48:
465-85 Aug 40
Burns and Mitchell on business cycles. R.
JPE 55:281-98 Aug 47
SHEA, JOHN LEO
Discussion: economics in social encyclicals.
RSE 1:19-22 Dec 42
SHEEHAN, JOHN HAROLD
An economist's comment on philosophico-
economic relationships. RSE 4:21-24
Jan 46
SHEFRIN, FRANK
Administration of Canadian wartime agricul-
tural policies. LE 21:167-80 May 45
SHELDON, CHARLES L.
Containers go to war. HBR 22:220-26
no.2, 44
SHENFIELD, A.
and Florence, P. S. Labour for the war in-
dustries: the experience of Coventry.
REStud 12:31-49 no.1, 44
and Florence, P. S. The economies and dis-
economies of industrial concentration:
the wartime experience of Coventry.
REStud 12:79-99 no.2, 45
SHENOY, BELLIKOTH RAGHUNATH
The new currency law in Ceylon. EJ 51:
512-15 Dec 41
[and others] Economic controls during the
war: discussion. IJE 24:535-44 Apr 44

SHENOY, BELLIKOTH RAGHUNATH (Cont.)
   The three phases of the transition from war
      to peace economy. IJE 25:201-07 Jan 45
   The classical theory of saving. IJE 28:
      223-36 Oct 47
SHEPARD, EARL FENTON
   and Horton, D. C. Federal aid to agriculture
      since World War I. AH 19:114-20 Apr 45
   Costs of federal agricultural activities: their
      meaning and classification for purposes of
      economic analysis. JFE 27:540-52
      Aug 45
SHEPARD, TIMOTHY MILLS
   The Starch application of the recognition
      technique. JM 6,no.4,pt.2:118-24 Apr 42
SHEPHARD, RONALD W.
   A mathematical theory of the incidence of
      taxation. Em 12:1-18 Jan 44
SHEPHERD, GEOFFREY SEDDON
   and Working, E. J. Notes on the discussion
      of the graphic method of correlation
      analysis. JFE 23:322-23 Feb 41
   Decentralization in agricultural marketing:
      causes and consequences. JM 6:341-48
      Apr 42
   Stabilization operations of the Commodity
      Credit Corporation. JFE 24:589-610
      Aug 42
   Bases for controlling agricultural prices.
      JFE 24:743-60 Nov 42
   Agricultural price policy: discussion.
      JFE 25:14-16 Feb 43
   Food price control: discussion. JFE 25:
      33-35 Feb 43
   Controlling hog prices during the transition
      from war to peace. JFE 25:777-92 Nov 43
   Changing emphases in agricultural price con-
      trol programs. JFE 26:476-502 Aug 44
   A price policy for agriculture, consistent
      with economic progress, that will promote
      adequate and more stable income from
      farming. JFE 27:886-94 Nov 45
   A rational system of agricultural price and
      income controls. JFE 28:756-72 Aug 46
   A farm income stabilization program could
      be self-financing. JFE 30:142-50 Feb 48
   The field of agricultural marketing research:
      objectives, definition, content, criteria.
      JFE 31:444-55 Aug 49
   The objectives, effects and costs of feed
      grain storage. JFE 31,pt.2:998-1007
      Nov 49
SHEPSTONE, D. G.
   Some reflections on the financial policy of
      certain municipalities toward the Natives
      within their boundaries. A criticism.
      SAJE 8:264-71 Sep 40
SHERE, LOUIS
   Taxation and inflation control. AER 38:
      843-56 Dec 48
   Federal corporate income tax: revenue and
      reform. NTJ 2:110-21 Jun 49

SHERWOOD, W. T.
   Tax administration in Mexico. NTJ 2:63-70
      Mar 49
SHIBATA, KEI
   Economic theory of planning. R. Kyo 18,
      no.4:19-41 Oct 43
SHIELDS, MURRAY
   A measure of purchasing power inflation
      and deflation. JASA 35:461-71 Sep 40
SHILLAND, PETER DAVID
   Problems in the teaching of economics.
      AER 30:350 Jun 40
   Wages, income, and compensation under un-
      employment insurance. ILRR 3:45-53
      Oct 49
SHILS, EDWARD A.
   Some remarks on "The theory of social and
      economic organization." R. Ec N.S.15:
      36-50 Feb 48
SHIMKIN, DIMITRI BORIS
   The entrepreneur in Tsarist and Soviet
      Russia. EEH 2:24-34 Nov 49
SHIOMI, SABURO
   The reform of the tax system. Kyo 15,no.2:
      34-70 Apr 40
   Economic fluctuations and public finance.
      Kyo 16,no.1:1-17 Jan 41
   The reform of the local tax system. [Pt.I-II]
      Kyo 16,no.3:51-67; no.4:42-57 Jul,Oct 41
   The taxation system of China. Kyo 17,no.4:
      1-26 Oct 42
SHIRRAS, GEORGE FINDLAY
   The position and prospects of gold. EJ 50:
      207-23 Jun-Sep 40
   James Bonar (1852-1941). [obit.] EJ 51:
      145-56 Apr 41
   The British Association conference and eco-
      nomic planning. EJ 51:515-23 Dec 41
   Methods of estimating the burden of taxation.
      JRSS 106:214-36 pt.3, 43
   The British Association conference and the
      place of science in industry. EJ 55:121-27
      Apr 45
   and Craig, J. H. Sir Isaac Newton and the
      currency. EJ 55:217-41 Jun-Sep 45
   Edwin Walter Kemmerer (1875-1945). [obit.]
      EJ 56:325-28 Jun 46
   Irving Fisher (1867-1947). [obit.] EJ 57:
      393-98 Sep 47
   The measurement of national wealth. Em 17,
      suppl.:247-53 Jul 49
   Planning towards recovery. ZN 12:475-82
      Dec 49
SHISHKIN, BORIS
   Labor problems: discussion. AER/S 33:
      249-51 Mar 43
SHISTER, JOSEPH
   The economics of collective wage bargaining:
      a case study. JPE 51:338-47 Aug 43
   The theory of union wage rigidity. QJE 57:
      522-42 Aug 43
   The theory of union bargaining power. SEJ 10:
      151-59 Oct 43

SHISTER, JOSEPH (Cont.)
A note on cyclical wage rigidity. AER 34: 111-16 Mar 44
The National War Labor Board: its significance. JPE 53:37-56 Mar 45
Trade-union government: a formal analysis. QJE 60:78-112 Nov 45
Collective bargaining and the competitive system: a comment. CJE 12:176-78 May 46
The locus of union control in collective bargaining. QJE 60:513-45 Aug 46
Trade union policies and non-market values. IRRA 2:85-99 Dec 49

SHONE, ROBERT M.
The iron and steel development plan: some statistical considerations. JRSS 110: 283-303 pt.4, 47

SHORT, JOHN A.
An engineer's appraisal of the Missouri Basin development program. JFE 31,pt.2: 1030-34 Nov 49

SHOU SHAN PU
see Pu, Shou Shan

SHOUP, CARL SUMNER
Defense financing and inflation: some comments on Professor Hansen's article, Choice of tax measures to avert inflation. REStat 23:88-90 May 41
Problems in war finance. AER 33:74-97 Mar 43
Postwar federal interest charge. AER/S 34, no.2:44-85 Jun 44
Three plans for post-war taxation. AER 34: 757-70 Dec 44
Résumé of remarks at the conference of the International Institute of Public Finance. PF 2:387-88 no.4, 47
Incidence of the corporation income tax: capital structure and turnover rates. NTJ 1:12-17 Mar 48

SHOUP, ELDON C.
Post-war marketing responsibilities need changed marketing executives. JM 7: 125-28 Oct 42

SHOVE, GERALD FRANK
The place of Marshall's Principles in the development of economic theory. EJ 52: 294-329 Dec 42
Lord Meston 1865-1943. [obit.] JRSS 106: 294-96 pt.3, 43
Mrs. Robinson on Marxian economics. R. EJ 54:47-61 Apr 44

SHREVE, EARL OWEN
Objective: industrial peace. ILRR 1:431-42 Apr 48

SHRYOCK, HENRY S., Jr.
Internal migration and the war. JASA 38: 16-30 Mar 43

SHRYOCK, RICHARD HARRISON
[What is economic history?] Comment. JEH/S 4:20-24 Dec 44

SHULTIS, ARTHUR
Farm management as an art: discussion. JFE 31,pt.2:889-90 Nov 49

SICKLE, JOHN VALENTINE VAN
see Van Sickle, John Valentine

SICKLER, BARCLAY J.
Bonneville resale rates pay out. LE 16: 487-91 Nov 40

SIEGEL, IRVING HERBERT
Hourly earnings and unit labor cost in manufacturing. JASA 35:455-60 Sep 40
and Evans, W. D. The meaning of productivity indexes. JASA 37:103-11 Mar 42
The measurement of capacity utilization. JASA 37:430-36 Dec 42
The concept of productive activity. JASA 39: 218-28 Jun 44
and Taylor, M. F. W. Public expenditures for veterans' assistance. JPE 56:527-32 Dec 48

SIELAFF, THEODORE JOHN
Postwar wholesale dry goods sales and stores. JM 10:60-62 Jul 45

SILCOCK, THOMAS HENRY
Professor Chamberlin and Mr. Smith on advertising. REStud 15:34-39 no.1, 47
A note on the working of rubber regulation. EJ 58:228-35 Jun 48
Accountants, economists and the valuation of fixed assets. EJ 59:343-59 Sep 49

SILVERMAN, ABNER D.
Housing needs and housing standards. LE 25: 130-31 Feb 49

SILVERMAN, HERBERT ALBERT
The optimum firm in the boot and shoe industry. OEP 6:95-111 Apr 42

SILVERMAN, HERBERT RALPH
Factoring as a financing device. HBR 27: 594-611 Sep 49

SILVERSTEIN, NATHAN L.
Some considerations on the management of commercial bank investments. JB 13: 136-45 Apr 40

SIMERL, LAWRENCE H.
A price policy for agriculture, consistent with economic progress, that will promote adequate and more stable income from farming. JFE 27:895-902 Nov 45
Discussion of price policy award papers. JFE 28:284-89 Feb 46
Farm attitudes and methods of supporting prices. JFE 29:246-49 Feb 47
Agricultural marketing research: discussion. JFE 31,pt.2:563-64 Feb 49

SIMHA, S. L. N.
The future of cheap money. IJE 28:113-20 Jul 47

SIMKIN, COLIN GEORGE FREDERICK
Budgetary reform. ER 17:192-209 Dec 41
Budgetary reform for New Zealand. ER 18: 16-30 Jun 42
Insulationism and the problem of economic stability. ER 22:50-65 Jun 46

SIMKIN, COLIN GEORGE FREDERICK (Cont.)

The nationalization of the Bank of New Zealand. ER 22:228-40 Dec 46

Economic planning and the N.Z. Ministry of Works. ER 23:103-07 Jun 47

Some aspects and generalisations of the theory of discrimination. REStud 15:1-13 no.1, 47

Wartime changes in the New Zealand economy. ER 24:18-31 Jun 48

SIMMONS, EDWARD CHRISTIAN

Treasury deposits and excess reserves. JPE 48:325-43 Jun 40

Federal Reserve policy and the national debt during the war years. JB 20:84-95 Apr 47

The relative liquidity of money and other things. AER/S 37:308-11 May 47

The position of the Treasury bill in the public debt. JPE 55:333-45 Aug 47

The role of selective credit control in monetary management. AER 37:633-41 Sep 47

SIMMONS, FRANCIS E.

Packaging aids to marketing. JM 13:512-17 Apr 49

SIMMONS, H. H.

Building an industrial advertising campaign. JM 5:446-49 Apr 41

SIMMONS, WILLARD and Deming, W. E.

On the design of a sample for dealers' inventories. JASA 41:16-33 Mar 46

SIMON, HERBERT ALEXANDER

The planning approach in public economy: further comment. QJE 55:325-30 Feb 41

The incidence of a tax on urban real property. QJE 57:398-420 May 43

Effects of increased productivity upon the ratio of urban to rural population. Em 15:31-42 Jan 47

and Hawkins, D. Note: some conditions of macro-economic stability. Em 17:245-48 Jul-Oct 49

SIMON, LESLIE E.

On the initiation of statistical methods for quality control in industry. JASA 36:53-60 Mar 41

SIMONS, GUSTAVE

Payroll flexibility through employee trusts. HBR 26:441-53 Jul 48

Economic and legal aspects of profit-sharing plans. ILRR 2:76-89 Oct 48

SIMONS, HENRY CALVERT

Incidence, theory and fiscal policy. [Summary] AER/S 30:242-44 Mar 40

Hansen on fiscal policy. R. JPE 50:161-96 Apr 42

Postwar economic policy: some traditional liberal proposals. AER/S 33:431-45 Mar 43

Some reflections on syndicalism. JPE 52:1-25 Mar 44

On debt policy. JPE 52:356-61 Dec 44

[and others] International monetary and credit arrangements: discussion. AER/S 35:289-96 May 45

The Beveridge program: an unsympathetic interpretation. R. JPE 53:212-33 Sep 45

Debt policy and banking policy. REStat 28:85-89 May 46

SIMONSEN, W.

On the reproduction of the trend by the method of simple moving averages. NTTO 12:229-39 no.37, 48

SIMPSON, FLOYD ROBERT

The handset telephone and monopoly price policy. LE 17:245-47 May 41

Price regulation and the public utility concept: the Sunshine Anthracite Coal case. LE 17:378-79 Aug 41

Price regulation and the public utility concept: Olsen v. Nebraska. LE 18:223 May 42

Public ownership of telephones in U.S. LE 19:99-103 Feb 43

Recent utility activities. LE 19:481-82 Nov 43

Cost trends in the telephone industry. LE 21:286-94 Aug 45

The war's impact on urban transit systems. HBR 23:460-68 no.4, 45

SIMPSON, GLENN D. and King, A. J.

New developments in agricultural sampling. JFE 22:341-49 Feb 40

SIMPSON, PAUL BYRON

Neoclassical economics and monetary problems. AER 39:861-82 Sep 49

SINDING, THOMAS

Some remarks on objectivity and subjectivity. NTTO 12:241-46 no.37, 48

SINGER, HANS WOLFGANG

The German war economy in the light of German economic periodicals. Pt.I-XII. EJ 50:534-46; 51:19-35; 192-215; 400-21; 52:18-36; 186-205; 377-99; 53:121-39; 243-59; 370-80; 54:62-74; 206-16 Dec 40-Jun/Sep 44

The coal question reconsidered: effects of economy and substitution. REStud 8:166-77 Jun 41

An index of urban land rents and house rents in England and Wales 1845-1913. Em 9:221-30 Jul-Oct 41

Some disguised blessings of the war. MS 12:49-56 Oct 41

The sources of war finance in the German war economy. REStud 10:106-14 no.2, 43

How widespread are national savings? A critique of the Madge enquiry. MS 13:61-79 Aug 44

Wage policy in full employment. EJ 57:438-55 Dec 47

--- A rejoinder. EJ 58:424-25 Sep 48

Profit measurement and the trade cycle. EJ 58:594-96 Dec 48

and Leser, C. E. V. Industrial productivity in England and Scotland. JRSS 111:309-21 pt.4, 48

Economic progress in underdeveloped countries. SR 16:1-11 Mar 49

SINGER, KURT
Landlords and tenant farmers of Japan.
ER 23:238-49 Dec 47
Robot economics: a critical introduction to
von Neumann's theory of general equilib-
rium. ER 25,(no.48):48-73 Jun 49
SINGER, RUSSELL E.
Guess again. Computing tourist expenditures
is tricky business with many pitfalls.
JM 5:279-80 Jan 41
SINGH, AMRITDHARI
Can we plan under Indian capitalism?
IJE 26:305-11 Oct 45
SINGH, ARJAN
A statistical analysis of factors affecting
gross return of some farms in the Punjab.
IJE 20:321-42 Jan 40
Principles of sampling as applied to investi-
gations in agricultural economics.
IJE 25:533-40 Apr 45
SINGH, BALJIT
Devaluation and India's balance of payments.
IJE 30:205-09 Oct 49
SINGH, V. B.
The nature of rent in India. IJE 30:77-78
Jul 49
SINGHAL, ANAND SWARUP
A note on conditions of cotton marketing at
Hathras in 1944. IJE 26:124-33 Jul 45
SINGHANIA, LALA LAKSMIPAT
Section 6(4) of the Excess Profit Tax Act.
IJE 25:164-65 Oct 44
SINHA, BIMAL CHANDRA
The basis of land tax: a problem in applied
economics. IJE 21:158-66 Oct 40
SINHA, HARIS CHANDRA
Teaching and research in economic statistics.
IJE 24:221-24A Jan 44
SINHA, JOGIS CHANDRA
Recent economic policy in India: presiden-
tial address. IJE 29:311-25 Jan 49
SINHA, MATHURA NAND
Indian currency and war. IJE 22:199-207
Oct 41
SINIGAGLIA, OSCAR
The future of the Italian iron and steel in-
dustry. BNL 1:240-45 Jan 48
SITARAMAYYA, M.
Recent developments in monetary practice.
IJE 22:1-37 Jul 41
Reserve Bank and the management of public
debt. Pt.I-II. IJE 26:597-621; 27:35-52
Apr,Jul 46
The land systems of the Madras Presidency
with special reference to inam tenures.
IJE 27:221-31 Oct 46
Cheap money policy. IJE 28:105-12 Jul 47
SITTERLEY, JOHN H.
Some factors affecting the rate of retirement
of farms in the submarginal land area of
Ohio. JFE 26:737-53 Nov 44
Farm abandonment in southeastern Ohio.
LE 21:34-44 Feb 45

SITTERSON, JOSEPH CARLYLE
The transition from slave to free economy
on the William J. Minor plantations.
AH 17:216-24 Oct 43
SKELTON, D. A.
Canada-United States trade relationships.
JFE 24:35-41 Feb 42
SKEOCH, LAWRENCE A.
Changes in Canadian wheat policy. CJE 9:
565-69 Nov 43
Agriculture's share of the national income
further considered. CJE 10:210-12 May 44
SKILBECK, DUNSTAN
War-time changes in British farming.
LBR 5:60-80 Jul 47
SKOVGAARD, KRISTEN
Utilisation of productive capacity and the
problem of intensity in agriculture.
NTTO 12:247-54 no.37, 48
SLAGSVOLD, PETER L. and Paschal, J. L.
Irrigation development and area adjustment
in the Great Plains. JFE 25:433-43
May 43
SLEEMAN, JOHN FREDERICK
Municipal transport costs and revenue:
1938-9 and 1945-6. MS 16:289-301 Sep 48
SLICHTER, SUMNER HUBER
The impact of social security legislation
upon mobility and enterprise. AER/S 30:
44-60 Mar 40
The conditions of expansion. AER 32:1-21
Mar 42
Postwar boom or collapse. HBR 21:5-42
no.1, 42
The responsibility of organized labor for
employment. AER/S 35:193-208 May 45
Comment on the Murray bill. REStat 27:
109-12 Aug 45
Adjustment of wages during conversion.
HBR 24:57-74 no.1, 45
Wage-price policy and employment.
AER/S 36:304-18 May 46
The problem of wage policy in the spring of
1947. REStat 29:139-45 Aug 47
[and others] Report to the Governor of
Massachusetts on labor-management rela-
tions. ILRR 1:110-28 Oct 47
The problem of inflation. REStat 30:3-5
Feb 48
The Taft-Hartley Act. QJE 63:1-31 Feb 49
Profits in a laboristic society. HBR 27:
346-61 May 49
Raising the price of labor as a method of
increasing employment. REStat 31:283-88
Nov 49
The social control of industrial relations.
IRRA 2:2-12 Dec 49
SLITOR, RICHARD EATON
The flexibility of income-tax yield under
averaging. JPE 54:266-68 Jun 46
The measurement of progressivity and built-
in flexibility. QJE 62:309-13 Feb 48

SLOAN, DOUGLAS
Full employment measures and the real
wage rate. SAJE 16:306-08 Sep 48
S[MAILS], R[EGINALD] G[EORGE HAMPDEN]
C. E. Walker, 1880-1942. [obit.] CJE 9:
75-76 Feb 43
SMELKER, MARY WISE
and Dean, J. An appraisal of index numbers
of prices farmers pay. JASA 36:210-18
Jun 41
Shifts in the concentration of income.
REStat 30:215-22 Aug 48
SMITH, A. H.
Evolution of the exchange control. Ec N.S.16:
243-48 Aug 49
SMITH, ABBOT EMERSON
Indentured servants: new light on some of
America's "first" families. JEH 2:40-53
May 42
SMITH, ALFRED GOUD
Synthetics versus Singapore. LE 24:89-94
Feb 48
SMITH, BLACKWELL
[Significance of size in our economic system]:
discussion. JM 4:378-81 Apr 40
SMITH, BRADFORD BIXBY
Functions of the economist. HBR 20:375-79
no.3, 42
SMITH, CALEB ALLEN
The cost-output relation for the U.S. Steel
Corporation. REStat 24:166-76 Nov 42
SMITH, DAN THROOP
Economic consequences of deficit financing:
a review. AER/S 30,no.5:88-98 Feb 41
and Mace, M. L. Tax uncertainties in corpo-
rate financing. HBR 20:315-26 no.3, 42
[Management of the public debt after the
war]: discussion. AER/S 34,no.2:133-34
Jun 44
Education for administration. HBR 23:
360-71 no.3, 45
Business profits during inflation. HBR 26:
216-29 Mar 48
SMITH, ELMER A.
A new price policy for the railroads: quan-
tity or multiple-car rates. LE 16:230-33
May 40
The Interstate Commerce Commission, the
Department of Justice, and the Supreme
Court. AER/S 36:479-93 May 46
SMITH, EVERETT R.
Buying power classifications: introduction.
JM 7:354-55 Apr 43
chairman. Report of AMA Committee on
Buying Power Classifications. JM 8:
329-30 Jan 44
and Himmel, C. Some major recent market
changes. JM 9:225-33 Jan 45
chairman. Design, size, and validation of
sample for market research. [Report of
Committee on Marketing Research Tech-
niques] JM 10:221-34 Jan 46

SMITH, FRANK G.
Handling labor grievances in the bituminous
coal industry. HBR 19:352-63, no.3, 41
SMITH, GEORGE CLINE, Jr.
Lorenz curve analysis of industrial decentral-
ization. JASA 42:591-96 Dec 47
SMITH, GEORGE WINSTON
A rising industry's battle for the Morrill
tariff. BHR 16:106-11 Dec 42
SMITH, HENRY
Reflections on the war-time control of food
prices. OEP 8:12-17 Nov 47
Advertising costs and equilibrium: a reply.
REStud 15:40-41 no.1, 47
SMITH, HOWARD FRANK
Food controls in occupied Japan. AH 23:
220-23 Jul 49
SMITH, HOWARD ROSS
The problem of evaluating regulatory policy.
SEJ 12:17-29 Jul 45
Capital and labor in the railroad industry.
HBR 23:144-56 no.2, 45
The role of science in the formulation of
economic policy. SEJ 12:331-47 Apr 46
The rise and fall of the public utility con-
cept. LE 23:117-31 May 47
The status of stagnation theory. Pt.I-II.
SEJ 15:191-204; 289-302 Oct 48, Jan 49
SMITH, Sir HUBERT LLEWELLYN
H. W. Macrosty. [obit.] EJ 51:156-57 Apr 41
SMITH, JOHN GEORGE
C. F. Bastable. [obit.] EJ 55:127-30 Apr 45
SMITH, JOHN HENRY
Constant-amplitude scales for plotting stock
prices. Em 14:316-19 Oct 46
SMITH, LINCOLN
Tidal power in Maine. LE 24:239-52 Aug 48
The regulation of some New England holding
companies. LE 25:289-303 Aug 49
SMITH, NELSON LEE
The outlook in regulation. Pt.I-II. LE 16:
386-92; 17:48-53 Nov 40, Feb 41
Rail and utility investments under expanding
public control. HBR 18:397-409 no.4, 40
Rate regulation by the Federal Power Com-
mission. AER/S 36:405-25 May 46
SMITH, R. H.
Some reflections on the economics of wage
fixation in South Africa. SAJE 8:91-116
Jun 40
[Financial policy of municipalities towards
Natives.] A criticism. SAJE 8:272-78
Sep 40
with Burrows, H. R. and Halliday, I. G. Price
control in war-time. [Pt.I] SAJE 8:
400-30 Dec 40
Native farm labour in Natal. SAJE 9:154-75
Jun 41
and Byron, F. A. The expansion of industry
and the supply of labour. SAJE 9:251-64
Sep 41
War-time control of prices in South Africa.
[Pt.II-III] SAJE 9:400-15; 11:11-23
Dec 41, Mar 43

SMITH, R. H. (Cont.)

[and others] Social security. SAJE 10:
193-247 Sep 42

A note on the meaning of the term "rationalisation." SAJE 11:210-17 Sep 43

The organisation of employment in the transition from war to peace. SAJE 13:91-116
Jun 45

The size of the South African industrial unit.
SAJE 13:263-303 Dec 45

SMITH, RAYMOND CHARLES

Social effects of the war and the defense program on American agriculture. JFE 23:
15-27 Feb 41

SMITH, REGINALD ANTHONY LENDON

Marsh embankment and sea defence in
medieval Kent. EHR 10:29-37 Feb 40

SMITH, RICHARD K.

State frontiers in agricultural statistics:
discussion. JFE 31,pt.2:304-08 Feb 49

SMITH, ROBERT SIDNEY

Spanish antimercantilism of the seventeenth
century: Alberto Struzzi and Diego Jose
Dormer. JPE 48:401-11 Jun 40

Life insurance in fifteenth-century Barcelona.
JEH 1:57-59 May 41

A method of comparing home-mortgage financing costs. JM 9:386-88 Apr 45

A note on mortgage loan interest. LE 24:
185-86 May 48

SMITH, ROBERT WORTHINGTON

Was slavery unprofitable in the ante-bellum
South? AH 20:62-64 Jan 46

SMITH, ROY JAMES

Fuller annual employment of farm labor.
JFE 26:514-28 Aug 44

Economic functions and units in farm organization. JFE 28:534-42 May 46

SMITH, RUSSELL

Government and the economy. JFE 29:77-83
Feb 47

SMITH, SYLVESTER R.

Current status of marketing agreements for
fruits and vegetables. JFE 31,pt.2:1228-36
Nov 49

SMITH, T. R.

Internal marketing of New Zealand primary
products. ER 19:171-84 Dec 43

SMITH, THOMAS LYNN

and Roberts, R. W. Sources and distribution
of the farm population in relation to farm
benefit payments. JFE 23:607-18 Aug 41

Land tenure in Brazil. LE 20:194-201
Aug 44

SMITH, TYNAN and Hengren, R. E.

Bank capital: the problem restated. JPE 55:
553-66 Dec 47

SMITH, VICTOR EARLE

Nonlinearity in the relation between input and
output: the Canadian automobile industry,
1918-1930. Em 13:260-72 Jul 45

The statistical production function. QJE 59:
543-62 Aug 45

Note on the kinky oligopoly demand curve.
SEJ 15:205-10 Oct 48

SMITH, WILLIAM J. J.

Milk price differentials in the Southeast.
JFE 28:742-55 Aug 46

SMITHIES, ARTHUR

and Savage, L. J. A dynamic problem in
duopoly. Em 8:130-43 Apr 40

Equilibrium in monopolistic competition.
QJE 55:95-115 Nov 40

Monopolistic price policy in a spatial market.
Em 9:63-73 Jan 41

Optimum location in spatial competition.
JPE 49:423-39 Jun 41

Professor Hayek on The pure theory of
capital. AER 31:767-79 Dec 41

Process analysis and equilibrium analysis.
Em 10:26-38 Jan 42

Equilibrium in monopolistic competition:
an addendum. QJE 56:332-36 Feb 42

The stability of competitive equilibrium.
Em 10:258-74 Jul-Oct 42

The behavior of money national income under
inflationary conditions. QJE 57:113-28
Nov 42

The dynamics of inflation: a comment.
REStat 24:189-90 Nov 42

Aspects of the basing-point system. AER 32:
705-26 Dec 42

The quantity of money and the rate of interest. REStat 25:69-76 Feb 43

Reply to Mr. Salera. AER 33:902 Dec 43

The international bank for reconstruction
and development. AER 34:785-97 Dec 44

Forecasting postwar demand: I. Em 13:
1-14 Jan 45

Full employment in a free society. R.
AER 35:355-67 Jun 45

The American economy in the thirties.
AER/S 36:11-27 May 46

The impact of the federal budget. REStat 29:
28-31 Feb 47

Economic forecasts: discussion. AER/S 37:
85 May 47

Multilateral trade and employment.
AER/S 37:560-68 May 47

The multiplier. AER/S 38:299-305 May 48

Fiscal aspects of preparedness for war.
AER/S 39:356-65 May 49

The effect of the role of government on international comparisons of national income.
Em 17,suppl.:242-46 Jul 49

SMULLYAN, EMILE BENOIT-
see Benoit, Emile

SNAVELY, TIPTON RAY

Round table on the incidence of taxation.
[Summary of discussion] AER/S 30:245-46
Mar 40

Abraham Berglund, 1875-1942. [obit.]
AER 33:238-40 Mar 43

The place of education in the developing economic structure of the South. SEJ 13:
404-15 Apr 47

SNEAD, ROSWELL P.
Problems of field interviews.  JM 7:139-45
Oct 42
SNEDEKER, G. B. and Rowland, B.
The United States Court of Claims and
French spoliation records.  BHR 18:
20-27 Apr 44
SNELL, HAMPTON KENT [and others]
Transportation and public utilities prob-
lems: discussion.  AER/S 37:478-97
May 47
SNIDER, DELBERT ARTHUR
French monetary and fiscal policies since
the liberation.  AER 38:309-27 Jun 48
SNIDER, JOSEPH LYONS
Symposium on the industrial economist.
[Introduction] HBR 20:375 no.3, 42
Management's approach to the annual wage.
HBR 24:326-38 no.3, 46
Looking ahead.  HBR 26:1-10 Jan 48
What's ahead for prices and business?
HBR 26:757-66 Nov 48
Facing the business future.  HBR 27:449-58
Jul 49
SNOW, ERNEST CHARLES
The international comparison of industrial
output.  JRSS 107:1-30 pt.1, 44
[and others] The statistical basis of export
targets.  JRSS 110:169-86 pt.3, 47
SNYDER, RICHARD C.
Commercial policy as reflected in treaties
from 1931 to 1939.  AER 30:787-802
Dec 40
SOGGE, TILLMAN MORRIS
Industrial classes in the United States in
1940.  JASA 39:516-18 Dec 44
SOLEM, MILLARD
Effect of land purchase by FSA standard loan
borrowers on agricultural production in
northern Great Plains.  LE 19:231-33
May 43
SOLLENBERGER, ISAAC J.
Estimated cost of Old-Age and Survivors
Insurance.  QJE 59:427-50 May 45
SOLOMON, EZRA
Are formula plans what they seem to be?
JB 21:92-97 Apr 48
SOLOMON, MORTON R.
The structure of the market in undeveloped
economies.  QJE 62:519-41 Aug 48
SOLOW, ANATOLE A.
Measuring the quality of urban housing en-
vironment: a new appraisal technique.
LE 22:282-93 Aug 46
SOMERS, HAROLD MILTON
Money wage cuts in relation to unemployment:
a rejoinder to Mr. Kaldor.  REStud 7:
136-37 Feb 40
and Fellner, W.  Alternative monetary ap-
proaches to interest theory.  REStat 23:
43-48 Feb 41
Monetary policy and the theory of interest.
QJE 55:488-507 May 41

The impact of fiscal policy on national in-
come.  CJE 8:364-85 Aug 42
and Fellner, W. J.  Comment on Dr. Lerner's
note.  REStat 26:92 May 44
An economic analysis of the capital gains tax.
NTJ 1:226-32 Sep 48
The multiplier in a tri-fiscal economy.
QJE 63:258-72 May 49
and Fellner, W. J.  Note on "stocks" and
"flows" in monetary interest theory.
REStat 31:145-46 May 49
The inflationary process: comments.
REStat 31:212-13 Aug 49
SOMERS, HERMAN MILES
Adequacy of data in the field of public aid.
JASA 36:81-90 Mar 41
SORRELL, LEWIS CARLYLE
Transportation and national defense. JB 14:
235-58 Jul 41
SOTH, LAUREN
Mr. Hoover's Department of Agriculture.
JFE 31:201-12 May 49
Economics for the farmer.  JFE 31,pt.2:
880-87 Nov 49
SOUTHWORTH, HERMAN M.
The economics of public measures to sub-
sidize food consumption.  JFE 27:38-66
Feb 45
Levels of food consumption, past and pros-
pective.  JFE 29:323-25 Feb 47
Poverty within agriculture: discussion.
JFE 31,pt.2:1117-18 Nov 49
SOUZA, VITUS LAWRENCE D'
see D'Souza, Vitus Lawrence
SOVANI, N. V.
A critique [of B. G. Ghate's Changes in the
occupational distribution of the population].
IJE 23:46-58 Jul 42
Transition from war to peace economy in
India.  IJE 25:207-23 Jan 45
The future of the rupee.  IJE 26:410-19
Jan 46
Population planning in India.  IJE 27:299-316
Jan 47; Errata. 432 Apr 47
SPAHR, WALTER EARL [and others]
Fiscal policy in prosperity and depression:
discussion.  AER/S 38:404-16 May 48
SPAL, SAM G.
The treatment of noncumulative preferred
stockholders with regard to dividends.
JB 15:248-65 Jul 42
Agreed charges in railway freight rates
abroad.  JB 16:100-06 Apr 43
SPANN, R. N.
A city plan [of Manchester, Eng.].  MS 14,
no.2:98-108 May 46
SPARLIN, ESTAL E.
Public ownership versus state purchasing:
the case of printing.  JPE 48:211-21
Apr 40

SPAULDING, RICHARD C.
    Pennsylvania amends permissive local tax
    law. NTJ 2:272-77 Sep 49
SPEAR, HARVEY MILTON
    Dividend policies under changing price levels.
    HBR 27:612-21 Sep 49
SPEARS, RICHARD F.
    Improving super market operating efficiency:
    a case study. JM 13:218-20 Oct 48
SPEERS, PETER C.
    Colonial policy of the British Labour Party.
    SR 15:304-26 Sep 48
SPEIER, HANS [and others]
    Economic power blocs and American capital-
    ism: discussion. IRRA 2:192-202 Dec 49
SPENCE-SALES, H.
    Physical planning in the region: British
    endeavours. CJE 13:507-13 Nov 47
SPENCER, CHARLES and Converse, P. D.
    What housewives think of the super-market.
    JM 6:371-74 Apr 42
SPENCER, JOSEPH EARLE
    The development of agricultural villages in
    southern Utah. AH 14:181-89 Oct 40
SPENCER, LELAND
    Marketing research under the Research and
    Marketing Act of 1946. [Summary of
    round table discussion] JFE 29:292-98
    Feb 47
SPENCER, MYRON JAY
    Government and private enterprise: discus-
    sion. AER/S 33:41-44 Mar 43
SPENGLER, EDWIN HAROLD
    The taxation of urban land-value increments.
    LE 17:54-58 Feb 41
SPENGLER, JOSEPH JOHN
    Population movements and economic equilib-
    rium. [Abstract] AER/S 30:383-84
    Mar 40
    Population movements and economic equilib-
    rium in the United States. JPE 48:153-82
    Apr 40
    Sociological presuppositions in economic
    theory. SEJ 7:131-57 Oct 40
    --- Reply to Mr. Beckwith. SEJ 7:339-401
    Jan 41
    Regional differences and the future of manu-
    facturing in America. SEJ 7:475-93
    Apr 41
    Some effects of changes in the age composi-
    tion of the labor force. SEJ 8:157-75
    Oct 41
    Political science, political economy, and
    values: discussion. AER/S 34:9-12
    Mar 44
    Pareto on population. Pt.I-II. QJE 58:
    571-601; 59:107-33 Aug,Nov 44
    Malthus's total population theory: a restate-
    ment and reappraisal. Pt.I-II. CJE 11:
    83-110; 234-64 Feb,May 45
    [and others] Consumption economics: dis-
    cussion. AER/S 35:56-66 May 45
    The physiocrats and Say's law of markets.

Pt.I-II. JPE 53:193-211; 317-47 Sep,
    Dec 45
    chairman. Final report of the Committee on
    Development of Economic Thinking and
    Information. AER/S 36:922-33 May 46
    and Burns, E. M. The proposed publication
    of a periodic review of economics. [Précis
    of the round table discussion] AER/S 36:
    784-88 May 46
    Undergraduate teaching of economics: dis-
    cussion. AER/S 36:860-63 May 46
    The future of prices. SEJ 13:1-35 Jul 46
    Monopolistic competition and the use and
    price of urban land service. JPE 54:
    385-412 Oct 46
    Aspects of the economics of population
    growth. Pt.I-II. SEJ 14:123-47; 233-65
    Oct 47, Jan 48
    The role of the state in shaping things eco-
    nomic. JEH/S 7:123-43 '47
    The problem of order in economic affairs.
    SEJ 15:1-29 Jul 48
    [and others] Possibilities for a realistic
    theory of entrepreneurship: discussion.
    AER/S 39:349-55 May 49
    [and others] Round table on economic re-
    search: discussion. AER/S 39:464-72
    May 49
    Laissez faire and intervention: a potential
    source of historical error. JPE 57:
    438-41 Oct 49
    Power blocs and the formation and content of
    economic decision. IRRA 2:174-91 Dec 49
SPERO, HERBERT and Leavitt, J. A.
    Inflation as a post-war problem. JPE 51:
    356-60 Aug 43
SPIEGEL, HENRY WILLIAM
    Wehrwirtschaft: economics of the military
    state. AER 30:713-23 Dec 40
    The war economy and the economic man.
    JB 16:1-6 Jan 43
    Economic theory and economic policy. R.
    JB 18:56-59 Jan 45
    The prospects of business in Brazil. JB 20:
    33-43 Jan 47
    A century of prices in Brazil. REStat 30:
    57-62 Feb 48
    [and others] Present issues of the Latin-
    American economy: discussion.
    AER/S 39:406-14 May 49
SPIEGELMAN, MORTIMER and Lotka, A. J.
    The trend of the birth rate by age of mother
    and order of birth. JASA 35:595-601
    Dec 40
SPIELMANS, JOHN V.
    Measurements of the effectiveness of the
    National Labor Relations Act. AER 30:
    803-13 Dec 40
    Strikes under the Wagner Act. JPE 49:
    722-31 Oct 41
    On strike analysis. JPE 50:750-60 Oct 42
    The dilemma of the closed shop. JPE 51:
    113-34 Apr 43

STEPHENSON, CHARLES A.
Methods of correlation analysis: reply.
AER 33:902-03 Dec 43

STEPHENSON, FRANCIS M.; Sufrin, S. C. and
Swinyard, A. W.
The North-South differential: a different
view. SEJ 15:184-90 Oct 48

STEPHENSON, WENDELL H.
Ante-bellum New Orleans as an agricultural
focus. AH 15:161-74 Oct 41

STEPP, JAMES M.
Postwar planning survey at Anderson, S.C.
LE 21:184-91 May 45
Southern agriculture's stake in occupational
freedom. SEJ 13:46-52 Jul 46

STERN, BERNARD J.
Income and health. S&S 5:193-206 no.3, 41
Science and war production. S&S 7:97-114
no.2, 43

STERN, ERNEST HENRY
Public expenditure in the national income.
Ec N.S.10:166-75 May 43
--- A reply. Ec N.S.11:23-26 Feb 44
The agreements of Bretton Woods. Ec N.S.11:
165-79 Nov 44
Capital requirements in progressive econ-
omies. Ec N.S.12:163-71 Aug 45
The problem of capital accumulation. AER 39:
1160-70 Dec 49

STERN, JOHN KENNETH
Unsettled questions relating to agricultural
cooperation. JFE 31,pt.2:567-74 Feb 49

STERNBERG, FRITZ
The United States in the future world econ-
omy. SR 11:285-304 Sep 44
Japan's economic imperialism. SR 12:328-49
Sep 45

STETTNER, WALTER FRITZ
Sir James Steuart on the public debt. QJE 59:
451-76 May 45

STEVENS, WILLIAM HARRISON SPRING
Railroad reorganizations under the Bankruptcy Act. Pt.I-II. JB 15:205-24; 361-81
Jul,Oct 42
[and others] Postwar railroad problems:
discussion. AER/S 36:494-519 May 46

STEWART, ANDREW
Edward Arthur George Luxton, 1914-1945.
[obit.] CJE 11:478-79 Aug 45
Stabilization of the income of the primary
producer. CJE 11:359-72 Aug 45
and Hanson, E. J. Some aspects of rural
municipal finance. CJE 14:481-90 Nov 48

STEWART, BRYCE MORRISON
War-time labour problems and policies in
Canada. CJE 7:426-46 Aug 41

STEWART, CHARLES DAVID
Degree and character of the wartime expansion of the national labor force. AER/S 33:
207-17 Mar 43
and Wood, L. Employment statistics in the
planning of a full-employment program.
JASA 41:313-21 Sep 46

STEWART, CHARLES LESLIE
Extended functions for institutional landowners. LE 16:357-62 Aug 40

STEWART, CLYDE E.
Can sufficient private credit be obtained for
FHA insured farm real estate loans?
JFE 30:561-66 Aug 48

STEWART, HUGH L. [and others]
Recent regional changes in farming and
probable future trends. JFE 24:256-79
Feb 42

STEWART, M. C.
Industrial assurance. OIS 5,suppl.4:18-24
Feb 20, 43

STEWART, MARGARET
The new railway agreement. OIS 3:300-04
Sep 20, 41

STEWART, SHEILA I.
Statutes, orders, and official statements relating to Canadian war-time economic
controls. CJE 13:99-114 Feb 47

STEWART, WILLIAM BLAIR
Shifts in the geographical and industrial pattern of economic activity. AER/S 36:
36-51 May 46
[and others] Does large-scale enterprise
lower costs? Discussion. AER/S 38:
165-71 May 48

STICE, LESLIE F.
Useful techniques in an extension marketing
program. JFE 31,pt.2:690-92 Feb 49

STIEBELING, HAZEL KATHERINE
Agricultural surpluses: discussion. JFE 22:
337-39 Feb 40

STIEBER, JACK
Minnesota Labor Relations Act: an opinion
survey. HBR 27:665-77 Nov 49

STIGLER, GEORGE JOSEPH
Agricultural surpluses and malnutrition:
discussion. JFE 22:339-40 Feb 40
Round table on cost functions and their rela-
tion to imperfect competition: [discussion].
AER/S 30:401-02 Mar 40
Notes on the theory of duopoly. JPE 48:
521-41 Aug 40
A note on discontinuous cost curves. AER 30:
832-35 Dec 40
The extent and bases of monopoly. AER/S 32,
no.2:1-22 Jun 42
A note on Price discrimination in steel.
AER 32:354-55 Jun 42
The new welfare economics. AER 33:355-59
Jun 43
The cost of subsistence. JFE 27:303-14
May 45
The economics of minimum wage legislation.
AER 36:358-65 Jun 46
Labor productivity and size of farm: a sta-
tistical pitfall. JFE 28:821-25 Aug 46
Professor Lester and the marginalists.
AER 37:154-57 Mar 47
Notes on the history of the Giffen paradox.
JPE 55:152-56 Apr 47

STIGLER, GEORGE JOSEPH (Cont.)
  Stuart Wood and the marginal productivity
    theory. QJE 61:640-49 Aug 47
  The kinky oligopoly demand curve and rigid
    prices. JPE 55:432-49 Oct 47
  [Notes on the history of the Giffen paradox]:
    a reply. JPE 56:61-62 Feb 48
  A survey of contemporary economics. R.
    JPE 57:93-105 Apr 49
  A theory of delivered price systems. AER 39:
    1143-59 Dec 49
STILLMAN, CALVIN WHITNEY
  Rural health and the Truman Plan. JFE 31:
    391-408 Aug 49
STINE, OSCAR CLEMEN
  Future of cotton in the economy of the South.
    JFE 23:112-21 Feb 41
  Parity prices. JFE 28:301-05 Feb 46
STITTS, T. G.
  Organization of agricultural markets: dis-
    cussion. JFE 22:185-87 Feb 40
STOCK, J. STEVENS and Frankel, L. R.
  On the sample survey of unemployment.
    JASA 37:77-80 Mar 42
STOCKING, GEORGE WARD
  [and others] The progress of concentration
    in industry: discussion. AER/S 38:109-20
    May 48
  The effectiveness of the federal antitrust
    laws: a symposium. AER 39:719-20
    Jun 49
STOCKING, SAMUEL B.
  Recent trends in consumption. CJE 7:371-81
    Aug 41
STODDARD, CHARLES H.
  Future of private forest land ownership in
    the northern Lake states. LE 18:267-83
    Aug 42
  Folweiler's Political economy of forestry.
    R. LE 21:65-68 Feb 45
STODDARD, WILLIAM LEAVITT
  Small business wants capital. HBR 18:
    265-74 no.3, 40
STOKDYK, ELLIS ADOLPH
  Trends in agricultural cooperation. JFE 24:
    857-65 Nov 42
  Supreme Court upholds state proration.
    JFE 25:504-06 May 43
STOKES, JOHN W.
  The new projective-type tests for selection
    of salesmen. JM 10:58-59 Jul 45
STOKES, R. S.
  A shipyard from within. MS 17:88-96 Jan 49
STOKES, WILLIAM S.
  The land laws of Honduras. AH 21:148-54
    Jul 47
STOLPER, GUSTAV and Doblin, E. M.
  The new Federal Reserve Board index of pro-
    duction. EJ 51:47-55 Apr 41
STOLPER, WOLFGANG FRIEDRICH
  The possibility of equilibrium under monopo-
    listic competition. QJE 54:519-26 May 40
  British monetary policy and the housing

  boom. QJE 56,no.1,pt.2:1-166 Nov 41
  and Samuelson, P. A. Protection and real
    wages. REStud 9:58-73 Nov 41
  Monetary, equilibrium, and business-cycle
    theory. REStat 25:88-92 Feb 43
  The volume of foreign trade and the level of
    income. QJE 61:285-310 Feb 47
  Purchasing power parity and the pound sterl-
    ing from 1919-1925. Kyk 2:240-69
    fasc.3, 48
  [and others] Problems of the ITO: discus-
    sion. AER/S 39:269-79 May 49
  American foreign economic policy, the dollar
    shortage, and Mr. Balogh. R. Kyk 3:
    160-72 fasc.2, 49
STONBOROUGH, THOMAS H. W.
  Fixed panels in consumer research. JM 7:
    129-38 Oct 42
STONE, JOHN RICHARD NICHOLAS
  see Stone, Richard
STONE, LAWRENCE
  State control in sixteenth-century England.
    EHR 17:103-20 no.2, 47
  The anatomy of the Elizabethan aristocracy.
    EHR 18:1-53 no.1-2, 48
  Elizabethan overseas trade. EHR II.2:30-58
    no.1, 49
STONE, RALEIGH WEBSTER
  Labor problems: discussion. AER/S 33:
    251-52 Mar 43
STONE, RICHARD
  and Meade, J. E. The construction of tables
    of national income, expenditure, savings
    and investment. EJ 51:216-33 Jun-Sep 41
  The national income, output and expenditure
    of the United States of America, 1929-41.
    EJ 52:154-75 Jun-Sep 42
  with Champernowne, D. G. and Meade, J. E.
    The precision of national income esti-
    mates. REStud 9:111-25 no.2, 42
  National income in the United Kingdom and
    the United States of America. REStud 10:
    1-27 no.1, 42
  The fortune teller. R. Ec N.S.10:24-33
    Feb 43
  Two studies on income and expenditure in
    the United States. R. EJ 53:60-75 Apr 43
  [U.S. national income statistics.] Comment.
    EJ 53:82-83 Apr 43
  Employment in U.S. manufacturing. R.
    EJ 54:246-52 Jun-Sep 44
  The analysis of market demand. JRSS 108:
    286-382 pt.3-4, 45
  and Jackson, E. F. Economic models with
    special reference to Mr. Kaldor's system.
    EJ 56:554-67 Dec 46
  The measurement of national income and ex-
    penditure: a review of the official esti-
    mates of five countries. EJ 57:272-98
    Sep 47
  The theory of games. R. EJ 58:185-201
    Jun 48
  The analysis of market demand; an outline

STONE, RICHARD (Cont.)
of methods and results. RIIS 16:23-34
no.1-4, 48
Prediction from autoregressive schemes and
linear stochastic difference systems.
Em 17,suppl.:29-37 Jul 49; Errata.
19:227 Apr 51
STONER, PAUL MATTHEW
The mortgage market: today and after World
War I. LE 19:224-30 May 43
STONIER, ALFRED W.
[Note on F. A. Hayek's "Scientism and the
study of society."] Ec N.S.10:188-89
May 43
STOUT, WHITNEY B.
Postwar Extension problems in agricultural
marketing. JFE 28:187-98 Feb 46
Marketing research contemplated by the
state experiment stations under the Re-
search and Marketing Act of 1946.
JFE 29:1385-88 Nov 47
STRAUS, EVERET M.
Cost accounting and statistical cost functions.
AER 35:430-32 Jun 45
Prices, income flow and employment.
QJE 60:600-11 Aug 46
STRAUSS, FREDERICK
The food problem in the German war econ-
omy. QJE 55:364-412 May 41
STRAYER, PAUL JOHNSTON
Public expenditure policy. AER 39:383-404
Mar 49
STREETEN, PAUL
The theory of profit. MS 17:266-96 Sep 49
STROHKARCK, FRANK and Phelps, K.
The mechanics of constructing a market
area map. JM 12:493-96 Apr 48
STRUNK, NORMAN
Low-cost housing under the USHA experi-
ment. LE 16:96-99 Feb 40
Progress in defense housing. LE 17:92-97
Feb 41
Housing priorities. LE 17:484-88 Nov 41
The improved investment position of savings
and loan associations. JF 2,no.2:1-21
Oct 47
STRUVE, GLEB
Peter Struve. [obit.] EJ 54:438-43 Dec 44
STUDENSKI, PAUL
Toward a theory of business taxation.
JPE 48:621-54 Oct 40
On some appendices to the Rowell-Sirois
report: III. The national income of Canada.
CJE 7:78-84 Feb 41
and Wyler, J. National income estimates of
Soviet Russia; their distinguishing char-
acteristics and problems. AER/S 37:
595-610 May 47
Federal grants-in-aid. NTJ 2:193-214 Sep 49
STURMTHAL, ADOLF
The crisis of the WFTU. ILRR 1:624-38
Jul 48
National patterns of union behavior. JPE 56:
515-26 Dec 48

STYKOLT, STEFAN
A note on economic activity in the adminis-
trative state. EEH 1,no.1:30-31 Jan 49
A note on the parametric approach. EEH 1,
no.2:25-26 Feb 49
SUBBA RAO, B. R.
see Rao, B. R. Subba
SUFRIN, SIDNEY CHARLES
The effects of minimum wages. AER 30:
576-78 Sep 40
Wage increases and employment: reply.
AER 31:838 Dec 41
with Swinyard, A. W. and Stephenson, F. M.
The North-South differential: a different
view. SEJ 15:184-90 Oct 48
SUITER, W. O.
Divergent theories of national debt. SEJ 13:
53-64 Jul 46
SUKHLA, S. S.
Some aspects of the Indian food problem.
IJE 27:427-31 Apr 47
SULLAM, VICTOR BENEDICT
Scientific progress as a cause of maladjust-
ment. SEJ 8:391-95 Jan 42
The Iowa statutory provisions for automatic
lease renewal. JFE 24:677-84 Aug 42
SULLIVAN, DAVID J.
The Negro market today and postwar.
JM 10:68-69 Jul 45; Errata. 179 Oct 45
SULLIVAN, RODMAN
The disposition of the United States Merchant
Marine. SEJ 11:369-75 Apr 45
The Southern passenger fare case. SEJ 13:
126-31 Oct 46
SUMBERG, THEODORE ABRAHAM
The government's role in export trade.
HBR 23:157-73 no.2, 45
Menace of export subsidies. HBR 23:420-32
no.4, 45
The Soviet Union's war budgets. AER 36:
113-26 Mar 46
Financing international institutions. SR 13:
276-306 Sep 46
Leakage problems in flexible taxation.
JPE 55:572-75 Dec 47
SUMMERS, CLYDE W.
Admission policies of labor unions. QJE 61:
66-107 Nov 46
SUMNER, JOHN DUNCAN
A note on cyclical changes in demand elas-
ticity. AER 30:300-08 Jun 40
The effects of the war on price policies and
price making. AER/S 32:404-15 Mar 42
Differential pricing in nonferrous metals.
AER/S 33:279-86 Mar 43
The disposition of surplus war property.
AER 34:457-71 Sep 44
[and others] Economic problems of foreign
areas: discussion. AER/S 36:650-60
May 46
SUNDARA RAJAN, V.
"Food planning in India." IJE 26:565-70
Jan 46

SURÁNYI-UNGER, THEO
Individual and collective wants. JPE 56:
1-22 Feb 48
Analytical notes on economic systems.
ZN 12:171-97 Dec 49
The concept of elasticity in economics.
WA 62:11-25 Hft.1, 49
Economic structure and planning. ZS 105:
251-82 Hft.2, 49

SURVEYER, ARTHUR
The Canadian economy and the encyclicals.
RSE 7,no.1:61-72 Mar 49

SUTCH, WILLIAM BALL
Marketing and price control in New Zealand.
ER 16:68-77 Jun 40
New Zealand's war controls. SAJE 8:136-44
Jun 40
New Zealand's war economy. ER 16:208-17
Dec 40
Changes in New Zealand's import structure.
ER 19:203-11 Dec 43

SUTHERLAND, ARTHUR E., Jr.
The constitutionality of the Taft-Hartley law.
ILRR 1:177-205 Jan 48

SUTHERLAND, LUCY STUART
Samson Gideon and the reduction of interest,
1749-50. EHR 16:15-29 no.1, 46
The East India Company in eighteenth-
century politics. EHR 17:15-26 no.1, 47

SUTTON, CHARLES T.
An enquiry into the assessing of salvage
awards. JRSS 108:41-84 pt.1-2, 45

SVEISTRUP, POUL PETER
Some problems in laying out a new traffic
line. NTTO 12:255-64 no.37, 48

SWAN, ELIOT J.
Financing social security. AER/S 37:345-50
May 47

SWAN, T. W.
Australian war finance and banking policy.
ER 16:50-67 Jun 40
Some notes on the interest controversy.
ER 17:153-65 Dec 41
Price flexibility and employment. R. ER 21:
236-53 Dec 45
--- Rejoinder. ER 22:282-84 Dec 46

SWANSON, ERNST WARNER
Some aspects of value and capital in a war
economy. AER 33:852-67 Dec 43

SWARDT, STEPHANUS JANSEN DE
see De Swardt, Stephanus Jansen

SWEEZY, ALAN RICHARDSON
[and others] Round table on population prob-
lems: [discussion]. AER/S 30:393-98
Mar 40
Population growth and investment opportunity.
QJE 55:64-79 Nov 40
Wages and investment. JPE 50:117-29 Feb 42
The government's responsibility for full em-
ployment. AER/S 33:19-26 Mar 43
[Net investment, consumption and full em-
ployment]: reply. AER 34:875-78 Dec 44
Social security and national prosperity.
S&S 8:193-204 no.3, 44

Fiscal and monetary policy. AER/S 36:
291-303 May 46

SWEEZY, MAXINE YAPLE
see Woolston, Maxine Yaple

SWEEZY, PAUL MARLOR
The illusion of the "managerial revolution."
S&S 6:1-23 no.1, 42
Professor Schumpeter's theory of innovation.
REStat 25:93-96 Feb 43
Rationing and the war economy. S&S 7:64-71
no.1, 43
John Maynard Keynes. S&S 10:398-405
no.4, 46
Marxian and orthodox economics. S&S 11:
225-33 no.3, 47
Fabian political economy. JPE 57:242-48
Jun 49

SWENSRUD, SIDNEY ANTON
Converting war pipe lines to natural gas.
HBR 22:459-74 no.4, 44

SWINYARD, ALFRED WILBUR; Sufrin, S. C.
and Stephenson, F. M.
The North-South differential: a different
view. SEJ 15:184-90 Oct 48

SWOPE, GERALD
Some aspects of corporate management.
HBR 23:314-22 no.3, 45

SYKES, JOSEPH
Some results of the Distribution of Industry
Act, 1945. MS 17:36-48 Jan 49
The development areas. MS 17:128-45
May 49
Postwar distribution of industry in Great
Britain. JB 22:188-99 Jul 49

SYKES, PAUL C.
An analysis of income and expenditure of a
sample of Indian families in the Clairwood
area of Durban. SAJE 9:45-65 Mar 41;
Errata. 207 Jun 41

SZATROWSKI, ZENON
Time series correlated with the beef-pork
consumption ratio. Em 13:60-78 Jan 45
The consistency of U.S.D.A. estimates of
possible consumption and prices of beef
and pork in 1950. JFE 27:984-89 Nov 45

SZELISKI, VICTOR VON
see Von Szeliski, Victor Spartan

TAEUBER, CONRAD
Rural-urban migration. AH 15:151-60 Jul 41
[and others] Need for a new classification of
farms. JFE 26:694-708 Nov 44
and Tolley, H. R. Wartime developments in
agricultural statistics. JASA 39:411-27
Dec 44
Farm wage statistics for a full employment
program. JASA 40:234-35 Jun 45
with Black, J. D. and Becker, J. A. The
reclamation of flooded areas of Holland.
JFE 28:1070-75 Nov 46
Some aspects of the statistics program in the
Department of Agriculture. JASA 42:41-45
Mar 47
and Taeuber, I. B. World population trends.

TAEUBER, CONRAD (Cont.)
(Food supply problems) JFE 31,pt.2:
237-50 Feb 49
TAEUBER, IRENE BARNES
see Taeuber, Conrad and Taeuber, I. B.
TAFT, PHILIP
Opposition to union officers in elections.
QJE 58:246-64 Feb 44
Judicial procedure in labor unions. QJE 59:
370-85 May 45
Dues and initiation fees in labor unions.
QJE 60:219-32 Feb 46
Democracy in trade unions. AER/S 36:
359-69 May 46
Understanding union administration. HBR 24:
245-57 no.2, 46
The constitutional power of the chief officer
in American labor unions. QJE 62:459-71
May 48
Attempts to "radicalize" the labor movement.
ILRR 1:580-92 Jul 48
Status of members in unions during appeal
from a penalty imposed by the local union.
QJE 62:610-16 Aug 48
The Association of Catholic Trade Unionists.
ILRR 2:210-18 Jan 49
TAGLIACARNE, GUGLIELMO
Cost of living, salaries, consumption and the
situation of the Italian middle classes.
BNL 1:75-85 Jul 47
Italian foreign trade in the framework of
world trade. BNL 1:228-39 Jan 48
TAGLIACOZZO, GIORGIO
Croce and the nature of economic science.
QJE 59:307-29 May 45
T'AI-CH'U LIAO
see Liao, T'ai-ch'u
TAITEL, MARTIN
Price indexes as viewed from the standpoint
of the national defense program. JASA 36:
201-09 Jun 41
Business-reporting under the defense pro-
gram. JB 14:284-93 Jul 41
TAKATA, YASUMA
Money, the economic veil. Kyo 15,no.4:25-43
Oct 40
TALMAGE, GEORGE E., Jr.
Transportation for war. HBR 21:336-43
no.3, 43
TAMAGNA, FRANK MARIUS
The fixing of foreign exchange rates. JPE 53:
57-72 Mar 45
The financial position of China and Japan.
AER/S 36:613-27 May 46
TANIGUCHI, KICHIHIKO
The theory of wider territory economy.
Kyo 16,no.4:20-41 Oct 41
The trade policy of East Asia wider territory
economy. Kyo 17,no.2:20-43 Apr 42
The formation of the Trade Corporation.
Kyo 18,no.3:26-45 Jul 43
TANNENBAUM, JUDITH
The neighborhood: a socio-psychological
analysis. LE 24:358-69 Nov 48

TANNENBAUM, ROBERT
Developments affecting cost under the unfair
practices acts. JB 13:118-35 Apr 40
The manager concept: a rational synthesis.
JB 22:225-41 Oct 49
TAPP, JESSE WASHINGTON
Significance of the general price level and
related influences to American agriculture:
further comment. JFE 31,pt.2:788-92
Nov 49
TARP, B. GLOERFELT-
see Gloerfelt-Tarp, B.
TARSHIS, LORIE
Real and money wage rates: further com-
ment. QJE 55:691-97 Aug 41
An exposition of Keynesian economics.
AER/S 38:261-72 May 48
TATE, WILLIAM EDWARD
Members of Parliament and the proceedings
upon enclosure bills. EHR 12:68-75
no.1-2, 42
The Commons' journals as sources of infor-
mation concerning the eighteenth-century
enclosure movement. EJ 54:75-95 Apr 44
Opposition to parliamentary enclosure in
eighteenth-century England. AH 19:137-42
Jul 45
Members of Parliament and their personal
relations to enclosure: a study with spe-
cial reference to Oxfordshire enclosures,
1757-1843. AH 23:213-20 Jul 49
TAUSSIG, FRANK WILLIAM
My father's business career. HBR 19:177-84
no.2, 41
TAWNEY, RICHARD HENRY
Dr. Eileen Power. [obit.] EHR 10:92-94
Nov 40
Professor W. R. Scott. [obit.] EHR 10:91-92
Nov 40
The rise of the gentry, 1558-1640. EHR 11:
1-38 no.1, 41
The abolition of economic controls 1918-1921.
EHR 13:1-30 no.1-2, 43
In memory of Sidney Webb. Ec N.S.14:
245-53 Nov 47
TAYLOR, ALONZO E.
Five postwar trade problems. HBR 21:
150-63 no.2, 43
TAYLOR, AMOS ELIAS
International economic problems; regional:
discussion. AER/S 34,no.1:370-71
Mar 44
TAYLOR, ARNOLD JOSEPH
Concentration and specialization in the Lan-
cashire cotton industry, 1825-1850.
EHR II.1:114-22 no.2-3, 49
TAYLOR, CHARLES THEODORE
Population increase, municipal outlays, and
debts. SEJ 9:327-34 Apr 43
Voluntary savings and consumer behavior.
SEJ 10:239-45 Jan 44
Some economic consequences of federal aid
and subsidies to southern agriculture.
SEJ 14:62-72 Jul 47

TAYLOR, EVA GERMAINE RIMINGTON
The surveyor. EHR 17:121-33 no.2, 47
TAYLOR, GEORGE ROGERS
State laws which limit competition in agri-
cultural products. JFE 22:241-48 Feb 40
TAYLOR, GEORGE WILLIAM
chairman. Round table on collective bargain-
ing and job security. AER/S 30:223-29
Mar 40
Wage regulation in postwar America.
AER/S 34:181-92 Mar 44
Is compulsory arbitration inevitable?
IRRA 1:64-77 Dec 48
TAYLOR, HENRY CHARLES
Early history of agricultural economics.
JFE 22:84-97 Feb 40
Training and recruitment of agricultural
economic personnel. I. A general view.
JFE 22:411-14 May 40
The farmer in the groupistic regime. LE 16:
253-61 Aug 40
and Wehrwein, G. S. Richard T. Ely. [obit.]
LE 19:389-90 Nov 43
World conditions in the postwar period that
will affect Mississippi Valley agriculture.
JFE 26:1-9 Feb 44
Richard Theodore Ely (April 13, 1854-
October 4, 1943). [obit.] EJ 54:132-38
Apr 44
TAYLOR, HORACE
Political science, political economy, and
values: discussion. AER/S 34:12-14
Mar 44
TAYLOR, J. G.
College revenue bonds to finance self-sup-
porting projects. JF 4:328-41 Dec 49
TAYLOR, KENNETH WIFFIN
Canadian war-time price controls, 1941-6.
CJE 13:81-98 Feb 47
TAYLOR, MALCOLM DEAN
Allocation of scarce consumers' goods to re-
tailers. JM 8:123-32 Oct 43
Appraisal of the BLS index of wholesale food
prices in wartime. JM 9:32-42 Jul 44
TAYLOR, MAURICE C.
An evaluation of "Evaluating soil conserva-
tion." JFE 29:966-73 Nov 47
TAYLOR, MAURICE FRANCIS WALKER and
Siegel, I. H.
Public expenditures for veterans' assistance.
JPE 56:527-32 Dec 48
TAYLOR, MORRIS HARDING
Selective selling and leasing of county land
in North Dakota. LE 19:238-42 May 43
TAYLOR, OVERTON HUME
Economic theory and the age we live in. R.
REStat 29:102-07 May 47
The economics of a "free" society: four
essays. R. QJE 62:641-70 Nov 48
TAYLOR, ROSSER H.
Post-bellum southern rental contracts.
AH 17:121-28 Apr 43

The sale and application of commercial
fertilizers in the south Atlantic states to
1900. AH 21:46-52 Jan 47
TAYMANS, ADRIEN C.
Facts and theory in entrepreneurial history.
EEH 1,no.1:15-20 Jan 49
George Tarde and Joseph A. Schumpeter: a
similar vision. EEH 1,no.4:9-17 Apr 49
TEAD, ORDWAY
Advancing the public interest in labor relations. ILRR 2:391-402 Apr 49
TEELE, STANLEY FERDINAND
with Gragg, C. I. and Grimshaw, A. Competition under rationing. HBR 20:141-55
no.2, 42
and Bursk, E. C. Marketing practices of
food manufacturers. HBR 22:358-76
no.3, 44
and Gragg, C. I. The proposed full employ-
ment act. HBR 23:323-37 no.3, 45
TEILHET, DARWIN and Franzen, R.
A method for measuring product acceptance.
JM 5:156-61 Oct 40
TEISER, RUTH
and Harroun, C. Origin of Wells, Fargo &
Company, 1841-1852. BHR 22:70-83
Jun 48
and Harroun, C. Wells, Fargo & Company:
the first half year. BHR 23:87-95 Jun 49
TEMPLE, ALAN H.
The business outlook. AER/S 37:64-70
May 47
TENNY, LLOYD STANLEY
The Bureau of Agricultural Economics: the
early years. JFE 29:1017-26 Nov 47
TEPER, LAZARE
Observations on the cost of living index of the
Bureau of Labor Statistics. JASA 38:
271-84 Sep 43
"Motivation analysis in market research":
a criticism. JM 13:524-27 Apr 49
The function of management in achieving
sound labor relations. ILRR 2:558-75
Jul 49
TERBORGH, GEORGE
Postwar surpluses and shortages of plant
and equipment. AER/S 32:360-68 Mar 42
[The doctrine of economic maturity.] Note.
AER 36:141 Mar 46
Dr. Hansen on "The bogey of economic
maturity." REStat 28:170-72 Aug 46
The January 1949 economic report of the
President: appraisal. REStat 31:176-78
Aug 49
TERRILL, ROBERT PHILIP
Cartels and the international exchange of
technology. AER/S 36:745-67 May 46
TETREAU, ELZER DES JARDINES
The location of heirs and the value of their
inheritances: farm and city estates. LE 16:
416-29 Nov 40

TETRO, ROBERT C.; Johnson, S. R. and
Johnson, N. W.
Resources available for agricultural produc-
tion in 1943. JFE 25:65-83 Feb 43

TEW, BRIAN
and Kalecki, M. A new method of trend
elimination. Em 8:117-29 Apr 40; Cor-
rection. 9:93-94 Jan 41
Reports on the iron and steel industry. R.
EJ 56:487-99 Sep 46
The direct control of interest rates. ER 23:
198-205 Dec 47
Sterling as an international currency.
ER 24:42-55 Jun 48
A note on the multiplier. ER 24:109-11
Jun 48

TEWARI, JAGDISH NARAIN
What is economics? IJE 27:421-25 Apr 47

THACKERAY, FREDERICK GORDON and
Martin, K.
The terms of trade of selected countries,
1870-1938. OIS 10:373-94 Nov 48

THARAKHAN, K. J. MATHEW
'Consumer's surplus': a rejoinder. IJE 21:
307-19 Jan 41

THARP, MAX M.
A reappraisal of farm tenure research.
LE 24:315-30 Nov 48

THATCHER, LIONEL WILMOT
Financial and depreciation history of the
Utah Power and Light Company. Pt.I-II.
LE 15:448-55; 16:89-95 Nov 39, Feb 40

THIN, MAUNG TUN and Musgrave, R. A.
Income tax progression, 1929-48. JPE 56:
498-514 Dec 48

THIRLBY, G. F.
The Industrial and Agricultural Requirements
Commission (First interim report).
(U.G. 33/1940) SAJE 8:185-94 Jun 40
The Report of the Railway Line Revision
Commission. (U.G. no.20, 1940) SAJE 8:
175-82 Jun 40
The Report of the Rural Industries Commis-
sion. (U.G. no.27, 1940) SAJE 8:303-11
Sep 40
A note on Dr. J. N. Reedman's remarks
upon the balance of external payments.
SAJE 9:100-02 Mar 41
Permanent resources. Ec N.S.10:238-50
Aug 43
The subjective theory of value and account-
ing "cost." Ec N.S.13:32-49 Feb 46
The ruler. SAJE 14:253-76 Dec 46
The marginal cost controversy: a note on
Mr. Coase's model. Ec N.S.14:48-53
Feb 47
Demand and supply of money. EJ 58:331-55
Sep 48

THOMAS, BRINLEY
Migration and the British Commonwealth.
EI 1:1147-56 Nov 48

THOMAS, DOROTHY SWAINE and Galbraith, V. L.
Birth rates and the interwar business cycles.
JASA 36:465-76 Dec 41

THOMAS, EUGENE P.
Shifting scenes in foreign trade. JM 4,no.4,
pt.2:51-58 Apr 40

THOMAS, PARAKUNNEL JOSEPH
The zamindari problem in Madras. IJE 21:
1-12 Jul 40
"The growth of federal finance." IJE 21:
210 Oct 40
The finances of Indian states. IJE 21:819-29
Apr 41
The prices of food grains in Madras in the
19th century. IJE 21:559-68 Apr 41
The late Professor V. G. Kale. [obit.]
IJE 27:333-34 Jan 47

THOMAS, ROLLIN GEORGE
100 per cent money: the present status of
the 100 per cent plan. AER 30:315-23
Jun 40

THOMAS, WOODLIEF
The heritage of war finance. AER/S 37:
205-15 May 47
Planning and forecasting in the transition
period. AER/S 37:51-57 May 47

THOMASINE, MARY, sister
see Cusack, Mary Thomasine, sister

THOMPSON, CECIL HARRY
"The United Kingdom Economic survey for
1948." R. SAJE 16:89-97 Mar 48

THOMPSON, CHARLES WOODY and Riggs, H. E.
Two commentaries on Anatomy of depreciation. R. LE 23:433-38 Nov 47

THOMPSON, D. O. and Glover, W. H.
A pioneer adventure in agricultural extension: a contribution from the Wisconsin
cut-over. AH 22:124-28 Apr 48

THOMPSON, DONALD SCOUGALL
Round table on bank deposits and the business
cycle. [Summary of remarks] AER/S 30:
82 Mar 40
Nonfarm real estate finance. JF 2,no.1:34-50
Apr 47
--- [idem] LE 23:105-16 May 47
Measuring effective demand in the housing
market. LE 25:108-11 Feb 49

THOMPSON, EDGAR T.
The climatic theory of the plantation. AH 15:
49-60 Jan 41

THOMPSON, MORRIS
Department store problems. JM 8:21-24
Jul 43

THOMPSON, ROBERT JOHN
Land utilization in rural areas. R. JRSS 105:
218-19 pt.3, 42
The future of agriculture. JRSS 106:32-42
pt.1, 43

THOMPSON, WALTER and Fainsod, M.
The OPA economy for victory program.
JM 7:319-24 Apr 43

THOMPSON, WOODY and Riggs, H. E.
Two commentaries on Anatomy of depreciation. R. LE 23:433-38 Nov 47

THOMSEN, FREDERICK LUNDY
Export-dumping plans. JFE 22:446-59
May 40

THOMSEN, FREDERICK LUNDY (Cont.)
The impact of war on marketing farm products. JFE 25:120-42 Feb 43
A critical examination of marketing research.
JFE 27:947-62 Nov 45
How good is marketing research? HBR 24:
453-65 no.4, 46
chairman. Technological developments in
agricultural marketing. Report of a sub-
committee. JFE 29:310-19 Feb 47

THORNDIKE, EDWARD LEE
The variation in wage-ratios. QJE 54:369-83
May 40
and Woodyard, E. The cost of living in cities
in relation to their size and latitude.
JASA 38:238-41 Jun 43

THORP, WILLARD LONG
and Crowder, W. F. Concentration and prod-
uct characteristics as factors in price-
quantity behavior. AER/S 30,no.5:390-408
Feb 41
Postwar depressions. AER/S 30,no.5:352-61
Feb 41
Paul T. Cherington, 1876-1943. [obit.]
JASA 38:471-72 Dec 43
Irving Fisher 1867-1947. [obit.] JASA 42:
311 Jun 47

THRELFELL, R. L.
The relative merits of tariffs and subsidies
as methods of protection. SAJE 14:
117-31 Jun 46
--- Reply. SAJE 14:225 Sep 46
Review of Board of Trade and Industries
Report no. 285 and Railway Administra-
tion White Paper of May 28, 1946.
SAJE 14:310-17 Dec 46
Some comments on secondary industry in
South Africa. SAJE 14:288-304 Dec 46

THRONE, MILDRED
Southern Iowa agriculture, 1833-1890: the
progress from subsistence to commercial
corn-belt farming. AH 23:124-30 Apr 49

THRUPP, SYLVIA LETTICE
Social control in the medieval town.
JEH/S 1:39-52 Dec 41
Medieval gilds reconsidered. JEH 2:164-73
Nov 42

THUNBERG, PENELOPE HARTLAND
Interregional payments compared with inter-
national payments. QJE 63:392-407
Aug 49

TIBBETTS, FRANK C.
The accounting period in federal income taxation. SEJ 7:362-79 Jan 41

TIERNEY, JOHN LESTER
"Fair value" and the deficiency judgment.
LE 16:181-95 May 40
War housing: the Emergency Fleet Corpora-
tion experience. Pt.I-II. LE 17:151-64;
303-12 May,Aug 41

TIFFIN, JOSEPH
The uses and potentialities of attitude surveys in industrial relations. IRRA 2:
204-11 Dec 49

TILAK, V. R. K.
Some aspects of price control in India.
IJE 24:323-29 Apr 44

TILTON, LEON DEMING
[The education of planners.] At the University of California, Berkeley. LE 21:
309-11 Sep 45

TIMLIN, MABEL FRANCES
The economics of control. R. CJE 11:
285-93 May 45
Price flexibility and employment. CJE 12:
204-13 May 46
General equilibrium analysis and public
policy. CJE 12:483-95 Nov 46
--- A rejoinder. CJE 13:285-87 May 47
John Maynard Keynes. [obit.] CJE 13:363-65
Aug 47
Theories of welfare economics. R. CJE 15:
551-59 Nov 49

TIMM, TYRUS R.
An introduction to Extension economics.
JFE 31,pt.2:682-86 Feb 49

TIMMERMAN, WILLEM ABRAM
Reply to Mr. Threlfell's review of the Board
of Trade & Industries' Report, no. 285.
SAJE 16:106-07 Mar 48

TIMMONS, JOHN FRANCIS
Land tenure policy goals. LE 19:165-79
May 43
and Johnson, V. W. Public works on private
land. JFE 26:665-84 Nov 44
Institutional obstacles to land improvement.
LE 22:140-50 May 46
with Johnson, V. W. and Howenstine, E. J., Jr.
Rural public works. Pt.I-II. LE 23:12-21;
132-41 Feb,May 47
Farm ownership in the United States: an
appraisal of the present situation and
emerging problems. JFE 30:78-100
Feb 48

TIMOSHENKO, VLADIMIR PZOKOP
The agrarian policies of Russia and the wars.
AH 17:192-210 Oct 43

TINBERGEN, JAN
Econometric business cycle research.
REStud 7:73-90 Feb 40
On a method of statistical business-cycle
research. A reply. EJ 50:141-54 Mar 40
Unstable and indifferent equilibria in eco-
nomic systems. RIIS 9:36-50 no.1-2, 41
Does consumption lag behind incomes?
REStat 24:1-8 Feb 42
Critical remarks on some business-cycle
theories. Em 10:129-46 Apr 42
Professor Douglas' production function.
RIIS 10:37-47 no.1-2, 42
Colin Clark's "Economics of 1960." RIIS 12:
1-4 no.1-4, 44
The economic situation in the Netherlands in
autumn, 1945. OIS 7:266-68 Nov 3, 45
Some measurements of elasticities of substi-
tution. REStat 28:109-16 Aug 46
Some problems in the explanation of interest
rates. QJE 61:397-438 May 47

TINBERGEN, JAN (Cont.)

The use of correlation analysis in economic research. ET 49:173-92 Sep 47

Some considerations on the problem of dollar scarcity. EI 1:562-67 May 48

Central planning in the Netherlands. REStud 15:70-77 no.2, 48

The equalisation of factor prices between free-trade areas. Met 1:39-47 Apr 49

and Derksen, J. B. D. Recent experiments in social accounting: flexible and dynamic budgets. Em 17,suppl.:195-203 Jul 49

Some remarks on the problem of dollar scarcity. Em 17,suppl.:73-95 Jul 49

[and others] Theory of choice and utilization of resources: discussion. Em 17, suppl.:173-78 Jul 49

Long-term foreign trade elasticities. Met 1:174-85 Dec 49

Government budget and central economic plan. PF 4:195-99 no.3, 49

TINLEY, JAMES MADDISON

Control of agriculture in South Africa. SAJE 8:243-63 Sep 40

George Martin Peterson, 1897-1940. [obit.] JFE 22:827-28 Nov 40

and Mirkowich, B. M. Control in the sugar-cane industry of South Africa. JFE 23: 537-49 Aug 41

Behavior of prices of farm products during World Wars I and II. JFE 24:157-67 Feb 42

TINTNER, GERHARD

The analysis of economic time series. JASA 35:93-100 Mar 40

The variate difference method: a reply. Em 9:163-64 Apr 41

The pure theory of production under technological risk and uncertainty. Em 9:305-12 Jul-Oct 41

The theory of choice under subjective risk and uncertainty. Em 9:298-304 Jul-Oct 41

A contribution to the non-static theory of choice. QJE 56:274-306 Feb 42

A "simple" theory of business fluctuations. Em 10:317-20 Jul-Oct 42

The theory of production under nonstatic conditions. JPE 50:645-67 Oct 42

A note on the derivation of production functions from farm records. Em 12:26-34 Jan 44

An application of the variate difference method to multiple regression. Em 12: 97-113 Apr 44

and Brownlee, O. H. Production functions derived from farm records. JFE 26: 566-71 Aug 44; Correction. 35:123 Feb 53

The "simple" theory of business fluctuations: a tentative verification. REStat 26:148-57 Aug 44

Multiple regression for systems of equations. Em 14:5-36 Jan 46

A note on welfare economics. Em 14:69-78 Jan 46

Some applications of multivariate analysis to economic data. JASA 41:472-500 Dec 46

Homogeneous systems in mathematical economics. Em 16:273-94 Oct 48

Static macro-economic models and their econometric verifications. Met 1:48-52 Apr 49

TIPPETT, LEONARD HENRY CALEB

The study of industrial efficiency, with special reference to the cotton industry. JRSS 110:108-16 pt.2, 47

TIRANA, RIFAT

Behavior of bank deposits abroad. AER/S 30:92-105 Mar 40

TIRUMALACHAR, B.

Deficit financing. IJE 20:567-86 Apr 40

Allocation of resources in a socialist economy. IJE 21:511-25 Apr 41

Economic organisation in ancient India. IJE 22:367-86 Jan 42

TIWARI, JAGDISH NARAYAN

Marshall and the theory of rent. IJE 26: 290-95 Oct 45

TOBBE, WALTER

Governmental measures to encourage large families. RSE 4:54-76 Jan 46

TOBEN, GEORGE E. and Dowell, A. A.

Some economic effects of graduated income tax rates on investors in farm capital. JFE 26:348-58 May 44

TOBIN, JAMES

A note on the money wage problem. QJE 55: 508-16 May 41

Liquidity preference and monetary policy. REStat 29:124-31 May 47

The fallacies of Lord Keynes' General theory: comment. QJE 62:763-70 Nov 48

[Monetary velocity and monetary policy.] A rejoinder. REStat 30:314-17 Nov 48

[and others] Liquidity and uncertainty: discussion. AER/S 39:196-210 May 49

Taxes, saving, and inflation. AER 39: 1223-32 Dec 49

TOKUNAGA, KIYOYUKI

The progress of monetary unification in the Meng Chiang provinces. Kyo 15,no.1: 30-44 Jan 40

Monetary and financial reorganization in North China. Kyo 15,no.2:71-100 Apr 40

The first phase of the Bank of China as a note-issuing bank. Kyo 16,no.1:32-48 Jan 41

The Chinese banks in malformed transition, with a special reference to their movement in the early period of the republican regime. Kyo 17,no.1:53-69 Jan 42

Characteristics of the security market in China: its special relations with Chinese native capital. Kyo 18,no.2:27-47 Apr 43

Adjustment of the Chinese banking business. Kyo 18,no.4:42-62 Oct 43

TOLLES, NEWMAN ARNOLD
Labor statistics for a full employment program. JASA 40:235-36 Jun 45
Conference on the teaching of economics. AER 36:908-10 Dec 46

TOLLEY, HOWARD ROSS
An appraisal of the national interest in the agricultural situation. AER/S 30,no.5: 108-26 Feb 41
[and others] Need for a new classification of farms. JFE 26:694-708 Nov 44
and Taeuber, C. Wartime developments in agricultural statistics. JASA 39:411-27 Dec 44
[and others] Agriculture in the transition from war to peace. AER/S 35:390-404 May 45

TOLMIE, J. ROSS
Excess profits taxation. I. The Canadian act and its administration. CJE 7:350-63 Aug 41

TOMAJAN, JOHN SARKIS
But who is to lead the leader? HBR 23: 277-82 no.3, 45

TONER, JEROME L.
The closed shop and the Taft Act. JPE 56: 258-62 Jun 48

TONGUE, WILLIAM WALTER
Postwar domestic monetary problems: discussion. AER/S 34:278-80 Mar 44

TONTZ, ROBERT L.
and Harrington, A. H. Significance of hog-feed price ratios, Alabama. JFE 28: 835-45 Aug 46
and Ross, E. D. The term "agricultural revolution" as used by economic historians. AH 22:32-38 Jan 48

TOOKER, ELVA
A merchant turns to money-lending in Philadelphia. BHR 20:71-85 Jun 46

TOOTELL, R. B.
Future of the Great Plains: discussion. JFE 31,pt.2:927-28 Nov 49

TORGERSON, HAROLD W.
Agricultural finance in the United States. Pt.I-II. LE 16:196-206; 318-24 May,Aug 40

TÖRNQVIST, LEO
An attempt to analyze the problem of an economical production of statistical data. NTTO 12:265-74 no.37, 48

TOSDAL, HARRY RUDOLPH
Significant trends in sales management. JM 5:215-18 Jan 41
Significant current trends in sales management. JM 6,no.4,pt.2:14-16 Apr 42
Sales management: retrospect and prospect. HBR 21:71-82 no.1, 42
Disposal of war surpluses. HBR 22:346-57 no.3, 44

TOSTLEBE, ALVIN SAMUEL
Estimate of Series E bond purchases by farmers. JASA 40:317-29 Sep 45

TOUGH, ROSALIND
and Weintraub, R. G. Federal housing and World War II. LE 18:155-62 May 42
and Robison, S. M. Toward post-war planning for Yorkville. Pt.I-IV. LE 18: 485-94; 19:354-63; 470-78; 20:156-63 Nov 42, Aug,Nov 43 May 44
and Weintraub, R. G. Farms and homes for veterans. LE 20:371-73 Nov 44
and Weintraub, R. G. Socialization in housing: Great Britain and the United States. LE 22:273-81 Aug 46
and Weintraub, R. G. The United Nations and changing land use in a metropolis. LE 24:186-90 May 48

TOUSAW, A. A.
Taxation problems of life insurance. CJE 6: 440-47 Aug 40

TOUSLEY, RAYBURN DEAN
The Federal Food, Drug, and Cosmetic Act of 1938. JM 5:259-69 Jan 41
Advertising fresh fruits and vegetables. Pt.I-II. HBR 22:447-58 no.4, 44; 23:79-94 no.1, 44
Reducing distribution costs in the grocery field: a case study. JM 12:455-61 Apr 48

TOUT, HERBERT
A statistical note on family allowances. EJ 50:51-59 Mar 40

TOWER, WALTER S.
Steel to meet our needs. HBR 20:34-42 no.1, 41

TOWLE, HERBERT L.
The new type of business cycle: an industrial interpretation. JB 13:360-86 Oct 40
Economic maturity: an industrial view. JB 19:224-31 Oct 46

TOWNSEND, MARY EVELYN
The economic impact of imperial Germany: commercial and colonial policies. JEH/S 3:124-34 Dec 43

TRACEY, MINNIE BEULAH
The present status of frozen food marketing. JM 13:470-80 Apr 49

TRACHTENBERG, I.
Soviet comment on Keynesian theories of full employment. S&S 10:405-09 no.4, 46

TRAYLOR, ORBA FOREST
State taxation of production of blended spirits. NTJ 2:179-84 Jun 49

TREFFTZS, KENNETH LEWIS
The regulation of loans to executive officers of commercial banks. JPE 50:377-96 Jun 42

TRELOGAN, HARRY CHESTER
Federal projects submitted under the Research and Marketing Act of 1946. JFE 29:1383-84 Nov 47

TREMELLONI, ROBERTO
Premises and tasks of the special fund for financing the Italian engineering industry. BNL 1:169-83 Oct 47

TREMELLONI, ROBERTO (Cont.)
The Italian long-term program submitted to
the O.E.E.C. BNL 2:12-24 Jan-Mar 49

TRESS, RONALD CHARLES
The practice of economic planning. MS 16:
192-213 May 48
The diagrammatic representation of national
income flows. Ec N.S.15:276-88 Nov 48

TREVELYAN, GEORGE MACAULAY
John Harold Clapham (1873-1946). [obit.]
EJ 56:499-507 Sep 46

TRICKETT, JOSEPH M.
Planning and controlling sales and production. JM 10:331-35 Apr 46

TRIFFIN, ROBERT
Monopoly in particular-equilibrium and in
general-equilibrium economics. Em 9:
121-27 Apr 41
[The classification of market positions.]
Reply. QJE 56:673-77 Aug 42
International versus domestic money.
AER/S 37:322-24 May 47
National central banking and the international
economy. REStud 14:53-75 no.2, 47

TRIVEDI, P. M.
Agricultural economy: some vital aspects.
IJE 22:189-98 Oct 41
Rural co-operation in India: a study in the
theory and practice of agricultural credit
co-operation. IJE 22:753-77 Jan 42

TROXEL, CHARLES EMERY
Indexes of construction cost for public utility
industries. LE 16:363-68 Aug 40
Capital structure control of utility companies
by the Securities and Exchange Commis-
sion. JB 15:225-47 Jul 42
Incremental cost determination of utility
prices. LE 18:458-67 Nov 42
Limitations of the incremental cost patterns
of pricing. LE 19:28-39 Feb 43
Incremental cost control under public owner-
ship. LE 19:292-99 Aug 43
Incremental cost pricing: a further comment.
LE 20:60-63 Feb 44
Financial management of gas and electric
utilities by the SEC: discussion. JF 3,
no.1:54-58 Feb 48
Holding company integration: several com-
ments. LE 24:86-89 Feb 48
Demand elasticity and control of public
utility earnings. AER 38:372-82 Jun 48
Price discrimination in space heating. LE 24:
281-92 Aug 48
Inflation in price-regulated industries.
JB 22:1-16 Jan 49
Cost behavior and the accounting pattern of
public utility regulation. JPE 57:413-27
Oct 49

TROXEL, EMERY
see Troxel, Charles Emery

TROXELL, JOHN PHILIP
Protecting members' rights within the union.
AER/S 32:460-75 Mar 42

TRUE, RODNEY H.
The Virginia Board of Agriculture, 1841-
1843. AH 14:97-103 Jul 40

TRUESDELL, LEON EDGAR
Population. JASA 40:232-33 Jun 45

TRYNIN, BEN
Cooperative marketing, good and bad.
JM 4:252-57 Jan 40

TSE-CHUN CHANG
see Chang, Tse-Chun

TSIANG, SHO-CHIEH
The effect of population growth on the gen-
eral level of employment and activity.
Ec N.S.9:325-32 Nov 42
A note on speculation and income stability.
Ec N.S.10:286-96 Nov 43
Prof. Pigou on the relative movements of
real wages and employment. EJ 54:
352-65 Dec 44
Rehabilitation of time dimension of invest-
ment in macrodynamic analysis.
Ec N.S.16:204-17 Aug 49

TSOU, P. W.
Modernization of Chinese agriculture.
JFE 28:773-90 Aug 46

TSURU, SHIGETO
Economic fluctuations in Japan, 1868-1893.
REStat 23:176-89 Nov 41

TUCK, WILLIAM R.
The Court of Arbitration in New Zealand.
ER 17:46-56 Jun 41

TUCKER, DONALD SKEELE
Capital money and revenue funds. AER 32:
468-85 Sep 42
and Rogers, B. A. Davis Rich Dewey, 1858-
1942. [obit.] AER 33:236-38 Mar 43
and Rogers, B. A. Davis Rich Dewey, 1858-
1942. [obit.] JASA 38:107-09 Mar 43
The interest rate and saving. JASA 38:
101-02 Mar 43

TUCKER, JAMES F. and Wasserman, M. J.
The U.S. tax treaty program. NTJ 2:33-50
Mar 49

TUCKER, ROBERT HENRY
Some aspects of intergovernmental tax exemption. SEJ 6:273-90 Jan 40

TUCKER, RUFUS STICKNEY
The growth of rigidity in business: discus-
sion. AER/S 30:315-16 Mar 40
Concentration and competition. JM 4:354-61
Apr 40
The frontier as an outlet for surplus labor.
SEJ 7:158-86 Oct 40
The degree of monopoly. QJE 55:167-69
Nov 40
The National Resources Committee's report
on distribution of income. REStat 22:
165-82 Nov 40
Estimates of savings of American families.
REStat 24:9-21 Feb 42
Distribution of income in 1935-36. JASA 37:
489-95 Dec 42

TUCKER, RUFUS STICKNEY (Cont.)
    The composition of income and ownership of
       capital by income classes in the United
       States in 1936. JASA 38:187-200 Jun 43
    [Industry and business statistics.] Discus-
       sion. JASA 40:231 Jun 45
    Postwar output at full employment: a rebut-
       tal. REStat 27:192-96 Nov 45
    [and others] The progress of concentration
       in industry: discussion. AER/S 38:109-20
       May 48
TUCKER, WILLIAM P.
    Populism up-to-date: the story of the
       Farmers' Union. AH 21:198-208 Oct 47
TUGWELL, REXFORD GUY
    A planner's view of agriculture's future.
       JFE 31:29-47 Feb 49
TUN THIN
    see Thin, Maung Tun
TURCK, FENTON B.
    Man-hours as a measurement of marketing
       efficiency. JM 12:499-500 Apr 48
TURNBULL, JOHN GUDERT
    The small business enterprise and the man-
       agement prerogative issue. ILRR 2:33-49
       Oct 48
TURNER, ALEXANDER H.
    Federal marketing and price support legis-
       lation in Canada. JFE 31:594-609 Nov 49
TURNER, CHARLES W.
    Railroad service to Virginia farmers, 1828-
       1860. AH 22:239-48 Oct 48
TURNER, RALPH E.
    Economic discontent in medieval western
       Europe. JEH/S 8:85-100 '48
TURRONI, COSTANTINO BRESCIANI
    see Bresciani-Turroni, Costantino
TURVEY, RALPH
    The inflationary gap. ET 50:10-17 Mar 48
    The multiplier. Ec N.S.15:259-69 Nov 48
    A further note on the inflationary gap.
       ET 51:92-97 Jun 49
    Period analysis and inflation. Ec N.S.16:
       218-27 Aug 49
    Three notes on "Expectation in Economics."
       I. Ec N.S.16:336-38 Nov 49
TVERDOKHLEBOV, V.
    A. Zaitzev (1888-1942). [obit.] EJ 54:138-39
       Apr 44
    T. Chr. Oserov. [obit.] EJ 55:297-98
       Jun-Sep 45
TYLER, PAUL M.
    Minerals and war. HBR 19:1-13 no.1, 40
TYNDALL, DAVID GORDON
    A note on "General equilibrium analysis and
       public policy." CJE 13:118-20 Feb 47
    The stabilization of investment in two public
       utility industries. LE 25:382-96 Nov 49
    A suggestion for the control of peacetime
       inflation. JF 4:315-27 Dec 49
TYSZYNSKI, H.
    Economics of the Wheat Agreement.
       Ec N.S.16:27-39 Feb 49

UCKER, PAUL
    Swiss retail trade and fascism. JM 6:50-53
       Jul 41
UHLMANN, RICHARD
    The war and the wheat market. JB 15:
       131-39 Apr 42
ULLAH, SHAIK ATA
    see Ataullah, Shaik
ULMER, MELVILLE J.
    On the economic theory of cost of living in-
       dex numbers. JASA 41:530-42 Dec 46
ULREY, ORION
    Unsettled questions relating to cooperatives
       and cooperation. JFE 31,pt.2:577-79
       Feb 49
UNDERHILL, HAROLD FABIAN
    Recent Canadian labor relations legislation.
       JPE 48:357-73 Jun 40
    The incidence of payroll taxes. QJE 57:
       160-62 Nov 42
    Pre-war personnel practices in Illinois.
       JB 16:14-27 Jan 43
UNGER, THEO SURÁNYI-
    see Surányi-Unger, Theo
UNTERBERGER, S. HERBERT
    and Henig, H. Wage control in wartime and
       transition. AER 35:319-36 Jun 45
    and Henig, H. Theory of wage control in the
       transition period. SEJ 12:283-89 Jan 46
UNWIN, Sir RAYMOND
    Land values in relation to planning and hous-
       ing in the United States. LE 17:1-9
       Feb 41. Reprinted. LE 27:280-86 Aug 51
UPADHYAYA, P. K.
    What farmers eat in Oudh. IJE 26:641-46
       Apr 46
UPCHURCH, MELVIN LEWIS
    Grazing development in western Oregon: an
       experiment in cooperative land develop-
       ment and control. LE 17:313-19 Aug 41
    The partido system. LE 18:218-19 May 42
    and Henderson, S. Relocation of manpower
       and zoning. LE 19:1-17 Feb 43
    Land economics research: discussion.
       JFE 31,pt.2:1054-55 Nov 49
UPGREN, ARTHUR REINHOLD
    and Hansen, A. H. Some aspects, near-term
       and long-term, of the international posi-
       tion of the United States. AER/S 30,no.5:
       366-72 Feb 41
    International trade: discussion. AER/S 34:
       354-55 Mar 44
    Economic proposals for the peace settlement.
       HBR 22:393-404 no.4, 44
    Fiscal problems of transition and peace:
       discussion. AER/S 35:353-54 May 45
    Objectives and guides to policy. AER/S 35:
       67-84 May 45
UPTON, ROBINSON MILLER
    Expanded cooperation between commercial
       banks and finance companies in financing
       consumer credits. JF 2,no.2:55-67 Oct 47

UPTON, ROBINSON MILLER (Cont.)
Conference on the teaching of business finance. JF 4:243 Sep 49

UQAILI, NABIBUX
Resurrection of banking in Western Pakistan. PEJ 1,no.11:109-11 Jul 49
Agricultural finance in Sind. PEJ 1,no.2: 25-31 Oct 49

URQUHART, MALCOLM C.
Public investment in Canada. CJE 11:535-53 Nov 45
[and others] Social security in a stable prosperity: discussion. AER/S 37:351-66 May 47
Post-war international trade arrangements. CJE 14:373-85 Aug 48

URQUIDI, VICTOR L. [and others]
Present issues of the Latin-American economy: discussion. AER/S 39:406-14 May 49

USEEM, JOHN
Changing economy and rural security in Massachusetts. AH 16:29-40 Jan 42

USHER, ABBOTT PAYSON
The influence of the cod fishery upon the history of the North American seaboard. R. CJE 6:591-99 Nov 40
Institutional methodology in economic history. R. JEH 1:88-96 May 41
[and others] Economic adjustments after wars: discussion. AER/S 32:31-36 Mar 42
The resource requirements of an industrial economy. JEH/S 7:35-46 '47
The role of monopoly in colonial trade and in the expansion of Europe subsequent to 1800. AER/S 38:54-62 May 48
The significance of modern empiricism for history and economics. JEH 9:137-55 Nov 49

USOSKIN, M.
Soviet banking system. PF 2:348-53 no.4, 47

VAILE, ROLAND SNOW
["Income and consumption" by Vaile and Canoyer]: discussion. JM 4,no.4,pt.2: 149-50 Apr 40
Efficiency within the marketing structure. JM 5:350-59 Apr 41
Cash and future prices of corn. JM 9:53-54 Jul 44
Speculation and the price of grain. JM 12: 497-98 Apr 48
Inverse carrying charges in futures markets. JFE 30:574-75 Aug 48
Federal Trade Commission v. Cement Institute. JM 13:224-26 Oct 48
Productivity in distribution. JM 13:385-86 Jan 49
Towards a theory of marketing: a comment. JM 13:520-22 Apr 49

VAKIL, CHANDULAL NAGINDAS
Teaching of economics: change in outlook. IJE 27:331-32 Jan 47

VALK, WILLEM LODEWIJK
The transfer problem and the idea of an international monetary union. EI 1: 246-50 Jan 48

VANCE, LAWRENCE LEE
Grain market forces in the light of inverse carrying charges. JFE 28:1036-40 Nov 46
The interpretation of consumer dis-saving. JM 11:243-49 Jan 47

VANCE, RUPERT BAYLESS
How can the southern population find gainful employment? JFE 22:198-205 Feb 40
and Danilevsky, N. Population and the pattern of unemployment in the Southeast, 1930-1937. SEJ 7:187-203 Oct 40

VANDENHAAG, ERNEST R. MELAMERSON-
see Melamerson-Vandenhaag, Ernest R.

VAN DER HORST, SHEILA T.
Financing the South African war effort. SAJE 9:66-84 Mar 41
[Financing the South African war effort.] II. A reply. SAJE 9:184-89 Jun 41
Inflation in South Africa: some comments on the annual address of the Governor of the Reserve Bank. SAJE 12:238-40 Sep 44
Some reflections on full employment. SAJE 14:1-16 Mar 46
The industrial council system and the community. SAJE 16:274-85 Sep 48
Native urban employment: a study of Johannesburg employment records, 1936-1944. R. SAJE 16:251-59 Sep 48

VAN HISE, CHARLES RICHARD
Science and pragmatics in the education of planners. [Reprinted from Science magazine, v.16, Aug.29, 1902] LE 24:209-20 Aug 48

VAN SICKLE, JOHN VALENTINE
Reform of the federal taxes on personal and corporate income. AER 34:847-49 Dec 44
Regionalism: a tool of economic analysis. AER/S 35:355-67 May 45
The International Labor Office: an appraisal. SEJ 12:357-64 Apr 46
Regional aspects of the problem of full employment at fair wages. SEJ 13:36-45 Jul 46
Geographical aspects of a minimum wage. HBR 24:277-94 no.3, 46
Industrialization and the South. SEJ 15: 412-24 Apr 49

VANVIG, ANDREW and Nodland, T.
The effect of a reduction in farm prices on farm earnings. JFE 31:544-48 Aug 49

VAN WAASDIJK, TOM
Investigation into the distributive trade in blankets (Transvaal), under conditions of controlled and free markets (1947-1948). SAJE 16:342-87 Dec 48
Some notes on price inflation in South Africa 1938-1948. Pt.I-II. SAJE 17:252-73; 380-415 Sep,Dec 49

VARGA, STEPHEN
  Hungary's monetary crisis: comment.
    AER 39:956-60 Sep 49
VASWANI, M. H.
  The theory of location of industries. IJE 27:
    149-56 Oct 46
  Policy of full employment. IJE 27:317-21
    Jan 47
  Scientific management and rationalisation.
    IJE 27:401-07 Apr 47
  Cheap money policy. IJE 28:61-66 Jul 47
  Mixed economy in theory and practice.
    IJE 30:161-66 Oct 49
VATTER, WILLIAM JOSEPH
  Accounting measurements of incremental
    cost. JB 18:145-56 Jul 45
  Cost accounting and statistical cost functions.
    AER 35:940-42 Dec 45
VAUGHAN, FLOYD LAMAR
  [and others] International cartels: discus-
    sion. AER/S 36:768-83 May 46
  Patent policy. AER/S 38:215-34 May 48
VEGH, IMRE DE
  see De Vegh, Imre
VENIT, ABRAHAM H.
  Isaac Bronson: his banking theory and the
    financial controversies of the Jacksonian
    period. JEH 5:201-14 Nov 45
VENKATACHALAM AYYAR, K. L.
  see Ayyar, K. L. Venkatachalam
VENKATASUBBIAH, HIRANYAPPA
  A note on institutionalism in Indian economic
    thought. IJE 22:394-99 Jan 42
  Structural changes in the capitalistic econ-
    omy in relation to its rationale. IJE 24:
    403-08 Apr 44
  [and others] Discussion on "India and inter-
    national economic co-operation." IJE 25:
    626-29 Apr 45
VENKATESAN, S.
  Nationalisation of industries: the role of
    local bodies (with special reference to
    Hyderabad State). IJE 29:301-06 Jan 49
VERDOORN, PETRUS JOHANNES
  Problems of recovery in the Netherlands.
    OIS 9:15-18 Jan 47
VERHULST, MICHEL J. J.
  The pure theory of production applied to the
    French gas industry. Em 16:295-308
    Oct 48
VERLINDEN, CHARLES
  The rise of Spanish trade in the Middle Ages.
    EHR 10:44-59 Feb 40
VERMILYA, HOWARD P.
  Building codes: administration vs. techniques.
    LE 17:129-37 May 41
VERNON, RAYMOND
  Postwar trends in international business or-
    ganization. AER/S 38:94-108 May 48
VIAL, EDMUND ELLSWORTH
  Some examples of differential pricing of
    milk. JM 6,no.4,pt.2:171-73 Apr 42

VICARY, JAMES M.
  Labor, management, and food. HBR 26:
    305-12 May 48
VICKERY, CHARLES WATSON
  Cyclically invariant graduation. Em 12:
    19-25 Jan 44
VICKERY, RAYMOND E.
  and Sant, P. T. Agricultural statistics in
    Germany. JFE 28:1061-69 Nov 46
  and Sant, P. T. The food and agricultural
    statistics of the Reich Food Administra-
    tion. AH 21:177-85 Jul 47
VICKREY, WILLIAM
  The effects of federal revenue acts of 1938,
    1939, and 1940 on the realization of gains
    and losses on securities: comment.
    JASA 36:431-33 Sep 41
  The rationalization of succession taxation.
    Em 12:215-36 Jul-Oct 44
  The effect of averaging on the cyclical
    sensitivity of the yield of the income tax.
    JPE 53:275-77 Sep 45
  Measuring marginal utility by reactions to
    risk. Em 13:319-33 Oct 45
  [and others] Fiscal policy in prosperity and
    depression: discussion. AER/S 38:
    404-16 May 48
  Some objections to marginal-cost pricing.
    JPE 56:218-38 Jun 48
  Limitations of Keynesian economics. SR 15:
    403-16 Dec 48
  Some limits to the income elasticity of in-
    come tax yields. REStat 31:140-44 May 49
VILLARD, HENRY HILGARD
  Further comment on "offset checks."
    AER 30:823-25 Dec 40
  Reply to H. G. Moulton and associates.
    AER 31:570-72 Sep 41
  The effect of the war upon capital markets.
    AER/S 32:369-81 Mar 42
  The problem of bank-held government debt:
    comment. AER 37:936-37 Dec 47
  The inflationary process: comments.
    REStat 31:213-16 Aug 49
VINER, JACOB
  The short view and the long in economic
    policy. AER 30:1-15 Mar 40
  Marshall's economics, in relation to the man
    and to his times. AER 31:223-35 Jun 41
  International relations between state-con-
    trolled national economies. AER/S 34:
    315-29 Mar 44
  Clapham on the Bank of England. R.
    Ec N.S.12:61-68 May 45
  International finance in the post-war world.
    LBR 2:3-17 Oct 46
  --- [idem] JPE 55:97-107 Apr 47
  The Employment Act of 1946 in operation.
    REStat 29:74-79 May 47
  The prospects for foreign trade in the post-
    war world. MS 15:123-38 May 47

VINER, JACOB (Cont.)
  An American view of the British economic
    crisis. LBR 6:28-38 Oct 47
  Bentham and J. S. Mill: the utilitarian back-
    ground. AER 39:360-82 Mar 49
VINING, RUTLEDGE
  A process analysis of bank credit expansion.
    QJE 54:599-623 Aug 40
  Regional variation in cyclical fluctuation
    viewed as a frequency distribution.
    Em 13:183-213 Jul 45
  Location of industry and regional patterns of
    business-cycle behavior. Em 14:37-68
    Jan 46
  The region as a concept in business-cycle
    analysis. Em 14:201-18 Jul 46
  Measuring state and regional business cycles.
    R. JPE 55:346-51 Aug 47
  Koopmans on the choice of variables to be
    studied and of methods of measurement.
    REStat 31:77-94 May 49
  The region as an economic entity and cer-
    tain variations to be observed in the study
    of systems of regions. AER/S 39:89-104
    May 49
VIRTUE, GEORGE OLIEN
  The Federal Coordinator's investigation of
    common carrier subsidies. LE 24:
    340-57 Nov 48
VISWANATHAN, T. V.
  Statistical study of the prices of foodgrains
    in the Madras Presidency. IJE 30:19-29
    Jul 49
VITON, ALBERT
  Trends in world food economy. JFE 29:
    1043-54 Nov 47
VLADECK, STEPHEN CHARNEY
  On the sovereignty of labor unions. ILRR 1:
    480-85 Apr 48
VOESENDORF, ALFRED BERGER-
  see Berger, Alfred Viktor
VOLIN, LAZAR
  The Russian peasant and serfdom. AH 17:
    41-61 Jan 43
  America looks at Russian agriculture.
    JFE 26:46-58 Feb 44
VON BECKERATH, HERBERT
  see Beckerath, Herbert von
VON HAYEK, FRIEDRICH AUGUST
  see Hayek, Friedrich August von
VON MERING, OTTO
  see Mering, Otto von
VON MISES, LUDWIG
  see Mises, Ludwig von
VON NEUMANN, JOHN
  A model of general economic equilibirum
    (translated by G. Morgenstern).
    REStud 13:1-9 no.1, 45
VON SZELISKI, VICTOR SPARTAN
  and Roos, C. F. The determination of inter-
    est rates. JPE 50:501-35 Aug 42
  and Roos, C. F. The demand for durable
    goods. Em 11:97-122 Apr 43

V[OORHIES], E[DWIN] C[OBLENTZ]
  Carl L. Alsberg, 1877-1940. [obit.] JFE 23:
    535-36 May 41
VORCE, CARA HASKELL
  What is the basic drug store pattern? JM 10:
    394-96 Apr 46
VOS, P. J. DE
  see De Vos, P. J.
VOSKUIL, WALTER H.
  and Weidenhammer, R. M. A national fuel
    policy. Pt.II. LE 19:436-51 Nov 43
  Coke: a key industrial material. LE 22:
    339-45 Nov 46
  Postwar Russia and her mineral deposits.
    LE 23:199-213 May 47
  Multiple fuel needs of the American economy.
    LE 24:370-83 Nov 48
VYVER, FRANK TRAVER DE
  see De Vyver, Frank Traver
WAASDIJK, TOM VAN
  see Van Waasdijk, Tom
WACHTEL, SIDNEY BARNETT
  Certain observations on seasonal movements
    in stock prices. JB 15:184-93 Apr 42
WADSWORTH, H. E.
  Utility cloth and clothing scheme.
    REStud 16:82-101 no.2, 49
WAGAR, J. V. K.
  Yellowstone's conception rethought. LE 20:
    55-58 Feb 44
WAGNER, LOUIS C.
  Advertising and the business cycle. JM 6:
    124-35 Oct 41
  Price control in Canada. JM 7:107-14
    Oct 42
WAGNER, MARTIN
  American versus German city planning.
    LE 22:321-38 Nov 46
W[AINES], W. J.
  [Robert McQueen, 1896-1941.] Bibliography.
    CJE 7:281-83 May 41
WAITE, WARREN CLELAND
  and Halvorson, H. W. Relative importance
    of changes in demand and quantity on
    producer revenues. JFE 22:776-79
    Nov 40
  Place of, and limitations to the method.
    JFE 23:317-22 Feb 41
  Indexes of the terms of trade between areas
    in the United States. REStat 24:22-30
    Feb 42
  Price fixing of agricultural products.
    JASA 37:13-21 Mar 42
  The pressure of red point rationing. JM 8:
    422-24 Apr 44
  and Cox, R. W. The influence of prices on
    agricultural production. JFE 26:382-88
    May 44
  A quantitative comparison of agricultural
    price plans. JFE 28:575-87 May 46
  State index numbers of agricultural prices.
    JFE 29:1250-56 Nov 47

WALCH, JACQUES W.
 A survey of the problems of reconstruction
 facing the Fourth Republic. JB 20:67-83
 Apr 47
WALD, ABRAHAM
 The approximate determination of indiffer-
 ence surfaces by means of Engel curves.
 Em 8:144-75 Apr 40
 and Mann, H. B. On the statistical treatment
 of linear stochastic difference equations.
 Em 11:173-220 Jul-Oct 43
 Foundations of a general theory of sequential
 decision functions. Em 15:279-313 Oct 47
WALD, HASKELL PHILIP
 A comparative analysis of three variations
 of retail sales taxes. AER 34:280-302
 Jun 44
 The classical indictment of indirect taxation.
 QJE 59:577-96 Aug 45
 Fiscal policy, military preparedness, and
 postwar inflation. NTJ 2:51-62 Mar 49
WALES, HUGH GREGORY
 The Kansas City wholesale fruit and vegetable
 market. JB 19:161-75 Jul 46
WALKER, CHARLES H.
 Unincorporated investment trusts in the
 nineteenth century. EH 4:341-55 Feb 40
WALKER, CHARLES L., Jr.
 Education and training at International
 Harvester. HBR 27:542-58 Sep 49
WALKER, CHARLES RUMFORD and Richard-
 son, F. L. W., Jr.
 Work flow and human relations. HBR 27:
 107-22 Jan 49
WALKER, EDWARD RONALD
 and Riley, M. E. Australia's war economy:
 developments from December, 1939, to
 May, 1940. ER 16:78-81 Jun 40
 War economy: the nature of the problem.
 ER 16:1-15 Jun 40
 and Osborne, R. G. Federalism in Canada.
 ER 16:245-59 Dec 40
 and Beecroft, R. M. New developments in
 Australia's war economy. ER 17:1-18
 Jun 41
 and Beecroft, R. M. Changes in the stock of
 Australian money. ER 17:210-17 Dec 41
 Total war, with reservations. (Australia's
 war economy, May to October, 1941)
 ER 17:166-79 Dec 41
 and Linford, R. J. War-time price control
 and price movements in an open economy:
 Australia 1914-20 and 1939-40. REStat 24:
 75-86 May 42
 The co-ordination problem in war economy.
 JPE 51:149-55 Apr 43
 War-time economic controls. QJE 58:503-20
 Aug 44
WALKER, GILBERT
 Road and rail: a transatlantic comparison.
 JPE 54:503-21 Dec 46
 The Transport Act 1947. EJ 58:11-30 Mar 48
 Transport in Ireland. R. EJ 59:443-44 Sep 49

WALKER, HERMAN, Jr.
 and Johnson, V. W. Centralization and co-
 ordination of police power for land-con-
 trol measures. LE 17:17-26 Feb 41
 Police power for counties. LE 17:367-72
 Aug 41
 Rural land-use legislation in the states: the
 war years. LE 22:232-58 Aug 46
WALKER, KENNETH FREDERICK
 The psychological assumptions of economics.
 ER 22:66-82 Jun 46
 The American city worker's standard of
 living: a note on technique and content.
 ER 24:250-53 Dec 48
WALKER, KENNETH O.
 The classical economists and the factory
 acts. JEH 1:168-77 Nov 41
WALKER, QUINTON FORREST
 with Collins, W. T. and Higgins, D. E. The
 effects of federal revenue acts of 1938,
 1939, and 1940 on the realization of gains
 and losses on securities. JASA 35:
 602-14 Dec 40; A correction. 36:122
 Mar 41
 --- Rejoinder. JASA 36:433-35 Sep 41
 The nature of the distribution cost problem.
 JM 11:151-58 Oct 46
WALKER, ROSS G.
 Explorations in accounting. HBR 18:384-96
 no.3, 40
 The misinformed employee. HBR 26:267-81
 May 48
WALKER, STUART B.
 Developing products to fit market needs.
 JM 8:268-73 Jan 44
WALL, NORMAN JULIAN
 Discussion of papers on social security for
 farm people. JFE 28:110-13 Feb 46
 Review of papers by R. I. Nowell and R. C.
 Engberg. JFE 29:163-66 Feb 47
WALLACE, DAVID
 Mail questionnaires can produce good
 samples of homogeneous groups. JM 12:
 53-60 Jul 47
WALLACE, DONALD HOLMES
 Kinds of public control to replace or supple-
 ment antitrust laws. AER/S 30:194-212
 Mar 40
 [Price control and rationing in the war-
 peace transition.] Introduction.
 AER/S 35:150-51 May 45
WALLACE, GEORGE S. and Hermens, F. A.
 Inflation and anti-inflation policies in the
 United States, 1939-1949. ZS 105:675-709
 Heft 4, 49
WALLACE, HENRY AGARD
 The use of statistics in the formulation of a
 national full employment policy. JASA 40:
 11-19 Mar 45
WALLACE, IRVING
 Individual firm sales forecasting. JM 13:
 183-88 Oct 48

WALLACE, K. J.
Australian Wool Realization Commission
wool price index. ER 25,(no.49):31-45
Dec 49

WALLICH, HENRY CHRISTOPHER
The future of Latin American dollar bonds.
AER 33:321-35 Jun 43
Income-generating effects of a balanced
budget. QJE 59:78-91 Nov 44
The outlook for Latin America. HBR 23:
65-78 no.1, 44
Effect of taxation on investment. HBR 23:
442-50 no.4, 45
Debt management as an instrument of eco-
nomic policy. AER 36:292-310 Jun 46
The current significance of liquidity prefer-
ence. QJE 60:490-512 Aug 46
The changing significance of the interest rate.
AER 36:761-87 Dec 46
Financing the International Bank. HBR 24:
164-82 no.2, 46

WALLIS, PETER FRANCIS DAINTREE
with Henderson, P. D. and Seers, D. Notes
on estimating national income components.
OIS 11:59-70 Feb-Mar 49
and Seers, D. Changes in real national income. OIS 11:163-76 Jun 49
and Seers, D. A national income matrix.
OIS 11:181-93 Jul-Aug 49

WALLIS, WILSON ALLEN
Compounding probabilities from independent
significance tests. Em 10:229-48
Jul-Oct 42
How to ration consumers' goods and control
their prices. AER 32:501-12 Sep 42
The temporal stability of consumption pat-
terns. REStat 24:177-83 Nov 42
Price control: discussion. AER/S 33:276-78
Mar 43

WALLRABENSTEIN, PAUL P. and Robinson,
T. C. M.
Estimates of agricultural employment and
wage rates. JFE 31:233-52 May 49

WALRATH, ARTHUR J. and Gibson, W. L., Jr.
Inheritance of farm property. JFE 29:
938-51 Nov 47

WALSH, JOHN RAYMOND
Labor's contribution to the war. S&S 7:72-79
no.1, 43

WALSH, ROBERT MERTON
Export market and price of lard. JFE 25:
487-94 May 43
Response to price in production of cotton and
cottonseed. JFE 26:359-72 May 44
Statistics and research in the field of price
analysis. JFE 31,pt.2:714-22 Feb 49

WALTER, GEORGE H.
Non-agricultural factors in land prices.
LE 22:173-76 May 46

WALTERS, ADELAIDE
The International Copper Cartel. SEJ 11:
133-56 Oct 44

WALTERS, PHILIP G. and Walters, R., Jr.
The American career of David Parish.
JEH 4:149-66 Nov 44

WALTERS, RAYMOND, Jr.
and Walters, P. G. (see preceding entry)
The origins of the second Bank of the United
States. JPE 53:115-31 Jun 45

WANG, FOH-SHEN and Ou, P. S.
Industrial production and employment in pre-
war China. EJ 56:426-34 Sep 46

WANTRUP, SIEGFRIED VON CIRIACY-
see Ciriacy-Wantrup, Siegfried von

WARBURTON, CLARK
Measuring the inflationary gap. AER 33:
365-69 Jun 43
Who makes the inflationary gap? AER 33:
607-12 Sep 43
Monetary expansion and the inflationary gap.
AER 34:303-27 Jun 44
Normal production, income, and employment
1945 to 1965. SEJ 11:219-45 Jan 45
Monetary theory, full production, and the
Great Depression. Em 13:114-28 Apr 45
The monetary theory of deficit spending.
REStat 27:74-84 May 45
The volume of money and the price level
between the world wars. JPE 53:150-63
Jun 45
Messrs. Mosak and Salant on wartime infla-
tion: a rejoinder. AER 35:658-60 Sep 45
[The monetary theory of deficit spending.]
A reply. REStat 28:92-94 May 46
[and others] The problem of "full employ-
ment": discussion. AER/S 36:319-35
May 46
The misplaced emphasis in contemporary
business-fluctuation theory. JB 19:199-220
Oct 46
Quantity and frequency of use of money in
the United States, 1919-45. JPE 54:
436-50 Oct 46
A suggestion for post-war taxes. AER 36:
882-91 Dec 46
Volume of savings, quantity of money, and
business instability. JPE 55:222-33 Jun 47
Hansen and Fellner on full employment
policies. AER 38:128-34 Mar 48
[and others] A consideration of the economic
and monetary theories of J. M. Keynes:
discussion. AER/S 38:291-98 Mar 48
Monetary velocity and monetary policy.
REStat 30:304-14 Nov 48
Bank reserves and business fluctuations.
JASA 43:547-58 Dec 48
The secular trend in monetary velocity.
QJE 63:68-91 Feb 49
Monetary policy and business forecasting.
Pt.I-II. JB 22:71-82; 178-87 Apr,Jul 49

WARD, LEWIS B.
Personnel testing. HBR 26:181-93 Mar 48
and Cheskin, L. Indirect approach to market
reactions. HBR 26:572-80 Sep 48

WARD, R. L.
    The taxation of land values in the Transvaal
        by local authorities. SAJE 10:16-35
        Mar 42
    A note on Cape Town's draft rating ordinance.
        SAJE 11:69-75 Mar 43
    The "Uthwatt" report in its relation to site
        value rating in the Transvaal. SAJE 11:
        279-81 Dec 43
WARD, RALPH E.
    Adjusting wheat acreage in the northern
        Great Plains to wartime demand. LE 20:
        344-60 Nov 44
WARE, CAROLINE FARRAR
    Trends in university programs for labor
        education, 1946-1948. ILRR 3:54-69
        Oct 49
WARK, J. M. and Hamilton, J. M.
    Building industry statistics. ER 24:204-17
        Dec 48
WARNE, COLSTON ESTEY
    [The corporation and the historian]: comment.
        JEH/S 4:42-46 Dec 44
WARNER, DONALD F.
    The Farmers' Alliance and the Farmers'
        Union: an American-Canadian parallel-
        ism. AH 23:9-19 Jan 49
WARNER, LUCIEN
    Estimating the character of unsampled seg-
        ments of a universe. JM 12:186-92
        Oct 47
WARREN, EDGAR L.
    Hired farm labor under minimum wage and
        maximum hours regulation. JFE 24:
        296-313 Feb 42
    The Conciliation Service: V-J day to Taft-
        Hartley. ILRR 1:351-62 Apr 48
    and Bernstein, I. The mediation process.
        SEJ 15:441-57 Apr 49
WARREN, STANLEY WHITSON
    Firm and farm management research: dis-
        cussion. JFE 22:118-23 Feb 40
    Farm-management research: discussion.
        JFE 23:237-39 Feb 41
    and Hardin, L. S. Maintaining farm output
        with a scarcity of production factors.
        JFE 25:95-100 Feb 43
    Forty years of farm management surveys.
        JFE 27:18-23 Feb 45
    and Cunningham, L. C. Sampling methods in
        use in some of the farm management re-
        search at Cornell. JFE 29:1267-70 Nov 47
    Size of farm in the Northeast. JFE 31,pt.2:
        596-98 Feb 49
WASSERMAN, MAX JUDD
    The new Ethiopian monetary system. JPE 54:
        358-62 Aug 46
    and Weyl, N. The International Bank, an in-
        strument of world economic reconstruc-
        tion. AER 37:92-106 Mar 47
    and Tucker, J. F. The U.S. tax treaty pro-
        gram. NTJ 2:33-50 Mar 49

WASSON, ROBERT GORDON
    Another view of the historian's treatment of
        business. BHR 18:62-68 Jun 44
    Beveridge's "Full employment in a free
        society." R. HBR 23:507-18 no.4, 45
WATERHOUSE, STUART G.
    An Englishman looks at American marketing
        and distribution policies. JM 12:305-10
        Jan 48
    British marketing today. JM 13:289-94
        Jan 49
WATERMAN, MERWIN H.
    Financial management of gas and electric
        utilities by the Securities and Exchange
        Commission. JF 3,no.1:41-50 Feb 48
WATKINS, D. W.
    [County planning product]: discussion.
        JFE 22:310-14 Feb 40
WATKINS, FREDERICK M.
    Proudhon and the theory of modern liberal-
        ism. CJE 13:429-35 Aug 47
WATKINS, LEONARD LYON, chairman
    Round table on banking reform through su-
        pervisory standards. AER/S 30:230-40
        Mar 40
WATKINS, MYRON WEBSTER
    Present position and prospects of antitrust
        policy. AER/S 32,no.2:89-135 Jun 42
    "Post-war plan and program." R. JPE 51:
        397-414 Oct 43
    Cushman on independent regulatory commis-
        sions. R. JPE 51:547-50 Dec 43
    Scarce raw materials: an analysis and a
        proposal. AER 34:227-60 Jun 44
    [and others] The Sherman Act and the en-
        forcement of competition: discussion.
        AER/S 38:203-14 May 48
    The effectiveness of the federal antitrust
        laws: a symposium. AER 39:720-21
        Jun 49
WATKINS, RALPH JAMES
    Statistical requirements for economic
        mobilization. JASA 44:406-12 Sep 49
WATSON, ALFRED NELSON
    and Lockley, L. C. Some fundamental con-
        siderations in the conduct of polls. JM 5:
        113-15 Oct 40
    Use of small area census data in marketing
        analysis. JM 6,no.4,pt.2:42-47 Apr 42
    Wartime incomes and consumer markets.
        JM 8:231-37 Jan 44
WATSON, JAMES A. S.
    Land ownership, farm tenancy, and farm
        labor in Britain. AH 17:73-80 Apr 43
WATSON, JOHN WHALEY
    Urban developments in the Niagara Peninsula.
        CJE 9:463-86 Nov 43
WAUGH, FREDERICK VAIL
    Programs for using agricultural surpluses
        to reduce malnutrition and to benefit
        farmers. JFE 22:324-34 Feb 40
    State protectionism as a menace to a sound
        agricultural program. JM 4,no.4,pt.2:
        5-10 Apr 40

WAUGH, FREDERICK VAIL (Cont.)
  Training and recruitment of agricultural eco-
    nomic personnel. II. The civil servant.
    JFE 22:415-17 May 40
  Regressions between sets of variables.
    Em 10:290-310 Jul-Oct 42
  Does the consumer benefit from price in-
    stability? QJE 58:602-14 Aug 44
  Food consumption programs as a part of a
    farm program. JFE 26:784-88 Nov 44
  [Does the consumer benefit from price in-
    stability?] Reply. QJE 59:301-03 Feb 45
  Agricultural marketing programs after the
    war. JFE 27:297-302 May 45
  Connecticut's research in milk marketing:
    another opinion. JFE 27:707-09 Aug 45
  A price policy for agriculture, consistent
    with economic progress that will promote
    adequate and more stable income from
    farming. (The third award paper)
    JFE 27:773-84 Nov 45
  What shall we do with surplus foods? JM 10:
    253-57 Jan 46
  Excise taxes and economic stability. JFE 30:
    399-410 Aug 48

WEAVER, ROBERT CLIFTON
  Race restrictive housing covenants. LE 20:
    183-95 Aug 44
  Recent events in Negro union relationships.
    JPE 52:234-49 Sep 44
  Negro employment in the aircraft industry.
    QJE 59:597-625 Aug 45
  Planning for more flexible land use. LE 23:
    29-41 Feb 47

WEBBER, HAROLD H.
  The consumer panel: a method of media
    evaluation. JM 9:137-40 Oct 44

WEBBINK, PAUL
  Unemployment in the United States, 1930-40.
    AER/S 30,no.5:248-72 Feb 41

WEBER, PAUL JOHN
  The economics department of one industrial
    company. HBR 20:381-85 no.3, 42

WEBSTER, BETHUEL MATTHEW
  The effectiveness of the federal antitrust
    laws: a symposium. AER 39:721-22
    Jun 49

WEBSTER, CHARLES K.
  Eileen Power (1889-1940). [obit.] EJ 50:
    561-72 Dec 40

WEEKS, DAVID
  Objectives of area analysis in the northern
    Sierra Nevada. LE 19:153-64 May 43
  European antecedents of land tenures and
    agrarian organization of Hispanic America.
    LE 23:60-75 Feb 47
  The agrarian system of the Spanish American
    colonies. LE 23:153-68 May 47
  Land tenure in Bolivia. LE 23:321-36 Aug 47

WEEKS, HUGH THOMAS [and others]
  Statistics and the statistician in industry.
    JRSS 110:95-107 pt.2, 47

WEHE, ROY A.
  Who will pay for the Central Valley Project
    of California? A reply. LE 23:87-88
    Feb 47

WEHRWEIN, GEORGE SIMON
  Institutional economics in land economic
    theory. JFE 23:161-70 Feb 41
  Changes in farms and farm tenure, 1935-1940.
    LE 17:372-74 Aug 41
  and Johnson, H. A. Zoning land for recrea-
    tion. LE 18:47-57 Feb 42
  and Johnson, H. A. A recreation livelihood
    area. LE 19:193-206 May 43
  The administration of rural zoning. LE 19:
    264-91 Aug 43
  and Taylor, H. C. Richard T. Ely. [obit.]
    LE 19:389-90 Nov 43

WEIDENHAMMER, ROBERT M.
  A national fuel policy. Pt.I-III. [Pt.II by
    Weidenhammer and W. H. Voskuil] LE 19:
    127-40; 436-51; 21:223-35 May,Nov 43,
    Aug 45
  The political economy of international car-
    tels: discussion. AER/S 35:324-28
    May 45

WEIL, FELIX JOSÉ [and others]
  Present issues of the Latin-American
    economy: discussion. AER/S 39:406-14
    May 49

WEIMER, ARTHUR MARTIN
  Federal inducements for small-house con-
    struction. LE 16:101-02 Feb 40
  Potential effects of the defense program on
    housing. LE 17:207-15 May 41
  Housing problems: discussion. AER/S 37:
    524-26 May 47
  Measuring effective demand in the housing
    market. LE 25:111-15 Feb 49

WEIN, HAROLD HERMAN
  Wages and prices: a case study. REStat 29:
    108-23 May 47

WEINBERG, SIDNEY JAMES
  A corporation director looks at his job.
    HBR 27:585-93 Sep 49

WEINBERGER, OTTO
  The importance of Francesco Ferrara in the
    history of economic thought. JPE 48:
    91-104 Feb 40

WEINER, ABRAHAM and Mayer, H.
  The New Jersey Telephone Company case.
    ILRR 1:492-99 Apr 48

WEINRYB, BERNARD D.
  Industrial development of the Near East.
    QJE 61:471-99 May 47

WEINSTEIN, HAROLD R.
  Land hunger and nationalism in the Ukraine,
    1905-1917. JEH 2:24-35 May 42

WEINTRAUB, DAVID
  and Ober, H. Union policies relating to tech-
    nological developments. [Abstract]
    AER/S 30:225-27 Mar 40
  and Magdoff, H. The service industries in
    relation to employment trends. Em 8:
    289-311 Oct 40

WEINTRAUB, RUTH GOLDSTEIN
  and Tough, R.  Federal housing and World
    War II.  LE 18:155-62 May 42
  and Tough, R.  Farms and homes for veter-
    ans.  LE 20:371-73 Nov 44
  and Tough, R.  Socialization in housing,
    Great Britain and the United States.
    LE 22:273-81 Aug 46
  and Tough, R.  The United Nations and chang-
    ing land use in a metropolis.  LE 24:
    186-90 May 48
WEINTRAUB, SIDNEY
  Inflation and price control.  HBR 18:429-36
    no.4, 40
  Compulsory savings in Great Britain.
    HBR 20:53-64 no.1, 41
  Price cutting and economic warfare.  SEJ 8:
    309-22 Jan 42
  Monopoly equilibrium and anticipated de-
    mand.  JPE 50:427-34 Jun 42
  The classification of market positions:
    comment.  QJE 56:666-73 Aug 42
  The foundations of the demand curve.
    AER 32:538-52 Sep 42
  Rationing consumer expenditure.  HBR 21:
    109-14 no.1, 42
  Monopoly pricing and unemployment.  QJE 61:
    108-24 Nov 46
WEISS, HARRY
  Economic coverage of the Fair Labor
    Standards Act.  QJE 58:460-81 May 44
WEISSKOPF, WALTER ALBERT
  Psychological aspects of economic thought.
    JPE 57:304-14 Aug 49
WEISZ, MORRIS
  Conciliation and arbitration in Australia and
    New Zealand.  Pt.II. An analysis of re-
    sults.  ILRR 2:105-12 Oct 48
WEITZELL, E. C.
  Economics of soil conservation.  Pt.I-II.
    LE 19:339-53; 20:330-43 Aug 43, Nov 44
  Maryland's forest conservation law.  LE 19:
    479-80 Nov 43
  Resource development in the Pacific Man-
    dated Islands.  LE 22:199-212 Aug 46
  Evaluating soil conservation.  JFE 29:475-94
    May 47
  --- A rejoinder.  JFE 29:974-76 Nov 47
  and Regan, M. M.  Economic evaluation of
    soil and water conservation measures
    and programs.  JFE 29:1275-94 Nov 47
WELBORN, ROLAND
  Feed grain storage: discussion.  JFE 31,pt.2:
    1008-09 Nov 49
WELCH, ALFRED C. and Root, A. R.
  The continuing consumer study: a basic
    method for the engineering of advertising.
    JM 7:3-21 Jul 42
WELCH, EMMETT H.
  and Haber, W.  The labor force during recon-
    version.  Estimated changes in employ-
    ment and labor force distribution during
    transition period.  REStat 26:194-205
    Nov 44

  and Bancroft, G.  Recent experience with
    problems of labor force measurement.
    JASA 41:303-12 Sep 46
WELCH, FRANK J.
  and Miley, D. G.  Mechanization of the cotton
    harvest.  JFE 27:928-46 Nov 45
  Some economic and social implications of
    agricultural adjustments in the South.
    JFE 29:192-99 Feb 47
WELCKER, JOHN WILLIAM
  The Federal budget: a challenge to business-
    men.  HBR 22:431-42 no.4, 44
  Fair profit?  HBR 26:207-15 Mar 48
  Divergent views on corporate profits.
    HBR 27:250-64 Mar 49
  The community relations problem of indus-
    trial companies.  HBR 27:771-80 Nov 49
WELD, LOUIS DWIGHT HARVELL
  The place of marketing research during a
    national emergency.  JM 4,no.4,pt.2:
    66-69 Apr 40
  Trends in advertising, 1940 [and 1941].
    JM 5:224-25; 6,no.4,pt.2:7-8 Jan 41,
    Apr 42
  chairman.  Report of the Committee on
    Income Classifications.  JM 6:375-79
    Apr 42
WELDEN, WILLIAM CLAYTON
  Formula pricing of class I milk under mar-
    ket orders.  JFE 31,pt.2:420-27 Feb 49
WELDON, JOHN CATHCART
  The multi-product firm.  CJE 14:176-90
    May 48
WELFLING, WELDON
  Some characteristics of savings deposits.
    AER 30:748-58 Dec 40
  Defense activity and coke prices.  SEJ 9:
    134-39 Oct 42
WELINDER, CARSTEN
  On the future of income tax.  NTTO 12:
    275-81 no.37, 48
WELLER, GEORGE ANTHONY
  Control of banking in war-time.  ER 18:
    87-93 Jun 42
WELLES, CHARLES BRADFORD
  The economic background of Plato's com-
    munism.  JEH/S 8:101-14 '48
WELLINGTON, STEPHEN
  Soviet agriculture: a discussion.  I. Queries.
    S&S 11:270-72 no.3, 47
WELLMAN, HARRY RICHARD
  Application and uses of the graphic method
    of multiple correlation.  JFE 23:311-16
    Feb 41
  and Mehren, G. L.  Some considerations of
    research in marketing horticultural
    products.  JFE 28:170-81 Feb 46
  and Mehren, G. L.  Some theoretical aspects
    of agricultural parity price policies and
    national employment.  JFE 28:563-71
    May 46
  chairman.  On the redefinition of parity price
    and parity income.  Report of a committee.
    JFE 29:1358-74 Nov 47

WELLS, ANITA
  Legislative history of treatment of capital
    gains under the federal income tax, 1913-
    1948. NTJ 2:12-32 Mar 49
WELLS, FREDERICK ARTHUR
  Voluntary absenteeism in the cutlery trade.
    REStud 9:158-80 no.2, 42
WELLS, ORIS VERNON
  Agricultural surpluses and nutritional defi-
    cits: a statement of the problem and some
    factors affecting its solution. JFE 22:
    317-23 Feb 40
  Agricultural prices following World War II.
    JFE 26:725-36 Nov 44
  Agricultural legislation: an appraisal of
    current trends and problems ahead.
    JFE 29:41-51 Feb 47
  Parity price and parity income: a dissenting
    comment. JFE 29:1374-76 Nov 47
  Significance of the "general price level" and
    related influences to American agricul-
    ture. JFE 31,pt.2:779-87 Nov 49
WELSH, CHARLES A.
  The Murray report on small business.
    ILRR 1:94-103 Oct 47
WENDT, PAUL FRANCIS
  The control of rubber in World War II.
    SEJ 13:203-27 Jan 47
  The availability of capital to small business
    in California in 1945-1946. JF 2,no.2:
    43-54 Oct 47
  Term loans to small business in California,
    1945-46. JF 3,no.2:45-58 Jun 48
  Administrative problems under the British
    Town and Country Planning Act of 1947.
    LE 25:427-32 Nov 49
WENGERT, NORMAN
  The land, TVA, and the fertilizer industry.
    LE 25:11-21 Feb 49
WENSLEY, A. J. and Florence, P. S.
  Recent industrial concentration, especially
    in the Midlands. REStud 7:139-58 Jun 40
WERNETTE, JOHN PHILIP
  Financing the defense program. AER 31:
    754-66 Dec 41
  Guns and butter? HBR 19:286-97 no.3, 41
  [and others] Effects of the war and defense
    program upon economic conditions and
    institutions: discussion. AER/S 32:
    426-31 Mar 42
WERNIMONT, KENNETH
  State rural land use legislation in 1939 [and
    1940]. LE 16:110-16; 17:103-08 Feb 40,
    Feb 41
  and Davidson, R. D. Tenure arrangements
    in Oklahoma oil fields. LE 19:40-58
    Feb 43
WESTCOTT, GEORGE WILLIAM
  Postwar extension problems in general agri-
    cultural economics. JFE 28:199-212
    Feb 46
  Research needed in economics for farm and
    home planning. JFE 29:175-82 Feb 47

WESTERFIELD, RAY BERT
  The objectives of monetary policy: discus-
    sion. AER/S 30:39-40 Mar 40
  [and others] Effects of the war and defense
    program upon economic conditions and in-
    stitutions: discussion. AER/S 32:382-90
    Mar 42
  chairman. The future of interest rates.
    [Abstract of specialized conference dis-
    cussion] AER/S 32:217-26 Mar 42
  Amortization of mortgage premiums. LE 20:
    316-29 Nov 44
  [and others] Banking problems: discussion.
    AER/S 37:289-98 May 47
  Irving Fisher. [obit.] AER 37:656-61 Sep 47
WESTERMANN, WILLIAM LINN
  Industrial slavery in Roman Italy. JEH 2:
    149-63 Nov 42
WESTON, JOHN FREDERICK
  Profit as the payment for the function of un-
    certainty-bearing. JB 22:106-18 Apr 49
  Enterprise and profit. JB 22:141-59 Jul 49
  Some theoretical aspects of formula timing
    plans. JB 22:249-70 Oct 49
  Incidence and effects of the corporate in-
    come tax. NTJ 2:300-15 Dec 49
WESTSTRATE, CORNELIS
  The economic and political implications of
    a customs union. QJE 62:362-80 May 48
WETTEREAU, JAMES O.
  The branches of the first Bank of the United
    States. JEH/S 2:66-100 Dec 42
WEXLER, HARVEY JOSEPH
  How to succeed in business, 1840-1860.
    EEH 1,no.1:26-29 Jan 49
  Business opinion and economic theory, 1840-
    1860. EEH 1,no.3:10-18 Mar 49
WEYL, NATHANIEL and Wasserman, M. J.
  The International Bank, an instrument of
    world economic reconstruction. AER 37:
    92-106 Mar 47
WHALE, PHILIP BARRETT
  A retrospective view of the Bank Charter
    Act of 1844. Ec N.S.11:109-11 Aug 44
WHEELER, RICHARD GIBBS and Brinser, A.
  Farm planning as a basis for extending ag-
    ricultural credit. JFE 30:243-58 May 48
WHEELER, WILLARD C.
  The victory merchandise bond plan. JM 8:
    58-61 Jul 43
WHELPTON, PASCAL KIDDER
  and Fels, B. An industrial classification for
    reports from individuals. JASA 35:74-85
    Mar 40
  Mr. Gottlieb on optimum population: an ob-
    jection. JPE 54:368 Aug 46
WHETHAM, EDITH H.
  War-time changes in agricultural marketing.
    LBR 7:33-46 Jan 48
WHITE, BENNETT SEXTON, Jr.
  The shrinking foreign market for United
    States cotton. QJE 54:255-76 Feb 40
  Cotton situation: discussion. JFE 23:131-37
    Feb 41

WHITE, BENNETT SEXTON, Jr. (Cont.)
  and Denhardt, E. T.  Chronic surpluses of
    agricultural commodities in the post-war
    period.  JFE 25:743-58 Nov 43
  Selecting marketing projects: discussion.
    JFE 31,pt.2:1224-27 Nov 49
WHITE, GERALD T.
  Financing industrial expansion for war: the
    origin of the Defense Plant Corporation
    leases.  JEH 9:156-83 Nov 49
WHITE, GILBERT F.
  State regulation of flood-plain use.  LE 16:
    352-57 Aug 40
WHITE, HARRY DEXTER
  Postwar currency stabilization.  AER/S 33:
    382-87 Mar 43
WHITE, HORACE GLENN, Jr.
  Foreign trading in American stock-exchange
    securities.  JPE 48:655-702 Oct 40
WHITE, JOHN W.
  Poverty within agriculture: discussion.
    JFE 31,pt.2:1118-20 Nov 49
WHITE, JOSEPH H.
  Measuring local markets.  JM 12:220-33
    Oct 47
  Discretionary spending power at multiple
    levels.  JM 13:1-11 Jul 48
WHITE, KENNETH D.
  The neglect of economic factors in the study
    of Roman history.  Pt.I-III.  SAJE 16:
    422-29; 17:194-201; 18:196-204 Dec 48,
    Jun 49, Jun 50
WHITE, MATILDA
  and Zeisel, J.  Reading indices.  JM 6:103-11
    Oct 41
  Ideal conditions for product testing.  JM 11:
    55-61 Jul 46
WHITE, MELVIN IRVIN
  Personal income tax reduction in a hypotheti-
    cal contraction.  REStat 31:63-68 Feb 49
WHITE, REVEL CLYDE
  The social insurance movement.  JASA 38:
    358-64; 39:520-21 Sep 43, Dec 44
WHITE, WILLIAM R. [and others]
  Banking problems: discussion.  AER/S 37:
    289-98 May 47
WHITEHILL, ARTHUR M., Jr.
  Location of potential labor reserves from
    published data.  SEJ 13:257-62 Jan 47
WHITLAM, A. G.
  Food and Agricultural Organization of the
    United Nations.  ER 22:289-92 Dec 46
WHITMAN, ROSWELL HARTSON
  A note on the concept of "degree of monopoly."
    EJ 51:261-69 Jun-Sep 41
WHITNALL, GORDON
  Urban disintegration and the future of land
    investments.  LE 17:440-51 Nov 41
WHITNEY, NATHANIEL R.
  The economist as adviser.  HBR 20:379-80
    no.3, 42
WHITTAKER, EDMUND
  Wealth and welfare.  AER 30:580-82 Sep 40

Professor Whittaker on indifference curves:
  a rejoinder.  AER 31:835-36 Dec 41
WHITTINGHILL, D. C.
  Manufacturer's sales research helps large
    customers to grow.  JM 7:203-05 Jan 43
WHITTLESEY, CHARLES RAYMOND
  Round table on problems of American com-
    mercial policy.  [Summary of remarks]
    AER/S 30:123 Mar 40
  Retirement of internally held debt.  AER 33:
    602-04 Sep 43
  Problems of our domestic money and bank-
    ing system.  AER/S 34:245-59 Mar 44
  Reserve requirements and the integration
    of credit policies.  QJE 58:553-70 Aug 44
  Federal Reserve policy in transition.
    QJE 60:340-50 May 46
  Memorandum on the stability of demand de-
    posits.  AER 39:1192-1203 Dec 49
  Political aspects of the gold problem.
    JEH/S 9:50-60 '49
WICKENS, ARYNESS JOY
  The meaning of unemployment statistics.
    JASA 36:167-74 Jun 41
  and Williams, F. M.  Notes on Mr. Teper's
    observations.  JASA 38:284-86 Sep 43
  What the cost-of-living index is.  JB 17:
    146-61 Jul 44
  The public debt and national income.
    AER/S 37:184-91 May 47
WIDENER, HOMER WILLIAM
  Marketing rewritten from the consumer's
    point of view.  R.  JM 4,no.4,pt.2:124-31
    Apr 40
WIGGLESWORTH, EDWIN
  International balance of payments, 1941.
    JM 6:290-92 Jan 42
WIJNHOLDS, H. W. J.
  Some observations on foreign exchange rates
    in theory and practice.  SAJE 15:235-47
    Dec 47
  --- Further observations.  SAJE 16:309
    Sep 48
WILBUR, CLARENCE MARTIN
  Industrial slavery in China during the
    former Han Dynasty (206 B.C.-A.D. 25).
    JEH 3:56-69 May 43
WILCOX, CLAIR
  Price control policy in the postwar transition.
    AER/S 35:163-74 May 45
  The London draft of a charter for an Inter-
    national Trade Organization.  AER/S 37:
    529-41 May 47
WILCOX, EMERY C. and Ebling, W. H.
  Presentation of agricultural data in the
    states.  JFE 31,pt.2:309-22 Feb 49
WILCOX, WALTER WILLIAM
  with Goodsell, W. D. and Jessen, R. J.  Pro-
    cedures which increase the usefulness of
    farm management research.  JFE 22:
    753-61 Nov 40
  and Bunce, A. C.  Neglected point in the eco-
    nomics of the soil: a reply.  JFE 23:
    475-77 May 41

WILCOX, WALTER WILLIAM (Cont.)
Regional changes in farming: discussion.
JFE 24:273-76 Feb 42
Capital in agriculture. QJE 58:49-64 Nov 43
Discussion of papers on postwar agricultural
problems. JFE 28:264-66 Feb 46
The economy of small farms in Wisconsin.
JFE 28:458-75 May 46
The wartime use of manpower on farms.
JFE 28:723-41 Aug 46
Research in economics of farm production.
JFE 29:632-43 Aug 47
The efficiency and stability of American
agriculture. JFE 30:411-21 Aug 48
and Rauchenstein, E. The effect of size of
herd on milk production costs. JFE 30:
713-23 Nov 48
High farm income and efficient resource use.
JFE 31:555-57 Aug 49
Comments on agricultural policy. JFE 31,
pt.2:806-13 Nov 49
WILCOXEN, LEWIS C.
The market forecasting significance of mar-
ket movements. JASA 37:343-51 Sep 42
WILLCOX, WALTER FRANCIS
Josiah Charles Stamp, 1880-1941. [obit.]
JASA 36:546-47 Dec 41
[Tribute to Walter F. Willcox.] Response.
JASA 42:7-10 Mar 47
WILLIAMS, BRUCE RODDA
Mr. Swan's theory of price flexibility. ER 22:
275-82 Dec 46
Further note on a homogeneous system.
ER 24:104-08 Jun 48
Types of competition and the theory of em-
ployment. OEP N.S.1:121-44 Jan 49
WILLIAMS, ELGIN
Nicholas Barbon: an early economic realist.
SEJ 11:45-55 Jul 44
WILLIAMS, ERNEST WILLIAM, Jr.
Railroad traffic and costs. AER 33:360-65
Jun 43
Railroad rate levels and earning power in an
era of competitive transport. LE 25:
405-13 Nov 49
WILLIAMS, FAITH MOORS
Factors to be considered in measuring inter-
city and interregional differences in living
costs. JASA 35:471-82 Sep 40
with Rice, F. R. and Schell, E. D. Cost of
living indexes in wartime. JASA 37:415-24
Dec 42
and Wickens, A. J. Notes on Mr. Teper's
observations. JASA 38:284-86 Sep 43
and Brady, D. S. Advances in the techniques
of measuring and estimating consumer expenditures. JFE 27:315-44 May 45
and Hoover, E. D. Measuring price and quality of consumers' goods. JM 10:354-69
Apr 46
WILLIAMS, J.
Professor Douglas' production function.
ER 21:55-63 Jun 45

WILLIAMS, JOHN HENRY
Deficit spending. AER/S 30,no.5:52-66
Feb 41
The implications of fiscal policy for monetary
policy and the banking system. AER/S 32:
234-49 Mar 42
The postwar monetary plans. AER/S 34:
372-84 Mar 44
An appraisal of Keynesian economics.
AER/S 38:273-90 May 48
WILLIAMS, MELVILLE C. and Musbach, W. F.
Rural zoning in Minnesota. LE 16:105-09
Feb 40
WILLIAMS, RANDALL SMALLWOOD, Jr.
Fiscal policy and the propensity to consume.
EJ 55:390-97 Dec 45
WILLIAMS, ROBERT MARTIN and Cassady,
R, Jr.
Radio as an advertising medium. HBR 27:
62-78 Jan 49
WILLIAMSON, HAROLD FRANCIS
[What is economic history?] Comment.
JEH/S 4:25-28 Dec 44
Prophecies of scarcity or exhaustion of
natural resources in the United States.
AER/S 35:97-109 May 45
WILLIAMSON, KOSSUTH MAYER
Connecticut state tax survey. NTJ 2:371-74
Dec 49
WILLIAMSON, LUCILLE and Williamson, P.
What we eat. JFE 24:698-703 Aug 42
WILLIAMSON, PAUL
see Williamson, Lucille and Williamson, P.
WILLIAMSON, WILLIAM F.
The place of coffee in trade with Latin
America. JM 6,no.4,pt.2:149-51 Apr 42
WILLIS, JOHN BROOKE
Secondary reserve requirements. JF 3,no.2:
29-44 Jun 43
The case against the maintenance of the war-
time pattern of yields on government se-
curities. AER/S 37:216-27 May 47
Postwar changes in commercial bank invest-
ments in U.S. government securities.
JF 4:140-55 Jun 49
WILLS, JOHN ELLIOT
Effects of technological changes on cost re-
duction in agriculture: effects in the
Midwest. JFE 31,pt.2:448-50 Feb 49
WILLS, JOHN HARVEY
Postwar monetary and credit policies: dis-
cussion. JF 4:114-18 Jun 49
WILMERDING, LUCIUS, Jr.
Public debt: history: discussion. AER/S 37:
151-54 May 47
WILSEY, HARRY LAWRENCE
The use of sinking funds in preferred stock
issues. JF 2,no.2:31-42 Oct 47
The Investment Advisers Act of 1949. JF 4:
286-97 Dec 49
WILSON, ARCHIE DELL
Settler relocation: a progress report on the
"Minnesota plan." LE 17:102-03 Feb 41

WILSON, C. F.
[The new wheat condition figures, based on weather factors, for the Prairie Provinces.] A reply. JASA 37:483-88 Dec 42

--- A further reply. JASA 39:99-100 Mar 44

WILSON, CHARLES
Treasure and trade balances: the mercantilist problem. EHR II.2:152-61 no.2, 49

WILSON, Sir DUNCAN
Factory inspection: a thirty-five years retrospect. JRSS 104:209-24 pt.3, 41

WILSON, EDWIN BIDWELL
and Worcester, J. Frequency functions fitted by moments. REStat 25:97-100 Feb 43

Pareto on Marshall's demand curve. QJE 58:141-45 Nov 43

On notation for utility theory. QJE 58:647-50 Aug 44

Hicks on perfect substitutes. QJE 59:134-40 Nov 44

and Worcester, J. The normal logarithmic transform. REStat 27:17-22 Feb 45

Consumption in fixed proportion. QJE 59:635-39 Aug 45

Notes on utility theory and demand equations. QJE 60:453-60 May 46

John Law and John Keynes. QJE 62:381-95 May 48

WILSON, ELEANOR MARY CARUS-
see Carus-Wilson, Eleanor Mary

WILSON, FRANCIS G.
Ethics in the study of democratic politics. AER/S 34:41-47 Mar 44

WILSON, GEORGE LLOYD
and Rose, J. R. Pacific Gas and Electric case: reply. AER 30:827-29 Dec 40

Railroad land-grant rates. JB 15:266-78 Jul 42

Freight rates in wartime. HBR 21:230-37 no.2, 43

and Kramer, R. L. Postwar shipping policy: discussion. AER/S 36:575-78 May 46

and Rose, J. R. "Out-of-pocket" cost in railroad freight rates. QJE 60:546-60 Aug 46

WILSON, JAMES HAROLD
Industrial activity in the eighteenth century. Ec N.S.7:150-60 May 40

WILSON, JOHN M.
How the National Cash Register Company views the responsibilities of sales management. JM 10:283-88 Jan 46

WILSON, JOHN ROBERTSON McKAY
Report of the Royal Commission on the taxation of annuities and family corporations, 1945. CJE 12:87-92 Feb 46

WILSON, JOHN STUART GLADSTONE
Further developments in Australia's war economy (October, 1941 to April, 1942). ER 18:43-57 Jun 42

The octopus of control. (Australia's war economy May to October, 1942) ER 18:192-208 Dec 42

The present versus the future. (Australia's war economy November, 1942, to May, 1943) ER 19:23-37 Jun 43

The Western Australian basic wage, 1926-42. ER 19:83-93 Jun 43

Prospects of full employment in Australia. ER 22:99-116 Jun 46

Australia's central bank. JPE 55:28-38 Feb 47

The future of banking in Australia. EJ 59:208-18 Jun 49

Investment in a monetary economy. Ec N.S.16:321-35 Nov 49

WILSON, MILBURN LINCOLN
Problem of poverty in agriculture. JFE 22:10-29 Feb 40

Nutritional science and agricultural policy. JFE 24:188-205 Feb 42

and Dixon, H. M. Farm and home planning: a new approach to farm management extension work. JFE 29:167-74 Feb 47

WILSON, R. F.
New Zealand production. ER 17:252-55 Dec 41

WILSON, THOMAS
Capital theory and the trade cycle. REStud 7:169-79 Jun 40

Price and outlay policy of state enterprise. EJ 55:454-61 Dec 45

A reconsideration of the theory of effective demand. R. Ec N.S.14:283-95 Nov 47

Private enterprise and the theory of value. MS 16:165-91 May 48

Programmes and allocations in the planned economy. OEP N.S.1:40-53 Jan 49

The January 1949 economic report of the President: appraisal. REStat 31:166-72 Aug 49

WINGATE, JOHN WILLIAMS
Current trends in retail distribution. JM 5:410-18 Apr 41

WINKLÉ, F. F.
Some aspects of the recent inflation and stabilization of the Hungarian currency. SAJE 15:178-91 Sep 47

WINN, WILLIS JAY
with Beale, W. T. M., Jr. and Kennedy, M. T. Commodity reserve currency: a critique. JPE 50:579-94 Aug 42

Commodity-reserve currency: a rejoinder. JPE 51:175-77 Apr 43

WINTERGALEN, EDWARD HENRY
Teachers' cooperative training courses. RSE 7,no.1:82-85 Mar 49

WINTERNITZ, J.
Values and prices: a solution of the so-called transformation problem. EJ 58:276-80 Jun 48

WINTERS, LAURENCE MERRIAM and Dowell, A. A.
Economic aspects of artificial insemination

WINTERS, LAURENCE MERRIAM and Dowell,
A. A. (Cont.)
    of commercial dairy cows. JFE 24:
    665-76 Aug 42
WINTERS, ROBERT ALONZO
    Aspects of joint bargaining in the rubber in-
    dustry. ILRR 3:3-16 Oct 49
WINTON, EILEEN MARIE
    "Wages fund theory and the popular influence
    of economists": a reply. AER 31:343-44
    Jun 41
WINTON, J. R.
    The value of the rupee. LBR 4:42-48 Apr 47
WIRTENBERGER, HENRY J.
    Public policy and postwar employment in the
    United States. RSE 3:45-52 Dec 44
WISE, HENRY LESLIE
    War-time price control in New Zealand.
    ER 17:180-91 Dec 41
    Some aspects of price stabilization in New
    Zealand. ER 18:180-91 Dec 42
    Price stabilization in New Zealand. ER 19:
    38-45 Jun 43
    Stabilization of land values in New Zealand.
    ER 19:225-30 Dec 43
WISE, MARY HILTON
    see Smelker, Mary Wise
WITNEY, FRED
    Union-shop and strike-vote elections: a
    legislative fallacy. ILRR 2:247-50 Jan 49
    The appropriate bargaining unit controversy.
    SEJ 16:170-88 Oct 49
WITT, LAWRENCE W.
    Changes in the agriculture of south central
    Brazil. JFE 25:622-43 Aug 43
    Some further world trade problems; a review
    of Professor Jesness' paper. JFE 31,pt.2:
    825-31 Nov 49
WITTAUSCH, WILLIAM KARL
    Used homes in the low-cost housing market.
    LE 18:350-56 Aug 42
    Postwar competition for mass-produced,
    low-cost housing. JM 8:375-81 Apr 44
    Marketing prefabricated houses. HBR 26:
    693-712 Nov 48
WITTE, EDWIN EMIL
    What's ahead in social security. HBR 19:
    311-25 no.3, 41
    A critique of Mr. Arnold's proposed antilabor
    amendments to the antitrust laws.
    AER/S 32:449-59 Mar 42
    American post-war social security proposals.
    AER 33:825-38 Dec 43
    What to expect of social security. AER/S 34:
    212-21 Mar 44
    1944-1945 programs for postwar social se-
    curity and medical care. REStat 27:
    171-88 Nov 45
    Steadying the worker's income. HBR 24:
    306-25 no.3, 46
    [and others] Social security in a stable pros-
    perity: discussion. AER/S 37:351-66
    May 47

The university and labor education. ILRR 1:
    3-17 Oct 47
Wartime handling of labor disputes. HBR 25:
    169-89 no.2, 47
Labor-management relations under the Taft-
    Hartley Act. HBR 25:554-75 no.4a, 47
An appraisal of the Taft-Hartley Act.
    AER/S 38:368-82 May 48
Where we are in industrial relations.
    IRRA 1:6-20 Dec 48
The Taft-Hartley Act in operation: a brief
    appraisal. ILRR 2:403-06 Apr 49
WOHL, RUBIN RICHARD
    An historical context for entrepreneurship.
    [Pt.I]-III. EEH 1,no.2:8-16; no.4:18-27;
    no.6:1-10 Feb,Apr,Jun 49
    [Aitken's Analysis of business decisions.]
    EEH 1,no.3:26-29 Mar 49
    A further note on Aitken's parametric ap-
    proach. EEH 2:51-53 Nov 49
WOLCOTT, LEON
    Regionalism: political implement.
    AER/S 35:368-76 May 45
WOLD, HERMAN OLE ANDREAS
    On Giffen's paradox. NTTO 12:283-93
    no.37, 48
    Statistical estimation of economic relation-
    ships. Em 17,suppl.:1-21 Jul 49; Errata.
    19:227 Apr 51
WOLF, ALOIS F.
    Measuring the effect of agricultural advertis-
    ing. JFE 26:327-47 May 44
WOLF, HARRY DeMERLE, chairman
    Wartime materials in the field of labor.
    [Report of a subcommittee] AER/S 37:
    671-80 May 47
WOLF, RICHARD BENJAMIN
    Collective bargaining in small-scale indus-
    try: a case study. HBR 27:706-14 Nov 49
WOLFBEIN, SEYMOUR L. and Jaffe, A. J.
    Internal migration and full employment
    in the U.S. JASA 40:351-63 Sep 45
WOLFE, ALBERT BENEDICT
    "Full utilization," equilibrium, and the ex-
    pansion of production. QJE 54:539-65
    Aug 40
    Schisms in agricultural policy: discussion.
    JFE 24:514-17 May 42
    Economy and democracy. AER 34:1-20
    Mar 44
    Price-making in a democracy. R. JPE 53:
    73-78 Mar 45
    Undergraduate teaching of economics: dis-
    cussion. AER/S 36:848-52 May 46
    The economic mind in American civilization.
    R. JPE 55:65-68 Feb 47
WOLFE, HARRY DEANE
    Grocery prices and marketing functions.
    JM 6:27-30 Jul 41
    Dispersion of consumer purchases among
    competing retail outlets. JB 15:160-65
    Apr 42
    Techniques of appraising brand preference

WOLFE, HARRY DEANE (Cont.)
 and brand consciousness by consumer
  interviewing. JM 6,no.4,pt.2:81-87 Apr 42
WOLFF, PIETER de
 Income elasticity of demand, a micro-eco-
  nomic and a macro-economic interpreta-
  tion. EJ 51:140-45 Apr 41
WOLFF, REINHOLD PAUL
 Foreign experience with retail price controls.
  JM 5:143-47 Oct 40
WOLL, MILTON
 The need for better rental data. LE 17:
  226-28 May 41
WOLMAN, LEO
 Labor policy and economic history.
  JEH/S 5:86-92 Dec 45
WOMER, STANLEY
 Some applications of the continuous consumer
  panel. JM 9:132-36 Oct 44
WOOD, ALBERT J.
 and Schreier, F. T.  Motivation analysis in
  market research. JM 13:172-82 Oct 48
 and Schreier, F. T.  Reply to criticism by
  Lazare Teper on "Motivation analysis in
  market research." JM 14:453-56 Oct 49
WOOD, ELIZABETH
 The role of the government in defense hous-
  ing. LE 16:382-85 Nov 40
WOOD, ELMER [and others]
 Domestic versus international equilibrium:
  discussion. AER/S 37:581-94 May 47
WOOD, G. BURTON
 Training agricultural economic majors for
  business careers. JFE 29:1341-54 Nov 47
WOOD, GORDON LESLIE
 The economic implications of peace for Aus-
  tralia. ER 16:82-95 Jun 40
 Federal finance in India. R. ER 17:106-09
  Jun 41
 Economic aspects of war damage compensa-
  tion. ER 18:77-82 Jun 42
 American thought on reconstruction. R.
  ER 18:228-31 Dec 42
 The future of federal aid. ER 21:197-211
  Dec 45
 Power or palsy in the federation? R. ER 23:
  90-95 Jun 47
 International economic co-operation and the
  Australian economy. ER 23:159-76 Dec 47
 Financial systems in federations. R. ER 24:
  235-37 Dec 48
WOOD, LORING and Stewart, C.
 Employment statistics in the planning of a
  full-employment program. JASA 41:
  313-21 Sep 46
WOOD, MARSHALL and Dantzig, G. B.
 Programming of interdependent activities. I.
  General discussion. Em 17:193-99
  Jul-Oct 49
WOOD, RALPH CLINTON
 The control of rubber: a case study. JM 7:
  99-106 Oct 42

WOOD, RICHARDSON
 The corporation goes into politics. HBR 21:
  60-70 no.1, 42
 The community goes into business. HBR 26:
  144-55 Mar 48
 Market research and industrial development.
  JM 12:503-04 Apr 48
WOODBURY, COLEMAN
 Objectives and accomplishments of the
  veterans' emergency housing program.
  AER/S 37:508-23 May 47
 Richard T. Ely and the beginnings of research
  in urban land and housing economics.
  LE 25:55-66 Feb 49
 Urban land economics: a new textbook. R.
  LE 25:313-15 Aug 49
 Housing in the redevelopment of American
  cities. LE 25:397-404 Nov 49
WOODBURY, ROBERT MORSE
 Quantity adjustment factors in cost-of-living
  ratios. Em 8:322-32 Oct 40
 Economic consumption scales and their uses.
  JASA 39:455-68 Dec 44
WOODCOCK, FRED
 The price of provisions and some social con-
  sequences in Worcestershire in the
  eighteenth and nineteenth centuries.
  JRSS 106:268-72 pt.3, 43
WOODEN, WALTER B.
 The cement basing point case. JM 13:220-22
  Oct 48
WOODS, H. D.
 The Dawson Report on Nova Scotia. R.
  CJE 12:496-505 Nov 46
WOODWARD, CARL R.
 Woodrow Wilson's agricultural philosophy.
  AH 14:129-42 Oct 40
WOODWARD, DONALD BOSLEY
 [and others] The changing structure of the
  American economy: discussion.
  AER/S 36:80-92 May 46
 Public debt and institutions. AER/S 37:
  157-83 May 47
WOODWELL, WILLIAM H.
 The Woodwell shipyard, 1759-1852. BHR 21:
  58-74 Jun 47
WOODWORTH, HARRY CLARK
 Land economics: discussion. JFE 24:
  251-53 Feb 42
 Farm management research needs in New
  England. JFE 26:503-13 Aug 44
WOODYARD, ELLA and Thorndike, E. L.
 The cost of living in cities in relation to
  their size and latitude. JASA 38:238-41
  Jun 43
WOOFTER, THOMAS JACKSON, Jr.
 A method of analysis of family composition
  and income. JASA 39:488-96 Dec 44
WOOLF, LEONARD
 Beatrice Webb. (1858-1943). [obit.] EJ 53:
  284-90 Jun-Sep 43
WOOLLEY, CATHERINE
 Companies never remember. BHR 15:62-64
  Oct 41

WOOLLEY, ELLIOTT BALLANTYNE
  The method of minimized areas as a basis
    for correlation analysis. Em 9:38-62
    Jan 41
WOOLLEY, HERBERT BALLANTYNE
  The anomalous case of the shifting cost
    curve. QJE 57:646-56 Aug 43
  The general elasticity of demand. Em 15:
    226-30 Jul 47
WOOLSTON, MAXINE YAPLE
  German corporate profits: 1926-1938.
    QJE 54:384-98 May 40
WOOSLEY, JOHN BROOKS
  The capital problem of small and medium-
    sized businesses. SEJ 7:461-74 Apr 41
WOOTEN, HUGH H.
  Farming opportunities for veterans. LE 21:
    259-67 Aug 45
  The agricultural flood control program. R.
    LE 22:35-47 Feb 46
WORCESTER, DEAN AMORY, Jr.
  Economics, politics, and consumer subsidies.
    SEJ 11:56-62 Jul 44
  Postwar markets for consumer goods. JM 9:
    234-38 Jan 45
  A reconsideration of the theory of rent.
    AER 36:258-77 Jun 46
  The dynamic theory of rents: a comment.
    CJE 13:283-85 May 47
  Justifiable price "discrimination" under con-
    ditions of natural monopoly: a diagram-
    matic representation. AER 38:382-88
    Jun 48
WORCESTER, JANE
  and Wilson, E. B. Frequency functions fitted
    by moments. REStat 25:97-100 Feb 43
  and Wilson, E. B. The normal logarithmic
    transform. REStat 27:17-22 Feb 45
WORKER, JOHN, pseud.
  My union: an inside story. HBR 26:108-14
    Jan 48
WORKING, ELMER JOSEPH
  Crop-yield index numbers. JFE 22:701-13
    Nov 40
  and Shepherd, G. S. Notes on the discussion
    of the graphic method of correlation analy-
    sis. JFE 23:322-23 Feb 41
  Some problems in the control of food prices.
    JM 6,no.4,pt.2:29-36 Apr 42
  Crop yield index numbers: some comments
    on Hirsch's views. JFE 25:874-81 Nov 43
  Price control and the wartime pricing of
    farm products. JFE 26:110-21 Feb 44
  Work of the Committee on Agricultural
    Price Supports and Their Consequences.
    AER/S 35:419-21 May 45
  Report of ad hoc Committee on Agricultural
    Price Supports. AER/S 36:817-26 May 46
  [and others] [Wage-price relations at high
    level employment]: discussion. AER/S 37:
    254-64 May 47
WORKING, HOLBROOK
  War and commodity prices. JASA 35:309-24
    Jun 40

Quotations on commodity futures as price
  forecasts. Em 10:39-52 Jan 42
Agricultural price policies in war time.
  JFE 24:557-70 Aug 42
Agricultural price policy: discussion.
  JFE 25:16-18 Feb 43
Statistical laws of family expenditure.
  JASA 38:43-56 Mar 43
Reflections on the President's Economic
  report. R. AER 37:383-86 Jun 47
Theory of the inverse carrying charge in
  futures markets. JFE 30:1-28 Feb 48
Professor Vaile and the theory of inverse
  carrying charges. JFE 31:168-72 Feb 49
The investigation of economic expectations.
  AER/S 39:150-66 May 49
The theory of price of storage. AER 39:
  1254-62 Dec 49
WORMSER, ALVIN R.
  A case study in the costs of distribution.
    JM 9:19-25 Jul 44
WORSDALE, J. E.
  The task before us; with special reference
    to industry: a comment. SAJE 13:63-64
    Mar 45
WORSWICK, GEORGE DAVID NORMAN
  The Area Organisation. OIS 2,no.4:10-11
    Jul 40
  and Bowen, I. The Prices of Goods Act.
    Pt.I-II. OIS 2,no.6:2-5; no.7:2-7
    Aug,Sep 40
  and Bowen, I. The controls and war finance.
    OEP 4:77-104 Sep 40
  and Bowen, I. The cotton industry.
    OIS 2,no.8:9-11 Oct 40
  Export policy since the outbreak of war.
    OIS 3:17-21 Feb 1, 41
  Notes on the cotton industry. I. The future
    of the industry. OIS 3:53-55 Feb 22, 41
  Concentration in the hosiery industry.
    OIS 3:97-98 Apr 5, 41
  Concentration in the Leicester hosiery in-
    dustry. OIS 3:118-23 Apr 26, 41
  The release of labour from the cotton indus-
    try. OIS 3:135-40 May 17, 41
  and Burchardt, F. Point rationing. OIS 3:
    183-89 Jun 28, 41
  Retail sales during the war. A. Turnover
    and population movements. OIS 3:207-13
    Jul 19, 41
  Rational retailing in war-time. OIS 3:287-94
    Sep 20, 41
  Concentration: success or failure? OIS 3:
    359-64 Nov 22, 41
  Notes on rationing. OIS 4:44-52 Jan 10, 42
  The Retail trade report. OIS 4:70-74
    Feb 21, 42
  British raw material controls. OEP 6:1-41
    Apr 42
  and Nicholson, J. L. Consumption and ration-
    ing. OIS 4:132-35 Apr 25, 42
  Costs and prices in government contracts.
    OIS 4:185-89 Jun 27, 42

WORSWICK, GEORGE DAVID NORMAN (Cont.)
and Balogh, T. The battle for fuel. OIS 4:
    261-69 Oct 10, 42
Prices and retail consumption in 1942.
    OIS 5:57-63 Mar 13, 43
Dual capacity. OIS 5:80-85 Apr 3, 43
Steel prices. OIS 5:151-55 Jun 26, 43
Aircraft production. OIS 5:211-16 Sep 18, 43
Note on steel prices. OIS 5:284-88 Dec 11, 43
Points, prices and consumers' choice. OIS 6:
    33-39 Feb 26, 44
Clothing shops in the United Kingdom. OIS 6:
    168-72 Jul 22, 44; Erratum. 192 Aug 12, 44
The T.U.C. and reconstruction. R. OIS 6:
    287-92 Dec 4, 44
A survey of war contract procedure. OIS 7:
    79-90 Apr 7, 45
Price stabilisation. OIS 7:173-80 Jul 21, 45
The Pottery Working Party Report. R.
    OIS 8:217-31 Jul 46
and Burchardt, F. A. Britain in transition:
    output and financial policy. OIS 9:74-103
    Mar, Apr 47
and Martin, K. Prices and wages policy.
    OIS 10:84-93 Mar 48
A fall in consumption: a reply. OIS 10:
    195-208 Jun 48
--- A further comment. OIS 10:284-90
    Sep 48
WOYTINSKY, WLADIMIR S.
Additional workers on the labor market in
    depressions: a reply to Mr. Humphrey.
    JPE 48:735-39 Oct 40
Controversial aspects of unemployment esti-
    mates in the United States. REStat 23:
    68-77 May 41
National product, war and prewar: some
    comments on Professor Kuznets' study.
    REStat 26:123-26 Aug 44
Relationship between consumers' expendi-
    tures, savings and disposable income.
    REStat 28:1-12 Feb 46
The maintenance of full employment after the
    transition period: notes on Mr. Kalecki's
    models. AER 36:641-45 Sep 46
What was wrong in forecasts of postwar de-
    pression? JPE 55:142-51 Apr 47
Consumption-saving function: its algebra
    and philosophy. REStat 30:45-55 Feb 48
[and others] Problems of timing and adminis-
    tering fiscal policy in prosperity and de-
    pression: discussion. AER/S 38:443-51
    May 48
WRATHER, S. E.
Adaptation of crop insurance to tobacco.
    JFE 25:410-18 May 43
WREN, MELVIN C.
The Chamber of London in 1633. EHR II.1:
    46-53 no.1, 48
WRIGHT, ALMON R.
World war food controls and archival sources
    for their study. AH 15:72-83 Apr 41
Food purchases of the Allies, 1917-1918.
    AH 16:97-102 Apr 42

WRIGHT, CHESTER WHITNEY
American economic preparations for war,
    1914-1917 and 1939-1941. CJE 8:157-75
    May 42
The more enduring economic consequences
    of America's wars. JEH/S 3:9-26 Dec 43
WRIGHT, DAVID McCORD
The economic limit and economic burden of
    an internally held national debt. QJE 55:
    116-29 Nov 40
A neglected approach to the acceleration
    principle. REStat 23:100-01 May 41
Internal inconsistency in D. H. Robertson's
    "Saving and hoarding" concepts. EJ 51:
    334-37 Jun-Sep 41
The interpretation of the Kuznets-Fabricant
    figures for "net" capital consumption.
    JFE 50:435-43 Jun 42
Mr. Ratchford on the burden of a domestic
    debt: comment. AER 33:115-19 Mar 43
Moulton's The new philosophy of public
    debt. R. AER 33:573-90 Sep 43
Professor Knight on limits to the use of
    capital. QJE 58:331-58 May 44
Interest-free deficit financing: a reply.
    QJE 58:637-46 Aug 44
Hopes and fears: the shape of things to
    come. R. REStat 26:206-15 Nov 44
The future of Keynesian economics. AER 35:
    284-307 Jun 45
Business and the radical indictment. HBR 23:
    393-414 no.4, 45
"The great guessing game": Terborgh
    versus Hansen. R. REStat 28:18-22
    Feb 46
[and others] New frontiers in economic
    thought: discussion. AER/S 36:139-53
    May 46
[and others] [The economic theory of im-
    perfect competition, oligopoly, and
    monopoly]: discussion. AER/S 38:19-32
    May 48
How much can planning do? JPE 56:337-41
    Aug 48
Inflation and equality. AER 38:892-97
    Dec 48
The economics of a classless society.
    AER/S 39:27-36 May 49
Inflation and equality: a rejoinder. AER 39:
    965-66 Sep 49
WRIGHT, JOHN W.
The competitive outlook for cotton. JM 10:
    258-64 Jan 46
WRIGHT, KARL T.
Basic weaknesses of the parity price formula
    for a period of extensive adjustments in
    agriculture. JFE 28:294-300 Feb 46
Should all farms be large? JFE 31,pt.2:
    592-95 Feb 49
WRIGHT, QUINCY
The international regulation of the air.
    AER/S 35:243-48 May 45

WRIGHT, WILSON
  [and others] Effects of the war and defense
    program upon economic conditions and in-
    stitutions: discussion. AER/S 32:382-90
    Mar 42
  The industrial economist as staff officer.
    HBR 20:385-86 no.3, 42
  Impact of the war on technical training and
    occupational mobility. AER/S 33:238-48
    Mar 43
WRIGLEY, ROBERT L., Jr.
  with Hall, K. S. and Mayer, H. M. Mapping
    Chicago's industrial and commercial land
    use. LE 20:365-70 Nov 44
  Organized industrial districts, with special
    reference to the Chicago area. LE 23:
    180-98 May 47
  The Sanborn map as a source of land use
    information for city planning. LE 25:
    216-19 May 49
WU, YUAN-LI
  A note on the post-war industrialisation of
    "backward" countries and centralist
    planning. Ec N.S.12:172-78 Aug 45
  International capital investment and the de-
    velopment of poor countries. EJ 56:
    86-101 Mar 46
WUBNIG, ARTHUR [and others]
  Postwar shipping policy: discussion.
    AER/S 36:575-602 May 46
WUELLER, PAUL HAHN
  Public finance: trends and issues. HBR 19:
    248-60 no.2, 41
  [and others] Problems of taxation: discus-
    sion. AER/S 32:102-11 Mar 42
WUNDERLICH, FRIEDA
  The Beveridge plan. SR 10:233-45 May 43
  The National Socialist conception of landed
    property. SR 12:60-76 Feb 45
  The National Socialist agrarian program.
    SR 13:33-50 Mar 46
  Social insurance versus poor relief. SR 14:
    75-94 Mar 47
  New trends in social insurance. SR 16:31-44
    Mar 49
WURM, F. J.
  Note on the French possessions in South &
    Central America. OIS 2,no.7:21-22 Sep 40
  Argentine trade policy. OIS 2,no.9:10-13
    Nov 2, 40; Errata. 3,no.1:16 Jan 11, 41
WYCKOFF, VERTREES JUDSON and Gray, S.
  The international tobacco trade in the seven-
    teenth century. SEJ 7:1-26 Jul 40
WYLER, JULIUS
  The share of capital in national income:
    United States, United Kingdom and Ger-
    many. SR 10:436-54 Nov 43
  The national income of Soviet Russia. SR 13:
    501-18 Dec 46
  and Studenski, P. National income estimates
    of Soviet Russia: their distinguishing
    characteristics and problems. AER/S 37:
    595-610 May 47

WYLIE, KATHRYN HULEN
  and Ezekiel, M. The cost curve for steel
    production. JPE 48:777-821 Dec 40
  and Ezekiel, M. Cost functions for the
    steel industry. JASA 36:91-99 Mar 41
WYNNE, WILLIAM HARRIS
  Industrial adjustment at the end of the war:
    discussion. AER/S 33:162 Mar 43
WYTHE, GEORGE
  International economic problems; regional:
    discussion. AER/S 34:368-70 Mar 44
  [and others] Present issues of the Latin-
    American economy: discussion. AER/S 39:
    406-14 May 49
YAGI, YOSHINOSUKE
  The planning of agricultural production in
    wartime. Kyo 15,no.1:1-15 Jan 40
  The co-operative movement under wartime
    economic control. Kyo 15,no.3:25-40
    Jul 40
  Japan's current rice policy. Kyo 16,no.2:
    1-21 Apr 41
  Two forms of agricultural management in
    the Tropics. Kyo 17,no.3:20-35 Jul 42
  The problem of agricultural labour-power in
    the South. Kyo 18,no.1:1-17 Jan 43
YAMEY, BASIL S.
  and Franklin, N. N. An enquiry into some
    effects of a wage determination in
    Grahamstown. SAJE 9:416-22 Dec 41
  The excess profits duty in South Africa.
    SAJE 10:263-81 Dec 42
  Scientific bookkeeping and the rise of capital-
    ism. EHR II.1:99-113 no.2-3, 49
YATES, PAUL LAMARTINE
  see Lamartine Yates, Paul
YATES, SIDNEY R.
  Design for Chicago transit: London style.
    LE 17:320-32 Aug 41
YNTEMA, DWIGHT B.
  Changing seasonal fluctuations in the amounts
    of public and private assistance and earn-
    ings on CWA and WPA projects in 116
    urban areas, 1929-38. JASA 35:644-52
    Dec 40
YNTEMA, THEODORE OTTE
  chairman. Round table on cost functions and
    their relation to imperfect competition.
    AER/S 30:400-02 Mar 40
  Some economic problems in the expansion
    of capacity to produce military goods.
    AER/S 30,no.5:373-78 Feb 41
  Competition as a norm of economic behavior.
    JB 14:270-83 Jul 41
  The future role of large-scale enterprise.
    JPE 49:833-48 Dec 41
  "Full" employment in a private enterprise
    system. AER/S 34:107-17 Mar 44
YODER, DALE
  Economic changes and industrial unrest in
    the United States. JPE 48:222-37 Apr 40
  The structure of the demand for labor.
    AER/S 32:261-74 Mar 42

YODER, DALE (Cont.)
Comment on Mr. Graham's note. AER 35:
436-37 Jun 45
YOLANDE, MARY, sister
see Schulte, Mary Yolande, sister
YOUNG, CHARLES E.
Duties of the economist. HBR 20:391-92
no.3, 42
Applications and problems of productivity
data. JASA 41:421-31 Dec 46
YOUNG, DUDLEY
Farm land values in the Southeast. LE 22:
213-22 Aug 46
YOUNG, ERNEST CHARLES
Use of the normal value concept as a
stabilizing influence in agriculture.
JFE 22:148-54 Feb 40
The function of credit in modern agriculture.
JFE 23:52-62 Feb 41
and Bottum, J. C. Agricultural programs
for the post-war period. JFE 24:17-26
Feb 42
Farm work simplification studies. JFE 26:
232-39 Feb 44
and Bierly, I. R. The future of farm work
simplification research. JFE 28:331-37
Feb 46
and Bergfeld, A. J. Methods employed in an
analysis of the spread between farm and
consumer milk prices in New York City.
JFE 31,pt.2:1194-1202 Nov 49
YOUNG, HAROLD NEWELL
Work simplification: review. JFE 29:
231-32 Feb 47
YOUNG, J. A. and Duckham, A. N.
Rural planning in the United Kingdom.
JFE 29:1075-88 Nov 47
YOUNG, JOHN PARKE
Problems of international economic policy
for the United States. AER/S 32:182-94
Mar 42
[and others] [The future of international in-
vestment]: discussion. AER/S 33:355-61
Mar 43
[and others] International investment: dis-
cussion. AER/S 36:710-16 May 46
Exchange rate determination. AER 37:
589-603 Sep 47
YOUNG, RALPH AUBREY [and others]
The changing structure of the American
economy: discussion. AER/S 36:80-92
May 46
YU-PIN, PAUL
The economic future of China. RSE 2:100-01
Jan 44
YUAN-LI WU
see Wu, Yuan-Li
YUGOW, ARON
Economic statistics in the U.S.S.R.
REStat 29:242-46 Nov 47
YUNG-YING HSU
see Hsu, Yung-Ying

ZACCHIA, C. and Pietranera, G.
Recent banking developments in Italy:
December 1947-September 1949. BNL 2:
225-37 Oct-Dec 49
ZACHARIAS, C. W. B.
The level of stabilization. IJE 27:21-34
Jul 46
Reform of land revenue with special refer-
ence to Madras. IJE 27:237-44 Oct 46
Inflation and monetary policy with special
reference to India. IJE 30:185-92 Oct 49
ZAGLITS, OSCAR
International price control through buffer
stocks. JFE 28:413-43 May 46
ZANDER, ARNOLD S. [and others]
Labor problems: discussion. AER/S 33:
197-206 Mar 43
ZASSENHAUS, HERBERT K. [and others]
The sociology and economics of class con-
flict: discussion. AER/S 29:37-46 May 49
ZAUBERMAN, ALFRED
Economic thought in the Soviet Union.
Pt.I-III. REStud 16:1-12; 102-16; 189-200;
no.1, 48, no.2-3, 49
ZEBOT, CYRIL
Evaluation of economic systems. RSE 7,no.2:
48-63 Sep 49
ZEISEL, HANS and Harper, V. E.
The advertising value of different magazines.
JM 13:56-61 Jul 48
ZEISEL, JOHN and White, M.
Reading indices. JM 6:103-11 Oct 41
ZEITLIN, LEON
Merits and demerits of German price-con-
trol during the last war. EJ 51:507-12
Dec 41
ZETTEL, RICHARD M.
Taxation for highways in California. NTJ 1:
207-25 Sep 48
ZEUTHEN, FREDERIK
A note about capital values. Met 1:53-56
Apr 49
ZIELSKE, HUGH
Tabulation planning. JM 14:458-59 Oct 49
ZIMMERMAN, MAX MANDELL
The supermarket and the changing retail
structure. JM 5:402-09 Apr 41
Super market sales and profit trends, 1941-
1943. JM 9:162-63 Oct 44
Tomorrow's super market. JM 10:384-88
Apr 46
ZIMMERMAN, ROBERT W.
Doing business in Mexico. HBR 20:508-16
no.4, 42
ZIMMERN, W. H.
Lancashire and Latin America. MS 13:45-60
Aug 44
ZINGLER, ERVIN KENNETH
Advertising and the maximisation of profit.
Ec N.S.7:318-21 Aug 40
The National Labor Relations Board and the
federal courts. SEJ 7:538-55 Apr 41

ZINKE, GEORGE WILLIAM
 Six letters from Malthus to Pierre Prévost.
  JEH 2:174-89 Nov 42
ZINNER, SHANDOR M.
 The contribution of commercial receivable
  companies and factors to financing small-
  and medium-sized business. JF 2,no.1:
  76-90 Apr 47
ZIVNUSKA, JOHN A.
 Some aspects of the economic theory of
  forestry. LE 25:165-72 May 49

ZUCKERT, EUGENE M
 and Abbott, C. C.  Venture capital and taxation. QJE 55:667-82 Aug 41
 and Bates, G. E.  Directors' indemnity:
  corporate policy or public policy?
  HBR 20:244-64 no.2, 42
ZVAVICH, ISAK
 Economic education and economic research
  in the Soviet Union.  EJ 53:415-18
  Dec 43

# INDEX TO THE CLASSIFICATION SCHEDULE

( This index refers only to major classes and subclasses containing specified materials. Users should note cross-references in the classification schedule, pp. xxi-lxvi. They should also refer to the <u>General</u> subclasses containing material relevant to any topic; see p. x for explanation. )

### Q

### R

### S

## T

TURNOVER: labor, 19.23; tax, 10.441

TYING contracts, 15.344

## U

UNCERTAINTY, 2.02; use of farm resources under, 16.43

UNDERCONSUMPTION theory, 2.333

UNDERDEVELOPED economies, theory of, 2.34; for empirical studies of particular countries, 5 and 6.

UNDEREMPLOYMENT, 2.311 and 19.202

UNEMPLOYMENT, 19.202; assistance, 21.6; structural, 2.343; technological, 2.223 and 19.202

UNION-MANAGEMENT relations see Industrial relations

UNIONS see Trade unions

URBAN: planning and development, 22.3; redevelopment, 22.31; transportation, 15.86

UTILITY theory, 2.11; interpersonal comparisons, 2.162; under uncertainty, 2.02

## V

VALUE theory, 2.1

VARIANCE, analysis of, 7.231

VEGETABLES, 16.011; marketing of, 16.542; retailing of, 15.544

VELOCITY of money, 2.323 and 9.22

VETERANS: benefits, 21.5; housing, 22.53; land settlement, 17.3421

VITAL statistics, 18.3; registration of, 18.5

VOCATIONAL: education, 19.24; rehabilitation, 19.23

## W

WAGE: aspects of employment theory, 2.318; determination, 2.222 and 19.592; differentials, 2.221 and 19.33; levels, 19.32; payment systems, 19.593; policies, 19.592; structures, 19.33; theory, 2.22

WAGES, 19.3; agricultural, 16.34; and growth, 2.343; and productivity, 19.301; and stabilization policy, 12.32; as share of national income, 8.2; guaranteed annual, 19.594; minimum, 2.224, 19.32, and 19.35

WAR: damage compensation, 13.34; debts, 11.3533; economics, 13

WATER: resources, 17.2 and 17.6; transportation, 15.83; use on the farm, 16.421; utilities, 15.6

WEALTH, national, 8.2

WELFARE economics, theory of, 2.16; in international trade theory, 11.231

WELFARE funds, union, 19.596

WELFARE programs, 21

WHOLESALE price index, 8.54

WHOLESALE trade, 15.542

WOMAN labor, 19.221; wages of, 19.334

WOOL: manufacturing, 15.526; marketing, 16.543; production, 16.013

WORK relief programs, 21.6

WORK rules, 19.598

WORKMEN'S compensation, 19.5731

## Z

ZONING: rural, 22.41; urban, 22.32

# Groupwork Skills
# and Theory

## Margaret Hough

Hodder & Stoughton
A MEMBER OF THE HODDER HEADLINE GROUP

Order queries: please contact Bookpoint Ltd, 130 Milton Park, Abingdon, Oxon OX14 4SB. Telephone: (44) 01235 827720, Fax: (44) 01235 400454. Lines are open from 9.00–6.00, Monday to Saturday, with a 24 hour message answering service. Email address: orders@bookpoint.co.uk

A catalogue record this title is available from The British Library

ISBN 0 340 79957 9

Typeset by Dorchester Typesetting Group Limited, Dorchester, Dorset
Printed in Great Britain for Hodder & Stoughton Educational, a division of Hodder Headline Plc, 338 Euston Road, London NW1 3BH by Martins the Printers Ltd.